Personal Finance

12e

E. Thomas Garman
Virginia Tech University

Raymond E. Forgue
University of Kentucky

CENGAGE
Learning·

Australia • Brazil • Japan • Korea • Mexico • Singapore • Spain • United Kingdom • United States

CENGAGE
Learning®

Personal Finance, Twelfth Edition
E. Thomas Garman, Raymond E. Forgue

Vice President, General Manager, Quantitative Business: Balraj Kalsi

Product Director: Joe Sabatino

Senior Product Manager: Mike Reynolds

Associate Content Developer: Conor Allen

Senior Product Assistant: Adele Scholtz

Marketing Director: Natalie King

Marketing Manager: Heather Mooney

Senior Marketing Coordinator: Eileen Corcoran

Art and Cover Direction, Production Management, and Composition: Lumina Datamatics, Inc.

Associate Media Developer: Mark Hopkinson

Senior Intellectual Property Director: Julie Geagan-Chevez

Intellectual Property Analyst: Christina Ciaramella

Intellectual Property Project Manager: Anne Sheroff

Manufacturing Planner: Kevin Kluck

Cover Images: © Peter Booth/Getty Images (Team Talk on colorful Talk Bubbles);

© S-F/Shutterstock.com (Isolated green grass on a blue background)

For product information and technology assistance, contact us at
Cengage Learning Customer & Sales Support, 1-800-354-9706

For permission to use material from this text or product, submit all requests online at **www.cengage.com/permissions**
Further permissions questions can be emailed to
permissionrequest@cengage.com

Library of Congress Control Number: 2014933479

ISBN-13: 978-1-133-59583-0

Cengage Learning
20 Channel Center Street
Boston, MA 02210
USA

Cengage Learning is a leading provider of customized learning solutions with office locations around the globe, including Singapore, the United Kingdom, Australia, Mexico, Brazil, and Japan. Locate your local office at: **www.cengage.com/global**

Cengage Learning products are represented in Canada by Nelson Education, Ltd.

To learn more about Cengage Learning Solutions, visit **www.cengage.com**

Purchase any of our products at your local college store or at our preferred online store **www.cengagebrain.com**

Printed in Canada
Print Number: 01   Print Year: 2014

Brief Contents

Contents

CHAPTER 3

Financial Statements, Tools, and Budgets   64

PART 2   MONEY MANAGEMENT   103

CHAPTER 4

Managing Income Taxes   104

CHAPTER 8

CHAPTER 9

PART 3   INCOME AND ASSET PROTECTION   287

CHAPTER 10
Managing Property and Liability Risk   288

PART 4   INVESTMENTS   379

CHAPTER 13

Investment Fundamentals   380

CHAPTER 14

Investing in Stocks and Bonds   410

CHAPTER 15

Preface

A NOTE TO THE STUDENT

The 12th edition of *Personal Finance* offers high confidence to readers on how to succeed financially in today's economy. All the tools—and we mean ALL—are here for you to learn to use to your advantage so you will do well. The stock market is up, housing prices are rising, unemployment is declining, and a wonderful and interesting knowledge base awaits your reading.

"You need skills," said one college senior. "You need skills to successfully manage your financial resources because so much of the responsibility of financial success today rests solely upon your shoulders." The student also said that the skills must be presented "in small portions and be easy to understand." Without skills you fail. Lucky you! You are holding the ultimate learning tool in your hands, *Personal Finance*.

Personal Finance carefully lays out your financial "marching orders" for challenging economic times. "What to do, when to do it, and how to do it" is the mantra for this book. We give you "prescriptions" to follow that will guide you to success in your personal finances.

Personal Finance reminds students of the values of their grandparents: "Work hard, study, save, invest, and live within your means." In chapter after chapter, the 12th edition demonstrates the fundamental principles of how to do well in the financial side of living life.

Personal finance is not rocket science. In fact, it is not very complicated. Making good personal financial decisions for you and your loved ones simply requires making informed choices. Learn the vocabulary of personal finance, consider our prescriptions, and then apply the principles in your everyday decision making. Sacrifice a little now and reap big benefits in the future.

Ignore these suggestions at your peril, because a lack of financial literacy will guarantee your financial failure. Our goal as authors is to give you the knowledge, tools, attitudes, and skills you need to become financially sound. Along with the text, we have developed a full, rich companion website that you can use to learn as much as possible from your efforts as well as to develop your own financial plans.

TO THE INSTRUCTOR

This 12th edition of *Personal Finance* has been heavily revised, and it sets a high standard in the field. Once again when revising we surprised ourselves: we revised a lot! We love working on this book because we know what it does for students.

The text involves the student in genuinely learning the subject, particularly through newly created information presented in boxes, enhanced end-of-chapter activities, and innovative "prescriptions" from the authors. Your authors are the "Doctors of Personal Finance"—with 80 years of teaching experience, 65 years of experience writing college textbooks, and writing over 200 research articles. By drawing on their years of experience, the authors have made the 12th edition more than just a compilation of what to know. This edition emphasizes the "right things to do in personal finance, why, and then how to do them."

Why this emphasis? Because today's students need more precise guidance than those of yesteryear, mostly because one's personal finances are much more complicated today. Plus, these are extremely challenging economic times. The book's many features consistently offer normative, value-laden suggestions on getting ahead in one's personal finances. The activities require the reader to think about and apply their personal values to the facts and opinions presented. In short, *Personal Finance* gets students to think!

Every chapter includes the doctors' "prescriptions" for the student. Early in each chapter we offer the readers tips for "Your Next Five Years," which focus on correct actions readers should do soon. Later we point out to the reader "Your Worst Financial Blunders in (name of chapter)." Also, each chapter begins with a brief case with questions that asks "What Do You Recommend?" and the student usually does not know much at that early point. At the end of the chapter, the question is repeated with "What Do You Recommend NOW?" and the student should know a lot more after reading and class discussion and thus can answer the question knowledgeably.

Each chapter further includes multiple "Financial Power Points" that offer practical information that can be used immediately, a robust list of appropriate "Money Websites," and a concrete list of good and bad habits illustrated in "Turn Bad Habits into Good Ones." "Sean's Success Story" also appears in every chapter; Sean is a person to emulate because he does everything well in personal finance. Each chapter closes with a "Do It NOW!" feature that highlights three key personal finance actions that smart students should take immediately.

This 12th edition balances all the pieces of wise financial planning. In addition to updating and enhancing the quality of the content, this edition stimulates student interest in several new ways. The revised end-of-chapter activities are phenomenal. One continuing case is that of "Julia Price," whose successful financial life evolves through challenging economic times. Her case always ends with a question to challenge the student: *"Offer your opinions about her thinking."*

This edition includes five or six case problems in each chapter. The "Be Your Own Financial Planner" feature focuses on personalizing the concepts and lessons contained in the student workbook. These activities are not busy-work. They are concrete questions and tasks that require applying the knowledge provided in each chapter at a personal level.

All of the "On the 'Net" activities have been designed to carefully direct students to online materials that are genuinely useful and appropriate for this time in their personal financial lives.

The 12th edition includes over 43 new headings, more than 106 new boxed inserts, 53 new terms, 7 tables, 9 figures, and lots of new and expanded material. This edition connects all the pieces of personal finance in a comprehensive manner, shows students the relevancy of the topics, and requires students to do a reality check on their own finances. As a result, your students will succeed!

Changes in This Edition

- Chapter 11, Planning for Health Care Expenses, is totally new because the Affordable Health Care Act, also known as Obamacare, mandates enormous changes in how Americans go about protecting themselves from high health care expenses. It also includes the information on using advance directives that formerly was in Chapter 18.

- Chapter 18 was deleted because Congress changed estate planning law so couples with estates valued at less than $10.5 million owe no taxes, and this impacts only about 1,300 families a year. The remaining content is contained in Chapter 17, Retirement and Estate Planning.

- Chapter 4 was updated to reflect the impact of the Congress passing a new tax bracket on higher-income earners and it reflects additional taxes on the top 3 percent of income earners to help pay for provisions of the Affordable Care Act.

- A new boxed feature is included in every chapter "Bias toward…." that gives examples of what people "tend to do wrong" in personal finance and what the actions the reader can take to avoid such threats.

- Another new feature is "Do It in Class." This new chapter feature uses icons that link key concepts and calculations to specific end-of-chapter exercises that are most suitable for an instructor to flip the classroom through in-class learning activities.

TOPICAL COVERAGE OF THE 12TH EDITION

We have carefully constructed the 12th edition to address instructors' concerns about getting through all the necessary material for this course. The table of contents outlines 17 chapters divided into four parts: Financial Planning, Money Management, Income and Asset Protection, and Investments. We also include a comprehensive chapter on "Career Planning" that provides students with innovative 21st century suggestions necessary to obtain and succeed in starting their careers. In every chapter where relevant, we place the material in the context of today's challenging economic times.

FEATURES

We have carefully designed pedagogical features to strengthen learning opportunities for students. Each feature is designed to communicate vital information meaningfully and to maintain student interest. The following features support student understanding and retention.

You Must Be Kidding, Right? If you typically skip the opening case, now is the time to change your ways. This feature opens every chapter with a short narrative about a financial topic and a question with four possible answers. The often surprising (and sometimes funny) answers provide an excellent opportunity to quickly engage students in a concept that is key to understanding the chapter.

Learning Objectives Concise behavioral objectives that can be measured against the content of each chapter, its activities, and then tested.

What Do You Recommend? These concise, realistic cases are pretests at the beginning of each chapter followed by leading questions asking about the most important fundamental concepts in the chapter. The case acts as a pretest because a student who has not read the chapter will be able to offer only simplistic, experience-based opinions and suggestions to respond to the questions. This will communicate to them how much they have to learn from an instructor-led classroom discussion of the chapter. A corresponding posttest, "What Do You Recommend NOW?" appears as part of the end-of-chapter pedagogy. At that point, after reading and classroom discussion, student responses should be very different: informed, practical, and action oriented.

Your Next Five Years "Your Next Five Years" boxes list the most important chapter-related actions students need to take to get off to a great start financially. These tips are sufficiently detailed to allow ready implementation. If students take these actions, they truly will become financially successful over the next five years!

The Tax Consequences of (name of chapter) This box focuses on the income tax aspects of each chapter, so the reader is pushed to always think of income taxes when making financial decisions.

Bias toward .... These new boxes appear in every chapter and give the reader a reality check on the behavioral economics biases that lead to common errors in personal finance. And the bias box narrative concisely tells what to do about it.

Financial Power Point These boxes provide concise, practical information on a variety of current financial issues and opportunities. Sometimes 6 or more appear in a chapter.

YOU MUST BE KIDDING, RIGHT?

The world of personal finances is getting more complicated and challenging each year. Recent economic times have been tough with some negative impacts on people's personal finances. Which one of the following statements is false?

A. Half of Americans have less than one month's income saved for a rainy day.

B. Half of adults say they do not budget.

C. Sixty percent of Americans say they live paycheck-to-paycheck.

D. Forty percent of Americans say they find it difficult to meet monthly expenses.

The answer is "none of the above" because all the statements are true. Clearly, many Americans are experiencing trouble with their personal finances. You can get smart about personal finances so these statements do not apply to you!

YOUR NEXT FIVE YEARS

In the next five years, you can start achieving financial success by doing the following related to financial statements, tools, and budgets:

1. *Develop financial goals and update them annually.*

2. *Develop a cash-flow statement and spending plan every month to ensure that you spend less than you make.*

FINANCIAL POWER POINT

Income Does Not Create Wealth, Investments Do

People do not get wealthy by earning an income. Real wealth comes from increases in the value of assets over time such as the growth of investments within a 401(k) retirement program.

DO IT IN CLASS

Run the Numbers   These boxes guide students to their best personal finance decisions that require mathematics or illustrate commonly confronted choices that follow a step-by-step process.

Do It in Class   This new feature highlights with icons the topics in the chapter that are most suitable for students to "turn the class upside down" by choosing to do in-class learning activities for 20 to 25 minutes.

Did You Know?   These boxes—sometimes a dozen in a chapter—have interesting, catchy titles that encourage students to actually read the information. Classroom research demonstrates that this technique works.

Concept Checks   At the end of each major segment of each chapter, we provide concept check questions tied to the major topics in that part. These aid classroom discussion, serve as student assignments, or simply provide students with a self-check for a fuller understanding of the material.

Advice from a Professional   These feature boxes—written by some of the nation's best personal finance experts—offer authoritative, real-world advice on getting out of credit card debt, making purchases online, buying a used car, and paying for retirement on the layaway plan, plus many other topics.

Do It NOW!   These boxes in each chapter list three key personal finance actions that smart students should take immediately. They focus primarily on implementing some of the most pressing "Next Five Years" tips from the chapter.

END-OF-CHAPTER PEDAGOGY   The end of chapter pedagogy—much of which is new—carefully directs student learning of the concepts and principles that are key to success in personal finance.

What Do You Recommend NOW?   This end-of-chapter section asks the same leading questions pertaining to the case at the beginning of the chapter. At this point, however, instructors can anticipate higher-quality responses and a deeper level of understanding because students have read the chapter and likely listened to instructor-led class discussion.

DID YOU KNOW ?

Your Worst Financial Blunders in Financial Statements, Tools, and Budgets

Based on others' financial woes, you will make mistakes in personal finance when you:

1. *Fail to plan for non-monthly irregular expenditures.*
2. *Underestimate how much you plan to spend each month.*
3. *Use credit card purchases to "balance" your budget.*

CONCEPT CHECK 3.1

1. Summarize the financial planning process.
2. Explain the relationships among financial values, goals, and strategies.

DO IT NOW!

You know more about personal finance after reading this chapter, so get started right now by:

1. *Putting a notepad in your pocket to record every single expense of $1 or more for one month.*
2. *Preparing a cash-flow statement at the end of the month.*
3. *Setting up a spending plan for next month that provides for savings for at least one of your goals.*

ADVICE FROM A PROFESSIONAL

Get-Tough Ways to Cut Spending

If you always run out of money before the month is over, you may need to take some drastic steps to get your finances under control. Consider the following:

1. Stop paying bank fees by maintaining minimum balances and eliminating overdrafts.
2. Stop making ATM withdrawals.
3. Stop getting cash back from debit or credit card purchases to use for pocket money.
4. Spend only cash or money that you have, and leave debit and credit cards at home.
5. Stop using credit cards.
6. Refinance credit card debt at a credit union.
7. Do not eat out.
8. Cut back on excessive telephone use.
9. Don't pay for entertainment; rather do activities that are free.
10. Reduce or stop spending on luxuries such as clothing, movies, entertainment, memberships, hobbies, CDs, DVDs, phones, and expanded cable channels.
11. Drop landline telephone service and use only a cell phone.
12. Find cheaper auto insurance.
13. Increase your 401(k) retirement contribution as it reduces income taxes.
14. Change income tax withholding to increase take-home pay.
15. Take a list when shopping, and stick to it.
16. Avoid shopping malls and discount stores.
17. Sell an asset, especially one that requires additional expenses, such as a boat or second car.
18. Build up an emergency fund of savings even if it means temporarily decreasing retirement-plan contributions.
19. Only buy used items.
20. Consider making Christmas a "nonspend" holiday.
21. Move to lower-cost housing.
22. Increase income by working overtime or finding a second job.

Alena C. Johnson
Utah State University

Big Picture Summary of Learning Objectives   Three to six sentences review the most important content cited in each of the chapter's learning objectives and explained in each section of the chapter.

Let's Talk about It   Students are given an opportunity to discuss their personal experiences related to the chapter by addressing these questions.

Do the Math   These questions apply the relevant quantitative mathematical calculations used in personal finance decision making. The companion website includes Excel calculators for these exercises.

Financial Planning Cases   Students must apply key concepts when analyzing typical personal financial problems, dilemmas, and challenges that face individuals and couples. Because some cases are designed to be both continuous and independent of the other chapters' cases, each case can be analyzed by itself. One continuing case is that of "Julia Price," whose sometimes complicated financial life evolves through challenging economic times, and each of her cases ends with a question for the student: *"Offer your opinions about her thinking."* Two other continuing cases are "Harry and Belinda Johnson," starting out married life as a young couple, and "Victor and Maria Hernandez," a family starting in middle age. This edition features five or six cases in each chapter. The series of case questions requires data analysis and critical thinking, and this effort reinforces mastery of chapter concepts.

Be Your Own Personal Financial Planner   This end of chapter section provides concrete, personalized activities that engage students in developing aspects of their own financial plans. Most are keyed to the online "My Personal Financial Planner" worksheets complete with interactive spreadsheets.

MYPERSONAL
FINANCIAL
PLANNER

On the 'Net   All of these exercises have been updated to carefully focus the student to online materials that are genuinely useful and appropriate for this time in their personal financial lives. Each chapter includes several Internet-based exercises, activities, and focused questions that expand the student's learning in a guided manner, allowing the student to research and apply chapter concepts while finding the answers.

Action Involvement Projects   Each out-of-class project points the student toward concrete steps that require applying the knowledge provided in each chapter at a personal level, particularly aiming to have an impact on their thoughts about personal finance.

Do It in Class Exercises for Instructors to "Flip the Classroom"   The traditional pattern of teaching and learning has been for instructors to assign students to read a textbook and have them work on problems, cases, and exercises outside of school. Then the students come to class to listen to lectures, participate in discussions, and take tests.

Flip teaching or a flipped classroom is a pedagogical model in which the typical lecture and homework elements of a course are reversed. It is a form of learning where students learn new content by what used to be class work (the "lecture") that is usually done online at home by students who watch video lessons and what used to be "homework" (assigned problems and cases) is now done in class with instructors who offer more personalized guidance and interaction with students.

In a flipped classroom, the instructor has decided that students will study the chapter before coming to class, often using video lessons, podcasts or screencasts prepared by the instructor or a third party. Sometimes these can be found online from YouTube, the Khan Academy, MIT's OpenCourseWare, Coursera, or other similar sources. As a result the students may watch, rewind, and fast-forward as needed. Then the students the come to class to apply their knowledge by working on problems, cases, and various exercises, including short discussions, for part or all of what used to be the usual class time.

In the flipped class the instructor tutors the students when they become stuck working on problems, rather than imparting the initial lesson by lecturing in person.

The flipped classroom frees up class time for hands-on work. Students learn by doing and asking questions. Students can also help each other, a process that benefits both the advanced and less advanced learners.

This *Personal Finance* book offers instructors a break-through approach to try out a flipped classroom. If instructors provide students some at-home video lessons or if they simply want to try out flipping the classroom, they may review the end-of-chapter "Do It in Class" icons and decide which questions might be most suitable for their students. They might plan for perhaps 20 to 25 minutes of class time for students to solve appropriate problems.

To assist with this endeavor we have placed several "Do It in Class" icons within each chapter that are suitable for students to "turn the class upside down" should they choose to do the related in-class learning activities marked with icons at the end of the chapter. The in-chapter icons have no meaning upon first reading the chapter. However, their importance become apparent when the student sees the selected end-of-chapter questions that are marked with the same icons. Each of these questions also has page numbers that direct the student to the appropriate section of the chapter (marked with the same icon) where the content exists for them to review and learn so they may perform the tasks requested. The instructor needs only to assign some end-of-chapter "Do It in Class" activities and supervise the student learning.

Glossary   A comprehensive end-of-text glossary includes precise definitions of all key terms and concepts.

COMPLETE INSTRUCTOR SUPPORT

- **Instructor's Manual**. Written by main text author, Ray Forgue, this ancillary includes a variety of useful components: suggested course syllabi to emphasize a general, insurance, or investments approach to personal finance; learning objectives; a summary overview for use as a lecture outline; and teaching suggestions including student application exercises and tips for bringing the Web into the classroom. This item is found on the Instructor's Resource CD and instructor website.
- **Solutions Manual.** Written by main text author, Ray Forgue. Answers and solutions to all end-of-chapter questions and problems are included. This item is found on the Instructor's Resource CD and on the instructor website.
- **PowerPoint Slides.** The PowerPoint slides contain chapter outlines, figures, and tables from the main text, which were written by main text author Ray Forgue. Lecture material is available within the PowerPoint slides.
- **Instructor Website.** The instructor website that accompanies *Personal Finance* provides a wealth of supplemental materials to enhance learning and aid in course management. Features of the site include PowerPoint slides, downloadable Instructor Manual and Solution Manual files, and test bank content.

COMPLETE STUDENT SUPPORT

- **My Personal Financial Planner** is a terrific workbook for students to use in planning and organizing their personal finances. This booklet contains over 60 useful worksheets, schedules, and planners for personal finance. They are not busywork for students. Some of the worksheets mimic the calculations and planning exercises covered in the book; others help students develop personal financial plans and actions. A student's use of this handbook virtually guarantees positive changes in personal financial behaviors and success in money matters.
- **Student Companion Website** is accessible *without* an access code. Among other assets, students can find a short interactive quiz for each chapter.

Acknowledgments

We would like to thank our reviewers and other experts, who offered helpful suggestions and criticisms to this and previous editions. This book is their book, too. We especially appreciate the assistance of the following individuals:

Tim Alzheimer, *Montana State University*

Gary Amundson, *Montana State University-Billings*

Jan D. Andersen, *California State University, Sacramento*

Dori Anderson, *Mendocino College*

Sophia Anong, *University of Georgia*

Robert E. Arnold, Jr., *Henry Ford Community College*

Bala Arshanapalli, *Indiana University Northwest*

Hal Babson, *Columbus State Community College*

Anne Bailey, *Miami University*

Rosella Bannister, *Bannister Financial Education Services*

Richard Bartlett, *Muskingum Area Technical College*

Anne Baumgartner, *Navy Family Service Center-Norfolk*

John J. Beasley, *Georgia Southern University*

Kim Belden, *Daytona Beach Community College*

Pamela J. Bennett, *University of Central Arkansas*

Daniel A. Bequette, *Harwell College*

Peggy S. Berger, *Colorado State University*

David Bible, *Louisiana State University-Shreveport*

George Biggs, *Southern Nazarene University*

Robert Blatchford, *Tulsa Junior College*

Susan Blizzard, *San Antonio College*

Karin B. Bonding, *University of Virginia*

Linda Bradley, *California State University-Northridge*

Dean Brassington, *Joint Expeditionary Base Little Creek-Fort Story*

Anne Bunton, *Cottey College*

Bruce Brunson, *Tidewater Community College*

Paul L. Camp, *Galecki Financial Management*

Chris Canellos, *Stanford University*

Andrew Cao, *American University*

Diana D. Carroll, *Carson-Newman College*

Gerri Chaplin, *Joliet Junior College*

Steve Christian, *Jackson Community College*

Ron Christner, *Loyola University*

Charlotte Churaman, *University of Maryland*

Carol N. Cissel, *Roanoke College*

Thomas S. Coe, *Xavier University of Louisiana*

Edward R. Cook, *University of Massachusetts-Boston*

Patricia Cowley, *Omni Travel*

Kathy Crall, *Des Moines Area Community College*

Sheran Cramer, *University of Nebraska-Lincoln*

Ellen Daniel, *Harding University*

Joel J. Dauten, *Arizona State University*

William Dean, *Southern University*

Lorraine R. Decker, *Decker & Associates Inc.*

Carl R. Denson, *University of Delaware*

Dale R. Detlefs, *William M. Mercer, Inc.*

A. Terrence Dickens, *California State University*

Charles E. Downing, *Massasoit Community College*

Alberto Duarte, *Access Counseling*

Dottie Durband, *Kansas State University*

Sidney W. Eckert, *Appalachian State University*

Marc Eiger, *Standard & Poor's*

Gregg Edwards, *Monroe Community College*

Jacolin P. Eichelberger, *Hillsborough Community College*

Gregory J. Eidleman, *Alvernia College*

Rchard English, *Augustana College*

Evan Enowitz, *Grossmont College*

Don Etnier, *University of Maryland-European Division*

Judy Farris, *South Dakota State University*

Vicki Fitzsimmons, *University of Illinois*

Jonathan Fox, *Iowa State University*

Fred Floss, *Buffalo State College*

Paula G. Freston, *Colby Community College*

H. Swint Friday, *University of South Alabama*

Caroline Fulmer, *University of Alabama*

Wafica Ghoul, *Davenport University*

Joel Gold, *University of South Maine*

Elizabeth Goldsmith, *Florida State University*

Joseph D. Greene, *Augusta State University*

Paul Gregg, *University of Central Florida*

Jeri W. Griego, *Laramie County Community College*

Michael P. Griffin, *University of Massachusetts-Dartmouth*

Rchard C. Grimm, *Grove City College*

David R. Guarino, *Standard & Poor's*

Hilda Hall, *Surry Community College*

Patty Hatfield, *Bradley University*

Andrew Hawkins, *Lake Area Technical Institute*

Janice Heckroth, *Indiana University of Pennsylvania*

Diane Henke, *University of Wisconsin-Sheboygan*

Roger P. Hill, *University of North Carolina-Wilmington*

Jeanne Hilton, *University of Nevada*

Laura Horvath, *University of Detroit Mercy*

David Houghton, *Northwest Nazarene College*

George Hruby, *University of Akron*

Holly Hunts, *Montana State University*

Samira Hussein, *Johnson County Community College*

Roger Ignatius, *University of Maine-Augusta*

James R. Isherwood, *Community College of Rhode Island*

Naheel Jeries, *Iowa State University*

Karen Jones, *SWBC Mortgage Corporation*

Marilyn S. Jones, *Friends University*

Ellen Joyner, *Liberty National Bank-Lexington*

Virginia W. Junk, *University of Idaho*

Peggy D. Keck, *Western Kentucky University*

Dennis Keefe, *Michigan State University*

Jim Keys, *Florida International University*

Haejeong Kim, *Central Michigan University*

Jinhee Kim, *University of Maryland-College Park*

Karen Eilers Lahey, *University of Akron*

Eloise J. Law, *State University of New Tork-Plattsburgh*

Andrew H. Lawrence, *Delgado Community College*

David W. Leapard, *Eastern Michigan State University*

Hongbok Lee, *Western Illinois University*

Charles J. Lipinski, *Marywood University*

Janet K. Lukens, *Mississippi State University*

Kenneth Marin, *Aquinas College*

Kenneth Mark, *Kansas Community College*

Julia Marlowe, *University of Georgia*

Allen Martin, *California State University Northridge*

Gerald J. Mellnick, *Schoolcraft College*

Lee McClain, *Western Washington University*

Billy Moore, *Delta State University*

John R. Moore, *Navy Family Services Center-Norfolk*

Diane R. Morrison, *University of Wisconsin-La Crosse*

Steven J. Muck, *El Camino College*

Randolph J. Mullis, *WEATrust*

James Nelson, *East Carolina State University*

Donald Neuhart, *Central Missouri State University*

Oris L. Odom II, *University of Texas-Tyler*

William S. Phillips, *Memphis State University*

John Piccione, *Rochester Institute of Technology*

Carl H. Pollock, Jr., *Portland State University*

Angela J. Rabatin, *Prince George's Community College*

Gwen M. Reichbach, *Dealers' Financial Services*

Mary Ellen Rider, *University of Nebraska*

Eloise Lorch Rippie, *Iowa State University*

Edmund L. Robert, *Front Range Community College*

Clarence C. Rose, *Radford University*

David E. Rubin, *Glendale Community College*

Michael Rupured, *University of Georgia*

Peggy Schomaker, *University of Maine*

Barry B. Schweig, *Creighton University*

Elaine D. Scott, *Bluefield State University*

James Scott, *Southwest Missouri State University*

Wilmer E. Seago, *Virginia Tech University*

Kim Simons, *Madisonville Community College*

Marilyn K. Skinner, *Macon Technical Institute*

Rosalyn Smith, *Morningside College*

Horacio Soberon-Ferrer, *University of Florida*

Edward Stendard, *St. John Fisher College*

Mary Stephenson, *University of Maryland-College Park*

Eugene Swinnerton, *University of Detroit Mercy*

Lisa Tatlock, *The Master's College*

Francis C. Thomas, *Port Republic, New Jersey*

Stephen Trimby, *Worcester State College*

John W. Tway, *Amber University*

Shafi Ullah, *Broward Community College*

Dick Verrone, *University of North Carolina-Wilmington*

Jerry A. Viscione, *Boston College*

Stephen E. Wagner, *Attorney at Law, Blacksburg, Virginia*

Rosemary Walker, *Michigan State University*

Grant J. Wells, *Michigan State University*

Jon D. Wentworth, *Southern Adventist University*

Dorothy West, *Michigan State University*

Gloria Worthy, *State Technical Institute-Memphis*

Rui Yau, *South Dakota State University*

Alex R. Yguado, *L.A. Mission College*

Robert P. Yuyuenyongwatana, *Cameron University*

Martha Zenns, *Jamestown Community College*

Larry Zigler, *Highland College*

Virginia S. Zuiker, *University of Minnesota*

This 12th edition also has benefited from the contributions of some of the best personal finance experts in the United States, who have shared some specialized expertise by contributing to a series of boxes titled "Advice from a Professional":

Dennis R Ackley, *Ackley & Associates*

Philip Corwin Bryant, *Ivy Tech Community College*

William Dean, *Southern University*

Brenda J. Cude, *University of Georgia*

Dorothy B. Durband, *Texas Tech University*

Patti Fisher, *Virginia Tech*

Elizabeth Fletcher, *Evangel University*

Jonathan Fox, *Iowa State University*

Carol S. Fulmer, *The University of Alabama*

Jordan E. Goodman, *MoneyAnswers.com*

Steve Holcombe, *North Greenville University*

Holly Hunts, *Montana State University*

Alena C. Johnson, *Utah State University*

Hyungsoo Kim, *University of Kentucky*

Joan Koonce, *University of Georgia*

Frances C. Lawrence, *Louisiana State University*

Irene Leech, *Virginia Tech*

Gerald J. Mellnick, *Schoolcraft College*

Diann Moorman, *University of Georgia*

Ann Ranczuch, *Monroe Community College*

Michael Ruff, *Monroe Community College*

Michelle Singletary, *The Washington Post*

Feliccia Smith, *North Greenville University*

Sherry Tshibangu, *Monroe Community College*

Robert O. Weagley, *University of Missouri-Columbia*

Jon Wentworth, *Southern Adventist University*

Mary Ann Whitehurst, *Southeastern Crescent Technical College*

James J. Williams, *Hudson Valley Community College*

Dana Wolff, *Southeast Technical Institute*

We definitely wish to thank the many students who had the opportunity to read, critique, and provide input for various components of the *Personal Finance* project. Please keep sending us your e-mails.

This edition of *Personal Finance* benefited enormously from the editorial efforts of Conor Allen. In addition to being a fine manager and editor, he brought much insight, creativity, intelligence, and wisdom to the project.

A project of this dimension could never have been completed without the patience, support, understanding, and sacrifices of our friends and families during the book's development, revision, and production. Tom Garman, professor emeritus and fellow at Virginia Tech University, retired to life in The Villages, Florida, and stays in contact with his children and their spouses and significant others: Scott and his husband Dave, Dana and her husband Tom with Julia, Alieu and his wife Isatou with Kumba, Alimatou, and Ousman. Thanks are owed to all. Tom also credits the mentors in his life—Ron West, Bill Boast, Bill McDivitt, and John Binnion—for guiding him along the way, particularly through their noble examples of compassion, commitment, and excellence. He also thanks Gerry Chambers, the love of his life for her laughter, love, and support, which guarantees that the fourth quarter of his life will continue to be blessed with more happiness than all the years before. Ray Forgue, retired from University of Kentucky, lives in Easley, South Carolina, with his wife Snooky and her son, Stuart, and proudly watches over his son Matthew and daughter Amy and her husband Mack Holly and Snooky's children Dru and Seth as they continue their working careers. Ray wishes to thank his mother, Mary, and brothers Bob, Gary, Joe, and Dave for their patience over the years as he spent time during vacation and holiday visits working on this book. Special thanks to Snooky, whose assistance on the first edition of *Personal Finance* continues to shine through to this current edition.

Finally, we wish to say "thank you" to the hundreds of personal finance instructors around the country who have generously shared their views, in person and by e-mail, on what should be included in a high-quality textbook and ancillary materials. Some of you thankfully have written multiple times. You demand the best for your students, and we've listened. *Personal Finance* is your book! The two of us and the 'top notch' team of people at Cengage Learning have tried very hard to meet your needs in every possible way. We hope we have exceeded your expectations. Why? Because we share the belief that students need to study personal finance concepts thoroughly and learn them well so that they will be truly successful in their personal finances.

E. Thomas Garman   Raymond E. Forgue
ethomasgarman@yahoo.com   perfinypm@yahoo.com

P.S. Dear students: If you are going to save any of your college textbooks, be certain to keep this one because the basic principles of personal finance are everlasting. Also, you might want to present the book as a gift to a significant other, spouse, sibling, or parent.

PART 1

1 Understanding Personal Finance

LEARNING OBJECTIVES

After reading this chapter, you should be able to:

1. Recognize the keys to achieving financial success.

2. Understand how the economy affects your personal financial success.

3. Apply basic economic principles when making financial decisions.

4. Perform time value of money calculations in personal financial decision making.

5. Make smart decisions about your employee benefits.

6. Identify the professional certifications of providers of financial advice.

MORTGAGE RETIREMENT

INSURANCE TAXES

401(k) VACATION

EDUCATION CREDIT CARDS

© S-E/Shutterstock.com;Peter Booth/E+/Getty Images

WHAT DO YOU RECOMMEND?

Na Yeon Choi, age 23, recently graduated with her bachelor's degree in library and information sciences. She is about to take her first professional position as an archivist with a large civil engineering firm in a rapidly expanding area in California. While in school, Na Yeon worked part time for that firm, earning about $10,000 per year. For the past two years, she has managed to put $1000 each year into an individual retirement account (IRA). Na Yeon owes $35,000 in student loans on which she is obliged now to begin making payments. Her new job will pay $55,000. Na Yeon may begin participating in her employer's 401(k) retirement plan immediately, and she can contribute up to 8 percent of her salary to the plan. Her employer will contribute 1/2 of 1 percent for every 1 percent that Na Yeon contributes.

© qingqing/Shutterstock.com

What do you recommend to Na Yeon on the importance of personal finance regarding:

1. **Participating in her employer's 401(k) retirement plan?**

2. **Understanding the effects of her marginal tax rate on her financial decisions?**

3. **Considering the current state of the economy in her personal financial planning?**

4. **Using time value of money considerations to project what her IRA might be worth at age 63?**

5. **Using time value of money considerations to project what her 401(k) plan might be worth when she is age 63 if she were to participate fully?**

YOUR NEXT FIVE YEARS

In the next five years, you can start achieving financial success by doing the following related to understanding personal finance:

1. *Stay up to date with current economic conditions.*

2. *Use marginal and opportunity costs and time value of money calculations when making financial decisions.*

3. *Harness the power of compounding by starting early to save a consistent amount each month for long-term goals.*

4. *Take responsibility for managing your own financial success.*

5. *Take advantage of tax sheltering through your employer's benefits program.*

personal finance

The study of personal and family resources considered important in achieving financial success; it involves how people spend, save, protect, and invest their financial resources.

financial literacy

Knowledge of facts, concepts, principles, and technological tools that are fundamental to being smart about money.

financial responsibility

Means that you are accountable for your future financial well-being and that you strive to make wise personal financial decisions.

LEARNING OBJECTIVE 1

Recognize the keys to achieving financial success.

Can you successfully manage your personal finances in today's economy? Yes you can. But it will be challenging. Most people now realize that consuming less, paying off credit cards, and saving and investing more are the keys to long-term financial stability and success. That is good advice for you, too. In the years ahead many opportunities will arise for you to take smart actions to help assure your future financial success. You can do these things if you put in practice what you will learn in your personal finance course.

Personal finance is the study of personal and family resources considered important in achieving financial success; it involves how people spend, save, protect, and invest their financial resources. Topics in personal finance include financial and career planning, budgeting, tax management, cash management, credit cards, borrowing, major expenditures, risk management, investments, retirement planning, and estate planning. A solid understanding of personal finance topics offers you a better chance of success in facing the financial challenges, responsibilities, and opportunities of life. The best of all the successes is the sense of freedom from financial worries that comes with effectively planning your personal finances.

You are fortunate to be reading this book as it provides prudent guidance for every step of the way. Careful study will enhance your **financial literacy**, which is simply your knowledge of facts, concepts, principles, and technological tools that are fundamental to being smart about money. Financial literacy empowers you. It improves your ability to handle day-to-day financial matters, helps you avoid the consequences of poor financial decisions that could take years to overcome, helps you make informed and confident personal money decisions, and makes you more financially responsible.

Financial responsibility means that you are accountable for your future financial well-being and that you strive to make good decisions in personal finance. The biggest example of not being financially responsible is to live like you are rich *before* you are. Being financially responsible means you will control your personal financial destiny and be successful. At the beginning of each chapter, we provide a short case vignette titled "What Do You Recommend?" Each story focuses on the financial challenges that can be experienced by someone who has not learned about the material in that chapter. You will be asked to think about what advice you might give the person as you study the chapter. Then at the end of each chapter, you will again be asked to provide more informed advice based on what you have learned. You will be much better informed then!

1.1 ACHIEVING PERSONAL FINANCIAL SUCCESS

Today's marketplace provides a constant barrage of messages suggesting that you can spend and borrow your way to financial success, security, and wealth. Well, they are wrong because you can't. These messages are very enticing for those starting out in their financial lives. In truth, overspending and overuse of consumer credit seriously impede financial success.

Many people think that being wealthy is a function of how much you earn or inherit. In reality, it is much more closely related to your ability to make good decisions that generate wealth for you.

Consider accepting some advice from your grandparent's generation: "Be responsible for yourself. Be frugal. Work hard. Keep a level head. Use common sense. And above all, never give up on what you love."

DID YOU KNOW

In Life and Career We Must Learn to "Focus"

Daniel Goleman's book *Focus: The Hidden Ingredient in Excellence* offers tips for getting more out of our lives and careers as well as our roles as parents and as partners. He argues that the secret to high performance and fulfillment is "attention." Goleman says that we must learn to sharpen our focus if we are to contend with, let alone succeed in, a complex world. We are overwhelmed by so much stuff in life (e.g., e-mails, texts, smart phones, Facebook) that we hardly enjoy a relaxed conversation, listening, and even quietly enjoy our meals. Goleman's research focuses on three types of listening: inner, other, and outer focus. Paying careful attention is a capability that can be learned because it will enhance one's emotional intelligence and performance.

You have to do only a *few* things right in personal finance during your lifetime, as long as you don't do too many things wrong. Personal finance is not rocket science. You can succeed very well in your personal finances by making appropriate plans and taking sensible actions to implement those plans.

1.1a Plan for Financial Success and Happiness

Financial success is the achievement of financial aspirations that are desired, planned, or attempted. Success is defined by the person who seeks it. Some define financial success as being able to actually live according to one's standard of living. Many seek **financial security**, which provides the comfortable feeling that your financial resources will be adequate to fulfill any needs you have as well as most of your wants. Others want to be **wealthy** and have an abundance of money, property, investments, and other resources.

Financial happiness encompasses a lot more than just making money. It is the experience you have when you are satisfied with your money matters. People who are happy about their finances are likely to be spending within a budget and taking steps to achieve their goals, and this happiness spills over in a positive way to feelings about their overall enjoyment of life. Financial happiness is in part a result of practicing good financial behaviors. Examples of such behaviors include paying bills on time, spending less than you earn, knowing where your money goes, and investing some money for the future. The more good financial behaviors you practice, the greater your financial happiness. In fact, simply setting financial goals contributes to financial happiness.

financial success
The achievement of financial aspirations that are desired, planned, or attempted, as defined by the person who seeks it.

financial security
The comfortable feeling that your financial resources will be adequate to fulfill any needs you have as well as most of your wants.

financial happiness
The experience you have when you are satisfied with your money matters, which is in part a result of practicing good financial behaviors.

DID YOU KNOW

Bias Toward Thinking Negatively

People engaged in the understanding personal finance have a bias toward certain behaviors that can be harmful, such as a tendency toward thinking negatively about their level of living. These people compare their personal finances to others a lot and care about the results. And, they tend to feel better when others are doing poorly. What to do? Focus on your own goals and resist comparing your situation to others.

The Five Fundamental Steps in the Financial Planning Process

There are five fundamental steps to the personal financial planning process: (1) Evaluate your financial condition relative to your education and career choice; (2) define your financial goals; (3) develop a plan of action to achieve your goals; (4) implement your plan; and

(5) review your financial progress and make changes as appropriate.

As indicated in step 5, this process is revisited periodically, ideally every year, and whenever your life takes a meaningful turn such as a new job, marriage, birth of a child, or even after a sad event such as a divorce or death of a family member.

1.1b Spend Less So You Can Save and Invest More

Financial objectives are rarely achieved without forgoing or sacrificing current **consumption** (spending on goods and services). This restraint is accomplished by putting money into **savings** (income not spent on current consumption) for use in achieving future goals. Some savings are actually **investments** (assets purchased with the goal of providing additional future income from the asset itself). By saving and investing, people are much more likely to have funds available for future consumption. If you save for tomorrow, you will be happier today *and* tomorrow.

Effective financial management often separates the *haves* from the *have-nots*. The haves are those people who learn to live on less than they earn and are the savers and investors of society. The have-nots are the spenders who live paycheck to paycheck, usually with high consumer debt. They fail to manage money and as a result money manages them.

Being frugal is not about abstinence. It is about being smart in personal finance. Saving money does not make you cheap; it makes you smarter than those who just spend

savings
Income not spent on current consumption.

investments
Assets purchased with the goal of providing additional future income from the asset itself.

Figure 1-1   Building Blocks to Achieving Financial Success

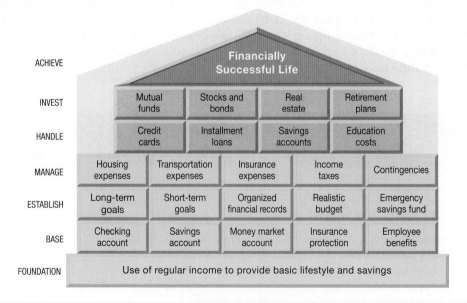

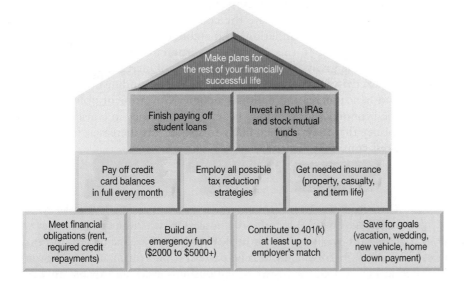

Figure 1-2   **How to Get Your Financial House in Order by Age 30**

Make plans for the rest of your financially successful life

Finish paying off student loans

Invest in Roth IRAs and stock mutual funds

Pay off credit card balances in full every month

Employ all possible tax reduction strategies

Get needed insurance (property, casualty, and term life)

Meet financial obligations (rent, required credit repayments)

Build an emergency fund ($2000 to $5000+)

Contribute to 401(k) at least up to employer's match

Save for goals (vacation, wedding, new vehicle, home down payment)

standard of living
Material well-being and peace of mind that individuals or groups earnestly desire and seek to attain, to maintain if attained, to preserve if threatened, and to regain if lost.

and spend. Spending less is about prioritizing your choices. You should think about making good choices in life when making every day spending decisions by asking yourself "What is most important to me?" This helps you get out of the habit of simply spending money and making choices that will enhance your life.

Saving for future consumption represents a good illustration of the human desire to achieve a certain **standard of living**. This standard is what an individual or group earnestly desires and seeks to attain, to maintain if attained, to preserve if threatened, and to regain if lost. Our standards include our wants and needs—our comforts and luxuries too. In contrast, individuals actually experience their **level of living** at any particular time. In essence, your standard of living is where you would like to be, and your level of living is where you actually are.

Figure 1-1 shows the building blocks to achieving financial success and how they fit together. Figure 1-2 shows how to get your financial house in order by age 30. Accomplish these steps and you will be financially successful.

FINANCIAL POWER POINT

Dreams Are Not Goals

Everybody has dreams about financial success. But only by setting clear financial goals with specific plans for their achievement will you achieve financial success in the future.

CONCEPT CHECK 1.1

1. Distinguish among financial success, financial security, and financial happiness.

2. Explain the five fundamental steps in the financial planning process.

3. What are the building blocks to achieving financial success?

1.2 THE ECONOMY AFFECTS YOUR PERSONAL FINANCIAL SUCCESS

LEARNING OBJECTIVE 2

Understand how the economy affects your personal financial success.

Your success in personal finance depends in part on how well you understand the economic environment; the current stage of the business cycle; and the future direction of the economy, inflation, and interest rates.

DID YOU KNOW

Your Worst Financial Blunders in Understanding Personal Finance

Based on other's financial woes, you will make personal finance mistakes when you:

1. *Only think about money matters when you have a financial problem*
2. *Spend more than you earn*
3. *Believe and act on financial advice from amateurs rather than trust professional sources*

economic growth

A condition of increasing production (business spending) and consumption (consumer spending) in the economy and hence increasing national income.

business cycle/economic cycle

Business cycles can be depicted as a wavelike pattern of rising and falling economic activity; the phases of the business cycle include expansion, peak contraction (which may turn into recession), and trough.

deleveraging

A time period when credit use shrinks in an economy instead of expanding as during normal economic times.

recession

A recurring period of decline in total output, income, employment, and trade, usually lasting from six months to a year and marked by widespread contractions in many sectors of the economy.

1.2a How to Tell Where We Are in the Business Cycle

An economy is a system of managing the productive and employment resources of a country, state, or community. The U.S. federal government attempts to regulate the country's overall economy to maintain stable prices (low inflation) and stable levels of employment (low unemployment). In this way, the government seeks to achieve sustained **economic growth**, which is a condition of increasing production (business activity) and consumption (consumer spending) in the economy—and hence increasing national income. Government policies also affect the economy. For example, tax cuts keep money in consumers' pockets, money that they are then likely to spend. Tax increases, in contrast, depress consumer demand.

1.2b The Business Cycle

Growth in the U.S. economy varies over time. The **business cycle** (also called the **economic cycle**) is a process by which the economy grows and contracts over time. It can be depicted as a wavelike pattern of rising and falling economic activity in which the same pattern occurs again and again over time. As illustrated in Figure 1-3, the phases of the business cycle are expansion (when the economy is increasing), peak (the end of an expansion and the beginning of a contraction), contraction (when the economy is falling), and trough (the end of a contraction and beginning of an expansion).

The preferred stage of the economic cycle is the **expansion phase**, where production is at high capacity, unemployment is low, retail sales are high, and prices and interest rates are low or falling. Under these conditions, consumers find it easier to buy homes, cars, and expensive goods on credit, and businesses are encouraged to borrow to expand production to meet the increased consumer demand. The stock market also rises because investors expect higher profits in the future.

As the demand for credit increases, short-term interest rates rise because more borrowers want money. Consumers and businesses purchase more goods, exerting upward pressure on prices. Eventually, prices and interest rates climb high enough to stifle consumer and business borrowing, send stock prices down, and choke off the expansion. One effect of such economic turmoil is **deleveraging**, meaning that instead of normal economic times when credit usage grows, it shrinks because companies and individuals pay down their debts. When businesses and consumers use less debt, home and car sales decline as does employment. The result is a period of negligible economic growth or even a decline in economic activity.

In such situations, the economy often contracts and moves toward a **recession**. During recessions, consumers become pessimistic about their future buying plans. The typical U.S. recession is marked by an average economic decline of 2 percent that lasts for ten months with an average unemployment rate exceeding 6 percent.

There have been five recessions since 1980. The federal government's Business Cycle Dating Committee of the National Bureau of Economic Research officially defines a recession as "a period of falling economic activity spread across the economy, lasting more than a few months, normally visible in real gross domestic product, real income, employment, industrial production, and wholesale-retail sales."

The Aftermath of the Great Recession The Great Recession began in December 2007 and ended in June 2009. The recession lasted 18 months, which makes it the longest of any recession since World War II.

The economy contracted 5.1 percent during the Great Recession, and it was of historic proportions. It was the worst economic contraction since the Great Depression of 1929–1941. During the Great Recession nine million people in the United States

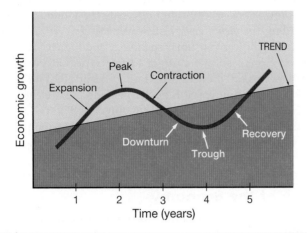

Figure 1-3   **Business Cycle Phases**

had their jobs disappear as unemployment surpassed 10 percent. Half of all American workers suffered job losses, pay cuts, or reduced hours at work, or they were forced into part-time employment.

Many people of your parents' ages saw the value of their homes shrink 25 to 65 percent while at the same time half of their retirement funds evaporated. The Great Recession destroyed 20 percent of American's wealth in home values and investments. Surveys revealed that over 60 percent of those between age 50 and 61 have had to delay their retirements, and the average retirement age rose three years since 2008. Consumer confidence dropped to an all-time low.

Years later the U.S. economy is still dealing with the aftermath of the Great Recession. We continue to experience slow economic growth and relatively high unemployment. It took four years (until 2013) for stock prices to recover and to see home prices recover in most communities.

FINANCIAL POWER POINT

Double Dip Recession

Some people fear that continued downward pressure from relatively weak wages and demand may result in a **double dip recession**. This occurs when the economy has a recession and then, soon after emerging from the recession with a short period of growth, falls back into recession.

The Economic Future . . . Eventually . . . Will Be Expansion   Despite the severity or length of any recession, eventually the economic contraction ends, and consumers and businesses become more optimistic. The economy then moves beyond the trough toward recovery and expansion, where levels of production, employment, and retail sales begin to improve, allowing the overall economy to experience some growth from its previously weakened state. The entire business cycle typically takes about six years.

Politicians and economic advisors struggle with which path to take to create economic growth. Most of the world has followed the Keynesian economic theory since the 1930s, which is to increase demand with stimulus spending even if it creates large temporary government deficits. The logic is that when consumers and businesses spend less, the economy will be depressed unless the government spends more. Such spending creates additional economic growth that results in increased tax revenues, thus resulting in budget surpluses that can be used to pay down the debts.* Now, however, the deficits themselves are seen as the problem by some U.S. politicians and in other countries resulting in calls to slash public outlays. Others say such an austerity approach will lead

* The last budget surpluses in the United States were during the last two years of the Clinton presidency (1999 and 2000). Every year since 1970, Congress has authorized more spending than projected revenue.

FINANCIAL POWER POINT

You Can Be Optimistic About Your Future

During slow or sluggish economic times people face uncertain financial futures. However, this does not mean that they should stop saving and investing for their futures. Every generation has faced similar uncertainties. You should be positive about the long-term economic future. Make sound, prudent decisions regarding spending, saving, and investing by putting in practice what you learn in this book.

economic indicator
Any economic statistic, such as the unemployment rate, GDP, or the inflation rate, that suggests how well the economy is doing now and how well it might be doing in the future.

gross domestic product (GDP)
The nation's broadest measure of economic health; it reports how much economic activity (all goods and services) has occurred within the U.S. borders during a given period.

leading economic indicators
Statistics that change before the economy changes, thus helping predict how the economy will do in the future, such as the stock market, the number of new building permits, and the consumer confidence index.

to lower demand, lower growth, lower tax revenues, stock market declines, and an even higher national debt, as has occurred in Greece, Ireland, Portugal, Spain, and Great Britain.

No matter what path is chosen, the 2007 to 2009 contraction of the economy will have costly after effects in the United States for years to come, including the *new normal* of slower job growth, slimmer paychecks, less borrowing, lower consumer spending, and higher savings.

The Congressional Budget Office says that given the severity of the Great Recession, it could take until 2022 or 2023 for unemployment to get back to the more typical 5 or 5½ percent and see the economy return to a healthy growth rate of 3+ percent annually. The U.S. economy has to grow around 2.5 percent a year just to keep up with rising productivity and population growth, and to keep unemployment from rising.

1.2c   How to Tell the Future Direction of the Economy

To make sound financial decisions, you need to know where we are in the business cycle, how well the economy is doing, and where the economy might be headed. You can do this by paying attention to some economic statistics that are regularly reported in the news as well as on cable TV business shows. Your knowledge can help guide your long-term financial strategy. An **economic indicator** is any economic statistic, such as the unemployment rate, GDP, or the inflation rate (terms discussed in the next few paragraphs), that suggests how well the economy is doing and how well the economy might do in the future.

Look at Procyclic Indicators, like GDP and Jobs   A **procyclic** (or **procyclical**) economic indicator is one that moves in the same direction as the economy. Thus if the economy is doing well, this number typically is increasing. If we are in a recession, this indicator is decreasing. Examples of procyclic indicators are retail sales, industrial production, new orders for durable goods (like household appliances), number of employees on nonagricultural payrolls, and the gross domestic product. Consumer spending accounts for about 70 percent of the total U.S. economy.

The best understood example of a procyclic economic indicator is the **gross domestic product (GDP)**, which is the broadest measure of the economic health of the nation because it reports how much economic activity (all goods and services) has occurred within the U.S. borders. The government regularly announces the rate at which the GDP has grown during the previous three months (www.bea.gov/newsreleases/rels.htm). In the United States, an annual rate of 2 percent or less is considered very low growth (not even enough to create jobs for new entrants to the job market such as college graduates), and 3 percent is considered growth occurring at a safe speed that is not likely to induce excessive inflation. A sustained rate of 4 percent or higher starts to worry economists and investors. The United States needs a GDP growth rate of about 2.5 percent just to keep unemployment from rising and much faster economic growth, such as a growth rate of 4 or 5 percent, to bring the unemployment rate significantly down.

Look at Countercyclic Indicators   A **countercyclic** (or **countercyclical**) economic indicator is one that moves in the opposite direction from the economy. For example, the unemployment rate is countercyclic because it gets larger as the economy gets worse. Similarly, the price of gold rises as the economy gets worse since some people see gold as a safe haven in bad times (even though it is not).

Look at Leading Indicators   **Leading economic indicators** are those that change before the economy changes; thus, they help predict how the economy will do in the future. The stock market is a leading economic indicator because it usually begins to decline shortly before the overall economy slows down. Then the stock market advances before the economy begins to pull out of a recession. Other examples of leading economic indicators are the number of new building permits, existing home sales, home prices, jobless claims (average number of weekly first-time filings for unemployment benefits), the Standard & Poor's 500 Stock Index, and the consumer confidence index.

The **consumer confidence index** is a widely watched leading economic indicator that gauges how consumers feel about the economy and their personal finances. It gives a sense of consumers' willingness to spend (www.conference-board.org). Growing confidence suggests increased consumer spending. Consumers worried about the future postpone purchases, and the reduced spending acts as a drag on the economy.

The **index of leading economic indicators (LEI)** is a composite index, reported monthly by the Conference Board, that suggests the future direction of the U.S. economy (www.conference-board.org). The LEI averages ten components of growth from different segments of the economy, such as building permits, factory orders, and new private housing starts. Leading economic indicators are very important to investors as they help predict what the economy will be like in the future.

index of leading economic indicators (LEI)
A composite index reported monthly by the Conference Board that suggests the future direction of the U.S. economy.

1.2d The Future Direction of Inflation and Interest Rates

Prices and interest rates typically move in the same direction. A steady rise in the general level of prices is called **inflation**. Inflation is measured by the changing cost over time of a "market basket" of goods and services that a typical household might purchase. Inflation often occurs when the supply of money (or credit) rises faster than the supply of goods and services available for purchases. It also may be attributed to excessive demand or sharply increasing costs of production.

inflation
A steady and sustained rise in general price levels across economic sectors; measured by the changing cost over time of a "market basket" of goods and services that a typical household might purchase.

Inflation Is the Typical Economic Condition Some level of inflation is the typical condition in any economy and can be beneficial in moderation as it encourages job creation and economic growth. But when there is high inflation in the United States, perhaps 5 or 6 percent workers begin to push for higher wages, thereby adding to the cost of production. In response to the increases in the costs of labor and raw materials, manufacturers will charge more for their products. Lenders, in turn, will require higher interest rates to offset the lost purchasing power of the loaned funds. Consumers will lessen their resistance to price increases because they fear even higher prices in the future. Thus, inflation can have a snowball effect. In times of moderate to high inflation, buying power declines rapidly, and people on fixed incomes suffer the most. A very negative complication of inflation that sometimes occurs is **stagflation**, which is the condition of stagnant economic growth and high unemployment accompanied by rising prices.

Here Is How Inflation Is Measured The U.S. Bureau of Labor Statistics measures inflation on a monthly basis using the **consumer price index (CPI)**. The CPI is a broad measure of changes in the prices of all goods and services purchased for consumption by urban households. The prices of more than 400 goods and services (a "market basket") sold across the country are tracked, recorded, weighted for importance in a hypothetical budget, and totaled. In essence, the CPI is a cost of living index. The index has a base time period—or starting reference point—from which to make comparisons. The 1982 to 1984 time period represents the base period of 100. For example, if the CPI were 234 on January 1, 2015, the cost of living would have risen 121 percent since the base period [$(234 - 100) / 100 = 1.34$ or 134%]*. Similarly, if the index rises from 234 to 242 on January 1, 2016, then the cost of living will have increased by 3.4 percent over the year [$(242 - 234) / 234 = 0.034$ or 3.4%].

consumer price index (CPI)
A broad measure of changes in the prices of all goods and services purchased for consumption by urban households.

Here Is How Inflation Affects Your Income From an income point of view, inflation has significant effects. Consider the case of Scott Wade of Chicago, a single man who took a job in retail management three years ago at a salary of $50,000 per year.

---

* This equation shows how the percentage change is calculated for any difference between two measurements. Divide the difference between measurement 1 and measurement 2 by the value of measurement 1. For example, a stock selling for $65 per share on January 1 and for $76 on December 31 of the same year would have risen 16.92 percent during the year: [($76 − $65) ÷ $65 = 0.1692 or 16.92%.]

Since that time, Scott has received annual raises of $1000, $1200, and $1500, but he still cannot make ends meet because of inflation. Although Scott received raises, his current income of $53,700 ($50,000 + $1000 + $1200 + $1500) did not keep pace with the annual inflation rate of 3.0 percent ($50,000 × 1.03 = $51,500; $51,500 × 1.03 = $53,045; $53,045 × 1.03 = $54,636). If Scott's own cost of living rose at the same rate as the general price level, in the third year he would be $936 ($54,636 − $53,700) short of keeping up with inflation. He would need $936 more in the third year to maintain the same purchasing power that he enjoyed in the first year.

real income

Income measured in constant prices relative to some base time period. It reflects the actual buying power of the money you have as measured in constant dollars.

nominal income

Also called money income; income that has not been adjusted for inflation and decreasing purchasing power.

Personal incomes rarely keep up in times of high inflation. Your **real income** (income measured in constant prices relative to some base time period) is the more important number. It reflects the actual buying power of the **nominal income** (also called money income) that you have to spend as measured in current dollars. Rising nominal income during times of inflation creates the illusion that you are making more money, when in actuality that may not be true.

To compare your annual wage increase with the rate of inflation for the same time period, you first convert your dollar raise into a percentage, as follows:

$$\text{Percentage change} = \frac{\text{nominal annual income after raise} - \text{nominal annual income last year}}{\text{nominal annual income last year}} \times 100$$

(1.1)

For example, imagine that Javier Gomez, a single parent and assistant manager of a convenience store in Windermere, Florida, received a $1600 raise to push his $37,000 annual salary to $38,600. Using Equation (1.1), Javier calculated his percentage change in personal income as follows:

$$\frac{(\$38,600 - \$37,000)}{\$37,000} = 0.043 \times 100 = 4.3\%^*$$

After a year during which inflation was 4.0 percent, Javier did better than the inflation rate because his raise amounted to 4.3 percent. Measured in real terms, his raise was 0.3 percent (4.3 − 4.0). In dollars, Javier's real income after the raise can be calculated by dividing his new nominal income by 1.0 plus the previous year's inflation rate (expressed as a decimal):

DO IT IN CLASS

$$\text{Real income} = \frac{\text{nominal annual income after raise}}{1.0 + \text{previous inflation rate}}$$

(1.2)

$$\frac{\$38,600}{1 + 0.040} = \$37,115$$

ADVICE FROM A PROFESSIONAL

Seven Money Mantras for a Richer Life

1. It's not an asset if you are wearing it!
2. Is this a need or is it a want?
3. Sweat the small stuff.
4. Cash is better than credit.
5. Keep it simple.
6. Priorities lead to prosperity.
7. Enough is enough!

Michelle Singletary

Nationally syndicated Washington Post *columnist ("The Color of Money") and author of* The Power to Prosper: 21 Days to Financial Freedom.

Reprinted with permission of the author.

Clearly, a large part of the $1600 raise Javier received was eaten up by inflation. To Javier, only $115 ($37,115 − $37,000) represents real economic progress, while $1485 ($1600 − $115) was used to pay the inflated prices on goods and services. The $115 real raise is equivalent to 0.31 percent ($115 / $37,000, or less than 1 percent) of his previous income, reflecting the difference between Javier's percentage raise in nominal dollars and the inflation rate.

Here Is How Inflation Affects Your Consumption When prices are rising, an individual's income must rise at the same rate to maintain its **purchasing power**, which is a measure of the goods and services that one's income will buy. When prices rise, the purchasing power of the dollar declines, but not by the same percentage. Instead, it falls by the *reciprocal amount* of the price increase (the counterpart ratio quantity needed to produce unity).

In the preceding illustration where prices increase between 2015 and 2016, prices rose 2.1 percent, whereas the purchasing power of the dollar declined 2.07 percent over the same period. [The previous year base of 237 divided by the index of 242 equals 0.9793; the reciprocal is 0.0207 (1 − 0.9793), or 2.07%.].

The **Rule of 70** can be used to determine how long it will take for the value of the dollar to go down by one-half. Simply divide 70 by the current inflation rate. In our example, a 2.1 percent inflation rate would reduce the value of a dollar by one-half in 33 years (70 / 2.1). As you can see, even a low inflation rate means that by the time a young worker retires, the purchasing power of their initial income will have dropped significantly.

Inflation pushes up the costs of the products and services we consume. If automobile prices rose 20 percent over the past five years, for example, then it will take $28,800 now to buy a car that once sold for $24,000 ($24,000 × 1.20). If your market basket of goods and services differs from that used to calculate the CPI, you might have a very different **personal inflation rate** (the rate of increase in prices of items purchased by a particular person). Inflation pushes up the cost of borrowing, so monthly car payments and home mortgage rates increase when inflation rises.

Deflation Can Be Bad, Too During a severe recession there is the possibility of **deflation**, which is a broad, sustained decline in prices of goods and services. Deflation last occurred in the United States in 2009 as prices declined 0.34 percent during the year, and prices continued to decline during the early months of 2010. When faced with deflation, government policymakers often embark on massive spending programs to stimulate the economy. Such spending, of course, creates high national liabilities that ideally could be repaid when the economy is strong.

You Can Track the Federal Funds Rate to Forecast Interest Rates and Inflation One of the mandates of the Federal Reserve Board (an agency of the federal government commonly referred to as the "**Fed**") is to "promote maximum employment and price stability." You can forecast interest rates and inflation by paying attention to changes in the **federal funds rate**, which is the short-term rate at which banks lend funds to other banks overnight so that the borrowing bank has sufficient reserves as mandated by the Fed. The federal funds rate is set by the Fed and is a benchmark for business and consumer loans and an indication of future Fed policy. The Fed lowers the federal funds rate to boost the economy in slow economic times and raises it to slow down an overheated economy. The Fed has kept the federal funds rate low for the past decade, but as the economy expands it will allow rates to go up. The Fed's goals are inflation at 2 percent or a bit lower, interest rates at 3 percent or a bit lower, and unemployment at 5 percent or a bit higher.

Here Is How Inflation Affects Your Borrowing, Saving, and Investing Interest is the price of money. During times of high inflation, interest rates on new loans for cars, homes, and credit cards rise. Even though nominal interest rates for savers rise as well, the increases do not provide "real" gains if the inflation rate is higher than the interest rate on savings accounts or certificates of deposit.

purchasing power

Measure of the goods and services that one's income will buy.

Rule of 70

A formula to determine how long it will take for the value of a dollar to decline by one-half.

DO IT IN CLASS

deflation

A broad, sustained decline in prices of goods and services that is hard to stop once it takes hold, causing less consumer spending, lower corporate profits, declining home values, rising unemployment, and lower incomes.

fed

The Federal Reserve Board, an agency of the federal government.

federal funds rate

The short-term rate at which depository institutions lend balances at the Federal Reserve to other depository institutions overnight.

interest

The price of borrowing money.

Xinhua/Sipa USA/Newscom

The Fed meets regularly to discuss the economy and review federal interest rates.

Smart investors recognize that the degree of inflation risk is higher for long-term lending (5 to 20 years, for example) than for short-term lending (such as a year) because the likelihood of error when estimating inflation increases when lots of time is involved. Therefore, long-term interest rates are generally higher than short-term interest rates. Similarly, stock market investors are negatively affected when inflation causes businesses to pay more when they borrow, thereby reducing their profits and depressing stock prices. When inflation is at 5 percent annually, a dollar of profit that a company will earn a year from now will be worth only 95 cents in today's prices. If instead inflation were only 2 percent, that dollar would be worth 98 cents today. Such differences add up to significant amounts over many years.

Throughout your financial life, you will want to factor the impact of inflation into your financial decisions in an effort to reduce its negative effects.

In summary, to assess the economic outlook for the United States, watch these indicators: (1) GDP and jobs, including unemployment rate changes; (2) procyclic items like inflation and interest rates; (3) countercyclic items like unemployment and gold prices; (4) leading indicators like the consumer confidence index, LEI, and the stock market; (5) interest rates; and (6) the federal funds rate.

DO IT IN CLASS

DID YOU KNOW

Bias Toward Thinking Things Will Continue as They Have

People engaged in the understanding personal finance have a bias toward certain behaviors that can be harmful, such as a tendency toward thinking things will go on as they have

recently. During a rising stock market people often will think that things will continue as they have for many more months. What to do? Watch for economic indicators that suggest that the economy and the stock market are reaching a peak and sell stocks that are likely to decline as the economy eventually slows.

CONCEPT CHECK 1.2

1. Summarize the phases of the business cycle.

2. Describe two statistics that help predict the future direction of the economy.

3. Give an example of how inflation affects income and consumption.

1.3 THINK LIKE AN ECONOMIST WHEN MAKING FINANCIAL DECISIONS

Understanding and applying basic economic principles will affect your financial success. The most important of these are opportunity costs, marginal utility and costs, and marginal income tax rate.

1.3a Consider Opportunity Costs When Making Decisions

The **opportunity cost** of a decision is the value of the next best alternative that must be forgone. A simple example of opportunity costs in personal finance is spending money on current living expenses, which, of course, reduces the amount you can save and invest and the opportunity to earn interest and dividends. Also, buying on credit results in monthly payments later, which reduces the opportunity to make desired purchases in the future. It is not just the payments and interest that is the cost of credit but other uses of those funds. If opportunity costs are underestimated, then decisions will be based on faulty information, and judgments may prove wrong. Properly valuing opportunity costs of alternatives represents a key step in rational decision making.

Using the concept of opportunity costs in your thinking allows you to address the personal consequences of choices because every decision inevitably involves trade-offs. A **trade-off** is giving up one thing for another. For example, it is wise to give up some current spending in order to enjoy a financially comfortable future. For example, suppose that instead of reading this book you could have gone to a movie or watched television, but mainly you wanted to sleep. The lost benefit of reading—the next best alternative—is the opportunity cost when you choose sleep. Similarly, keeping the money in a savings account has the opportunity cost of the higher return on investment that a stock market mutual fund might pay. This opportunity to earn a higher rate of return is a primary opportunity cost when making low-risk investment decisions. Other challenging opportunity cost decisions are renting versus buying housing, buying a new or used car, working or borrowing to pay for college, and starting early or late to save and invest for retirement.

opportunity cost
The opportunity cost of any decision is the value of the next best alternative that must be forgone.

trade-off
Giving up one thing for another.

FINANCIAL POWER POINT

Save $4.66 for Every $1 Not Saved Earlier

If you want to retire at age 65, you will have to save about $4.66 beginning at age 42 to make up for every dollar you did not save at age 22.

1.3b Identify Marginal Utility and Costs in Your Decision Making

Utility is the ability of a good or service to satisfy a human want. A key task in personal finance is to determine how much utility you will gain from a particular decision. For example, if you decide to spend $90 on a ticket to a concert, you might begin by thinking about what you might gain from the expenditure. Perhaps you'll enjoy a nice evening, good music, and so on.

Marginal utility is the extra satisfaction derived from having one more incremental unit of a product or service. **Marginal cost** is the additional (marginal) cost of one more incremental unit of some item. When known, this cost can be compared with the marginal utility received. Thinking about marginal utility and marginal cost can help in decision making because it reminds us to compare only the most important variables. It requires that we examine what we will really gain if we also experience a certain extra cost.

To illustrate this idea, assume that you will consider spending $150 instead of $90 (an additional $60) for a ground floor seat at the concert. What marginal utility will you gain from that decision? Perhaps it is the ability to see and hear more or the satisfaction of having one of the best seats in the house. You would then ask yourself whether those extra benefits are worth 60 extra dollars. In practice, people are inclined to seek additional utility as long as the marginal utility exceeds the marginal cost.

marginal utility
The extra satisfaction derived from gaining one more incremental unit of a product or service.

marginal cost
The additional (marginal) cost of one more incremental unit of some item.

In another example, imagine that two new automobiles are available on a dealership lot in Ferndale, Michigan, where chemical engineer Pamela Hicks is trying to make a purchase decision. The first, with a sticker price of $29,100, has a moderate number of options; the second, with a sticker price of $32,800, has numerous options. Marginal analysis suggests that Pamela does not need to consider all of the options when comparing the vehicles. Instead, the concept of marginal cost says to compare the benefits of the additional options with the additional costs—$3700 in this instance ($32,800 − $29,100). Pamela needs to decide if the additional options are worth $3700.

1.3c   Factor Your Marginal Income Tax Rate When Making Financial Decisions

marginal tax rate

The tax rate at which your last dollar earned is taxed.

Financial decisions often have an impact on the income taxes one must pay. Of particular importance is your **marginal tax rate**, which is the tax rate at which your last dollar earned (not all your income) is taxed. As income rises, taxpayers pay progressively higher marginal income tax rates. Financially successful people often pay U.S. federal income taxes at the 25 percent, or higher, marginal tax rate on the top segment of their income. For example, if Juanita Martinez, an unmarried office manager working in Atlanta, Georgia, has a taxable income of $66,000 and receives a $1000 bonus from her employer, she has to pay an extra $250 in taxes on the bonus income ($1000 × 0.25 = $250). Juanita also has to pay state federal income taxes of 6 percent, or $60 ($1000 × 0.06 = $60), local income taxes of 2 percent and Social Security and Medicare taxes of 7.65 percent, or $76.50 ($1000 × 0.0765 = $76.50). Therefore, Juanita pays an effective marginal tax rate of just over 40 percent (25% + 6% + 2% + 7.65% = 40.65%), or $406.50, on the extra $1000 of earned income.

tax-exempt income

Income that is totally and permanently free of taxes.

The Very Best Kind of Income Is Tax-Exempt Income   The best kind of income, as this discussion implies, is **tax-exempt income**, which is income that is totally

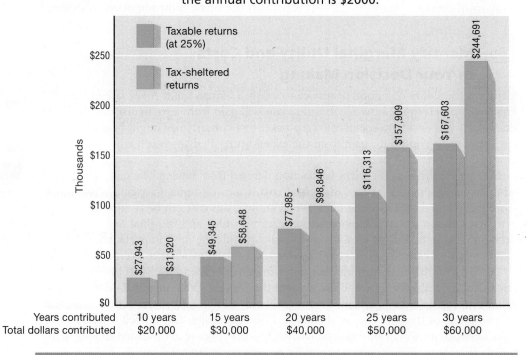

Figure 1-4   Tax-Sheltered Returns Are Greater Than Taxable Returns

In the illustration, the annual return is 8 percent and the annual contribution is $2000.

	10 years	15 years	20 years	25 years	30 years
Taxable returns (at 25%)	$27,943	$49,345	$77,985	$116,313	$167,603
Tax-sheltered returns	$31,920	$58,648	$98,846	$157,909	$244,691
Years contributed	10 years	15 years	20 years	25 years	30 years
Total dollars contributed	$20,000	$30,000	$40,000	$50,000	$60,000

and permanently free of taxes. People who pay high marginal tax rates often seek out tax-exempt investments, such as buying bonds issued by various agencies of states and municipalities. For example, Serena Miller, a married chiropractor with two children from Prescott, Arizona, currently earns $250 per year on $5000 in stocks and pays $62.50 in federal income tax on that income at her 25 percent marginal tax rate ($250 × 0.25). Alternatively, a tax-exempt $5000 state bond paying 4 percent will provide Serena with a better after-tax return, $200.00 instead of $187.50.

The Second Best Kind of Income Is Tax-Sheltered Income The second best kind of income for individuals is **tax-sheltered (or tax-deferred) income**—that is, income that is exempt from income taxes in the current year but that will be subject to taxation in a later tax year. Figure 1-4 shows that tax-sheltered returns on savings and investments provide much greater returns than returns on which income taxes have to be paid because more money remains available to be invested. In addition, tax-sheltered funds grow more rapidly because compounding (the subject of the next section in this chapter) is enhanced when larger dollar amounts continue to grow especially during the latter years of an investment.

tax-sheltered (or tax-deferred) income

Income exempt from income taxes in the current year but that will be subject to taxation in a later tax year.

CONCEPT CHECK 1.3

1. Define *opportunity cost* and give an example of how opportunity costs might affect your financial decision making.

2. Explain and give an example of how marginal analysis makes some financial decisions easier.

3. Describe and give an example of how income taxes can affect financial decision making.

1.4 PERFORM TIME VALUE OF MONEY CALCULATIONS

A dollar in your pocket today is worth more than a dollar to be received five years from now. Why? Time is money.

The **time value of money** (TVM) is perhaps the single most important concept in personal finance. **TVM** is the cost of money that is borrowed or lent, and it commonly referred to as interest. TMV adjusts for the fact that dollars to be received or paid out in the future are not equivalent to those received or paid out today. It is easy to understand that a dollar received today is worth more than a dollar received five years from now because today's dollar can be saved or invested and earn some kind of return, such as interest, so that in five years you expect it to be worth more than a dollar. The time value of money involves two components: future value and present value.

LEARNING OBJECTIVE 4

Perform time value of money calculations in personal financial decision making.

time value of money

A method by which one can compare cash flows across time, either as what a future cash flow is worth today (present value) or what an investment made today will be worth in the future (future value). Also, the cost of money that is borrowed or lent; it is commonly referred to as interest and adjusts for the fact that dollars to be received or paid out in the future are not equivalent to those received or paid out today.

1.4a There Are Only Two Common Questions About Money

To illustrate the time value of money, two questions in personal finance are commonly asked:

1. What will an investment (or a series of investments) be worth after a period of time? This question asks for a future value, which is referred to as compounding.

2. How much has to be put away today (or as a series of investments) to provide some dollar amount in the future? This question asks for a present value.

As you can see from these two questions, comparisons between time periods cannot be made without making adjustments to money values. Accordingly, time value of money calculations compare future and present values by taking into account the interest rate (or investment rate of return) and the time period involved.

principal

The original amount invested.

compound interest

Compound interest is earning of interest on interest and arises when interest is added to the principal so that, from that moment on, the interest that has been added also earns interest.

compounding

The addition of interest to principal; the effect of compounding depends on the frequency with which interest is compounded and the periodic interest rate that is applied.

Simple Interest The calculation of interest involves (1) the dollar amount, called the **principal**, (2) the rate of interest earned on the principal, and (3) the amount of time the principal is invested. One way of calculating interest is called simple interest and is illustrated by the simple interest formula

$i = prt$ where
p = the **principal** set aside
r = the **rate** of interest   (1.3)
t = the **time** in years that the funds are left on deposit

If someone saved or invested $1000 at 8 percent for four years, he would receive $320 in interest ($1000 $\times$ 0.08 $\times$ 4) over the four years.

Compounding Is the Basis of All Time Value of Money Considerations

But something is missing in the simple interest calculation. The simple interest formula assumes that the interest is withdrawn each year and only the $1000 stays on deposit for the entire four years, and thus interest is not added to the principal. Most people do not invest this way. Instead, they leave the interest earned in the account so that it will earn additional interest. This earning of interest on interest is referred to as **compound interest**. It arises when interest is added to the principal, so that from that moment on the interest that has been added also itself earns interest. This addition of interest to the principal is called **compounding**. The effect of compounding depends on the frequency with which interest is paid and the periodic interest rate that is applied. Compound interest is always assumed in time value of money calculations.

Compounding is the best way to build investment values over time. Because of compounding, money grows much faster when the income from an investment is left in the account. In fact, the deposit of $1000 in our example would grow to $4,661 after 20 years (the calculation is described in the following paragraph). Many of the techniques for building wealth that we describe in this book are based on compounding. The way to build wealth is to make money on your money, not simply to put money away. Yes, you need to put money away first, but compounding over time is what really builds wealth.

Compounding serves as the basis of all time value of money considerations. To see how this works, let us look again at our example in which $1000 is invested at 8 percent for four years. Here is how the amount invested (or principal) would grow using compounding:

At the end of year 1, the $1000 would have grown to
    $1080 [$1000 + ($1000 $\times$ 0.08)].
At the end of year 2, the $1080 would have grown to
    $1166.40 [$1080 + ($1080 $\times$ 0.08)].
At the end of year 3, the $1166.40 would have grown to
    $1259.71 [$1166.40 + ($1166.40 $\times$ 0.08)].
At the end of year 4, the $1259.71 would have grown to
    $1360.49 [$1259.71 + ($1259.71 $\times$ 0.08)].

Due to the effects of compounding, this investor would have earned an additional $40.49 ($360.49 − $320). While this amount might not seem like much, realize that a $1000 investment for a longer period—say, 40 years—earning 8 percent interest would grow to $21,724.52, providing $20,724.52 in interest over that time period. Simple interest would have resulted in only $3200 in interest ($1000 $\times$ 0.08 $\times$ 40). The benefit of compounding over that time period is an additional $17,524.52 in interest ($20,724.52 − $3200).

The results are even more dramatic if $1000 is invested at the end of each year for 40 years. The total at the end of 40 years would be $259,056, with $219,056 representing the interest on the invested funds. This illustration suggests one of the cardinal rules of personal financial planning: Getting rich is not a function of investing a lot of money. It is the result of investing regularly for long periods of time. The greatest investment strategy of all is compounding. Only through compounding will you attain the serious growth of your wealth over time.

1.4b Calculating Future Values

Future value (FV) is the valuation of an asset projected to the end of a particular time period in the future. You can calculate the future value of a lump sum or the future value of a series of deposits.

future value
The valuation of an asset projected to the end of a particular time period in the future.

Future Value of a Lump Sum Equation (1.4) can be used to calculate the future value of a lump sum:

$$FV = (\text{Present value of sum of money})(1.0 + i)^n \quad \textbf{(1.4)}$$

where i represents the interest rate and n represents the number of time periods. Applying this formula to our earlier example of investing $1000 at 8 percent for four years, we obtain

$$\$1360.49 = (\$1000)(1 + 0.08)^4$$

or

$$\$1360.49 = (\$1000)(1.08)(1.08)(1.08)(1.08)$$

While mathematically correct, these calculations can be cumbersome when using long time periods. Table 1-1 provides a quick and easy way to determine the future dollar value of an investment. For the preceding example, use the table in the following manner: Go across the top row to the 8 percent column. Read down the 8 percent column to the row for four years to locate the factor 1.3605 (at the intersection of the dark brown column and row). Multiply that factor by the present value of the cash asset ($1000) to arrive at the future value ($1360.50).

Appendix A.1 provides an even more complete table for calculating the future value of lump-sum amounts. Figure 1-5 demonstrates the importance of higher yields and longer time horizons by showing the effects of various compounded returns on a $10,000 investment. The $10,000 will grow to $57,435 in 30 years with an interest rate of 6 percent. Compounding $10,000 at 10 percent yields $174,494 over the same time period; at 14 percent, it yields a whopping $509,502! For practice you might want to confirm these results using Appendix A.1.

DO IT IN CLASS

Table 1-1 Future Value of $1 After a Given Number of Periods

Periods	1%	2%	3%	4%	5%	6%	7%	8%	9%	10%
1	1.0100	1.0200	1.0300	1.0400	1.0500	1.0600	1.0700	1.0800	1.0900	1.1000
2	1.0201	1.0404	1.0609	1.0816	1.1025	1.1236	1.1449	1.1664	1.1881	1.2100
3	1.0303	1.0612	1.0927	1.1249	1.1576	1.1910	1.2250	1.2597	1.2950	1.3310
4	1.0406	1.0824	1.1255	1.1699	1.2155	1.2625	1.3108	1.3605	1.4116	1.4641
5	1.0510	1.1041	1.1593	1.2167	1.2763	1.3382	1.4026	1.4693	1.5386	1.6105
6	1.0615	1.1262	1.1941	1.2653	1.3401	1.4185	1.5007	1.5869	1.6771	1.7716
7	1.0721	1.1487	1.2299	1.3159	1.4071	1.5036	1.6058	1.7138	1.8280	1.9487
8	1.0829	1.1717	1.2668	1.3686	1.4775	1.5938	1.7182	1.8509	1.9926	2.1436
9	1.0937	1.1951	1.3048	1.4233	1.5513	1.6895	1.8385	1.9990	2.1719	2.3579
10	1.1046	1.2190	1.3439	1.4802	1.6289	1.7908	1.9672	2.1589	2.3674	2.5937

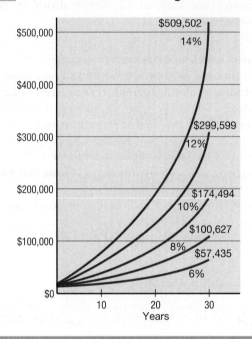

Figure 1-5   **The Importance of Higher Yields and More Time (Future Value of a Single Investment of $10,000)**

annuity

A stream of payments to be received in the future.

Future Value of a Stream of Payments (an Annuity) People often save for long-term goals by putting away a series of payments. Appendix A.3 provides a complete table for calculating the future value of a stream of deposited amounts, referred to as an **annuity**. You can use it to determine the effects of various compounded returns on a $2000 annual investment made at the end of each year. The $2000 will grow to $91,524 in 20 years (read across the interest rate row in Appendix A.3 to 8 percent and then down the column to 20 years to obtain the factor of 45.762 to multiply by $2000) and to $226,566 in 30 years at an 8 percent rate. Compounding $2000 at 10 percent yields $114,550 in 20 years and $328,988 over 30 years; at 14 percent, it becomes $713,574 after 30 years! As you can see, time builds wealth.

1.4c   Finding Present Values Is Called Discounting

Present value (or discounted value) is the current value of an asset (or stream of assets) that will be received in the future. **Discounting** is the process of reducing future values to present values. You can calculate the present value of a lump sum to be received in the future or the present value of a series of payments to be received in the future.

Present Value of a Single Lump Sum The present value of a lump sum is the current worth of an asset to be received in the future. Alternatively, it can be thought of as the amount you would need to set aside today at a given rate of interest for a given time period so as to have some desired amount in the future. Suppose you want to have $20,000 for the down payment on a new home in ten years. What would you need to set aside today to reach this goal if you could invest your money and receive a 7 percent return? Using Appendix A.2 you could look across the interest rate rows to 7 percent and then down to ten years to obtain the factor of 0.5083. Multiplying $20,000 by this factor reveals that $10,166 set aside today would allow you to reach your goal.

A simple formula for figuring the number of years it takes to double the principal using compound interest is the **Rule of 72**. Simply divide the interest rate that the money will earn into the number 72.

Present Value of a Stream of Payments (an Annuity) The present value of an annuity is the current worth of a stream of payments to be received in the future. Alternatively, it can be thought of as the amount you would need to set aside today at a given rate of interest for a given time period so as to receive that stream of payments. Suppose you want to have $30,000 per year for 20 years during your retirement. What amount would you need to have invested at retirement to reach this goal if you could invest your money and receive a 7 percent return? Using Appendix A.4 you could look across the interest rate rows to 7 percent and then down to 20 years to obtain the factor of 10.5940. Multiplying $30,000 by this factor reveals that $317,820 (10.5940 × $30,000) set aside at retirement would fund this stream of payments. Note the beauty of compound interest in this result. It takes only $317,820—not $600,000—to fund a $30,000 per year retirement for 20 years if you can earn 7 percent on your financial nest egg.*

CONCEPT CHECK 1.4

1. Explain the difference between simple interest and compound interest, and describe why that difference is critical.

2. What are the two components used when figuring the time value of money?

3. Use Table 1-1 to calculate the future value of (a) $2000 at 5 percent for four years, (b) $4500 at 9 percent for eight years, and (c) $10,000 at 6 percent for ten years.

1.5 MAKE SMART MONEY DECISIONS AT WORK

Smart decisions about your employee benefits can increase your actual income by 30 percent or more each year. An **employee benefit** is compensation for employment that does not take the form of wages, salaries, commissions, or other cash payments. Your benefits package might also include paid vacations and sick days, health insurance, a retirement plan, child care, and an educational assistance program.

LEARNING OBJECTIVE 5

Make smart decisions about your employee benefits.

employee benefit

Compensation for employment that does not take the form of wages, salaries, commissions, or other cash payments.

1.5a Choosing Tax-Free Cafeteria Plan Benefits

A **cafeteria** (or **flexible benefits**) **plan** is a type of employee benefit plan where employees choose their benefits from a "menu" of both taxable and one or more qualified nontaxable or tax-sheltered benefits, thereby providing a funding mechanism by which employees may pay for some of the benefits they choose on a pretax basis. For example, an employer might offer $4000 annually to each employee to spend on benefits. The plan might offer health insurance, life insurance, sick leave or disability benefits, medical expense reimbursement, vacation days, dependent care, adoption assistance, and orthodontia treatments. Employees choose the benefits they want and can design their own benefits package.

cafeteria plan (flexible benefits plan)

A type of employee benefit plan where employees choose their benefits from a "menu" of taxable and tax reducing benefits, thereby providing a funding mechanism by which employees may pay for some of the benefits they choose on a pretax basis.

* If you are using a financial calculator for time value of money calculations, see "How to Use a Financial Calculator" on the *Gorman/Forgue* companion website, or you can use the present and future value calculators also found on the *Garman/Forgue* companion website, www.cengagebrain.com.

1.5b   Making Decisions About Employer's Flexible Spending Accounts

flexible spending account (FSA)

An employer-sponsored account that allows employee-paid expenses for medical or dependent care to be paid with an employee's pretax dollars rather than after-tax income.

pretax dollars

Money income that has not been taxed by the government.

DO IT IN CLASS

Some employee benefits are tax-sheltered. A **flexible spending account (FSA)**, also called a flexible spending arrangement, is an employer-sponsored account that allows employee-paid expenses related to health and dependent care to be paid with **pretax dollars** (money income that has not been taxed by the government) rather than after-tax income. Under a typical FSA, the employee agrees to have a certain amount deducted from each paycheck that is then deposited into a separate account. There are two types of flexible spending accounts; the *medical and dental expense FSA* and the *dependent care FSA*. FSA contributions are limited to $2500. Dependent care FSA contributions are limited to $5000 per year. As eligible expenses are incurred, the employee requests and receives reimbursements from the account.

Because many workers pay combined effective marginal income tax rates (discussed earlier) of about 40 percent, that same percentage can be *saved* by not giving it to the government in taxes. The worker who contributes $5000, for example, to a flexible spending account (FSA) saves approximately $2000 ($5000 × 0.40) in taxes, further reducing his or her overall expenses.

Funds in a dependent care FSA account may be used to pay for the care of a dependent younger than age 13 or the care of another dependent who is physically or mentally incapable of caring for himself or herself and who resides in the taxpayer's home. Funds in a medical care FSA account may be used to pay for qualified, unreimbursed out-of-pocket expenses for health care, but they may not be used for over-the-counter medicines unless specifically prescribed by a doctor.

Before enrolling in an FSA, you need to estimate your expenses carefully so that the amount in the FSA does not exceed anticipated expenses. According to Internal Revenue Service (IRS) regulations, unused amounts are forfeited and are not returned to the employee—a condition called the "use it or lose it" rule. However, employers may choose to offer a 2½-month grace period during which time you can continue to spend up to $500 of the previous year's FSA money. Many employers offer debit cards that withdraw money directly from an employee's FSA. Only about 20 percent of eligible employees participate in flexible spending accounts, even though doing so saves money.

DID YOU KNOW

A Baker's Dozen of Good Financial Behaviors

Good financial behaviors to follow include these:

1. Develop a plan for your financial future.
2. Saving regularly and increase savings as income grows.
3. Follow a budget or spending plan to control and/or reduce living expenses.
4. Keep personal debts to a minimum.
5. Pay credit card bills in full each month.
6. Sign up to participate in employer's retirement plan.
7. Calculate how much money is needed for retirement and then save for it through your employer's plan and/or an individual retirement account (IRA).
8. Comparison shop for purchases.
9. Use a credit/budget counselor if debt becomes unmanageable.
10. Contemplate how economic events will affect personal financial decision making.
11. Consult a financial planner when faced with complicated financial questions.
12. Set aside an emergency fund sufficient to live on for three to six months.
13. Contribute to a flexible spending account at work.

1.5c Making Decisions About Employer-Sponsored Health Care Plans

Many employers offer employees a choice of **health care plans** to assist employees with their health care expenses. The premium for an employee's individual or family plan could be as high as $10,000 annually depending upon the amount of coverage selected. The premiums for employees are often either paid for entirely or partially by the employer. For example, some employers pay the first $3000 of annual premiums for employee health care coverage and require that employees pay the remainder. Employees usually can make a decision to change health plans once a year as well as when one's family situation changes, such as getting married.

Employers often offer multiple options for health care plans. These may include an expensive traditional health plan, perhaps with a high annual premium that offers comprehensive coverage requiring little out-of-pocket health care spending by the employee. Also frequently available is a less expensive **high-deductible health plan (HDHP)**, which has lower premiums and higher deductibles than a traditional health plan. The **deductible** is the amount paid to cover health care expenses before benefits begin. A policy with perhaps a $3500 premium might require larger out-of-pocket health care spending by the employee.

Younger employees, particularly those who are typically healthy, often select high-deductible plans to save on the cost of premiums. For example, if an employer pays only the first $3000 in health care premiums for employees, an employee selecting the high-cost plan described previously has to pay $6000 ($9000 premium − $3000 employer contribution) annually, or $500 a month in premiums. This contrasts with only a $500 total annual premium for employees who select the high-deductible plan ($3500 premium − $3000 employer contribution). The maximum out-of-pocket limit for HDHPs is $6250 for self-only coverage and $12,500 for self-and-family coverage, after which the policy is supposed to pay for all health expenses.

Some employers also offer **health savings accounts (HSAs)**. This special savings account is intended for people who have a high-deductible health care plan. Employees make tax-deductible contributions to a savings account to be used for eligible expenses. Employers may also contribute. The employee invests HSA funds, and the money in the account grows tax free. Withdrawals are made to pay for medical expenses. The limits on contributions to an HSA are $3300 per year for individuals and $6550 for families. The money in the account remains there even if you don't spend it within a certain time period.

health care plans
An employee benefit designed to pay all or part of the employee's medical expenses.

high-deductible health plan (HDHP)
A plan that requires individuals to pay a higher deductible to cover medical expenses before insurance plan payments begin; chosen to save money on premiums.

deductible
An initial portion of any loss that must be paid before collecting insurance benefits.

health savings accounts (HSAs)
Special savings account intended for people who have a high-deductible health care plan (with annual deductibles of at least $1000 for individuals and $2000 for families).

1.5d Making Decisions About Participating in Employer Insurance Plans

Life, disability, and long-term care insurance coverages are often available through employers. While the premiums charged for the group of employees for life insurance are rarely as low as those available in the general marketplace, some employers pay for part or all of employees' premiums. Coverage is typically one or two times the employee's salary. So, always sign up for free or subsidized life insurance at work. The premiums for disability and long-term care insurance are often less expensive when purchased through one's employer rather than in the general marketplace. See Chapters 10, 11, and 12 to begin to purchase any needed insurance coverage.

1.5e Making Decisions About Participating in Your Employer's Retirement Plan

More than half of all workers are covered by an employer-sponsored, defined-contribution retirement plan, also called a **tax-sheltered retirement plan**. These include 401(k) plans and similar 403(b) and 457 plans, as discussed in Chapter 17, "Retirement and Estate Planning." Employer-sponsored retirement plans provide four distinct advantages.

tax-sheltered retirement plan
Employer-sponsored, defined-contribution retirement plans including 401(k) plans and similar 403(b) and 457 plans.

DID YOU KNOW

Turn Bad Habits into Good Ones

Do You Do This?

Ignore news about the economy

Buy lots of extra features on products

Focus only on take-home pay

Don't know how much to save for retirement

Have not yet started to invest for retirement

Pay out-of-pocket expenses for health care

Get financial advice from friends

Do This Instead!

Watch business news on cable television

Use marginal costs in buying decisions

Sign up for employer tax-advantaged saving plans

Calculate future values

Begin investing as soon as possible

Use employer's cafeteria benefits plan for expenses

Seek advice of fee-only financial planner

First Advantage: Tax-Deductible Contributions Tax-sheltered retirement plans provide tremendous tax benefits compared with ordinary savings and investment plans. Because pretax contributions to qualified plans reduce taxable income, the current year's tax liability is lowered. The money saved in taxes can then be used to partially fund a larger contribution, which creates even greater returns. The 401(k) plan lets the IRS help employees finance their retirement plans because of the income taxes saved.

As Table 1-2 illustrates, you can save substantial sums for retirement with minimal effects on your monthly take-home pay. For example, a married man like Hongbok Lee of Macomb, Illinois, with a monthly taxable income of $4000 paying taxes at the 25 percent marginal tax rate who forgoes some spending and places $500 into a tax-sheltered retirement plan every month reduces monthly take-home pay from $3345 to $2970, or $375—that is certainly not an enormous amount.

The net effect is that it costs Hongbok only $375 to put away that $500 per month into a retirement plan. The immediate "return on investment" equals a fantastic 25 percent ($125 / $500). In essence, the taxpayer puts $375 into his or her retirement plan and the government contributes $125. (Without the plan, the taxpayer would pay the $125 directly to the government.) A taxpayer paying a higher marginal tax rate realizes even greater gains. Because a substantial part of your contributions to a tax-sheltered retirement plan comes from money that you would have paid in income taxes, it costs you less to save more. In addition, the Social Security Administration credits Hongbok with an earned income of $4000 a month rather than $3500.

Table 1-2   It Costs Only $375 a Month (or $4500) to Save $6000 a Year for Retirement

Monthly Taxable Income	$4000	Monthly Taxable Income	$4000
Pretax retirement plan contribution	0	Monthly Taxable Income	500
Monthly Taxable Income	4000	Monthly Taxable Income	3500
Federal taxes*	655	Federal taxes	530
Monthly take-home pay	3345	Monthly take-home pay	2970
		Cost to put away $500 per month ($3345 − $2970)	375
Amount put away for retirement	0	Annual amount put away for retirement	6000

* From Chapter 4; 25 percent income tax rate, single.

Second Advantage: Employer's Matching Contributions To retain employees and encourage saving for retirement, many employers also offer employer-paid **matching contributions** in addition to amounts contributed by the employee. Employers may match all or part of their employees' contributions. An employee who saves $250 might receive an additional $250 a month from his/her employer. That's a 100 percent return on the employee's $250! More typically, employer's match fifty percent of an employee's contributions up to a certain maximum—still, a nice 50 percent return.

Third Advantage: Employer's Contributions Are Not Income You will pay income taxes on any employer's contributions to your 401(k) retirement plan only when you withdraw from the account. That may not be until you retire and perhaps are in a lower tax bracket than you were in when the contributions were made.

Careful planning can result in a much more comfortable life when you retire.

Fourth Advantage: Tax-Deferred Growth Because interest, dividends, and capital gains from qualified plans are taxed only after funds are withdrawn from the plan, investments in tax-sheltered retirement plans grow tax-deferred. The benefits of tax deferral can be substantial.

For example, if a person in the 25 percent tax bracket invests $2000 at the end of every year for 30 years and the investment earns an 8 percent taxable return compounded annually, the fund will grow to $158,116 at the end of the 30-year period. As shown in Figure 1-5 on page 20, if the same $2000 invested annually were instead compounded at 8 percent within a tax-deferred program, it would grow to $226,566! The higher amount results from compounding at the full 8 percent and not paying any income taxes on investment income over the years. When the funds are finally taxed upon their withdrawal some years later, the taxpayer may be in a lower marginal tax bracket.

Fifth Advantage: Borrowing Lets You Tap Your Funds Without Income Taxes If you have an immediate need for cash, you can get it quickly by borrowing from your own 401(k) account. Your credit score doesn't matter and interest rates are low. All you need to do is ask your plan administrator for a loan and you do not have to explain why you need the money.

The most you can borrow is 50% of your account balance or $50,000, whichever is less. You have to repay the loan in level amounts over no more than five years (longer if the funds are used to buy a home), but you can pay it off more quickly with no penalty. If you're married, you must obtain your spouse's consent to the loan.

Sixth Advantage: Starting Early Really Pays Off Big Recall the rule of 72, which can be used to calculate the number of years it would take for a lump-sum investment to double. An 8 percent rate of return doubles an investment every nine years. Waiting eight years to begin saving (starting at age 31 instead of 22) results in the loss of one doubling. Unfortunately, it is the *last* doubling that is lost, as illustrated in Table 1-3. In the example, $48,000 ($96,000 − $48,000) is lost due to a hesitancy to invest $3000. That is a tremendously negative opportunity cost for waiting nine years to start. The financial gains in a 401(k) or other tax-sheltered retirement account will work best for you only if you begin to invest early in life. You cannot wait until your 40s to begin to save because the compounding boat will have sailed and you will have missed it.

Table 1-3	Starting to Save Early Versus Starting Late

Starting Earlier		Starting Later	
Age	$ Value	Age	$ Value
22	$ 3,000	22	$ 0
31	6,000	31	3,000
40	12,000	40	6,000
49	24,000	49	12,000
58	48,000	58	24,000
67	$ 96,000	67	$ 48,000

Starting to save $3000 eight years earlier (age 22 instead of 31) earns the investor an extra $48,000 ($96,000 − $48,000) assuming a compound growth rate of 8 percent.

The gains are awesome when you start early and make regular, continuing investments instead of delaying. The amounts invested do not have to be large to have a big impact. For example, a worker who starts saving $50 per week in a qualified retirement plan starting at age 22 will have a million dollars ($1,052,740) by age 66, assuming an annual rate of return of 8 percent. Waiting until age 30 to start saving, instead of beginning at age 23, results in a retirement fund of *only* about $540,950; about one-half of the larger amount. The benefit of starting to invest early is about $512,000 yet the total extra dollars invested over the ten years was only about $21,000! This effect occurs because most of the power of compounding appears in the last years of growth.

CONCEPT CHECK 1.5

1. Summarize the benefits of participating in a high-deductible health care plan at work.

2. Create a math example of why many employees participate in a tax-sheltered employee benefit plan, such as an HSA or 401(k) plan.

3. List two ways you can maximize the benefits from a tax-sheltered retirement program.

DID YOU KNOW

Sean's Success Story

Sean appears in every chapter of this book. Sean always makes good decisions in personal finance, and he aims to be financially successful and happy. Following graduation during his first year of work as a public relations analyst earning $60,000, Sean signed up for his employer's low-premium, high-deductible health care plan. Within his employer cafeteria benefits plan, he chose the tax-free options of excellent vacation days, maximum sick leave and disability benefits, and a dollar limit of medical expense reimbursements. Sean did some future value calculations on the cost of his eventual retirement and then filled out the forms to contribute

the maximum possible to his 401(k) retirement plan ($3000), and since he is in the 25 percent tax bracket, he saved $750 ($3000 × 0.25) in income taxes. His $3000 was fully matched by his employer, thus giving him $6000 to invest within his retirement plan. Since he expects the economy to expand in the coming years, Sean concluded this was an excellent time to invest in stocks as values will probably rise, so he put the full $6000 into those kinds of investments. Sean decided that when his retirement account reaches $50,000 (probably in about five years with continuing contributions and values growing at 8 percent), he will contact a fee-only financial planner for investment advice.

1.6 WHERE TO SEEK EXPERT FINANCIAL ADVICE

At various points in their lives, many people rely on the advice of a professional to make comprehensive financial plans and decisions. Most often financial planning advice is focused on a narrow area of one's finances. Professional advisers, such as lawyers, tax preparers, insurance agents, credit counselors, or stockbrokers, are often relied upon for advice. Much too often, however, these people are salespeople for specific financial services and receive compensation if they make a sale and as a result may not have your best interests at heart.

People often find it helpful to obtain the services of more broadly qualified financial experts. A **financial planner** is an investment professional who evaluates the personal finances of an individual or family and recommends strategies to set and achieve long-term financial goals. The most recognized professional designation for financial planners is the Certified Financial Planner (CFP®).

A good financial planner should be able to analyze a family's total needs in such areas as investments, taxes, insurance, education goals, and retirement and pull all of the information together into a cohesive plan. The planner may help a client select and prioritize goals and then rearrange assets and liabilities to fit the client's lifestyle, stage in the life cycle, and financial goals. Where appropriate, planners should make referrals to outside advisers, such as attorneys, accountants, trust officers, real estate brokers, stockbrokers, and insurance agents. Effective financial advice helps you make better day-to-day financial decisions so you have more to spend, save, invest, and donate. About half of large employers offer discounted visits to a financial planner.

The shape of the relationship between you and your financial advisor should be clear from the beginning. It should be spelled out in writing, and both you and the advisor should have a copy of the document. When the nature of the advice includes investments an **investment policy statement** is a must. Such a statement details your investment philosophy, your financial situation, and the risks you are willing to take, as well as what the advisor will do for you. It provides a road map of how he/she will guide the investing of your money.

Always ask if a financial advisor adheres to a **fiduciary standard** meaning that they must always act in the best interest of the client regardless of how it might affect the advisor. If the advisor says that such a standard is unnecessary be very wary of the advice given especially if it involves buying financial products through the advisor.

You can check the background of the planner you are considering. Self-regulatory organizations and government agencies are available to help.

- The Certified Financial Planner Board of Standards (CFP Board) assists those searching for a CFP as well as accepts complaints. Contact www.cfp.net or (800)487-1497.
- The National Association of Insurance Commissioners (NAIC) directs inquiries to the appropriate state agency where you can check on planners who also sell insurance products. Contact www.naic.org or (816)842-3600.
- The Financial Industry Regulatory Authority (FINRA) regulates U.S. security firms. Contact www.finra.org or (301)590-6500.
- The National Association of Personal Financial Advisors (NAPFA) assists those searching for a fee-only financial planner and sets standards for CFPs who are NAPFA Registered Financial Planners. Contact www.napfa.org or (847)483-5400.
- The Securities and Exchange Commission (SEC) regulates investment advisers and all securities dealers. Contact www.sec.gov or (800)732-0330.

1.6a How Financial Planners Are Compensated

One way or another, you will pay to get financial advice—commissions, fees, or lousy financial decisions—so assess the total costs up front as well as the opportunity costs. Financial planners earn their income in one of four ways:

1. **Commission-only financial planners and brokers** live solely on the commissions they receive on the financial products (such as investments or insurance) they sell to their clients. In this case, the plan will be "free," but a commission will be paid

---

LEARNING OBJECTIVE 6

Identify the professional certifications of providers of financial advice.

financial planner
An investment professional who evaluates the personal finances of an individual or family and recommends strategies to set and achieve long-term financial goals.

investment policy statement
A written document that spells out the relationship between an investor and his or her financial advisor and guides how the advisor will invest the person's money; it should detail the person's investment philosophy, financial situation, and the risks he or she is willing to take, as well as what tasks the advisor will perform.

fiduciary standard
A financial advisor must always act in the best interest of the client regardless of how it might affect the advisor.

ADVICE FROM A PROFESSIONAL

Questions to Ask a Financial Planner

Financial planners will influence your life and your future, so be sure to ask them these questions:

1. What experience do you have, such as work history and companies with which you have been associated?
2. Am I permitted a no-cost, initial consultation, and how much time is allowed?
3. What are your qualifications to practice financial planning, such as education, formal training, licenses, and credentials, and who can vouch for your professional reputation including some of your long-term clients?
4. Will you be the only person working with me or will an associate be involved in evaluating and updating the plan you suggest, and how often are formal reviews held with the client?

5. How do you evaluate my investment performance, and how often?
6. What process do you follow to identify a client's financial goals and may I see representative examples of financial plans, monitoring reports, and portfolios or actual case studies of your clients?
7. How much do you charge, what is your fee structure, how are you personally compensated, and if you earn commissions, how are they earned and from whom?
8. To whom would I take a complaint, if I had one?
9. Do you adhere to a fiduciary standard when working with your clients? Why or why not?
10. May I have a written agreement that details the points above and the services to be provided?

Joan Koonce
University of Georgia

to the adviser by the source of the financial product, such as an insurance company or mutual fund. Advantage: Save money if you make only a few transactions.

2. **Fee-based financial planners** charge an up-front fee for providing services and charge a commission on any securities trades or insurance purchases that they conduct on your behalf. Advantage: Unlimited consultations with broker.
3. **Fee-offset financial planners** charge an annual or hourly fee. That fee will be reduced by any commissions earned off the purchase of financial products sold to the client. Advantage: Fee will be reduced as you trade investments.

DID YOU KNOW

A Baker's Dozen of Bad Financial Behaviors

Poor financial behaviors to avoid include the following:

1. *Purchasing things in order to feel good or important*
2. *Reaching the maximum limit on a credit card*
3. *Spending more money than you make*
4. *Making a credit purchase after running out of money*
5. *Obtaining a cash advance on a credit card after running out of money or to pay on another credit card*
6. *Ignoring an overdue notice from a creditor*

7. *Paying a credit card, utility, or any other bill late*
8. *Borrowing money from a coworker or employer*
9. *Borrowing from 401(k) retirement plan at work*
10. *Taking an old employer's 401(k) money in cash when changing jobs*
11. *Using a debit card (or writing a check) with insufficient funds, incurring hefty overdraft fees*
12. *Lending to or borrowing money from friends or family*
13. *Following the financial advice of family or friends rather than qualified financial advisors*

Table 1-4 Financial Planner Professional Certifications

Many financial planners have voluntarily undergone training and satisfied various qualifications for particular professional certifications. Related work experience is often required.

Certification	Description	Contact Information
Accredited Estate Planner	Estate planning	(866) 226-2224 www.naepc.org
Certified Financial Planner (CFP®)	Best-known financial planning certification	(800) 487-1497 www.cfp.net
NAPFA Registered Financial Advisor (NRFA)	Source for fee-only financial advisors	(847) 483-5400 www.napfa.org
Chartered Financial Consultant (ChFC®)	Financial planning in insurance	(888) 263-7265 www.theamericancollege.edu
Chartered Life Underwriter (CLU®)	Life insurance	(888) 263-7265 www.theamericancollege.edu
Certified Public Accountant (CPA)	Income tax and estate planning	(888) 777-7077 www.aicpa.org
Personal Financial Specialist (PFS)	Personal finance credential for CPAs	(888) 777-7077 www.aicpa.org
Certified Trust and Financial Advisor (CTFA)	Trusts and taxes	(800) 226-5377 www.aba.com
Accredited Financial Counselor (AFC)	Financial counseling and money management	(614) 485-9650 www.afcpe.org
Chartered Mutual Fund Counselor (CMF®)	Mutual funds	(800) 237-9990 www.cffpinfo.com/cmfc.html
Registered Investment Adviser (RIA)	Investment adviser	(202) 551-6999 www.sec.gov

4. **Fee-only financial planners** earn no commissions and work solely on a fee-for-service basis—that is, they charge a specified fee (typically $50 to $200 per hour or 1 percent of the client's assets annually) for the services provided. They usually need five or more one-hour appointments to analyze a client's financial situation and to present a thorough plan. Fee-only planners do not sell financial products, such as stocks or insurance. As a result and unlike other financial planners/ brokers, they do not recommend products that earn them a commission at the lowest cost. Using a true fee-only financial planner has one big advantage; unbiased advice.

Remember, it's your money and your financial future. So when you use the services of a financial planner, don't be intimidated. Ask the hardest questions and don't leave the planner's office until you understand the answers.

DO IT NOW!

You know more about personal finance after reading this chapter, so get started right now by:

1. *Searching the Internet to identify the current stage in the business cycle;*

2. *Visiting www.bls.gov to determine the current inflation rate;*

3. *Going to www.conference-board.org to assess expectations for economic growth for the next 12 months.*

CONCEPT CHECK 1.6

1. What are the four ways financial planners may be compensated?

2. Describe two professional certification programs for financial planners.

WHAT DO YOU RECOMMEND *NOW?*

Now that you have read the chapter on the importance of personal finance, what do you recommend to Na Yeon in the case at the beginning of the chapter regarding:

1. Participating in her employer's 401(k) retirement plan?
2. Understanding the effects of her marginal tax rate on her financial decisions?
3. Considering the current state of the economy in her personal financial planning?
4. Using time value of money considerations to project what her IRA might be worth at age 63?
5. Using time value of money considerations to project what her 401(k) plan might be worth at age 63 if she were to participate fully?

© qinqqing/Shutterstock.com

BIG PICTURE SUMMARY OF LEARNING OBJECTIVES

LO1   **Recognize the keys to achieving financial success.**

Financial success and happiness come from spending less and saving and investing more. The goal is to achieve a level of living that is very close to your standard level of living. You can do so by applying the five fundamental steps in the financial planning process.

LO2   **Understand how the economy affects your personal financial success.**

Using your knowledge of where we are in the business cycle and tracking a few economic statistics will guide you to make appropriate adjustments in your long-term financial strategy. Also recognize how inflation and deflation will affect your finances.

LO3   **Apply economic principles when making financial decisions.**

Understanding and applying the basic economic principles of opportunity cost, marginal utility and cost, and marginal income tax rate will affect your financial success. The opportunity cost of a decision is the value of the next best alternative that must be forgone. Marginal cost is the additional (marginal) cost of one more incremental unit of some item. When known, this cost can be compared with the marginal utility received. One's marginal tax rate is the tax rate at which your last dollar is taxed.

LO4   **Perform time value of money calculations in personal financial decision making.**

Dollars to be received or paid out in the future are not equivalent to those received or paid out today. A dollar received today is worth more than a dollar received a year from now because today's dollar can be saved or invested; by next year, you expect it to be worth more than a dollar. The time value of money involves two components: future value and present value.

LO5   **Make smart decisions about your employee benefits.**

Smart decisions can increase your actual income by thousands of dollars each year. You need to select wisely among choices within employer-sponsored cafeteria plans; health care; flexible spending accounts; life, disability, and long-term care insurance; and retirement. These decisions often require you to calculate the tax-sheltered aspects of the employee benefits.

LO6   **Identify the professional certifications of providers of financial advice.**

When choosing a financial planner, know that many professional designations are meaningful in this field, such as CFP and ChFC. Costs may be charged on a fee-only, commission-only, fee-based, or fee-offset basis.

3. **Future Values of a Lump Sum.** Complete Worksheet 2: Calculating the Future Value of a Lump Sum from "My Personal Financial Planner" for the following three questions: (a) $10,000, 2 years, 6%; (b) $22,500, 20 years, 8%; (c) $5000, 10 years, 7%. Fill out the worksheet including the last two columns.

MY PERSONAL FINANCIAL PLANNER

4. **Future Value of an Annuity.** Complete Worksheet 3: Calculating the Future Value of an Annuity from "My Personal Financial Planner" for the following three questions: (a) $3000 annually, 5 years, 6%; (b) $1000 annually, 20 years, 8%; (c) $5000 annually, 30 years, 7%. Fill out the worksheet including the last two columns.

MY PERSONAL FINANCIAL PLANNER

5. **Present Value of a Lump Sum.** Complete Worksheet 4: Calculating the Present Value of a Lump Sum from "My Personal Financial Planner" for the following three questions: (a) lump sum needed $10,000, 5 years, 6%; (b) lump sum needed $250,000, 30 years, 8%; (c) lump sum needed $30,000, 10 years, 7%. Fill out the worksheet including the last two columns.

MY PERSONAL FINANCIAL PLANNER

6. **Present Value of an Annuity.** Complete Worksheet 5: Calculating the Present Value of an Annuity from "My Personal Financial Planner" for the following three questions: (a) withdraw $12,000 annually for 5 years at 6%; (b) withdraw $2000 annually for 15 years at 8%; (c) withdraw $3000 annually for 10 years at 7%. Fill out the worksheet including the last two columns.

MY PERSONAL FINANCIAL PLANNER

ON THE NET

Go to the Web pages indicated to complete these exercises.

1. **Inflation.** Visit the Bureau of Labor Statistics Consumer Price Index homepage at www.bls.gov/cpi/ and link to information for various areas of the country and metropolitan areas of various sizes. Describe how prices have been changing for your area and community during the past year.

2. **Future Direction of the Economy.** Visit the Conference Board website, www.conference-board.org and click on "U.S. Indicators" for the latest information on the consumer confidence index and the index of leading economic indicators. What do the indexes suggest about the direction of the economy over the next six months to one year?

3. **Economic Trends.** Scan the top four economic trends at the Economic Policy Institute (www.epi.org/) for insights on the future of the economy.

4. **NAPFA Financial Planners' Code of Ethics.** Visit the website of the National Association of Personal Financial Advisors at www.napfa.org/about /FiduciaryOath.asp. Read through the code of ethics for members of the organization. What does the code tell you about the members?

5. **Financial Planning Careers.** Visit the website of the Certified Financial Planner Board of Standards at www.cfp.net and read about "Become a CFP™ Professional." Summarize your findings.

ACTION INVOLVEMENT PROJECTS

1. **Interview a Financial Planner.** Use the Internet and/or Yellow Pages to find a fee-only or fee-based financial planner in your community and telephone that person to ask if he/she would agree to an interview. Take the list of questions in the box "Advice from a Professional ... Questions to Ask a Financial Planner" on page 28, and use it as an outline for your interview. Ask the professional to pick the three questions that he/she considers the most important. Write a summary of your findings.

2. **Smart Money Decisions at Work.** Survey three employed relatives or friends to determine whether or not they take advantage of certain employee benefits at work, such as a cafeteria plan, health care plan, high-deductible health care plan, health savings account, flexible spending account, life insurance, and tax-sheltered retirement plan. Make a written summary of your findings.

3. **Opportunity and Marginal Costs.** Survey three relatives or friends and ask about their decision-making process when they most recently bought a vehicle. Find out if they thought about the opportunity costs when making the purchase. Also ask if they used marginal costs in their thinking. Make a written summary of your findings.

4. **Research Future Direction of the Economy.** Survey five people to determine their opinions on the direction of the economy over the next 12 months. Even though they may not know the meaning of these exact terms, ask about their perceptions on such indicators as the (a) gross domestic product, (b) consumer confidence, (c) inflation and deflation, (d) interest rates, and (e) federal fund rate. Make a table that summarizes your findings.

Visit the Garman/Forgue companion website at www.cengagebrain.com.

2 Career Planning

LEARNING OBJECTIVES

After reading this chapter, you should be able to:

1 Identify the key steps in successful career planning.

2 Analyze the financial and legal aspects of employment.

3 Practice effective employment search strategies.

MORTGAGE RETIREMENT

INSURANCE TAXES

401(k) VACATION

EDUCATION CREDIT CARDS

© S-F/Shutterstock.com-Peter Booth/E+/Getty Images

WHAT DO YOU RECOMMEND?

Nicole Linkletter, age 21, expects to graduate next spring with a bachelor's degree in business administration. Nicole's grades are mostly As and Bs, and she has worked part time throughout her college career. Nicole is vice president of the Student Marketing Association on her campus. She would like to work in management or marketing for a medium- to large-size employer. Because she loves the outdoors, Nicole thinks she would prefer a job in the Northwest, perhaps in northern California, Oregon, or Washington.

© Tyler Olson/Shutterstock.com

What would you recommend to Nicole on the importance of career planning regarding:

1. Clarifying her values and lifestyle trade-offs?
2. Enhancing her career-related experiences before graduation?
3. Creating career plans and goals?
4. Understanding her work-style personality?
5. Identifying job opportunities?

career

The lifework chosen by a person to use personal talent, education, and training.

career planning

Can help you identify an employment pathway that aligns your interests and abilities with the tasks and responsibilities expected by employers over your lifetime.

You *can* control much of your financial future with effective career planning. A **career** is the lifework chosen by a person using his or her personal talent, education, and training. **Career planning** can help you identify an employment pathway that aligns your interests and abilities with the tasks and responsibilities expected by employers. Career planning has always been important, but with today's level of unemployment and slow economy, it is absolutely crucial. You must plan your career because failure awaits those who do not.

Your focus should not be simply a "job" but a career. The general progression of one's career will include a number of related jobs. Indeed, the average tenure at a job for U.S. workers is about three years. A career translates into a base of income, employee benefits, additional educational experiences, advancement opportunities, and a secure financial future. Career planning is a high-priority, do-it-yourself project, allowing you to take control of where you are going and how you are going to get there.

2.1 DEVELOPING YOUR CAREER PLAN

LEARNING OBJECTIVE 1

Identify the key steps in successful career planning.

career plan

A strategic guide for your career through short-, medium-, longer-, and long-term goals as well as future education and work-related experiences.

Your **career plan** provides a strategic guide for your career through short-, medium-, longer-, and long-term goals as well as future education and work-related experiences. You can't advance very far in planning your financial life without also planning a career that will earn you an adequate income. A career that suits you will give you opportunities to display your abilities in jobs you find satisfying while providing balance between work and your personal life.

In many parts of the country a slow job market may mean that neither the pay nor the geographic location opportunities for employment are quite what you expect. Realize, too, that the rest of your life will not be determined by your first professional job. No matter what job you choose, consider it a chance to do the required tasks effectively and learn more about yourself and your career field.

Career planning is a continuous process that lasts throughout your life. Every time your life circumstances change, you will likely reconsider your career plan. Figure 2-1 provides an illustration of the steps in career planning.

2.1a Clarify Your Values and Interests

Thinking about and discovering what you want out of life gives you guidance for what to do to lead a satisfying life. Understanding yourself enables you to select a career path that best suits you. This requires understanding your values and interests.

Values are the principles, standards, or qualities considered worthwhile or desirable. Values provide a basis for decisions about how to live, serving as guides we can use to direct our actions. For something to be a value, it must be prized, publicly affirmed, chosen from alternatives, and acted upon repeatedly and consistently. Values are not right or wrong, or true or false; they are personal preferences.

People may place value on family, friends, helping others, religious commitment, honesty, pleasure, good health, material possessions, financial security, and a satisfying career. Examples of conflicting values are family versus satisfying career, privacy

values

The principles, standards, or qualities that you consider desirable.

Figure 2-1   Steps in Career Planning

Finalize your career plan
Align yourself with tomorrow's employment trends
Take advantage of professional and social networking
Review your abilities, experiences, and education
Identify one or more desired career fields
Clarify your values and interests

versus social networking, and material possessions versus financial security. When you make important decisions, you might be wise to think carefully to clarify your values before taking action. Consider making a list of your ten most important values.

Your **professional interests** are topics and activities about which you have feelings of curiosity or concern. Interests engage or arouse your attention. They reflect what you like to do. Interests, including occupational interests, are likely to vary over time.

You might consider making a list of your top ten interests. On that list will probably be some things you enjoy but have not done recently. Because of conflicting interests and alternative claims on your time, you cannot pursue all your interests. It is important in career planning to evaluate your interests; if you plan your career with your interests in mind, you will increase the likelihood of career satisfaction.

Interest inventories are measures that assist people in assessing and profiling the interests and activities that give them satisfaction. They compare how your interests are similar or dissimilar to the interests of people successfully employed in various occupations. The theory behind these interest inventories is that individuals with similar interests are often attracted to the same kind of work. These inventories can help you identify possible career goals that match your strongest personal interests.

The Strong Interest Inventory assessment is considered by many to be the gold standard of career exploration tools. The opportunity to take one or more interest inventory assessments, usually for free or at a nominal cost, is available at most colleges and state-supported career counseling facilities. These assessments can also be completed online for a fee. (See, for example, www.cpp .com/products/strong/index.aspx.)

2.1b Identify One or More Desired Career Fields

People used to take a single job and remain at the same company until they retired. Now, people often change jobs five to ten times during their working years, about 4.4 years on average. Surveys show that 35 percent of employees change jobs at least every 5 years, 18 percent change between 6 and 10 years, and nearly half stay more than 10 years. In contrast, young adults average six jobs before age 26.

Thinking about a career goal helps you focus on what you want to do for a living. A **career goal** can be a specific job (e.g., cost accountant, teacher, human resources manager) or a particular field of work (e.g., health care, communications, green engineering). It helps guide you to do the kind of work you want in life rather than drift from job to job. You should focus on a series of jobs that form a career ladder. A **career ladder** typically describes the progression from entry-level positions to higher levels of pay, skill, responsibility, or authority. Formulating a career goal requires thinking about your interests, skills, and experiences and learning about different careers and employment trends. The process of establishing a career goal motivates you to consider career possibilities that you may not have thought of otherwise.

To create a career goal, explore the jobs, careers, and trends in the employment marketplace that fit your interests and skills. Ask people you trust about their careers. Search websites such as those for the *Occupational Outlook Handbook* (www.bls.gov /ooh/) and the *Occupational Outlook Quarterly* (www.bls.gov/opub/ooq/home.htm). Research the occupational groups that interest you, median pay, education, and projected growth.

Benefits and Costs When making career choices, you must weigh the benefits against the costs. The benefits could include a big salary, likelihood of personal growth and job advancements, and high job satisfaction. For some, the pluses might include the psychic benefit of a prestigious job with a high income. The costs might include living in a less desirable geographic area and climate, being far from friends and family, sitting at a desk all day, working long hours, and/or doing too much traveling.

YOUR NEXT FIVE YEARS

In the next five years, you can start achieving financial success by doing the following related to career planning:

1. *Continue to enhance your education and professional training.*
2. *Seek out mentors and sponsors on the job and in other professional settings.*
3. *Join and be active in the professional associations relevant to your career.*
4. *Identify your career planning values and live them in your selection of jobs and in your performance at work.*
5. *Map out your career plan by setting benchmarks as you move up the career ladder.*

professional interests
Long-standing topics and activities that engage your attention.

interest inventories
Scaled surveys that assess career interests and activities.

career goal
Identifying what you want to do for a living, whether a specific job or field of employment.

career ladder
Describes the progression from entry-level positions to higher levels of pay, skill, responsibility, or authority.

lifestyle trade-offs
Weighing the demands of particular jobs with your social and cultural preferences.

Lifestyle Trade-offs A **lifestyle trade-off** is weighing the demands of particular jobs with your social and cultural preferences. When you consider a career, think about what lifestyle trade-offs are important to you. For example, if access to big-name live entertainment, museums, and artistic activities is important, then working and living in a rural area may not be appropriate. If you like to visit new places, you may choose a career that involves frequent travel or the chance to work overseas.

Consider the following lifestyle options in your decision making:

- Urban/rural setting
- Close/far from work
- Own/rent housing
- City/suburban life
- Warm/cold climate
- Constant/variable climate
- Near/far from relatives

DO IT IN CLASS

The Price of Career Coaching Privately available career coaching experts are available. For $600 you can buy 5 hours of basic services including identifying career goals, targeting companies, and practicing interviewing skills. For $3000 you can get customized preparation before each job interview. For $8000 you get 24/7-access to coaching, mock interviews, and one-on-one advice on salary and benefits.

2.1c   Review Your Abilities, Experiences, and Education

Reviewing your abilities, aptitudes, experiences, education, and work style are key steps in career planning. The purpose is to see how well they match up with your career-related interests.

DECISION-MAKING WORKSHEET

Your Career Field Research

Selecting a career field should be based on solid research. It helps to have a set of questions prepared in advance. Use this worksheet to gather data about one or more career fields and use the results to compare fields against your values and interests. Various sources of data for your research are located throughout this chapter.

Career field	Comments on research results
General nature of work performed	
Working conditions such as typical hours, degree of travel required, physical activities, and work locations and surroundings	
Educational level, certifications, and training required for an entry-level position	
Typical employee benefits provided	
Typical career ladder including any geographical relocations that are likely to be required as one advances up the ladder	
Educational level, certifications, and training required for career advancement	
Earnings initially and as career progresses	
Career field outlook in terms of employment growth and likely technological advances	

Abilities and Aptitudes Your professional abilities are the qualities that allow you to perform job-related tasks physically, mentally, artistically, mechanically, or financially. Most of us think of *ability* as a word describing how well we do something, a proficiency, dexterity, or technique, particularly one requiring use of the mind, hands, or body. Other examples of abilities include being skilled in working with people, being able to easily meet the public, and being good at persuading people.

Employer surveys indicate that the single most important ability needed for career success in the twenty-first century is computer skills. Also very highly ranked are communication skills and honesty/integrity. Consider making a list of your top ten professional abilities.

Aptitudes are the natural abilities and talents that people possess. Aptitudes suggest that you have a tendency or inclination to learn and develop certain skills or abilities. Are you good with numbers? Do you find public speaking easy to do? Do you enjoy solving problems? What are your natural talents? Consider making a list of your top ten aptitudes.

Experiences Most college graduates have much more going for them than a degree and a string of part-time job experiences. Reviewing your experiences is a step in career planning. Evaluate what you have been doing in your life, including jobs, participation in student organizations and community and church groups, leadership on school projects, volunteer activities, and internships. Hiring managers say college grads need two internships to be competitive.

Those still in college can enhance their job opportunities by learning as much as possible in school, participating in clubs and other student organizations (including volunteering for committees and campus projects), getting involved in a faculty research project, and attending off-campus professional meetings related to their major. Academic advisers can provide suggestions.

Education and Professional Training Going to college is excellent preparation for your career and your life. But college may not have provided you with all the skills and abilities to be successfully employed. A review of your abilities, experiences, and education may suggest you need to seek additional education and professional training.

Know Your Preferred Work-Style Personality Every job requires the worker to function in relation to data, people, and things in differing work environments and corporate cultures. Your work-style personality is a unique set of ways of working with and responding to your job requirements, surroundings, and associates. When making a career selection, you must balance your work-style personality against the demands of the work environment.

You can begin by rating each work value as shown in the Decision-Making Worksheet "What Is Your Work-Style Personality?" Put a check mark in the appropriate column in terms of importance in your career. Armed with this information, you can now more clearly decide on careers that are most suitable for you.

professional abilities
Job-related activities that you can perform physically, mentally, artistically, mechanically, and financially.

aptitudes
The natural abilities and talents that individuals possess.

work-style personality
Your own ways of working with and responding to job requirements, surroundings, and associates.

Career planning should reflect your lifestyle preferences.

ADVICE FROM A PROFESSIONAL

Competencies of Successful People

People who are successful in their chosen careers, with their finances, and/or in life in general often possess and exhibit certain competencies.

1. *Set goals in the various aspects of life and track progress toward attaining goals.*
2. *Use organizational tools such as making lists as well as using time management techniques.*
3. *Exhibit integrity.*
4. *Understand personal motives and behave ethically.*
5. *Make a quality effort every time.*
6. *Accept accountability for their decisions and actions.*
7. *Exhibit good written and oral communication skills.*
8. *Demonstrate strong computer skills.*
9. *Remain open to new ideas.*
10. *Adapt easily to change.*
11. *Share knowledge to assist and mentor others.*
12. *Acquire advanced education and technical training.*
13. *Be a life-long learner.*
14. *Willingly take on new assignments and capitalize on the new skills learned.*
15. *Anticipate problems and work proactively to implement solutions.*
16. *Work well in teams and know when to lead and when to follow.*
17. *Project an image consistent with organizational values.*
18. *Understand the operations, structure, and culture of the organization.*
19. *Are loyal to and supportive of the company and boss.*

Caroline S. Fulmer
The University of Alabama

2.1d   Take Advantage of Professional and Social Networking

professional networking
Making and using contacts with individuals, groups, and other firms to exchange career information.

Professional networking is the process of making and using contacts, such as individuals, groups, or institutions, to obtain and exchange information in career planning. Also use social-networking sites, including Facebook, LinkedIn, and Twitter. Spend a few minutes on the site each day making new connections, and keeping your profile up to date. Always send a personal message with all connection requests. Every person you know or meet is a possible useful contact. Don't forget that a single crude quote or photo on a social-networking site could eliminate you from a job interview, therefore, be thoroughly professional at all times.

job referral
The act recommending someone to another by sending a reference for employment.

Job referrals are critical in professional networking. A **job referral** is the act of recommending someone to another for possible employment. This helps your résumé get a close look from a hiring manager. When you're referred for a position, and you mention it in your cover letter, you've got a built in recommendation for the job in the first paragraph of your cover letter. It's even better when the person referring you can take a couple of minutes to personally refer you for the job. A referral generally does not include a letter of recommendation. Companies find one-third of new hires through referrals. Thus you must make a conscious effort to use people you know and meet to maximize your job search process. Networking involves utilizing your social contacts, taking advantage of casual meetings, and asking for personal referrals. Most of your contacts will not be able to hire you, but they could refer you to the people who can, or they may be able to give you useful information about a potential employer.

Maintain a continually growing list of people who are family, neighbors, friends, college associates, coworkers, previous supervisors, teachers, professors, alumni, business contacts, and others you know through civic and community organizations such as churches and business and social groups. Take note of where your contacts work and what types of jobs they have. Ask these people for 10 to 20 minutes of their time so you can share a copy of your résumé and in an effort to seek information and suggestions from them. Perhaps meet at their workplaces (where you might meet other potential networking contacts), and afterward send them thank-you notes.

DECISION-MAKING WORKSHEET

What Is Your Work-Style Personality?

It would be useful for you to consider a number of work values critical to the process of career selection, particularly in the areas of work conditions, work purposes, and work relationships. Rate how you value the following work values as either very important in your choice of career, somewhat important, or unimportant.

Work-Style Factor	Your Rating of Importance		
	Very Important	**Somewhat Important**	**Unimportant**
1. Work Conditions			
Independence and autonomy			
Time flexibility			
Change and variety			
Stability and security			
Physical challenge			
Mental challenge			
Pressure and time deadlines			
Decision making			
2. Work Purposes			
Material gain			
Truth and knowledge			
Expertise and authority			
Achievement and recognition			
Ethical and moral			
3. Work Relationships			
Working alone			
Public contact			
Close friendships			
Influencing others			
Supervising others			

For additional values clarification, go back to the list and *circle the activities* that you want to do more often. The goal is to match your highest work-style values to career choices with similar work-style requirements.

As many as three-quarters of all job openings may never be listed in want ads, so the people in your network become a vital source of information about employment opportunities. For this reason, expanding the number of people in your network is advantageous; some of the people you know will also likely share their networking contacts. Don't forget to keep them informed of your progress and eventual success in obtaining employment.

2.1e Align Yourself with Tomorrow's Employment Trends

What are the trends in employment? The aging U.S. population will create jobs in the service industries of finance, insurance, health care, recreation, and travel. Jobs are gravitating to existing population centers, particularly in warmer climates that have superior transportation systems. Jobs in manufacturing continue to go overseas to Mexico, Asia, Europe, and other countries, with the U.S. job market primarily demanding highly skilled workers in the service industries.

Table 2-1   Projected High-Growth Occupations

Job Title	Employment in 2017	Median Annual Income
Accountants/auditors	1,440,000	$76,000
Advertising promotions managers	77,000	$95,000
Business operations specialists	396,000	$79,000
Child and social workers	324,000	$51,000
Compensation benefits managers	70,000	$100,000
Computer system design	2,100,000	$100,000
Green construction	400,000	$75,000
Home health care services	1,900,000	$70,000
Human resource managers	72,000	$122,000
Industrial engineers	205,000	$98,000
Market research analysts	227,000	$81,000
Marketing managers	228,000	$153,000
Media and communications	46,000	$61,000
Medical/health service managers	305,000	$102,000
Property association managers	454,000	$60,000
Public relations specialists	231,000	$66,000
Sales managers	403,000	$122,000
Retail stores	2,100,000	$60,000
Social networking	400,000	$85,000
Training and development specialists	261,000	$74,000

Sources: Bureau of Labor Statistics, Table 15, High-growth occupations, by educational attainment cluster and earnings; authors' income projections to 2017.
www.bls.gov/ooh/fastest-growing.htm and
www.bls.gov/news.release/ecopro.t05.htm; authors' projections to 2017.

DID YOU KNOW

The No-Limits Job

Many younger workers are employed in entry-level positions where they are expected to be on-call via a mobile device at all hours of the day and night. They face stressful demands from their companies, such as 300 or 400 daily e-mails and tweets and only a few less on weekends. These jobs encourage them to knock down the boundaries between life and work. This is affecting millennials, the creative class, and the workforce at large. Ask about these things during an interview and decide about the job based on the answers you receive.

High-demand occupations tend to pay high salaries and offer career advancement opportunities. Majors in engineering can yield starting salaries of $90,000 and above. Accountants, actuaries, nurses, pharmacists, and software engineers are also in high demand and they, too, are highly compensated. Your academic choices should, at least in part, be based upon employment trends. If you have the aptitude, you might pursue a degree in a field that pays well. Table 2-1 shows the projected job opportunities in high-growth occupations in the United States.

2.1f Finalize Your Career Plan

As you near graduation, you will be ready to develop a formal career plan. Figure 2-2 provides an illustrative career plan. Your career plan should be realistic and flexible. Your career interests and goals will change over time, especially as you continue your education, gain work experience, and see how your friends fare with their jobs and avocations. Teaching music education might be your first career, but you may eventually realize that the accompanying small income could keep you on a tight financial budget forever. This issue might encourage you to consider a total career change—perhaps to sales in the music industry or a related field, where incomes are higher.

Assessing yourself and your career plans every few years is important to achieving success in your working life. What do you find satisfying and not so satisfying? Honest answers will help you, particularly as your interests evolve. Your work experiences should hone your abilities and skills. Learning new skills on the job is common, and if that is not happening in a job, move on and change employers and perhaps careers.

Figure 2-2   Career Goals and Plans for Harry Johnson

Harry Johnson began his working career following graduation from college by obtaining employment with a small commercial interior design firm. He has an undergraduate degree from a university accredited by the American Society of Interior Designers. He is happy that his first professional job is in his major field of interest.

Initial career goal: To become an interior designer. To design, plan, and supervise commercial/contract design projects.

Long-term career goal (20-plus years): Own or become a partner in a medium- to large-size commercial/contract interior design firm.

Short-term plans and goals in career establishment stage (3 to 6 years): Gain work experience in current job; receive employer compliments on quality of work; obtain continuing education credits for professional growth and development; secure higher-level design responsibilities, such as lead professional design team; volunteer for committee responsibilities in local and state professional associations; obtain substantial increases in income; receive promotions; learn operational aspects and marketing of the company.

Medium-term plans and goals in professional growth stage (7 to 12 years): Be promoted to the level of senior designer; consider going to work for another employer as a senior designer and, if necessary, move to another community; volunteer for higher-level service in professional associations; obtain a master of fine arts degree in interior design; become assistant to the firm's general manager.

Longer-term plans and goals in advancement stage (13 to 20 years): Become general manager of commercial design firm; seek out potential partners and sufficient financing to either buy out or start up a medium-size design firm.

DID YOU KNOW

Entrepreneurship May Be Your Best Way

Starting a company out of a perceived opportunity occurs when people are hopeful about their situations. They are making a choice between working for someone or working for themselves. Participating in a new business creation is a common activity among U.S. workers over the course of their careers.

An **entrepreneur** is someone who organizes, manages, and assumes the risks of a business or enterprise. Don't be afraid to take the chance to be part of a start-up company, especially while you are young because if you fail you can always return to the normal working world. If you succeed, well, the world is yours.

CONCEPT CHECK 2.1

1. Distinguish between a job and a career.

2. How do your values affect your trade-offs in career planning?

3. What can be done to enhance your abilities and experiences without working in a job situation?

2.2 FINANCIAL AND LEGAL ASPECTS OF EMPLOYMENT

This section examines financial and legal aspects of employment to consider when analyzing your career plans.

2.2a Is College Worth the Cost?

STEM majors

Academic majors in science, technology, engineering, and mathematics.

Concerns regarding educational quality and student indebtedness are good ones. Only you—the student—can answer the question: "Is college worth the cost?" While in school avoid a major with a vague credential, appears low in knowledge and skills, and results in a crippling amount of debt. Besides the **STEM majors** (science, technology, engineering, and mathematics), there are numerous academic majors that teach employable skills and also pay good salaries upon graduation.

Education is more than an investment; it is a treasure. It is priceless. College is a place to think, to contemplate, to find out what is valuable, and question the value of what is made. You should be a reasonably literate citizen of the world who had some intelligent understanding of the larger-than-local interests.

Going to college does not require $25,000 or $50,000 in debt. It does not mean you borrow to pay for your rent and food as well as your tuition. If necessary, attend a less expensive school, live at home, work part-time, go to school part-time, and ask parents and other relatives for some financial assistance. Borrow as little money for tuition as possible. And no matter what, do not drop out of school before you graduate. Nearly 9 out of 10 graduates say their college expenses have been a good investment. College graduates also earn twice as much per hour as high school graduates. The return on investment for a bachelor's degree is about 15 percent a year.

employee benefits

Forms of remuneration provided by employers to employees that result in the employee not having to pay out-of-pocket money for certain expenses; also known as nonsalary benefits.

2.2b Place Dollar Values on Employee Benefits

Employee benefits are tremendously important to employees, especially when comparing the benefits provided by one employer with another. **Employee benefits** (or **nonsalary**

DID YOU KNOW

Do Not Give Up $160,000 When Changing Employers

When changing jobs, nearly half of workers unwisely cash out all the money in their employer-sponsored retirement plan instead of roll it over to a new employer's 401(k) plan, moving it to an IRA rollover account, of leaving it with the old employer (if that is allowed). If an individual has $50,000 in a 401 (k) account and cashes it out, that person gives up $160,000 in future dollars over the following 20 years earning 6 percent annually.

DO IT IN CLASS

	If you cash out $50,000:	If you roll over $50,000:
20% required federal income tax withholding	−$10,000	
5% additional tax (in 25% tax bracket)	−$ 2,500	
10% required early-withdrawal penalty	−$ 5,000	
5% state/local income tax	−$ 2,500	
Total withdrawn	−$20,000	+$50,000
Money spent on new car, TV, home repair, vacation, etc.	−$30,000	Money invested in another tax-deferred retirement account that earns 6 percent annually
Total	−$50,000	+$50,000
Additional investment actions taken	None	Money grows for 20 years
Investment balance after 20 years	$ 0	$160,000

DID YOU KNOW

Value of Additional Education

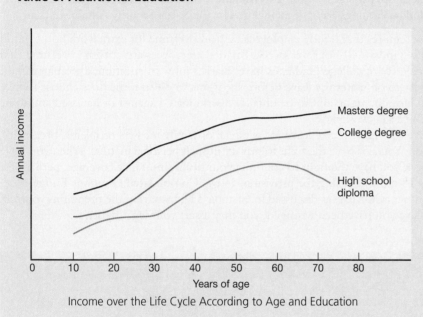

Income over the Life Cycle According to Age and Education

Income varies over the life cycle. Higher incomes typically go to those with more education or more specialized education. The U.S. Census Bureau reports that young adults (ages 25–34) with a bachelor's degree earn an average of $47,000 compared to $31,000 for a high school graduate and $80,000 for those with advanced degrees.

benefits) are forms of remuneration provided by employers to employees that result in the employee not having to pay out-of-pocket money for certain expenses. Examples include paid vacations, health care, paid sick leave, child care, tuition reimbursement, and financial planning services.

To put monetary values on employee benefits, you may (1) place a market value on the benefit or (2) calculate the future value of the benefit.

Place a Market Value on the Benefit If instead of enjoying a certain employee benefit, you had to pay out-of-pocket dollars for it, you can easily determine its market value. Private child care might cost $300 a week in your community; thus, when child care is provided free from your employer, that is a whopping $15,000 ($300 × 50 weeks) saved annually. Actually, it is more because after paying $7000 in income and Social Security taxes you would likely have to earn perhaps $22,000 to have $15,000 left over. An employer-provided paid-for life insurance policy with a face value of $50,000 might cost $100 to $400 if you had to buy it yourself.

Calculate the Future Value of the Benefit An employer that provides a 401(k) retirement plan offers a valuable benefit. If an employer provides a match of $1200 a year to your $1200 in contributions, all the money in the account will grow free of income taxes until the funds are withdrawn. Over 20 years, the annual employer contributions of $1200 growing at 6 percent annually to more than $44,000 (using Appendix A.3). That is in addition to your $1200 a year contributions for a total of over $88,000.

2.2c Know Your Legal Employment Rights

You have legal rights both during the hiring process and after you are hired. When selecting employees, employers may not discriminate based on age, gender, race, color, sex, marital/family status, religion, national origin, birthplace, age, and disability (if the person can perform the essential job tasks). Laws in many states and cities also prohibit discrimination against gays and lesbians in the hiring process. Once hired, you have many rights. Employers must do the following:

- Pay the minimum wage established by federal, state, or local laws
- Provide unemployment insurance
- Provide workers' compensation benefits for job-related injuries or illness
- Pay Social Security taxes to the government, which are then credited to the employee's lifetime earnings account maintained by the Social Security Administration

The law requires that hourly employees be paid overtime for extra work hours put in beyond the standard 40-hour workweek. Salaried employees are not paid overtime, and the vast majority of college graduates have salaried jobs. In addition, a woman cannot be forced to go on maternity leave before she wants to do so if she does choose to take leave. You have the rights not to be unfairly discriminated against or harassed and to be employed in a safe workplace.

You have the right to take leave for personal or family medical problems, pregnancy, or adoption. You also have the right to privacy in such personal matters. When you leave an employer, you have the right to continue your health insurance coverage, perhaps for as long as 18 months [using the provisions in the Consolidated Omnibus Budget Reconciliation Act (COBRA) as discussed in Chapter 11], by paying the premiums yourself. If you believe you have been wronged, you may assert your legal rights.

RUN THE NUMBERS

Assessing the Benefits of a Second Income

A second income might add surprisingly little to your total earnings because of all the costs associated with earning it. In this example, a nonworking spouse is considering a job that pays $30,000 annually. The total net amount of the extra $30,000 income is a mere $8805, thus adding only *$734 ($8805/12 = $767)* a month to total earnings.

DO IT IN CLASS

1. Second Income	
Annual earnings	$30,000
Value of benefits (life insurance)	300
Total 1	$30,300
2. Expenses	
Federal income taxes (25% rate × $30,000)	$ 7,500
State/local income taxes (6% rate × $30,000)	1,800
Social Security taxes (7.65% × $30,000)	2,295
Transportation and commuting (50 weeks @ $40)	2,000
Child care (9 months after-school only)	3,600
Lunches out (50 weeks, twice a week at $10)	1,000
Work wardrobe (including dry cleaning)	1,200
Other work-related expenses (magazines, dues, gifts)	300
Take-out food for supper (too tired to cook; $100 per month)	1,200
Guilt complex purchases (to make up for time lost with others)	600
Total 2	$21,495
3. Net Value of Second Income	
Total of 1 from above	$30,300
Subtract total of 2 from above	21,495
Total accurate net amount of second income	$ 8,805

DID YOU KNOW

What to Do When You Lose Your Job

What should you do when you are laid off from your job?

1. **Think of yourself as being employed.** *Your job is to find a new job. Set a work schedule for yourself and a location at home from which to do the work.*

2. **Get your finances in order.** *Determine how much money you have and the level of unemployment benefits you might be able to receive. Determine how long you can continue to pay your bills in the usual fashion.*

3. **Tap into your network.** *Let people know that you are looking for work. Rebuild your network if necessary. Build contacts with other unemployed persons in your field so that you can share successful and unsuccessful strategies.*

4. **Take a hard look at the prospects for a possible rebound of employment opportunities in your career field.** *Some of the jobs lost in the recent economic turmoil are the result of temporary sluggishness in an industry. Others will never come back.*

5. **Get retrained.** *This is especially important if your career field will see permanent reductions in the needed level of workers. Local community colleges are especially focused on retraining programs and may have financial assistance to help you.*

6. **Be prepared to move.** *Some geographic areas of the country are poised to rebound faster than others. Those which will grow fastest are places with strong public schools and colleges, highly educated workers, and emerging high-tech and information-age industries.*

7. **Don't be afraid to be a temp.** *Many firms will hire temporary workers at first when recovering so that they can quickly downsize if necessary. They will look first to hire the temporary workers into their permanent work force.*

CONCEPT CHECK 2.2

1. Summarize how education level and age affect income.

2. What two techniques can be used to place monetary values on employee benefits?

3. Choose three career advancement tips and explain how each one might apply in someone's personal situation.

2.3 EFFECTIVE EMPLOYMENT SEARCH STRATEGIES

Once you have undertaken some career planning, you will want to start the process of getting a job in your preferred career field. This is an effort that takes much effort. A successful job search might require 25 to 40 hours per week of your time. Effective search strategies follow.

LEARNING OBJECTIVE 3

Practice effective employment search strategies.

2.3a Assemble an Attention-Getting Resume

The Internet is a valuable resource for you in all aspects of career planning, including preparing a résumé. A **résumé** is a summary record of your education, training, experience, and other qualifications. It is often submitted with a job application. Your résumé, usually one or two pages in length, should be carefully written and contain zero errors or inconsistencies in message, content, and appearance. A survey of top executives reveals that 75 percent will not even consider an applicant whose résumé has one or more typos. Resumes should be in PDF format so they can be viewed on a variety of mobile devices.

résumé
Summary record of your education, training, experience, and other qualifications.

DID YOU KNOW

Prospective Employers Can Check Your Credit Report

Thirteen percent of employers obtain the credit reports of prospective job candidates. A lousy credit history can suggest a lot about a person's inability to manage important tasks. Federal law requires that individuals (1) are aware that consumer credit reports may be used for employment purposes and must agree to such use and (2) are to be notified promptly if information in a consumer report may result in a negative employment decision. About 20 states prohibit employers from using credit reports when hiring.

Its primary function is to provide a basis for screening people out of contention for jobs. When you supply a résumé, you are providing documentation for some kind of subjective evaluation against unknown criteria. Large employers, recruiters, and local and national websites screen resumes using an applicant tracking software system, also known as APS, to screen online resumes.

We live in a world of income inequality based in part on what is known as **skill-based-technological-change (SBTC)**, and if you do not have the skills you better get some. If you do have the skills, show them off in your résumé. Use nouns and noun phrases, such as "Microsoft Office" or "Excel" so the scanning process picks them up. A good place to find keywords is to review 10 employment ads with similar job titles in your field and see which words are repeatedly mentioned.

A Harvard professor observed that, "The world no longer cares about what you know; the world only cares about what you can do with what you know." Thus, you should focus your résumé on skills and competencies that are most relevant to the position you aspire to hold. When it is necessary to technically fulfill a requirement in the employment process, tailor a special edition of your résumé to fit that special set of circumstances. Resumes are usually presented in a **chronological format** (information in reverse order with the most recent first), **skills format** (aptitudes and qualities), or **functional format** (career-related experiences). See Figures 2-3, 2-4, and 2-5 for sample resumes. The most

chronological format
Resume that provides your information in reverse order, with the most recent first.

skills format
Resume that emphasizes your aptitudes and qualities.

functional format
Resume that emphasizes career-related experiences.

DO IT IN CLASS

Figure 2-3   **Sample Chronological Resume**

GORDON CATHEY

SCHOOL ADDRESS:
2824 West Street
Ames, IA 50211
(401) 555-1212
E-mail: cgordo@yahoo.com

HOME ADDRESS:
3055 Vallejo Street, Apt.12
Denver, CO 80303
(303) 333-4141

CAREER OBJECTIVE	Entry-level position as a metallurgical engineer.
EDUCATION	Bachelor of Science, Metallurgical Engineering, Iowa State University, Ames, IA, June 2014.
	Associate of Arts, Kishwaukee Community College, Malta, IL, June 2012.
EXPERIENCE	August 2012–May 2014 (academic year, part time), Iowa State University, Ames, IA, Research Assistant to Professor John Binnion on metals and plastics, conducted research, performed statistical analyses, wrote reports, led group of interns.
	Summer 2011 and Summer 2012 (full time), EMD Electro-Motive Division, Metallurgical Engineering Department, Chicago, IL, Internship (paid), tested materials, prepared reports, participated in team efforts.
	September 2010–April 2011, Volunteer, Village Nursing Home, Denver, CO, updated some resident activities, organized weekend volunteers.
CAMPUS ACTIVITIES	Associate Editor college newspaper, Iowa State Daily; Vice President, ISU Metallurgical Society; Hispanic Club; Singer, University Chorale; Tutor for College of Engineering computer laboratory; Attended two national conferences of American Society for Metals International.
HONORS	Etta Mae Johnson Scholarship; College of Engineering Academic Scholarship; Most Valuable Member, ISU Metallurgical Society; Julie Lynn Marshall Scholarship.
REFERENCES	Available upon request.

| *Figure 2-4* | **Sample Functional Resume** |

Elizabeth Anklin
12144 Southwest 174th Loop
Tupelo, MS 38803
School: (662) 844-5698
Home: (662) 921-1213
Eanklin@hotmail.com

CAREER OBJECTIVE
Public relations or communications department with opportunities to contribute and learn.

EDUCATION
Bachelor of Science, University of Georgia, Financial Planning, Housing and Consumer Economics with a minor in communications, Athens, GA, May 2014; Associate of Arts, Mississippi Valley Community College, Booneville, MS, August 2012.

CAREER-RELATED EXPERIENCES
Organized breakfast meetings, supervised new members, updated membership records, led annual auction, created administrative procedures, Chamber of Commerce, Athens, GA, part time.
Maintained inventory records, monitored reordering systems, JC Penney Company, Athens, GA, part time.
Updated merchandising records, redesigned sales floor layout, Johnson's Shoes, Booneville, MS, part time.
Overseas experience building a school in Botswana, Africa.
Translated Spanish and French for Atlanta Translation Services.

CAMPUS CAREER-RELATED ACTIVITIES
Vice president, Sales and Merchandising Club; Treasurer, Aces Chorale Club; Secretary, National Honor Society; Secretary, Alpha Kappa Alpha Sorority; Co-coordinator Speaker's Committee, Consumer Club; Debate Club; attended SOCAP meetings in Atlanta; intramural hockey; campus church choir.

COMPUTER SKILLS
Microsoft Office, Corel WordPerfect Office, Corel Paint Shop Pro X, Adobe Acrobat, Dazzle Video Creator, QuickBooks Pro, Computer Assisted Design, Macromedia, FrontPage.

HONORS
Hanna Pallagrosi Academic Scholarship; Modu Samega-Janneh Service Award, College of Family and Consumer Sciences, University of Georgia; Highest Monthly Sales Award, JC Penney; Employee of the Month (twice), JC Penney.

REFERENCES
Furnished upon request.

| *Figure 2-5* | **Sample Skills Resume** |

Ji-hoon Hyun
2122 South 141th Street West, Apt. 340
San Antonio, TX 78204
School: (210) 207-5454
Home: (210) 419-1445
jhyun@hotmail.com

CAREER OBJECTIVE:
Professional position in human development with administrative responsibilities.

EDUCATION:
Master of Science, 2014, University of Texas at San Antonio, Human Development, San Antonio, TX; Bachelor of Science, 2012, University of Texas at San Antonio, Education and Human Development, San Antonio, TX; Associate of Arts, 2010, San Antonio College, San Antonio, TX.

CAREER-RELATED LEADERSHIP EXPERIENCES
- Organized and coordinated student session at national Family Relations Conference
- Hosted student session at Texas Family Relations Conference
- Led departmental graduate student study committee
- Treasurer of honor society Kappa Omicron Nu
- Organized speaker series for Kappa Omicron Nu
- Chaired Graduate Student Recruitment committee
- Vice President Study Body, San Antonio College
- Volunteer coordinator for neighborhood Meals-on-Wheels for adults

CAREER-RELATED WORK EXPERIENCE
- Administered intake procedures at Humanas Family Center
- Updated record-keeping systems for Humanas Family Center
- Planned learning activities for Gonzales Child Center
- Supervised parental security for Gonzales Child Center
- Presented research paper at Texas Family Relations Conference
- Attended two state Texas Family Relations Conferences
- Attended University of Utah summer seminar on human development
- Planned curriculum updates for Alamo Elder Center
- Trained and managed interns at campus family counseling center

CAREER-RELATED COMPUTER SKILLS
Word, Excel, Corel Graphics, Adobe Acrobat, SPSS, SAS.

HONORS
Henry B. Gonzales Public Service Scholarship, Lane Johnson Memorial Scholarship, Outstanding Member of Kappa Omicron Nu.

common mistake in a résumé is to fill it up with a long list of functions and responsibilities that you had in your previous jobs instead of evidencing the specific accomplishments that made a difference in the companies for which you worked.

Colleges have career centers with sample resumes and professional staff who can offer personal advice. You can also find examples of resumes on the Internet. Monster.com has 500,000 online resumes, and it's easy to find resume templates by searching for them online. However, posting your résumé on an Internet site or sending out resumes is not conducting a significant job search. Realize also that if your résumé is posted on the Internet your current employer can view it.

Some high-tech and marketing companies are skipping resumes altogether and hiring based solely on tweets, the online text-based messaging service of up to 140 characters. A tweet or two or five over five days may provide the company with everything they need to know about you and your online personality. But most jobs will still require resumes.

2.3b Target Your Preferred Employers

A key step in the job search process is to think about both the industries in which you would prefer employment and which employers might be best for you. If, for example, you want to work in the health care

ADVICE FROM A PROFESSIONAL

Career Advancement Tips

The essence of career advancement is to build your job-related knowledge and skills for the future by learning. You do not want to fall behind your coworkers and those who work for other employers, as they may be your future job market competitors. Change jobs when appropriate to obtain a different or better position that advances your career or when deemed necessary to entirely alter your career. To advance in your career, consider the following:

- **Mentors and Sponsors.** Ask one or two people to serve as your mentors, people with whom you can regularly discuss your career progress. A **mentor** is an experienced person, often a senior coworker, who offers friendly career-related advice, guidance, and coaching to a less experienced person. Getting someone to sponsor you is even better. A **sponsor** is a powerfully positioned champion who "leans in" with you by advocating on their proteges' behalf and guiding them toward key players and assignments.

- **Traits.** Exhibit passion, self-discipline, confidence, and determination in your everyday responsibilities.

- **Volunteer.** Volunteer for new assignments.

- **Training.** Sign up for employer-sponsored seminars and training and certification opportunities.

- **Conferences.** Attend meetings and conferences in your field. Become a member of your local professional association and become active in its leadership.

- **College Courses.** Take advanced college courses and complete a graduate degree.

- **Professional Reading.** Stay alert to what is happening in your career field by reading professional and trade publications.

- **Current Events.** Be up to date on current events and business and economic news by reviewing websites and reading newspapers, news magazines, and business periodicals.

- **Nonwork Activities.** Be actively involved in something besides work, such as coaching children's athletics, playing softball, singing in a choral group, or teaching reading to illiterate adults.

Dana Wolff
Southeast Technical Institute, Sioux Falls, SD

industry, you must visit the websites of health trade associations and various health care firms. Learn as much as you can about the health care industry. How broad is the industry? What types of companies are at the retail level? At the wholesale level? What kinds of firms provide services to the industry? Which companies are the largest? Which have the fastest growth rates? Which employers have employment facilities in geographic areas that are of interest to you? What are the leading companies? Which are the "employers of choice" that are family friendly or offer especially good benefits? What are the employee benefits at different companies? Knowing the industry and specific employers of interest to you tells you whom to target for employment in your career path. "Liking" a company can mean receiving early notices of job openings and other news.

2.3c Identify Specific Job Opportunities

The next step is to identify specific job openings that fit your skill set and provide opportunities for advancement in your career. Record your job search progress below using the Decision-Making Worksheet "Keeping Track of Your Job Search."

Internet, Career Websites and Job Boards You can use the Internet to obtain career advice, review job opportunities by industry and company, and conduct specialized job searches. You also can review resumes, create your résumé, create a cover letter, and post your résumé. The Internet allows you to review salary information, calculate living costs in different communities, and research career fairs. Just about all your search information on the Web can be saved for your future use.

Use **job boards** in your search, too. These are websites devoted to helping employers find suitable new employees by providing job listings, job sites, job search tips, job search engines, and related articles; some allow posting of resumes. Check out targeted industry sites, such as SalesJobs.com, Indeed.com, or Bridgespan.org. Also search Google for "niche job websites" in specific industries.

Career Fairs Career fairs are university-, community-, and employer-sponsored opportunities for job seekers to meet with perhaps dozens or even hundreds of potential employers over one or more days. Here you can schedule brief screening interviews with a half-dozen or more employers in a single day. Career fairs are advertised in local newspapers, on television, and on the Internet. Search "career fairs" on the Internet as well as at CareerBuilder.com and NationalCareerFairs.com. There usually are not many jobs at career fairs but participating definitely will help you practice your interviewing skills.

Classified Advertisements Advertisements in newspapers and professional publications usually are not very important in the job search process. However, big newspapers, such as the *Atlanta Journal-Constitution* and *Chicago Tribune*, advertise many jobs in large geographic areas. Others such as the *New York Times* and *The Wall Street Journal* have jobs for the whole country. And others like the *Financial Times* (aboutus.ft.com/careers) describe overseas opportunities.

Employment Agencies An **employment agency** is a firm specializing in locating employment positions for certain types of employees, such as secretaries, salespeople, engineers, managers, and computer personnel. Most employment agencies are paid fees by organizations that hire them to find new employees. Others charge the job hunter fees, sometimes very high amounts. Only talk with those firms whose companies pay the fees. Governments also have state or city employment offices that offer free services. Often these are not the best ways to find a good job, although sometimes they are very successful.

---

mentor
An experienced person, often a senior coworker, who offers friendly career-related advice, guidance, and coaching to a less experienced person.

sponsor
A powerfully positioned champion who "leans in" with an employee by advocating on their proteges' behalf and guiding them toward key players and assignments.

job boards
A website devoted to helping employers find suitable new employees by providing job listings, job sites, job search tips, job search engines, and related articles; some allow posting of resumes.

career fairs
University-, community-, and employer-sponsored events for job seekers to meet with many employers quickly to screen potential employers.

employment agency
Firm that locates employment for certain types of employees.

DID YOU KNOW

Money Websites for Career Planning

Informative websites for career planning, including job boards and sites that account for 30 percent of newly hired people are:

CareerBuilder.com (www.careerbuilder .com)

CareerBuilder.com key résumé words (www.careerbuilder.com/Article/CB-464-Cover-Letters-Resumes-What-are-Resume-Keywords/)

FlipDog (www.flipdog.com)

LinkUp (www.linkup.com)

Monster (www.monster.com)

NationJob (www.nationjob.com)

ResumeMachine.com (www.resume machine.com)

RileyGuide (www.rileyguide.com)

SimplyHired (www.simplyhired.com)

DECISION-MAKING WORKSHEET

DO IT IN CLASS

Keeping Track of Your Job Search

Below is a list of task areas in worksheet format that you can use to help keep track of your job search progress. Create more columns to the right so you can input important information, such as dates when you completed each effort.

	Date Done	Deadline to Do More
1. Identify your values.	_____	_____
2. Decide on economic, psychic, and lifestyle trade-offs.	_____	_____
3. Clarify career-related interests.	_____	_____
4. Assess abilities, experiences, and education.	_____	_____
5. Identify employment trends.	_____	_____
6. Create career goals and plans.	_____	_____
7. Target preferred employers.	_____	_____
8. Analyze your work-style personality.	_____	_____
9. Compare salary and living costs in different cities.	_____	_____
10. Calculate values on employee benefits.	_____	_____
11. Create an expanding list of networking contacts.	_____	_____
12. Obtain excellent letters of reference.	_____	_____
13. Compile revealing personal stories.	_____	_____
14. Assemble a résumé.	_____	_____
15. Prepare a cover letter.	_____	_____
16. Identify job opportunities:		
a. Career websites	_____	_____
b. Job boards	_____	_____
c. Career fairs	_____	_____
d. Classified advertisements	_____	_____
e. Employment agencies	_____	_____
17. Interviewing:		
a. Research the company.	_____	_____
b. Create responses for anticipated interview questions.	_____	_____
c. Create positive responses to list of negative questions.	_____	_____
d. Evaluate your interview performance.	_____	_____
18. Send thank-you notes.	_____	_____
19. Negotiate for salary.	_____	_____
20. Accept the job.	_____	_____

2.3d   Write an Effective Cover Letter

cover letter

A letter of introduction sent to a prospective employer to get an interview.

A **cover letter** is a letter of introduction sent to a prospective employer designed to express your interest in obtaining an interview. An effective cover letter helps introduce and sell you to the prospective employer. The cover letter should be specifically written for each position for which you are applying. See Figure 2-6 for an example. Expand upon a couple of details from your résumé, explaining how your talents and experience can benefit the employer. Communicate your enthusiasm for the job. When appropriate, mention a networking contact.

Address your cover letter, written on high-quality paper, to a specific person and request a brief meeting. If the hiring manager's name is not in the job announcement, telephone the employer and speak with a receptionist in the correct department. Be candid about your reason for needing a specific person's name. Your letter should try to secure a face-to-face meeting to obtain more information and gather impressions. End the letter with a sentence stating that you will be telephoning or e-mailing within two

Figure 2-6   Sample Cover Letter

June 23, 2014

Mrs. Juanita M. Pena, President
Pena Public Relations Agency, Inc.
4235 International Blvd NW
Atlanta, GA 30303

Dear Mrs. Pena:

We met briefly in Atlanta at last January's luncheon meeting of the Society of Consumer Affairs Professionals in Business. My professor at that time, Sarah Marlowe, introduced us and stated that your company was "undoubtedly one of the most successful creative agencies" in the Atlanta community.

My work experience in public relations and sales, academic background in consumer economics and communications, and research about your firm has led me to the conclusion that I am very interested in seeking employment in your organization. Also, a former employee of yours, Brittany Allyson, now with Hewitt Advertising, told me that you were a fine boss and encouraged me to join your fast-growing company.

My abilities to research, organize, communicate, and lead can provide Pena Public Relations with a person with multiple skills who can adapt to fast-changing needs. My strengths include fluency in three languages, serious computer skills, technical writing, persuasion, and ease in meeting new people. Attending two colleges and living in three states has broadened my perspectives as has studying public relations from the consumer perspective. See my enclosed résumé for more details.

I look forward to the opportunity to meet with you to better communicate my qualifications and evaluate how they might fit the Pena Public Relations Agency. You may contact me at (662) 921-1213 or Eanklin@hotmail.com. Also, I will telephone you in two weeks.

Sincerely,

Elizabeth Anklin
Elizabeth Anklin
12144 Southwest 174th Loop
Tupelo, MS 38803

Enclosure

weeks to reassert your interest in the position. Then, do so! Be sure to use a professional and nondescript e-mail address (like Jsmith@yahoo.com or Jsmith@aol.com) instead of something like cutelady@cutelady.com. Your cover letter should include a signature block that provides a link to your online résumé.

2.3e   Obtain Strong Reference Letters

College students too often simply ask a couple of professors they like to write them a letter of recommendation. Professors typically give their best judgments in these letters. This may include identifying some student weaknesses as well as strengths. Students who ask for a letter from an instructor who does not know them well also risk receiving a bland, boilerplate, or average kind of reference.

Ask only those professors who know you and your schoolwork well and give them a copy of your résumé. Approach them with a request similar to "Are you willing to give me a strong, *positive* letter of recommendation? I need one that points out my better qualities and performance here at college." If the instructor hesitates too long or gives you some negative feedback, consider asking a different professor for a recommendation. If your recommenders are willing to give you a separate copy of their letters, you will have them in your personal files to photocopy for future use.

2.3f   Formally Apply for the Job

You can't get a job without applying for it. Personalize your cover letter and résumé to fit the specific job of interest. Send it to the prospective employer. Many large employers prefer to receive job inquiries via the Internet, often through their website. If so, follow the application instructions perfectly. Other employers prefer a written letter and résumé. It may be smart to do both.

DID YOU KNOW

Sean's Success Story

Sean began his college career without a specific major in mind, although he knew he was interested in working with people. During his sophomore year, Sean took a class in public relations. He enjoyed the class immensely and realized that the public relations field fit his interests, abilities, and aptitudes. He declared a major in communications and talked to his advisor about jobs he could take to help him understand the field better and make good contacts for the future. Sean volunteered at his local chamber of commerce and signed up for an internship at a public relations firm between his junior and senior years. At graduation, he mapped out a career plan and soon found a job in a small public relations firm that would help him learn all of the various aspects of working in such a firm. Sean has been with the company for two years and was promoted to project manager. His long-term goal is to one day own his own public relations firm.

Stay Positive in a Sluggish Job Market

In many parts of the country a sluggish job market is causing financial strains for many and can delay career advancement. It has psychological impacts as well. Here are strategies that can help you cope.

1. *Stay physically active and eat well. Exercise and staying fit have both physical and psychological benefits.*

2. *Be up front about your anxiety, frustration, stress, and even fears. Share your concerns with family and friends.*

3. *Maintain a positive frame of mind. Delays are not permanent and the job market will turn around.*

4. *Stay involved in your professional network.*

5. *Volunteer both for the good you will be doing and for the possibilities for networking it provides.*

Bias Toward Underestimating Incomes

People engaged in career planning have a bias toward certain behaviors that can be harmful, such as a tendency toward underestimating the fair value of their labor in the future. This suggests that people overvalue the pay of a new job and undervalue the value of future economic benefits. What to do? Consider staying at the employer a long time to enjoy the higher pay later on in life.

job interview
Formal meeting between employer and potential employee to discuss job qualifications and suitability.

If you have not received a response to a job inquiry within two or three weeks, send a follow-up inquiry by adding a brief new opening sentence to your cover letter and send the revised letter with your résumé. When employers express interest in you as a prospective employee, they may request that you complete their official job application form. Be accurate in your responses.

2.3g Interview for Success

The interview is the single most important part of your search for employment. A **job interview** is a formal meeting to discuss an individual's job qualifications and suitability for an employment position. When you are invited for an interview, be prepared. This is a sales event in a traditional environment, so be professional. To succeed you should have an up-to-date haircut and wear clothes that are in fashion. Look the interviewer in the eye and lean forward as this suggests you are interested. When talking focus on the company's needs not yours. Be sure to bring up how you have been keeping up with technology and changes in your field of work.

Malcolm Gladwell, author of *Blink*, argues that when you meet someone for the first time, "your mind takes about two seconds to jump to a series of conclusions." It is not intuition or a snap judgment; it is rapid rational thinking. A human resources manager can read you the moment you walk into the door from your smile, first few sentences, tone of voice, the way you walk, the clothes you wear, how you stand, the grip of your handshake, and how you sit. You must present yourself as a confident and energetic professional.

Practice your "blink" before every interview, so you will be ready for a conversation on Skype instead of a traditional face-to-face interview. If this happens to you, get ready. If interviewing at home, make the background neat, make sure your face is well lit, eliminate the chance of interruptions, sit still, and practice beforehand. Professional recruiters estimate that perhaps only 20 percent of college seniors adequately prepare for their interviews.

Five Good Points to Raise in an Interview Make five key points during your interview: (1) "Let me tell you about the time that I solved a similar problem" (and then tell a story), (2) "Does that make sense, please clarify" (demonstrates that you are thorough and accurate), (3) "I saw that announcement about your company on a website" (shows off your genuine interest in the firm), (4) "Why did you come to work here?" (shows that you are curious about the company), (5) "I'd love the opportunity to join this company" (implies that you will accept an offer, if made).

Do Lots of Research Before the Interview Before the interview, research the company. Try to know more about it than the interviewer. Learn how the company makes money, its operations and history, profitability, expansion plans, and other recent developments. Research the company's history. Also research the company's competitors and the industry. You cannot spend enough hours on this effort!

Know the major industry trends and news and be able to talk about how they could affect the company. Know what the company is good at and how this relates to your skills. Be familiar with the job description. Find out what it is like to work at the specific company. When you do a background check on companies, you might seek out candid posts from current or former employees about salaries, company culture, and lousy bosses. However, be wary about unsubstantiated information. See CareerBuilder (www.careerbuilder.com), Glassdoor (www.glassdoor.com), Jobster (www.jobster.com), PayScale (www.payscale.com), LinkedIn (www.linkedin.com), and Vault (www.vault.com).

Prepare Responses for Anticipated Interview Questions Your responsibilities during the interview are to remain calm, reveal your personality, be honest, convey your best characteristics, handle questions well, and communicate your enthusiasm about the job. Always answer in a controlled manner. During the interview, be confident that you are the best person for the job and project yourself accordingly.

Job interviewers seem to ask similar questions. You know they are coming so prepare good, personal responses for the following inquiries:

1. Tell me about yourself.
2. How would your instructors and previous employers describe you?
3. What did you like the most about college, and the least?
4. Tell me what you know about our company.
5. Why are you interested in working for this company?
6. What unique abilities and experiences qualify you for the job?
7. Describe some of your strengths and weaknesses.
8. What experiences have you had working with teams and coordinating such efforts?
9. Give an example of an ethical challenge you faced and tell how you handled it.
10. Relate a time when you were faced with a very difficult problem and how you handled it.
11. Describe the supervisors who motivated you to do your best work.
12. What were some of the best and worst aspects of your last job?
13. What do you do in your leisure time?
14. Describe your career plans for two and five years from now.

Create Positive Responses to Negative Questions Be prepared to "turn any negative into a positive" when asked such questions. One popular negative question is, "What are your weaknesses?" Interviewers who ask this type of question want to determine whether the applicant possesses certain qualities such as honesty, self-awareness, humility, sincerity, zest, and skill in managing shortcomings and mistakes. Denying weakness or being evasive means you don't get the job.

Practice your interview skills beforehand. Practice your responses, especially to negative questions. Perhaps make a videotape of a mock interview, and after evaluating your performance, do it again.

Compile Revealing Personal Stories Assemble some personal stories about yourself that reveal some of your better characteristics. For a single job at a company you could have five or more interviews in one day, and during the interview process, you are expected to talk about yourself. Therefore, prepare by writing down some concise stories or statements, perhaps about the time you took over caregiver duties for your siblings while your mother was hospitalized, or facilitated resolving some internal conflicts among the officers in your student club, or assisted a high school teacher to coordinate and supervise 20 students on a field trip, or worked 14 straight hours at Walmart during a weather emergency. Preparing as many as a dozen stories will give you many ways to talk about your positive qualities without just saying, "I'm good." Everyone else says that! Communicate that message about yourself in part by telling stories to illustrate your better qualities.

You need not volunteer information in an interview that might hurt you, but respond to questions accurately. Misrepresenting facts, making even small distortions, will cast doubt on everything in your résumé and on everything you said in the interview, and you will not be hired.

Be certain to ignore tweets and do no texting at any time during an interview visit. Even better, turn off your cellphone. Your entire focus should be on the interview experience.

Prepare Questions to Ask the Interviewer A key to success in any interview is to show your enthusiasm and interest in the position and organization. Compliment the

DID YOU KNOW

Your Worst Financial Blunders in Career Planning

Based on others' financial woes you will make mistakes career planning when you:

1. *Neglect to fully research a company before going for an interview.*
2. *Fail to match your interests and preferred work style with the requirements of the career.*
3. *Disregard networking by not getting involved in local career-related professional associations.*

interviewer's company based on some facts learned in your pre-interview research. Also, prepare some questions to ask, perhaps about future company plans, company policies, employee benefits, specific duties, and job expectations. You will want to inquire about the corporate culture, too. Write down your questions so you will have your thoughts clear in your mind. Consider the following questions:

- "What qualifications make for an ideal candidate?"
- "What attracted you to this company?"
- "If you hire me, what can I accomplish in the next six months that will make you glad you did?"
- Toward the end of the interview and after restating your interest in the position, ask, "What is the next step?"

Personality Tests One-third of employers give job candidates personality tests assessing team orientation, strengths important to a job, emotional intelligence, motivation, and true work-style inclinations. Don't try to game the employer by telling them what they want to hear—the "right" answer. Being honest confirms what the prospective employer already knows about you.

Be Ready for Telephone Interviews When returning a telephone call or engaging in an interview present yourself in a professional manner. Have a pen or pencil and paper handy. Be aware of distractions in your surroundings, such as traffic noise. If necessary, arrange to call the interviewer back when you find a quiet place. Speak clearly, and eliminate the "uhs" and "umms." The interviewer will notice if you take a sip of coffee or a bite out of a bagel.

After the Interview, Evaluate It and Send Thank-You Notes After a job interview, take a few minutes to objectively evaluate your performance. Write down any

DID YOU KNOW

How to Interview Over a Meal

More people lose a job interview over lunch than during the formal interview because they fail to realize that going to lunch is a continuation of the interview rather than a social situation. Employers want to hire people with some degree of refinement, people who will mix well with clients and executives. It is smart to engage in conversation over a meal, of course, but let the host do most of the talking. Good etiquette tips include the following:

- Order something that is less expensive than what the host has ordered.
- Keep your elbows off the table.
- Break (don't cut) your bread or roll before buttering.
- Use the bread knife (the small knife to the right of your plate).
- Use the small fork outermost from the plate for the first course.

- Don't salt and pepper your meal before tasting it.
- Cut your meat one bite at a time.
- Don't talk with food in your mouth.
- Don't order beer, wine, or liquor.
- Avoid ordering soup or pastas because they can be too messy.
- Be extremely polite and respectful of the servers.
- Never complain about a meal.
- Leave it to your host to signal the server.
- If confused, be patient and follow the lead of the host.
- Leave your napkin on your chair when excusing yourself.
- When the meal is over, thank the host and state that you want the job.

questions you were asked that were different from what you expected and make some notes about ways to improve in your next interview. The more interviews you have, the better you will be able to present yourself. Also, immediately mail thank-you notes expressing your appreciation for the opportunity to interview and restate your interest in the position. Four out of five successful job seekers send thank-you notes to *everyone* they meet.

2.3h **Negotiate and Accept the Job**

Wait until after the job has been firmly offered to discuss salary. Ask for the salary range for the position. Do not be the first to give a definitive dollar amount. Your objective in negotiating is to obtain a salary 20 percent above the highest figure because you are an exceptional candidate and you will perform at the highest level anticipated. Don't sell yourself short. Even if the job posting states "salary is not negotiable," do so. Your competitors will.

Focus on both gross and net pay. A gross income of $60,000 shrinks to about $40,000 after subtracting federal income, Social Security, and Medicare taxes. Additional deductions for contributions for medical care, retirement, and flexible benefits may drop the take-home pay to $37,000, or $3083 a month. You can then add back the value of employer-paid benefits such as life insurance and the employer match in their retirement plan, but you cannot take that money home.

Compare Salary Offers Comparing salary offers from employers located in different cities can be tricky without sufficient information on the approximate cost of living in each community. Sometimes those costs vary drastically. Information from the Internet reveals, for example, that life in a high-cost city such as Seattle is more expensive than life in a lower-cost city such as Portland, Oregon. The data are reported in index form, with the "average cost" community being given a rating of 100.

The following example demonstrates how to compare salary offers in two cities. Assume the Seattle (city 1) index is 138, and Portland's (city 2) is 114. You want to compare the buying power of a salary offer of $52,000 in Portland with a $65,000 offer in Seattle. The costs can be compared using Equations (2.1) and (2.2).

$$\text{Salary in city 1} \times \frac{\text{index city 2}}{\text{index city 1}} = \text{equivalent salary in city 2}$$

(2.1)

$$\text{Seattle salary of } \$65,000 \times \frac{114}{138} = \$53,695 \text{ in buying power in Portland}$$

Thus, the $65,000 Seattle salary offer would buy $53,695 of goods and services in Portland, an amount more than the Portland offer of $52,000. All things being equal (and they are both nice cities), the Seattle offer is slightly better ($53,695 − $52,000 = $1,695).

To compare the buying power of salaries in the other direction, reverse the formula:

$$\text{Salary in city 2} \times \frac{\text{index city 1}}{\text{index city 2}} = \text{equivalent salary in city 1}$$

(2.2)

$$\text{Portland salary of } \$52,000 \times \frac{138}{114} = \$62,947 \text{ in buying power in Seattle}$$

Thus, the $52,000 Portland offer can buy only $62,947 of goods and services in Seattle—an amount less than the $65,000 Seattle salary offer. All things being equal, the Seattle offer is still better. For fairer comparisons, add the value of employee benefits and redo the calculations. Note that non salary benefits for college graduates are typically valued at 25 to 30 percent of the salary.

FINANCIAL POWER POINT

Common Job Interview Mistakes

1. Inappropriate attire
2. Being late or at the wrong time/date
3. Displayed little knowledge of employer or industry
4. Poorly prepared to discuss abilities, skills, and experience
5. Unable to discuss career plans and goals
6. Overly aggressive/entitled about job expectations
7. Demonstrated little enthusiasm
8. Poor eye contact
9. Use slang or overly casual language
10. Checking phone/texting/tweeting

DO IT IN CLASS

DID YOU KNOW

How to Deal with Rejection

The job search process is filled with rejections. Before you land a job, you might have 5 or even 100 potential employers say "No!" Don't let employment rejections strip you of your self-esteem, or you will begin to falsely think that there is something wrong with you. A rejection is simply an indicator that there is an inadequate match between your qualities and the employer's needs as perceived in the interview.

After a turndown, when possible, ask the company for a review of the strengths and weaknesses of your interview. Make an effort to improve for the next interview. Then, forget the disappointment and move on with your job search.

DID YOU KNOW ?

Happiness Peaks at $75,000

Researchers at Harvard and Princeton find that happiness peaks at an income of about $75,000. Once you reach $75,000 in the United States the beneficial aspects of more money taper off. More stuff does not make you happier either. To be happier, shift spending from buying stuff, like cars and electronics, to experiences, like trips and special evenings out. Buying for others increases happiness, too.

DO IT IN CLASS

DID YOU KNOW ?

How to Get a Raise

Find out what people in your field earn by talking with others, reviewing trade publications, and checking online at sites such as Glassdoor.com, vault.com, payscale .com, salary.com, and HotJobs.com. Then talk with your boss and write down well-defined, achievable, and measurable goals that you can work toward. This may occur during a formal annual review. Document your accomplishments in writing and keep records. Throughout the year, perhaps on a quarterly basis, discuss these with your boss. Do so in sit-down meetings rather than in brief hallway conversations.

Schedule a meeting with your boss before the scheduled time for the annual personnel review. Never mention how much you need a big raise and instead focus on your performance. If the boss cannot give you all the money you deserve, ask for a bigger bonus, enhanced health or retirement benefits, a more flexible work schedule, a change in work hours, permission to occasionally telecommute, or more vacation time.

Compare Salary and Cost of Living You may compare salary figures and the cost of living in different communities at the following websites [most use the ACCRA Cost of Living data (www.coli.org/)]:

- CityRating.com (www.cityrating.com/costofliving.asp).
- CNNMoney.com (cgi.money.cnn.com/tools/costofliving/costofliving.html)
- Moving.com (www.moving.com/real-estate/compare-cities/index.asp)
- Realtor.com (www.homefair.com/real-estate/cost-of-living.asp)
- Salary.com (swz.salary.com/costoflivingwizard/layoutscripts/coll_start.aspx)

Compare Other Community Resources Comparing salary offers among various cities where you might work is only part of the decision where and whether to relocate. Here are some resources for other important aspects of the decision:

The cost of housing—www.zillow.com

Quality of life issues—money.cnn.com/magazines/moneymag/best-places/

Moving costs—www.citytocitymoving.us/

Wait and Negotiate Be comfortable with silence, and wait for a response. If the offer is less than what you were expecting, explain that point. Be firm but amicable. This will enhance the employer's respect for you. Tell the employer that you are not willing to start at the bottom or middle of the salary ladder. Reiterate your two or three strongest selling points. Be certain to make a short list of these points beforehand. If the employer states that the offer is final, reply that you need a day or two to think it over. Never turn down an offer until you are absolutely positive you must do so.

Seattle has a lot to offer, but it comes at a price.

© Rigucci/Shutterstock.com

DID YOU KNOW

Turn Bad Habits into Good Ones

Do You Do This?	*Do This Instead!*
Avoid getting to know your professors	Visit one professor in his/her office on a regular basis
Ignore student professional associations	Join and take a leadership role in at least one association
Use an old résumé	Update your résumé frequently
Simply change the name/address when writing a cover letter	Write a new cover letter for each job application
Plan to move back to your hometown after graduation	Explore employment opportunities in several new cities
Focus primarily on gross pay when deciding on a job opportunity	Factor take-home pay, employee benefits, and cost of living into your job decisions

If the terms are right, accept the job. Give your new employer your acceptance orally as well as in writing. Obtain a letter confirming your acceptance of the job at the agreed-upon salary with benefits, such as moving expenses, flexible hours, and extra vacation days.

2.3i At Work Practice the Four Rules of Career Success

Experts say you should focus on just four things.

1. **Competence:** Be as good at your job as possible.
2. **Confidence:** Be able to formulate and communicate your ideas in a way that inspires others.
3. **Caring:** Put the interests of your company, coworkers, and customers ahead of your own.
4. **Come:** Arrive early and stay late—every day—even at least for 10 to 15 minutes.

2.3j Periodically Update Your Career Plan

Getting that desired job does not mean that your career planning efforts are over. Indeed, they have only just begun. You know that employers formally evaluate their employees on a regular basis and you should do the same for your career plan.

DO IT NOW!

You know more about personal finance after reading this chapter, so get started right now by:

1. *Preparing your résumé.*
2. *Contacting your school's placement office to explore careers in your field.*
3. *Visiting one of your professors to seek a mentoring relationship.*

CONCEPT CHECK 2.3

1. Offer suggestions on correctly assembling a résumé and cover letter, and explain how the two documents differ.
2. Explain how to compare salary and living costs in different cities.
3. Summarize the best methods to identify job opportunities.
4. List five suggestions to interview for success.

WHAT DO YOU RECOMMEND *NOW?*

Now that you have read the chapter on the importance of career planning, what do you recommend to Nicole in the case at the beginning of the chapter regarding:

1. Clarifying her values and lifestyle trade-offs in career planning?
2. Enhancing her career-related experiences before graduation?
3. Creating career plans and goals?
4. Understanding her work-style personality?
5. Identifying job opportunities?

© Tyler Olson/Shutterstock.com

BIG PICTURE SUMMARY OF LEARNING OBJECTIVES

LO1   Identify the key steps in successful career planning.

Career planning is identifying an employment pathway that aligns with your interests and abilities and that is expected to provide the lifestyle and work style you find enjoyable and satisfying. It includes clarifying your values; identifying one or more desired career fields; reviewing your abilities, experiences and education; taking advantage of networking; aligning yourself with tomorrow's employment trends; and finalizing your career plan and beginning your career.

LO2   Analyze the financial and legal aspects of employment.

The financial side of career planning includes placing dollar values on employee benefits and knowing your legal employment rights.

LO3   Practice effective employment search strategies.

Smart job search strategies include assembling an attention-getting résumé, targeting your preferred employers, identifying specific job opportunities, writing an effective cover letter, obtaining strong reference letters, formally applying for the job, interviewing for success, negotiating and accepting the job, practicing the four rules of career success, and periodically updating your career plans. This includes comparing salary offers in different cities.

LET'S TALK ABOUT IT

1. **Interviewing Tips.** List three interviewing tips for new college graduates looking for employment when in many parts of the country a sluggish job market exists.

2. **Interview Mistakes.** Thinking about some common mistakes that people make in job interviews, which five are the worst? Make a list often things people should do to improve success in an interview.

3. **Career Trade-offs.** People regularly make decisions in career planning that have trade-offs. Identify some benefits and costs people are faced with as well as two lifestyle trade-offs.

4. **Keeping Track Topics.** Review the task areas in the Decision-Making Worksheet "Keeping Track of Your

Job Search" on page 52, and identify what you think are the five that likely are the most difficult for people to accomplish. For each of the five, offer a suggestion that might help people accomplish the task.

5. **Assessing the Benefits of a Second Income.** Adding a second income to a family either by having another person work or by working two jobs often seems to be a good way to add financial resources. But the impact is not always as large as people hope. Review the example given in the "Run the Numbers" box on page 46 and discuss the pros and cons of a second income in that example.

**DO IT IN CLASS
PAGE 46**

DO THE MATH

1. **Economic Trade-off of Graduate School.** Jessica Sotomajor hopes to earn an extra $600,000 over her remaining 40-year working career by going to night school to obtain a master's degree. If her income projection is correct, that's an average of $15,000 more money a year. Jessica's employer is willing to pay 75 percent, or $45,000, toward the $60,000 schooling costs, so she must pay out $15,000 of her own money.

   DO IT IN CLASS
   PAGE 19

   (a) What is the forgone lost future value of her $15,000 over the 40 years at 6 percent? (Hint: See Appendix A.1.)

   (b) What would be the forgone lost future value of $60,000 over 40 years if Jessica had to pay all the costs for her master's degree? (Hint: See Appendix A.1.)

2. **Comparing Salary Offers.** Using Equations (2.1) or (2.2), if the cost-of-living index was 132 for Chicago and 114 for San Antonio, compare the buying power

   DO IT IN CLASS
   PAGE 57

   of a $50,000 salary in Chicago with a $47,000 offer in San Antonio.

3. **Future Value of Employer's Match.** Tyler Winkle's employer makes a matching contribution of $1200 a year to his 401(k) retirement account at work. If the dollar amount of the employer's contribution increases 4 percent annually, how much will the employer contribute to the plan in the twentieth year from now? (Hint: See Appendix A.1.)

   DO IT IN CLASS
   PAGE 19

4. **Cashing Out 401(k) Plan.** Emily Amarrada has accepted a new job and is thinking about cashing out the $30,000 she has built up in her employer's 401(k) plan to use to buy a new car. If, instead, she left the funds in the plan and they earn 6 percent annually for the next 30 years, how much would Emily have in her plan? (Hint: See Appendix A.1.)

   DO IT IN CLASS
   PAGE 19

FINANCIAL PLANNING CASES

CASE 1

Harry and Belinda Johnson Consider Inflation and Children

Throughout this book, we will present a continuing narrative about Harry and Belinda Johnson. Following is a brief description of the lives of this couple.

Harry graduated with a bachelor's degree in interior design last spring from a large Midwestern university near his hometown. Belinda has a degree in information technology from a university on the West Coast and is employed in a medium-size public relations firm. Harry and Belinda both worked on their school's student newspapers and met at a conference during their junior year in college. They were married last June and live in an apartment in Kansas City. They will face many financial challenges over the next 20 years, as they buy their first home, decide on life insurance needs, begin a family, change jobs, and invest for retirement.

(a) Harry receives $3000 in interest income annually from a trust fund set up by his deceased father's estate. The amount will never change. What will be the buying power of $3000 in ten years if inflation rises at 3 percent a year? (Hint: Use Appendix A.2.)

(b) Belinda and Harry have discussed starting a family but decided to wait for perhaps five years in order to get their careers off to a good start and organize

their personal finances. They also know that having children is expensive. They figure that the extra expense of a child would be about $5000 annually until high school graduation. How much money will they likely cumulatively spend on a child over 18 years assuming a 3 percent inflation rate? (Hint: Use Appendix A.3.)

CASE 2

Victor and Maria Hernandez Consider a Career Change

Throughout this book, we will present a continuing narrative about Victor and Maria Hernandez. Following is a brief description of the lives of this couple.

Victor and Maria, both in their late 30s, have two children: Jacob, age 13, and Nicholas, age 15. Victor has had a long sales career with a retail appliance store. Maria works part time as a medical records assistant. Victor is somewhat satisfied with his career but has always wondered about a career as a teacher in a public school. He would have to take a year off work to go to college to obtain his teaching certificate, and that would mean giving up his $43,000 salary for a year. Victor expects that he could earn about the same income as a teacher.

(a) What would his annual income be after 20 years as a teacher if he received an average 3 percent raise every year? (Hint: Use Appendix A.1.)

(b) Victor could earn $4000 each year teaching during the summers. What is the accumulated future value of earning those annual amounts over 20 years assuming a 5 percent raise every year? (Hint: Use Appendix A.3.)

CASE 3

Julia Price's Career Plans Change

Julia has recently undergone a severe career crisis. After nearly ten years as a professional engineer, her position was phased out by her company due to a loss of government contracts, and she has been offered a position in the marketing department. The new job will require that she interact with purchasing agents for various companies that are current and potential customers of her company. The job pays more but will require considerable travel. She will be using her engineering background, but the primary tasks all will relate to presenting herself and her company in the best possible light to these other firms. Julia thinks she should take the new job and make a personal commitment to doing it for one year and, if she does not truly enjoy the work, seek a new engineering job within her company or at another employer. Offer your opinions about her thinking.

CASE 4

Matching Yourself with a Job

After completing his associate of arts degree four months ago from a community college in Rochester, New York, Juan Ramirez has answered more than a two dozen advertisements and interviewed several times in his effort to get a sales job, but he has had no success. Juan has never done sales work before, but he did take some business classes in college, including "Personal Selling." After some of the interviews, Juan telephoned some of those potential employers only to find that even though they liked him, they said they typically hired only those people with previous sales experience or who seemed to possess terrific potential.

(a) If Juan actually were well suited for sales, which work values and work-style factors do you think he would rate as "very important"?

(b) What would you recommend to Juan regarding how to find out about the depth of his interest in a sales career?

(c) Assuming Juan has appropriate personal qualities and academic strengths to be successful in a sales career, what additional strategies should he consider to better market himself?

CASE 5

Career Promotion Opportunity

DO IT IN CLASS PAGE 57

Nina and Ting Guo of Lima, Ohio, have been together for eight years, having married just after completing college. Nina has been working as an insurance agent ever since. Ting began working as a family counselor for the state of Ohio last year after completing his master's degree in counseling. Recently Nina's boss commented confidentially that he was going to recommend Nina to be the next person promoted, given a raise of about $15,000, and relocated to the home office in St. Louis, Missouri. Nina thinks that if offered the opportunity she would like to take it, even if it means that Ting will have to resign from his new job.

(a) What suggestions can you offer Nina when she gets home from work and wants to discuss with her husband her likely career promotion?

(b) What lifestyle factors and benefits and costs issues should Nina and Ting probably discuss?

BE YOUR OWN PERSONAL FINANCIAL MANAGER

1. **Work-Style Personality.** Do you know your preferred work-style personality? Take the time to complete the worksheet on page 41 or you can use Worksheet 6: What Is My Work-Style Personality from "My Personal Financial Planner."

MY PERSONAL FINANCIAL PLANNER

2. **Values Clarification.** Go online and do a Web search or "values clarification assessment" to bring up a long list of possible values clarification exercises. Complete one or more exercises and then compare the results to what you have been thinking in terms of your academic major in college and possible careers.

3. **Career Field Exploration.** Visit the Career Guide to Industries at www.bls.gov/ooh/about/career-guide-to-industries.htm to determine the earnings, benefits, and employment outlook for a position in a career field that interests you. Complete Worksheet 7: Career Field Research from "My Personal Financial Planner" to write up your results including an assessment of how well your work-style personality and values fit the career field that you researched.

4. **Compare Salary Offers.** Use two actual salary offers or two desired offers in two cities of your choosing to compare the salary offers based on the different costs of living in the two cities. See Worksheet 8: Comparing Salary Offers in Two Different Cities from "My Personal Financial Planner" as a guide for your analysis.

5. **Assess the Benefits of a Second Income.** Using real or example data assess the benefits of a second income for a dual-earner household in your salary range. Use the example provided in the text on page 46 or Worksheet 9: Assessing the Benefits of a Second Income from "My Personal Financial Planner" for your assessment.

ON THE NET

Go to the Web pages indicated to complete these exercises.

1. **Research the Occupational Outlook Handbook.** Go to the website for the *Occupational Outlook Handbook* at www.bls.gov/oco/home.htm. Select two occupational areas that are of interest to you, and for each, determine the likely starting salary, career path, future salary expectations, and demand for people with the skills appropriate for the occupation.

2. **Research the National Unemployment Rate.** Go to the website for the Bureau of Labor Statistics' assessment of the labor outlook in the United States at www.bls.gov /bls/employment.htm. Browse through the information provided to determine the current national unemployment rate for the nation as a whole and for a city or area of interest to you. Compare current statistics with those of one year ago and with projections for five and ten years in the future.

3. **Research a Career of Interest.** Check the U.S. Department of Labor's Career Guide to Industries at www .bls.gov/oco/cg to learn about the earnings, benefits, educational requirements, and employment outlook for a career of interest to you. Make a written summary of your findings.

4. **Check Out Income Levels.** Are your current perceptions about the income level typical for various career fields correct? Visit www.payscale.com and research salary data on five to seven fields including your own.

ACTION INVOLVEMENT PROJECTS

1. **Interview a Human Resource Manager.** Use the Internet and/or Yellow Pages to find a local company that employs people in your prospective career field. Request an interview with the human resource manager. Ask about salary levels, employee benefits, and the career ladder. Make a written summary of your findings.

2. **Prepare a Resume.** Using the newspaper want ads or Monster.com find a job listing for a position in your career field. Prepare a résumé for the job. Review Figures 2-3, 2-4, and 2-5 on pages 48 and 49 and create or update your résumé accordingly. Take the job listing and documents to your faculty advisor and ask him or her for feedback. **DO IT IN CLASS PAGE 48**

3. **Cover Letter.** Review Figure 2-6 on page 53 and create or update a sample cover letter to accompany your résumé when applying for a job. **DO IT IN CLASS PAGE 48**

4. **Where Do You Want to Live?** It is highly likely that one of the best job opportunities for you at graduation will require that you move away from your hometown and/or where you went to college. While that new location is unknown now, it is not too early to begin thinking of where you might need and/ or want to live. Use the list of websites on page 58 to compare housing costs, quality of life issues, and moving costs for three cities of interest to you. **DO IT IN CLASS PAGE 58**

5. **Clarify Your Values.** To help you clarify your values, review the section titled "Clarify Your Values and Interests" on page 36 and make a list of your 10 most important ones. **DO IT IN CLASS PAGE 36**

6. **Trade-Offs.** To clarify your lifestyle trade-offs, review the section titled "Lifestyle Trade-offs" on page 38 and given the list and make a list of your choices for trade-offs. **DO IT IN CLASS PAGE 38**

7. **Anticipated Interview Questions.** Review the questions in the section on "Prepare Responses for Anticipated Interview Questions" on page 55 and write out concise sample responses to each question. **DO IT IN CLASS PAGE 55**

Visit the Garman/Forgue companion website at www.cengagebrain.com.

3 Financial Statements, Tools, and Budgets

LEARNING OBJECTIVES

After reading this chapter, you should be able to:

1 Identify your financial values, goals, and strategies.

2 Use balance sheets and cash-flow statements to measure your financial health and progress.

3 Collect and organize the financial records necessary for managing your personal finances.

4 Achieve your financial goals through budgeting.

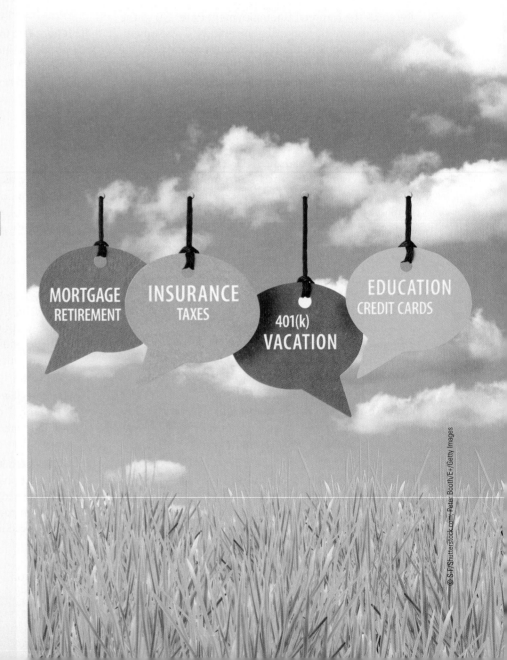

MORTGAGE
RETIREMENT

INSURANCE
TAXES

401(k)
VACATION

EDUCATION
CREDIT CARDS

© S-F/Shutterstock.com-Peter Booth/E+/Getty Images

WHAT DO YOU RECOMMEND?

Austin and Rachel Patterson, both age 26, have been married for four years and have no children. Austin is a licensed electrician earning $46,000 per year, and Rachel earns $41,000 annually as a middle-school teacher. Austin would like to go to half time on his job and return to school on a part-time basis; he is one year short of finishing his bachelor's degree in engineering. His education expenses would be about $20,000 for the year, which could be partially covered by student loans. He has not yet discussed his plans with Rachel.

Austin and Rachel have recently started saving for retirement through their employment and have set aside some savings for emergencies. They have substantial credit card debt and are still paying off their student loans. The couple rents a two-bedroom apartment. Austin always thought it smart to save all of their receipts, bank statements, and other financial documents. His system for organizing their records is very simple; each month he puts everything in a manila envelope and then puts the 12 envelopes into a box at the end of the year.

Austin knows that his educational plans will have financial implications for the couple. He wants to factor these financial issues into his discussion with Rachel about his plans. To this point, they have never developed financial statements or explicit financial goals.

© auremar/Shutterstock.com

What do you recommend to Austin for his talk with Rachel on the subject of financial planning regarding:

1. **Setting financial goals?**
2. **Determining what they own and owe?**
3. **Using the information in Austin's newly prepared financial statements to summarize the family's financial situation?**
4. **Evaluating their financial progress?**
5. **Setting up a record-keeping system to better serve their needs?**
6. **Starting a budgeting process to guide saving and spending?**

Sixty percent of all adults say they do not budget. Four in ten say they are living beyond their means and rate themselves as fair or poor in managing money. A similar percentage say they find it difficult to meet monthly expenses. They live paycheck-to-paycheck, and they often turn to credit cards. They are incompetent in money matters, and their choices will forever make them the "have nots" in society rather than the "haves." Living above your means can lead to financial ruin at a young age. If you always live below your means, you will always have means. That's the secret.

To not mess up your financial life you must avoid living paycheck-to-paycheck because this lets your spending dictate your savings. Save first so you can spend later. To succeed you need to follow a spending plan that includes savings, take appropriate actions to achieve results, and regularly measure your financial strength and progress. No matter what your previous financial background, applying the knowledge within this chapter will help you enjoy financial decision making and be successful in managing your money.

What is important is not how much money you have. It is how well you spend your money. At its essence wealth is not measured by how much you make, rather it is how much you hang onto.

3.1 FINANCIAL VALUES, GOALS, AND STRATEGIES

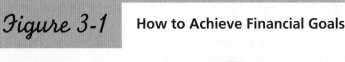

LEARNING OBJECTIVE 1

Identify your financial values, goals, and strategies.

Identifying your financial values and goals sets the stage for financial success. Values and goals help you keep a balance between spending and saving and make you stay committed to your financial plans. Once goals are set, you can develop the strategies necessary for their achievement. **Financial planning**, which is the process of developing and implementing a coordinated series of financial plans, can help you achieve financial success. By planning your personal finances, you seek to manage your income and wealth so that you reach your financial goals throughout your lifetime.

Figure 3-1 provides an overview of effective personal financial planning. Table 3-1 illustrates one couple's (Harry and Belinda Johnson) overall financial plan.

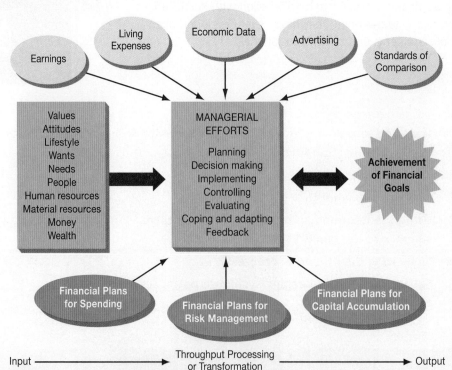

Figure 3-1   **How to Achieve Financial Goals**

Table 3-1	**Financial Plans, Goals, and Objectives for Harry (Age 23) and Belinda (Age 22) Johnson, Prepared in February 2015**	

Financial Plan Areas	Long-Term Goals and Objectives	Short-Term Goals and Objectives
FOR SPENDING		
Evaluate and plan major purchases	Purchase a new car in two years.	Begin saving $200 a month for a downpayment for a new car.
Manage debt	Keep installment debt under 10 percent of take-home pay.	Pay off charge cards at the end of each month and do not finance any purchases of appliances or other similar products.
FOR RISK MANAGEMENT		
Medical costs	Avoid large medical costs.	Maintain employer-subsidized medical insurance policy by paying $135 monthly premium.
Property and casualty losses	Always have renter's or homeowner's insurance. Always have maximum automobile insurance coverage.	Make semiannual premium payment of $220 on renter's insurance policy. Make premium payments of $440 on automobile insurance policy.
Liability losses	Eventually buy $1 million liability insurance.	Rely on $100,000 policy purchased from same source as automobile insurance policy.
Premature death	Have adequate life insurance coverage for both as well as lots of financial investments so the survivor would not have any financial worries.	Maintain employer-subsidized life insurance on Belinda. Buy some life insurance for Harry. Start some investments.
Income loss from disability	Buy sufficient disability insurance.	Rely on sick days and seek disability insurance through private insurers.
FOR CAPITAL ACCUMULATION		
Tax fund	Have enough money for taxes (but not too much) withheld from monthly salaries by both employers to cover eventual tax liabilities.	Confirm that employer withholding of taxes is sufficient. Have extra money withheld to cover additional tax liability because of income on trust from Harry's deceased father.
Revolving savings fund	Always have sufficient cash in local accounts to meet monthly and annual anticipated budget expense needs.	Develop cash-flow calendar to ascertain needs. Put money into revolving savings fund to build it up quickly to the proper balance. Keep all funds in interest-earning accounts.
Emergency fund	Build up monetary assets equivalent to three months' take-home pay.	Put $150 per month into an emergency fund until it totals one month's take-home pay.
Education	Maintain educational skills and credentials to remain competitive. Have employer assist in paying for Belinda to earn a master of business administration (MBA). Have Harry complete a master of fine arts (MFA), possibly a PhD in interior design.	Both take one graduate class per term.
Savings	Always have a nice-size savings balance. Regularly save to achieve goals. Save a portion of any extra income or gifts. Save $26,000 for a down payment on a home to be bought within five years.	Save enough to pay cash for the newest smart phone. Pay off Visa credit card balance of $390 soon. Begin saving $400 per month for a down payment on a new home.
Investment	Own substantial shares of a conservative mutual fund that will pay dividends equivalent to about 10 percent of family income at age 45.	Start investing in a mutual fund before next year.
Retirement	Own some real estate and common stocks. Retire at age 60 or earlier on income that is the same as the take-home pay earned just before retirement.	Establish individual retirement accounts (IRAs) for Harry and Belinda before next year. Contribute the maximum possible amount to employer-sponsored retirement accounts.
Estate planning	Provide for surviving spouse.	Each spouse makes a will.

YOUR NEXT FIVE YEARS

In the next five years, you can start achieving financial success by doing the following related to financial statements, tools, and budgets:

1. *Develop financial goals and update them annually.*

2. *Develop a cash-flow statement and spending plan every month to ensure that you spend less than you make.*

3. *Track your net worth and financial ratios annually to assess your financial progress.*

4. *Use an uncomplicated but effective personal financial record-keeping system.*

5. *Openly and honestly communicate about money matters with key loved ones on a regular basis.*

values
Fundamental beliefs about what is important, desirable, and worthwhile.

financial goals
Specific objectives addressed by planning and managing finances.

Such excellent managerial efforts help push them toward achieving financial success. The couple has made plans in 15 specific areas spread across three broad categories: (1) spending, (2) risk management, and (3) capital accumulation. Some people choose not to make a financial plan. The fact is that not having a financial plan is still a plan, it is just a really bad plan.

3.1a Values Define Your Financial Success

Your **values** provide the underlying support and rationale for your financial and lifestyle goals. Your values are your fundamental beliefs about what is important, desirable, and worthwhile. They serve as the basis for your goals. All of us differ in the ways we value education, spiritual life, health, employment, credit use, family life, and many other factors. Personal financial goals grow out of these values because we inevitably consider some things more important or desirable than others. We express our values, in part, by the ways we spend, save, invest, and donate our money.

3.1b "Sacrifice Now or Suffer Later" Is a Key Value

One major benefit of financial planning is using money wisely. People who are smart about personal finance typically value saving some of their income. They adhere to the personal finance philosophy of "Pay myself first." If you earn money, shouldn't you be "paid" first? Successful money managers do this instead of spending it all or, even worse, spending even more than they earn by using credit. They establish a current spending level based on the necessities of life. They set aside money for future spending, such as for a vehicle purchase, home, child's education, vacation home, and living expenses during the years of retirement. They live well while preparing for the future. If you do not save early in life, you definitely will have a lower level of living later.

3.1c Financial Goals Follow from Your Values

Successful financial planning evolves from your financial goals. **Financial goals** are the specific long-, intermediate-, and short-term objectives to be attained through financial planning and management efforts. Financial and lifestyle goals should be consistent with your values. To serve as a rational basis for financial actions, they must be stated explicitly in terms of purpose, dollar amounts, and the projected dates by which they are to be achieved.

Set Specific Goals Setting goals helps you visualize the gap between your current financial status and where you want to be in the future. Make a list of your goals. Examples of general financial goals include finishing a college education, paying off credit card debts, repaying education loans, meeting financial emergencies, taking a vacation, owning a home, accumulating funds to send children through college, owning your own business, creating peace of mind, ensuring family harmony, and having financial independence at retirement.

The path toward turning a wish into reality begins with writing it down. If buying a condo is your goal, tape a photograph of a beautiful one onto your refrigerator. Then tell others about your financial goal. The public affirmations and constant reminders will help you make it into a reality.

Put Target Dates on Your Financial Goals Setting target dates for financial goals is important for success. Consider the example of Stephanie Vogel, a dance instructor from Champaign, Illinois. Stephanie has just made the last $347 payment on her four-year car loan. She does not like being in debt, so she does not want to take out such a large loan again. Stephanie would like to put at least part of the money she has been paying monthly for the loan into a savings account, which would allow her to replace her current vehicle in four or five years. Stephanie figures that it would take about $22,500 to buy a similar inexpensive high-mileage used vehicle in five years. She assumes she could earn a 2 percent return on her savings and, using Appendix A.3, has determined that she would need to save $4323 per year ($22,500 ÷ 5.2040 for five years at 2 percent interest), or roughly $360 per month.

Stephanie's thinking offers a good example of how proper financial goal setting works. She recognized the value she put on staying out of debt and proceeded to the general goal of trying to pay cash for her next car. After determining an overall dollar amount needed, she broke that amount down into first annual and then monthly amounts. For only $13 more per month than she has been paying on her loan ($360−$347), Stephanie will be able to pay cash for her next car. This is the sacrifice she is willing to make to avoid using credit to buy a vehicle in the future.

Prioritize Your Goals Once your financial goals are clearly identified, you can decide which are the most important. You simply prioritize the list by making trade-off decisions on what you can do with your finances in the near term as well as in the more distant future.

3.1d Financial Goals Require Wealth-Building Principles

Following are several wealth-building principles that may help you achieve your financial goals:

1. Set clear financial goals both in the short and long term.
2. Save by paying yourself first out of your paycheck.
3. Pay credit card balances in full each month.
4. Spend less than you earn.
5. Participate in the retirement plan at work.
6. Take full advantage of your employer's match on retirement savings.
7. Buy a home for the tax advantages.
8. Pay off your home before retirement.
9. Be patient when investing for the long term.
10. Live every day knowing that your financial future is under control.

3.1e Financial Strategies Guide Your Financial Success

Financial strategies are pre-established plans of action to be implemented in specific situations. Stephanie Vogel implemented an effective strategy in the preceding example. That is, when a loan has been repaid, start a savings program with the same monthly payment amount. Saving may be easier for Stephanie if she arranges for the amount she would like to save to be automatically deposited from her paycheck into her savings account. Another useful savings strategy is to arrange for as much as 75 percent of any raises or bonuses to go into savings before you become accustomed to the additional income.

financial strategies
Pre-established action plans implemented in specific situations.

CONCEPT CHECK 3.1

1. Summarize the financial planning process.
2. Explain the relationships among financial values, goals, and strategies.

3.2 FINANCIAL STATEMENTS MEASURE YOUR FINANCIAL HEALTH AND PROGRESS

LEARNING OBJECTIVE 2
Use balance sheets and cash-flow statements to measure your financial health and progress.

Financial statements are compilations of personal financial data that describe an individual's or family's current financial condition. They present a summary of assets and liabilities as well as income and spending of an individual or family. The two most useful statements are the balance sheet and the cash-flow statement.

financial statements
Snapshots that describe an individual's or family's current financial condition.

DID YOU KNOW

Money Topics to Discuss with Your Partner

When you find the right partner, it is smart to do the following:

- **Change beneficiaries.** Life insurance policies, mutual fund accounts, and retirement accounts all have beneficiaries (the people who will receive the funds at your death) named when you set them up. (See Chapters 12, 15, and 17.)

- **Coordinate employee benefits.** Couples often have two incomes today, so each has a menu of employee benefits from which to choose. As a result, one spouse may drop a benefit that is being received via the other's plan. (See Chapter 1.)

- **Update life insurance coverage.** Focus on term life insurance for the bulk of your needs. (See Chapter 12.)

- **Review auto and homeowner's insurance coverages.** Also inventory your personal property. (See Chapter 10.)

- **Update names with government agencies.** If one or both partners' names are changed as a result of your new status, you need to notify the Social Security Administration and driver's licensing office of that change. You will need to show your marriage certificate as proof of the change.

- **Close redundant bank accounts.** Reducing the number of accounts that each partner brings into the marriage can save money on account fees. Decide which accounts

are "yours, mine, or ours." (See Chapters 5 and 6 for more on managing accounts.)

- **Get out of debt.** One or both of you may bring debts into the new family. Because a couple can live together a little more cheaply than two individuals who live apart, funds can be freed up to pay off credit cards, student loans, and other borrowing. (See Chapters 6, 7, and 9.)

- **Decide on how to manage money.** Decide on who pays what bills and makes investment decisions. Decide on whether or not each person will have individual control over certain money. Decide on who pays for the debt that precedes the relationship. Decide on who pays for gift giving. Decide on what money tasks you will do together, such as establishing annual financial goals, making purchases with debt, and agreeing on which expenditures require joint agreement, like an expense over $300. (See Chapter 5 for how to effectively discuss money matters.)

- **Save for retirement separately.** Day-to-day living expenses will go down somewhat when you team up as a couple. Use some of that money to allocate additional amounts to your individual retirement plans. (See Chapter 17.)

- **Update estate transfer plans.** With a new "number one" in your life, you should change (or set up) your will, durable power of attorney, living will, and health care proxy. (See Chapter 11.)

---

balance sheet or net worth statement

Snapshot of assets, liabilities, and net worth on a particular date.

A **balance sheet** (or **net worth statement**) describes an individual's or family's financial condition on a specified date (often January 1) by showing assets, liabilities, and net worth. It provides a current status report and includes information on what you own, what you owe, and what the net result would be if you paid off all of your debts. It answers the question, "Where are you financially right now?"

cash-flow statement or income and expense statement

Summary of all income and expense transactions over a specific time period.

A **cash-flow statement** (or **income and expense statement**) lists and summarizes income and expense transactions that have taken place over a specific period of time, such as a month or a year. It tells you where your money came from and where it went. It answers the question, "Where did your money go?"

3.2a The Balance Sheet Is a Snapshot of Your Financial Status Right Now

To benchmark where you are on the wealth-building scale, determine your net worth. If you are indeed serious about your financial success, then you will sit down soon with pencil and paper or at your computer to see exactly where you stand. You do so by preparing your balance sheet, which summarizes the value of what you own minus what you owe. Your balance sheet should be updated at least once each year and compared to previous ones, so save all your old financial statements. Then you can assess your progress over the years. Net worth grows slowly, but it definitely increases over time. If you are successful in your career and follow the basic principles outlined in this book, there is no reason why you cannot have a net worth of $1 million, or $2 million or more, later in your life. Net worth typically peaks for people in their 50s or 60s (see Figure 3-2 on page 73) and declines thereafter as one lives off their financial nest egg in retirement.

Components of the Balance Sheet A balance sheet consists of three parts: assets, liabilities, and net worth. Your **assets** include everything you own that has monetary value. Your **liabilities** are your debts—amounts you owe to others. Your **net worth** is the dollar amount left when what is owed is subtracted from the dollar value of what is owned—that is, if all the assets were sold at the listed values and all debts were paid in full. Your net worth is the true measure of your financial wealth.

assets
Everything you own that has monetary value.

liabilities
What you owe.

net worth
What's left when you subtract liabilities from assets.

What Is Owned—Assets Are "The Things You Own." The assets section of the balance sheet lists items valued at their fair market value—what a willing buyer would pay a willing seller, not the amount originally paid or what it might be worth a year from now. It is useful to classify assets as monetary, tangible, or investment assets.

    Monetary assets (also known as **liquid assets** or **cash equivalents**) include cash and low-risk near-cash items that can be readily converted to cash with little or no loss in value such as checking and savings accounts. They are primarily used for maintenance of living expenses, emergencies, savings, and payment of bills.

monetary assets/liquid assets/ cash equivalents
Assets that can be used as cash.

    Tangible (or **use** or **lifestyle**) assets are personal property whose primary purpose is to provide maintenance of one's everyday lifestyle. Tangible assets, such as furniture and vehicles, generally depreciate in value over time.

tangible/use/lifestyle assets
Personal property used to maintain your everyday lifestyle.

    Investment assets (also known as **capital assets**) include tangible and intangible items that have a relatively long life and high cost and that are acquired for the monetary benefits they provide, such as generating additional income and appreciation (or increasing in value). Examples include stocks and bonds. Investment assets generally appreciate and are dedicated to the maintenance of one's future level of living.

investment/capital assets
Tangible and intangible items acquired for their monetary benefits.

    Following are some examples of each kind of asset.

Monetary Assets

- Cash (including cash on hand, checking accounts, savings accounts, savings bonds, certificates of deposit, and money market accounts)
- Tax refunds due
- Money owed to you by others

Tangible Assets

- Automobiles, motorcycles, boats, bicycles
- House, condominium, mobile home
- Household furnishings and appliances
- Personal property (jewelry, furs, tools, clothing)
- Other "big ticket" items

Investment Assets

- Stocks, bonds, mutual funds, gold, partnerships, art, IRAs
- Life insurance and annuities (cash values only)
- Real property (and anything fixed to it)
- Personal and employer-provided retirement accounts

short-term (current) liability
Obligation paid off within one year.

long-term (noncurrent) liability
Debt that comes due in more than one year.

What Is Owed—Liabilities Are "The Money You Owe" The liabilities section of the balance sheet summarizes debts owed, including both personal and business-related debts. The debt could be either a **short-term** (or **current**) **liability**, an obligation to be paid off within one year, or a **long-term** (or **noncurrent**) liability, debts that do not have to be paid in full until more than a year from now. To be accurate, record debt obligations at their current payoff amounts (excluding future interest payments). Following are some examples of items to include in the liabilities section of a balance sheet, with some suggested subheadings.

Short-Term (or Current) Liabilities

• Personal loans owed to other people

• Credit card and charge account balances

• Other open-end credit obligations

• Professional services unpaid (doctors, dentists, chiropractors, lawyers)

• Taxes unpaid

• Past-due rent, utility bills, and insurance premiums

Long-Term Liabilities

• Automobile loans

• Real estate mortgages

• Home equity (second mortgage) loan

• Consumer installment loans and leases (although a lease is technically not a debt)

• Education loans

• Margin loans on securities

DO IT IN CLASS

Net Worth—What Is Left Is "A Measure of Your Financial Worth" Net worth is determined by subtracting liabilities from assets, as indicated in (Equation 3.1) the *net worth formula*:

$$\text{Assets} - \text{liabilities} = \text{net worth} \quad \textbf{(3.1)}$$

or

$$\text{What is owned} - \text{what is owed} = \text{net worth}$$

This formula assumes that if you converted all assets to cash and paid off all liabilities, the remaining cash would be your net worth. For example, if your items of value had a fair market value of $8000 and the amount you owe to others is $4500, your net worth, or wealth, is $3500($8000−$4500). Figure 3-2 shows household net worth figures by age group. College students typically have more debts than assets; thus they are technically **insolvent** because they have a negative net worth. When students graduate and take on full-time jobs, typically their balance sheets change dramatically after a few years.

insolvent
When a person owes more than he or she owns and the person has a negative net worth.

Sample Balance Sheet The total assets on a balance sheet must equal the total liabilities plus the net worth. Both sides must balance, which is the source of the name "balance sheet." You decide how much detail to include to show your financial condition accurately on a given date. The balance sheet shown in Table 3-2 (page 74) reflects the degree of detail and complexity that might be included for a couple with two children (Victor and Maria Hernandez).

3.2b Strategies to Increase Your Net Worth

You can increase your net worth by increasing assets, decreasing liabilities, or doing both. One way to increase assets and net worth is to cut back on spending. Perhaps consider forgoing the cup of coffee or soda you buy each day as you head to class, as any decrease in spending leaves money in the bank as an asset ($5 day × 200 days = $1000). Reducing expenses on high-cost items, such as housing and transportation, will have an even greater effect on assets. A second way to increase net worth is to increase income

Figure 3-2 **Median Net Worth by Age**

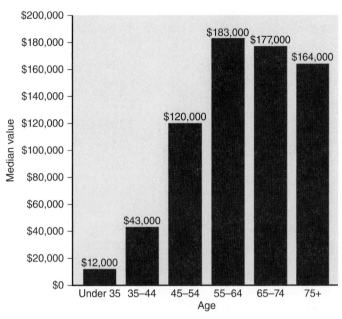

Source: Basic data from *Federal Reserve Bulletin.* Authors' estimates for 2015.

to build assets or pay down debts. For example, as you earn more money, perhaps consider saving half or more of the difference between your new income and your old income rather than using the added money for more spending. Third, paying off debt, especially high-interest credit card balances, can quickly increase net worth.

3.2c The Cash-Flow Statement Tracks Where Your Money Came From and Went

The cash-flow (or income and expense) statement summarizes the total amounts that have been received and spent over a period of time, usually one month or one year. It shows whether you were able to live within your income during that time period. It reflects the flow of funds in and out.

A cash-flow statement includes three sections: **income** (total income received); **expenses** (total expenditures made); and **surplus** (or **net gain** or **net income**), when total income exceeds total expenses, or **deficit** (or **net loss**), when expenses exceed income. Such statements are usually prepared on a **cash basis**,* meaning the only transactions recorded are those involving actual cash received or cash that was spent.

Income/Cash Coming In: Where Your Money Comes From You may think of income as simply what is earned from salaries or wages, but there are other types of income that you should include on a cash-flow statement, such as the following:

- Bonuses and commissions
- Child support and alimony
- Public assistance
- Social Security benefits

* An alternative method is **accrual-basis budgeting** that recognizes earnings and expenditures when money is earned and expenditures are incurred, regardless of when money is actually received or paid.

expenses
Total expenditures made in a specified time such as reported on a cash-flow statement.

surplus (or net gain or net income)
When total income exceeds total expenses such as reported on a cash-flow statement.

cash basis
Only transactions involving actual cash received or cash spent are recorded.

FINANCIAL POWER POINT

Income Does Not Create Wealth, Investments Do

People do not get wealthy by earning an income. Real wealth comes from increases in the value of assets over time such as the growth of investments within a 401(k) retirement program.

Table 3-2 — Balance Sheet for a Couple with Two Children— Victor and Maria Hernandez, January 1, 2015

ASSETS			
Monetary Assets			
	Cash on hand	260	0.07%
	Savings account	1,500	0.40%
	Victor's checking account	2,700	0.72%
	Maria's checking account	3,300	0.89%
	Tax refund due	700	0.19%
	Rent receivable	660	0.18%
	Total Monetary Assets	$ 9,120	2.45%
Tangible Assets			
	Home	176,000	47.23%
	Personal property	9,000	2.42%
	Automobiles	11,500	3.09%
	Total Tangible Assets	$196,500	52.73%
Investment Assets			
	Fidelity mutual funds	4,500	1.21%
	Scudder mutual fund	5,000	1.34%
	Ford Motor Company stock	2,800	0.75%
	New York 2018 bonds	1,000	0.27%
	Life insurance cash value	5,400	1.45%
	IRA accounts	34,300	9.21%
	Real estate investment	114,000	30.59%
	Total Investment Assets	$167,000	44.82%
	Total Assets	$372,620	100.00%
LIABILITIES			
Short-Term Liabilities			
	Dentist bill due	120	0.03%
	Credit card debt	1,545	0.41%
	Total Short-Term Liabilities	$ 1,665	0.45%
Long-Term Liabilities			
	Sales finance company: auto	7,700	2.07%
	Savings bank: real estate	92,000	24.69%
	Total Long-Term Liabilities	$ 99,700	26.76%
	Total Liabilities	$101,365	27.20%
	Net Worth	$271,255	72.80%
	Total Liabilities and Net Worth	$372,620	100.00%

DO IT IN CLASS

- Pension and profit-sharing income
- Scholarships and grants
- Interest and dividends received (from savings accounts, investments, bonds, or loans to others)
- Income from the sale of assets
- Other income (gifts, tax refunds, rent, royalties, capital gains)

Expenses/Cash Going Out: Where Your Money Goes All expenditures made during the period covered by the cash-flow statement should be included in the expenses section. The number and type of expenses shown will vary for each individual and family. Many people categorize expenses according to whether they are fixed or variable.

Fixed expenses are usually paid in the same amount during each time period; they are typically inflexible and often contractual. Examples of such expenses include rent payments and automobile installment loans. It usually takes quite an effort to reduce a fixed expense.

Variable expenses (or **flexible expenses**) are expenditures over which an individual has considerable control. Food, entertainment, and clothing are variable expenses, for example. Some categories, such as savings, can be listed twice, as both fixed and variable expenses. The following are examples of fixed and variable expenses that you might include in a cash-flow statement:

fixed expenses
Expenses that recur at fixed intervals.

variable expenses (or flexible expenses)
Expenses over which you have substantial control.

Fixed Expenses

- Savings and investments
- Retirement contributions (employer's plan, IRA)
- Housing (rent, mortgage, loan payment)
- Automobile (installment payment, lease)
- Insurance (health, life, liability, disability, renter's, homeowner's, automobile)
- Installment loan payments (appliances, furniture)
- Internet service
- Taxes (federal income, state income, local income, real estate, Social Security, Medicare, personal property)

Variable Expenses

- Meals (at home and away)
- Utilities (cell phone, electricity, water, gas)
- Transportation (gasoline and maintenance, licenses, registration, public transportation, tolls)
- Medical expenses
- Child care (nursery, baby-sitting)
- Clothing and accessories (jewelry, shoes, handbags)
- Snacks (candy, soft drinks, other beverages)
- Education (tuition, fees, books, supplies)
- Household furnishings (furniture, appliances, curtains)
- Cable television (beyond basic services)
- Personal care (beauty shop, barbershop, cosmetics, dry cleaner)
- Entertainment and recreation (hobbies, socializing, health club, downloads/tapes/CDs, movie rentals, movies)
- Charitable contributions (gifts, church, school, charities)
- Magazine subscriptions
- Vacations and long weekends
- Credit card payments
- Savings and investments
- Miscellaneous (postage, books, magazines, newspapers, personal allowances, domestic help, membership fees)

There is no rigid list of categories to be used in the expenses section, but you do need to classify all of your expenditures in some way that suits your needs. Rather than just use fixed and variable expenses categories, you might also separate expenditures into savings/investments,

When reducing variable expenses, cut back or eliminate overpriced items like café' lattes and make bigger budget cuts elsewhere.

© Rido/Shutterstock.com

debts, insurance, taxes, and household expenses. The more specific your categories, the deeper your understanding of your outlays.

Cash Surplus (or Cash Deficit) The surplus (deficit) section shows the amount of cash remaining after you have itemized income and subtracted expenditures from income, as illustrated by the following calculations using Equation (3.2), the **surplus/deficit formula**. A business would call this amount its net profit or net loss.

$$\text{Surplus (deficit)} = \text{total income} - \text{total expenses}$$

or

$$\$1100 \text{ surplus} = \$12{,}500 - \$11{,}400 \tag{3.2}$$

$$(\$800 \text{ deficit}) = \$14{,}900 - \$15{,}700$$

A surplus demonstrates that you are managing your financial resources successfully and do not have to use savings or borrow money to make financial ends meet. When the calculation shows a surplus, that amount is then available (in your checking and savings accounts) to spend, save, invest, or donate. A surplus is not really cash lying around on the kitchen table; it is the cash value reflected in the accounts on your balance sheet. Figure 3-3 shows the typical personal financial situation over the life cycle in present value dollars, from the wealth accumulation years through retirement.

Sample Cash-Flow Statements Table 3-3 shows the cash-flow statement for a couple with two children (Victor and Maria Hernandez). It vividly highlights the additional income needed to rear children and shows the increased variety of expenditures that characterize a family's (rather than an individual's) lifestyle. As a person earns more income, the cash-flow statement usually becomes more involved and detailed.

𝓕𝓲𝓰𝓾𝓻𝓮 3-3   Personal Finance over the Life Cycle

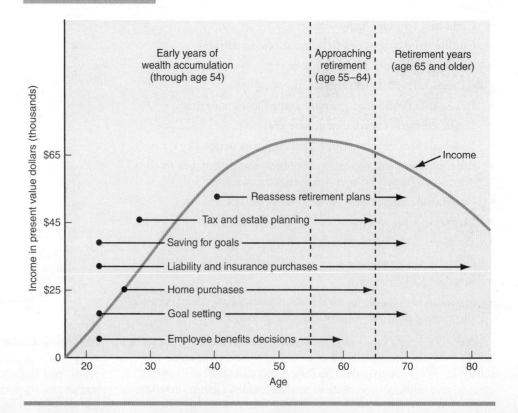

Table 3-3 — Cash Flow Statement for a Couple with Two Children—Victor and Maria Hernandez, January 1–December 31, 2015

	Dollars	Percent
INCOME		
Victor's gross salary	63,180	70.99%
Maria's gross salary	15,500	17.42%
Interest and dividends	1,800	2.02%
Bonus	600	0.67%
Tax refunds	200	0.22%
Net rental income	7,720	8.67%
Total Income	89,000	100.00%
EXPENDITURES		
Fixed Expenses		
Mortgage loan payments	14,400	16.18%
Real estate taxes	2,400	2.70%
Homeowner's insurance	1,200	1.35%
Automobile loan payments	4,400	4.94%
Automobile insurance and registration	2,190	2.46%
Life insurance premiums	1,200	1.35%
Medical insurance (employee portion)	2,980	3.35%
Emergency fund savings	2,400	2.70%
Revolving savings fund	1,800	2.02%
Federal income taxes	11,300	12.70%
State income taxes	4,200	4.72%
City income taxes	1,600	1.80%
Social Security taxes	6,020	6.76%
Personal property taxes	950	1.07%
Retirement IRAs	6,000	6.74%
Total Fixed Expenses	$63,040	70.83%
Variable Expenses		
Food	4,900	5.51%
Utilities	2,100	2.36%
Gasoline and maintenance	3,100	3.48%
Medical expenses	3,400	3.82%
Medicines	1,750	1.97%
Clothing and upkeep	1,950	2.19%
Church	2,400	2.70%
Gifts	1,400	1.57%
Personal allowances	2,400	2.70%
Children's allowances	2,080	2.34%
Miscellaneous	480	0.54%
Total Variable Expenses	$25,960	29.17%
Total Expenses	$89,000	100.00%
SURPLUS (DEFICIT)	$0	0.00%

CONCEPT CHECK 3.2

1. Distinguish between the balance sheet and cash-flow statement.

2. How should assets and liabilities be valued for the balance sheet?

3. Distinguish between fixed and variable expenses.

DID YOU KNOW

Ratios for Evaluating One's Financial Progress

Financial ratios are numerical calculations designed to simplify the process of evaluating your financial strength and the progress of your financial condition. Ratios serve as tools or yardsticks to develop saving, spending, and credit-use patterns consistent with your goals. They are illustrated below using data from the Hernandez family shown in Table 3-2 and Table 3-3. Calculators for these ratios can be found on the **Garman/Forgue** companion website.

DO IT IN CLASS

Ratio	Question It Answers	Calculation	Example	Explanation
Liquidity Ratio	Do I have enough liquidity to pay for emergencies?	Monetary assets divided by monthly expenses	$9120/$7417 = 1.23 ratio or 1 and 2/10th of a month	The number of months in which living expenses can be paid should an emergency arise; 3 to 6 months is preferred.
Asset-to-Debt Ratio	Do I have enough assets to meet my debt obligations?	Total assets/total debt	$372,620/$101,365 = 3.676 or a 3.7 to 1 ratio	Provides a broad measure of one's financial liquidity; a high ratio is desirable.
Debt-to-Income Ratio	Is my total debt burden too high?	Annual debt repayments/gross income × 100	$18,800/$89,000 = 21.12%	Compares amount spent on debt repayments to gross income; should be 36 or less and it should decline as one grows older.
Debt Payments-to-Disposable Income Ratio	Is my non-mortgage debt too stressful?	Monthly non-mortgage debt payments/monthly disposable (not gross) income	$366.67/5242.67 = 6.99	Estimates funds available for debt repayment; 14 percent or less is desirable and 16 percent or more is problematic.
Investment Assets-to-Total Assets Ratio	Am I saving/investing enough?	Investment assets/total assets	$167,000/$372,620 = 0.448 or 44.8%	How well is one advancing toward their financial goals; ratio of 10 for people in their 20s, 11 to 30 for those in their 30s, and 31 or higher for older adults.

financial ratios
Calculations designed to simplify evaluation of financial strength and progress.

financial records
Documents that evidence financial transactions.

LEARNING OBJECTIVE 3

Collect and organize the financial records necessary for managing your personal finances.

3.3 COLLECT AND ORGANIZE YOUR FINANCIAL RECORDS TO SAVE TIME AND MONEY

Financial records are documents that evidence financial transactions, such as bills, receipts, credit card receipts and statements, bank records, tax returns, brokerage statements, and paycheck stubs. Your financial records will help determine where you are, where you have been, and where you are going financially. They also help you save money as well as make money. Good records enable you to review the results of financial transactions as well as permit other family members to find them in an emergency. Organized records help you take advantage of all available tax deductions when filing income taxes and provide you with more dollars to spend, save, invest, or donate.

Table 3-4 shows categories of financial records and the contents that might be included in each. Many people keep duplicates of important records in an envelope at their workplace or with relatives because the likelihood of records at both locations being stolen or destroyed simultaneously is very small. You can purge or shred some of your records when you no longer need them, such as non-tax-related checks and credit card receipts more than a year old, out-of-date warranties, expired insurance policies for which there will be no claims, records from automobiles you no longer own, and financial reports when replaced with updated reports.

Some records may be safely stored at home in a fire-resistant file cabinet or a safe. Other records should be kept in a **safe-deposit box**. Safe-deposit boxes are secured lock boxes available for rent ($25 to $250 per year) in banks. Two keys are used to open such a box. The customer keeps one key, and the bank holds the other.

FINANCIAL POWER POINT

Before You Buy, Ask Yourself These Questions

If you want to *save $1,000* this year, ask yourself these questions before you buy!

1. Did I plan to buy this?
2. If I have to pay cash, do I still want it?
3. What will happen if I don't buy this?
4. Do I need this... or just want it?

Source: Created by the LFE Institute, a corporate skills-based financial literacy curriculum developer. Copyright © LFE Institute, www.lfeinstitute.com.

ADVICE FROM A PROFESSIONAL

Get-Tough Ways to Cut Spending

If you always run out of money before the month is over, you may need to take some drastic steps to get your finances under control. Consider the following:

1. Stop paying bank fees by maintaining minimum balances and eliminating overdrafts.
2. Stop making ATM withdrawals that assess fees.
3. Stop getting cash back from debit or credit card purchases to use for pocket money.
4. Spend only cash or money that you have, and leave debit and credit cards at home.
5. Stop using credit cards.
6. Refinance credit card debt at a credit union.
7. Do not eat out.
8. Cut back on telephone use if it costs money.
9. Avoid paying for entertainment; rather do activities that are free.
10. Reduce or stop spending on luxuries such as clothing, movies, entertainment, memberships, hobbies, CDs, DVDs, phones, and expanded cable channels.
11. Drop landline telephone service and use only a cell phone.
12. Find cheaper auto insurance.
13. Increase your 401(k) retirement contribution as it reduces income taxes.
14. Change income tax withholding to increase take-home pay.
15. Take a list when shopping, and stick to it.
16. Avoid shopping malls and discount stores.
17. Sell an asset, especially one that requires additional expenses, such as a boat or second car.
18. Build up an emergency fund of savings even if it means temporarily decreasing retirement-plan contributions.
19. Only buy used items.
20. Consider making Christmas a "nonspend" holiday.
21. Move to lower-cost housing.
22. Increase income by working overtime or finding a second job.

Alena C. Johnson
Utah State University

Table 3-4	**Financial Records: What to Keep and Where**

	Contents	
Category	**In Home Files and Fireproof Home Safe**	**In Safe-Deposit Box**
Financial plans/ budgeting	Financial plans Balance sheets and cash-flow statements Current budget List of safe-deposit box contents Names and contact information for financial advisers	Names and contact information for financial advisers Copy of written financial plans, goals, and budgets
Career and employment	Current resume College transcripts Letters of recommendation Employee benefits descriptions Written career plans	Employer retirement plan correspondence
Banking and financial services	Checkbook, unused checks, and canceled checks List of locations and account numbers for all bank accounts Checking and savings account statements Locations and access numbers for safe-deposit boxes Account transaction receipts	List of financial institutions and account numbers for all financial services accounts Certificates of deposit
Taxes	Copies of all income tax returns, both state and federal, for the past three years, including all supporting documentation Receipts for all donations of cash or property Log of volunteer expenses Receipts for property taxes paid	Copies of all income tax filings, both state and federal, for the past three years Records of securities purchased and sold
Credit	Utility and telephone bills Monthly credit card statements Receipts of credit payments List of credit accounts and telephone numbers to report lost/stolen cards Unused credit cards Credit reports and scores	List of credit accounts and telephone numbers to report lost/stolen cards Loan discharge notice when it is paid off Credit card bills for seven years if they support tax deductions
Housing, vehicles, and consumer purchases	Copies of legal documents (leases, mortgage, deeds, titles) Property appraisals and inspection reports Home repair/home improvement receipts Warranties Owner's manuals for purchases Auto registration records Vehicle service and repair receipts Receipts for important purchases	Original legal documents (leases, mortgage, deeds, titles) Copies of property appraisals Vehicle purchase contracts (until vehicle is sold) Photographs or videos of valuable possessions
Insurance	Original insurance policies List of insurance policies with premium amounts and due dates Premium payment receipts Calculation of life insurance needs Insurance claims forms and reports Medical records for family, including immunization records and list of prescription drugs	List of all insurance policies with company and agent names and addresses and policy numbers Listing with photographs or videotape of personal property

Table 3-4	Financial Records: What to Keep and Where (*Continued*)

	Contents	
Category	**In Home Files and Fireproof Home Safe**	**In Safe-Deposit Box**
Investments	Records of stock, bond, and mutual fund transactions and certificate numbers Mutual fund statements Statements from brokers Reports from financial planner Company annual reports Retirement plan quarterly and annual reports Documents on business interests Written investment philosophy Written investment strategies	Contact information for all investment needs Stock and bond certificates Rare coins, stamps, and other collectibles
Retirement and Estate Planning	Pension and retirement plan information Retirement statements Copies of all retirement plan transactions Copy of Social Security card Trust agreements Information on Social Security Copy of current will Copies of advance directives (wills, living wills, medical powers of attorney, durable powers of attorney with originals with physician/attorney) Copies of trust documents (originals with executor, trustees/attorney)	Extra copy of all retirement plan transactions and statements Social Security statements (newest one) Copy of will (original of all estate planning documents should be placed in attorney's office)
Personal information	Copy of birth certificate and marriage license Religious documents Copy of divorce decree, property settlement, and custody agreement Receipts for alimony and child support payments Custodial information for your children, relatives, and/or elderly parent	Passports while not being used Military and adoption papers Originals of birth, marriage, death certificates Originals of Social Security cards Originals of divorce decrees, property settlements, and custody agreements Master list of all important documents and their location Flash drive or CD containing soft copies of many financial records (update once a year)

CONCEPT CHECK 3.3

1. List some advantages of keeping good financial records.

2. Name three financial records that might be best kept in a safe-deposit box.

3.4   REACHING YOUR GOALS THROUGH BUDGETING: YOUR SPENDING/ SAVINGS ACTION PLAN

budget
Paper or electronic document used to record both planned and actual income and expenditures over a period of time.

long-term goals
Financial targets to achieve more than five years in the future.

Your financial success is largely a matter of choice, not a matter of chance. Your budget is where you make and implement those choices. Your budget is your plan for spending and saving. Budgeting forces you to consider what is important in your life, what things you want to own, how you want to live, what it will take to do that, and, more generally, what you want to achieve in life. The budgeting process gives you control over your finances, and it empowers you to achieve your financial goals while simultaneously (and successfully) confronting any unforeseen events. In short, budgeting answers the question, "What is my spending/savings action plan?" Another advantage of budgeting is that it reduces stress because making and following a budget helps you get more of what you want.

Some people do all their budgeting mentally—and do so successfully. Good for them! Many of us, however, need to see the actual numbers on paper or on a computer screen. A **budget** is a paper or electronic document used to record both planned and actual income and expenditures over a period of time. Your budget represents the major mechanism through which your financial plans are carried out and goals are achieved.

Figure 3-4 illustrates how to think about financial statements and budgeting. The cash-flow statement focuses on *where you have been* financially, the balance sheet shows *where you are* financially at the current time, and the budget indicates *where you want to go* in the future. Creating and following a spending plan has three stages: before, during, and after.

3.4a   Action Before: Set Financial Goals

Before establishing your budget, take action to set financial goals. **Long-term goals** are financial targets or ends that an individual or family wants to achieve perhaps more than five years in the future. Such goals provide direction for overall financial planning as well as shorter-term budgeting. An example of a long-term goal is to create a $1 million retirement fund by age 60. Goals must be specific. They should contain dollar-amount targets and specific dates for achievement.

If you have a small income or large debts, it may be unrealistic to think of long-term goals until any current financial difficulties are resolved. You may be unable to do

---

Figure 3-4   **About Financial Statements and Budgets**

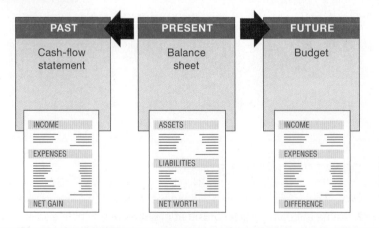

much more than take care of immediate necessities, such as housing and vehicle expenses, food, and utility bills. In such instances, you need to focus on short-term efforts to improve your financial situation. You may need to focus on paying down debt, not adding to it.

Establishing unrealistic short-term goals sets up a high likelihood of failure. Instead, set financial targets that are almost too easy to meet. For example, you may want to save $350 per month to use as a down payment on a home in five years. That may seem like a lot. Start perhaps painlessly by saving $100 per month for a few months. Then put away $150 for two months, $200 for two months, then $250, then $300, and finally $350 so that by the end of the first year you are on target.

Intermediate-term goals are financial targets that can be achieved between one year and perhaps three to five years. Examples of intermediate-term goals are creating an emergency fund amounting to three months of income within four years, saving $22,500 within three years for a down payment on a home, taking a $4000 vacation to Asia in two years, paying off $8000 in credit card debt in one-and-a-half years, and paying off a $12,000 college loan in five years. **Short-term goals** are financial targets or ends that can be achieved in less than a year, such as finishing college, paying off an auto loan, increasing savings, purchasing assets (i.e., vehicle, furniture, television, stereo, clothes), reducing high-interest debt, taking an annual vacation, attending a wedding, buying life insurance, and making plans for retirement.

You need to be as clear as possible about what your financial goals are. The goals worksheet in Figure 3-5 provides examples of how much to save to reach long-, intermediate-, and short-term goals. People can view such savings as a fixed expenditure (such as withholding from a paycheck to contribute to an employer's retirement plan or to transfer to a savings account). Additional savings, such as saving what is left over after all expenditures are made, will be a variable expense.

Prioritizing your goals makes sense. But what are your most important goals? One certain priority should be to pay off high-interest credit cards as soon as possible because paying 18 percent interest is foolish. Another is to contribute as much as you can afford to a retirement plan at least up until you receive the employer's full matching contribution. Many college graduates buy a new car soon after getting their first job to celebrate having "made it." Before you're lured into following suit, give careful consideration to your priorities and remember that every action carries not only the dollar cost of the action taken but also the opportunity cost of the alternatives forgone. To achieve your long-term goals, you may have to sacrifice by deferring some of your short-term desires. Thus, you might consider buying a used car or a lower-cost new one.

3.4b Action Before: Make and Reconcile Budget Estimates

Before the month begins, you identify how you are spending money now in the process of making and reconciling budget estimates of income and expenditures. Here you resolve conflicting needs and wants by revising estimates as necessary. You can't have everything in life—especially this month—even though you might want it.

Budget Estimates Gets You from Gross Income to What's Available for Variable Expenses **Budget estimates** are the projected dollar amounts in a budget that one plans to receive or spend during the period covered by the budget. Begin by estimating total gross income from all sources. For example, Jonathan Depp's annual gross income is $60,000. Typical withholdings from your paycheck and noted as percentages of gross income are: federal income taxes (12%), Social Security taxes (7%), state income taxes (6%), employer retirement plan (6%), health insurance premiums (10%), and Roth IRA (5%). This totals 46% leaving Jonathan with 54% in **take-home pay** (also called **disposable income**). This is the pay received after employer withholdings for such things as taxes, insurance, and union dues, and it is available for budgeting for spending, saving, investing, and donating.

intermediate-term goals
Financial targets that can be achieved within one to five years.

short-term goals
Financial targets or ends that can be achieved in less than a year.

budget estimates
Projected dollar amounts to receive or spend in a budgeting period.

take-home pay/disposable income
Pay received after employer withholdings for such things as taxes, insurance, and union dues, and it is available for budgeting for spending, saving, investing, and donating.

Figure 3-5 Goals Worksheet for Harry and Belinda Johnson

Date worksheet prepared *January 1, 2015*

1 LONG-TERM GOALS	2 AMOUNT NEEDED	3 MONTH & YEAR NEEDED*	4 MONTHS TO SAVE	5 DATE START SAVING	6 MONTHLY AMOUNT TO SAVE (2 ÷ 4)
European vacation	$3,000	Aug. 2018	30	Feb. '15	$100
Down payment on new auto	5,000	Oct. 2019	45	Jan. '15	111

Date worksheet prepared *January 1, 2015*

1 INTERMEDIATE-TERM GOALS	2 AMOUNT NEEDED	3 MONTH & YEAR NEEDED*	4 MONTHS TO SAVE	5 DATE START SAVING	6 MONTHLY AMOUNT TO SAVE (2 ÷ 4)
Down payment on home	$18,900	Dec. 2020	60	Jan. '15	$315

Date worksheet prepared *January 1, 2015*

1 SHORT-TERM GOALS	2 AMOUNT NEEDED	3 MONTH & YEAR NEEDED*	4 MONTHS TO SAVE	5 DATE START SAVING	6 MONTHLY AMOUNT TO SAVE (2 ÷ 4)
House fund	$3,600	Dec. '15	12	Jan. '15	315
Holiday vacation	1,200	Dec. '15	12	Jan. '15	100
Summer vacation	1,200	Aug. '15	6	Mar. '15	100
Anniversary dinner party	500	June '15	5	Jan. '15	50

*Goals requiring five years or more to achieve require consideration of investment return and after-tax yield, which will be presented in Chapter 4.

discretionary income

Money left over after necessities such as housing and food are paid for.

Now Jonathan subtracts money for fixed expenses, such as rent (4%), emergency savings (2%), student loans (2%), auto loan (1%), and auto insurance (1%). This totals (10%) for **discretionary** or **controllable expenses**, which make up the bulk of money available to pay for one's various expenses. After paying his fixed expenses Jonathan has 44% of his pay left to spend (100%−46%−10%) for such variable items as food, electricity, Internet, cable television, phone, gasoline and maintenance, church and charity, entertainment, and miscellaneous.

Table 3-5 presents budget estimates for a college student, a single working person, a young married couple, a married couple with two young children, and a married couple with two college-age children. The college student's budget requires monthly withdrawals of previously deposited savings to make ends meet. The single working person's budget allows for an automobile loan, but not much else. The young married couple's budget permits one automobile loan, an investment program, contributions to retirement accounts, and significant spending on food and entertainment. The budget of the married couple with two young children allows for only an inexpensive automobile loan payment even though one spouse has a part-time job to help with the finances.

Table 3-5   Sample Monthly Budgets for Various Family Units

Classifications	College Student	Single Working Person	Young Married Couple	Married Couple with Two Young Children	Married Couple with Two College-Age Children
INCOME					
Salary	300	2,800	2,200	3,500	4,400
Salary	0	0	2,100	860	1,600
Interest and dividends	5	15	15	15	80
Student loans	300	0	0	0	0
Savings withdrawals	570	0	0	0	500
Total Income	$1,175	$2,815	$4,315	$4,375	$6,580
EXPENSES					
Fixed Expenses					
Retirement contributions	$ 0	$ 20	$ 360	$ 180	$ 340
IRA	0	20	160	180	200
Savings (withheld)	0	20	20	10	100
Housing	350	750	900	1,100	1,300
Health insurance	0	0	60	150	140
Life and disability insurance	0	0	20	60	40
Homeowner's or renter's insurance	0	0	40	60	80
Automobile insurance	0	80	90	60	140
Automobile payments	0	280	345	220	0
Loan 1 (TV and stereo)	0	80	80	40	0
Loan 2 (other)	0	40	40	0	50
Federal and state taxes	30	455	715	600	710
Social Security taxes	23	210	330	305	385
Real estate taxes	0	0	0	0	40
Investments	0	0	60	100	300
Total fixed expenses	$ 403	$1,955	$3,220	$3,065	$3,825
Variable Expenses					
Other savings	$0	$ 60	$ 150	$0	$ 0
Food	180	230	270	340	350
Utilities	40	80	90	140	145
Automobile gas, oil, maintenance	0	90	110	90	100
Medical	10	30	40	70	50
Child care	0	0	0	260	0
Clothing	20	50	60	50	40
Gifts and contributions	10	20	40	60	80
Allowances	20	75	60	100	180
Education	400	0	0	0	1,500
Furnishing and appliances	10	10	30	20	20
Personal care	10	45	25	30	30
Entertainment	40	120	100	60	120
Vacations	17	30	40	30	60
Miscellaneous	15	20	80	60	80
Total variable expenses	$ 772	$ 860	$1,095	$1,310	$2,755
Total Expenses	$1,175	$2,815	$4,315	$4,375	$6,580

FINANCIAL POWER POINT

Cut the Dollars and the Pennies

If you are often spending $5 per day (rather than $1.50) on fancy coffee, you end up spending $700 more per year ($5 − $1.50 = $3.50 × 200 workdays). So, when reducing variable expenses, cut back or eliminate things like café lattes, overpriced vitamin water, and energy drinks, and make bigger budget cuts elsewhere, like housing, care, preschool, health care, and frequent treats.

The budget of the married couple with two college-age children permits a home mortgage payment, ownership of two paid-for automobiles, savings and investment programs, and a substantial contribution for future college expenses.

It is essential to make reasonable budget estimates. If you have seven holiday gifts to buy and expect to spend $50 for each, it's easy to make an estimate of $350. If you want to go out to dinner once each week with a friend at $60 per meal, estimate an expense of $240 per month. Avoid using unrealistically low figures by simply being fair and honest in your estimates. Then add up your totals.

Revise Budget Estimates to Create a "Balanced Budget" When trying to make your spending conform to your budget goals, sometimes you will find the math is alarming! When initial expense estimates exceed income estimates, three choices are available: (1) earn more income, (2) cut back on expenses, or (3) try a combination of more income and fewer expenses. The process of reconciling needs and wants is a healthy exercise. It helps identify your priorities by telling you what is important in your life at the current time, and it identifies areas of sacrifice that you might make. Revising your short-term financial goals may also be required.

You must reconcile conflicting wants to revise your budget until total expenses do not exceed income. You have no choice! Perhaps you can change some "must have" items to "maybe next year" purchases. Perhaps you can keep some quality items but reduce their quantity. For example, instead of $240 for four meals for you and a friend at restaurants each month, consider dining out twice each month at $70 per evening out. You'll save $100 a month and still have two really nice meals. Your actions on money matters override your words, so act accordingly. Eventually you will finalize your "balanced budget" by making sure planned income equals or exceeds projected expenses.

Unfinished Budget Estimates for Harry and Belinda   Table 3-6 presents the projected annual budget for Harry and Belinda Johnson and reflects their efforts to reconcile their budget estimates. Wisely Harry and Belinda are "paying themselves first." They plan to save $100 a month in a savings/emergency fund, put away $300 per month to save to buy their own home, and contribute to both their retirement plans at work. However, the Johnsons have failed to complete their budget because their total planned expenses are $1310 more than their total planned income. The Johnsons have a little ways to go to fully reconcile their annual budget estimates.

3.4c   Action Before Budgeting Period: Plan Cash Flows

Before the month begins, you plan your cash flows or where the money will go. Income usually remains somewhat constant month after month, but expenses do rise and fall, sometimes sharply. As a result, people occasionally complain that they are "broke, out of money, and sick of budgeting." This challenge can be anticipated by using a cash-flow calendar and eliminated by using a revolving savings fund.

cash-flow calendar

Budget estimates for monthly income and expenses.

Cash Flow Calendar for Harry and Belinda Johnson   The budget estimates for monthly income and expenses in Table 3-6 have been recast in summary form in Table 3-7, providing a **cash-flow calendar** for the Johnsons. Annual estimated income and expenses are recorded in this calendar for each budgeting time period in an effort to identify surplus or deficit situations. In the Johnsons' case, planned annual expenses still exceed income. The couple starts out the year with five months of income meeting expenses, and then they face planned monthly deficits for the remainder of the year.

Table 3-6 — 2015 Unfinished Annual Budget Estimates for Harry and Belinda Johnson

	Jan.	Feb.	Mar.	Apr.	May	June	July	Aug.	Sept.	Oct.	Nov.	Dec.	Yearly Total	Monthly Totals
INCOME														
Harry's salary	3,250	3,250	3,250	3,250	3,250	3,250	3,250	3,250	3,250	3,250	3,250	3,250	39,000	3,250.00
Belinda's salary	4,750	4,750	4,750	4,750	4,750	4,750	4,750	4,750	4,750	4,750	4,750	4,750	57,000	4,750.00
Interest	12	12	13	13	14	14	15	15	15	16	16	16	171	14.25
Trust	0	0	0	0	0	0	0	3,000	0	0	0	0	3,000	250.00
TOTAL INCOME	$8,012	$8,012	$8,013	$8,013	$8,014	$8,014	$8,015	$11,015	$8,015	$8,016	$8,016	$8,016	$99,171	$8,264.25
EXPENSES														
Fixed Expenses														
Rent	1,100	1,100	1,100	1,100	1,100	1,100	1,200	1,200	1,200	1,200	1,200	1,200	13,800	1,150.00
Health insurance	200	200	200	200	200	200	250	250	250	250	250	250	2,700	225.00
Life insurance	15	15	15	15	15	15	15	15	15	15	15	15	180	15.00
Home purchase fund	300	300	300	300	300	300	300	300	300	300	300	300	3,600	300.00
Renter's insurance	0	0	0	0	0	220	0	0	0	0	0	0	220	18.33
Automobile insurance	0	0	0	0	0	850	0	0	0	0	0	850	1,700	141.67
Auto loan payments	497	497	497	497	497	497	497	497	497	497	497	497	5,964	497.00
Student loan	300	300	300	300	300	300	300	300	300	300	300	300	3,600	300.00
Savings/emergencies	100	100	100	100	100	100	100	100	100	100	100	100	1,200	100.00
Harry's retirement plan	195	195	195	195	195	195	195	195	195	195	195	195	2,340	195.00
Belinda's retirement	190	190	190	190	190	190	190	190	190	190	190	190	2,280	190.00
Cable TV and Internet	120	120	120	120	120	120	120	120	120	120	120	120	1,440	120.00
Federal income taxes	1,210	1,210	1,210	1,210	1,210	1,210	1,210	1,210	1,210	1,210	1,210	1,210	14,520	1,210.00
State income taxes	400	400	400	400	400	400	400	400	400	400	400	400	4,800	400.00
Social Security	535	535	535	535	535	535	535	535	535	535	535	535	6,420	535.00
Auto registration	0	0	0	0	0	0	0	0	0	0	300	0	300	25.00
Total fixed expenses	$5,162	$5,162	$5,162	$5,162	$5,162	$6,232	$5,312	$5,312	$5,312	$5,312	$5,612	$6,162	$ 65,064	$5,422.00
Variable Expenses														
Savings/investments	0	0	0	0	0	0	0	2,000	0	0	0	0	2,000	166.67
Revolving savings fund	250	250	250	250	250	0	240	0	200	190	0	0	1,880	156.67
Food (groceries)	440	440	440	440	440	440	440	440	440	440	440	440	5,280	440.00
Food (out)	300	300	300	300	300	300	300	300	300	300	300	300	3,600	300.00
Utilities	125	150	150	150	100	100	100	100	100	125	125	150	1,475	122.92
Cell phones	75	75	75	75	75	75	75	75	75	75	75	75	900	75.00
Gas and maintenance	120	120	120	120	120	120	120	120	120	120	120	120	1,440	120.00
Doctor and dentist bills	100	100	100	100	100	100	100	100	100	100	100	100	1,200	100.00
Medicines	60	60	60	60	60	60	60	60	60	60	60	60	720	60.00
Clothing and upkeep	170	170	170	170	170	170	170	170	170	170	170	170	2,040	170.00
Church and charity	100	100	100	100	100	100	100	100	100	100	100	100	1,200	100.00
Gifts	80	80	110	75	140	20	20	60	60	50	400	300	1,395	116.25
Public transportation	60	60	60	60	60	60	60	60	60	60	60	60	720	60.00
Personal allowances	720	720	720	720	720	720	720	720	720	720	720	720	8,640	720.00
Entertainment	150	150	150	150	150	150	150	150	150	150	150	150	1,800	150.00
Holiday vacation	0	0	0	0	0	0	0	0	0	0	0	600	600	50.00
Summer vacation	0	0	0	0	0	0	0	1,200	0	0	0	0	1,200	100.00
Anniversary party	0	0	0	0	0	500	0	0	0	0	0	0	500	41.67
Miscellaneous	100	75	46	81	67	67	48	48	48	44	44	39	707	58.92
Total variable expenses	$2,850	$2,850	$2,851	$2,851	$2,852	$2,982	$2,703	$5,703	$2,703	$2,704	$2,864	$3,384	$37,297	$3,102.08
TOTAL EXPENSES	$8,012	$8,012	$8,013	$8,013	$8,014	$9,214	$8,015	$11,015	$8,015	$8,016	$8,476	$9,546	$102,361	$8,530.08
Difference (available for spending, saving, and investing)	$ 0	$ 0	$ 0	$ 0	$ 0	−1,200	$ 0	$ 0	$ 0	$ 0	−460	−1,530	−3,190	
Revolving savings withdrawals	0	0	0	0	0	1200	0	0	0	0	460	220	1,880	
Uncovered shortfall	$ 0	$ 0	$ 0	$ 0	$ 0	$ 0	$ 0	$ 0	$ 0	$ 0	$ 0	$1,310	$ 1,310	

Table 3-7	Cash-Flow Calendar for Harry and Belinda Johnson

	1	2	3	4
Month	Estimated Income	Estimated Expenses	Surplus/ Deficit (1-2)	Cumulative Surplus/Deficit
January	$8,012	$8,012	0	0
February	8,012	8,012	0	0
March	8,013	8,013	0	0
April	8,013	8,013	0	0
May	8,014	8,014	0	0
June	8,014	9,214	−1,200	−1,200
July	8,015	8,015	0	−1,200
August	11,015	11,015	0	−1,200
September	8,015	8,015	0	−1,200
October	8,016	8,016	0	−1,200
November	8,016	8,476	−460	−1,660
December	8,016	9,546	−1,530	−3,190
Total	$99,171	$102,361	−$3,190	

Effective management of cash flow can involve curtailing expenses during months with financial deficits, increasing income, using savings, or borrowing. If you borrow money and pay finance charges, the credit costs will further increase your monthly expenses.

Revolving Savings Fund for Harry and Belinda Johnson For this reason alone, it is smart to "borrow from yourself" by using a **revolving savings fund**. This is a variable expense classification budgeting tool into which funds are allocated in an effort to create savings that can be used to balance the budget later so as to avoid running out of money. Establishing such a fund involves planning ahead—much like a college student does when saving money all summer (creating a revolving savings fund) to draw on during the school months.

revolving savings fund

Variable budgeting tool that places funds in savings to cover emergency or higher-than-usual expenses.

You establish a revolving savings fund for two purposes: (1) to accumulate funds for large nonmonthly irregular expenses, such as automobile insurance premiums, medical costs, holiday gifts, and vacations; and (2) to meet occasional deficits due to income fluctuations.

Table 3-8 shows the Johnsons' revolving savings fund. When preparing their budget, the Johnsons realized that in June, November, and December they were going to have significant deficits. Thus they decided to begin setting aside $250 per month to cover the June deficit, so by June they had $1250 in their revolving savings fund to cover that amount. Continued use of the revolving savings fund helped them meet the November deficit as well.

Harry and Belinda Argue About Budgeting Alternatives The Johnsons will still be $1530 short in December. Lacking that much money, the couple has a number of alternatives: (1) reduce some planned spending throughout the year to create sufficient surpluses, (2) use some of Harry's trust fund interest income to cover the deficit, (3) dip into their emergency savings in December, and/or (4) utilize credit cards to get through the end-of-year expenses. Ideally, the Johnsons want to have sufficient emergency funds by the end of the year to establish their revolving savings fund for the following 12 months.

Table 3-8	Revolving Savings Fund for Harry and Belinda Johnson				
Month	**Large Expenses**	**Amount Needed**	**Deposit into Fund**	**Withdrawal from Fund**	**Fund Balance**
January		$0	$250	$0	$250
February		0	250	0	500
March		0	250	0	750
April		0	250	0	1,000
May		0	250	0	1,250
June	Party/ insurance	1,200	0	1,200	50
July		0	240	0	290
August		0	0	0	290
September		0	200	0	490
October		0	190	0	680
November	Holiday gifts	460	0	460	220
December	Gifts/vacation	1,530	0	220	0
Total		$3,190	$1,880	$1,880	−$1,310

The Johnsons disagree about their budget priorities. Belinda wants to spend less on food out and to open a credit card account to pay for the deficits later in the year, while Harry wants to spend less on clothing and entertainment and to skip their planned anniversary dinner party. They both wonder how they can earn so much money and still have such challenging budgeting problems. The Johnsons might benefit by considering the suggestions in Chapter 5 (see pages 159–163) on how to talk with a significant other about financial matters. The Johnsons need to discuss their spending priorities and make decisions so they can reconcile their budget estimates for the year.

3.4d   Action During the Budgeting Period: Control Spending

Budget controls are techniques to maintain control over personal spending so that planned amounts are not exceeded. They give feedback on whether spending is on target and provide information on overspending, errors, emergencies, and exceptions or omissions. Following are several examples of budget controls:

Budget for Shopping Trips Set a budget for every shopping trip, and don't spend a penny more.

Record the Purpose of Expenditures Checks contains a space to record the purpose of expenditures. The check stub or register also provides a place to record explanations of expenditures. If you use automatic teller machines (ATMs) to withdraw cash or use debit cards to pay for day-to-day expenditures, record these withdrawals in the check register *immediately*. Retain the paperwork, and write the purpose of each expense on the back of each. Deposit all checks received to your checking account without receiving a portion in cash; if you need cash, write a check or make an ATM withdrawal. If you get cash back when using a credit card, be sure to record why on the receipt.

Keep Track of Credit Transactions People often do not record their credit transactions until they receive a statement. Then it is easy to continue buying on credit without recognizing the amount of indebtedness until the statement arrives. Instead you should record each credit transaction when it occurs. If you spend $40 on clothing using a credit card, record the expenditure as clothing expenditure and reduce the amount you have remaining to spend for the month in that category.

ADVICE FROM A PROFESSIONAL

Secrets of Super Savers

How do some people enjoy the good comfortable life and still find ways to save 20 to 30 percent or more of their incomes? Like most many people, such super savers have home mortgages, pay tuition bills, and take vacations. And they tend to have peace of mind about their finances because they have built up a sizeable cushion of savings and investments. Some of their secrets include:

- Be goal-oriented about savings and investments to achieve results.

- Ignore impulses to spending (ask "Do I *really* need it?") and choose to postpone buying anything expensive for a few months to see if the "need" is still strong.

- Avoid debt (auto loans and installment loans for computers, TVs, cell phones, and furniture) and using credit cards so you will not spend money you do not have.

- Cut back on spending on expensive items such as homes (not the largest in the neighborhood) and cars (drive older ones), and enjoy creative vacations that are not too pricey.

- Choose to spend wisely on everyday expenses by comparison shopping, clipping and using coupons, buying cheaper discounted goods and services, and being careful and mindful about entertainment expenses.

- Track spending by writing down every purchase, perhaps on a small tablet, so you know where money goes.

- Make savings automatic by diverting the maximum contribution to your employer's retirement plan, and sign up for automatic transfers from a checking to a savings account as well as to a brokerage account, a 529 plan, a Roth IRA, and/or a high-yield savings account. Save more as income rises.

Dorothy B. Durband
Kansas State University

To help keep to a budget, write checks as often as possible instead of using cash. Also record the purpose of the expenditure on the lower left of the check.

Monitor Unexpended Balances to Control Overspending the Number
One method to control overspending is to monitor unexpended balances in each of your budget classifications. You can accomplish this task by using a budget design that keeps a declining balance, as illustrated by parts (a) and (b) of Figure 3-6. Other budget designs, such as those shown in parts (c) and (d) of Figure 3-6, need to be monitored differently. As illustrated in parts (c) and (d) of the figure, simply calculate subtotals every week or so, as needed, during a monthly budgeting period. You can also track your spending using Quicken software or an online program.

DO IT IN CLASS

Justify Exceptions to Avoid Lying to Yourself **Budget exceptions** occur when budget estimates in various classifications differ from actual expenditures. Exceptions usually take the form of overexpenditures but can also occur in the over- or underreceipt of earnings. Simply spending extra income instead of recording it is not being honest with yourself. Recording the truth—by writing a few words to explain the exception—gives you the information to control your finances. If the exception is an expenditure, then immediately determine how to make up for the overexpenditure by trying to reduce other expenses in your spending plan.

budget exceptions
When budget estimates differ from actual expenditures.

Use a Subordinate Budget A **subordinate budget** is a detailed listing of planned expenses within a single budgeting classification. For example, an estimate of $1200 for a vacation could be supported by a subordinate budget as follows: motels, $700; restaurants, $300; and entertainment, $200.

subordinate budget
Detailed listing of planned expenses within a single budgeting classification.

Use the Envelope System for the Strongest Control The **envelope system** of budgeting entails placing exact amounts of money into envelopes for purposes of strict budgetary control. Here you place money equal to the budget estimate for the various expenditure classifications in envelopes at the start of a budgeting period and write the classification name and the budget amount on the outside of each envelope. As expenditures are made, record them on the appropriate envelope and remove the proper amounts of cash. When an envelope is empty, funds are exhausted for that classification. Of course, you must safeguard your cash.

envelope system
Placing exact amounts into envelopes for each budgetary purpose.

3.4e Action After: Evaluate Budgeting Progress to Make Needed Changes

Evaluation occurs at the end of each budgeting cycle. The purpose is to determine whether the earlier steps in your budgeting efforts have worked, and it gives you feedback to use for the next budget cycle. You review by comparing actual amounts with budgeted amounts, evaluating whether your objectives were met, and assessing the success of the overall process as well as your progress toward your short- and long-term goals. The evaluation process helps you to make any needed changes.

budget variance
Difference between amount budgeted and actual amount spent or received.

In some budget expenditure classifications, the budget estimates rarely agree with the actual expenditures—particularly in variable expenses. A **budget variance** is the difference between the amount budgeted and the actual amount spent or received. The remarks column, as illustrated in parts (c) and (d) of Figure 3-6, can help clarify why variances occurred. Overages on a few expenditures may cause little concern. If large variances have prevented you from achieving your objectives or making the budget balance, then take some action. Serious budget controls might have to be instituted or current controls tightened.

Whatever your goals, it feels good when you make progress toward them, and it is thrilling to achieve them. If you did not achieve some of your objectives, you can determine why and then adjust your budget and objectives accordingly. It is okay to revise your plans. Suppose at the end of the month Robert Chen finds that he is unable to set aside a planned amount of $250 in monthly savings. By evaluating his budget,

DID YOU KNOW

Your Worst Financial Blunders in Financial Statements, Tools, and Budgets

Based on others' financial woes, you will make mistakes in personal finance when you:

1. *Fail to plan for non-monthly irregular expenditures.*

2. *Underestimate how much you plan to spend each month.*

3. *Use credit card purchases to "balance" your budget.*

Figure 3-6 Record-Keeping Formats

(a)

Food Budget: $400			
DATE	ACTIVITY	AMOUNT	BALANCE
2-6	Groceries	$80	$320
2-9	Dinner out	45	275
2-14	Groceries	60	

(b)

DATE	ACTIVITY	AMOUNT BUDGETED	EXPENDITURES	BALANCE
2-1	Food Budget	$400		$400
2-6	Groceries		$80	320
2-9	Dinner out		45	230
2-14	Groceries		60	170
2-20	Groceries		50	120
2-28	February Totals	$400	$800	$400

(c)

DATE	ACTIVITY	Food Budget: $400	Clothing Budget: $30	EXPENDITURES Auto Budget: $200	Rent Budget: $800	Savings Budget: $90	Utilities Budget: $60	TOTAL Budget: $1580	REMARKS
2-1	Gasoline			40				40	
2-6	Groceries	80						80	Had friends over
2-8	Gasoline			37				37	Good price
2-9	Dinner out	45						45	
2-14	Groceries	60						60	Pepsi on sale
2-15	Subtotals	185/400		77/200				262/1580	

(d)

DATE	ACTIVITY	CASH IN	INCOME Salary	Other	TOTAL	EXPENDITURES Food	Clothing	Auto	Rent	Savings	Utilities	TOTAL	REMARKS
Estimates			800	40	840	400	30	200	800	90	60	1580	
Balance forwarded from January						6		14			2	22	
Sum			800	40	840	406	30	214	800	90	62	1602	
2-1	Paycheck	800	800									800	
2-1	Texaco-gasoline							40				40	
2-6	Safeway-groceries					80						80	Had friends over
2-8	7/11-gasoline							37				37	Good price
2-9	Dinner out					45						45	
2-14	Giant-groceries					60						60	Pepsi on sale
2-15	Paycheck	800	800										
2-28	Totals	1600	1600		800	400	30	195	800	90	65	1580	Good month

perhaps Robert will find that unexpected emergency car repairs led him to spend more than budgeted for the month. Because Robert understands why the objective was not achieved, he can set his sights on reaching the goal during the next budgeting time period.

DID YOU KNOW

Turn Bad Habits into Good Ones

Do You Do This?

Spend all your income

Overspend

Can't find financial records

Do not know how much you owe

Can't pay for auto insurance premium or vacation

Run out of money every few months

Do This Instead!

Save 10 percent or more

Utilize budget controls to reduce spending

Create a record-keeping system

Make a balance sheet

Save for large irregular expenses

Create a cash-flow calendar

Record Keeping In the process of budgeting, **record keeping** is the process of recording the sources and amounts of dollars earned and spent. Recording the estimated and actual amounts for both income and expenditures helps you monitor your money flow. Keeping track of income and expenses is the only way to collect sufficient information to evaluate how close you are to achieving your financial objectives. For those who keep records on paper, Figure 3-6 shows four samples of self-prepared recordkeeping formats that vary in complexity. Most people record earnings and expenditures when they occur. When writing in the "activity" and "remarks" columns in your record, be descriptive because you may need the information later.

record keeping
Recording sources and amounts of dollars earned and spent.

Adding Up Actual Income and Expenditures After the budgeting period has ended—usually at the beginning of a new month—you need to add up the actual income received and expenditures made during that period. You can perform this calculation on a form for each budget classification, as shown in parts (a) and (b) of Figure 3-6 or on a form with all income and expenditure classifications, as in parts (c) and (d) of Figure 3-6. Such calculations indicate where you may have overspent within your budget categories. If you are new at budgeting, do not be too concerned about overspending.

It occurs in some classifications almost always, only to be balanced by underspending in other categories. Use such information to refine your budget estimates in the future. In three or four months, you will be able to estimate your expenses much more accurately. The *Garman/Forgue* companion website provides budgeting software as well as numerous other templates, calculators, and worksheets that you can use in your own personal financial planning.

What to Do with Budgeted Money Left Over at the End of the Month At the end of the budgeting time period, some budget classifications may still have a positive balance. For example, perhaps you estimated the electric bill at $100, but it was only $80. You may then ask, "What do I do with the $20 surplus?" You also may ask, "What happens to budget classifications that were overspent?"

People handle the **net surplus** (the amount remaining after all budget classification deficits are subtracted from those with surpluses) in any of the following ways:

net surplus
Amount remaining after all budget classification deficits are subtracted from those with surpluses.

- Put the money into savings (and this allows the budget to total out to zero)

- Carry the surpluses forward to the following month

DID YOU KNOW

Save Money When Shopping by Using Coupons

You can save hundreds of dollars every year by taking advantage of coupons and discounts. It's fun getting a "$25-off coupon at Ruby Tuesdays," a "$5-off coupon for Pepsi or Coke at Walgreens," or "$50 off a phone." Try the following:

- Take advantage of Facebook or Twitter to sign up for coupons and discounts by liking your favorite brands.

- Receive daily coupon notices on local deals at BuyWithMe, groupon.com, and livingsocial.com.

- Use your phone to check out ShopSavy's app that scans an item barcode, sees who has it for less, and locates those sellers.

- In addition, it can send price alerts when items drop below the prices you've already seen.

- Utilize the Google Shopper app, which uses your phone's camera to recognize products by cover art, barcode scanning, voice, and text, and then provides reviews and specs. Also try Coupon Sherpa, Shopkick, and Scoutmob for your phone.

- Search for air, car rental, and hotel coupon codes at promotional/codes.com or couponwinner.com.

- Try out "price comparison" programs such as bizrate.com, InvisibleHand, nextag.com, price-grabber.com, and RedLaser.

- Redeem Sunday newspaper coupons that provide discounts for hundreds of products.

- Stop by the U.S. Post Office for an envelope of coupons if you are moving from one address to another or if you think you might move.

- Take grocery store coupons attached to products, on tear pads, and on bottlenecks as well as from cashiers upon checkout.

- Go online to obtain coupons and do so by setting up a separate e-mail account for coupons and then registering at the sites. Examples are restaurant.com, coupons.com, coolsavings.com, smartsource.com, grocerycoupons.com, couponmom.com, retailmenot.com, and grocerysmarts.com.

- Go to the websites for local radio stations, where they may have downloadable coupons for local restaurants and entertainment venues.

- Purchase valid coupons on eBay for only 10 to 25 cents on the dollar.

- Pay toward credit card debt
- Put surpluses toward a mortgage or other loan
- Put the money into a retirement account
- Spend surpluses like "mad money" on anything you want

DID YOU KNOW

Sean's Success Story

Sean has done well financially since he started working for his current employer three years ago. In addition to earning better-than-average raises, he has received an annual bonus of $3000 each year. One of Sean's major life goals is to enjoy an early retirement, perhaps beginning at age 55. He creates financial statements every year to track his progress. Sean now has a net worth of over $20,000 because he saved the after-tax amount of each bonus ($2500) and contributed the maximum amount to his employer's 401(k) retirement plan ($3000), which includes a 100 percent match ($3000 a year). Sean uses Quicken software to manage his personal finances. He lives below his income and is saving about $300 a month for emergencies, irregular expenses, and occasional splurges.

The budgeting form in part (d) of Figure 3-6 (page 92) allows for carrying balances forward to the next period. Some people carry forward deficits, with the hope that having less available in a budgeted classification the following month will motivate them to keep expenditures low. Because variable expense estimates are usually averages, it is best not to change the estimate based on a variation that occurs over just one or two months. If estimates are too high or low for a longer period, you will want to make adjustments.

Using financial software for budgeting, like Quicken, takes the drudgery out of making and using a spending plan. And it gets to be easy after a few months.

3.4f Some Final Suggestions

Here are some final suggestions for successful budgeting: (1) Keep it simple, (2) make it personal, (3) keep it flexible, and (4) keep a positive attitude. A smart thing to do is to list the benefits to yourself that will occur when you reach a particular financial goal. You are likely to achieve a financial goal when you are convinced that it is your own goal, when you make an emotional commitment to the goal, when your short-term goals lead to your long-term goals, and when you can visualize receiving the benefits of your goals.

DO IT NOW!

You know more about personal finance after reading this chapter, so get started right now by:

1. *Putting a notepad in your pocket to record every single expense of $1 or more for one month.*

2. *Preparing a cash-flow statement at the end of the month.*

3. *Setting up a spending plan for next month that provides for savings for at least one of your goals.*

CONCEPT CHECK 3.4

1. Identify two actions that should be performed before establishing a budget.

2. What are budget estimates? Offer some suggestions on how to go about making budget estimates for various types of expenses.

3. Distinguish between a cash-flow calendar and a revolving savings fund, and tell why each is important.

4. Offer three suggestions for effective budget controls.

DID YOU KNOW ?

Income Inequality Continues

Rising income inequality worries many Americans. Continuing a three-decade trend, the wealthiest Americans—the richest 1 percent who have a pre-tax family income above $394,000—earned more than 23 percent of the country's household income in a recent year. And they earned 95 percent of the increase in income in the post-crisis recovery. The top 10 percent of earners—those with pre-tax income exceeding $114,000—captured 48 percent of total earnings. Reasonable people can be fairly certain that there is a problem here.

WHAT DO YOU RECOMMEND *NOW?*

Now that you have read the chapter on financial planning, what do you recommend to Austin for his talk with Rachel on the subject of financial planning regarding:

1. Setting financial goals?
2. Determining what they own and owe?
3. Using the information in Austin's newly prepared financial statements to summarize the family's financial situation?
4. Evaluating their financial progress?
5. Setting up a record-keeping system to better serve their needs?
6. Starting a budgeting process to guide saving and spending?

BIG PICTURE SUMMARY OF LEARNING OBJECTIVES

LO1 Identify your financial values, goals, and strategies.

By identifying your financial values, goals, and strategies, you can always keep a balance between spending and saving and stay committed to your financial success. You may create financial plans in three broad areas: plans for spending, plans for risk management, and plans for capital accumulation.

LO2 Use balance sheets and cash-flow statements to measure your financial health and progress.

Financial statements are compilations of personal financial data designed to furnish information on money matters. The balance sheet provides information on what you own, what you owe, and what the net result would be if you paid off all your debts. The cash-flow statement lists income and expenditures over a specific period of time, such as the previous month or year.

LO3 Collect and organize the financial records necessary for managing your personal finances.

Your financial records will help determine where you are, where you have been, and where you are going financially. They also help you make money.

LO4 Achieve your financial goals through budgeting.

Budgeting is all about logical thinking about your finances. Budgeting forces you to consider what is important in your life, what things you want to own, how you want to live, what it will take to do that, and, more generally, what you want to achieve in life. A budget is a process used to record both projected and actual income and expenditures over a period of time, and it represents the major mechanism through which your financial plans are carried out and goals are achieved.

LET'S TALK ABOUT IT

1. **Families.** During sluggish economic times, the federal government's budgeting priority is to borrow so it can spend much more money than it takes in. What happens to families that try that, and why?

2. **Your Values.** What are your three most important personal values? Give an example of how each of those values might influence your financial plans.

3. **Cash Flow.** College students often have little income and many expenses. Does this reduce or increase the importance of completing a cash-flow statement on a monthly basis? Why?

4. **Financial Ratios.** Of the financial ratios described in this chapter, which two might be most revealing for the typical college student? Which two might be the most revealing for a retiree?

5. **Why Budget.** Do you have a budget? Why or why not? What do you think are the major reasons why people do not make formal written budgets?

6. **Control Spending.** What can a person do to control spending to better achieve financial success?

7. **Budgeting Mistake.** What is the biggest budget-related mistake that you have made? What would you do differently now?

8. **Personal Finances over the Life Cycle.** Areas of financial decision making change over one's life-cycle. Based on the information provided in Figure 3-3 on page 76 contrast your own areas of concern with those of your parents.

DO IT IN CLASS
PAGE 76

DO THE MATH

1. **Ratio Analyses for Victor and Maria.** Review the financial statements of Victor and Maria Hernandez (Table 3-2 and Table 3-3) and respond to the following questions:

   (a) Using the data in the Hernandezes' balance sheet, calculate an investment assets-to-net worth ratio. How would you interpret the ratio? The Hernandez family appears to have too few monetary assets compared with tangible and investment assets. How would you suggest that they remedy that situation over the next few years?

   (b) Comment on the couple's diversification of their investment assets.

   (c) Calculate the asset-to-debt ratio for Victor and Maria. How does this information help you understand their financial situation? How do their total assets compare with their total liabilities?

   (d) The Hernandezes seem to receive most of their income from employment rather than investments. What actions would you recommend for them to remedy that imbalance over the next few years?

   (e) The Hernandezes want to take a two-week vacation next summer, and they have only eight months to save the necessary $2400. What reasonable changes in expenses might they consider to increase net surplus and make the needed $300 per month?

2. **Calculating Net Worth and Net Surplus.** Jennifer Pontesso wants to better understand her financial situation. Use the following balance sheet and cash-flow statement information to determine her net worth and her net surplus for a recent month. Liquid assets: $10,000; home value: $210,000; monthly mortgage payment: $1300 on $170,000 mortgage; investment assets: $90,000; personal property: $20,000; total assets: $330,000; short-term debt: $5500 ($250 a month); total debt: $175,500; monthly gross income: $9000; monthly disposable income: $6800; monthly expenses: $6000.

DO IT IN CLASS
PAGE 72

3. **Ratio Analyses.** Now that Jennifer better understands her situation she wants to do some analysis of what she has found. Given her balance sheet and cash-flow statements calculate the following ratios:

   (a) Liquidity ratio
   (b) Asset-to-debt ratio
   (c) Debt-to-income ratio
   (d) Debt payments-to-disposable income ratio
   (e) Investment assets-to-total assets ratio

DO IT IN CLASS
PAGE 76

4. **Cash Flow Surplus/Deficit.** Cody Sebastion earns $40,000 a year. He pays 30 percent of his gross income in federal, state, and local taxes. He has fixed expenses in addition to taxes of $1200 per month and variable expenses that average $900 per month. What is his net cash flow (surplus or deficit) for the year?

5. **Construct Financial Statements.** Thomas Green has been a retail salesclerk for six years. At age 35, he is divorced with one child, Amanda, age 7. Thomas's salary is $36,000 per year. He regularly receives $400 per month for child support from Amanda's mother. Thomas invests $100 each month ($50 in his mutual fund and $50 in U.S. savings bonds). Using the following information, construct a balance sheet and a cash-flow statement for Thomas.

DO IT IN CLASS
PAGE 78

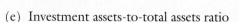

ASSETS	Amount
Vested retirement benefits (no employee contribution)	$3,000
Money market account (includes $150 of interest earned last year)	5,000
Mutual fund (includes $200 of reinvested dividend income from last year)	4,000
Checking account	1,000
Personal property	5,000
Automobile	3,000
U.S. savings bonds	3,000

LIABILITIES	Outstanding Balance
Dental bill (pays $25 per month and is included in uninsured medical/dental)	$ 450
Visa (pays $100 per month)	1,500
Student loan (pays $100 per month)	7,500

ANNUAL EXPENSES	Amount
Auto insurance	$ 780
Rent	9,100
Utilities	1,200
Phone	680
Cable	360
Food	3,000
Uninsured medical/dental	1,000

ANNUAL EXPENSES	Amount
Dry cleaning	480
Personal care	420
Gas, maintenance, license	2,120
Clothes	500
Entertainment	1,700
Vacations/visitation travel	1,300
Child care	3,820
Gifts	400
Miscellaneous	300
Taxes	4,600
Health insurance	2,440

6. **Budgeting and Income Projections.** Leyia and Aldolfo DeVaney of Monument, Colorado, have decided to start a family next year, so they are looking over their budget (illustrated in Table 3-5 as the "young married couple"). Leyia thinks that she can go on half-salary ($1050 instead of $2100 per month) in her job as a graduate assistant for about 18 months after the baby's birth; she will then return to full-time work.

(a) Looking at the DeVaneys' current monthly budget, identify categories and amounts in their $4315 budget where they realistically might cut back $1050. (Hint: Federal and state taxes should drop about $290 as their income drops.)

(b) Assume that Leyia and Aldolfo could be persuaded not to begin a family for another two to three years until Leyia finishes graduate school. What specific budgeting recommendations would you give them for handling (i) their fixed expenses and (ii) their variable expenses to prepare financially for an anticipated $1050 loss of income for 18 months as well as the expenses for the new baby?

(c) If the DeVaneys' gross income of $4315 rises 3 percent per year in the future, what will their income be after five years? (Hint: See Appendix A.1 or the *Garman/Forgue* companion website.)

FINANCIAL PLANNING CASES

CASE 1

The Financial Statements of Harry and Belinda Johnson Suggest Budgeting Problems

Harry graduated with a bachelor's degree in interior design last spring from a large Midwestern university near his hometown. Belinda has a degree in information technology from a university on the West Coast and is employed in a medium-size public relations firm. Harry and Belinda both worked on their schools' student newspapers and met at a conference during their junior year in college. They were married last June and live in an apartment in Kansas City. They will face many financial challenges over the next 20 years, as they buy their first home, decide on life insurance needs, begin a family, change jobs, and invest for retirement.

Harry works at a medium-size interior design firm and, during the last half of last year, earned a gross salary of $3100 per month. He also receives $3000 in interest income per year from a trust fund set up by his deceased father's estate; the trust fund will continue to pay that amount until 2028. He anticipates a raise of $150 a month in his salary by next January. Belinda works as a salesperson for a regional stock brokerage firm.

She earned a salary of $4750 per month last year. Belinda has many job-related benefits, including life insurance, health insurance, a retirement plan, and a credit union. Since she is a new employee Belinda does not expect a raise at the end of the year. The Johnsons live in an apartment located approximately halfway between their places of employment; however, their rent will increase by $100 a month next July. Harry drives about ten minutes to his job, and Belinda travels about 15 minutes via public transportation to reach her downtown job. Harry and Belinda's apartment is very nice, but small, and it is furnished primarily with furniture given to them by their families. Soon after starting their first jobs, Harry and Belinda decided to begin their financial planning. Fortunately each had taken a college course in personal finance. After initial discussion, they worked together for two evenings to develop the two financial statements presented below.

(a) Briefly describe how Harry and Belinda probably determined the fair market prices for each of their tangible and investment assets.

(b) Using the data from the cash-flow statement developed by Harry and Belinda, calculate a liquidity ratio, asset-to-debt ratio, debt-to-income ratio, debt payments-to-disposable income ratio, and investment assets-to-total assets ratio. What do these ratios tell you about the Johnsons' financial situation? Should Harry and Belinda incur more debt, such as credit cards or a new car loan?

(c) The Johnsons enjoy a high income because both work at well-paying jobs. They have spent parts of three evenings over the past several days discussing their financial values and goals together. As shown in the upper portion of Figure 3-5, they have established three long-term goals: $3000 for a European vacation to be taken in 2018, $5000 needed in October 2019 for a down payment on a new automobile, and $18,900 for a down payment on a home to be purchased in December 2020. As shown in the lower portion of the figure, the Johnsons did some calculations to determine how much they had to save for each goal—over the near term—to stay on schedule to reach their long-term goals as well as pay for two vacations and an anniversary party. After developing their balance sheet and cash-flow statement (shown below), the Johnsons made a budget for the year (shown in Table 3-6 on page 87). They then reconciled various conflicting needs and wants until they found that total annual income was close to the total of planned expenses. Next, they created a revolving savings fund (Table 3-8 on page 89) in which they were careful to include enough money each month to meet all of their short-term goals. When developing their cash-flow calendar for the year (Table 3-7 on page 88), they noticed a problem: substantial cash deficits toward the end of the year. In fact, despite their projected high income, they anticipate a deficit of $1530 for the year. To solve this problem, they do not anticipate increasing their income, using savings, or borrowing. Instead, they are considering modifying their needs and wants to reduce their budget estimates to the point where they would have a positive balance for the year. Make specific recommendations to the Johnsons on how they could make reductions in their budget estimates. Do not offer suggestions that would alter their new lifestyle drastically, as the couple would reject these ideas.

Balance Sheet for Harry and Belinda Johnson

January 1, 2015

ASSETS

Monetary Assets

Cash on hand	1,178	5.48%
Savings (First Federal Bank)	890	4.14%
Savings (Far West Savings Bank)	560	2.60%
Savings (Homestead Credit Union)	160	0.74%
Checking (First Federal Bank)	752	3.50%
Total monetary assets	$3,540	16.45%

Tangible Assets

Automobile (3-year-old Toyota)	11,000	51.13%
Personal property	2,300	10.69%
Furniture	1,700	7.90%
Total tangible assets	$15,000	69.72%
Investment Assets		
Harry's retirement account	1,425	6.62%
Belinda's retirement account	1,550	7.20%
Total investment assets	$ 2,975	13.83%
Total Assets	$21,515	100.00%

LIABILITIES

Short-Term Liabilities

Visa credit card	390	1.81%
Target credit card	45	0.21%
Dental bill	400	1.86%
Total short-term liabilities	$ 835	3.88%
Long-Term Liabilities		
Vehicle loan (First Federal Bank)	3,800	17.66%
Student loan (Belinda)	8,200	38.11%
January 1, 2015		
Total long-term liabilities	$12,000	55.78%
Total Liabilities	$12,835	59.66%
Net Worth	$ 8,680	40.34%
Total Liabilities and Net Worth	$21,515	100.00%

Cash-Flow Statement for Harry and Belinda Johnson July 1–December 31, 2014 (First Six Months of Marriage)

Cash Flow	Dollars	Percent
INCOME		
Harry's gross income ($3100×6)	18,600	37.11%
Belinda's gross income ($4750×6)	28,500	56.86%
Interest on savings account	24	0.05%
Harry's trust fund	3,000	5.99%
Total Income	$50,124	100.00%
EXPENDITURES		
Fixed Expenses		
Rent	6,600	13.17%
Renter's insurance	220	0.44%
Automobile loan payments	2,980	5.95%
Automobile insurance	850	1.70%
Health insurance (withheld from salary)	1,200	2.39%
Student loan payments	3,600	7.18%
Life insurance (withheld from salary)	90	0.18%
Cable TV and Internet	720	1.44%
Health club	420	0.84%
Savings/emergencies	600	1.20%
Harry's retirement plan (6% of salary)	1,115	2.22%
Belinda's retirement plan (4% of salary)	1,140	2.27%
Federal income tax (withheld from salary)	4,600	9.18%
State income tax (withheld from salary)	1,600	3.19%
Social Security (withheld from salary)	3,600	7.18%
Automobile registration	300	0.60%
Total Fixed Expenses	$29,635	59.12%
Variable Expenses		
Food (groceries)	2,600	5.19%
Food (out)	1,800	3.59%
Utilities	750	1.50%

Cash Flow	Dollars	Percent
Cell phones	450	0.90%
Gasoline and maintenance	700	1.40%
Doctor's and dentist's bills	710	1.42%
Medicines	350	0.70%
Clothing and upkeep	1,200	2.39%
Church and charity	1,200	2.39%
Gifts	1,070	2.13%
Public transportation	720	1.44%
Personal allowances	4,160	8.30%
Entertainment	960	1.92%
Vacation (holiday)	600	1.20%
Vacation (summer)	1,200	2.39%
Miscellaneous	480	0.96%
Total Variable Expenses	$18,950	37.81%
Total Expenses	$48,585	96.93%
SURPLUS (DEFICIT)	$1,539	3.07%

CASE 2

Victor and Maria Hernandez

Victor and Maria, both in their late 30s, have two children: John, age 13, and Joseph, age 15. Victor has had a long sales career with a major retail appliance store. Maria works part-time as a medical records assistant. The Hernandezes own two vehicles and their home, on which they have a mortgage. They will face many financial challenges over the next 20 years, as their children drive, go to college, and leave home and go out in the world on their own. Victor and Maria also recognize the need to further prepare for their retirement and the challenges of aging.

Victor and Maria spent some time making up their first balance sheet, which is shown in Table 3-2. Victor and Maria are a bit confused about how various financial activities can affect their net worth.

(a) Assume that their home is now appraised at $192,000 and the value of their automobile has dropped to $9500. Calculate and characterize the effects of these changes on their net worth and on their asset-to-debt ratio.

(b) If Victor and Maria take out a bank loan for $1545 and pay off their credit card debts totaling $1545, what effects would these changes have on their net worth?

(c) If Victor and Maria sell their New York 2028 bond and put the cash into the savings account, what effects would this have on their net worth and liquidity ratio?

CASE 3

Julia Price Thinks About Financial Statements, Tools, and Budgets

Julia graduated six years ago in aeronautical engineering and changed job once. Her income is more than sufficient for her needs. Julia contributes the maximum into her employer's retirement account and additionally saves about $400 a month. She has only about $1000 in credit card debt and makes a monthly car payment of $520. With such a strong financial position, she thinks it would be a waste of time to prepare financial statements and create a budget. Offer your opinions about her thinking.

CASE 4

Budget Control for a Recent Graduate

Seo-yeon, a political scientist from Lubbock, Texas, graduated from college eight months ago and is having a terrible time with his budget. Seo-yeon has a regular monthly income from her job and no really large bills, but she likes to spend. She exceeds her budget every month, and her credit card balances are increasing. Choose three budget control methods that you could recommend to Seo-yeon, and explain how each one could help her gain control of her finances.

DO IT IN CLASS
PAGES 89–91

CASE 5

A Couple Creates an Educational Savings Plan

Stanley Marsh and Wendy Testaburger of South Park, Colorado, have two young children and have been living on a tight budget. Their monthly budget is illustrated in Table 3-5 on page 85 as the "married couple with two young children." Wendy and Stanley are nervous about not having started an educational savings plan for their children. Wendy has just begun working on a part-time basis at a local accounting firm and earns about $860 per month; this income is reflected in the Marsh-Testaburgers' budget. They have decided that they want to save $200 per month for the children's education, but Wendy does not want to work more hours away from home.

(a) Review the family's budget and make suggestions about how to modify various budget estimates so that they could save $200 per month for the education fund.

(b) Briefly describe the effect of your recommended changes on the Marsh-Testaburgers' lifestyle.

BE YOUR OWN PERSONAL FINANCIAL MANAGER

1. **Financial Plan.** Use Table 3-1 on page 67 as a guide to making your financial plans, goals, and objectives for spending, risk management, and capital accumulation. Write up your findings.

2. **Balance Sheet.** Use Table 3-2 on page 74 as a guide to create a balance sheet or complete Worksheet 10: My Balance Sheet from "My Personal Financial Planner" to create your own detailed annual balance sheet. Write up your findings.

   MY PERSONAL FINANCIAL PLANNER

3. **Cash-Flow Statement.** Use Table 3-3 on page 77 as a guide to create a cash-flow statement or complete Worksheet 11: My Cash-Flow Statement from "My Personal Financial Planner" to create your own cash-flow statement. Write up your findings.

   MY PERSONAL FINANCIAL PLANNER

4. **Evaluate Your Financial Ratios.** Use the financial ratios on pages 78 to help evaluate your personal financial condition or complete Worksheet 12: My Financial Ratios from "My Personal Financial Planner" to record your financial ratios.

   MY PERSONAL FINANCIAL PLANNER

5. **Categorize Your Financial Records.** Review Table 3-4 "Financial Records: What to Keep and Where" on pages 80–81 to develop a system for your own records or complete Worksheet 13: My Financial Records from "My Personal Financial Planner" to record what records will be placed in your home file, safe-deposit box, or another place.

   MY PERSONAL FINANCIAL PLANNER

6. **Monthly Saving to Reach Your Goals.** Use Figure 3-5 "Goals Worksheet for Harry and Belinda Johnson" on page 84 as a guide to develop your own personal savings goals or complete Worksheet 14: Monthly Savings to

   MY PERSONAL FINANCIAL PLANNER

Reach My Financial Goals from "My Personal Financial Planner" to record the dollar amount, time, and interim short-term goals.

7. **Nonmonthly Expenses.** Complete Worksheet 15: Determining Monthly Budget Amounts for My Nonmonthly Expenses from "My Personal Financial Planner" to carefully plan for your nonmonthly expenses over the year.

   MY PERSONAL FINANCIAL PLANNER

8. **Revolving Savings Fund.** Review Table 3-8 "Revolving Savings Fund for Harry and Belinda Johnson" on page 89 to develop a plan for yourself or complete Worksheet 16: My Revolving Savings Fund from "My Personal Financial Planner" to record how you can save to pay for irregular expenses throughout the year.

   MY PERSONAL FINANCIAL PLANNER

9. **Create Your Budget.** Use Table 3-6 on page 87 as a guide to create a 12-month budget or complete Worksheet 17: My Budget from "My Personal Financial Planner" to do so.

   MY PERSONAL FINANCIAL PLANNER

10. **Control Spending with Budget Worksheets.** Complete Worksheet 18: My Budget Category Ledger Worksheets from "My Personal Financial Planner" to create a system to monitor and control spending.

    MY PERSONAL FINANCIAL PLANNER

11. **Organize Your Financial Records.** Use Table 3-4 on pages 80–81 as a guide to helping you get your financial records in order. Write down some notes about your thinking on what documents you will need and where to keep them.

ON THE NET

Go to the Web pages indicated to complete these exercises.

1. **Online Calculators.** Visit MoneyChimp's website (www .moneychimp.com/). There you will find an assortment of calculators that can be used in various present and future value calculations. Select three that you believe would be particularly useful in the aspects of personal financial planning that were discussed in this chapter.

2. **More Online Calculators.** Visit CNNMoney's website (cgi.money.cnn.com/tools/). Select three calculators to try out that you think would be useful in personal finance.

3. **Input Your Budget and Compare to Your Projected Expenditures.** Visit the website www.kiplinger.com /tool/spending/T007-S001-budgeting-worksheet-a-household-budget-for-today-a/index.php and use the budgeting worksheet and input your projected monthly living costs in various categories. It will compare your projections to what you actually spent.

4. **Can You Make It Through the Month?** "Spent" is an online game that simulates the struggles of homelessness. Accept the challenge and take 10 minutes to play Spent (playspent.org/).

ACTION INVOLVEMENT PROJECTS

1. **Money Discussion Topics.** Use the list in the box "Did You Know? Money Topics to Discuss with Your Partner" as a guide to interview three married couples. Ask them which of the topics they discussed with their partners within the first year of marriage. Make a table that summarizes your findings.

2. **Financial Mistakes.** Survey five people to learn about their financial mistakes in life. Ask each person to cite two financial mistakes he/she has made. Make a table that summarizes your findings.

3. **Short-Term Financial Goals.** Survey five people to ascertain their financial goals. Ask each person, "What are your top two short-term financial goals?" Make a table that summarizes your findings.

4. **Long-Term Financial Goals.** Survey five people to ascertain their financial goals. Ask each person, "What are your top three long-term financial goals?" Make a table that summarizes your findings.

Visit the Garman/Forgue companion website at www.cengagebrain.com.

PART 2

4 Managing Income Taxes

YOU MUST BE KIDDING, RIGHT?

Bharat Persaud's employer gave him a $2000 bonus last year, and when Bharat was filling out his federal income tax form, he discovered that $1000 of it moved him from the 15 percent marginal tax rate to 25 percent. How much additional income tax will Bharat pay on the $2000?

A. $150   **C.** $250

B. $180   **D.** $400

The answer is C. The federal marginal tax rate is applied to your last dollar of earnings. The first $1000 of Bharat's bonus is taxed at the marginal tax rate of 15 percent ($150), but the second $1000 is taxed at 25 percent ($250). Be aware of your marginal tax rate!

LEARNING OBJECTIVES

After reading this chapter, you should be able to:

1. Explain the nature of progressive income taxes and the marginal tax rate.

2. Differentiate among the eight steps involved in calculating your federal income taxes.

3. Use appropriate strategies to avoid overpayment of income taxes.

MORTGAGE
RETIREMENT

INSURANCE
TAXES

401(k)
VACATION

EDUCATION
CREDIT CARDS

WHAT DO YOU RECOMMEND?

Zero Creatives/Cultura/Jupiter Images

Timothy Edgar and Amber Szpanka plan to get married in two years. Timothy earns $44,000 per year managing a fast-food restaurant. He also earns about $10,000 per year selling jewelry that he designs at craft shows held monthly in various nearby cities. Right after they get married, Timothy plans to go back to college full time to finish the last year of his undergraduate degree. Amber earns $58,000 annually working as an institutional sales representative for an insurance company. Both Timothy and Amber each contribute $100 per month to their employer-sponsored 401 (k) retirement accounts. Timothy has little additional savings, but Amber has accumulated $18,000 that she wants to use for a down payment on a home. Amber also owns 300 shares of stock in an oil company that she inherited six years ago when the price was $90 per share; now the stock is worth $130 per share. Timothy and Amber live in a state where the state income tax is 6 percent.

What would you recommend to Timothy and Amber on the subject of managing income taxes regarding:

1. **Using tax credits to help pay for Timothy's college expenses?**

2. **Determining how much money Amber will realize if she sells the stocks, assuming she pays federal income taxes at the 25 percent rate?**

3. **Buying a home?**

4. **Increasing contributions to their employer-sponsored retirement plans?**

5. **Establishing a sideline business for tax purposes for Timothy's jewelry operation?**

In the next five years, you can start achieving financial success by doing the following related to managing income taxes:

1. *Sign up for tax-advantaged employee benefits at your workplace.*

2. *Contribute to your employer-sponsored 401(k) retirement plan at least up to the amount of the employer's matching contribution.*

3. *Buy a home to reduce income taxes.*

4. *Prepare your own tax return so you can learn how to reduce your income tax liability.*

5. *Maintain good tax records.*

tax planning
Seeking legal ways to reduce, eliminate, or defer income taxes.

taxable income
Income upon which income taxes are levied.

LEARNING OBJECTIVE 1
Explain the nature of progressive income taxes and the marginal tax rate.

taxes
Compulsory government-imposed charges levied on citizens and their property.

progressive tax
A tax that progressively increases as a taxpayer's taxable income increases.

marginal tax bracket (MTB)/ marginal tax rate
One of seven income-range segments at which income is taxed at increasing rates. Also known as marginal tax rate.

Managing your money includes not paying unnecessary sums to the government in taxes. Learning about tax-saving techniques will provide you with more money to do with what you want. "The avoidance of taxes is the only intellectual pursuit that carries any reward," wrote economist John Maynard Keynes.

You should pay your income tax liabilities in full, but that's all—there is no need to pay a dime extra. To achieve this goal, you need to adopt a **tax planning** perspective designed to eliminate, reduce, or defer some income taxes. To get started, you should recognize that you pay personal income taxes only on your **taxable income**. This amount is determined by subtracting various exclusions, adjustments, exemptions, and deductions from total income, with the result being the income upon which the tax is actually calculated. Details for these calculations are provided later. For now, simply remember that the main idea in managing income taxes is to reduce your taxable income as much as possible while maintaining a high level of total income. The result will lower your actual tax liability. Then you will have more money available every year to manage, spend, save, invest, and donate—activities that are the focus of this whole book.

4.1 PROGRESSIVE INCOME TAXES AND THE MARGINAL TAX RATE

Taxes are compulsory charges imposed by a government on its citizens and their property. The U.S. Internal Revenue Service (IRS) is the agency charged with the responsibility for collecting federal income taxes based on the legal provisions in the *Internal Revenue Code*.

4.1a The Progressive Nature of the Federal Income Tax

Taxes can be classified as progressive or regressive. The federal personal income tax is a **progressive tax** because the tax rate progressively increases as a taxpayer's taxable income increases. A higher income implies a greater ability to pay. As Table 4-1 shows, the higher portions of a taxpayer's taxable income are taxed at increasingly higher rates under the federal income tax.

A **regressive tax** operates in the opposite way. It is a tax imposed in such a manner that the tax rate stays the same for all income with the result that lower-income people pay proportionately more in taxes. An example is the state sales tax, since a rate of perhaps 7 percent might have to be paid by everyone regardless of income. One who earns \$30,000 and spends \$6,000 on food pays 1.5 percent on food purchases (7% × \$6000 = \$420/\$30,000 = 1.4%). This compares to another person who earns \$80,000 and spends \$10,000 on food, thus paying less than 1 percent on sales tax on food purchases (7% × \$10,000 − \$700/\$80,000 = 0.87%).

4.1b The Marginal Tax Rate Is Applied to the Last Dollar Earned

Note that the marginal tax brackets are progressive. The first portion of someone's income is taxed at the rate in the lowest bracket; the next portion is taxed at the next lowest rate; and the final portion of income is taxed an even higher rate. Because our tax system has graduated tax rates, you do not pay the same tax rate on every dollar subject to tax.

The **marginal tax bracket (MTB)** (or **marginal tax rate**) is illustrated with the seven income-range segments are taxed at increasing rates as income goes up. The tax rates apply only to the income within each tax bracket range. Recall from Chapter 1 that your marginal tax rate is the one that is applied to your last dollar of earnings.

Depending on their income, taxpayers fit into one of the brackets (as shown in Table 4-1) and, accordingly, pay at one of those marginal tax rates: 10 percent,

Table 4-1   The Progressive Nature of the Federal Income Tax

Single Individuals	
If taxable income is:	**Marginal Tax Rate**
Up to $9,075	10%
Over $9,075 but not over $36,900	15%
Over $36,900 but not over $89,350	25%
Over $89,350 but not over $186,350	28%
Over $186,350 but not over $405,100	33%
Over $405,100 but not over $406,750	35%
Over $406,750	39.6%

15 percent, 25 percent, 28 percent, 33 percent, 35 percent, or 39.6 percent.* In addition, each year the dollar amounts for the taxable income brackets are adjusted for inflation to reduce the effects of inflation in a process called **indexing**. This keeps taxpayers from being forced to pay more taxes as they receive raises.

Your marginal tax rate is perhaps the single most important concept in personal finance. It tells you the portion of any extra taxable earnings—from a raise, investment income, or money from a second job—you must pay in income taxes. It also measures the tax reduction benefits of a tax-deductible expense that allows you to reduce your taxable income.

Consider this example of how the marginal tax rate might apply. Victoria Bassett is from Syracuse, New York (see Figure 4-1). Because of the progressive provisions in the tax laws, part of her $60,000 income ($10,150 [$6200 + $3950]) is not taxed, the next $9075 is taxed at 10 percent, the next $27,825 is taxed at 15 percent, and the remaining $12,950 of Victoria's $60,000 income is taxed at 25 percent. Thus, Victoria is in the 25 percent marginal tax bracket because the *last* dollar that she earned is taxed at that level. Her tax liability is $8,318.75 based on her $60,000 in income.

indexing
Yearly adjustments to tax brackets that reduce inflation's effects on tax brackets.

DO IT IN CLASS

Figure 4-1   How Your Income Is Really Taxed (Example: Victoria Bassett with a $60,000 Gross Income, and she is in the 25% marginal tax bracket)

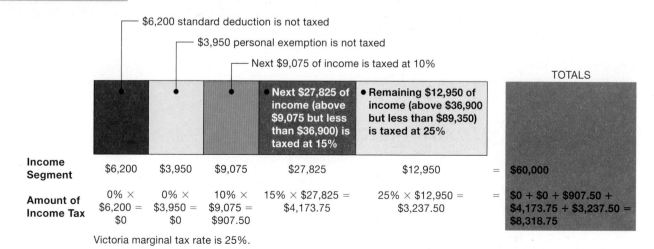

---

* The history of the latest year when the highest federal marginal tax rates in the United States was applied to taxable income is as follows: 1953 (92%); 1980 (70%); 1986 (50%); 2000 (39.6%); and 2012 (35%).

The United States Is Not a High-Tax Country

The tax burden in the United States is the lowest among industrialized countries in the world. Compared to countries that are members of the Organization for Economic Cooperation and Development (OECD), combined taxes in the United States are 33.4 percent. Seventeen countries have higher rates including Denmark (47.6%), Belgium (43.5%), France (42%), Australia (42.0%), Hungary (37.9%), Germany (36.1%), and United Kingdom (34.9%). The United States is far from a high-tax country. In fact, federal taxes on middle-income Americans are near historic lows.

effective marginal tax rate
The total marginal rate reflects all taxes on a person's income, including federal, state, and local income taxes as well as Social Security and Medicare taxes.

The mathematics shown in Figure 4-1 is based either on the **IRS tax table** (used for tax returns with incomes up to $100,000) or the **tax-rate schedules** (used for tax returns with incomes above $100,000). All information cited in this chapter is for income tax returns filed in 2015 for the previous year's income, unless otherwise noted.

4.1c Use Your Marginal Tax Rate to Help Make Financial Decisions

The marginal tax rate can affect many financial decisions that you make. Consider, for example, what happens if you are in the 25 percent marginal tax bracket and you make a $100 tax-deductible contribution to a charity. The charity receives the $100, and you deduct the $100 from your taxable income. This deduction results in a $25 reduction in your federal income tax ($100 × 0.25). In effect, you give only $75 (not $100) because the government, in effect, "gives" $25 to the charity.

4.1d Your Effective Marginal Tax Rate Is Higher

The **effective marginal tax rate** describes a person's total marginal tax rate on income after including federal, state, and local income taxes as well as Social Security and Medicare taxes. To determine your effective marginal tax rate on income, add all of these other taxes to your federal marginal tax rate.

For example, a single taxpayer earning a taxable income between $36,900 and $89,350 will pay federal income taxes at a marginal rate of 25 percent, a combined Social Security 6.2%* and Medicare tax rate of 1.45%** that totals 7.65 percent,*** a state income tax rate of 6 percent,**** and a city income tax rate of 2 percent. These taxes result in an effective marginal tax rate of 40 percent (25 + 7.65 + 6 + 2 = 40.65, about 40). Most employed taxpayers pay an effective marginal tax rate of 40 percent.

How to Determine Your Marginal Tax Rate

You can determine your marginal tax rate by following this example.

1. *Start with a single person who has a taxable income of $39,600, and looking at the illustrated tax table (Table 4-3 on page 119), he/she finds his tax on that amount of income ($5763).*

2. *Add $100 to that income for a total of $39,700, and find the tax on that amount ($5788).*

3. *Calculate the difference between the two tax amounts ($5788–$5763). The extra $25 in taxes from a $100 increase in income reflects a federal marginal tax rate of 25 percent.*

CONCEPT CHECK 4.1

1. Distinguish between a progressive and a regressive tax.

2. What is a marginal tax bracket, and how does it affect taxpayers?

3. Explain why some taxpayers have a marginal tax rate as high as 40 percent.

---

* The 6.2 percent Social Security tax is applied to wages up to $117,000.

** The Medicare tax is applied to all wages regardless of amount.

*** "Higher-income" taxpayers earning $200,000+, about 4.7 million returns, which is 3.2 percent of all returns, also must pay two additional Medicare taxes: A 3.8 percent surtax on net investment income and a 0.9 percent Medicare contributions tax on self-employment earnings. Those earning $400,000+ also pay a 20 percent rate on all long-term capital gains.

**** Check income tax rates in various states at www.bankrate.com/taxes.aspx

4.2 EIGHT STEPS IN CALCULATING YOUR INCOME TAXES

There are eight basic steps in calculating federal income taxes:

1. Determine your total income.
2. Determine and report your gross income after subtracting exclusions.
3. Subtract adjustments to income.
4. Subtract either the IRS's standard deduction amount for your tax status or your itemized deductions.
5. Subtract the value of your personal exemptions.
6. Determine your preliminary tax liability.
7. Subtract tax credits for which you qualify.
8. Calculate the balance due the IRS or the amount of your refund.

LEARNING OBJECTIVE 2

Differentiate among the eight steps involved in calculating your federal income taxes.

Figure 4-2 graphically depicts these eight steps in the overall process of federal income tax calculation. The idea is to reduce your income so that you pay the smallest amount possible in income taxes. You do so by reducing total income by removing nontaxable income and then subtracting exclusions, deductions, exemptions, and tax credits, as indicated in the unshaded boxes in Figure 4-2.

4.2a Determine Your Total Income

Practically everything you receive in return for your work or services and any profit from the sale of assets is considered income, whether the compensation is paid in cash, property, or services. Listing these earnings will reveal your **total income**—compensation from all sources—and much of it, but not all, will be subject to income taxes.

total income
Compensation from all sources.

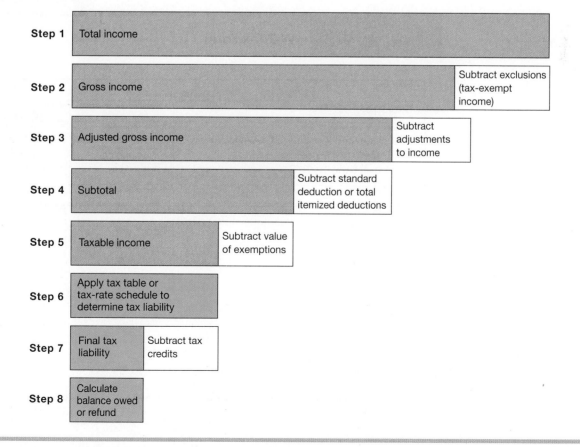

Figure 4-2 **The Steps in Calculating Your Income Taxes**

Step 1 — Total income

Step 2 — Gross income — Subtract exclusions (tax-exempt income)

Step 3 — Adjusted gross income — Subtract adjustments to income

Step 4 — Subtotal — Subtract standard deduction or total itemized deductions

Step 5 — Taxable income — Subtract value of exemptions

Step 6 — Apply tax table or tax-rate schedule to determine tax liability

Step 7 — Final tax liability — Subtract tax credits

Step 8 — Calculate balance owed or refund

earned income

Compensation for performing personal services.

For most people, **earned income** is income derived from active participation in a trade or business, including wages, salary, tips, commissions, and bonuses. It is reported to them annually on a Form W-2, Wage and Tax Statement. Employers must provide W-2 information (see Figure 4-3) by January 31 of the year following the earned income. If you also receive income from interest or dividends or other sources, you will receive a Form 1099-INT or 1099-DIV, providing appropriate details. The IRS also receives the information on their Form 1099s, which it uses to verify the income you report.

Income to Include The following types of income are included when you report your income to the IRS:

- Wages and salaries
- Commissions
- Bonuses
- Professional fees earned
- Hobby income
- Tips earned
- Severance pay
- Medical insurance rebates because of Patient Protection and Affordable Care Act
- Fair value of anything received in a barter arrangement
- Forgiven or cancelled debt (unless borrower is insolvent or bankrupt)
- Alimony received
- Scholarship and fellowship income spent on room, board, and other living expenses
- Grants and the value of tuition reductions that pay for teaching or other services
- Annuity and pension income received

Figure 4-3 **W-2 Tax Form**

a Control number					
	22222	OMB No. 1545-0008			
b Employer identification number (EIN) 37-12345678			1 Wages, tips, other compensation 65,000.00	2 Federal income tax withheld 10,400.00	
c Employer's name, address, and ZIP code Financial Knowledge Communications 1245 Oak Street Oak Park, IL 60302			3 Social security wages 65,000.00	4 Social security tax withheld 4,030	
			5 Medicare wages and tips 65,000.00	6 Medicare tax withheld 76.25	
			7 Social security tips	8 Allocated tips	
d Employee's social security number 123-45-6789			9 Advance EIC payment	10 Dependent care benefits	
e Employee's first name and initial Last name Suff. Yasuo Konami			11 Nonqualified plans	12a	
			13 Statutory employee Retirement plan Third-party sick pay	12b	
			14 Other	12c	
				12d	
f Employee's address and ZIP code					
15 State Employer's state ID number IL 37-14119877	16 State wages, tips, etc.	17 State income tax 1,950.00	18 Local wages, tips, etc.	19 Local income tax	20 Locality name

Form **W-2** Wage and Tax Statement   Department of the Treasury—Internal Revenue Service

Copy 1—For State, City, or Local Tax Department

- Withdrawals and disbursements from retirement accounts, such as an individual retirement account (IRA) or 401(k) retirement plan (discussed in Chapter 17, "Retirement and Estate Planning")
- Military retirement income
- Social Security income (a portion is taxed above certain income thresholds)
- Disability payments received if you did not pay the premiums
- Damage payments from personal injury lawsuits (punitive damages only)
- Value of personal use of employer-provided car
- State and local income tax refunds (only if the taxpayer itemized deductions during the previous year)
- Employee productivity awards
- Awards for artistic, scientific, and charitable achievements unless assigned to a charity
- Prizes, contest winnings, and rewards
- Gambling and lottery winnings
- All kinds of illegal income
- Fees for serving as a juror or election worker
- Unemployment benefits
- Net rental income
- Royalties
- Investment, business, and farm profits
- Interest income (this includes credit union dividends)
- Dividend income (including mutual fund capital gains distributions even though they are reinvested)

Capital Gains and Losses Are Taxed at Special Low Rates An **asset** is property owned by a taxpayer for personal use or as an investment that has monetary value. Examples of assets include stocks, mutual funds, bonds, land, art, gems, stamps, coins, vehicles, and homes. The net income received from the sale of an asset above the costs incurred to purchase and sell it is a **capital gain**.

A **capital loss** results when the sale of an asset brings less income than the costs of purchasing and selling the asset. Capital gains and losses on investments must be reported on your tax return. Capital gains from the sale or exchange of property held for personal use, such as on a vehicle or vacation home, must be reported as income, but losses on such property are not deductible. There is no tax liability on any capital gain until the stock, bond, mutual fund, real estate, or other investment is sold.

A **short-term gain** (or **loss**) occurs when you sell an asset that you have owned for one year or less; it is taxed at the same rates as ordinary income, which is all income other than capital gains. A **long-term gain** (or **loss**) occurs when you sell an asset that you have owned for more than one year (at least a year and a day), and it is taxed at special low rates. The long-term capital gains rate is zero for taxpayers in the 15 percent marginal tax bracket. The rate is 15 percent for those in the 25, 28, 33, and 35 percent brackets. It is 20 percent for those in the 39.6 percent tax bracket.

Capital losses may be used first to offset capital gains on your tax return. If there are no capital gains, or if the capital losses are larger than the capital gains, you can deduct the capital loss against your other income, but only up to a limit of $3000 in one year. If your net capital loss is more than $3000, the excess may be carried forward to be deducted on the next tax year's form, again up to an annual $3000 maximum.

Dividends and Interest Are Treated Differently Owners of stocks in a corporation may receive dividends quarterly. These payments to shareholders are made out of current or accumulated earnings of a corporation and are taxable. Shareholders are

capital gain
The net income received from the sale of an asset above the costs incurred to purchase and sell it.

long-term gain/loss
A profit or loss on the sale of an asset that has been held for more than a year.

annually sent tax forms 1099-DIV that explains what amounts must be reported to the IRS when taxes are filed. Dividends from most domestic corporations and many foreign companies are subject to the same favorable rates as capital gains. Dividends in the form of shares of stock are generally not taxable.

So called dividends are actually "interest" reported to taxpayers on Form 1099-INT when received from credit unions, cooperative banks, savings and loan associations, building and loan associations, and mutual savings banks. They are subject to ordinary income taxes. Dividends received from a life insurance policy are actually a refund of your premium and are not taxed.

4.2b Determine and Report Your Gross Income After Subtracting Exclusions

gross income

All income in the form of money, goods, services, and/or property.

exclusions

Income not subject to federal taxation.

DO IT IN CLASS

Gross income consists of all income (both earned and unearned) received in the form of money, goods, services, and property before exclusions and deductions that a taxpayer is required to report to the IRS. To determine gross income, you need to determine which kinds of income are not subject to federal taxation and, therefore, need not be reported as part of gross income. These amounts are called **exclusions**.

Income to Exclude The more common exclusions (some are subject to limits) are as follows:

- Gifts
- Inherited money or property
- Income from a carpool
- Income from items sold at a garage sale for a sum less than what you paid
- Cash rebates on purchases of new cars and other products
- Tuition reduction, if not received as compensation for teaching or service
- Federal income tax refunds
- State and local income tax refunds for a year in which you claimed the standard deduction
- Scholarship and fellowship income spent on course-required tuition, fees, books, supplies, and equipment (degree candidates only)
- Withdrawals from state-sponsored Section 529 plans (prepaid tuition and savings) used for education
- Prizes and awards made primarily to recognize artistic, civic, charitable, educational, and similar achievements
- Return of money loaned
- Withdrawals from medical savings accounts used for qualified expenses
- Earnings accumulating within annuities, cash-value life insurance policies, Series EE bonds, and qualified retirement accounts
- Interest income received on tax-exempt government bonds issued by states, counties, cities, and districts
- Life insurance benefits received
- Combat zone pay for military personnel
- Welfare, black lung, workers' compensation, and veterans' benefits
- Value of food stamps
- First $500,000 ($250,000 if single) gain on the sale of a principal residence
- Disability insurance benefits if you paid the insurance premiums
- Social Security benefits (except for high-income taxpayers)

- Rental income from a vacation home if not rented for more than 14 days
- First $5000 of death benefits paid by an employer to a worker's beneficiary
- Travel and mileage expenses reimbursed by an employer (if not previously deducted by the taxpayer)
- Employer-provided per diem allowance covering only meals and incidentals
- Amounts paid by employers for premiums for medical insurance, workers' compensation, and health and long-term care insurance
- Moving expense reimbursements received from an employer (if not previously deducted by the taxpayer)
- Employer-provided payments of $130 per month for transit passes and $250 a month for parking
- Value of premiums for first $50,000 worth of group-term life insurance provided by an employer
- Employer payments (up to $5000) for dependent care assistance (for children and parents)
- Benefits from employers that are impractical to tax because they are so modest, such as occasional supper money and taxi fares for overtime work, company parties, holiday gifts (not cash), and occasional theater or sporting events
- Employer contributions for employee expenses for education (up to $5250 annually)
- Employee contributions to flexible spending accounts
- Reimbursements from flexible spending accounts
- Interest received on Series EE and Series I bonds used for college tuition and fees
- Child support payments received
- Property settlement in a divorce
- Compensatory damages in physical injury cases

4.2c Subtract Adjustments to Income

In the process of determining your taxable income, you make **adjustments to income** (or **adjustments**). These are allowable subtractions from gross income, and include items such as moving expenses to a new job location (including college graduates who move to take their first job as long as it is at least 50 miles from their old residence); higher-education expenses for tuition and fees (up to $4000); student loan interest for higher education, including that paid by a parent ($2500 maximum); military reservists' travel expenses (for more than 100 miles); contributions to qualified personal retirement accounts (IRA and 401[k] accounts) and health savings accounts (up to $3300 for singles and $6550 for family coverage); alimony payments; interest penalties for early withdrawal of savings certificates of deposit;; and certain expenses of self-employed people (such as health insurance premiums). Adjustments are subtracted from gross income to determine **adjusted gross income (AGI)**. Subtracting adjustments to income from gross income results in a subtotal.

To illustrate the value of adjustments to income, consider that Jose Martinez from Columbia, South Carolina, has a gross income of $50,000. This past year he spent $1200 moving to Nashville, Tennessee, for a new job, and he also paid $2000 in higher-education expenses working on a graduate degree. The $3200 in adjustments reduces his gross income to $46,800, and therefore Jose saves $800 in income taxes because he is in the 25 percent marginal tax bracket ($3200 × 0.25).

Adjustments are called **above-the-line deductions** because they may be subtracted from gross income even if itemized deductions are not claimed. Adjustments may be taken regardless of whether or not the taxpayer itemizes deductions or takes the standard deduction amount (discussed next).

adjustments to income
Allowable subtractions from gross income.

adjusted gross income (AGI)
Gross income less any exclusions and adjustments.

above-the-line deductions
Adjustments subtracted from gross income whether taxpayer itemizes deductions or not.

ADVICE FROM A PROFESSIONAL

A Sideline Business Can Reduce Your Income Taxes

A sideline business can open many doors to tax deductions. You should never spend money simply for a tax deduction; however, if you're going to spend the money anyway, you should do everything you can to make it tax deductible.

By having your own business, every dollar you spend attempting to make a profit becomes tax deductible. While no deduction is allowed for personal expenses, you can deduct expenses for auto, travel, office, office equipment (e.g., desk, chair, computer), contributions to self-funded

retirement accounts, health insurance premiums, educational expenses, entertainment, business gifts, and more. You can deduct salaries of employees, even if they are your children, other relatives, or friends.

The business does not have to be your primary employment. If you lose money in the business, you can deduct those losses from your other income. The IRS says that you must do what a "reasonable business person" would do to make a profit. If you do not meet that test, the IRS will classify the operation as a hobby, require you to report the income, and disallow all deductions.

James J. Williams
Hudson Valley Community College, Troy, New York

Table 4-2   Tax Rate Schedules

Single Individuals		
If taxable income is over—	**But not over—**	**The tax is—**
$ 0	$ 9,075	10% of the taxable income
$ 9,075	$ 36,900	$907.50 plus 15% of the amount over $9,075
$ 36,900	$ 89,350	$5,081.25 plus 25% of the amount over $36,900
$ 89,350	$186,350	$18,193.75 plus 28% of the amount over $89,350
$186,350	$405,100	$45,353.75 plus 33% of the amount over $186,350
$405,100	$406,750	$117,541.25 plus 35% of the amount over $405,100
Over $406,750	No limit	$118,118.75 plus 39.6% of the amount over $406,750
Married Couples Filing Jointly		
If taxable income is over—	**But not over—**	**The tax is—**
$ 0	$ 18,150	10% of the taxable income
$ 18,150	$ 73,800	$1815 plus 15% of the amount over $18,150
$ 73,800	$148,850	$10,162 plus 25% of the amount over $73,800
$148,850	$226,850	$28,925 plus 28% of the amount over $148,850
$226,850	$450,100	$50,765 plus 33% of the amount over $226,850
$405,100	$457,600	$109,587.50 plus 35% of the amount over $405,100
$457,600	No limit	$127,962.50 plus 39.6% of the amount over $457,600

DO IT IN CLASS

itemized deductions
Tax-deductible expenses.

<u>4.2d</u>   Subtract Either the IRS's Standard Deduction for Your Tax Status or Your Itemized Deductions

Taxpayers may reduce income further by the amount of the standard deduction. Or they can list their **itemized deductions**, which are specific items that may be used to directly reduce income that may reduce the amount of your income subject to tax.

You can itemize or use the standard deduction, and you want to use the larger of the two. The **standard deduction** is a fixed amount that all taxpayers (except some dependents) who do not itemize deductions regardless of their actual expenses may subtract from their adjusted gross income. In effect, it consists of the government's permissible estimate of any likely tax-deductible expenses these taxpayers might have. Two out of three taxpayers take the standard deduction.

The standard deduction amount depends on **filing status**, a description of your marital status on the last day of the year. A return can be filed with a status of a single person, a married person (filing separately or jointly), a head of household, or qualifying widow or widower. Certain tax benefits apply to each filing status. For example, the standard deduction amounts are $6200 for single individuals and twice as much, $12,400, for married people filing jointly.

Additional standard deductions if age 65 or blind are permitted. The additional standard deduction for those age 65 or older or who are blind is $1200 for married individuals and surviving spouses. It is $1550 for singles age 65 or older or blind filers.

Taxpayers can take the greater of the standard deduction or itemizations but not both. For example, a single person might list all of his or her tax deductions and find that they total $6800, which is more than the standard deduction amount of $6200, so he or she takes the $6800. Someone else with calculated deductions of $4900 can instead take the standard deduction of $6200.

The tax form lists the following six classifications of itemized deductions:

1. Medical and Dental Expenses
2. Taxes You Paid
3. Interest You Paid
4. Gifts to Charity
5. Casualty and Theft Losses
6. Job Expenses and Most Other Miscellaneous Deductions

Examples of deductions in each of these categories follow. Note that the deduction amounts allowed are reduced for very high income taxpayers.

standard deduction

Fixed amount that all taxpayers may subtract from their adjusted gross income if they do not itemize their deductions.

filing status

Description of a taxpayer's marital status on the last day of the tax year.

DID YOU KNOW

Income Taxes and Same-Sex Couples

Same-sex couples who are legally married in a state are treated as married for all federal income tax purposes. Thus, they may file joint federal income tax returns in all 50 states. State income forms may be filed only in those states that recognize their marriages.

1. Medical and Dental Expenses (Not Paid by Insurance) in Excess of 10.0 Percent of Adjusted Gross Income*

- Medicine and drugs
- Insurance premiums for medical, long-term care, and contact lenses
- Medical services (doctors, dentists, nurses, hospitals, long-term health care, acupuncture, chiropractor)
- Sterilizations and prescription contraceptives
- Costs of a physician-prescribed course of treatment for obesity
- Expenses for prescription drugs/ programs to quit smoking
- Medical equipment and aids (contact lenses, eyeglasses, hearing devices, orthopedic shoes, false teeth, wheelchair lifts)

Charitable contributions—even in cash—are typically tax deductible if you itemize deductions.

Lynn Goldsmith/Documentary/Corbis

* If you or your spouse is age 65 or older, medical expenses exceeding 7.5 percent of AGI may be claimed.

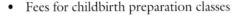

- Fees for childbirth preparation classes
- Costs of sending a mentally or physically challenged person to a special school
- Home improvements made for the physically disabled (ramps, railings, widening doors)
- Travel and conference registration fees for a parent to learn about a child's disease
- Long-term care policy premiums and nursing home expenses
- Transportation costs to and from locations where medical services are obtained, using a standard flat mileage allowance

2. Taxes You Paid

- Real estate property taxes (such as on a home or land)
- Personal property taxes (such as on an automobile or boat when any part of the tax is based on the value of the asset)
- State, local, and foreign income taxes
- Health care penalty tax, which is the greater of a flat dollar amount per individual of $325 or 2 percent of the individual's MAGI in 2015 or $695 or 2.5 percent of MAGI in 2016; afterwards it is indexed to inflation.

3. Interest You Paid

- Interest paid on home mortgage loans
- "Points" treated as a type of prepaid interest on the purchase of a principal residence
- "Points" paid when refinancing a home mortgage (portion deducted over life of the loan)
- Interest paid on home-equity loans
- Interest paid on loans used for investments

DO IT IN CLASS

4. Gifts to Charity

- Cash contributions to qualified organizations such as churches, schools, and charities (receipt required for $250 or more)
- Noncash contributions at **fair market value** (what a willing buyer would pay to a willing seller); IRS says that personal property must be in "good used condition or better" to qualify
- Mileage allowance for travel and out-of-pocket expenses for volunteer charitable work
- Charitable contributions made through payroll deduction
- Contributions to charity up to $100,000 from one's individual retirement account (IRA) for those age 70½ or older

5. Casualty and Theft Losses (Not Paid by Insurance) in Excess of 10 Percent of Adjusted Gross Income

- Casualty losses (such as from storms, vandalism, and fires) in excess of $100
- Theft of money or property in excess of $100
- Mislaid or lost property if the loss results from an identifiable event that is unexpected or unusual (such as catching a diamond ring in a car door and losing the stone)

6. Job Expenses and Most Other Miscellaneous Deductions in Excess of 2 Percent of Adjusted Gross Income (Partial Listing)

- Union or professional association dues and membership fees
- Subscriptions to magazines, journals, and newspapers used for business or professional purposes
- Books, software, tools, and supplies used in a business or profession
- Cost of computers and cell phones required as a condition of your job
- Clothing and uniforms not suitable for off-the-job usage as ordinary wearing apparel (protective shoes, hats, safety goggles, gloves, uniforms), laundering and cleaning
- Unreimbursed employee business expenses (but only a portion of the cost of meals and entertainment), including long-distance telephone calls, cleaning and laundry, and car washes of business vehicle
- Investment-related expenses (e.g., computer software, fees for online trading, adviser fees, investment club expenses, IRA fees, safe-deposit box rental, subscriptions to investment magazines and newsletters, tax preparation charges)
- Legal fees that pertain to tax advice in a divorce or alimony payments
- Travel costs between two jobs, using a flat mileage allowance
- Job-related car expenses (but not commuting to a regular job), using a flat mileage allowance or actual expenses
- Commuting costs to a temporary workplace
- Commuting costs that qualify as a business or education expense
- Medical examinations required (but not paid for) by an employer to obtain or keep a job
- Appraisal fees for charitable donations or casualty losses
- Education expenses if required to keep your job or improve your job or professional skills (but not if the training readies you for a new career)

DID YOU KNOW

Deduction for Work-Related Education as a Business Expense

If you are an employee and can itemize your deductions, you may be able to claim a deduction for the expenses you pay for your work-related education. Your deduction will be the amount by which your qualifying work-related education expenses plus other job and certain miscellaneous expenses is greater than 2% of your adjusted gross income.

Work-related education is that which meets at least one of the following two tests: (1) The education is required by your employer or the law to keep your present salary, status or job, and the required education must serve a bona fide business purpose of your employer, and (2) The education maintains or improves skills needed in your present work. However, even if the education meets the above tests, it is not qualifying work-related education if it: (1) Is needed to meet the minimum educational requirements of your present trade or business, or (2) Is part of a program of study that will qualify you for a new trade or business. You can deduct the costs of qualifying work-related education as a business expense even if the education could lead to a degree.

If you are self-employed, you deduct your expenses for qualifying work-related education directly from your self-employment income.

The Best Tax Guides and Other Help

Your Federal Income Tax: For Individuals, Publication 17, is the IRS's detailed 100-plus-page book for preparing your income taxes. A good, readable tax guide is the annual *J. K. Lasser's Your Income Tax* (www .jklasser.com/). All federal income tax forms, regulations, guides, and answers to frequently asked questions can be obtained from the IRS at (800) TAX-3676, or at www .irs.gov. The IRS help line is (800) TAX-1040. Most taxpayers can obtain free tax preparation from the Volunteer Income Tax Assistance (VITA) program (www.vita-volunteers .org/index.htm, or call (800) 906-9887).

exemption (or personal exemption)

Legally permitted amount deducted from AGI based on the number of people that the taxpayer's income supports.

dependent

A relative or household member for whom an exemption may be claimed on one's income taxes.

DO IT IN CLASS

tax credit

Dollar-for-dollar decrease in tax liability; also known as credit.

nonrefundable tax credit

A tax credit that can reduce one's tax liability only to zero; however, if the credit is more than the tax liability, the excess is not refunded.

refundable tax credit

A tax credit that can reduce one's income tax liability to below zero with the excess being refunded to the taxpayer.

- Job-hunting expenses for typing, printing, resume advice, career counseling, want ads, telephone calls, mailing costs, job placement agency fees, and travel for seeking a job in your current career field

- 50 percent of food and 100 percent of transportation and entertainment costs for job hunting (which does not have to be successful) in your current career

- 100 percent of gambling losses that offset reported gambling income (not subject to 2% AGI floor)

- 100 percent of business expenses for workers with disabilities (not subject to 2% AGI floor)

4.2e Subtract the Value of Your Personal Exemptions

An **exemption** (or **personal exemption**) is a legally permitted amount deducted from adjusted gross income based on the number of people supported by the taxpayer's income. A **dependent** is a relative or household member for whom an exemption may be claimed. Thus, exemptions may be claimed for the taxpayer and qualifying dependents, such as a spouse (if filing jointly), children, parents, and other dependents earning less than a specific income and for whom the taxpayer provides more than half of their financial support. For example, a husband and wife with two young children would have four exemptions.

A person can serve as an exemption on only one tax return—his or her own or another person's (usually a parent). Each exemption reduces taxable income by $3950. The value of an exemption is phased out for those with extremely high incomes.

4.2f Determine Your Preliminary Tax Liability

The steps detailed to this point have explained how to determine your taxable income. Taxable income is calculated by taking the taxpayer's gross income, subtracting the adjustments to income, subtracting the amount permitted for the number of exemptions allowed, and subtracting either the standard deduction or total itemized deductions.

The amount of taxable income is then used to determine taxpayers' preliminary tax liability via the tax tables or tax-rate schedules for his or her filing status (such as single or married filing jointly). The following examples illustrate how to determine tax liability. Table 4-3 shows segments of the tax table.

1. A married couple filing jointly has a gross income of $50,000, adjustments of $4700, two exemptions ($3950 each), and itemized deductions of $8285. They take the standard deduction of $12,400 because their itemized deductions do not exceed that amount.

Gross income	$50,000
Less adjustments to income	−4,700
Adjusted gross income	45,300
Less standard deduction for married couple	−12,400
Subtotal	32,900
Less value of two exemptions	−7,900
Taxable income	25,000
Tax liability (from Table 4-3)	$ 2,846

2. A single person has a gross income of $56,000, adjustments of $4050, one exemption, and itemized deductions of $8400. She subtracts her itemized deductions because the amount exceeds the $6200 standard deduction value.

Gross income	$56,000
Less adjustments to income	−4,050
Adjusted gross income	51,950
Less itemized deductions	−8,400
Subtotal	43,550
Less value of one exemption	−3,950
Taxable income	39,600
Tax liability (from Table 4-3)	$ 5,763

3. A married couple with a gross income of $137,000 has adjustments of $4000, two exemptions, and itemized deductions of $9800. The standard deduction value for a married couple is taken because it exceeds the itemized deductions.

Gross income	$137,000
Less adjustments to income	−4,000
Adjusted gross income	133,000
Less standard deduction	−12,400
Subtotal	120,600
Less value of two exemptions	−7,900
Taxable income	112,700
Tax liability (from Table 4-2)*	$ 19,887.50

*The tax liability is calculated from the tax-rate schedules in Table 4-2 because the taxable income exceeds $100,000. The tax liability is computed on taxable income as follows: $112,700 − $73,800 = $38,900 × 0.25 = $9,725 + $10,162.50 = $19,887.50.

4.2g Subtract Tax Credits for Which You Qualify

You may be able to lower your preliminary tax liability through tax credits. A **tax credit** reduces your tax liability dollar for dollar whereas a tax deduction reduces the amount of your taxable income, which is used to calculate your tax liability. Tax credits are more valuable because they reduce your tax liability by one dollar for every dollar of the credit. Tax deductions, on the other hand, reduce your tax liability by your tax rate for every dollar of the deduction. A $1000 tax deduction saves $250 in taxes if you are in the 25 percent bracket, but a $1000 tax credit saves you $1000.

You may take tax credits regardless of whether you itemize deductions. A **nonrefundable tax credit** may reduce your tax liability to zero (0), but not below. Thus if the nonrefundable credit amount exceeds the tax you owe, you are not given a refund of the difference. A **refundable tax credit** can reduce your tax liability to below zero (0), and the excess amount will be refunded. To get a refundable tax credit, you must file an income tax return. Credits are often subject to income limits, meaning that high-income taxpayers may not be eligible for a particular credit.

Health Insurance Premium Tax Credit The **Health Insurance Premium Tax Credit** is part of the Affordable Care Act provisions, and it provides that individuals and families may take a tax credit to help them afford health insurance coverage purchased through an Affordable Insurance Exchange offered through the federal and/or state government. The health insurance premium tax credit is refundable so taxpayers who have little or no income tax liability can still benefit. The credit also can be paid in advance to a taxpayer's insurance company to help cover the cost of premiums.

Table 4-3

Tax Table*

If Taxable Income is		Your Tax Is	
At Least	But Less Than	Single	Married Filing Jointly
25,000	25,050	3,300	2,846
25,050	25,100	3,508	2,854
25,100	25,150	3,315	2,861
27,850	27,900	3,728	3,274
27,900	27,950	3,735	3,281
30,000	30,050	4,050	3,596
30,050	30,100	4,058	3,604
30,100	30,150	4,065	3,611
30,150	30,200	4,073	3,619
39,600	39,650	5,763	5,036
39,650	39,700	5,775	5,044
39,700	39,750	5,788	5,051
39,750	39,800	5,800	5,059
40,200	40,250	5,913	5,126
40,250	40,300	5,925	5,133
47,800	47,850	7,813	6,266
47,850	47,900	7,825	6,273
48,900	48,950	8,088	6,431
48,950	49,000	8,100	6,439
49,200	49,250	8,162	6,476
49,250	49,300	8,175	6,484
53,050	53,100	9,125	7,054
53,100	53,150	9,138	7,061
56,050	56,100	9,875	7,504
56,100	56,150	9,888	7,511
59,000	59,050	10,613	7,946
59,050	59,100	10,625	7,954
74,100	74,150	14,388	10,244
74,150	74,200	14,400	10,256
90,200	90,250	18,439	14,269
90,250	90,300	18,453	14,281

*These segments of the tax table are derived from the IRS tax-rate schedule illustrated in Table 4-2.

DID YOU KNOW

About the Alternative Minimum Tax

The **alternative minimum tax (AMT)** takes back some of the tax breaks allowed for regular tax purposes for very high-income taxpayers who previously were entirely escaping paying income taxes through legitimate means. Some high-income taxpayers are pushed into paying the higher AMT tax instead of the regular tax when claiming excess itemized deductions, certain tax-exempt interest, and/or a substantial number of exemptions. When the value of those benefits is added back to one's income, it may result in an AMT calculation that exceeds one's regular tax. About four million taxpayers pay the AMT tax rate at 26 or 28 percent, which typically amounts to an additional tax liability of about $3900.

American Opportunity Tax Credit

A partially refundable tax credit of up to $2500 a year to help defray college expenses for the first four years of postsecondary education.

American Opportunity Tax Credit The **American Opportunity Tax Credit** provides an up to $2500 per student tax credit to help defray college expenses for the first four years of postsecondary education. The tax credit is for 100 percent of qualified tuition, fees, books, and course materials paid by the taxpayer during the taxable year not to exceed $2000, plus 25 percent of the next $2000 in qualified tuition, fees, and course materials. The maximum total credit is $2500. The money must have been spent for qualified tuition and expenses for textbooks, supplies, equipment, and student activity fees if required as a condition of enrollment. The credit can be claimed in two taxable years for individuals enrolled on at least a half-time basis during any part of the year. Forty percent of the credit (up to $1000) is refundable.

lifetime learning credit

A nonrefundable tax credit that may be claimed every year for tuition and related expenses paid for all years of postsecondary education undertaken to acquire or improve job skills.

Lifetime Learning Credit The **lifetime learning credit** (nonrefundable) may be claimed every year for tuition and related expenses paid for all years of postsecondary education undertaken to acquire or improve job skills. The expenses for one or more courses may be for yourself, your spouse, or your dependents. The student need not be pursuing a degree or other recognized credential. This credit amounts to 20 percent of the first $10,000 paid, for a maximum of $2000 for all eligible students in a family. There is no limit on the number of years the credit may be taken for the student. The Lifetime Learning and American Opportunity credits may not be claimed for the same student expenses for the same tax year.

earned income credit (EIC)

A refundable tax credit that may be claimed by workers with a qualifying child and in certain cases by childless workers.

Earned Income Credit The **earned income credit (EIC)** (or **earned income tax credit [EITC]**) is refundable, and it may be claimed not only by workers with a qualifying child but also, in certain cases, by childless workers. The maximum credit is $496 with no qualifying children, $3305 with one child, $5460 with two children, and $6143 with three or more children. For married taxpayers with one child, the credit begins to phase out if adjusted gross income is $23,260.

child and dependent care credit

A nonrefundable tax credit that may be claimed by workers who pay employment-related expenses for care of a child or other dependent if that care gives them the freedom to work seek work, or attend school full time.

Child and Dependent Care Credit The **child and dependent care credit** is for workers who pay employment-related expenses if the care for children under age 13 and/or other dependents gives them the freedom to work. Depending on your income, the credit may be up to 35 percent of qualifying care expenses of up to $3000 (or a credit of $1050) for one dependent and of up to $6000 of care expenses for two or more dependents (or a credit of $2100). The credit is limited to the liability, but part or all of the credit may be refundable as an "additional child tax credit," which is discussed below.

Child Tax Credits Taxpayers can claim a **child tax credit (CTC)** of up to $1000 per child under age 17. The child tax credit is nonrefundable. Some parents also may qualify for a refundable **additional child tax credit** if the child portion of the child and dependent care tax credit exceeds their tax liability.

Adoption Credit An **adoption tax credit** (refundable) of up to $13,190 is available for the qualifying costs of an adoption.

DID YOU KNOW

Nearly Half of Households Pay No Income Tax

The Tax Policy Center reports that between 40 and 50 percent of all households paid no federal income tax in recent years. Thus millions of Americans paid nothing toward our national defense, foreign aid, or federal parks.

Of those not paying federal income taxes, 57 percent did not earn enough to pay Social Security payroll and Medicare taxes, 21 percent are elderly, 14 percent earn less than $20,000, and 8 percent are others, which totals

100 percent. The households qualified for enough credits, deductions, and exemptions to eliminate their federal tax liability. These people do pay excise taxes on gasoline and various taxes on telephone services, gasoline, tires, aviation, alcohol, and tobacco, and they may pay state and local income taxes as well as sales taxes.

Most Americans work and pay federal income taxes. Three-quarters of them pay more in payroll taxes that fund Social Security and Medicare than they do in federal income taxes.

Mortgage Interest Credit A **mortgage interest tax credit** (nonrefundable) of up to $2000 for mortgage interest paid may be claimed under special state and local government programs that provide a "mortgage credit certificate" for people who purchase a principal residence or borrow funds for certain home improvements. The home must not cost more than 90 to 110 percent of the average area purchase price.

Retirement Savings Contribution Credit A nonrefundable **retirement savings contribution credit** (also known as a **saver credit**) of up to $1000 is available. The tax credit is calculated based on a percentage of your retirement contributions. For single individuals, a 50 percent credit applies on the amount saved (up to $2000) if AGI does not exceed $18,000, a 20 percent rate applies if AGI does not exceed $19,500, and a 10 percent rate applies if AGI does not exceed $30,000. For married persons, the thresholds are $36,000, $39,000, and $60,000.

Elderly or Disabled Tax Credit Lower income individuals who are age 65 or older or who are permanently and totally disabled may claim a nonrefundable federal tax credit that can be as much as $1125.

4.2h Calculate the Balance Due the IRS or the Amount of Your Refund

After taking all your tax credits, if the amount withheld (shown on your W-2 form) plus any estimated tax payments you made is greater than your final tax liability, then you are entitled to receive a **tax refund**.

If the amount is less than your final tax liability, then you have a **tax balance due**. If you owe money, you pay by check, money order, or credit card. The IRS imposes a convenience fee of 2.5 percent of the amount charged on a credit card.

tax refund
Amount the IRS sends back to a taxpayer if withholding and estimated payments exceed the tax liability.

4.2i Which Tax Form Do You Use to File?

To file your income tax return, you record all your tax information on the correct tax form and submit it to the Internal Revenue Service by mail or electronically. Use the IRS tax form that is appropriate for your circumstances:

- **Form 1040EZ.** You are single or married, under age 65, and have no dependents; your income consists of less than $100,000 in wages, salary, and tips, and no more than $1500 in interest; and you do not claim any tax credits or adjustments or itemize deductions.
- **Form 1040A.** Your income is less than $100,000 and you use the standard deduction and/or take adjustments to income or tax credits.
- **Form 1040.** You itemize your deductions and you do or do not make contributions to a qualified retirement plan or take adjustments to income or tax credits. Figure 4-4 shows a completed 1040 Form for a taxpayer.
- **Form 1040X.** You are eligible for a deserved refund or refundable tax credit, or you want to correct any tax filing mistake(s) or claim overlooked deductions for any of the past three years.

4.2j File on Time and Check the Status of Your Refund

You should file your return on time—usually by April 15—to avoid a penalty. If you owe the IRS and you are broke, you can borrow to pay the taxes or contact the IRS about setting up an installment plan to repay the debt within three years.

Taxpayers hear from the IRS within three weeks if they have failed to sign the return, neglected to attach a copy of the Form W-2, made an error in arithmetic, owe a tax penalty, or figured the tax incorrectly. Once taxpayers file their federal return, they can track the status of their refunds by using the "Where's My Refund?" tool, located on the front page of www.irs.gov.

DID YOU KNOW

Sean's Success Story

Sean is one smart fellow. After learning a lot about how to avoid income taxes, he took action. Sean recently made a down payment and bought a foreclosed home with a $120,000, 4 percent, 20-year mortgage. The more than $14,000 in interest (from Table 9-4 on page 273) and $1500 in real estate property taxes together put him well over the $6200 standard deduction threshold. Therefore, he can take all kinds of other deductions on his tax return, such as cash and non-cash charitable contributions, mileage allowance and out-of-pocket expenses for volunteer charitable work, personal property taxes on his auto and boat, expenses for business magazines and newspapers to better manage his investments, and software to help prepare his income taxes. He started to contribute the maximum $3000 annually to his retirement account. Now Sean is researching all the tax credits to determine if he qualifies for any of them.

DID YOU KNOW

Money Websites for Managing Income Taxes

Informative websites for managing income taxes, including preparing your own income tax form are:

Bankrate.com's tax estimator (www.bankrate.com /calculators/tax-planning/1040-form-tax-calculator.aspx)

Bankrate.com (www.bankrate.com/finance/taxes/check-taxes -in-your-state.aspx)

Center for American Progress (www.americanprogress .org/issues/2012/02/corporate_profits.html)

Dinkytown's tax estimator (www.dinkytown.net/java /Tax1040.html)

H&R Block's TaxCut (www.hrblock.com/tax-software /index.html)

Internal Revenue Service (www.irs.gov)

IRS *Publication 17* (www.irs.gov/publications/p17/)

Lasser's Your Income Tax (www.jklasser.com/)

Quicken's TurboTax (turbotax.intuit.com/)

TaxACT (www.taxact.com)

Volunteer Income Tax Assistance (www.irs.gov/Individuals /Free-Tax-Return-Preparation-for-You-by-Volunteers)

Worldwide-Taxes.com (www.worldwide-tax .com/#partthree)

---

payroll withholding

The IRS requirement that an employer withhold a certain amount from an employee's income as a prepayment of that individual's tax liability for the year. It is sent to the government where it is credited to the taxpayer's account.

estimated taxes

People who are self-employed or receive substantial income from an employer that is not required to practice payroll withholding (such as lawyers and owners of rental property) are required by the IRS to estimate their tax liability and pay their taxes in advance in quarterly installments.

4.2k   File Your Income Taxes Electronically for Free and Get Your Refund Within Ten Days

Over 70 percent of taxpayers pay someone to prepare the return, even though it is not complicated for most taxpayers. To file your income taxes online by yourself, visit the website of the Internal Revenue Service (www.irs.gov) and click on "IRS E-file." Alternatively, you may choose to click on "IRS Free File" because it provides options for free brand-name tax software or online fillable forms plus free electronic filing for most taxpayers. E-filers may request that their refund be deposited directly into their bank account, and it usually will be deposited within ten days of filing. Ninety percent of taxpayer's returns are filed electronically. The average refund last year was just over $3000.

4.2l   People Pay Their Income Taxes in One or Two Ways

The federal income tax is a "pay as you go" tax. Through **payroll withholding**, an employer takes a certain amount from an employee's income as a prepayment of an individual's tax liability for the year and sends those dollars to the IRS, where they are credited to that particular taxpayer's account. People who are self-employed or who receive substantial income from an employer that is not required to practice payroll withholding, such as lawyers, accountants, consultants, and owners of rental property, must pay **estimated taxes**. They are required to estimate their tax liability and pay their estimated taxes in advance in quarterly installments on April 15, June 15, September 15, and the following year's January 15.

CONCEPT CHECK 4.2

1. Give five examples of income that must be included in income reported to the Internal Revenue Service.

2. How are long-term and short-term capital gains treated differently for income tax purposes?

3. Give five examples of income that is excluded from IRS reporting.

4. List three examples of adjustments to income.

5. Distinguish between a standard deduction and a personal exemption.

6. What advice on filing a Form 1040X can you offer someone who did not file a federal income tax return last year or in any one of the past three years?

7. List five examples of tax credits.

Figure 4-4   Federal Income Tax Form 1040 (Yasuo Konami)

Form 1040 Department of the Treasury—Internal Revenue Service   (99)
U.S. Individual Income Tax Return

OMB No. 1545-0074   IRS Use Only—Do not write or staple in this space.

See separate instructions.

Your first name and initial	Last name	Your social security number
Yasuo	Konami	123 : 45 : 6789

If a joint return, spouse's first name and initial	Last name	Spouse's social security number

Home address (number and street). If you have a P.O. box, see instructions.   Apt. no.
1245 Oak Street

▲ Make sure the SSN(s) above and on line 6c are correct.

City, town or post office, state, and ZIP code. If you have a foreign address, also complete spaces below (see instructions).
Oak Park, FL 60302

Presidential Election Campaign
Check here if you, or your spouse if filing jointly, want $3 to go to this fund. Checking a box below will not change your tax or refund. ☐ You ☐ Spouse

Foreign country name	Foreign province/state/county	Foreign postal code

Filing Status

Check only one box.

1 ☒ Single
2 ☐ Married filing jointly (even if only one had income)
3 ☐ Married filing separately. Enter spouse's SSN above and full name here. ▶
4 ☐ Head of household (with qualifying person). (See instructions.) If the qualifying person is a child but not your dependent, enter this child's name here. ▶
5 ☐ Qualifying widow(er) with dependent child

Exemptions

6a ☒ **Yourself.** If someone can claim you as a dependent, **do not** check box 6a . . . . .
b ☐ **Spouse** . . . .

c Dependents:	(2) Dependent's social security number	(3) Dependent's relationship to you	(4) ✓ if child under age 17 qualifying for child tax credit (see instructions)
(1) First name Last name			
			☐
			☐
			☐
			☐

If more than four dependents, see instructions and check here ▶ ☐

Boxes checked on 6a and 6b   1
No. of children on 6c who:
• lived with you
• did not live with you due to divorce or separation (see instructions)
Dependents on 6c not entered above
Add numbers on lines above ▶

d   Total number of exemptions claimed . . . .

Income

Attach Form(s) W-2 here. Also attach Forms W-2G and 1099-R if tax was withheld.

If you did not get a W-2, see instructions.

7	Wages, salaries, tips, etc. Attach Form(s) W-2	7	65,000 —
8a	**Taxable** interest. Attach Schedule B if required	8a	200 —
b	Tax-exempt interest. **Do not** include on line 8a . . . 8b		
9a	Ordinary dividends. Attach Schedule B if required	9a	
b	Qualified dividends 9b		
10	Taxable refunds, credits, or offsets of state and local income taxes .	10	
11	Alimony received	11	
12	Business income or (loss). Attach Schedule C or C-EZ	12	
13	Capital gain or (loss). Attach Schedule D if required. If not required, check here ▶ ☐	13	
14	Other gains or (losses). Attach Form 4797	14	
15a	IRA distributions . 15a	b Taxable amount . . .	15b	
16a	Pensions and annuities 16a	b Taxable amount . . .	16b	
17	Rental real estate, royalties, partnerships, S corporations, trusts, etc. Attach Schedule E	17	
18	Farm income or (loss). Attach Schedule F	18	
19	Unemployment compensation	19	
20a	Social security benefits 20a	b Taxable amount . . .	20b	
21	Other income. List type and amount _____	21	
22	Combine the amounts in the far right column for lines 7 through 21. This is your **total income** ▶	22	65,200 —

Adjusted Gross Income

23	Educator expenses	23	
24	Certain business expenses of reservists, performing artists, and fee-basis government officials. Attach Form 2106 or 2106-EZ	24	
25	Health savings account deduction. Attach Form 8889 .	25	
26	Moving expenses. Attach Form 3903	26	
27	Deductible part of self-employment tax. Attach Schedule SE .	27	
28	Self-employed SEP, SIMPLE, and qualified plans .	28	
29	Self-employed health insurance deduction	29	
30	Penalty on early withdrawal of savings	30	
31a	Alimony paid b Recipient's SSN ▶ _____	31a	
32	IRA deduction	32	4,000 —
33	Student loan interest deduction	33	1,100 —
34	Tuition and fees. Attach Form 8917	34	
35	Domestic production activities deduction. Attach Form 8903	35	
36	Add lines 23 through 35	36	5,100 —
37	Subtract line 36 from line 22. This is your **adjusted gross income** . . . . . ▶	37	60,100 —

For Disclosure, Privacy Act, and Paperwork Reduction Act Notice, see separate instructions.   Cat. No. 11320B   Form **1040** (2013)

(Continued)

Figure 4-4 **Federal Income Tax Form 1040 (Yasuo Konami)**
(*Continued*)

Form 1040 (2013)   Page **2**

Tax and Credits	38	Amount from line 37 (adjusted gross income)	38	60,100 —
	39a	Check if: ☐ **You** were born before January 2, 1949, ☐ Blind. ☐ **Spouse** was born before January 2, 1949, ☐ Blind. } Total boxes checked ▶ 39a		
Standard Deduction for—	b	If your spouse itemizes on a separate return or you were a dual-status alien, check here ▶ 39b ☐		
• People who check any box on line 39a or 39b **or** who can be claimed as a dependent, see instructions.	40	**Itemized deductions** (from Schedule A) **or** your **standard deduction** (see left margin)	40	6,950 —
	41	Subtract line 40 from line 38	41	53,150 —
	42	**Exemptions.** If line 38 is $150,000 or less, multiply $3,900 by the number on line 6d. Otherwise, see instructions	42	3,950 —
	43	**Taxable income.** Subtract line 42 from line 41. If line 42 is more than line 41, enter -0-	43	49,200 —
• All others: Single or Married filing separately, $6,200	44	**Tax** (see instructions). Check if any from: **a** ☐ Form(s) 8814 **b** ☐ Form 4972 **c** ☐ _____	44	8,162 —
	45	**Alternative minimum tax** (see instructions). Attach Form 6251	45	
Married filing jointly or Qualifying widow(er), $12,400	46	Add lines 44 and 45 ▶	46	
	47	Foreign tax credit. Attach Form 1116 if required	47	
Head of household, $9,100	48	Credit for child and dependent care expenses. Attach Form 2441	48	
	49	Education credits from Form 8863, line 19	49	
	50	Retirement savings contributions credit. Attach Form 8880	50	
	51	Child tax credit. Attach Schedule 8812, if required	51	
	52	Residential energy credits. Attach Form 5695	52	
	53	Other credits from Form: **a** ☐ 3800 **b** ☐ 8801 **c** ☐	53	
	54	Add lines 47 through 53. These are your **total credits**	54	
	55	Subtract line 54 from line 46. If line 54 is more than line 46, enter -0- ▶	55	
Other Taxes	56	Self-employment tax. Attach Schedule SE	56	
	57	Unreported social security and Medicare tax from Form: **a** ☐ 4137 **b** ☐ 8919	57	
	58	Additional tax on IRAs, other qualified retirement plans, etc. Attach Form 5329 if required	58	
	59a	Household employment taxes from Schedule H	59a	
	b	First-time homebuyer credit repayment. Attach Form 5405 if required	59b	
	60	Taxes from: **a** ☐ Form 8959 **b** ☐ Form 8960 **c** ☐ Instructions; enter code(s) _____	60	
	61	Add lines 55 through 60. This is your **total tax** ▶	61	
Payments	62	Federal income tax withheld from Forms W-2 and 1099	62	
	63	2013 estimated tax payments and amount applied from 2012 return	63	
If you have a qualifying child, attach Schedule EIC.	64a	**Earned income credit (EIC)**	64a	
	b	Nontaxable combat pay election	64b	
	65	Additional child tax credit. Attach Schedule 8812	65	
	66	American opportunity credit from Form 8863, line 8	66	
	67	Reserved	67	
	68	Amount paid with request for extension to file	68	
	69	Excess social security and tier 1 RRTA tax withheld	69	
	70	Credit for federal tax on fuels. Attach Form 4136	70	
	71	Credits from Form: **a** ☐ 2439 **b** ☐ Reserved **c** ☐ 8885 **d** ☐	71	
	72	Add lines 62, 63, 64a, and 65 through 71. These are your **total payments** ▶	72	10,400 —
Refund	73	If line 72 is more than line 61, subtract line 61 from line 72. This is the amount you **overpaid**	73	2,232 —
	74a	Amount of line 73 you want **refunded to you.** If Form 8888 is attached, check here ▶ ☐	74a	
Direct deposit? See instructions.	b	Routing number _____ ▶ c Type: ☐ Checking ☐ Savings		
	d	Account number _____		
	75	Amount of line 73 you want **applied to your estimated tax** ▶ 75		
Amount You Owe	76	**Amount you owe.** Subtract line 72 from line 61. For details on how to pay, see instructions ▶	76	
	77	Estimated tax penalty (see instructions) 77		

Third Party Designee	Do you want to allow another person to discuss this return with the IRS (see instructions)? ☐ **Yes.** Complete below. ☐ **No**			
	Designee's name ▶	Phone no. ▶	Personal identification number (PIN) ▶	

Sign Here

Under penalties of perjury, I declare that I have examined this return and accompanying schedules and statements, and to the best of my knowledge and belief, they are true, correct, and complete. Declaration of preparer (other than taxpayer) is based on all information of which preparer has any knowledge.

Joint return? See instructions. Keep a copy for your records.

Your signature	Date	Your occupation	Daytime phone number
Yasuo Konami	04-15-15	Media Specialist	630-555-1234
Spouse's signature. If a joint return, **both** must sign.	Date	Spouse's occupation	If the IRS sent you an Identity Protection PIN, enter it here (see inst.)

Paid Preparer Use Only

Print/Type preparer's name	Preparer's signature	Date	Check ☐ if self-employed	PTIN
Firm's name ▶			Firm's EIN ▶	
Firm's address ▶			Phone no.	

Form **1040**

4.3 STRATEGIES TO REDUCE YOUR INCOME TAXES

While the U.S. tax laws are strict and punitive about compliance (although the IRS audits less than 0.5 percent of all returns), they remain neutral about whether the taxpayer should take advantage of every "tax break" and opportunity possible. The strategies described here will help you to reduce your tax liability.

LEARNING OBJECTIVE 3
Use appropriate strategies to avoid overpayment of income taxes.

4.3a Practice Legal Tax Avoidance, Not Tax Evasion

Tax evasion involves deliberately and willfully hiding income, falsely claiming deductions, or otherwise cheating the government out of taxes owed. It is illegal. A waiter who does not report tips received and a babysitter who does not report income are both evading taxes, as is a person who deducts $150 in charitable contributions but who does not actually make the donations.

Tax avoidance means reducing tax liability through legal techniques. It involves applying knowledge of the tax code and regulations to personal income tax planning. Tax evasion results in penalties, fines, interest charges, and a possible jail sentence. In contrast, tax avoidance boosts your income because you pay less in taxes. As a result, you will have more money available to spend, save, invest, and donate.

tax evasion
Deliberately and willfully hiding income from the IRS, falsely claiming deductions, or otherwise cheating the government out of taxes owed; it is illegal.

tax avoidance
Reducing tax liability through legal techniques.

4.3b Strategy: Reduce Taxable Income via Your Employer

It may seem illogical to suggest that to lower your tax liability you should reduce your income. But it is not. The objective is to reduce *taxable* income. Reducing your federal taxable income also will reduce the personal income taxes imposed by state and local governments. Four useful ways of reducing taxable income are premium-only plans, transit spending account, dependent care flexible spending accounts, and defined-contribution retirement plans.

Premium-Only Plan Many large employers offer a **premium-only plan (POP)** that allows employees to withhold a portion of their pretax salary to pay their premiums for employer-provided health benefits. Benefits could include health, dental, vision, and disability insurance. Amounts withheld are not reported to the IRS as taxable income. For example, if Nhon Ngo, a restaurant manager in Dallas, has $400 per month ($4800 annually) withheld through his employer to pay for his share of the employer-sponsored health insurance premium, he saves as much as $1920 ($4800 × 0.40 [his effective marginal tax rate]) a year because he does not have to send that amount to the government in taxes.

amended return
A special tax return form (Form 1040X) that may be filed to obtain a deserved refund or correct any tax filing mistakes on an original or previously filed return for the previous three years.

Transit Spending Account A transportation reimbursement plan is a similar pretax program. This employer plan allows you the opportunity to save money by using payroll deduction with pretax salary dollars to pay for work-related transportation expenses, such as transit passes ($130) and qualified parking ($250). If Nhon contributes $380 in pretax income to his employer's transportation plan, he saves as much as $152 ($380 + $130 = $380 × 0.40).

Flexible Spending Account A benefit for employees who pay for child care or provide care for a parent is a salary reduction plan known as a **flexible spending account (FSA)**, also called a **flexible spending arrangement**. An FSA allows an employee (and an employer) to fund qualified expenses on a pretax basis through salary reduction to pay for out-of-pocket unreimbursed expenses for medical and dental expenses (maximum for employees is $2500 annually) and dependent care (maximum is $5000 annually). The expenses are those that are not covered by insurance. Examples are annual deductibles, office co-payments, orthodontia, prescriptions, and

FINANCIAL POWER POINT

File IRS Form 1040X to Obtain Refunds for Previous Years

Anyone who was eligible for a refundable tax credit or neglected to take a deduction may file an **amended return** to receive it retroactively for the previous three tax years using Form 1040X. Use this easy-to-complete form to obtain a deserved refund or correct any tax filing mistakes on an original or previously filed return.

FSA debit card (also known as Flexcard)
A card used to access and spend funds from a flexible spending account.

use-it-or-lose-it rule
An IRS regulation requiring that unspent dollars in a flexible spending account at the end of a calendar year be forfeited, unless the employer allows a 2 1/2-month grace period for spending the funds.

defined-contribution retirement plan
IRS-approved retirement plan sponsored by employers that allows employees to make pretax contributions that lower their tax liability.

matching contributions
Employer programs that match employees' 401 (k) contributions up to a particular percentage.

after-tax dollars
Money on which an employee has already paid taxes.

tax-sheltered investments
A financial arrangement that results in a reduction or elimination of taxes due.

over-the-counter drugs for which one has a doctor's prescription. Paper forms or an **FSA debit card**, sometimes known as a **Flexcard**, may be used to spend the funds. The salary reductions are not included in the individual's taxable earnings reported on Form W-2, and reimbursements from an FSA account are tax free.

FSAs are subject to a "**use-it-or-lose-it rule**," which means that any unspent dollars in the account at the end of the year are forfeited and not returned to the employee. As a result, you should make conservative estimates of your expenses when you elect your FSA choices. For example, if you had $1000 withheld for medical expenses but spent only $700 over the year, the balance of $300 will go back to your employer, not to you. The IRS does allow a 2½-month additional "grace period" if one's employer permits such an extension.

In summary, suppose Nhon in the preceding example has $4800 annually withheld through his employer's premium only plan to be used to pay out-of-pocket medical expenses, another $380 to the transit reimbursement plan, plus another $3000 to pay out-of-pocket expenses for dependent care of his child.

Defined-Contribution Retirement Plan   Contributing money to a qualified employer-sponsored retirement plan also reduces income taxes. A **defined-contribution retirement plan** (discussed in Chapter 17) is an IRS-approved retirement plan sponsored by an employer to which employees may make pretax contributions that lower their tax liability. The most popular plan is known as a 401(k) retirement plan, although other variations exist as well.

The amount of money that an employee contributes to his or her individual account via salary reduction also does not show up as taxable income on the employee's W-2 form. For example, if you contribute $2000 to your employer's retirement plan and you are in the 25 percent tax bracket, this immediately saves you at least $500 ($2000 × 0.25) that you will not have to pay in taxes.

An extra benefit of a defined-contribution retirement plan is that employers often offer full or partial **matching contributions** to employees' accounts up to a certain proportion. For example, if you invest $2000 into your 401(k) plan and your employer matches half of what you contribute, that is an immediate return of 50 percent ($1000 / $2000) on your investment! The employer's "match" is essentially free money.

All of the dollars in a qualified retirement plan are likely to be invested in mutual funds where they will grow free of income taxes. Income taxes must eventually be paid when withdrawals are made, presumably during retirement when the marginal tax rate may be lower than during one's working years.

4.3c   Strategy: Prune Taxable Investments

If you have some investments in your portfolio that have lost value, you may want to sell them before the end of the a year. Then you can use those capital losses to offset any capital gains earned that year from other investments. If you do not have gains to offset, you can deduct up to $3000 annually in losses against your regular income. Another strategy is to donate stocks that have appreciated in value to charity. In addition to obtaining the substantial charitable tax deduction, you avoid having to pay taxes on the gain.

4.3d   Strategy: Make Tax-Sheltered Investments

Investments are often made with **after-tax dollars**, which means that the individuals earned the money and paid income taxes on it. Then they take their after-tax money and invest it. The returns earned from these investments typically again result in taxable income. Investment alternatives are examined in Chapters 13 through 16.

Tax laws encourage certain types of investments or other taxpayer behaviors by giving them special tax advantages over other activities, and as a result, numerous **tax-sheltered investments** exist. A tax shelter is any financial arrangement (as a certain kind of investment) that results in a reduction or elimination of taxes due. The tax laws allow certain income to be exempt from income taxes in the current year or permit an adjustment, reduction, deferral of income tax liability. When making investment decisions, investors should consider tax-sheltered investments.

Invest with Pretax Income Making an investment contribution with **pretax income** means that you do not have to pay taxes this year on the income. In effect, investing with pretax income is an interest-free deferral of income taxes to another year. Examples include contributions to work-related retirement plans and flexible spending arrangements.

Make Your Investments Grow Tax Sheltered When income, dividends, or capital gains are **tax sheltered**, the investor does not pay the current-year tax liability on the income and instead shifts the income and any tax liability to a later year. This benefit is substantial. Investments can grow faster because the money that would have gone to the government in taxes every year can remain in the investment for many years to accumulate. In effect, the government "loans" tax-free money to taxpayers to help fund their investment and retirement plans. The tax-free growth of such investments is called **tax-sheltered compounding**.

Seven Examples of Tax-Sheltered Investments Numerous tax-sheltered investments exist, and some popular ones follow.

Roth IRA Accounts Contributions (up to $5500 annually) to a **Roth IRA** accumulate tax-free and withdrawals are tax-free. There is no tax break on contributions, as they are made with after-tax money. This is an excellent investment vehicle for people with a long-term investment horizon who want to save more money for retirement than they can through an employer-sponsored retirement plan. All types of IRA accounts and other retirement plans are examined in Chapter 17. IRAs are examined in Chapter 17.

Individual Retirement Accounts The amount contributed (up to $5500 annually) to a traditional **individual retirement account (IRA)** is considered an adjustment to income, which reduces your current-year income tax liability. Investments inside the IRA (such as stocks and stock mutual funds) accumulate tax sheltered. Income taxes are owed on the eventual withdrawals, likely during retirement.

Coverdell Education Savings Accounts Contributions of up to $2000 per year of after-tax money may be made to a **Coverdell education savings account** (also known as an **education savings account** and formerly known as an "education IRA") to pay future education costs. Earnings accumulate tax-free, and withdrawals for qualified expenses are tax-free. The money can be used to pay for public, private, or religious school expenses, in college or graduate school. It can pay for tuition, fees, room and board, tutoring, uniforms, home computers, Internet access and related technology, transportation, and extended day care.

Qualified Tuition Programs There are two types of **qualified tuition programs**, and these are known as **529 plans**. Under the **prepaid educational service plan**, an individual purchases tuition credits today for use in the future. Also known as a state-sponsored **prepaid tuition plan**, this program allows parents, relatives, and friends to purchase a child's future college education at today's prices by guaranteeing that amounts prepaid will be used for the future tuition at an approved institution of higher education in a particular state. The funds may be used to pay for tuition only—not room, board, or supplies.

tax sheltered
Income, dividends, or capital gains that are allowed to grow without taxes until distributions are taken.

Roth IRA
An individual retirement account of investments made with after-tax money; the interest on such accounts is allowed to grow tax-free, and withdrawals are also tax-free.

individual retirement account (IRA)
Investment account that reduces current year income, and the funds in the account accumulate tax-free.

Coverdell education savings account (or education savings account)
An IRS-approved way to pay the future education costs for a child younger than age 18 whereby the earnings accumulate tax-free and withdrawals for qualified expenses are tax-free.

The second qualified IRS Section 529 tuition program, called a **college savings plan**, is set up for a designated beneficiary. You may contribute up to $14,000 per year per child of after-tax money to a 529 college savings plan. Withdrawals are tax-free if made for qualified education expenses such as tuition, room, and board. If one child does not go to college, the funds may be transferred to another relative. One may contribute to both a Section 529 plan and a Coverdell education savings account for the same beneficiary in the same year.

Government Savings Bonds Series EE and Series I **government savings bonds** are promissory notes issued by the federal government. The income is exempt from state and local taxes. You may defer the income tax until final maturity (30 years) or report the interest annually. Reporting the interest in a child's name is advisable especially when it can be offset totally by the child's standard deduction. You may exclude accumulated interest from bonds from income tax in the year you redeem the bonds to pay qualified educational expenses. (See Chapter 14 for information on similar bonds.)

Tax-Exempt Municipal Bonds Tax-exempt **municipal bonds** (also called **munis**) are long-term debts issued by local governments and their agencies that are used to finance public improvement projects. Interest is free from federal and state taxes if the bond is purchased in one's state of residence. Taxpayers in higher-income brackets (28 percent or more) often take advantage of these kinds of investments. (See Chapter 14.) Smart investors choose the bonds that pay the better return after payment of income taxes. The formula to decide whether a taxable investment or nontaxable investment is better for you appears in the box "How to Compare Taxable and After-Tax Yields" on page 129.

DID YOU KNOW

Saving for a Child's College Education

Good ways to save for a child's college education while taking advantage of some income tax breaks are as follows:

The **Section 529 College Savings Plan** is named after the related section of the Internal Revenue Service Code, and all states have established at least one **Section 529 college savings plan**. Deposits into a 529 plan are not deductible, but withdrawals (including tax-free growth) for qualified educational expenses are tax-free.

A **Coverdell Education Savings Account** accepts nondeductible contributions up to a maximum of $2000 per year for a child younger than 18 to pay his or her future education costs. The money and earnings on the account may be withdrawn tax-free to pay for qualified expenses.

Individual Retirement Accounts (IRAs) are designed primarily for retirement savings but under certain circumstances withdrawals can be used to pay for qualified college expenses for the account holder, child or grandchild. Early withdrawal penalties are waived if the funds are used for education expenses.

A **custodial account** may be opened in the name of a child younger than age 14 under the provisions of the Uniform Gifts to Minors Act. College students usually are in the 10 or 15 percent tax bracket and they may be able to sell assets given to them without paying any capital gains taxes. The **kiddie tax** also applies to income of a minor child earned off the assets (such as interest and dividends). For children younger than age 18, the first $1000 of unearned income (the income earned from an investment) earned on custodial account assets is tax-free to the child. The next $1000 is taxed at the child's tax rate. Income in excess of $2000 is taxed at the parent's (likely higher) rate. When a child is age 18, he or she pays taxes based on his or her own income tax bracket.

Discount bonds (also called **zeroes** or **zero coupon bonds**) are corporate and government bonds that pay no annual interest. Instead, discount bonds are sold to investors at sharp discounts from their face value, which may be redeemed at full value upon maturity. For example, a $10,000 **Series EE savings bond** sold by the federal government can be purchased for $5000, one-half its face amount. The interest accumulates within the bond itself, and this phantom income earned by a child is generally so small that little, if any, income taxes are due each year as the bond matures. Taxes on the interest earned each year may be deferred until redemption and are tax-free when the proceeds are used to fund a child's college education.

DID YOU KNOW

How to Compare Taxable and After-Tax Yields

Investors may choose to put their money into vehicles that provide taxable income, such as stocks, corporate bonds, and stock mutual funds. Taxpayers also have the opportunity to lower their income tax liabilities by investing in tax-exempt municipal bonds, money market funds that invest in municipal bonds, and other tax-exempt ventures. (These investment alternatives are discussed in Chapter 14.)

Because of their tax-exempt status, these investments offer lower nominal returns than taxable alternatives. But after considering the effects of taxes, the actual return to an investor on a tax-exempt investment may be higher than the after-tax yield on a taxable corporate bond.

To find out whether a taxable investment pays a higher after-tax yield than a tax-exempt alternative, the investor must determine the after-tax yield of each alternative. The **after-tax yield** is the percentage yield on a taxable investment after subtracting the effect of federal income taxes that will need to be paid on the investment. The after-tax yield on a tax-exempt investment is the same as the nominal yield because you do not have to pay income taxes on income from this kind of investment. So the question is, "How does the investor calculate the after-tax yield on a taxable investment?"

DO IT IN CLASS

When you know the taxable yield, use Equation (4.1) to determine the equivalent after-tax yield on a taxable investment. Only then can you decide which investment is better.

For example, suppose Bobby Bigbucks pays income taxes at the 35 percent combined federal and state marginal tax rate and is considering buying either a municipal bond that pays a 3.5 percent yield or a taxable corporate bond that pays a 5.7 percent yield. Equation (4.1) calculates the equivalent after-tax yield on the corporate bond:*

$$
\begin{aligned}
\text{After-tax yield} &= \text{taxable yield} \\
&\quad \times (1 - \text{federal marginal tax rate}) \\
&= 5.7 \times (1.00 - 0.35) \qquad \textbf{(4.1)}^\dagger \\
&= 5.7 \times 0.65 \\
&= 3.71
\end{aligned}
$$

The answer is 3.71 percent. Thus, a 5.7 percent taxable yield is equivalent to an after-tax yield of 3.71 percent. Eureka! Bobby now knows that he should buy the corporate bond paying 5.7 percent because its after-tax yield of 3.71 percent is higher than the 3.5 percent paid by the municipal bond. These differences may look small, and they are, but over time they add up. For example, the extra 0.21 percent (3.71 − 3.50) yield on a $20,000 bond investment for 20 years amounts to $840 [$20,000 × 0.0021 × 20 (bond interest is not compounded)]. That's real money!

The higher your federal tax rate, the more favorable tax-exempt municipal bonds become as an investment compared with taxable bonds. The tax-exempt status of municipal bonds does not apply to capital gains. When you sell an investment for more than what you paid for it, you will owe federal income taxes on the capital gain.

* This and similar equations can be found and used on the *Garman/Forgue* companion website.

† The formula can be reversed to solve for the equivalent taxable yield when one knows the tax-exempt yield. To continue the example, the return for Bobby on a 3.71 percent tax-exempt bond is equivalent to a taxable yield of 5.7 percent [3.71 ÷ (1.00 − 0.35)]. If Bobby finds a tax-exempt bond paying more than 3.71 percent, he should consider buying it.

Capital Gains on Housing A big tax shelter is available to homeowners when they sell their homes. Those with appreciated principal residences are allowed to avoid taxes on capital gains of up to $500,000 if married and filing jointly and on gains up to $250,000 if single. The home must have been owned and used as the taxpayer's private residence for two out of the five years immediately prior to the date of the sale.

after-tax yield
The percentage yield on a taxable investment after subtracting the effect of federal income taxes that will need to be paid on the investment.

4.3e   Strategy: Defer Income

A popular way to reduce income tax liability is to shelter income by deferring it. You will not have to pay taxes on income earned after December 31st until April the following year or 15 months in the future. This goal is achieved by purposefully making arrangements to receive some of this year's income in the next year, when your marginal tax rate might be lower, perhaps only 25 percent rather than 28 percent. A 3 percent tax savings (paying at the 25 percent rate rather than 28 percent) on $3000 of income is $90 ($3000 × 0.03), enough to pay for a good meal in a restaurant. Your employer

DID YOU KNOW

Tax Reform Proposals: Flat Tax and Value-Added Tax

Politicians and pundits are talking about tax reform that overhauls the huge and complicated U.S. tax code. Many want to eliminate certain tax deductions and simplify the tax code. This is difficult to do since the vested interests that obtained a deduction in the first place will fight to maintain the popular deductions for interest paid on home loans, contributions to charity, interest on loans for investing, contributions to retirement plans, and tax credits for child and dependent care.

Some call for a **flat tax** as a substitute for our current tax system. This is an income tax having but a single rate for all taxpayers regardless of income level and type. Economists suggest that a single rate, perhaps 22 percent, might replace the revenue currently derived from the present multiple tax rates. However, for most taxpayers this would result in a tax increase.

Another idea is a federal **value-added tax (VAT)**, which is essentially a federal retail sales tax. It is a tax, perhaps 10 percent, on the calculated "value added" to a product or material at each stage of manufacture or distribution; thus it is a form of consumption tax paid by consumers. Even though every company that handles a product from raw material to finished goods must pay a VAT to the government, businesses would actually pay nothing since they receive tax credits for all the VAT they pay to suppliers. Over 40 industrialized countries have VATs.

flat tax

An income tax having but a single rate for all taxpayers regardless of income level and type.

value-added tax

A federal retail sales tax on the estimated "value added" to a product or material at each stage of manufacture or distribution.

Capital gains are taxable income but up to $500,000 for couples might be exempt on a profitable sale.

might be willing to give you a bonus or commission check in January rather than in December, and those who are self-employed can ask clients and customers to wait until January to pay their bills.

You might expect to be in a lower tax bracket in the following year because you anticipate fewer sales commissions or know that you will not work full time. For example, if you return to school, have a child, or decide to travel. Retired people may be able to postpone withdrawals of income from retirement plans, and entrepreneurs may delay billing customers for work.

ADVICE FROM A PROFESSIONAL

Consider the Tax Consequences of Buying a Home to Reduce Income Taxes

Brianna Pallagrosi of Rome, New York, took a sales position at a retail chain store two years ago, where she earned a gross income of $46,736. Brianna wisely made a $1000 contribution to her IRA. Her itemized deductions came to only $4400, so she took the standard deduction and personal exemption amounts. The result was a tax liability of $5425. Brianna was not happy about paying what she thought was a large tax bill that year.

Gross income	$46,736
Less adjustment to income	−1,000
Adjusted gross income	45,736
Less value of one exemption (old figure)	−3,800
Subtotal	41,936
Less standard deduction (old figure)	−5,950
Taxable income	35,986
Tax liability (from old tax table not shown)	$ 5,425

Last year, Brianna did not receive a raise. Nonetheless, Brianna continued to contribute $1000 into her IRA. To reduce her federal income taxes, she also became a homeowner after using some inheritance money to make the down payment on a condominium. During the year,

she paid out $9126 in mortgage interest expenses and $1995 in real estate taxes. After studying various tax publications, Brianna determined that she had $3814 in other itemized deductions that, when combined with the interest and real estate taxes, then came to a grand total of $14,935. These deductions reduced Brianna's tax liability dramatically.

Gross income	$46,736
Less adjustment to income	−1,000
Adjusted gross income	45,736
Less itemized deductions	−14,935
Subtotal	30,801
Less value of one exemption	−3,950
Taxable income	26,851
Tax liability (from Table 4-3)	$ 3,573

Brianna correctly concluded that the IRS "paid" $1852 ($5425 − $3573) toward the purchase of her condominium and her living costs because she did not have to forward those dollars to the government. An additional benefit for Brianna is that she now owns a home whose value could appreciate in the future. Buying a home often reduces one's income taxes.

Frances C. Lawrence
Louisiana State University

4.3f   Strategy: Accelerate Deductions

This strategy allows you to lower your taxable income sooner rather than later, which is usually a good idea. Many people find that they do not have enough itemized deductions to exceed the standard deduction amount. By shifting the payment dates of some deductible items, you can increase your deductions. For example, if a single person has about $6000 of deductible expenses this year, she could prepay some items in December to push the total over the $6200 threshold and benefit by taking the excess deductions now. The next year, she can take the standard deduction amount instead of itemizing.

This process is known as **accelerating deductions**. Items that may be prepaid include medical expenses, dental bills, real estate taxes, state and local income taxes, the January payment of estimated state income taxes, personal property taxes that have been billed (e.g., on autos and boats), dues in professional associations, and charitable contributions. You may mail the payments or charge them on credit cards by December 31.

4.3g   Strategy: Take All of Your Legal Tax Deductions

Although you should not spend money just to create a tax deduction, you are encouraged to take all of the deductions to which you are entitled. One way to increase itemized deductions, for example, is to

DID YOU KNOW

Bias Toward Avoiding Risk

People engaged in managing income taxes have a bias toward certain behaviors that can be harmful, such as a tendency toward avoiding risk. People often are worried that taking too many deductions on their income tax return will risk an audit so they do not take deductions they actually deserve. What to do? Reject this tendency and take your deductions because the odds of an audit for most of us is well under 1 percent, and even then the IRS is likely to accept all of one's deductions.

purchase a home with a mortgage loan. The large amounts of money homeowners expend for both interest and real estate taxes are deductible. Plus, if your property taxes and interest exceed the standard deduction amount, then you are able to take additional deductions that were ineligible because of the threshold.

Here are some other approaches to increase your deductions and keep more tax dollars in your pocket. Assume you are in the 25 percent marginal tax bracket and itemize deductions. Cash contributions made to people collecting door to door or at a shopping center during holidays are deductible, even though receipts are not given. Fifty dollars in contributions deducted can save you $12.50 in taxes. Instead of throwing out an old television set, donate it. An $80 charitable contribution for a TV will save you $20 in taxes. These amounts may sound like "small change," but lots of little tax deductions can quickly add up to more than $100, and that soon becomes real money!

Expenses for business-related trips can be a fruitful area for tax deductions. If you are in the 25 percent tax bracket and take one business trip per year, perhaps incurring $800 in deductible expenses, you will save $200 in taxes, assuming your miscellaneous deductions already exceed 2 percent of your AGI. The IRS also permits tax deductions for the costs expended on occasional job-hunting trips. In other words, depending on your tax bracket, the U.S. government pays the bill for 25 percent of such expenditures.

4.3h Strategy: Shift Income to a Child

A parent who runs his or her own business may pay a child up to $10,150 ($6200 [value of standard deduction]) + $3950 [value of exemption]) in "earned income" before any income tax liability occurs. This assumes the child has no other income. Thus, the parent can deduct the payments as business expenses.

However, giving unearned income to children is treated differently by the IRS. **Unearned income** is interest from a savings account, bond interest, alimony, and dividends from stock that comes from investments. This excludes income from wages or self-employment.

The **kiddie tax** is applied to a child's unearned income of more than $2,000, and it impacts children under age 19 (or up to 24 for full-time students). The tax is meant to discourage parents from reducing their own taxes by shifting lots of investment income to their children, who generally have lower tax brackets.

unearned income
Investment returns in the form of rents, dividends, capital gains, interest, or royalties.

Under the Kiddie tax, a parent can shift income-generating investment assets to the name of a child who then may receive $1000 tax-free. The next $1000 of such unearned income is taxed at the child's tax rate, often only 10 percent. All of the child's unearned income in excess of $2000 is taxed at the parent's tax rate, which could be as high as 39.6 percent.

4.3i Strategy: Buy and Manage a Real Estate Investment

Tax losses are paper losses in the sense that they may not represent actual out-of-pocket dollar losses, and they are created when deductions generated from an investment (such as depreciation and net investment losses) exceed the income from an investment.

Taxpayers are allowed to deduct certain real estate losses against ordinary taxable income, such as salary, interest, dividends, and self-employment earnings. Deductions are allowed for real estate investors who (1) have an adjusted gross income of $150,000 or less and (2) actively participate in the management of the property. Here the investor may deduct up to $25,000 of net losses from a "passive investment," such as real estate, against income from "active" sources, such as salary. For example, a residential real estate investment property might generate an annual cash income $1000 greater than the out-of-pocket operating costs associated with it. However, after depreciation expenses on the building are taken as a tax deduction, the resulting $1500 tax loss may then be used to offset other income. (For more details, see Chapter 16, "Real Estate and High-Risk Investments.")

DO IT NOW!

You know more about personal finance after reading this chapter, so get started right now by:

1. *Projecting your taxable income and total withholding for this year.*
2. *Estimating your federal tax liability based on your income projection using this year's tax tables or schedules.*
3. *Revising your W-4 form with your employer as necessary to withhold more if you estimate owing more in taxes or to withhold less.*

tax losses
Created when deductions generated from an investment (such as depreciation and net investment losses) exceed the income from an investment.

CONCEPT CHECK 4.3

1. Distinguish between two types of tax-sheltered investment returns.
2. Explain how to reduce income taxes via your employer, and name three employer-sponsored plans to do so.
3. Summarize the differences between an individual retirement account (IRA) and a Roth IRA.
4. Identify three strategies to avoid overpayment of income taxes, and summarize the essence of each.

WHAT DO YOU RECOMMEND *NOW?*

Now that you have read the chapter on managing income taxes, what advice can you offer Timothy and Amber in the case at the beginning of the chapter regarding:

1. Using tax credits to help pay for Tom's college expenses?
2. Determining how much money Amber will realize if she sells the stocks, assuming she pays federal income taxes at the 25 percent rate?
3. Buying a home?
4. Increasing contributions to their employer-sponsored retirement plans?
5. Establishing a sideline business for Tom's jewelry operation?

BIG PICTURE SUMMARY OF LEARNING OBJECTIVES

LO1 **Explain the nature of progressive income taxes and the marginal tax rate.**

The federal personal income tax is a progressive tax because the tax rate increases as a taxpayer's taxable income increases. The marginal tax rate is applied to your last dollar of earnings. Your effective marginal tax rate is probably 40 percent.

LO2 **Differentiate among the eight steps involved in calculating your federal income taxes.**

There are eight steps in calculating your income taxes. Certain types of income may be excluded. Regulations permit you to subtract adjustments to income, exemptions, deductions, and tax credits before determining your final tax liability.

LO3 **Use appropriate strategies to avoid overpayment of income taxes.**

You can reduce your tax liability by following certain tax avoidance strategies, such as putting your money in tax-sheltered investments, reducing taxable income via your employer, and investing pretax money for tax-deferred compounding. Other strategies are to postpone income, accelerate deductions, take all your legal deductions, and buy and manage a real estate investment.

LET'S TALK ABOUT IT

1. **During Slow Economic Times.** Congress reduced taxes on middle- and low-income taxpayers with the expectation that they will spend most of that money and help create more economic growth. Was this idea good or not, and why?

2. **Filing a Tax Return.** Many college students choose not to file a federal income tax return, assuming that the income taxes withheld by employers "probably" will cover their tax liability. Is such an assumption correct? What are the negatives of this practice if the employers withheld too much in income taxes? What are the negatives if the employers did not withhold enough in income taxes? Will any tax credits be lost?

3. **Fairness of Capital Gains.** Long-term capital gains are taxed at a rate of 20, 15 or 5 percent, or zero (0). What is your opinion on the fairness of these lower capital gains tax rates as compared with the marginal rates applied to income earned from employment that range as high as 39.6 percent?

4. **Reporting Cash Income.** Some college students earn money that is paid to them in cash and then do not include this as income when they file their tax returns. What are the pros and cons of this practice?

5. **Sideline Business.** Identify one possible sideline business that you might engage in to reduce your income tax liability.

6. **Tax Credits.** Name three tax credits that a college student might take advantage of while still in school or during the first few years after graduation.

7. **Reduce Tax Liability.** Identify five strategies to reduce income tax liability that you may take advantage of in the future.

8. **Taxable Income or Exclusions?** Review the list of exclusions on pages 112 and 113 and select 3 you think ought to be classified as taxable income rather than exclusions.

9. **Eliminate Tax Credits.** Review the list of tax credits on pages 119 and 121 and select 2 you think ought to be eliminated, and explain your reasoning.

10. **Strategies to Reduce Income Taxes.** Review the list of strategies to reduce your income taxes on pages 125 through 133 and select 2 you think you might use in the future, and explain your reasoning.

DO THE MATH

1. **Calculate Tax Liability.** What would be the tax liability for a single taxpayer who has a gross income of $39,700? (Hint: Use Table 4-2, and don't forget to first subtract the value of a standard deduction and one exemption.)

2. **Marginal Tax Rate.** What would be the marginal tax rate for a single person who has a taxable income of

(a) $40,210, (b) $47,800, (c) $56,100, and (d) $90,230? (Hint: Use Table 4-2.)

3. **Determine Tax Liability.** Find the tax liabilities based on the taxable income of the following people: (a) married couple, $74,125; (b) married couple,

DO IT IN CLASS
PAGE 118

$53,077; (c) single person, $27,880; (d) single person, $59,000. (Hint: Use Table 4-3.)

4. **Use Tax Rate Schedule.** Benjamin Addai determined the following tax information: gross salary, $60,000; interest earned, $90; IRA contribution, $1000; personal exemption, $3950; and itemized deductions, $5900. Calculate Benjamin's taxable income and tax liability filing single. (Hint: Use Table 4-2.)

DO IT IN CLASS
PAGE 114

5. **Use Tax Rate Schedule.** Samual Clark determined the following tax information: salary, $144,000; interest earned, $2000; qualified retirement plan contribution, $7000; personal exemption, $3950; itemized deductions, $10,000. Filing single, calculate Samual's taxable income and tax liability. (Hint: Use Table 4-2.)

DO IT IN CLASS
PAGE 114

6. Review Figure 4-1 on page 107 and comment on the logic of how different segments of Victoria's income is taxed.

DO IT IN CLASS
PAGE 107

FINANCIAL PLANNING CASES

CASE 1

The Johnsons Calculate Their Income Taxes

Several years have gone by since Harry and Belinda graduated from college and started their working careers. They both earn good salaries. They believe that they are paying too much in federal income taxes. The Johnsons' total income last year included Harry's salary of $63,000 and Belinda's salary of $84,000. She contributed $3000 to her 401 (k) for retirement. She earned $400 in interest on savings and checking and $3000 interest income from the trust that is taxed in the same way as interest income from checking and savings accounts. Harry contributed $3000 into a traditional IRA.

(a) What is the Johnsons' reportable gross income on their joint tax return?

(b) What is their adjusted gross income?

(c) What is the total value of their exemptions?

(d) How much is the standard deduction for the Johnsons?

(e) The Johnsons are buying a home that has monthly mortgage payments of $3000, or $36,000 a year. Of this amount, $32,800 goes for interest and real estate property taxes. The couple has a $14,000 in other itemized deductions. Using these numbers and Table 4-2, calculate their taxable income and tax liability.

(f) Assuming they had a combined $22,000 in federal income taxes withheld, how much of a refund will the Johnsons receive?

(g) What is their marginal tax rate?

(h) List three additional ways that the Johnsons might reduce their tax liability next year.

CASE 2

Victor and Maria Reduce Their Income Tax Liability

The year before last, Victor earned $51,000 from his retail management position, and Maria began working full-time and earned $45,000 as a medical technician. After they took the standard deduction and claimed four exemptions (themselves plus their two children), their federal income tax liability was about $12,000. After hearing from friends that they were paying too much in taxes, the couple vowed to try to never again pay that much. Therefore, the Hernandezes embarked on a yearlong effort to reduce their income tax liability. This year they tracked all of their possible itemized deductions, and both made contributions to qualified retirement plans at their places of employment.

DO IT IN CLASS
PAGE 114

(a) Calculate the Hernandezes' income tax liability for this year as a joint return (using Table 4-2) given the following information: gross salary income (Victor, $56,000; Maria, $51,000); state income tax refund ($400); interest on checking and savings accounts ($250); holiday bonus from Maria's employer ($375); contributions to qualified retirement accounts ($5500); itemized deductions (real estate taxes, $2600; mortgage interest, $6300; charitable contributions, $2500); and exemptions for themselves and their two children ($3950 each).

(b) List five additional strategies that Victor and Maria might consider for next year's tax planning to reduce next year's tax liability.

CASE 3

Julia Price Thinks About Reducing Her Income Taxes

Julia does well financially because she earns a good salary as an engineer, is somewhat frugal, and is making the maximum contribution to her employer-sponsored retirement plan. After reading about ways to decrease her income tax liability, she has some thoughts. Buying a home is an option, but Julia is worried about the changing prices of housing. As an accomplished sculptural artist, she is thinking about creating a sideline business to sell some of her work and convert some everyday expenses into business expenses. She is considering taking a tax-deductible job-hunting trip and then stretching the trip into a vacation. Also on her possibilities list is to start a master's degree program in engineering to enhance her skills. Finally, Julia figures she could contribute $200 a month to a Roth IRA account. Offer your opinions about her thinking.

CASE 4

A New Family Calculates Income and Tax Liability

Jerri Nichols and her two children, Austin and Alexandra, moved into the home of her new husband, Samuel Glenner, in Ames, Iowa. Jerri is employed as a librarian, and her husband sells cars. The Glenner family income consists of the following: $40,000 from Jerri's salary; $42,000 from Samuel's salary; $10,000 in life insurance proceeds from a deceased aunt; $140 in interest from savings; $4380 in alimony from Jerri's ex-husband; $14,200 in child support from her ex-husband; $500 cash as a Christmas gift from Samuel's parents; and a $1600 tuition-and-books scholarship Jerri received to go to college part time last year.

(a) What is the total of the Glenner reportable gross income?

(b) After they put $5600 into qualified retirement plan accounts last year, what is their adjusted gross income?

(c) How many exemptions can the family claim, and how much is the total value allowed the household?

(d) How much is the allowable standard deduction for the household?

(e) Their itemized deductions are $13,100, so should they itemize or take the standard deduction?

(f) What is their taxable income for a joint return?

(g) What is their final federal income tax liability, and what is their marginal tax rate? (Hint: Use Table 4-2.)

(h) If Jerri's and Samuel's employers withheld $18,000 for income taxes, does the couple owe money to the government or do they get a refund? How much?

CASE 5

Taxable Versus Tax-Exempt Bonds

Dario Flores, radio station manager in Franklin County, New Jersey, is in the 25 percent federal marginal tax bracket and pays an additional 5 percent in income taxes to the state of New Jersey. Dario currently has more than $20,000 invested in corporate bonds bought at various times that are earning differing amounts of taxable interest: $10,000 in ABC earning 5.9 percent; $5000 in DEF earning 5.5 percent; $3000 in GHI earning 5.8 percent; and $2000 in JKL earning 5.4 percent. What is the after-tax return of each investment? To calculate your answers, use the after-tax yield formula (or the reversed formula) on page 129, or the *Garman/Forgue* companion website.

DO IT IN CLASS
PAGE 129

CASE 6

Taxable Versus Nontaxable Income

Identify each of the following items as either part of taxable income or an exclusion, adjustment, or an allowable itemized deduction from taxable income for Brian Collins and Morgan Smithfield, a married couple from San Diego:

DO IT IN CLASS
PAGES 112
AND 116

(a) Brian earns $45,000 per year.

(b) Brian receives a $1000 bonus from his employer.

(c) Morgan receives $40,000 in commissions from his work.

(d) Morgan receives $300 in monthly child support from his ex-wife.

(e) Brian pays $200 each month in alimony.

(f) Brian contributes $2000 to his retirement account.

(g) Morgan inherits a car from his aunt that has a fair market value of $3000.

(h) Morgan sells the car and donates $1500 to his aunt's church.

(i) Brian receives a $5000 gift from his mother.

BE YOUR OWN PERSONAL FINANCIAL MANAGER

1. **Keep Track of Your Sources of Income.** Complete Worksheet 19: My Sources of Taxable Income from "My Personal Financial Planner" to record all of your various income sources throughout the tax year so that you will not forget to report them to the Internal Revenue Service. Record the names

MY PERSONAL FINANCIAL PLANNER

of the income sources in the spaces provided. Record the amounts in the appropriate spaces.

2. **Estimate Your Income Tax Liability.** Complete Worksheet 20: Estimate Your Income Tax Liability from "My Personal Financial Planner" to determine an estimate of your income tax liability (for either last year or next year).

MY PERSONAL FINANCIAL PLANNER

3. **Should You File an Income Tax Return to Obtain a Refund?**

MY PERSONAL FINANCIAL PLANNER

Complete Worksheet 21: Determining Whether I Should File for a Refund from "My Personal Financial Planner." Even if you are not required to file a return perhaps because you did not earn enough money, you should file if you have a refund coming—that is, if you had more taxes withheld from your paychecks than you ultimately owed. Follow the steps to make the determination.

4. **Strategies to Reduce Your Income Tax Liability.**

MY PERSONAL FINANCIAL PLANNER

Complete Worksheet 22: Strategies to Reduce My Income Tax Liability from "My Personal Financial Planner." There are several ways to reduce your income tax liability. For each strategy that might be of interest, make checkmarks to identify what characteristics you like about each and which strategies you might follow during your tax-paying life.

ON THE NET

Go to the Web pages indicated to complete these exercises.

1. **IRS Publication 17.** Go to the Internal Revenue Service website address www.irs.gov/publications/p17/. There you will find the IRS's entire Publication 17 online. This is the government's detailed explanation of all aspects of federal income taxes where you can look up almost any possible tax question. Summarize your observations about this publication.

2. **Estimate Your Tax Refund.** Visit the website for BankRate.com (www.bankrate.com/calculators/tax-planning/1040-form-tax-calculator.aspx)to estimate your tax refund. Fill in a few numbers and get an answer.

3. **Estimate Your Income Taxes.** Enter your filing status, income, deductions and credits and the calculator at Dinkytown (www.dinkytown.net/java/Tax1040.html) and based on your inputs (filing status, income, deductions, and credits) and projected withholdings for the year, it can estimate your tax refund or amount you may owe the IRS next year.

4. **Check Taxes in Your State to Determine Your Effective Tax Rate.** Visit Bankrate.com's website www.bankrate.com/finance/taxes/check-taxes-in-your-state.aspx. There you will find a map of states. Click to find your state income tax, if applicable. What is your combined federal and state marginal tax rate? Add in another 7.65 percent for Social Security and Medicare taxes to determine your effective marginal tax rate.

ACTION INVOLVEMENT PROJECTS

1. **Telephone the Internal Revenue Service.** Dial 1 (800) TAX-3676 (or 1 (800) 829-3676) to pose a question for an IRS spokesperson. Think of a question before you call. Perhaps it has to deal with whether or not you qualify for a specific tax credit, can deduct expenses for a sideline business, or can make Roth IRA contributions. Write a summary of your findings.

2. **Tax Reform Proposals.** Type "tax reform" into your browser and skim read what you find of interest on three websites. Write a summary of your findings and include your views of what reform(s) you might prefer.

3. **Who Pays Income Taxes?** Type "income taxes, who pays" into your browser and skim read what you find of interest on three websites. For starters, you will discover that close to half of Americans do not pay any federal income taxes at all and that the top 1 percent of earners pay close to 40 percent of all personal income tax revenues. Write a summary of your findings, and cite your sources.

4. **Tax Bills Lowest Since 1950s.** Read the FactCheck.org article on taxes in the United States at factcheck.org/2012/07/tax-facts-lowest-rates-in-30-years/. In addition, search the Web for a more recent report on the same topic and write a summary of your findings.

5. **Corporate and Individual Tax Rates Around the World.** Comparing taxes on individuals and businesses around the world is extremely challenging. Some countries have a value-added tax paid by consumers. Others provide free health care to citizens, while people in some countries have to pay health care premiums. Review the table provided by Worldwide-Taxes.com at www.worldwide-tax.com/#partthree, and write a brief summary of your impressions.

6. **Corporate Tax Avoidance.** Read the article on the Center for American Progress (www.americanprogress.org/issues/2012/02/corporate_profits.html) to discover how many billions the large multinational corporations in the United States do or do not pay in income taxes in this country. Write a summary of your findings.

Visit the Garman/Forgue companion website at www.cengagebrain.com.

5

Managing Checking and Savings Accounts

YOU MUST BE KIDDING, RIGHT?

Kayla Patterson realized about two weeks ago that she had misplaced her debit card. At first she was not worried because she reasoned that it had to be somewhere at home. Last week she received her account statement. She looked at her statement today and found that $200 had been withdrawn from her account on five different occasions ($1000 total). She immediately called her bank to report the fraudulent withdrawals. How much of this money will Kayla lose because of the unauthorized withdrawals?

A. $0   **C.** $500

B. $50   **D.** $1000

The answer is C, $500. Because Kayla waited more than two days after realizing the card was lost to report it to her financial institution, federal law states that she is liable for the first $500 in unauthorized uses. If she had notified the bank within two days, her loss would have been only $50. If Kayla failed to notify her bank of the loss within 60 days, the law states that she would lose all of the money taken fraudulently. Immediately report a lost debit card!

LEARNING OBJECTIVES

After reading this chapter, you should be able to:

1 Identify the goals of monetary asset management and sources of such financial services.

2 Understand and employ the various types of accounts available to meet the goals of monetary asset management.

3 Describe your legal protections when conducting monetary asset management electronically.

4 Discuss your personal finances and money management more effectively with loved ones.

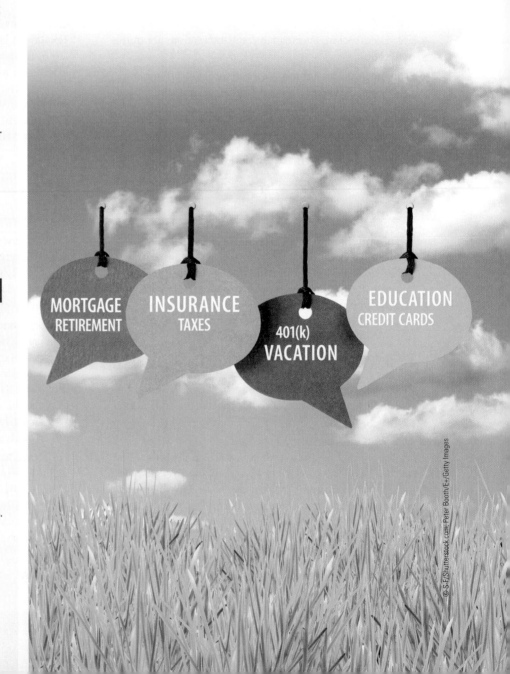

MORTGAGE RETIREMENT

INSURANCE TAXES

401(k) VACATION

EDUCATION CREDIT CARDS

©S-F/Shutterstock.com; Peter Booth/E+/Getty Images

WHAT DO YOU RECOMMEND?

© iStockphoto.com/Sturti

Nathan Rosenberg and Alyssa Adams are to be married in two months. Both are employed full time and currently have their own apartments. Once married, they will move into Alyssa's apartment because it is larger. They plan to use Nathan's former rent money to begin saving for a down payment on a home to be purchased in four or five years. Nathan has a checking account at a branch of a large regional commercial bank near his workplace where he deposits his paychecks. He also has three savings accounts—one at his bank and two small accounts at a savings and loan association near where he went to college. Nathan pays about $30 per month in fees on his various accounts. In addition, he has a $10,000 certificate of deposit (CD) from an inheritance; this CD will mature in five months. Alyssa has her paycheck directly deposited into her share draft account at the credit union where she works. She has a savings account at the credit union as well as a money market account at a stock brokerage firm that was set up years ago when her father gave her 300 shares of stock. She also has $9300 in an individual retirement account invested through a mutual fund.

What would you recommend to Alyssa and Nathan on the subject of managing checking and savings accounts regarding:

1. Where they can obtain the services that they need for managing their monetary assets?

2. Their best use of checking accounts and savings accounts as they begin saving for a home?

3. The use of an asset management account for managing their monetary assets?

4. Their use of electronic banking?

5. How they can best discuss the management of their money and finances?

YOUR NEXT FIVE YEARS

In the next five years, you can start achieving financial success by doing the following related to checking and savings accounts:

1. *Use a free, interest-earning checking account for your day-to-day spending needs.*

2. *Start now to build an emergency fund sufficient to cover three months of living expenses.*

3. *Use a pay-yourself-first approach as you begin to build other savings and investments.*

4. *Secure your electronically accessible accounts with strong user IDs, PINs and passwords.*

5. *Use all your checking and savings accounts appropriately by never overdrawing the accounts and by reconciling them monthly.*

Your financial success will depend in part on how well you manage your **monetary assets**. These assets were defined in Chapter 3 as cash and low-risk, near-cash items that can be readily converted to cash with little or no loss in value. If you are a college student, your monetary assets are probably the largest component of your net worth and are the major focus of the activities you consider "personal finance." Monetary assets represent *all* your money.

People use monetary assets in one of two ways. First, they use them for day-to-day spending. They buy food, clothing, entertainment, and many products and services. Spending usually requires cash or the use of a check or a debit card to access funds in a checking account. (Using credit is covered in Chapters 6 and 7.) Checking accounts are appropriate places to keep money that you will spend within the next three to six months or so. The second way that people use monetary assets is to accumulate funds to meet needs that will occur six months to, perhaps, three to five years in the future. You could keep these funds in a checking account, but various types of savings accounts pay more interest. With savings accounts, the focus is on holding money safely until needed in the future for spending or investing. The money in most checking and savings accounts is fully insured by the federal government.

The third way that people use monetary assets is to make investments. Investments are the best places to put money you will not need for 5, 10, or even 20 years in the future. The magic of the world of investments is that over long periods of time, it is quite possible to watch your money triple or quadruple over the original amount invested. Investments are examined in Chapters 13 through 16.

5.1 WHAT IS MONETARY ASSET MANAGEMENT?

LEARNING OBJECTIVE 1

Identify the goals of monetary asset management and sources of such financial services.

monetary asset (cash) management
How you handle your monetary assets.

liquidity
Ease with which an asset can be converted to cash.

financial services industry
Companies that provide monetary asset management and other services.

depository institutions
Organizations licensed to take deposits and make loans.

Monetary asset (cash) management encompasses how you handle cash on hand, checking accounts, savings accounts and certificates of deposit, money market accounts, and other monetary assets.

5.1a The Goals of Monetary Asset Management

The goals of monetary asset management are to maximize interest earned and to minimize fees while keeping funds safe and readily available for living expenses, emergencies, and saving and investment opportunities. Successful monetary asset management allows you to earn interest on your money while maintaining reasonable liquidity and safety. **Liquidity** refers to the speed and ease with which an asset can be converted to cash. **Safety** means that your funds are free from financial risk.

5.1b Who Provides Monetary Asset Management Services?

The **financial services industry** comprises companies that provide checking, savings, and money market accounts and possibly credit, insurance, investment, and financial planning services. These companies include depository institutions such as banks and credit unions, stock brokerage firms, mutual funds, financial services companies, and insurance companies. Table 5-1 matches these various types of firms with the financial products and services that they offer. As you can see, there is considerable overlap. For example, State Farm, which most people recognize as an insurance company, also owns a mutual fund and a bank.

Depository Institutions **Depository institutions** are financial institutions in the United States that are legally allowed to accept monetary deposits from consumers and make loans. They all can offer some form of government account insurance on deposited funds and are government regulated. They offer a wide range of financial services,

Table 5-1	Today's Providers of Monetary Asset Management Services	
Providers	**What They Sell**	**Examples of Well-Known Company Names**
Depository institutions (banks, mutual savings banks, and credit unions)	Checking, savings, lending, credit cards, investments, and trust advice	Citibank, Chase, Bank of America, Wells Fargo
Mutual funds	Money market mutual funds, tax-exempt funds, bond funds, and stock funds	Fidelity, T. Rowe Price, Vanguard
Stock brokerage firms	Securities investments (stocks and bonds), mutual funds, and real estate investment trusts	Schwab, Fidelity
Financial services companies	Checking, savings, lending, credit cards, securities investments, real estate investments, insurance, accounting and legal advice, and financial planning	American Express, Edward Jones, Raymond James
Insurance companies	Property and liability, health and life insurance, credit services, financial planning services	Allstate, Aetna, State Farm

including loans. Examples of depository institutions are commercial banks, savings banks, and credit unions. Although each is a distinct type of institution, people often call them all simply *banks*. Internet banks are similarly regulated and operate entirely online, and because they avoid the "bricks and mortar" costs of conventional institutions they often pay higher interest rates.

Commercial banks are a type of bank that provides services such as accepting deposits, making business loans, and offering basic investment products. They are under federal and state regulations. They offer numerous consumer services, such as checking, savings, loans, safe-deposit boxes, investment services, financial counseling, and automatic payment of bills.

Savings banks (or **savings and loan associations-S&Ls**) focus primarily on accepting savings and providing mortgage and consumer loans. They offer checking services through interest-earning NOW accounts (discussed later in this chapter). Savings banks generally pay depositors an interest rate about 0.10 to 0.20 percentage points higher than the rate found at commercial banks.

Accounts in federally chartered commercial banks and savings banks are insured against loss by the **Deposit Insurance Fund (DIF)** of the **Federal Deposit Insurance Corporation (FDIC)**, which is an agency of the federal government. The regulator of these banking entities is the **Office of the Comptroller of the Currency**.

A **credit union (CU)** also accepts deposits and makes loans. Credit unions operate on a not-for-profit basis and are owned by their members. The members/owners of the credit union all share some common bond, such as the same employer, church, trade union, fraternal association, or neighborhood. People in the family of a member are also eligible to join.

Federally chartered credit unions have their accounts insured through the **National Credit Union Share Insurance Fund (NCUSIF)**, which is administered by the National Credit Union Administration (NCUA). State-chartered credit unions are often insured by NCUSIF, and most others participate in private insurance programs. Credit unions usually pay higher interest rates and charge lower fees than commercial banks or savings banks.

A **mutual savings bank (MSB)** is similar to a savings bank in that it also accepts deposits and makes housing and consumer loans. State laws permit these banks to

commercial banks

A type of bank that provides services such as accepting deposits, making business loans, and offering basic investment products.

credit union (CU)

Member-owned, not-for-profit, insured financial institutions that provide checking, savings, and loan services to members.

DID YOU KNOW ?

Bias Toward the Familiar and Comfortable

People engaged in managing checking and savings accounts have a bias toward certain behaviors that can be harmful, such as a tendency toward sticking with the familiar and comfortable. Young adults often bank where their parents do and will stay with that bank for years. What to do? Look for the depository institution that charges the lowest fees and pays the highest interest, which is probably a credit union.

DO IT IN CLASS

federal deposit insurance

Insures deposits, both principal amounts and accrued interest, up to $250,000 per account for most accounts.

mutual funds

Investment companies that raise money by selling shares to the public and then invest that money in a diversified investment portfolio.

operate in only 17 states, primarily those in the eastern United States. They are called "mutual" because the depositors own the institution and share in the earnings. Generally, MSBs have the DIF insurance coverage. Like savings banks, they offer interest-earning checking accounts.

Deposit Insurance Protects Your Money Deposits in depository institutions are insured against loss of both the amount on deposit and the accrued interest by various insurance funds. Not a single depositor has lost a dime of insured funds since the inception of deposit insurance during the Great Depression of the 1930s. This **federal deposit insurance** for your deposits at any one institution works as follows:

1. The maximum insurance on all of your single-ownership (individual) accounts (held in your name only) is $250,000.
2. The maximum insurance on all of your joint accounts (accounts held with other individuals) is $250,000.
3. The maximum insurance on all of your retirement accounts is $250,000.
4. A maximum of $250,000 in insurance per beneficiary is available on **payable at death accounts** (accounts set up so that the funds go to a designated person[s] upon the death of the account holder).

Thus, individuals might have several increments of insurance for their accounts at any one institution. Funds on deposit at other institutions will also have these same limits. So if your rich uncle had $140,000 in individual accounts at each of two different institutions, you would have a total of $280,000 of deposit insurance.

Other Financial Services Providers Depository institutions are not the only providers of monetary asset management services. Mutual funds, stock brokerage houses, and insurance companies provide some monetary asset management services as well. The services they do not provide are government-insured checking and savings accounts; however, many of these companies also own banks and thus do provide insured deposits through their banking entities.

Mutual funds are investment companies that raise money by selling shares to the public and then invest that money in a diversified portfolio of investments. Most have created cash management accounts to provide a convenient and safe place to keep money while awaiting alternative investment opportunities. Money deposited in a mutual fund is not insured by the federal government, although some mutual fund companies purchase insurance privately for the noninvestment portions of customers' accounts. Mutual funds are the subject of Chapter 15.

Stock brokerage firms are licensed financial institutions that specialize in selling and buying stocks, bonds, and other investments and providing advice to investors. They earn commissions based on the buy and sell orders that they process. Stock brokerage firms typically offer cash or mutual fund accounts into which clients may place money while waiting to make investments. The noninvestment portion of an account (for example, cash held in the account prior to making an investment) is protected by the Securities Investor Protection Corporation (SIPC), a nongovernment entity. **Insurance companies** provide property, liability, health, life, and other insurance products (These topics are covered in Chapters 10–12.). Many offer monetary asset services, such as money market accounts.

CONCEPT CHECK 5.1

1. Identify the primary goals of monetary asset management.
2. Explain the circumstances when it would be appropriate to have funds in a checking account, a savings account, or in investments.
3. Describe your insurance protections when you have funds on deposit in a depository institution as opposed to other financial services providers.

5.2 CHOOSE APPROPRIATE MONETARY ASSET ACCOUNTS

There are various categories monetary asset accounts. Each has its own costs and benefits. Depending on the complexity of your mix of monetary assets you can select the tools that meet your needs: (1) Low-cost, interest-earning checking accounts from which to pay ongoing, current living expenses, and (2) Interest-earning savings accounts in financial institutions in which you accumulate and hold funds for upcoming expenditures or investments.

LEARNING OBJECTIVE 2

Understand and employ the various types of accounts available to meet the goals of monetary asset management.

5.2a Conduct Day-to-day Spending Using Interest-earning Checking Accounts

A **checking account** at a depository institution allows you to write paper checks against amounts you have on deposit. **Checks** transfer your deposited checking account funds to other people and organizations. Checking accounts also can be accessed by using a **debit card** (or **check card**) in an automated teller machine (ATM), a point-of-sale (POS) terminal at a retail store or on your cell phone, tablet or computer. When you use a debit card, funds are instantaneously removed from your account.

Whenever you deposit money into, withdraw funds from, or make any payment out of a checking account, you should record the transaction. To do so record the date, amount, and purpose of the transaction in the **check register** provided with your paper checks or in an electronic recordkeeping software program and calculate your new account balance. Failure to know your available account balance can lead to costly fees when you overdraw your account.

checking account
At depository institutions, allows depositors to write checks against their deposited funds, which transfer deposited funds to other people and organizations.

Types of Checking Accounts at Depository Institutions Checking accounts may or may not pay interest. **Demand-deposit accounts** are checking accounts that pay no interest. Instead, select an **interest-earning checking account** (also called a **negotiable order of withdrawal [NOW] account**). A share draft **account** is the credit-union version of a NOW account. NOW accounts and share draft accounts may pay higher interest rates on larger balances (such as amounts above $1000). The combination of a base rate and a higher rate is called **tiered interest**. For example, an account might pay 0.30 percent on the first $2000 and 0.50 percent on any additional funds in the account. **Super NOW accounts** are also available, and they pay slightly higher interest rates but place a limit on the number of checks that can be written each month.

interest-earning checking account
Any account on which you can write checks that pays interest.

tiered interest
A way to calculate interest where the account that pays lower interest on smaller deposits and higher interest on larger balances.

Figure 5-1 The Relationship Among Checking, Savings, and Investment Accounts

	Checking	Saving	Investments
Purpose	Funds for day-to-day spending up to 3 to 6 months in advance	Accumulate and hold funds for goals 6 months to 3 to 5 years in the future	Grow your money for goals that are 5 to 20 or more years in the future
Basic Types	-Regular Checking and Share Draft -NOW Accounts -Money Market Mutual Funds (MMMFs)	-Statement Savings -Certificates of Deposit -Money Market Accounts	-Securities (Stocks and Bonds) -Mutual Funds -Real Estate
Protections	Typically insured except for MMMFs	Typically insured	Not insured

ADVICE FROM A PROFESSIONAL

Protect Yourself from Overdraft Fees

An **overdraft**, or bounced check, occurs any time you write a check or use a debit card when there are insufficient funds in the account. If funds to cover the usage are not available, the bank will charge you a fee that averages $33 nationally. And the merchant to whom a bad check was written will charge you a similar fee. The costs could total $60 to $80 for one bad check or overdraft!

It is easy to fall victim to these charges if you are not careful. One reason is that banks can choose the order in which they process checks/debits. Let's say you write a large check one day. The next day you use your debit card for three small purchases and the check shows up at your bank for payment. There might be enough money in your account to cover the three small items but not the check. The bank can choose to process the check first. You are now overdrawn and the three debit card items are overdrafts, as well. You now have four overdrafts. If the bank had cleared the debits first you would only have had one overdraft.

Almost $40 billion dollars in overdraft fees were collected by banks in a recent year. Such fees are one of their biggest profit centers. Don't be part of this equation. Your financial institution likely offers three ways to avoid overdraft fees:

1. ***Automatic funds transfer agreement.*** The amount necessary to cover an overdraft will be transmitted from your savings account to your checking account, as long as you keep sufficient funds in your savings account. An automatic funds transfer agreement is the least expensive of these alternatives.

2. ***Automatic overdraft loan agreement.*** The needed funds will be automatically loaned to you by your bank if you have an overdraft line of credit or will be charged as a cash advance to your Visa or MasterCard credit card account with the same bank. Note that the loan may be advanced in fixed increments of $100. If you need only $10, for example, you will consequently be responsible for paying interest on amounts not needed. A cash advance fee of $10 or $20 may also be assessed by the credit card company and a high interest rate starts just as soon as you access the funds.

3. ***"Opt-in" overdraft/bounce protection.*** The bank will honor overdrafts up to a certain limit, such as

$1000, by loaning the money to the account holder. In return, the customer must pay a $25 to $40 fee for each overdraft. Then, the customer must repay the funds usually within a month. With some plans, the money is repaid as soon as any money is deposited back in the account.

The Dodd-Frank Wall Street Reform and Consumer Protection Act requires that you "opt in" for the opt-in protection. Think twice before you do so. Many new users of checking accounts rack up high levels of fees because they do not really understand opting-in. **Opting in** means that the bank will not alert or stop you when you use your debit card or write a check when there are insufficient funds. Use of a debit card for $3.50 for a drink and some chips could trigger a fee ten times as high.

You must keep track of your own account balance and ensure that you have enough in your account each and every time you access the funds. Banks love it when people opt-in and they receive about 25 percent of their revenue from overdraft fees. Opting in is a high-risk and high-cost way to cover overdrafts. You should be able to get by with options 1 or 2 above. If you do want to opt in, read the rules of the plan before you make the decision.

Of the billions of dollars in overdraft fees assessed each year, most were to young and low-income customers. Will you be a victim? The choice is yours. Consider these ways to deal with overdrafts listed from best to worst:

Ways to cover your overdrafts	Examples of possible cost for each overdraft. You should know what your bank charges
Practice good account management	$0; you have no overdrafts
Automatic funds transfer agreement	$0 to $5 transfer fee
Overdraft line of credit	$15 annual fee +18% APR
Automatic overdraft cash advance from a credit card	$3 to $10 cash-advance fee + 18% APR
"Opt-in" overdraft/ bounce protection	$20 to $30

Patti Fisher and Irene Leech
Virginia Tech, Blacksburg, Virginia

College students can sometimes benefit from a **lifeline banking account** that offers access to certain minimal financial services that every consumer needs—regardless of income—to function in our society. An applicant's income and net worth determine acceptance into a lifeline program. The cost of lifeline banking accounts is extremely low, often about $5 per month, although they do not pay interest.

Checking Account Balance Requirements and Fees Most interest-earning checking accounts have a balance requirement that, if not met, will result in the assessment of a monthly fee and, often, forfeiture of any interest earned for the month. An account with no balance requirement is preferable but these are increasingly rare in today's banking world.

Balance requirements are structured as either a minimum-balance or average-balance requirement. With a **minimum-balance account**, the customer must keep a certain amount (perhaps $500 or $1000) in the account throughout a specified time period (usually a month or a quarter) to avoid a flat service charge (usually $5 to $15). A fee is assessed whenever the triggering event occurs—that is, when the balance drops below the specified minimum. With an **average-balance account**, a service fee is assessed only if the average daily balance of funds in the account drops below a certain level (perhaps $800 or $1200) during the specified time period (usually a month or a quarter).

Most depository institutions will waive the assessment of monthly fees for depositors who have their paychecks or other regular deposits made electronically via **direct deposit** from the payer into the depositor's account. People interested in getting their money's worth in banking would be wise to avoid as many of the charges shown in Table 5-2 as possible.

Free Checking Is Not Really Free Lots of banks offer "free" checking accounts. What this typically means is that there is no minimum-balance requirement or monthly maintenance fee on the account. However, there can be fees for writing checks when there are insufficient funds in the account, using another bank's ATM, inactivity on the account, and other events. Make sure you understand how and when your bank assesses fees.

minimum-balance account
Checking account that requires customers to keep a certain minimum amount for a specified time period to avoid fees.

average-balance account
Checking account for which service fees are assessed if the account's average daily balance drops below a certain level during a specified time.

DO IT IN CLASS

ADVICE FROM A PROFESSIONAL

Endorse Your Checks Properly

Endorsement is the process of writing on the back of a check to legally transfer its ownership, usually in return for the cash amount indicated on the face of the check. Choosing the proper type of endorsement can protect you from having the check cashed by someone else against your wishes.

A check with a **blank endorsement** contains only the payee's signature on the back. Such a check immediately becomes a bearer instrument, meaning that anyone who attempts to cash it will very likely be allowed to do so, even if the check has been lost or stolen.

A **special endorsement** can be used to limit who can cash a check. To make this kind of endorsement, you write the phrase *Pay to the order of [person's name]* on the back along with your signature. The person named in such a "two-party check" will likely only be able to deposit it in an account at a financial institution.

A **restrictive endorsement** uses the phrase *For deposit only* written on the back along with the signature and can only be deposited into an account. For further safety, you can include the name of your financial institution and account number as part of the endorsement.

Mary Ann Whitehurst
Southeastern Crescent Technical College, Griffin, Georgia

Table 5-2	Costs and Penalties on Checking and Savings Accounts

Account Activity	Reasons for Assessing Costs or Penalties	Assessed on Checking or Savings
Automated teller machine (ATM) transactions	A customer's account is assessed a fee (often $1 to $3) for each transaction on an ATM; an additional fee may be charged for using an ATM not owned by the financial institution.	Checking, savings
Telephone, computer, or teller information	Fees are assessed for access or requests for account information by telephone, by computer, or in person (often $2 per transaction) after a number of free requests (perhaps three) have been made.	Checking, savings
Maintenance fees on a minimum-balance account (often waived if paychecks are directly deposited electronically)	The account balance falls below a set minimum amount, such as $300. A set fee of $10 to $20 per month is often charged.	Checking
Maintenance fees on an average-balance account (often waived if paychecks are directly deposited electronically)	The average daily account balance for the month falls below a set amount, such as $500. The cost is usually based on a set fee, a scaled amount (the more the account falls below the average, the greater the cost), or a percentage of the amount the account falls below the average.	Checking
Stop-payment order	A customer asks the financial institution to not honor a particular check; the fee is $25 to $30 per check.	Checking
Bad check "bounced" for insufficient funds	Charges of $25 to $40 or more are assessed for each check written or deposited to your account marked "insufficient funds."	Checking
Early account closing	Charges are assessed if a customer closes an account within a month or quarter of opening it. Charges range from $10 to $20.	Checking, savings
Delayed use of funds	Amounts deposited by check cannot be withdrawn until rules allow it.	Checking, savings
Inactive accounts	A monthly penalty may be assessed for inactive accounts (ones with no activity for six months to a year), sometimes $10 monthly.	Checking, savings
Excessive withdrawals	Some savings institutions assess a penalty ($2 to $5) when withdrawals exceed a certain number per month.	Savings
Early withdrawal	Amounts withdrawn before the end of a quarter earn no interest for that quarter.	Savings
Deposit penalty	Deposits made during the current quarter earn no interest until the beginning of the next quarter.	Savings

What Happens When You Write a Check? When you write a paper check, you either simultaneously make a copy that serves as your record that the check was written or make a note of the transaction in your check register. When the check is paid by your bank, it is said to have **cleared** the bank.

The check itself is treated in one of two ways. In the traditional method, a **canceled check** is sent to your bank so that the funds can be paid to whomever you had written the check. Typically today, the check is scanned by the receiving bank or the business to which you wrote it and an electronic **substitute check** is created and transmitted immediately to your bank. As a result, the check can clear your bank in a matter of minutes or hours. Under the Check Clearing for the 21st Century Act, your bank must quickly correct any errors in the processing of paper and substitute

stop-payment order

Notifying your bank not to honor a check when it's presented for payment.

checks. Check your statement each month to ensure that errors have not occurred.

Stop-Payment Order A **stop-payment order** is a notice made by a depositor to his or her bank directing the bank to refuse payment on a specific check drawn by the depositor. To issue such an order, you can telephone your bank and stop payment on the check or you may do it online if your bank allows it. You will need the check number, which is in the upper right hand corner, the dollar amount of the check, the date on the check or the date the check was issued, the person the check is payable to and finally the reason for issuing a stop payment.

A stop-payment order works only if the check has not yet cleared. A fee of $15–$35 will be charged. If the stop payment order is issued on time the person in receipt of the check will not be able to cash it.

FINANCIAL POWER POINT

Don't Pay for an Idle Account

If you have money untouched in an account for too long of a time period (such as 6 months) the bank may assess you with an "inactivity fee" of perhaps $10 per monthly statement. One way to beat the fee is to have another account automatically deposit a small amount into the account each month so it won't be idle.

DID YOU KNOW ?

How to Reconcile Your Bank Accounts

It is good to maintain records of the activities occurring in your various banking accounts. You should record all checks written, debit card transactions, and deposits in your check register as they take place. It is also smart to go online every few days to confirm your deposits, withdrawals, and checking transactions.

DO IT IN CLASS

You also should conduct an **account reconciliation** in which you compare your records with your bank's records, checking the accuracy of both sets of records and identifying any errors. The best time to do so is when you receive your monthly account statement from your bank. Account reconciliation is a three-step process:

1. *Bring your own records up to date.*
2. *Bring the bank's records up to date.*
3. *Reconcile the results from Steps 1 and 2.*

If the revised balance in your records and the revised balance from the bank statement differ, you will need to find where the error occurred. First, check the additions and subtractions in your records. Next, make sure that all previous entries in your records are properly reported on the account statement.

Looking for errors when Steps 1 and 2 yield differing results is a necessary but tedious task. Fortunately, it is less likely to be necessary today because of electronic banking. Many people go online frequently to check their balances and review their account activity for accuracy. In this way, they can catch errors early and are always very confident that their balances are exactly as shown in their own records. Here is a table you can use to guide your reconciling efforts.

STEP 1: Bring Your Own Records Up to Date	Amount
1. Enter balance from your check register.	$
2. Add deposits not yet recorded.	$
3. Subtract checks and other withdrawals not yet recorded.	$
4. Subtract bank fees and charges included in the monthly statement and not yet recorded.	$
5. Add interest earned.	$
ADJUSTED CHECKBOOK REGISTER BALANCE	$

STEP 2: Bring the Account Statement Up-to-Date	
1. Enter ending balance from bank statement.	$
2. Add deposits made since bank statement closing date.	$
3. Subtract outstanding checks written since bank statement closing date.	$
ADJUSTED BANK STATEMENT BALANCE	$

STEP 3: Compare adjusted checkbook register balance and adjusted bank statement balance. If the two balances do not match, identify where the error occurred.

You should reconcile your bank account monthly.

DID YOU KNOW

About Special Purpose Payment Instruments

There are some payment instruments that you might find useful from time to time.

Certified Checks

A **certified check** is a personal check drawn on your account on which your financial institution imprints the word *certified*, signifying that the account has sufficient funds to cover its payment. The financial institution simultaneously places a hold on that amount in the account until the check clears. The fee for a certified check is usually $10 to $15.

Cashier's Checks

Some payees insist on receiving payment in the form of a **cashier's check** drawn on the account of the financial institution itself and, thus, backed by the institution's finances. To obtain such a check, you would pay the financial institution the amount of the cashier's check and pay a fee of $10 to $15.

Money Orders

A **money order** is a checking instrument bought for a particular amount with a fee assessed based on the amount of the order. Many financial institutions, including retailers such as Wal-Mart and the U.S. Postal Service, sell money orders.

<u>5.2b</u> Money Market Accounts Offer Limited Check Writing

When income begins to exceed expenses on a regular basis, perhaps by $300 or $500 each month, a substantial amount of excess funds can quickly build up. Although this situation is a comfortable one, it is wise from a monetary asset management point of view to move some of the excess funds into an account that pays more interest.

A **money market account** is any of a variety of interest-earning accounts that pays relatively high interest rates (compared with regular savings accounts) that are based on current interest rates in the money markets, and they offer some limited check-writing privileges.

money market account

Interest-earning accounts that pay relatively high interest rates and offer limited check-writing privileges.

The funds on deposit are not loaned out to consumers but instead are invested in the "money market" for short-term loans to businesses. Money market accounts are offered by depository institutions (where they are called **money market deposit accounts (MMDA)**), stock brokerage firms, financial services companies, and mutual funds.

5.2c Money Market Mutual Funds Also Have Checking Privileges

A **money market mutual fund (MMMF)** is a money market account in a mutual fund investment company (rather than at a depository institution) where the funds are invested in short-term debt securities such as US Treasury bills and commercial paper. Money market accounts can be used much like a checking account.

MMMFs pool the cash of thousands of investors and earn a relatively safe return by buying the highest rated debt, which matures in under 13 months. The portfolio must maintain a weighted average maturity (WAM) of 60 days or less and not invest more than 5% in any one issuer, except for government securities and repurchase agreements. Interest is calculated daily, and an investor can withdraw funds at any time. Money market mutual funds historically pay the highest rate of return that can be earned on a daily basis by small investors.

MMMFs require a minimum deposit ranging from $500 to $1000. Dozens of mutual fund companies offer unlimited check writing with no minimums on the amount of each check. Electronic transfers are permitted, but ATMs cannot be used. Although MMMFs are not insured by any federal agency, they are considered extremely safe. To open an MMMF account, you can contact a mutual fund company online. A few of the more prominent MMMFs are managed by American Century (www.americancentury.com), Dreyfus (www.dreyfus.com), Fidelity (www.fidelity.com), T. Rowe Price (www.troweprice.com), and Vanguard (www.vanguard.com).

5.2d Accumulate and Hold Funds Using Savings Accounts

When you are trying to accumulate and hold funds you want to take advantage of the time element to earn more interest than a checking account would pay. Most people start out by opening a **savings account**; sometimes called a **statement savings account**. Funds on deposit in a savings account are considered **time deposits**, which require that account holders give 30 to 60 days notice for withdrawals (although this restriction is almost never enforced). Although savings account deposits are extremely safe, the interest rate paid is only slightly higher than on a checking account. The actual dollar amount of interest you will earn depends on four variables:

1. Amount of money on deposit
2. Method of determining this balance
3. Interest rate applied to the balance
4. Frequency of compounding (such as annually, semiannually, quarterly, monthly, or daily)

The Truth in Savings Act requires depository institutions to disclose a uniform, standardized rate of interest so that depositors can easily compare various checking and savings options that pay interest. This rate, called the **annual percentage yield (APY)**, is a percentage based on the total interest that would be received on a $100 deposit for a 365-day period given the institution's annual rate of simple interest and frequency of compounding. The more frequent the compounding, the greater the effective return for the saver.

A **grace period** is the time in days during which deposits or withdrawals can be made and still earn interest from a given day of the interest period. For example, if deposits are made by the tenth day of the month, interest

---

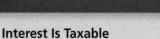

FINANCIAL POWER POINT

How to Find a Better Bank

The largest and most well-known national banks have some of the worst fee assessments. For a better deal check out small local banks, credit unions, and online banks that meet your needs at, www.creditunion.coop, and www.bankrate.com. Make sure the institution provides federally insured accounts.

---

money market deposit accounts

Government-insured money market account with minimum-balance requirements and tiered interest rates.

money market mutual fund (MMMF)

Money market account in a mutual fund rather than at a depository institution.

annual percentage yield (APY)

Return on total interest received on a $100 deposit for 365-day period, given the institution's simple annual interest rate and compounding frequency.

FINANCIAL POWER POINT

Interest Is Taxable

Any interest earned on your checking and savings accounts must be reported as income on your federal and state income tax returns. Your financial institutions should send you a Form 1099 statement that reports your interest income for the previous year; that information also is sent to the IRS. Failure to receive a Form 1099 does not absolve you of the requirement to report the earnings.

DID YOU KNOW

Be a Better Saver

When asked, Americans typically complain that they cannot save because "there simply is no money left over at the end of the month." This is evidence that these people are thinking about savings in the wrong way. Instead, they should follow the adage "**pay yourself first**," which means to treat savings as the first expenditure every payday. This builds savings into your budget right from the beginning.

Your first "pay yourself first" goal should be to create an emergency fund in case of job layoff, long illness, or other serious financial calamity. Most people do not have a sufficient emergency savings fund. Instead, they rely on credit cards when an emergency or unforeseen need arises. For a person with a $42,000 in take home pay, the recommended three-month emergency fund might be $10,500 ($42,000/12 = $3500 for each month).

People who should consider keeping more funds available—perhaps income to cover six months to a year of living expenses—are those who depend heavily on commissions or bonuses or who own their own businesses. Next, save funds to meet short-term goals. Then, you can save for retirement, a down payment on a home, or a child's college education by breaking your long-term goals into short-term benchmarks. Saving is not glamorous; slow and steady wins the race.

Super smart savers have as much as 20 percent of their paychecks directly deposited to savings, and they save as much as 75 of any raises or bonuses. Such people find that savings is liberating. When you have money when you need it you are independent. Then you do not owe any credit card debt or owe money to your parents. Your financial life is good.

---

pay yourself first

Treating savings as the first expenditure after—or even before—getting paid rather than simply the money left over at the end of the month.

certificate of deposit (CD)

An interest-earning savings instrument purchased for a fixed period of time.

FINANCIAL POWER POINT

Millenials Are Good Savers

Young adults between 18 and 34 seem to be better savers than their parents. They save a higher percentage of their income and have higher retirement account balance than predecessors at the same age. They must be getting the message about wise management of their personal finances.

might be earned from the first day of the month. For withdrawals, the grace period generally ranges from three to five days. Thus, if a saver withdrew money from an account within three to five days of the end of the interest period, the savings might still earn interest as if the money remained in the account for the entire period.

5.2e Certificates of Deposit

Some time deposits, such as a certificate of deposit, are classified as a **fixed-time deposit**. As such, they have a specific time period that the savings must be left on deposit. A **certificate of deposit (CD)** is an interest-earning savings instrument purchased for a fixed period of time. The required deposit amounts range from $100 to $100,000, while the time periods range from seven days to eight years. The interest rate in force when the CD is purchased typically remains fixed for the entire term of the deposit. Depositors collect their principal and interest when the CD expires. Certificates of deposit are insured similarly to checking and savings accounts.

Variable-rate (or **adjustable-rate**) **certificates of deposit** pay an interest rate that is adjusted (up or down) periodically. Typically, savers are allowed to "lock in," or fix, the rate at any point before their CDs mature.

A **bump-up CD** is one where the interest rate can go up. Thus, if interest rates in general go up, the holder can elect to increase the interest rate to the now higher going rate. If interest rates don't rise, there is the opportunity cost of having to keep the lower interest rate for the term of the CD. When purchasing a bump-up CD, be sure to find out how many times you are allowed to bump-up the interest rate, and whether you have to extend the term of the CD with each bump-up.

Brokered certificates of deposit often pay the highest yields and are available through stockbrokerage firms. Brokered CDs are bought by a brokerage firm in bulk for the purpose of reselling to brokerage customers. They are FDIC insured and usually do not have sales commissions.

Avoid "investment certificates" because they are not CDs. They are not insured and can be recalled by the financial institution and reissued at a lower interest rate prior to their maturity. Sometime the issuer goes bankrupt and the saver loses 100 percent of his or her money. Always ask "Is this a CD or an investment certificate?" If it's a CD, then verify that information.

Money withdrawn from a CD before the end of the specified time period is subject to interest penalties, and these vary by institution. The most common penalty is still three months' interest for CDs with maturities of less than one year, and six months' interest for CDs with maturities of one year and longer. If the penalty exceeds the interest amount, you will get back less than you deposited. The institution, if necessary, will take the penalty from your principal. Consequently, before putting money into a CD, make sure that it is appropriate to tie up your funds in this way.

CDs might appear to be a low-risk place to hold funds. But, there is a risk if interest rates in general go up while your money is in the CD. The risk is that you have the opportunity cost of not being able to move your money to an account that is paying the newer higher interest rate. The uncertainty about changing rates is referred to as **interest-rate risk**. Bump-up CDs discussed above help reduce this risk.

CD laddering is a technique that smoothes out the fluctuations in interest rates and lowers interest-rate risk. Here's how laddering works. Let's say you have $10,000 you would like to put into a CD. To start, simply go to www.bankrate.com and find the best rate you can get at the time. Then you purchase five CDs: CD #1 for $2000 for a one-year term, CD #2 for $2000 for a two-year term, CD #3 for $2000 for a three-year term, CD #4 for $2000 for a four-year term, and CD #5 for $2000 for a five-year term.

As the CDs mature, you renew each of them for five years. After five years, you continue to have one CD mature each year, and you renew at the highest current market rate you can find. You do not have to stay with the same financial institution. As interest rates fluctuate over time, you always have some CDs at lower rates and some at higher rates. As a result, you are always earning an average rate overall, thus avoiding the possibility of having of your money earning very low rates. And you always will be able to access at least some of your money within a relatively short time frame.

5.2f Asset Management Accounts Can Serve Both Checking and Savings Functions

An **asset management account (AMA)** is a multiple-purpose, coordinated package that gathers most of the customer's monetary asset management vehicles into a unified account and reports them on a single monthly statement. Included in this package might be transactions in a money market mutual fund and in checking, credit card,

FINANCIAL POWER POINT

Use a Savings Calculator

An easy-to-use savings calculator can be found at www.bankrate.com/calculators /savings/compound-interest-calculator-tool.aspx. You can determine how much to save to reach your goal or find out what your savings will be worth at a future date.

asset management account (AMA, or central asset account)
Multiple-purpose, coordinated package that gathers most monetary asset management vehicles into a unified account and reports activity on a single monthly statement to the client.

DID YOU KNOW ?

Turn Bad Habits into Good Ones

Do You Do This?	*Do This Instead!*
Ignore your account statements	Read each statement for completeness and accuracy
Talk about money only when there is a problem	Schedule regular "money talks" with your family
Pay fees every month for checking	Explore low- or no-fee accounts at a credit union
Overdraw your checking account	Keep track of your balance online and reconcile your account monthly
Keep most of your money in your checking account	Earn higher returns in a savings account, money-market account, or certificate of deposit

DID YOU KNOW

How Ownership of Accounts (and Other Assets) Is Established

When you open a new account, you will be asked to sign a **signature card** that can be used to verify the signatures of the owners of the account. Accounts can be owned either individually or jointly.

An **individual account** has one owner who is solely responsible for the account and its activity. At the death of the individual owner, the account becomes part of his or her estate and will go to heirs in accordance with the owner's will. If desired, individual accounts can be set up with a **payable at death designation** whereby a person is named in the account to receive the funds upon the death of the individual owner. This allows that person to gain quick access to the funds after the owner's death but does not give the person any rights to the account while the owner is still alive.

A **joint account** has two or more owners, each of whom has legal rights to the funds in the account. The forms of joint ownership discussed here apply to all types of property, including automobiles and homes, as well as checking and savings accounts. Three types of joint ownership exist:

1. ***Joint tenancy with right of survivorship*** *(also called simply **joint tenancy**) is the most common form of joint ownership, especially for husbands and wives. In this case, each person owns the whole of the asset and can dispose of it without the approval of the other(s). With accounts at financial institutions, the financial institution will honor checks or withdrawal slips possessing any of the owners' signatures. An advantage of a joint account is that in case of death of*

DO IT IN CLASS

one of the owners, the property continues to be owned by the surviving account holder(s).

2. ***Tenancy in common*** *is a form of joint ownership in which two or more parties own the asset, but each retains control over a separate piece of the property rights. In most states, the ownership shares are presumed to be equal unless otherwise specified. When one owner dies, however, his or her share in the asset is distributed to his or her heirs according to the terms of a will (or if no will exists, according to state law) instead of automatically going to the other co-owners.*

3. ***Tenancy by the entirety***, *which is recognized in about 26 states, is restricted to property held between a husband and a wife. Under this arrangement, no one co-owner can sell or dispose of his or her portion of an asset without the permission of the other. This restriction prevents transfers by one owner without the knowledge of the other. It takes both signatures to write a check.*

Dual-earner couples often prefer to own some property together and some property separately. If you own a business and default on a loan, for example, your creditors usually cannot attach your home if it is in your spouse's name. Nonworking spouses, however, should get their name on all deeds and investments; in the event of divorce, courts typically award property to the people who legally own it.

In **community property states**—in which all of the money and property acquired during a marriage is legally considered the joint property of both spouses—the rights of both husbands and wives are equally protected. Likewise, all debts are jointly owed. These jurisdictions include Arizona, California, Idaho, Louisiana, Nevada, New Mexico, Texas, Washington, and Wisconsin.

loan, and stock brokerage accounts. Also known as **central-asset accounts**, AMAs are offered through depository institutions, stock brokerage firms, financial services companies, and mutual funds. The mutual fund sweeps your funds into and out of an account with a depository institution on your behalf. AMAs enable you to conduct all of your financial business with one institution.

Typically, $10,000, spread across all subaccounts, is required to open an AMA. AMAs assess an annual fee, usually $100. If the account fee is 1 percent, this would reduce your return by 1 percentage point ($100/$10,000). AMAs usually have other features that attract investors as well—for example, free credit and debit cards, a rebate of 2 percent on credit card purchases, free traveler's checks, free bill-pay services, inexpensive term life insurance, inexpensive stock trades, and an investment advisory newsletter.

CONCEPT CHECK 5.2

1. Distinguish among the time-frame differences for checking, savings, and investment accounts.

2. Explain why is there no such thing as *free* checking and list two checking account fees that you could avoid by using your account appropriately.

3. Describe reasons to keep money in a savings account rather than a checking account.

4. Explain the benefits of a pay-yourself-first approach to saving.

5. Explain the benefits and drawbacks of certificates of deposit.

5.3 ELECTRONIC MONEY MANAGEMENT

Monetary asset management can be summed up today with the phrase "paper, plastic, or neither." "Paper" comprises the traditional cash- and check-based systems. "Plastic" is the use of a debit or other type of card to access your funds. You should always make a photocopy of both sides of your cards should it be lost or stolen. "Neither" is the use of your computer or smartphone to access and use your accounts.

Electronic money management occurs whenever transactions are conducted without using paper documents. Most of these activities involve **electronic funds transfers (EFTs)**, in which funds are shifted electronically (rather than by check or cash) among your various accounts and to and from other people and businesses.

5.3a Using "Plastic" in Monetary Asset Management

There are many types of plastic devices used to access your money.

1. **ATM cards** allow you to withdraw money from or transfer money among your checking and savings accounts at an automatic teller machine. You must use a **personal identification number (PIN)** to use the card.

2. **Debit cards** do ATM cards one better—you can also use them to make purchases via a point-of-sale (POS) terminal at retail outlets. Using a debit card to make a purchase immediately transfers money from your account. You typically use a PIN or provide your signature when using a debit card. Some merchants will also provide a discount when you use a debit, rather than credit, card.

3. **Prepaid cards** allow users to function as though they have a bank account, providing services through its mobile app such as direct deposit, online bill pay, and check deposits. The card can be used at ATMs as well as purchases online and at retail cash registers. Walmart offers the American Express Bluebird prepaid card. T-Mobile and Sprint offer similar cards. Fees are low, and the companies provide private insurance rather than FDIC insurance.

4. **Preloaded debit cards** are cards that are tied to funds in an account at a financial institution and are used much like an ordinary debit card. Parents might use such a card to provide funds to a child away at college. Employers sometimes use such a card to pay their employees.

5. **Stored-value cards** contain a magnetic strip or bar code that encrypts the amount of money stored via the card. Some stored-value cards can be "reloaded" with additional funds. A **gift card** is an example of such a stored-value card. Others, such as those offered at some colleges, can be used for student meal plans and at participating retailers on- and off-campus.

   There are risks associated with some stored value cards since many have an activation fee, expiration date (no shorter than five years), and an inactivity fee if there is no activity within a 12-month time period. Cards that can only be used at one retailer carry risk should the retail company go bankrupt.

LEARNING OBJECTIVE 3
Describe electronic money management, including your legal protections.

electronic funds transfers (EFTs)
Funds shifted electronically (rather than by check or cash) among various accounts or to and from other people and businesses.

DID YOU KNOW

ATM transaction fee

Payments levied each time an automated teller machine (ATM) is used.

6. **Electronic benefits transfer (EBT) cards** are used by the government to pay military personnel and provide Social Security and other government benefits.

7. **Credit cards** allow you to make purchases or obtain cash with credit from the bank or retailer that issued the cards. These are debts that must be paid back, often with interest. In some states, merchants are allowed to charge a higher price when a credit card is used, such as for gasoline.

Regardless of the type of card you are using, you should always make a photocopy of both sides of your card for verification should the card ever be lost or stolen.

5.3b Electronic Money Management Can Be Easy but Is Not Always Free

There are costs assessed with the use of some electronic banking. An **ATM transaction fee** may be assessed for using an ATM. Fees may be levied by your financial institution as well as by the institution that provides the ATM if you are using an ATM linked to a national network.

Retail transaction fees of $1 to $3 also may be assessed whenever you make a purchase via a POS terminal at a retail store. This is most likely to happen when you use a PIN number. Such a usage occurs when you hit the "debit" button on the terminal. You can usually avoid the fee if you hit "credit" instead. Rather than use your PIN, you sign for the purchase. The transaction is still a debit transaction but is processed in a way that costs less for your bank. You also have additional legal protections for signed debit transactions as discussed later.

Fees can be assessed for other uses of electronic money management. Some banks charge for online banking services such as bill paying and verification of your account balances. Often the fees for these services are a fixed monthly rate for all usage that may be cheaper than writing checks and mailing payments. These paper-based services are often free. **Smartphone Apps** let you use your phone to pay for everything. Transactions are fee-free when paired with your bank account or debit card. You can avoid almost all such fees by shopping for an account that matches your banking habits. Otherwise you will waste money on unnecessary banking fees.

5.3c Use Electronic Banking Safely

Federal and state regulations have been adopted to provide protections for the use of debit cards and other electronic banking. The Electronic Funds

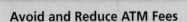

FINANCIAL POWER POINT

Avoid and Reduce ATM Fees

You can avoid ATM fees altogether by banking at an institution that does not charge ATM fees at its banks. The average ATM fee for using another bank's ATM is over $4.

You can minimize your ATM fees by writing a check for cash and simply managing your money. You also may make a few large withdrawals rather than more frequent small withdrawals. A $3 fee on a $20 withdrawal is 15 percent; on a $100 withdrawal it is 3 percent. Do you really want to give 15 percent, or even 3 percent, of your money to your bank? The annual percentage rates for each of these transactions is well over 400 percent.

Transfer Act is the governing law, and the Federal Reserve Board's Regulation E provides specific guidelines on ATM and debit card liability. When you sign up for electronic banking services, the depository institution must inform you of your rights and responsibilities in a written disclosure statement.

Users also must be provided with written receipts when using an ATM or POS terminal. These receipts show the amount of the transaction, the date on which it took place, and other pertinent information. General protection of a customer's account takes the form of a **periodic statement** sent by the financial institution that shows all electronic transfers to and from the account, fees charged, and opening and closing balances. Users of electronic banking services and electronic funds transfers (EFTs) should regularly compare the information on this periodic statement with their written receipts.

Fixing Account Errors If you find an error in your periodic statement, notify the issuing organization in writing as soon as possible. Use the notification procedures found in the disclosure statement accompanying your monthly statement. If the institution needs more than ten business days to investigate and correct a problem, generally it must return the amount in question to your account while it conducts the investigation.

If an error did occur, the institution must permanently correct it promptly. If the institution decides that no error occurred, it must explain its decision in writing and let you know that it has deducted any amount temporarily credited during the investigation. In such a case, the institution must honor withdrawals against the credited amount for five days, allowing you time to deposit additional funds. You may ask for copies of the documents on which the institution relied in its investigation and again challenge the outcome if you believe that a mistake was made.

Protections for Lost ATM and Debit Cards The sooner you report the loss of an ATM or debit card, the more likely you will be to limit your liability if someone uses the card without your permission. Cardholders are liable for only the first $50 of unauthorized use if they notify the issuing company within two business days after the loss or theft of their card or PIN.

Note that fraudulent debit card transactions using a PIN are *not* afforded this protection! After two days, cardholder liability for unauthorized use rises to $500. Some issuers, including Visa and MasterCard, have usually have policies that voluntarily waive enforcement of this liability. However, you risk unlimited loss for the card's misuse if, within 60 days after the institution sends your financial statement to you, you do not report an unauthorized transfer or withdrawal. Thus, you could lose all of the money in your account.

periodic statements
Monthly reports that show all electronic transfers to and from accounts, fees charged, and opening and closing balances.

DO IT IN CLASS

DID YOU KNOW

How to Protect Against the Privacy Risks from Using Your Mobile Device to Manage Money

People today are using their smartphones, ipads, and tablet computers for managing money and transferring personal financial data. Yet many underestimate the degree to which the data transmitted and stored via the device is ripe for identity theft. Here are some things you can do to protect yourself:

1. *Do not store ID numbers and passwords* in your phone.

2. *Use the blocking mechanism* such as a password (and make it complex) provided with your device.

3. *Erase the flash-chip memory* using the "hard reset" function (or destroy the chip and/or SIM card) when discarding, trading-in, or recycling your phone.

These regulations apply to debit cards and other cards used to make electronic funds transfers (EFTs). The protections offered for fraudulent use of debit cards are not as strong as when your credit card is used fraudulently. It is much safer to use a credit card for certain transactions, especially those made online. States may have laws that provide additional protection for consumers in EFT transactions.

Most homeowner's and renter's insurance policies (discussed in Chapter 10) already cover your liability for theft of both debit and credit cards. If you are not currently protected, such insurance coverage generally can be added for $15 or $20 a year. Many companies sell similar insurance as a separate policy for an annual premium of $30 to $99.

card registration service

Firm that will notify all companies with which you have debit and credit cards if your cards are lost or stolen.

Some firms sell a **card registration service** that will notify all companies with which you have debit and credit cards in the event of loss. For $50 to $100 a year, you need make only one telephone call to report all card losses. Of course, you can also notify debit and credit card companies yourself at no cost.

Protect Your Privacy Yourself Having the law and insurance on your side when banking electronically or online is a good thing, but it is better to not have problems in the first place. Most victims of identity theft are between the ages of 20 and 29. Here are some tips for reducing the risk:

- Study your statements. Ask about anything that looks unusual or the least bit in error. A small $1 charge to a debit or credit card is a red flag that someone is checking to see if an account number is valid and hoping that you won't notice. Big charges may come later.

- Avoid banking via computer or mobile device on a public or unsecured wireless system away from home. Use your wireless system at home only if it is fully protected.

- Be cautious about social networking and job search sites. Would you put personal information on a sign outside your home? Of course not, so avoid doing so where all the world can see on your social networking pages.

- Never provide account information if you get an e-mail from your bank. It's likely from a scam artist, because banks never email customers seeking information.

- When finished banking via computer, always hit the log off button at the top of the page and then close the browser window.
- Avoid using someone else's computer to manage your account. If you do, shut down the computer completely when finished.
- Regularly change your passwords and keep them to yourself.
- Keep your financial papers away from the eyes of roommates and houseguests.
- Buy a shredder and use it.
- Make and save paper copies of all your electronic transactions until you can verify their accuracy on your next account statement.

CONCEPT CHECK 5.3

1. Distinguish among credit cards, debit cards, and a stored-value card.
2. List the steps you should take if you find an error in your periodic statement regarding an electronic transaction.
3. Summarize the rules that apply if you lose your ATM or debit card and it is used without your authorization.

5.4 THE PSYCHOLOGY OF MONEY MANAGEMENT

A common cause of tension in personal relationships is conflict over money. Mutual trust in money matters can be developed—and must be—to have happy relationships and achieve financial success.

5.4a Managing Money and Making Financial Decisions Are Different

Managing money includes such tasks as handling the checkbook, overseeing the budget, and doing the household shopping. Couples should agree on who will carry out these day-to-day chores and then carry through on their responsibilities. Financial experts recommend that each person in a relationship keep some money of his or her own. This can encourage independence and self-control in a relationship rather than dependency on the other person. This can be accomplished by setting up three checking accounts: a discretionary account for each individual (two accounts) and a third, joint account. Then clearly specify the budget categories for spending related to each account.

While managing family money is a significant task, decision making is where most disagreements arise. Shared decision making is the best model when defining goals and setting up a budget; when contemplating any major expense, such as buying vehicles and housing; and when conferring on key topics such as insurance, estate planning and investments, and long-term financial plans.

5.4b People Connect Strong Emotions to Money

People often attach a number of emotions to money, including freedom, trust, self-esteem, guilt, indifference, envy, security, comfort, power, and control. They bring with them the patterns, beliefs, and attitudes that were prevalent in their family of origin.

DID YOU KNOW

The Financial Side of Popping the Question

Before you pop the question about marriage, or say "yes!" if asked, stop to consider the following financial questions. If you haven't discussed them or, worse, have been afraid to bring them up, perhaps it is time to take a big step back before you take the big step forward.

1. *Do you know how much your sweetie owes including student loans, to whom, and his/her plan for paying the debts off and when?*

2. *Have you seen each other's credit reports and know each other's credit score?*

3. *Do you know what type of wedding you would like (and your sweetie would like), how much it would cost, and from where the money will come?*

4. *Do you have any concerns about how your sweetie spends money, and have you discussed the concerns and resolved them to your joint satisfaction?*

5. *Do you budget? Does your sweetie budget? Have you discussed your budgets?*

And for those of you who are thinking that these questions aren't important because you plan to live together before marriage, you should think again. Money issues are the number one problem area for both cohabiting couples and newlyweds.

Author Judith Viorst suggests that becoming responsible and adept at managing one's financial matters represents a true passage into adulthood. This evolution involves communicating effectively with others on money matters. Addressing questions openly and calmly helps keep emotions in check. Separately writing down the answers to the following questions and then bringing the answers to the table in a meeting can be an effective way to discuss money matters.

1. What is my biggest money worry today?
2. What are we doing well financially?
3. Is there an issue in our finances that I would like to understand better?
4. If we needed to cut back our spending, what three areas are off limits and what three are fair game?
5. What money issues do we avoid and how can we bring them out into the open?

DID YOU KNOW

How to Develop Money Sense in Children

A major theme of this chapter is that checking and savings accounts and investments are an integral part of reaching your financial goals. By progressively building savings funds and then investing, you can achieve financial success. Parents can help children develop money sense by providing them with opportunities to manage their own money while still young and guiding this behavior toward appropriate patterns. Financially clueless parents beget financially clueless children. Do not let this happen. Instead, do the following to increase your children's ease in handling money:

1. ***Give an allowance.*** *Even children as young as 5 years old should have some money of their own.*

An allowance should be the source of these funds in the preteen years. The amounts of allowance should fit the family income level. Allowances are a means for teaching money management.

2. ***Encourage work.*** *Once children reach their preteen years, there are many opportunities to earn their own money. When children see what it takes to make money, it is easier for them to know the real cost of spending.*

3. ***Set reasonable limits.*** *Children should be given age-appropriate limits for spending in various categories and should be required to save a portion of their money. However, parents should not stop children from*

"wasting their money" or bail them out of every mistake. We often learn best from experience, not from what someone else tells us is best.

4. **Teach them to make good choices through increasingly complex activities.** *The dollar amounts and the areas of discretionary spending can increase as the child becomes older. A 7-year-old might be allowed to spend a portion of his or her own money on toys, snacks, and gifts to charity at church or school. A 14-year-old might be allowed to buy meals and clothing as well. More responsibility and autonomy should be given only as the child exhibits the ability to handle less complicated tasks.*

5. **Help them learn to wait.** *Children should have autonomy over at least some of their own money. But the remainder, perhaps 50 percent, should be saved. Then when children desire some high-cost item, they* can see that saving for a while can help them reach their goal.

6. **Talk about family finances with children.** *In many families, money matters are a taboo subject. Children need to see that parents must work at managing the family finances. They should know what it costs to raise a family and to make ends meet. Otherwise, kids will grow up with unrealistic expectations and behaviors that will be passed on to their children.*

7. **Be a role model.** *Children learn more from what they see than what they are told. Avoid borrowing money from, or loaning money to, children. They will learn that credit is easy. And, certainly, all intrafamily loans should be paid back on time. Otherwise, they will think people can borrow without paying back. Save money yourself, and tell your children that saving means that you can't have something you, or they, want right away.*

5.4c How to Talk About Financial Matters

Discussions about money matters are not always easy. Some people who are entirely rational about other issues are unpredictable or even careless in money matters. Adults need to accept that honest differences may exist among people and respect these values. The following ideas will help you discuss money with more confidence and candor.

Get to Know Yourself The first step in learning to talk with others about financial matters is to understand your own approach to money. Consider the emotions described earlier to help you get started. It is constructive to discuss any differences in how you view yourself as compared with how your partner views you. Write these down.

Focus on Commonalities Successful communication about money requires that the effort be aimed toward agreeing on common goals and reaching a consensus of opinion without substantially compromising the views of others.

Learn to Manage Financial Disagreements Give all family members time to express their views when discussing financial matters. Each also needs to listen to what others are saying and feeling. If talking proves too difficult, have each person separately write down his or her concerns. By swapping notes, ideas and concerns can be shared. Schedule a time and place for financial talks, decide on agenda items, and leave other conflicts outside the door.

Recall from Chapter 3 that Harry and Belinda Johnson had a significant disagreement when setting up their budget to allow for their anniversary party and spending for holiday gifts at the end of the year. As a result, they ended up with a draft budget that did not balance for the year as planned expenses exceeded anticipated income. They agreed to disagree and postponed decisions that will need to be made on how to cover their shortfalls. They will need to do better in the future.

Use Positive "I" Statements Messages focusing on "I" describe the behavior in question, the feelings you experienced because of the behavior, and any tangible effect on you. For example, a spouse might say, "I feel upset when we use credit cards because I do not know where we will find the money to pay the bills at the end of the month." "I" messages say three things: what (the behavior), I feel (feelings), and because (reason). Using "I" messages helps build stronger relationships

Each member of the family should be aware of and involved with important financial decisions.

because they tell the other person "I trust you to decide what change in behavior is necessary."

Beware of "I" statements that begin with "I need you to...." "You" statements are blaming statements, such as "You always ...," "You never ...," and "If you don't, I will...." These statements have a high probability of being condescending to other people, of making them feel guilty, and of implying that their needs and wants are not as important as yours.

Be Honest and Talk Regularly   Achieving consensus requires that each person be honest when talking about money matters. It further demands that couples regularly talk about finances. Perhaps begin by deciding to talk about money matters for only ten minutes at a time. Also be prepared to compromise. When you make decisions together, take action on them. Focus attention on current financial activities and issues as well as long-term financial planning. Use these discussions to forge overall long-term strategies for dealing with your family finances. Once the proper base has been established, short-term issues are more likely to fall into place.

DID YOU KNOW

Money Topics to Discuss with Your Partner

When you find the right partner, it is smart to do the following:

- **Change beneficiaries.** Life insurance policies, retirement accounts, and mutual fund accounts all have beneficiaries (the people who will receive the funds at your death) named when you set them up. (See Chapters 12, 15, and 17.)

- **Coordinate employee benefits.** Couples often have two incomes today, so each has a menu of employee benefits from which to choose. As a result, one spouse may drop a benefit that is being received via the other's plan. (See Chapter 1.)

- **Update life insurance coverage.** Focus on term life insurance for the bulk of your needs. (See Chapter 12.)

- **Review auto and homeowner's insurance coverages.** Also inventory your personal property. (See Chapter 10.)

- **Update names with government agencies.** If one or both partners' names are changed as a result of your new status, you need to notify the Social Security Administration and driver's licensing office of that change. You will need to show your marriage certificate as proof of the change.

- **Close redundant bank accounts.** Reducing the number of accounts that each partner brings into the marriage can save money on account fees. Decide which accounts are "yours, mine, or ours." (See Chapters 5 and 6 for more on managing accounts.)

- **Get out of debt.** One or both of you may bring debts into the new family. Because a couple can live together a little more cheaply than two individuals who live apart, funds can be freed up to pay off credit card, student, and other loans. (See Chapters 6, 7, and 9.)

- **Decide on how to manage money.** Decide on who pays what bills and makes investment decisions. Decide on whether or not each person will have individual control over certain money. Decide on who pays for the debts that precedes the relationship. Decide on who pays for gift giving. Decide on what money tasks you will do together, such as establishing annual financial goals, making purchases with debt, and agreeing on which expenditures require joint agreement, like expenses over $300.

- **Save for retirement separately.** Day-to-day living expenses will go down somewhat when you team up as a couple. Use some of that money to allocate additional amounts to your retirement plans. (See Chapter 17.)

- **Update estate transfer plans.** With a new "number one" in your life, you should change (or set up) your will, durable power of attorney, living will, and health care proxy. (See Chapter 11.)

5.4d Complications Brought by Remarriage

Remarriage merges financial histories, values, and habits as well as households. Some remarried couples—and those choosing to live together following a previous relationship—may have substantial combined incomes bolstered by child-support payments from a former spouse. In many cases, at least one person may be paying (instead of receiving) alimony and child support. When "his," "her," and "our" children are included in the household, living expenses can be quite steep.

Special concerns for blended families include determining who assumes financial responsibility for biological offspring and stepchildren; handling resentment over alimony and child-support payments; and managing unequal assets, incomes, responsibilities, and debts. Even gift giving can become a quandary. These challenges can be mitigated with effective communication.

Many remarried people use "his" and "her" funds and require the legally responsible parent owing financial support to a previous spouse or to children to make such payments out of his or her own money. Professor Jean Lown of Utah State University suggests that, "What is best is what the couple can agree on."

DO IT NOW!

Guard Your Monetary Assets

You know more about personal finance after reading this chapter, so get started right now by:

1. *Use complicated passwords, vary them among accounts, and change them regularly.*

2. *Go on-line two or three times each week to monitor activity and accuracy of your checking account balances.*

3. *Use a shredder to destroy paper account documents no longer needed for transaction verification or tax records.*

CONCEPT CHECK 5.4

1. Explain why it is difficult for many people in relationships to talk about money matters.

2. Identify four ways you could more effectively communicate about money matters.

3. List four things that parents can do to help their children be better money managers.

WHAT DO YOU RECOMMEND *NOW?*

Now that you have read the chapter on managing checking and savings accounts, what would you recommend to Nathan Rosenberg and Allysa Adams in the case at the beginning of the chapter regarding:

1. Where they can obtain the monetary asset management services that they need?
2. Their best use of checking accounts and savings accounts as they begin saving for a home?
3. The use of a money market account for their monetary asset management?
4. Their use of electronic banking in the future?
5. How they can best discuss the management of their money and finances?

BIG PICTURE SUMMARY OF LEARNING OBJECTIVES

LO1 Identify the goals of monetary asset management and sources of such financial services.

Maximizing interest earnings and minimizing fees on savings and checking accounts is the goal of monetary asset management. The primary providers of monetary asset management services include depository institutions (such as insured accounts at banks and credit unions), stock brokerage firms, mutual funds, financial services companies, and insurance companies.

LO2 Understand and employ the various types of accounts available to meet the goals of monetary asset management.

Day-to-day monetary asset management is conducted best via an interest-earning checking account that is used to pay monthly living expenses. Money market accounts provide similar functions and, though not insured, are extremely safe. When setting up an account, consider charges, fees, and penalties. For funds not needed for six months to five years into the future you can use some type of savings oriented accounts that allow you to accumulate and hold funds and earn higher rates of interest. Savings accounts are where most people start. Certificates of deposit (CDs) allow you to

safely earn even higher returns if you are willing to forgo liquidity. When your income begins to exceed expenses on a regular basis, it is wise to move excess funds into a money market account. Asset management accounts combine the functions of checking and savings and more into one package account at many of the providers of monetary asset management services.

LO3 Describe your legal protections when conducting monetary asset management electronically.

Electronic money management occurs whenever banking transactions are conducted via computers without the customer using paper documents. Electronic banking includes the use of automatic teller machines (ATMs), point-of-sale (POS) terminals, debit cards, and stored-value cards. The Electronic Funds Transfer Act protects consumers who use electronic money management.

LO4 Discuss your personal finances and money management more effectively with loved ones.

Recognize the psychological and emotional aspects of money, and identify your own approaches to money. Communicate openly and frequently about money matters by using "I" statements.

LET'S TALK ABOUT IT

1. **Bank Account Fees.** Describe some examples of checking and savings account transactions that result in assessment of fees or penalties. Which are the least and most avoidable?

2. **Avoiding Overdraft Fees.** You know someone who recently had $90 in overdraft fees for two small debit card transactions. Explain to him why such high fees resulted from such small transactions and the relative benefits of having an automatic funds transfer agreement versus an automatic overdraft loan agreement versus overdraft protection.

3. **Forms of Account Ownership.** When would you recommend using an individual account, a joint tenancy with right of survivorship account, and a tenancy by the entirety account for your monetary assets?

4. **Opting in.** Many people desire protection from the possibility of overdrawing their checking account. Banks make it easy by allowing you to opt into overdraft

protection. Explain how this and other overdraft protections work and why the true cost of opting in may exceed the benefits.

5. **Earning Higher Interest on Your Savings.** When might it be appropriate for you to save via a certificate of deposit versus a money market account?

6. **Lost/Stolen Debit Cards.** What should you do if your ATM or debit card is lost or stolen? Why?

7. **Talking About Money.** Have you ever had a disagreement with a friend or family member over a money issue? How might you communicate differently now?

8. **Money Issues for Young Couples.** Review the questions for those contemplating marriage that are listed on page 158. Discuss the importance of these questions. Most couples do not discuss these issues early in a relationship. Why do you think that is so, and what do you think you will do should the challenge arise for you?

DO THE MATH

1. **Invest Now or Later? Twins Kimberly and Kaitlyn are both age 27.** Beginning at age 27, Kimberly invests $2000 per year for ten years and then never sets aside another penny. Kaitlyn waits ten years and then invests $2000 per year for the next 30 years. Assuming they both earn 7 percent, how much will each twin have at age 67? (Hint: Use Appendixes A.1 and A.3 or visit the *Garman/ Forgue* companion website.)

2. **The Benefit of a Higher APY.** Isabel Lopez, age 18, recently received an inheritance of $50,000 from her grandmother's estate. She plans to use the money for the down payment on a home in ten years when she finishes her education. Right now the funds are in a savings account paying 1.0 percent APY. How much would Isabel have in ten years if instead she purchased a ten-year CD paying 3.0 percent? (Hint: Use Appendix A.1 or visit the *Garman/ Forgue* companion website.)

3. **Reconciling a Checking Account.** Andrew Parker has a checking account at the credit union affiliated with his university. Illustrated below are his check register and monthly statement for the account. Reconcile the checking account and answer the following questions.

DO IT IN CLASS
PAGE 147

(a) What is the total of the outstanding checks?

(b) What is the total of the outstanding deposits?

(c) Why is there a difference between the uncorrected balance in the check register and the balance on the statement?

(d) What is the updated and correct balance in the check register to the right?

Account Name	Andrew Parker		Period of Activity	11/2/15–12/01/15
Account #	123–45678			
Summary of Your Activity This Month				
Date	Activity		Amount	Balance
11/02				$ 412.66
11/04	Debit Card POS Transaction		$17.46	395.20
11/09	Check #237		33.33	361.87
11/12	Direct Deposit		876.99	1238.86
11/13	Debit Card POS Transaction		84.56	1154.30
11/13	EFT		22.00	1132.30
11/15	Check#238		645.00	487.30
11/23	Debit Card POS Transaction		68.87	418.43
11/27	Debit Card POS Transaction		43.00	375.43
11/28	Deposit		200.00	575.43
11/30	Check#239		125.00	450.43
11/30	Service Charge		4.50	445.93
11/30	ATM Withdrawal		100.00	345.93
12/01	Check #240		46.00	299.93

Date	Check #	Payee/ Payor	For	Amount	Balance
11/01					412.66
11/03	Debit Card	CVS	Cold Meds	$ 17.46	395.20
11/05	237	Univ. Book-store	Of Mice and Men	33.33	361.87
11/12	Deposit	PNC Bank	Payday-Yeah!	876.99	1238.86
11/12	238	ABC Property Mgmt.	Rent	645.00	593.86
11/13	Debit Card	Kroger's	Groceries	84.56	509.30
11/13	Electronic Payment	Maysville Water	Water Bill	22.00	487.30
11/23	Debit Card	Kroger's	Groceries	67.88	419.42
11/23	Debit Card	Applebee's	Dinner with Karen	43.00	376.42
11/27	Deposit	Mom	For Utilities	200.00	576.42
11/27	239	Duke Power	Electric/ Heat Bill	125.00	451.42

Date	Check #	Payee/ Payor	For	Amount	Balance
11/27	240	Conoco	Gas	46.00	405.42
11/30	Debit Card	ATM With-drawal	Carry Around Money	100.00	305.42
12/01	241	Comcast	Cable Bill	53.88	252.54

4. **Saving for College.** You want to create a college fund for a child who is now 3 years old. The fund should grow to $30,000 in 15 years. If an investment available to you will yield 6 percent per year, how much must you invest in a lump sum now to realize the $30,000 when needed? (Hint: Use Appendix A.2 or visit the *Garman/Forgue* companion website.)

5. **Saving for Retirement.** You plan to retire in 40 years. To provide for your retirement, you initiate a savings program of $4000 per year yielding 7 percent. What will be the value of the retirement fund after 40 years? (Hint: Use Appendix A.3 or visit the *Garman/Forgue* companion website.)

FINANCIAL PLANNING CASES

CASE 1

How Should the Johnsons Manage Their Cash?

In January, Harry and Belinda Johnson had $3540 in monetary assets (see page 99): $1178 in cash on hand; $890 in a statement savings account at First Federal Bank earning 1.0 percent interest compounded daily; $560 in a statement savings account at the Far West Savings and Loan earning 1.1 percent interest compounded semiannually; $160 in a share account at the Smith Brokerage Credit Union earning a dividend of 1.3 percent compounded quarterly; and $752 in their non-interest-earning regular checking account at First Interstate.

(a) What specific recommendations would you give the Johnsons for selecting checking and savings accounts that will enable them to effectively use the first and second tools of monetary asset management?

(b) Their annual budget, cash-flow calendar, and revolving savings fund (see Tables 3-6, 3-7, and 3-8 on pages 87–89) indicate that the Johnsons will have additional amounts to deposit in the coming year. What are your recommendations for the Johnsons regarding use of a money market account? Why?

(c) What savings instrument would you recommend for their savings, given their objective of saving enough to purchase a new home? Support your answer.

(d) If the Johnsons could put most of their cash on hand ($1000) into a money market account earning 1.4 percent, how much would they have in the account after one year?

(e) Recall from Chapter 3 that Harry and Belinda had significant disagreements regarding their anniversary dinner and holiday gift spending and ended up not having a draft balanced budget for the year. Provide some advice for the couple about how to resolve or, better, prevent such disagreements in the future.

CASE 2

Victor and Maria Hernandez Need to Save Money Fast

The Hernandez family is experiencing some financial pressures, even though the couple has a combined income of $66,000. Also, their eldest son, Joseph, will start college in only three years. Maria is contemplating going to work full time to add about $25,000 to the family's annual income.

(a) How will this change in income affect the family's emergency fund needs?

(b) How much should they save annually for the next three years if they want to build up Joseph's college fund to $20,000, assuming a 3 percent rate of return and ignoring taxes on the interest? (Hint: Use Appendix A.1 or visit the *Garman/Forgue* companion website.)

(c) Given their 25 percent marginal tax rate, what is the Hernandezes' after-tax return on their savings and how would that affect the amount they would need to save each year?

(d) What savings options are open to the Hernandezes that could reduce or eliminate the effects of taxes on their savings program?

CASE 3

Julia Price Thinks About Using Checking and Savings Accounts

Julia's six-figure salary has allowed her to build up a considerable cash reserve of over $20,000. She initially had basic checking and savings accounts. She also has a credit card with her bank that she uses to make most of her purchases, thereby earning reward points. She is careful to pay the account balance in full each month. Over time, she purchased several CDs. About three years ago, she also opened a money market deposit account at her bank in which she keeps almost $10,000. Last week she got a call from the bank suggesting that she open a cash management account to coordinate her accounts and maximize her overall earnings. She is hesitant to do so as she feels her current arrangement meets her needs. Offer your opinions about her thinking.

CASE 4

Liability for a Lost ATM Card

DO IT IN CLASS PAGE 155

Joshua Franz earned $4600 during the summer and put $3500 of the money in a newly opened savings account for use during the school year. It is now November 4th and Joshua went to the bank to withdraw $1000. The teller informed him that there was only $200 in the account. When Josua protested, the teller informed him that there had been three ATM $1100 withdrawals from the account on the last day of the month in August, September and October. Joshua typically neglects to open the statements he had received on the third day of each month. When he got home he could not find the ATM card he had received when he opened the account in mid-August and recalled that he had found his car door open in his parking lot in late August but had thought nothing was taken. When he opened the statements he saw the record of each of the withdrawals. He went immediately back to the bank to tell them of the loss. How much money will Joshua lose because of these fraudulent transactions?

CASE 5

The Impact of Federal Deposit Insurance

Alexandra Bronson, age 58, has done a very good job of accumulating savings over the years. She has all of her

accounts at the same depository institution and has multiple accounts. Her balances are as follows:

DO IT IN CLASS PAGE 142

$130,000 in a joint-checking account with her husband; $145,000 in a joint-savings account with her sister from an inheritance they received; $100,000 in a savings account in her own name with her sister as the payable at death party (also from the inheritance); and $75,000 in a savings account in her own name. She also has an individual retirement account (IRA) in her own name with a balance of $459,000. How much federal deposit insurance does Alexandra have in these accounts, and how much of her funds remain uninsured?

CASE 6

How Ownership Affects Who Will Receive Assets After a Death

DO IT IN CLASS PAGE 152

Bang Liu passed away recently at age 67. Among his assets where the following items. 1) Checking and savings accounts with a total balance of $45,000 with his widow, Fen, held in joint tenancy with right of survivorship. 2) A paid-for $330,000 home with his widow, Fen, held in joint tenancy with right of survivorship. 3) A $144,000 vacation cottage owned equally with his brother held in tenancy in common. 4) A dry cleaning business valued at $280,000 owned equal shares with his business partner, Fai, held in tenancy in common. 5) An automobile valued at $14,000 owned individually. 6) Two savings accounts of $20,000 each with his daughter named as payable at death party on one and his son named as payable at death party on the other. Bang's will names his widow as his sole heir. For each asset, identify who will receive all, or what portions, of the asset.

CASE 7

Which Is Better: A Minimum-balance Account or an Average-balance Account?

DO IT IN CLASS PAGE 145

Aaron Searle, a service station owner from Moscow, Idaho, has been paying $30 per month in fees on his checking account for about a year. He is considering changing banks but fears that the fees will be similar no matter where he banks. He has tracked his high-, low- and average-balance on his account for the last six months and found the following:

Month	Highest Balance	Lowest Balance	Average Balance
1	$4800	$1200	$2400
2	$4300	$300	$1700
3	$3600	$900	$1200
4	$5100	$1700	$2700
5	$3500	$400	$900
6	$4100	$1200	$2100

In your opinion, would Aaron be better off with a minimum-balance account or an average-balance account to minimize his fees? What other advice would you have for Aaron regarding the avoidance of a monthly fee on his account?

CASE 8

Deciding Among the Tools of Monetary Asset Management

Kwaku Addo, a licensed physical therapist from Columbia, Missouri, earns $4200 per month take-home pay and has the funds directly deposited in his checking account. He spends only about $3500 per month, and the excess funds have been building up in his account for about two years.

(a) What other types of accounts are available to Kwaku?

(b) How might he manage his accounts to earn as much interest as possible and keep his money safe?

(c) How might he use electronic money management to accomplish these tasks?

BE YOUR OWN PERSONAL FINANCIAL MANAGER

1. **Checking and Savings Accounts.** Create a table outlining the rates, rules, and fees of your checking and savings accounts. Use Table 5-2 on page 146 as a guide for the types of information to include. Assess the appropriateness of the accounts for you and shop for more appropriate accounts if necessary using Worksheet 23: Selecting a Checking Account That Meets My Needs from "My Personal Financial Planner" as a guide for your selection process.

   MY PERSONAL FINANCIAL PLANNER

2. **Keep Your Accounts Current.** Go online every few days to monitor checking account activity. Use the "Did You Know?" box on page 147 or Worksheet 24: Reconciling My Checking Account from "My Personal Financial Planner" to help reconcile your account monthly.

   MY PERSONAL FINANCIAL PLANNER

3. **Protect Your Privacy.** Confirm the existence and amount of each transaction in your checking and savings accounts soon after receiving your account statements. Report any discrepancies immediately.

4. **Prepare for Possible Identity Theft.** Create a table listing all of your checking, savings, and credit card accounts. For each, list the account number and customer service address and telephone number. Store the document in a safe location for easy access should you find that any unauthorized use has occurred or that the account "plastic" has been lost or stolen.

5. **Talk About Money.** If married or cohabiting, schedule a regular time to discuss finances with your partner. Use the material on pages 157–161 as a guide for the topics and tone of the discussions. To get your conversation started, you might pose the following questions: If we unexpectedly received $10,000 tax free, what would we do with it? If we had to cut our spending by 10 percent, where would we make the reductions?

ON THE NET

Go to the Web pages indicated to complete these exercises.

1. Visit the website for the Federal Reserve Board, where you will find articles (www.federalreserve.gov/consumer info/bankaccountservices.htm) on checking accounts. Browse through the articles to find five things you could do that would help you get the most out of your checking account.

2. Visit the website for Bankrate.com at www.bankrate .com/checking.aspx for information about checking accounts. Use the search box to find articles on "Check 21," which governs check clearing and processing. How might the rules of Check 21 affect your use of your checking account?

3. Visit the Bankrate.com website at www.bankrate.com/ compare-rates.aspx where you will find information about rates of return on certificates of deposit. What is the best rate for a one-year CD and a five-year CD in a large city near your home (look in the state, then the city)? How do these rates compare with the average rates nationally and the highest rates nationally?

4. Visit the website for FDIC at www.fdic.gov. Use the search box to find articles on "internet banking." Read the article titled "Safe Internet Banking." After reading the information, make a list of important positive and negative aspects of Internet banking. Is Internet banking right for you?

ACTION INVOLVEMENT PROJECTS

1. **Checking Accounts Where You Live.** Select several banks, savings banks, or credit unions in your community. Contact each to gather information on the types of checking accounts they offer and the basic rules of the accounts, including overdraft protections, fees, and interest rates. Make a table that summarizes your findings, and identify one institution that best meets your needs.

2. **Account Monitoring.** Survey five of your friends about their patterns of monitoring their checking and savings accounts. Compare what they do to your own pattern.

3. **Debit and ATM Activity.** Survey five of your friends about the patterns and amounts of their typical debit and ATM card usage. Compare their patterns to your own and those recommended in this chapter.

4. **Money Talk.** Survey five couples to ascertain their patterns of money talk. Ask each the following questions: "What are the areas of your finances that are easiest to discuss?" "What are your areas of most difficulty?" "How do you resolve disagreements?" Make a table that summarizes your findings and identify one institution that best meets your needs.

Visit the Garman/Forgue companion website at www.cengagebrain.com.

6 Building and Maintaining Good Credit

YOU MUST BE KIDDING, RIGHT?

People with no prior credit history or those who show poor repayment patterns in the past often wonder if they will ever be able to get credit, especially during economic times when credit is difficult to obtain. Simply put, will any lender want to trust them? Which of the following is true about the availability of credit for people in such situations?

A. Sadly, they will be doomed to a lifetime of no access to credit.

B. There are a few lenders who will be happy to provide credit to such borrowers.

C. Most of the "big name" banks will grant them credit.

D. Credit will be relatively easy to obtain for such borrowers just about anywhere.

The answer is B. It is difficult for people with poor or no credit to obtain credit from most banks and credit unions. But some lenders do accept such applicants, and they will charge high interest rates. Building and maintaining a good credit history does more than get you access to credit. It will also get you low interest rates!

LEARNING OBJECTIVES

After reading this chapter, you should be able to:

1 Explain reasons for and against using credit.

2 Establish your own debt limit.

3 Achieve a good credit reputation.

4 Describe the common sources of consumer credit.

5 Identify signs of over indebtedness, and describe the options that are available for debt relief.

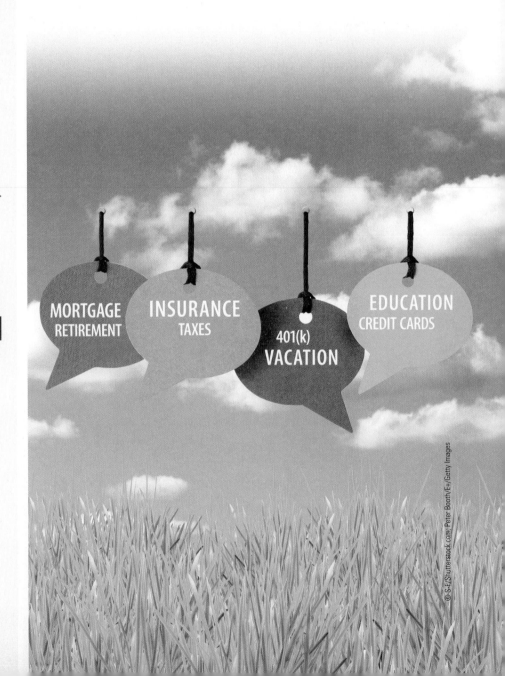

MORTGAGE RETIREMENT

INSURANCE TAXES

401(k) VACATION

EDUCATION CREDIT CARDS

WHAT DO YOU RECOMMEND?

Hanna Savarin, age 25, is a nurse practitioner with the local health department in Collegedale, Tennessee. She earns $65,000 per year, with about $9000 of her income coming from overtime pay. Her disposable income is about $3800 per month. Her employer provides a qualified tax-sheltered retirement plan to which Hanna contributes 4 percent of her salary and for which she receives an additional 4 percent matching contribution from her employer. (She could contribute up to 6 percent with an equal employer match.) Hanna has $29,000 in outstanding student loans on which she will pay $454 per month over the next five years, and her total credit card debt is $3000 on which she has been paying $120 per month. Otherwise, she is debt free. Hanna would like to purchase a new or late-model used car to replace the car she has been driving since her senior year in high school. She has $2000 to use as a down payment.

Barry Austin Photography/Getty Images

What would you recommend to Hanna on the subject of building and maintaining good credit regarding:

1. **Factors she should consider regarding her ability to take on additional debt?**

2. **The impact of her current debt on her ability to obtain a loan to buy a vehicle?**

3. **Where she might obtain financing for a vehicle loan?**

4. **The effect of taking on a loan on her overall financial planning?**

LEARNING OBJECTIVE 1

Explain reasons for and against using credit.

credit cards
Cards that allow repeated use of credit as long as the consumer makes regular monthly payments.

credit
An arrangement in which goods, services, or money is received in exchange for a promise to repay at a future date.

loan
Consumer credit that is repaid in equal amounts over a set period of time.

credit card blocking
Occurs when hotel or other service providers place a hold on a card holder's account to reflect the anticipated cost of services.

Your financial success depends heavily on your ability to make the sacrifices necessary to spend less than you earn. This allows you to save money for future uses. Yet, you are likely to use credit to buy housing and vehicles as well as use **credit cards**. However, paying high interest rates and overuse of credit impedes your financial success.

The term **credit** describes an arrangement in which goods, services, or money is received in exchange for a promise to repay at a future date. Consumer credit usually takes the form of a **loan** that is repaid in equal payments over a set period of time. You also are likely to use **revolving credit**, which allows repeated use of credit as long as regular, monthly payments are maintained. Credit cards are an example of revolving credit.

There are valid reasons for using credit. You should use credit only when necessary, pay low interest rates, make repayments on time, and repay amounts owed as quickly as possible.

6.1 REASONS FOR AND AGAINST USING CREDIT

Credit represents a form of trust established between a lender and a borrower. If the lender believes that a prospective borrower has both the ability and the willingness to repay money, then credit will be extended. The borrower is expected to live up to that trust by repaying the lender. For the privilege of borrowing, a lender requires that a borrower pay interest and sometimes other charges.

You can distinguish between good and bad uses of credit. Among the good uses are a mortgage loan to buy a home, a loan to open a business, and to finance education expenses. These purposes have benefits because the funds are invested in ways that can have a long-term payoff. Bad uses of credit include using a credit card or student loans money to support a better lifestyle than really needed and loans for extravagant homes and vehicles.

6.1a Good Uses of Credit

There are good reasons for using credit:

1. **For convenience.** Using credit cards simplifies the process of making many purchases. Convenience use is justified *only* if the card balance is paid in full each month, however. You do not want to be paying for today's restaurant meal for months or years in the future.

2. **For emergencies.** Consumers use credit to pay for unexpected expenses such as emergency medical services and automobile repairs.

3. **To make reservations.** Most motels, hotels, and car rental agencies require some form of deposit to hold a reservation. A credit card number can serve as such a deposit, allowing guaranteed reservations to be made over the telephone. In many cases, the hotel will notify the credit card issuer to put a hold on your account for the anticipated total amount of the charge. This common practice is called **credit card blocking**.

4. **To own expensive products sooner.** Buying "big ticket" items such as a home or automobile on credit allows the consumer to enjoy immediate use of the product. Many expensive items would not be purchased (or would be bought only after several years of saving) without the opportunity to pay for them over time. The expected life of the product should be at least as long as the repayment period on the debt.

5. **To take advantage of free credit.** Merchants sometimes offer "free" credit for a period of time as an inducement to buy. Free credit, however, should not be used to buy a more expensive item than you can afford. Known as "same as cash" or "interest-free" terms, these programs allow the buyer to pay later without incurring finance charges.

The free credit lasts for a defined time period, but interest may be owed for the entire time period if the buyer repays even one day after the allotted free-credit period ends.

6. **For protection against rip-offs and frauds.** Internet and telephone purchases made on a credit card can be contested with the credit card issuer under the guidelines of the Fair Credit Billing Act (FCBA), as discussed more fully in Chapter 7. The protections afforded by the FCBA are not available when using a debit card.

7. **To obtain an education.** The high cost of education has forced many students to use student loans. This may be one of the better uses of credit, as the borrower is investing in himself or herself to raise the quality of life and/or income in the future. The amount borrowed should be compared to the projected extra income provided by the education to be obtained.

FINANCIAL POWER POINT

Debt Has Enormous Opportunity Costs

When people take on debt they often neglect to save or invest. Taking on too much debt early in life, instead of saving and investing, can compromise your goal of being financially successful.

6.1b The Downside of Credit

Despite its benefits, the use of credit has significant negatives.

1. **Credit reduces your financial flexibility and buying power.** The greatest disadvantage of credit use comes from the loss of financial flexibility in personal money management. As the old proverb states, "He who borrows sells his freedom." The money that you pay each month on your debt is money you could have spent elsewhere on other opportunities. Also, credit can be seen as a promise for you to "work for the creditor" in the future to pay off your debt. People rarely go through life without taking on debt from time to time, but repaying debt for years and years is not a smart move. Mortgage debt reduces significantly the flexibility you will need at that time in your life, so make paying off your home before retirement an important financial priority.

2. **Interest itself is costly.** Interest represents the price of credit. It is the "rent" you pay while you use someone else's money. When stated in dollars, interest makes up the **finance charge**, which is the total dollar amount paid to use credit (including interest and any other required charges such as a loan application fee). The Truth in Lending Act requires lenders to state the finance charge both in dollars and as an **annual percentage rate (APR)**. The APR expresses the cost of credit on a yearly basis as a percentage rate. For example, a one-year, single-payment loan for $1000 with a finance charge of $140 has a 14 percent APR.

3. **It is tempting to spend more money.** A major disadvantage of credit is that its use can lead to overspending. Using a credit card to buy $425 worth of new clothes and paying off $25 per month over 20 months costs and extra $75 in interest (20 × $25 = $500 − $425) may seem less painful than paying cash or spending less money, perhaps only $300, on clothing. This tendency to spend more is why sellers promote buying on credit so heavily.

4. **Overindebtedness is a real possibility.** Consumers with monthly nonmortgage debt repayments amounting to 15 percent of monthly take-home pay or more are considered to be precariously in debt. They teeter on the brink of disaster. If they begin missing payments, they run a high risk of a poor credit reputation, damage to employment prospects, an increase in rates paid for insurance, difficulty in renting or buying a home, and the possible repossession of some purchased items.

interest
In this context, interest is the "rent" you pay for using credit.

finance charge
Total dollar amount paid to use credit.

annual percentage rate (APR)
Expresses the cost of credit on a yearly basis as a percentage rate.

CONCEPT CHECK 6.1

1. Which two good uses of credit seem most reasonable to you? Which do not?

2. Explain the two downsides of credit that would be most worrisome for you.

3. Distinguish between the APR and the finance charge on a debt.

6.2 SET YOUR OWN DEBT LIMIT

debt limit
Overall maximum you believe you should owe based on your ability to meet repayment obligations.

DO IT IN CLASS

You should set your **debt limit**, which is the overall maximum you believe you should owe based on your ability to meet the repayment obligations. Most people's debt limit is and should be lower than what lenders are willing to offer. Lenders are willing to take chances that some borrowers will not repay, knowing that some of the interest paid by other borrowers will cover the unpaid debts. There are four methods to determine your debt limit.

6.2a Method 1: Debt-to-Income Method

The **debt-to-income method (DTI)** was introduced in Chapter 3 on page 78. Using the debt-to-income method your monthly debt repayments (including your prospective mortgage, and any other loan or alimony payments you must make) are divided by your gross monthly income (your income before taxes) and multiplied by 100. A ratio of 36 percent or less is desirable. Home loan seekers may not exceed 43 percent to obtain a qualified residential mortgage (details in Chapter 9).

6.2b Method 2: Debt Payments-to-Disposable Income Method

debt payments-to-disposable income method
Percentage of disposable personal income available for regular debt repayments aside from set obligations.

disposable income
Amount of income remaining after taxes and withholding for such purposes as insurance and union dues.

DO IT IN CLASS

The **debt payments-to-disposable income method** uses the **debt-payments-to-disposable income ratio** also introduced in Chapter 3 on page 78. Recall that this ratio excludes the first mortgage loan on a home and credit card charges that are paid in full each month. **Disposable income** is the amount of your income remaining after taxes and withholding for such purposes as insurance and union dues. Note that the debt payments-to-disposable income method focuses on the amount of monthly debt repayment—not the total debt. As a result, it also would be wise to consider the length of time that the severe financial situation caused by high debt payments might last. You could get yourself into financial trouble for many years.

Table 6-1 shows some monthly debt-payment limits expressed as a percentage of disposable personal income. As the table indicates, with monthly payments representing 15 to 18 percent of monthly disposable personal income, a borrower is precariously overindebted and fully extended; taking on additional debt would be unwise.

Table 6-2 shows the effects on a budget of increasing one's level of debt. In the table, after deductions, disposable personal income amounts to $2200 per month. Current budgeted expenses (totaling the full $2200) are allocated in a sample distribution throughout the

---

Table 6-1 Debt-Payment Limits as a Percentage of Disposable Personal Income*

Percent	Current Debt Situation	Borrower's Feelings	Take on Additional Debt?
0	No debt at all	No stress about personal finances	Taking on some consumer debt is fine
10 or less	Little debt	Borrower feels no stress from debt repayment obligations	More debt could be undertaken cautiously
11 to 14	Safe debt limit but fully extended financially	Borrower is moderately stressed about pressure from debt repayment obligations	Should not acquire more debt
15 to 18	Precariously overindebted	Borrower starts to feel seriously stressed about debts and hopes no emergency arises	Absolutely should not take on more debt
19 to 28	Seriously overindebted	Borrower feels overwhelming stress and is desperate about debts	Contact a nonprofit credit counseling company
29+	Excessively overindebted	Borrower feels hopeless or knows his or her debts are so large that he or she is doomed to financial failure	Contact a bankruptcy attorney

*Excluding home mortgage loan repayments and convenience credit card purchases to be repaid in full when the monthly bill arrives.

various categories. As you can see, increasing debt payments to 25 percent of disposable income ($550 per month; perhaps to buy a new automobile) has dramatic effects on this budget.

Where would you make reductions as debt load grows? Spending a few minutes changing the figures in Table 6-2 will give you an idea of your priorities and the size of the debt limit that you might establish.

DO IT IN CLASS

Table 6-2   Effects of Increasing Debt Payments on a Budget*

Gross income	$34,000				
Deductions for taxes, insurance	$ 7,600				
Disposable personal income	$26,400				
Monthly disposable income	$ 2,200				
	No Debt	**10% Debt**	**15% Debt**	**20% Debt**	**25% Debt**
Rent	$ 700	$ 700	$ 700	$ 700	$ 700
Savings and investments	250	180	120	80	50
Food	280	250	240	220	210
Utilities (telephone, electricity, heat)	130	130	130	120	120
Insurance (automobile, renter's, and life)	80	80	80	80	80
Transportation expenses	100	90	90	80	80
Charitable contributions	60	50	50	40	40
Entertainment	140	120	110	100	80
Clothing	50	40	30	20	20
Vacations and long weekends	60	50	40	40	30
Medical/dental expenses	60	50	50	50	50
Newspapers and magazines	40	30	30	30	0
Cable TV	50	50	40	40	30
Personal care	30	20	20	20	20
Gifts and holidays	40	30	30	30	30
Health club	60	60	60	60	60
Miscellaneous	70	50	50	50	50
Debt repayments	0	220	330	440	550
TOTAL	$2,200	$2,200	$2,200	$2,200	$2,200

*One person's decisions on where to cut back expenses to make increasing monthly debt payments.

DID YOU KNOW

Bias Toward Overconfidence

People engaged in building and maintaining good credit have a bias toward certain behaviors that can be harmful, such as a tendency toward overconfidence. Examples are young adults who take on heavy student loan debt and people who finance large sums to buy a large new home or expensive vehicle. What to do? Calculate your current debt load ratios before taking on new debt and also calculate what they will be with the new debt; then, if necessary, adjust the borrowed amount down appropriately.

6.2c   Method 3: Compare Debt-to-Equity

Another method for determining your debt limit involves calculating the ratio of your consumer debt to your assets. The **debt-to-equity ratio** compares the **equity** in a person's assets (the amount by which the value of those assets exceeds debts) with amounts owed. This ratio excludes first mortgage assets and debt because the total amount of mortgage debt usually does not get people into trouble; it is the payments themselves that do so. The ratio of debt-to-equity method provides a quick idea of one's financial solvency. A ratio in excess of 0.33 is considered high.

6.2d   Method 4: Continuous-Debt Method

Another approach for determining your debt limit is the **continuous-debt method**. If you are unable to get completely out of debt every four years (except for a mortgage loan), you probably lean on debt too heavily. You could be developing a credit lifestyle in which you will never eliminate debt and will continuously pay out substantial amounts of income for finance charges—likely $1200 or more per year, and that is like throwing away $100 every month!

6.2e   Dual-Earner Households Should Set a Lower Debt Limit

Having two incomes in a household has its benefits. Two people, each of whom earns $42,000 per year, will gross $84,000, with a disposable personal income of around $63,000, or $5250 monthly. It may seem that the couple can afford a much higher level of debt than before the incomes were combined, but beware.

DID YOU KNOW

How to Manage Student Loan Debt

Total student loan debt outstanding now exceeds $1 trillion, more than that owed on all credit cards combined. Two-thirds of students borrow for school costs, and the average student with such debt owes more than $27,000 at graduation; this is double what it was 20 years ago. Such student loan debt makes it very difficult to buy a vehicle, a home, and save for retirement. While in school, strive to keep your student debt down. Here are some tips for managing the student debt:

1. *Always know your outstanding debt and required monthly payment. Both while in school and after graduation you should fully understand how much you owe and your future or current payment based on a ten-year payoff. The payment can calculated at www.bankrate.com/calculators/managing-debt/loan-calculator.aspx. If you do not know your interest rate, ask your loan servicer or use 5 percent as an estimate.*

2. *Choose your most advantageous repayment pattern allowed. The standard repayment plan for student loan debt calls for equal monthly installments paid over ten years, but to pay the debt off faster, you* can establish a graduated repayment plan whereby the payments are lower in the early years but then increase in later years.

3. *Make your repayments on time, every time. In some programs, if you make the first 48 payments on time, the interest rate will be reduced by 2 percentage points. Failing to repay in a timely manner can have dire consequences, including forfeiture of federal and state income tax refunds, as well as Social Security and veterans' benefits.*

4. *Pay electronically. Make arrangements to have the monthly payment transferred electronically out of a checking account and you can receive a small reduction in the interest rate.*

5. *Consolidate your student loans. Consolidating your education loans means that all your existing loans are paid off and one new loan is created. This strategy may allow for a much more convenient repayment schedule. The interest rate may be lower, and the amount of time for repayment may be longer, resulting in a lower monthly payment under the new loan. Loans can be*

consolidated through a private bank or through one of two government programs: Sallie Mae (www.salliemae .com) or Federal Direct Consolidation Loans (www .loanconsolidation.ed.gov).

6. *If desired, sign up for the Federal government's income-based repayment plan.* If your student loan debt is very high compared to your salary, you may qualify for a plan that has low payments and the

remaining debt is forgiven after 25 years if you have made payments consistently up to that point. See www.studentaid.ed.gov/. You may also qualify for reduced payments if you work in a public-service job, in an underserved profession, or for a national service organization such as AmeriCorps. Go to www.finaid .org/loans/forgiveness.phtml.

Two incomes should not mean a doubled debt limit.

Many young couples adopt a lifestyle based on two incomes. Their spending grows in tandem with their rising incomes. After a while, they are spending and borrowing to the limit. This situation cannot go on forever, of course. Eventually they may begin to feel financially stressed and wonder, "How can we be so broke when we make so much money?" When a child comes along or one partner loses a job or overtime pay, they may quickly get into deep financial trouble as debts that had been manageable with two incomes quickly become overwhelming.

Couples would be wise to set a debt limit based on the higher of their two incomes and use the second income to build savings accounts and make investments early in their lives together. That will truly protect their future financial security. This is one of the smartest financial actions a couple can make—save and invest extra money early in a relationship.

CONCEPT CHECK 6.2

1. Distinguish among the debt payments-to-disposable income, debt-service-to-income, debt-to-equity ratios, and continuous-debt methods for setting your debt limit.

2. What are the threshold levels for both the debt payments-to-disposable income, debt-service-to-income and ratio of debt-to-equity ratios that would indicate that a person is carrying too much debt?

3. Discuss how dual-earner households should consider their ability to carry additional debt.

Tips for Keeping Student Loan Debt Down

You should try to limit your total student loan debt to no more than the average of your projected annual take-home pay over the first ten years after you graduate. That way, you can repay your loan in ten years by using about 10 percent of your income each year.

Here's how you can keep student debt from becoming too much to handle:

1. Work part-time or increase your work hours to lower the amount you must borrow.

2. Set aside funds to pay down the debt as soon as you graduate.

6.3 OBTAINING CREDIT AND BUILDING A GOOD CREDIT REPUTATION

LEARNING OBJECTIVE 3

Achieve a good credit reputation.

Credit is widely and readily available to most of us today. It is not unusual for a customer to walk into a retail store such as Target or Home Depot and be offered a credit card account that can be used immediately. However, if the applicant has not used credit previously (no credit), or has bounced a lot of checks, or has failed to honor credit agreements in the past (bad credit), the offer may be withdrawn or changed after the credit check to a much higher interest rate. Your success in obtaining credit at a low interest rate depends on an understanding of the credit approval process and having a good credit reputation.

6.3a The Credit Approval Process

To obtain credit, you must first complete a credit application. Based on the information in this application, the lender will investigate your credit history. The information is then evaluated (sometimes instantly via computer), and the lender decides whether to extend credit. When an application is approved, the rules of the account are established.

Turn Bad Habits into Good Ones

Do You Do This?

Ignore the list of transactions in your credit card account statements

Assume your credit bureau files are correct and up to date

Borrow from your own bank when you need new credit

Assume you are doing fine if you can make your monthly debt payments

Do This Instead!

Inspect your statements for errors and signs of identity theft

Check your file for free with one of the three credit bureaus alternating every four months

Shop at various lenders for the best credit terms and lowest APR

At least once a year, calculate your debt limit using appropriate ratios

You Apply for Credit A **credit application** is a form or an interview that requests information that sheds light on your ability and willingness to repay debts. This information helps lenders make informed decisions about whether they will be repaid by borrowers. Answering questions completely and honestly both on an application form and during an interview (if any) is important. If inconsistencies arise during the lender's subsequent investigation of the applicant's credit history, the lender could refuse the request for credit or charge a higher interest rate. At the time of application, ask for a copy of the rules governing the account, including the APR and repayment terms. However, the offered terms are not final and can change when the actual decision to lend is made. This is one reason why you should read all credit contracts before signing.

The Lender Obtains Your Credit Report Upon receiving your completed credit application, the lender conducts a **credit investigation** and compares the findings with the information on your application. The goal of the investigation is to assess the applicant's creditworthiness. Lenders want to know the applicant's prior credit usage and repayment patterns, income, length of employment, and home ownership status.

To conduct its investigation, the lender obtains a **credit report** from a **credit bureau** that keeps records of many borrowers' credit histories. Credit bureaus compile information from merchants, utility companies, banks, court records, and creditors. There are three major national credit-reporting bureaus: Experian, TransUnion, and Equifax. A lender may consult one or all of the bureaus when you apply for credit.

The Lender Also Obtains Your Credit Score Lenders use a **credit score** (also known as a **risk score**) in which a statistical measure is used to rate applicants on the basis of various factors deemed relevant to creditworthiness and the likelihood of repayment. All three of the major credit reporting bureaus also calculate and report credit scores to lenders and there are more than 50 versions of the scores from the three credit bureaus.

The most well-known score is the FICO score developed by Fair Isaac Corporation. The generic FICO score ranges from 300 to 850. FICO and other brand credit scores have been developed for many specific uses such as vehicle loans, mortgages, and credit cards, and the range of scores differs somewhat on each. Lenders are free to use whatever scoring system they prefer. So the odds are slim that the score you obtain on your own will be the exact score the lender will use. It is a good idea when you have applied for credit to ask the lender for the score it used as well as the source.

The Lender Decides Whether to Accept the Application and Under What Terms The approval or rejection of credit is based on the lender's judgment of the willingness and ability of the applicant to repay the debt. If the application is accepted, a contract is created that outlines the rules governing the account. For credit cards, this contract is called a **credit agreement**. For loans, the contract is called a **promissory note** (or simply, the **note**).

Approximately 15 percent of all people who apply for credit are denied. Half of the unsuccessful applicants have no established **credit history** (a continuing record of a person's credit usage and repayment of debts) or their credit history contains negative information. The other half have low credit scores or are attempting to take on too much debt.

Credit scoring simply allows lenders to categorize credit users according to the perceived level of risk. Under the concept of **tiered pricing**, lenders may offer lower interest rates to applicants with the highest credit scores while charging steeper rates to more risky applicants. The difference in rates is modest except for those with scores below 620. People with such low credit scores can often find some lender that will say yes. However, the interest rates will be higher. The lender (not a credit bureau) always makes the decision about whether to grant credit.

FINANCIAL POWER POINT

What to Do Before You Apply for Credit

To get the lowest interest rates possible, you should make sure that your credit bureau file is accurate before filling out a credit application. If possible, you should do this at least three months in advance to allow time for you to correct any errors or omissions in your file.

---

credit application

Form or interview that provides information about your ability and willingness to repay debts.

credit report

Information compiled by a credit bureau from merchants, utility companies, banks, court records, and creditors about your payment history.

credit bureau

Firm that collects and keeps records of many borrowers' credit histories.

credit score (risk score)

Statistical measure used to rate applicants based on various factors deemed relevant to creditworthiness and the likelihood of repayment.

credit agreement

Contract that stipulates repayment terms for credit cards.

promissory note (note)

Contract that stipulates repayment terms for a loan.

credit history

Continuing record of a person's credit usage and repayment of debts.

DID YOU KNOW

Making Sense of Credit Scores

Although the credit-scoring systems in use today go by a number of brand names, the most widely known is the generic **FICO score** developed by Fair Isaac Corporation (www.myfico.com). Because your credit file and the method of calculating the score may differ at each of the three major credit bureaus, your credit score at each may differ as well. (See "Access Your Credit Bureau File for Free" on page 180.) Under the Fair and Accurate Credit Transactions Act, credit bureaus must provide consumers with their credit scores upon request. A nominal fee of about $20 is charged for a credit score report. However, if you are denied credit altogether or at less than favorable rates you must be told why, and if the reason was your credit score you may request a credit score report at no charge.

Credit scores are produced via complex statistical models that correlate certain borrower characteristics with the likelihood of repayment. The exact methodologies employed in the models, though similar, are closely held secrets. The factors used in the FICO score system are shared openly by Fair Isaac Corporation on the company's website:

1. **Payment history.** Are you late with your payments? How late? How often? On how many of your accounts?

2. **Amounts owed.** What is the balance on each of your credit obligations? (Even if you pay in full each month, there might be a balance on a given date.) How do the amounts owed vary on various types of accounts, such as credit cards versus loans? How many accounts have balances? Are you maxed out or nearly so on your cards, regardless of the dollar amount of your balances? (Credit scores are negatively affected if you have a balance on any card in excess of 30 percent of the credit limit on that card.) On loans, how much of the original loan is still owed?

3. **Length of credit history.** How long have you had each account? How long has it been since you used the accounts?

4. **Taking on more debt.** How many new accounts do you have? How long has it been since you opened a new account? How many recent inquiries have been made by lenders to which you have made application? If you had a period of poor credit usage in the past, for how long have you been in good standing?

5. **Types of credit used.** Do you have a good mix of credit usage, with reliance on multiple types depending on the purpose of the credit (for example, not using a credit card to buy a boat)? How many accounts in total do you have?

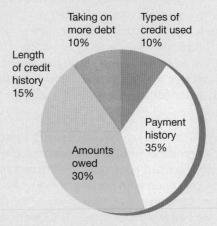

The median FICO score is about 736. About one-fourth of consumers have a FICO score below 620, making it nearly impossible to get a loan from all but the most expensive types of lenders. The FICO website provides suggestions on how to improve your FICO score. For example, if you are maxed out on two cards and have low balances on others, you might shift some of the large balances to other cards so that you owe no more than 30 percent of the debt limit on any of your cards. This percentage, known as the **credit utilization ratio**, contributes almost one-third of the weight of your credit score. The chart above indicates the relative importance of each of the five factors in the development of FICO scores.

6.3b Your Credit Reputation

The information about you that is contained in credit bureau files is one of the most important aspects of your financial life. It is used not only when lenders decide whether to approve your applications for credit but also when you apply for a job, insurance, and rent or buy housing. Thus, it is important that you build a good credit reputation and ensure that the information in your file is as accurate as possible and up to date.

DID YOU KNOW

Unfair Credit Discrimination Is Unlawful

The Equal Credit Opportunity Act (ECOA) prohibits certain types of **unfair discrimination** (making distinctions among individuals based on unfair criteria) when granting credit. Under this law, a lender must notify an applicant within 30 days about the lender's acceptance or rejection of a credit application.

The ECOA also requires the creditor to provide the applicant with a written statement, if requested, detailing the reasons for refusing credit. Rejecting a credit application due to poor credit history is legal. Conversely, it is illegal to reject applicants on the basis of gender, race, age, national origin, religion, marital status, or receipt of Social Security income, child-bearing plans, or public assistance. (Applicants may offer such information voluntarily, however.) Always request that a lender who turns you down

for credit provide you with the credit score it used in the decision and the name of the credit bureau that provided the score.

A creditor cannot require an applicant to disclose income from alimony, separate maintenance payments, or child support payments. If the borrower wants this income to be counted during the lender's evaluation of the application, the creditor can consider whether that income stream is received consistently. Information about a spouse or former spouse may not be requested unless the spouse will use the account, it is a joint account, or repayment of debts will rely on the spouse's income or other financial support. The law requires that credit granted in both spouses' names be used to build a credit history for the parties as a couple as well as for each individual spouse.

Build a Strong Credit History Some people who are new to the world of credit wonder whether they will ever get credit when they need it. They will if they establish a good credit history. This is what is meant when someone is said to have "good credit." The following steps can help you build a strong credit history:

1. **Establish both a checking account and a savings account.** Lenders see people who can handle these accounts as being more likely to manage credit usage properly.
2. **Have your cell phone and utilities billed in your name.** The fact that you can maintain a good payment pattern on your utility bills indicates that you can manage your money wisely and will do the same with your credit repayments.
3. **Request, acquire, and use a retail credit card.** These cards are relatively easy to obtain. Use the credit sparingly, and the entire balance in full and on time each month as these card have high APRs.
4. **Apply for a bank credit card.** Your own bank is the best place to start your search for a credit card. If not successful there, you usually can find some bank that will issue you a card (search at www.bankrate .com). The credit limit may be low (perhaps $1000) and the APR high (perhaps 27 percent), but at least the opportunity exists to establish a credit history. Later, you can request an increase in the credit limit and a lower APR.
5. **Ask a bank for a small, short-term cash loan.** Putting these borrowed funds into a savings account at the bank will almost guarantee that you will make the required three or four monthly payments. In addition, the interest charges on the loan will be partially offset by the interest earned on the savings.

FINANCIAL POWER POINT

Closing Accounts Does Not Help Your Credit Score

Many people incorrectly think that closing some existing credit card accounts will help raise their credit score. This is not usually the case unless you have a very large number of accounts that you do not use. When accounts are closed, it reduces the ratio between what you owe to the total amount of credit available on all credit cards, and that smaller window of credit available is what reduces your credit score. Also, credit scores are higher when accounts have been open for longer periods of time. Therefore, if you feel you must close accounts, close your newest accounts, not the oldest. Also take care to ensure that closing accounts does not raise your credit utilization ratio above 30 percent.

6. **Stay current on your student loans.** Many young adults have their first exposure to credit through the student loans. Making payments on time and paying off these loans quickly will show prospective lenders that you are a responsible borrower.

Access Your Credit Bureau File for Free Federal law requires credit bureaus to provide consumers with their credit reports upon request. You can obtain one report for free each year from each of the national credit bureaus. In addition, consumers must be notified if merchants report negative information to a credit bureau. You should request a report periodically (certainly every year) and whenever you move, have a change in family status (marry, get divorced, or become widowed), or after resolving any credit billing errors or disputes.

Only One Website Is Truly Free To obtain a free credit report, simply contact www.annualcreditreport.com. This is the *only* site that links you directly to the mechanism for obtaining a free report.

www.annualcreditreport.com

For a free credit report, visit www.annualcreditreport.com.

DID YOU KNOW

Credit Monitoring Is Costly and Unnecessary

If you go to websites other than annualcreditreport.com to obtain a copy of your credit report for a "free" credit score you will be enticed to sign up for a **credit-monitoring service**. Such services allow you to access your report as often as daily and perhaps even obtain a generic personal credit score, supposedly for free for a month or two.

However, these offers always are **negative option plans**. Thus you will be automatically signed up for a plan costing as much as $100 or more per year and your membership will renew automatically unless you notify them that you want to renew at the end of the free period. This is a bad deal, especially when you can obtain the information in your files for free.

Actually, You Can Obtain a Free Report Every Four Months The free annual credit report law allows you to check your credit for free every four months. How? By staggering your requests across the three national bureaus. For example, in January you can request a report from Experian through www.annualcreditreport.com. Then, in May you can order a report from TransUnion. In September you can request a report from Equifax. Then in January, it's back to Experian. Because the bureaus all gather information from essentially the same sources, you can have some confidence that what appears on one file will be present in the others. If you find an error, contact all three to make the correction. The major credit bureaus often sell lists of consumer names in their files (but not each consumer's specific credit history information) for credit card marketing purposes. To have your name withheld for two years from this practice, call (888) 567-8688 or go online at www.optoutprescreen.com.

ADVICE FROM A PROFESSIONAL

Guard Your Privacy

Identity theft is a form of stealing someone's identity in which someone pretends to be someone else by assuming that person's identity, usually as a method to gain access to resources or obtain credit and other benefits in that person's name. It is the fastest growing crime in America. Over 17 million Americans each year fall victim to identity theft and lose over $25 billion. Fortunately, a vigilant watch over personal documents can greatly reduce the risk of becoming a victim of identity theft.

Identify theft thieves can take bills and account information out of mailboxes, steal wallets, memorize debit card information from watching victims at ATMs, and piece together bills and bank account statements found in the trash. With a Social Security number, they can steal from already established bank and credit accounts, open new credit accounts, rent or buy housing, obtain a new driver's license or passport, obtain a tax refund, and utilize medical services. All this can saddle the victim with thousands of dollars in legal fees to restore their identity.

YOU SHOULD NEVER:

- Carry anything in your wallet that contains your Social Security number.

- Write your Social Security number or other identifying information like a credit card number on a check, and realize that merchants are prohibited from recording such information on a check.

- Keep Social Security numbers, bank account, medical insurance, or other sensitive information on hard drives, tablets, or cell phones, because even a so-so hacker can obtain quick access to the sensitive information.

- Give your credit card or bank information numbers over the telephone unless you initiated the contact with the merchant.

- Respond to emails claiming that your bank or a government agency is trying to reach you.

YOU SHOULD ALWAYS:

- Use hard to crack PINs and passwords and make sure that no two accounts share the same PIN number or password.

- Consider using "password generating software" to create unique passwords.

- Ask insurance companies (and others) to assign each customer a randomly generated "ID" instead of using Social Security numbers.

- Ask financial institutions for "two-factor authentication" for online transactions, which makes hacking into accounts more difficult.

- Shred sensitive documents before recycling or throwing them away.

- Consider using automatic bank deposits, filing income taxes electronically, and paying bills online to minimize opportunities for thieves.

- Consider placing a **security freeze** on your credit report, which for a small fee is an effective way to prevent unauthorized credit accounts from being opened in your name. With a freeze, you tell the credit bureaus not to release your financial records to anyone without specifically obtaining your written consent.

- Remember the Federal Trade Commission's "Identity Theft" website www.consumer.ftc.gov/articles /0277-create-identity-theft-report/.

Holly Hunts
Montana State University

Fair Credit Reporting Act (FCRA)

Requires that credit reports contain only accurate relevant information and allows consumers to challenge errors or omissions of information in their reports.

Here's How to Fix Errors in Your Report When you obtain your report, you should thoroughly inspect it for accuracy. If you find an error, the **Fair Credit Reporting Act (FCRA)** allows you to challenge the error as it requires that reports contain accurate information. It also requires that only bona fide users be permitted to review your file for approved purposes. The FCRA governs both lenders and credit bureaus.

If you find an error or omission in a credit report from a particular credit bureau, you should immediately take steps to correct the information since the FCRA is partially enforced by consumers and also by the Consumer Financial Protection Bureau (CFPB) Here is how to assert your rights:

1. Simultaneously notify both the credit bureau and the original lender of the error and ask the original lender for confirmation of the debt. State that you wish to exercise your right to a reinvestigation under FCRA. Specifically, you should ask the bureau to "reaffirm" the item or delete it.
2. The bureau and lender must reinvestigate the information within 45 days. If the bureau cannot complete its investigation within 45 days, it must drop the information from your credit file.
3. If the information was erroneous, it must be corrected. If a report containing the error was sent to a creditor investigating your application within the past six months, a corrected report must be sent to that creditor.

consumer statement

Your version of disputed information in your credit report when the credit bureau refuses to remove the disputed item.

4. If the credit bureau refuses to make a correction (perhaps because the information was "technically correct"), you may wish to provide your version of the disputed information (in 100 words or less) by adding a **consumer statement** to your credit bureau file. This statement will be included with any credit reports by that bureau.
5. Also obtain a report from the other two bureaus to ensure that the error does not also appear in their files. If an error appears, correct it beginning at step #2.
6. If you have trouble getting erroneous information removed, contact the CFPB.

DID YOU KNOW

The Effects of Divorce on Your Credit

The breakup of a marriage affects the creditworthiness of both partners. The Federal Trade Commission offers the following suggestions for individuals seeking a divorce.

Pay careful attention to credit accounts held jointly, including mortgages, second mortgages, and credit cards. The behavior of one divorcing spouse will continue to affect the other individual as long as the accounts are held in both names. One party could make credit card charges, for example, and refuse to pay the debt, leaving the financial burden on the other party. Ask creditors to close joint accounts. Then, if possible reopen them as individual accounts. Never accept a creditor's verbal assurance, either over the telephone or in person, that an account has been closed. Always insist on written confirmation, including the effective date of the account closure.

When debts were accumulated in both names, a divorce decree has no legal effect on who technically owes the debts. Creditors can legally collect from *either* of the divorcing parties when the accounts were held jointly. If the person absolved of responsibility for the debt under the divorce decree is forced by a creditor to pay off the account, he or she must then go to court to seek enforcement of the divorce decree and collect reimbursement from the former spouse.

Both before and after a divorce, get copies of your credit report from all three credit bureaus. Check them for accuracy and challenge any problem areas, such as accounts, that continue to be shown in both names.

CONCEPT CHECK 6.3

1. Summarize the basic steps that occur when someone applies for credit.
2. What is a credit history, and what role do credit bureaus play in the development of your credit history?
3. What is a credit score, and what five major factors go into its calculation?
4. Identify five actions you can take to build a good credit reputation.
5. Summarize the protections provided under the Fair Credit Reporting Act.

6.4 SOURCES OF CONSUMER LOANS

Today's consumers have many sources of consumer loans from which to choose. Most lending to consumers occurs through depository institutions and sales finance companies. Other sources include consumer finance companies, stockbrokers, and insurance companies. Table 6-3 shows the interest rates charged and example payment amounts and finance charges were you to borrow $1,000 from these various sources of consumer loans.

LEARNING OBJECTIVE 4
Describe the common sources of consumer credit.

6.4a Depository Institutions Lend Money to Their Customers

Depository institutions include commercial banks, mutual savings banks, savings banks, and credit unions (see Chapter 5 on pages 140 and 141 for more-detailed descriptions of these institutions). They tend to make loans to their own customers and to noncustomers with good credit histories. Depository institutions offer highly competitive rates, partly because the funds loaned are obtained primarily from their depositors. The interest rate commonly ranges from 4 to 18 percent. Research indicates that many people who go elsewhere for loans actually meet the qualifications for depository institution lending and as a result end up paying a higher interest rate than necessary.

6.4b Sales Finance Companies Lend Money to Purchasers of Consumer Products

A **sales finance company** is a seller-related lender (such as Ally Financial for General Motors and Ford Credit for Ford vehicles) whose primary business is financing the sales

sales finance company
Seller-related lender whose primary business is financing sales for its parent company.

Table 6-3 Estimating What It Costs to Borrow Money ($1,000)

Lender	Annual Percentage Rate	Two-Year Loan		Five-Year Loan	
		Monthly Payment	Finance Charge	Monthly Payment	Finance Charge
Life insurance company	4	$43.42	$ 42.19	$18.42	$104.99
Sales finance company	6	44.32	63.68	19.33	159.80
Credit union	8	45.23	85.52	20.28	216.80
Commercial bank	10	46.14	107.36	21.25	275.00
Mutual savings bank	10	46.14	107.36	21.25	275.00
Savings and loan association	10	46.14	107.36	21.25	275.00
Bank credit card	18	49.92	198.08	25.39	523.40
Consumer finance company	24	52.87	268.88	28.77	726.20

Credit costs money. Just how much can be seen by considering the cost of borrowing $1000 for two years and for five years from various sources at various interest rates.

DID YOU KNOW

Compare APRs Not Lenders

Knowing the APR simplifies making comparisons among credit arrangements. The lower the APR the lower the true cost of the credit. The APR can be used to compare credit contracts from different sources, with different time periods, finance charges, repayment schedules, and amounts borrowed.

All states have **usury laws** (sometimes called **small loan laws**) that establish the maximum loan amounts, interest rates, and credit-related fees for different types of loans from various sources. These maximum rates may vary from 18 percent to as much as 54 percent. These laws also apply to bank credit card fees, such as annual fee and late payment fees.

of its parent company. Such state licensed firms specialize in making purchase loans, often with the item being bought serving as the collateral for the loan. Because the seller often works in close association with the sales finance company, credit can be approved on the spot.

Sales finance companies require collateral and deal only with customers who are considered medium to good risks. Thus, their interest rates are often competitive with those offered by depository institutions. Their interest rates may be even lower than those offered by other sources when the seller subsidizes the rate to encourage sales—as with the special low-APR financing often offered on new cars, for example. Most new-car loans today are made by sales finance companies.

6.4c Consumer Finance Companies Make Small Cash Loans

consumer finance company/ small-loan company

Firm that specializes in making relatively small secured or unsecured loans that require monthly installment payments.

A **consumer finance company** specializes in making relatively small loans and is, therefore, also known as a **small-loan company**. These state licensed lenders range from the well-recognized large corporations to many local neighborhood lenders. Such companies make both secured and unsecured loans at relatively high interest rates and require repayment on a monthly installment basis. They focus mainly on the **subprime lending** market. This market focuses on lending to people who have FICO scores of less than 620 and normally would not qualify for any credit elsewhere.

DID YOU KNOW

Alternative Lenders Offer High-Priced Credit

High-priced credit can come from alternative lenders such as payday lenders, rent-to-own stores, and pawnshops.

Payday lenders (which are illegal in some states) are businesses that grant credit when they honor a personal check but agree not to deposit the check for a week or longer. The fees for check cashing are often 20 percent or more of the amount of the check, pushing the annual percentage rate from 20 to 300 to 700 percent. Eighty percent of payday borrowers either roll over their loans or take out larger loans further escalating the cost of borrowing.

A **rent-to-own program** offered through a rent-to-own store provides a mechanism for buying an item with little or no down payment by renting it for a period of time, after which it is owned. Furniture, appliances, and electronic entertainment items are commonly sold via the rent-to-own approach.

These programs have two big drawbacks for consumers. First, the renter does not own the item until the final payment is made. Paying late or stopping payments will cause the products to be seized with no allowance being made for the previous "rental" payments. Second, the actual cost for renting items is often exorbitantly high. For example, a TV worth $1000 might be rented for $39 per week for one year, producing a finance charge of $1028 [(52 × $39) − $1000].

A **pawnshop** is a business that offers secured loans to people, with items of personal property used as collateral that the borrower turns over to the pawnshop. The lender offers single-payment loans, often ranging from $100 to $500, for short time periods (typically two to six months). The dollar amount loaned is typically equal to one-third or less of the value of the item pawned. In most states, to get the cash a borrower need merely turn over the item, present identification, and sign on the dotted line.

The pawnshop owner can legally sell the item if the borrower fails to redeem the property by paying the amount due, plus interest, within the time period specified. The pawnshop commonly charges an interest rate of about 5 percent per month plus a 2 percent monthly storage fee; thus, the annual combined "interest" amounts to 84 percent $[(5 + 2) \times 12]$.

Approximately one-fifth of all loans granted by consumer finance companies are for the purpose of **debt consolidation**. Here the borrowed takes out one new loan to pay off many others. This is often done to secure a lower interest rate, secure a fixed interest rate or for the convenience of servicing only one loan. Other common uses of such loans are for travel, vacations, education, automobiles, and home furnishings. Some small-loan companies specialize in making loans by mail. They advertise on the Internet as well as in newspapers and magazines to attract borrowers, who complete a credit application and receive approval via e-mail or mail.

6.4d Stockbrokers and Employers Lend Money to Their Clients

People build significant assets in investment accounts that may be earmarked for their children's college education, their own retirement, or other purposes. If you have a margin account (see Chapter 14), you can borrow from your stockbroker using your investments as collateral. Although many people prefer not to tap into these investment funds directly, it is possible to borrow from these accounts.

Also, it usually is possible to borrow from one's employer-sponsored, tax-sheltered retirement account (see Chapter 17), depending on the rules of the plan. Care must be taken to ensure that the loan plus interest is repaid so that the savings goal can still be met. Serious consequences may arise if one changes employers or the retirement account loan is not repaid. (See Chapter 17 for details.)

6.4e Insurance Companies Lend Money to Their Policyholders

Insurance companies, such as State Farm or Allstate, offer credit cards to their policyholders. Policyholders who have cash-value life insurance policies also can obtain loans based on the cash values built up in their policies. An advantage to borrowing on a cash-value life insurance policy is that the interest rates are low, ranging from 4 to 9 percent even though the policyholders actually are borrowing their own money. Many people fail to pay back such loans because no fixed schedule of repayment is established and insurance companies do not pressure borrowers to repay the debt. If the insured person dies before repaying the loan, the life insurance company will deduct the amount of the loan from the amount that would otherwise be paid on the policy.

6.4f Choose Your Source of Credit Wisely

Figure 6-1 provides a representation of various lenders with those with the highest standards at the top of the pyramid and those with the lowest standards at the bottom. Try to borrow from lenders as high on the pyramid as possible.

DID YOU KNOW

Money Websites for Building and Maintaining Good Credit

Informative websites for building and maintaining good credit, including credit scores are:

Bankrate.com (www.bankrate.com /debt-management.aspx)

Center for Responsible Lending (www .responsiblelending.org/)

Consumer Financial Protection Bureau (www.consumerfinance.gov/)

Federal Reserve Board (www.federal reserve.gov/creditreports/default.htm)

Federal Trade Commission (www .consumer.ftc.gov/topics/money-credit)

FICO (www.myfico.com)

MyMoney.gov (www.mymoney.gov /borrow/Pages/borrow.aspx)

National Foundation for Credit Counseling (www.nfcc.org/)

NOLO (www.nolo.com/legal-encyclopedia /collection-agencies)

Sallie Mae (www.salliemae.com/)

Figure 6-1 **The Credit Pyramid**

Source: Michael Rupured, © University of Georgia Cooperative Extension. Used with permission.

CONCEPT CHECK 6.4

1. List the types of depository institutions that are sources of credit for consumers.

2. Distinguish between a sales finance company and a consumer finance company.

3. Summarize how stockbrokers and insurance companies serve as sources of consumer credit.

4. Explain where you would go to obtain credit at the lowest cost.

6.5 DEALING WITH OVERINDEBTEDNESS

LEARNING OBJECTIVE 5

Identify signs of overindebtedness, and describe the options that are available for debt relief.

overindebted

When one's excessive personal debts make repayment difficult and cause financial distress.

People become **overindebted** when their excessive personal debts make repayment difficult and cause financial distress.

6.5a Ten Signs of Overindebtedness

1. **Not knowing how much you owe.** Have you lost track of how much you owe? Do you avoid reality by not adding up the total? Are you afraid to add up how much debt you have?

2. **Running out of money.** Are you using credit cards on occasions when you previously used cash? Are you borrowing to pay insurance premiums, taxes, or other large, predictable bills? Are you borrowing to pay for regular expenses such as food or gasoline? Do you try to borrow from friends and relatives to carry you through the month?

DID YOU KNOW

Sean's Success Story

Sean's success as a personal financial manager is reflected in his debt situation. While in college, Sean worked part-time for his living expenses and only used student loans to pay for his tuition and fees. He had a credit card that provided cash-back rewards. He used the card for most of his expenses and paid the balance due in full each month. He used the cash-back amount each year to help pay for a road trip during spring break. During his senior year, Sean checked his credit report with all three national bureaus.

He found one or two mistakes in each and had the errors corrected. He now checks one of the files every four months. Sean has been considering the purchase of a new vehicle so he purchased his FICO score and was pleased to see that the score was above 800, indicating that he would qualify for a loan at the lowest possible rates. He plans to seek preapproval from at least three sources including his credit union before visiting a dealership. Sean's approach to building and maintaining good credit will benefit him for years to come.

3. **Paying only the minimum amount due.** Do you pay the minimum payment—or just a little more than the minimum—on your credit cards instead of making large payments to more quickly reduce the balance owed?

4. **Exceeding debt limits and credit limits.** Are you spending 15 percent or more of your take-home pay on nonmortgage credit repayments? Do you sometimes reach the maximum approved credit limits on your credit cards?

5. **Requesting new credit cards and increases in credit limits.** Have you applied for additional credit cards to increase your borrowing capacity? Have you asked for increases in credit limits on your current credit cards?

6. **Using cash advances to pay other credit cards.** Have you obtained a cash advance on one credit card to make a payment due on another card? Have you used a cash advance to pay other bills?

7. **Paying late or skipping credit payments.** Are you late once or more a year in paying your mortgage, rent, vehicle loan or lease, or utility bills? Do you sometimes pay late charges? Are you juggling bills to pay the utilities, rent, or mortgage? Are creditors sending overdue notices?

8. **Taking add-on loans.** Taking **add-on loans**, also called **flipping**, occurs when you refinance or rewrite a loan for an even larger amount before it has been completely repaid. Suppose that a loan of $1000 has been repaid down to $400. You decide to refinance the debt balance of $400 by borrowing $2000 and using the additional $1600 ($2000 − $400) for other purposes.

9. **Using debt-consolidation loans.** Are you borrowing, perhaps from a new source, to pay off old debts? Such action may temporarily reduce pressure on your budget, but it also indicates that you are overly indebted.

10. **Experiencing garnishment.** **Garnishment** is a court-sanctioned procedure by which a portion of the debtor's wages are set aside by the debtor's employer to pay money owed. Wages and salary income, including that of military personnel, can be garnished. The Truth in Lending Act prohibits more than two garnishments of one person's paycheck. The total amount garnished cannot represent more than 25 percent of a person's disposable income for the pay period or more than the amount by which the weekly disposable income exceeds 30 times the federal minimum wage (whichever is less). In addition, the law prohibits garnishment from being used as grounds for employment discharge.

garnishment
Court-sanctioned procedure by which a portion of debtors' wages are set aside by their employers to pay debts.

11. **Experiencing repossession or foreclosure.** **Repossession** is a legal proceeding by which the lender seizes an asset (called **foreclosure**, if the property is a home)

repossession/foreclosure
Legal proceeding by which the lender seizes an asset.

FINANCIAL POWER POINT

Old Debts May Never Die

It is not uncommon for a credit collector to contact someone who thought a debt was written off by a lender and demand repayment. This may occur years later. A single dollar of repayment by you will start the clock ticking again, because if you make a partial payment you "reaffirm" the debt as valid; thus you will owe the whole balance all over again.

for nonpayment of a loan. When a lender repossesses property, the borrower may still owe some money on the debt. A **deficiency balance** occurs when the sum of money raised by the sale of the repossessed collateral fails to cover the amount owed on the debt plus any repossession expenses (collection, attorney, and court costs) paid by the creditor.

To illustrate this point, consider what happened to Maria Peterson, a staff sergeant in the army from San Diego, California, whose husband lost his civilian job. In an attempt to reduce expenditures, Maria voluntarily turned her Chevrolet Malibu back to the finance company while still owing $11,000 on the debt. A month later, she was notified that the vehicle had been sold at auction for $7800; the proceeds were reduced to only $7100, however, due to collection and selling costs of $500 and attorney fees of $200. Maria was billed for a deficiency balance of $3900 ($11,000 − $7100). She would have been much better off had she sold the vehicle herself, as vehicles at auction usually sell for much less than their book values.

deficiency balance

Occurs when money raised by the sale of repossessed collateral doesn't cover the amount owed on the debt plus any repossession expenses.

Fair Debt Collection Practices Act (FDCPA)

Prohibits third-party debt collection agencies from using abusive, deceptive, or unfair practices to collect past-due debts.

debt collection agency

Firm that specializes in collecting debts that the original lender could not collect.

6.5b   Federal Law Regulates Debt Collection Practices

The federal **Fair Debt Collection Practices Act (FDCPA)** prohibits third-party debt collection agencies from using abusive, deceptive, and unfair practices in the legitimate effort to collect past-due debts. **Debt (or credit) collection agencies** are firms that specialize in making collections that could not be obtained by the original lender. In some cases, they assist the original lender (for a fee); in other cases, they take over (purchase) the debt and become a new creditor. When a debtor offers to make payment for several debts, the FDCPA requires that the amount paid must be applied to whichever debts the debtor desires. Banks, dentists, lawyers, and others who conduct their own collections (second-party collectors) are exempt from the provisions of the FDCPA. Nevertheless, many states have enacted similar laws that govern these second-party collectors.

Collection agencies are prohibited from telephoning the debtor at unusual hours, making numerous repeated telephone calls during the day, not applying payments to amounts under dispute, using deceptive practices (such as falsely claiming that their representatives are attorneys or government officials), making threats, or using abusive language. They also cannot telephone a debtor's employer.

Even with these limitations, collection agencies can be irritatingly persistent when collecting past-due accounts. If the collection effort is not successful, the creditor may take the debtor to court to seek a legal judgment against the debtor; this judgment may be collected by repossessing some of the debtor's property or garnishing wages. More than one third of Americans have been reported to collection agencies for unpaid bills.

6.5c   Steps to Take to Get Out from Under Excessive Debt

Even the most well-meaning credit user can become overextended as a result of illness, unemployment, or divorce. What should you do if you realize that you are overly indebted?

1. **Determine your account balances and the payments required.** Find out exactly what it would take to pay off your balances today. This amount is not the same as the total of your remaining payments and very likely includes additional fees, penalties and late charges if you have been late in your payments.

2. **Focus your budget on debt reduction.** Calculate the percentage of your budget necessary to make the payments on your debts, and then add 5 percent. Use this extra money to help pay your creditors by applying the extra money to the debt with the highest APR. Paying off small debts might give a psychological boost but it is the high APR largest debts that are the most expensive. And remember, paying off debts provides a higher "rate of return" than money in savings and investments, so "invest" your money in debt repayment first.

3. **Contact your creditors.** Try to work out a new payment plan with your creditors. Many lenders, including those that finance vehicles, may let you skip a payment. They want to see you solve your financial problems so you can avoid bankruptcy. Creditors are more likely to work with borrowers who come to them first rather than after collection efforts begin.

4. **Take on no new credit.** Return your credit cards to the issuer or lock them up so that you cannot use them. Disciplined action to reduce debt should show results in only a few months. If progress does not occur, seek professional help.

5. **Refinance.** Determine whether some loans can be refinanced to obtain a lower interest rate, especially mortgage loans. (See Chapter 9 for details.) Even if you refinance, keep making the same payment so you will pay the new loan off more quickly. Consumers who have difficulty making credit repayments may resort to a **debt-consolidation loan**, through which the debtor exchanges several smaller debts with varying due dates and interest rates for a single large loan. You should avoid the temptation to use this strategy simply to lower your total monthly payments.

6. **Avoid credit repair and debt settlement companies.** Many companies claim that they want to help people in debt. A **credit repair company** (also known as a **credit clinic**) is a firm that offers to help improve or clean up a person's credit history for a fee. Experts say that none are reputable. The Credit Repair Organization Act (CROA) makes it illegal for credit repair companies to lie about what they can do for you, and to charge you before they've performed their services. The CROA is enforced by the Federal Trade Commission and requires credit repair companies to explain your legal rights in a written contract. The contract must specify the cost, services they will perform, how long it will take to get results, and explain your three-day right to cancel without any change.

    In reality, no company can remove or "fix" accurate but negative information in anyone's credit history. You can improve your future credit history by making on-time repayments. And you can correct errors in your credit bureau files on your own for free with little effort.

    Debt settlement companies also are to be avoided. These firms promise to reduce your debt by negotiating with your creditor. Debt settlement programs typically are offered by for-profit companies and involve the company negotiating with your creditors to allow you to pay a "settlement" to resolve your debt. The settlement is another word for a lump sum that is less than the full amount you owe. To make that lump sum payment, the company asks that you stop making monthly payments to your creditors. Instead you are supposed to set aside a specific amount of money every month in a savings account and you are to transfer this amount every month into an escrow-like account to accumulate enough savings to pay off a settlement that is reached eventually.

    One of your problems is that those creditors will have reported late payments to the credit bureaus, which will stay on your credit file for up to seven years. Also, no "paid in full" notations will be in your credit report, and the IRS may assess you for income taxes due on the debts cancelled.

7. **Find good help.** You may be able to obtain free budget and credit advice from your employer, credit union, or labor union. Also, many banks and consumer finance companies offer advice to help financially distressed debtors, as do nonprofit **credit counseling agencies (CCAs)**. Such an agency can make arrangements with unsecured creditors to collect payments from overly indebted consumers to repay debts, and it can provide individuals with credit counseling, assistance with financial problems, educational materials on credit and budgeting, and a **debt management plan (DMP)**.

    A DMP is an arrangement whereby the consumer provides one monthly payment (usually somewhat smaller than the total of previous credit payments) that is distributed to all creditors. Creditor concessions, such as reduced interest rates, may also allow debtors to repay what they owe more quickly than would otherwise be possible.

DO IT IN CLASS

debt-consolidation loan
A loan taken out to pay off several smaller debts.

credit repair company (credit clinic)
Firm that offers to help improve or fix a person's credit history for a (usually hefty) fee.

credit counseling agency (CCA)
Agency that can arrange payment schedules with unsecured creditors for overly indebted consumers and can provide individuals with credit counseling.

debt management plan (DMP)
Arrangement whereby the consumer provides one monthly payment (usually somewhat smaller than the total of previous credit payments) that is distributed to all creditors.

FINANCIAL POWER POINT

Debt Management Plans Do Not Impact Your Credit Score

Entering into a debt management plan with a nonprofit credit counseling company will not lower your credit score. A future lender may look at debt management plans unfavorably and either deny credit or charge a higher APR for a DMP participant.

bankruptcy
Constitutionally guaranteed right that permits people (and businesses) to ask a court to wipe out all their debts.

discharged debts
Debts (or portions thereof) that are excused as a result of a bankruptcy.

Chapter 13 of the Bankruptcy Act (wage earner or regular income plan)
Bankruptcy plan designed for individuals with regular incomes who might be able to pay off some or all of their debts given certain court protections.

DID YOU KNOW

Your Worst Financial Blunders in Building and Maintaining Good Credit

Based on others' financial woes, you will make mistakes in personal finance when you:

1. *Fail to regularly check the accuracy of your credit bureau files.*
2. *Let a lender's willingness to grant credit be an indicator that you can afford to repay the debt.*
3. *Pay more than 14 percent of your disposable income toward nonmortgage debt payments.*

Credit counseling services are provided at a nominal cost on a face-to-face basis, online, or via the telephone. Seek a non profit agency that will do a full budget review for you. Make sure the agency is a member of the Association of Independent Consumer Credit Counseling Agencies ([866] 703-8788; www.aiccca.org) or the National Foundation for Credit Counseling ([800] 388-2227; www.nfcc.org). Contact the Better Business Bureau for a reputation report as well.

6.5d Bankruptcy as a Last Resort

When debts are so overbearing that life seems really bleak—a situation that may be aggravated by recent unemployment, illness, hospital bills, disability, death in the family, divorce, or small-business failure—many people consider filing a petition in federal court to declare bankruptcy. **Bankruptcy** is a constitutionally guaranteed right that permits people (and businesses) to ask a court to find them officially unable to meet their debts.

The court will designate some debts as **discharged debts** that are excused. Some debts are never excused through bankruptcy. These include education loans that have come due within the previous seven years, fines, alimony, child support, income taxes for the most recent three years, and debts for causing injury while driving under the influence of alcohol or drugs. Bankruptcy is not a do-it-yourself project. Use a lawyer who specializes in consumer bankruptcies.

Before you can file for bankruptcy, you must complete credit counseling with an agency approved by the United States Bankruptcy Trustee's office. The purpose of this counseling is to give you an idea of whether you really need to file for bankruptcy or whether an informal repayment plan could get you back on your feet financially. Also, you will have to attend another counseling session, this time to learn more about the fundamentals of personal financial management. Only after you submit proof to the court that you have fulfilled this requirement can your attorney request a bankruptcy discharge wiping out many of your debts.

Chapter 13—Regular Income Plan **Chapter 13 of the Bankruptcy Act** (also known as the **wage earner** or the **regular income plan**) is designed for individuals with regular incomes who might be able to pay off some or all of their debts given certain protections of the court. Under this plan, the debtor submits a debt repayment plan to the court that is designed to repay as much of the debt as possible, typically in three to five years. After the debtor files a petition for bankruptcy, the court issues an **automatic stay**—a court order that temporarily prevents all creditors from recovering claims arising from before the start of the bankruptcy proceeding. This action protects the debtor from collection efforts by creditors, including garnishments. Typically, no assets may be sold by the debtor or repossessed by the lender after a stay is granted.

After the court notifies all creditors of the petition for bankruptcy, a hearing is scheduled. With the help of a **bankruptcy trustee** (an agent of the bankruptcy court), who verifies the accuracy of a bankruptcy petition at a hearing and who distributes the assets according to a court-approved plan, the proposed repayment plan is reviewed (and modified, if necessary) and finally approved by the court. The debtor must then follow a strict budget while repaying the obligations. During this time, the bankrupt person cannot obtain any new credit without the permission of the trustee. If the debtor makes all scheduled payments, he or she is discharged of any remaining amounts due that could not be repaid within the repayment period.

Chapter 7—Immediate Liquidation Plan **Chapter 7 of the Bankruptcy Act**, also called **straight bankruptcy**, provides for an immediate liquidation of assets and discharge of debts. This option is permitted

DID YOU KNOW

Don't Wait Too Long to Declare Bankruptcy

The thought of declaring bankruptcy is so onerous for many that some people wait too long to seek its protection. Both Chapter 7 and 13 bankruptcies allow debtors to keep a portion of their assets. For example, 401(k) retirement accounts are 100 percent protected from creditors in bankruptcy. If a debtor begins taking money out of a retirement plan when faced with mounting debt and ultimately declares bankruptcy, the debtor would have used up an asset that could have been fully protected had he or she filed sooner. If the only way you can pay your debts or home mortgage is to tap your retirement plan, you should consult a lawyer about whether the time already has come to seek bankruptcy protection.

when it would be highly unlikely that substantial repayment could ever be made. Petitioners seeking to file Chapter 7 must pass a "means test." Those who fail this test because their income is too high must file Chapter 13 instead.

When Chapter 7 is allowed, most of the bankrupt person's assets are given over to the bankruptcy trustee. Any assets that serve as collateral for loans are turned over to the appropriate secured creditors. Most of the remaining assets are sold, and the proceeds of the sales are distributed to the unsecured creditors of the bankrupt person.

A debtor may choose to sign a **reaffirmation agreement** and become legally obligated again to pay all or a portion of a debt that would have been discharged in the bankruptcy case, such as for a vehicle. Any leftover debt is usually discharged by the court when the debtor emerges from bankruptcy.

State and federal laws govern what assets the debtor can keep. In general, bankrupt people are allowed to keep a small amount of equity in their homes, an inexpensive vehicle, and limited personal property. Discharged debtors usually emerge with little, if any, debt and a much improved net worth and, of course, a lower credit score.

Bankruptcy should be used as a last resort rather than as a quick fix or cure-all for overuse of credit. Bankruptcy remains on one's credit record for ten years. People who have declared bankruptcy typically face years of trouble when renting housing, obtaining home loans, buying insurance, obtaining employment, and getting new credit cards. They also cannot use Chapter 7 bankruptcy again for at least six years. Therefore, some creditors will lend to such individuals, but at much higher interest rates than usual.

Chapter 7 of the Bankruptcy Act (straight bankruptcy)
Provides for the liquidation of assets with proceeds applied to paying off excusable debts to the degree possible.

DO IT NOW!

You know more about personal finance after reading this chapter, so get started right now by:

1. *Obtaining a free copy of your credit report (www.annualcreditreport.com) from one of the three national credit bureaus.*

2. *Confirming the accuracy of the report and, if there are errors or omissions, challenging them.*

3. *Repeating step two every four months, staggering the bureaus to ensure that each request is free.*

 ## CONCEPT CHECK 6.5

1. Identify four signs of overindebtedness.

2. List the major provisions of the Fair Debt Collection Practices Act.

3. What services are provided by a credit counseling agency, and how might a debt management plan work to provide relief for someone who is having debt problems?

4. Distinguish between Chapter 7 and Chapter 13 bankruptcy, and explain who might be forced to use Chapter 13 rather than Chapter 7.

WHAT DO YOU RECOMMEND *NOW?*

Now that you have read this chapter on building and maintaining good credit, what would you recommend to Hanna Savarin regarding:

1. Factors she should consider regarding her ability to take on additional debt?
2. The impact of her current debt on her ability to obtain a loan to buy a vehicle?
3. Where she might obtain financing for a vehicle loan?
4. The effect of taking on a loan on her overall financial planning?

Barry Austin Photography/Getty Images

BIG PICTURE SUMMARY OF LEARNING OBJECTIVES

LO1   **Explain reasons for and against using credit.**

People borrow for a variety of reasons—for example, to deal with financial emergencies, to have goods immediately, and to obtain discounts in the future. Perhaps the greatest disadvantage of using credit is the ensuing loss of financial flexibility in personal money management. The annual percentage rate (APR) provides the best approximation of the true cost of credit.

LO2   **Establish your own debt limit.**

It is important to establish your own debt limit. There are three approaches you can take to do this. One, you can compare debt payments to income. Two, you can compare debt load to your assets. Three, you can determine how long it should take for you to get out of all your debts other than your home mortgage.

LO3   **Achieve a good credit reputation.**

In the process of opening a credit account, the lender investigates your credit history, obtains a credit score (such as a FICO score) from a credit

bureau, and then determines whether to grant credit and under what conditions.

LO4   **Describe the common sources of consumer credit.**

Major sources of consumer loans include depository institutions (commercial banks, savings and loan associations, and credit unions), sales finance companies, and consumer finance companies. Loans are also available through insurance companies and stockbrokers. Depository institutions typically offer the lowest interest rates, although sales finance companies sometimes offer very low rates to increase sales of the products being financed. Only those people with high credit scores qualify for the best rates from any source.

LO5   **Identify signs of overindebtedness, and describe the options that are available for debt relief.**

Among the signals of being overly indebted are exceeding credit-limit guidelines and running out of money too often. People experiencing serious financial difficulties can obtain professional assistance through nonprofit credit counseling agencies or by contacting an attorney about bankruptcy.

LET'S TALK ABOUT IT

1. **Good Versus Bad Debt.** If there is such a thing as good debt, what types of debt do you consider to be "good"? What types do you consider to be "bad"?

2. **Your Creditworthiness.** What aspects of your financial life make you creditworthy? What aspects would make it difficult for you to obtain credit?

3. **Assessing Your Debt Load.** How might students judge whether they are taking on too high a level of student loan debt?

4. **Managing Student Loan Debt.** Use the information on pages 174 and 175 to discuss how best to deal with student loan debt.

5. **Sources to Borrow for a Vehicle.** If you wanted to borrow money to buy a new or used car, where would you turn? Why?

6. **Your Privacy.** Are you concerned that the major national credit bureaus may have files containing information about you? What do you think about the process required to correct errors in those files?

7. **Easy Credit.** Is it too easy for college students to get credit cards? Who do you know who has gotten into financial difficulty because of overuse of credit cards?

8. **Feelings About Bankruptcy.** How do you feel about bankruptcy? When might bankruptcy be justified in your opinion? When might it not be justified?

DO THE MATH

1. **Taking Out a Motorcycle Loan.** Kevin Jones is single and recently graduated from law school. He earns $9000 per month, an awesome salary for someone only 26 years old. He also has $1400 withheld for federal income tax, $540 for state income taxes, $688 for Medicare and Social Security taxes, and $230 for health insurance every month. Kevin has outstanding student loans of almost $80,000 on which he pays about $900 per month and a 0% auto loan payment of $300 on a Ford Fusion Hybrid he purchased new during law school. He is considering taking out a loan to buy a Kawasaki motorcycle.

   DO IT IN CLASS PAGE 172

   (a) What is Kevin's debt payments-to-disposable income ratio?

   (b) Based on your answer to (a), how would you advise Kevin about his plan?

2. **Buying a Vacation Home.** Carmen and Juan Montoya have just finished putting their three daughters through college. As empty-nesters, they are considering purchasing a vacation home on a nearby lake because prices have dropped in recent years. The house might also serve as a retirement home once they retire in 12 years. The Montoyas' net worth is $283,000 including their home worth about $265,000 on which they currently owe $143,000 for their first mortgage. Their outstanding debts in addition to their

   DO IT IN CLASS PAGE 174

mortgage include $12,500 on one car loan, $13,700 on a second car loan, and a $25,500 second mortgage on their home taken out to help pay for college expenses.

   (a) Calculate the Montoyas' debt-to-equity ratio.

   (b) Advise them as to the wisdom of borrowing for a vacation home at this time.

3. **A Recent Graduate's Debt Status.** Chelsea Menken recently graduated with a degree in food science and now works for a major consumer foods company earning $20K per year with about $36,000 in take-home pay. She rents an apartment for $1040 per month. While in school, she accumulated about $38,000 in student loan debt on which she pays $385 per month. During her last fall semester in school, she had an internship in a city about 100 miles from her campus. She used her credit card for her extra expenses and has a current debt on the account of $8000. She has been making the minimum payment on the account of about $320. She has assets of $14,000.

   DO IT IN CLASS PAGES 172 AND 174

   (a) Calculate Chelsea's debt payment-to-disposable income and debt-service-to-income ratios.

   (b) Calculate Chelsea's debt-to-equity ratio.

   (c) Comment on Chelsea's debt situation and her use of student loans and credit cards while in college.

FINANCIAL PLANNING CASES

CASE 1

The Johnsons Attempt to Resolve Their Credit and Cash-Flow Problems

Harry and Belinda have a substantial annual joint income—more than $95,000, in fact. Nevertheless, they expect to experience some cash-flow deficits during several months of the upcoming year (see Tables 3-6 and 3-7 on pages 87–88).

   To resolve this difficulty, the couple is considering opening a credit card account and using it exclusively for those expenditures that will cause the deficits they face. They could also open a line of credit that would

allow them to borrow money by simply going online and having money placed in their checking account.

   (a) What are the advantages and disadvantages of the Johnsons opening these accounts?

   (b) What financial calculations should Harry and Belinda undertake to see whether they could afford to borrow more money at this time?

   (c) What might Harry and Belinda do before applying for credit to ensure that they will pay the lowest interest rate possible?

CASE 2

Victor and Maria Advise Their Niece

Victor and Maria have always enjoyed a close relationship with Maria's niece Teresa, who graduated from college with a pharmacy degree. Teresa recently asked Maria for some assistance with her finances now that her education debts are coming due. She owes $19,000 in student loans and earns $44,000 per year in disposable income. Teresa would like to take on additional debt to furnish her apartment and buy a better car.

(a) What advice might Maria give Teresa about managing her student loan debt?

(b) If next year Teresa were to consolidate her loans into one loan at 6 percent interest, what advice might Maria give regarding Teresa's overall debt limit using both the debt payments-to-disposable income method and the continuous-debt method? (Hint: Use Table 6-3 on page 183 or visit the *Garman/Forgue* companion website to calculate monthly payments for various time periods.)

CASE 3

Julia Price Thinks About a Loan to Buy a Ski Boat

Julia has been thinking about the purchase of a boat. As a teenager, she was an avid water skier at her parents' summer home. Now that she has moved away, she wants to renew her hobby at a lake nearby. Julia recently received a raise of $200 per month and plans to visit a dealership nearby to see what kind of boat she can buy with that level of payment. Based on the information in this chapter, including Table 6-3 on page 183, offer your opinions about her thinking.

CASE 4

Reducing Expenses to Buy a New Car

DO IT IN CLASS
PAGE 173

Courtney Bennett recently graduated from college and accepted a position in Manhattan, Kansas, as an assistant librarian in the public library. Courtney has no debts, and her budget is shown in the first column (no debt) of Table 6-2 on page 173. She now faces the question of whether to trade in her old car for a new one requiring a monthly payment of $330. Taking the role of a good friend of Courtney, suggest how Courtney might cut back on her expenses so that she can afford the vehicle.

(a) What areas might be cut back?

(b) How much in each area might be cut back?

(c) After finishing your analysis, what advice (and possibly alternatives) would you offer Courtney about buying the new car?

CASE 5

Cousins Discuss Their Debt Situations

DO IT IN CLASS
PAGE 172

Melinda Dennis from Troy, New York, just graduated from college and is concerned about her student loan debts. While at her graduation party she got to talking with three of her cousins, Kyle, Mariah, and Hadrian who have been out of school for several years and found they each have had somewhat different pattern with using credit and carrying debt. Kyle, who had taken a personal finance class, said he felt good about his credit management and mentioned he has a debt payments-to-disposable income ratio of 7 percent. None of the other three cousins even knew what such ratio was. Kyle offered to do the calculations for the other three cousins. After doing so, he found ratios of 20 percent for Melinda due to her student loan debt, 12 percent for Mariah due primarily to a car loan, and 16 percent for Hadrian due to both a car loan and credit card debt. The cousins are planning to get together next week and discuss what Kyle has found. What assessment and advice should Kyle give to his cousins?

CASE 6

Preparation of a Credit-Related Speech

Jacob Marchese of Auburn, Alabama, is the credit manager for a regional chain of department stores. He has been asked to join a panel of community members and make a ten-minute speech to graduating high-school seniors on the topic "Using Credit Wisely." In the following outline that Jacob has prepared, provide him with some suggested comments.

(a) What is consumer credit?

(b) Why might graduates use credit?

(c) How can graduates use credit wisely?

CASE 7

Debt Consolidation as a Debt Reduction Strategy

DO IT IN CLASS
PAGE 189

Justin Granovsky, an assistant manager at a small retail shop in Lubbock, Texas, had an unusual amount of debt. He owed $5400 to one bank, $1800 to a clothing store, $2700 to his credit union, and several hundred dollars to other stores and individuals. Justin was paying more than $460 per month on the three major obligations to pay them off when due in two years. He realized that his take-home pay of slightly more than $2100 per month did not leave him with much excess cash. Justin discussed a different way of handling his major payments with his bank's loan officer. The officer suggested that he pool all of his debts and take out an $11,000 debt-consolidation loan for seven years at 21 percent. As a result, he would pay only $250 per month for all his debts. Justin seemed ecstatic over the idea.

(a) Is Justin's enthusiasm over the idea of a debt-consolidation loan justified? Why or why not?

(b) Why can the bank offer such a "good deal" to Justin?

(c) What compromise would Justin make to remit payments of only $250 as compared with $460?

(d) How much total interest would Justin pay over the seven years, and what would be a justification for this added cost?

BE YOUR OWN PERSONAL FINANCIAL MANAGER

1. **Your Credit Report.** Visit the website for obtaining a free credit report at www.annualcreditreport.com to order a copy of your credit report. Check the accuracy of the report and follow the directions provided to correct any errors. If no report is available on you, it should be because you have never used credit. If you have used credit and there is no report, you should notify the credit bureaus of this error and ask them to create a file on you.

2. **Set Your Debt Limit.** Based on your personal balance

MY PERSONAL FINANCIAL PLANNER

sheet and cash-flow statement, calculate your debt payments-to-disposable income and debt-to-equity ratios. Do you feel that you are overly indebted by these measures? Also consider the continuous-debt method in your considerations. Use Worksheet 25: The Effect of Taking on Additional Debt on My Financial Ratios from "My Personal Financial Planner" to determine if you could take on any debt at this time.

3. **List Your Outstanding Installment Loans.** Make an inventory of your installment loans including each loan's purpose, to whom the debt was owed, payoff date, monthly payment, and monthly due date using Worksheet 26: My Installment Loan Inventory from "My Personal Financial Planner."

MY PERSONAL FINANCIAL PLANNER

4. **Protect Your Privacy.** A lost or stolen debit or credit card can cost you money and time. Using your credit report and other information from various billing statements, compile a list of all your debit and credit accounts including the telephone number and address of where to send notification if the card is lost or stolen.

5. **List Your Student Loans.** Make an inventory of your student loans including source, amounts currently owed, current

MY PERSONAL FINANCIAL PLANNER

APR, when payments must begin, approximate monthly payment, and the maximum number of years you will have to repay the loan using Worksheet 27: My Student Loan Inventory from "My Personal Financial Planner."

ON THE NET

Go to the Web pages indicated to complete these exercises.

1. Visit the website for the Federal Reserve Board at www.gulletttitle.com/Forms/FRB_CHB_YourCredit.pdf. Locate its online copy of the *Consumer Handbook on Credit Protection Laws.* Identify one additional protection not discussed in this book that is provided by each of the following laws: the Fair Credit Billing Act, the Equal Credit Opportunity Act, and the Fair Credit Reporting Act.

2. Visit the website for Fair Isaac Corporation at www.myfico.com/crediteducation/articles/. Read up on how credit scoring works. Identify three actions you could take to improve your credit score.

3. Visit the website for the Center for Responsible Lending at www.responsiblelending.org/. Read about the various ways that lenders design onerous credit products and efforts to reign in those products.

ACTION INVOLVEMENT PROJECTS

1. **Understanding Credit Applications.** Visit a local bank or credit union and ask for an application for a credit card. Read through the items of information that are requested in the application. Why do you think that the lender asks for the information requested? Do you think the lender would view the information that you would provide positively?

2. **Good Uses of Credit.** Survey five of your friends about their perceptions of when it is appropriate to use credit. Compare their views to your own.

3. **The Downside of Credit.** Survey five of your friends about their three most negative aspects of using credit. Compare their three aspects to your own views and those listed in this chapter.

4. **Perceptions of Bankruptcy.** Survey five of your friends about their feelings about and understanding of bankruptcy. Do their feelings conflict with yours? Is their understanding of bankruptcy accurate?

Visit the Garman/Forgue companion website at www.cengagebrain.com.

7

Credit Cards and Consumer Loans

LEARNING OBJECTIVES

After reading this chapter, you should be able to:

1. Compare the common types of consumer credit, including credit cards and installment loans.

2. Describe the types and features of credit card accounts.

3. Manage your credit card accounts to avoid fees and finance charges.

4. Describe the important features of consumer installment loans.

5. Calculate the interest and annual percentage rate on consumer loans.

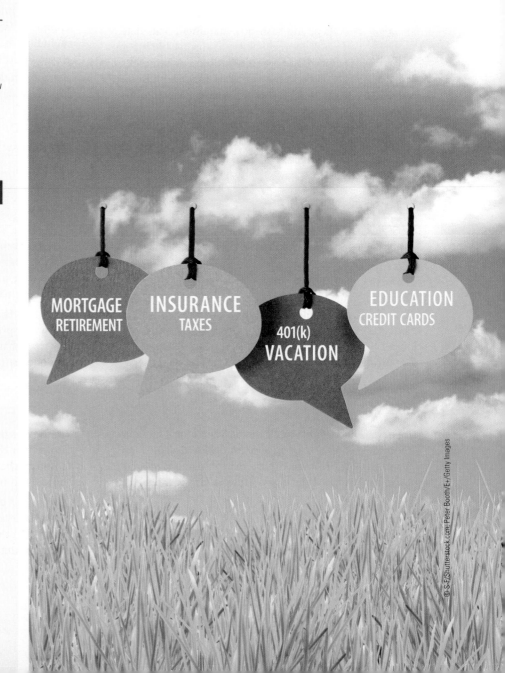

© S.F./Shutterstock.com; Peter Booth/E+/Getty Images

WHAT DO YOU RECOMMEND?

© iStockphoto.com/serts

Zachary Cochrane, a 31-year-old food scientist in Jackson, Tennessee, made $62,000 last year. Zachary avoided using credit and credit cards until he was 28 years old, when he missed three months of work due to a water-skiing accident. He made ends meet by obtaining two bank credit cards that, because of his lack of a credit history, carry 19.6 and 24 percent annual percentage rates (APRs). Zachary now has 11 credit card accounts open: five bank cards and six retail store cards. He uses them regularly, presenting whatever card a store will honor. He owes $13,000 on the 24 percent APR card and $4400 on the 19.6 percent APR card. His other three bank cards carry APRs of 11 percent, 12 percent, and 15 percent, and he owes $500 to $700 on each one. For the past year, Zachary has been making only the minimum payments on his bank cards. His retail cards all carry APRs in excess of 21 percent. Although he has managed to keep from running a balance on those cards during most months, occasionally these accounts have balances as well.

What would you recommend to Zachary on the subject of credit cards and consumer loans regarding:

1. His approach to using credit cards, including the number of cards he has?

2. Estimating the credit card interest charges he is paying each month?

3. How he might lower his interest expense each month?

4. Consolidating his credit card debts into one installment loan?

YOUR NEXT FIVE YEARS

In the next five years, you can start achieving financial success by doing the following related to credit cards and consumer loans:

1. *Pay all your credit card balances in full each month, or certainly no longer than two or three months later.*

2. *Move credit card balances you do carry to lower-interest accounts and never make convenience purchases on the accounts on which you carry a balance.*

3. *Use only credit cards with chip and pin technology as soon as they become available.*

4. *Use student loans for direct education expenses only rather than to maintain a better lifestyle.*

5. *Choose installment loans based on the lowest annual percentage rate (APR) rather than monthly payment and years to repay.*

LEARNING OBJECTIVE 1

Compare the common types of consumer credit, including credit cards and installment loans.

---

installment credit (closed-end credit)

Credit arrangement in which the borrower must repay the amount owed plus interest in a specific number of equal payments.

open-ended (revolving) credit

Arrangement in which credit is extended in advance of any transaction so that borrowers do not need to reapply each time they need to use credit.

credit limit

Maximum outstanding debt that a lender will allow on an open-ended credit account.

You cannot borrow your way to financial success. Using credit requires deliberate thinking and planning so you do not become overextended. You need to first consider whether the reason you are borrowing is sound and then decide in advance how you will repay the debt. This is especially true for credit cards. Credit card usage can be managed so that you pay no interest at all. This occurs if you pay your balance in full every month, and more than 4 in 10 cardholders do it. Also, to succeed in personal finance you might consider leading a life so that you avoid getting into the situation that the average household credit card holder face: over $7,000 in credit card debt.

Planning how to repay an installment loan is also important because you commit to making a series of monthly payments for one to seven or more years. Smart borrowers understand the mathematics behind the calculation of the finance charges on these installment loans. They always focus on the **annual percentage rate (APR)** when comparing among various sources of credit. The APR is the cost of credit on a yearly basis stated as a percentage rate.

7.1 TYPES OF CONSUMER CREDIT

Consumer credit is nonbusiness debt used by consumers for expenditures other than home mortgages. (Borrowing for housing has investment aspects that result in a separate classification and is discussed in Chapter 9.)

There are two types of consumer credit: installment credit and noninstallment credit.

- With **installment credit** (also called **closed-end credit**), the borrower must repay the amount owed plus interest in a specific number of equal payments, usually monthly. For example, an $18,000 used vehicle loan might require monthly payments of $356 for 60 months at 7 percent interest.

- **Noninstallment credit** includes single-payment, open-ended credit, and service credit. **Single-payment loans** are the easiest of the three to understand. As an example, a borrower might take out a loan of $2000 at 12 percent interest for one year. If so, a single payment of $2240 ($2000 + $240 interest; $2000 × 0.12) would be due at the end of one year.

Credit cards are an example of open-ended credit. With **open-ended credit** (also called **revolving credit**), credit is extended in advance of any transaction so that the borrower does not need to reapply each time credit is desired. Any amounts owed will be repaid in full in a single payment or via a series of equal or unequal payments, usually made monthly. The borrower can use the account as long as the total owed does not exceed his or her **credit limit**. This credit limit amount is set by the lender and is the maximum outstanding debt allowed on the credit account. Credit limits vary with the perceived creditworthiness of the borrower.

Open-ended credit can be used to make purchases and, in some cases, to obtain cash advances. It is the most convenient type of credit, and it is also the most abused. Many open-ended accounts—but not all—use a credit card. A **credit** (or **charge**) **card** is a plastic card identifying the holder as a participant in the charge account plan of a lender, such as a retailer or financial institution.

A **charge card** charges no interest but requires the user to pay his/her balance in full upon receipt of the statement, usually on a monthly basis. The major benefit offered by a charge card is that it has much higher, often unlimited, spending limits. **Travel and entertainment (T&E) cards** are charge cards and are often used by businesspeople for food and lodging expenses while traveling; however, they are not accepted at as many outlets as bank credit cards. Applicants must have higher-than-average incomes to qualify, and applicants must pay an annual membership fee of $90+ annually. Examples are American Express and Diner's Club.

DID YOU KNOW

How to Avoid Using Credit Cards in College

Those who use credit card debt sometimes find that its use can quickly spiral out of control. Instead some college students plan ahead and find other ways to manage money. Consider using the following: prepaid cards, a no-fee checking account, a charge card, and gift cards.

Cash advances may be obtained at any financial institution that issues the type of card (e.g., Visa, MasterCard, Discover) being used. A cash advance is a cash loan from a credit card account. The borrower can receive a cash advance from an ATM or the funds may be transferred electronically into the cardholder's checking account.

A **personal line of credit** is a form of open-ended credit that allows the borrower access to a prearranged revolving line of credit provided by the lender (usually a commercial bank, savings bank, credit union, or brokerage firm). Like credit card accounts, a personal line of credit includes a credit limit and a flexible repayment schedule. The essence of a line of credit is that borrowers can obtain a cash advance when needed and not have to reapply for a loan each time they need money. Some people use the equity in their home as collateral for a line of credit. This arrangement is referred to as a home-equity line of credit.

Service credit is granted to consumers by public utilities, physicians, dentists, and other service providers that do not require full payment when services are rendered. For example, your electric company allows you to use electricity all month and then sends you a bill that may not be due for 10 to 15 days. Service credit usually carries no interest, although penalty charges and interest may apply if payments are made late. Service may be cut off for continued slow payment or nonpayment of the debt.

 CONCEPT CHECK 7.1

1. Distinguish between installment credit and open-ended credit.

2. Explain the basic features of revolving credit.

3. Describe how someone might use a personal line of credit.

7.2 CREDIT CARD ACCOUNTS PROVIDE INSTANT ACCESS TO CREDIT

Once a credit card account is opened, it can be used at any time. Credit card accounts allow the borrower to pay the balance in full at any time or carry over a balance owed from month to month (travel and entertainment cards are an exception). If a balance is carried over, a **minimum payment** must be made each month to cover interest and a small payment on the amount owed (the **principal**). If at least the minimum payment amount is not received by the **payment due date** (the specific day by which the credit card company should receive payment from you), the cardholder must pay a **late payment fee** and may be declared in **default**. Default occurs when a borrower has failed to make a payment of principal or interest when due or failed to meet any other requirement of a credit agreement. Credit card companies often cancel the accounts of customers who are delinquent or in default.

LEARNING OBJECTIVE 2

Describe the types and features of credit card accounts.

minimum payment

Payment that must be made to a credit account each month to cover interest and a portion of the amount owed.

default

Occurs when a borrow fails to make a payment when due or fails to meet other requirements of the credit agreement (contract).

bank credit card account
Open-ended credit account with a financial institution that allows the holder to make purchases almost anywhere.

cash advance (or **convenience**) **checks**
A check-equivalent way to take a cash advance on a credit card.

retail credit cards
Allow customers to make purchases on credit at any of the outlets of a particular retailer.

7.2a Who Pays How Much Every Month?

Credit cards are the primary source of consumer credit other than home mortgages. About two-thirds of American adults have a credit card account. About 18 percent repay the minimum amount due each month and 40 percent pay a partial amount but more than the minimum payment due. About 42 percent pay their monthly balances in full. Those who never pay off the balance can do so for years, even as other charges and interest are added to the account. As long as the total debt remains below the credit limit, the user may continue to make charges on the account. A credit card borrower may also ask a creditor to increase his or her credit limit.

7.2b Bank Credit Cards

A **bank credit card** is a credit card issued by a financial institution that allows the cardholder to pay for goods and services based on the holder's promise to pay for them. The issuer of the card creates a revolving account and grants a line of credit to the user for use in making purchases or to obtain a cash advance.

Visa, MasterCard, Discover, and Optima are the most commonly recognized bank card names. However, the actual lender is the bank, savings bank, or credit union through which the card is offered. Visa and MasterCard are service providers that maintain the electronic network through which transactions are communicated.

Participating merchants pay fees that average 2 percent to these companies based on the dollar amounts charged, although they can be as high as 6 percent. Virtually all financial institutions offer bank credit cards as do a number of consumer products companies, such as AT&T, Allstate Insurance, and Verizon. These companies contract with Visa, MasterCard, and a bank to offer these **cobranded credit cards**.

Many bank credit card issuers periodically send **cash advance** (or **convenience**) **checks** to their cardholders. These instruments are not genuine checks but simply a check-equivalent way to take a cash advance. Customers can use these "checks" to make payments to others or themselves. If you receive convenience checks but do not want to use them, either put them in a safe place or destroy them immediately because they easily could be used fraudulently by someone else.

7.2c Retail Credit Card Accounts

A **retail credit card** allows a customer to make purchases on credit at any of the outlets of a particular retailer or retail chain. Examples of credit card accounts at retail stores include those offered by Kohl's, REI, and Shell Oil. Many retailers have alliances with a financial institution to offer a bank credit card that carries the retailer's logo and can also be used anywhere the bank credit card can be used.

Some smaller retail establishments offer open-ended accounts that do not use a credit card as the vehicle for using the account. With these retail credit accounts, customers simply ask to have the purchase put on their account for repayment at a later date. Repayment may be required in full monthly or allowed to be spread over time.

7.2d Common (But Not Always Beneficial) Aspects of Credit Card Accounts

Federal law requires credit card lenders to disclose all the rules governing the account to borrowers before they sign up for any card. Some of that information must be displayed in a uniform manner, as illustrated in the sample credit card disclosure box in Figure 7-1. The remainder of the information appears in the **credit card agreement** (**contract**).

DID YOU KNOW ?

Credit Card Security Chip Update

The increasing frequency of cases where hackers have stolen consumers' credit card data from retailers and others has sped up efforts to introduce "Chip and PIN technology" in the United States. The standards leader is EMV, which is an abbreviation for Europay, MasterCard, and Visa. Cards with this technology cannot be counterfeited and are more secure than magnetic stripe credit cards because personal data is encrypted on the card rather than in a retailer's database and are accessible only with a PIN.

Figure 7-1 Sample Credit Card Disclosure Box

Federal law requires that key pieces of information be disclosed in direct-mail advertising and when applying for credit cards and any time the rules of an account are changed. To search for the best offers on credit cards, you can visit www.bankrate.com or www.cardtrack.com.

CARD DISCLOSURES		
Annual Percentage Rate (APR) for purchases	2.90% for 6 months from date of account opening. After that, 19.2% variable.	
Other APRs	Cash advance APR: 21.99% variable.	
Variable rate information	Your APRs may vary each billing period as published in the *Wall Street Journal* The purchase APR equals the Prime Rate plus 13.99%. The cash advance APR equals the Prime Rate plus 21.99%.	
Grace period for repayment of the balance for purchases	At least 23 days if you pay the total balance in full by the due date every billing period. If you do not, you will not get a grace period.	
Method of computing the balance for purchases	Average daily balance. This includes new purchases.	
Penalty APR	Up to 28.99% and may be applied to your account if you make a late payment, go over your credit limit, make a payment that is returned or do any of these with any other account you have with us.	
Annual fees	None.	
Fee for foreign purchases	3% of the U.S. dollar amount of each purchase made outside the United States whether made in U.S. dollars or in a foreign currency.	
Other fees	Balance transfer fee:	• 4% of each balance transfer; $10 minimum.
	Cash advance fee:	• 4% of each cash advance; $10 minimum.
	Late fee:	• $25 on balances up to $100.
	Over-the-credit-line fee:	• $25.
**When can we change the rates, fees, and terms of your card agreement? We may change the rates, fees, and terms of your card agreement from time to time as permitted by law. We will give you 45-day advance notice of the changes and a right to opt out to the extent required by law.		

Credit Card Offers Often Come "Preapproved" Credit card companies often send applications to consumers who have been preapproved. It is important to understand that being **preapproved** means only that you will be granted credit. Both the credit card debt limit and APR will be determined after you apply for an account.

DID YOU KNOW

How to Close a Credit Card Account Wisely

Credit card accounts can remain open for decades even if you never use the card or stopped using it at some point. Accounts are not closed if you cut up the cards. The lender must be formally notified of your request before the account will be officially closed. Here's what to do:

1. *Pay off your balance in full.* Accounts cannot be truly closed until they are paid off. You can, however, ask an issuer to stop honoring a card.

2. *Obtain the customer service telephone number* for the lender from your most recent monthly statement. If you do not have a recent bill, obtain a free copy of your credit report, which will list the contact information for the lender.

3. *Contact the lender* to request the address to which you should send your cancellation request. It will not be the same address to which you send your monthly payment. Confirm that there is no longer a balance owed as sometimes a very small amount of interest may still be owed for the last month when an account is paid off.

4. *Send a written request* to close the account and request that the creditor send a confirmation that the account is, indeed, closed.

5. *Obtain a copy of your credit report,* after 90 days, from one of the three national credit bureaus (pay if necessary). If the account shows as closed, obtain free copies from the other two bureaus as confirmation at the next opportunity. If the account shows as still open at any of the bureaus use the procedures outlined in Chapter 6 on page 182 to correct the error.

---

annual fees

Charges levied against cardholders for the privilege of having an open account but that are not included in the advertised APR.

transaction fee

A small charge levied each time certain types of transactions occur, such as for cash advances and balance transfers.

balance transfer

Full or partial payment on the balance of one credit card using a cash advance from another.

Annual and Transaction Fees Can Be Avoided Some bank credit card lenders assess **annual fees** ranging from $25 to $100+. In addition, lenders may charge a **transaction fee** (a small charge levied each time certain types of transactions occur). The card illustrated in Figure 7-1 assesses transaction fees for cash advances and **balance transfers**, which are full- or partial-payments on one credit card by using a cash advance from another. Some lenders even charge a fee for printing the monthly credit bill. As you can see, an apparently low-rate card may turn into a higher-cost card when all fees are considered.

Liability for Lost or Stolen Cards Is Limited The Truth in Lending Act limits a cardholder's **credit card liability** for lost or stolen credit cards. Under the law, if you notify the card issuer within two days of a loss or theft, you are not legally responsible for any fraudulent usage of the card. After two days, your maximum liability for fraudulent usage of the card prior to your notification is $50.

Although your financial liability is low, many companies nevertheless sell credit card insurance (for an annual premium ranging from $15 to $49) that will cover the first $50 of unauthorized use of an insured person's lost or stolen credit cards. Such insurance is profitable for the sellers but a wasteful expense for you. If you are insistent and talk with a credit card company supervisor, she/he will waive the $50 fee for unauthorized use as a gesture of goodwill to keep you as a good credit card customer. Also you should know that most homeowner's and renter's insurance policies will pay the $50 fee you might be charged for unauthorized use of a lost or stolen credit card.

Late-Payment, Bounced-Check, and Over-the-Limit Fees Are Very Costly The fees assessed by credit card issuers can be expensive. Late-payment fees are limited by law to $25 in most cases. Card issuers also assess fees if you write a bad check when making your monthly payment or you exceed your credit limit. This latter fee can only be assessed if the cardholder agrees to allow the lender to accept over-the-limit usage. If this agreement has not been given, over-the-limit usage will be blocked. Each of these fees is much higher than necessary in terms of the actual cost to the

DID YOU KNOW

Credit Card Rules Can Change at Any Time

When you open a credit card account, the account rules and interest rate are determined based on two groups of factors. The first consists of your credit history and information in your application form. The second group relates to conditions in the economy as a whole and the policies of the issuer of the card.

Over time, these sets of information can change, and as a result, the card issuer may wish to make amendments to the interest rate, credit limit, and other card rules or

features. The law requires card holders be given 45 days of advance notice. However, interest rates cannot be changed on existing balances. Therefore, the issuer must give you the option of rejecting or accepting a change in interest rates. If you reject the change, the card will be blocked for further usage, and you may repay any balance according to the old rules. Once you have repaid the balance owed, your card is cancelled. If you accept the changes, they will take effect 45 days after notification.

lender for these rule violations. Indeed, they represent a significant source of profits for credit card issuers. The account illustrated in Figure 7-1 assesses a maximum fee of $25 for each of these offenses.

Teaser Interest Rates May Be Appealing Some cards carry a temporarily low **teaser rate (introductory rate)** to entice borrowers to apply for an account. Teaser rates must stay in effect for six months after the account is opened unless the cardholder violates a rule of the account such as being late with a payment by more than 60 days. Teaser APRs of 0 to 3.9 percent are common. In Figure 7-1, the teaser rate is 2.9 percent for purchases and 0.0 percent for cash advances. The APR typically reverts to a much higher fixed or variable interest rate (19.2% in the example in Figure 7-1) after the introductory period ends. Some credit card borrowers take advantage of teaser rates by opening new accounts regularly and transferring the balances from other accounts to the new account to take advantage of the low introductory rate despite any high balance transfer fee that might exist.

Higher Penalty APRs Can Be Assessed A serious downside to many credit card accounts is the assessment of a **penalty APR** that can be 8 to 10 percentage points higher that the normal APR. The penalty APR is assessed whenever a borrower fails to uphold certain rules of the account, such as being more than 60 days late on the minimum payments or making a payment by check that is returned for insufficient funds. The disclosure notice in Figure 7-1 indicates a penalty APR of 28.99 percent for violation of the listed rules. By law, penalty rates must be reviewed after six months and rescinded if all payments have been made on time in that period. Some credit card issuers simply cancel the account when the rules are violated rather than assess the penalty APR.

Variable Interest Rates Can Easily Go Up Credit card accounts (and installment loans) carry either fixed or variable interest rates. **Variable interest rates** go up and down, usually monthly or annually, often according to changes in interest rates in the economy as a whole. The example in Figure 7-1 has a variable interest rate with the prime rate used as a base rate. The **prime rate** is a key measure of interest rates in the economy, and its fluctuations drive the changes in rates for all types of variable-rate credit. In recent years, the prime rate has ranged from 3 to 4 percent. As indicated in Figure 7-1, the card company uses the prime rate as published in *The Wall Street Journal* to determine interest rates for purchases, cash advances, and balance transfers on the card.

FINANCIAL POWER POINT

Paying Cash Instead of Using a Credit Card Might Save You 2 or 3 Percent

The Federal Reserve says that merchants are allowed to give discounts for those who pay cash or use a debit card rather than use a credit card. If the availability of such a discount is not obvious, just ask. You might save 2 to 3 percent on a purchase, such as for gasoline purchases.

FINANCIAL POWER POINT

Be Smart When Using a Rewards Credit Card

Credit cards that provide airline miles or cash-back bonuses can be a good idea. However, the benefits will be lost if the card has a high APR and/or substantial fees. And it absolutely makes no sense to use a rewards card if you are going to carry a balance on the card.

variable interest rates
Interest rates that change monthly or annually according to general interest rate changes in the economy as a whole.

Extremely low APRs are usually temporary. Read the rules of your account carefully.

Credit Card Insurance Is Overpriced Many lenders encourage borrowers to sign up for **credit life insurance** that pays the unpaid balance of a loan—to the lender—in the event of the borrower's death. Credit life insurance is grossly overpriced (and very profitable) and is a cost that can be avoided. The same can be said for **credit disability insurance**, which repays the outstanding loan balance if the borrower becomes disabled (with "disability" usually being very narrowly defined). The companies also sell unneeded **credit unemployment insurance**.

7.2e Prestige and Affinity Cards

Some bank credit cards are a form of **prestige card**, often with a precious metal in the brand name such as "gold," "silver," or "platinum." These accounts require that the user probably possess high credit qualifications and they offer enhancements such as higher credit limits. Prestige cards sometimes carry higher annual fees.

Some Visa and MasterCard credit cards are identified as **affinity cards**— that is, they are standard bank cards but with the logo of a sponsoring organization imprinted on the face of the card. The issuing financial institution often donates a portion of the annual fee and a small percentage of the amounts charged (perhaps 0.25, 0.5, or 1 percent) to the sponsoring organization. Sponsors may include charitable, political, sports, or other organized groups, such as the Sierra Club or Mothers Against Drunk Driving. Supporters of the sponsoring organization may be motivated to use an affinity card because the organization receives money from each transaction. Creditors rightly calculate that fewer delinquencies will occur among the particular group of people, so they can afford to transfer some income to the named organization.

DID YOU KNOW

Prepaid Cards Are Mainstream

Prepaid cards (or **reloadable cards**) are stored value cards that are used like credit cards. These were once marketed to low-income consumers but today they are mainstream. You choose the dollar amount to put on the card and as you spend, your purchases are deducted from the total balance. When the balance gets low, you can reload with more money. People without banking or a standard credit card account and those with little or no credit history often choose to use prepaid cards as an alternative to cash.

Since prepaid cards are associated with one of the major card networks, such as Visa, MasterCard, and Discover, they can be used anywhere those cards are accepted. They can be used to purchase groceries, buy merchandise on eBay, pay bills online, and withdraw cash from an ATM machine. Almost all of them come with FDIC insurance as well as the full theft and loss protections of the Fair Credit Billing Act. High fees can be avoided if you shop carefully online for the best accounts.

CONCEPT CHECK 7.2

1. Distinguish among bank credit cards, retail credit cards, and travel and entertainment cards.

2. What are the differences and similarities between a cash advance and a balance transfer using a bank credit card?

3. Describe the positive and negative aspects of having a variable interest rate on a credit card.

4. Briefly describe five common fees assessed on credit card accounts and how they can be avoided.

7.3 YOU MUST MANAGE YOUR CREDIT CARDS WISELY

Credit cards can be a positive tool in personal financial management—but only when used appropriately. To do so, you must understand and monitor your credit statements, correct any billing errors quickly, and verify the computation of any finance charges. Your goal should be to use the credit card in a manner that avoids all fees, including finance charges. This means paying your balance in full every month. Otherwise, credit card debt likely will be your most expensive form of debt. As one personal finance expert observed, "You want to earn a 21% risk-free return on your money? Pay off your credit cards."

If you do not manage your credit cards wisely, you will unnecessarily pay hundreds or even thousands of dollars every year in interest, penalties, and fees to credit card companies. You also may mess up your credit rating and, as a result, will wind up paying higher interest rates than normal for all your credit transactions including rented and owned housing, vehicle purchases, and insurance. You might even miss out on a job opportunity because employers sometimes turn down applicants who have poor credit histories.

> **LEARNING OBJECTIVE 3**
> Manage your credit card accounts to avoid fees and finance charges.

7.3a Credit Statements

Active charge account holders receive a monthly **credit statement** (also called a **periodic statement**) that summarizes the charges, payments, finance charges, and other activity on the account. Figure 7-2 shows an example monthly statement for a credit card.

Statement Date The **statement date** (sometimes called the **billing date** or **closing date**) is the last day of the month for which any transactions are reported on the statement. Any transactions or payments made after this date will be recorded on the following month's credit statement. The statement is mailed to the cardholder a day or so after the statement date. It is generally the same day of each month, and the time period between statement dates is referred to as the **billing cycle**.

credit (or periodic) statement
The monthly bill on a credit card account showing the charges and payments made, minimum payment required, and due date among other information.

statement/billing/closing date
The last day of the month for which any transactions are reported on the credit statement.

DID YOU KNOW

Bias Toward an Easy Solution

People engaged in credit cards and consumer loans have a bias toward certain behaviors that can be harmful, such as a tendency toward taking the easiest solution. People who owe on multiple credit cards often want to pay off the card with the lowest balance first regardless of the APR. What to do? Repay just the minimum repayment amounts on the cards with the lowest APR and pay as much as possible on the highest APR card.

ADVICE FROM A PROFESSIONAL

Get Rid of Your Credit Card Debt

If your credit card debt rises to a hard-to-manage level, consider the following suggestions:

1. **Immediately stop using your credit cards**. And avoid the temptation to open new credit card accounts or accept any new offers.

2. **Get organized**. Gather your more recent outstanding credit card statements. Using Excel, or other financial software, list each credit card's balance with its interest rate, in order from highest interest rate to lowest. Then calculate the total balance owed on all cards and the total monthly payment required.

3. **Set a goal and stick with it.** Determine a reasonable pay-off date. Calculate the monthly payment you will need to pay off the debt. You may visit www.bankrate .com/calculators/credit-cards/credit-card-payoff-calculator .aspx or similar online tools for calculators.

4. **Develop a new budget.** Evaluate all of your budgeted expenditures and streamline your new budget so you can repay the largest possible amounts toward paying off your credit card balances. Now, it is time to take action!

5. **Create a plan of action.** You may use one or more of the following options:

a. Pay the minimum amount due on the card with the lowest interest rate and pay as much as possible on the card with the highest interest rate until it is paid in full. Repeat the process in the same manner for additional cards and continue until all of the credit card debts are paid in full.

b. Consider transferring existing balances on high interest rate accounts to an account with a lower interest rate. Pay attention to brief introductory periods, transaction fees, and penalties that may eliminate the potential savings.

c. Work overtime or take another job. Devote any extra income, such as overtime pay, a tax refund, or a bonus toward paying down the credit card debt.

d. Consider seeking professional assistance from a reputable nonprofit credit counseling agency. They may be able to negotiate with your creditors to lower payments, interest rates, and reduce or eliminate late fees and over-the-limit charges. You may do this at any time during the process. (See Chapter 6.)

e. Make timely payments to prevent fees and penalties. You can do it and you will.

Steve Holcombe and Feliccia Smith
North Greenville University, Tigerville, South Carolina

FINANCIAL POWER POINT

Consider Using Two Credit Cards

It is a smart financial move to use one credit card for convenience items that are paid in full each month and another credit card for items for which paying off the balance each month is impossible. Use a no-annual-fee card for the convenience purchases and a low-APR card for purchases for which you carry a balance.

Payment Due Date The **payment due date** is the specific day by which the credit card company should receive payment from you. Federal law states that bills must be mailed to cardholders at least 21 days before payments are due. Your payment due date must be the same each month, and if it falls on a weekend or holiday, you have until the following business day to pay. Payments received by 5 p.m. on the due date are considered to be on time.

Transaction and Posting Dates The date on which a credit cardholder makes a purchase (or receives a credit, as described later in this chapter) is known as the **transaction date** ("Trans Date" in Figure 7-2). Any interest is usually charged from the posting date ("Post Date" in Figure 7-2).

Grace Period A **grace period** is the time period between the posting date of a transaction and the due date, within which any new credit card purchases made during the billing cycle will avoid finance charges. Grace periods are offered only if the previous month's total balance was paid in full and on time. In Figure 7-2, the cardholder has a previous unpaid balance, $535.07, and was charged interest on the unpaid balance as well as on the new charges made within the billing cycle, starting from the date they were posted to the account. Thus, this example lacks a grace period because of the unpaid balance on the card.

Figure 7-2 Sample Statement for a Bank Credit Card Account

XXX Bank Credit Card Account Statement
Account Number XXXX XXXX XXXX XXXX
February 21, 2015 to March 22, 2015
Statement Date 03/22/15

Summary of Account Activity

Previous Balance	$535.07
Payments	−$450.00
Other Credit	−$0.00
Purchases	+$529.57
Balance Transfers	+$785.00
Cash Advances	+$318.00
Past Due Amount	$0.00
Fees Charged	**+$69.45**
Interest Charged	**+$11.05**
New Balance	$1,798.14
Credit limit	$2,000.00
Available credit	$201.86
Statement closing date	3/22/2015
Days in billing cycle	30

Questions?

Call Customer Service	1-XXX-XXX-XXXX
Lost or Stolen Credit Card	1-XXX-XXX-XXXX

Payment Information

New Balance	$1,798.14
Minimum Payment Due	$53.00
Payment Due Date	4/20/15

Late Payment Warning: If we do not receive your minimum Payment by the date listed above, you may have to pay a $25 late fee and your APRs may be increased up to the Penalty APR of 28.99%

Minimum Payment Warning: If you make only the minimum payment each period, you will pay more in interest and it will take you longer to pay off your balance. For example:

If you make no additional charges using this card and each month you pay...	You will pay off the balance shown on this statement in about...	And you will end up paying as estimated total of...
Only the minimum payment	10 years	$3,284
$62	3 years	$2,232 (Savings = $1,052)

If you would like information about credit counseling services, call 1-800-XXX-XXXX

Please send billing inquiries and correspondence to:
PO Box XXXX, Anytown, Anystate XXXXX

Transactions

Reference Number	Trans Date	Post Date	Description of Transaction or Credit	Amount
5884186PS0388W6YM	2/22	2/23	Store #1	$146.19
854338203FS8OO0Z5	2/25	2/25	Pymt Thank You	–
564891561545KOSHD	2/25	2/26	Store #2	$247.36
1542202074TWWZV48	2/26	2/26	Cash Advance	$318.00
4545754784KOHUIOS	2/27	3/1	Balance Transfer	$785.00
2564561023184102315	2/28	3/1	Store #3	$ 34.32
045148714518979874	3/4	3/5	Store #4	$ 29.45
0547810544898718AF	3/15	3/17	Store #5	$ 72.25

Fees				
9525156489SFD4545Q	2/23	2/23	Late Fee	$25.00
84151564SADS874H	2/27	2/27	Balance Transfer Fee	$23.55
256489156189451516L	2/28	2/28	Cash Advance Fee	$20.90
			TOTAL FEES FOR THIS PERIOD	**$69.45**

Interest Charged		
Interest Charge on Purchases		$ 6.40
Interest Charge on Cash Advances		$ 4.65
TOTAL INTEREST FOR THIS PERIOD		**$11.05**

2015 Totals Year-to-Date	
Total fees charged in 2015	$90.14
Total interest charged in 2015	$18.27

Interest Charge Calculation

Your Annual Percentage rate (APR) is the stated interest rate on your account.

Type of Balance	Annual Percentage Rate (APR)	Balances Subject to Interest Rate	Interest Charge
Purchases	14.99% (V)	$512.14	$6.40
Cash Advances	21.99% (V)	$253.50	$4.65
Balance Transfers	0.00%	$637.50	$0.00
Penalty APR	28.99%	$ 0.00	$0.00

(V) = Variable Rate

DID YOU KNOW

Secured Credit Cards Are Usually a Very Bad Deal

A **secured credit card** (or **collateralized credit card**) is a type of credit card that requires a fee to open, and it is backed by a savings account used as collateral on the credit available with the card. Money is deposited and held in the account backing the card. The limit, often

$500 to $1000, will be based on both your previous credit history and the amount deposited in the account. The limit as a percent of the deposit tends to range between 50 and 100 percent. Most people do not need a secured credit card, but those who have no alternative should consider obtaining one from a reputable institution, as scams abound in this market.

minimum payment

Lowest allowable monthly payment required by the lender.

credit receipt

Written evidence of any items returned that notes the specific amount and date of the transaction.

average daily balance

Sum of the outstanding balances owed each day during the billing period divided by the number of days in the period.

DID YOU KNOW

Money Websites for Credit Cards and Consumer Loans

Informative websites for credit cards and consumer loans, including how to correct billing errors are:

Center for Responsible Lending (www.responsiblelending.org/)

Consumer Financial Protection Bureau (www.consumerfinance.gov/)

Bankrate.com (www.bankrate.com /credit-cards.aspx)

NOLO (www.nolo.com/legal-encyclopedia /credit-cards)

Federal Reserve Board (www.federal reserve.gov/consumerinfo/default.htm)

Federal Trade Commission (www .consumer.ftc.gov/topics/money-credit)

MyMoney.gov (www.mymoney.gov /borrow/Pages/borrow.aspx)

Bankrate.com (www.bankrate.com/calculators /index-of-credit-card-calculators.aspx)

Minimum Payment Due To meet their obligations, borrowers must make a **minimum payment** due monthly that is no smaller than the amount required by the creditor. In Figure 7-2, the cardholder has two options: pay the total amount due, known as the "new balance," of $1798.14 or make at least the minimum payment of $53. If the borrower pays the total amount due, finance charges on new purchases in the next billing cycle generally can be avoided. If a partial payment, such as $53, is made, additional finance charges will be assessed and will be payable the following month.

The Credit Card Accountability, Responsibility and Disclosure Act requires that your credit card statement include the number of months it will take to pay off your card balance if you make only the minimum payment with no additional charges. In the example, it would take ten years to pay off the balance making only the minimum payments, resulting in estimated total payments of $3284.

Transaction Fees Credit card companies usually charge **transaction fees** whenever the card is used for a balance transfer or cash advance.

Credit for Merchandise Returns and Errors If you return merchandise bought on credit, the merchant will issue you a **credit receipt**—written evidence of the items returned that notes the specific amount of the transaction. In essence, the amount of the merchandise credit is charged back to the credit card company and eventually to the merchant. A credit may also be granted by the card issuer when a billing error has been made and when an unauthorized transaction appears. Credits obtained in the current month should appear on the next monthly statement as a reduction of the total amount owed.

Computation of Finance Charges Companies that issue credit cards must tell consumers the APR applied as well as the method used to compute the finance charges. Mathematically the APR translates into a periodic rate, which is the APR for a charge account divided by the number of billing cycles per year (usually 12). For example, a periodic rate of 1½ percent per month would result from an APR of approximately 18 percent (actually a bit higher because of compounding); both figures must be disclosed.

The finance charge is typically calculated by first computing the **average daily balance**—the sum of the outstanding balances owed each day during the billing period divided by the number of days in the period. The periodic rate is then applied against that balance. For example, a card with an 18 percent APR, a 1½ percent periodic rate, and an average daily balance of $1000 would have a finance charge for the month of $15 ($1000 × 0.015). As shown at the bottom on the statement in Figure 7-2, differing APRs apply for purchases, balance transfers, and cash advances.

7.3b How Credit Card Average Daily Balances Are Calculated

Three methods can be used to calculate the average daily balance on a credit card billing statement.

1. **Average daily balance including new purchases with a grace period.** The balance calculation includes the balance from the previous month and any new charges made during the billing cycle. The grace period allows for the exclusion of new charges made during the billing cycle only if the balance from the previous billing cycle was zero. This is the most commonly used method.

2. **Average daily balance excluding new purchases.** The cardholder pays interest only on any balance left over from the previous month. Good for consumers.

3. **Average daily balance including new purchases with no grace period.** The balance from the previous month and any new charges made during the billing cycle are included in the balance calculation, even if the previous month's balance was paid in full. This is the worst method for consumers.

FINANCIAL POWER POINT

How Your Credit Card Payment Is Applied

Under the Credit Card Accountability, Responsibility and Disclosure (CARD) Act, whenever you make more than a minimum payment on your credit card account, the lender must apply any excess above the minimum payment to the portion of the card debt that carries the highest APR, and this is usually for cash advances.

DO IT IN CLASS

ADVICE FROM A PROFESSIONAL

Avoid the Minimum Payment Trap

Do you currently have balances outstanding on your credit cards? If so, how long have you carried those balances? If you open an account in college and already have an unpaid balance of $2500 upon your graduation, you may find that the balance owed will not drop below $2500 for many years. This situation occurs when you continue to make purchases with the card but continue to pay only the amounts charged each month. If $2500 is still owed on the account years later, then you have "permanent debt." In essence, you have never repaid the college charges. With an 18 percent APR, the finance charges on a debt principal of $2500 for 15 years will total $6750 (0.18 × $2500 × 15), almost three times as much as the debt itself!

The outlook is similarly bleak if you discontinue using the card for new purchases but still remit only the required minimum repayment amount. Credit card issuers often require a minimum monthly payment as low as

3 to 5 percent of the outstanding balance. This small payment requirement is mathematically guaranteed to keep the user in debt for many years. To illustrate, a minimum payment of $75 (3 percent) on an outstanding balance of $2500 with a 1½ percent monthly periodic rate results in only one-half of the payment ($37.50 = $2500 × 0.015) going to reduce the actual debt (the principal). The other $37.50 is used to pay the monthly interest. At this rate of repayment, it will take more than six years to repay the $2500.

A ploy that card issuers frequently use is to allow cardholders to "skip a payment"—in essence, to make "a zero-dollar minimum payment." Interest will continue to accrue for the month during which no payment is made and the unpaid interest simply adds to the unpaid balance.

To avoid paying credit card charges for six to ten years, or even longer, you must make much larger monthly payments that go toward retiring your credit card balances more quickly.

Jonathan J. Fox
Iowa State University

Fair Credit Billing Act (FCBA)

Helps people who wish to dispute billing errors on revolving credit accounts and permits chargebacks.

chargeback

The amount of the transaction is charged back to the business where the transaction originated in the case of a dispute or challenge by the cardholder.

DO IT IN CLASS

dunning letters

Notices that make insistent demands for repayment.

How to Correct Errors on Your Credit Card Billing Statement The **Fair Credit Billing Act (FCBA)** helps people who wish to dispute billing errors on revolving credit accounts. In effect, the FCBA permits a **chargeback**; that is, the amount of the transaction is charged back to the business where the transaction originated.

Withholding payment to a credit card company is permitted when the cardholder alleges an error. For example, a mathematical error has been made in a billing statement or when fraudulent use of the card appears to have occurred. Also when (within certain reasonable limitations) a **goods and services** dispute asserts that the charges were for faulty, damaged, shoddy, defective, or poor-quality goods and services and you made a good-faith effort to try to correct the problem with the merchant. For goods and services disputes, the FCBA applies only to charges of more than $50 made in your home state or within 100 miles of your current mailing address. Most lenders apply the spirit of the FCBA to any goods and services disputes, regardless of the geographic distances involved.

Your Time Limits You must make your billing error complaint within 60 days after the date on which the first bill containing the error was mailed to you. The lender then has 30 days to acknowledge your notification and, within 90 days, must either correct the error permanently, return any overpayment (if requested), or provide evidence of why it believes the bill to be correct (such as a copy of a charge slip you supposedly signed).

Lender Responsibilities While the dispute is being investigated, creditors cannot assess interest on or apply penalties for nonpayment of the disputed amount, send **dunning letters** (notices that make insistent demands for repayment), or send negative information about your account to a credit bureau without stating that "some items are in dispute." A lender that does not follow the procedures correctly cannot collect the first $50 of the questioned amount, even if the bill was correct. Back interest and penalties may be charged if the disputed item is shown to be legitimately owed.

Your Action Steps Take several actions when disputing an item on a billing statement:

1. **Notify the merchant** involved of the error. Although the FCBA does not apply to merchants, it is often the merchant that caused the error and who is in the best position to clear up the error. Be sure to tell the merchant that you also are asserting your rights under the FCBA with the card issuer.

2. **Send a written notice** of the error to the credit card issuer. The notice must be in writing to qualify for the protections provided under the FCBA. Instead of sending the notice to the same address where repayments are normally remitted, examine the billing statement thoroughly, looking for an address under the heading "Send Inquiries to" or something similar. If the error is an "unauthorized use," make sure you indicate this as these disputes have added protections.

3. **Provide photocopies** (not originals) of any necessary documentation. Keep the originals to challenge any finding by the company that no error occurred.

4. **Withhold payment for disputed items**. If possible, pay the remaining amount owed in full to isolate a disputed item. Under the provisions of the FCBA, the card company must immediately credit your account for the amount in dispute.

5. **Review your credit bureau file** after the dispute has been settled to ensure that it does not include information regarding your refusal to repay the disputed amount.

Shoppers frequently rely on purchase loans when buying big ticket items such as furniture and TVs.

CONCEPT CHECK 7.3

1. Describe how the finance charge is typically calculated on a credit card account.

2. What is the major benefit of having a credit card with a grace period?

3. Briefly summarize the steps you should take if you find an error on your credit card account billing statement.

7.4 UNDERSTANDING CONSUMER INSTALLMENT LOANS

Consumers obtain installment credit in two ways. With a **cash loan**, the borrower receives cash and then uses it to make purchases, pay off other loans, or make investments. With a **purchase loan** (also called **sales credit**), the consumer makes a purchase on credit with no cash transferring from the lender to the borrower. Instead, the funds go directly from the lender to the seller. For example, a car buyer might obtain a purchase loan from the Ford Credit to buy a new Ford Fiesta. With some purchase loans, the seller is also the lender. For all consumer loans, the borrower will sign a formal **promissory note** (a written installment loan contract) that spells out the terms of the loan.

7.4a Installment Loans Can Be Unsecured or Secured

Credit can either be unsecured or secured. An **unsecured loan** is granted solely based on the good credit character of the borrower. Sometimes unsecured loans are called **signature loans** because they are backed up by only the borrower's signature. Because unsecured loans carry higher risk than secured debts, the interest rate charged on them is substantially higher.

A **secured loan** requires a cosigner or collateral. A **cosigner** agrees to pay the debt if the original borrower fails to do so. Being a cosigner is a major responsibility because a cosigner has the same legal obligations for repayment as the original borrower does. In case of default, a lender will go after the party—either the borrower or the cosigner—from whom it is more likely to collect the funds. Remember that when people require a cosigner, it means that the lender feels that the borrower is not creditworthy on his or her own, and that judgment is usually quite correct. A good rule in life is to never cosign for a loan, even for relatives.

> **LEARNING OBJECTIVE 4**
> Describe the important features of consumer installment loans.
>
> **promissory note**
> *Written installment loan contract that spells out the terms of the loan.*
>
> **unsecured loan/signature loan**
> *Loan granted based solely on borrower's good creditworthiness.*
>
> **secured loan**
> *Loan that is backed by collateral or a cosigner.*

DID YOU KNOW

Sean's Success Story

Sean has been very careful about his use of credit since he graduated and began working full time for a marketing firm. He purchased a two-year-old used car soon after taking his job. He shopped thoroughly for the lowest APR and, so far, has made all of his payments on time. He also has three credit cards. One is a rewards card that he uses for most of his day-to-day spending, and he pays the card balance off in full every month. He has used his rewards bonuses to buy some cameras that he uses in his photography hobby. Sean has a second card that he uses when he travels on business.

This is also a rewards card, and it provides air miles that he has used for personal travel. He pays this card off with his travel reimbursement checks from his employer. He doesn't use his third card very often as it is used to charge items that he figures he might not be able to pay in full when the monthly bill is received. Sean is careful to make certain that he pays off the card balance before using it again for another purchase. He also does not carry this card with him so that he must return home before fully deciding to take on more debt that he cannot repay in full when the bill is received.

A loan secured with **collateral** means that the lender has a security interest in the property that is pledged as collateral. For example, the vehicle itself is the collateral on an automobile loan. The item of collateral does not necessarily need to be the property purchased with the loan. Typically, the lender records a lien in the county courthouse to make the security interest known to the public. A **lien** is a legal right to seize and dispose of (usually sell) property to obtain payment of a claim. When the loan is repaid, the lien will be removed. The borrower should double check to make sure this removal occurs.

In the event that the borrower fails to repay a loan, the creditor can exercise the lien and seize the collateral through repossession, sometimes without notice. Almost all credit contracts contain an **acceleration clause** stating that after a specific number of payments are unpaid (often just one), the loan is considered in default and all remaining installments are due and payable upon demand of the creditor. These clauses protect the lender's interest but can prove very difficult for borrowers. Don't be fooled if you miss a payment and the lender does not exercise the acceleration clause immediately. It can do so at any time after default occurs. Therefore, never ignore a warning letter from a creditor!

7.4b Purchase Loan Installment Contracts

Two kinds of contracts are used when purchasing goods with an installment loan:

- **Installment purchase agreements** (also called **collateral installment loans** or **chattel mortgage loans**), in which the title of the property passes to the buyer when the contract is signed. An installment purchase agreement provides a measure of protection for the borrower, as the creditor must follow all legal procedures required by state law when repossessing the property. Some state laws permit the lender to take secured property back as soon as the buyer falls behind in payments, possibly by seizing a car right from a person's driveway.

- **Conditional sales contracts** (also known as **financing leases**), in which the title does not pass to the buyer until the last installment payment has been paid. Thus it may be repossessed as soon as any payment is missed.

lien

A legal right to seize and dispose of (usually sell) property to obtain payment of a claim. Once the loan is paid, the lien is removed.

acceleration clause

Part of a credit contract stating that after a specific number of payments are unpaid (often just one), the loan is considered in default, and all remaining installments are due and payable upon demand of the creditor.

CONCEPT CHECK 7.4

1. Describe how a cash loan and a purchase loan differ.

2. Distinguish between a secured and an unsecured loan.

3. Describe when a lender might enforce an acceleration clause on a loan, and explain the impact of such an action by the lender.

4. Differentiate between an installment purchase agreement and a conditional sales contract.

7.5 CALCULATING INTEREST ON CONSUMER LOANS

The federal **Truth in Lending Act (TIL)** requires lenders to disclose to credit applicants both the interest rate expressed as an APR and the finance charge. Always inquire about the APR if it is not readily apparent, and use it to compare rates from other lenders to obtain the best deal. The finance charge is the cost of credit expressed in dollars. The finance charge plus the original amount borrowed must be paid.

7.5a Calculating an Installment Loan Payment

Installment credit typically comes with a **fixed interest rate**, meaning that the rate will not change over the life of the loan. Lenders may offer **variable-rate loans** (also called **adjustable-rate loans**) to borrowers. When the loan rate varies, the monthly payment

LEARNING OBJECTIVE 5

Calculate the interest and annual percentage rate on consumer loans.

Truth in Lending Act (TIL)

Requires lenders to disclose to credit applicants both the interest rate expressed as an annual percentage rate (APR) and the finance charge.

Table 7-1 — Monthly Installment Payment (Principal and Interest) Required to Repay $1000*

APR†	Number of Monthly Payments						
	12	**24**	**36**	**48**	**60**	**72**	**84**
5	$85.61	$43.87	$29.97	$23.03	$18.87	$16.10	$14.13
6	86.07	44.32	30.42	23.49	19.33	16.57	14.61
7	86.53	44.77	30.88	23.95	19.80	17.05	15.09
8	86.99	45.23	31.34	24.41	20.28	17.53	15.59
9	87.45	45.68	31.80	24.88	20.76	18.03	16.09
10	87.92	46.14	32.27	25.36	21.25	18.53	16.60
11	88.38	46.61	32.74	25.85	21.74	19.03	17.12
12	88.85	47.07	33.21	26.33	22.24	19.55	17.65
13	89.32	47.54	33.69	26.83	22.75	20.07	18.19
14	89.79	48.01	34.18	27.33	23.27	20.61	18.74
15	90.26	48.49	34.67	27.83	23.79	21.14	19.27
16	90.73	48.96	35.16	28.34	24.32	21.69	19.86
17	91.20	49.44	35.65	28.85	24.85	22.25	20.44
18	91.68	49.92	36.15	29.37	25.39	22.81	21.02
19	92.16	50.41	36.66	29.90	25.94	23.38	21.61
20	92.63	50.90	37.16	30.43	26.49	23.95	22.21

* To illustrate, assume an automobile loan of $14,000 at 8 percent for five years. To repay $1000, the monthly payment is $20.28; therefore, multiply $20.28 (8% row and 60-month column) by 14 to give a monthly payment of $283.92. For amounts other than exact $1000 increments, simply use decimals. For example, for a loan of $14,500, the multiplier would be 14.5.

† For fractional interest rates of 5.5, 6.5, 7.5, and so on, simply take a monthly payment halfway between the whole-number APR payments. For example, the payment for 48 months at 9.5 percent is $25.12 ($25.36 − $24.88 = $0.48; $0.48/2 = $0.24; $0.24 + $24.88 = $25.12).

will go up or down, allowing the loan to be paid off by the same date as originally established in the contract.

To help you figure out the required monthly payment for different loan amounts, Table 7-1 shows various monthly installment payments used to repay a $1000 loan at commonly seen APR interest rates and time periods. For loans of other dollar amounts, divide the borrowed amount by 1000 and multiply the result by the appropriate figure from the table. For example, an automobile loan for $12,000, financed at 10 percent interest, might be repaid in 36 equal monthly payments of $387.24 ($32.27 × 12). A loan for $3550 at 16 percent for 24 months will require monthly payments of $173.81 ($48.96 × 3.550).

The finance charge must include all mandatory charges to be paid by the borrower. In addition to interest, lenders may charge fees for a credit investigation; a loan application; or credit life, credit disability, or credit unemployment insurance. When fees are required, the lender must include them in the finance charge in dollars and as part of the APR calculations. When the borrower elects these options voluntarily, the fees are not included in the finance charge and APR calculations, even though they raise the actual cost of borrowing.

It is easy to calculate the finance charge on a consumer loan. First, multiply the monthly payment by the number of months and subtract the original amount borrowed. In the 36-month automobile loan example given earlier, the finance charge would be $1940.64 [($387.24 × 36) − $12,000]. Second, add any other mandatory charges.

variable-rate (adjustable-rate) loans

Loans for which the interest rate varies with the monthly payment going up or down, allowing the loan to be paid off by the original end date.

DO IT IN CLASS

7.5b Calculation of the Finance Charges and APR for Installment Loans

Interest accounts for the greatest portion of the finance charge. Three methods are used to calculate interest on installment and noninstallment credit: the declining-balance (sometimes called the simple-interest) method, the add-on interest method, and the discount method. The declining-balance method is widely used by credit unions to calculate interest on all loans, and it is always used for credit cards and home mortgages. The add-on method predominates on installment loans at banks, savings banks, and consumer finance companies when financing automobiles, furniture, electronics, and other credit requiring collateral. The following discussion illustrates the calculation of the APR for installment loans using each of the three methods.

1. The Declining-Balance Method Is Fair to Both Lender and Borrower With the **declining-balance method**, the interest assessed during each payment period (usually each month) is based on the current outstanding balance of the installment loan. The lender initially calculates a schedule (such as that given in Table 7-2) to have the balance repaid in full after a certain number of months. The borrower may vary the rate of repayment by making payments larger than those scheduled or may repay the loan in full at any time.

Here is an illustration of the declining-balance method for an installment loan. As shown in Table 7-2, at the end of the first month, a **periodic interest rate** (the monthly rate applied to the outstanding balance of a loan) of 1½ percent (18 percent annually divided by 12 months) is applied to the beginning balance of $1000, giving an interest charge of $15. Of the first monthly installment of $91.68, $15 goes toward the payment of interest and $76.68 ($91.68 − $15.00) goes toward payment of the principal.

For the second month, the outstanding balance is reduced to $923.32 ($1000 − $76.68). Since the balance is $78.68 lower, the interest portion of the payment drops to $13.85 (0.015 × $923.32). Because the declining-balance method applies the periodic interest rate to the outstanding loan balance, the APR and the simple interest rate will differ only if fees (such as an application fee) boost the finance charge. (This method of paying off a loan, called **amortization**, is also discussed in

declining-balance method

Interest calculation method in which interest is assessed during each billing period (usually each month) based on the outstanding balance of the installment loan that billing period.

periodic interest rate

The monthly rate applied to the outstanding balance of a loan.

amortization

Loan repayment method in which part of the payment goes to pay interest and part goes to repay principal. Extra payments toward principal shorten the life of the loan and decrease the total amount of interest paid.

Table 7-2	Sample Repayment Schedule for $1000 Principal Plus Interest Using the Declining-Balance Method (1½ Percent per Month)				
Month	Outstanding Balance	Payment	Interest	Principal	Balance
1	$1,000.00	$91.68	$15.00	$76.68	$923.32
2	923.32	91.68	13.85	77.83	845.49
3	845.49	91.68	12.68	79.00	766.49
4	766.49	91.68	11.50	80.18	686.31
5	686.31	91.68	10.29	81.39	604.92
6	604.92	91.68	9.07	82.61	522.31
7	522.31	91.68	7.83	83.85	438.46
8	438.46	91.68	6.58	85.10	353.36
9	353.36	91.68	5.30	86.38	266.98
10	266.98	91.68	4.00	87.68	179.30
11	179.30	91.68	2.69	88.99	90.31
12	90.31	91.66	1.35	90.31	0

Chapter 9 when we examine home mortgage loans.) Note that declining-balance loans carry no prepayment penalties.

2. The Add-On Method Favors the Lender The add-on method is also widely used for computing interest on installment loans. With this method, the interest is calculated and added to the amount borrowed to determine the total amount to be repaid. Equation (7.1) is used to calculate the dollar amount of interest. Note that the interest rate used in this equation for the add-on method is an add-on rate and should not be confused with the APR.

With the **add-on interest method**, interest is calculated by applying an interest rate to the amount borrowed times the number of years. The add-on interest formula given in Equation (7.1) is used as follows:

$$I = PRT \quad \text{(7.1)*}$$

where

add-on interest method
Interest is calculated by applying an interest rate to the amount borrowed times the number of years to arrive at the total interest to be charged.

DO IT IN CLASS

I = Interest or finance charges
P = Principal amount borrowed
R = Rate of interest (simple, add-on, or discount rate)
T = Time of loan in years

For example, assume that Graciela Lopez of New York City borrows $2000 for two years at 9 percent add-on interest to be repaid in monthly installments. Using Equation (7.1), her finance charge in dollars is $360 ($2000 × 0.09 × 2). Adding the finance charge ($360) to the amount borrowed ($2000) gives a total amount of $2360 to be repaid. When this amount is divided by the total number of scheduled payments (24), we find that Graciela must make 24 monthly payments of $98.33.

Calculating the APR When the Add-On Method Is Used Add-on rates and APRs are not equivalent. This is because the add-on calculation assumes the original debt is owed for the entire period of the loan. But of course the debt does go down as the debt is repaid. In the example just given, Graciela does not have use of the total amount borrowed for the full two years. Equation (7.2) shows the *n*-ratio method of estimating the APR on her add-on loan.

$$\begin{aligned}
APR &= \frac{Y(95P + 9)F}{12P(P + 1)(4D + F)} \quad \text{(7.2)*} \\
&= \frac{(12)(95 \times 24 + 9)(360)}{12(24)(24 + 1)[(4 \times 2000) + 360]} \\
&= \frac{(12)(2289)(360)}{(288)(25)(8360)} \\
&= \frac{9,888,480}{60,192,000} \\
&= 16.4\%
\end{aligned}$$

Where

APR = Annual percentage rate
Y = Number of payments in one year
F = Finance charge in dollars (dollar cost of credit)
D = Debt (amount borrowed or proceeds)
P = Total number of scheduled payments

Using Equation (7.2), the APR is 16.4 percent. Note that the APR is approximately double the add-on rate because, on average, Graciela has use of only half of the borrowed money during the entire loan period.

DID YOU KNOW

Your Worst Financial Blunders in Credit Cards and Consumer Loans

Based on others' financial woes, you will make mistakes in personal finance when you:

1. *Fail to shop for the lowest APR on credit cards and consumer loans.*
2. *Regularly carry balances on credit card accounts.*
3. *Use a credit card rather than lower interest rate installment loans to make expensive purchases.*

*Calculations involving Equation (7.1) and (7.2) can be found on the *Garman/Forgue* companion website.

DID YOU KNOW

Turn Bad Habits into Good Ones

Do You Do This?

Skim read your credit card billing statements

Pay with whatever card you pull out first from your wallet or purse

Make only the minimum payment on your credit card

Ignore the potential to earn rewards on your credit cards

Focus on the size of the monthly payment when you take out loans

Do This Instead!

Read each statement for completeness and accuracy

Avoid making purchases that you plan to pay off with a credit card on which you carry a balance

Set a date for paying off that card balance in full and make the payments required to meet your goal

Open an account that provides rewards and make day-to-day purchases paying balances in full when billed

Focus on the annual percentage rate and length of loan

DO IT NOW!

You know more about personal finance after reading this chapter, so get started right now by:

1. *Making a list of all your debts currently outstanding, the amounts owed, to whom, and at what interest rates.*

2. *Projecting any money you might borrow between now and graduation.*

3. *Using the calculator at finance .yahoo.com/calculator/loans/det03/ to determine your monthly payments if you were to pay off your total debt owed at graduation within 3 years, 5 years, and 10 years.*

prepayment penalty

Special charge assessed to the borrower for paying off a loan early.

rule of 78s method/sum of the digits method

A common method of calculating the prepayment penalty on a loan that uses the add-on method for calculating the interest.

The Rule of 78s Determines the Prepayment Penalty When an Add-On Loan Is Repaid Early Most installment loan contracts that use the add-on method include a **prepayment penalty**—a special charge assessed to the borrower for paying off a loan early. Prepayment penalties take into consideration the reality that borrowers should pay more in interest early in the loan period when they have the use of more money and increasingly less interest as the debt shrinks over time. With an add-on method loan, however, the interest is spread evenly across all payments rather than declining as the loan balance falls. If an add-on method loan is paid off early, the lender will use some penalty method to compensate for the lower interest component applied in the early months.

The **rule of 78s method** (also called the **sum of the digits method**) is the most widely used method of calculating a prepayment penalty. Its name derives from the fact that, for a one-year loan, the numbers between 1 and 12 for each month add up to 78 ($12 + 11 + 10 + 9 + 8 + 7 + 6 + 5 + 4 + 3 + 2 + 1$). For a two-year loan, the numbers between 1 and 24 would be added, and so on for loans with longer time periods.

To illustrate the use of the rule of 78s method, consider the case of Devin Grigsby from West Lafayette, Indiana. He borrowed $500 for 12 months plus an additional $80 finance charge and is scheduled to pay equal monthly installments of $48.33 ($580 ÷ 12). Assume Devin wants to pay the loan off after only six months. He might assume—incorrectly—that he would owe only $250 more because after six months he had paid $250 (one-half) of the $500 borrowed and $40 (one-half) of the finance charge, for a total of $290 in payments ($48.33 × 6). Actually, Devin still owes $268.46, including a prepayment penalty of $18.46. To calculate this amount using the rule of 78s method, the lender adds together all of the numbers between 12 and 7 (12 for the first month, 11 for the second, and so on for six months): $12 + 11 + 10 + 9 + 8 + 7 = 57$. The lender assumes that during the first six months $58.46 [(57 ÷ 78) × $80]—not $40—of the finance charges was received from the $290 in payments Devin had made on the loan.*

* If the loan was paid off after one month, the amount of interest paid is assumed to be 12/78 of the $80 finance charge, or $12.31. For a loan paid in full after two months, the amount of interest paid is assumed to be 23/78 of the total (12/78 for month 1 plus 11/78 for month 2), or $23.59.

Consequently, only $231.54 ($290.00 − $58.46) was paid on the $500 borrowed, leaving $268.46 ($500.00 − $231.54) still owed, for a prepayment penalty of $18.46 ($268.46 − $250.00).

3. With the Discount Method, Interest Is Paid Up Front The **discount method** is sometimes used by creditors to compute the interest on an installment loan. Here the interest is calculated based on a discount rate that is multiplied times the amount borrowed and multiplied by the number of years to repay. The interest is then subtracted from the amount of the loan, and only the difference is given to the borrower. Thus, the interest is paid up front.

When this method is applied to our earlier example involving Graciela Lopez, she would receive only $1640 [$2000 − ($2000 × 2 × 9%)] at the beginning of the loan period. Her monthly payment would be $83.33 ($2000 ÷ 24). Using Equation (7.2), the APR would be 19.8 percent (the APR rises because only $1640 is obtained while $2000 is repaid).

DO IT IN CLASS

discount method
Interest is calculated based on a discount rate multiplied by the amount borrowed and by the number of years to repay. Interest is then subtracted from the amount of the loan and the difference is given to the borrower. In this method, interest is paid up front before any part of the payment is applied to the principal.

CONCEPT CHECK 7.5

1. Explain how the interest is calculated on a consumer loan that uses the declining-balance method.

2. Summarize how interest is calculated on a consumer loan that uses the add-on method.

3. What is the effect of the rule of 78s when a borrower repays an add-on method loan early?

4. Explain how the interest is calculated on a consumer loan that uses the discount method.

WHAT DO YOU RECOMMEND *NOW?*

Now that you have read this chapter on credit cards and consumer loans, what would you recommend to Zachary Cochrane regarding:

1. His approach to using credit cards, including the number of cards he has?
2. Estimating the credit card interest charges he is paying each month?
3. How he might lower his interest expense each month?
4. Consolidating his credit card debts into one installment loan?

© iStockphoto.com/serts

BIG PICTURE SUMMARY OF LEARNING OBJECTIVES

L01 **Compare the common types of consumer credit, including credit cards and installment loans.**

Borrowers can use both installment and noninstallment credit. Open-ended credit is an example of noninstallment credit. It permits the customer to gain repeated access to credit without having to fill out a new application each time one borrows money. The consumer may choose either to repay the debt in a single payment or to make a series of payments of varying amounts. Bank credit cards and travel and entertainment credit cards are the most commonly used open-ended credit accounts.

LO2 **Describe the types and features of credit card accounts.**

Credit card borrowers must adhere to all the rules of the account or risk being charged a number of fees such as late-payment and bounced-check fees.

LO3 **Manage your credit card accounts to avoid fees and finance charges.**

Credit card statements provide a monthly summary of account activity, the calculation of any finance charges, and how long it will take to pay off the card balance if you only pay the minimum payment required. Credit card issuers compute finance charges by multiplying the average daily balance by the periodic interest rate.

LO4 **Describe the important features of consumer installment loans.**

Consumer loans, also called installment loans, have several features that distinguish them from credit

card accounts. Loans usually have a fixed payment for a fixed number of months. Once the loan is paid off, the account is closed and a new account would need to be opened if the person wanted to take out another loan.

LO5 **Calculate the interest and annual percentage rate on consumer loans.**

Both the declining-balance and add-on methods are used to calculate the interest on installment loans, although the annual percentage rate (APR) formula gives the correct rate in all cases. With declining-balance loans, the dollar amount of interest incorporated in each monthly payment declines as the loan balance declines.

LET'S TALK ABOUT IT

1. **Learning More About Credit.** Most young adults form their opinions about credit and debt from what they see in their parents' experiences. How has your perception of carrying credit card debt, student loans, and other borrowing changed as a result of reading Chapters 6 and 7?

2. **What Type of Borrowing Might Be Best?** If you wanted to borrow money to study abroad for a semester and could pay it back within two years after returning, would you prefer a single-payment loan, an installment loan, or a cash advance on a credit card? Why?

3. **Are Rewards Cards a Good Idea?** Some credit cards offer rewards points or a 1 percent or higher cash back reward for all purchases made on the card. How would you feel about using such a card to get those rewards with the intention of paying the balance off in full each month?

4. **The Declining-Balance Method.** How do you feel about the fact that interest costs are higher in the early months of a declining-balance loan than they are in the later months?

5. **The Rule of 78s.** Are prepayment penalties such as that applied with the rule of 78s justified? Why or why not?

DO THE MATH

1. **Monthly Payments and Finance Charges or an Add-on Rate Loan.** Zachary Porter of Highland Heights, Kentucky, is contemplating borrowing $10,000 from his bank. The bank could use add-on rates of 6.5 percent for 3 years, 7 percent for 4 years, and 8 percent for 5 years. Use Equation 7.1 to calculate the finance charge and monthly payment for these three options.

    DO IT IN CLASS
    PAGE 215

2. **Monthly Payments and Finance Charges.** Kimberly Jensen of Griffin, Georgia, wants to buy some living room furniture for her new apartment. A local store offered credit at an APR of 16 percent, with a maximum term of four years. The furniture she wishes to purchase costs $2800, with no down payment required. Using Table 7-1 or the *Garman/Forgue* companion website, make the following calculations:

    DO IT IN CLASS
    PAGE 213

    (a) What is the amount of the monthly payment if she borrowed for four years?

    (b) What are the total finance charges over that four-year period?

    (c) How would the payment change if Kimberly reduced the loan term to three years?

    (d) What are the total finance charges over that three-year period?

    (e) How would the payment change if she could afford a down payment of $500 with four years of financing?

    (f) What are the total finance charges over that four-year period given the $500 down payment?

3. **Average Daily Balance and Finance Charges.** Kayla Sampson, an antiques dealer from Great Bend, Kansas,

received her monthly billing statement for April for her MasterCard account. The statement indicated that she had a beginning balance of $600, on day 5 she charged $150, on day 12 she charged $300, and on day 15 she made a $200 payment. Out of curiosity, Kayla wanted to confirm that the finance charge for the billing cycle was correct.

DO IT IN CLASS
PAGE 209

(a) What was Kayla's average daily balance for April without new purchases?

(b) What was her finance charge on the balance in part (a) if her APR is 19.2 percent?

(c) What was her average daily balance for April with new purchases?

(d) What was her finance charge on the balance in part (c) if her APR is 19.2 percent?

4. **Average Daily Balance.** Alexis Monroe, a biologist from Storm Lake, Iowa, is curious about the accuracy of the interest charges shown on her most recent credit card billing statement, which appears in Figure 7-2 on page 207. Use the average daily balances provided to recalculate the interest charges, and compare the result with the amount shown on the statement.

5. **Comparing APRs.** James Sprater of Conway, South Carolina, has been shopping for a loan to buy a new car. He wants to borrow $18,000 for four or five years. James's credit union offers a declining-balance loan at 9.1 percent for 48 months, resulting in a monthly payment of $448.78. The credit union does not offer five-year auto loans for amounts less than $20,000,

however. If James borrowed $18,000, this payment would strain his budget. A local bank offered current depositors a five-year loan at a 9.34 percent APR, with a monthly payment of $376.62. This credit would not be a declining-balance loan. Because James is not a depositor in the bank, he would also be charged a $25 credit check fee and a $45 application fee. James likes the lower payment but knows that the APR is the true cost of credit, so he decided to confirm the APRs for both loans before making his decision.

(a) What is the APR for the credit union loan?

(b) Use the n-ratio formula to confirm the APR on the bank loan as quoted for depositors.

(c) What is the add-on interest rate for the bank loan?

(d) What would be the true APR on the bank loan if James did not open an account to avoid the credit check and application fees?

6. **Rule of 78s.** Miguel Perez of Norfolk, Nebraska, obtained a two-year installment loan for $1500 to buy some furniture eight months ago. The loan had a 12.6 percent APR and a finance charge of $204.72. His monthly payment is $71.03. Miguel has made eight monthly payments and now wants to pay off the remainder of the loan. The lender will use the rule of 78s method to calculate a prepayment penalty.

DO IT IN CLASS
PAGE 217

(a) How much will Miguel need to give the lender to pay off the loan?

(b) What is the dollar amount of the prepayment penalty on this loan?

FINANCIAL PLANNING CASES

CASE 1

The Johnsons' Credit Questions

Harry and Belinda need some questions answered regarding credit. Their three-year-old car has been experiencing mechanical problems lately. Instead of buying a new set of tires, as planned for in March, they are considering trading the car in for a newer used vehicle so that Harry can have dependable transportation for commuting to work. The couple still owes $3600 to the bank for their current car, or $285 per month for the remaining 18 months of the 48-month loan. The trade-in value of this car plus $1000 that Harry earned from a freelance interior design job should allow the couple to pay off the auto loan and leave $1250 for a down payment on the newer car. The Johnsons have agreed on a sales price for the newer car of $14,250. The money planned for tires

will be spent for other incidental taxes and fees associated with the purchase.

(a) Make recommendations to Harry and Belinda regarding where to seek financing and what APR to expect.

(b) Using the *Garman/Forgue* companion website or the information in Table 7-1, calculate the monthly payment for a loan period of three, four, and five years at 8 percent APR. Describe the relationship between the loan period and the payment amount.

(c) Harry and Belinda have a cash-flow deficit projected for several months this year (see Table 3-6 and Table 3-7 on pages 87–88). Suggest how, when, and where they might finance the shortages by borrowing.

CASE 2

Victor and Maria Have a Billing Dispute

Maria Hernandez was reviewing her recent bank credit card account statement when she found two charges that she and Victor could not have made. The charges were for rental of a hotel room and purchase of a meal on the same day in a distant city. These charges totaled $219.49 out of the couple's $367.89 balance for the month.

(a) What payment should Maria make on the account?

(b) How should she notify her credit card issuer about the unauthorized use?

(c) Once the matter is resolved, what should Maria do to ensure that her credit history is not negatively affected by this error?

CASE 3

Julia Price Thinks About Her Use of Credit Cards

Julia has been thinking about how she uses credit cards. She has two bank cards and three store cards. The APRs on the cards range from 10.5 to 24.9 percent, with the store cards being among the highest. She uses the cards often and picks whatever card she comes to first in her wallet. Most months she pays the balance off in full. However, sometimes she is unable to pay the balance on one or more of the cards, and so she only pays the minimum balance. Julia feels she is doing her best on managing her cards but wants to do better. She is thinking about using just one of her bank cards for any purchases that she thinks she will be unable to pay at the end of the month. Offer your opinions about her thinking.

CASE 4

A Delayed Report of a Stolen Credit Card

Jia Li Sun, took her sister-in-law Ah-Iam Johnson out for an expensive lunch. When it came for the time to

pay the bill, Jia Li noticed that her Visa credit card was missing, so she paid the bill with her MasterCard. While driving home, Jia Li remembered that she had last used the Visa card about a week earlier. She became concerned that a sales clerk or someone else could have taken it and might be fraudulently charging purchases on her card.

DO IT IN CLASS
PAGE 210

(a) Summarize Jia Li's legal rights in this situation.

(b) Discuss the likelihood that Jia Li must pay Visa for any illegal charges to the account.

CASE 5

Clauses in a Car Purchase Contract

Lauren Rowland is a dentist in Saint Charles, Missouri, who recently entered into a contract to buy a new automobile. After signing to finance $18,000, she hurriedly left the office of the sales finance company with her copy of the contract. Later that evening, Lauren read the contract and noticed several clauses—an acceleration clause, a repossession clause, and a rule of 78s clause. When she signed the contract, Lauren was told these standard clauses should not concern her.

(a) Should Lauren be concerned about these clauses? Why or why not?

(b) Considering the rule of 78s clause, what will happen if Lauren pays off the loan before the regular due date?

(c) If Lauren had financed the $18,000 for four years at 7 percent APR, what would her monthly payment be, using the information in Table 7-1 or on the *Garman/Forgue* companion website?

BE YOUR OWN PERSONAL FINANCIAL MANAGER

1. **List Your Credit Card Accounts.** Complete Worksheet 28:

   MY PERSONAL FINANCIAL PLANNER

   My Credit Card Inventory from "My Personal Financial Planner," which asks you to make an inventory of your credit cards including the name of the card (Visa, Discover, etc.); issuer (bank, retailer, etc.); account number; the current APRs for purchases, balance transfers, and cash advances; outstanding balance, if any; usual due dates; and phone numbers to use if the card is lost/stolen or there is a billing error.

2. **Shop for a New Credit Card.** Complete Worksheet 29: Comparing My Credit Card Offers from "My Personal

   MY PERSONAL FINANCIAL PLANNER

   Financial Planner," which asks you to shop for a new credit card from two different sources. If you already have a credit card, include the information on that card in the third column in the worksheet. Determine whether your current card is the best of the three, or if you have no current card, choose among the two you have researched.

3. **Monitor Your Credit Card Statements.** Review your most recent credit card statements for accuracy. List the steps you would take if you found an error in the statement.

4. **Compare Hypothetical Vehicle Loans.** Assume you have decided to buy a used car by borrowing $6000 and you have offers for loans at 6, 8, and 10 percent and each can be for 3, 4, or 5 years. Complete

MY PERSONAL FINANCIAL PLANNER

Worksheet 30: Monthly Installment Loan Payment Calculator from "My Personal Financial Planner" to determine the monthly payment for each of the six loan arrangements. Which loan is most attractive to you and why?

ON THE NET

Go to the Web pages indicated to complete these exercises.

1. **Review Current Market Interest Rates.** Visit the website for Bankrate.com at www.bankrate.com/credit-cards.aspx, where you will find information on bank credit card interest rates around the United States. View the information for the lenders in a large city nearest your home. How does the information compare with the interest rates charged on your own credit card account(s)? How do the rates in the city you selected compare with those found elsewhere in the United States?

2. **Explore the Impact of Varying Interest Rates and Time Periods on a Loan Payment Amount.** Visit the website for Interest.com at www.interest.com/auto /calculators/auto-loan-calculator/. There you will find an auto loan calculator that determines the monthly payment for any declining-balance loan given a specified time period, interest rate, and loan amount. Assume you wish to borrow $12,000 to buy a car. Vary the time period and interest rate of the loan to see how these variations affect your monthly payment.

3. **How Long Will It Take to Pay Off Your Credit Card?** Do you owe money on one or more credit cards? Visit the Bankrate.com website at www.bankrate.com and click on "Calculators" to find a calculator that will tell you how long it will take to pay off your balances given various monthly payment amounts.

ACTION INVOLVEMENT PROJECTS

1. **Comparing Credit Card Offers.** Select two local retailers, a local bank, and a local credit card and request credit card applications from all four. Compare the applications for the types of information they require. Compare the APRs offered among the cards and others that you may already hold. Make a table that summarizes your findings and write some brief reactions to what you found.

2. **Credit Card Repayment Patterns.** Survey five of your friends about their patterns of using their credit card accounts including their choice to make the minimum payment rather than pay off the balance in full each month. Compare what they do to your own pattern, and write a summary of your findings.

3. **Credit Card Billing Errors.** Survey five of your friends about experiences they have had concerning a billing error on their credit cards. Compare the steps they took to resolve the error(s) with those recommended in this chapter. Write a summary of your findings.

4. **Installment Loan Interest Methods.** Visit a bank and a credit union in your community and your own bankers. Tell them that you are considering taking out a loan to purchase a vehicle. Inquire whether they offer declining-balance or add-on method loans and which approach they would recommend. Compare the responses to the information provided in this chapter, and write a summary of your findings.

Visit the Garman/Forgue companion website at www.cengagebrain.com.

8

Vehicle and Other Major Purchases

YOU MUST BE KIDDING, RIGHT?

When Dora Marquez graduated from college three years ago, she really wanted a fully equipped Honda Civic. Her monthly payment would be about $350 per month, about $70 more than she could afford. To help Dora meet her budget, the dealer suggested that she lease the vehicle and offered a 42-month lease option at $270 per month with a driving maximum of 12,000 miles per year. The contract had a $0.30 per mile fee at the end of the lease for any excess mileage. Now, with six more months on her lease, Dora is already 1500 miles over the 42,000 (3.5 × 12,000) mileage limit in her contract. What is Dora's best option at this point?

A. Turn back the vehicle now and pay the $450 (1500 × $0.30) for excess mileage.

B. Try to cut back on her driving to minimize her excess mileage fee, which could be higher than $2500 if she keeps driving at the same rate as she has been.

C. Stop driving the car and pay $450 for excess mileage when she turns it back at the end of the lease.

D. Continue driving the vehicle and buy it at the end of the lease by paying the residual value agreed upon when she entered into the contract.

The answer is D. None of the other options is financially practical. Dora learned a hard lesson. Leases may have a lower monthly payment but have hidden costs that often are not known until the very end of the contract!

LEARNING OBJECTIVES

After reading this chapter, you should be able to:

1 Explain the first three steps in the planned buying process that occur prior to interacting with sellers.

2 Describe the process of comparison shopping.

3 Negotiate and decide effectively when making major purchases.

4 Use effective complaint procedures.

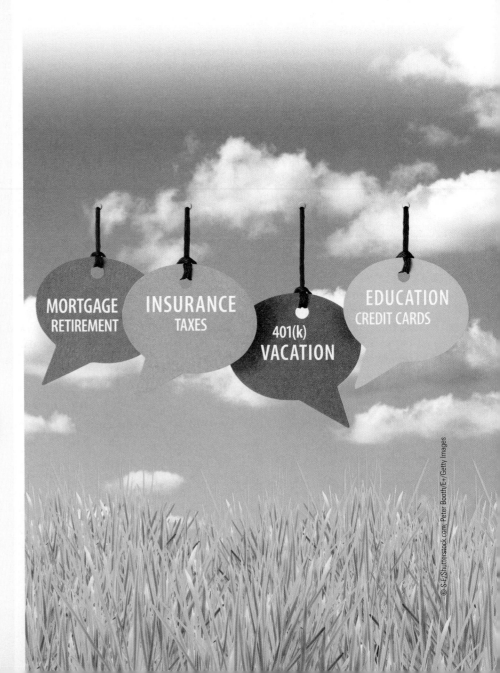

© S-F/Shutterstock.com; Peter Booth/E+/Getty Images

WHAT DO YOU RECOMMEND?

David and Lisa Cosgrove of Tacoma, Washington, are in their early 40s and have three children. They own three vehicles. Lisa drives an almost-new Toyota Camry; David uses a five-year-old Ford pickup; and Alyssa, the couple's 17-year-old daughter, drives a ten-year-old Dodge. Recently, a fire in their garage destroyed both the Dodge and the Camry. The Cosgroves received an insurance settlement of $21,900 on Lisa's car, although the loan payoff amount was $22,800. Alyssa's Dodge was not insured for fire. The couple wants to obtain replacement cars that are similar to those destroyed.

What do you recommend to David and Lisa on automobiles and other major purchases regarding:

1. How to search for two vehicles to replace those destroyed?

2. Whether to replace Lisa's vehicle with a new or used vehicle?

3. Whether to lease or buy a vehicle?

4. How to decide between a rebate and a special low APR financing opportunity if they decide to purchase a new vehicle for Lisa?

5. How to negotiate with the sellers of the vehicles?

YOUR NEXT FIVE YEARS

In the next five years, you can start achieving financial success by doing the following related to vehicle and other major purchases:

1. *Check repair ratings history in the April issue of* Consumer Reports *magazine when planning to buy vehicles.*

2. *Purchase late-model, high-quality used vehicles and obtain a vehicle history report at www.carfax.com and www .autocheck.com and any recall history at www.nhtsa.gov.*

3. *Obtain price information from at least three sources and aggressively negotiate prices and financing terms for major purchases.*

4. *Never tell a seller what payment you can afford.*

5. *Promptly and firmly seek redress when dissatisfied with purchases or services.*

LEARNING OBJECTIVE 1

Explain the first three steps in the planned buying process that occur prior to interacting with sellers.

need
Item thought to be necessary.

want
Item not necessary but desired.

Planned buying entails thinking about the details of a purchase from the initial desire to buy to your satisfaction after the purchase. You should use planned buying principles any time, but they are especially important when you are buying a vehicle or making other major purchases. You can save thousands of dollars when buying a car and hundreds of dollars when purchasing a television. You just need to learn how to do it. If you do not plan your buying in such circumstances, you will waste money, and this will detract from your overall financial success in life.

The seven distinct steps that lead you through the planned buying process are illustrated in Figure 8-1. Steps 1, 2, and 3 occur before you interact with sellers: determining your needs and wants, performing preshopping research, and fitting a purchase into your budget. Comparison shopping and other interactions with sellers comprise the 4th step in the buying process. Steps 5 and 6—negotiating and making the decision—follow. The 7th and final step—evaluation of the decision—is taken after making the purchase. After reading this chapter, you will understand enough about the planned buying process to save money when buying expensive goods while still meeting your needs and many of your wants.

8.1 DO YOUR HOMEWORK BEFORE YOU BUY

Let's look now at the first three steps in planned buying, all of which should occur before you actually interact with sellers. They are, in a sense, the homework you do when preparing to buy.

8.1a Wants Versus Needs

A **need** is something thought to be a necessity; a **want** is unnecessary but desired. In truth, very few needs exist. Yet in everyday language, people talk too often of "needing" certain things. Calling something a need makes it no longer open to careful consideration. Instead, consider all purchase options to be wants. Of course, some wants are more important than others. That is why you must prioritize your wants and consider the benefits and costs of each want. Costs should include opportunity costs as measured by some other want or goal that will become less attainable if a given want is

Figure 8-1 **The Steps in Planned Buying**

7	Evaluating the decision
6	Making the decision
5	Negotiating
4	Comparison shopping
3	Fitting your budget
2	Preshopping research
1	Prioritizing wants

satisfied. For example, buying a car with a retractable sunroof might mean that you cannot afford to purchase one with a remote start feature.

Setting priorities becomes difficult when a decision is complex such as when buying a car or home. Consider the case of Haley Wilson, a physical therapist from St. Paul, Minnesota. Haley has been late to work several times in the past few months because her 12-year-old car has been having too many mechanical problems. Haley wants to avoid being late. But how? Should she buy a new car or a used car, lease a new car, repair her current car, or take the bus to work? After considering these options, Haley decided to buy a new car. Now she must determine which features are of high or low priority. To do so, Haley developed the worksheet shown in Figure 8-2. Such a worksheet makes it easier to formalize her wants.

8.1b Get Smart and Conduct Some Preshopping Research

Smart shoppers learn as much as they can about a product or service before buying. This process starts with **preshopping research**—gathering information before actually beginning to interact with sellers. Manufacturers, sellers, and service providers are all important sources of information about products and services during preshopping research. Two other sources are friends and consumer information in print and on the Internet.

FINANCIAL POWER POINT

Avoid Impulse Buying

Buying too quickly without fully considering priorities and alternatives is called **impulse buying**. It wastes money, and impulse buyers often do not buy what they really want and later on they too often regret their decisions.

impulse buying
Buying too quickly without fully considering priorities and alternatives.

preshopping research
Gathering information before actually beginning to interact with sellers.

Figure 8-2   Priority Worksheet (for Haley Wilson)

AUTOMOBILE FEATURE	PRIORITY LEVEL		
	1	2	3
Adaptive front lighting		✔	
Adaptive cruise control (uses radar to keep a safe distance)		✔	
Air conditioning	✔		
Aluminum wheels		✔	
Automatic transmission	✔		
Backing-up cross-path monitoring		✔	
Blind-spot monitoring			✔
Capless fuel filler	✔		
Forward-collision warning system		✔	
4-wheel ABS		✔	
4-wheel drive		✔	
Lane departure warning			✔
Leather seats	✔		
Infotainment system		✔	
Pedestrian detection			✔
Power windows	✔		
Pass-through rear seat		✔	
Satellite radio	✔		
Seat belt tightening when braking		✔	
Sun/moon roof			✔
Top-level sound system	✔		

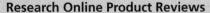

manufacturer's suggested retail price (MSRP)

The retail price set by the manufacturer and posted on the federally required side window sticker.

dealer invoice price (base invoice price)

The amount the automaker charges the dealership for new vehicles at the time the dealer buys them; it does not reflect some discounts that the dealer gets.

When buying vehicles you should always research vehicle reviews in *Consumer Reports*, which is the only magazine that objectively tests and reports on numerous product categories. Monthly issues of *Consumer Reports* generally provide a two- to five-page narrative analyzing the products and summarizing the information in chart form. *Consumer Reports Buying Guide*, which is published every December, lists facts and figures for all kinds of products. And each year, the April issue of *Consumer Reports* is devoted entirely to the purchase of automobiles. All this and more can be seen at www.ConsumerReports.org.

Know the Price You Should Expect to Pay Advertising is often a key source of information about prices. You can also obtain price information through catalogs, on the telephone, and over the Internet. This situation differs for big-ticket items. While the prices of furniture, appliances, and vehicles may be advertised, that price is almost never the lowest price you can expect to pay. This is because sellers of big-ticket items typically have the authority to negotiate an even lower price, if necessary, to make a sale. You should have a clear understanding what price to expect to pay before going out to shop. Otherwise, you risk negotiating a price higher than necessary.

Break the Dealer's Code on New Vehicle Prices You will see two prices when you walk into a vehicle dealer's showroom: (1) manufacturer's suggested retail price, and (2) dealer invoice price. Both are artificial numbers; thus your negotiation effort should not be to get close to the dealer invoice price but to a lower *real price* you may decide to pay. The **manufacturer's suggested retail price (MSRP)** is the retail price set by the manufacturer and posted on the federally required side window sticker. The dealership wants you to pay full MSRP plus any miscellaneous charges.

The **dealer invoice price** (or **base invoice price**) is the amount the automaker charges the dealership for new vehicles at the time the dealer buys them, and it does not reflect some discounts that the dealer gets. The invoice price typically has some additional charges tacked on by the dealer, which are attempts to generate additional revenue.

Web Sources Are Best for Price Information on Vehicles Edmunds.com reports that the average price for new cars and trucks is over $32,000. Smart buyers can research the average retail and wholesale prices on new and used vehicles by visiting the websites for Edmunds (www .edmunds.com), Kelley Blue Book (www.kbb.com), or the National Automobile Dealers Association (www.nadaguides.com).

Know the Value of Your Trade-in Vehicle When buying vehicles, it is common but not always advantageous, to trade in an old model when buying a new one. Vehicle buyers should know the true value of any vehicle they will trade in. Using the websites mentioned earlier, you may find the likely trade-in value of your vehicle (the wholesale price) as well as the amount you could sell it for yourself (the retail price). Armed with this information, you can more effectively negotiate a good trade-in allowance on your existing vehicle with a dealer. If you don't get a good offer on your vehicle from the dealer, shop at another dealer or consider selling it yourself.

Gauge Environmental Impact Many products such as vehicles, electronic equipment and household appliances have an impact on the environment. This factor is part of many people's purchase decisions and relevant information is often available. For example, window stickers on new vehicles include both estimated annual fuel costs and the vehicle's overall environmental impact. The labels also compare vehicles across classes so potential buyers can make more informed decisions.

8.1c Know What You Can Afford

When considering a big-ticket item everyone wonders, "Can I afford it?" An unaffordable cash purchase can wreck your budget for one or two months. However, the negative effects of an ill-advised credit or lease contract may last for years.

Consider the Cost per Use One way to view the cost of a major expenditure is to consider the cost per use of the product. For example, Dylan Lenz, an engineer from Dothan, Alabama, is considering buying a hot tub spa. He has researched several models and knows he would pay about $5000 for a model he likes including installation. Dylan figures that he would use the spa about 100 times per year and expects the spa to last about ten years, giving him 1000 uses. Dividing this figure into the price of a $5000 model yields a cost per use of $5($5000/1000), excluding the cost of chemicals, maintenance, and electricity to heat the unit. Dylan must consider if it is worth more than $5 each time he uses the spa and whether he will really use it about twice per week year in and year out.

Fit the Payment into Your Monthly Budget Many big-ticket items require the use of credit resulting in an impact on one's budget for many months in the future. To gauge this impact, consider how Haley Wilson (see Table 8-1) might fit a new car into her budget. She estimates that the dealer invoice price of the car she wants will be about $28,000. This price does not include her highest-priority wants. These options will likely add about $3300 more to the dealer invoice price: air conditioning, $700; automatic transmission, $600; leather seats, $700; capless fuel filler, $100; power windows, $400; top-level sound system, $600; and satellite ratio, $200. Buying a car with these features will run the cost up to $31,300 ($28,000 + $3300 for the options). She expects to use $3500 from her savings account as a down payment, receive $2000 for trading in her old car, and borrow the remaining amount.

The actual price she will pay for the car will depend on her ability to negotiate the final price down from the dealer invoice price. From her preshopping research, Haley knows that the final agreed upon price should be about 12 percent less than the dealer invoice price. Haley figures she should be able to negotiate the price of the purchase down by at least 10 percent from $31,300 to $28,170 ($31,300 − $3130 [$31,300 × 0.10]).

The final cost Haley will pay depends on (1) the price she actually pays for the car, (2) the amount of the down payment, (3) the time period for payback of the loan, (4) the amount she receives in trade for her old car, and (5) the interest rate on the vehicle loan. Assuming a car price of $28,170 and another $830 for sales tax and title fees to register the vehicle, Haley will need to finance about $29,000 ($28,170 + $830). The monthly payment over 48 months for a 5 percent loan could be about $668 a month (from Table 7-1 on page 213 [$23.03 × 29]).

Fit the Vehicle Payment into a Monthly Budget The next challenge is to determine if a possible vehicle payment is truly affordable. Haley tried to fit the $668 car payment into her budget as shown in Table 8-1.

Table 8-1 shows Haley's monthly budget. She started with the fact that her

DO IT IN CLASS

ConsumerReports | Subscribe to Consumer Reports

Get instant access to thousands of expert Reviews and Ratings.

New Subscribers

○ $30.00
ConsumerReports.org yearly

○ $6.95
ConsumerReports.org monthly

I accept the terms of the User Agreement and would like to subscribe with the convenience of automatic renewal.

[Next]

Current Subscribers

Active Consumer Reports Magazine subscribers click here for magazine subscriber rate.

NetPhotos2/Alamy

Time invested in preshopping research pays off in better purchase decisions.

	Table 8-1	Fitting a Vehicle Payment into a Monthly Budget (Haley Wilson's $2440 Disposable Income)		

	Prior Budget	Possible Cutbacks	New Budget
Food	$ 350	$ −30	$ 320
Clothing/laundry	120	−50	70
Vehicle maintenance/repairs/tires	80	−30	50
Auto insurance	80		80
Gasoline	160	−20	140
Housing	800		800
Utilities	150		150
Telephone	70		70
Entertainment	150	−50	100
Gifts	50	−10	40
Church and charity	60		60
Personal care	100	−20	80
Savings	200	−100	100
Miscellaneous	70	−20	50
TOTAL	**$2,440**	**$ 330**	**$2,110**
Car payment			668
TOTAL WITH CAR PAYMENT			**$2,778**

FINANCIAL POWER POINT

How Many Hours of Work Will This Item Cost?

When buying a new vehicle, computer, television, or any big-ticket item, divide the cost of the item by your hourly take-home pay. For example, if you divide the cost of a $360 camcorder by $15 take-home pay ($22 hourly minus taxes), that tells you that you must work 24 hours to pay for it.

take-home pay of $2440 is totally committed, including $200 in monthly savings. So she juggled the numbers to see if she could finance a new car and found she could only find $330. That's far short of the $668 needed for a monthly payment. By taking out a longer, 60-month 5 percent loan, she could reduce her payments to about $547 per month (29 × $18.87 from Table 7-1 on page 213). Haley's choices are to make more cutbacks in her budget, work overtime, get a part-time job, or buy a less expensive vehicle.

Alternatively, Haley could finance the car over more months. Thirty-three percent of new cars are financed for 73 to 84 months and over 20 percent are financed over 61 to 72 months. While this lowers the monthly payment, it extends the loan for a long time (perhaps longer than you want to drive the vehicle) and it costs a lot more in total interest. Perhaps she might qualify for a lower interest rate, maybe 3½ percent, at the new car dealer. Then again, Haley could forget the new car entirely and look for a used vehicle that is affordable.

CONCEPT CHECK 8.1

1. What is planned buying?

2. Distinguish between *needs* and *wants,* and explain why it may be better to act as if no needs exist.

3. Describe the types of information you need to be your own expert when making big-ticket purchases.

4. Summarize the process to determine whether you can afford a particular purchase.

8.2 USE COMPARISON SHOPPING TO FIND THE BEST BUY

Comparison shopping is the process of comparing products or services to find the best buy. A **best buy** is a product or service that, in the buyer's opinion, represents acceptable quality at a fair or low price for that level of quality. Purchasing the product with the lowest price does not necessarily ensure a best buy because quality and features count, too.

Prices on big-ticket items such as autos, furniture, appliances, and electronic equipment are rarely the same from seller to seller and vary from week to week. You can begin your comparison shopping online, but most likely you will need to visit different stores to see the products. Experts recommend that consumers use the **"rule of three"** when shopping at stores. This means comparing at least three alternatives before making a decision.

8.2a Compare Financing Options

The lowest payment does not mean the best credit plan. Better credit terms are frequently available at lenders not associated with sellers such as your credit union or bank that can lend money to make purchases for vehicles and household appliances and other big-ticket items. Also check rates on websites such as www.bankrate.com or www.interest.com.

Avoid Long-term Borrowing Beware of taking out a longer loan on a vehicle purchase, such as for five or more years, because the value of your vehicle may be less than the amount you owe for half or more of those years. This is known as being **upside down** due to negative equity. If you default on the loan or sell the vehicle, you will have to make up the difference. Rolling the negative equity forward into the car financing of the next vehicle purchase means that the amount will be added to the price of the new car.

When talking with sellers, consider "same as cash" offers on furniture, appliances, and electronics that allow you to delay interest or payment for, perhaps, 90 days to one year. If the product is paid off during this time period, you will not incur any finance charges. Be wary, however, because interest will be charged retroactively if a payment is late or if the purchase isn't fully paid off during the required time period.

When shopping for an automobile and going on a test-drive, tell the seller not to use your Social Security number or driver's license number to access your credit report and estimate how much you can afford to pay and your ability to obtain financing elsewhere.

What Is a Fair Interest Rate? A borrower with a high credit score who can get a 1 percentage point reduction in interest for a $15,000 loan over 48 months can save hundreds of dollars in interest paid over the life of the loan. You should note that the credit score used on vehicle loans will be different than the one you might obtain on your own. Credit bureaus have developed specialty scores for vehicle lending that have a heavier weighting placed on past experiences the borrower has had for those types of loans. Buyers should obtain multiple quotes from credit unions and banks. When shopping for a major purchase, ask your local credit union or bank for a **loan preapproval** before you visit sellers. This preshopping step will let you know how much you can borrow and at what interest rate.

Choose Between a Low Interest Rate and a Rebate Often a good source of loans for new vehicles is sales financing arranged through the dealer or manufacturer. The interest rate on this credit is usually low when manufacturers or dealers want to generate additional sales volume.

Many sellers also offer rebates to encourage people to buy. With a **rebate**, the seller refunds a portion of the purchase price of the product either as a direct payment or a credit against future purchases (often through a gift card). Vehicle manufacturers offer

LEARNING OBJECTIVE 2

Describe the process of comparison shopping.

comparison shopping
Process of comparing products or services to find the best buy.

best buy
Product or service that, in the buyer's opinion, represents acceptable quality at a fair or low price for that quality level.

upside down
A situation where the owner of a financed asset owes more than it is worth, thus creating negative equity.

DID YOU KNOW

Seven Things to Buy Used

Most everyone knows that used vehicles are a good option when the time comes to make a purchase. But a number of other products can be bought used as well with good quality for a low price. Sources such as eBay, Craig's List, Amazon, Goodwill Industries, the Salvation Army, consignment shops, and even garage sales can be a good source for used:

1. Fitness equipment—many people buy treadmills, elliptic trainers, stationary bikes and other such items and rarely use them. When the time comes to sell they are selling almost new items.

2. Furniture and appliances—Serviceable used furniture can be a good buy for young people just starting out or people who have moved into a larger dwelling and want to wait to furnish it fully.

3. Baby gear and clothing—Why buy new when the baby will outgrow the items in a few short months?

4. Jewelry—Buying wedding bands at a pawnshop may not be romantic but when money is tight nice items can be had at a fraction of the cost of new.

5. Electronics—many people want the very newest electronics and trade in or sell items that are technologically current.

6. Tools—many do-it-yourselfers buy tools for jobs they will not do again and will sell items that have used only a few times.

7. Sporting equipment—Golf clubs, skis, bicycles, and roller blades have winning prices at stores specializing in used equipment.

FINANCIAL POWER POINT

People Waste Rebates

Only about half of people who buy manufacturers' products that offer rebates actually take the time to complete and mail in the forms to obtain the money. The rate is even lower on items costing less than $50. Advice: Complete and mail such forms as soon as you return home with the purchase.

rebates of $1000 to $5000 to purchasers of new vehicles as a way to generate more sales volume or to help sell slow-selling models. In most cases, the buyer must choose between the rebate and a low APR loan offer also being offered by the manufacturer. Some people choose to borrow the full price elsewhere and receive the rebate in cash. In effect, this option means that they are borrowing more money than the vehicle actually costs. Plus, the buyers also lose out on the opportunity for the low APR offer.

The Run the Numbers worksheet on page 231 provides a way to calculate whether a rebate or low APR financing is the better option. If you do decide to take the rebate on a new vehicle, you should apply the money to the down payment on the vehicle or pay extra on the first monthly payment on the loan. Rebates are common when purchasing products such as vehicles, cell phones, and computers. The most current details on manufacturers' rebates to both consumers and auto dealers can be found at Edmunds.com (www .Edmunds.com). Just type in "rebates" on the Internet for others.

8.2b Compare Leasing to Buying

Leasing a new vehicle is an increasingly attractive option to people who are in the market for a car. More than 28 percent of the new cars "sold" in a recent year were actually leased. A person leasing a vehicle does not actually own the vehicle. With a **lease** on a vehicle or any other product, you are, in effect, renting the product while the ownership title remains with the lease grantor.

Is leasing a better deal than financing? It could be. Note first that the monthly cost of leasing is always lower than a purchase. This is because the payment is primarily based on the depreciation of the vehicle over the lease time period and also because in most states the sales tax is calculated on the monthly lease payment rather than the full purchase price. Still, you cannot answer this question until you understand some rules and risks of leasing.

Regulation M issued by the Federal Reserve Board governs lease contracts. A requirement of this regulation is a mandatory disclosure of pertinent information about the lease that the consumer is considering. The disclosure form must summarize the offer of the **lessor** (leasing agency) to the **lessee** (consumer). The information in this form should be compared with the actual lease contract prior to signing to ensure that the lease signed is actually what was agreed upon verbally.

lease

Rental of a product while ownership title remains with the lease grantor.

RUN THE NUMBERS

Choosing Between Low-Interest-Rate Dealer Financing and a Rebate

Advertisements for new vehicles often offer low APRs for dealer-arranged loans. A cash rebate of $1000 to $3000 (or more) off the price of the car may be offered as an alternative to the low interest rate. If you intend to pay cash, then the cash rebate obviously represents the better deal. But which alternative is better when you can arrange your own financing?

To compare the two APRs accurately, you must add the opportunity cost of the forgone rebate to the finance charge of the dealer financing. The worksheet provides an example of this process. Suppose a dealer offers 2.9 percent financing for three years with a $907 finance charge. Alternatively, you can receive

a $3000 rebate if you arrange your own financing. The price of the car before the rebate is $22,000. Assume you can make a $2000 down payment and that you can get a 6.5 percent loan on your own. This worksheet can be found on the *Garman/Forgue* companion website, or you can find similar worksheet at www .bankrate.com/calculators/auto/car-rebates-calculator.aspx.

DO IT IN CLASS

The lower of the values obtained in steps 3 and 4 is the better deal. In this instance, the financing that you arranged on your own is more attractive. In fact, any loan you arrange that carries an APR lower than 12 percent compares favorably with the dealer-arranged financing in this case.

Step	Example	Your Figures
1. Determine the dollar amount of the rebate.	$3000	_____
2. Add the rebate amount to the finance charge for the dealer financing (dollar cost of credit).	+$ 907	_____
3. Use the formula from Chapter 7 (Equation [7.2] on page 215 and used here as Equation [8.1]) to calculate an adjusted APR for the dealer financing.		

$$\text{APR} = \frac{Y(95P+9)F}{12P(P+1)(4D+F)} \quad \textbf{(8.1)}$$

where
APR = Annual percentage rate
   Y = Number of payment periods in one **year**
   F = **Finance** charge in dollars
   D = **Debt** (amount borrowed)
   P = Total number of scheduled **payments**

$$\text{APR} = \frac{(12)[(95 \times 36) + 9]($3000 + $907)}{12 \times 36(36+1)[(4 \times $20,000) + ($3000 + $907)]} = 12\%$$

4. Write in the APR that you arranged on your own.	6.5%	_____

Leasing Terminology Five terms are important in leasing:

1. The **gross capitalized cost (gross cap cost)** includes the price of the vehicle plus what the lessee paid to finance the purchase plus any other items the lessee agreed to pay for over the life of the lease, including insurance or a maintenance agreement.
2. **Capitalized cost reductions (cap cost reductions)** are monies paid on the lease at its inception, including any down payment, trade-in value, or rebate.
3. The **adjusted capitalized cost (adjusted cap cost)** is determined by subtracting the capitalized cost reductions from the gross capitalized cost.
4. The **residual value** is the projected value of a leased asset at the end of the lease time period.
5. The **money factor** (or **lease rate** or **lease factor**) measures the rent charge portion of your payment. Although the money factor is sometimes described by dealers as a figure for comparing leases, lease forms must carry the following disclosure about the money factor: "This percentage may not measure the overall cost of financing this lease."

gross capitalized cost (gross cap cost)
Includes vehicle price plus the cost of any extra features such as insurance or maintenance agreements.

adjusted capitalized cost (adjusted cap cost)
Subtracting the capitalized cost reductions from the gross capitalized cost.

residual value
Projected value of a leased asset at the end of the lease time period.

What is most important when considering leasing? Always negotiate the purchase price before discussing a lease! Leasing requires an initial outlay of cash to pay for the first month's lease payment and a security deposit. Payments are based on the capitalized cost of the asset minus any capitalized cost reductions and the residual value. This difference represents the cost of using the asset during the lease period; when divided by the number of months in the contract, it serves to establish the base for the monthly lease payment. (Some new vehicles are offered with single-payment leases in which the entire difference between the capitalized cost and residual value is paid up front.) With monthly payment leases, the payments are lower than monthly loan payments for equivalent time periods because you are paying for only the reduction in the asset's value—not its entire cost. To compare the costs of leasing versus buying, use the Run the Numbers worksheet, "Comparing Automobile Financing and Leasing." Also see www.leasecompare.com.

Open- and Closed-End Leases A lease may be either open end or closed end. In an **open-end lease**, you must pay any difference between the projected residual value of the vehicle and its actual market value at the end of the lease period. When a vehicle depreciates more rapidly than expected, the holder of an open-end lease has to pay extra money when the lease expires. For example, a vehicle with an $11,000 residual value but a $10,250 market value would require an end-of-lease payment of $750 ($11,000 − $10,250). The Consumer Leasing Act limits this end-of-lease payment to a maximum of three times the average monthly payment.

Most vehicle leases are closed-end leases. In a **closed-end lease** (also called a **walkaway lease**), the holder pays no charge if the end-of-lease market value of the vehicle is lower than the originally projected residual value. However, closed-end leases may

closed-end lease/walkaway lease

Agreement in which the lessee pays no charge if the end-of-lease market value of the vehicle is lower than the originally projected residual value.

RUN THE NUMBERS

Comparing Vehicle Financing and Leasing

This worksheet can be used to compare leasing and borrowing to buy a vehicle. Remember that the cost of credit is the finance charge—the extra that you pay because you borrowed. Leases also carry costs, but they are hidden within the contract. Indeed, some may remain unknown until the end of the lease period. These lease costs, which are indicated by an asterisk (*), are negotiable and are defined in the text. Ask the dealer for the price of each item, as these fees must be disclosed by dealers. Then complete the worksheet and compare the dollar cost of leasing with the finance charge on a loan for the same time period.

To make the comparison accurately, you must know the underlying price of the car as if you were purchasing it. Often you are not offered this value with a lease arrangement, so you should *always* negotiate a price for the vehicle before mentioning your interest in leasing.

 DO IT IN CLASS

Also, shop for a lease through dealers and independent leasing companies because costs vary widely. This worksheet can be found on the *Garman/Forgue* companion website, or you can find a similar worksheet at www.bankrate.com /calculators/auto/buy-or-lease-calculator.aspx.

Step		Example	Your Figures
1.	Monthly lease payment (36 payments of $375, for example)	$13,500	
2.	Plus acquisition fee* (if any)	300	
	Plus disposition charge* (if any)	300	
	Plus estimate of excess mileage charges* (if any)	0	
	Plus projected residual value of the vehicle	4,500	
3.	Amount for which you are responsible under the lease	18,600	
4.	Less the adjusted capitalized cost (gross capitalized cost* less the capitalized cost reductions*)	16,000	
5.	Dollar cost of leasing to be compared with a finance charge if you purchased the vehicle	2,600	

carry some type of end-of-lease charge if the vehicle has greater than normal wear or excess mileage. For example, a four-year closed-end lease might require a $0.30 per mile **excess mileage charge** in excess of 55,000 miles. If you actually drove the vehicle 60,000 miles during the four years, you would be charged an extra $1500 [$0.30 × 5000 (60,000 − 55,000)].

With either an open- or closed-end lease, you may purchase the vehicle at the end of the lease period. With an open-end lease, you would pay the actual cash value. With a closed-end lease, you would pay the residual value.

Understand Common Leasing Fees Other charges are possible with a lease. An acquisition fee is either paid in cash or included in the gross capitalization cost. It pays for a credit report, application fee, and other paperwork. A **disposition fee** is assessed when you turn in the vehicle at the end of the lease and the lessor must prepare it for resale. An **early termination charge** may also be levied if you decide to end the lease prematurely. Be wary of a lease with an early termination charge, even if you do not plan to end the lease early, because termination also occurs when a leased vehicle is traded in or is totally wrecked or stolen. Make sure you obtain a written disclosure of these charges well before you actually make your decision. The **early termination payoff** is the total amount you would need to repay if you end the lease agreement early; it includes both the early termination charge and the unpaid lease balance. In its early years, your lease may be financially upside down, which means that you owe more on the vehicle than it is worth.

Be Cautious About Leasing Getting a good deal on a leased vehicle can be very complicated. Therefore, be cautious if you talk about buying the vehicle all through the negotiation process only to be offered a lease at the last minute. The seller might realize that the purchase price is too high for you and can get you into the same vehicle for a lower monthly payment. But you may be tempted to sign a deal that actually costs considerably more. In addition, make sure all oral agreements related to trade-in value, mileage charges, and rebates are included in the lease contract.

Avoid Balloon Loans One option for people considering leasing versus buying is a balloon automobile loan. You can arrange this type of financing through your bank or credit union. With a **balloon automobile loan**, you actually buy the vehicle with the last monthly payment equaling the projected residual value of the vehicle at the end of the loan period. This arrangement effectively lowers all the other earlier monthly payments to make them more competitive with lease payments. When the final balloon payment is due, perhaps one to several thousand dollars, the borrower generally has three options:

1. Sell the car and pay the balloon payment with the proceeds (with luck, the vehicle will sell for a high enough amount).
2. Pay the balloon payment and keep the vehicle.
3. Return the vehicle to the lender to cover the balloon payment.

Be Cautious About "Gap" Insurance New cars and low-mileage used cars depreciate (go down in value) very quickly after purchase, often as much as 25 percent after leaving the dealer's lot. If you take out a vehicle loan with a low down payment, it is possible that the value of the vehicle will go down faster than the amount owed. As a result, you can owe more on the vehicle than it is worth. This situation is referred to as being upside down and can easily last for up to two years following the initial purchase.

Being upside down can be a big problem when a newer vehicle is totaled in an accident. In such cases, the insurance company will reimburse for the value of the vehicle, not the amount owed on the loan. Car dealers sell **gap insurance** that pays off the remainder of the loan if the insurance payment is insufficient to do so. While gap insurance is attractive, it is very profitable for the dealer and not such a good deal for the buyer. You should consider the possibility of being upside down as a sign that you are not making a large enough down payment or that you are buying a vehicle that is too expensive for you.

FINANCIAL POWER POINT

Do Not Lease Just to Drive a Better Vehicle

Leases work best for people who wish to drive a new vehicle every two or three years and, thus, have decided that they will always have a car payment. If you do choose a leasing option, your goal should be to lower your monthly cost rather than to "buy more car." Otherwise, in just a few years, you will find that you have spent big bucks for a vehicle you must turn back in or have to pay extra to buy as a used vehicle.

excess mileage charge
Fees assessed at the end of a lease if the vehicle was driven more miles than originally specified in the lease contract.

balloon automobile loan
A loan that has a low monthly payment similar in amount to that required if the vehicle had been leased and with a large final payment similar in amount to the residual value under a lease.

FINANCIAL POWER POINT

It Is Possible to Get out of a Lease Early

People eager to get out of a lease might consider a lease-swapping website such as leasetrader.com and swapalease.com. These companies try to match people who want to get out of a lease early with those who want to assume a short-term lease. They charge fees to post your vehicle's information, and your original leasing company likely charges a transfer fee.

8.2c Compare Warranties

Warranties are an important consideration in comparison shopping. Almost all products have **warranties**—assurances by sellers that goods are as promised and that certain steps will be taken to rectify problems—even if only in the form of implied warranties. The longer the warranty is and the more it covers, the better the warranty.

warranty

Sellers' assurances that goods are as promised and that certain steps will be taken to rectify problems if they arise.

Implied and Express Warranties Under an **implied warranty**, the product sold is warranted to be suitable for sale (a **warranty of merchantability**) and to work effectively (a **warranty of fitness**) whether or not a written warranty exists. Implied warranties are required by state law. The only way to avoid them is if the seller states in writing that the product is sold **as is**. If you buy any product as is, you have no legal recourse if it fails to perform, even if the salesperson made verbal promises to take care of any problems. Used cars are often sold as is.

as is

Way for the seller to get around legal requirements for warranties; the buyer takes all risk of nonperformance or other problems despite any salesperson's verbal assurances.

Written and oral warranties are called **express warranties**. Companies that offer written express warranties must do so under the provisions of the federal Magnuson-Moss Warranty Act if the product is sold for more than $15. This law provides that any written warranty offered must be classified as either a full warranty or a limited warranty.

Full and Limited Warranties A **full warranty** includes three stringent requirements:

full warranty

Warranty that meets three stringent promises: the product must be fixed at no cost to the buyer within a reasonable time, the owner will not have to undertake an unreasonable task to return the product for repair, and a defective product will be replaced with a new one or the buyer's money will be returned if the product cannot be fixed.

1. A product must be fixed at no cost to the buyer within a reasonable time after the owner has complained.
2. The owner will not have to undertake an unreasonable task to return the product for repair (such as ship back a refrigerator).
3. A defective product will be replaced with a new one or the buyer's money will be returned if the product cannot be fixed after a reasonable number of attempts.

A **limited warranty** offers less protection than a full warranty. For example, it may offer only free parts, not labor. Note that one part of a product could be covered by a full warranty (perhaps the engine on a lawnmower) and the rest of the unit by a limited warranty. Read all warranties carefully, and note that both full and limited warranties are valid for only a specified time period.

limited warranty

Any warranty that offers less protection than the three conditions for full warranty.

8.2d Extended Warranties (Service Contracts) Are Overpriced

extended warranty/service contract/maintenance agreement/buyer protection plan

Agreement between the seller and buyer of a product to repair or replace covered product components for some specified time period; purchased separately from the product itself.

An **extended warranty** (or **service contract**) is an agreement between the contract seller (the dealer, manufacturer, or an independent company) and the buyer of a product to provide repair or replacement for covered components of the product for some specified time period. Extended warranties are sometimes given names such as **maintenance agreement** or **buyer protection plan**. These service contracts are purchased separately from the product itself (such as a vehicle, appliance, or electronics equipment). The cost is paid either in a lump sum or in monthly payments.

Extended warranties are not insurance but act similarly. For example, a 42-inch LCD/LED flat panel high-definition television could have an extended warranty that promises to fix anything that goes wrong during the third and fourth years of ownership; the manufacturer's warranty covers the first two years. This contract might cost $120 for each year, or $10 per month.

Although buying an extended warranty might provide peace of mind, it is unwise financially because it makes no economic sense to insure against risks that can, if necessary, be paid for out of current income or savings. Plus extended warranties are horribly overpriced. More than 80 percent of all service contracts are never used, and total payouts to consumers to make repairs amount to less than 10 percent of all money spent on the contracts. More than half the profits of some electronics dealers come from extended warranty sales, not the products themselves.

Extended warranties are not a good choice when buying electronics because the products rarely have problems beyond the warranty period. Products that do seem to break down frequently are cell phones, laptops, treadmills, and elliptical trainers. These contracts are prevalent in the vehicle, appliance, and electronics markets because of the high profits involved and the persuasiveness of salespeople, who typically earn an extra high commission on the sale of an extended warranty.

Automobile manufacturers and dealers offer extended warranties as do a number of independent companies that offer service contracts for new vehicles. A deductible of about $100 usually must be paid with each use of the contract. Repairs are usually covered and may include preventive maintenance for certain covered components. The cost for an extended warranty averages $1800, and $800 of that is dealer profit, with $250 going to the salesperson. Sellers can afford to be more generous on a deal if they know that most of the money will be made back on the service contract. About one-third of people buy an extended warranty on their new vehicles, and three-fourths of those who haggled over price received a discount from the quoted price.

CONCEPT CHECK 8.2

1. What is the goal of comparison shopping?

2. Explain why lease payments for a new vehicle are lower than loan payments for the same vehicle.

3. Describe the relationships among capital cost, capital cost reductions, and residual value in a lease.

4. Explain the difference between an implied warranty and an express warranty. How do they relate to the term *as is?*

5. What is an extended warranty? What is a disadvantage of such a contract?

ADVICE FROM A PROFESSIONAL

Tips for Buying Online

People use the Internet to shop for appliances, vehicles, furniture, and other big-ticket items. Here's how you can become a better online shopper:

1. **Use only secure sites.** *A secure site will feature a key or lock symbol on its screens or have a URL starting with "https" ("s" for secure). Sites displaying the VeriSign symbol must meet certain security standards.*

2. **Only do business** *with sellers for which you have complete contact information, including a "snail mail" (postal) address and telephone number. To avoid bogus websites, verify any bargain website deal at the company's headquarters.*

3. **Review shipping policies** *and costs as well as return policies before placing your order.*

4. **Do not use your regular e-mail address.** *Set up a separate address at Yahoo!, Gmail, or other provider and use it solely for online transactions. This will reduce the spam coming into your everyday e-mail account.*

5. **Never use a debit card** *for online purchasing. When the debit card transaction is executed, your cash is immediately transferred from your account to the seller's account. Using a credit card allows you to request a chargeback (see Chapter 7) from the credit card company if there is a problem with the product.*

6. **Use only one particular credit card** *for online purchases. This practice will serve you well if your account number is stolen. In such a case, you can notify the one credit card issuer of the theft and block the card's future use without affecting your other accounts.*

7. **Print and keep copies** *of all purchase documents, warranties, credit card authorizations, and shipping notices.*

8. **Check the site's privacy policy.** *Sites that display the TRUSTe symbol or Better Business Bureau Online seal have agreed to meet certain privacy standards.*

9. **Opt out** *of any list sharing that the seller might conduct with other merchants.*

Brenda J. Cude
University of Georgia

8.3 NEGOTIATE EFFECTIVELY

Negotiating and decision making follow comparison shopping in the buying process. If you move through these steps too quickly, you may pay too much even when you have done a great job with your preshopping research and comparison shopping. Sellers of such products sell every day, and they are highly skilled; in contrast, consumers are amateurs when it comes to buying big-ticket items. Smart shoppers learn to negotiate.

DID YOU KNOW

Bias Toward Overconfidence

People engaged in understanding vehicle and major purchases have a bias toward certain behaviors that can be harmful, such as a tendency toward overconfidence. When negotiating the purchase of a major item like a vehicle people will assume they have sufficient information and skills to obtain the best buy. What to do? Arm yourself with tons of information about the price, interest rate, trade-in value, and dealer holdbacks before negotiating. And, remember that salespeople are professionals at selling and you are a relative amateur at buying.

negotiating/haggling
Process of discussing actual terms of agreement with a seller, usually on higher-priced items.

dealer holdback/dealer rebate
A percentage of the total MSRP that the manufacturer holds and then gives back to the dealer, often at the end of the year or quarter.

8.3a Successful Negotiators Are Armed with Information

Negotiating (or **haggling**) is the process of discussing the actual terms of an agreement with a seller. Consumers skip this step when making day-to-day purchases because prices in most stores are firm. With high-priced items—especially appliances, furniture, fine jewelry, and vehicles—there is an opportunity, and often an expectation, that offers and counteroffers will be made before arriving at the final price.

Negotiating is challenging for consumers when buying vehicles because many variables must be considered, including the price of the vehicle, the trade-in value (if any), the possibility of a rebate, the prices of options, the interest rate, and possibly a service contract. The dealer can appear to be cooperative on one aspect and make up the difference elsewhere. The key to successful negotiation is to be armed with accurate information on all variables, especially the price, interest rate, trade-in value, and dealer holdbacks.

Discover the Dealer Holdback Consumers have caught on to the fiction of new-car prices and now focus on the dealer invoice price, which reflects the price the dealer has been billed from the manufacturer. But this may not be the price the dealer truly will have to pay when the vehicle is sold. This occurs because manufacturers often offer a **dealer holdback** (or **dealer rebate**) to dealers. A dealer holdback is a percentage of the total MSRP that the manufacturer holds and then gives back to the dealer, often at the

Always obtain a firm price for a vehicle before negotiating financing or a trade-in.

© Monkey Business Images/Shutterstock.com

end of the year or quarter. Potential buyers often do not know about holdbacks. Here the dealer can hold back a sum of money from (instead of paying to) the manufacturer, thereby providing the dealer with additional profit on the vehicle.

Because of holdback incentives, dealers can sell a vehicle at or below dealer invoice price and still make a good profit. For example, a vehicle might have a sticker price of $27,890, an invoice price of $24,600, and a dealer holdback of 5 percent, or $1230. A negotiated price of $24,500 will still net the dealer a profit of $1130 [$1230 − ($24,600 − $24,500)]. Remember both the MSRP and dealer invoice price are artificial numbers set by the manufacturer and dealer to allow lots of room to negotiate a profitable price to the seller. For this reason, do not hesitate to negotiate for a price that is below the dealer invoice price. Visit www.edmunds.com/car-incentives/ for a listing of current dealer incentive offers on various makes and models of vehicles.

Negotiate Your Price The complexity and uncertainty involved in negotiating the price of a new vehicle have inspired the development of special services to assist buyers. A **new-vehicle buying service** is an organization that arranges discount purchases for buyers of new cars who are referred to nearby participating automobile dealers that have agreed to charge specific discount prices. After you sign up, a local dealer will call you to offer a no-haggle price, which is often within 4 percent of the dealer invoice price. The buying service earns its income by collecting a finder's fee from the dealer. One of the most popular is online at www.TrueCar.com. **Professional shoppers**, in exchange for a fee (perhaps $150 to $450) based on the dealer invoice price, will find the best available price from a nearby dealer and finalize the sale. Alternatively, for a lower fee, they will obtain price quotes so you can finalize the deal yourself. Two of the most popular buying services are CarBargains.com and Authority Auto (www.authorityauto.com). Also see car buying programs at Costco, Edmunds, and TrueCar.

When negotiating a vehicle purchase, the key is to obtain a firm price from a dealer for the vehicle and optional equipment desired before discussing *any other* aspects of the deal. Rule number one in auto buying: Do not mention financing or a trade-in until you have pinned the salesperson down to a price! You will know from your preshopping research and comparison shopping what a good price for the vehicle in question would be.

Start your bargaining from this low price rather than the asking price or dealer invoice price on the vehicle. Obtain prices from three or more dealers and then let each know that you have done so and whether or not their price is low compared with the others. The dealer will then have the chance to reduce the asking price to meet the competition. This smart strategy pressures the dealer to meet your needs rather than the other way around.

Negotiate Your Interest Rate Negotiating the interest rate, or APR, on a vehicle loan is not only possible but also essential to getting a good deal overall. Most vehicle borrowers accept that the dealer-arranged financing is the best they can find. However, buyers may not know that the dealer benefits from having the borrower agree to pay a higher interest rate.

Here is how the process works. The dealer asks the buyer to complete a simple loan application. The application is submitted to one or more lenders with whom the dealer has a pre-existing affiliation. The lenders will assess the application and, if approved, suggest an APR. However, if the dealer suggests and gets an acceptance for a higher rate by the buyer (perhaps by telling the prospective buyer that his or her credit score is low), the dealer (and salesperson) receives a higher fee for arranging the higher APR loan. In this way, the dealer can make money even if the profit off

DID YOU KNOW ?

Money Websites for Vehicles and Other Major Purchases

Informative websites for vehicles and other major purchases, including tips on buying safe vehicles are:

AutoTrader (www.autotrader.com)

CarGurus (www.cargurus.com)

CarFax (www.carfax.com)

CarsDirect (www.carsdirect.com)

Consumer Reports (www.consumerreports.org)

Edmunds (www.edmunds.com)

Insurance Institute for Highway Safety (www.iihs.org)

Kelly Blue Book (www.kbb.com)

Kiplinger's Personal Finance (kiplinger.com/fronts/channels/cars/)

MSN (home.autos.msn.com/)

MoneyCNN.com (money.cnn.com/pf/savvy_spending/?iid=PF_Sub)

National Highway Traffic Safety Administration (www.SaferCar.gov)

new-vehicle buying service
Organization that arranges discount purchases for new-car buyers who are referred to nearby participating automobile dealers that have agreed to charge specific discount prices.

high-balling
Sales tactic in which a dealer offers a trade-in allowance that is much higher than the vehicle is worth.

the sale of the vehicle itself is minimal. This is why it is so important to have a good credit history, know your credit score, and arrange the best financing you can on your own and accept the dealer financing only if it can beat your deal.

Negotiate Your Trade-in   Getting a good deal on a vehicle purchase typically requires one more negotiation—your trade-in. You can pay a low price for the car you are buying, arrange a low-rate loan, and still not have a good deal if you do not receive what your trade-in is worth. Success here depends on knowing the value of your vehicle as a trade-in based on your preshopping research. The same online sources you used to get that information also have information on the average price at which similar vehicles are selling via private individuals. While it is true that trade-in values are usually lower than private sale values, you also have the costs of selling and the time involved if you decide not to accept the dealer's offer for your vehicle.

Trade-ins are another way for a seller to make more money on the transaction. In one common sales technique, called **high-balling**, a dealer offers a trade-in allowance that is much higher than the vehicle is worth. This apparent generosity may look very good to a buyer. But beware; the dealer may be making up for this elsewhere, possibly in a higher-than-necessary price for the purchased vehicle. You will not know whether you are being high-balled unless you know the value of your trade-in.

Play "Good Cop-Bad Cop" When Buying a Vehicle   Many people are uncomfortable negotiating with sellers. Sellers understand this and are very good at putting people at ease with friendly talk and a supportive tone. But underneath, they are all business. How should you play the game? If you are a good negotiator, bring a friend along to be the friendly good cop while you focus on the deal and ask the hard questions. If you dislike negotiating, you can be the good cop, while your friend can ask the hard questions and focus on getting a good deal.

8.3b   Make the Decision at Home Using a Decision-Making Grid

It is unwise to make buying decisions for expensive purchases inside a retail store or showroom. By waiting until you get home to make the final decision, you are free of pressure from a salesperson and free of your own need to "get it over with." After taking some time to rationally consider all of the consequences of the purchase, you can return to the dealer's showroom and close the sale.

A **decision-making grid** allows you to visually and mathematically weigh the decision you are about to make. Table 8-2 depicts a grid for someone deciding among three different washing machines. The first task in developing such a grid is to determine the various attributes for making the decision. In Table 8-2, these factors include price, durability, and styling. Each attribute is assigned a weight that reflects the importance each has in the mind of the purchaser. Each alternative under consideration is then given a score (from 1 to 10 in this case) that indicates how well it performs on that attribute.

The rating (R) is multiplied by the weight (W) to obtain a weighted score. The total of the weighted scores for each alternative can then be compared with the totals for the other choices to determine which one "wins." In Table 8-2, Alternative C, which has a total score of 8.0, scores the best.

A grid of this type helps bring objectivity to your decision-making process and can be of benefit when buying big-ticket items. Also, you may consider other factors in your decision, such as seller reputation.

Table 8-2 — Decision-Making Grid (Illustrated for a Washing Machine)

Attribute	Weight (W)	Alternative A		Alternative B		Alternative C	
		Rating (R)*	Weighted Rating W × R	Rating (R)*	Weighted Rating W × R	Rating (R)*	Weighted Rating W × R
Price	30%	9	2.7	7	2.1	5	1.5
Durability	25%	6	1.5	8	2.0	10	2.5
Features	20%	6	1.2	8	1.6	10	2.0
Warranty	15%	6	0.9	10	1.5	8	1.2
Styling	10%	10	1.0	6	0.6	8	0.8
TOTAL	**100%**		**7.3**		**7.8**		**8.0**

*Using a 10-point scale where 10 is the highest score.

8.3c Finalizing a Car Deal

After negotiating a good deal and making your final decision, it would be nice if you could simply return to the dealer and sign the necessary papers. But even then there is opportunity for the dealer to push for a little more profit. One technique that is used at this point is called **low-balling**. This involves quoting and getting a verbal agreement from a buyer for an artificially low price. Then the salesperson attempts to raise the already negotiated price when it comes time to finalize the written contract. For example, after agreeing on the price of a vehicle with a buyer, the salesperson states that, as a formality, the approval of a manager is necessary. While the buyer is dreaming of driving home in the new car, the salesperson and the manager are talking about how much more they can get for the vehicle. When the salesperson returns, he or she indicates that there is a problem. Perhaps the trade-in value is too high, or the dealer invoice price can't be discounted by quite as much as planned, or the price of a certain option has increased. In reality, of course, low-balling is simply a ruse to allow the dealer to get more money. Smart buyers stand firm and insist on the deal that had been negotiated; otherwise, they walk out the door.

Finally, it is time to sign the papers. Commonly at this point the salesperson turns the buyer over to another member of the sales team whose specific job it is to have all the papers signed to finalize the sale, the loan, and the transfer of the title and registration of the vehicle. Sign only a **buyer's order** that names a specific vehicle and all charges, and do so only after the salesperson and sales manager have signed *first*. Then verify that all aspects of the deal are as originally agreed, sign your name, and drive away in your new vehicle.

8.3d The So-Called Buyer's Remorse "Legal Right" Is False

Buyer's remorse is a myth pertaining to the buyer's supposed legal right to change his or her mind and return a vehicle after signing a purchase contract. This is a popular misconception—that consumers always have what is referred to as a three-day "cooling-off period," or three days to decide whether the consumer wants to honor a signed vehicle purchase contract. It simply is not true.

low-balling
A sales tactic where the seller quotes an artificially low price to obtain a verbal agreement from a buyer and then attempts to raise the negotiated price when it comes time to finalize the written contract.

buyer's order
Written offer that names a specific vehicle and all charges; only sign such offers after the salesperson and sales manager have signed first.

buyer's remorse
A myth pertaining to the buyer's supposed legal right to change his or her mind and return a vehicle after signing a purchase contract.

FINANCIAL POWER POINT

Purchase Used Vehicles and Drive Them Forever

The best way to buy vehicles with the lowest overall cost is to buy late-model used vehicles and drive them for ten or more years or 200,000 miles or more. New cars lose about 25 percent of their value in the first year and 40 percent or more by the end of the second year. The average vehicle on the road today is over 11 years old so there are many from which to choose.

ADVICE FROM A PROFESSIONAL

How to Buy a Used Vehicle

Most experts recommend purchasing late-model used vehicles to get the most from your vehicle-buying dollar. Following are some steps that can help you get a good vehicle for the money:

1. ***Budget automotive expenditure.*** *Discuss your transportation budget with a spouse, significant other, or family member. Compare the cost for public transportation to that of vehicle ownership. Determine the amount you can afford for vehicle payments, insurance, fuel, and maintenance.*

2. ***Value shop.*** *Remain flexible concerning auto make, model, and options. The most practical and affordable vehicle may not contain every feature you desire. Write down the top five "must have" features you want, such as power locks and windows, air conditioning, aluminum wheels. And prioritize the list (see Figure 8-2). Consider all vehicles in a particular class regardless of manufacturer. Consider choosing an older model to obtain more of the features you value.*

3. ***Search for reliable makes and models.*** *The Internet is an excellent source of used-vehicle information. You also should examine the most recent April issue of* Consumer Reports *for its lists of recommended used vehicles in various price ranges, especially those with excellent repair records. Research Kelly Blue Book (www.kbb.com) and Edmunds (www.edmunds.com/appraisal) websites for pricing information. Obtain a* **vehicle history report**, *available from Carfax.com and other companies, which has odometer readings, accident reports, flood damage, total-loss information, ownership history. For example, a vehicle operated near salt water may have undercarriage corrosion. Also look at the federal government's online report for vehicles at www .vehiclehistory.gov/.*

4. ***Go shopping.*** *New-car dealerships and private parties tend to offer the nicer, more reliable, and more expensive used vehicles. Dealerships often verify reliability of their vehicles and offer warranties. Used-car dealerships tend to have the worst quality. Private individuals deserve your attention because they usually own the vehicle and know its history. Used vehicles sold by rental agencies such as Hertz and Avis can be good choices because their vehicles have been regularly maintained.*

5. ***Evaluate prior to purchase.*** *Take along a friend who is knowledgeable about vehicles if you are not car savvy. Immediately rule out any vehicle that seems to have a problem or raises a question in your mind. Test drive all vehicles. Review the maintenance records when available and, if necessary, communicate with previous owners. Take final choice(s) to a trusted repair specialist for inspection. This investment of time and money may help you avoid purchasing a vehicle with problems and save many dollars in repair bills later.*

6. ***Negotiate the details.*** *The asking price is the beginning point for negotiation. Decide on your final price and stick to it. Begin by making your opening offer substantially lower than what you expect to pay. Then negotiate. Do not give in to the pressure to buy an extended warranty and other items. If appropriate, obtain a smog certification from the seller. Be certain that all spoken assurances are written into the sales contract. If necessary, walk away and go home to consider your alternatives and to make your final decision. It may be necessary to place a refundable deposit (and get it in writing) to hold the vehicle for a day or two while you make your decision.*

7. ***Get insurance and a good title.*** *Before driving your purchased vehicle, telephone your auto insurance company to add the vehicle to your policy. Be certain to obtain a good title to the vehicle before giving the seller your money.*

Elizabeth Fletcher
Evangel University, Springfield, MO

8.3e   Evaluate Your Decision

The planned buying process is complete after you evaluate your decision. The purpose of this step is to think about where things went well and where they went less smoothly. The lessons learned will prove useful when you make a similar purchase in the future. Sometimes the buying process turns out to be so successful that you may want to compliment the seller.

Sean's Success Story

When shopping for a new car, Sean ran the numbers on leasing versus buying only to determine that he really could not afford the kind of vehicle he truly wanted. Therefore, he decided to buy a used car. He found a nice two-year-old Ford with only 21,000 miles on the odometer and bargained the price down to $19,000; thus, he avoided two years of heavy depreciation. Sean searched online for financing deals and then discovered an excellent rate at a nearby credit union. He paid the $5 credit union membership fee and deposited $5 to open an account, and they gave him a loan over 36 months. Sean considered buying an extended warranty but decided it would be too expensive. He has had the car for over two years now, and it has proved to be a reliable vehicle.

CONCEPT CHECK 8.3

1. List some of the complexities in vehicle buying, and offer your advice on how to get a best buy.

2. What three aspects of a vehicle purchase should be negotiated? In what order?

3. Why should you make major purchase decisions at home?

4. Summarize how to use a decision-making grid.

8.4 UTILIZE EFFECTIVE COMPLAINT PROCEDURES

Despite your efforts to make good consumer buying decisions, not all purchases turn out as well as you want. You may want to try to return goods, get out of a contract, file a complaint, or seek to right a wrong using an alternative dispute resolution program or using small claims court.

8.4a Use the Cooling-Off Rule to Cancel a Contract

If you buy something at a store and later change your mind, you may or may not be able to return the merchandise. However, if you buy an item in your home or at a location that is not the seller's permanent place of business, you may have that option. The Federal Trade Commission's (FTC's) **cooling-off rule** gives you three days to cancel a contract of $25 or more after signing it for a sale made anywhere other than a seller's normal place of business. The right to cancel for a full refund extends until midnight of the third business day after the sale.

The FTC's cooling-off rule applies to sales at the buyer's home, workplace, or dormitory, or at facilities rented by the seller on a temporary or short-term basis, such as hotel or motel rooms, convention centers, fairgrounds, and restaurants. The rule applies even when you invite the salesperson to make a presentation in your home. The cooling-off rule does not apply to sales made entirely by mail or telephone, sales that are needed to meet an emergency, or to real estate, insurance, or securities.

Under the FTC rule, the salesperson must tell you about your cancellation rights at the time of sale. In addition, the salesperson also must give you two copies of a cancellation form (one to keep and one to send) and a copy of your contract or receipt. The contract or receipt should be dated, show the name and address of the seller, and explain your right to

cooling-off rule
A Federal Trade Commission rule that gives consumers three days to cancel a contract of $25 or more after signing it for a sale made anywhere other than a seller's normal place of business.

Your Worst Financial Blunders in Vehicle and Other Major Purchases

Based on others' financial woes, you will make mistakes in personal finance when you:

1. *Tell a seller what you can afford to pay.*

2. *Rely solely upon the seller for information on price, financing terms, or trade-in value.*

3. *Fail to complain when products fail to perform as expected.*

DID YOU KNOW

Turn Bad Habits into Good Ones

Do You Do This?	*Do This Instead!*
Buy on impulse	Create and stick to a shopping list
Buy too much stuff	Write down your needs versus your wants
Get persuaded by ads to "buy now and save"	Realize you are still spending money
Ignore interest rates when financing a purchase	Shop for the best financing terms
Pay too much for vehicle purchases	Learn to comparison shop and get rebates
Can't decide on leasing a vehicle or not	Run the numbers on financing versus leasing
Buy overpriced extended warranties	Avoid buying such unneeded products

redress
Process of righting a wrong.

alternative dispute resolution programs
Industry- or government-sponsored programs that provide an avenue to resolve disputes outside the formal court system.

DO IT IN CLASS

cancel. The contract or receipt must be in the same language that is used in the sales presentation.

The best way to avoid problems is to read the contract carefully and to fully inspect a new or used product or service before taking ownership. Various states have cooling-off rules that apply even longer cancellation periods to specific types of sales, such as dancing lessons, buying clubs, and timeshares.

Sometimes you may want to complain about the product or service so as to obtain **redress**—that is, to right the wrong. This process should start with the actual seller, as indicated in Table 8-3. Seeking redress through the first three channels in the complaint procedures as shown in the table can rectify almost all consumer complaints.

8.4b   Mediation and Arbitration

Alternative dispute resolution programs are industry- or government-sponsored programs that provide an avenue to resolve disputes outside the formal court system. Vehicle manufacturers utilize these programs as part of their warranty procedures. **Mediation** is a procedure in which a neutral third party works with the parties involved in the dispute to arrive at a mutually agreeable solution. In **arbitration**, a neutral third party hears (or reads) the claims made and the positions taken by the parties to the dispute and then issues a ruling that may or may not be binding on one or both parties.

Table 8-3   Complaint Procedure (Levels and Channels of Complaining)

Levels to Bring Your Complaint	Channels for Complaint
1. Local business	Salesperson → supervisor → manager/owner
2. Manufacturer	Consumer affairs department → president/chief executive officer
3. Self-regulatory organizations	Better Business Bureau → trade associations → mediation/arbitration panels
4. Consumer action agencies	Private consumer action groups → media action lines → government agencies
5. Small-claims or civil court	Small-claims court → civil court

8.4c Lemon Laws and Small-Claims Courts

All states have new-vehicle **lemon laws** that provide guidelines for arbitrators to use to order a dealer's buyback of a "lemon." A common definition of a lemon in these laws is a vehicle that was in the shop for repairs four times for the same problem in the first year after purchase. (For the specific definition in your state, visit www.carlemon.com.) To enforce a lemon law, the buyer must go through the warranty process specified in the owner's manual. Eventually, if the problem is not resolved, an arbitration hearing will be held through which the owner can request a buyback. Some states have also enacted used-vehicle lemon laws.

Sometimes your best efforts at redress may not prove successful. As a result, you might consider taking legal action in **small-claims court**. In this state court, civil matters are often resolved without the assistance of attorneys (in some states, attorneys are actually prohibited from representing clients in small-claims courts). Small-claims courts usually place restrictions on the maximum amount under dispute, typically ranging from $500 to $5000, for which a claim may be made in those courts. To file a small-claims court action, contact your local county courthouse and ask which court hears small claims or check it out on-line.

DO IT NOW!

You know more about personal finance after reading this chapter, so get started right now by:

1. Setting up a filing system for the warranty information and receipts for all products you own that have a warranty.

2. Decide on a big-ticket item you would like to own in the near future and create a decision-making worksheet for it similar to Table 8-2, using your criteria and weights.

3. Keep a monthly budget and fit all payments for big-ticket items into your budget before making any purchase decision.

CONCEPT CHECK 8.4

1. Outline the steps to go through to seek redress.

2. Summarize the FTC's cooling-off rule to cancel a contract.

3. Distinguish between mediation and arbitration.

4. How do lemon laws work?

lemon laws
State laws that provide guidelines for arbitrators to use to order a dealer's buyback of a "lemon" as defined under the law—commonly a car that has been in the shop four or more times to fix the same problem.

WHAT DO YOU RECOMMEND *NOW?*

Now that you have read this chapter on vehicle and other major purchases, what do you recommend to David and Lisa Cosgrove regarding:

1. How to search for two vehicles to replace those destroyed?

2. Whether to replace Lisa's vehicle with a new or used vehicle?

3. Whether to lease or buy a vehicle?

4. How to decide between a rebate and a special low APR financing opportunity if they decide to purchase a new vehicle for Lisa?

5. How to negotiate with the sellers of the vehicles?

BIG PICTURE SUMMARY OF LEARNING OBJECTIVES

LO1 Explain the first three steps in the planned buying process that occur prior to interacting with sellers.

The planned buying process includes three steps that occur prior to interacting with sellers: prioritizing wants, obtaining information during preshopping research, and fitting the planned purchase into the budget. These steps represent the homework needed when preparing to buy.

LO2 Describe the process of comparison shopping.

To interact effectively with sellers, you should comparison shop to find the best buy. When purchasing vehicles and other big-ticket items, this shopping process includes comparing prices, financing

arrangements, leasing options, warranties, and extended warranties.

LO3 Negotiate and decide effectively when making major purchases.

Negotiating with sellers involves obtaining a fair price, low-cost financing, and a high trade-in allowance. After negotiating, the final decision should be made at home.

LO4 Use effective complaint procedures.

When the buying process has not gone well, you can use a variety of effective complaint procedures including the FTC's cooling-off rule, mediation, arbitration, lemon laws, or a small-claims court to try to resolve the situation.

LET'S TALK ABOUT IT

1. **Steps in the Planned Buying Process.** Do you think all of the steps in the planned buying process are used when buying simple everyday products (such as a loaf of bread or a half-gallon of milk), or are they used only when buying big-ticket items? Why, or why not?

2. **Positives and Negatives of Leasing.** What benefits do you see in leasing a vehicle? What negatives exist when leasing?

3. **A Bad Purchase Decision.** What is the worst purchase decision you have ever made? What step(s) in the planned buying process could you have done better in that situation?

4. **Do You Complain?** When was the last time you were seriously dissatisfied with a purchase? Did you complain? Why or why not? If you complained, what was the outcome?

DO THE MATH

1. **Future Value on Cost of Extended Warranty.** Allison Jones of Jonesboro, Arkansas, is considering paying $150 a year for an extended warranty on several of her major appliances. If the appliances are expected to last for five years and she can earn 2 percent on her savings, what would be the future value of the amount she will pay for the extended warranty?

2. **Value of Shopping Carefully.** James Canter of Dallas, Texas, is a good shopper. He always comparison shops and uses coupons every week. James figures he saves at least $40 a month as a result. Assuming an interest rate of 2 percent, what is the future value of this amount over ten years?

3. **Buy Versus Lease.** Amanda Forsythe of Tampa, Florida, must decide whether to buy or lease a car she has selected. She has negotiated a purchase price of $24,700 and could borrow the money to buy from her credit union by putting $3000 down and paying $515 per month for 48 months at 6.5 percent APR. Alternatively, she could lease the car for 48 months at $310 per month by paying a

$3000 capital cost reduction and a $350 disposition fee on the car, which is projected to have a residual value of $8100 at the end of the lease. Use the Run the Numbers worksheet on page 232 to advise Amanda about whether she should buy or lease the car.

DO IT IN CLASS
PAGE 232

4. **Rebate Versus Low Interest Rate.** Kyle Parker of Fayetteville, Arkansas, has been shopping for a new car for several weeks. So far, he has negotiated a price of $27,000 on a model that carries a choice of a $2500 rebate or dealer financing at 2 percent APR. The dealer loan would require a $1000 down payment and a monthly payment of $564 for 48 months. Kyle has also arranged for a loan from his bank with a 7 percent APR. Use the Run the Numbers worksheet on page 231 to advise Kyle about whether he should use the dealer financing or take the rebate and use the financing from the bank.

DO IT IN CLASS
PAGE 231

FINANCIAL PLANNING CASES

CASE 1

The Johnsons Decide to Buy a Car

After three years of riding a bus to work, Belinda finds that she can no longer do so because her employer moved to a location that is not convenient for public transportation. Thus the Johnsons are in the market for another car. Harry and Belinda estimate that they could afford to spend about $10,000 on a good used car by making a down payment of $2000 and financing the remainder over 24 months at $355 per month.

(a) Make suggestions about how the $355 might be integrated into the Johnsons' budget (Table 3-6 on page 87) by making reductions in certain expense categories.

(b) If they cannot make room in their budget for a $355 monthly car payment, would you recommend they finance a vehicle for 36 or 48 months? Why or why not?

(c) Which sources of used cars should they consider? Why?

(d) Assume that the Johnsons have narrowed their choices to two cars. The first car is a five-year-old Chevrolet Malibu with 77,000 miles; it is being sold for $10,000 by a private individual. The seller has kept records of all maintenance and repairs. The second car is a five-year-old Ford Fusion with 70,000 miles, being sold by a used-car dealership. Harry contacted the previous owner and found that the car was given in trade on another car about three months ago. The previous owner cited no major mechanical problems but simply wanted a bigger car. The dealer is offering a written 30-day warranty on parts only. The asking price is $10,400. Which used car would you advise the Johnsons to buy? Why?

(e) Would you recommend that they purchase or lease a low-priced new vehicle instead of buying a used vehicle? Why or why not?

CASE 2

Victor and Maria Hernandez Buy a Third Car

The Hernandezes' older son, Jacob, has reached the age at which it is time to consider purchasing a car for him. Victor and Maria have decided to give Maria's old car to Jacob and buy a later-model used car for Maria.

(a) What sources can Victor and Maria use to access price and reliability information on various makes and models of used cars?

(b) What sources of used cars might be available to Victor and Maria, and what differences might exist among them?

(c) How might Victor and Maria check out the cars in which they are most interested?

(d) What strategies might Victor and Maria employ when they negotiate the price for the car they select?

CASE 3

Julia Price Wants to Drive a BMW

It has been almost 15 years since Julia graduated with a major in aeronautical engineering, and now she makes "buckets of money" working as a project manager for a large defense contracting company. While she is not very thrifty, she does like a good deal, especially on expensive purchases. Julia recently compared new models of the BMW 4-Series, Jaguar F-type, Audi A7, and Infiniti Q50. She checked out reviews in *Consumer Reports* and other magazines and test drove each vehicle. After deciding on the BMW, Julia shopped online for dealers beyond her community. Julia thinks that she will save about $3800 if she buys her car and an extended warranty on it from a dealer located 40 miles from her home instead of her hometown seller. She is not sure whether she should take advantage of the dealer's 3 percent financing versus a $4000 rebate, take the rebate and get a 6 percent loan from a nearby credit union, or lease the vehicle. Offer your opinions about her thinking.

CASE 4

Purchase of a New Refrigerator

DO IT IN CLASS
PAGE 227

Gary Joseph, a financial consultant from Spokane, Washington, is remodeling his kitchen. Gary, who lives alone, has decided to replace his refrigerator with a new model that offers more conveniences. He has narrowed his choices to two models. The first is a basic 16-cubic-foot model with a bottom freezer for $799. The second is a 25.4-cubic-foot model with side freezer for $999. Additional features for this model include icemaker, textured enamel surface, and ice and water dispenser. Gary's credit union will lend him the necessary funds for one year at a 12 percent APR on the installment plan. Following is his budget, which includes $2140 in monthly take-home pay.

Food	$ 300
Entertainment	120
Clothing	60
Gifts	70
Charities	75
Car payment	330
Personal care	60
Automobile expenses	120
Savings	130
Housing	825
Miscellaneous	50
Total	**$2,140**

(a) What preshopping research might Gary do to select the best brand of refrigerator?

(b) Using the information in Table 7-1 on page 213 or the *Garman/Forgue* companion website, determine Gary's monthly payment for the two models.

(c) Fit each of the two monthly payments into Gary's budget.

(d) Advise Gary to help him make his decision.

CASE 5

A Dispute over New-Car Repairs

DO IT IN CLASS PAGE 242

Christopher Hardison, a high school football coach from Oklahoma City, Oklahoma, purchased a new SUV for $28,000. He used the vehicle often; in fact, in less than nine months, he had put 14,000 miles on it. A 24,000-mile, two-year warranty was still in effect for the power-train equipment, although Christopher had to pay the first $100 of each repair cost. After 16,500 miles and in month 11 of driving, the car experienced some severe problems with the transmission. Christopher took the vehicle to the dealer for repairs. A week later he picked the car up, but some transmission problems remained. When Christopher took the car back to the dealer, the dealer said that no further problems could be identified. Christopher was sure that the problem was still there, and he was amazed that the dealer would not correct it. The dealer told him he would take no other action.

(a) Was Christopher within his rights to take the car back for repairs? Explain why or why not.

(b) What logical steps might Christopher follow if he continues to be dissatisfied with the dealer's unwillingness or inability to repair the car?

(c) Should Christopher seek any help from the court system? If so, describe what he could do without spending money on attorney's fees.

BE YOUR OWN PERSONAL FINANCIAL MANAGER

1. **Can You Afford a Vehicle Payment?** Review Table 8-1, "Fitting a Vehicle Payment into a Monthly Budget," and reflecting upon your own likely financial situation following graduation, write down a few notes explaining how following such an approach might be appropriate for you.

2. **Priority Worksheet.** Review Figure 8-2, "Priority Worksheet (for Haley Wilson)," on page 225 to help you think through the options that you desire in a new vehicle. Tentatively decide on the top five options you would prefer on a new vehicle and write up your findings or complete Worksheet 31: My Top Priority Motor Vehicle Features from "My Personal Financial Planner" to establish your priorities.

MY PERSONAL FINANCIAL PLANNER

3. **Comparing Vehicle Purchase Contracts.** To avoid simply focusing on one or two aspects of buying a vehicle, such as the monthly payment or the trade-in value, complete Worksheet 32: Comparing Vehicle Purchase Contracts from "My Personal Financial Planner" to help you focus on effectively comparing what is most important to you.

MY PERSONAL FINANCIAL PLANNER

4. **Lease or Buy a Vehicle?** Review the Run the Numbers worksheet, "Comparing Automobile Financing and Leasing," on page 232 to help to decide which choice is better for you or complete Worksheet 33: Should I Lease or Buy a Vehicle? from "My Personal Financial Planner."

5. **Rebate or Low-Rate Financing?** Review the Run the Numbers worksheet, "Choosing Between Low- Interest-Rate Dealer Financing and a Rebate," on page 231 to help to decide which alternative is better for you when you can arrange your own financing or complete Worksheet 34: Should I Take a New Vehicle Rebate or Low-Rate Financing Offer? from "My Personal Financial Planner."

MY PERSONAL FINANCIAL PLANNER

6. **Major Purchase Decision-Making Grid.** Review Table 8-2, "Decision-Making Grid (Illustrated for a Washing Machine)," on page 239 and think about a purchase you might make. Then complete Worksheet 35: Decision-Making Worksheet for a Major Product Purchase from "My Personal Financial Planner" and insert the weighted scores you think appropriate.

MY PERSONAL FINANCIAL PLANNER

7. **Sample Complaint Letter.** Review Table 8-3, "Complaint Procedure (Levels and Channels of Complaining)," on page 242 to draft a letter to seek redress for a deficient product or service you may have had in the past using Worksheet 36: Sample Product or Service Complaint Letter from "My Personal Financial Planner" as a guide.

MY PERSONAL FINANCIAL PLANNER

ON THE NET

Go to the Web pages indicated to complete these exercises.

1. **Keys to Vehicle Leasing.** Visit the website of the Federal Reserve Board at www.federalreserve.gov/pubs/leasing/ where you will find a link titled "Keys to Vehicle Leasing" that expands on the information in this book. Use this information to generate a list of pros and cons of leasing versus purchasing a vehicle. By clicking on "sample leasing form" on this Web page, you can view and print a copy of the required vehicle leasing disclosure form.

2. **Car Buying Advice.** Visit the website of *Consumer Reports* magazine at www.consumerreports.org and click on the "Cars" tab and then see the "Car Buying Advice" section. There you will find lots of information on how to buy cars as well as reliability data. In what ways are the strategies similar and in what ways do they differ from the tips offered in this book for buying a used car?

3. **Consumer Protection Organizations.** Search Google for "consumer protection organizations" that assist consumers with complaints. Create a table showing your findings for three organizations, and include the name, telephone number, Web address, main purpose, and types of problems addressed for each.

4. **Visit Edmunds.com.** Go online to Edmunds.com and search the site carefully. Write a report of your findings.

5. **Value of Used Cars.** Visit the website for the Kelly Blue Book at www.kbb.com to determine the market price of three used cars that might be of interest to you. Determine their "used car retail value," "trade-in value," and "private party value." Why do the three values differ?

ACTION INVOLVEMENT PROJECTS

1. **Needs and Wants.** Using Figure 8-2 on page 225 as a guide, make a list of the options in the first column that you would want if you could have any car you wanted. Realizing that getting all the options would be a dream (these are wants), go back to the list, move the priority level on certain items, and move the checkmarks to the second or third priorities. Your needs should now be in column one with wants in the other columns.

2. **Price Available Vehicles.** Telephone two new car dealers to determine if they have a particular make and model of vehicle that is of interest to you, for example, a two-year-old Toyota Prius. Inquire about number of vehicles available of the make and model of interest, colors, options of interest, and asking prices. Make a table of your findings.

3. **Compare Financing Terms.** Telephone two new car dealers to determine some financing details on used vehicles. Inform the dealers that your FICO credit score is above 750 and that you want to finance $12,000 after making a $4000 down payment. Find out the interest rate, number of years one could finance, and the monthly payments. Make a table of your findings.

Visit the Garman/Forgue companion website at www.cengagebrain.com.

9

Obtaining Affordable Housing

YOU MUST BE KIDDING, RIGHT?

Kelvin Lattimore bought a new home and borrowed $230,000 at 4.75 percent interest for 30 years. His monthly payment for interest and principal will be $1200. A friend suggested that Kelvin should have been able to find a loan at 4.5 percent with a monthly payment of $1165. Kelvin dismissed his friend's comments, arguing that the difference in the monthly payments was no big deal. His friend replied, "Kelvin, it's not the monthly payment, it's the interest." How much more in interest will Kelvin pay over the life of the loan because he took a loan with the higher rate?

A. $3600

C. $9600

B. $6600

D. $12,600

The answer is D. Kelvin will be making a higher payment each and every month for 30 years. While the difference in the monthly payment seems small [$35 ($1200 − $1165) per month in this example], even such a little difference in the interest rates on mortgage loans can add up to thousands of dollars in extra interest over the life of the loan. Searching for the lowest possible interest rate is very important when buying a home!

LEARNING OBJECTIVES

After reading this chapter, you should be able to:

1. Decide whether renting or owning your home is better for you.

2. Explain the up-front and monthly costs of buying a home.

3. Describe the steps in the home-buying process.

4. Understand the mathematics of mortgage loans and distinguish among ways of financing the purchase of a home.

5. Identify some key considerations when selling a home.

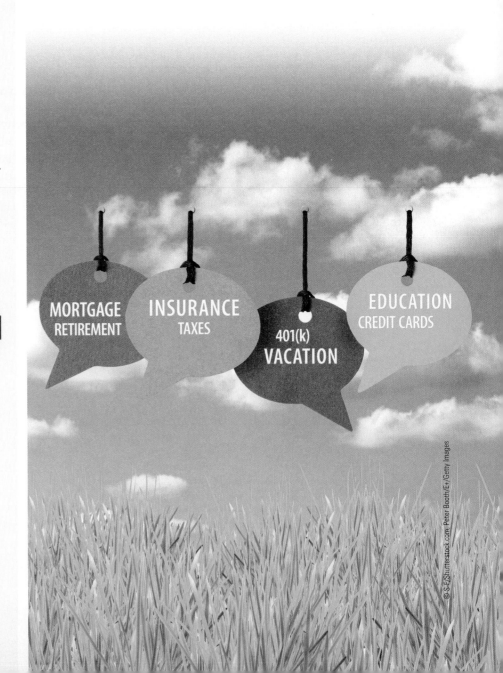

© S-F/Shutterstock.com; Peter Booth/E+/Getty Images

WHAT DO YOU RECOMMEND?

AP Images/Larry Macdougal

Shelby Clark has worked for a major consumer electronics retailer since graduating from college. The company has operations across the country with regional headquarters in Atlanta, Denver, Minneapolis, and Boston. She has been based in the Atlanta area for the past three years, and has begun to think about buying a home rather than renting her townhouse apartment. Then, last month, Shelby was promoted to deputy regional director for the Denver office. The promotion represents a key step for becoming a regional director in four or five years.

What do you recommend to Shelby on the subject of buying a home regarding:

1. **Buying or renting housing in the Denver area?**

2. **Steps she should take prior to actively looking at homes?**

3. **Finding a home and negotiating the purchase?**

4. **The closing process in home buying?**

5. **Selecting a type of mortgage to fit her needs?**

6. **Things to consider regarding the sale of her new home should she ultimately be promoted to a position in another of the four regions?**

YOUR NEXT FIVE YEARS

In the next five years, you can start achieving financial success by doing the following related to obtaining affordable housing:

1. *Read your leases and other real estate contracts thoroughly before signing.*

2. *Save the money for a home down payment within a tax-sheltered Roth IRA account.*

3. *Get your finances in order before shopping for a new home by reducing debt, budgeting better, and clearing up anything that keeps you from having a high credit score.*

4. *Buy a home as soon as it fits your budget and lifestyle so you can take advantage of special income tax deductions and price appreciation over time.*

5. *If you make a down payment of less than 20 percent on a home, cancel private mortgage insurance as soon as the equity in your home pushes the loan-to-value ratio down to 80 percent.*

The housing market bubble of the last decade was the largest in history. A **housing bubble** is a run-up in housing prices fueled by demand, speculation and the belief that recent history is an infallible forecast of the future. It can be identified through rapid increases in valuations of real property until they reach unsustainable levels and then decline.

Housing prices rose 50 to 100 percent or more in just a few years and then sharply crashed. This occurred partly because millions of Americans took out complicated mortgages that they did not understand. And they often bought too expensive a home. Mortgages that seemed affordable at first turned out later to be unaffordable as the monthly repayment amounts increased because the contracts allowed for increasing interest rates. The resulting rising payments and declining home values were a disaster and especially for those who lost their jobs in the Great Recession. Only recently has the housing market rebounded in most communities to pre-bubble prices.

The lingering effects of the economic downturn include the fact that today three in ten people in their 20s and early 30s are currently living with their parents. And 60 percent of all young adults are receiving financial assistance from them. This contrasts to a generation ago when only one in ten young adults moved back home and very few received financial support.

About 90 percent of all independent young adults rent their housing. In contrast, approximately 80 percent of people aged 55 to 64 are homeowners. Given these statistics, it is likely that one day you will want to buy a home. At that point, you should be able to mathematically evaluate the financial benefits of renting versus buying and take a hard look at what it really costs to buy a home. If you decide to buy, you will likely obtain a **mortgage loan**—a loan to purchase real estate in which the property itself serves as collateral. There are many types of mortgage loans, and you will need to fully understand your mortgage options before you obligate yourself for 15 to 30 years.

mortgage loan
Loan to purchase real estate in which the property itself serves as collateral.

LEARNING OBJECTIVE 1
Decide whether renting or owning your home is better for you.

9.1 SHOULD YOU RENT OR BUY YOUR HOME?

Whether to rent or buy depends on your preferences and what you can afford. In the short run, renting is usually less expensive than buying. In the long run, the opposite is usually true.

9.1a Renting Housing May Be Less Expensive in the Short Term

People may choose to rent their housing for many reasons. The large down payment and high monthly loan payments are barriers to buying a home. Some may simply prefer the easy mobility of renting or want to avoid many of the responsibilities associated with buying. Prospective renters need to consider the monthly rental fees, damage and security deposits, the lease agreement and restrictions, and tenant rights.

rent
Cost charged for using an apartment or other housing space.

Rent, Deposit, and Related Expenses Rent is the cost charged for using an apartment or other housing space. It is usually due on a specific day each month, with a late penalty being assessed if the tenant is tardy in making the payment. Other fees could be assessed for features such as use of a clubhouse and pool, exercise facilities, WIFI, cable television, Internet service, and space for storage and parking.

A **damage deposit** is an amount given in advance to a landlord to pay for repairing the unit beyond the damage expected from normal wear and tear. It is often charged before the tenant moves in, is often equal to one month's rent, and is refundable if at the end of the lease the tenant leaves the home in good condition. You may also be required to pay a **security deposit** to provide some assurance that you will not move

DID YOU KNOW

How to Make Sure Your Damage Deposit Is Returned

If you leave a rental unit clean and undamaged, you have a legal right to a refund of your damage deposit when you move out. Several steps will help ensure that you receive a full refund:

- Make a list of all damages and defects when you first move into the unit. Have the landlord sign this list.
- Maintain the unit and keep it clean.
- Notify the landlord promptly (in writing, if necessary) of any maintenance problems and malfunctions.

- Give proper written notice of your intention to move out at least 30 days in advance of the lease expiration.
- Make a written list of all damages and defects after moving out but prior to turning over the keys. Have the landlord sign this second list.
- Use certified mail (with a return receipt) to request the return of your security deposit and to inform the landlord of your new address.
- Use small-claims court (see Chapter 8, page 243), if necessary, to obtain a court-ordered refund.

without paying your rent. Again, this amount is often equal to the last month's rent payment. It too is refundable or is applied to the last month's rent. Thus, to rent an apartment might require payment of $900 for the first month's rent, a $900 security deposit, and a $900 damage deposit for a total of $2700.

Written Lease Contracts Protect All Parties A **lease** is a contract specifying the legal responsibilities of both the tenant and the landlord. It identifies the amount of rent and security deposit, the length of the lease (typically one year), payment responsibility for utilities and repairs, penalties for late payment of rent, eviction procedures for nonpayment of rent, and procedures to follow when the lease ends. Leases often state whether the security deposit accumulates interest, how soon the unit must be inspected for cleanliness after the tenant vacates the premises, and when the security deposit (or the balance) will be forwarded to the tenant. Illustrative leases may be found at Nolo. com. Renting housing without a formal, written lease may seem like an easy and congenial way to do business, but it is fraught with potential for disagreements later.

lease
In this context, a contract specifying both tenant and landlord legal responsibilities.

Two Types of Leases Two types of leases generally govern tenant-landlord relationships. The first provides for **periodic tenancy** (for example, week-to-week or month-to-month residency), where the agreement can be terminated by either of the parties if they give proper notice in advance (for example, one week or one month). Without such notice, the agreement stays in effect. This arrangement also typically applies in situations in which no written lease is established. The second type of lease provides for **tenancy for a specific time**, usually for one year. When this period expires, the agreement terminates unless prior notice is given by both parties that the agreement will be renewed.

Lease Restrictions Lease agreements may contain a variety of restrictions that are legally binding on tenants. For example, pets may or may not be permitted; when they are permitted, landlords often require a larger security deposit. Excessive noise from home entertainment systems or loud parties may be prohibited as well. To protect renters from overcrowding, a clause may limit the number of overnight guests.

An important restriction applies to **subleasing** (wherein an original tenant leases the property to another tenant). Here a tenant who moves before the lease expires may need to obtain the landlord's permission before someone else can take over the rental unit. The new tenant may even have to be approved, and the original tenant often retains some financial liability until the term of the original lease expires.

subleasing
An arrangement in which the original tenant leases the property to another tenant.

9.1b Tenants Have Rights Even in the Absence of a Written Lease

Tenants have a number of legal rights under laws in most states and many local communities. Some important rights are as follows:

- Prohibitions against retaliatory actions such as rent increases, eviction, or utility shut-off for reporting building-code violations or otherwise exercising a tenant's legal rights.

- Assurances of some legally prescribed minimum standard of **habitability** for items such as running water, heat, and a working stove and the safety of access areas such as stairways.

- The right to make minor repairs and deduct the cost from the tenant's next rent payment. This right is subject to certain restrictions, such as giving sufficient prior written notification to the landlord.

- Prompt return of a security deposit, with limits placed on the kinds of deductions that can be made. Landlords must explain specific reasons for deductions. Some state laws require that interest be paid on security deposits.

- The right to file a lawsuit against a landlord for nonperformance. Such suits can be brought in a small-claims court.

9.1c Owned Housing May Be Less Expensive in the Long Term

Americans have historically chosen single-family dwellings to satisfy their owned-housing desires. Other alternatives are popular, too, such as condominiums, cooperatives, manufactured housing, and mobile homes.

Single-Family Dwellings A **single-family dwelling** is a housing unit that is detached from other units. Buyers have many choices available for both new and existing homes with varying floor plans and home features. Some people prefer the modern kitchens and other features found in newer homes; others prefer the larger rooms, higher ceilings, and completed landscaping of older homes.

Condominiums and Cooperatives The terms condominium and cooperative describe forms of ownership rather than types of buildings. These forms of ownership typically cost less than single-family dwellings, offer recreation facilities, and have few if any resident maintenance obligations.

With a **condominium** (or **condo**), the owner holds legal title to a specific housing unit within a multiunit building or project and owns a proportionate share in the common grounds and facilities. The entire development is run by the owners through a **homeowners association**. Besides making monthly mortgage payments, the condominium owner must pay a monthly **homeowners association fee** that is established by the homeowners association. This fee covers expenses related to the management of the common grounds and facilities and insurance on the building.

Some areas of concern for condominium owners include potential increases in homeowner's fees and

single-family dwelling

Housing unit that is detached from other units.

condominium (condo)

Form of ownership with the owners holding legal title to their own housing unit among many, with common grounds and facilities owned by the developer or homeowners association.

Be sure to factor homeowners association fees into the monthly income needed to purchase a condominium.

limited resale appeal of the unit. Condo market prices are much more volatile than for single-family dwellings and condos don't increase as much in value as single-family dwellings. In addition, during a housing downturn, their values decline more than single-family homes.

With a **cooperative** (or **co-op**), the owner holds a share of the corporation that owns and manages a group of housing units. The value of this share is equivalent to the value of the owner's particular unit. The owner also holds a proportional interest in all common areas. A monthly fee for the cooperative covers the same types of items as does a condominium fee and also includes an amount to cover the professional management of the complex as well as payments on the cooperative's mortgage debt. (The pro rata share for interest and property taxes is deductible on each shareholder's income tax return.)

Manufactured Housing and Mobile Homes **Manufactured housing** consists of fully or partially factory-built housing units designed to be transported (often in portions) to the home site. Final assembly and readying of the housing for occupancy occurs at the home site. **Mobile homes**, in contrast, are fully factory-assembled housing units that are designed to be towed on a frame with a trailer hitch. Mobile homes depreciate in value every year just like automobiles.

9.1d So Who Pays More—Renters or Owners?

According to conventional wisdom, homeowners enjoy a financial advantage over renters when total housing costs are calculated over many years. Renters generally pay out less money in terms of annual cash flow, but owners receive annual income tax advantages and they can see increases in the value of their homes over time that can improve their financial situation. However, as evidenced by events of recent years, there is no guarantee that housing values will increase in a uniform fashion over time; they might even decline.

Ask your real estate agent for the **price-to-rent ratio** in your community. This ratio shows the average home price divided by annual rent in a community. The national average is 11. The higher the ratio number, especially above 15, is more attractive for renting a home versus buying similar housing. (See Chapter 16, page 483 for more information on price-to-rent ratios.)

Based on Initial Cash Flow, Renters Appear to Win The Run the Numbers worksheet "Should You Buy or Rent?" on page 254 illustrates a comparison between a condominium and an apartment with similar space and amenities. For the apartment, rent would total $1000 per month. Assume you could buy the condominium for $180,000 by using $36,000 in savings as a down payment and borrowing the remaining $144,000 for 30 years at 6.0 percent interest. As the worksheet shows, renting would have a cash-flow cost of $11,640 after a reduction for the interest that could be earned on your savings (after taxes). Buying requires several expenses beyond the monthly mortgage payment, including a monthly $150 homeowner's fee ($1800 annually) in our example. In this case, the cash-flow cost of buying is $16,485, or $4,845 more than renting.

After Taxes and Appreciation, Owners Usually Win To make the comparison more accurate, you must also consider the tax and appreciation aspects of the two options. If you rent, you would pay $180 ($720 × 0.25) in income taxes on the interest on the amount in your savings account ($36,000) not used for a down payment. If you buy the condominium, $1768 of the $10,360 in annual mortgage loan payments during the first year will go toward the principal of the debt, and the remainder—$8592 ($10,360−$1768)—will go toward interest. Both mortgage interest and

cooperative (co-op)
Form of ownership in which the owner holds a share of the corporation that owns and manages a group of housing units as well as common grounds and facilities.

real estate property taxes qualify as income tax deductions. If you are in the 25 percent marginal tax bracket, your taxes would be reduced by $2148 ($8592 × 0.25) as a result of deducting the mortgage interest and by $750 ($3000 × 0.25) as a result of deducting the real estate tax. In effect, every time you make a payment you will get some of it back from the government.

Condominiums also have a possibility of appreciation, or increase, in the home's value. A conservative assumption would be that the condominium will increase in value by 1 percent per year since condo values do not usually rise as fast as single family

RUN THE NUMBERS

Should You Buy or Rent?

This worksheet can be used to estimate whether you would be better off renting housing or buying. If you are renting an apartment and planning to buy a house, qualitative differences will enter into your decision. This worksheet

will put the financial picture into focus. A similar worksheet can be found at www. finance.yahoo.com/calculator/real-estate/hom06/

DO IT IN CLASS

	Example Amounts		Your Figures	
	Rent	Buy	Rent	Buy
Annual Cash-Flow Considerations				
Annual rent ($1000/month) or mortgage payments ($863.35/month)*	$12,000	$10,360	_____	_____
Property and liability insurance	360	725	_____	_____
Private mortgage insurance	N/A	0	N/A	_____
Real estate taxes	0	3,000	_____	_____
Maintenance	0	600	_____	_____
Other housing fees	0	1,800	_____	_____
Less interest earned on funds not used for down payment (at 2%)	720	N/A	_____	N/A
Cash-Flow Cost for the Year	**$11,640**	**$16,485**	_____	_____
Tax and Appreciation Considerations				
Less principal[†] repaid on the mortgage loan	N/A	1,768	N/A	_____
Plus tax on interest earned on funds not used for down payment (25% marginal tax bracket)	180	N/A	_____	N/A
Less tax savings due to deductibility of mortgage interest[‡] (25% marginal tax bracket)	N/A	2,148	N/A	_____
Less tax savings due to deductibility of real estate property taxes (25% marginal tax bracket)	N/A	750	N/A	_____
Less appreciation on the dwelling (2.5% annual rate)	N/A	1,800	N/A	_____
Net Cost for the Year	**$11,820**	**$10,019**	_____	_____

*Calculated from Table 9-4 on page 273
[†](Calculated according to the method illustrated in Table 9-2 on page 271
[‡]Mortgage interest tax savings equal total mortgage payments minus principal repaid multiplied by the marginal tax rate.

DID YOU KNOW

Walking Out on a Mortgage Is Usually a Bad Idea

In recent years some home borrowers have decided to take a **strategic default**. When the value of their homes decreased, they found themselves horribly **upside down** (also known as **under water**) meaning that they owed more than the homes were worth. Some financially strapped borrowers in such a situation choose to stop paying on

their mortgage and let the lender take back the home. This is attractive because mortgages are **nonrecourse loans**. With such loans, the lender may not go after other assets if the foreclosed home brings an insufficient amount to cover the outstanding debt when sold at auction. Given the moral issue this is a difficult decision for the underwater homeowner.

dwellings. A condominium valued at $180,000 would, therefore, be worth $181,800 ($180,000 × 1.01) after one year, a gain of $1800. In this case, buying is financially better than renting by approximately $1801 ($11,820−$10,019).

Note that the calculations above compare somewhat equivalent housing types. The process is more complicated when you want to compare renting an apartment with buying a house. You definitely should still do the math but recognize that you are comparing unlike

foreclosure

Process in which the lender sues the borrower to prove default and asks the court to order the sale of the property to pay the debt.

DID YOU KNOW

About Buying a Foreclosed Property

Any slip-up in making mortgage repayments may result in **foreclosure**. This is a specific legal process in which a lender attempts to recover the balance of a loan from a borrower who has stopped making payments to the lender by forcing the sale of the asset used as the collateral for the loan. Foreclosed properties are sometimes viewed as a way to buy a home for a low price. If interested in buying such a property you should understand the basic aspects of foreclosed properties:

1. *Short Sale. A short sale* occurs when a home sale is negotiated with the owner at a price below the actual balance of the debt. The property may or may not be in foreclosure as yet but the seller is trying to get out from under the debt. The lender must approve the short sale. Lenders are tough negotiators as they want to get as much money as possible for the property but may be willing to waive closing costs and other fees, making the overall cost more affordable.

2. *Preforeclosure. Preforeclosure* is the time between when the homeowner has been notified by the lender that he or she is in default and the actual foreclosure has been completed. To purchase such a property, you would

negotiate a price directly with the owner The owner may be willing to take a price lower than the market value especially if the offer is above the mortgage balance. Here the owner can get out of the loan and avoid foreclosure and perhaps still recoup some money. Or the purchase may be a short sale.

3. *Bank-owned property.* Once the foreclosure process has been completed, the lender typically takes ownership of the property. The lender then will attempt to sell the property on its own, through a real estate agent, or at a **foreclosure auction**. Most of the people bidding on these homes at auction are professionals and the buyer must come up with the cash immediately.

There are many potential pitfalls when buying a foreclosed residence. The property is likely to need repairs, so insist upon a professional home inspection. Also, taxes and other assessments may be owed. Foreclosure properties can be found on such websites as www.Foreclosure.com, www.Foreclosures.com, and www.RealtyTrac.com, which charge monthly subscription fees for access to their databases. Use a licensed real estate agent and hire a real estate attorney to help when making an offer and for the closing process.

properties. It is probable that you will find that buying a home is significantly more expensive than renting for the first few years. But if you stay in the home for five years or longer, the financial situation generally improves for the homeowner, especially for one with a fixed interest rate loan. This assumes you do not pay too much for it in the first place.

CONCEPT CHECK 9.1

1. Explain the purpose and value of a lease for both the renter and the landlord.

2. Distinguish between periodic tenancy and tenancy for a specific time when renting housing.

3. Identify three ways that home buyers can save on their income taxes.

4. Illustrate how housing buyers can pay less than renters when taxes and appreciation of housing values are considered.

9.2 WHAT DOES IT COST TO BUY A HOME?

LEARNING OBJECTIVE 2

Explain the up-front and monthly costs of buying a home.

Buying housing represents the largest outlay of funds over most people's lifetime. Some of these costs occur up front. The largest of these is usually the down payment. Others, such as the mortgage payment, occur monthly. A few items, such as real estate property taxes, require both an initial outlay and recurring monthly payments. Table 9-1 illustrates these outlays for the purchase of a $185,000 single-family dwelling with $25,000 down financed by a 30-year mortgage at 6.0 percent interest. (We have used a 6.0 percent rate for illustration purposes. Rates may be lower or higher depending on your credit score and market conditions.) This same example is used repeatedly throughout this chapter to illustrate the costs of home buying as it is near the median price for first-time buyers.

9.2a Pay Up-Front Costs at the Closing

closing costs

Include fees and charges other than the down payment and typically vary from 2 to 7 percent of the mortgage loan amount.

First-time home buyers are faced with substantial initial costs when buying a home. These include the down payment and closing costs. **Closing costs** include fees and charges other than the down payment and typically vary from 2 to 7 percent of the mortgage loan amount. The down payment and closing costs must be paid at a meeting called the **closing** at which ownership of the property is transferred. All the parties to the purchase, sale, and the mortgage loan are represented at the closing. Up-front costs are indicated on page 257 in Table 9-1.

down payment

An initial payment made in the context of buying expensive items on credit, such as a vehicle or home.

The Down Payment The **down payment** is an initial payment made in the context of buying expensive items on credit, such as a vehicle or home. When buying a home, the buyer actually writes a check to the seller for that amount. In this example, we assume that the prospective homeowner has $25,000 saved to use as a down payment on a $185,000 home and will, therefore, need to borrow $160,000.

point/interest point

Fee equal to 1 percent of the total mortgage loan amount.

Points A **point** (or **interest point**) is a fee equal to 1 percent of the total loan amount. Any charges for points must be paid in full when the home is bought, although sometimes they can be added to the amount borrowed. Lenders use points to increase their income return on loans. For example, a lender might advertise a loan as having an interest rate 0.25 percentage point below prevailing rates but then charge 1 point. Points are, in effect, prepaid interest and compensate the lender for having a lower interest rate. In our example, the lender charged 1 point on the $160,000 loan, resulting in a charge of $1600. By law, interest points must be included when calculating the APR for the loan because they really are interest. Interest points are deductible on federal income tax returns.

Attorney Fees Home buyers should hire an attorney to review documents and advise and represent them prior to and during closing. Attorney fees commonly amount to

Table 9-1	Illustrated Up-Front and Monthly Costs When Buying a Home (Purchase Price of a Home, $185,000 with $25,000 Down; Closing on July 1)

Home-Buying Costs	At Closing	Monthly
Payments Required Up Front		
Down payment	$25,000	
Points (1)	1,600	
Attorney's fee	500	
Title search	200	
Title insurance (to protect lender)	320	
Title insurance (to protect buyer)	320	
Loan origination fee	800	
Credit reports	60	
Home inspection	400	
Deed recording fees	250	
Appraisal fee	250	
Termite and radon inspection fee	130	
Lot survey fee	100	
Pro-rata interest	435	
Home title transfer fee	1,180	
Notary fee	150	
Payments Required Monthly		
Principal and interest (from Table 9-3 for a $160,000 loan for 30 years at 6.0%)		$ 959.28
Mortgage insurance		53.33
Warranty insurance		30.00
Payments Required Up Front and Then Monthly		
Property taxes ($2160 for the entire year, $1080 for first half-year, then $180 monthly)	1,080*	180.00
Homeowner's insurance ($1200 for the entire year; $600 for first half-year, then $100 monthly)	600†	100.00
Subtotal	**$33,375**	**$1,322.61**
Less amount owed by seller	−1,080*	
Total	**$32,295**	**$1,322.61**

*Would be received from seller, who legally owes these taxes, and then deposited in escrow account to be available when the tax bill comes due at the end of the year.
†Would be paid to escrow account to be available when the premium for the next year is due.

0.5 percent of the purchase price of the home, although some attorneys do this work for a flat fee ($500 in our example).

Title Search and Insurance The **title** to real property is the legal right of ownership interest. In real estate transactions, the title is transferred to a new owner through a **deed**, which is a written document used to convey real estate ownership. Although there are several types of deeds, a **warranty deed** is the safest as it guarantees that the title is free of any previous mortgages.

A title search and the purchase of title insurance protect the buyer's title to the property. Your attorney or title company will conduct a **title search** by inspecting court

title
Legal right of ownership interest to real property.

deed
Written document used to convey real estate ownership.

title insurance

Protects the lender's interest if the title search is later found faulty.

home inspection

Conducted to ensure that the home is physically sound and that all operating systems are in proper order.

appraisal fee

Fee charged for a professionally prepared estimate of the fair market value of the property by an objective party.

PITI

Elements of a monthly real estate payment consisting of principal, interest, real estate taxes, and homeowner's insurance.

loan-to-value (LTV) ratio

Original or current outstanding loan balance divided by the home value.

mortgage insurance

Insures the difference between the amount of down payment required by an 80 percent LTV ratio and the actual, lower down payment.

records and prepare a detailed written history of property ownership called an **abstract**. The fees for this process can be paid by the seller or buyer ($200 paid by buyer in our example). Lenders often require buyers to purchase **title insurance** because it protects the lender's interest if the title is later found faulty. Premiums for title policies vary among title companies. The one-time charge at closing may amount to 0.20 percent of the amount of the loan for each policy ($320 [$160,000 × 0.002] in our example). Homeowners who wish to insure their own interest must purchase a separate title insurance policy (another $320 in our example).

Miscellaneous Fees When a prospective mortgage borrower applies for a loan, the lender may charge a **loan origination fee** at the closing to process the loan ($800 or half of a point in our example). In addition, credit reports ($75 in our example) are needed before a home buyer can obtain a loan—and the borrower pays the fee for this report as well. Another important up-front cost is the **home inspection** ($400 in our example) conducted to ensure that the home is physically sound and that all operating systems are in proper order. Title and deed recording fees ($250 in our example) are charged to transfer ownership documents in the county courthouse. An **appraisal fee** ($250 in our example) may be required to obtain a professionally prepared estimate of the fair market value of the property by an objective party. If you are charged an appraisal fee, you have the right to receive a copy of the appraisal. Occasionally, termite and radon inspections ($130 in our example) are required by local laws, and these are a good idea even when not required. A **survey** ($100 in our example) is sometimes required to certify the specific boundaries of the lot. Finally, separate **notary fees** ($150 in our example) may be charged for the services of those legally qualified to certify (or notarize) signatures. Some communities also charge a **home title transfer fee**, which is simply a tax imposed to support community services such as police, fire, and schools. **Pro-rata interest** may be required if the closing does not occur on the due date of the mortgage payment and interest will accrue before the first payment is due.

9.2b   Your Monthly Costs Include Both Principal and Interest

Once a home is purchased, the monthly costs can consume as much as 30 or 40 percent of your disposable income. These costs include the portion of your monthly payment that goes to principal (the amount you owe) and interest. Additional monthly costs can include mortgage insurance, home warranty insurance, property taxes, and homeowner's insurance. Monthly costs are indicated 259 in Table 9-1.

Mortgage Principal and Interest A mortgage loan requires repayment of both principal (*P*) and interest (*I*), which are the first two letters of the acronym **PITI**, which real estate agents and lenders often use to indicate a mortgage payment that includes principal, interest, real estate taxes, and homeowner's insurance. In the example in Table 9-1, the mortgage payment for principal and interest on a 30-year mortgage for $160,000 at 6.0 percent is $959.28. (Later in this chapter, you will learn how the P and I components for any mortgage loan are calculated).

Mortgage Insurance Lenders today expect a 70 to 80 percent **loan-to-value (LTV) ratio** when a home is purchased. The LTV ratio is simply the loan amount divided by the value of the home (the purchase price initially). An 80 percent LTV ratio translates into a 20 percent down payment, an amount that is difficult to come by for many first-time buyers. When a buyer makes a lower down payment that results in an LTV higher than that desired by the lender, the lender requires that the borrower purchase mortgage insurance.

Mortgage insurance insures the difference between the amount of down payment required by the lender's desired LTV ratio and the actual, lower down payment. In this way, the lender is assured of payment of the loan balance if the home were later foreclosed for default and sold for less than the amount owed. Mortgage insurance may be obtained from several sources and can be canceled when the LTV ratio reaches the desired percent as the loan is paid down. You can obtain mortgage insurance from the following three sources.

- **Private Mortgage Insurance.** Private mortgage insurance (PMI) is obtained from a private company. The largest private mortgage insurer is the Mortgage Guaranty Insurance Corporation (MGIC, pronounced "magic"). The cost of PMI varies from 0.25 to 2.0 percent of the debt, depending on the degree to which the LTV ratio exceeds the lender-desired percentage. In our example, the LTV ratio is 86.5 percent ($160,000 ÷ $185,000), and the lender required 80 percent (20 percent down). As a result, the annual private mortgage insurance premium is 0.4 percent of the mortgage loan (0.004 × $160,000) and is $640, or $53.33 per month ($640 ÷ 12). It may be possible to obtain lender-paid mortgage insurance in return for paying a fractionally higher interest rate. The downside is that the insurance cannot be canceled when the LTV ratio hits the desired percentage without completely refinancing the loan.

private mortgage insurance (PMI)
Mortgage insurance obtained from a private company.

- **FHA Mortgage Insurance.** The Federal Housing Administration (FHA) of the U.S. Department of Housing and Urban Development (HUD) insures loans that meet its standards. FHA-insured loans can allow you to borrow with as little as 3.5 percent down. The insurance is paid for by a combination up-front charge ranging from 1.00 to 2.25 percent of the amount borrowed and a monthly charge of up to 1.15 percent. The maximum amount of the loan varies by geographic region. To obtain such mortgage insurance, the borrower must be creditworthy and the home must meet the FHA's minimum-quality standards.

Federal Housing Administration (FHA)
Part of the U.S. Department of Housing and Urban Development (HUD) that insures loans that meet its standards to encourage home ownership.

  (For information on HUD mortgage programs, visit www.hud.gov/buying /index.cfm.)

- **VA Mortgage Insurance-** The federal **Department of Veterans Affairs (VA)** promotes home ownership among military veterans (active-duty, reserve, and National Guard veterans may qualify) by providing the lender with a guarantee against buyer default. In effect, the VA (www.benefits.va.gov/homeloans/) guarantee operates much like FHA or private mortgage insurance—that is, the lender is guaranteed a portion of the loan's value in the event that the home must be foreclosed and sold below the outstanding balance on the loan.

Home Warranty Insurance All homes for sale carry some type of implied warranty (see page 234 Chapter 8). In most states, home sellers must complete and sign a form required by state law to verify the condition of home features and major mechanical equipment at the time of sale. A seller who knowingly hides serious defects might be liable, but the buyer may have to hire an attorney and sue to prove this point. Also, many new-home builders provide an express warranty good for one year on the new homes they sell.

Home warranty insurance, another option for the homeowner, operates much like a service contract (also discussed in Chapter 8 on pages 234–235). Insurance companies sell this type of insurance on existing homes through real estate agents and builders. The example in Table 9-1 has a $30-per-month home warranty insurance protection for one year. Typically, the homeowner must pay the first $100 to $500 of any repair.

9.2c Taxes and Insurance Are Paid Both Up Front and Monthly

Some home-buying costs do not fit neatly into an up-front or monthly pattern. This is because they are billed annually, although they often can be paid monthly. Examples are **taxes (T)** and **insurance (I)**, which represent the last two letters of PITI. To ensure that these are paid when due, the lender usually requires that monthly installments be paid into an escrow account. An **escrow account** is a special reserve account at a financial

escrow account
Special reserve account at a financial institution in which funds are held until they are paid to a third party—in this case, for home insurance and for property taxes.

institution in which funds are held until they are paid to a third party. When the insurance and tax bills are due, the institution pays them out of the escrow account.

Real Estate Property Taxes   **Real estate property taxes** (the T in PITI) must be paid to local governments annually and may range from 1 to 4 percent of the value of the home. The total property tax ($2160 in our example) is due once a year when the government mails out its tax bill. However, if a buyer takes possession during the tax year, the buyer must pay the taxes accrued so far into the escrow account at the closing ($1080, or $6 \times \$180$ here) to ensure that sufficient funds will be available when the bill comes due at the end of the year. Then the monthly amount ($180 in our example) is paid thereafter into the escrow account. (Because it is the seller who really owed the taxes for the six months prior to the sale, the seller will pay the buyer $1080 on the day of the closing.)

Real estate property taxes are based on the value of buildings and land. To calculate these taxes, local government officials first establish a **fair market value** which is what a willing buyer would probably pay a willing seller for the owner's home and land. Next, the **assessed value** of the property is calculated. This is the dollar value assigned for the purposes of measuring applicable taxes. A home with a fair market value of $160,000, for example, might have an assessed value of $120,000. Some government officials establish the assessed value of a property as the same as the fair market value. You might reduce your property taxes by claiming that the assessed valuation of your home is too high. If successful, your tax bill will be lowered. About one-half of all appeals succeed.

Homeowner's Insurance   Lenders always require homeowners to insure the home itself in case of fire or other calamity. Both the home and its contents can be covered in a typical homeowner's insurance policy (the second I in PITI). (Chapter 10 covers this information in detail.) The annual premium for such insurance must be paid each year in advance ($1200 in this example). Lenders require prepayment of the estimated insurance premium each month ($100 here) into the escrow account. In our example illustrated in Table 9-1, the purchaser must be prepared to pay one-half year's premium ($600 here) on the closing day so that there will be sufficient funds in the account to pay the next year's full premium in six months when it is due.

9.2d   Make a Decision Based on All Costs

The wise financial planner will carefully estimate all initial and monthly costs of housing. Focusing only on the down payment and the monthly payment for principal and interest does not tell the whole story.

In our example, the borrower was able to put less than 20 percent down ($13.5\% = \$25,000 \div \$185,000$). However, with points and other up-front costs, actually had to come up with $32,295 at the closing. Similarly, the monthly payment for principal and interest was $959.28, but the actual monthly outlay will be $1322.61. This is the real dollar amount that this buyer must fit into his or her budget when trying to determine whether he or she can afford to buy a home.

CONCEPT CHECK 9.2

1. What is the standard down payment amount on a mortgage loan?

2. If you make a down payment that is lower than standard, identify the extra cost you will be required to pay.

3. Why do lenders use points in home loans, and who is responsible for paying points?

4. Explain why the down payment and mortgage principal and interest understate the actual up-front and monthly costs of home ownership.

5. When should you request that private mortgage insurance be canceled if such insurance was required at the time of purchase of a home?

6. Identify the components of PITI.

9.3 THE STEPS IN HOME BUYING

Do not be in a hurry. Buying a home is the biggest purchase you will likely ever make and **special** attention needs to be paid to the seven steps outlined in Figure 9-1.

9.3a 1. Get Your Finances in Order

You need to be financially ready to buy a home. The first three steps ease the home buying process: doing a credit checkup, accurately estimating all monthly housing costs, and fitting projected housing costs into your budget.

Clean Up Your Credit History Your credit history can make or break your chances of buying the home of your dreams. The average FICO credit score for home loan borrowers is above 730. Obtain copies of your credit report and your credit scores from all

LEARNING OBJECTIVE 3

Describe the steps in the home-buying process.

Figure 9-1 **Steps in the Process of Buying a Home**

You should plan on it taking about 6 months to buy a home from the time you begin your efforts until you actually move in.

6 months before moving in	**1. Get your finances in order.** • Ensure that your credit bureau file is accurate and request any updates or corrections as necessary. • Estimate all your expected monthly housing costs. • Adjust your budget to fit the costs expected.
3 to 5 months before moving in	**2. Prequalify for a mortgage.** • Shop for best rates. • Estimate affordability using front- and back-end ratios. • Consult several lenders and mortgage brokers.
2 to 4 months before moving in	**3. Search for a home online and in person.**
2 months before moving in	**4. Agree to terms with a seller.** • Negotiate a price with the seller and give the seller earnest money. • Have your lawyer go over the purchase contract with you. • Sign the purchase contract. • Have the home inspected by someone you hire.
1 to 2 months before moving in	**5. Obtain a mortgage loan. Decide on the best type of mortgage loan for you.** • Formally apply for a mortgage from the desired lender. • Consider locking-in an interest rate if rates are likely to go up before the closing. • Arrange for a lawyer to help you go over the contract and the good-faith estimate of closing costs.
2 to 4 weeks before moving in	**6. Prepare for the closing.** • Make moving arrangements. • Activate all utilities. • Initiate the change of address process.
The Big Day	**7. Attend the closing.** • Correct any errors in the contract or uniform settlement statement. • Sign your name. Write the big checks. • Celebrate!

three major credit reporting agencies (lenders use all three) about six months in advance of starting to buy a home. That way you will have time to clear up any errors and problems before the loan application process begins. To finance a home purchase you also will need a sufficient and steady earnings history.

Use Internet Resources to Estimate Your Monthly Housing Costs It is vital to have an accurate estimate of what you will have to pay on a monthly basis for your new home. You should include all likely components of the monthly payment into your budget: the principal and interest, property taxes, homeowner's insurance, mortgage insurance, and perhaps a home warranty fee. You should also consider any additional costs you might pay for utilities. Heating, air-conditioning, electric, and water are all areas for which homeowners generally pay more than renters. Estimating a 50 percent increase from what you are currently spending might be a starting point.

1. Resources are available on the Internet to help estimate housing costs (www.cgi.money.cnn.com/tools/houseafford/houseafford.html and www.homes.yahoo.com/calculators/afford.html).
2. Then choose the type of home you would like to own and the neighborhoods in which you would like to live.
3. Go to the www.realtor.com website to search for housing that matches your interests. You will be able to estimate the selling price of similar housing and, by subtracting your available down payment amount, estimate the amount you will need to borrow.
4. Go to the www.bankrate.com website to estimate the current interest rates on mortgage loans in your market.
5. Use the calculator at www.bankrate.com/calculators/mortgages/mortgage-calculator.aspx to estimate the monthly payment for a loan of the amount you need at the prevailing interest rates. Or use Table 9-4 on page 273.
6. Add an additional 30 to 40 percent (it was 39 percent in the Table 9-1 example) to the monthly payment on the loan itself for such things as homeowner's insurance, property taxes, private mortgage insurance, and warranty insurance.

Fit the Housing Costs into Your Budget Once you have an estimate of the monthly costs associated with buying a home, you will need to see how these costs fit into your budget. You can follow a similar process as outlined in Chapter 8 on pages 227 to 228 to fit your payment into your budget. Base the budget on only one person's income. A young couple who buys a home based on their combined incomes is locked into a full-time, dual-income lifestyle to pay the loan. Family obligations or a job loss may later disrupt their ability or willingness to continue that lifestyle. Instead, base your housing affordability on just one income. Or, perhaps include part-time work income for the second person.

DID YOU KNOW

Bias toward Having the Best

People engaged in obtaining affordable housing have a bias toward certain behaviors that can be harmful, such as a tendency toward wanting to have the best. Many first-time homebuyers want to purchase a home that has all the most desirable features but doing so stretches their budgets. What to do? When purchasing your first home, buy it thinking "to get started" by making sure it easily fits your budget. Don't make your first home a really large "dream home."

DID YOU KNOW

Special Insurance Programs for Those Who Can Only Afford a Low Down Payment

Many state and local governments provide support for first-time homebuyers through various housing agencies. These supports often take the form of special low down payment loan programs, forgivable down payment loans, and certain guarantees that encourage lenders to accept lower than usual down payments or mortgage interest rates. Lenders in your area can provide you with information about programs that target these special-needs groups. Or go to www.hud.gov/buying/localbuying.cfm for links to programs in each state.

9.3b   2. Prequalify for a Mortgage

Before you even start looking at specific homes you should look into whether you will prequalify for a mortgage loan given the price range of homes that you like and your intended down payment. To **prequalify** means that a lender believes it is likely that a loan would be granted based on preliminary information provided such as a credit report, amount borrowed and likely down payment. It tells you if you can obtain a loan and the tentative APR. Make a list of three or four possible lenders at this point including your own bank (see www.bankrate.com). If your budget cannot accommodate the estimate of monthly costs you find in the pre-qualification, you may need to revise your goals by downsizing the type of home you desire or choose housing in a less expensive neighborhood. Helpful information can be found at the websites for the U.S. Department of Housing and Urban Development (www.hud.gov/buying/booklet.pdf) and the Federal National Mortgage Association (www.homepath.com/financing.html).

Consult Multiple Lenders Once you have an idea of the interest rate you might pay, you can consult other lenders to determine whether you would actually qualify for a mortgage in the amount you would like. Be aware that prequalifying for a loan carries no guarantee that you will be able to get a loan on a specific property. The purpose of the prequalification is to help you set the price range when you start looking for particular homes.

Perhaps Use a Mortgage Broker A **mortgage broker** is an individual or company that acts as an intermediary between borrowers and lenders. In other words, a broker helps lenders find borrowers and borrowers find lenders. Either the lender or the borrower may pay the fee charged by the broker. If the lender pays this fee, the broker legally represents the lender. If the borrower pays it, the broker legally represents the borrower. Thus, if you want the broker to work to find you the lowest possible rate, you should be prepared to pay for the service. On-line services such as at www.lendingtree.com make your application information available to multiple lenders who then contact you with loan offers. About 10 percent of all mortgage loans today are arranged through a mortgage broker.

mortgage broker
Individual or company that acts as an intermediary between borrowers and lenders.

Lenders Use Two Rule of Thumb for Home Loans To estimate the maximum affordability of housing expenses for a home loan applicant lenders use two rules of thumb.

- The **front-end ratio** compares the total annual expenditures for housing (the principal and interest on the mortgage plus the real estate taxes and insurance) with the loan applicant's gross annual income (before taxes). Generally, the total annual expenditures should not exceed 25 to 29 percent of gross annual income. Applying a 28 percent front-end ratio, a young couple with a combined gross annual income

front-end ratio
Compares the total annual PITI expenditures for housing with the loan applicant's gross annual income to assess the borrower's ability to pay the mortgage.

DID YOU KNOW

The Income Needed to Qualify for a Mortgage

The table below gives you a quick idea of how much income you need to buy a home at a certain price using a front-end ratio of 28 percent. The illustration is for a 30-year loan with a 20 percent down payment. For each home price, the top figure in each row shows the monthly payment for principal, interest, real estate taxes, and homeowner's insurance for the interest rates; the bottom figure shows the required

gross annual income to qualify for the loan. For example, a 6 percent loan on a $180,000 home requires a monthly payment of $1088 plus an income of $46,600 to qualify. Taxes and insurance are assumed to be 1.5 percent of the purchase price (divided by 12 months). Visit the *Garman/Forgue* companion website to perform these calculations for a variety of home prices and interest rates.

DO IT IN CLASS

	Price of Home						
Interest Rate	$120,000	$150,000	$180,000	$210,000	$240,000	$270,000	$300,000
3.0	555	693	832	971	1,109	1,248	1,387
	23,800	29,700	35,700	41,600	47,500	53,500	59,400
3.5	581	726	872	1,017	1,162	1,307	1,453
	24,900	31,100	37,400	43,600	49,800	56,000	62,300
4.0	608	760	912	1,064	1,217	1,368	1,520
	26,100	32,600	39,100	45,600	52,100	58,700	65,200
4.5	636	795	954	1,114	1,272	1,432	1,591
	27,300	34,100	40,900	47,700	54,600	61,400	68,200
5.0	665	832	998	1,164	1,331	1,497	1,663
	28,500	35,700	42,800	49,900	57,000	64,200	71,300
5.5	695	869	1,043	1,216	1,390	1,564	1,737
	29,800	37,200	44,700	52,100	59,600	67,000	74,500
6.0	725	907	1,088	1,269	1,451	1,634	1,814
	31,100	38,900	46,600	54,400	62,200	70,000	77,700
6.5	757	946	1,135	1,324	1,514	1,703	1,892
	32,400	40,600	48,700	56,800	64,900	73,000	81,100
7.0	789	986	1,183	1,380	1,577	1,775	1,971
	33,800	42,300	50,700	59,200	67,600	76,100	84,500
7.5	821	1,027	1,232	1,437	1,642	1,848	2,053
	35,200	44,000	52,800	61,600	70,400	79,200	88,000
8.0	854	1,068	1,282	1,495	1,709	1,922	2,136
	36,600	45,800	54,900	64,100	73,200	82,400	91,500

of $84,000 could qualify for a mortgage requiring total annual expenditures of less than $23,520 (0.28 × $84,000), or $1960 per month.

back-end ratio

Compares the total of all monthly PITI expenditures plus auto loans and other debts with gross monthly income.

DO IT IN CLASS

- The **back-end ratio** is also known as the **debt-to-income ratio**. To calculate divide the total of all monthly debt repayments (for the mortgage, real estate taxes, and insurance, plus auto loans and other debts) by one's gross monthly income (before taxes) and multiply by 100. A ratio of 0.36 or less is desirable. Home loan seekers may not exceed 43 percent to obtain a qualified mortgage, according to the Dobb-Frank law. Applying a back-end ratio of 38 percent, the same couple could qualify for any loan that does not result in total monthly debt repayments exceeding $2660 (their monthly income of $7000 [$84,000 ÷ 12] × 0.38). The fastest way to improve (or lower) your back-end ratio is to pay down your debts.

DID YOU KNOW

About Parental Help for Buying a Home

Many young, first-time home buyers look to family members, usually parents, to help them buy a home. Typically they need money to help make the required down payment. If the assistance is a gift to be paid at the closing, the lender will usually require a gift letter with the mortgage application stating that the funds will truly be a gift and from the giver's own funds.

Loans from parents are more complicated. The lender will require that the loan terms be put in writing and the payment amounts will be included when determining mortgage affordability.

Interest paid to any down payment lender will be considered taxable income for the lender. If there is no interest or the rate is below current market interest rates, and the buyer's tax return is audited, the IRS will determine the **imputed interest** amount that would otherwise have been paid, and that amount will be taxable for the lender of the down payment.

Interest paid by the borrower will not be tax deductible unless the down payment loan is secured by a lien on the home. Mortgage lenders will rarely agree to have a second lien holder, however. It may also be possible to borrow the entire amount from a family member. The paperwork must be drawn up carefully to ensure that the loan is secured and tax-advantages are safeguarded. For details visit www .nationalfamilymortgage.com/.

9.3c   3. Search for a Home Online and in Person

Searching for a home requires a commitment of time. You do not want to be impulsive when you will be committing yourself to many thousands of dollars of expense. You can find housing in any number of ways, but the Internet is most helpful. You can narrow your choices to excellent prospects without ever leaving home. Simply go to www.realtor.com and search for homes in your community. Never buy without knowing the typical prices for homes in the area in which you wish to buy; not just a particular home of interest. Use Zillow.com or Truvia.com to determine prices for homes that have sold recently in the area. You will be able to see floor plans, photos, descriptions of features and condition, and price-related information. Once you have found some homes you would like to see, you can contact the seller or the real estate agent handling the properties. Make a list of questions to ask including recent repairs such as to the roof, the cost of utilities over the past year, and many others. A convenient checklist can be found at www.hud.gov/buying/checklist.pdf.

FINANCIAL POWER POINT

Keep Your Debts Low if You Want to Buy a Home

High student loan, car loan, or credit card payments can easily disqualify a potential home buyer based on a lender's use of the back-end ratio. If you plan on buying a home, you need to be very careful about taking on too much debt while in school and after graduation.

9.3d   4. Agree to Terms with the Seller

Once you have your finances in order and have received assurances that you can qualify for a mortgage, you can start looking for a home in earnest.

Make an Offer to Buy   The written offer to purchase real estate is called a **purchase offer** (or an **offer to purchase**). Sellers generally put a price on the property that is 5 to 15 percent higher than the amount that they actually expect to receive. Therefore, you may want to make an offer to buy that is somewhat lower than the asking price. How much lower is a big question. If you have done your homework and know what homes have been selling for (not *offered* for) in the area, you will be able to make a knowledgeable offer slightly below what you have found. For more on making an offer to buy consult www.new.realtor.com/basics/buy/chooseoffer/makeoffer.asp?source=web

purchase offer/offer to purchase
Written offer to purchase real estate.

Earnest Money   Other aspects of the sale should be included in your offer as well. Examples of conditions include successful termite and radon inspections; a home inspection of the plumbing, heating, cooling, and electrical systems; and inclusion of the living room drapes and kitchen and other appliances. When you make an offer, you need to

DID YOU KNOW

How to Search for a Home

You can be a more effective home shopper if you do the following:

- **Make a list** in advance of special features and "must have" items that you are looking for in your new home.

- **Drive around desirable neighborhoods** before you visit a property. Look at the condition and upkeep of the homes and yards. Are there many homes for sale in the area? Get out of the car and listen. Are there industrial noises or excessive highway noises? Any pet noises from neighbors? Look at the availability and quality of parks and schools.

- **Look at only two or three properties** in one day at most. Looking at too many homes at one time can be confusing and exhausting.

- **Bring a notepad and tape measure** with you. Make sketches of the floor plans that you like. Bring along a camera or video equipment. Photos and videos you see on-line are taken from the most advantageous camera angles.

- **Use a checklist** to record, describe, and evaluate features of the home. These can be found on line such as at www.hud.gov/buying/checklist.pdf.

- **Check for slope and sags** by setting a small rubber ball at various places on floors, countertops, and door frames. The ball should not move.

- **Walk around the outside of the property** to assess the external condition of the home and yard. Look for signs of water damage to the home or drainage issues in the yard.

---

earnest money

Funds given to the seller as a deposit to hold the property until a purchase contract can be negotiated.

give the seller some **earnest money** as a deposit; 2 or 5 percent of the purchase price should be sufficient to show your good faith when making an offer to purchase the seller's property. This money is returned if the seller rejects the offer.

Respond to a Counteroffer Most home sellers do not accept the first offer from a prospective buyer. Instead, they usually make a **counteroffer**, which is a legal offer to sell (or buy) a home at a different price and perhaps with different conditions from those outlined in the original offer. You can assume that a seller who is willing to make a counteroffer may also be willing to sell at a slightly lower price. Thus, if you make a counteroffer falling between the two prices, a sale will usually result. But, it is common to have other offers outstanding on a home of choice. So, if you push the seller too far, you risk having the seller back out of the negotiations altogether.

purchase contract/sales contract

Formal legal document that outlines the actual agreement that results from the real estate negotiations.

real estate broker (agent)

Person licensed by a state to provide advice and assistance, for a fee, to buyers or sellers of real estate.

Negotiate a Price and Sign a Purchase Contract A **purchase contract** (or **sales contract**) is the formal legal document that outlines the actual agreement that results from the real estate negotiations. It includes the final negotiated price and a list of conditions that the seller has agreed to accept. When the purchase contract is signed, the seller keeps the earnest money as a deposit. If at this point you simply change your mind about buying, you will forfeit your earnest money and may be sued for damages.

DID YOU KNOW

The Role of Real Estate Agents

A **real estate broker** (agent) is a person licensed by a state to provide advice and assistance, for a fee, to buyers or sellers of real estate. Real estate brokers who are members of the National Association of Realtors often use the registered trademark of **Realtor**® to describe themselves. Brokers typically earn a commission of 6 to 7 percent on the sale price of a home. The seller—not the buyer—usually pays this commission. **Flat-fee brokers,** who charge a flat fee for their services rather than a percentage-based commission, are also available in most real estate markets.

Almost any agent can show you housing that is **listed** (under contract with the seller and the broker) by the realty firm.

Buyers should understand that a real estate agent can play various roles. The **listing agent** is the party with whom the seller signs the listing agreement. Listing agents advertise the property, show it to prospective buyers, and assist the seller in negotiations. They receive a commission when the home is sold and owe the seller undivided loyalty. A **selling agent** is any real estate agent that seeks out buyers for a home. Listing agents also play this role, but any real estate agent can search for buyers to whom to sell a property.

Most home buyers use a real estate agent in their search for a home. They should understand that the agent's legal obligation is to the party who will pay his or her fee or commission—generally the seller! Buyers should be wary of this potential conflict of interest and hire their own broker if they need such services. That is, home buyers who want an agent to represent their interests should obtain the services of a **buyer's agent**. This person serves as the buyer's representative in the real estate negotiations and transaction. You can find reputable buyer's agents at www.rebac.net /buyers-rep or www.naeba.org.

Why is the distinction among the three types of agents important? Consider the example of a buyer who has asked a selling agent to help him find a home. During negotiations, the potential buyer decides to offer $175,000 for a property with an asking price of $189,000 but tells the selling agent that he would be willing to go as high as $180,000. The selling agent would then be legally obligated to tell the seller about this $180,000 figure. The seller's agent is not your friend.

Contingency Clauses These are very important to a potential buyer because you want to make sure that your earnest money is protected by including one or more clauses in the purchase contract. These clauses specify that certain conditions must be satisfied before a contract is binding. One recommended clause would stipulate that the seller must refund the earnest money if the buyer cannot obtain satisfactory financing within a specified time period, usually 30 days. Other important **contingency clauses** should allow the buyer to opt out of the deal if the appraisal comes in below the agreed upon price or the home fails to pass certain aspects of the home inspection (for example, the inspection uncovers a major structural defect).

contingency clauses
Specify that certain conditions must be satisfied before a contract is binding.

9.3e 5. Formally Apply for a Mortgage Loan

Only after you sign a purchase contract do you formally apply for a mortgage loan on the specific home you have selected. Mortgage loan applications are complicated, and providing false information on the form can be considered fraud. Lenders all use the same form found at www.fanniemae.com/content/guide_form/1003rev.pdf. The potential lender usually pre approves or turns down this request within a few days A **loan preapproval** means that the lender agrees to grant a loan subject to verification of the information provided in the application.

The **loan officer** assigned to manage your application must mail you a **good-faith estimate** of all costs associated with the loan within three days of your application. The format for this document as shown at www.hud.gov/offices/hsg/ramh/res/gfestimate. pdf. The good-faith estimate lists the annual percentage rate, application and processing fees, and any other charges that must be paid when the deal is legally consummated. Almost all the items listed on the good-faith estimate are negotiable so be sure to do so.

good-faith estimate
Lender's list of all the costs associated with the loan, including the annual percentage rate (APR), application and processing fees, closing costs, and any other charges that must be paid when the deal is legally consummated.

Table 9-1 provides an example of the type of information in the good-faith estimate. Do not be afraid to shop around for a lender at this stage. Show the good-faith estimate to other lenders you have identified to see if they can give you better terms.

The exact interest rate on your mortgage may be the current rate at the time of application or the rate in force at the time of closing. If you expect rates to rise between the time you apply for the loan and the actual closing, you may wish to pay a small fee to obtain a **mortgage lock-in**. This agreement includes a lender's promise to hold a certain interest rate for a specified period of time, such as 30 or 60 days. Make sure you receive a written **lock confirmation** of the lender's promise. If needed, a **lock extension** can be obtained for an additional fee. A mortgage lock-in may be part of, but is not the same as, a **loan commitment**, which is a lender's promise to grant a loan.

loan commitment
Lender's promise to grant a loan.

DID YOU KNOW

What to Do if You Are Turned Down for a Mortgage Loan

A common nightmare of most first-time homebuyers: being denied a mortgage, What should you do if you get turned down for a mortgage loan?

1. **Find out specifically why you were turned down.** Request a written explanation from your lender as to why you were turned down for a mortgage. By law, your lender must provide you with this information within 30 days from your request. This explanation is called an **adverse action notice**, and it will detail the reasons why you were refused a mortgage.

2. **Try again with better information.** The adverse action notice may contain reasons for the turndown that can be corrected. Perhaps your income was too low. Did you include all sources and correct amounts of income? Perhaps your employment history was the problem. Can you provide additional information that would improve the assessment?

3. **Revisit a too-low appraisal.** If the appraisal on the home came in too low, the lender will be concerned that you were planning to pay too much for the home. It is against the law for you or your loan officer to obtain a new appraisal with a different appraiser. Occasionally,

though, the first appraiser will reconsider when given new evidence such as the sales prices of recent sales for higher prices in the neighborhood.

4. **Repair your credit.** If your credit score was too low to qualify, you may be able to improve your credit scores by correcting errors and rearranging credit accounts. See www.myfico.com/CreditEducation/ImproveYourScore .aspx for suggestions. Also see Chapter 6, page 182 for the steps to take to correct errors in your credit report and how to do so for free.

5. **Take steps to improve your front- and back-end ratios.** These ratios are based on your income, current debts, debt payments, and projected cost of the home you are considering. Changing any of these three items may help you qualify when you reapply. You may need to pay down some debt. Perhaps you should consider a still nice home in a lower price range.

6. **Save more.** Being turned down because of a too-low down payment, can be a sign that you need to wait to save more to afford the home you want.

7. **Try another lender.** Credit unions and small local banks often have more freedom to work with a client who has been turned down elsewhere. Understand, though, that a second turn-down may mean that the timing is just not right for you to buy.

DID YOU KNOW

Your Credit Score Affects the Mortgage Rate You Pay

Mortgage lenders charge interest rates based on your credit score. Illustrative FICO credit scores and the corresponding mortgage loan interest rates can be found at www.myfico .com/myfico/CreditCentral/LoanRates.aspx. Loan applicants whose scores are lower than desired are turned down. At that point the borrower may seek a lender in the

subprime market, which serves higher-risk applicants with low credit scores. Borrowers who are placed in this market are often happy to have obtained a loan. However, such loans carry higher interest rates that may lead to future repayment difficulties. Therefore, it might be better for people with low credit scores to wait and build up their scores before applying for conventional mortgages.

9.3f   6. Prepare for the Closing

After you have obtained a mortgage, you are not yet finished. Of course, you will want to do all the usual tasks associated with moving: giving notification of your change of address, hiring a moving company (or not), and getting your utilities shut off at your old residence and on at your new one are examples. However, there are two very important additional steps to take that can save you thousands of dollars and many headaches.

Hire Your Own Home Inspector Recall that you should always have a contingency clause included in your purchase contract so that you can back out of the deal if the house fails to pass the home inspection. The licensed or certified inspector should look for termite infestation, wood rot, mold, and radon gas as well as examine the general condition of the home, including heating/cooling, plumbing, and electrical. You should pay the inspector yourself ($250 to $350 is the typical fee) and should not choose one based on the recommendation of the seller's real estate agent. You want an independent person who is well qualified to look out for your interests (See www.ashi.org/find/default.aspx.) If the inspector finds problems, you can negotiate with the seller for an adjustment in the purchase price of the home or use the contingency clause to back out of the deal.

Hire an Attorney The good-faith estimate that you receive is a legal document outlining your entire up-front and monthly home-buying costs. Hiring an attorney to go over the estimate and your purchase contract to ensure that everything is in order is money well spent. Many of the closing costs are negotiable, and your attorney can advise on how to keep these costs to a minimum. If you are buying a home that was previously foreclosed, it is absolutely critical that you hire an attorney well experienced in these transactions. Some unfortunate buyers of foreclosed properties have later found serious defects in their titles as well as claims against the home.

9.3g 7. Sign Your Name on Closing Day

To complete the sale, the buyer, the seller, and their chosen representatives generally gather in the lender's office for the closing. At the closing, all required documents are signed and payments are made. A key document is the **uniform settlement statement**, which lists all of the costs and fees to be paid at the closing. You have the right to see this statement one business day before the closing and again at the closing so that you can avoid surprises and can compare the fees with the good-faith estimate provided earlier. Challenge any discrepancy. You can negotiate every closing cost item. A full description of the required disclosures can be found by going to www.hud.gov/respa to learn more about your rights under the Real Estate Settlement Procedures Act.

FINANCIAL POWER POINT

Protect Your Credit Score while Waiting for Your Mortgage to Close

In the weeks leading up to the closing for a home purchase, it may be tempting to begin buying furniture, appliances, outdoor equipment, and other costly items for the home. Think twice if doing so means racking up high balances on your credit cards. Your mortgage lender will raise your interest rate if you significantly change your credit score before closing.

uniform settlement statement
Lists all of the costs and fees to be paid at the closing.

DID YOU KNOW

Money Websites for Obtaining Affordable Housing

Informative websites for obtaining housing, including current prices on homes in your community are:

Bankrate.com (www.bankrate.com/mortgage.aspx)

Department of Housing and Urban Development (portal.hud.gov/hudportal/HUD)

Federal Housing Administration (www.fha.gov)

FSBO.com (www.fsbo.com)

Kiplinger's Personal Finance (www.kiplinger.com/fronts/channels/real-estate/)

MoneyCNN (www.money.cnn.com/real_estate/?iid=PF_Subr)

NOLO (www.nolo.com/legal-encyclopedia/real-estate-rental-property)

Trulia (www.trulia.com)

Veteran's Administration (www.benefits.va.gov/homeloans/)

Yahoo Finance (www.finance.yahoo.com/real-estate/)

Zillow (www.zillow.com)

DID YOU KNOW ?

Sean's Success Story

Sean knew that he could not afford to buy a home for a few years after he took his first job following college. Nonetheless, he began saving for this goal by using direct deposit to put 5 percent of his salary into a Roth IRA account set up exclusively as a home-buying savings fund. At the end of each year, he used the funds to buy certificates of deposit designed to mature six years after his graduation. Now after six years, he has a fund exceeding $20,000 and has begun taking steps to buy a condominium. Sean's first step was to obtain his credit reports and credit score to ensure that his

financial history was accurate. He then contacted multiple lenders to determine the interest rate and monthly payment he could expect on a property costing about $200,000. His good credit allowed him to be preapproved at that amount so he reworked his budget to see if he could afford the required monthly payment including an estimate for homeowner's insurance and property taxes. He was happy to see that he could do so. He has begun shopping for condos in the $180,000 range to give him a budget cushion once mortgage payments begin. Sean is excited about buying his first home.

CONCEPT CHECK 9.3

1. Distinguish between the two rules of thumb that lenders use to assess housing affordability.

2. What services does a mortgage broker offer?

3. What services do real estate agents provide for buyers?

4. Why should a buyer be cautious about working with a seller's agent?

5. Explain the benefits of having contingency clauses in a home purchase agreement

9.4 FINANCING A HOME

People often rent housing for five years or more while they save enough to make a down payment to purchase a home. Before buying, you must become knowledgeable about mortgage loans and learn how they are used to purchase a home.

9.4a The Mathematics of Mortgage Loans

Mortgage loans are available from depository institutions (described in Chapters 5 and 7) and **mortgage finance companies** that focus specifically on making mortgage loans. (To find approved lenders in your area go to www.hud.gov/ll/code/llslcrit .cfm.) In exchange for the loan, the lender (**mortgagee**) has a **lien** on the real estate—that is, the legal right to take and hold property or to sell it in the event the borrower (**mortgagor**) defaults on the loan.

The term **mortgage** receives its name from the concept of amortization, which is the process of gradually paying off a loan through a series of periodic payments to a lender. Each payment is allocated in two ways:

1. A portion goes to pay the simple interest on outstanding debt for that month multiplied by the periodic (monthly) interest rate.

2. The remainder goes to repay a portion of the principal, which is the debt remaining from the original amount borrowed.

As the principal is paid down, increasingly smaller portions of the payments will be required to pay interest while the portion of the payments devoted to the principal will grow larger. These changes in the allocation of each payment are illustrated

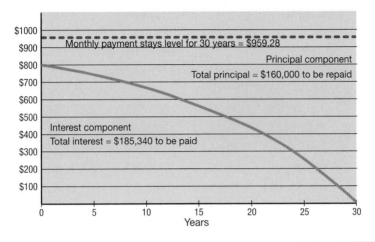

Figure 9-2 | Change in Principal and Interest Components of the Monthly Payment on a $160,000 Mortgage Loan at 6.0 Percent Interest Rate for 30 Years

in Figure 9-2. Note the very slow decline in the amount of each monthly payment going toward interest. It takes 7 years before the $800 going toward interest drops to $700. A high proportion of each monthly payment during the early years of a mortgage loan is allocated to interest.

Table 9-2 shows the interest and principal payment amounts for the first three months of a $160,000, 30-year, 6.0 percent mortgage loan. For the first month, $800 goes for interest costs, and only $159.28 goes toward retirement of the principal of the loan. Table 9-3 provides a partial **amortization schedule** for the same loan. When you take out a mortgage loan, you will receive a full amortization schedule for each month of the loan listing each and every monthly payment, which will show the portions that will go toward interest and principal, and the debt remaining after each payment is made.

It takes many years of monthly payments to significantly reduce the outstanding balance of the loan. At any point, the amount that has been paid off (including the down payment) plus any appreciation in the value of the home represents the **homeowner's equity** (the dollar value of the home in excess of the amount owed on it).

amortization schedule
List that shows all the monthly payments, the portions that will go toward interest and principal, and the debt remaining after each payment is made throughout the life of the loan.

homeowner's equity
Dollar value of the home in excess of the amount owed on it.

DO IT IN CLASS

Table 9-2 | Amortization Effects of Monthly Payment of $959.28 on a $160,000, 30-Year Mortgage Loan at 6.0 Percent

First Month	$160,000 × 6.0% × 1/12	=	$800.00 Interest payment
	$959.28 − 800.00	=	$159.28 Principal repayment
	$160,000 − 159.28	=	$159,840.72 Balance due
Second Month			
	$159,840.72 × 6.0% × 1/12	=	$799.20 Interest payment
	$959.28 − 799.20	=	$160.08 Principal repayment
	$159,840.72 − 160.08	=	$159,680.64 Balance due
Third Month			
	$159,680.64 × 6.0% × 1/12	=	$798.40 Interest payment
	$959.28 − 798.40	=	$160.88 Principal repayment
	$159,680.64 − 160.88	=	$159,519.76 Balance due

Table 9-3	Partial Amortization Schedule for a $160,000, 30-Year (360-Payment) Mortgage Loan at 6.0 percent

Payment Number (Month)	Monthly Payment Amount	Portion to Interest	Portion to Principal Repayment	Total of Payments to Date	Outstanding Loan Balance
1	$959.28	$800.00	$159.28	$ 959.28	$159,840.72
2	959.28	799.20	160.08	1,918.56	159,648.94
3	959.28	798.40	160.88	2,877.84	159,472.20
12	959.28	791.02	168.26	11,511.36	158,035.18
24	959.28	780.64	178.64	23,022.72	155,949.18
60	959.28	745.50	213.78	57,566.80	148,886.97
120	959.28	670.93	288.35	115,113.60	133,897.16
180	959.28	570.34	388.95	172,670.40	113,678.15
240	959.28	434.65	524.63	230,227.20	86,405.74
300	959.28	251.63	707.65	287,784.00	49,619.34
360	959.28	4.77	954.51	345,340.80	0

Figure 9-3	Change in Loan Balance and Owner's Equity for a $185,000 Home Purchased with $25,000 Down at a 6.0 Percent Interest Rate for 30 Years (Assumes a 3% Annual Market Price Increase)

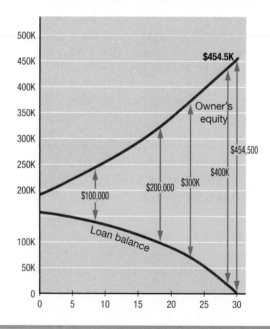

Figure 9-3 illustrates the buildup of equity in a home that results from reductions in the amount owed and the growth in the home's value. Note that the bulk of the increase in equity is a result of increases in the market value of the home. You want to buy a home based on its features and location, not as an investment. Nonetheless, equity buildup over the long run is a definite plus. If desired, additional payments can be directed toward the principal at any time to reduce the amount owed, increase equity, and reduce the eventual total amount of interest paid on the loan. The equity portion of a mortgage payment is a type of forced savings and helps explain why homeowners typically have a higher net worth than renters.

9.4b Three Factors That Affect the Mortgage Payment

Three factors affect the monthly payment on a mortgage loan: the amount borrowed, the interest rate charged, and the length of maturity of the loan.

1. Amount Borrowed The payment schedule illustrated in Table 9-4 gives the monthly payment required for each $1000 of a mortgage loan at various interest rates. Using this table, you can calculate the monthly payment for mortgage loans of different amounts. For example, the $160,000 mortgage loan described earlier (6.0 percent for 30 years) costs $5.9955 per $1000 per month. Thus, 160 × $5.9955 equals $959.28.

Making a down payment that is larger than required lowers the borrower's monthly payments. For example, a down payment of 30 percent, or $55,500, would lower the monthly payment on the loan to $776.42 [$5.9955 × ($185,000 − $55,500) ÷ 1000]. A smaller loan also carries lower total interest costs and may qualify for an interest rate that is perhaps 0.5 percentage points lower. In that case, the payment for the same loan would amount to only $735.29 [$5.6779 × ($185,000 − $55,500) ÷ 1000].

2. Interest Rate The higher the interest rate, the higher the monthly payment on a mortgage loan (see Table 9-4). For example, a $959.28 monthly payment is required for a $160,000 mortgage loan taken out for 30 years at 6.0 percent. If the interest rate were 7.0 percent, the monthly mortgage payment would be $1064.48 (160 × $6.6530), an increase of over $100. The effects are even greater when you consider the total of all the monthly payments and the total interest paid over the life of the loan. The 6.0 percent loan will have total payments of $345,340.80 (360 × $959.28) with total interest of $185,340.80 ($345,340.80 − $160,000.00). For the 7.0 percent loan, total payments are $383,212.80 (360 × $1064.48), and total interest is $223,212.80 ($383,212.80 − $160,000.00). Thus, the added cost for the 30-year loan at 7.0 percent is $37,872 over the life of the loan.

DO IT IN CLASS

Table 9-4	Estimating Mortgage Loan Payments for Principal and Interest (Monthly Payment per $1000 Borrowed)

Interest Rate (%)	Payment Period (Years)			
	15	20	25	30
3.0	$6.9058	$5.5460	$4.7421	$4.2160
3.5	7.1488	5.7996	5.0062	4.4904
4.0	7.3969	6.0598	5.2783	4.7742
4.5	7.6499	6.3265	5.5583	5.0669
5.0	7.9079	6.5996	5.8459	5.3682
5.5	8.1708	6.8789	6.1409	5.6779
6.0	8.4386	7.1643	6.4430	5.9955
6.5	8.7111	7.4557	6.7521	6.3207
7.0	8.9883	7.7530	7.0678	6.6530
7.5	9.2701	8.0559	7.3899	6.9921
8.0	9.5565	8.3644	7.7182	7.3376

Note: To use this table to figure a monthly mortgage payment, divide the amount borrowed by 1000 and multiply by the appropriate figure in the table for the interest rate and time period of the loan. For example, a $160,000 loan for 30 years at 6.0 percent would require a payment of $959,280 [($160,000 ÷ 1000) × 5.9955]; over 20 years, it would require a payment of $1146.29 [($160,000 ÷ 1000) × 7.1643]. For calculations for different interest rates, visit the *Garman/Forgue* companion website.

ADVICE FROM A PROFESSIONAL

Cancel Mortgage Insurance as Soon as Possible

Most first-time home buyers cannot make the standard loan-to-value ratio of 80 percent (20 percent down) and must buy mortgage insurance. As the borrower makes mortgage payments over time, the amount of principal remaining to be paid will decline until eventually the 80 percent threshold is reached. At that point, the lender must notify the borrower of the opportunity to drop the insurance. And, by law, the lender must terminate the PMI when the loan-to-value ratio reaches 78 percent based on the market value of the home at the beginning of the mortgage.

But there is no need to wait that long. In this chapter's example mortgage, the borrower starts out owing $160,000 or 86.5 ($160,000/$185,000) percent of the value of the home. It takes about five and one-half years to reach the 80 percent threshold ($148,000 = 0.80 × $185,000) simply by making loan payments. The good news is that the value of the home may increase faster than the loan principal declines. In the example the 80 percent threshold will be reached in about three years if the value of the home increases at 3 percent per year. When that threshold is attained, the borrower can ask the lender to cancel the mortgage insurance. Lenders usually require an appraisal of the property before doing so, but the cost of the appraisal (perhaps $300) represents money well spent. It is a smart move to make such a request, and it is even smarter to continue making the same monthly payment on the mortgage after the insurance is removed. The extra amount will be applied to the principal of the loan, thereby paying it off even sooner.

Michael Ruff and Sherry Tshibangu
Monroe Community College, Rochester, NY

3. Length of the Loan Table 9-5 illustrates the relationships among maturity length, monthly payment, and interest cost for a $100,000 loan at various interest rates. A longer term of repayment results in a smaller payment (for loans with the same interest rate). More total interest is paid over the longer repayment time period despite the lower monthly payment. For example, the monthly payment on a 5.5 percent loan is $688 for 20 years but only $568 for 30 years. When the loan is paid back in 20 years, the total interest costs are much lower ($65,100 rather than $104,400, for a savings of $39,300).

Some borrowers choose a mortgage loan with a comparatively short 15-year maturity. The advantages include a faster buildup of equity, lower total interest, and a quicker payoff of the loan. These advantages can also be gained with a 20- or 30-year mortgage by simply paying additional amounts toward the principal during the time period of the loan. It is wise to take a longer repayment period, such as 30 years, even if you plan to pay off the loan in 15 (or fewer) years. This way the faster payoff is optional rather than mandatory.

9.4c Conventional Mortgage and Adjustable Mortgage Loans

conventional mortgage
A fixed-rate, fixed-term, fixed-payment mortgage loan.

adjustable-rate mortgage (ARM)/variable-rate mortgage
Mortgage in which the borrower's interest rate fluctuates according to some index of interest rates based on the rising or falling cost of credit in the economy—thus transferring interest rate risk to the borrower.

A **conventional mortgage** is a fixed-rate, fixed-term, fixed-payment mortgage loan. Borrowers like conventional mortgages because they are so predictable. For example, a $160,000 loan could be granted at a 6.0 percent annual interest rate over a period of 30 years with a fixed monthly payment of $959.28. The payment is the same for month after month and year after year. Most borrowers see a conventional fixed-rate loan as the best possible choice because the amount of all future payments is known in advance.

With an **adjustable-rate mortgage (ARM)**—sometimes called a **variable-rate mortgage**—the borrower's interest rate fluctuates according to some index of interest rates based on the rising or falling cost of credit in the economy. With an ARM, the risk of interest rate changes is assumed by the borrower, not the lender. As a consequence, the monthly payment could increase or decrease, usually on an annual basis.

Table 9-5	Monthly Payment and Total Interest to Repay a $100,000 Loan				

	Interest Rate (%)				
Length of Loan	**5.0**	**5.5**	**6**	**6.5**	**7**
30 years	$ 537	$ 568	$ 600	$ 632	$ 665
	93,300	104,400	116,000	127,500	139,400
25 years	585	614	644	675	707
	75,500	84,200	93,200	102,500	112,100
20 years	660	688	716	745	775
	58,400	65,100	71,800	78,800	86,000
15 years	791	817	844	871	899
	42,300	47,100	51,900	56,800	61,800

Note: Figures are rounded. The top figure in each pair is the monthly payment, and the bottom figure is the total interest paid to the nearest $100.

You can use this table to estimate the monthly payment and total interest on any loan at these same interest rates. Simply divide the amount of the loan by $100,000 and multiply that figure by the amounts shown in the table. For example, the loan of $160,000 at 6.0% for 30 years illustrated in this chapter has a monthly payment of $960 (1.6 × $600) and total interest of $185,600 (1.6 × $116,000). Note that these figures differ slightly from those earlier due to rounding.

Some adjustable-rate loans may have a fixed rate for the first 3 or 5 years after which the rate can vary. Borrowers with ARMs should always determine the "worst case" scenario for interest rate increases under their loan contract and calculate the monthly payment that would result.

ARM rates are usually 1 to 2 percentage points below conventional mortgage rates. Lenders sometimes offer an even lower **teaser rate** to entice people to borrow using an ARM. If you do not feel you can afford even a minimal increase in the rate, you should not take out this type of loan.

ARMs have an **interest-rate cap** limit the amount by which the interest rate can increase to no more than 2 percent per year and no more than 6 percent over the life of the loan. This may not seem like much, but if the 6 percent loan we have been using as an example in this chapter were to go up 5 points after ten years because of rising inflation, the new payment would be almost $1300, which would be $340, or 35 percent more than the original $959 payment. While such an increase is unlikely, it could happen under the terms of the agreement.

When mortgage rates are low or rising, borrowers are wise to look for a fixed-rate loan. If rates are headed down, get an adjustable mortgage loan.

teaser rate
Low interest rate that lenders sometimes use to lure buyers; these rates will be low for the first year or so and then will rise to more realistic rates.

DID YOU KNOW

About Qualified Residential Mortgages

A **qualified residential mortgage (QRM)** is a descriptor placed on a home loan that meets strict underwriting guidelines and a specified set of product features built into the loan. The QRM was designed to set the standard for residential mortgages and to minimize the risk that borrowers may default. It requires that debt-to-income ratios be limited to 43 percent and loan fees limited to 3 percent, and interest-only loans and negative amortization are not allowed in most cases. A QRM does not require a special down payment requirement, such as 20 percent. To obtain a QRM, documentation of income must be verified. The lowering of debt-to-income limits on most loans will force some buyers to wait longer and save more to make that first purchase. As a result, these loans will have a lower risk of default compared to a decade ago.

DID YOU KNOW

The Tax Consequences of Buying a Home

Home ownership makes you eligible for three big tax breaks.

1. ***Mortgage interest and real estate taxes are tax deductible on federal (and most state) income tax returns.*** *These amounts often exceed the IRS's standard deduction (see Chapter 4). You can then take advantage of even more deduction opportunities that are available to taxpayers who itemize.*

2. ***You can save the funds to buy a home in a tax-sheltered account.*** *Individuals can use Roth IRAs (see Chapter 17) to save for retirement. Once the account is five years old, as much as $10,000 may be withdrawn tax free and penalty free, provided that a qualifying, first-time home buyer uses the funds for home-buying costs.*

3. ***The profits made by selling a home can be tax free.*** *If you sell a home for more than you originally paid, you have a **capital gain**. Gains are ordinarily taxable, but homeowners can avoid paying taxes on gains by buying a home that is more expensive, thus rolling the gain into the new home. Also, capital gains of up to $500,000 if married and filing jointly and up to $250,000 if single may be avoided. To qualify, the home must have been owned and used as the principal residence for two of the last five years prior to the date of the sale.*

9.4d Other Housing Financing Arrangements

There are other ways to finance a home purchase.

biweekly mortgage

A form of growing-equity mortgage (GEM) that calls for payments of half of the normal payment to be made every two weeks; the borrower thus makes 26 payments a year and reduces the principal amount by one full payment each year; this reduces the mortgage term to about 20 years on a 30-year mortgage.

Growing-Equity Mortgage The **growing-equity mortgage (GEM)** is a fixed rate mortgage on which the monthly payments increase over time. The interest rate on the loan does not change and as the payments increase the additional amounts are applied to the remaining balance, thus shortening the life of the mortgage and increasing interest savings.

One form of GEM is the **biweekly mortgage**, which calls for payments to be made every two weeks that represent half of the normal monthly payment. The borrower, therefore, makes 26 payments per year. For example, a $160,000, 6 percent, 30-year loan requires a $959.28 monthly payment for a total of $11,511.36 (12 × $959.28) paid in one year. On a biweekly basis with payments of $479.64

DID YOU KNOW

Turn Bad Habits into Good Ones

Do You Do This?

Think a verbal lease for renting is just fine

Move into an apartment without inspecting for defects and damages

Make your rent payment late from time to time

Hope, rather than plan, to buy a home

Want a home just like your parents' home

Do This Instead!

Get all terms in writing

Make a written list of all defects and damages at both move-in and move-out and get lists co-signed by landlord

Make all payments on time; your landlord may report patterns to a credit bureau

Start saving for a down payment as soon as you get a job after graduation

Recognize that buying a small starter home is just fine

($959.28 ÷ 2), the total amount paid each year would be $12,470.64 ($479.64 × 26). The difference of $959.28 ($12,470.64 − $11,511.36) is equivalent to one extra monthly payment per year and is applied to the principal of the loan. Under the biweekly repayment plan, a loan will be repaid in approximately 20 years, rather than the 30 years dictated by the monthly payment plan.

All mortgages use the declining-balance method of calculating interest (see Chapter 7 page 214), thus permitting payment of additional amounts toward principal at any time. Thus, you can voluntarily pay additional amounts on the principal without being locked into it as you would with a growing equity mortgage.

Assumable Mortgage With an **assumable mortgage**, the buyer pays the seller a down payment generally equal to the seller's equity in the home and takes responsibility for the mortgage loan payments for the remaining term of the seller's existing mortgage loan. The buyer's goal is to obtain the loan at the original interest rate, which should be below current market rates. This approach will work only if the original mortgage loan agreement does not include a **due-on-sale clause**. Such a clause requires that the mortgage loan be fully paid off if the home is sold. It can impose a burden on the seller because it prohibits a buyer from assuming the mortgage loan.

Seller Financing **Seller financing** occurs whenever the seller of a home agrees to accept all or a portion of the purchase price in installments rather than as a lump sum. Usually seller financing is a short-term arrangement, however, with payments based on amortization occurring over perhaps 20 years but with a final single **balloon payment** of the total remaining unpaid principal that is due after perhaps five years. Since, the remaining debt is due all at once, the buyer might typically take out a conventional mortgage to finish paying off the purchase.

FINANCIAL POWER POINT

Reasons Not to Pay Off a Mortgage Early

Many people want to pay their mortgage off as soon as possible, but is this a good idea? Perhaps not if you:

1. Can invest the money and get a better rate of return on your money than the after-tax interest rate you pay on your mortgage.

2. Are paying a higher interest rate on other debts you owe.

3. Have an inadequate amount of emergency funds.

4. Are not contributing the maximum amount allowed in your 401(k) accounts at work or an IRA account.

5. Are not adequately covered by property, liability, disability, and life insurance.

Moreover, consider taking any excess money available and spend it on these five unmet alternatives instead of paying off your mortgage loan early.

DID YOU KNOW

About Second Mortgage Loans

A **second mortgage** is an additional loan on a residence besides the original mortgage. Because the amount owed on the original mortgage must be paid first the interest rate on a second mortgage is often 2 to 3 percentage points higher than current market rates for first mortgages.

Historically, people have used second mortgages to pay for major remodeling projects, finance college costs for children, pay off medical bills, or start a business. Some people use these funds for everyday living expenses, an unwise practice dubbed "eating one's house."

Two types of second mortgages exist:

- The **home-equity installment loan**, where a specific amount of money is borrowed for a fixed time period with fixed monthly payments.

- The **home-equity line of credit**, where a maximum loan amount is established and the loan operates as open-ended credit, much like a credit card account. These line-of-credit loans often have variable interest rates and flexible repayment schedules.

The credit limit on a second mortgage loan is usually set at 80 to 90 percent of the home's appraised value minus the amount owed on the first mortgage. For example, a person with a home appraised at $200,000 with a balance owed of $100,000 on a first mortgage might be allowed to take out a $60,000 second mortgage [($200,000 × 0.80) − $100,000].

RUN THE NUMBERS

When You Should Refinance Your Mortgage

It is sometimes advantageous to refinance an existing mortgage when interest rates decline. In **mortgage refinancing**, a new mortgage is obtained to pay off and replace an existing mortgage. Most often it is undertaken to lower the monthly payment on the home by taking out a loan with a lower interest rate.

DO IT IN CLASS

The example here illustrates how to determine whether refinancing your mortgage is a wise choice. The original mortgage for $160,000 was obtained seven years ago at a 5.5 percent interest rate for 30 years. The monthly payment is $908. After seven years, the principal owed has declined to $142,100. If interest rates for new mortgages have declined to 4.5 percent, the owner could take out a new mortgage at the lower rate for a monthly payment of $827. Borrowing $142,100 for 23 years at 4.5 percent saves approximately $81 per month ($908 − $827). However, refinancing may have some up-front costs, including a possible prepayment penalty on the old mortgage and closing costs for the new mortgage. The question then becomes, will these costs exceed the monthly savings gained with a lower payment?

The following worksheet provides a means for estimating whether refinancing offers an advantage. It compares the future value of the reduced monthly payments (line 5) with the future value of the money used to pay the up-front costs (estimated here at 2%) of refinancing (line 8). The homeowner would need to estimate the number of months he or she expects to own the home after refinancing. Given an estimate of four years in this example, the net savings would be $977 (subtracting line 8 from line 5), and refinancing would benefit the owner. In this example, planning to live in the home only three more years would result in it not being financially advantageous to refinance. A similar worksheet can be found at www.bankrate.com/calculators /mortgages/refinance-calculator.aspx.

Decision Factors	Example	Your Figures
1. Current monthly payment	$ 908	_____
2. New monthly payment	827	_____
3. Monthly savings (line 1 − line 2)	81	_____
4. Additional years you expect to live in the house	4	_____
5. Future value of an account balance after 4 years if the monthly savings were invested at 3% after taxes (using the calculator on the *Garman/Forgue* companion website)	4,175	_____
6. Prepayment penalty on current loan (0%)	0	_____
7. Points and fees for new loan (2%)	2,842	_____
8. Future value of an account balance after 4 years if the prepayment penalty and closing costs ($4263) had been invested instead at 3% after taxes (using the calculator on the *Garman/Forgue* companion website)	3,198	_____
9. Net saving after 48 months (line 5 − line 8)	$ 977	_____

It may also be possible to borrow more than the current balance owed on the existing loan, thereby utilizing some of the equity built up in the home. Borrowers refinancing for more than the amount owed should understand that rebuilding the equity to its previous level may take many years. This also is dangerous because if home prices decline the borrower will owe more on the home than it is worth.

In most seller financing, the buyer obtains the title to the property when the deal is closed and the contract is signed. In contrast, a **land contract** (or **contract for deed**) brings greater risk for the buyer because all terms in the contract (including payment of the debt) must be satisfied before transfer of tide will occur. As a result, if you move before paying off the contract in full, you forfeit all money paid in installments to the seller and any appreciation in the home's value. You build no equity until the contract is completed.

Reverse Mortgage A **reverse mortgage**, also known as a **home-equity conversion loan**, allows a homeowner older than age 61 to borrow against the equity in a home that is fully or mostly paid for and to receive the proceeds in a lump sum or a series of monthly payments. The contract allows the person to continue living in the home. Essentially, the borrower trades his or her equity in the home in return for the funds. The most likely prospects for such loans are elderly people who have paid off their mortgages but need income. The mortgage does not have to be paid back until the last surviving owner sells the house, moves out permanently, or dies. There are some worries in this industry, so for more information on reverse mortgages, go to www .hud.gov/offices/hsg/sfh/hecm/rmtopten.cfm.

> **reverse mortgage/home-equity conversion loan**
>
> *Allows a homeowner older than age 61 to continue living in the home and to borrow against the equity in a home that is fully paid for and to receive the proceeds in a series of monthly payments, often for life.*

CONCEPT CHECK 9.4

1. Explain why the portions of a monthly mortgage payment that are allocated toward interest and toward principal will vary as the loan is repaid.

2. Distinguish between a conventional mortgage loan and an adjustable-rate loan.

3. Identify the two ways that homebuyers build equity in their property.

9.5 SELLING A HOME

While most of this chapter deals with buying a home, important considerations also arise when you are selling a home. It is extremely important to do minor painting, cleaning, and repairing before listing your home for sale. When selling your home, you may be obligated to disclose problems that could affect the property's value or desirability using a state required **defect disclosure form**. In most states, it is illegal to fraudulently conceal major physical defects in your property such as a basement that floods in heavy rains. And many states now require sellers to take a proactive role by making written disclosures about the condition of the property.

> **LEARNING OBJECTIVE 5**
>
> Identify some key considerations when selling a home.

> **defect disclosure form**
>
> *A state required form that discloses problems that could affect the property's value or desirability, such as a basement that floods in heavy rains.*

9.5a Should You List with a Broker or Try to Sell a Home Yourself?

Knowing that the sales commission to a broker on a $200,000 home could be $12,000 to $14,000 provides motivation for some homeowners to consider selling their homes themselves. The key to success in a **FSBO** (for sale by owner; commonly pronounced "fizbo") is to know what price to ask for your home. Asking too little could cost you much more than the commission paid to a broker. Setting the price too high keeps potential buyers away.

Many homeowners begin by contacting a few real estate agents to get their opinions on how much the home is worth. Agents are often quite willing to give their opinions because the homeowner might list the home with them if it does not sell quickly. Placing a for-sale sign on your lawn and spending about $500 on advertising the property should keep your telephone ringing with inquiries. If your home does not sell after a few months while other similar properties are selling, you might want to list it with a broker. For more information on selling your own home, visit www.fsbo.com, or www.forsalebyowner.com.

Brokers require that homeowners sign a **listing agreement** permitting them to list the property exclusively or with a multiple-listing service. A **multiple-listing** (or **open-listing**) **service** is an information and referral network among real estate brokers allowing properties listed with a particular broker to be shown by all other brokers. Brokers "qualify" prospective buyers—distinguishing between serious buyers and people who

> **FSBO**
>
> *For sale by owner; commonly pronounced "fizbo"; home sold directly by the homeowner to save on sales commission paid to a real estate broker.*

> **listing agreement**
>
> *Agreement that brokers require homeowners to sign that permits the broker to list the property exclusively or with a multiple-listing service.*

FINANCIAL POWER POINT

How to Sell a Home in a Hurry

What if you want to sell your home in a declining market with lots of properties that have further depressed home values? Tell your real estate agent that you are willing to pay a commission of 8 or even 10 percent rather than 6 percent. This will motivate the agent to show your home by bringing lots of people to see it. The agent's broker will also insist that all his or her agents show the property because the broker will earn more money too. The extra you pay in commission (about $4000 to $6000 on a $200,000 house) is probably much less than the money you would lose if you are forced to reduce your asking price one, twice, or even more.

Stockbyte/Jupiter Images

FSBOs can save a home seller money but usually take longer to sell.

are just looking or cannot afford the home. If your broker cannot find a buyer within 60 days, consider signing an agreement with another broker who might prove more aggressive in advertising and selling your property. If a sale occurs (or begins) during the time period of the listing agreement, you must pay a commission to the broker for any sale to a buyer not listed as an exception in the listing agreement.

9.5b   Selling Carries Its Own Costs

broker's commission

Largest selling cost in selling a home; these commissions often amount to 6 percent of the selling price of the home.

The largest selling cost is the **broker's commission**. These commissions often amount to 6 to 7 percent of the selling price of the home. Sellers are often unaware that brokers may negotiate their commission. Smart sellers also pay for a title search, a professional appraisal, and their own home inspection.

Most mortgage loans are paid off before maturity because people move and sell their homes. Mortgage loan contracts sometimes have a clause that specifies a **prepayment fee** or **prepayment penalty**. A prepayment penalty on a mortgage essentially

DID YOU KNOW

Your Worst Financial Blunders in Obtaining Affordable Housing

Based on others' financial woes, you will make mistakes in personal finance when you:

1. *Take out a mortgage loan with payments that you really cannot afford.*

2. *Fail to take steps to increase your credit score in the months prior to applying for a mortgage loan.*

3. *Fail to request that private mortgage insurance be canceled when the LTV ratio drops to 80 percent.*

charges you extra if you pay off the mortgage early. What is considered early, however, will be laid out in your loan documents and therefore must be scrutinized carefully. Not all mortgages come with them, and they are certainly not required. Prepayment penalties can range from 1 to 3 percent of the original mortgage loan. On a $160,000 mortgage loan, for example, the charge might vary from $1200 to $4800. Usually, the penalty is only for an early payoff in the first 2–5 years of the loan for the purposes of refinancing rather than because the home was sold.

Local communities may assess **real estate transfer taxes**. These taxes are paid by the seller and also possibly the buyer, and they are usually based on the selling price of the home. These tax rates can be as high as 2 or 4 percent, that is, $4000 or $8000 on a $200,000 home but are typically less than 1 percent. When paid by the seller, they may affect the offer that the seller is willing to accept for the home.

CONCEPT CHECK 9.5

1. List some disadvantages of trying to sell a home yourself.

2. List one advantage and one disadvantage of using a real estate broker to sell a home.

3. Describe two costs associated with selling a home in addition to the real estate commission.

DO IT NOW!

You know more about personal finance after reading this chapter, so get started right now by:

1. *Talking to family members or friends who have bought a home to obtain their insights into the process including any not-so-pleasant surprises.*

2. *Exploring the housing market at www .realtor.com for the geographic area where you might live if you get a job offer in that location.*

3. *Setting a reasonable goal for a down payment amount and calculating how much you would have to save per month to reach it at www .bankrate.com/calculators/savings /saving-goals-calculator.aspx.*

WHAT DO YOU RECOMMEND *NOW?*

Now that you have read the chapter on buying housing, what do you recommend to Shelby Clark regarding:

1. Buying or renting housing in the Denver area?

2. Steps she should take prior to actively looking at homes?

3. Finding a home and negotiating the purchase?

4. The closing process in home buying?

5. Selecting the type of mortgage to fit her needs?

6. Things to consider regarding the sale of her home should she ultimately be promoted to a position in another of the four regions?

BIG PICTURE SUMMARY OF LEARNING OBJECTIVES

L01 **Decide whether renting or owning your home is better for you.**

When choosing housing, renters must consider the costs of rent, a security deposit, and renter's insurance. Home buyers can choose among single-family dwellings, condominiums, cooperative housing, manufactured housing, and mobile homes. Renters generally pay out less money in terms of cash flow in the short run, whereas owners enjoy tax advantages and generally see an increase in the market value of their homes, making them better off financially in the long run.

LO2   **Explain the up-front and monthly costs of buying a home.**

Home buyers understand that they will make a down payment and then make monthly principal and interest payments on their mortgage. What many don't understand is that closing costs for interest points and other aspects of the purchase can add 2–7 percent or more to the amount needed up front at the closing. Similarly, monthly charges for private mortgage insurance (PMI), homeowner's insurance, and real estate property taxes can add 25 percent or more to their monthly payment.

LO3   **Describe the steps in the home-buying process.**

The home-buying process includes (a) getting your finances in order, (b) prequalifying for a mortgage, (c) searching for a home online and in person, (d) agreeing to terms with a seller, (e) formally applying for a mortgage loan, (f) preparing for the closing, and (g) signing your name on closing day.

LO4   **Understand the mathematics of mortgage loans and distinguish among ways of financing the purchase of a home.**

Mortgage loans for homes are amortized. Amortization is the process of gradually paying off a mortgage through a series of periodic payments to a lender, with a portion of each payment going toward the principal and another portion going toward the interest owed. The mathematics of buying a home shows how loan payments are calculated and how the portion of each monthly payment that goes toward interest declines, resulting in the portion that goes toward the principal increasing with each subsequent payment.

Conventional mortgages and adjustable-rate mortgages are the most common types of housing loans. Growing appreciation mortgages are designed for early pay-off.

LO5   **Identify some key considerations when selling a home.**

When selling a home, it is wise to consider the pros and cons of listing with a real estate broker versus selling the home yourself, the transaction costs of selling, and the pitfalls of seller financing.

LET'S TALK ABOUT IT

1. **The Housing Collapse.** How has the foreclosure crisis and collapse in home values in the last decade affected your thinking about buying a home someday?

2. **Renting Versus Buying.** What do you see as the advantages and the disadvantages for you of renting or buying housing at the current time? How might your feelings change in the future, such as within five years?

3. **Feelings About Long-Term Debt.** In the early years of the standard 30-year mortgage loan, as little as 10 percent of the monthly payment actually goes toward repaying the debt. As a result, it takes many, many years for the loan balance to come down to any significant extent. Explain how that affects your feelings about taking on such a long-term obligation.

4. **Alternative Mortgages.** Would you prefer a conventional mortgage, an adjustable-rate mortgage, or one of the other alternatives described in this chapter to finance a home purchase? Why?

5. **Negotiating the Purchase of a Home.** Almost all closing costs on a home purchase are negotiable. Would you feel comfortable entering into a discussion of these items? Why or why not?

DO THE MATH

1. **Deciding to Buy.** Adam and Laura Jensen of Atlanta, Georgia, both of whom are in their late 20s, currently are renting an unfurnished two-bedroom apartment for $880 per month, plus $130 for utilities and $34 for insurance. They have found a condominium they can buy for $170,000 with a 20 percent down payment and a 30-year, 5 percent mortgage. Principal and interest payments are estimated at $730 per month, with property taxes amounting to $150 per month and a homeowner's insurance premium of $720 per year. Closing costs are estimated at $3200. The monthly homeowners association fee is $275, and utility costs are estimated at $160 per month. The Jensens have a combined income of $57,000 per year, with take-home pay of $4100 per month. They are in the 15 percent tax bracket, pay $225 per month on an installment loan (ten payments left), and have $39,000 in savings and investments outside of their retirement accounts.

(a) Can the Jensens afford to buy the condo? Use the results from the *Garman/Forgue* companion website or the information on page 264 to support your answer. Also, consider the effect of the purchase on their savings and monthly budget.

(b) Adam and Laura think that their monthly housing costs would be lower the first year if they bought the condo. Do you agree? Support your answer. Assume that they currently have $10,000 in tax deductible expenses.

(c) If they buy, how much will Adam and Laura have left in savings to pay for moving expenses?

(d) Available financial information suggests that mortgage rates might increase over the next few months. If the Jensens wait until the rates increase 1 more percent, how much more will they spend on their monthly mortgage payment? Use the information in Table 9-4 or the *Garman/Forgue* companion website to calculate the payment.

2. **Mortgage Affordability.** Seth and Alexandra Moore of Berrien Spring, Michigan have an annual income of $78,000 and want to buy a home. Currently, mortgage rates are 6 percent. The Moores want to take out a mortgage for 30 years. Real estate taxes are estimated to be $4800 per year for homes similar to what they would like to buy, and homeowner's insurance would be about $1500 per year.

DO IT IN CLASS PAGES 263 AND 264

(a) Using a 28 percent front-end ratio, what are the total annual and monthly expenditures for which they would qualify?

(b) Using a 36 percent back-end ratio, what monthly mortgage payment (including taxes and insurance) could they afford given that they have an automobile loan payment of $470, a student loan payment of $350, and credit card payments of $250? (Hint: Subtract these amounts from the total monthly affordable payments for their income to determine the amount left over to spend on a mortgage.)

(c) If mortgage interest rates are around 5 percent and the Moores want a 30-year mortgage, use the information in the Did You Know box on page 264 to estimate how much they could borrow given your answer to part a. (Hint: Subtract the monthly real estate taxes and homeowner's insurance from your part a answer first.)

3. **Rent Versus Buy.** Alex Guadet of Forrest City, Arkansas, has been renting a small, two-bedroom house for several years. He pays $900 per month in rent for the home and $300 per year in property and liability insurance. The owner of the house wants to sell it, and Phillip is considering making an offer. The owner wants $130,000 for the property, but Phillip thinks he could get the house for $125,000 and use his $25,000 in 3 percent certificates of deposit that are ready to mature for the down payment. Alex has talked to his

banker and could get a 5.5 percent mortgage loan for 25 years to finance the remainder of the purchase price. The banker advised Alex that he would reduce his debt principal by $2200 during the first year of the loan. Property taxes on the house are $1800 per year. Phillip estimates that he would need to upgrade his property and liability insurance to $800 per year and would incur about $1500 in costs the first year for maintenance. Property values are increasing at about 2.5 percent per year in the neighborhood. Alex is in the 25 percent marginal tax bracket.

DO IT IN CLASS PAGE 254

(a) Use Table 9-4 to calculate the monthly mortgage payment for the mortgage loan that Phillip would need.

(b) How much interest would Alex pay during the first year of the loan?

(c) Use the Run the Numbers worksheet, "Should You Buy or Rent?" on page 254 to determine whether Alex would be better off buying or renting.

4. **Refinancing a Mortgage.** Kevin Tutumbo of Middletown, Ohio, has owned his home for 15 years and expects to live in it for five more years. He originally borrowed $105,000 at 6 percent interest for 30 years to buy the home. He still owes $65,750 on the loan. Interest rates have since fallen to 5.0 percent, and Kevin is considering refinancing the loan for 15 years. He would have to pay 2 points on the new loan with no prepayment penalty on the current loan.

DO IT IN CLASS PAGE 278

(a) What is Kevin's current monthly payment?

(b) Calculate the monthly payment on the new loan.

(c) Advise Kevin on whether he should refinance his mortgage using the Run the Numbers worksheet, "When You Should Refinance Your Mortgage" on page 278.

5. **Illustrating Amortization.** Heather McIntosh of DeKalb, Illinois, recently purchased a home for $165,000. She put $25,000 down and took out a 25-year loan at 5.4 percent interest.

DO IT IN CLASS PAGE 271 AND 273

(a) Use Table 9-4 to determine her monthly payment.

(b) How much of her first payment will go toward interest and principal and how much will she owe after that first month?

(c) How much will she owe after three months. Hint: Use the logic of Table 9-2 on page 271.

FINANCIAL PLANNING CASES

CASE 1

The Johnsons Decide to Buy a Home

Belinda Johnson's parents and maternal grandmother have combined their finances and presented Harry and Belinda with $35,000 with which to purchase a home. The Johnsons have shopped and found a house in a new housing development that they like very much. They could either borrow from the developer or obtain a loan from one of three other mortgage lenders. The financial alternatives and data for the home are summarized in the table below.

(a) Which plan has the lowest total up-front costs? The highest?

(b) What would be the full monthly payment for PITI and PMI for each of the options?

(c) If the Johnsons had enough additional cash to make the 20 percent down payment, would you recommend lender 1 or lender 2? Why?

(d) Assuming that the Johnsons will need about $3000 for moving costs (in addition to closing costs), which financing option would you recommend? Why?

Financing Details on a Home Available to the Johnsons

Price: $190,000. Developer A will finance the purchase with a 10 percent down payment and a 30-year, 5 percent ARM loan with 2 interest points. The initial monthly payment for principal and interest is $917.96 ($171,000 loan after the down payment is made; 171 × $5.3682). After one year, the rate rises to 5.5 percent, with a principal plus interest payment of $961.15. At that point, the rate can go up or down as much as 2 percent per year, depending on the cost of an index of mortgage funds. There is an interest-rate cap of 5 percent over the life of the loan. Taxes are estimated to be about $1800, and the homeowner's insurance premium should be about $700 annually. A mortgage insurance premium of $88 per month must be paid monthly on the two 10 percent down options.

Home: Price, $190,000; Taxes, $1800; Insurance, $700				
	Developer A	Lender 1	Lender 2	Lender 3
Loan term and type	30-year ARM*	30-year CON†	15-year CON	20-year REN‡
Interest rate	5.0%	5.5%	6%	5.5%
Down payment	$ 19,000	$ 38,000	$ 38,000	$ 19,000
Loan amount	171,000	152,000	152,000	171,000
Points	3,420	1,520	0	5,130
Principal and interest payment	917.96	863.04	1282.66	1176.29
PMI	88	0	0	88

*Adjustable-rate mortgage.
†Conventional.
‡Renegotiable every five years.

CASE 2

Victor and Maria Hernandez Learn About Real Estate Agents

Victor and Maria have been thinking about selling their home and buying a house with more yard space so that they can indulge their passion for gardening. Before they make such a decision, they want to explore the market to see what might be available and in what price ranges. They will then list their house with a real estate agent and begin searching in earnest for a new home.

(a) What services could a real estate agent provide for the couple, and what types of agents could represent them as they sell their current home?

(b) A friend has advised them that they really need a buyer's agent for the purchase of a new home. Explain to the Hernandez the difference between buyer's and seller's agents.

CASE 3

Julia Price Contemplates Buying a Home

Julia has been thinking about buying a home. For several months, she has been watching real estate shows on television and visiting open houses in her community. She thinks it is time to take the plunge and buy a much larger home since she can genuinely afford it. She also thinks that housing prices will rise substantially in the next five years. She has explored the interest rates currently being charged for mortgages and has calculated the amount of money she can afford to pay given her income. She is thinking that her next step would be to call a real estate agent and begin looking in earnest. Offer your opinions about her thinking.

CASE 4

Michael and Maggi Weigh the Benefits and Costs of Buying Versus Renting

Michael Joseph and Maggi Lewis of Biloxi, Mississippi, are trying to decide whether to rent or purchase housing. Michael favors buying and Maggi leans toward renting, and both seem able to justify their particular choice. Michael thinks that the tax advantages are a very good reason for buying. Maggi, however, believes that cash flow is so much better when renting. See whether you can help them make their decision.

(a) Does the home buyer enjoy tax advantages? Explain.

(b) Discuss Maggi's belief that cash flow is better with renting.

**DO IT IN CLASS
PAGE 254**

(c) Suggest some reasons why Michael might consider renting rather than purchasing housing.

(d) Suggest some reasons why Maggi might consider buying rather than renting housing.

(e) Is there a clear-cut basis for deciding whether to rent or buy housing? Explain why or why not.

CASE 5

Jeremy Decides to Sell His Home Himself

Jeremy Jorgensen of Tucson, Arizona, is concerned about the costs involved in selling his home, so he has decided to sell his home himself rather than pay a broker to do it.

(a) How would you advise Jeremy if he asked you whether he should sell the house himself or list with a broker? Explain your answer.

(b) Would Jeremy really save money by selling his home himself if he considers his time as part of his costs? Why or why not?

(c) Can you suggest any ways that Jeremy might reduce his selling costs without doing the selling himself? Explain.

BE YOUR OWN PERSONAL FINANCIAL MANAGER

1. **Are You Ready to Buy a Home?** Review the material in the Run the Numbers worksheet "Should You Buy or Rent?" on page 254. Then using dollar amounts that fit your situation, complete Worksheet 37: Should I Rent or Buy Housing from "My Personal Financial Planner."

MY PERSONAL FINANCIAL PLANNER

2. **Save to Buy a Home.** Review the material on "Financial Goals Follow From Your Values" on page 68–69 and on "Be a Better Saver" on page 150 and then complete Worksheet 14: Monthly Savings Needed to Reach My Goals from "My Personal Financial Planner," which allows you to determine the monthly savings amount you would need to reach a goal of having a down payment on a home.

MY PERSONAL FINANCIAL PLANNER

3. **Can You Afford a Mortgage?** Review the material on "The Income Needed to Qualify for a Mortgage" on page 264. Then using dollar amounts that fit your situation, complete

MY PERSONAL FINANCIAL PLANNER

Worksheet 38: Income Needed to Qualify for a Mortgage from "My Personal Financial Planner." What price range of home could you afford given the results of your analysis?

4. **Shop for a Mortgage.** If you are ready to buy a home, review the material on "The Conventional Mortgage and Adjustable Mortgage Loans" and "Other Housing Financing Arrangements" on pages 274–279. Then using that information complete Worksheet 39: Mortgage Shopping Worksheet from "My Personal Financial Planner" to begin your search for a mortgage.

MY PERSONAL FINANCIAL PLANNER

5. **Should You Refinance Your Mortgage?** Do you have an existing mortgage? Review the material on "When You Should Refinance Your Mortgage" on page 278. Then using dollar amounts that fit your situation, complete Worksheet 42: Should I Refinance My Mortgage? from "My Personal Financial Planner."

MY PERSONAL FINANCIAL PLANNER

ON THE NET

Go to the Web pages indicated to complete these exercises.

1. **Current Interest Rates.** Visit the website for Bankrate .com (www.bankrate.com/mortgage.aspx), where you will find information on mortgage interest rates around the United States. View the information for the lenders in a large city near your home. How does the information compare with the interest rates on your own credit card account(s)? How do the rates in the city you selected compare with other rates found in the United States?

2. **Can You Afford to Buy?** Visit the website for Bankrate .com, where you will find a calculator (www.bankrate .com/calculators/mortgages/new-house-calculator.aspx) that helps you determine the amount you can afford for the purchase of a home given your income and funds available for a down payment, closing costs, and other home-buying expenses. Enter the data requested for your current situation. What does the calculator tell you about your housing affordability? Change the entered data for some point in the future when you project a better financial situation for yourself. How do the results change?

3. **Searching for a Home to Buy.** Visit the website for the National Association of Realtors (www.realtor.com), where you can search for owned housing in various locales around the United States. Look for housing in your community. Were you able to find housing that meets your price range and other criteria? Also search for similar housing in the San Fransico, CA (high-cost) and Ocala, FL (low-cost) metropolitan areas. Compare these cost results with the housing found in your area.

ACTION INVOLVEMENT PROJECTS

1. **Do Some Home Shopping.** Realtors often open homes for sale to the public on Sunday afternoons. Spend an afternoon looking at housing that is for sale in a neighborhood near your campus. Gather the information sheets that are provided at the homes and take notes during your visits. Prepare a brief report that summarizes what you have learned about housing costs, features, and locations in the community.

2. **Comparing Leases.** Survey five of your friends who live in rental housing about their feelings about written leases. For those who have written leases, compare some of them for the rights and responsibilities of tenants outlined in the leases. Write a summary of your findings.

3. **Assess the Real Estate Market.** Make an appointment to talk with a real estate agent in your community. Ask whether home sales are slow or brisk, how long it typically takes for buyers to find a desirable home, whether home values are rising or declining, and tips the agent would give to people in your situation who hope to own their own homes one day. Write a summary of your findings.

4. **See How Others Go About Buying a Home.** Ask friends and relatives for the names of one or two people who have bought a home in recent years. Contact the home-buyers and ask them for an interview in person or over the phone to discuss how they went about buying a home and their feelings about how the process turned out for them. Compare their procedures and experiences with what you have learned in this chapter.

Visit the Garman/Forgue companion website at www.cengagebrain.com.

PART 3

© S. Dashkevych/Shutterstock.com

10

Managing Property and Liability Risk

YOU MUST BE KIDDING, RIGHT?

Megan Blake recently caused an automobile accident when she had a blowout on the freeway. The cost of repairs to Megan's car will be $13,200. The damage to the other vehicle was $37,900, although no one was injured in the accident. Megan had purchased an auto insurance policy with a $500 collision deductible and liability limits of $25,000/$50,000/$15,000; the legal minimums in her state. What dollar amount of the losses will Megan have to pay?

A. $500   **C.** $22,900

B. $13,400   **D.** $23,400

The answer is D. Megan will be personally responsible for the $23,400. That's the balance remaining after the insurance company payments ($500 + $22,900 [$37,900 − $15,000]). The company will pay her $12,700 after her $500 deductible for the loss of her vehicle. The company will also pay $15,000 for the damage to the other vehicle as that is the limit for property damage liability under her policy. Like most people, Megan did not carry sufficient liability protection. You should!

LEARNING OBJECTIVES

After reading this chapter, you should be able to:

1. Apply the risk-management process to address the risks to your property and income.

2. Explain how insurance works to reduce risk.

3. Design a homeowner's or renter's insurance program to meet your needs.

4. Design an automobile insurance program to meet your needs.

5. Describe other types of property and liability insurance.

6. Summarize how to make an insurance claim.

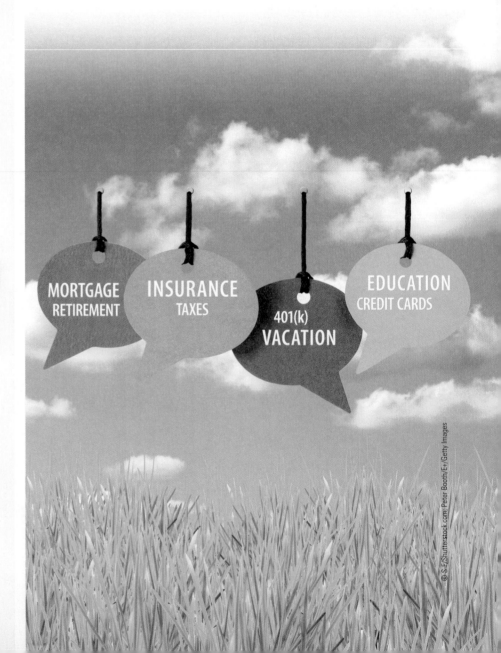

© S f/Shutterstock.com; Peter Booth/E+/Getty Images

WHAT DO YOU RECOMMEND?

© iStockphoto.com/janaiv

Nick and Amber Chandler of Nacogdoches, Texas, recently had a fire in their garage that destroyed two of their cars and did considerable damage to the garage and to the outside of their home. After receiving their reimbursements from their homeowner's and automobile insurance policies, the Chandlers realized that they were seriously underinsured. One vehicle was not insured for fire, and the insurance on their dwelling amounted to only 60 percent of its current replacement value.

What do you recommend to Nick and Amber about managing property and liability risk regarding:

1. **The risk-management steps they should take to update their insurance coverages?**

2. **The relationship between severity and frequency of loss when deciding whether to buy insurance?**

3. **Adequately insuring their home?**

4. **The use of deductibles and policy limits to keep their automobile insurance premiums at a manageable level while still maintaining vital coverage?**

LEARNING OBJECTIVE 1

Apply the risk-management process to address the risks to your property and income.

risk
Uncertainty about the outcome of a situation or event.

risk management
Process of identifying and evaluating purely risky situations to determine and implement appropriate management.

perils
Any event that can cause a financial loss.

property insurance
Protection from financial losses resulting from the damage to or destruction of your property or possessions.

liability insurance
Protection from financial losses suffered when you are held liable for others' losses.

It is important to protect your income, property and possessions from the possibility of financial loss from accidents, acts of nature, illness or injury, and death. An uninsured loss can lead to overuse of credit that can easily get-out of control. It could lead to repossession and bankruptcy. You can manage the risk of such losses through the use of insurance.

Learning what insurance is, how to use it wisely, and how to collect on a loss are examples of smart money management. You can waste hundreds of dollars buying too much or the wrong kind of homeowners, renters and auto insurance. Purchasing insurance policies wisely will give you more money to spend, save, invest and donate.

10.1   RISK AND RISK MANAGEMENT

10.1a   People Often Misunderstand the Concept of Risk

Risk is uncertainty about the outcome of a situation or event. It arises out of the possibility that the outcome will differ from what is expected. In the area of financial losses, risk consists of uncertainty about both whether the financial loss will occur and how large it might be. There are two types of risk. **Speculative risk** exists in situations where there is potential for gain as well as for loss. Investments such as those made in the stock market involve speculative risk. **Pure risk** exists when there is no potential for gain, only the possibility of loss. Fires, automobile accidents, illness, and theft are examples of events involving pure risk. Insurance only addresses pure risk.

Many people think of "odds" or games of chance when they hear the word risk. In fact, risk and chance are different concepts. The difference between the two is subtle but very important. An event with a 95 percent chance of occurring is highly likely to occur. Thus, both uncertainty and risk are low. An event with a 0.000001 percent chance of occurring is highly likely *not* to occur. Thus, both uncertainty and risk are low. When an event has a moderate chance of occurring—5 percent, for example—the uncertainty and risk are relatively high because it is difficult to predict the one person in 20 who will experience the event. In such cases, insurance often represents a wise choice for reducing risk.

10.1b   Apply the Five-Step Risk-Management Process

Risk management is the process of identifying and evaluating situations involving pure risk to determine and implement the appropriate means for its management. Risk management entails making the most efficient arrangements *before* a loss occurs. Risk management usually requires the purchase of insurance, although insurance is only one of the ways to handle risk, and it is not always the best choice.

The risk-management process involves five steps:

Step 1: Identify Your Risk Exposures Sources of risk are called **exposures** and these include the items you own and the activities in which you engage that expose you to potential financial loss. Owning and/or driving an automobile are common exposures. To determine your exposures to risk, you should take an inventory of what you own and what you do. You also need to identify the **perils** that you face, which are any events that can cause a financial loss. Fire, wind, theft, vehicle collision, illness, and death are examples of perils.

The items you own and your day-to-day activities expose you to two types of losses: property and liability. **Property insurance** protects you from financial losses resulting from the damage to or destruction of your property or possessions. **Liability insurance** protects you from financial losses suffered by others for which you are held responsible (**legally liable**). Coverage includes your legal fees if you are sued but does not include coverage for your intentional acts and contractual obligations. The most commonly purchased forms of property and liability insurance are insurance for your home and its contents and insurance for your use and ownership of vehicles.

Step 2: Estimate Your Risk and Potential Losses Next you estimate loss frequency and severity. **Loss frequency** is the likely number of times that a loss might occur over a period of time. **Loss severity** describes the potential magnitude of a loss.

Many people wonder whether they should buy insurance when loss frequency is low, for example, if they are young and healthy or if they live in a safe neighborhood. This is not a good way to think about potential losses because they still could occur, and if loss frequency is low, the cost of insurance would be small. Figure 10-1 illustrates the relationship between loss frequency and loss severity in risk management.

What is most important is loss severity. "How much might I lose?" is the question to ask. When considering possible property losses, you simply make an estimate of the value of the property. Liability losses are more complicated because the severity of the loss depends on the circumstances of the person you harm. For example, if you caused an accident that permanently disabled a young heart surgeon with three small children, you would be liable for the surgeon's care, lost earnings over his or her lifetime, and future care and education of the children. A loss of several million dollars is not out of the question in such a situation.

DID YOU KNOW

Bias toward Underestimating Risk

People engaged in managing property and liability risk have a bias toward certain behaviors that can be harmful, such as a tendency toward underestimating risk. Many fail to buy insurance for events that are rare and think that a catastrophe will not happen to them. What to do? Recognize that the cost of insurance is very low for rare events and adding to our policy limits is inexpensive.

Step 3: Choose How to Handle Your Risk of Loss The risk of loss may be handled in five ways: risk avoidance, risk retention, loss control, risk transfer, and **risk reduction**. Each strategy may be appropriate for certain circumstances, and the mix that you choose will depend on the source of the risk, the size of the potential loss, your personal feelings about risk, and the financial resources you have available to pay for losses.

- **Risk avoidance.** The simplest way to handle risk is to avoid it. For example, choosing not to own an airplane or not to sky-dive limits your exposures.

- **Risk retention.** A second way to handle risk is to retain or accept it. For example, you can use a **deductible clause** in an insurance policy to retain an initial portion of the risk. In this way, you pay the first dollars of a loss (perhaps $200 or $500) before the insurance company will reimburse for a loss.

- **Loss control.** Loss control is designed to reduce loss frequency and loss severity. For example, installing heavy-duty locks and doors may reduce the *frequency* of theft losses. Installing fire alarms and smoke detectors cannot prevent fires but should reduce the *severity* of losses from them. Insurance companies often require

risk reduction
Includes mechanisms, such as insurance, that reduce the overall uncertainty about the magnitude of loss.

risk retention
Accepting that some risks simply arise in the course of one's life and consciously retaining that risk.

deductible clause
Requires that the policyholder pays an initial portion of any loss.

loss control
Designing specific mechanisms to reduce loss frequency and loss severity.

Figure 10-1 **The Relationship Between Severity and Frequency of Loss**

	HIGH SEVERITY	LOW SEVERITY
LOW FREQUENCY	Purchase insurance to cover the potentially large losses. Their infrequency will make premiums affordable.	Consider retaining risk because the frequency and severity of loss are both low.
HIGH FREQUENCY	Purchase insurance. Loss control efforts can be useful in reducing the necessarily high premiums.	Retain risk but also budget for losses that are likely to be frequent.

Renters need insurance too.

Tom Carter/PhotoEdit

loss-control efforts or give discounts to policyholders who implement them.

- **Risk transfer**. Another way to handle risk is to transfer it to an insurance company.

- **Reduce Risk to Acceptable Levels**. The final way to handle risk is to reduce it to acceptable levels. Insurance is used by policyholders when they arrange for all or a portion of their risk to be covered by an insurance company, thereby reducing their personal level of risk.

Step 4: Implement Your Risk-Management Program The next step in risk management is to implement the risk-handling methods you have chosen. For most households, this means buying insurance to transfer and reduce risk. This involves selecting types of policies and coverages, dollar amounts of coverage, and sources of insurance protection. Always remember that your goal is to "buy" the insurance you need at a fair price. Do not let yourself be "sold" more or less insurance coverage than you need at unnecessary prices.

People often wonder what types of insurance to buy and how much coverage they should have. You should use the maximum possible loss as a guide for the dollar amount of coverage to buy. This way of thinking makes use of the **large-loss principle**, which states: "Insure the risks that you cannot afford and retain the risks that you can reasonably afford." In other words, pay for small losses out of your own pocket and purchase as much insurance as necessary to cover large, catastrophic losses that might ruin you financially. The example earlier of an auto accident that injures a heart surgeon would bring you such financial ruin because a court would hold you responsible for those losses. Consequently, you would want high dollar amounts of liability coverage on your auto insurance.

Step 5: Evaluate and Adjust Your Program The final step in risk management entails periodic review of your risk-management efforts. The risks people face in their lives change continually. Therefore, no risk-management plan should be put in place and then ignored for long periods of time. An annual review is certainly important but also check your insurance needs when you move, make a major purchase, or if your family situation changes. Many people simply keep old insurance policies that no longer fit their needs (too little or too much coverage) and then find they are inappropriately covered when a loss occurs.

large-loss principle

A basic rule of risk management that encourages us to insure the risks that we cannot afford and retain the risks that we can reasonably afford.

CONCEPT CHECK 10.1

1. Distinguish between pure risk and speculative risk.

2. Explain the distinctions between risk and odds.

3. Distinguish among the five common risk exposures that most people face.

4. Describe the five steps of risk management.

5. When considering likelihood of loss and severity of loss, explain which one of these two concepts is more important when deciding whether to buy insurance and why.

10.2 UNDERSTANDING HOW INSURANCE WORKS

Insurance is a mechanism for transferring and reducing pure risk through which a large number of individuals share in the financial losses suffered by members of the group as a whole. Insurance protects each individual in the group by replacing an uncertain— and possibly large—financial loss with a certain but comparatively small fee called the **premium**. Insurance premiums are paid for in advance and have four components:

LEARNING OBJECTIVE 2
Explain how insurance works to reduce risk.

1. The individual's share of the group's losses
2. A share of the company's expenses for administering the insurance plan
3. Insurance company reserves set aside to pay future losses
4. Profit when the plan is administered by a profit-seeking company

The **insurance policy** is the contract between the person buying insurance (the **insured**) and the insurance company (the **insurer**). It contains language that describes the rights and responsibilities of both parties. Most people do not take the time to read and understand their insurance policies. As a result, insurance remains one of the least understood purchases people make. You can do a much better job of managing your risks if you understand the basic terms and concepts used in the field of insurance, and reading this chapter will improve your understanding.

insurance
Mechanism for transferring and reducing pure risk through which a large number of individuals share in the financial losses suffered by members of the group as a whole.

premium
The fee paid for insurance.

insurance policy
Contract between the person buying insurance (the insured) and the insurance company (the insurer).

10.2a Hazards Make Losses More Likely to Occur

A **hazard** is any condition that increases the probability that a peril will occur. Driving under the influence of alcohol and/or texting represent especially dangerous hazards. Three types of hazards exist:

hazard
Any condition that increases the probability that a peril will occur.

- A **physical hazard** is a particular characteristic of the insured person or property that increases the chance of loss. An example of a physical hazard is high blood pressure in a person covered by health insurance.

- A **morale hazard** exists when a person is indifferent to a peril. For example, a morale hazard exists if the insured party, knowing that theft insurance will pay for the loss, becomes careless about locking doors and windows.

- A **moral hazard** relates to the possibility that the insured person will want or even cause a peril to occur in order to collect reimbursement from the insurance company.

Insurance companies often limit or deny coverage if a loss occurs as a result of a morale or moral hazard. An investigation often reveals the truth.

principle of indemnity
Insurance will pay no more than the actual financial loss suffered.

10.2b Only Fortuitous and Financial Losses Are Insurable

Certain minimum requirements must be met for a loss to be considered insurable—in particular, the loss must be fortuitous and financial. **Fortuitous losses** are unexpected in terms of both their timing and their magnitude. A loss caused by a lightning strike and fire to your home is fortuitous; a loss caused by a decline in the market value of your home is not because it is reasonable to expect home values to rise and fall over time. A **financial loss** is any decline in the value of income or assets in the present or future. Financial losses can be measured objectively in dollars and cents.

10.2c The Principle of Indemnity Limits Insurance Payouts

The **principle of indemnity** states that insurance will pay *no more* than the actual financial loss suffered. For example, an automobile insurance policy will pay

FINANCIAL POWER POINT

Your Credit Report Affects Your Insurance Rates

It is common for insurance companies to use an applicant's credit rating to provide information in order to help set their premiums. This is another reason for maintaining good credit and for making sure your credit bureau files are accurate!

policy limits
Specify the maximum dollar amounts that will be paid under the policy.

coinsurance
Method by which the insured and the insurer share proportionately in the payment for a loss.

only the actual cash value of a stolen automobile. This principle prevents a person from gaining financially from a loss (certainly a moral hazard). The principle of indemnity *does not* guarantee that insured losses will be totally reimbursed. Every policy includes **policy limits** that specify the maximum dollar amounts that will be paid under the policy. As a result, insurance purchasers must carefully select policy limits sufficient to cover their potential losses.

10.2d   Ways to Pay Less for Insurance and Still Maintain Sufficient Coverage

Some features of insurance policies can lower your premiums without significantly reducing the protection offered. These features include deductibles, coinsurance, hazard reduction, and loss reduction.

1. **Pay the first dollars of a loss yourself. A deductible** is an initial portion of any loss that must be paid before the insurance company will provide coverage. For example, automobile collision insurance often includes a $500 deductible and that means that the first $500 of loss to the car must be paid by the insured. The insurer then pays the remainder of the loss, up to the limits of the policy. The higher the deductible, the more you will save on your premium.

2. **Pay a share of any loss yourself. Coinsurance** is a method by which the insured and the insurer share proportionately in the payment for a loss. For example, a health insurance policy may require that the insured pay 20 percent of a loss and the insurer pay the remaining 80 percent. Substantial premium reductions can be realized through coinsurance, but you must be prepared to pay your share of losses. The following **deductible and coinsurance reimbursement formula** can be used to determine the amount of a loss that will be reimbursed when the policy includes both a deductible and a coinsurance clause:

$$R = (1 - CP)(L - D) \quad \textbf{(10.1)}$$

where

R = Reimbursement
CP = Coinsurance percentage required of the insured
L = Loss
D = Deductible

As an example, assume you have a health insurance policy with a $100 deductible per hospital stay and a 20 percent coinsurance requirement. If the hospital bill is $1350, the reimbursement will be $1000, calculated as follows:

$$R = (1.00 - 0.20)(\$1350 - \$100)$$
$$= (0.80)(\$1250)$$
$$= \$1000$$

3. **Reduce the chances that a loss will occur. Hazard reduction** is action taken by the insured to reduce the probability of a loss occurring. Quitting smoking is an example of hazard reduction related to life and health insurance.

4. **Reduce the dollar amount of a loss. Loss reduction** is action taken by the insured to lessen the severity of loss if a peril occurs. Smoke alarms and fire extinguishers in the home are examples of loss reduction efforts. These items will not prevent fires, but their use may lead to less severe damage.

10.2e   Risk Is Reduced for the Insurer through the Law of Large Numbers

Insurance consists of two basic elements: (1) the reduction of risk and (2) the sharing of losses. When you buy insurance, you exchange the uncertainty of a potentially large financial loss for the certainty of a fixed insurance premium, thereby reducing your risk.

DID YOU KNOW

How to Read an Insurance Policy

Insurance policies do not invite casual reading. Consequently, many people neglect to thoroughly examine their policies until a loss occurs, only to find that they had misunderstood the terms of the agreement. You can avoid such problems by systematically reading a policy before you purchase it, focusing on eight points:

1. **Perils covered.** *Some policies list only the perils that are covered; others cover all perils except those listed. The definition of certain perils may differ from that used in everyday language.*

2. **Property covered.** *Like perils, the property covered under a policy may be listed individually, or only the excluded property may be listed. When the property is listed individually, any new acquisitions must be added to the policy.*

3. **Types of losses covered.** *Three types of property losses can occur: (a) the loss of the property itself, (b) extra expenses that may arise because the property is rendered unusable for a period of time, and (c) loss of income if the property was used in the insured's work.*

4. **People covered.** *Insurance policies may cover only certain individuals. This information usually appears* on the first page of the policy but may be changed subsequently in later sections.

5. **Locations covered.** *Where the loss occurs may have a bearing on whether it will be covered. It is especially important to know which locations are not covered.*

6. **Time period of coverage.** *Policies are generally written to cover specific time periods. Restrictions may exclude coverage during specific times of the day or certain days of the week or year.*

7. **Loss control requirements.** *Insurance policies often stipulate that certain loss control efforts must be maintained by the insured. For example, coverage for a vehicle may be denied if the owner knowingly allows it to be driven by an unlicensed person.*

8. **Amount of coverage.** *All insurance policies specify the maximum amount the insurer will pay for various types of losses.*

The information on these eight points may be spread throughout a policy. In fact, coverage that appears to be provided in one location actually may be denied elsewhere. Carefully review the entire policy to determine the protection it provides. If necessary, telephone the salesperson or company to obtain clarification.

As the former baseball player Yogi Berra once said, "It is tough to make predictions, especially about the future." But predictions are much easier for an insurance company than for an individual. This is because risk is reduced for the insurer through the **law of large numbers**: As the number of members in a group increases, predictions about the group's behavior become increasingly more accurate. This greater accuracy decreases uncertainty and, therefore, risk.

law of large numbers
As the number of members in a group increases, predictions about the group's behavior become increasingly accurate.

10.2f Each Insured Benefits Even if One Does Not Suffer a Loss

Individual insurance purchasers benefit regardless of whether they actually suffer a loss because of the reduction of risk. This is the essence of insurance. Reduced risk gives one the freedom to drive a car, own a home, start a business, and plan financially for the future with the knowledge that some unforeseen event will not result in financial disaster.

10.2g How Companies Select among Insurance Applicants

The purchase of insurance begins with an offer by the purchaser in the form of a written or oral policy application. The insurer typically issues a temporary insurance contract, called a **binder**, which is replaced at a later date with a written policy. The application then goes through a process of **underwriting**—that is, the insurer's procedure for deciding which insurance applicants to accept. To describe the process of underwriting, it is necessary to first understand how insurance rates are set.

An **insurance rate** is the price charged for each unit of insurance coverage. Rates represent the average cost of providing coverage to various **classes of insureds**. These classes consist of insureds who share similar characteristics. For example, automobile insurance policyholders may be classified by age, gender, marital status, and driving record, as well as by the make and model of vehicle that they drive.

When underwriters receive an application, they assign the applicant to the appropriate class. They then determine whether the rates established for that class are sufficient to provide coverage for that specific applicant. Underwriters divide insurance applicants into four groups:

1. *Preferred* applicants have lower-than-average loss expectancies and save money because they typically qualify for lower premiums.
2. *Standard* applicants have average loss expectancies for their class and pay the standard rates.
3. *Substandard* applicants have higher-than-average loss expectancies and may be charged higher premiums and have restrictions placed on the types or amounts of coverage they may purchase.
4. *Unacceptable* applicants have loss expectancies that are much too high and are rejected.

You might save money by confirming with your insurance agent that you have been placed in the proper class for premium-determination purposes.

10.2h Who Sells Insurance?

insurance agents

Representative of an insurance company authorized to sell, modify, service, and terminate insurance contracts.

Sellers of insurance, called **insurance agents**, represent one or more insurance companies. They have the power to enter into, change, and cancel insurance policies on behalf of these companies. Two types of insurance agents exist: independent agents and exclusive agents.

Independent insurance agents are independent businesspeople who act as third-party links between insurers and insureds. Such agents earn commissions from the companies they represent and will place each insurance customer with the company that they believe best meets that customer's particular needs.

Exclusive insurance agents represent only one insurance company for a specific type of insurance. They are employees of the insurance company they represent. Life insurance, for example, is often sold through exclusive insurance agents.

direct sellers

Companies that market insurance policies through salaried employees, mail-order promotions, newspapers, the Internet, and even vending machines.

Direct sellers are companies that market their policies through salaried employees, mail-order promotions, newspapers, the Internet, and even vending machines. Any type of insurance can be sold directly.

Each type of seller presents both advantages and disadvantages. Independent agents may provide more personalized service and can select among several companies to meet a customer's needs. Exclusive agents can provide personalized service as well but are limited to the policies offered by the one company they represent but their sales commissions tend to be low. For people who know what coverage they need, the lowest-cost insurance premiums can be found with direct sellers.

CONCEPT CHECK 10.2

1. Define *insurance*.
2. Distinguish among the three types of hazards.
3. Why is the principle of indemnity so important to insurance sellers?
4. Identify four key points to review when reading an insurance policy.
5. Summarize how to use deductibles, coinsurance, hazard reduction, and loss reduction to lower the cost of insurance.
6. Differentiate among independent agents, exclusive agents, and direct sellers.

10.3 HOMEOWNER'S INSURANCE

Whether you own or rent housing, you face the possibility of suffering property and liability losses.

10.3a Coverages

Homeowner's insurance combines the liability and property insurance coverages needed by homeowners and renters into a single-package policy.

Property Coverage Homeowner's insurance provides protection for various types of property damage losses, including the following: (1) damage to the dwelling, (2) damage to other structures on the property—referred to as **appurtenant structures**, (3) damage to personal property and dwelling contents, and (4) expenses arising out of a loss of use of the dwelling (for example, food and lodging). Additional coverages are usually provided for such items as debris removal, trees and shrubs, and fire department service charges.

The property protection in a homeowner's policy is written on a named-perils or open-perils basis. **Named-perils policies** cover only those losses caused by perils that are specifically mentioned in the policy. **Open-perils** (or **all-risk**) **policies** cover losses caused by all perils other than those specifically *excluded* by the policy. All-risk policies provide broader coverage because hundreds of perils can cause property losses, but only a few would be excluded. Common exclusions are flood, earthquake, and mold unless caused by some nonexcluded event such as burst water pipes. Coverage for excluded perils can often be purchased for an additional premium if desired.

Liability Coverage Whenever homeowners are negligent or otherwise fail to exercise due caution in protecting visitors, they may potentially suffer a liability loss. Liability insurers have three major duties: (1) the duty to indemnify, and (2) the duty to settle a reasonably claim, and when appropriate (3) the duty to defend. **Homeowner's general liability protection** applies when you are legally liable for the losses of another person and can include legal fees and damages assessed up to the limits of the policy.

Homeowners often wish to take responsibility for the losses of another person regardless of the legal liability. Consider, for example, a guest's child who suffers burns from touching a hot barbecue grill. **Homeowner's no-fault medical payments protection** will pay for bodily injury losses suffered by visitors regardless of who was at fault. In the preceding example, such coverage would help pay for the medical treatment of the visitor's burns. **Homeowner's no-fault property damage protection** will pay for property losses suffered by visitors to your home. An example of such a loss might be damage to a friend's leather coat that was chewed by your dog.

10.3b Types of Homeowner's Insurance Policies

Six distinct types of homeowner's insurance policies exist: HO-1 through HO-3 and HO-8, HO-4 and HO-6, as described in Table 10-1. Each is a standardized package of protections designed to cover the perils that commonly affect homeowners and renters. The same terms and identifying numbers are generally used by most insurance companies.

Policies for Owners of Single-Family Dwellings The **basic form (HO-1)** is a named-perils policy that covers 11 property-damage-causing perils and liability-related exposures. The **broad form (HO-2)** is a named-perils policy that covers not 11 but 18 property-damage-causing perils and liability-related exposures. There are special limits on certain classes of personal property, such as loss of jewelry or money. The **special form (HO-3)** is the most common type purchased by homeowners. It provides all 18-perils protection (except for glass breakage) and protection from liability-related exposures. There are special limits on certain classes of personal property, such as loss of jewelry or money. The **older home form (HO-8)** is a named-perils policy that provides actual-cash-value protection on the dwelling; not replacement protection. The replacement value of older home may be much higher than its market or actual cash value. Thus, the policy only provides that the dwelling be rebuilt to make it serviceable; not rebuilt to the same standards of style and quality.

homeowner's insurance
Combines liability and property insurance coverages that homeowners and renters typically need into single-package policies.

named-perils policies
Cover only losses caused by perils that the policy specifically mentions.

all-risk (open-perils) policies
Cover losses caused by all perils other than those that the policy specifically excludes.

homeowner's general liability protection
Applies when you are legally liable for another person's losses, other than those that arise out of use of vehicles or your professional duties.

special (homeowner's insurance) form (HO-3)
Provides open-perils protection (except for the commonly excluded perils of war, earthquake, and flood) for four types of property losses.

DO IT IN CLASS

Table 10-1   Summary of Homeowner's Insurance Policies

	HO-1 (Basic Form)	HO-2 (Broad Form)	HO-3 (Special Form)
Perils covered (descriptions are given below)	Perils 1–11	Perils 1–18	All perils except those specifically excluded for buildings; perils 1–18 on personal property (does not include glass breakage)
House and any other attached buildings	Amount based on replacement cost, minimum $15,000	Amount based on replacement cost, minimum $15,000	Amount based on replacement cost, minimum $20,000
Detached buildings (appurtenant structures)	10 percent of insurance on the home (minimum)	10 percent of insurance on the home (minimum)	10 percent of insurance on the home (minimum)
Trees, shrubs, plants, etc.	5 percent of insurance on the home, $500 maximum per item	5 percent of insurance on the home, $500 maximum per item	5 percent of insurance on the home, $500 maximum per item
Personal property	50 percent of insurance on the home (minimum)	50 percent of insurance on the home (minimum)	50 percent of insurance on the home (minimum)
Loss of use and/or additional living expense	10 percent of insurance on the home	20 percent of insurance on the home	20 percent of insurance on the home
Credit card, forgery, counterfeit money	$1000	$1000	$1000

Liability coverage/limits (for all policies)		**Special limits of liability**
Comprehensive personal liability	$300,000	For the following classes of personal property, special limits apply on a per-occurrence basis (e.g., per fire or theft): money, coins, bank notes, precious metals (gold, silver, etc.), $200; computers, $5000; securities, deeds, stocks, bonds, tickets, stamps, $1000; watercraft and trailers, including furnishings, equipment, and outboard motors, $1000; trailers other than for watercraft, $1000; jewelry, watches, furs, $1000; silverware, goldware, etc., $2500; guns, $2000.
No-fault medical payments	$1000	
No-fault property damage	$500	

List of perils covered

1. Fire, lightning
2. Windstorm, hail
3. Explosion
4. Riots
5. Damage by aircraft
6. Damage by vehicles owned or operated by people not covered by the homeowner's policy
7. Damage from smoke
8. Vandalism, malicious mischief
9. Theft
10. Glass breakage
11. Volcanic eruption
12. Falling objects (external sources)

13. Weight of ice, snow, sleet
14. Collapse of building or any part of building (specified perils only)
15. Leakage or overflow of water or steam from a plumbing, heating, or air-conditioning system
16. Bursting, cracking, burning, or bulging of a steam or hot water heating system, or of appliances for heating water
17. Freezing of plumbing, heating, and air-conditioning systems and home appliances
18. Injury to electrical appliances and devices (excluding tubes, transistors, and similar electronic components) from short circuits or other accidentally generated currents

Table 10-1   **Summary of Homeowner's Insurance Policies (*Continued*)**

HO-4 (Renter's Contents Broad Form)	HO-6 (For Condominium Owners)	HO-8 (For Older Homes)
Perils 1-9,11-18	Perils 1-18	Perils 1-11
10 percent of personal property insurance on additions and alterations to the apartment	$1000 on owner's additions and alterations to the unit	Amount based on actual cash value of the home
Not covered	Not covered (unless owned solely by the insured)	10 percent of insurance on the home (minimum)
10 percent of personal property insurance, $500 maximum per item	10 percent of personal property insurance, $500 maximum per item	5 percent of insurance on the home, $500 maximum per item
Chosen by the tenant to reflect the value of the items, minimum $6000	Chosen by the homeowner to reflect the value of the items, minimum $6000	50 percent of insurance on the home (minimum)
20 percent of personal property insurance	40 percent of personal property insurance	20 percent of insurance on the home
$1000	$1000	$1000

This table describes the standard policies. Specific items differ from company to company and from state to state. When you want a limit that exceeds the standard limit for your company, you usually can increase the limit by paying an additional premium.

Policies for Renters The **renter's contents broad form (HO-4)** is a named-perils policy that protects the insured from losses to the contents of a dwelling rather than the dwelling itself. It covers 17 perils (except for glass breakage) and provides some liability protection. HO-4 also provides for living expenses if the dwelling is rendered uninhabitable by one of the covered perils.

Policies for Condominium Owners The **condominium form (HO-6)** is a named-perils policy protecting condominium owners from the three principal losses they face: losses to contents and personal property, losses due to the additional living expenses that may arise if one of the covered perils occurs, and liability losses. (The building itself is insured by the management of the condominium.)

FINANCIAL POWER POINT

Renter's Insurance Is Very Inexpensive

Renter's insurance can cost as little as $20 a month and discounts are available if you buy from the same company that provides your auto coverage.

10.3c Buying Homeowner's Insurance

In keeping with the large loss principle you need to select appropriate amounts of coverage on your dwelling and its contents as well as to protect you from liability losses.

How Much Coverage Is Really Needed on Your Dwelling? If you own your home, your first step is to determine the dwelling's replacement value. You could either use the services of a professional liability appraiser and/or consult with your insurance agent to determine replacement value. Note that over one-half of the homes in the United States are said to be underinsured.

Homeowner's insurance policies usually contain a **replacement-cost requirement** that stipulates that a home must be insured for a specified percentage of its replacement value (historically, 80 percent, and companies are increasingly requiring 100 percent). Thus, a home with a replacement value of $200,000 would need to be insured for $160,000 (or perhaps $200,000), and this amount would be the maximum that the insurance company would be obligated to pay for a total loss (after payment of the deductible by the policyholder). If you fail to meet your replacement-cost

renter's contents broad form (HO-4)
Named-perils policy that protects the insured from losses to the contents of a rented dwelling rather than to the dwelling itself.

replacement-cost requirement
Stipulates that a home must be insured for 80 percent of its replacement value (some companies require 100 percent) in order for any loss to be fully covered.

requirement, you will not be considered fully insured and must coinsure partial losses as well. The amount of reimbursement for partial losses will be calculated using the **replacement-cost-requirement formula**:

$$R = (L - D) \times [I \div (RV \times 0.80 \text{ or } 1.00)] \quad \textbf{(10.2)}$$

DO IT IN CLASS

where
- R = Reimbursement payable
- L = Amount of loss
- D = Deductible, if any
- I = Amount of insurance actually carried
- RV = Replacement value of the dwelling

Consider the example of Selena Torres from Las Cruces, New Mexico, who owns a home with a replacement value of $200,000 with a $500 deductible. Selena had insured her home for $144,000, even though the policy required coverage of 80 percent of the replacement cost. Last month a fire in her home caused damage amounting to $80,500. Applying Equation (10.2), Selena's calculations are as follows:

$$R = (\$80,500 - \$500) \times [\$144,000 \div (\$200,000 \times 0.80)]$$
$$= \$80,000 \times (\$144,000 \div \$160,000)$$
$$= \$80,000 \times 0.90 = \$72,000$$

As this calculation shows, Selena will be reimbursed for only $72,000 of her loss. Her failure to insure her house for 80 percent of its replacement cost, or $160,000 ($200,000 × 0.80), means she will be covered for only 90 percent ($144,000/$160,000) of its value, and she must pay 10 percent of any partial loss—in this case, $8000.

Meeting an 80 percent replacement-cost requirement enables you to avoid coinsurance on small losses but might still result in inadequate coverage on large losses that, though rare, exceed the policy limit. Thus, it is wise to insure your dwelling for 100 percent of its replacement cost. You will also want to sign up for **inflation guard protection** to have your insurance company increase your coverage automatically each year to keep up with inflation.

A standard property insurance policy will replace a damaged property so that it is the same or similar as before. If a house was built a long time ago, building a similar structure as a replacement may not satisfy new building code regulations that will be required in the rebuild. This is especially true in areas that may have experienced natural disasters such as wildfires, windstorms, and flooding. **Law and ordinance protection** is a special insurance endorsement that pays for demolishment and/or repairs to meet modern building standards.

DID YOU KNOW ?

How to Insure High-Value Items

Some high-value items of personal property are subject to specific item limits in the homeowner's policy. For example, the typical policy provides maximum coverages of $200 for cash, $5000 for personal computers, and $1000 for jewelry. This is because most people do not have such items above these values and do not need higher levels of coverage. If your home inventory reveals a higher valuation on such items, you can simply ask your company for extra coverage and pay the higher premium required.

How Much Coverage Is Needed on Your Personal Property? Making a **personal property inventory** of, and placing a value on, all the contents of your home are time-consuming but important tasks. Table 10-2 shows the inventory and valuation for the contents of and personal property in a typical living room. You should conduct such an inventory for each room, the basement, garage, shed, and yard possessions. When totaled, these values will enable you to select proper policy coverage limits. Most homeowner's policies are designed to automatically cover contents and personal property for up to 50 percent of the coverage on the home. For example, if your home is insured for $240,000, you automatically would have $120,000 in personal property insurance. If you need more coverage, simply notify your agent.

Notice that Table 10-2 lists three estimates for the value of the contents of a room: the purchase price, the actual cash value, and the replacement cost. Historically, property insurance policies paid only the **actual cash value** of an item of personal property, which represents the purchase price of the property less depreciation. The **actual-cash-value (ACV) formula** is:

$$ACV = P - [CA \times (P \div LE)] \qquad (10.3)$$

where

   P = Purchase price of the property
CA = Current age of the property in years
 LE = Life expectancy of the property in years

Consider the case of Marianna Kinard, a music teacher from Joanna, South Carolina, whose nine-year-old heating/air-conditioning unit was struck by lightning. The unit cost $2400 when new and had a total life expectancy of 12 years. Its actual cash value when it was struck by lightning was:

$$\begin{aligned} ACV &= \$2400 - [9 \times (\$2400 \div 12)] \\ &= \$2400 - (9 \times \$200) \\ &= \$600 \end{aligned}$$

Marianna could not replace the unit for $600. A more realistic replacement cost might be $3000. **Contents replacement-cost protection** is an option sometimes available in homeowner's insurance policies that pays the full replacement cost of any

actual cash value (of personal property)
Represents the purchase price of the property less depreciation.

contents replacement-cost protection
Option sometimes available in homeowner's insurance policies (including the renter's form) that pays the full replacement cost of any personal property.

Table 10-2   Personal Property Checklist: Living Room

Item	Date Purchased	Purchase Price	Actual Cash Value	Replacement Cost
Furniture				
Sofa	8/10	$ 750	$ 375	$ 950
Chair	11/08	250	100	375
Lounger	12/11	575	300	695
Ottoman	12/11	100	50	120
Bookcase	4/13	275	225	300
End table (two)	7/14	300	250	300
Appliances				
TV	1/14	550	500	600
DVD	6/13	400	300	400
Wall clock	7/08	60	10	100
Furnishings				
Carpet	6/07	375	50	600
Painting	12/11	125	225	225
Floor lamp	4/09	150	50	225
Art (three items)	10/13	600	600	800
Table lamp	4/09	75	40	100
Table lamp	5/13	125	100	135
Throw pillows	7/10	45	20	60
TOTAL		**$4,755**	**$3,195**	**$5,985**

DID YOU KNOW

What's Covered while You Are Away at College

College students and their parents sometimes wonder about the student's insurance coverage while attending school away from home. Students who have moved into their own residence to live year-round need to buy their own renter's and automobile insurance policies. This is because the family's homeowner's and auto coverages will only apply if the student (1) lives in a dorm or fraternity/sorority house or (2) lives in off-campus housing in what is clearly a temporary arrangement (that is, the student returns home during semester breaks and over the summer).

If you are covered by your family's policies, here are some guidelines to remember:

1. *Property stored away from home is often only covered for up to 10 percent of the coverage on the home.*

If the family home is insured for $150,000, for example, then $15,000 of total coverage applies regardless of how many students are in the family.

2. *Expensive items such as jewelry or computers are subject to specific limits in the homeowner's insurance policy. Auto insurance rates are based on where the vehicle is garaged (or parked) at night. The insurance agent should be notified if a covered vehicle is used while away at school. It is better to pay a slightly higher rate than to face denial of coverage for a loss because of misinformation. A discount is common for a college student listed on a parent's policy if the student does not have a car at school and the school is at least 100 miles from the parent's home.*

FINANCIAL POWER POINT

Stay out of the Doghouse

One-third of homeowner's insurance liability claims are associated with dog bites. Notify your insurance company that you have a dog, because they might not renew your policy if you make a claim and did not tell them about the animal. And raise your liability limits for better protection.

personal property. The standard limitation that applies to contents (50 percent of insured value of the dwelling) remains in effect if contents replacement-cost protection is purchased. The overall limit on contents may need to be raised, as it is easy to reach the 50 percent figure when replacement-cost valuation is used.

How Much Coverage Is Needed for Liability Losses? Newly written standard homeowner's policies provide $300,000 ($100,000 for older policies unless amended) of personal liability coverage, $1000 of no-fault medical expense coverage, and $500 of no-fault property damage coverage. It is smart to apply the large-loss principle here and increase the policy limits for all three of these coverages (or consider an umbrella liability policy discussed later). The extra cost is small because the odds of such larger losses are low.

CONCEPT CHECK 10.3

1. Describe the types of losses covered under the property insurance portion of a homeowner's policy.

2. Give three examples of liability protection under homeowner's insurance policies.

3. Name the three types of homeowner's insurance policies for most residences; HO-3, HO-4, and HO-6.

4. Identify four types of personal property for which the covered loss is limited to a specific dollar amount under standard homeowner's insurance policies (see Table 10-1).

5. List the three questions you should ask yourself when determining the policy limits for a homeowner's insurance policy.

10.4 AUTOMOBILE INSURANCE

Driving a car is the largest single exposure to catastrophic losses for most Americans. A split-second error in driving judgment or bad luck can result in many tens of thousands of dollars of automobile-related property damage and personal injury losses. Automobile insurance combines the liability and property insurance coverages needed by automobile owners and drivers into a single-package policy. It is illegal to operate a motor vehicle without assuming financial responsibility for any losses you might cause; therefore, most states require automobile owners to purchase automobile insurance to meet this responsibility (although because of lack of enforcement there are millions of illegally uninsured drivers on the roads).

10.4a Losses Covered

Automobile insurance combines four distinct types of coverage: (1) liability insurance, (2) medical payments insurance, (3) protection against uninsured and underinsured motorists, and (4) insurance for physical damage to the insured automobile. Each coverage has its own policy limits, conditions, and exclusions. Table 10-3 summarizes the coverage provided by automobile insurance policies for people not specifically excluded in the policy.

Coverage A—Liability Insurance Liability insurance covers the insured when he or she is held responsible for losses suffered by others. Two types of liability can arise out of the ownership and operation of an automobile. **Automobile bodily injury liability** occurs when a driver or car owner is held legally responsible for bodily injury losses suffered by other people, including pedestrians. **Automobile property damage liability**

> **LEARNING OBJECTIVE 4**
>
> Design an automobile insurance program to meet your needs.

automobile insurance
Combines the liability and property insurance coverages that most car owners and drivers need into a single-package policy.

automobile bodily injury liability
Occurs when a driver or car owner is held legally responsible for bodily injury losses that other people, including pedestrians, suffer.

automobile property damage liability
Occurs when a driver or car owner is held legally responsible for damage to others' property.

Table 10-3 Summary of Automobile Insurance Coverages

Section	Type of Coverage	People Covered	Property Covered	Recommended Limits
A	LIABILITY INSURANCE (1) Bodily injury liability	Relatives living in insured's household driving an owned or nonowned automobile	Not applicable	At least legally required minimums or $250,000/$500,000, whichever is greater
	(2) Property damage liability	Relatives living in insured's household driving an owned or nonowned automobile	Automobiles and other property damaged by insured driver while driving	At least legally required minimum or $100,000, whichever is greater
B	MEDICAL PAYMENTS	Passengers in insured automobile or nonowned automobile driven by insured family member	Not applicable	$50,000 or higher
C	UNINSURED AND UNDERINSURED	Anyone driving insured car with permission and insured family members driving nonowned automobiles with permission	Not applicable	$50,000/$100,000 or higher, if available
D	PHYSICAL DAMAGE (1) Collision	Anyone driving insured car with permission	Insured automobile	Actual cash value less deductible
	(2) Comprehensive	Not applicable	Insured automobile and its attached contents	Actual cash value less deductible

FINANCIAL POWER POINT

Bodily Injury Liability Losses Can Be Very High

A one-day stay in a hospital intensive care unit can cost more than $50,000. An accident with multiple injuries can result in liability losses in excess of $300,000. When buying auto insurance policy, always select very high liability limits.

occurs when a driver or car owner is held legally responsible for damage to the property of others. Such damage can include damage to another vehicle, a building, or roadside signs and utility poles.

The most common type of automobile insurance policy is the **family auto policy (FAP)**. The policy limits for FAPs are quoted as **split liability limits**, usually three numbers such as 100/300/50, with each number representing a multiple of $1000 (Figure 10-2). The first number gives the maximum that will be paid for liability claims for *one* person's bodily injury losses resulting from an automobile accident ($100,000 in our example). The second number indicates the overall maximum that will be paid for bodily injury liability losses to *any number* of people resulting from an automobile accident ($300,000 in our example). The third number specifies the maximum that will be paid for property damage liability losses resulting from an accident ($50,000 in our example).

In some auto insurance policies, the liability limits are stated as a **single liability limit** such as $250,000. Under such policies, all property and bodily injury liability losses resulting from an accident would be paid until the limit is reached. Liability insurance covers only the insured for losses suffered by others. It does not pay for bodily injury losses suffered by the insured or for property damage to the insured's car. Injured passengers of an at-fault driver may collect under the driver's liability coverage, but only after exhausting the coverage provided under medical payments (discussed below) and only after reimbursement is made to people injured in other vehicles or as pedestrians.

Driving a rental car exposes you to the same potential liabilities as driving your own vehicle. If you have automobile liability insurance, such liabilities will usually be covered while you drive a rented car. Check your coverage before you rent a car so you can avoid buying overpriced insurance from the rental agency.

Figure 10-2 Automobile Liability Insurance Policy Limits

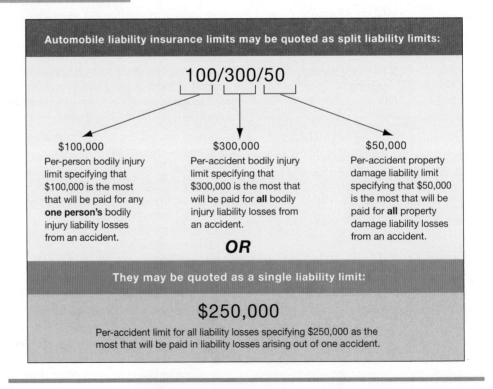

Automobile liability insurance limits may be quoted as split liability limits:

100/300/50

$100,000
Per-person bodily injury limit specifying that $100,000 is the most that will be paid for any **one person's** bodily injury liability losses from an accident.

$300,000
Per-accident bodily injury limit specifying that $300,000 is the most that will be paid for **all** bodily injury liability losses from an accident.

$50,000
Per-accident property damage liability limit specifying that $50,000 is the most that will be paid for **all** property damage liability losses from an accident.

OR

They may be quoted as a single liability limit:

$250,000
Per-accident limit for all liability losses specifying $250,000 as the most that will be paid in liability losses arising out of one accident.

Drivers need to make sure they have sufficient liability coverage in the event of an accident—the person at fault is typically responsible for all damages.

Coverage B—Medical Payments Insurance Automobile medical payments insurance can help pay medical expenses no matter who's at fault. It covers you, your passengers, and any family members driving or riding in the insured vehicle at the time of the accident.

Medical payments coverage is subject to a single policy limit, which is applied per person, per accident. Medical payments also protect insured family members who are injured while passengers in any car or who are injured by a car when on foot or riding a bicycle.

Under medical payments, drivers and their injured passengers collect directly from the driver's insurance. If the driver was not at fault, then the driver's insurer pays the claims and subsequently may choose to exercise subrogation rights against the at-fault party. **Subrogation rights** allow an insurer to take action against a negligent third party (and that party's insurance company) to obtain reimbursement for payments made to an insured.

Some states have adopted a version of no-fault automobile insurance where insureds collect first (and possibly *only*) from their own insurance companies for bodily injury losses. In these states, the medical payments coverage is often referred to as **personal injury protection (PIP)** covers the driver and any passengers for bodily injury losses as well as possibly lost wages and rehabilitation expenses. Subrogation rights are limited in no-fault states.

Coverage C—Uninsured and Underinsured Motorist Insurance What if you are injured in an accident caused by a driver who has no or insufficient auto liability insurance? You would first be covered by your own medical payments auto insurance but that almost surely will not cover all of the losses. **Uninsured motorist insurance** protects you and your passengers from bodily injury losses (and, in a few states, property damage losses) resulting from an automobile accident caused by an uninsured motorist. **Underinsured motorist insurance** protects the insured and his or her passengers from bodily injury losses (and, in some cases, property damage losses) when the at-fault driver has insurance but that coverage is insufficient to reimburse the losses. This insurance is a smart risk-management choice and carries a very low premium—often less than $75 per year.

Coverage D—Physical Damage Insurance Automobile physical damage insurance provides protection against losses caused by damage to your vehicle.

Collision insurance reimburses an insured for losses resulting from a collision with another car or object or from a rollover. The insurer pays the cost of repairing or replacing the insured's car, regardless of who is at fault. When the other driver is at fault, subrogation rights may allow the insurer to obtain reimbursement through that driver's property damage

automobile medical payments insurance

Insurance that covers bodily injury losses suffered by the driver of the insured vehicle and any passengers, regardless of who is at fault.

subrogation rights

Allow an insurer to take action against a negligent third party (and that party's insurance company) to obtain reimbursement for payments made to an insured.

uninsured and underinsured motorist insurance

Coverage that an insured can purchase as part of automobile insurance that covers the insured in an accident when an uninsured or underinsured driver is at fault.

collision insurance

Reimburses insureds for losses to their vehicles resulting from a collision with another car or object or from a rollover.

DID YOU KNOW

Turn Bad Habits into Good Ones

Do You Do This?

Assume your parents' homeowner's policy covers you at school

Base your potential auto liability losses on your own financial status

Base your insurance decisions on how much coverage will cost

Buy low limits on your liability coverages

Buy policies with the lowest possible deductibles

Do This Instead!

Confirm that you are correct and, if not, buy your own renter's policy

Estimate the maximum loss others could suffer if you caused an accident

Base your decisions on the potential losses you could suffer

Buy higher limits and or an umbrella liability policy

Raise the deductibles on your policies and apply the savings toward higher limits

DID YOU KNOW

Quick and Easy Steps Can Cut Your Auto and Homeowner's Insurance Bill

There is no point in paying more for insurance than necessary. Here are some suggestions for achieving this goal.

Select Appropriate Coverages and Limits. Buy only needed coverages but be certain to select policy limits appropriate for the largest potential losses. Choosing low limits is unwise, as you will be personally liable if an accident exceeds those limits. Elimination of some coverages, such as comprehensive or uninsured/underinsured motorist insurance, would yield little savings while sharply reducing protection.

Take Advantage of Discounts. Most insurance companies offer discounted premiums for policyholders who insure multiple vehicles or buy multiple policies (for example, both automobile and homeowner's insurance) from them.

Engage in Loss Control. Many companies charge lower premiums to policyholders who take steps to reduce the probability or severity of loss. For example, discounts are available if you install dead-bolt door locks or a fire extinguisher in your home. Ask your agent what you need to do to qualify.

Raise Your Deductible. Raising your deductible can save you hundreds of dollars per year. You may even wish to eliminate this coverage altogether for cars having a book value of less than $2000.

Shop Around for the Lowest-Cost Coverage. Insurance premiums from one company can be two or three times as much as those charged by another company for essentially the same coverage, so considerable savings can be realized by seeking quotes from multiple agents and direct sellers. To obtain a quote, go on the Internet and provide some companies your information. You can also telephone an agent or a direct seller. Also see a quote service such as www.insure.com or www.insweb.com. Make sure you provide sufficient accurate information in your request to obtain the best quote possible.

Become Insurance Wise. The insurance regulatory agency in your state (to find yours, visit www.naic.org /state_web_map.htm) may publish helpful insurance buyer's guides that discuss how to buy specific types of insurance, compare premiums, and rate the companies providing such insurance. In addition, *Consumer Reports* magazine periodically publishes feature articles that discuss insurance.

---

comprehensive automobile insurance

Protects against property damage losses to an insured vehicle caused by perils other than collision and rollover.

liability protection. Collision insurance is written with a deductible that usually ranges from $100 to $1000. If you carry collision insurance coverage on your own car, you are generally covered when you drive someone else's car with that person's permission. Most automobile insurance policies provide for collision coverage on rental cars if such coverage applies to your owned vehicle. Check with your agent before you rent a car.

Comprehensive automobile insurance helps pay for damages that are not caused by a collision or rollover. Covered perils include fire, theft, vandalism, hail, and wind, among many others, and it typically carries a deductible ranging from $100 to $1000.

When you have a loss that qualifies under collision or comprehensive insurance, an estimate of the repair cost will be made. If this estimate exceeds the value that the insurance company puts on the vehicle, the lower of the two figures is paid, less any deductible. Insurance companies set vehicle values based on the average current selling price of vehicles of the same make, model, and age. Insurance companies will not give you more money because your wrecked vehicle had very low mileage and was in near-perfect condition.

Other Valuable Protections Two other low- or no-cost, but helpful, coverages are available to automobile insurance buyers. **Towing coverage** pays the cost of having a disabled vehicle transported for repairs. It usually pays only the first $25 or $50 per occurrence but will cover any towing need—not just assistance needed due to an accident. **Rental reimbursement** coverage provides a rental car when the insured's vehicle is being repaired after an accident or has been stolen. It often has a daily payout limit of $20 to $30 and, therefore, may provide only part of the funds needed to obtain replacement transportation.

DID YOU KNOW

You Can Change Insurers at Any Time

You do not have to wait until renewal time to change insurance companies. If shopping around reveals that you can save money and/or improve your coverage with a new company, consider doing so right away. Contact the new company first to ensure that you have been accepted and then contact the old company. You will receive a refund of the unused premium less a minor processing charge when you cancel.

DID YOU KNOW

Money Websites for Managing Property and Liability Risk

Informative websites for managing property and liability risk, including sites that compare policies and prices are:

Insure.com (www.insure.com/home-insurance/ and www.insure.com/car-insurance//)

Insurance Institute for Highway Safety (www.iihs.org/ratings/default.aspx)

Insweb (www.insweb.com)

Kiplinger's Personal Finance (www.kiplinger.com/fronts/channels/insurance/)

National Association of Insurance Commissioners (www.naic.org/store_home.htm)

National Flood Insurance Program (www.FloodSmart.gov)

New York Times (www.topics.nytimes.com/your-money/insurance/home-insurance/index.html)

MSN Money (www.money.msn.com/insurance/)

DID YOU KNOW

The Best Way to Title Vehicles

Couples may be tempted to put major assets in both their names, and sometimes this is the best way to go. For automobiles, however, the decision is different because the owner of a vehicle is legally liable for accidents caused by the driver. If both partners own an automobile, both could be sued. Thus, it is smart to title an automobile in only one name. For couples with two vehicles, each could be owned separately.

CONCEPT CHECK 10.4

1. Identify the four types of automobile insurance coverage.

2. Explain the meaning of the numbers 100/200/75.

3. Identify who is protected by medical payments coverage.

4. Distinguish between collision and comprehensive insurance.

5. Explain why selecting a policy with a high deductible and high liability limits is better than one with a low deductible and low liability limits.

10.5 BUY SPECIALIZED PROTECTION FOR OTHER LOSS EXPOSURES

LEARNING OBJECTIVE 5

Describe other types of property and liability insurance.

umbrella (excess) liability insurance

Catastrophic liability policy that covers liability losses in excess of those covered by any underlying homeowner's, automobile, or professional liability policy.

Some people need protection against property and liability losses that are not covered by or exceed the limits of the standard homeowner's or automobile insurance policies.

10.5a Umbrella Liability Insurance

Umbrella liability insurance is a catastrophic liability policy that covers liability losses over and above those covered by any underlying homeowner's, automobile, or professional liability policy. Such policies provide two benefits. First, the types of losses covered are broader than those recognized by comprehensive personal liability insurance. Second, umbrella policies provide for high dollar amounts of coverage over and above the basic policies. To be covered for these higher limits, you must carry the basic coverages as well.

Figure 10-3 shows how umbrella policies work. In this example, the insured has an automobile insurance policy with total liability limits of $600,000 (the total liability coverage for one accident is $500,000 per accident plus $100,000 for property damage), a homeowner's insurance policy with liability protection of $200,000, and a $500,000 professional liability insurance policy. If the insured bought an umbrella policy with a $1 million limit and then experienced a $750,000 professional liability loss, the umbrella policy would provide protection of $250,000 after the professional liability policy limits were exceeded. Umbrella policies are relatively low in cost when purchased to supplement basic policies (perhaps $150 to $200 per year for an additional $1 million of protection) and protect against virtually all liability exposures that a person might face.

Figure 10-3   **How Umbrella Liability Policies Work**

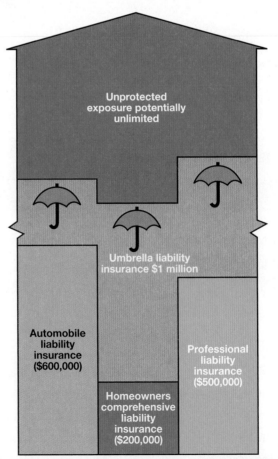

Types of Exposures

DID YOU KNOW

How Automobile Insurance Would Apply to an Accident

DO IT IN CLASS

Just how the many provisions in an automobile insurance policy apply to a specific accident mystifies many people. As a result, the claims process may generate considerable dissatisfaction after an accident. The example given here and outlined in the following chart is intended to clarify the application of the multiple coverages and limits.

In September of last year, Olivia Redman, a college student from Itta Benna, Mississippi, caused a serious accident when she failed to yield to an approaching vehicle while attempting to make a left turn. Olivia suffered a broken arm and facial cuts, resulting in medical costs of $5254. Her passenger, Philip Windsor, was seriously injured with head and neck wounds requiring surgery, a two-week hospital stay, and rehabilitation. Philip's injuries generated medical costs of $137,650. The driver of the other car, Patrick Monk, suffered serious back and internal injuries and facial burns that resulted in some disfigurement. His medical care costs totaled $122,948. His passenger, Annette Monk, suffered cuts and bruises requiring minor medical care at a cost of $1423.

Both cars were completely destroyed in the accident. Olivia's 10-year-old Buick was valued at $2150. Patrick's Mazda Miata was valued at $19,350. The force of the impact spun Patrick's car around, causing it to destroy a traffic-signal control box (valued at $3650).

Both Olivia and Patrick were covered by family automobile policies with liability limits of $50,000/$10,000/$25,000 and medical payment limits of $10,000 per person and $100 collision coverage deductibles. In total, Olivia had to pay $11,048 out of her own pocket, as the policy limits were exceeded by Patrick's and Phillip's medical costs.

An additional point needs to be raised concerning situations in which an accident victim suffers serious, permanent injuries that are not fully reimbursed by the insurance policy protecting the driver at fault. In our example, Patrick suffered very painful injuries resulting in permanent disfigurement. He may wish to sue Olivia for his pain and suffering and for his unpaid medical expenses. If he were to file such a suit, Olivia would be provided with legal assistance by her insurance company. Any judgment that exceeds the policy limits (remember that Olivia's per-person policy limit has already been reached) will be Olivia's responsibility, however. Both Olivia and Patrick were terribly underinsured.

Olivia Redman's Accident: Who Pays What?

Coverage	Olivia's Policy	Patrick's Policy
Liability (limits)	(50/100/25)	(50/100/25)
Bodily injury:		
Patrick Monk	$50,000	
Annette Monk	1,423	
Philip Windsor	43,577**	
Property damage:		
Patrick Monk's car	19,350	
Traffic-signal control box	3,650	
Medical payments (limits):	($10,000)	($10,000)
Patrick Monk		10,000*
Annette Monk		1,423
Olivia Redman	5,254	
Philip Windsor	10,000	
Collision coverage (limits):	(ACV, $100 deductible)	(ACV, $100 deductible)
Olivia's car	2,050	
Patrick's car		19,250*
Olivia's out-of-pocket expenses:		
Patrick Monk's bodily injury	72,948	
Phillip Windsor's bodily injury	84,073	
Olivia's collision insurance deductible	100	
TOTAL	**$157,121**	

* Also, included in Olivia's column because Patrick's company filed a claim against Olivia by exercising its subrogation rights.

** Olivia's liability policy paid a total of $55,423 to the passengers in the other car leaving only $43,577 of the $100,000 per accident limit remaining to reimburse Phillip for his medical care that exceeded the medical payments limit of $10,000.

10.5b　Flood and Earthquake Insurance

Standard homeowner's insurance policies exclude losses caused by flood, sinkholes, and earthquakes. This is because these types of losses are subject to **adverse selection**. This occurs when people who are most likely to suffer such losses will know that. And those that are least likely to suffer a loss will know that, too. As a result, those people with high probabilities of loss will want to buy the coverage and those will extremely low probabilities will not, thereby violating the law of large numbers. But if you live in a flood-prone area or earthquake zone, your risk of loss should be addressed. The **National Flood Insurance Program** is a federal government program that makes flood insurance available in counties where flood is common (see www.FloodSmart.gov).

Earthquake insurance can be purchased only from a private insurance company either as a separate policy or as an endorsement (an addition to a standard policy) to an existing homeowner's or renter's insurance policy. **Sinkhole insurance** covers damage to your home due to ground collapse. Coverage and availability varies by state but is especially important consideration in Florida, Tennessee, and other states where sinkholes are possible.

endorsement

An addition to a standard insurance policy designed to expand coverage for a special area of need.

professional liability insurance/malpractice insurance

Protects individuals and organizations that provide professional services when they are held liable for their clients' losses.

10.5c　Professional Liability Insurance

Professional liability insurance (sometimes called **malpractice insurance** or **errors and omissions insurance**) protects individuals and organizations that provide professional services (physician, lawyers, psychologists, etc.) when they are held liable for the financial losses suffered by their clients due to professional mistakes

RUN THE NUMBERS

Buying Automobile Insurance

Even though automobile insurance premiums can vary by hundreds of dollars annually among companies, only 40 percent of consumers shop around when they buy or renew coverage. It is especially important to re-shop for automobile insurance after you have had an accident or major ticket or before purchasing

a vehicle. Insurance companies differ in how they handle these changes and a new company might be a better option for you.

You can use Worksheet 45 available in the *My Personal Financial Planner* workbook accompanying this text to record automobile insurance premium quotations obtained from insurers.

DID YOU KNOW

Sean's Success Story

Sean's success as a personal financial manager is reflected in his tangible assets. He owns a two-year-old luxury vehicle and a motorcycle. He has all the latest home entertainment equipment in his condo in an upscale neighborhood. He also has substantial coin and stamp collections as both hobbies and investments. He recently undertook a thorough risk-management process to assess his exposures

to risk and assess the ways to best address the risks he faces. As a result, he bought additional insurance to cover his personal property and stamps and coins. He also raised his automobile insurance deductible to $1000 and used the savings to raise his liability limits to 250/500/100. He also purchased a $2 million umbrella liability policy. Sean feels more secure now and plans to reassess his risk-management efforts every year.

or omissions. Policy limits, deductibles, premiums, and other characteristics of such policies vary widely depending on the profession involved. A $1 million professional liability policy written for a family therapist may cost as little as $500 per year; in contrast, some surgeons pay $60,000 or more per year for professional liability insurance. In some state and for certain professions, professional liability insurance may be required by law.

10.5d Floater Policies

Floater policies provide all-risk protection for accident and theft losses to movable property (such as cameras, sporting equipment, MP3 players, and clothing) regardless of where the loss occurs. Limited floater protection for personal property is part of the standard homeowner's insurance policy. Automobile insurance policies only cover portable personal property that is permanently installed in the vehicle. Property owned for business purposes is excluded from both types of insurance. This means that a mechanic's tools, a lawyer's books, and a karaoke DJ's equipment, for example, would not be covered. A separate floater policy would be required if you have extensive portable property whether for personal or business use.

floater policies
Provide all-risk protection for accident and theft losses to movable property regardless of where the loss occurs.

CONCEPT CHECK 10.5

1. Explain how purchasing an umbrella liability insurance policy applies the large-loss principle.

2. Are you preparing for a professional career that might expose you to liability losses? How might you protect yourself from such losses?

3. Give two examples of someone who might want to purchase a floater insurance policy.

10.6 HOW TO COLLECT ON YOUR PROPERTY AND LIABILITY LOSSES

The direct benefit of owning insurance becomes evident when a loss occurs and it is time to file a claim. Even when you have a legitimate claim, however, you may want to consider whether you should do so. A small claim might be best ignored as it may increase your rates, as one claim increases premiums, on average, 9 percent the following year. Of course, if you have a large claim, you would want to file for its recovery. Here are the four steps that you should take when you have a loss.

10.6a 1. Contact Your Insurance Agent about Your Loss

If you decide to file a claim, the first step—contacting your agent—should be taken as soon as possible. Follow the agent's instructions regarding who to contact next (including filing a written police report) and what to do to minimize the loss. Then keep the company informed of everything relevant to the loss in a timely manner until the claim is settled. The tenacious claimant is more likely to collect fully on a loss.

LEARNING OBJECTIVE 6
Summarize how to make an insurance claim.

FINANCIAL POWER POINT

Check Your Home's Claims History because It Affects Your Rates

Much like an individual's credit history, a home has a history, too, of its insurance claims. Claims that have occurred in the last seven years are included. You can check your home's claims history at www.personalreports.lexisnexis.com /homesellers_disclosure_report/landing.jsp.

ADVICE FROM A PROFESSIONAL

Applying the Large-Loss Principle to Property and Liability Insurance

You should always select insurance coverage limits for the highest possible loss. Although rare, such losses can destroy your financial future. That thinking underlies the large-loss principle discussed earlier. Here is how to apply the principle to property and liability insurance.

For your personal property insurance, you should select limits that equal the value of the property involved. A $240,000 home should be insured for $240,000. Better yet, you can add **extended-replacement coverage**, which covers the difference if the price to rebuild exceeds your dwelling limit. Select all-risk policies rather than named-peril policies. Yes, the cost may be higher, but the loss of your property could be much worse.

The purchase of an umbrella liability policy is the best way to apply the large-loss principle to liability insurance. Never buy the legal minimums for auto insurance. Causing an accident that destroys one newer-model vehicle can exceed most state minimum limits.

You can afford to apply the large-loss principle through the use of higher deductibles. Ask yourself: "What is the largest loss I can afford to cover myself?" Then choose the highest deductible that does not exceed what you can afford to cover. The money saved by selecting a higher deductible can be used to pay for higher policy limits. For example, on a 100/300/50 auto policy with a $100 deductible, you can save as much as $300 per year by simply raising the deductibles to $1000! Then you can apply some of those savings to buy a $1,000,000 umbrella policy to protect yourself from a catastrophe.

Gerard J. Mellnick
Schoolcraft College, Livonia, Michigan

DID YOU KNOW

Your Worst Financial Blunders in Managing Property and Liability Risk

Based on others' financial woes, you will make mistakes in personal finance when you:

1. *Buy only the legally required minimum liability coverage on your vehicle.*

2. *Pay high premiums because you select low deductibles on property insurance for your home and car.*

3. *Fail to keep good records (e.g., lists, photos, videos, receipts) that could serve to document insured property losses.*

FINANCIAL POWER POINT

Use Your Company's Claims Phone App

Many insurance companies have developed mobile device apps for the reporting of losses covered by their policies. Contact your agent to see if such an app is available. A similar app is available from the National Association of Insurance Commissioners at www.insureuonline.org/auto_page.htm.

10.6b 2. Document Your Loss

You carry the burden of proof whenever a property or liability loss occurs. Adequate documentation of the circumstances and the amount of the loss is essential. In the absence of such documentation, the insurance company will generally interpret the situation in the manner most favorable to its interests, not yours.

The best way to document a theft, fire, or other personal property loss is with a visual inventory. Photographs or videotapes of all valuable property including a written record of the date of purchase, price paid, description, model name and number, and serial number (if any) is very helpful. Keep such records in a safe-deposit box, in a file cabinet at work, or with a relative. If a loss occurs, present a *copy* of your documentation to the agent or insurance company.

You should always file a police report if you become involved in an automobile accident. Make a written record of the accident giving the time and place of the accident, the direction of travel and estimated speed of the cars involved, the road and weather conditions, the behavior of all parties involved and a diagram of the accident scene. Also, obtain the names, driver's license numbers and contact information for witnesses. Police reports are also advisable (and often required) when filing a theft claim of any type.

10.6c 3. File Your Claim

An **insurance claim** is a formal request to the insurance company for reimbursement for a covered loss. All of the documentation and information will be requested by the insurance agent or a **claims adjuster** (the person designated by the insurance company to assess whether the loss is covered and to determine the dollar amount that the company will pay). Insurance companies require that claims be made in writing, although the adjuster may assist you in completing the necessary forms.

10.6d 4. Sign a Release

Part of the final step in the claims-settlement process is to sign the **release** which is an insurance document affirming that the dollar amount of the loss settlement is accepted as full and complete reimbursement and that the insured will make no additional claims for the loss against the insurance company. Signing the release absolves the insurance company of any further responsibility for the loss. Resist the temptation to sign a release until you are sure that the full magnitude of the loss has become evident.

insurance claim
Formal request to the insurance company for reimbursement for a covered loss.

claims adjuster
Person designated by the insurance company to assess whether the loss is covered and to determine the dollar amount that the company will pay.

release
Insurance document affirming that the dollar amount of the loss settlement is accepted as full and complete reimbursement.

DO IT NOW!

You know more about personal finance after reading this chapter, so get started right now by:

1. *Identifying your exposures to risk and the magnitude of the losses that could occur.*

2. *Assessing your automobile insurance coverage and making changes as necessary.*

3. *Buying renter's insurance if you rent your housing.*

CONCEPT CHECK 10.6

1. What is the best way to establish documentation for potential losses to your personal property?

2. Describe what you should do to file a claim most effectively when involved in an automobile accident.

3. Describe the term *release* and explain why signing a release too soon might work to your disadvantage.

WHAT DO YOU RECOMMEND *NOW?*

Now that you have read the chapter on risk management and property liability insurance, what would you recommend to Nick and Amber in the case at the beginning of the chapter regarding:

1. The risk-management steps they should take to update their insurance coverages?

2. The relationship between severity and frequency of loss when deciding whether to buy insurance?

3. Adequately insuring their home?

4. The use of deductibles and policy limits to keep their automobile insurance premiums at a manageable level while still maintaining vital coverage?

© iStockphoto.com/Janalva Design

BIG PICTURE SUMMARY OF LEARNING OBJECTIVES

LO1 **Apply the risk-management process to address the risks to your property and income.**

Personal financial managers practice risk management to protect their present and future assets and income. Risk management entails identifying the sources of risk, evaluating risk and potential losses, selecting the appropriate risk-handling mechanism, implementing and administering the risk-management plan, and evaluating and adjusting the plan periodically.

LO2 **Explain how insurance works to reduce risk.**

Insurance is a mechanism for reducing pure risk by having a larger number of individuals share in the financial losses suffered by all members of the group. It is used to protect against pure risk but cannot be used to protect against speculative risk, which carries the potential for gain as well as loss. Likewise, insurance cannot be used to provide payment in excess of the actual financial loss suffered. Insurance consists of two elements: the reduction of pure risk through application of the law of large numbers, and the sharing of losses.

LO3 **Design a homeowner's or renter's insurance program to meet your needs.**

Homeowner's insurance is designed to protect homeowners and renters from property and liability losses. Six types of homeowner's insurance are available, including one geared toward renters. Homeowner's policies can be purchased on a named-perils or an open-perils basis.

LO4 **Design an automobile insurance program to meet your needs.**

Automobile insurance is designed to protect the insured against property and liability losses arising from use of a motor vehicle. These policies typically provide liability insurance (both bodily injury and property damage liability), medical payments or personal injury protection insurance, property insurance on your car, and underinsured and uninsured motorist insurance. The most commonly purchased type of automobile insurance is the family automobile policy. The premium for automobile insurance is based on the characteristics of the insured driver, including age, gender, marital status, and driving record.

LO5 **Describe other types of property and liability insurance.**

Other important types of property and liability insurance include floater policies (to protect personal property regardless of its location), professional liability insurance, and umbrella liability insurance.

LO6 **Summarize how to make an insurance claim.**

The insured is responsible for documenting and verifying a loss. Photographs or videotapes of the insured property are ideal for documenting claims made under a homeowner's insurance policy. A police report provides the best documentation for claims made under an automobile insurance policy.

LET'S TALK ABOUT IT

1. **Insurance Underwriting.** How do you feel about being grouped into classes in the insurance underwriting process? Do you feel that insurance companies should treat all such groups of people alike?

2. **Actual Cash Value.** Many people complain that property insurance policies should pay more than what the insurance companies say is the actual cash value of the property, such as for a used motor vehicle with low mileage that is in near-perfect condition. How do you feel about this issue, and what would happen if insurance companies were more generous in their reimbursements?

3. **Auto Liability Limits.** Do you know the liability limits on the automobile insurance policy under which you are covered? Are the limits appropriate?

4. **Personal Property Protection.** Is your personal property, such as furniture and computer, covered under a homeowner's or renter's insurance policy? If not, why not? If so, what are the policy limits?

5. **Auto Insurance Claims.** What experiences have you or a family member had with the automobile insurance claims process? What if anything might have been done differently or better?

DO THE MATH

1. **How Much of Fire Loss Will Be Covered?**
Toula and Ian Miller of Lincoln, Nebraska, recently suffered a fire in their home. The fire, which began in a crawl space at the back of the house, caused $24,000 of damage to the dwelling. The garage, valued at $18,400, was totally destroyed but did not contain a car at the time of the fire. Replacement of the Millers' personal property damaged in the home and garage amounted to $18,500. In addition, $350 in cash and a stamp collection valued at $3215 were destroyed. While the damage was being repaired, the Millers stayed in a motel for one week and spent $1350 on food and lodging. The house had a value of $195,000 and was insured for $150,000 under an HO-3 policy with a $250 deductible. Use Table 10-1 on page 298 to answer the following questions. (Hint: You must first determine whether the Millers have adequate dwelling replacement coverage and, if not, what percentage of the necessary 80 percent coverage they do have. The resulting answer will determine the percentage of the loss to the dwelling covered, and consequently the amount to be reimbursed by the insurance company.)

   DO IT IN CLASS PAGES 297–300

   (a) Assuming that the deductible was applied to the damage to the dwelling, calculate the amount covered by insurance and the amount that the Millers must pay for each loss listed: the dwelling, the garage, the cash and stamp collection, and the extra living expenses.

   (b) How much of the amount of the personal property loss would be covered by the insurance policy? Paid for by the Millers?

   (c) Assuming that they have contents replacement-cost protection on the personal property, what amount and percentage of the total loss must be paid by the Millers?

2. **Sufficient Dwelling Coverage?** Colton Gentry of Atlanta, Georgia, has owned his home for ten years. When he purchased it for $178,000, Colton bought a $160,000 homeowner's insurance policy. He still owns that policy, even though the replacement cost of the home is now $300,000.

   DO IT IN CLASS PAGE 300

   (a) If Colton suffered a $20,000 fire loss to the home, what percentage and dollar amount of the loss would be covered by his policy?

   (b) How much insurance on the home should Colton carry now to be fully reimbursed for a fire loss?

3. **Coverage on a One-Vehicle Accident.** Bill Converse of Birmingham, Alabama, recently had his truck slide off a gravel road and strike a tree. Bill's vehicle suffered $17,500 in damage. The truck has a book value of $40,000. Bill carried collision insurance with a $500 deductible. How much will Bill be reimbursed by his policy?

4. **How Much of a Major Auto Accident Loss Will Be Covered?** Ashley Diamond of Griffin, Georgia, drives an eight-year-old Toyota valued at $5600. She has a $75,000 personal automobile policy with $10,000 per-person medical payments coverage and both collision ($200 deductible) and comprehensive coverage. David Smith of Bristol Virginia, drives a four-year-old Chevrolet Malibu valued at $9500. He has a 25/50/15 family automobile policy with $20,000 in medical payments coverage and both collision ($100 deductible) and comprehensive insurance. Late one evening, while he was driving back from Rocky Mountain National Park, David's car crossed the centerline of the road, striking Ashley's car and forcing it into a ditch. David's car also left the road and did extensive damage to the front of a roadside store. The following table indicates the damages and their dollar amounts.

   DO IT IN CLASS PAGE 309

Item	Amount
Bodily injuries suffered by Ashley	$ 6,800
Bodily injuries suffered by Fran, a passenger in Ashley's car	28,634
Ashley's car	9,600
Bodily injuries suffered by David	2,700
Bodily injuries suffered by Cecilia, a passenger in David's car	12,845
David's car	9,500
Damage to the roadside store	14,123

Complete the following chart and use the information to answer these questions:

(a) How much will Ashley's policy pay Ashley and Fran?

(b) Will subrogation rights come into play? In what way?

(c) How much will David's bodily injury liability protection pay?

(d) To whom and how much will David's property damage liability protection pay?

(e) To whom and how much will David's medical protection pay?

(f) How much reimbursement will David receive for his car?

(g) How much will David be required to pay out of his own pocket?

David Smith's Accident: Who Pays What?

COVERAGE	David's Policy	Ashley's Policy
Liability (limits)	___	___
Bodily injury		
Ashley	___	___
Fran	___	___
Cecilia	___	___
Medical payments (limits)	___	___
David	___	___
Ashley	___	___
Fran	___	___
Cecilia	___	___
Collision coverage (limits)	___	___
David's car	___	___
Ashley's car	___	___
David's out-of-pocket expenses	___	___
Fran's bodily injury	___	___
Excess property damage losses	___	___
Collision insurance deductible	___	___
TOTAL	___	___

FINANCIAL PLANNING CASES

CASE 1

The Johnsons Decide How to Manage Their Risks

Six years have passed since the Johnsons were married, and their financial affairs have become much more complicated. Both Harry and Belinda are earning about 30 percent more at work. They have purchased a $140,000 condominium that has added about $400 per month to their housing expense. And they have purchased a second car for $3200. As a result of these changes, Harry and Belinda realize that they now face greater risks in their financial affairs. They have decided to review their situation with an eye toward managing their risks more effectively. Use the steps in the risk-management process (pp. 290–292), their net worth and income and expense statements at the end of Chapter 3 (on pages 99–100), and other information in this chapter to answer the following questions:

(a) What are Harry and Belinda's major sources of risk from home and automobile ownership, and what is the potential magnitude of loss from each?

(b) Given the choices listed in Step 3 of the risk-management process, how should the Johnsons handle the sources of risk listed in part a?

CASE 2

The Hernandezes Consider Additional Liability Insurance

Victor and Maria's next-door neighbor, Jasmine Saunders, was recently sued over an automobile accident and eventually was held liable for $437,000 in damages. Jasmine's automobile policy limits were 100/300/50. Because of the shortfall, she had to sell her house and move into an apartment. Victor and Maria are now concerned that a similar tragedy might potentially befall them. They have a homeowner's policy with $100,000 in comprehensive personal liability coverage and an automobile policy with 50/100/25 limits, and Maria has a small ($100,000) professional liability policy for her work as a medical records assistant.

(a) How might Victor and Maria more fully protect themselves through their homeowner's and automobile insurance policies?

(b) What additional benefits would they receive in buying an umbrella liability policy?

CASE 3

Julia Price Thinks About Managing Her Property and Liability Risk

Julia has always tried to keep her insurance spending under control by purchasing low limits on her policies. Now that her assets and income have grown, she is beginning to reconsider the wisdom of this approach when buying insurance. Julia knows she has a lot more to lose in terms both of property and liability exposures. Last week, she called her insurance agent to discuss raising her policy limits on her homeowner's and automobile insurance policies. The agent suggested she consider an umbrella liability policy. Julia still wants to be frugal and is considering simply raising the limits on the policies she already has rather than obtaining another policy. Offer your opinions about her thinking.

CASE 4

The Princes' Auto Insurance Is Not Renewed

Mark and Kelly Prince of Hattiesburg, Mississippi, face a crisis. Their automobile insurance company has notified them that their current coverage expires in 30 days and will not be renewed. Mark and the Princes' younger son each had a minor, at-fault accident during the past year. Their children are otherwise good drivers, as are both parents. The Princes are confused because they know families whose members have much worse driving records but still have insurance.

(a) Explain to Mark and Kelly why their policy might have been canceled.

(b) Use the box on page 306 to give Mark and Kelly some pointers on how to save money when shopping for a new auto insurance policy.

CASE 5

A Student Buys Insurance for a Used Car

Makiko Iwanami, a student from Osaka, Japan, is in one of your classes. She is considering the purchase of a used car and has been told that she must buy automobile insurance to register the car and obtain license plates. Makiko has come to you for advice, and you have decided to focus on three aspects of automobile insurance.

(a) Explain how liability insurance works in the United States. Advise Makiko about which liability insurance limits she should select.

(b) Makiko is especially impressed that automobile insurance includes medical payments coverage because she has no health insurance. Explain why the medical payments coverage does not actually

solve her health insurance problem, and describe the type of coverage it provides.

(c) Makiko plans to pay cash for the car and doesn't want to spend more than $5000. Outline the coverage provided by collision insurance and factors that might make such coverage optional for Makiko.

CASE 6

An Argument About the Value of Insurance

You have been talking at a party to some friends about insurance. One young married couple in the group believes that insurance is almost always a real waste of money. They argue, "The odds of most bad events occurring are so low that you don't need to worry." Furthermore, they say, "Buying insurance is like pouring money down a hole; you rarely have anything to show for it in the end." Based on what you have learned from this chapter, how might you argue against this couple's point of view?

CASE 7

Enlai Contemplates a New Homeowner's Insurance Policy

Enlai Li Zhang of Lancaster, California recently bought a home for $700,000. The previous owner had a $600,000 HO-1 policy on the property, and Enlai can simply pay the premiums to keep the same coverage in effect. Her insurance agent called her and cautioned that she would be better off to upgrade the policy to an HO-2 or HO-3 policy. Enlai has turned to you for advice. Use the information in Table 10-1 to advise her.

DO IT IN CLASS
PAGES 297–300

(a) What additional property protection would Enlai have if she purchased an HO-2 policy?

(b) What additional property protection would Enlai have if she purchased an HO-3 policy?

(c) What property protection would remain largely the same whether Enlai had an HO-1, HO-2, or HO-3 policy?

(d) Advise Enlai on what differences in liability protection, if any, exist among the three policies.

BE YOUR OWN PERSONAL FINANCIAL PLANNER

1. **Property Loss Exposures.** Use Worksheet 43: My Home Inventory from "My Personal Financial Planner" to develop a list of your personal property items, including items you keep at school and those at other locations such as the home of a family member. Use Table 10-2 on page 301 as guides for the types of information to include. Assess the appropriateness of insurance to protect these items from loss.

   MY PERSONAL FINANCIAL PLANNER

2. **The Risk-Management Process.** Build upon your list of property loss exposures to develop a complete risk-management assessment. Use the risk-management information on pages 290–292 as a guide and use Worksheet 44: My Insurance Inventory from "My Personal Financial Planner" to record the results of your efforts.

   MY PERSONAL FINANCIAL PLANNER

3. **Evaluate Your Need for Homeowner's or Renter's Insurance.** Determine whether or not you are currently covered by a homeowner's or renter's insurance policy. If you are, determine whether the policy is adequate for your needs. If you are not, decide what coverage levels you will need.

4. **Evaluate Your Automobile Insurance.** If you drive a vehicle owned by a family member or yourself, you are covered by the insurance policy on that vehicle. Use Table 10-3 on page 303 as a guide to assess the coverage under that policy. Determine whether the policy adequately protects you from loss, and if not, identify what changes you want to make in the policy.

5. **Shop for Automobile Insurance.** Use Worksheet 45: My Comparison of Auto Insurance Providers from "My Personal Financial Planner" to shop for vehicle insurance based on your analysis in item 4 above. Use your current policy for Company A in the worksheet. Then contact two additional companies to obtain quotes on similar coverage to determine whether you are receiving a good value for your current policy or would benefit from switching companies.

   MY PERSONAL FINANCIAL PLANNER

ON THE NET

Go to the Web pages indicated to complete these exercises.

1. **Minimum Liability Limits.** Visit the website for the National Association of Insurance Commissioners at www.naic.org/state_web_map.htm, where you will find a map where you can link to the Insurance Commission in your state. Determine the minimum automobile insurance liability limits in your state. How well-insured do you feel someone would be if he or she carried only these minimums?

2. **Insurance Buyer's Guides.** Visit the website for the National Association of Insurance Commissioners, where you will find a map at www.naic.org/state_web_ map.htm through which you can link to your state insurance regulator's website. If available in your state, obtain an insurance buyer's guide for automobile and homeowner's insurance that describes policy provisions and compares insurance rates. Use these rate comparisons to select two automobile insurance companies that would be appropriate for your needs. E-mail or telephone the companies to obtain specific premium quotations for the desired insurance protection. Do the same for single-family dwelling, condominium, or renter's insurance, depending on your circumstances.

3. **Safe Cars Save Money.** Visit the website for the Insurance Institute for Highway Safety at www.iihs .org/ratings/default.aspx. For your own vehicle and one or two you would like to own, check how the vehicles stack up against the competition in terms of injury protection.

ACTION INVOLVEMENT PROJECTS

1. **The Benefits of Renter's Insurance.** Identify three to five of your friends who currently live in rental housing. Ask them if they are covered by a renter's insurance policy. If not, ask them why they have not decided to buy such coverage. If they are covered, ask them to give their assessment of the costs and benefits of having a policy.

2. **Independent Versus Exclusive Insurance Agents.** Interview two insurance agents, one who is an independent

agent and one who is an exclusive agent. Ask each to describe the benefits to a customer who buys insurance from that type of agent.

3. **Automobile Insurance Claims.** Interview three or four people who have been involved as an insured party in an automobile accident. Ask them to summarize the claims process as they experienced it and how they now view the process compared to what they expected.

Visit the Garman/Forgue companion website at www.cengagebrain.com.

11 Planning for Health Care Expenses

LEARNING OBJECTIVES

After reading this chapter, you should be able to:

1. Explain how the Affordable Care Act works, and how consumers shop and pay for health insurance coverage.

2. Distinguish among the types of health care plans.

3. Describe the typical features and limitations of health care plans.

4. Explain the fundamentals of planning for long-term custodial care.

5. Develop a plan to protect your income when you cannot work due to disability.

6. Summarize the benefits of preparing advance medical directive documents.

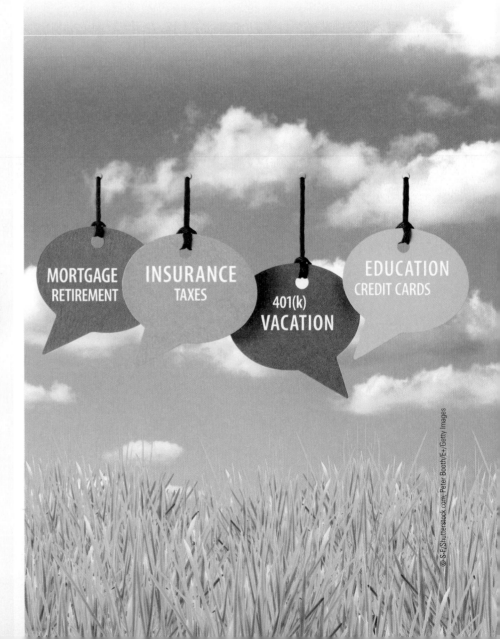

MORTGAGE RETIREMENT   INSURANCE TAXES   401(k) VACATION   EDUCATION CREDIT CARDS

© S-F/Shutterstock.com; Peter Booth/E+/Getty Images

WHAT DO YOU RECOMMEND?

Danielle DiMartino is a 36-year-old single mother with two children, ages 10 and 14. Her 10-year-old daughter has a history of ear infections that require doctor's office visits four or five times per year. Danielle's 71-year-old mother lives with the family for financial reasons; she has hereditary high blood pressure and high cholesterol as well as diabetes. Danielle's mother has enrolled in Medicare Parts A and B.

Danielle's employer pays all or a portion of the cost for a health care plan to cover the company's workers, their spouses, and their dependents. Danielle has four options: (1) the basic HMO managed by a local university medical school/hospital with no additional cost for Danielle, but with additional cost of $122 per month to cover her children, (2) a health insurance plan with a PPO at that same medical center for an additional cost of $245 per month, (3) a traditional health insurance plan that provides access to virtually all health care providers in her community for $455 per month, and (4) a health plan with a $5000 deductible at no additional cost. Danielle's employer offers no disability income or long-term care group plan. She does receive ten sick days per year, which can accumulate if not taken. Danielle has accumulated 30 days.

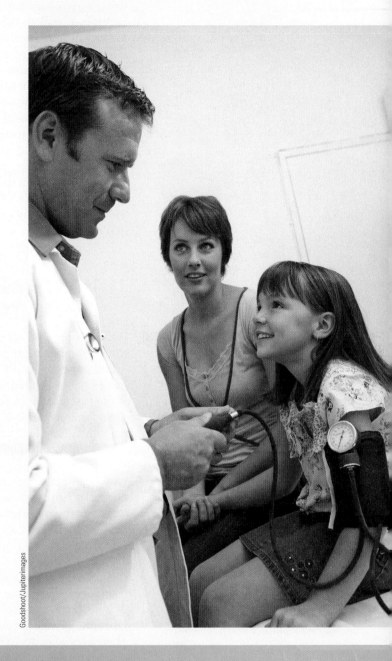

Goodshoot/Jupiterimages

What do you recommend to Danielle DiMartino on the subject of managing health expenses regarding:

1. **Choosing among the four alternatives available to her?**

2. **Danielle's concerns about providing for her mother's health care needs?**

3. **Danielle's need for disability income insurance?**

4. **How Danielle can cover her long-term care risk?**

Few things in life are more important than your good health. When illness or injuries strike, three issues may affect your finances. First, there is the direct cost of the required health care, such as the cost of hospital stay and surgery. Second, there is the potential for lost income when you cannot work. And third, there are the costs of any rehabilitation. Health care events can quickly wipe out much or all of your assets. More than half of all credit collections are health care related and 60 percent of all personal bankruptcies are caused by health care bills.

Such extreme health care costs now can be avoided because there are programs available to address all of these problems. Now you have no choice! You must learn how to protect your health and personal finances by purchasing the best policy for yourself. That could be mean staying on your parent's health care policy until you are age 26 or by signing up for a policy through your employer. Or, you could buy a price-subsidized policy in the private marketplace. Health illiteracy is no longer acceptable. You have no choice. Today you must know what the insurance vocabulary means as well as all about any exclusions, deductibles, co-pays, and out-of-pocket limits. If you don't, you will lose.

11.1 THE AFFORDABLE CARE ACT AND YOU

LEARNING OBJECTIVE 1

Explain how the Affordable Care Act works, and how consumers shop and pay for health insurance coverage.

premiums
The monthly or annual cost of a health care plan.

When people who are uninsured suffer any insurable loss, such as a vehicle crash, lost ring, or home fire, they typically bear the full cost of the loss themselves. Health care losses, however, are different. Because federal law requires it, when an uninsured person becomes ill or injured they may obtain care by going to a public hospital for treatment. If they are unable to pay, the costs are primarily shifted first to hospitals because the 1986 Emergency Medical Treatment and Active Labor Act requires hospitals participating in Medicare (and nearly all do) to provide emergency care to anyone who needs it.

That pushes hospitals costs up. Those costs are then shifted to people who do have health insurance in the form of higher costs to insurance companies. The insurers then raise health care insurance **premiums** (the monthly or annual cost for a health care plan) that partially "cover" those without insurance.

Before the Affordable Care Act went into effect the United States of America was the only industrialized country in the world that did not provide universal access to health care to all citizens. This continued despite the fact that every U.S. president in the past 70 years pushed their Congresses to pass a universal health care law.

Such legislative failures also meant that about 45 million Americans had no health insurance. Every year among the 45 million uninsured men, women, and children 272,000 cancers were diagnosed and 92,000 died. Ever year another 95,000 died of heart diseases and yet another 22,000 died of respiratory diseases. Strokes killed 20,000. Many lives were devastated because a loved one died by a freak accident or an infectious disease. Or they died from an unexpected diagnosis of a disease like diabetes, nephritis, or influenza. And none had health insurance. These deaths happened every year to those individuals without insurance.

Until 2014 when the ACA went into effect there were two nations in this country: One with the security of health care and one with no security at all. In the eyes of many, including the religious as well as non-believers, their consciences told them that this history was a moral disgrace. Passage of the ACA has made progress in changing the old status quo.

11.1a The Affordable Care Act

The ACA aims to pool risk and share the costs as broadly as possible so that everyone is protected by affordable health insurance throughout their lives. Thus, everyone benefits if all people are covered by a health plan because each person's costs are lowest when you are sharing risk with others. The insurance idea works because most people are mostly healthy most of the time.

However, no one is guaranteed good health forever. And the reality is most people need to see health providers to stay healthy or at least monitor their health. That is why we buy insurance. Just like auto insurance you have to have health insurance as a "what if" something happens. We all wish we could avoid buying any kind of insurance until after the vehicle crashes, or the storm hits, or the home catches on fire, or we get very sick, but that is not how insurance works.

The goal of the 2010 **Patient Protection and Affordable Care Act (PPACA)**, commonly known as the **Affordable Care Act (ACA)**, is to provide affordable health insurance for all U.S. citizens and reduce the growth in health care spending. The ACA aims to reform U.S. health insurance industry and the American health care system as a whole. In essence, the ACA begins to fix our broken health care system.

The current $2.8 trillion U.S. healthcare system costs almost $9000 a year for every man, woman, and child. A more accurate figure is about $16,300 a year for employed workers in America whose employers pay $11,700 for their insurance and their employees pay about $4600.

These costs amount to 18 percent of gross domestic product spent on health care, which is the highest percentage spent on health care of any country in the world. The people of Britain, Canada, Germany, and Norway, to name a few industrialized countries that provide health care to all citizens, spend only about half as much on health care but their citizens live longer than those in the United States.

The health care system in the USA is not a **single-payer health system**, like in many nations worldwide, where the government, rather than private insurers, pays for all health care costs. Instead we have a highly fragmented system of private and public payers. Thus the USA system is more inefficient and more costly than others, and despite the ACA it remains so.

11.1b   The ACA Does Not Impact the 85 Percent of Americans Who Already Have Insurance

The 85 percent of Americans who were already covered by a health care plan prior to the law's implementation were not impacted by the Affordable Care Act because they already had insurance that meets the law's requirements. They already had a group health care plan offered by an employer, already had private insurance, or were enrolled in a government provided insurance plan (e.g., Medicare Part A, Medicaid, CHIP, and TRICARE).

11.1c   The ACA Does Impact Individuals without Health Insurance

The 15 percent without health insurance are required to purchase coverage or pay a penalty tax. These 45 million Americans who did not have health insurance at the beginning of 2014 were impacted under new health care law. By 2015, 8 million of those people bought health insurance, 3 million were added to Medicaid, and 3 million more who were under age 26 were added to their parent's health plan. That's 14 million now with health insurance. By 2016 25 million people will have insurance who would not have had it otherwise, predicts the non-partisan Congressional Budget Office. Hospitals, doctors, and health insurance companies like the ACA because it creates more customers and additional income.

11.1d   The ACA Is Based on RomneyCare and the Heritage Foundation's Ideas

The ACA, commonly known as ObamaCare, is based on health reform in Massachusetts, signed into law in 2006 by the state's then governor, Mitt Romney, which is informally called RomneyCare. Today the law provides coverage for 98.1 percent

YOUR NEXT FIVE YEARS

In the next five years, you can start achieving financial success by doing the following related to managing health expenses:

1. *Sign up for an employer-sponsored premium conversion plan and a flexible spending arrangement for medical and dental expenses, whenever they are available, to save money on taxes.*

2. *Consider using a bronze-level health plan and health savings account if you are unable to afford the high costs of an HMO or traditional health insurance plan.*

3. *Consider maintaining coverage for health care expenses when changing employers using the COBRA law or a plan offered through the Affordable Care Act.*

4. *Take advantage of employer-sponsored long-term disability income insurance if available or consider purchasing protection individually.*

5. *Create your advance medical directive documents so your family will know your wishes.*

Patient Protection and Affordable Care Act (ACA)

The law passed by Congress in 2010 to provide affordable health insurance for all US citizens and reduce the growth in health care spending.

of Massachusetts residents with satisfaction rates over 96 percent. The law mandates that nearly every resident obtain a state-government-regulated minimum level of health care insurance coverage and provides free health care insurance for residents earning less than 150 percent of the federal poverty level (FPL). RomneyCare has proved cost effective, sharply reduced health insurance costs, and it provides better quality affordable health care to more people. And the law is creating jobs.

The concept behind both RomneyCare and the ACA was originally purposed by the conservative Heritage Foundation in 1989 as a traditional, market-based reform of health care, suggested in contrast to a single-payer health care system. It was strongly supported for a while by conservative economists and Republican senators as a conservative approach to health care reform, particularly on the basis of individual responsibility.

11.1e   The ACA Provides Benefits, Rights, and Protections

The ACA offers a lot of new benefits, rights, and protections to 25 to 30 million uninsured Americans who will buy health insurance policies in the individual market. The benefits include a mandate for health insurance companies to cover everyone regardless of pre-existing conditions (which 1 in 2 Americans have), stops insurers from charging women more than men, prohibits dropping coverage for any reason except for fraud, eliminates annual and lifetime limits on health care, mandates that insurers cover 10 essential health benefits, wellness visits and preventative services with no out-of-pocket costs, and generally increases the quality of American's health care. The only way health insurance providers can afford all of this is if everyone buys insurance.

You Must Have a Health Care Plan If You Are Uninsured   The Affordable Care Act regulates health insurance, not health care. The law includes over 2700 pages of reforms to the insurance and health care industries in order to cut health care costs, provide affordable health insurance to all Americans, and reduce wasteful spending. The law focuses on prevention and primary care to help people stay healthy and to manage chronic medical conditions before they become more complex and costly to treat. Provisions of the ACA and answers to many questions may be found at www.irs.gov.aca. Step-by-step help on the law is offered by *Consumer Reports* at HealthLawHelper.org.

The government wants you to have a health care plan. The ACA law requires that all Americans and legal residents no matter how sick and regardless of any pre-existing health problems, buy health coverage. This is known as the **individual mandate**.

Almost everyone is required to obtain a **quality healthcare plan** that meets the government's standard for its required "10 essential benefits" of adequate coverage (see next page) either through a private provider, their employer, through a state or federally assisted program or pay a tax penalty.

If you do not have health care, you will be assessed a tax penalty. The IRS calls the tax penalty an **individual shared responsibility fee**. It goes toward funding the ACA, subsidizing hospitals (which will still have to cover unpaid emergency room visits for those not covered by Medicaid programs in states that do not offer expanded Medicaid [discussed below] and undocumented immigrants), and as a down payment on other uninsured people's almost inevitable use of the health care system. The tax penalty will be assessed when filing your income tax return. It will offset any refund that would otherwise be due or will add to any balance due.

Health insurance coverage gaps of up to three months are allowed and will not violate the individual mandate. But after that, the tax applies to each month within a calendar year that you did not have coverage for yourself or a member of your household. Health insurance plans will provide documentation to prove you had insurance, which is filed with your income tax return.

DID YOU KNOW ?

Protections and Benefits of the Affordable Care Act

- **Ban on Denial for Pre-exisiting Conditions and Cancellation of Policies**. You cannot be denied coverage because of **pre-exisiting health conditions** diagnosed prior to signing up for a plan, and this impacts half of all Americans. Nor can an insurer cancel your policy if you get sick or make an honest mistake on your application. Policies can only be canceled for customer fraud.

- **Prohibits Charging Women and Men Different Prices.** The law stops discrimination based on gender, income, and health issues.

- **Prohibits Rationing Health Care.** The law protects consumers from the health care rationing insurance companies have been doing for ages.

- **Lousy Health Policies Are Prohibited.** Prior to passage of the law, the nation saw a race to the bottom as insurers cut benefits to lower premiums. Any policy today offering less than the federal government's "10 Essential Benefits" are prohibited.

- **Required Free Preventive Care and Annual Checkups Without Co-pays.** Plans must eliminate cost-sharing (co-payment, coinsurance, or deductible) for proven preventive measures such as immunizations, mammograms, cancer screenings, well-woman visits, screening for gestational diabetes, colonoscopies, domestic violence screening, breast-feeding supplies, and contraception.

- **Requires Lower Premiums for Prescriptions via Medicare.** The law provides lower prescription drug costs for people on Medicare.

- **Payout Maximums Prohibited.** Major or long-term illness can rack up serious medical bills and health insurance policies may no longer set annual and lifetime limits on how much they would pay for an individual's medical bills.

- **Remain on Parent's Plan Until Age 26.** Young adults may remain as dependents on their parent's policy until they turn 26, regardless of whether they live at home, attend school, or are married, unless they can get coverage at work.

- **Prohibits Overcharging Older Consumers.** Prohibit insurers from charging older people more than three times the amount they charge younger policyholders or vary premiums based on gender; but premiums are allowed to be higher for tobacco users.

- **Rapid Appeals.** People can appeal insurance company decisions to an independent reviewer and receive a response in 72 hours for urgent medical situations.

- **Required Standard Disclosure Forms.** All plans must use a standardized form to summarize benefits and coverage, including co-payments, deductibles, and out-of-pocket limits, and they must disclose typical out-of-pocket costs for having a baby and treating type 2 diabetes.

- **Requires Justification of Rate Hikes.** The law requires health insurance companies to justify any rate increases above 10 percent to a state agency.

- **Promotes Choice Without a Referral.** Plans must allow people to choose any available participating primary care provider, OB-GYN, or pediatrician in their health plan's network, or emergency care outside of the plan's network, without a referral.

- **Required Premium Rebates If Companies Underspend on Care.** Insurers must spend at least 80 percent (85 percent for insurers covering large employers) of the premiums on medical care, and if insurers spend too much on salaries, bonuses, or administrative costs, instead of health care, they must issue refunds to policyholders.

- **Required Hospital Grading.** Doctors and hospitals are being moved to a system where they are rewarded for providing quality care not quantity. The Medicare Value-Based Purchasing Program means hospitals can lose or gain up to 1 percent of Medicare funding based on a number of quality measures related to treatment of patients with heart attacks, heart failures, pneumonia, certain surgical issues, re-admittance rate, as well as patient satisfaction.

11.1f   Ten Essential Benefits of All New Health Care Plans

Health coverage available in the exchanges is better than the substandard polices that were typically available to individuals in the health insurance marketplace before because it was dominated by bare-bones, limited-coverage plans. Older policies usually did not cover prescription drugs, mental health, maternity, and rehabilitative care. These lousy policies worked fine for many people as long as they did not discover the limitations of

essential health benefits

A list of ten categories of benefits that all health care plans sold on the health insurance exchanges must Provide.

their policies by getting sick, going to the hospital or requiring some other excluded health care services.

The ACA established ten comprehensive **essential health benefits** for adequate coverage that all health care plans now must include:

- Ambulatory patient services, such as doctor's visits and outpatient services
- Emergency services
- Hospitalization
- Maternity and newborn care
- Mental health and substance use disorder services, including behavioral health treatment
- Prescription drugs
- Rehabilitative and rehabilitative services and devices
- Laboratory services
- Preventive and wellness services and chronic disease management
- Pediatric services, including oral and vision care

11.1g   Paying for the Cost of Health Insurance

If you do not have health insurance you must pay a penalty tax equal to the greater of 1 percent of your income or $325 (up to a family maximum of $975) in 2015; 2.5 percent or $695 (up to a family maximum of $2085) in 2016. Penalties for children are half the amount for adults. Beginning in 2017 the numbers are indexed to inflation.

Recall from Chapter 4, Managing Income Taxes, that before you calculate your income tax liability you are allowed to reduce your income using exclusions, deductions, and personal exemptions. This results in your **taxable income**, which for most of us is the same as your **modified adjusted gross income (MAGI)**. This is the total of adjusted gross income plus any additional tax-exempt interest income you might have. On a MAGI of $50,000 the maximum tax penalty for a single person amounts to $1000 in 2015 or $2500 in 2016.

In contrast, a subsidized health insurance policy for a young person might cost $1200 to $1500 annually. Six in 10 adults who are receiving subsidies now pay less than $100 a month for their ACA policies, and almost half of young, single individuals pay $50 or less a month. For people qualifying for subsidies that amount is less than their cell phone bill or their cable bill.

Depending upon the state in which you live, the premium could be nearly double that charged in a less expensive state. The first-year premium in Colorado was $844 and in New York it was only $255. Price is determined by supply, demand, geographic location, and competition. Predictions are for low premium increases as health care costs are the lowest in more than a decade. These prices are before subsidies, which are provided for three-quarters of the uninsured because of their incomes.

About 1.5 million people do not qualify for subsidies. They will pay much more for health insurance. Rates are lower in states with vigorous competition in their insurance markets and have robust programs to review rates.

Choosing to pay the penalty tax and forego health insurance means that you are responsible for paying all of your health care costs, from visits to the doctor's office for vaccinations, health screenings, and check-ups to ambulance rides and emergency room visits for life-threatening situations. You also will not have any protection against enormous medical bills. A two-hour emergency room visit can cost $10,000. It costs about $30,000 to stay in the hospital for three days or to have a baby, and cancer treatments can run $100,000 or more.

health insurance exchange (HIX)

Stat-by-state mechanisms established by the ACA through which consumers can purchase a health care plan.

Knowing that health care is expensive, the ACA subsidizes middle- and low-income people thus helping them purchase health insurance at a lower cost so that coverage is more affordable. Americans may purchase federally regulated and subsidized insurance in their states through **health insurance exchanges (HIX)** (also known as the

health insurance marketplace), and these are run by the states and/or federal governments. This is where the insurance companies compete to sell you their policies. Find your state's shopping portal at www.healthcare.gov.

Affordable health insurance is a policy that costs 8 percent of your income for health care premiums or 9.5 percent of family income if insurance is obtained through an employer. Those who cannot afford health insurance will either qualify for Medicare, Medicaid, or enhanced Medicaid government insurance programs or obtain financial help in the form of tax credits.

11.1h How Premium Credits Work under the ACA

Under the Affordable Care Act there are numerous tax credits and other assistance for low- and moderate-income people. The credit is based on household income and the number of people (adults and children) in the household. Premium subsidies in the form of federal tax credits are available for people buying their own insurance in the exchanges who have incomes from 100 percent up to 400 percent of the federal poverty level (about $24,500 annually for an individual to about $95,900 annually for a family of four). Middle-income people under age 65, who are not eligible for coverage through their employer or Medicaid, may apply for tax credit subsidies available through state-based exchanges. More than half of these Americans qualify for income-based tax credits to help pay the premiums. While premiums are not cheap, they are a lot lower than they used to be.

The exact amount of the credit is based on a **benchmark premium**, which is the cost of the second-lowest-cost silver plan (described below) in the area where a person lives. The tax credit equals that benchmark premium minus what the individual is expected to pay based on his or her family income. This is calculated on a sliding scale from 2 percent to 9.5 percent of income. The individual can choose to have some, all, or none of the credit applied toward insurance premiums. Any reconciliation may be done on the income tax return when it is filed the following April.

Here is an example from the Kaiser Foundation of how the calculation of the credit might work for a 40-year-old individual making $30,000 a year:

- Estimated benchmark premium for a 40-year-old is $3857 per year (which varies from state to state)
- Person is responsible for paying 8.37 percent of their income, or $2512 per year
- Tax credit equals $1345

The tax credit may be used in any plan offered in the exchanges. Thus, the person would end up paying $2512 ($209 a month) to enroll in the low-cost silver plan or a lower-cost bronze plan, or more to enroll in a higher cost plan. A calculator from the Kaiser Family Foundation (www.kff.org/interactive/subsidy-calculator/) provides subsidy estimates for families of varying characteristics.

The Kaiser Family Foundation figures that more than half the individuals who buy insurance on their own are eligible for subsidies, which are worth an average of $5,550 per household. This would effectively discount the projected price of insurance premiums by two-thirds, on average. Seventy percent of consumers who bought subsidized ACA health policies paid $100 or less in monthly premiums.

The Congressional Budget Office (CBO) projects that the ACA will not increase the national debt. Rather it is expected to cut the deficit by more than a trillion dollars over the next two decades. The cost of subsidies would be paid for by revenues from taxing the most expensive health plans, a small tax on the highest-income earners, tax penalties on people who do not sign up for policies, and lowering payments to hospitals.

11.1i Uninsured Individuals Shopping for Health Coverage

Individuals, families, and small business owners may shop for health plans in online marketplaces, similar to travel websites. These marketplaces make it possible to compare and buy private insurance and to be able to understand the plan you are buying, as well as determine if you qualify for financial help. Health insurance for uninsured people can be

FINANCIAL POWER POINT

Practicing a Healthy Lifestyle Can Reduce the Cost of Your Health Care Plan

Health care plans are increasing discounts to people who maintain a healthy lifestyle. Most common are discounts for nonsmokers. Discounts also are offered those who drink alcohol in moderation, exercise regularly, and meet good health-risk assessment targets for weight, blood pressure, and cholesterol levels.

purchased using tax credits. You may choose the provider you want for you, your family, or business based on of who offers the most attractive package in terms of affordability and quality of coverage. You may choose among federally regulated and subsidized health plans with high or low premiums using side-by-side benefits and rates.

Today only three factors can affect the cost of your health insurance: (1) age, (2) place of residence, and (3) number of people in your family. Your health history and current illnesses may no longer be used to set premiums. Once you input your information on your state exchange the system will automatically calculate your subsidies. Now insurance companies are required to provide essential health benefits that previously were not covered and to take on people who were rejected before because of poor health.

11.1j Health Care Plans on the Government Exchanges

There are a number of different tiers of plans available on the exchanges that meet the government's 10 essential minimum requirements. Plans on the federal and state exchanges are grouped into four categories that cover 60 to 90 percent of **out-of-pocket expenses**, which is the most you pay during a policy period (usually a year) before your health insurance or plan begins to pay 100 percent of the allowed amount. Plans range from bare bones "bronze" plans which cover 60 percent of out of pocket medical costs leaving the other 40 percent to be paid by you (but the deductibles could be $5000), to "silver," which is a standard plan familiar to most insured Americans that covers 70 percent (a deductible of about $3000), to "gold" that pays 80 percent, and "platinum" plans that cover 90 percent of the costs. An inexpensive "catastrophic" plan is available only to those under age 30 and it also covers close to 60 percent of initial annual costs. Comparison shop common health care procedures in your area at www.opscost.com.

All plans have **exclusions**, or a list of services that are not typically covered in the policy, but they do include all ten essential benefits. The types of health care plans available on the exchanges include most of those described in the next section.

11.1k Opposition to the ACA

The legislatures and governors in states not participating in the ACA are generally opposed to the law and want to see the whole health care program fail, ostensibly because it is a large federal government program. Similar conservative complaints were made about other social welfare programs, including Social Security, Medicare, Medicaid, Medicare Part D (prescription drug coverage for the elderly), CHIP (Children's Health Insurance Program), food stamps (Supplemental Nutrition Assistance Program and Special Supplemental Nutrition Program for Women, Infants and Children), general welfare/public assistance (Temporary Assistance for Needy Families and Supplemental Security Income), and public housing.

While the debate over the ACA continues most people recognize that social welfare is one of the accepted goals of the United States and of the entire industrialized free world. Jim Yong Kim, President of the World Bank, says that proving universal health coverage is vital for economic development as it alleviates poverty.

CONCEPT CHECK 11.1

1. Summarize what the Affordable Care Act is supposed to accomplish.

2. How much is the penalty if you do not purchase health insurance and your income is $40,000?

3. If you choose a "silver" health insurance plan, how much of your out-of-pocket medical costs will be paid by the plan?

11.2 TYPES OF HEALTH CARE PLANS

11.2a **Types of Health Care Plans**

A **health care plan** is a generic name for any program that pays or provides reimbursement for health care expenditures. There are several types of health care plans available to Americans, and the major ones are described below.

Employer-Provided Group Health Care Plan When a **group health plan** is available as an benefit for active employees, the employer typically pays the cost for the workers (and often subsidizes the costs for other members of the workers' immediate family) typically for the lowest-cost plan the employer offers. Employees can choose a higher-priced plan or add family members to the coverage by paying an additional charge. These plans are provided by employers to 170 million employees.

health care plan
Generic name for any program that pays or provides reimbursement for health care expenditures.

group health plan
Sold collectively to an entire group of people rather than to individuals, such as the group health care policies offered by employers.

New employees often must choose from among a menu of health care plans soon after being hired.

© Goodluz/Shutterstock.com

DID YOU KNOW

Private Exchanges for Employee Group Plans

Many employers will no longer offer fully paid health care as an employee benefit, rather they will subsidize it. Some companies have dropped offering their health care plan and are instead offering employees a sum of money—perhaps $500 a month in financial assistance—to purchase insurance on their private exchange. Examples are Darden Restaurants, IBM, Trader Joe's, Sears Holdings, and Walgreens. Within five years it is estimated that more than a quarter of all workers who formerly had an employer-provided group health care plan will get their benefits through private exchanges.

These are employer-based exchanges that provide eligible workers with an employer subsidy to purchase health care policies. The benefits company Aon Hewitt invented the private exchange concept last year. These private exchanges are a new trend away from defined-benefit health coverage offered by employers to defined-contribution coverage. Thus, these exchanges are sometimes called **defined contribution health care**.

health insurance

Provides protection against direct medical expenses resulting from illness and injury based on the concept of payment after an expense occurs.

Traditional Health Insurance Plan A **traditional** health insurance plan provides protection against direct medical expenses resulting from illness and injury based on the concept of payment after an expense occurs. The insurer pays all or most of a portion of the "usual, customary, and reasonable fees" directly with the insured patient being billed for any remainder. These health insurance plans are often referred to as a **fee-for-service health plan**.

Basic Indemnity Plan A more limited type of traditional health insurance plan is a **basic indemnity plan**. Here they compensate the insured for only a part of the cost of care received. The insured receives the benefit amount that is usually fixed without regard to the actual expenses incurred. It might, for example, provide a set cash amount of $150 a day for hospital care. This amount is woefully inadequate.

deductibles

Clauses in health care plans that require the participant to pay an additional portion of health expenses annually before receiving reimbursement.

High-Deductible Health Insurance Plan A deductible is a clause in health care plan contracts that require you to pay an initial portion of medical expenses annually before receiving reimbursement. A **high-deductible plan** has a high deductible that you must meet before the insurance will start paying for your office visits, lab tests, and prescriptions. In order to qualify as a high-deductible plan the deductible must be at least $1000. The average deductible is $5000. Often once you have reached the deductible the insurance will kick in with coverage.

High-deductible plans typically have a lower premium than traditional health plans. If you are healthy, and are looking for a way to reduce costs this may be an option to consider.

health maintenance organizations (HMOs)

Health insurance plans that provide a broad range of health care services for a set monthly fee on a prepaid basis.

Health Maintenance Organizations Health maintenance organizations (HMOs) provide a wide array of health care services, including hospital, surgical, and preventive health care. A goal of HMOs is to catch any medical problem early, which helps keep overall costs low by reducing the probability of subsequent high-cost medical treatment.

Such plans control the conditions under which health care can be obtained. Examples include preapproval of hospital admissions and restrictions on which hospitals or doctors may be used. If the HMO itself does not provide a particular type of care, the primary care physician may refer the patient to a local hospital or clinic for those services. Most participants are assigned a **primary-care physician** by the HMO or choose one from a list of physicians employed by the HMO. The primary-care physician usually must order all procedures and approve referrals to specialized health care providers (for example, a cardiologist) within the HMO.

Such plans typically have **co-pays**, which are when the insured pays a specified amount of out-of-pocket expenses for health care services such as doctor visits and prescriptions drugs at the time the service is rendered, with the insurer paying the remaining costs. These differ from coinsurance, where the insured is required to pay a certain percentage of the covered costs.

preferred provider organization (PPO)

Group of health care providers (doctors, hospitals, and other health care providers) who contract with a health insurance company to provide services at a discount.

Preferred Provider Health Care Organization A preferred provider organization (PPO) is a managed care organization of medical doctors, hospitals, and other health care providers who have contracted with an insurer or a third-party administrator to provide health care at reduced rates to the insurer clients. A PPO is similar to a HMO, but you pay for care when it is received rather than in advance. This discount is then passed along to the policyholders in the form of reductions or elimination of deductibles and coinsurance requirements. These are sometimes referred to as a **participating provider organization** or **preferred provider option**.

Provider-Sponsored Network A **provider-sponsored network (PSN)** health care plan identifies a group of cooperating physicians and hospitals who have banded together to offer a health insurance contract. Such networks operate primarily in rural areas, where access to HMOs may be limited. As a group, the members of the PSN coordinate and deliver health care services and manage the insurance plan financially. They also contract with outside providers for health services that are not available through members of the group.

ADVICE FROM A PROFESSIONAL

Maintain Your Health Care Plan between Jobs

What happens when you no longer work for an employer that offers a group health care plan and you want to continue the coverage? You can assert your **COBRA rights** (Consolidated Omnibus Budget Reconciliation Act of 1985). These rules allow you to remain a member of a group health plan for as long as 18 months if you worked for an employer with more than 20 workers. COBRA applies to you and to any of your dependents who had been covered under the employer's plan. COBRA rights apply to your dependents for 36 months. These rights must be exercised within 60 days after the termination of employment, and you must pay the full premiums (including both the employee's and the employer's portions) plus a 2 percent administrative fee.

You might be tempted to go without coverage for a time because of the high cost of converting your previous plan, you expect to have a job soon that will provide coverage, or simply because you are willing to pay the penalty. This latter reason is shortsighted because young people do get sick and are injured.

So what should you do? Buy a health plan using the government health exchange in your state. Coverage for a premium of perhaps $150 to $250 per month is available. About half of COBRA users are expected to move to the government exchanges.

William Dean
Southern University, Baton Rouge, Louisiana

Medicare is a Government Health Care Plan for the Elderly

Over fifty million people are enrolled in the **Medicare** program, which is the federal government's single-payer health care program for the elderly. It costs only 6 cents on the dollar for the government to run this single-payer system, which is less than one-third that of commercially available health plans. Medicare's primary beneficiaries are people age 65 and older who are eligible for Social Security retirement benefits. Medicare is funded by means of the Medicare payroll tax. This tax for most American workers is 1.45 percent of earned income. Both employees and employers pay the 1.45 percent. The nation's top 3 percent of income earners pay an additional 2.35 percent Medicare surtax on incomes over $200,000. In addition, their unearned income (e.g., interest, dividends, capital gains, annuities, rental income) is taxed at a 3.8 percent rate [1.45 + 2.35].

Medicare is divided into two parts. **Medicare Part A** is the hospitalization portion of the program; it requires no premium. Most people do not pay a monthly Part A premium because they or a spouse has 40 or more quarters of Medicare-covered employment.

Medicare Part B is the supplementary health expense insurance portion for outpatient care, doctor office visits, or certain other services of the Medicare program; it requires payment of a monthly premium of about $105 (but more for higher income older people). Both components require patients to pay a portion of their costs, recently $147 a year. The federal government pays 75 percent of Part B costs and beneficiaries pay 25 percent.

Medicare also includes an optional prescription coverage plan under **Medicare Part D**. Participants pay an initial portion of prescription costs annually depending on their level of income and a portion of the cost for each prescription.

Medicare's Competitors Some programs compete with Medicare to serve the elderly and their programs are approved by the government. **Medicare Advantage Plans** are health care plans that offer Medicare benefits through private health plans, such as HMOs and PPOs. Medicare pays Medicare Advantage plans a lump sum annually to provide Plan A and B coverages. The also offer annual financial incentives for

COBRA rights
The Consolidated Omnibus Budget Reconciliation Act of 1985 allows a former employee to remain a member of a group health plan for as long as 18 months if the employee worked for an employer with more than 20 workers.

Medicare
The federal government's health care program for the elderly.

DID YOU KNOW

Workers' Comp Pays if You Are Hurt on the Job

If you are injured on the job or become ill as a direct result of your employment, state law requires your employer to pay any resulting medical costs. **Workers' compensation insurance** covers employers for liability losses for injury or disease suffered by employees that result from employment-related causes. The benefits to the employee include health care, recuperative care, replacement of lost income, and, if necessary, rehabilitation. Thus, workers' compensation insurance covers the full range of health-related losses.

FINANCIAL POWER POINT

Making Changes in Your Health Care Plan

In almost all health care plans, you must wait until the next **open-enrollment period** to make changes in coverage or switch among alternative plans. Open-enrollment periods are one to two months long. Open-enrollment period for the Affordable Care Act is October 15 to December 7. Plan rules allow changes at other times during the open year if the participant experiences certain family events such as births, adoptions, divorce, and marriage.

Medicaid

A government health care program for low-income people funded jointly by the federal and state governments.

the better plans. Medicare Advantage plans replace Medicare for ¼ of the nation's elderly population. Medicare Advantage plans provide broader coverage than Medicare and some plans also provide prescription drug benefits.

Choosing a Medicare Advantage Plan typically results in lower out-of-pocket costs. The features of Medicare Advantage and prescription drug plans, including premiums as well as other costs and benefits may be compared using HealthPocket's free Medicare comparison tool at www .healthpocket.com/medicare.

Medicaid and Expanded Medicaid are Government Programs for Lower-Income Americans Medicaid is a joint federal and state funded program that provides health care for over 60 million low-income Americans, mostly children, pregnant women, people with disabilities and elderly people who need help or live in nursing homes. Medicaid programs must follow federal guidelines, but they vary somewhat from state to state. Eligibility for Medicaid is based on both household income and family size, and it is either free or costs very little.

More than half the states have adopted a voluntary **expanded Medicaid** program, which expands Medicaid eligibility to all individuals (who were not previously eligible) and households with incomes below 138 percent of the Federal Poverty Level. Five million poor families living in states that decided not to offer expanded Medicaid will have no affordable health care option, even though the federal government paid 100 percent of the costs for 3 years and 90 percent after that. Thus that 7 percent of the population remains uninsured. Instead they will use emergency services and drive up costs for all taxpayers.

CONCEPT CHECK 11.2

1. Distinguish between health maintenance organizations (HMOs) and traditional health insurance.

2. Identify two benefits of selecting a preferred provider organization (PPO) when seeking health care.

3. List three ways you can save on taxes when paying for health care or insurance.

DID YOU KNOW ?

The Tax Consequences of Managing Health Expenses

The Internal Revenue Code allows several avenues for reducing income taxes when you spend your own money on health care plan premiums and health care expenses, and all plans must be integrated with employer's plans and the Affordable Care Act:

1. *Many employees may save on taxes when they use* **premium conversion plans** *to pay their health care insurance premiums (discussed in Chapter 1). With premium conversion, the employee's share of the premiums is paid with pretax dollars, and those amounts are not included when the employer reports the employee's taxable income to the IRS.*

DO IT IN CLASS

2. *A* **flexible spending arrangement (FSA)** *is a plan that allows an employee to fund qualified expenses on a pretax basis through salary reduction to pay for out-of-pocket unreimbursed medical and dental expenses for health care expenditures. Employees can contribute $2,500 to a FSA. (This was discussed in Chapter 1.)*

3. *A* **health savings account (HSA)** *is a tax-deductible savings account into which individuals and/or their employers can deposit tax-sheltered funds to use later to pay medical bills including the deductibles and other out-of-pocket costs for health plans. The maximum annual savings deposit is $3300 for an individual or $6550 for a family plan.*

4. *A* **health reimbursement arrangement (HRA)** *consists of funds set aside solely by employers to reimburse employees for qualified medical expenses. Thus, the employer helps employees pay their medical bills. There is no limit on the employer's contributions, which are excluded from an employee's taxable income.*

5. **Employee contributions to private exchanges** *are covered under IRS Section 125. The employee contributions are pretax, just like today.*

6. **Health care expenditures can be used as itemized deductions** *on one's income tax return to the extent that they exceed 10 percent of adjusted gross income. Self-employed people may deduct (as a business expense, not an itemized deduction) the cost of health care plan premiums for themselves and their dependents.*

11.3 YOUR HEALTH PLAN BENEFITS AND LIMITS

LEARNING OBJECTIVE 3

Describe the typical features and limitations of health care plans.

You can save yourself considerable confusion, delay, and money if you understand your health plan benefits before illness or injury strikes. If you have a group insurance plan, you will receive a **certificate of insurance** that outlines your benefits. HMO participants can obtain a copy of the plan contract. You should become familiar with the details of your health insurance plan. Below are some questions to ask yourself and background information to understand what you find in these documents.

health savings account (HSA)
Tax-deductible savings accounts into which individuals or employers can deposit tax-sheltered funds to pay medical bills.

certificate of insurance
Document or booklet that outlines group health insurance benefits.

11.3a What Types of Care Are Covered?

The typical health care plan covers hospital room and board expenses, surgical procedures both as an inpatient and outpatient, prescription drugs, diagnostic tests, visits to the doctor's office, and many other aspects of health care. Dental and vision care are now covered as they are part of the required 10 essential benefits.

11.3b Who Is Covered?

A family generally consists of a parent or parents and dependent children. Are the children of a divorced parent who does not have custody covered under that parent's group plan?

What about stepchildren? These questions must be answered to ensure that all family members are covered under some plan.

11.3c How Much Must You Pay out of Your Own Pocket?

Health care plans contain provisions that specify the level of coverage for your expenses and the portion that you must pay yourself.

How Much Is Your Deductible? An **annual deductible** is a clause in health care plans that require you to pay an initial portion of medical expenses annually before receiving reimbursement. A deductible of $200 per year, for example, would mean that the patient must pay the first $200 of the medical costs for the year. Family plans generally include a deductible for each family member (again, perhaps $200 per year) with a maximum family deductible (perhaps $500 per year). Once the deductible payments for individual family members reach the maximum family deductible ($500 in this example), further individual deductibles will be waived.

How Much Is the Co-payment? A **co-payment** requires you to pay a specific dollar amount each time you have a specific covered expense item. A co-payment is often required for visits to the doctor's office and prescription drugs. For example, you might have to pay $25 for each prescription, with the insurer paying the remainder. A co-payment differs from a deductible in that it might require that you pay $35 for each office visit even after the annual deductible is met.

How Much Is the Coinsurance Payment? A **coinsurance clause** requires you to pay a proportion of any loss suffered. The typical share is 80/20, with the insurer paying the larger percentage. Usually, a coinsurance cap limits the annual out-of-pocket payments required of the patient when meeting the coinsurance.

The following example illustrates how a deductible of $250 and an 80/20 coinsurance provision with a $1000 coinsurance cap work together to determine the coverage for an $8760 health care bill. Because the deductible is the responsibility of the insured party, the patient pays the first $250. The coinsurance ratio is applied to the remaining $8510 ($8760 − $250) until the portion paid by the patient reaches the coinsurance cap. Thus, $1000 is covered by the insured and $4000 by the insurer. The additional expenses of $3510 ($8510 − $1000 − $4000) are covered 100 percent by the insurance company. In this example, the insured party will pay $1250 ($250 deductible + $1000 coinsurance) and the insurer will pay $7510 ($4000 coinsurance + $3510 remaining charges).

co-payment

A variation of a deductible that requires you to pay a specific dollar amount each time you use your benefits for a specific covered expense item.

DO IT IN CLASS

coinsurance clause

A clause in a health care plan that requires the participant to pay a proportion of any loss suffered.

DID YOU KNOW

Dual-Income Couples Should Coordinate Their Employee Health Care Benefits

Dual-income households often have overlapping health care benefits. For example, both Harry and Belinda Johnson's employers provide partially subsidized family health insurance plans as employee benefits. The Johnsons chose to be covered under Belinda's policy because it provides more protection and is less expensive. Belinda's coverage is fully paid for, and she can add Harry to the plan for only $125 per month. Harry can then drop his health plan through his employer and sign up instead for another benefit such as disability income insurance or education reimbursement for additional training.

CONCEPT CHECK 11.3

1. Distinguish among a deductible, a co-payment, and coinsurance.

2. Explain COBRA rights and portability rights that apply when you leave a job that has a group health care plan.

3. Explain the linkages among premium conversion plans, flexible savings arrangements and health savings accounts (HSAs) and **health reimbursement accounts (HRAs)**.

11.4 PLANNING FOR LONG-TERM CUSTODIAL CARE

Many health care episodes include a period of time when the patient no longer needs skilled medical care but does need assistance to a degree that requires confinement in a nursing home or special help at home. This impacts about 4 percent of the population. This need is especially prevalent with the extremely elderly and patients with certain conditions such as Alzheimer's disease. The cost for such nonmedical assistance is typically not covered by HMOs, health insurance, or Medicare. The elderly who have spent down their assets then may be eligible to receive Medicaid reimbursement for a portion of their custodial nursing home care and custodial assistance at home. But for others, a long-term care policy may be an important part of one's health care planning. **Long-term care insurance** provides reimbursement for costs associated with custodial care in a nursing facility or at home.

Factors to assess when considering a long-term care policy include the following:

1. **The degree of impairment required for benefits to begin.** Insurance companies use the inability to perform a certain number of **activities of daily living (ADLs)** as a criterion for deciding when the insured becomes eligible for long-term care benefits. Typically, a policy pays benefits when a person cannot perform two or three ADLs without assistance. The ADLs commonly used in this type of decision making are bathing, bladder control, dressing oneself, eating without assistance, toileting (moving on and off the toilet), and transferring (getting in and out of bed). Because bathing is often one of the first ADLs that is lost, a policy that does not list bathing as a criterion makes it more difficult to reach the threshold at which benefits become available.

2. **The level of care covered.** The levels of nursing home care are usually categorized three ways. **Skilled nursing care** is intended for people who need intensive care, meaning 24-hour-a-day supervision and treatment by a registered nurse, under the direction of a doctor. **Intermediate care** is appropriate for people who do not require around-the-clock nursing but who are not able to live alone. **Custodial care** is suitable for many people who do not need skilled nursing care but who nevertheless require supervision (for example, help with eating or personal hygiene). Insurance companies' definitions of these levels of care may differ and must be considered when policies are evaluated. Although the largest expenses related to long-term care result from a stay in a nursing home, many people are able to remain in their homes with the assistance of visiting nurses, therapists, and even housekeepers. Long-term care policies can be written to cover such in-home care.

3. **The person's age.** The younger the person is when the policy is purchased, the lower the premium as the odds of needing care increase with age. The trade-off lies between buying young and paying premiums for many years versus waiting to purchase a policy, at which

LEARNING OBJECTIVE 4
Explain the basics of planning for long-term custodial care.

long-term care insurance
Provides reimbursement for costs associated with custodial care in a nursing facility Or at home.

activities of daily living (ADLs)
Insurance companies use the inability to perform a certain number of such activities as a criterion for deciding when the insured becomes eligible for long-term care benefits.

DO IT IN CLASS

custodial care
Suitable for people who do not need skilled nursing care but who nevertheless require supervision (for example, help with eating or personal hygiene).

FINANCIAL POWER POINT

Who Most Needs Long-Term Care Insurance

Low-wealth, low-income individuals can be covered for long-term care expenses under the Medicaid program. Those who have built-up accumulated retirement nest eggs of $500,000 or more generally can afford the cost of long-term care. Thus middle-income people most need long-term care insurance.

time it may be difficult to afford coverage because of pre-existing conditions and consequently high policy costs.

4. **The benefit amount.** Long-term care plans are generally written to provide a specific dollar benefit per day of care. If the cost per day for nursing homes in your geographic area is typically $200, you can pay lower premiums by choosing to buy a policy for $160 per day, thereby coinsuring for a portion of the expenses.

benefit period

The maximum period of time for which benefits will be paid under a disability income or other insurance policy.

5. **The benefit period.** The **benefit period** in a long-term care policy is the maximum period of time for which benefits will be paid; typically stated in years. Although it is possible to buy a policy with lifetime benefits, this option can be very expensive. The average nursing home stay is about two-and-one-half years. A policy with a three-year limit might cost one-third less than a policy with a lifetime benefit period.

waiting period (elimination period)

The time period between the onset of a disability and the date that disability benefits begin.

6. **The waiting period.** The **waiting period (elimination period)** in a long-term care policy is the time period between the onset of the need for care and the date that benefits begin. Policies can pay benefits from the first day of nursing home care or they can include a waiting period. Selecting a 30-day or 90-day waiting period can significantly reduce premiums.

7. **Inflation protection.** If a policy is purchased prior to age 60, the buyer faces a significant risk in that inflation may render the daily benefit woefully inadequate when care is ultimately needed. Some policies increase the daily benefit by 4 or 5 percent per year to adjust for inflation, but this protection adds considerably to the premium. The younger your age when a policy is purchased, the more you need inflation protection.

DID YOU KNOW

Money Websites

Informative websites for those planning health care expenses, including those that explain the Affordable Care Act are:

ACA provisions (www.irs.gov/uac/Affordable-Care-Act-Tax-Provisions)

AARP (www.healthlawanswers.aarp.org/)

Centers for Medicare & Medicaid Services (www.cms.gov)

Department of Health and Human Services (www.longtermcare.gov/)

Department of Labor (www.dol.gov/ebsa/)

EHealth (www.ehealthinsurance.com) to compare individual policies

Healthcare portal for states (www.healthcare.gov)

Kaiser Family Foundation subsidy calculator (www.kff.org/interactive/subsidy-calculator/)

National Association of Insurance Commissioners (www.insureuonline.org/health_page.htm)

NOLO (www.nolo.com/legal-encyclopedia/medicare-long-term-care)

Social Security Administration (www.ssa.gov/disability/ and www.ssa.gov/pgm/medicare.htm)

CONCEPT CHECK 11.4

1. Describe the protections provided by long-term care insurance.

2. Distinguish between the benefit period and the waiting period for a long-term care policy.

3. List three aspects of long-term care insurance that affect the cost of a policy.

11.5 PROTECT YOUR INCOME DURING DISABILITY

Anyone with a job can lose income when he or she becomes sick or is injured. Many employers offer sick days and other time off that can be used as necessary. Some employers may offer **disability income insurance** that replaces a portion of the income lost when you cannot work because of illness or injury. These plans come in two forms. A **short-term disability income insurance plan** replaces a portion of one's income for a short period of time, usually from two weeks up to two years. Short-term plans are sometimes partially paid for by the employer. Employers may also offer a group **long-term disability income insurance plan** for coverage periods of five or more years. The employee is usually required to pay the full premium for such coverage. If your employer does not offer either of these plans, you may buy them on your own.

Workers who are eligible can collect **Social Security Disability Income Insurance** benefits from the federal government if their disability is total (meaning they cannot work at any job) and is expected to last one year (or until death if that is anticipated within one year). The amount of these benefits is based on the worker's average lifetime earnings subject to Social Security tax and, thus, might not be sufficient to adequately support young workers and their families.

Long-term disability income loss is often overlooked, though it is vitally important for all workers including young single adults. A male worker has a 21 percent chance of becoming disabled for three months or longer at some point during his working career. Older workers who become disabled may have retirement money available because

LEARNING OBJECTIVE 5

Develop a plan to protect your income when you cannot work due to disability.

disability income insurance
Insurance that covers a portion of the income lost when you cannot work because of illness or injury.

Social Security Disability Income Insurance
Under this government program, eligible workers can receive some income if their disabilities are total, meaning that they cannot work at any job.

DO IT IN CLASS

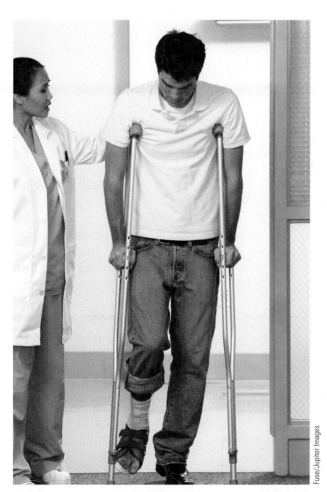

A young person needs disability income insurance even with no dependents.

certain types pension plans (not 401(k) plans or IRAs for workers under age 55) provide benefits to workers who become disabled while still employed. However, such benefit plans fall far short of fully meeting the needs of most workers.

11.5a What Is Your Level of Need?

The first question to ask when contemplating disability income insurance is, "How much protection do I need?" The dollar limits on disability income policies are written either in increments of $100 per month or as a percentage of monthly income. Policy coverage is limited to 60 to 80 percent of the insured's after-tax earnings. The government's Social Security disability income program pays an average of $13,560 annually in tax-free income to the family of a fully insured disabled worker. See Appendix B at the end of the book or the *Garman/Forgue* companion website for an illustration of how to estimate these benefits.

Determining the amount of additional protection needed is challenging because some sources of help may not actually be available for all disabilities. It is smart to complete the calculations in the Run the Numbers feature, "Determining Disability Income Insurance Needs." You can use the figure obtain from the worksheet as a starting point when shopping for disability income insurance protection.

11.5b What Disability Income Insurance Policy Provisions Best Meet Your Needs?

Once you have estimated your level of need, you can begin your search for a disability income insurance policy. Look first for the major policy provisions discussed in the following paragraphs that meet your needs. Disability income insurance policies are complicated so avoid relying on the verbal assurances of the agent selling the policy, do your own analysis, and also seek the advice of a financial planner before making a decision.

Waiting Period Disability income policies will have a waiting period between the onset of the disability and the date that disability benefits begin. Because disability

RUN THE NUMBERS

Determining Disability Income Insurance Needs

The determination of disability insurance needs begins with your current monthly after-tax income. From this figure, subtract the amounts you would receive from Social Security disability and other sources of disability income. The resulting figure will provide an estimate of extra coverage needed.

Decision Factor	Example	Your Figures
1. Current monthly after-tax income	$3,200	_____
2. Minus previous established disability income protections		_____
(a) Monthly Social Security disability benefits	−$1,250	_____
(b) Monthly benefit from employer-provided disability insurance	−$ 600	_____
(c) Monthly benefit from private disability insurance	_____	_____
(d) Monthly benefit from other government disability insurance	_____	_____
Total Subtractions	−$1,850	_____
3. Estimated monthly disability income insurance needs	$1 350	_____

DID YOU KNOW

Bias toward Minimizing Losses

People engaged in managing for health care events have a bias toward certain behaviors that can be harmful, such as a tendency towards minimizing even small, initial losses. An example is wanting a short waiting period on disability and long-term care insurance. Many people fail to understand that having a short waiting period usually means that you are at greater risk of catastrophic losses. This is because the high cost of the short waiting period makes it difficult to afford a long benefit period. What to do? Purchase policies with six-month or one-year waiting period and apply the premium savings to getting a five-year or longer benefit period.

---

income benefits are paid monthly, the first check will not arrive until 30 days after the end of the waiting period.

Benefit Period The benefit period in a disability income policy is the maximum period of time for which benefits will be paid. It begins when the elimination period ends. The benefit period is usually stated in years but may instead state a specific age when benefits will cease. Most disability income policies will not pay past age 65.

Degree of Disability Policies can be written on an "own-occupation" or "any-occupation" basis. An **own-occupation policy** will provide benefits if you can no longer perform the occupation you had at the time you became disabled. An **any-occupation policy** will provide full benefits only if you cannot perform any occupation. In effect, an any-occupation policy is an income replacement policy, as it makes up a portion of the difference between what you were earning prior to becoming disabled and what you can earn while disabled. Own-occupation policies are more generous and, therefore, cost more. Some policies provide own-occupation coverage during the first two years of a disability, and then switch to an any-occupation basis with income replacement for the remaining years of the benefits. Such **split-definition policies** are likely to provide benefits for rehabilitation and retraining at insurance company expense.

A **residual clause** is a feature of own-occupation policies that allows for some reduced level of disability income benefits when a partial—rather than full—disability occurs. Consider the case of Françoise LaDeux, a criminal lawyer in Athens, Alabama,

any-occupation policy
Provides full benefits only if the insured cannot perform any Occupation.

residual clause
Feature of own-occupation policies that allows for some reduced level of disability income benefits when a partial—rather than full—disability strikes.

DID YOU KNOW

Sean's Success Story

Early in his working life, Sean recognized that financial success is not simply a matter of making more money and building assets. He also focused on protecting his assets and income through the purchase of insurance. Sean has always been healthy but knew that illness and accidents happen all the time. His first step was to sign up for the health care plan offered by his employer. He selected an expensive health plan to keep his costs under control and signed up for a health savings account to accumulate funds for his out-of-pocket health care expenses. In addition, Sean used a premium conversion option to pay his portion of the plan's cost on a pretax basis, and he set up a flexible spending arrangement with his employer. Sean also considered the risk of being unable to work due to illness or injury. Fortunately his employer offered a group disability income insurance plan, and Sean signed up for the plan and selected a 120-day waiting period and a ten-year benefit that would pay 60 percent of his salary should he not be able to work.

DID YOU KNOW

Your Worst Financial Blunders in Managing Health Expenses

Based on others' financial woes, you will make mistakes in personal finance when you:

1. *Pay the tax-penalty assessed under the Affordable Care Act because you fail to enroll in a health care plan.*

2. *Duplicate employer-provided health care protection with your employed spouse.*

3. *Ignore your need for disability income insurance.*

---

who purchased a disability policy offering a benefit of $3000 per month. Françoise later developed multiple sclerosis and was forced to cut back her workload by 50 percent, thereby taking a 50 percent pay cut. Her disability policy had a residual clause, so she received $1500 (0.50 × $3000) per month during her disability.

A Social Security Rider Provides Additional Protection If you have figured your disability income insurance needs assuming that you would receive Social Security benefits, you will find yourself with inadequate protection if your Social Security application is denied (65 percent of all applicants are rejected). To provide an extra dollar amount of protection if you fail to qualify for Social Security disability benefits, a **Social Security rider** may be added to your policy.

Consider the case of Heather Gifford, a florist from Springfield, Missouri. Heather determined that her disability insurance needs would be $1400 per month after assuming that she would receive $1000 from Social Security if she were to become disabled. She could have purchased a $2400-per-month policy and removed all uncertainty, but the premium would have been more than she could afford. Instead, she bought a $1400 policy with a $1000 Social Security rider for a premium savings of 30 percent.

Cost-of-Living Adjustments You are wise to seek out a policy with a **cost-of-living clause**, which will increase your benefit amount to keep up with inflation. You

Social Security rider

Provides an extra dollar amount of protection if a person fails to qualify for Social Security disability benefits (70 percent of all applicants are rejected).

DID YOU KNOW

Turn Bad Habits into Good Ones

Do You Do This?	*Do This Instead!*
Simply assume your health care plan provides the coverage you want	Read the plan documents and make any changes desired
Pay all of your medical expenses with after-tax dollars	Sign up for a premium conversion plan for your health insurance payments, a flexible savings arrangement, and a health savings account to save on taxes
Ignore the potential for lost income if you became sick or injured	Explore the purchases of disability income insurance through your employer or on your own.
Ignore your employer's open-enrollment period	Use open enrollment to reassess all of your employee benefits including those related to health care
Have no advance medical directive documents	Go online and fill out online forms

might also consider buying a policy that limits benefits to a percentage of income rather than a specific dollar amount per month. With such a policy, your potential monthly benefit would increase automatically as your income increases.

CONCEPT CHECK 11.5

1. Explain how you determine your level of need for disability income insurance.

2. Identify the major policy provisions to consider when purchasing disability income insurance.

3. Distinguish between any-occupation and own-occupation disability income insurance plans.

4. Describe how you might adjust the waiting period on a disability income insurance policy in order to affordably obtain a longer benefit period.

11.6 CREATE ADVANCE DIRECTIVE DOCUMENTS IN CASE YOU BECOME INCAPACITATED

LEARNING OBJECTIVE 6

Summarize the benefits of preparing advance medical directive documents.

Advance medical directives refers to treatment preferences and the designation of a surrogate decision maker in the event that a person should become unable to make decisions on her or his own behalf as a result of coma, dementia, brain tumor, or other serious medical condition. These documents may be used to retain your dignity and save your loved ones the burden of making some very challenging and difficult decisions. In essence, you sign legal documents stating exactly what you want to happen if you become incapacitated. Four out of five adults have no advance directive documents.

There are three types of advance directives: (1) health care proxy, (2) living will, and (3) durable power of attorney for legal and financial matters. Once you have created advance directive documents, give copies to members of your family and other responsible people in your life, and your wishes in these matters may then be controlled as you desire.

11.6a A Health Care Proxy Designates One to Make Health Care Decisions

A **health care proxy** is a legal document in which individuals designate another person to make health care decisions on their behalf if they are rendered incapable of making their wishes known. The authorized person executes such decisions or tries to make sure that health care professionals follow the maker's intentions. The person who is authorized is called a proxy or agent. Filling out a health care proxy form does not deprive the creator of the right to make decisions about medical treatment as long as he or she is able to do so.

11.6b A Living Will Specifies End-of-Life Medical Treatments

A **living will** allows you to document in advance your specific wishes concerning medical treatments in an emergency or during end-of-life health care. The document sets forth one's wishes in case of terminal illness or persistent unconsciousness where the individual is no longer capable of participating in his or her health care decisions.

advance medical directives

Treatment preferences and the designation of a surrogate decision maker in the event that a person should become unable to make decisions on her or his own behalf.

health care proxy

A legal document in which individuals designate another person to make health care decisions on their behalf if they are rendered incapable of making their wishes known.

living will

Allows you to document in advance your specific wishes concerning medical treatments in an emergency or during end-of-life health care.

FINANCIAL POWER POINT

Advanced Directives for Unmarried Couples

While state laws are evolving on the rights of unmarried couples, a loved one can be protected and have some legal power. To do so, name each other as your durable power of attorney for finances and health care proxy.

DO IT NOW!

You know more about personal finance after reading this chapter, so get started right now by:

1. *Learning exactly what group health care coverage you actually do have through your job, your school, and/or your family.*

2. *Investigating the possibility of saving on income taxes via a premium conversion plan, flexible spending arrangement, or health savings account (HSA).*

3. *Create living will and health care proxy documents.*

11.6c   A Durable Power of Attorney Appoints Someone to Handle Legal and Personal Finances

Everyone should create a **durable power of attorney** in advance of the onset of any incapacitating medical condition. A durable power of attorney gives the designated person virtually absolute power to manage your financial affairs, so choose a trusted individual who knows your wishes. It allows the named individual to make bank transactions, collect Social Security payments, apply for disability, and pay bills while an individual is medically incapacitated. Understand, too, that you may revoke your power of attorney and/or give it to another person as long as you are mentally capable to do so. A **limited (or special) power of attorney** is narrower in scope and could be restricted to one specified act or a certain time period, such as signing the maker's name at the closing of the sale of a home or managing the maker's investment accounts.

CONCEPT CHECK 11.6

1. Offer three reasons why people should create advance medical directive documents.

2. What does a health care proxy achieve, and how does it differ from a living will?

3. What does a durable power of attorney provide?

WHAT DO YOU RECOMMEND *NOW?*

Now that you have read the chapter on health care planning, what do you recommend to Danielle DiMartino in the case at the beginning of the chapter regarding:

1. Choosing among the four alternatives available to her?

2. Danielle's concerns about providing for her mother's health care needs?

3. Danielle's need for her own disability income insurance?

4. How Danielle can cover her long-term care risk?

Goodshoot/Jupiterimages

BIG PICTURE SUMMARY OF LEARNING OBJECTIVES

LO1 Explain how the Affordable Care Act works and how consumers shop and pay for health insurance coverage.

The Patient Protection and Affordable Care Act of 2010 was designed to provide affordable health insurance for all US citizens and reduce the growth in health care spending. Americans already covered by a plan prior to 2014 saw little change as a result of the law. The uninsured had to have a health care plan or pay a tax penalty. The law provides for health insurance exchanges to allow consumers to find and select a quality health care plan. It also provides subsidies for families whose incomes are up to 400 percent of the poverty level to assist them in buying a health care plan.

LO2 Distinguish among the types of health care plans.

Traditional health insurance and HMOs address the need for health care. Health insurance will reimburse you or pay your medical bills directly. HMOs provide health care on a prepaid basis.

LO3 Describe the benefits and limitations of health care plans.

Health care policies contain language that outlines coverage in general and, more important, describes the limitations and conditions that determine the level of protection afforded under the plan. Some of the more important plan provisions include what types of care are covered and who is covered under the plan. Important limitations on coverage include deductibles and co-payments, and coinsurance requirements.

LO4 Explain the fundamentals of planning for long-term custodial care.

Long-term care insurance provides a per-day dollar reimbursement when the insured person must stay in a nursing home or other long-term care facility. It is not designed to provide health care protection, as that coverage is available through other plans such as an HMO, private insurance, or Medicaid.

LO5 Develop a plan to protect your income when you cannot work due to disability.

Disability income insurance replaces a portion of the income lost when you cannot work as a result of illness or injury. The amount you need is equal to your monthly after-tax income less any benefits to which you are entitled (for example, Social Security). By selecting among various policy provisions, you can tailor a policy that fills any gaps in your existing disability protection.

LO6 Summarize the benefits of preparing advance medical directive documents.

Making advance medical directives can save your loved ones the burden of making some challenging decisions in case you become incapacitated. These documents include health care proxy, living will, and durable power of attorney.

LET'S TALK ABOUT IT

1. **The Affordable Care Act and You.** Were you affected directly by the Affordable Care Act? If so, in what ways.

2. **Your Health Care Plan.** Are you covered by a health care plan? If so, what do you see as the largest potential for losses if you become ill or injured? How well do you understand the plan?

3. **HMOs Versus Health Insurance.** HMO plans and health insurance plans take different approaches to health care. What are the major differences between the two types of plans? Which plan would you prefer for your own health care protection?

4. **Long-Term Care Insurance.** Are you covered by a long-term care insurance plan? What would happen if you became so incapacitated that such care was necessary? What could you do?

5. **Disability Income Insurance.** Are you covered by disability income insurance? What would happen if you were unable to work for two or three years because of illness or injury?

6. **Advance Medical Directive Documents.** Give some thought to naming a health care proxy, signing a living will and a durable power of attorney. What are some specific provisions that you might put into the documents, and who might you name as your proxy and power of attorney?

DO THE MATH

1. **Health Care Coverage Amounts.** Michael Howitt of Berkley, Michigan, recently had his gallbladder removed. His total bill for this surgery, which was his only health care expense for the year, came to $13,890. His health insurance plan has a $500 annual deductible and an 80/20 coinsurance provision. The cap on Michael's coinsurance share is $2000.

 DO IT IN CLASS PAGE 334

   (a) How much of the bill will Michael pay?

   (b) How much of the bill will be paid by Michael's insurance?

2. **Health Care Event Protection.** Christina Haley of San Marcos, Texas, age 57, recently suffered a stroke. She was in intensive care for 3 days and was hospitalized for 10 more days. Her total bill for this care was $125,500.

After being discharged from the hospital, she spent 25 days in a nursing home at a cost of $170 per day. Christina, who earns $4,500 per month, missed two months of work. Christina had a health insurance plan through her employer. The policy had a $1000 deductible and an 80/20 coinsurance clause with a $2000 coinsurance cap. She had also accumulated 21 sick days (equivalent to one month) at work. Otherwise she had no long-term care or disability income insurance.

DO IT IN CLASS PAGES 334, 335, 337

   (a) How much of Christina's direct medical expenses was paid by her insurance policy?

   (b) What did Christina have to pay for her nursing home care?

   (c) How much income did Christina lose?

FINANCIAL PLANNING CASES

CASE 1

The Johnsons Consider Buying Disability Insurance

Although Belinda's employer offers a generous employee benefit program, it does not provide disability income protection other than 8 sick days per year, which may accumulate to 20 days if Belinda does not use them. Harry also has no disability income insurance. Although both have worked long enough to qualify for Social Security disability benefits, Belinda has estimated that Harry would receive about $640, and she would receive about $800 per month from Social Security. Harry and Belinda realize that they could not maintain their current living standards on only one salary. Thus, the need for disability income insurance has become evident even though they probably cannot afford such protection at this time. In fact, they chose not to purchase the disability waiver of premium option when they purchased their life insurance. Advise them on the following points:

DO IT IN CLASS PAGE 337

   (a) Use the Run the Numbers worksheet on page 338 to determine how much disability insurance Harry and Belinda each need. Use the December salary figures from Table 3-6 on page 87. To determine the amount of taxes and Social Security paid by each, assume that Harry, whose salary represents approximately 40 percent of their total income, paid a comparable percentage of the taxes.

   (b) Use the information on pages 336–344 to advise the Johnsons about their selections related to the following major policy provisions:

   1. Elimination period
   2. Benefit period
   3. Residual clause
   4. Social Security rider
   5. Cost-of-living adjustments

CASE 2

The Hernandezes Face the Possibility of Long-Term Care

Victor Hernandez recently learned that his uncle has Alzheimer's Disease. While discussing this tragedy with Maria, he realized that both of his grandparents probably had the disease, although no formal diagnosis was ever made. As a result, Victor and Maria have become interested in how they might protect themselves from the financial effects of long-term health care.

   (a) What factors should the Hernandezes consider as they shop for long-term care protection?

   (b) Victor is still in his 40s. How does his age affect their decisions related to long-term care protection?

CASE 3

Julia Price Assesses Her Health Care Plan

Julia is about to change jobs. Her new employer offers several different health care plans including a traditional fee-for-service plan with a PPO, and an HMO. Her employer will pay the first $300 per month for any plan she chooses.

DO IT IN CLASS
PAGE 333

This means that Julia will have to pay the remainder of the premium for the plan plus the deductible and coinsurance and co-payments. These costs are higher than they were at her previous employer's, and she is concerned about the added expenses. After talking with the employee benefits office at the new firm, she is considering saving money by opting for the medium cost plan and signing up for a health savings account, a premium conversion plan, and a flexible spending arrangement. Offer your opinions about her thinking.

CASE 4

A New Employee Ponders Disability Insurance

Charles Napier of Indiana, Pennsylvania, recently took a new job as a manufacturer's representative for an aluminum castings company. While looking over his employee benefits materials, he discovered that his employer would provide 10

DO IT IN CLASS
PAGE 337

sick days per year, and he can accumulate these to a maximum of 60 sick days if any go unused in a given year. In addition, Charles's employer provides a $1000-per-month, short-term, one-year total disability policy. When he called the employee benefits office, Charles found that he might qualify for $500 per month in Social Security disability benefits if he became unable to work. Charles earns a base salary of $2000 per month and expects to earn about that same amount in commissions, for an average after-tax income of $3100 per month. After considering this information, Charles became understandably concerned that a disability might destroy his financial future.

(a) What is the level of Jim's short-term, one-year disability insurance needs?

(b) What is the level of Jim's long-term disability insurance needs?

(c) Help Jim select from among the important disability insurance policy provisions to design a disability insurance program tailored to his needs.

CASE 5

A CPA Selects a Health Care Plan

Your friend Taliesha Jackson of Stillwater, Oklahoma, recently changed to a new job as a CPA in a moderate-size accounting firm. Knowing that you were taking a personal finance course, she asked your advice about selecting the best health insurance plan. Her employer offered five options. In addition, she could open a flexible spending arrangement and pay any premiums she must pay through a premium conversion plan:

- **Option A:** A standard health insurance plan with a $500 annual deductible and an 80 percent/20 percent coinsurance clause with a $2000 out-of-pocket limit. Taliesha must pay $80 per month toward this plan.

- **Option B:** Same as option A except that a PPO is associated with the plan. If Taliesha agrees to have services provided by the PPO, her annual deductible drops to $200 and the coinsurance clause is waived. As an incentive to get employees to select option B, Taliesha's employer will provide dental expense insurance worth about $40 per month.

- **Option C:** Another health insurance plan with a $200 annual deductible and a 90 percent/10 percent coinsurance clause with a $1000 out-of-pocket limit. Taliesha must pay $170 per month toward the cost of this plan.

- **Option D:** Membership in an HMO. Taliesha will have to contribute $40 extra each month if she chooses this option.

(a) To help her make a decision, Taliesha has asked you to list two positive points and two negative points about each plan. Prepare such a list.

(b) Why might Taliesha's employer provide an incentive of dental insurance if she chooses option B?

(c) Which plan would you recommend to Taliesha? Why?

BE YOUR OWN PERSONAL FINANCIAL MANAGER

1. **How Do You Pay for Your Health Care?** Make a list of the health care services that you used last year and estimate the cost of each of those services. Then indicate how these costs were paid, whether by yourself, by a health plan, or shared. Write a summary of what you have learned about how your health care expenses are paid.

2. **Analyze Your Health Care Plan!** Obtain a copy of your health insurance policy or the explanation of benefits brochure if you are covered by a group plan. Analyze the plan by focusing on the types of care covered, persons covered, its deductibles, coinsurance, and co-pay amounts, and any restrictions on providers of your health care.

3. **What Level of Social Security Disability Benefits Is Available to You?** Visit the website for the Social Security Administration and use its online calculator at www.ssa.gov/planners/benefitcalculators.htm to determine whether you are currently eligible to receive Social Security disability insurance benefits if you become disabled and the projected level of those benefits.

4. **Calculate Your Need for Disability Income Insurance.**

   MY PERSONAL FINANCIAL PLANNER

   Use the Run the Numbers worksheet and material on page 338 or Worksheet 46: Determining My Disability Income Insurance Needs from "My Personal Financial Planner" to estimate the amount you would need to replace should you become disabled.

5. **Explore Your Options for Saving on Taxes via Your Health Care Plan.** Are you currently employed and eligible to participate in an employer-sponsored health care plan? Use the material on page 333 to assess the opportunities you have to make use of premium conversion, a flexible spending account, high-deductible health care plan, and a health savings account to lower your after-tax cost of health care.

6. **Develop Advance Medical Directive Documents.**

   MY PERSONAL FINANCIAL PLANNER

   Complete Worksheet 47: My Advance Directive Documents in "My Personal Financial Planner" by recording which of the three advance medical directives documents the date you prepared and the names of those who know about their location or have a copy.

ON THE NET

Go to the Web pages indicated to complete these exercises.

1. **Understanding Health Care Reform.** Visit the website for U.S. Department of Health and Human Services at www.healthcare.gov/law/introduction/index.html and the Kaiser Family Foundation at www.kff.org for information on the health care reform law. What provisions in the law will be most beneficial to you in your current life situation? How might the law affect you once you graduate?

2. **Benefiting from Long-term Care Insurance.** Visit the website for U.S. Department of Health and Human Services at www.longtermcare.gov and read its information on long-term care insurance. How might such protection fit into your risk-management program or that of your family?

3. **Selecting a Disability Income Insurance Policy.** Visit the website for the U.S. Department of Agriculture at www.publications.usa.gov/USAPubs.php?PubID=6042 and read its information on disability income insurance. How might such protection fit into your plans for protecting your income should you become sick or be injured and unable to work?

ACTION INVOLVEMENT PROJECTS

1. **Assessment of Your State's Health Insurance Exchange.** Visit your state's health insurance exchange (www.kff.org/state-health-exchange-profiles). How easy was it to navigate through the information provided? Would you feel comfortable using the state or the federal health exchange to obtain coverage?

2. **Views Concerning Having Health Care Protection.** Talk to five fellow students who are not taking your personal finance class. Ask them to explain their feelings about their health care plan. Then ask them how they plan to meet their health care needs once they graduate. Make a table that summarizes your findings.

3. **What Is It Like to Choose Among an Employer's Health Care Options?** Survey three individuals or couples who are covered by a group health care plan at work. Ask them how they went about making the choice among the plans the employer offered. Include a discussion of how they approach the same decisions when the open-enrollment period occurs with the plan each October. Write a summary of their responses and how their experiences affected your thinking about an employer-provided plan.

4. **Applying the Large-Loss Principle to Health Care Planning.** The large-loss principle says that one is better off paying a higher initial portion of any loss and expanding the coverage for the largest and most catastrophic losses. In health care planning, this would mean selecting a health care plan with a high deductible for your health care expenses and a longer waiting period and longer benefit period for your disability income and long-term care insurance plans. Talk to three students in your personal finance class on their views of this approach. Also talk to three people outside of your class who are covered by a health care plan for their views. Write a summary of the responses of these two groups and how their views affect your own thinking about the large-loss principle.

5. **Addressing the Need for Disability Income Insurance.** Talk to a family member who has gone through the process of deciding about disability income insurance. Ask what motivated him or her to decide to buy or not buy such insurance. Also ask about which aspects were the most difficult part of the process. Write a summary of the responses and how your family member's efforts, or lack thereof, affect your thinking about disability income insurance.

6. **Planning for Long-Term Care.** Talk to a family member who has had to decide how to meet the long-term care needs of a loved one. Ask what aspects were the most difficult part of the process. Also ask your family member how going through the process affected his or her thinking about planning for their own long-term care needs. Write a summary of your family member's responses and how his or her efforts, or lack thereof, affect your thinking about long-term care.

Visit the Garman/Forgue companion website at www.cengagebrain.com.

12

Life Insurance Planning

YOU MUST BE KIDDING, RIGHT?

Michelle and Jason Bailey are in their early 30s and expecting their first child next month. Each earns about $60,000 per year. Currently, they have $50,000 life insurance policies on each of their lives with the other named as the beneficiary. They bought these policies a few years ago to pay for death-related expenses if tragedy struck. With the baby coming, they are thinking about buying $300,000 in life insurance coverage on each of their lives so the proceeds could be used to replace the income lost if one of them died. How much will Michelle and Jason each pay for this additional protection?

A. About $25 per month

B. About $50 per month

C. About $100 per month

D. About $200 per month

The answer is A. Term life insurance for people in their 30s can cost about $1 (or less) per $1000 of coverage per year. Thus, Michelle and Jason could each easily buy this insurance for $300 each or about $25 per month—a small price to pay for the security provided. Always buy inexpensive term life insurance so that you replace the lost income needed by your dependents if you were to pass away!

LEARNING OBJECTIVES

After reading this chapter, you should be able to:

1 Understand why you might need life insurance and calculate the appropriate amount of coverage.

2 Distinguish among types of life insurance.

3 Explain the major provisions of life insurance policies.

4 Apply a step-by-step strategy for implementing a life insurance plan.

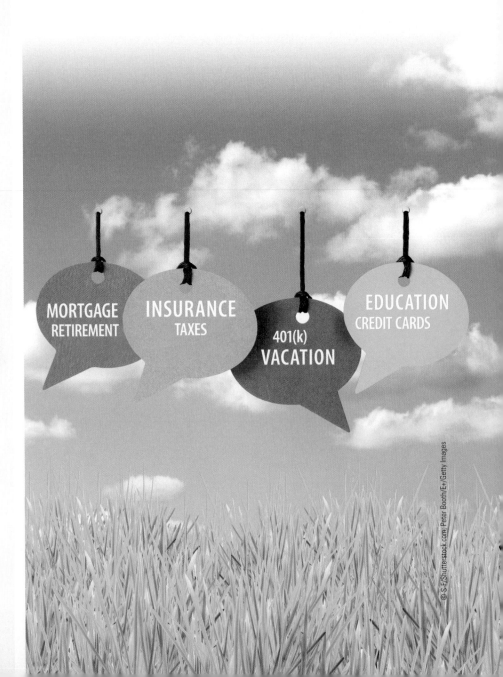

© S-F/Shutterstock.com; Peter Booth/E+/Getty Images

WHAT DO YOU RECOMMEND?

Stephanie Bridgeman, age 28, and her husband Will, age 30, recently had their first child. Both have small cash-value life insurance policies ($25,000 and $50,000, respectively) that their parents purchased when they were children. Stephanie is a real estate attorney and earns $90,000 per year. She has continued working after having the baby. Stephanie's employer offers a 401(k) plan into which she contributes a maximum of 6 percent of her salary each year matched by her employer one-half of 1 percent for each 1 percent that Stephanie contributes. Her employer does not offer employer-paid life insurance. Will is a high-school teacher and track coach and makes $49,000 per year. His employer pays the full cost of his retirement pension plan. An optional supplemental retirement plan is available into which Will can contribute 5 percent of his salary, but he has not done so as yet. Will has an employer-provided life insurance policy equal to twice his annual salary. Will and Stephanie have no other life insurance.

© Nikolay Mamluke/Dreamstime.com

What do you recommend to Stephanie and Will on the subject of life insurance planning regarding:

1. **Their changing need for life insurance now that they have a child?**

2. **What types of life insurance they should consider and whether they should purchase multiple policies?**

3. **Coordinating their retirement savings and other investments with their life insurance program?**

4. **Shopping for life insurance?**

YOUR NEXT FIVE YEARS

In the next five years, you can start achieving financial success by doing the following related to life insurance planning:

1. *Calculate your life insurance needs every three years or when major life events occur, such as the birth of a child.*

2. *Comparison-shop for term life insurance on the Internet to obtain the lowest possible rates.*

3. *Protect against health-related premium increases by selecting guaranteed renewable term policies and cash-value policies that have a guaranteed insurability option.*

4. *Employ the principle of "buy term life insurance and invest the rest" by purchasing guaranteed renewable term life insurance.*

5. *Partially fund your tax-sheltered retirement plan with the money saved by purchasing term rather than cash-value life insurance.*

LEARNING OBJECTIVE 1

Understand why you might need life insurance and calculate the appropriate amount of coverage.

---

life insurance
An insurance contract that promises to pay a dollar benefit to a beneficiary upon the death of the insured person.

final expenses
One-time expenses occurring just prior to or after a death.

Two financial problems arise because you do not know when you will die. The first problem is the risk of living too long. This raises the possibility that you will outlive your savings during retirement. Life insurance is the wrong way to address the living-too-long problem. For that problem you should invest through tax-sheltered retirement savings plans (discussed in Chapter 17) and over time create a substantial amount of wealth.

The second problem is the risk of dying too soon. This is the possibility that you might die before adequately providing for the financial well-being of loved ones, especially your spouse and children. **Life insurance** protects your loved ones against the possibility that you may die too soon. As you will see, term life insurance does this best.

The need for life insurance is greatest during the child-rearing years because the income of one or more adults is needed to support a child financially. As children get into their teenage years, they need fewer additional years of financial support. Thus the necessity of life insurance on the income earner begins to decline. And eventually, the children leave home for employment, school, or whatever. Over time, the need for life insurance for the family is eliminated because sufficient funds should be available for survivors through savings and investments that will build up over time, primarily through a retirement plan.

12.1 HOW MUCH LIFE INSURANCE DO YOU NEED?

The primary reason for buying life insurance is to allow your family members to continue with their lives free from the financial burdens that your death would bring. Your purchase of life insurance is to benefit your loved ones, not yourself. So if you are young, unmarried, and childless, you need little, if any, any life insurance.

12.1a What Financial Needs Must Be Met upon Your Death?

Financial losses that arise from dying too soon include expenditures for final expenses; the lost income of the deceased; and funds for a readjustment period, debt repayment, and possibly education expenses for a surviving spouse and children.

- **Final-Expense Needs** **Final expenses** are one-time expenses occurring just prior to or after a death. The largest of these expenses is for the funeral and burial or cremation of the deceased, which could cost as little as $2000 or as much as $15,000. In addition, there also travel and food for mourners and costs of settling the estate.

- **Income-Replacement Needs** Once someone else becomes financially dependent on you, your income and employee benefits will be the major financial loss resulting from your premature death.

- **Readjustment-Period Needs** Families often need a period of readjustment after the death of a loved one. This period may last for several months to two or three years and may require the surviving spouse to forgo employment for a time or obtain further education.

- **Debt-Repayment Needs** A family that has bought sufficient life insurance for the replacement of lost income probably will not need to make specific insurance provisions for the repayment of most debts. It is sometimes helpful, however, to buy an additional amount of life insurance to pay off all nonmortgage debt in order to simplify the finances of the survivors.

- **College-Expense Needs** Death of a parent can impede planning for children's college expenses. A suggested amount of additional life insurance would be the current cost of tuition and room and board and expenses for four years at a desired institution.

- **Other Special Needs** Many families have special needs that must be considered in the life insurance-planning process. For example, a family might have a child with special needs who will require medical or custodial care as an adult. Extremely wealthy families might need extra life insurance to pay federal estate taxes and state inheritance taxes (covered in Chapter 17).

12.1b There Are Three Ways You Can Meet These Financial Needs

There are three ways you can meet your need for protection from losses described earlier: existing assets, government benefits, and life insurance.

1. Existing Assets Can Help Meet the Need The funds held in savings accounts, certificates of deposit, stocks, bonds, and mutual funds often are specifically earmarked for some special goal, such as retirement, travel, or college for children. These could be used by survivors, even though it might be wiser to retain these funds for their originally intended purposes. Retirement accounts, such as 401(k) plans and IRAs (discussed in Chapter 17), will go to the survivor named as the beneficiary on the account. Younger families should not use these funds earlier in life because such action will jeopardize the surviving spouse's retirement.

2. Government Benefits May Help Meet Some of the Needs Widows, widowers, and their dependents may qualify for various government benefits—most notably **Social Security survivor's benefits**, which are paid to a surviving spouse with minor children or to the children directly if there is no surviving spouse. These benefits generally cease when the youngest child reaches age 18. The level of benefits depends on income earned during the lifetime of the deceased and could be as high as $2500 per month although they average less than $1000.

3. Life Insurance Can Close Any Remaining Gap in Needs Life insurance is the simplest form of insurance because it protects against only one peril—death. The benefit the policy will pay in cash is known in advance. This payment to the **beneficiary** (the person named in the policy to receive the funds) will occur within a few days once a death certificate is presented to the insurance company. Some people have existing life insurance that was purchased previously or provided through their employer. These coverages can reduce or eliminate the need for additional life insurance purchases.

12.1c What Dollar Amount of Life Insurance Do You Need?

Determining the magnitude of the losses resulting from a premature death can be complicated. Two methods are commonly used: a multiple-of-earnings approach and a needs-based approach. The needs-based approach is more accurate.

The Multiple-of-Earnings Approach Uses Flawed Logic The **multiple-of-earnings approach** estimates the amount of life insurance needed by multiplying your income by some number, such as 5, 7, or 10. Thus, someone with an annual income of $40,000 would need $200,000 to $400,000 in life insurance. Life insurance agents often suggest this simplistic approach. However, it addresses only one of the factors affecting life insurance needs—income-replacement needs—and does not take into

FINANCIAL POWER POINT

Buying Life Insurance versus Investing

Most college students will live well into their 80s, although about 20 percent will die before retirement. Buy term life insurance to protect against an early death and make investments to prepare for a long life.

FINANCIAL POWER POINT

Partners Both Need a Life Insurance Plan

Both married and co-habitating couples should coordinate their life insurance planning and they also need individual policies. This is true even if one partner makes the bulk of the family income. When appropriate, the cost of replacing the household labor of a stay-at-home spouse should be included in life insurance planning.

Social Security survivor's benefits
Government program benefits paid to a surviving spouse and children.

beneficiary
Person who receives life insurance proceeds, as per the policy.

FINANCIAL POWER POINT

Social Security Survivor Benefits Have a Blackout Period

Once the youngest child reaches age 18, a surviving spouse enters the **Social Security blackout period** and is ineligible for Social Security survivor benefits. The blackout period ends when the surviving spouse reaches age 60. The surviving spouse may then collect survivor's benefits until age 62, and then may begin collecting Social Security retirement benefits based on his or her own or the deceased spouse's retirement account, whichever provides the higher payment.

Adequate life insurance can ensure that important goals, such as paying for a child's education, are met should a parent die.

consideration such factors as age, family situation, and other assets that could cover the lost income.

The Needs-Based Approach Is the Best Method The **needs-based approach** for estimating life insurance needs considers all of the factors that might potentially affect the level of need. The Run the Numbers worksheet below, "The Needs-Based Approach to Life Insurance," illustrates calculations made via the needs-based approach. You would be wise to calculate your current needs for life insurance and then to revisit those calculations every few years and when changes occur in your employment, family situation or your health status.

Calculating Life Insurance Needs for a Couple with Small Children Consider the example of Gene Thomas, a 35-year-old chef from Denver, Colorado, who has a spouse Candice (age 30) and three children (ages 8, 7, and 3 years). Gene earns $56,000 annually and desires to replace his income for 30 years, at which time his spouse would be approaching retirement. The "Example" column of the Run the Numbers worksheet, "The Needs-Based Approach to Life Insurance," expands on the situation faced by Gene.

1. **Final-expense needs.** Gene estimates his final expenses for funeral, burial, and other expenses at $12,000.
2. **Income-replacement needs.** Gene's income of $56,000 is multiplied by 0.75 and the interest factor of 19.6004 (from Appendix A-4). This factor was used because Gene decided that it would be best to replace his lost income for 30 years or until Candice, his wife, reached age 60 and passed through the Social Security blackout period. Gene and Candice are moderate-risk investors and believe that she could earn a 3 percent after-tax, after-inflation rate of return on life insurance proceeds. Income-replacement needs based on these conditions amount to $823,217.
3. **Readjustment-period needs.** Candice is a reporter for a local newspaper, earning an annual income of $38,000. Allocating $19,000 for readjustment-period needs would allow her to take a six-month leave of absence from her job or meet other readjustment needs.
4. **Debt-repayment needs.** Gene and Candice owe $10,000 on various credit cards and an auto loan. They also owe about $128,000 on their home mortgage. Candice would like to pay off all debts except the mortgage debt if Gene dies. The mortgage debt would be affordable if Gene's income were adequately replaced.
5. **College-expense needs.** Gene estimates that it would currently cost $25,000 for each of his sons to attend the local community college. If he dies, $25,000 of the life insurance proceeds could be invested for each child. If invested appropriately, the funds should grow at a rate sufficient to keep up with increasing costs of a college education.
6. **Other special needs.** Gene and Candice do not have any unusual needs related to life insurance planning, so they entered zero for this factor.

RUN THE NUMBERS

The Needs-Based Approach to Life Insurance

This worksheet provides a mechanism for estimating life insurance needs using the needs-based approach. The amounts needed for final expenses, income replacement, readjustment needs, debt repayment, college expenses, and other special needs are calculated and then reduced by funds available from government benefits and any current insurance or assets that could cover the need. This worksheet is also available on the *Garman/Forgue* companion website.

Factors Affecting Need	Example	Your Figures
1. Final-expense needs Includes funeral, burial, travel, and other items of expense just prior to and after death	$ 12,000	$_____
2. Income-replacement needs Multiply 75 percent of annual income* by the interest factor from Appendix A-4 that corresponds to the number of years that the income is to be replaced and the assumed after-tax, after-inflation rate of return. ($42,000 × 19.6004 for 30 years at a 3% rate of return)	+ 823,217	+_____
3. Readjustment-period needs To cover employment interruptions and possible education expenses for surviving spouse and dependents	+ 19,000	+_____
4. Debt-repayment needs Provides repayment of short-term and installment debt, including credit cards and personal loans	+ 10,000	+_____
5. College-expense needs To provide a fund to help meet college expenses of dependents	+ 75,000	+_____
6. Other special needs	+ 0	+_____
7. Subtotal (combined effects of items 1–6)	+$939,217	+_____
8. Government benefits Present value of Social Security survivor's benefits and other benefits. Multiply monthly benefit estimate by 12 and use Appendix A-4 for the number of years that benefits will be received and the same interest rate that was used in item 2. ($2725 × 12 × 11.9379 for 15 years of benefits and a 3% rate of return)	− 390,369	−_____
9. Current insurance assets	− 100,000	−_____
10. Life insurance needed	$ 448,848	$_____

*Seventy-five percent is used because about 25 percent of income is used for personal needs.

7. Subtotal. The Thomases total items 1 through 6 on the worksheet and determine that the family's financial needs arising out of Gene's death would amount to $939,217. Although this sum seems large to them, they have access to two resources that can reduce this figure, as indicated in items 8 and 9.

8. Government benefits. Gene determined from his Social Security Benefits Statement that his family would qualify for monthly Social Security survivor's benefits of $2725, or $32,700 a year.* These benefits would be paid for 15 years,

DO IT IN CLASS

needs-based approach
A superior method of calculating the amount of insurance needed that considers all of the factors that might potentially affect the level of need.

* Your personal Social Security benefits can be estimated by requesting a Social Security Statement from the Social Security Administration (www.ssa.gov) or see Appendix B.

until his youngest son turns 18. The present value of this stream of benefits is $390,369 (from Appendix A-4), assuming a 3 percent return for 15 years.

9. **Current insurance and assets.** Gene has a $50,000 life insurance policy purchased five years ago. His employer also pays for a group policy with a face amount of $50,000. Gene's major assets include his home and his retirement plan. Because he does not want Candice to have to liquidate these assets if he dies, he includes only the $100,000 insurance coverage in item 9.

10. **Life insurance needed.** After subtracting worksheet items 8 and 9 from the subtotal, Gene estimates that he needs an additional $448,848 in life insurance. This amount may large, but Gene can meet this need through term life insurance for as little as $30 per month.

Because Candice earns an income that is about two-thirds of Gene's, her life insurance needs may be about one-third percent lower. To determine the specific amount, the couple must complete a worksheet for her as well. Next, the Thomases will need to decide what type of life insurance is best and from whom to buy the additional life insurance needed. These topics are covered later in this chapter.

Calculating Life Insurance Needs for a Young Professional Baomei Zhao of Akron, Ohio, recently graduated with a degree in tourism management and has accepted a position paying $43,000 per year. Baomei is single and lives with her sister. She owes $14,500 on a car loan and $21,800 in education loans. She has about $7000 in the bank. Among her employee benefits is an employer-paid term insurance policy equal to her annual salary.

Baomei has been approached by a life insurance agent who used the multiple-of-earnings approach to suggest that she needs $215,000 in life insurance, or about five times her income. Does she? If you apply the needs-based approach to Baomei's situation, you will see the following:

- Baomei estimates her final expenses at $12,000, which she entered for item 1.

- Items 2, 3, 5, and 6 in the needs-based approach worksheet on page 353 are zero because Baomei has no dependents.

- Baomei would like to see her $14,500 automobile loan and $21,800 education loans repaid in the event of her death. She feels better knowing that her younger sister could inherit her car free and clear. She entered $36,300 for item 4.

- Baomei's survivors will not qualify for any government benefits, so item 8 will also be zero.

- Baomei has other life insurance and certain assets worth a total of $50,000, so she entered that amount for item 9.

DID YOU KNOW

Bias toward Avoiding Difficult Subjects

People engaged in life insurance planning have a bias toward certain behaviors that can be harmful, such as a tendency toward avoiding discussing difficult topics. Many people avoid planning for the possibility of death. What to do? Force yourself to do a life insurance needs assessment and purchase the insurance you need.

The resulting calculations show that Baomei needs no additional life insurance ($12,000 + $36,300 − $50,000 = − $1700). The agent also suggested that Baomei buy now while she is young and rates are low. This is not a smart idea because you should never buy life insurance simply to lock in low rates. That would be like buying car insurance before you own a car. Besides, life insurance prices are declining. Unless you have a personal or family-based medical history that might interfere with the purchase of life insurance when needed later, you, like Baomei, should wait until you actually need life insurance before buying a policy.

DO IT IN CLASS

CONCEPT CHECK 12.1

1. Distinguish between the dying-too-soon problem and the living-too-long problem and the best ways to address each.

2. List five types of needs that can be addressed through life insurance.

3. Explain why the multiple-of-earnings approach is less accurate than a needs-based approach to life insurance planning.

4. Identify two periods in a typical person's life cycle when the need for life insurance is low and one when it is high.

12.2 THERE ARE ONLY TWO BASIC TYPES OF LIFE INSURANCE

LEARNING OBJECTIVE 2
Distinguish among types of life insurance.

Many people are confused by the wide variety of life insurance plans available. But, in reality, there are only two types of life insurance: term life insurance and cash-value life insurance. **Term life insurance** is often described as "pure protection" because it pays benefits only if the insured person dies within the time period (term) covered by the policy. The policy must be renewed if coverage is desired for another time period. In this way, it acts much like car or homeowner's insurance.

All the other life insurance policies are variations of **cash-value life insurance**. These policies pay benefits at death (like term policies) but also include a savings/ investment element that can provide benefits to the policyholder prior to the death of the insured person. This **cash value** factor represents the value of the investment aspect of the life insurance policy. Because of the investment aspect of cash-value policies, many people automatically believe cash value life insurance is the better option, but this is false. Cash-value life insurance costs much more than term insurance, and there are much better options for investing than life insurance, as you will learn in upcoming chapters

term life insurance
"Pure protection" against early death; pays benefits only if the insured dies within the time period (term) that the policy covers.

cash-value life insurance
Pays benefits at death and includes a savings/investment element that can provide a level of benefits to the policyholder prior to the death of the insured person.

12.2a Term Life Insurance Is Pure Protection

Term life insurance contracts are most often written for time periods (or terms) of 1, 5, 10, or even 20 years. If the insured survives the specified time period, the beneficiary receives no monetary benefits. Term insurance can be purchased in contracts with face amounts in multiples of $1000, usually with a minimum face amount of $50,000. The **face amount** is the dollar value of life insurance protection as listed in the policy and used to calculate the premium. Variations on term life insurance include decreasing term insurance, guaranteed renewable term insurance, convertible term insurance, and credit (term) life insurance.

face amount
Dollar value of protection as listed in the policy and used to calculate the premium.

DID YOU KNOW

The Tax Consequences of Life Insurance

Life insurance proceeds paid to a beneficiary are not subject to income taxes and may be used in any way the beneficiary wishes. If the funds are put in the bank or invested in some way, any interest or dividends earned will be subject to income taxation.

Unless otherwise stipulated by the original contract, to renew the policy you must apply for a new contract and may be required to undergo a medical examination. The premium will increase slightly with each renewal, reflecting your increasing age, of course. For example, a $100,000 five-year renewable term policy for a man age 25 might have an annual premium of $100; at age 35, the policy might cost $135; and at age 45, it might cost $220. Term policies are much less expensive than a new cash-value policy at any given age because they do not include a savings/investment element.

Guaranteed Renewable Term Insurance Proving insurability at renewal of a term policy may be difficult if you develop a serious health problem. To avoid this dilemma, term life insurance policies are usually written as **guaranteed renewable term insurance**. The guarantee protects you against the possibility of becoming uninsurable due to health status reasons. The number of renewals you can make without proving insurability may be limited to two or three, and a maximum age may be specified for these renewals (usually 65 or 70 years). Unless you are positive that you will not need a renewal, guaranteed renewable term insurance is recommended. The additional cost for this guarantee is negligible but the coverage is critically important.

guaranteed renewable term insurance
Protects you against the possibility of becoming uninsurable.

level-premium term insurance
Term policy with a long term under which premiums remain constant. Also called guaranteed level-premium term insurance.

convertible term insurance
Offers policyholders the option of exchanging a term policy for a cash-value policy without evidence of insurability.

Level-Premium Term Insurance As you grow older, you can avoid term insurance premium increases in part by buying **level-premium (or guaranteed level-premium) term insurance**. This is is a term policy with a long time period. Under such a policy, the premiums remain constant throughout the entire life of the policy, perhaps 5, 10, or 20 years. Premiums charged in early years are higher than necessary to balance out the lower-than-necessary premiums in later years covered by the policy. Premiums on policies written for ten or more years usually remain constant for a five-year interval, and then might increase to a new constant rate for another five- or ten-year interval.

Decreasing Term Insurance With **decreasing term insurance**, the face amount of coverage declines annually, while the premiums remain constant. The buyer chooses an initial face amount and a contract period, after which the face amount of the policy gradually declines (usually each year) to some minimum in the last year of the contract. For example, a woman age 35 might buy a 30-year $200,000 decreasing term policy that declines by $5000 each year to a minimum of $50,000.

Convertible Term Insurance **Convertible term insurance** offers the policyholder the option of exchanging a term policy for a cash-value policy without evidence of insurability. Usually, this conversion is available only during the first five years of the policy. There are two ways to convert a term policy to a cash-value policy. First, you can simply request the conversion and begin paying the higher premiums required for the cash-value policy.

FINANCIAL POWER POINT

Millions of Families Have No Life Insurance

Surveys show that only 44 percent of families have an individual life insurance policy. Most people think that life insurance is expensive but that is false. On the contrary, term life insurance is very affordable, costing as little as $40 per month for a $500,000 policy and $70 per month for a $1 million policy on a person under age 45.

Second, you can pay the company the cash value that would have built up had the policy originally been written on a cash-value basis.

Group Term Life Insurance **Group term life insurance** is issued to people as members of a group, typically through an employer, rather than as individuals. Group life insurance premiums are average rates based on the characteristics of the group as a whole and, therefore typically, cost *more* than individually purchased plans for healthy individuals. If you are insured under a group plan, however, you do not need to prove your insurability. This is a major benefit for people whose health status makes individual life insurance unaffordable or unattainable.

Credit and Mortgage Term Life Insurance **Credit term life insurance** will pay the remaining balance of a specific loan if the insured dies before repaying the debt. **Mortgage life insurance** specifically pays off a mortgage debt. In essence, both of these types of term insurance are decreasing term insurance with the creditor named as beneficiary. These products are grossly overpriced, and the only people who should consider their purchase are those who are truly uninsurable because of a serious health condition.

12.2b Cash-Value Life Insurance Has a Savings Element

Cash-value life insurance pays benefits upon the death of the insured and also incorporates a savings/investment element. This cash value belongs to the owner of the policy rather than to the beneficiary. While the insured is alive, the owner may obtain the cash value by borrowing some of it from the insurance company or by surrendering and canceling the policy. Cash-value insurance is referred to as **permanent insurance** because coverage is maintained for the entire life of the insured as long as premiums are paid. The annual premiums for cash-value policies usually remain constant.

The premiums for newly written cash-value policies are always much higher than those for term policies providing the same amount of coverage. This difference arises because only a portion of the premium is used to provide the death benefit; the remainder is used to keep the premium level and to build the cash value. Figure 12-1 illustrates the premium differences between cash-value and term life insurance policies.

Figure 12-1 **Comparison of Premium Dollars for Cash-Value and Term Life Insurance**

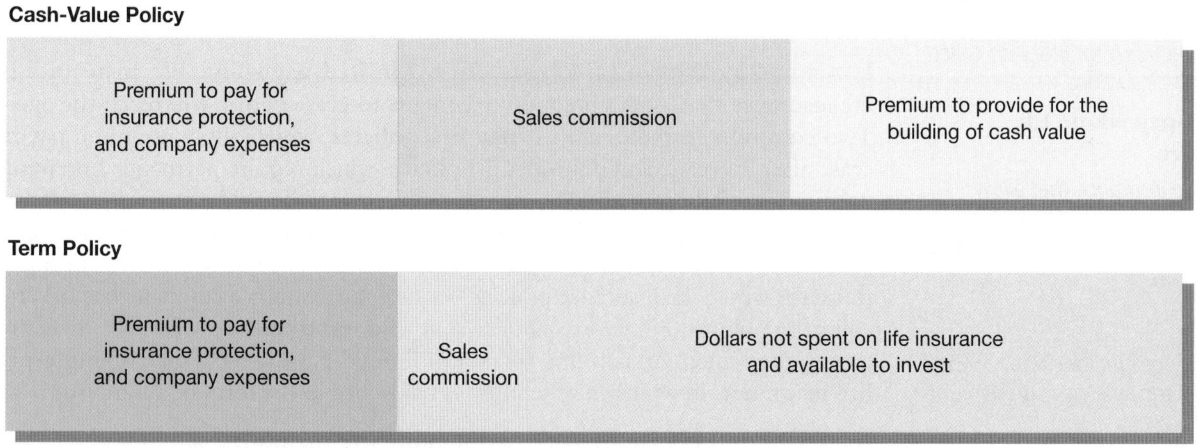

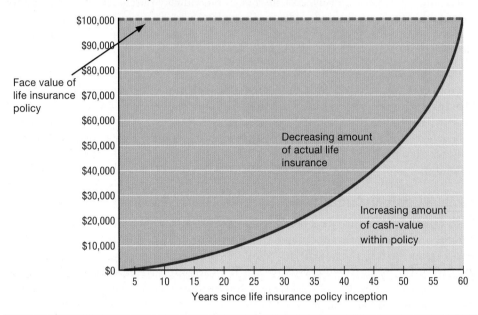

Figure 12-2 The Fundamental Nature of Cash-Value Life Insurance

The $100,000 death benefit (face value) paid to the beneficiaries comprises a decreasing amount of life insurance and the policyholder's returned built-up cash values.

Cash-value life insurance represents a combination of decreasing term insurance and an investment account that adds up to the face amount of the policy. Figure 12-2 illustrates this concept. Initially, for example, you might have $100,000 of insurance and no savings. About a decade later, you might have built up $2000 in savings within the policy. In the event of your death, your beneficiary would collect $100,000, of which $2000 would be your own money. If you lived long enough, the cash value could equal the $100,000 figure. In effect, your beneficiary would then collect your "savings account" rather than an insurance payment. Discussed below are 5 types of of cash-value life insurance.

Whole Life Insurance **Whole, or straight, life insurance** is the most popular form of cash-value life insurance, and it provides lifetime life insurance as long as the premiums are paid every year the person is alive. The policy remains in effect and does not need to be renewed.

Limited-Pay Whole Life Insurance **Limited-pay whole life insurance** is whole life insurance that allows premium payments to cease before you reach the age of 100. Two common examples are **20-pay life policies**, which allow premium payments to cease after 20 years, and **paid-at-65 policies**, which require payment of premiums only until the insured turns 65. Although premiums need be paid only for the specified time period in limited-pay policies, the insurance protection lasts for your entire life.

Of course, the annual premiums for limited-pay insurance policies are higher than those for whole life insurance policies because the insurance company has fewer years to collect premiums. Limited-pay policies are said to be **paid up** when the owner can stop paying premiums. An extreme version of limited-pay life insurance is **single-premium life insurance**, in which the premium is paid once in the form of a lump sum.

Adjustable Life Insurance **Adjustable life insurance** allows you to modify any one of the three components of life insurance (premium, the face amount of the policy,

whole life insurance

Form of cash-value life insurance that provides lifetime life insurance protection and expects the insured to pay premiums for life. Also called straight life insurance.

limited-pay whole life insurance

Whole life insurance that allows premium payments to cease before the insured reaches the age of 100.

paid up

Point at which the owner of a whole life policy can stop paying premiums.

and the rate of cash-value accumulation) with corresponding changes occurring in the other two. These changes may be made without providing new proof of insurability.

Modified Life Insurance **Modified life insurance** is whole life insurance for which the insurance company charges reduced premiums in the early years and higher premiums thereafter. The premiums are lower in early years because some of the protection during the early years is provided by term insurance. Because modified life insurance uses term insurance in the early years, it accumulates cash value extremely slowly.

12.2c Some Cash-Value Life Policies Earn a Variable Return

The rate at which the cash value accumulates in a cash-value policy depends on the rate of return paid by the company. All of the cash-value policies described above earn a guaranteed minimum rate of return, often 2 to 4 percent and are known as **fixed-rate policies**. Some cash-value policies, however, may instead pay a higher rate depending on the success of the investments made by the insurance company. Table 12-1 illustrates these rates.

A drawback of policies with a variable return is the high expense loadings and fees they carry. A 2 percent annual fee would change a policy with an annual return of 5 percent on its investments to one with a net 3 percent return. Discussed below are 3 types of cash-value life insurance policies.

Universal Life Insurance **Universal life insurance** provides both the pure protection of term insurance and the cash-value buildup of whole life insurance, along with variability in the face amount, rate of cash-value accumulation, premiums, and rate of return. Initially, the purchaser selects a face amount, and the company quotes an annual premium. The annual premium goes into the cash-value fund, from which the company deducts the cost of providing the insurance protection and charges for company expenses.

As time goes by, the owner of the policy may choose to pay a smaller are larger premium, with corresponding changes occurring in the insurance protection or amount

universal life insurance
Provides the pure protection of term insurance and the cash-value buildup of whole life insurance, along with face amount variability, rate of cash-value accumulation, premiums, and rate of return.

Table 12-1	Cash-Value Buildup Illustration—Guaranteed Versus Current Rates*

Policy Year	"Guaranteed" Cash-Surrender Value (2.0% rate)	"Current Rate" Cash-Surrender Value (3.1% rate)
1	$ 0	$ 0
2	0	96
3	289	354
4	640	730
5	995	1,152
6	1,310	1,475
7	1,730	1,910
8	2,100	2,365
9	2,567	3,420
10	2,910	4,123
15	5,050	6,780
20	7,300	9,355
25	$10,200	$13,630

*Figures are illustrative for a $50,000 universal life policy; the annual premium is $684.

ADVICE FROM A PROFESSIONAL

Don't Be Fooled by "Return-of-Premium" Riders

A feature of some term life insurance that is sometimes promoted as a great idea is **return-of-premium (ROP) rider**. Here the salesperson selling the policy promises that it will return all the premiums paid if the insured person maintains the policy and lives past a certain number of years—usually 30. These term policies cost much more in order to provide for the return of premiums. Insurance companies promote these policies as a way to avoid "wasting" your money.

In reality, what they are trying to do is entice you to pay more with the difference becoming analogous to an investment with the profit being the returned premium. Of course, most policyholders do not keep their policies for 30 years. And if you die during the policy term you receive nothing on your "investment." Finally, the extra costs may prevent you from buying enough life insurance. This is definitely not a good idea.

Hyungsoo Kim
University of Kentucky

DO IT IN CLASS

added to cash value. If premiums drop below the amount necessary to cover the insurance protection and expenses, funds are removed from the cash-value account to cover the shortfall. Essentially, universal life insurance combines annual term insurance with a type of investment program. A popular version of universal life insurance is the **indexed universal life insurance** policy where the investments portion is invested in an index mutual fund (see Chapter 15).

Variable Life Insurance **Variable life insurance** allows you to choose the investments made with your cash-value accumulations and to share in any gains or losses. The face amount of your policy and the policy's cash value may rise or fall based on changes in the returns earned on the invested funds. The face amount of the policy usually will not drop below the originally agreed-upon amount, however. Instead, the cash value will fluctuate. Variable life insurance policies are complicated and should be read and analyzed very carefully before purchase.

variable-universal life insurance

Form of universal life insurance that gives the policyholder some choice in the investments made with the cash value accumulated by the policy. Also called flexible-premium variable life insurance.

Variable-Universal Life Insurance **Variable-universal life insurance** is a form of universal life insurance that gives the policyholder some choice in the investments made with the cash value accumulated by the policy. It is sometimes called **flexible-premium variable life insurance**. It is no longer a popular type of cash-value life insurance even though it appears to embody the philosophy of "buy term and invest the rest." In fact, it does not do this very well as you will read later in this chapter on page 368. Variable-universal life policies usually provide no minimum guaranteed rate of return.

CONCEPT CHECK 12.2

1. Distinguish between term life insurance and cash-value life insurance.
2. Explain why the premiums for term insurance are so much lower than those of cash-value life insurance.
3. Describe the benefit of buying guaranteed renewable term insurance.
4. Explain why the amount of "insurance" declines over time under a cash-value life insurance policy.
5. Distinguish between cash-value life insurance with a fixed return and with a variable

12.3 UNDERSTANDING YOUR LIFE INSURANCE POLICY

A **life insurance policy** is a contract between an insurance policy holder/owner and an insurance company, where the company promises to pay a designated beneficiary a sum of money (the "benefits") upon the death of the insured person. It contains all of the information relevant to the agreement. Several parties will be named in the life insurance contract. The **owner,** or **policyholder**, retains all rights and privileges granted by the policy, including the right to amend the policy and the right to designate who receives the proceeds. The **insured** is the person whose life is insured. In addition to the beneficiary, the owner will name a **contingent beneficiary** who will become the beneficiary if the original beneficiary dies before the insured. The same person may be one or more of these parties.

12.3a Policy Terms and Provisions Unique to Life Insurance

Life insurance policies define the terminology used in the policy and outline the basic provisions of such insurance. This information serves to clarify the meaning of the policy and the protection afforded the insurer and the policyholder.

The Application The **life insurance application** is the policyholder's offer to purchase a policy. It provides information and becomes part of the life insurance policy. Any errors or omissions in the application may allow the insurance company to deny a request for payment (usually within the first year) of the death benefit and instead any premiums will be refunded.

Lives Covered Most life insurance policies cover the life of a single person—the insured. **First-to-die policies** cover more than one person but pay only when the first insured dies. These policies are less costly than separate policies written on each person, but the survivor then has no coverage after the first person dies. An alternative is the **survivorship joint life policy**, which pays when the last person covered dies.

life insurance policy
A contract between an insured (insurance policy holder) and an insurer or assurer, where the insurer promises to pay a designated beneficiary a sum of money (the "benefits") upon the death of the insured person.

owner/policyholder
Retains all rights and privileges granted by the policy, including the right to amend the policy and the right to designate who receives the proceeds.

insured
Individual whose life is insured.

DID YOU KNOW

How Insurance Policies Are Organized

All insurance policies have five basic components including declarations, insuring agreements, exclusions, conditions, and endorsements. In order of their usual location in the policy, these five elements contain information as follows:

1. **Declarations** provide the basic descriptive information about the insured person or property, the premium to be paid, the time period of the coverage, and the policy limits. Also included may be promises by the insured to take steps to control the losses associated with a specific peril, such as not smoking.

2. **Insuring agreements** are the broadly defined coverages provided under the policy. The insurer makes these promises in return for the premium paid by the insured. For example, in life insurance, the insurer promises to pay the death benefit amount to the beneficiary upon proof of the insured's death.

3. **Exclusions** narrow the focus and eliminate specific coverage broadly stated in the insuring agreements. The insurer makes no promise to pay for these exceptions and special circumstances. For example, suicide is commonly excluded during the first two years of a life insurance policy. People who do not understand the exclusions in their policies may believe they are covered for a loss when, in fact, they are not.

4. **Conditions** impose obligations on both the insured and the insurer by establishing the ground rules of the agreement. For example, they might include procedures for making a claim after a loss, rules for cancellation of the policy by either party, and procedures for changing the terms of the policy.

5. **Endorsements** (or **riders**) are amendments and additions to the basic insurance policy that can both expand and limit coverage or raise the policy limits to accommodate specific needs.

incontestability clause

Places a time limit on the right of the insurance company to deny a claim.

Incontestability Clause Life insurance policies generally include an **incontestability clause** that places a time limit—usually two years after issuance of the policy—on the right of the insurance company to deny a claim. This clause addresses the problems arising out of erroneous statements that may have been made by the insured on the application.

Suicide Clause Life insurance policies always include a **suicide clause** that allows the life insurance company to deny coverage (although all premiums will be refunded) if the insured commits suicide within the first two years after the policy is issued. If the specified number of years has elapsed, the full death benefit will be paid.

insurance dividends

Surplus earnings of the insurance company when the difference between the total premium charged exceeds the cost to the company of providing insurance.

participating policies

Life insurance policies that pay dividends.

death benefit

Amount that will be paid to the beneficiary when the insured dies.

Cash Dividends **Insurance dividends** are defined by the Internal Revenue Service as a return of a portion of the premium paid for a life insurance policy; they are not considered taxable income. They represent the surplus earnings of the company when the difference between the total premium charged exceeds the cost to the company of providing insurance. Policies that pay dividends are called **participating policies**, and policies that do not pay dividends are called **nonparticipating policies**. Both term and cash-value policies may pay dividends.

Death Benefit The **death benefit** of a life insurance policy is the amount that will be paid upon the death of the insured person. The amount of the death benefit may be either higher or lower than the face amount. It can be higher due to such items as earned dividends not yet paid or premiums paid in advance. Or it can be lower due to outstanding policy loans or unpaid premiums. Consider a $100,000 participating whole life policy with annual premiums of $1380. If the insured died halfway through the policy year, with an outstanding cash-value loan of $5000 and earned but unpaid dividends of $4000, the death benefit would be $99,690, calculated as follows:

DO IT IN CLASS

$100,000	Face amount
4,000	Unpaid dividends
+690	Premiums paid in advance (one-half year)
$104,690	Subtotal
−5,000	Outstanding cash-value loan
$ 99,690	Death benefit

Grace Period Prompt payment of the premium is crucial to the continuation of coverage provided by any insurance policy. A **lapsed policy** is one that has been terminated because of nonpayment of premiums. More than one-half of all whole life policies lapse within ten years of being issued!

DID YOU KNOW

Turn Bad Habits into Good Ones

Do You Do This?

Assume that you have life insurance set up by your parents

Put off thinking about life insurance because you are young

Assume a cash-value life insurance policy is the best way to buy life insurance

Rely on a life insurance agent to determine how much and what type of insurance to buy

Do This Instead!

Confirm that you are covered and for how much

Determine the dollar amount of insurance that you need and buy insurance to cover any shortfall

Explore term life insurance as the lowest cost and most appropriate means of protection

Make your own assessments based on your income and family obligations

To help prevent a lapse, state laws generally require that cash-value and multiyear term policies include a grace period, that is, a period of time (usually 30 days following each premium due date) during which an overdue premium may be paid without a lapse of the policy. During the grace period, all provisions of the policy remain intact if payment is made before the grace period ends.

grace period
Period of time during which an overdue premium may be paid without a lapse of the policy.

Reinstatement If your life insurance policy lapses, it may be possible to reinstate it. To do so, you typically must prove insurability and pay any missed premiums, plus interest, to be reinstated.

Multiple Indemnity A **multiple indemnity clause** provides for a doubling or tripling of the face amount if death results from certain accidents. It is most often used to double the face amount if death results from an accident. Such a clause is often included automatically as part of the policy at no extra cost.

12.3b Policy Features Unique to Cash-Value Life Insurance

Cash-value life insurance policies carry special features that all relate to the cash values built up in the policies.

The Policy Illustration Cash-value life insurance policies generally provide a **policy illustration** that charts the projected growth in the cash value. Table 12-1 (on page 359) provides an example of a policy illustration.

Policy illustrations can be somewhat helpful, but you should only rely on the **guaranteed minimum rate of return** (the minimum rate that, by contract, the company is legally obligated to pay) and understand that the **current rate** (the rate of return recently paid by the company to policyholders) is an estimate of future returns and is quickly outdated. For this reason, it is smart to periodically ask your agent for an **in-force illustration** that shows the cash-value status of the policy and projections for the future given the current rate of return at the time of the illustration (rather than the rate used at the inception of the policy). Reading the middle and right columns in the policy illustration in Table 12-1 reveals that a cash-value policy has very little cash surrender value unless you have held it for ten years or more.

Asking a few pertinent questions can help cut through some of the misconceptions:

guaranteed minimum rate of return
Minimum rate that, by contract, the insurance company is legally obligated to pay.

current rate
Rate of return the insurance company has recently paid to policyholders.

1. Is the "current rate" illustrated actually the rate paid recently? What was the current rate in each of the past five years?
2. What assumptions have been made regarding company expenses, dividend rates, and policy lapse rates?
3. Does all of my cash value earn a return at the current rate? (If not, the current rate is misleading.)
4. Is the illustration based on the "cash surrender value" or the "cash value"? (The cash surrender value is usually the lower value and reflects what will actually be paid if the policy is cashed in.)

Nonforfeiture Values Nonforfeiture values are important for consumers. These are amounts stipulated in a life insurance policy that protect the cash value, if any has accumulated, in the event that the policyholder chooses at some point to not pay or fails to pay the premiums. The policy owner can receive the accumulated cash-value funds in one of three ways. First, the policy owner may continue the policy with the original face amount but for a time period shorter than the original policy. Second, he or she may simply surrender the policy and receive the **cash surrender value**, which represents the cash value minus any surrender charges. Third, the policy may be continued on a paid-up basis, with a new and lower face amount being established based on the amount that can be purchased with the accumulated funds.

nonforfeiture values
Amounts stipulated in a life insurance policy that protect the cash value, if any, in the event that the policyholder chooses not to pay or fails to pay required premiums.

cash surrender value
Represents the cash value of a policy minus any surrender charges.

Policy Loans The owner of a cash-value policy may borrow all or a portion of the accumulated cash value. Interest rates charged for the loan will range from 2 to 8 percent, depending on the terms of the policy. In addition, the interest rate earned

DID YOU KNOW

Money Websites for Life Insurance Planning

Informative websites for life insurance planning, including sites that compare policies and prices are:

Accuquote (www.accuquote.com/)

Insweb (www.insweb.com)

Kiplinger's Personal Finance (www.kiplinger.com/fronts /channels/insurance/index.html)

National Association of Insurance Commissioners
(www.naic.org/store_home.htm)

New York Times (topics.nytimes.com/your-money /insurance/life-and-disability-insurance/index.html)

CNN Money www.money.cnn.com/magazines/moneymag/ money101/lesson20/index.htm

Your State's Department of Insurance (www.naic.org /state_web_map.htm)

DID YOU KNOW

Your Worst Financial Blunders in Life Insurance Planning

Based on others' financial woes, you will make mistakes in personal finance when you:

1. *Let a life insurance agent tell you how much and what type of life insurance to buy.*
2. *Buy cash-value life insurance rather than term policies.*
3. *Ignore your changing need for life insurance as your get older.*

automatic premium loan
Provision that allows any premium not paid by the end of the grace period to be paid automatically with a policy loan if sufficient cash value or dividends have accumulated.

waiver of premium
A clause in an insurance policy that waives the policyholder's obligation to pay any further premiums should he or she become seriously ill or disabled.

guaranteed insurability (guaranteed purchase option)
Permits the cash-value policyholder to buy additional stated amounts of cash-value life insurance at stated times in the future without evidence of insurability.

on the remaining cash value typically reverts to the guaranteed minimum rate while the loan remains outstanding. As a result, the cash value ultimately accumulated may be significantly reduced. At a minimum, you must pay the interest on the amount borrowed and any amount owed will be subtracted from the face amount of the policy if you die while the debt remains outstanding.

An **automatic premium loan** provision allows any premium not paid by the end of the grace period to be paid automatically with a policy loan if sufficient cash value or dividends have accumulated. In the first few years of a policy, this provision may not offer much benefit because cash value and dividends accumulate slowly. Eventually these funds may grow enough to pay premiums for a considerable length of time, thereby effectively preventing the lapse of the policy.

Some life insurance policies have a **living benefit clause** (or **accelerated death benefits rider**) that allows the payment of a portion of the death benefit prior to death if the insured contracts a terminal illness or requires long-term medical care such as in a nursing home. These early payments are not cash-value loans but do reduce the death benefit ultimately paid. **Viatical companies** specialize in buying life insurance policies from terminally ill insureds for a percentage of the death benefit in return for being named owner and beneficiary on the policy. The viatical company continues to pay the premiums on the policy.

Waiver of Premium A **waiver of premium** is a clause in an insurance policy that waives the policyholder's obligation to pay any further premiums should he or she become seriously ill or disabled. It usually applies when a policyholder becomes totally and permanently disabled, but it may also apply under other conditions, depending on the policy provisions. In effect, the waiver-of-premium option (for an extra cost) protects against the risk of becoming disabled and being unable to pay premiums.

Guaranteed Insurability The **guaranteed insurability (or guaranteed purchase)** option permits the cash-value policyholder to buy additional stated amounts of cash-value life insurance at stated times in the future without taking a health exam. This option differs from the guaranteed renewability option for term insurance in that it enables the owner to increase the face amount of the policy or to buy an additional policy. The policy might allow the exercise of these options when the insured turns age 30, 35, or 40, or when he or she marries or has children. The added cost of this option is nominal and worthwhile.

12.3c Settlement Options Specify How the Death Benefit Will Be Paid

Settlement options are the choices that the life insurance policyholder has in determining how the death benefit will be paid. The owner may choose the option before death, or the beneficiary may select the option after the insured's death. The five settlement options are as follows:

settlement options
Choices from which the policyholder can choose in how the death benefit payment will be structured.

1. **Lump sum.** The death benefit may be received as a lump-sum cash settlement immediately after death. This is often the best approach to take because the beneficiary can invest the proceeds and earn a return higher than the insurance company would pay.

2. **Interest income.** The beneficiary can receive the annual interest earned from the death benefit. For example, the beneficiary would receive $4000 each year from a $100,000 death benefit earning 4 percent interest. The $100,000 principal would remain intact and would continue to earn interest until the death of the beneficiary, when it becomes part of his or her estate.

3. **Income of a specific amount.** The beneficiary may receive a specific amount of income per year from the death benefit. Under this option, payments cease when the death benefit and interest are exhausted. For example, a $100,000 death benefit earning 4 percent interest would provide a $15,000 annual income for approximately eight years.*

4. **Income for a specific period.** The beneficiary may receive an income from the death benefit for a specific number of years. For example, a widow with small children may choose to receive an income for 18 years. The insurance company would calculate a level of income that would allow for equal proceeds each year, with all funds, including interest, being exhausted at the end of the 18th year.

5. **Income for life.** The beneficiary may elect to receive an income for life. In such a case, the insurance company would use the life expectancy of the beneficiary to calculate the level of income that would allow for equal annual payments so that funds would be exhausted by the expected date of the beneficiary's death. If the beneficiary lives longer than expected, the income payments would continue.

CONCEPT CHECK 12.3

1. Distinguish among the owner, the insured, the beneficiary, and the contingent beneficiary of a life insurance policy.

2. Briefly describe each of the five components of all insurance policies.

3. Identify the five settlement options for the payment of the proceeds of a life insurance policy to its beneficiary.

4. Besides taking the cash value as a lump sum, what are some additional ways a cash-value policyholder may take the proceeds of the policy at cancellation?

5. Distinguish between an automatic premium loan and a waiver-of-premium option in a life insurance policy.

6. Explain how guaranteed renewability for term life insurance and guaranteed insurability for cash-value insurance protect insured people who develop serious health conditions.

---

* This option and options 4 and 5 are variations of an annuity and are covered further in Chapter 17.

DID YOU KNOW

About Life Insurance after Divorce

If you receive income from a former spouse either through alimony or child support, life insurance on that person is strongly advised. If a policy that was purchased while a couple was married remains in effect, it is smart to keep it. To be certain that the correct beneficiary is named, have that requirement stated in a court order and/or made part of the divorce decree. The custodial parent should be named as owner of the policy, thereby preventing the noncustodial parent from making any changes in the policy. Also require written confirmation from the insurance company each year that the premium has been paid and the policy is in force. Noncustodial parents will also need life insurance on their former spouses because they will probably receive custody of the children if the former spouse dies and he or she may need additional income to support the larger household.

12.4   HOW TO BUY LIFE INSURANCE

Your life insurance needs vary over your life cycle and so should your insurance plan.

LEARNING OBJECTIVE 4

Apply a step-by-step strategy for implementing a life insurance plan.

12.4a   Integrate Your Life Insurance into Your Overall Financial Planning

Figure 12-3 depicts a life insurance and investment plan recommended over an individual's life cycle. This plan is built on two foundations: (1) the purchase of term insurance for all or major portion needs because term insurance is more flexible than cash-value insurance and provides more protection for each premium dollar and (2) a systematic, regular investment program.

As a family ages, life insurance needs typically decrease.

Figure 12-3 Wisely Using Life Insurance and Investments over the Life Cycle

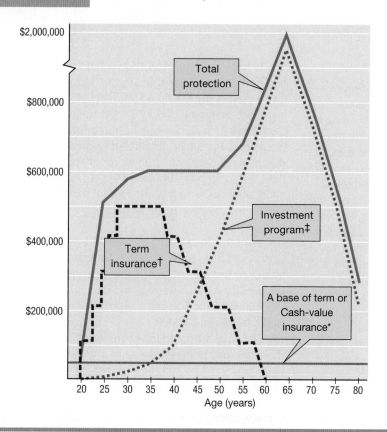

† Layered term insurance policies.
‡ Includes vested employer-sponsored retirement (e.g., 401[k]) plans. (See Chapter 17.)

A base of insurance can provide for funeral, burial, and other final expenses. A $20,000 to $50,000 guaranteed-renewable term or guaranteed-insurable, cash-value policy is sufficient. The remainder of your life insurance should consist of multiple term insurance policies that you start buying when you begin to have dependents. These should be five-or ten-year, level-premium, guaranteed renewable policies in increments of $100,000 or more. The policies should be layered so that you can drop policies as your need declines. By the time you reach retirement, you can drop all your policies as your retirement investment plan can provide for your survivor's needs.

12.4b Get a Great Price Buying Life Insurance Online

Smart personal financial managers take a do-it-yourself approach to life insurance. They regularly calculate their needs and decide what types of insurance to buy and cancel in what increments. This allows them to use a **premium quote service** that offers computer-generated comparisons from among 20 to 80 different companies. Premium quote services can be found at www.insure.com, www.quotescout.com, and www.accuquote.com. These websites also offer online life insurance needs calculators and a wealth of information on life insurance from an unbiased perspective. In addition, all the major life insurance companies have an online purchase system. Term insurance is easiest to buy this way, but even cash-value insurance can be purchased online.

DO IT IN CLASS

premium quote service
Offers computer-generated comparisons from among 20 to 80 different companies.

ADVICE FROM A PROFESSIONAL

Buy Term Insurance and Invest the Rest

Americans tend to buy the wrong type of life insurance—cash-value—when term insurance policies cost about 80 percent less. They incorrectly think of life insurance as an investment and not as an expense. And the life insurance industry likes it that way. Be smart and spend as little money as possible to buy the coverage you need. One way to do this is to use the strategy to "buy term and invest the rest." If you invest the money difference between the cost of premiums for a term life insurance policy and the cost of premiums for a more expensive cash-value policy, you will always come out ahead financially. To see why, consider the buildup of protection for Seth Cameron, a 30-year-old art gallery administrator from New York City who is considering life insurance policies. Seth could pay an $870 annual premium to buy a $100,000 whole life policy. Alternatively, he could spend $130 for the first-year premium of a $100,000 five-year renewable term policy and invest the $740 difference ($870−$130) in through a tax-sheltered retirement account (assuming a 5 percent after-tax rate of return).

If Seth were to die tomorrow, the policy's beneficiary would receive both the $100,000 in insurance proceeds and the $740 in savings. After five years (age 35), Seth's annual $740 in savings would have grown to $4293; if he were to die at that time, the total death benefit would be $104,293. If Seth dies years into the future, the estate is even further ahead because of the growing principal in the account. By age 60, Seth's mutual fund investment would have grown to $58,052. If the account earned higher than 5 percent annually, the amount would be much greater. By the time Seth reached age 60, the term insurance premiums would exceed the premiums for the cash-value policy. However, his need for life insurance would presumably be eliminated or greatly reduced at that point. If Seth's children were self-supporting by then, he could probably drop the term insurance policy altogether. Nevertheless, his mutual fund account would remain to provide a financial nest egg of $58,052 or more to his heirs.

With the "buy term and invest the rest" strategy, Seth would have been insured more than 30 years at total premium cost of just $7350. By contrast, the cash-value policy would have required total premiums of $26,100 ($870 × 30), and the policy's cash value at year 30 would be about $44,000.

For "buy term and invest the rest" to work, however, the difference between the term and cash-value policy premiums must, in fact, be invested on a regular basis. Many people say that they will invest this money but then fail to follow through on that promise. You can, like Seth, succeed with a little discipline. The easiest way to ensure that your money is actually invested is to set up an automatic investment program (AIP) in which a mutual fund is authorized to withdraw money from your checking account, perhaps monthly, to buy mutual fund shares. When you agree to invest the "difference" automatically, the strategy will work well for you.

Estate Buildup If a Term Life Insurance Buyer Invests the Difference

Age	Premium for Five-Year Renewable Term	Difference (Not Spent on Whole Life)	Total Investment and Earnings* at 5%	Total Estate
30	$130	$740	$ 740	$100,740
35	150	720	4,293	104,293
40	180	690	9,657	109,657
45	210	660	16,328	116,328
50	240	630	24,668	124,668
60			$58,052	58,052

* This illustration makes the following assumptions: The whole life policy premium for the same $100,000 in coverage is fixed at $870 every year; the buyer pays the five-year renewable term premium at the beginning of each year; and the difference is invested. Those amounts stay in the investments account all year, as does the previous year's ending balance. Investments earn a compounded 5 percent after-tax annual rate of return. Upon the insured's death, the beneficiary would receive the $100,000 face amount of the term life insurance policy plus the amount built up in the investments account earning 5 percent.

Source: Jordan E. Goodman "America's Money Answers Man" (www.MoneyAnswers.com) and author of *Everyone's Money Book and Everyone's Money Book* series

DID YOU KNOW

Buy Life Insurance from a Financially Strong Company

The most important feature of any life insurance company is its ability to pay its obligations. The company you choose must have the stability and financial strength to survive for the many years your policy will remain in force. Ratings of the financial strengths of insurance companies are available from A.M. Best Company (www.ambest.com), Standard & Poor's (www.standardandpoors.com). Weiss Ratings (www.weissratings.com/), Moody's Investor Services (www.moodys.com/), Duff and Phelps (www.duffandphelps.com/)

12.4c Or Contact a Local Insurance Agent

An **insurance agent** is a representative of an insurance company authorized to sell, modify, service, and terminate insurance contracts. In the United States, life insurance is typically sold through exclusive agents who represent only one company.

The life insurance agent must be qualified to design a program tailored to your specific needs and should understand all life insurance needs. The agent should have earned the professional designations chartered life underwriter (CLU) and either the certified financial planner (CFP) or chartered financial consultant (ChFC) designation. In addition, you should check your agent's reputation with your state's insurance and securities investment regulatory agencies. See www.naic.org/state_web_map.htm.

insurance agent
Representative of an insurance company who is authorized to sell, modify, service, and terminate insurance contracts.

layering term insurance policies
Purchasing level-premium term policies so that coverage grows when you need it most and then can be decreased as your needs change.

DID YOU KNOW

Layer Your Term Insurance Policies and Never Pay More than $60 per Month

You can meet your life insurance needs by **layering term insurance policies** so that coverage grows and then can be decreased as your needs change. An example is provided in the following chart. It assumes that the person is age 25 when a first child is born and age 30 when a last child is born. In this example, the parents buy several level-premium term policies near the birth of the first child, with the policies having differing time periods. They buy another policy when their last child is born and another as the first child gets close to college age. As the children go out on their own, some of the earliest policies expire, thereby reducing the overall amount of insurance as the parents' needs decline.

One benefit of layering is affordability. Based on premium rates for healthy nonsmokers, the cost for the plan illustrated here would never be more than $60 per month.

Age	Buy	Policies in Force at Each Age	Total Coverage at Each Age
25	Policy 1, $100,000, 30 years	#1, #2, #3	$450,000
	Policy 2, $150,000, 25 years		
	Policy 3, $200,000, 20 years		
30	Policy 4, $150,000, 25 years	#1, #2, #3, #4	600,000
35		#1, #2, #3, #4	600,000
40	Policy 5, $50,000, 20 years	#1, #2, #3, #4, #5	650,000
45		#1, #2, #4, #5	450,000
50		#1, #4, #5	300,000
55		#5	50,000
60			0

12.4d   Sales Commissions Can Amount to 90 Percent of the Annual Premium

Part of the premium you pay for life insurance each year goes toward the sales commissions that are paid to the selling insurance agent. Ssales commissions on term insurance policies are very low—often no more than 10 percent of the premium if the policy is purchased directly rather than through an agent.

Cash value policies are different, and that is a major reason why agents try to sell them instead of term policies: They make more money. Sales commissions are as much as 90 to 100 percent of the first-year premium paid for a cash-value life insurance policy. Over the following years, commissions decline annually to 50, 40, 30, 20, and eventually 10 percent. Then more of the premium each year builds cash value.

You can buy life insurance policies with low sales commissions. Such **low-load life insurance** can be bought on the Internet at such sites such as www.llis.com. You can also do so through fee-only financial planners and **fee-for-service insurance agents** who charge a set fee rather than a percentage commission.

DO IT IN CLASS

12.4e   Fair Prices for Term Life Insurance

The price people pay for life insurance depends on their age, health, occupation, and lifestyle. Life insurance companies offer their lowest prices to "preferred" applicants whose health status and lifestyle (for example, nonsmokers) suggest longevity. "Standard" and "impaired" applicants would pay more. Because companies differ in how they assign these labels to applicants, you should comparison-shop for the best treatment. For example, some companies allow an occasional (monthly) cigar smoker to qualify for non-smoker rates.

Term life insurance premiums are usually quoted in dollars per $1000 of coverage. Generally, the higher the face amount of the policy, the lower the rate per $1000. For example, a company might sell term life insurance for $1 per $1000 per year when purchased in face amounts of $100,000 or more and for $1.25 per $1000 per year for policies of less than $100,000. Policies with face amounts of $1 million can cost less than $0.50 per $1000 per year for people younger than age 35.

It is easy to pay too much for term life insurance, especially if you do not comparison-shop. Table 12-2 on page 371 shows fair prices for term life insurance based on price per $1000 of coverage. Note that smokers pay much higher premiums than nonsmokers because, as a group, smokers die ten years earlier than nonsmokers. Men pay more than women because they typically die three years earlier.

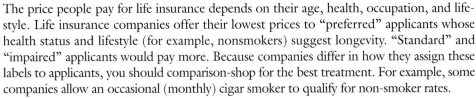

DID YOU KNOW

Sean's Success Story

Sean has always felt that life insurance planning is an important part of his overall financial well-being. When he graduated from college, his first job provided him with a term-life insurance policy equal to his annual salary. He calculated his need for life insurance and found that this amount was more than adequate. He has been in a steady relationship for almost two years and has begun to think about how his life insurance needs might change should he get married. Last week, he met with a life insurance agent who

suggested that Sean buy a $50,000 whole life policy with annual premium of $587. He shopped around on his own and realized he could buy as much as $1 million of term insurance for the same money. After more research, he plans to buy multiple guaranteed-renewable, level-premium term policies that he can add and discard in a layering process. The money he saves by purchasing term insurance will be invested in a Roth IRA retirement account that he can use to pay for his children's college or his own retirement when the time comes.

DID YOU KNOW

Signs of an Unethical Life Insurance Agent

In an effort to earn maximum commissions and fee revenues, some agents act unethically, and may do any of the following:

1. **Seven times your salary should do the trick.** To assess your insurance needs the agent uses the multiple earnings approach rather than the needs approach.

2. **Cash-value is a great investment.** The agent discourages you from buying a term policy and instead pressures you to buy a cash-value policy.

3. **I have a better policy for you.** The agent encourages you to replace an existing cash-value policy with another (this is illegal in some states).

4. **The policy pays for itself.** The agent focuses strongly on the net cost of the policy rather than how the policy genuinely meets the needs of your family.

5. **Look at how much you will make.** The agent suggests that the high current rate of return is all but guaranteed and unlikely to go down.

6. **I can make you even more money.** The agent says it is a good idea to borrow from a policy to make some other investment such as an annuity.

7. **Hurry, act now.** The agent pressures you to sign and pay for a policy without giving you ample time to read it and compare the policy to others.

8. **I will keep your situation to myself.** The agent tells you to misstate your health status or age in order to lower your premium a bit.

9. **You get a rebate.** It is illegal for the insurance agent to give you a rebate of premium out of his commission as an inducement for you to buy a policy.

10. **Talk, talk, talk.** The agent does all the talking and uses lots of insurance jargon rather than addresses your issues in understandable language.

12.4f Two Methods May Be Used to Compare Similar Life Insurance Policies

It is much more difficult when comparing different types of cash-value policies. The cost of insurance measured in dollars per $1000 is not an appropriate way to compare term with cash-value insurance or when examining different types of cash-value insurance. Also inappropriate is the **net cost** of a life insurance policy which equals

Table 12-2 Fair Prices for Term Life Insurance*

| | Based on Price Per $1000 of Coverage | | | |
| | Nonsmokers | | Smokers | |
Age	Male	Female	Male	Female
18–30	$0.70	$0.67	$1.00	$0.95
35	$0.83	$0.74	$1.25	$1.15
40	$1.08	$1.00	$1.95	$1.60
45	$1.67	$1.60	$2.80	$2.40
50	$2.30	$2.20	$4.00	$3.25

* Multiply the rate by each $1000 of coverage and add $60 for estimated administrative fees. For example, a fair annual premium for a $50,000 policy for a 36-year-old male nonsmoker might be $101.50 ($0.83 × 50 = $41.50; $41.50 + $60 = $101.50).

Table 12-3   Premiums for a $100,000 Life Insurance Policy (Typical annual premiums for various types of policies)

Policy Type	Policy Year							
	1	2	3	5	10	11	20	Age 65
Annual renewable term (guaranteed renewability to age 70)	$ 80	$ 81	$ 82	$ 83	$ 90	$ 92	$110	$2,400
Decreasing term (over 20 years)	160	160	160	160	160	160	160	0
Convertible term (within 5 years)	170	170	170	170	940	940	940	940
Whole life	870	870	870	870	870	870	870	870
Universal life	590	590	590	590	680	730	760	790
Limited-pay life (paid-at-age65)	920	920	920	920	920	920	920	0

* Premiums quoted are for a 21-year-old male nonsmoker.

DO IT NOW!

You know more about personal finance after reading this chapter, so get started right now by:

1. *Finding out if you currently have life insurance and, if so, what type you have.*

2. *Using the needs approach (a calculator can be found on this book's website) to determine your present need for life insurance.*

3. *Discussing the results of the above with your closest family members.*

interest-adjusted net payment index (IANPI)

If a policy will remain in force until death, this method allows you to effectively measure the cost of cash-value insurance. The lower the IANPI, the lower the cost of the policy.

the total of all premiums to be paid minus any accumulated cash value and accrued dividends. The net cost is often a negative figure, giving a false impression that the policy will pay for itself. You should ignore net cost calculations provided by a life insurance agent.

There are two methods suitable for comparisons. Table 12-3 shows illustrative premiums for various types of life insurance policies. These range from annual renewable term to a paid-at-age-65 policy.

1. **Interest-adjusted cost index method.** A **cost index** is a numerical method used to compare the costs of similar plans of life insurance. The **interest-adjusted cost index (IACI)** measures the cost of life insurance, taking into account the interest that would have been earned had the premiums been invested rather than used to buy insurance. The lower the IACI, the lower the cost of the policy. Ask for 5-, 10-, 20-, and 30-year IACI values as well because companies have been known to manipulate their dividend and cash-value accumulations to look especially good at the 20-year point. You should insist on being told the index before you agree to buy a policy, and you should shop elsewhere if the agent refuses, resists, or implies that the index has little value.

2. **Interest-adjusted net payment index method.** The IACI assumes that the policy will be cashed in and surrendered at the end of a certain period (usually 20 years) rather than remaining in force until the death of the insured. If the policy will remain in force until death, you can use the **interest-adjusted net payment index (IANPI)** to effectively measure the cost of cash-value insurance. The lower the IANPI, the lower the cost of the policy.

CONCEPT CHECK 12.4

1. List the benefits of buying term and investing the rest.

2. Explain how the pattern of one's life insurance program should vary from young adulthood through retirement years.

3. Explain how you can benefit by layering your term insurance policies.

WHAT DO YOU RECOMMEND *NOW?*

Now that you have read the chapter on protecting loved ones through life insurance, what would you recommend to Stephanie and Will Bridgeman in the case at the beginning of the chapter regarding:

1. Their changing need for life insurance now that they have a child?
2. What types of life insurance they should consider and whether they should purchase multiple policies?
3. Coordinating their retirement savings and other investments with their life insurance program?
4. Shopping for life insurance?

© Nikolay Mamluke/Dreamstime.com

BIG PICTURE SUMMARY OF LEARNING OBJECTIVES

LO1 **Understand why you might need life insurance and calculate the appropriate amount of coverage.**

Life insurance is designed to provide protection from the financial losses that result from death. The reasons to purchase life insurance change over the life cycle. The need for this type of protection is nonexistent or very small for children and single adults. Factors affecting life insurance needs include the need to replace income, final-expense needs, readjustment-period needs, debt-repayment needs, college-expense needs, availability of government programs, and ownership of other life insurance and assets. Two methods to calculate life insurance needs are the multiple-of-earnings approach and the needs-based approach. The needs-based approach is the more accurate of the two and should be conducted every three years or whenever your family situation changes.

LO2 **Distinguish among types of life insurance.**

Two basic types of life insurance exist: term life insurance and cash-value life insurance. Variations on term life insurance include decreasing term insurance, guaranteed renewable term insurance, convertible term insurance, and credit life insurance. Variations on cash-value insurance include whole life insurance, limited-pay life insurance, and universal and variable life insurance.

LO3 **Explain the major provisions of life insurance policies.**

A **life insurance policy** is a contract between an insurance policy holder/owner and an insurance company, where the company promises to pay a designated beneficiary a sum of money (the "benefits") upon the death of the insured person when buying life insurance, you should pay attention to the policy's general terms and conditions, the special features of cash-value life insurance, and settlement options.

LO4 **Apply a step-by-step strategy for implementing a life insurance plan.**

Life insurance should be purchased to address the dying-too-soon problem. Your investments should manage the living-too-long problem. Addressing these two problems appropriately requires high amounts of term insurance while you are raising children, and a sound investment program to prepare for your retirement years. You should not purchase life insurance until you have determined the actual dollar amount and type of policy you need and compared premiums using various life insurance cost indices.

LET'S TALK ABOUT IT

1. **Thinking About Life Insurance.** What were your feelings about the need for life insurance before you read this chapter? What are they now?

2. **Are You Insured?** Are you covered by life insurance? If so, how much? Do you feel that you are over- or under-insured?

3. **Term Versus Cash-Value Insurance.** Why do you think people persist in buying cash-value life insurance when,

in most cases, they would be better off buying term insurance and investing the money saved into a retirement account.

4. **Life Insurance for Unmarried Couples.** Many people today choose to cohabitate rather than marry (at least for some time period). How might this affect their thinking about life insurance?

DO THE MATH

1. **Life Insurance Needs for a Young Single.** Matthew Paul of Sisseton, South Dakota, is single and has been working as an admissions counselor at a university for five years. Matthew owns a home valued at $156,000 on which he owes $135,000. He has a two-year-old vehicle valued at $12,500 on which he owes $8000. He has about $13,800 remaining on his student loans. His retirement account has grown to $7800, and he owns some stock valued at $4400. Matthew has no life insurance and is considering buying some. How much should he buy?

DO IT IN CLASS
PAGES 353 AND 355

2. **Life Insurance Needs for a Young Married Couple.** Amy and Mack Holly from Macomb, Illinois, have been married for three years. They recently bought a home costing $212,000 using a $190,000 mortgage. They have no other debts. Mack earns $42,000 per year, and Amy earns $41,000. Each has a retirement plan valued at approximately $10,000. They recently received an offer in the mail from their mortgage lender for a mortgage

life insurance policy of $190,000. Their only life insurance currently is a $20,000 cash-value survivorship joint life policy. They each would like to provide the other with support for five years if one of them should die.

(a) Assuming $10,000 in final expenses and $20,000 allocated to help make mortgage payments, calculate the amount of life insurance they need using the needs-based approach.

(b) How would their needs change if Amy became pregnant?

3. **Calculating a Death Benefit.** Alexandra Cunningham of College Park, Maryland, has a $100,000 participating cash-value policy written on her life. The policy has accumulated $4700 in cash value; Alexandra has borrowed $3000 of this value. The policy also has accumulated unpaid dividends of $1666. Yesterday Alexandra paid her premium of $1200 for the coming year. What is the current death benefit from this policy?

DO IT IN CLASS
PAGE 362

FINANCIAL PLANNING CASES

CASE 1

The Johnsons Change Their Life Insurance Coverage

Harry and Belinda Johnson spend $15 per month on life insurance in the form of a premium on a $10,000, paid-at-65 cash-value policy on Harry. Belinda has a group term insurance policy from her employer with a face amount of $85,500. By choosing a group life insurance plan from his menu of employee benefits, Harry now has $39,000 of group term life insurance. Harry and Belinda have decided that, because they have no children, they could reduce their life insurance needs by protecting one another's income for only four years, assuming the survivor would be able to fend for himself or herself after that time. They also realize that their savings fund is so low that it would have no bearing on

their life insurance needs. Harry and Belinda are basing their calculations on a projected 4 percent rate of return after taxes and inflation. They also estimate the following expenses: $10,000 for final expenses, $6000 for readjustment expenses, and $5000 for repayment of short-term debts.

(a) Should the $3000 interest earnings from Harry's trust fund be included in his annual income for the purposes of calculating the likely dollar loss if he were to die? (See the discussions about the Johnsons in Chapter 3 beginning on page 86.) Explain your response.

(b) Based on your response to the previous question, how much more life insurance does Harry need? Use the Run the Numbers worksheet on page 353 to arrive at your answer.

(c) Repeat the calculations to arrive at the additional life insurance needed on Belinda's life.

(d) How might the Johnsons most economically meet any additional life insurance needs you have determined they may have?

(e) In addition to their life insurance planning, how might the Johnsons begin to prepare for their retirement years?

CASE 2

Victor and Maria Hernandez Contemplate Switching Life Insurance Policies

Victor and Maria Hernandez have a total of $200,000 in life insurance. Victor has a $50,000 cash-value policy purchased more than 20 years ago when the couple was first married and a $100,000 group term policy through his employer. Maria has a $50,000 group term insurance policy through her employer. The couple has been approached by a life insurance agent who thinks that they need to change their policy mix because, he says, they are inadequately insured. Specifically, the agent has suggested that Victor cash in his cash-value policy and buy a new variable-universal life insurance policy.

(a) If Victor cashes in his policy, what options would he have when receiving the cash value?

(b) Determine what the $16,000 in cash value in Victor's life insurance policy would be worth in 20 years if that sum were invested somewhere else and earned an 8 percent annual return. (Hint: Use the *Garman/Forgue* companion website.)

(c) Would cashing in the policy be a wise decision? Why or why not?

(d) As the Hernandezes' children are now grown and out on their own, and both Victor and Maria are employed full time, give general reasons why Victor may need more or less insurance.

(e) Explain why it would be a bad idea for Victor to buy a variable-universal life insurance policy.

CASE 3

Julia Starts Thinking About Life Insurance

Julia Price is now in her late 30s and has always wanted children. She has arranged to adopt two siblings from overseas, ages 2 and 4. Julia is happy that she earns enough money to support the children adequately, but the agency sponsoring the adoption also requires that adoptive parents purchase sufficient life insurance. Julia currently has a $20,000 paid-up cash-value life insurance policy purchased by her parents when she was a child. In addition, Julia's employer provides

DO IT IN CLASS
PAGE 367

term insurance that matches her salary as an employee benefit. She talked with the agency, and they suggested that she buy a whole life insurance policy in the amount of $450,000 based on her current salary of $150,000. Julia isn't sure this is the way to go. For one thing, the policy would cost about $5000 per year. Further, she realizes that the amount the agency requires would not maintain the children's lifestyle for long and not be sufficient to help pay for their college educations. Julia is thinking that guaranteed renewable term insurance would be a better way to go. Offer your opinion about her thinking.

CASE 4

Life Insurance for a Newly Married Couple

Just-married couples sometimes overindulge in the type and amount of life insurance that they buy. Jason and Nicole Greenwood of Walnut, California, took a different approach. Both were working and had a small

DO IT IN CLASS
PAGE 367

amount of life insurance provided through their respective employee benefit programs: Jason, $40,000, and Nicole, $50,000. During their discussion of life insurance needs and related costs, they decided that if Nicole completed her master's degree in industrial psychology, she would have better employment opportunities. Consequently, they decided to use money they had available for additional life insurance to pay for Nicole's education. They both feel, however, that they do not want to have inadequate life insurance.

(a) In what way does Nicole's return to school alter the Greenwoods' life insurance needs?

(b) Would you agree that the amount of life insurance provided by the Greenwoods' respective employers is adequate while Nicole is in school? Explain your response.

(c) Summarize how the Greenwoods' life insurance needs might change over their life cycle.

CASE 5

Fraternity Members Contemplate Permanent Life Insurance

Zachary Chen is a college student from Waterville, Maine. Soon to graduate, Zachary was approached recently by a life insurance agent, who set up a group meeting for several members of his fraternity. During the meeting, the agent presented six life insurance plans

DO IT IN CLASS
PAGES 360
AND 370

and was very persuasive about the benefits of a universal life insurance plan that his company calls Affordable Life II. Under the plan, the prospective graduate can buy $100,000 of permanent life insurance for a very low premium during the first five years and then pay a higher premium later when income presumably will have increased. Zachary was confused after the meeting, as were his friends. Armed with your knowledge from this personal finance book, you have been asked to respond to some of their questions.

(a) Do you think universal life insurance is a good deal for these people? Why or why not?

(b) How can the individual fraternity members decide how much life insurance they need?

(c) Life insurance cannot be as confusing as the agent made it seem. What clearer explanation would you give to the fraternity members?

(d) What type of life insurance, if any, would you advise for the fraternity brothers?

(e) How would they know if a life insurance policy is offered at a fair price?

CASE 6

A Married Couple with Children Address Their Life Insurance Needs

Joseph and Marcia Michael of Troy, New York, are a married couple in their mid-30s. They have two children, ages 5 and 3, and Marcia is pregnant with their third child. Marcia is a part-time book indexer who earned $15,000 after taxes last year. Because she performs much of her work at home, it is unlikely that she will need to curtail her work after the baby is born. Joseph is a family therapist; he earned $68,000 last year after taxes. Because both are self-employed, Marcia and Joseph do not have access to group life insurance. They are each covered by $50,000 universal life policies they purchased three years ago. In addition, Joseph is covered by a $50,000, five-year guaranteed renewable term policy, which will expire next year. The Michaels are currently reassessing their life insurance program. As a preliminary step in their analysis, they have determined that Marcia's account with Social Security would yield the family about $1094 per month, or an annual benefit of $13,128, if she were to die. For Joseph, the figure would be $2072 per month, or an annual benefit of $24,864. Both agree that they would like to support each of their children to age 22, but to date, they have been unable to start a college savings fund. The couple estimates that it would cost $40,000 to put each child through a regional university in their state as measured in today's dollars. They expect that burial expenses for each spouse would total about $12,000, and they would like to have a lump sum of $50,000 to help the surviving spouse make payments on their home mortgage. They also feel that each spouse would want to take a three-month leave from work if the other were to die.

(a) Calculate the amount of life insurance that Marcia needs based on the information given. Use the Run the Numbers worksheet on page 353 or the *Garman/Forgue* companion website. Assume a 3 percent rate of return after taxes and inflation and an income need for 22 years because the unborn child will need financial support for that many years.

(b) Calculate the amount of life insurance that Joseph needs based on the information given. Use the Run the Numbers worksheet on page 353 or the *Garman/Forgue* companion website. Assume a 3 percent rate of return after taxes and inflation and an income need for 22 years because the unborn child will need financial support for that many years.

BE YOUR OWN PERSONAL FINANCIAL MANAGER

1. **Calculating Life Insurance Need.** Review the material

MY PERSONAL FINANCIAL PLANNER
in "How Much Life Insurance Do You Need?" on pages 351–354. Then using dollar amounts that fit your personal situation, complete Worksheet 48: Determining My Life Insurance Needs from "My Personal Financial Planner." If you are currently single and childless, for the purposes of this activity, assume that you are 30 years old, have two children under age 5, are married, and earn $60,000 per year and redo the estimate of need. How would having a family change your need for life insurance?

2. **Review Your Life Insurance Program.** Review the material in "There Are Only Two Basic Types of Life Insurance" and "Understanding Your Life Insurance Policy" on pages 355–356 and 361–365. Then examine any life insurance policies on your life. Given what you learn from those policies and your own need for life insurance as determined in item 1 above, decide on the amount and type(s) of additional life insurance you probably need and any appropriate policy features, such as who should own the policy(s) and be named as beneficiaries.

3. **Name Your Beneficiary.** Review the information in "Understanding Your Life Insurance Policy" on pages 361–365. Then revisit the naming of the beneficiary on any policies currently in force on your life and make any changes desired. If you are not currently covered by an insurance policy, assume that you have taken a job after graduation and your employer offers free life insurance as an employee benefit. Who would you name as your beneficiary?

4. **Life Insurance Settlement Options.** Review the material in "Settlement Options Specify How the Death Benefit Will Be Paid" on page 365. If you were the beneficiary on another person's life insurance policy in the amount of $100,000, how would you choose to receive the benefits if you were to receive the proceeds of the policy?

5. **Life-Cycle Life Insurance Planning.** Review the information in "Integrate Your Life Insurance into Your Overall Financial Planning," including Figure 12-3 on pages 367–368. Then map out a plan for yourself that integrates life insurance and investments. The plan should protect you from both the dying-too-soon and living-too-long risks outlined on page 350. Make appropriate assumptions for your plans regarding

marriage and having children and project your plan out to age 65.

6. **Set Up a Layered Term Insurance Program.** Review the material in the Did You Know? box titled "Layer Your Term Insurance Policies and Never Pay More than $60 per Month" on page 369, and then complete Worksheet 49: Layering Term Insurance Policies from "My Personal Financial Planner," which allows you to set up a term insurance program until age 60. Use your current personal situation if you currently have dependents, or assume that you will earn an annual salary of $45,000 at age 25 and plan to have at least two children.

MY PERSONAL FINANCIAL PLANNER

ON THE NET

Go to the Web pages indicated to complete these exercises.

1. **Obtain a Quote on Your Life Insurance.** Visit the website for AccuQuote at www.accuquote.com to obtain a quote for the annual premium on a $200,000 guaranteed renewable, ten-year term policy for you. Then call a life insurance agent in your community to obtain a quote on the same term insurance coverage. How do the term rates quoted by your local agent compare with the rates found over the Internet? Also, ask for the quote on a $100,000 universal life policy with guaranteed insurability and waiver-of-premium options. Ask the agent to explain why the quotes for the two types of policies differ. Analyze his or her response based on what you learned in this chapter.

2. **Check an Insurance Company's Financial Strength.** Visit the websites for A.M. Best Company at www.ambest.com/ratings/guide.asp and Moody's Investor Services (www.moodys.com/) to check the ratings for the insurance company recommended by the agent in Exercise 1 as well as the company with the lowest cost for term insurance that you found on the Web. What do the ratings tell you about the relative strengths of those companies?

3. **Determine Your Need for More Life Insurance.** Visit the Life and Health Insurance Foundation for Education website at www.lifehappens.org/life-insurance-needs-calculator. Calculate your current need for life insurance. Then recalculate your need for five years from now given your estimates of your income and family situation.

ACTION INVOLVEMENT PROJECTS

1. **Review Life Insurance Company Websites.** Visit the websites of two large life insurance companies. Focus on how their approaches to educating the public about life insurance are similar to or different from the information provided in this chapter. Write a summary of your findings.

2. **Talk to a Life Insurance Agent.** Visit a life insurance agent and ask for an assessment of your life insurance needs given your current situation. Compare the information you receive with what you have learned in this chapter and write a summary of your findings.

3. **How Others Approach the Need for Life Insurance.** Talk to three friends and/or relatives below age 30 who are

married. Ask about their approach to life insurance and how they have gone about setting up a life insurance program. Write a summary of your findings and compare what they have done to what you would do if you were in a similar situation.

4. **Term Versus Cash-Value Life Insurance.** Talk to three of your friends or acquaintances who have never purchased life insurance. Explain to them the differences between term and cash-value life insurance. Then inquire about which type they would prefer to buy. Write a summary of your findings and compare their views with yours.

PART 4

© S. Dashkevych/Shutterstock.com

13 Investment Fundamentals

YOU MUST BE KIDDING, RIGHT?

Twins Tiffany and Taylor Jackson have worked for the same employer for many years. Tiffany started early to save and invest for retirement by putting $5000 away each year for 15 years starting at age 25 and never added any more money to the account. Taylor waited until age 40 to begin saving for retirement and he invested $5000 per year for 25 years until retirement at age 65. Assuming that they both earn a 6 percent annual return, how much more money will Tiffany have accumulated for retirement than Taylor by the time they reach age 65?

A. $ 98,919   C. $274,323

B. $174,231   D. $373,242

The answer is A, $98,919. Tiffany's account balance at age 65 is projected at $373,242 and Taylor's is $274,323. Even though Tiffany saved for only 15 years compared with Taylor's 25 years of saving, Tiffany's long-term investment approach had her starting to save early in her working career for retirement. Thus, she accumulated 36 percent more money than her brother ($373,242 − $274,323 = $98,919/$274,323). Starting early on long-term investment goals is a money-winning idea!

LEARNING OBJECTIVES

After reading this chapter, you should be able to:

1 Explain how to get started as an investor.

2 Identify your investment philosophy and invest accordingly.

3 Describe the major risk factors that affect the rate of return on investments.

4 Decide which of the four long-term investment strategies you will utilize.

5 Create your own investment plan.

6 Use Monte Carlo Advice when investing for retirement.

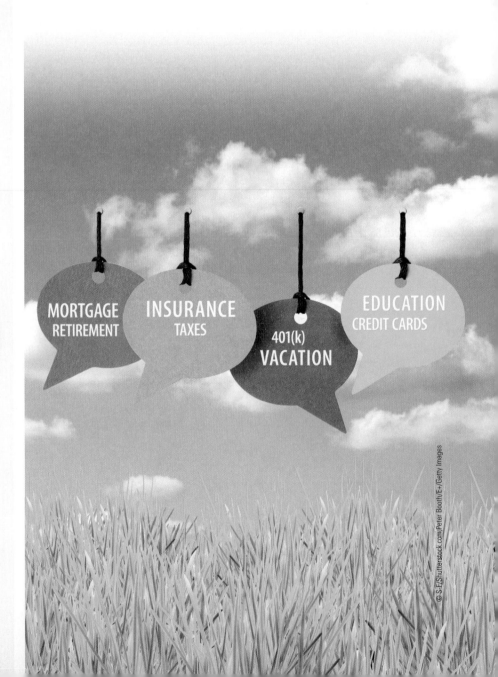

MORTGAGE RETIREMENT
INSURANCE TAXES
401(k) VACATION
EDUCATION CREDIT CARDS

© S-E/Shutterstock.com/Peter Booth/E+/Getty Images

WHAT DO YOU RECOMMEND?

© istockphoto.com/peepo

Shavenellyee and Sarena are sisters, both in their 20s. Shavenellyee drives a leased BMW convertible, and she makes about $42,000, including tips, as a part-time bartender at two different restaurants. Although she has no employee benefits, she enjoys having flexible work hours so that she can go to the beach and the local nightspots. Currently, Shavenellyee has $10,000 in credit card debt. She has $1500 in a bank savings account, and two years ago she opened an individual retirement account (IRA) with a $1000 investment in a mutual fund. Her sister Sarena drives a paid-for Honda CR-V, pays her credit card purchases in full each month, and sacrifices some of her salary by putting $100 per month into her employer's company stock through her 401(k) retirement account. Over the past seven years, the stock price, which was once about $40, has risen to almost $70, and Sarena's 401(k) plan is now worth about $16,000. Sarena also has invested about $14,000 in a Roth IRA mutual fund account that is currently invested in an aggressive growth mutual fund, and she plans to use that money for a down payment on a home purchase. She earns $58,000 as a manager of a restaurant, plus she receives an annual bonus ranging from $2000 to $4000 every January that she uses for a spring vacation in Mexico. Sarena's employer provides many employee benefits.

What do you recommend to Shavenellyee and Sarena on the subject of investment fundamentals regarding:

1. **Portfolio diversification for Sarena?**
2. **Dollar-cost averaging for Shavenellyee ?**
3. **Investment alternatives for Sarena?**

YOUR NEXT FIVE YEARS

In the next five years, you can start achieving financial success by doing the following related to investment fundamentals:

1. *Start investing early in life by sacrificing some income and putting some cash into a diversified investment portfolio for the future.*

2. *Avoid thinking about short-term results and accept substantial risk when investing for the long term.*

3. *Invest regularly through your employer's retirement plan.*

4. *Invest no more than 5 or 10 percent of your portfolio in any single company stock, including that of your employer.*

5. *Rebalance your portfolio at least once a year based on your chosen asset allocation strategy.*

LEARNING OBJECTIVE 1

Explain how to get started as an investor.

investing

Putting saved money to work so that it makes you even more money.

securities

Assets suitable for investment, including stocks, bonds, and mutual funds.

stocks

Shares of ownership in a corporation.

bond

A debt instrument issued by an organization that promises repayment at a specific time and the right to receive regular interest payments during the life of the bond.

portfolio

Collection of investments assembled to meet your investment goals.

At many points in this book, we have encouraged you to set aside funds for the future, especially by accumulating funds through regular savings. Financial writer Andrew Tobias argues that saving more is the smartest, safest investment move you will ever make. Save every nickel you can. Then you will have funds for investing.

Investments can be tricky, of course. When the stock market crashed in 2008, millions of American investors lost 40 to 50 percent of their investment assets and some lost even more. The biggest declines occurred in portfolios that were poorly diversified, as their money was not spread among various types of investments. Those who had a well-diversified portfolio lost only about 20 percent. People who remained invested (instead of selling while the market was declining week after week) were happy when the market started its rebound only 2 years later. Within another year the market doubled and those who remained in the market recovered all their losses. Since then they made even more gains, plus an additional 29 percent return last year. Patience is critically important when investing.

Despite the ups and downs of the world's stock markets, one of the best ways to make money over the long term—especially for retirement—is to invest in stocks, bonds, and mutual funds. This remains the best advice! The earning power of the U.S. and world economies, even with occasional serious fluctuations, endures. This chapter explains both why this is true and how to succeed during an economic recession; in an economy growing at a slow pace; or in the course of a rapidly growing economy.

13.1 STARTING YOUR INVESTMENT PROGRAM

To help secure a desirable future lifestyle, you cannot spend every dollar that you earn today. Instead, you must sacrifice by setting aside some of your current income and invest it. You postpone the pleasure of using money for here-and-now consumption so you can have more in the future. To be financially successful, you are wise to start investing early in life, invest regularly, and stay invested. Why? Because, for every five years you delay investing, you will have to double your monthly investment amount to achieve the same goals. Remember: You—and no one else—are responsible for your own financial success.

13.1a Investing Is More than Saving

Savings is the accumulation of excess funds by intentionally spending less than you earn. Investing is more. **Investing** is taking some of the money you are saving and putting it to work so that it makes you even more money. Your goals and the time it will take to reach those goals dictate the investment strategies you follow and the investment alternatives you choose.

The most common ways that people invest are by putting money into assets called **securities**, such as stocks, bonds, and mutual funds (often purchased through their employer-sponsored retirement accounts), and by buying real estate. **Stocks** are shares of ownership in a corporation, and **bonds** represent loans to companies and governments. Essentially, they are IOUs that are bought and sold among investors. All of your investment assets make up your **portfolio**, which is the collection of multiple investments in different assets chosen to meet your investment goals.

13.1b What Investment Returns Are Possible?

Figure 13-1 shows the long-term rates of return on some popular investments. While stock market returns have averaged about 9.6 percent over the long term, the returns in the first decade of the millennium were extremely low and then much higher in more recent years.

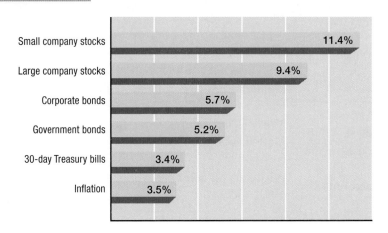

Figure 13-1

Long-Term Rates of Return on Investments (Annualized returns since 1926)

Since 1927, the *worst* 20-year performance for stocks was a gain of 3 percent annually. Over the past 80 years, the chance of making money during any one year in the stock market has been 66 percent. Over five years, the probability increases to 81 percent; over ten years, it increases to 89 percent.

DO IT IN CLASS

13.1c Gains (and Losses) Plus Dividends Equals One's Total Return

When people invest their money, they take a **financial risk** (also called **business risk**)—namely, the possibility that the investment will fail to pay any return to the investor. At the extremes, a company could have a very good year earning a considerable profit, or it could go bankrupt, causing investors to lose all of their money.

Investors hope that their investments will earn them a positive **total return**, which is the income an investment generates from a combination of current income and capital gains. **Current income** is money received while you own an investment. It is usually received on a regular basis as interest, rent, or dividends.

As we have noted elsewhere in the text, **interest** for an investor is the return earned for lending money. **Rent** is payment received in return for allowing someone to use your real estate property, such as land or a building. A **dividend** is a portion of a company's earnings that the firm pays out to its shareholders. For example, Eliza Rodriguez from Ypsilanti, Michigan, purchased 100 shares of H&M stock at $45 per share ($4500) last year. The company paid dividends of $3 per share during the year, so Eliza received $300 in cash dividends as current income.

total return

Income an investment generates from current income and capital gains.

current income

Money received while you own an investment; usually received regularly as interest, rent, or dividends.

interest

Charge for borrowing money; investors in bonds earn interest.

DID YOU KNOW

Bias toward Minimizing Investment Losses

People engaged in the understanding investment fundamentals have a bias toward certain behaviors that can be harmful, such as a tendency toward forgetting about their

investment losses. People usually forget about losses and instead remember more clearly their successes, convinced that they are above-average investors. What to do? When one has investment losses, stop and think, and learn from mistakes.

DID YOU KNOW

Money Websites for Investment Fundamentals

Informative websites for investment fundamentals, including tips for young adults are:

Bankrate.com' risk tolerance quiz (www.bankrate.com /finance/financial-literacy/quiz-what-is-your-risk-tolerance.aspx)

Fundamentals of Investing (www.financialwisdom .com)

Financial Soundings' limited management accounts (www.financialsoundings.com)

How To Be Set For Life (www.howtobesetforlife.com /articles/6-investment-fundamentals/)

Kiplinger.com's risk tolerance quiz (www.kiplinger.com /quiz/investing/T031-S001-the-investor-psychology-quiz /index.html)

Motley Fool (www.fool.com/how-to-invest/thirteen-steps /index.aspx)

Wikipedia on asset allocation (en.wikipedia.org/wiki /Asset_allocation)

---

capital gain

Increase in the value of an initial investment (less costs) realized upon the sale of the investment.

capital loss

Decrease in paper value of an initial investment; only realized if sold.

rate of return/yield

Total return on an investment expressed as a percentage of its price.

A **capital gain** occurs only when you actually sell an investment that has increased in value. It is calculated by subtracting the total amount paid for the investment (including purchase transaction costs) from the higher price at which it is sold (minus any sales transaction costs). For example, if the price of H&M company stock rose to $52 during the year, Eliza could sell it for a capital gain. If Eliza paid a transaction cost of $1 per share at both purchase and time of sale, her capital gain would be $500 [($5200 − $100) − ($4500 + $100)].

Capital losses can occur as well. For most investments, a trade-off arises between capital gains and current income. Investments with potential for high capital gains often pay little current income, and investments that pay substantial current income generally have little or no potential for capital gains. Long-term investors are often willing to forgo current income in favor of possibly earning substantial future capital gains.

The **rate of return**, or **yield**, is the total return on an investment expressed as a percentage of its price. It is usually stated on an annualized basis, and it includes dividends and capital gains. For example, if Eliza sells the H&M stock for $52 per share after one year, she will have a total return of $800 ($300 in dividends plus $500 in capital gains). Her yield would be 17.78 percent ($800 ÷ $4500).

FINANCIAL POWER POINT

Out of the Market? You Missed a 45 Percent Gain

If you had been out of stocks during the market's ten best days in the past decade, according to Charles Schwab, you would have missed out on 45 percent of the gains.

13.1d Your Investing Future Looks Promising

Corporate profits—and investor's returns—are difficult to earn when the United States and the world's large economies are struggling. During such challenging economic times, one's average investment returns from stocks are likely to be about 6 percent. This is likely to come from a 2 percent dividend yield for stocks and an earnings growth rate of around 4 percent. These are still good returns when inflation is low.

CONCEPT CHECK 13.1

1. How does savings differ from investing?

2. Why were returns so poor for the first decade of the millennium?

3. What are the two parts of an investor's total return?

4. What stock market returns can be anticipated in the near- to mid-term, and why?

13.2 IDENTIFY YOUR INVESTMENT PHILOSOPHY AND INVEST ACCORDINGLY

Achieving financial success requires that you understand your investment philosophy and adhere to it when investing. Thus, you also need to know about investment risk and what to do about it. Keep in mind the advice offered by investment guru Warren Buffett, "The first rule of investing is don't lose money; the second rule is don't forget Rule No. 1."

13.2a You Can Learn to Handle Investment Risk

Pure risk, which exists when there is no potential for gain, only the possibility of loss, was discussed in Chapter 10. Investments, in contrast, are subject to **speculative risk**, which exists in situations that offer potential for gain as well as for loss. **Investment risk** represents the uncertainty that the yield on an investment will deviate from what is expected. For most investments, the greater the risk is, the higher the potential return. This potential for gain is what motivates people to accept increasingly greater levels of risk, as illustrated in Figure 13-2. Nevertheless, many people remain seriously averse to risk.

Figure 13-2 also provides insight about possible investment choices. Don't be overwhelmed because these investments are explained in the following chapters. You *will* learn how to make informed investment decisions for yourself.

speculative risk
Involves the potential for either gain or loss; equity investments might do either.

investment risk
The possibility that the yield on an investment will deviate from its expected return.

13.2b Investors Demand a Risk Premium

One popular investment is the short-term Treasury bill, or **T-bill**, which is a government IOU of less than one year. Because T-bills are risk-free investments, they pay too low a return for most people, perhaps only 0.25 or 0.35 percent. Some people invest in T-bills to safeguard their money until it can be invested at a later time.

DO IT IN CLASS

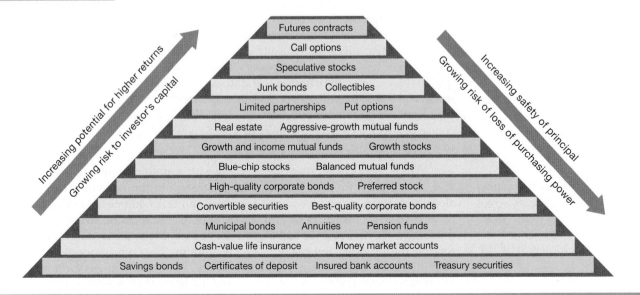

Figure 13-2 **Risk Pyramid Reveals the Trade-Offs Between Risk and Return**

risk premium (or equity risk premium)

The difference between a riskier investment's expected return and the totally safe return on the T-bill.

risk tolerance

An investor's willingness to weather changes in the value of your investments, that is, to weather investment risk.

investment philosophy

Investor's general approach to tolerance for risk in investments, whether it is conservative, moderate, or aggressive, given the investor's financial goals.

conservative investment philosophy (risk aversion)

Investors with this philosophy accept very little risk and are generally rewarded with relatively low rates of return for seeking the twin goals of a moderate amount of current income and preservation of capital.

risk averse

In investments, one who tends to dislike risk and is unable to put money into investments that seem risky.

moderate investment philosophy (risk indifference)

Investors with this philosophy accept some risk as they seek capital gains through slow and steady growth in investment value along with current income.

Investors need the promise of a high return to warrant placing their money at risk in an investment. When making investments, people demand a **risk premium (or equity risk premium)** for their willingness to make investments for which there is no guarantee of future success. This risk premium constitutes the difference between a riskier investment's expected return and the totally safe return on the T-bill.

If the expected return is 8 percent on stocks and 2 percent on ten-year Treasury securities, the risk premium is 6 percent. Industry experts figure that the amount of the risk premium for most investors is 3 to 6 percent, although the long-term average is 8 percent. Higher-risk investments carry higher-risk premiums.

13.2c   What Is Your Investment Philosophy?

Investors have to take risks that are appropriate to reach their financial goals. The task is to find the right balance and make choices accordingly. You must weigh the risks of an investment with the likelihood of not reaching your goal.

Your **risk tolerance** is your willingness to weather changes in the values of your investments. This is not the same as your capacity to take risk. To be successful in investing, your risk tolerance must be factored into your investment philosophy. If you lose sleep over your investments, you know it is time to reduce your risk and adjust your investment philosophy.

An **investment philosophy** is one's general approach to tolerance for risk in investments, whether it is conservative, moderate, or aggressive, given the financial goals to be achieved. The more risk you take, within reason, the more you can expect to earn and accumulate over the long term. However, just because you are comfortable with a risky portfolio does not mean that you actually need one. By the same token, you still need to be aggressive enough to meet your financial goals. Wise investors follow their investment philosophy without wavering; they do not change course unless their basic objectives change.

Are You a Conservative Investor?   If you have a **conservative investment philosophy**, you accept very little risk and are generally rewarded with relatively low rates of return for seeking the twin goals of a moderate amount of current income and preservation of capital. **Preservation of capital** means that you do not want to lose any of the money you have invested. In short, you could be characterized as an investor who is **risk averse**. This is one who tends to dislike risk and is unable to put money into investments that seem risky.

Conservative investors focus on protecting themselves. They do so by carefully avoiding losses and trying to stay with investments that demonstrate gains, often for long time periods (perhaps for five or ten years). Tactically, they rarely sell their investments. Investors who are approaching retirement or who are planning to withdraw money from their investments in the near future often adhere to a conservative investment philosophy.

Conservative investors typically consider investing in obligations issued by the government. Examples include Treasury bills, notes, and bonds, municipal bonds, high-quality (blue-chip) corporate bonds and stocks, balanced mutual funds (which own both stocks and bonds), certificates of deposit, and annuities. A bond is essentially a loan that the investor makes to a government or a corporation. It is a debt of the issuer. Over the course of a year, a conservative investor with $1000 could possibly lose $20 and is likely to gain $20 to $30.

Are You a Moderate Investor?   People with a **moderate investment philosophy** seek capital gains through slow and steady growth in the value of their investments along with some current income. They invite only a fair amount of risk of capital loss. Most have no immediate need for the funds but instead focus on laying the investment foundation for later years or building on such a base. Moderate investors are fairly comfortable during rising and falling market conditions. They remain secure in the knowledge that they are investing for the long term. Their tactics might include spreading investment funds among several choices and adjusting their portfolio by trading some assets perhaps once or twice a year.

People seeking moderate returns consider investing in dividend-paying common stocks, growth and income mutual funds, high-quality corporate bonds, government bonds, and real estate. Over the course of a year, a moderate investor with $1000 could possibly lose $150 and is likely to gain $40 to $60.

Are You an Aggressive Investor? If you choose to strive for a very high return by accepting a high level of risk, you have an **aggressive investment philosophy**. As such, you could be characterized as a risk seeker. Aggressive investors primarily seek capital gains. Many such investors take a short-term approach, remaining confident that they can profit substantially during major upswings in market prices.

People seeking exceptionally high returns consider investing in common stocks of new or fast-growing companies, high-yielding junk bonds, and aggressive-growth mutual funds. Such investors also may put their money into limited real estate partnerships, undeveloped land, precious metals, gems, commodity futures, stock-index futures, and collectibles. Devotees of this investment philosophy sometimes do not diversify by spreading their funds among many alternatives. Also, they may adopt short-term tactics to increase capital gains. For example, aggressive investors might place most of their investment funds in a single stock in the hope that it will rise 10 percent over 90 days, giving a yield of more than 30 percent annually. Those shares could then be sold and the money invested elsewhere. Investment tactics for aggressive investors are discussed in Chapter 16.

Aggressive investors must be emotionally and financially able to weather substantial short-term losses—such as a downward swing in a stock's price of 30 or 40 percent—even though they might expect that an upswing in price will occur in the future. Over the course of a year, an aggressive investor with $1000 could possibly lose $300 and could gain $100, $200, $300, or even more.

aggressive investment philosophy (risk seeker)
Investors with this philosophy primarily seek capital gains, often with a short time horizon.

FINANCIAL POWER POINT

Take a Risk-Tolerance Quiz

Find out how much risk you can comfortably tolerate by taking a risk-tolerance quiz at one of the following websites:

- Bankrate.com: www.bankrate.com/finance/financial-literacy/use-investments-to-reach-your-goals-2.aspx.
- Kiplinger: www.kiplinger.com/quiz/investing/T031-S001-the-investor-psychology-quiz/.

13.2d Should You Take an Active or Passive Investing Approach?

Another aspect of your personal investment philosophy is your level of involvement in investing. That is, do you want to be an active or passive investor?

Active Investing An active investor carefully studies the economy, market trends, and investment alternatives; regularly monitors these factors; and makes decisions to buy and sell, perhaps three or four or more times a year, with or without the advice of a professional. In addition, active investors stay alert because the prices of many investments vary with certain news events, world happenings, and economic and political variables. Knowing what is going on in the larger world helps active investors understand when to buy or to sell investments quickly so as to reap profits and/or reduce losses.

Passive Investing Succeeds over the Long Term A passive investor does not actively engage in trading of securities or spend large amounts of time monitoring his or her investments. Such an individual may make regular investments in securities, such as mutual funds (described in Chapter 15), and his or her assets are rarely sold for short-term profits. Instead, passive investors simply aim to match the returns of the entire market. They ignore "hot" tips and the investment of the day touted in the financial press. They keep their emotions in check, and they earn higher returns than active investors over the long term. Most long-term investors utilize a passive approach.

An active investor keeps a close watch on the economy and financial markets.

Tom Grill/Photographer's Choice RF/Getty Images

13.2e   Identify the Kinds of Investments You Want to Make

The investments you choose should match your interests. Before investing, think about lending versus owning, short term versus long term, and how to select investments that are likely to provide your desired potential total return.

Do You Want Lending Investments or Ownership Investments?   You can invest money in two ways, by lending or by owning. When you lend your money, you receive some form of IOU and the promise of repayment plus interest. The interest is a form of current income while you hold the investment.

You can lend by depositing money in banks, credit unions, and savings and loan associations (via savings accounts and certificates of deposit) or by lending money to governments (via Treasury notes and bonds as well as state and local bonds), businesses (corporate bonds), mortgage-backed bonds (such as Ginnie Maes), and life insurance companies (annuities).

debts

Lending investments that typically offer both a fixed maturity and a fixed income.

These lending investments, or **debts**, generally offer both a fixed maturity and a fixed income. With a **fixed maturity**, the borrower agrees to repay the principal to the investor on a specific date. With a **fixed income**, the borrower agrees to pay the investor a specific rate of return for use of the principal. Such investments allow lenders to be fairly confident that they will receive a certain amount of interest income for a specified period of time and that the borrowed funds will eventually be returned. Thus, the return is somewhat assured.

fixed maturity

Specific date on which a borrower agrees to repay the principal to the investor.

No matter how much profit the borrower makes with your funds, the investing lender at best receives only the fixed return promised at the time of the initial investment. Lending investments rarely result in capital gains.

fixed income

Specific rate of return that a borrower agrees to pay the investor for use of the principal (initial investment).

Alternatively, you may invest money through ownership of an asset. Ownership investments are often called **equities**. You can buy common or preferred corporate stock (to obtain part ownership in a corporation) in publicly owned companies, purchase shares in a mutual fund company (which invests your funds in corporate stocks and bonds), put money into your own business, purchase real estate, buy commodity futures (pork bellies or oranges), or buy investment-quality collectibles (such as rare antiques or gold). Ownership investments have the potential for providing current income; however, the emphasis is usually upon achieving substantial capital gains.

equities

Ownership equities such as common or preferred stocks, equity mutual funds, real estate, and so on that focus on capital gains more than on income.

Making Short-, Intermediate-, and Long-Term Investments   When investing for a short-term goal, such as less than one year, you would want to be very conservative to ensure that a sudden drop in the market would not jeopardize your reaching the goal before the market has time to recover. You want to be confident that you preserve the value of what you have. After all, you don't want to lose money in an investment when you need to use that money for a near-term goal, such as college tuition, or be forced to sell an investment because you need cash in a hurry. People with a short or intermediate time horizon require investments that offer some predictability and stability. As a result, these investors are usually more interested in current income than capital gains.

By contrast, if you are investing to achieve long-term goals, you want your money to grow. Long-term investors usually invite more risk by seeking capital gains as well as current income.

When investing for long-term goals, you can afford to be more aggressive. That is one reason why the stock market is a good place to save for retirement. After you retire, you can leave a portion of your portfolio in stocks or stock mutual funds since you likely will still have 20 to 25 years before you need the last dollars in your nest egg.

real rate of return

Return on an investment after subtracting the effects of inflation and income taxes.

Long-term investors seek growth in the value of their investments that exceeds the rate of inflation. In other words, they want their investments to provide a positive **real rate of return**. This is the return after subtracting the effects of both inflation and income taxes.

DID YOU KNOW

Calculate the Real Rate of Return (After Taxes and Inflation) on Investments

1. **Identify the rate of return before income taxes.** Perhaps you think that a stock will offer a return of 10 percent in one year, including current income and capital gains.

2. **Subtract the effects of your marginal tax rate on the rate of return to obtain the after-tax return.** If you are in the 25 percent federal income tax bracket,

the calculation is $(1 - 0.25) \times 0.10 = 0.075 = 7.5$ percent.

3. **Subtract the effects of inflation from the after-tax return to obtain the real rate of return on the investment after taxes and inflation.** If you estimate an annual inflation of 4 percent, the calculation gives 3.5 percent (7.5 percent − 4.0 percent). Thus, your before-tax rate of return of 10 percent provides a real rate of return of 3.5 percent after taxes and inflation.

13.2f Choose Investments for Their Components of Total Return

When investing, you want to build a portfolio of investments that will provide the necessary potential total return through current income and capital gains in the proportions that you desire. One stock might provide an anticipated cash dividend of 1.5 percent and an expected annual price appreciation of 6 percent, for a total anticipated return of 7.5 percent. Another choice offering the same projected total return might be a stock with expected annual cash dividends of 2.5 percent and capital gains of 5 percent.

13.2g What Should You Do Next?

Once you have clarified your investment philosophy, whether to lend or own, active or passive, understand the investment timeline of your financial goals, and accept the components of your anticipated total return, you will be able to make investing decisions with confidence and conviction. You will be able to show patience by following your long-term views rather than making emotional and wrong decisions—in other words, mistakes—about your money. The investments you choose and the returns earned will match your investment philosophy.

CONCEPT CHECK 13.2

1. Summarize your investment philosophy and general approach to tolerance for risk.

2. Indicate whether you view yourself as an active or passive investor, and explain why.

3. Summarize your personal views on lending or owning investments.

4. Which type of investment return—current income or capital gains— seems more attractive to you? Why?

13.3 RISKS AND OTHER FACTORS AFFECT THE INVESTOR'S RETURN

LEARNING OBJECTIVE 3

Describe the major factors that affect the rate of return on investments.

To be a successful investor, you must understand the major factors that affect the rate of return on investments. Being informed, you can then take the appropriate risks when making investment decisions.

random/unsystematic risk

Risk associated with owning only one investment of a particular type (such as stock in one company) that, by chance, may do very poorly in the future due to uncontrollable or random factors that do not affect the rest of the market.

diversification

Process of reducing risk by spreading investment money among several different investment opportunities.

Random Risk Is Reduced by Diversification, Eventually   **Random risk** (also called **unsystematic risk**) is the risk associated with owning only one investment of a particular type (such as stock in one company) that, by chance, may do very poorly in the future because of uncontrollable or random factors, such as labor unrest, lawsuits, and product recalls. If you invest in only one stock, its value might rise or fall. If you invest in two or three stocks, the odds are lessened that all of their prices will fall at the same time. Such **diversification**—the process of reducing risk by spreading investment money among several different investment opportunities—provides one effective method of managing random risk as it reduces the ups and downs of a portfolio.

The principle holds that when you own different types of investment assets in a portfolio, some assets should be rising when others are falling. It results in a potential rate of return on all of the investments that is *lower* than the potential return on a single alternative, but the return is more predictable and the risk of loss is lower. Diversification does not mean that you will not lose money. Diversification averages out the high and low returns. While investors might be disappointed with a lower return from a diversified portfolio, they would be even more disappointed by the return in a down market from one that is poorly diversified.

Research suggests that you can cut random risk in half by diversifying into as few as five stocks or bonds; you can eliminate random risk by holding 15 or more stocks or bonds. Rational investors diversify so as to reduce random risk, and over the long term—as little as a decade—it works. You also can diversify by investing in foreign stocks.

13.3a   Market Risk and the Great Recession

Diversification among stocks or bonds cannot eliminate all risks. Some risk would exist even if you owned all of the stocks in a market because stock prices in general move up and down over time. **Market risk** (also known as **systematic** or **nondiversifiable risk**) is the possibility for an investor to experience losses due to unknown factors that affect the overall performance of the financial markets.

In this case, the value of an investment may drop due to influences and events that affect all similar investments. Examples include a change in economic, social, political, or general market conditions; fluctuations in investor preferences; or other broad market-moving factors, such as a recession political turmoil, changes in interest rates, and terrorist attacks. Market risk cannot be eliminated but it can be reduced by dividing your portfolio among several different markets.

market risk/systematic risk/ undiversifiable risk

The possibility for an investor to experience losses due to unknown factors that affect the overall performance of the financial markets.

The Great Recession   Not all markets normally will decline at the same time, but it can happen. The Great Recession of December 2007 through March of 2009 impacted the whole world and it demonstrates the possibility of a mistake in the logic of efficient markets as all types of investments (e.g., credit, investments, and real estate) fell in unison. The systemic collapse proves that once-in-a-lifetime financial disasters not only can occur, but do. The mission of the Financial Stability Oversight Council is to identify financial companies in need of government intervention before they collapse and negatively affect the American economy.

The Congressional Budget Office (CBO) predicts that the U.S. economy will continue to crawl along at a 2.4 percent rate of annual growth through 2022, rather than a more typical growth rate of 3.0 percent or higher.

U.S. and world markets are continuing to recover in today's challenging economic environment. Over the short term, diversification cannot protect your investments against market declines. Over the long term, and this suggests that if you remain invested in the market during your entire lifespan, you will likely experience a significant down market that will take back a sizable chunk of your wealth. But in time you will get it all back and then some.

Market Risk in an Investor's Portfolio   Market risk remains after an investor's portfolio has been fully diversified within a particular market. Over the years, market risk for all investments has averaged about 8 percent. As a consequence of this risk, the return on any single securities investment (such as a stock), through no fault of its own, might vary up and down about 8 percent annually. The total risk in an investment consists of the sum of the random risk and the market risk.

13.3b Types of Investment Risks

A number of other investment risks affect investor returns:

- **Business failure risk. Business failure risk**, also called **financial risk**, is the possibility that the investment will fail, perhaps go bankrupt, and result in a massive or total loss of one's invested funds.

- **Inflation risk.** Inflation risk may be the most important concern for the long-term investor. **Inflation risk**, also called **purchasing power risk**, is the danger that your money will not grow as fast as inflation and therefore not be worth as much in the future as it is today. Over the long term, inflation in the United States has averaged 3.1 percent annually. Historically, common stocks and real estate have reduced inflation risk, as their values tend to rise with inflation over many years. However, all ownership investments are also subject to **deflation risk**. This is the chance that the value of an investment will decline when overall prices decline. Housing prices declined 30 to 60 percent in many U.S. communities as a result of the Great Recession.

- **Time horizon risk.** The role of time affects all investments. The sooner your invested money is supposed to be returned to you—the **time horizon** of an investment—the less the likelihood that something could go wrong. The more time your money is invested, the more it is at risk. For taking longer-term risks, investors expect and normally receive higher returns.

- **Business-cycle risk.** As we discussed in Chapter 1, economic growth usually does not occur in a smooth and steady manner and this affects profits as well as investment returns. This is known as **business-cycle risk**. Instead, periods of expansion lasting three or four years are often followed by contractions in the economy, called **recessions**, that may last a year or longer. The profits of most industries follow the business cycle. Some businesses do not experience business-cycle risk because they continue to earn profits during economic downturns. Examples are gasoline retailers, supermarkets, and utility companies.

- **Market-volatility risk.** All investments are subject to occasional sharp changes in price as a result of events affecting a particular company or the overall market for similar investments, and this is **market-volatility risk**. For example, the value of a single stock, such as that of a technology company like Apple, might change 10 or even 20 percent in a single day. Also, all technology stocks could decline 2 or perhaps 5 percent if two or three competitors announce poor earnings. In recent years the number of days with a 4 percent swing in the overall stock market prices ranged from 2 to 11.

- **Liquidity risk. Liquidity** is the speed and ease with which an asset can be converted to cash. You can sell your stock investments in one day, but rules state that it may take up to four days to have the proceeds available in cash. You will never truly know the value of liquidity until you need it and you do not have it. **Liquidity risk** is the risk that a given security or asset cannot be traded quickly enough in the market to prevent a loss (or make the required profit). Real estate is **illiquid** because it may take weeks, months, or even years to sell.

- **Marketability risk.** When you have to sell a certain asset quickly, it may not sell at or near the market price. This possibility is referred to as **marketability risk**. Selling real estate in a hurry, for example, may require the seller to substantially reduce the price in order to sell to a willing buyer.

- **Reinvestment risk. Reinvestment risk** is the risk that the return on a future investment will not be the same as the return earned by the original investment.

13.3c Commission Costs Reduce Returns

Buying and selling investments may result in a number of transaction costs. Examples include "fix-up costs" when preparing a home for sale, appraisal fees for collectibles, and storage costs for precious metals. **Commissions** are usually the

financial risk

Possibility that an investment will fail to pay a return to the investor.

business-cycle risk

The fact that economic growth usually does not occur in a smooth and steady manner, and this impacts profits as well as investment returns.

market-volatility risk

The fact that all investments are subject to occasional sharp changes in price as a result of events affecting a particular company or the overall market for similar investments.

liquidity

The speed and ease with which an asset can be converted to cash.

liquidity risk

The risk that a given security or asset cannot be traded quickly enough in the market to prevent a loss (or make the required profit).

commissions

Fees or percentages of the selling price paid to salespeople, agents, and companies for their services in buying or selling an investment.

DID YOU KNOW

"Improve Returns by Minimizing Expenses"

Vanguard's Total Stock Index mutual fund charges a mere 0.17% in management expenses while the typical actively managed mutual fund charges 1.4%. The results after 30 years of investing $4000 annually with both accounts earning 5 percent: Low management fee: $270,594 ; high management fee: $217,479. An extra $53,115 is a big difference!

leverage
Using borrowed funds to invest with the goal of earning a rate of return in excess of the after-tax costs of borrowing.

largest transaction cost in investments. These are fees or percentages of the units or selling price paid to salespeople, agents, and companies for their services—that is, to buy or sell an investment. The commission charged to buy an investment (one commission) and then later sell it (a second commission) is partially based on the value of the transaction.

Commission ranges are as follows: stocks, 1.5 to 2.5 percent (although trades can be made on the Internet for less than $10); bonds, 0 to 2.0 percent; mutual funds, 0 to 8.5 percent; real estate, 4.5 to 7.5 percent; options and futures contracts, 4.0 to 6.0 percent; limited partnerships, 10.0 to 15.0 percent; and collectibles, 15.0 to 30.0 percent.

13.3d   Leverage May or May Not Increase Returns

Another factor that can affect return on investment is **leverage**. In the leveraging process, borrowed funds are used to make an investment with the goal of earning a rate of return in excess of the after-tax costs of borrowing. You can become financially overextended by using leverage, a factor you should not ignore. For example, housing investors during the last decade were shocked when home values declined 5, 10, or even 15 percent in a year, thus forcing many real estate investors into bankruptcy. In many U.S. cities housing prices dropped 50 percent or more. Now prices are rising in most markets.

CONCEPT CHECK 13.3

1. Distinguish between random risk and market risk.

2. Summarize three other types of investment risks that may affect returns.

3. Explain how transactions costs and leverage may increase or decrease investment returns.

13.4   ESTABLISHING YOUR LONG-TERM INVESTMENT STRATEGY

securities markets
Places where stocks and bonds are traded (or in the case of electronic trading, the way in which securities are traded).

bull market
Market in which securities prices have risen 20 percent or more over time.

bear market
Market in which securities prices have declined in value by 20 percent or more from previous highs, often over the course of several weeks or months.

Investing is not rocket science! Anyone reading this book and following its recommendations for making long-term investments can become a successful investor.

13.4a   Long-Term Investors Understand Bull and Bear Markets and Corrections

Long-term investors understand how the **securities markets** (places where stocks and bonds are traded) are performing as a whole. That is, are the markets moving up, moving down, or remaining stagnant?

Bull Markets Are Profitable for Investors A **bull market** results when securities prices have risen 20 percent or more over time. Historically, the more than 20 bull markets averaging 55 months in length have seen an average gain of 159 percent.

Bear Markets Turn into Bull Markets A securities market in which prices have declined in value by 20 percent or more from previous highs, often over the course of several weeks or months, is called a **bear market**. Four bear markets have occurred since 1980. Bear markets are what clear the decks for a longer-lasting recovery and drives valuations down to truly low levels from which bigger gains can spring.

The bear market that started in October 2007 saw stock prices decline 55 percent by March 2009. Then the optimistic bull buyers took over thinking that surely the U.S. economy had already reached rock bottom and that stock prices were certain to rise as the economy recovered. Since March 9, 2009 when stock prices stopped falling the U.S. bull market saw a 100+ percent rally in just a few years, a gigantic move, and tech stocks rose an amazing 200+ percent in 5 years.

A **bull** in the market is a person who expects securities prices to go up; a **bear** expects the general market to decline. The origin of these terms is unknown, but some suggest that they refer to the ways that the animals attack: Bears thrust their claws downward, and bulls move their horns upward. Historically, bear markets last, on average, about 9 months; bull markets average 55 months in length.

Market Corrections Also Occur Another type of short-term market trend is called a market correction, which typically occur every 18 months. A **market correction** is a reverse movement of at least 10 percent in a stock, bond, commodity, or index to adjust for recent price rises. They interrupt an uptrend in the market or an asset.

market correction

A short term price decline in the stock markets of at least 10 percent in a stock, bond, commodity or index to adjust for a recent price rises.

13.4b Long-Term Investors Accept Substantial Market Volatility

In an average year, the price of a typical stock fluctuates up and down by about 50 percent; thus, the price of a stock selling for $30 per share in January might range from $15 to $45 before the end of the following December. It is not unusual for overall stock market prices to fall (or rise) 3, 4, or 5 percent in a single day. In a recent year the stock market fluctuated 11 times by more than 4 percent in *one day*. That tells us that today's stock markets are riskier than yesterday's. Terrifying daily swings are likely to remain a constant during these turbulent economic times. Such swings are today's "new normal."

Long-term investors who get scared during market downturns and withdraw most or all of their investing dollars miss out on the subsequent increase in prices during the next up market. Long-term investors must learn to accept **market volatility** by ignoring short-term market movements.

market volatility

The likelihood of large price swings in securities due to a company's success (or lack of it) and various market conditions.

13.4c Long-Term Investors Do Not Practice Market Timing

Investors get into trouble when they start to think too much like traders. **Market timers** attempt to predict the short-term movements of various markets (or market segments) and, based on those predictions, move capital from one segment to another in order to capture market gains and avoid market losses. Essentially, market timers try to outguess the trend of stocks or other prices. For example, an investor worried about the future might sell his or her stock investments and move to cash. Another investor who anticipates increasing future stock prices might get 100 percent invested in stocks.

market timers

Investors who attempt to predict the short-term movements of various markets (or market segments) and, based on those predictions, move capital from one segment to another in order to capture market gains and avoid market losses.

To succeed in timing the market, you need to know just the right time to buy and just the right time to sell, know what signals suggest you take action, and exhibit the discipline to do it. Market timers often sell at the first sign of trouble and then keep their money out of the market until better opportunities are apparent. If you try to time the market, you are just as likely to miss an upswing as you are to avoid a downswing. Note that market timers are competing against graduates from Chicago, Stanford, and Wharton who do the same job full time for big paychecks.

Market Timing Loses Money **Market efficiency** has to do with the speed at which new information is reflected in investment prices. The theory is that security prices are reflective of their true value at all times because publicly available information has driven market prices to the correct level.

market efficiency

The speed at which new information is reflected in investment prices suggesting that security prices are reflective of their true value at all times because publicly available information has driven market prices to the correct level.

When information is reported in the financial press, it is already too late for the typical investor to act and make a profit. And individuals don't always even know which information is relevant. Therefore, individual investors cannot pursue an active investment strategy that beats the market because they are just as likely to invest in an overpriced security rather than one that is undervalued. Thus, these investors typically earn substantially less than average market returns every year.

Not surprisingly, stock analysts and investment managers believe they can make better choices than the average investor in part because they can act on information more quickly than other investors. The reality, however, is that 70 to 80 percent of investment managers, and oftentimes 90 percent in any given year fail to beat the average returns of the stock market.

DID YOU KNOW ?

Women Are Better Investors than Men

Research suggests that women are better investors than men. The big reason is that men are overconfident about their financial prowess and as a result they make more mistakes. A woman's investment portfolio exceeds a man's by about 1 percentage point every year. Investing $4000 annually for 30 years earning 6 percent shows that a woman's portfolio will amount to $316,000 and the man's earning 5 percent will be $266,000, a $50,000 difference, which adds up to 18.8 percent more.

© iStockphoto.com/bedo

Long-Term Investors Avoid Too Many "Facts."

herd behavior

When emotion, not logic, rules investing decisions and investors decide to copy the observed decisions of other investors or movements in the markets rather than follow their own beliefs and information.

13.4d Long-Term Investors Avoid Trading Mistakes

Long-term investors avoid trading mistakes by not trading too much, buying high and selling low, and by avoiding herd behavior.

Trading Too Much Loses Money One cause of lower returns is trading too much. The more you trade, the more likely you are to make a wealth-destroying mistake. Such investors also often sell winners too soon and keep losers too long. Don't make the mistake of trading when you should be investing.

Buying High and Selling Low Loses Money Emotion, not logic, often rules investing decisions. Investors often overreact when buying and selling as their thinking goes through alternating times of panic and euphoria. When plunging portfolio values become too much to accept, investors just want the pain to end so they sell, which presumably means big losses. This is "buying high and selling low," which is the opposite of what investors should do.

Herd Behavior Loses Money At the other extreme, when the market prices are rapidly rising, people are fooled into thinking that it is safe to invest more ("I've got to put more money in there") and lose their sense of caution because it must be safe if everyone else is buying. People follow the crowd and tend to push stock prices too far up or down. They look at behavior and assume it is based on knowledge, but often it's not. This is an illustration of **herd behavior**, which arises when investors decide to copy the observed decisions of other investors or movements in the markets rather than follow their own beliefs and information.

Herd behavior happens in part because people feel compelled to look at prices in the newspaper every day or watch the 24-hour financial news chatter, such as CNBC and CNN, whose TV talking heads spew financial factoids with minute-by-minute updates and sensationalize every blip in the stock markets. Such arcane and sometimes meaningless information creates anxiety or mania that can lead to bad decision making. Acquiring more "facts" is not the same as gaining knowledge or expertise.

The kinds of news and information on cable news and the blogosphere is not designed to appeal to our long-term, rational thought processes. It excites our emotions and fears, and sometimes stokes our prejudices and cynicism. It compels action, not patience. Therefore, ignore that kind of news and information. Stay focused on your long-term investing strategy and make decisions accordingly; otherwise, your returns will be less than the averages, like those of most American investors.

13.4e There Are Only Four Strategies for Long-Term Investors

To succeed financially, you must establish your own long-term investment strategies. And follow them! Don't sabotage your plan by doing stupid thing like those described above. There are only four long-term investment strategies to follow, and they all hang together.

Strategy 1: Buy-and-Hold Anticipates Long-Term Economic Growth The secret to long-term investing success is benign neglect. Long-term investors need to relax with the confidence and knowledge that investing regularly and not trading frequently will create a substantial portfolio over time. Long-term investors do not follow or react emotionally to the day-to-day changes that occur in the market. Ignoring them is the best advice. Because most people are overly sensitive to short-term losses, daily monitoring could motivate one to make shortsighted buying and selling decisions.

Selling high-quality assets in a bear market is a poor strategy because sellers lock in their losses, plus they fail to realize that bear markets are typically short in duration (about 9 months). It is smart to buy more shares when prices are lower during market downturns because rising prices in a bull market always follow a bear market.

Most long-term investors use the investment strategy **buy and hold** (also called **buy to hold**). That is, they buy a widely diversified mix of stocks and/or mutual funds, reinvest the dividends by buying more stocks and mutual funds, and hold on to those investments almost indefinitely. With this approach, the investor expects that the values of the assets will increase over the long run in tandem with the growth of the U.S. and world economies. The investments may pay some current income as well. The investor's emphasis is on holding the assets through both good and bad economic times with the confidence that their values will go up over the long term. This is a wise strategy.

Some critics argue that "buy and hold" is a discredited concept. But they are wrong because this remains the best approach for investing over 20 years or longer. Long-term investors must have the patience and fortitude necessary to tolerate bear markets, no matter how severe.

Buy and hold does not mean buy and ignore. Review your whole portfolio once a year to make sure that each remains a good investment. Questions to ask include: "Is the valuation too high?"; "Has the fundamental outlook of the company changed?"; "Does this asset still fit my investment plan?"; "Would I buy it today?" If necessary, sell the asset and keep the remainder of your portfolio.

Strategy 2: Dollar-Cost Averaging Buys at "Below-Average" Costs **Dollar-cost averaging** (or **cost averaging**) is a systematic program of investing equal sums of money at regular intervals regardless of the price of the investment. In this approach, the same fixed dollar amount is invested in the same stock or mutual fund at regular intervals over a long time. Since investments generally rise more than they fall, the "averaging" means that you purchase more shares when the price is down and fewer shares when the price is high. Most of the shares are, therefore, purchased at **below-average costs**.

This strategy avoids the risks and responsibilities of investment timing because the stock purchases are made regularly (usually every month) regardless of the price. It also ignores all outside events and short-term gyrations of the market, providing the investor with a disciplined buying strategy.

Table 13-1 shows the results of dollar-cost averaging for a stock under varying market conditions (commissions are excluded). As an example, assume that you invest $300 into a stock every three months. Notice that dollar-cost averaging is successful in all three scenarios illustrated.

Dollar-Cost Averaging in a Fluctuating Market To illustrate the effects of dollar-cost averaging, assume that you first invested funds during the "fluctuating market" shown in Table 13-1. Because the initial price is $15 per share, you receive 20 shares

buy and hold/buy to hold
Investment strategy in which investors buy a widely diversified mix of stocks and/or mutual funds, reinvest the dividends by buying more stocks and mutual funds, and hold onto those investments almost indefinitely.

dollar-cost averaging/cost averaging
Systematic program of investing equal sums of money at regular intervals, regardless of the price of the investment.

below-average costs
Average costs of an investment if more shares are purchased when the price is down and fewer shares are purchased when the price is high.

DID YOU KNOW

Sean's Success Story

Sean's financial life continues successfully. Only six years past college graduation, he has a retirement plan at work now worth over $90,000. He continues to have an aggressive investment philosophy and is invested in six mutual funds through his job. After paying off his car three years ago, Sean continued to make payments to himself, thus building up his savings account

as well, which now is over $20,000. He is worried about the economy even though it has been rising recently, so he is keeping those dollars out of the stock market for the time being. Sean's employer recently announced that employees may now contribute up to 8 percent of their salaries to their retirement plan with a full match, so he is going online this weekend to bump up his contribution from 6 to 8 percent.

Table 13-1 Dollar-Cost Averaging for a Stock or Mutual Fund Investment

Fluctuating Market			Declining Market			Rising Market		
Regular Investment	Share Price	Shares Acquired	Regular Investment	Share Price	Shares Acquired	Regular Investment	Share Price	Shares Acquired
$ 300	$15	20	$ 300	$15	20	$ 300	$ 6	50
300	10	30	300	10	30	300	10	30
300	15	20	300	10	30	300	12	25
300	10	30	300	6	50	300	15	20
300	15	20	300	5	60	300	20	15
Totals $1,500	$65	120	$1,500	$46	190	$1,500	$63	140
Average share price: $13.00 ($65 ÷ 5)* Average share cost: $12.50 ($1500 ÷ 120)†			Average share price: $9.20 ($46 ÷ 5)* Average share cost: $7.89 ($1500 ÷ 190)†			Average share price: $12.60 ($63 ÷ 5)* Average share cost: $10.71 ($1500 ÷ 140)†		

*Sum of share price total ÷ number of investment periods.

† Total amount invested ÷ total shares purchased.

average share price

Calculated by dividing the share price total by the number of investment periods.

average share cost

Actual cost basis of the investment used for income tax purposes, calculated by dividing the total amount invested by the total shares purchased.

for your investment of $300. Then the market drops—an extreme but easy-to-follow example—and the price falls to $10 per share. When you buy $300 worth of the stock now, you receive 30 shares. Three months later, the market price rebounds to $15 and you invest another $300, receiving 20 shares. The price then drops and rises again.

You now own 120 shares, thanks to your total investment of $1500. The **average share price** is calculated by averaging the amounts paid for the investment: Simply divide the share price total by the number of investment periods. In this example, the average share price is $13 ($65 ÷ 5). The **average share cost**, a more meaningful amount, is the actual cost basis of the investment used for income tax purposes. It is calculated by dividing the total amount invested by the total shares purchased. In this example, it is $12.50 ($1500 ÷ 120). Based on the recent price of $15 per share, each of your 120 shares is worth on average $2.50 ($15 − $12.50) more than you paid for it. Thus, your gain is $300 (120 × $2.50; or $15 × 120 = $1800, $1800 − $1500 = $300).

Dollar-Cost Averaging in a Declining Market Markets may also decline over a time period. The "declining market" columns in Table 13-1 (representing a prolonged bear market of 15 months) show purchases of 190 shares for increasingly lower prices that eventually reach $5 per share at the bottom of the business cycle. In a declining market, if you keep investing using dollar-cost averaging, you will purchase a large volume of shares. If you sell when the market is down substantially, you will not profit. In this example, you have purchased 190 shares at an average cost of $7.89, and they now have a depressed price of $5. Selling at this point would result in a substantial loss of $550 [$1500 − (190 × $5)]. Investing during a lousy market can be a benefit because shares are accumulated at low prices.

Dollar-Cost Averaging in a Rising Market During the "rising market" in Table 13-1, you continue to invest but buy fewer shares. The $1500 investment during the bull market bought only 140 shares for an average cost of $10.71. In this rising market, you profit because your 140 shares have a recent market price of $20 per share, for a total value of $2800 (140 × $20).

Almost anyone can profit in a rising market. If you use dollar-cost averaging over the long term, you will continue to buy in rising, falling, and fluctuating markets. The overall result will be that you buy more shares when the cost is down, thereby lowering the average share cost to below-average prices. The totals in Table 13-1, for example, reveal an overall investment of $4500 ($1500 + $1500 + $1500) used to purchase 450 shares (120 + 190 + 140) for an average cost of $10 per share ($4500 ÷ 450). With the recent market price at $20, you will realize a long-term gain of $4500 ($20 current market price × 450 shares = $9000; $9000 − $4500 invested = $4500 gain). Note that the dollar-cost averaging method would remain valid if the time interval for investing were monthly, quarterly, or even semiannually. The benefits of dollar-cost averaging are derived, in part, from the regularity of investing.

ADVICE FROM A PROFESSIONAL

Use a Dividend-Reinvestment Plan to Dollar-Cost Average

Many well-known companies allow investors to purchase shares of stock on a dollar-cost basis directly from them without the assistance of a stockbroker and then to continue to invest on a regular basis with low or no brokerage commissions. Such a program is known as a **dividend-reinvestment plan (DRIP)**. You simply sign up with the company, agreeing to buy a certain number of shares and to reinvest cash dividends into more shares of stock for little or no transaction fees. Investors' accounts are credited with fractional shares, too.

The Direct Stock Purchase Plan Clearinghouse at www.dripinvestor.com/clearinghouse/home.asp manages the **DRIP** for many companies. Coca Cola (stock symbol KO) is illustrative. It requires a minimum investment of $500 or minimum monthly investments of $50 each for at least 10 months. The enrollment fee is $10. Coca Cola will buy back shares for a transaction fee of only $15. Other companies offering DRIPs include AT&T, ExxonMobil, Home Depot, McDonald's, Johnson & Johnson, Verizon, and Chevron.

Jon Wentworth
Southern Adventist University, Collegedale, Tennessee

Dollar-Cost Averaging Offers Two Advantages The first advantage is that it reduces the average cost of shares of stock purchased over a relatively long period. Profits occur when prices for an investment fluctuate and eventually go up. Although this approach does not eliminate the possibility of loss, it does limit losses during times of declining prices. And profits accelerate during rising prices.

The second advantage is that dollar-cost averaging dictates investor discipline. This strategy of investing is not particularly glamorous, but it is the only approach that is almost guaranteed to make a profit for the investor. It takes neither brilliance nor luck, just discipline. People who invest regularly through individual retirement accounts (IRAs), employee stock ownership programs, and 401(k) retirement plans (all discussed in Chapter 17) enjoy the benefits of dollar-cost averaging. Dollar-cost averaging is a systematic strategy that will eventually get your portfolio where you want it to be.

Strategy 3: Portfolio Diversification Reduces Portfolio Volatility Owning too much of any one investment creates too great a financial risk. Experts advise that you never keep more than 5 or 10 percent of your assets in one investment, including

DID YOU KNOW

The Tax Consequences in Investment Fundamentals

There are some favorable aspects to income taxes to think about when making investments.

1. ***Income versus capital gain.*** *Current investment income, such as dividends and interest, is taxed at one's marginal tax bracket, likely 25 percent. Capital gains are taxed at special lower rates, likely at 10 or 15 percent.*

2. ***Tax-deferred investments.*** *The income and capital gains from investments within employer-sponsored retirement accounts are not subject to income taxes until the*

funds are withdrawn. Thus such investments rise in value much more quickly than those that are taxed.

3. ***After-tax return.*** *When comparing similar investments, your objective is to earn the best after-tax return. This return is the net amount earned on an investment after payment of income taxes. (See Equation 4.1 on page 129.)*

4. ***Tax-exempt income.*** *Income earned from municipal bonds is exempt from federal income taxes.*

5. ***Tax-exempt investments.*** *The income and capital gains from investments within Roth IRA accounts are not subject to income taxes, unless the funds are removed from the account within five years of opening it.*

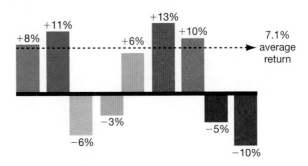

Figure 13-3 Diversification via Asset Allocation Averages Out An Investor's return

This chart represents a hypothetical mix of winning and losing various investments after one year. One investment, for instance, increased in value 13 percent; another declined 6 percent. While some investments lost value, over the year those losses were offset with the gains of others, and the overall portfolio earned a 7.1 percent average return.

your employer's stock. Many workers who invested too much in their employer's stock have seen their retirement funds disappear or be drastically reduced in value when their employers' stocks plunged in price.

Diversification is the single most important rule in investing. **Portfolio diversification** is the practice of selecting a collection of different asset classes of investments (such as stocks, bonds, mutual funds, real estate, and cash) that are chosen not only for their potential returns but also for their dissimilar risk-return characteristics.

The goal of portfolio diversification is to create a collection of investments that will provide an acceptable level of return and an acceptable exposure to risk. This outcome can be achieved because asset classes typically react differently to economic and market-place changes. The major benefit of having a diversified portfolio is that when one asset class performs poorly, there is a good chance that another will perform well, and vice versa, thus this strategy helps control your exposure to risk.

As shown in Figure 13-3 diversification reduces portfolio volatility while averaging out an investor's return. If you were totally invested in the investment that rose 13 percent, you would be happy; if you were totally invested in the investment that declined 10 percent, you would be sad. Instead your diversified portfolio over 9 investments averaged 7.1 percent, which is a respectable return. Diversification lowers the odds that you will lose money investing and increases the odds that you will make money.

The lack of diversification can quickly destroy one's investment portfolio. All stock prices dropped dramatically (actually 55%) during the Great Recession. Table 13-2 illustrates the point demonstrating that when stocks crash 50 percent, a $200,000 portfolio that is poorly diversified (too heavy on equities in this case) is devastated, in this case down $85,000.

Strategy 4: Asset Allocation Keeps You in the Right Investment Categories for Your Time Horizon

Asset allocation, a form of diversification, is deciding on the proportions of your investment portfolio that will be devoted to various categories of assets. Asset allocation helps preserve capital by selecting assets so as to protect the entire portfolio from negative events while remaining in a position to gain from positive events. This strategy helps control your exposure to risk.

Asset allocation rather than your choice of specific securities is the most important determinant of financial success. Research shows that more than 90 percent of returns earned by long-term investors result from having one's assets allocated in a diversified portfolio. Thus you must strive to own the right asset categories at the right time.

Your allocation proportions and investment choices need to reflect your age, income, family responsibilities, financial resources, risk tolerance, goals, retirement plans, and investment time horizon. You need not change the proportions of your asset allocation until your broad investment goals change—possibly not for another five or ten years.

Table 13-2	The Great Recession Devastated Portfolios That Were Not Well Diversified			

Beginning Portfolio Values ($200,000 each)			Ending Portfolio Values	
Portfolio A—Nicely Balanced Between Bonds and Stocks			Stocks Jump 10%	Stocks Crash 50%*
Cash	Bonds	Equities†		
10%	45%	45%		
$20,000	$90,000	$90,000	+$9,000	−$45,000
Portfolio B—Light on Bonds and Heavy on Equities				
Cash	Bonds	Equities†		
5%	10%	85%		
$10,000	$20,000	$170,000	+$17,000	−$85,000

*Decline from previous high in stock market prices during severe economic recession.
†Equity portion of portfolio rises or falls with changes in stock market prices.

When your investment objectives change, perhaps because of marriage, birth of a child, child graduating from college, loss of employment, divorce, or death of a spouse, you may need to change your asset allocation as well. Otherwise, stay the course.

Asset Allocation Requires Only Three Types of Investments To achieve an appropriate mix of growth, income, and stability in your portfolio, you need a combination of three investments: (1) stocks and/or stock mutual funds (equities), (2) bonds (debt), and (3) cash (or cash equivalents like Treasury securities). You need a little cash or cash equivalents in your portfolio because this allows you to move more money into stocks when appropriate. Asset allocation requires that you keep your equities, debt, and cash at a fixed ratio for long time periods, occasionally rebalancing the allocations, perhaps quarterly or annually, so as to continue to meet your investment objectives.

Asset Allocation Rules of Thumb Consider these two rules of thumb to guide the stock and bond allocation of your portfolio:

1. The percent to invest in equities is 110 minus your age, multiplied by 1.25. For example, if you are 40 years old, calculate as follows: $110 - 40 = 70$; $70 \times 1.25 = 87.5$. Therefore, a 40-year-old investor is advised to maintain a portfolio where 87.5 percent of the assets are in equities and 12.5 percent are in bonds and cash equivalents.

2. The percent to invest in equities is found by subtracting your age from 120. Put the resulting number in the form of the percentage of your portfolio to invest in stocks. Put the remainder in bonds. So if you are age 30, put 90 percent $(120 - 30)$ in stocks and 10 percent in bonds and cash. Every year, subtract your age from 120 again and rebalance your portfolio as needed.

Know Your Risk Tolerance and How Much Time You Have to Invest Figure 13-4 illustrates model portfolios that reflect varying degrees of risk tolerance and time horizons. A young, risk-tolerant, long-term investor with an aggressive investment philosophy might have a portfolio that is 100 percent in equities because equities offer the highest return over the long term. Younger investors also have ample time to ride out market fluctuations and make up any major losses. A moderate approach with a time horizon of six to ten years might have an equities-bond-cash portfolio of 60/30/10 percent.

Rebalance Your Investments at Least Once a Year Portfolio **rebalancing** is the process of bringing the different asset classes back into proper relationship following a significant change in one or more of them. You must reset your asset allocation to return your portfolio to the proper mix of stocks, bonds, and cash when they no longer conform to your plan. Here is why.

Figure 13-4 — Asset Allocation and Time Horizons

0–5 Years	6–10 Years	11+ Years	Risk Tolerance/ Investment Philosophy
10% Cash 30% Bonds 60% Equities	20% Bonds 80% Equities	100% Equities	High Risk/Aggressive
20% Cash 40% Bonds 40% Equities	10% Cash 30% Bonds 60% Equities	20% Bonds 80% Equities	Moderate Risk/Moderate
35% Cash 40% Bonds 25% Equities	20% Cash 40% Bonds 40% Equities	10% Cash 30% Bonds 60% Equities	Low Risk/Conservative

Assume you have a moderate investment philosophy and started out with a 50/40/10 bond-equities-cash portfolio, as shown in Figure 13-5, and a year later, stock values increased to 49 percent of your portfolio's value while bonds dropped to 42 percent. The result: Your portfolio is now too heavy in stocks and too light in bonds. It is too risky. As shown in Figure 13-5, this suggests that you sell some of your equities and use the proceeds to buy more bonds, thus rebalancing your portfolio according to your previously determined asset allocations.

When rebalancing, you will be selling high and buying low—the goal of all investors. It is temperamentally difficult for investors to rebalance. They don't like to sell assets that have increased in value because they hope those values will continue to increase. Rebalancing is an appropriate form of market timing as it provides some of the benefits of market timing without the risk.

Figure 13-5 — Rebalance Assets in Your Investment Portfolio Even Though Values Increased

DO IT IN CLASS

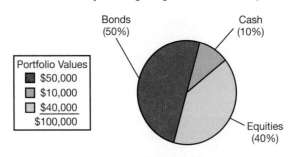

Day 1 — Beginning asset allocation of portfolio

Bonds (50%) Cash (10%)

Portfolio Values
- $50,000
- $10,000
- $40,000
$100,000

Equities (40%)

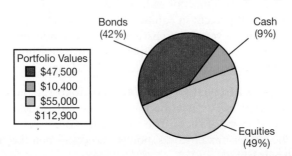

One year later — This allocation needs rebalancing to original percentages

Bonds (42%) Cash (9%)

Portfolio Values
- $47,500
- $10,400
- $55,000
$112,900

Equities (49%)

ADVICE FROM A PROFESSIONAL

When to Sell an Investment

It is time to consider selling an investment when one of the following conditions has been met:

- Something significant about the company's business or its earnings has changed dramatically for the worse since you bought the company's stock.

- The stock is doing so well that it is overvalued, and the share price is much higher than what you believe the company is worth.

- The investment is performing poorly and causing you undue anxiety. The great financier Bernard Baruch advised, "Sell down to the level where you are sleeping well."

- You need cash for a worthwhile purpose, and this investment appears the most fully priced.

- The investment no longer fits your situation or goals, and you have a more promising place to invest your money.

Diann Moorman
University of Georgia

About half of employees who participate in their employer-sponsored retirement plan have access to paid services that automatically rebalance employees' retirement assets. A worker can sign up for the services of a **limited managed account**. Once you have signed a contract with a vendor approved by your employer, you decide on your preferred asset allocation. Then under supervision by the limited managed account contract the company sells and buys your mutual fund assets, usually quarterly, on your behalf each time adjusting your portfolio back to your specified asset allocation percentages.

The service may be paid for entirely or just subsidized by the employer. A study by Financial Engines and Aon Hewitt of 425,000 savers over 5 years found that the median annual returns of those workers who got these services was almost 3 percentage points higher than those who invested on their own. Financial Soundings charges $20 annually, and both Betterment and SigFig Wealthfront charge 0.25 percent annually. Similar programs are offered by Morningstar and Financial Engines.

limited managed account
An account at an investment firm whereby, for a fee, they sell and buy your mutual fund assets, usually quarterly, on your behalf to automatically rebalance your portfolio back to your specific standards.

DID YOU KNOW

Bias toward Not Selling

People engaged in the understanding investment fundamentals have a bias toward certain behaviors that can be harmful, such as a tendency toward refusing to sell poorly performing investments that have lost value, clinging to the hope that the assets will eventually regain their old values. What to do? Regularly monitor your portfolio and sell investments that are no longer providing the desired return and then reinvest the money elsewhere.

CONCEPT CHECK 13.4

1. Summarize what the buy-and-hold strategy is all about.

2. Explain the concept of dollar-cost averaging including why one invests at below-average costs.

3. What is the goal of portfolio diversification, and how is this accomplished?

4. What is asset allocation, and why does it work?

5. What happens to a worker's 401(k) retirement account if he or she signs up for a limited management account service?

13.5 USE MONTE CARLO ADVICE TO HELP YOU INVEST FOR RETIREMENT

Monte Carlo analysis

Technique that performs a large number of trial runs of a particular portfolio mix of investments, called simulations, to find an optimal allocation for a particular investor's goals and risk tolerance.

Employer-based financial advice must follow the requirements of the Pension Protection Act. The advice must be based on computer simulations of projected investment performance using **Monte Carlo analysis**, an evolution of the long-term strategy of asset allocation. Here, the goal is to identify the investor's acceptable level of risk tolerance and then find an optimal portfolio of assets that may reduce overall portfolio volatility while providing the highest expected returns for that level of risk. This technique performs a large number of trial runs of a particular portfolio mix of investments, called simulations.

13.5a Monte Carlo Simulations

Monte Carlo simulations, named for the famous casino site, can be used to model the performance of hundreds or even thousands of individual mutual funds and stocks through thousands of fluctuating securities markets. The simulations allow you to estimate the probability of reaching your financial goals, such as a specific retirement income at a certain point in the future.

The mathematical simulations are based on long-term historical risk and return characteristics for various mixes of stock, bond, and short-term investment asset classes. Each simulation estimates how much you need to save—the accumulation phase—of your investments performed better or worse than expected, and it gives the odds that your assets will last throughout the retirement time period—the distribution phase—after you choose a given set of investments and establish a withdrawal amount. These calculations are probabilities, not certainties.

By using Monte Carlo simulations, investors can get a fairly realistic view of how much their current investments may yield in retirement. Investors often learn that they are playing it too safe by investing too conservatively, and this may prevent them from reaching their goals. By evaluating the trade-offs among various combinations of retirement plan contribution levels, diverse investment mixes, overall portfolio risk, projected retirement age, and retirement income goals, Monte Carlo simulations let you understand how certain changes in these factors will affect the chance that you will have enough money in retirement. Some investors may have to learn to be comfortable with increased risk, while others may have to save more or work longer. See Figure 13-6 for illustrative Monte Carlo calculations.

13.5b Monte Carlo Software Programs Available

Software programs can be used to assist investors in creating an efficient portfolio using Monte Carlo simulations. Products are available from Financial Engines, Financial Soundings, Morningstar, and Vanguard. Many employers offer employees free or low-cost access to Monte Carlo analysis as an employee benefit for retirement planning, often through an outside firm that offers limited management accounts.

DID YOU KNOW

Your Worst Financial Blunders in Investment Fundamentals

Based on others' financial woes, you will make mistakes in personal finance when you:

1. *Buy and sell more than you should.*
2. *Diversify less than you should.*
3. *Hold on to a bad investment long after evidence shows it was a bad decision.*

Figure 13-6 Monte Carlo Simulation from Financial Engines

You're on track!

The Forecast for your new strategy looks good! Click the **Next** button to receive your Advice Action Kit.

Your decisions

	Current	New
Your contribution	$3,400/year	$6,100/year
Employer contribution	$1,300/year	$1,300/year
Your investments	Current	Advice
Your risk level	Mod. conserv.(0.82)	Mod. aggr.(1.25)
Retirement age	65	67
Desired income	$59,000	$59,000
Minimum income	$42,000	$42,000

Your outlook at age 65

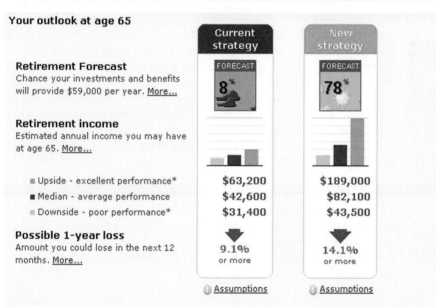

Retirement Forecast
Chance your investments and benefits will provide $59,000 per year. More...

Retirement income
Estimated annual income you may have at age 65. More...

- ■ Upside - excellent performance*
- ■ Median - average performance
- ■ Downside - poor performance*

Possible 1-year loss
Amount you could lose in the next 12 months. More...

	Current strategy	New strategy
FORECAST	8%	78%
Upside - excellent performance*	$63,200	$189,000
Median - average performance	$42,600	$82,100
Downside - poor performance*	$31,400	$43,500
Possible 1-year loss	9.1% or more	14.1% or more
	Assumptions	Assumptions

*Note: There is a 5% chance you'll have less than the downside amount and a 5% chance you'll have more than the upside amount. Amounts shown are in pre-tax dollars and have been adjusted for inflation.

Your personalized investment advice is based on your decisions. How we created your investment advice.

Investment advice

	Current strategy	New strategy
401(k) Account		
Redwood Money Market	5%	0%
Platinum Growth	17%	10%
Cypress Balanced Fund	11%	0%
Maple Bond Market	13%	13%
Sequoia Small Cap	25%	0%
Granite S&P 500 Index	29%	30%
Silver Growth and Income	0%	23%
Chestnut Idx:500 Idx	0%	24%

CONCEPT CHECK 13.5

1. Review Figure 13-6, Monte Carlo Simulation from Financial Engines, and give your impressions of the "New Strategy" recommendations.

2. What do you think about paying $20 a year for Monte Carlo simulations through your employer from a limited management company?

LEARNING OBJECTIVE 6

Create your own investment plan.

investment plan

An explanation of your investment philosophy and your logic on investing to reach specific goals.

FINANCIAL POWER POINT

Create Your Financial Plan on the Web

To obtain an overall assessment of your financial progress and advice on how to achieve your goals, you may want to consult an online financial advisor to construct a financial plan. Prices vary from $250 to $500 or more. Check out Fidelity .com, Schwab.com, TRowePrice.com, and Vanguard.com.

13.6 CREATING YOUR OWN INVESTMENT PLAN

To create an **investment plan**, which is a reflection of your investment philosophy and your logic on investing to reach specific goals, see the illustrated plan for Christina Garcia in Figure 13-7. Christina's plan includes saving for retirement as well as to buy a vehicle. You can begin creating your own investment plan by identifying your financial goals and explaining your investment philosophy as called for in Steps 1 and 2 in Figure 13-7.

To help in your thinking for Step 3 in Figure 13-7, consider the time horizons of various investments. (Terms new to you are explained in the chapters that follow.) What are the time horizons for your investment goals? Are you building up an amount for a down payment on a home, creating a college fund for a child, or putting away money for retirement? Or are all three time horizons relevant? Keep in mind why you are investing and proceed accordingly. Now calculate the numbers. How much money do you need to achieve each goal, and by when? What is the total of your current investment assets? Do the math.

Step 4 in Figure 13-7 asks about investment alternatives. Review Figure 13-1 on the long-term rates of return on various investments. Then examine Figure 13-2 because it shows the trade-offs between risk and return on investment alternatives. Next take a pencil or pen and delete some investment choices that do not appeal to you or match your investment philosophy. You will be left with alternatives that better fit your investment goals and philosophy.

DID YOU KNOW

Turn Bad Habits into Good Ones

Do You Do This?

Make small contribution to employer's retirement plan

Invest conservatively for retirement

Try to time investments to market ups and downs

Ignore transaction costs on investments

Invest mostly in employer's stock

Do This Instead!

Contribute the maximum

Invest aggressively for long-term goals

Stay invested for the long term

Hold down transaction costs

Reduce holding to 5 or 10 percent

$\mathcal{F}igure$ 13-7   **Christina Garcia's Investment Plan**

After some thinking and reading, Christina, age 24, jotted down some investment plan notes.

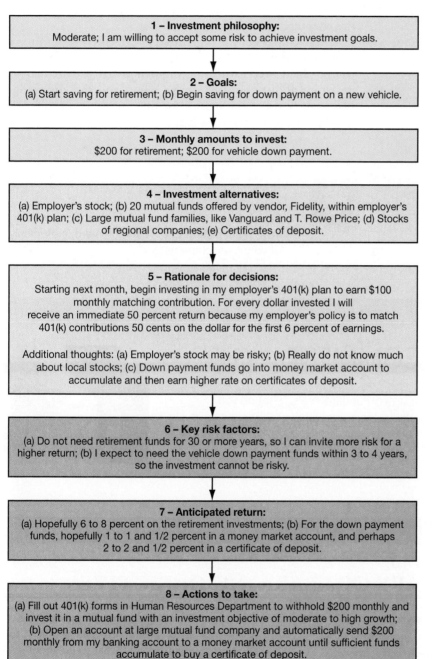

1 – Investment philosophy:
Moderate; I am willing to accept some risk to achieve investment goals.

2 – Goals:
(a) Start saving for retirement; (b) Begin saving for down payment on a new vehicle.

3 – Monthly amounts to invest:
$200 for retirement; $200 for vehicle down payment.

4 – Investment alternatives:
(a) Employer's stock; (b) 20 mutual funds offered by vendor, Fidelity, within employer's 401(k) plan; (c) Large mutual fund families, like Vanguard and T. Rowe Price; (d) Stocks of regional companies; (e) Certificates of deposit.

5 – Rationale for decisions:
Starting next month, begin investing in my employer's 401(k) plan to earn $100 monthly matching contribution. For every dollar invested I will receive an immediate 50 percent return because my employer's policy is to match 401(k) contributions 50 cents on the dollar for the first 6 percent of earnings.

Additional thoughts: (a) Employer's stock may be risky; (b) Really do not know much about local stocks; (c) Down payment funds go into money market account to accumulate and then earn higher rate on certificates of deposit.

6 – Key risk factors:
(a) Do not need retirement funds for 30 or more years, so I can invite more risk for a higher return; (b) I expect to need the vehicle down payment funds within 3 to 4 years, so the investment cannot be risky.

7 – Anticipated return:
(a) Hopefully 6 to 8 percent on the retirement investments; (b) For the down payment funds, hopefully 1 to 1 and 1/2 percent in a money market account, and perhaps 2 to 2 and 1/2 percent in a certificate of deposit.

8 – Actions to take:
(a) Fill out 401(k) forms in Human Resources Department to withhold $200 monthly and invest it in a mutual fund with an investment objective of moderate to high growth; (b) Open an account at large mutual fund company and automatically send $200 monthly from my banking account to a money market account until sufficient funds accumulate to buy a certificate of deposit.

DO IT NOW!

You know more about investment fundamentals after reading this chapter, so get started right now by:

1. *Writing down your investment philosophy.*

2. *Recording the percentages you would allocate to stocks, bonds, and cash equivalents using an asset allocation strategy to save for retirement.*

3. *Starting to save even a small amount perhaps by signing up to automatically transfer some money every payday to a savings or investment account.*

Now you have started to create an investment plan, so record your responses to Steps 5, 6, and 7. Then create an investment portfolio appropriate for your life now using Figure 13-4 as a model. All that remains is to put your plan into action. That means filling out forms to open an investment account, selecting your investments, writing checks for your first investing dollars, and monitoring your investments. These topics are examined in the chapters that follow.

When you take the appropriate retirement planning action steps, including a moderate amount of risk when investing, you will be able to relax with the confidence that you are making wise decisions about your investment assets and the knowledge that your money will grow and will be there to fund your lifestyle during the last quarter of your life.

CONCEPT CHECK 13.6

1. Review Figures 13-1 and 13-2, and record in writing an investment plan to fund your retirement, presumably one of your own long-term goals.

WHAT DO YOU RECOMMEND *NOW?*

Now that you have read the chapter on investment fundamentals, what do you recommend to Shavenellyee and Sarena on the subject regarding:

1. Portfolio diversification for Shavenellyee?

2. Dollar-cost averaging for Shavenellyee?

3. Investment alternatives for Shavenellyee?

BIG PICTURE SUMMARY OF LEARNING OBJECTIVES

LO1   Explain how to get started as an investor.

Before investing, think about how investing is more than savings, the investment returns which are possible, and the long-term rates of return on investment choices. Investors hope that their investments will earn them a positive total return, which is the income an investment generates from current income and capital gains.

LO2   Identify your investment philosophy and invest accordingly.

Achieving financial success requires that you understand your investment philosophy and adhere to it when investing. An investment philosophy is one's general approach to tolerance for risk in investments, whether

it is conservative, moderate, or aggressive, given the financial goals to be achieved. You also need to know about investment risk and what to do about it. Before investing your money, you need to think about lending versus owning, short term versus long term, and how to select investments that are likely to provide your desired potential total return.

LO3   Describe the major risk factors that affect the rate of return on investments.

Because of the uncertainty that surrounds investments, people often follow a conservative course in an effort to keep their risk low. Being too conservative when investing means that they risk not reaching their financial goals. To be a successful investor, you must understand the major risk factors that affect the rate of return on investments so you can then take the appropriate risks when making investment decisions. Key concepts include random and market risk.

LO4   **Decide which of the four long-term investment strategies you will utilize.**

To succeed as an investor, you must establish your own long-term investment strategy. Most investors accept the fact that they cannot time the market with any consistency. Most long-term investors are passive investors. They wisely ignore the ups and downs of the stock market and the business cycle and simply use the four investment strategies of buy and hold, dollar-cost averaging, diversification, and asset allocation. Rebalancing your portfolio at least once a year is critical to success.

LO5   **Use Monte Carlo Advice when investing for retirement.**

By using Monte Carlo simulations, investors can get a more realistic view of how much their current investments may yield later on during retirement. Investors may learn that they are playing it too safe by investing too conservatively today, and this may prevent them from reaching their long-term goals. Some investors may have to learn to be comfortable with increased risk, while others may have to save more or work longer.

LO6   **Create your own investment plan.**

An investment plan is an explanation of your investment philosophy and your logic on investing to reach specific goals. Steps include identifying your goals, contemplating which types of investments might best fit your investment goals, clarifying your investment philosophy, learning about investment alternatives, and narrowing down your choices.

LET'S TALK ABOUT IT

1. **Why Invest.** Why should people invest? Give three reasons each for college students, young college graduates in their 20s, couples with young children, and people in their 50s.

2. **Long-Term Rates of Return.** Review Figure 13-1, "Long-Term Rates of Return on Investments" on page 383. and offer your views on which two investment types would be most suitable for yourself.

3. **Market Risk.** What do you think is the likelihood of years of poor stock market returns.

4. **What Is Your Tolerance for Risk in Investing?** Is it the same as for other members of your class? Why or why not?

5. **Risk and Return Trade-Offs.** Review Figure 13-2, "The Risk Pyramid Reveals the Trade-Offs Between Risk and Return" on page 385 and give your views on which three investments would be most suitable for you.

6. **Your Investment Philosophy.** Is your investment philosophy conservative, moderate, or aggressive? Give two reasons to support the adoption of your philosophy. How does your view compare with the philosophies of other members of your class?

7. Review the section on "Types of Investment Risks" on page 391, and note two that might worry you the most in the world of investing.

DO IT IN CLASS PAGE 391

8. **Invest How Much?** Assume you have graduated from college and have a good-paying job. If you had to commit to investing regularly right now, how much money would you put away every month? Explain why. How does your view compare with the views of other members of your class?

DO THE MATH

1. **Annual Investments.** Sheldon Cooper and Amy Farrah live in Pasadena, California, have as a new investment goal to create a college fund for their newborn daughter. They estimate that they will need $200,000 in 18 years. Assuming that the Cooper-Fowler family could obtain a return of 5 percent, how much would they need to invest annually to reach their goal? Use Appendix A-3 or the *Garman/Forgue* companion website.

2. **Number of Years.** Mary Cooper, Sheldon's mother, who lives in Texas, wants to help pay for her grandchild's education. How long will it take Mary to reach her goal of $200,000 if she invests $10,000 per year, earning 6

percent? Use Appendix A-3 or the *Garman/Forgue* companion website.

3. **Future Cost.** If one year of college currently costs $15,000, how much will one year cost Michelle Spindle's newborn daughter, Melissa, in 18 years, assuming a 5 percent annual rate of inflation? Use Appendix A-1 or the *Garman/Forgue* companion website.

4. **Returns and Actions.** Kunal Nayyar from California, had $50,000 in investments at the beginning of the year that consisted of a diversified portfolio of stocks (40 percent), bonds (40 percent), and cash equivalents

DO IT IN CLASS PAGE 400

(20 percent). His returns over the past 12 months were 13 percent on stocks, 6 percent on bonds, and 1 percent on cash equivalents.

(a) What is Kunal's average return for the year?

(b) If Kunal wanted to rebalance his portfolio to its original position, what specific actions should he take?

5. **Early Investor Wins.** Jordan and Jeremy, who are twins living in Rexburg, Idaho, took different approaches to investing. Jordan saved $2000 per year for ten years starting at age 23 and never added any more money to the account. Jeremy saved $2000 per year for 20 years starting at age 35. Assuming that the brothers earned a 6 percent return, who had accumulated the most by the time they reached age 63? Use Appendix A-1 and Appendix A-3 or the *Garman/Forgue* companion website.

FINANCIAL PLANNING CASES

CASE 1

The Johnsons Embark on a Solid Investment Program

After nearly eight years of marriage, Harry and Belinda's finances have improved, even though they have incurred debts for an automobile loan and a condominium. Because they did not contribute very much to their retirement plans every year, Harry's account is currently worth only $28,000 and Brenda's is $31,000, but they do have $12,000 in investments outside their employers' retirement plans.

DO IT IN CLASS
PAGES 383
AND 385

Therefore, the Johnsons have decided to seriously forgo some current spending for the next three years to concentrate on getting a solid investment program under way while they still have two incomes available and before they start a family. They are willing to accept a moderate amount of risk and expect to invest between $600 and $800 per month over the next three years. Respond to the following questions:

(a) In what types of investments (choose only two) might the Johnsons place the first $2000? (Review Figures 13-1 and 13-2 for ideas and available options, and consider the types of investment risks inherent in each choice.) Give reasons for your selections.

(b) In what types of investments might they place the next $4000? Why?

(c) What types of investments should they choose for the next $10,000? Why?

CASE 2

Victor and Maria Hernandez Try to Catch Up on Their Investments

The expenses associated with sending two children through college prevented Victor and Maria Hernandez from adding substantially to their investment program. Now that their younger son, Joseph, has completed school and is working full time, they would like to build up their investments quickly. Victor is 47 years old and wants to retire early, perhaps by age 60. In addition to the retirement program at his place of employment, Victor believes that their investment portfolio, currently valued at $70,000, will need to triple to $210,000 by retirement time. He and Maria realize that they will have to sacrifice a lot of current spending to save and invest for retirement.

(a) What rate of return is needed on the $70,000 portfolio to reach their goal of $210,000 (assuming no additional contributions)? Use Appendix A-3 or visit the *Garman/Forgue* companion website.

(b) Victor and Maria think they will need a total of $400,000 for a retirement financial nest egg. Therefore, they will need to create an additional sum of $190,000 through new investments. Assuming an annual return of 8 percent, how much do the Hernandezes need to invest each year to reach their goal of $190,000? Use Appendix A-3 or visit the *Garman/Forgue* companion website.

(c) If they assume a 6 percent annual return, how much do the Hernandezes need to invest each year to reach their goal of $190,000? Use Appendix A-3 or visit the *Garman/Forgue* companion website.

CASE 3

Julia Price's Goal Is to Buy a Luxury Condominium

It has been about 20 years since Julia graduated with a major in aeronautical engineering, and she has been quite successful in her career and her personal finances. Accordingly she wants to sell her home and buy a luxury condominium. She has $40,000 in savings, and she figures that she can continue her savings and investment program for three more years before making a 20 percent down payment on a luxury condominium. The home that she wants to purchase is currently priced at $450,000. Julia thinks she should invest her $40,000 and additional savings during the next three years by using lending investments like certificates of deposit and bonds rather than owning stocks or stock mutual funds. Offer your opinions about her thinking.

CASE 4

A First-Time Investor Gets a Head start

Lucia Gomez, a flight attendant from Indiana, Pennsylvania, is thinking about jump-starting a retirement savings plan by investing the $50,000 gift that her elderly uncle gave her. She also wants to invest $1000 a month for the next 25 years for retirement. Lucia knows little about investments and does not seem to have a big desire to learn.

(a) What can you suggest to Lucia about figuring out her investment philosophy? (Hint: Mention the information in Figure 13-2 in your response.)

(b) Would you recommend active or passive investing for her, and why?

(c) Should Lucia be a lender or owner?

(d) Identify three risks to her retirement investments that Lucia should try to avoid, and explain how she can avoid them.

(e) Select two of the four recommended investment strategies to recommend to Lucia, and explain why she should follow them.

(f) If Lucia's $50,000 is invested in a standard investment account and her $1000 monthly is invested in a tax-sheltered account, with each account growing at 5 percent annually for 25 percent in 25 years, how much money will she have accumulated in each account? (Hint: Adjust the lump-sum investment for 25 percent taxes.)

BE YOUR OWN PERSONAL FINANCIAL MANAGER

1. **Your Personal Risk Pyramid.** Review Figure 13-2, "The Risk Pyramid Reveals the Trade-Offs Between Risk and Return," and record your opinions on which types of risk you are probably willing to take over the next ten years in the world of investing by listing the names of the investments with which you would be comfortable.

2. **What Is Your Investment Philosophy?** Review the section titled "Identify Your Investment Philosophy and Invest Accordingly" and then complete Worksheet 50: My Investment Philosophy from "My Personal Financial Planner" to record various aspects of your approach to investing.

3. **Your Long-Term Investment Strategies.** Complete Worksheet 51: My Preferred Long-Term Investment Strategies from "My Personal Financial Planner" by check marking the strategies you like and that you might follow during your investing life.

4. **Real Return on Investments.** Review the box "Did You Know? Calculate the Real Rate of Return (After Taxes and Inflation) on Investments" and complete Worksheet 53: The Real Return on My Investments from "My Personal Financial Planner" by inserting some realistic numbers next to the examples.

ON THE NET

Go to the Web pages indicated to complete these exercises.

1. **Why Invest?** Visit the John Hancock website www.jhinvestments.com/Article.aspx?ArticleID={79432E5F-30DF-4624-94F8-FC319EA99D71} and read the article titled "Why Invest?" Compare what you read there with what is in this chapter.

2. **Investing for Beginners** Visit the Investing for Beginners website invest-for-beginners.blogspot.com/ and read the series of short articles on that page. Compare what you read there with what is in this chapter.

3. **Herd Behavior** Visit the Investopedia website www.investopedia.com/university/behavioral_finance

/behavioral8.asp#axzz1yB21OU00 and read the article on herd behavior on that page. Compare with what you read in this chapter.

4. **Asset Allocation** Visit the Wikipedia website en.wikipedia.org/wiki/Asset_allocation and read it's contents. Compare with what you have read in this chapter.

5. **Monte Carlo Simulation** Visit the Financial Engines website corp.financialengines.com/. Click on "How We Help You" and read the links that are there. Compare with what you have read in this chapter.

ACTION INVOLVEMENT PROJECTS

1. **Your Investment Strategy.** The text discusses four strategies for long-term investors on pages 394–401. Which one appeals to you most and why?

2. **Risk-Tolerance Quiz.** Go to two of the risk-tolerance quiz websites listed in "Financial Power Point: Take a

Risk-Tolerance Quiz" on page 387 and offer some comments on how they differ.

3. **Current Investment Magazine Article.** Obtain a current issue of *Money* or *Kiplinger's Personal Finance* and summarize an article that offers suggestions on investing.

Visit the Garman/Forgue companion website at www.cengagebrain.com.

14 Investing in Stocks and Bonds

YOU MUST BE KIDDING, RIGHT?

Brothers Michael and Christopher Morton differ in investment philosophies—Michael is a conservative investor and Christopher holds a moderate investing outlook. Their father left each of them $100,000 when he died ten years ago, and Christopher invested in common stocks while Michael invested in corporate bonds. After ten years, how much more money is Christopher likely to have in his account than Michael?

A. $12,000   **C.** $148,000

B. $21,000   **D.** $179,000

The answer is B, $21,000. One could expect in today's times to obtain a long-term average annual return of perhaps 6 percent on U.S. common stocks compared with about 4 percent on corporate bonds. A $100,000 common stock portfolio that returned 6 percent annually would accumulate to $179,000 in ten years while a bond portfolio earning 4 percent annually over the same time period would grow to $148,000. Christopher's willingness to accept more risk by investing in common stocks may provide him with a balance bigger than his brother's by a whopping $31,000 or 21 percent ($31,000/$148,000)!

LEARNING OBJECTIVES

After reading this chapter, you should be able to:

1 Explain how stocks and bonds are used as investments.

2 Describe ways to evaluate stock prices, and calculate a stock's potential rate of return.

3 Use the Internet to evaluate common stocks in which to invest.

4 Summarize how to buy and sell stocks, as well as the techniques of margin buying and selling short.

5 Describe how to invest in bonds.

MORTGAGE RETIREMENT

INSURANCE TAXES

401(k) VACATION

EDUCATION CREDIT CARDS

© S-F/Shutterstock.com/Peter Booth/E+/Getty Images

WHAT DO YOU RECOMMEND?

Ashley Diaz, age 42, is a senior Web designer for a communications company in Lansing, Michigan. She earns $92,000 annually. From her salary, Ashley contributes $200 per month to her 401(k) retirement account, matched by her employer, through which she invests in the company's stock. Ashley is divorced and has custody of her three children, 10-year-old twins and a 6-year-old. Her ex-husband pays $1500 per month in child support. Ashley and her former spouse contribute $3000 each annually to a college fund for their children. Over the past 15 years, Ashley has built a $300,000 portfolio of investments after starting by investing the proceeds of a $50,000 life insurance policy following the death of her first husband. Currently, her portfolio is allocated 40 percent into preferred stocks (paying 4.5 percent); 30 percent into cyclical, blue-chip common stocks (P/E ratio of 14); 10 percent into Treasury bonds (paying 2.2 percent); 10 percent into municipal bonds (paying 1.7 percent); and 10 percent into AAA corporate bonds (paying 4.6 percent). Ashley's total return in recent years has been about 6 percent annually. Her investment goals are to have sufficient cash to pay for her children's education and to retire in about 18 years.

© Golden Pixels LLC/Shutterstock.com

What do you recommend to Ashley on the subject of stocks and bonds regarding:

1. **Investing for retirement in 18 years?**

2. **Owning blue-chip common stocks and preferred stocks rather than other common stocks given Ashley's investment time horizon?**

3. **The wisdom of owning municipal bonds rather than corporate bonds?**

4. **The likely selling price of her corporate bonds, if sold today?**

5. **Investments that might be appropriate to fund her children's education?**

LEARNING OBJECTIVE 1

Explain how stocks and bonds are used as investments.

securities

Negotiable instruments of ownership or debt, including common stock, preferred stock, and bonds.

stocks

Shares of ownership in a business corporation's assets and earnings.

common stock

Most basic form of ownership of a corporation.

cash dividends

Cash profits that a firm distributes to stockholders.

market price

The current price of a share of stock that a buyer is willing to pay a willing seller.

To earn a larger return than offered by conservative investments, you must accept more risk. Historically, common stocks, for example, have earned substantially more than bonds, often twice as much. When you invest in stocks, you can increase returns significantly while increasing risk only slightly. These investments belong in everyone's investment portfolio because they provide opportunities for moderate and aggressive investors alike. Your task when selecting stocks is to find the right balance between safety and risk.

The principles of long-term investing remain valid because over time turbulent stock and bond markets calm down and provide investors fairly predictable returns. In fact, a good time to invest is when the share prices of high-quality firms have been beaten down to affordable levels. When the stock markets are down that means that stocks are "on sale," as prices are lower than usual.

You should welcome the fact that economic slumps always spark a powerful market recovery. The typical post-recession rally in prices on the stock market is a 50 percent increase over the following 18 months. In fact, the Great Recession stock market that started in October 2007 saw stock prices decline 55 percent by March 2009, and the subsequent bull market more than doubled prices in less than four years. Investing is an act of faith and confidence in the future of the U.S. and global economies. History argues that by the time students in college are ready to retire, stock market prices will have tripled or quadrupled.

14.1   THE ROLE OF STOCKS AND BONDS IN INVESTMENTS

Individual investors provide the money corporations use to create sales and earn profits. The investor shares in those profits. A **corporation** is a state-chartered legal entity that can conduct business operations in its own name. A **public corporation** is one that issues stock purchased by the general public and traded on stock markets such as the New York Stock Exchange. In contrast, the stock of a **privately held corporation** is held by a relatively small number of people and is not traded on a public stock exchange. The ability to sell shares of ownership to investors offers a corporation the opportunity to develop into a firm of considerable size. It can continue to exist even as ownership of its shares changes hands. For example, the owners of AT&T are the holders of its more than 5.38 million shares of stock.

A corporation's financial needs will vary over time. To begin its operations, a new corporation needs **start-up capital** (funds initially invested in a business enterprise). During its life, a corporation may need additional money to grow. To raise capital and finance its goals, it may issue three types of **securities** (negotiable instruments of ownership or debt): common stock, preferred stock, and bonds.

14.1a   Common Stock

Stocks are shares of ownership in the assets and earnings of a business corporation. Each stock investor is a part owner in a corporation. **Common stock** is the most basic form of ownership of a corporation. For the investor, stocks represent potential income because the investor owns a piece of the future profits of the company. Investors usually have two expectations: (1) the corporation will be profitable enough that income will exceed expenses, thereby allowing the firm to pay **cash dividends** (a share of profits distributed in cash); and (2) the **market price** of a share of stock, which is the current price that a buyer is willing to pay a willing seller, will increase over time.

Stocks usually require a low minimum investment. Investors expect to earn annual returns of 6 percent or higher on average over time from the combination of dividends and capital gains.

Each person who owns a share of stock—called a **shareholder** or **stockholder**—has a proportionate interest in the ownership (usually a very small slice) and, therefore, in the assets and income of the corporation. This **residual claim** means that common stockholders have a right to share in the income and assets of a corporation only after higher-priority claims are satisfied. These higher-priority claims include interest payments to those who own company bonds and preferred stocks.

Stockholders have a **limited liability**, as their responsibility for business losses is limited to the amount invested in the shares of stock owned. These amounts may be small or large, but the most the shareholder can lose is the original amount invested. If the corporation becomes bankrupt, the common stockholder's ownership value consists of the amount left per share after the claims of all creditors are satisfied first. Each common stockholder has **voting rights**: the proportionate authority to express an opinion or choice in matters affecting the company. Stockholders vote to elect the company's **board of directors**. This group of individuals sets policy and names the principal officers of the company—**management**—who run the firm's day-to-day operations. The number of votes cast by each shareholder depends on the number of shares he or she owns. Stockholders attend an annual meeting or vote by **proxy**— shareholders' written authorization to someone else to represent them and to vote their shares at a stockholder's meeting.

14.1b Preferred Stock

Preferred stock is a type of fixed-income ownership security in a corporation. Owners of a preferred stock receive a fixed dividend per share that corporations are required to distribute before any dividends are paid out to common stockholders. They receive no extra income from the stock other than their fixed dividend, even when the firm is highly profitable. The regular dividend payments appeal to those who desire a reliable stream of income, such as retired investors. While the income stream may be consistent, the market price of preferred stock is sensitive to changes in interest rates. Preferred stockholders rarely have voting privileges.

Sometimes a corporation decides not to pay dividends to preferred stockholders because it lacks profits or simply because it wants to retain and reinvest all of its earnings. When the board of directors votes to skip (**pass**) making a cash dividend to preferred stockholders, holders of **cumulative preferred stock** must be paid that dividend before any future dividends are distributed to the common stockholders. For example, assume that a company passes on the first two quarterly dividends of $2.25 each to preferred stockholders, who expect to receive $9 each year ($2.25 × 4 quarters).

If the company prospers and wants to give a cash dividend to its common stockholders in the third quarter, it must first pay the passed $4.50 to the cumulative preferred stockholders. Furthermore, the usual third-quarter cash dividend of $2.25 has to be made to the preferred stockholders before the common stockholders can receive any dividends. In the case of **noncumulative preferred stock**, the preferred stockholders would have no claim to previously skipped dividends. **Convertible preferred stock**, a unique security occasionally sold by companies, can be exchanged at the option of the stockholder for a specified number of shares of common stock.

14.1c Bonds

Individuals who want to invest by loaning their money can do so by buying bonds and becoming a creditor of the business (again a very small one). A **bond** is an interest-bearing negotiable certificate of long-term debt issued by a corporation, the U.S. government, or a municipality (such as a city or state). Bonds are basically IOUs. Corporations and governments often use the proceeds from bonds to finance expensive construction projects and to purchase costly equipment.

With bonds, investors lend the issuer a certain amount of money—the **principal**— with two expectations: (1) they will receive regular interest payments at a fixed rate of return for many years, and (2) they will get their principal returned at some point in the

shareholder (stockholder)

Each person who owns a share of a company's stock holds a proportionate interest in firm ownership and, therefore, in the assets and income of the corporation.

residual claim

Common stockholders have a right to share in the income and assets of a corporation after higher-priority claims are satisfied.

voting rights

Proportionate authority to express an opinion or choice in matters affecting the company.

DO IT IN CLASS

preferred stock

Type of fixed-income ownership security in a corporation that pays fixed dividends.

cumulative preferred stock

Preferred stock for which dividends must be paid, including any skipped dividends, before dividends go to common stockholders.

convertible preferred stock

Can be exchanged at the option of the stockholder for a specified number of shares of common stock.

principal

Face amount of a bond.

maturity date

Date upon which the principal is returned to the bondholder.

future, called the **maturity date**. The regular pattern of interest appeals to those who desire a reliable stream of income, again retired investors. The market price of bonds is sensitive to changes in interest rates.

DID YOU KNOW

Don't Get Scared Out of Buying Stocks and Stock Mutual Funds

Investment expert Peter Lynch says, "The real key to making money in stocks and stock mutual funds is not to get scared out of them." Investing based on the recent past is like driving a car while focused on the rear view mirror: it is stupid and dangerous. Therefore, remain optimistic about stocks and look for gains of 4 to 6 percent annually for the next 10 or 20 years.

profit

Money left over after a firm pays all expenses and interest to bondholders.

after-tax profit

Money left over after a firm has paid expenses, bondholder interest, and taxes.

retained earnings

Money left over after a firm has paid expenses, bondholder interest, taxes, preferred stockholder dividends, and common stockholder dividends.

FINANCIAL POWER POINT

Assume Your Investment Portfolio Will Earn 5 Percent to 6 Percent

When planning for long-term financial goals, assume your investments will conservatively earn 3 percent after inflation or at least 5 percent to 6 percent a year. Your investment returns could be higher.

14.1d　An Illustration of Stocks and Bonds: Running Paws Cat Food Company

To better understand how a corporation finances its goals by issuing common and preferred stock while also paying returns for stockholders, consider the example of Running Paws Cat Food Company. When reading through the example, imagine that the numbers have many more zeros to better visualize a company the size of Google or Microsoft.

Running Paws Is Born　Running Paws began as a small family business in Lincoln, Nebraska, started by Linda Webtek. She developed a wonderful recipe for cat food that contained no corn, corn meal, or corn gluten meal and sold the product through a local grocery store. As sales increased, Linda decided to incorporate the business, expand its operations and share ownership of the company with the public by asking people to invest in the company's future. Running Paws issued 10,000 shares of common stock at $10 per share. Three friends each bought 2500 shares, and Linda signed over the cat food recipe and equipment to the corporation itself in exchange for the remaining 2500 shares. At that point, Running Paws had $75,000 in working capital (7500 shares sold at $10 each), equipment, a great recipe, and a four-person board of directors. Each of the directors worked for the firm, although they paid themselves very low salaries.

Running Paws Begins to Grow　The sales revenues of a corporation like Running Paws are used to pay (1) expenses, (2) interest to bondholders, (3) taxes, (4) cash dividends to preferred stockholders, and (5) cash dividends to common stockholders, in that order. If money is left over after items 1 and 2 are paid, the corporation has earned a **profit**. If funds are available after item 3 is paid, the company has an **after-tax profit**. The average corporation pays out 40 to 60 percent of its after-tax profit in cash dividends to stockholders. The remainder, called **retained earnings**, is left to accumulate and finance the company's goals—often expansion and growth. In its early years, Running Paws retained all of its profits and distributed no dividends.

Common stockholders, such as the stockholders of Running Paws Cat Food Company, are not guaranteed dividends. However, most profitable companies do pay common stockholders a small dividend on a quarterly basis until increased earnings justify paying out a higher amount.

Given that Running Paws retained all its earnings, you might wonder why people would invest in such a company. Two reasons explain the attraction. First, as a company becomes more efficient and profitable, cash dividends to common stockholders may not only begin but also become significant. Second, the market price of the stock may increase sharply as more investors become interested in the future profitability of a growing company. Common stock constitutes a share of ownership; thus as the company grows, the price of its common stock follows suit.

Increasing sales meant more production for Running Paws. Soon more orders were coming in from Chicago than the firm could handle. After three years, the owners of Running Paws decided to expand once again. They wanted to borrow an additional $100,000, but their business was so new and its future so uncertain that lenders demanded an extremely high interest rate. To raise the needed funds, the owners decided to issue 5000 shares of preferred stock at $20 per share, promising to pay a cash dividend of $1.80 per share annually, providing a 9 percent yield to investors. The preferred stock was sold to outside investors, but the original investors retained control of the company through their common stock.

Running Paws Becomes a National Company Following its pattern of expanding into new markets, Running Paws soon developed additional lines of cat food that sold well. With the proceeds from the sale of preferred stock, and after a new plant in Brooklyn, New York, opened, the income of the four-year-old business finally exceeded expenses, and it had a profit of $13,000. The board of directors declared the promised preferred stock dividend of $9000 (5000 preferred shares × $1.80) but no dividend for common stockholders. In the following year, net profits after taxes amounted to $28,000. Once again the board paid the $9000 dividend to preferred stockholders but retained the remainder of the profits to finance continued expansion and improved efficiency.

Then one of the original partners wanted to exit the business and needed to sell her 2500 shares of stock, for which she had originally paid $25,000. Because Running Paws was beginning to show some profits, two other private investors recommended by a local stockbroker made offers to purchase her shares. The shares were sold at $16 per share, with 1500 shares going to one investor and 1000 shares to another investor. Thus, this original investor gained $15,000 in price appreciation ($16 × 2500 = $40,000; $40,000 − $25,000 = $15,000) when she sold out. (Running Paws did not profit from this transaction.) Now five owners of the common stock, including the two new ones, voted for the board of directors, with each share representing one vote.

During the sixth year, the company's sales again increased and its earnings totaled $39,000. This time the board voted $9000 for the preferred stockholders and $5000 ($0.50 per share) for the common stockholders but retained the remaining $25,000. With the $5000 distribution, the common stockholders finally began to receive cash dividends.

Even with its success, Running Paws faced another decision. To distribute its products nationally would require another $400,000 to $500,000 for expansion costs. After much discussion, the board voted to sell additional shares of stock and issue some bonds. The company planned to sell 10,000 shares of common stock at $25 per share. This would dilute the owners' proportion of ownership by half. Common stockholders, however, have a **pre-emptive right** to purchase additional shares before new shares are offered to the public. Thus, each current stockholder retained the legal right to maintain proportionate ownership by being allowed to purchase more shares.

Bonds were sold, too.* Running Paws issued two hundred $1000 bonds with a coupon rate of 8 percent. After several months, all of the new stock and bond shares were sold. After brokerage expenses, the company netted more than $190,000 from the bonds to help finance the expansion. On the stock sales, various local stockbrokers took selling commissions totaling $16,000, leaving $234,000 available for the company to use for expansion. These and other investors will follow the progress of Running Paws and buy and sell shares accordingly. The company will not benefit from this trading. Running Paws and its shareholders will benefit from a rising stock price because ownership in a growing company becomes increasingly valuable. If Running Paws continues to prosper, its board of directors might work toward having its stock listed on a regional stock exchange (discussed later in this chapter) to facilitate trading of shares and to further enhance the company's image.

pre-emptive right
Right of common stockholders to purchase additional shares before a firm offers new shares to the public.

DID YOU KNOW

Money Websites Investing in Stocks

Informative websites for investing in stocks and bonds, including online screens to compare stocks are:

AOL Money Basics (www.dailyfinance .com/?icid=navbar_Finance)

BloombergBusinessWeek (www.business week.com/markets-and-finance)

CNN Money (www.money.cnn.com /magazines/moneymag/money101/)

Kiplinger's Personal Finance (www .kiplinger.com/fronts/channels/investing/)

MarketWatch (www.marketwatch .com/personal-finance?showsmscrim =true)

Morningstar (www.morningstar.com)

Motley Fool (www.fool.com)

NASDAQ (www.nasdaq.com)

Yahoo! Finance on stocks (www.finance .yahoo.com/marketupdate?u)

Zacks Investment Research (www .zacks.com)

---

* Companies that need capital to begin or expand their operations sell new issues of stocks, bonds, or both to the investing public. New issues of stock are referred to as **initial public offerings (IPOs)**. **Investment banking firms** serve as intermediaries between companies issuing new stocks and bonds and the investing public.

CONCEPT CHECK 14.1

1. Distinguish between common stocks and bonds.

2. How do public corporations use stocks and bonds?

3. Why do individuals invest in stocks?

14.2　HOW TO EVALUATE COMMON STOCKS

LEARNING OBJECTIVE 2

Describe ways to evaluate stock prices, and calculate a stock's potential rate of return.

beta value (beta coefficient)

A measure of stock volatility; that is, how much the stock price varies relative to the rest of the market.

DID YOU KNOW ?

Reasons to Invest in Dividend-Paying Stocks

When you invest in companies that pay dividends, odds are that they will continue to pay the dividend even when the company is not doing well financially. Dividend-paying companies typically outperform other firms and provide a greater total return than the return on the S&P 500 index. Firms that pay dividends typically boost them about 3.2 percent annually. When inflation is low a dividend of 2 to 4 percent is an excellent return. Finally, dividend-paying companies are less volatile than other stocks often with a beta of 1.0 or less.

fundamental analysis

School of thought in market analysis that assumes each stock has an intrinsic (or true) value based on its expected stream of future earnings.

When thinking about investing in a stock it is helpful to begin by reviewing Table 14-1, which shows the types of stocks and their characteristics.

14.2a　Use Beta to Compare a Stock to Similar Investments

Beta is a number widely used by investors to predict future stock prices. The **beta value** (or **beta coefficient**) is a measure of an investment's volatility compared with a broad market index for similar investments over time. For large-company stocks, the S&P 500 Stock Index often serves as a benchmark. The average for all stocks in the market is a beta of +1.0, thus a stock with a beta of +1.0 typically moves in lockstep with the S&P and a beta greater than 1.0 indicates higher-than-market volatility. Recall from Chapter 13 that market risk is assumed to be 8 percent; thus when the overall stock market increases 8 percent a stock with a 1.0 beta is likely to increase the same amount. A stock with a beta of 1.2 will move 20 percent high and lower than the index.

Most stocks have positive betas between 0.5 and 2.0. A beta of less than 1.0 (0.0 to 0.9) indicates that the stock price is less sensitive to the market. This is because the price moves in the same direction as the general market, but not to the same degree. A beta of more than +1.0 to +2.0 (or higher) indicates that the price of the security is more sensitive to the market because its price moves in the same direction as the market but by a greater percentage. Higher betas mean greater risk relative to the market. A beta of zero suggests that the price of the stock is independent of the market, much like that of a risk-free U.S. Treasury security. You may look up betas for stocks (just input the stock's symbol) at Calculator Edge (www.calculatoredge.com/finance/betas.htm) or Yahoo! Finance (screener.finance.yahoo.com/stocks.html). Stocks with a negative beta move in the opposite direction of the market.

14.2b　Most Use Fundamental Analysis to Evaluate Stocks

The theory underlying **fundamental analysis** is that each stock has an intrinsic (or true) value based on its expected stream of future earnings. Most professional stock analysts and investors take this approach to investing as they research corporate and industry financial reports. Fundamental analysis suggests that you can identify some stocks that will outperform others given the state of the economy. The fundamental approach presumes that a stock's basic value is largely determined by its current and future earnings trends, assets and debts, products, competition, and management's expertise to assess its growth potential. The aim is to seek out sound stocks—perhaps even unfashionable ones—that are priced below what they ought to be.

Fundamental analysis suggests that you should consider investing only in companies that will likely be industry leaders—not necessarily the largest firms and fastest-growing industries, but the pacesetters in terms of profitability. You should invest in a stock because you have good reasons related to earnings and profitability, such as a new division in a firm that soon is expected to be quite profitable, a firm is starting to outsell its competitors, product research looks promising, or the firm is a leader in an industry that

Table 14-1 Characteristics of Stocks

Type of Stock	Characteristics
Income Stock	Company that pays a cash dividend higher than that offered by most companies. Stocks issued by telephone, electric, and gas utility companies; beta often less than 1.0.
Growth Stock	Corporations that are leaders in their fields, that dominate their markets, and that have several consecutive years of above-industry-average earnings are considered; pays some dividends. Investor awareness of such corporations is widespread, and expectations for continued growth are high. The P/E ratio is high; betas of 1.5 or more.
Blue-Chip Stock	A company that has been around for a long time, has a well-regarded reputation, dominates its industry (often with annual revenues of $1 billion or more), and is known for being a solid, relatively safe investment; betas are usually around 1.0.
Countercyclical Stock	A company whose profits are greatly influenced by changes in the economic business cycle in consumer-dependent industries, like automobiles, housing, airlines, retailing, and heavy machinery; betas of about 1.0. A stock with a beta that is less than 1.0 is called a **countercyclical** (or **defensive**) because it exhibits price changes contrary to movements in the business cycle, thus prices remain steady during economic downturns. Examples are cigarette manufacturers, movies, soft drinks, cat and dog food, electric utilities, and groceries.
Value Stock	A company that grows with the economy and tends to trade at a low price relative to its company fundamentals (dividends, earnings, sales, and so on) and thus is considered under-priced by a value investor; beta 1.0 to 2.0.
Large-Cap, Small-Cap, and Mid-Cap stocks	A company's size classification in the stock market is based on market capitalization. **Large caps** are those firms valued at or more than $10 billion. **Mid-caps** are $2 billion to $10 billion. **Small caps** is $300 million to $2 billion.
Tech Stock	A company in the technology sector that offer technology-based products and services, biotechnology, Internet services, network services, wireless communications, and more.
Speculative Stock	A company that has a potential for substantial earnings at some time in the future but those earnings may never be realized; betas above 2.0. Examples: computer graphics firms, Internet applications firms, small oil exploration businesses, genetic engineering firms, and some pharmaceutical manufacturers.

will be a future driver of profits in the economy. Several numerical measures are used to evaluate stock performance, and these are readily available to investors on the Internet to help you assess future stock prices.

14.2c Some Investors Use Technical Analysis to Evaluate Stocks

An opposing and minority theory on valuing common stocks is advocated by proponents of **technical analysis**, often investment newsletter authors. This method of evaluating securities analyzes statistics generated by market activity, such as past prices and volume. Technical analysts do not attempt to measure a security's intrinsic value but instead use charts, graphs, mathematics, and software programs to identify and predict future price movements. Technical analysis has proved to be of little value, although some investors find technical analysts' logic appealing.

income stock
A stock that may not grow too quickly, but year after year pays a cash dividend higher than that offered by most companies.

growth stock
The stock of a company that offers the promise of much higher profits tomorrow and has a consistent record of relatively rapid growth in earnings in all economic conditions.

blue-chip stocks
Stocks that have been around for a long time, have a well-regarded reputation, dominate its industry, and are known for being solid, relatively safe investments.

Countercyclical Stock
The stock of a company whose profits are greatly influenced by changes in the economic business cycle.

value stock
A stock that tends to trade at a low price relative to its company fundamentals (dividends, earnings, sales, and so on) and thus is considered undervalued by a value investor.

technical analysis
Method of evaluating securities that uses statistics generated by market activity, such as past prices and volume, over time to determine when to buy or sell a stock.

DO IT IN CLASS

corporate earnings

The profits a company makes during a specific time period that indicate to many analysts whether to buy or sell a stock.

earnings per share (EPS)

A firm's profit divided by the number of outstanding shares.

price/earnings (P/E ratio) (or multiple)

The current market price of a stock divided by earnings per share (EPS) over the past four quarters; used as the primary means of valuing a stock.

earnings yield

The earnings per share of a stock divided by its price; an inversion of the price/earnings ratio; helps investors more clearly see investment expectations.

trailing P/E ratio

Calculated using recently reported earnings, usually from the previous four quarters.

projected P/E ratio (forward price/earnings ratio)

Because investors need to look to the future rather than the past, this measure divides price by projected earnings over the coming four quarters. Also known as forward price/earnings ratio.

14.2d You Should Use Corporate Earnings and Other Measures

Those who use fundamental analysis use several numerical measures to evaluate stock performance. These numbers are readily available to investors on the Internet that will help you assess future stock prices.

Corporate Earnings **Corporate earnings** are the profits a company makes during a specific time period. If a company cannot generate earnings now or in the future, stock market analysts and investors are not going to be impressed. As people reach this conclusion, there quickly will be more sellers than buyers of the company's common stock, and that will depress the stock's market price. Corporate earnings are at the core of fundamental analysis.

Earnings Per Share A company's **earnings per share (EPS)** is annual profit divided by the number of outstanding shares. It indicates the income that a company has available, on a per-share basis, to pay dividends and reinvest as retained earnings. The EPS is a measure of the firm's profitability on a common-stock-per-share basis, and it is helpful because investors can use it to compare financial conditions of many companies. The EPS is reported in the business section of many newspapers as well as online.

In our example, assume that next year, after payment of $9000 in dividends to preferred stockholders, Running Paws had a net profit of $32,000. With 20,000 shares of stock, the company's EPS would be $1.60 ($32,000 ÷ 20,000).

Price/Earnings Ratio The **price/earnings ratio (P/E ratio)** (or **multiple**) is the current market price of a stock divided by earnings per share (EPS) over the past four quarters. This ratio is the primary means of valuing a stock. It demonstrates how expensive the stock is versus the company's recently reported earnings, by revealing how much you are paying for each $1 of earnings. For example, if the market price of a share of Running Paws stock is currently $25 and the company's EPS is $1.60, the P/E ratio will be 16 ($25 ÷ $1.60 = 15.6, which rounds to 16). This value can also be called a 16-to-1 ratio or multiple, or a P/E ratio of 16. The P/E ratios of many corporations are widely reported on the Internet and in the financial section of newspapers. Stocks with low P/E ratios tend to have higher dividend yields, less risk, lower prices, and slower earnings growth.

To assess a company's financial status, you could compare that firm's P/E ratio with the P/E ratios for other similar stocks. The P/E ratios for corporations typically range from 5 to 25.

The historical average P/E ratio for stocks is 15, although it varies for different industries. Financially successful companies that have been paying good dividends through the years might have a P/E ratio ranging from 7 to 10. Rapidly growing companies would likely have a much higher P/E ratio—13 to 20. Speculative companies might have P/E ratios of 25 or 50 or even higher because they have low earnings now but anticipate much higher earnings in the future. Firms that are expected to have strong earnings growth generally have a high stock price and a correspondingly high P/E ratio.

Inverting a P/E ratio of 12 reveals that stocks have an **earnings yield** of 8.5 percent. In other words, each $100 of stocks is backed by $8.50 in expected earnings. During times of low interest rates, an 8.5 percent yield on stocks looks terrific.

Trailing and Projected Price/Earnings Ratios The standard P/E ratio is, in fact, called a **trailing P/E ratio** measure because it is calculated using recently reported earnings, usually from the previous four quarters.

Investors need to focus on future prospects when analyzing the value of a stock. A **projected P/E** or **forward price/earnings ratio** divides price by projected earnings over the coming four quarters, an estimate available via online stock quote providers. The **earnings yield**, which is the inverse of the P/E ratio (Running Paws' earnings yield

Being invested in the stock market is an excellent way to create wealth.

is 6.4 percent [$1.60 ÷ $25]), helps investors think more clearly about expectations for investments.

PEG Ratio Critics of the price-earnings ratio argue that because of fundamentals sometimes they should pay more for a stock. Those firms with high levels of growth should not be penalized for having high P/E ratios. **PEG ratio**, or **price-earnings growth**, is a way to adjust for this. Divide the P/E ratio by the company's projected growth rate. Going back to Running Paws, divide the firm's P/E ratio of 16 by its projected growth rate of 15 percent (16/15 = 1.07). Investors think a PEG ratio of 1 is fairly priced while a value of 2 or more is too high.

Price/Sales Ratio The **price/sales ratio (P/S ratio)** indicates the number of dollars it takes to buy a dollar's worth of a company's annual revenues. The P/S is obtained by dividing a company's total market capitalization by its sales for the past four quarters. For example, if Running Paws Cat Food Company's common stock currently sells for $25 per share and 20,000 shares of the company's stock are outstanding, its total capitalization is $500,000. If company revenues (sales of dog and cat food) were $750,000 over the past year, the stock's P/S would be 0.67 ($500,000 ÷ $750,000). Stock analysts suggest investors avoid companies with a P/S greater than 1.5 and favor those having a P/S of less than 0.75. Many investors ignore the P/S, but it works better than the highly acclaimed P/E ratio in predicting which companies provide the best return, as explained in James P. O'Shaughnessy's *What Works on Wall Street*.

Cash Dividends Stocks usually pay dividends. Cash dividends are distributions made in cash to holders of stock. They are the current income that you receive while you own shares in the company. The firm's board of directors usually declares a dividend on a quarterly basis (four times per corporate year), typically at the end of March, June, September, and December. Dividends are ordinarily paid out of current earnings, but in the event of unprofitable times (low earnings or none), the money might come from cash reserves held by the company. Occasionally, a company will borrow to pay the dividend so as to maintain its reputation of consistently paying dividends. Later profits can be used to repay any funds borrowed for this purpose.

PEG ratio (price-earnings growth)
A way to rationalize buying a stock that has high growth is to calculate by dividing the P/E ratio by the company's projected growth rate.

price/sales ratio (P/S ratio)
Tells the number of dollars it takes to buy a dollar's worth of a company's annual revenues; calculated by dividing company's total market capitalization by its sales for the past four quarters.

dividends per share

Translates the total cash dividends paid out by a company to common stockholders into a per-share figure.

dividend payout ratio

Dividends per share divided by earnings per share (EPS); helps judge the likelihood of future dividends.

dividend yield

Cash dividend to an investor expressed as a percentage of the current market price of a security.

book value (shareholder's equity)

Net worth of a company, determined by subtracting total liabilities from assets.

book value per share

Reflects the book value of a company divided by the number of shares of common stock outstanding.

price-to-book ratio (P/B ratio)

Current stock price divided by the per-share net value of a firm's plant, equipment, and other assets (book value).

Dividends per Share   The **dividends per share** measure translates the total cash dividends paid out by a company to common stockholders into a per-share figure. For example, Running Paws might elect to declare a total cash dividend of $8000 for the year to common stockholders. In that case, cash dividends per share would amount to $0.40 ($8000 ÷ 20,000 shares).

Dividend Payout Ratio   The **dividend payout ratio** is the dividends per share divided by EPS. It helps you judge the likelihood of future dividends. For example, imagine that Running Paws Cat Food Company earned $32,000 (after paying preferred stockholders), paid out a cash dividend of $8000 to company stockholders, and retained the remaining $24,000 to facilitate growth of the company. In this case, the dividend payout ratio equals 0.25 ($8000 ÷ $32,000). For that year, Running Paws paid a dividend equal to 25 percent of earnings.

Newer companies usually retain most, if not all, of their profits to facilitate growth. An investor interested in growth would, therefore, seek a company with a low payout ratio. The lower the payout ratio the greater the likelihood that the company will grow, which results in later capital gains for investors. Examples of companies that historically have a high payout ratio are AT&T (T), Chevron (CVX), Exelon (EXC), Home Depot (HD), Intel (INTC), Merck (MRK), Pfizer (PFE), and Verizon (VZ).

Dividend Yield   The **dividend yield** is the cash dividend paid to an investor expressed as a percentage of the current market price of a security. For example, the $0.40 cash dividend of Running Paws divided by the current $25 market price for its stock reveals a dividend yield of 1.6 percent ($0.40 ÷ $25). Growth and speculative companies typically pay little or no cash dividends, so they have limited dividend yields. Such companies are attractive to investors who are interested in capital gains.

Book Value   **Book value** (also known as **shareholder's equity**) is the net worth of a company, which is determined by subtracting the company's total liabilities from its assets. It theoretically indicates a company's worth if its assets were sold, its debts were paid off, and the net proceeds were distributed to the investors who own the outstanding shares of common stock.

Book Value per Share   The **book value per share** reflects the book value of a company divided by the number of shares of common stock outstanding. Running Paws has a net worth of $230,000, which, when divided by 20,000 shares, gives a book value per share of $11.50.

Often little relationship exists between the book value of a company and its earnings or the market price of its stock. A stock's price usually exceeds its book value per share. The reason is that stockholders bid up the stock price because they anticipate earnings and dividends in the future and expect the market price to rise even more. When the book value per share exceeds the price per share, the stock may truly be underpriced.

Price-to-Book Ratio   The **price-to-book ratio (P/B ratio)**, also called the **market-to-book ratio**, identifies firms that are asset rich, such as many banks, brokerage firms, and insurance companies. The P/B ratio is the current stock price divided by the per-share net value of the company's plant, equipment, and other assets (book value). It tells you the premium that you are paying for the net assets of the company.

In the Running Paws example, the book value per share of $11.50 would be divided into the recent price at which the stock was sold ($25 in this case); thus, the P/B ratio for Running Paws is 2.17. The current P/B ratio for most stocks lies between 2.1 and 1.0. The lower the ratio, the less highly a company's assets have been valued, indicating that the stock may be currently under-priced. If the ratio is less than 1, the assets may be utilized ineffectively. In such cases, an under-performing and undervalued company may become a target of a corporate takeover; where the company may be broken up and sold.

DID YOU KNOW

Bias toward Following the Bandwagon

People engaged in investing in stocks and bonds have a bias toward certain behaviors that can be harmful, such as a tendency toward getting on the "bandwagon" when investments are headed down. What to do? Remember that markets that go down will definitely come up again, so stay in the market and continue to invest or you will miss the big upswing that sure will follow.

14.2e Calculating a Stock's Potential Rate of Return Takes Five Steps

There is but a single reason to make an investment: to obtain a positive return. Although you cannot know the exact performance of any investment in advance, you certainly will want to pay no more than the "right price" for the investment given its potential rate of return. Calculating returns on a potential investment involves five steps. Armed with these data, you will be better positioned to make informed decisions:

1. Use beta to estimate the level of risk of the investment.
2. Estimate the market risk.
3. Calculate the required rate of return.
4. Calculate the potential rate of return on the investment.
5. Compare the required rate of return with the potential rate of return on the investment.

1. Use Beta to Estimate the Risk of the Investment Beta is a useful piece of information when you want to estimate the rate of return you require on an investment in a stock, bond, or mutual fund before putting your money at risk. Betas for individual stocks, mutual funds, and other investments are available online from brokerage firms, advisory services, and investment magazines.

The following example illustrates how to use beta to estimate the amount of risk in an investment portfolio. Assume you are willing to accept more risk than the general investor and that you buy a stock with a beta of 1.5. If the average price of all stocks rises by 20 percent over time, the price of the stock you chose might rise by 30 percent, which is the beta of 1.5 multiplied by the increase in the market (1.5 × 20%). If the average price of all stocks drops in value by 10 percent, the price of the stock you chose might drop by 15 percent (1.5 × 10%).

2. Estimate the Market Risk To estimate the required rate of return on an investment, you need to quantify the market risk. **Market risk**, also known as **systematic risk**, which we discussed in Chapter 13, is the risk associated with the effects of the overall economy on securities markets. It often causes the market price of a particular stock or bond to change, even though nothing has changed in the fundamental values underlying that security. Historical records indicate that 8 percent represents a realistic estimate of market risk for U.S. stocks. Market risk is high during turbulent times in stock markets, and in the near term, it remains elevated.

DO IT IN CLASS

3. Calculate Your Required Rate of Return The return on short-term U.S. Treasury bills has historically exceeded the rate of inflation by a slight degree (but not always as sometimes it is lower). Thus, when T-bills pay 2 percent interest, the inflation rate might hover around 1.7 percent. (The various interest rates in this chapter are chosen to be instructive. Note that the government's real T-bill rate is currently much lower than 1 percent.) This circumstance provides almost no gain for the investor because the combination of inflation and income taxes reduce the return to about zero. For this reason, investors often use the yield on Treasury bills as a base number that provides a zero **real rate of return**—that is, a zero return on investment after inflation and income taxes.

To calculate your required rate of return on an investment, multiply the beta value of an investment by the estimated market risk and then add the risk-free T-bill rate, as shown in Equation (14.1). For recent T-bill rates, see www.treasurydirect.gov/indiv /research/indepth/tbills/res_tbill_rates.htm. Use Equation (14.1) to determine an **estimate of the required rate of return on an investment**.

> **estimate of the required rate of return on an investment**
>
> *A calculation that multiplies the beta value of an investment by the estimated market risk and adds the risk-free T-bill rate that suggests to investors the return required to put their money at risk.*

$$\text{Estimate of the required rate of return on an investment} = \text{T-bill rate} + (\text{beta} \times \text{market risk}) \quad \textbf{(14.1)}$$

For example, assume you are considering investing in Running Paws Cat Food Company, which has a beta of 1.5. If you assume a market risk of 8 percent and the current T-bill rate is 2.0 percent, the total rate of return you will require on this investment is 14.0 percent $[2.0 + (1.5 \times 8.0)]$. Investors need the promise of a return higher than 14 percent to put their money at risk in this investment.

4. Calculate the Stock's Potential Return The **potential return** for any investment over a period of years can be determined by adding anticipated income (from dividends, interest, rents, or other sources) to the future value of the investment and then subtracting the investment's original cost. The investor using fundamental analysis can obtain the figures needed to construct the expected stream of future earnings for a company from a variety of sources. For example, you can use estimates for earnings and dividends gathered from large investment data firms such as Value Line, Standard & Poor's, MarketWatch, or Reuters, and then obtain an individual stock analyst's projections or you can create your own numbers.

> **potential return**
>
> *Determined by adding anticipated income (from dividends, interest, rents, or other sources) to the future value of investment and then subtracting the investment's original cost.*

Add Up Projected Income and Price Appreciation Table 14-2 illustrates how to sum up the projected income (dividend income) and price appreciation (earnings). You can convert these figures into a potential rate of return by calculating the approximate compound yield, as shown in Equation (14.2). This figure can then be compared with returns on other investments.

Table 14-2 One Investor's Projections of the Earnings and Dividends for Running Paws Cat Food Company

End of Year	Earnings	Dividend Income
1	$2.76	$0.76
2	3.17	0.87
3	3.65	1.00
4	4.20	1.15
5	4.83	1.33
Total dividends		$5.11
Average annual dividend ($5.11 ÷ 5)		$1.02

$$ACY = \cfrac{\text{average annual} \atop \text{dividend} + \cfrac{{\text{projected price} \atop \text{of stock}} - {\text{current price of} \atop \text{stock}}}{\text{number of years projected}}}{\cfrac{{\text{projected price} \atop \text{of stock}} + {\text{current price} \atop \text{of stock}}}{2}} \quad \text{(14.2)}$$

$$= \cfrac{\$1.02 + \cfrac{\$60.38 - \$30.00}{5}}{\cfrac{\$60.38 + \$30.00}{2}}$$

$$= \cfrac{\$1.02 + \$6.08}{\$45.19}$$

$$= 15.7\%$$

Example: Running Paws Cat Food Company Based on a recommendation from his stockbroker, Izzle Stevens, who lives in Seattle, is considering Running Paws Cat Food Company as a potential investment. Izzle figures that the company's stock might provide a better return than inflation and income taxes for about five years. He has determined the following information about this stock investment: It is currently priced at $30 per share, its most recent 12-month earnings amounted to $2.40 per share, and the cash dividend for the same period was $0.66 per share.

Izzle began the task of projecting the future value of one share of the stock by using the EPS information. He first calculated the P/E ratio to be 12.5 ($30 ÷ $2.40). Next, as illustrated in Table 14-2, Izzle applied a 15 percent rate of growth estimate (the same rate that occurred in previous years, according to Running Paws' annual report) for the EPS for each year ($2.40 × 1.15 = $2.76; $2.76 × 1.15 = $3.17; and so forth). Using a P/E ratio of 12.5 (the same as the current ratio), Izzle estimated the market price at the end of the fifth year to be $60.38 (12.5 × $4.83). This calculation gives a projected net appreciation in stock price over five years of $30.38 ($60.38 minus the current price of $30).

To project the future income of the investment in Running Paws—the anticipated cash dividends—Table 14-2 shows that Izzle estimated a 15 percent growth rate in the cash dividend ($0.66 × 1.15 = $0.76; $0.76 × 1.15 = $0.87; and so forth). Adding the projected cash dividends over five years gives a total of $5.11. Izzle obtained the potential return for one share of Running Paws over five years by adding anticipated dividend income ($5.11) to the future value of the investment ($60.38) less its original cost ($30.00), for a result of $35.49 ($5.11 + $30.38). Thus, Izzle has projected that $30 invested in one share of Running Paws will earn a potential total return of $35.49 in five years.

What is the ACY? The question now becomes, what is the percentage yield for this dollar return? The **approximate compound yield (ACY)** provides a measure of the annualized compound growth of any long-term investment. You can determine this value by using Equation (14.2). The calculation requires use of an *annual average* dividend rather than the specific projected dividends. In this example, the annual average dividend of $1.02 is computed by dividing the $5.11 in dividend income by five years. Substituting the data from Table 14-2 into Equation (14.2) and using the average annual dividend figure results in an approximate compound yield of 15.7 percent on the potential investment in one share of Running Paws stock for five years. (This formula can be found on the *Garman/Forgue* companion website.)

5. Compare the Required Rate of Return with the Potential Rate of Return on the Investment Now the moment of decision making is at hand. You compare the estimated required rate of return on an investment (given its risk) with the investment's

approximate compound yield (ACY)

A measure of the annualized compound growth of any long-term investment stated as a percentage.

DID YOU KNOW

potential projected rate of return. In our example involving Running Paws Cat Food Company, the risk suggested a required rate of return of 14.0 percent. The investment's potential rate of return was projected to be 15.7 percent, which suggests that Running Paws is a good buy for Izzle at the current selling price of $30—that is, the stock is under priced. Once armed with projected rate of return information for an investment, you can compare it with other investments.

CONCEPT CHECK 14.2

1. Distinguish between the terms *income stocks* and *growth stocks*.

2. Explain how a stock with a beta of 1.0 differs from ones with a beta of 1.2 and 2.5.

3. What is the focus of *fundamental analysis*?

4. Summarize the meanings of the terms *trailing* and *projected price/earnings ratio*.

5. List the five steps to calculate a stock's potential rate of return.

14.3 USE THE INTERNET TO EVALUATE AND SELECT STOCKS

An overwhelming amount of information is available on stock investments. With about 5000 U.S. public companies to choose from and another 33,000 stocks in other countries, stock selection takes time. Hundreds of investment resources exist, including television and radio shows, books, websites, blogs, and newsletters. What approach should you take? Use the Internet because everything you need is online.

14.3a Begin by Setting Criteria for Your Stock Investments

The process of setting criteria for a stock investment starts with a review of your investment plan, as discussed in Chapter 13 and illustrated in Figure 13-7 on page 405. To make informed selections of the stock investments that match your investment goals, philosophy, and time horizon, begin by making decisions on criteria for your stock investments:

• What classifications of stocks are best suited for your goals?

• What market capitalization size company meets your desires?

• What specific numeric measures do you require on beta, sales, profitability, P/E ratio, dividends, payout ratio, and market price?

• What projected EPS growth do you require?

• Do you want to invest in an industry leader?

14.3b Investor Education Is Widely Available Online

Comprehensive investment websites provide updated news headlines; market overviews; market statistics; industry statistics; industry trends; corporate stock symbols; current stock market prices; specific company profiles, history, financials, prices, and outlook for the future; tips on how to build a portfolio; and stock-screening tools with search capabilities. Following are some popular websites on investor education:

- The Investor's Clearinghouse (investoreducation.org/release032013.cfm)
- FINRA Investor Education Clearinghouse (www.finrafoundation.org /resources/education/modules/)
- US Securities and Exchange Commission (investor.gov/)
- The Motley Fool (www.fool.com/how-to-invest/index.aspx?source =ifltnvpnv0000001)

14.3c Set Up Your Portfolio Online

You can set up a portfolio through an online brokerage account or by using any of several websites. For example, see WikiHow at www.wikihow.com /Build-a-Stock-Portfolio and JP Morgan at www.jpmorganfunds.com/cm /Satellite?pagename=jpmfVanityWrapper&UserFriendlyURL=buildyourportfolio. Both let you insert the number of shares you own and at what price. The sites then track stock quotes to update the value of your holdings.

14.3d Use Stock Screening Tools

You can research stocks, bonds, and mutual funds by using **stock-screening tools** available on the Internet. Screening enables you to quickly sift through vast databases of numerous companies to find those that best suit your investment objectives. For example, you can use the Kiplinger screening tool to filter thousands of stocks using 27 search criteria, and you can use Kiplinger's or another company's tools to identify dividend-paying stocks, small companies, and growth companies. You simply set the standard for screening, such as high P/E ratios, and the program sorts out the investment choices, including five-year EPS growth projections by professional stock analysts. You may be surprised to find how easy it is to screen stocks. The following websites offer stock-screening tools:

- Kiplinger (www.kiplinger.com/tools/stockscreener/index.html)
- MSN Money (investing.money.msn.com/investments/stockscouter-top-rated -stocks?sco=10)
- MarketWatch (www.marketwatch.com/tools/stockresearch/screener//)

stock-screening tools
Enable you to quickly sift through vast databases of hundreds of companies to find those that best suit your investment objectives.

14.3e Get a Sense of the History of a Stock

You can study the price of stock movements over different time frames, including bull and bear markets, as well as make comparisons to various benchmarks such as the S&P 500 Index. See Market Watch (bigcharts.marketwatch.com/historical//).

14.3f Go to the Source for Company Information

Corporate filings required by the Securities and Exchange Commission are available on the Internet from the Electronic Data Gathering and Retrieval (EDGAR) project (www.sec.gov/edgar/searchedgar/webusers.htm#.U2p5IaJn34g). Top online sources for stock, bond, and mutual fund information include Morningstar (www .morningstar.com) and Bloomberg (www.bloomberg.com). Each public company has its own website that offers insights from management about the future of the firm, and it is easy to request a company's annual report.

Every company registered with the Securities and Exchange Commission (SEC) is required to file once each year to ensure public availability of accurate current information about the firm. The company summarizes its financial activities for the year. The

FINANCIAL POWER POINT

Phone Apps for Investing

Vanguard's Phone app users can access their stock brokerage accounts and mutual fund accounts, read market news, listen to podcasts, and watch videos. Scores of apps for investing are available including those from Bloomberg, Chase, CNBC Real-Time, EFFdb, Mint, Morningstar, Fidelity, Forbes, Charles Schwab, StockTwits, Wikinvest Portfolio Manager, and Yahoo! Finance.

There are numerous websites that offer fundamental and technical analysis of stocks. The Motley Fool does so with humor.

10-Q report

A report required by the SEC prepared by the company showing its financial results for the quarter, a discussion from management, a list of material events and other risk factors that have occurred, forecasts of the company's future, and notes of any significant changes or events in the quarter.

annual report

Legally required yearly report about financial performance, activities, and prospects sent to major stockholders and made available to the general public.

prospectus

Highly legalistic information presented by a firm to the SEC and to the public with any new issue of stock.

10-Q report includes the financial results for the quarter, a discussion from management, a list of material events and other risk factors that have occurred (such as legal problems and loss of a large customer), a forecast of the company's future, and any significant changes or events in the quarter. A similar 10-K report is filed annually. You can obtain both 10-Q and 10-K reports from the SEC online (www.sec.gov). You can find executive compensation details on Form DEF 14A.

The company's **annual report** is mostly a numbers-free publication that looks like a slick marketing magazine. While annual reports do contain some summarized financial information, they serve more as promotional corporate brochures.

When a company issues any new security, it files a **prospectus** with the SEC. This disclosure describes the experience of the corporation's management, the company's financial status, any anticipated legal matters that could affect the company, and potential risks of investing in the firm. The language is legalistic and full of technical jargon, but the interested investor may find it useful to sift through the details.

14.3g Use Stock Analysts' Research Reports

Stock analysts working for independent stock advisory firms or stock brokerages write research reports on companies and industries, as illustrated in Figure 14-1 with a report from Standard & Poor's. Reports based on fundamental analysis are quite informative. The quality of advice is uneven, ranging from brilliant to pedestrian as analysts have a tendency to run with the herd and make similar recommendations. They often recommend buying certain stocks and rarely suggest selling. The prudent investor interprets "hold" recommendations as a signal to sell.

14.3h Read Research Newsletters

The most popular firms that offer stock advisory research services on a subscription basis to individual investors are Morningstar (www.morningstar.com), Value Line (www.valueline.com), MarketWatch (www.marketwatch.com), and Reuters (reuters.com/finance/markets). The cost for some of these services is in the hundreds of dollars per year.

Figure 14-1   Illustrative Stock Analyst's Report

Stock Report | March 1, 2014 | NNM Symbol: **GOOG** | **GOOG** is in the S&P 500

Google Inc

S&P CAPITAL IQ
McGRAW HILL FINANCIAL

S&P Capital IQ Recommendation	**HOLD** ★★★☆☆
S&P Capital IQ Equity Analyst Scott Kessler	

Price	12-Mo. Target Price	Report Currency	Investment Style
$1,215.65 (as of Feb 28, 2014 4:00 PM ET)	$1,300	USD	Large-Cap Growth

UPDATE: PLEASE SEE THE ANALYST'S LATEST RESEARCH NOTE IN THE COMPANY NEWS SECTION

GICS Sector Information Technology
Sub-Industry Internet Software & Services

Summary Google is the world's largest Internet company, specializing in search and advertising.

Key Stock Statistics (Source S&P Capital IQ, Vickers, company reports)

52-Wk Range	$1,228.88–761.26	S&P Oper. EPS 2014E	40.74	Market Capitalization(B)	$340.240	Beta		0.88
Trailing 12-Month EPS	$38.02	S&P Oper. EPS 2015E	46.12	Yield (%)	Nil	S&P 3-Yr. Proj. EPS CAGR(%)		15
Trailing 12-Month P/E	32.0	P/E on S&P Oper. EPS 2014E	29.8	Dividend Rate/Share	Nil	S&P Quality Ranking		B+
$10K Invested 5 Yrs Ago	$35,967	Common Shares Outstg. (M)	336.1	Institutional Ownership (%)	84			

Price Performance

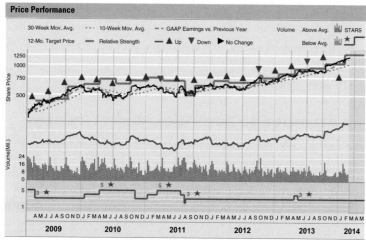

30-Week Mov. Avg. — 10-Week Mov. Avg. — GAAP Earnings vs. Previous Year — Volume Above Avg. STARS — 12-Mo. Target Price — Relative Strength — ▲ Up ▼ Down ► No Change — Below Avg.

Past performance is not an indication of future performance and should not be relied upon as such.

Analysis prepared by Equity Analyst **Scott Kessler** on Feb 13, 2014 09:20 PM, when the stock traded at **$1,199.90**.

Analyst's Risk Assessment

LOW **MEDIUM** HIGH

Our risk assessment reflects what we see as significant competition, substantial and increasing investment and related new offerings, considerable ongoing legal and regulatory matters, and potential issues related to the pending sale of Motorola Mobility.

Revenue/Earnings Data

Revenue (Million U.S. $)

	1Q	2Q	3Q	4Q	Year
2013	13,969	14,105	14,893	16,858	59,825
2012	10,645	11,807	13,304	14,419	50,175
2011	8,575	9,026	9,720	10,584	37,905
2010	6,775	6,820	7,286	8,440	29,321
2009	5,509	5,523	5,945	6,674	23,651
2008	5,186	5,367	5,541	5,701	21,796

Earnings Per Share (U.S. $)

2013	9.87	7.55	8.71	9.91	36.05
2012	8.75	8.42	6.48	8.68	32.46
2011	5.51	7.68	8.33	8.22	29.76
2010	6.06	5.71	6.72	7.81	26.31
2009	4.49	4.66	5.13	6.13	20.41
2008	4.12	3.92	4.06	1.21	13.31

Fiscal year ended Dec. 31. Next earnings report expected: Mid April. EPS Estimates based on S&P Capital IQ Operating Earnings; historical GAAP earnings are as reported in Company reports.

Dividend Data

Amount ($)	Date Decl.	Ex-Div. Date	Stk. of Record	Payment Date
Stk.	Jan 31	Apr 3	Mar 27	Apr 2 '14
Stk.	Jan 31	Apr 3	Mar 27	Apr 2 '14

Source: Company reports.

Past performance is not an indication of future performance and should not be relied upon as such.

Highlights

➤ We believe revenues will rise 17% in 2014 and 18% in 2015, reflecting the purchase of Motorola Mobility in May 2012, and related completed divestiture and restructuring actions. Our estimates do not reflect the pending sale of Motorola announced in January 2014. In April 2013, GOOG sold Motorola's Home unit Arris (ARRS 28, Buy), in a transaction valued at $2.4 billion in cash and stock. We project growth in the Google segment of 19% in both 2014 and 2015, owing to growth in online advertising and increasing traction for GOOG's display offerings. We think uncertain global economies pose some difficulties.

➤ Pro forma operating margins narrowed notably in 2012, due to the Motorola purchase. We see improvements in 2014 and 2015, reflecting Motorola-focused efforts. We also see continuing spending related to new offerings and government inquiries/investigations.

➤ In May 2012, GOOG acquired Motorola Mobility for $12.5 billion. We believe the pursuit of Motorola was motivated by GOOG's interest in fortifying its patent portfolio and protecting its key Android franchise.

Investment Rationale/Risk

➤ In January 2014, GOOG announced the planned sale of Motorola to Chinese hardware company Lenovo, in a transaction valued at $2.9 billion. We had been skeptical about the Motorola purchase. We see regulatory challenges to consummating the deal, but believe it would be fundamentally positive for GOOG. Nonetheless, we see healthy growth from GOOG's namesake business unit, with opportunities related to mobile, video and international. Concerns related to mobile advertising pricing persist.

➤ Risks to our recommendation and target price include possible challenges in the selling Motorola, market share losses, new offerings succeeding less than we expect, excess expenditures associated with expansion, and adverse legal/regulatory developments.

➤ Our 12-month target price of $1,300 reflects our discounted cash flow analysis. Our DCF model assumes a WACC of 8.5%, five-year average annual free cash flow (FCF) growth of 15%, and a perpetuity growth rate of 2%. Motorola has restrained FCF growth, reflecting a less profitable business model and the potential need for greater investment.

Please read the Required Disclosures and Analyst Certification on the last page of this report.
Redistribution or reproduction is prohibited without written permission.
This document is not intended to provide personal investment advice and it does not take into account the specific investment objectives, financial situation and the particular needs of any specific person who may receive this report. Investors should seek independent financial advice regarding the suitability and/or appropriateness of making an investment or implementing the investment strategies discussed in this document and should understand that statements regarding future prospects may not be realized. Investors should note that income from such investments, if any, may fluctuate and that the value of such investments may rise or fall. Accordingly, investors may receive back less than they originally invested. Investors should seek advice concerning any impact this investment may have on their personal tax position from their own tax advisor. Please note the publication date of this document. It may contain specific information that is no longer current and should not be used to make an investment decision. Unless otherwise indicated, there is no intention to update this document.

A Google search for "stock advisory newsletters" will reveal several dozen firms that offer guidance on stock selections, market updates, and investment advice. You may wish to avoid those that offer suggestions based on a "technical" or "chartist" approach to analyzing stocks; instead select one that uses a mainstream approach emphasizing fundamental research.

14.3i Be Aware of Economic Trends

You need to know the stage of the business cycle (recession or prosperity) and the current interest and inflation rates. You also need to understand how economic conditions are likely to change over the next 12 to 18 months. (These topics were examined in Chapter 1.) Economic information is available through almost all media:

- Search engines: Yahoo!, Google, and Momma
- Big newspapers: *USA Today, Los Angeles Times, The Wall Street Journal*
- Business news: *Business Week Fortune, Forbes Financial World*
- Personal finance: *Money* magazine and *Kiplinger's Personal Finance*
- Investment sources: *The Wall Street Journal, Barron's, Investor's Business Daily, Market Watch, Reuter's*
- News magazines: *U.S. News & World Report, Time*

14.3j Pay Attention to Securities Market Indexes

Reports on securities market indexes are provided around the clock in almost every media. "The Dow went up 80 points today." "The S&P 500 rose 68 points." When it is reported that "the Dow rose 80 points today in heavy trading," realize that these "points" are changes in the index, not actual dollar changes in the value of the stocks. A **securities market index** is an indicator of market performance. It measures the average value of a number of securities chosen as a sample to reflect the behavior of a more general market. Popular indexes include the following.

securities market index

Measures the average value of a number of securities chosen as a sample to reflect the behavior of a more general market.

Dow Jones Industrial Average (DJIA)

The most widely reported of all stock market indexes that tracks prices of only 30 actively traded blue-chip stocks, including well-known companies such as American Express and AT&T.

Dow Jones Industrial Averages The **Dow Jones Industrial Average (DJIA)** is the most widely reported of all indexes. The most popular DJIA industrial average, also called the "Dow," follows prices of only 30 actively traded blue-chip stocks, including well-known companies such as American Express, AT&T, Caterpillar, Coca-Cola, Nike, Visa, Walmart, and Walt Disney. The average is calculated by adding the closing prices of the 30 stocks and dividing by a number adjusted for splits, spin-offs, and dividends.* The DJIA also produces a transportation average based on 20 stocks, a utility average based on 15 stocks, and a composite average based on all 65 industrial, transportation, and utility stocks.

Standard & Poor's 500 Index The popular **Standard & Poor's (S&P) 500 Index** reports price movements of 500 stocks of large, established, publicly traded firms. It includes stocks of 400 industrial firms, 40 financial institutions, 40 public utilities, and 20 transportation companies. Companies with the highest market values influence the index the greatest.

NASDAQ Composite Index The **NASDAQ Composite Index** takes into account virtually all U.S. stocks (about 3700) traded in the over-the-counter market in the automated quotations system operated by the National Association of Securities Dealers.

---

* A **stock split** occurs when the shares of a stock owned by existing shareholders are divided into a larger number of shares. This may be an indicator that management expects better profits in the years ahead. Many companies provide a cash dividend to stockholders, and sometimes companies declare a noncash dividend in the form of a **stock dividend**. Here the shareholder receives additional shares of the company's stock.

It provides a measure of companies not as popular or as large as those traded on the popular exchanges, including price behavior of many smaller, more speculative companies, although some big companies (such as Cisco Systems, Intel, Microsoft, and Staples) are listed as well. It is often used as a benchmark for the performance of high-tech stocks.

Dow Jones Wilshire 5000 Index The **Dow Jones Wilshire 5000 Index** represents the total market value of all the publically traded stocks in the United States, about 3776. One point in the index is worth $1 billion; thus when the index is 20,200, that translates into a U.S. stock market valued at over $20 trillion.

Russell 2000 Index The **Russell 2000 Index** is a small-cap stock market index of relatively small capitalized companies and is the most widely quoted measure of the overall performance of the small-cap to midcap company shares.

Foreign Stock Exchanges Stock exchanges are located in major cities throughout the world, including London, Sydney, Tokyo, Toronto, Frankfort, Mumbai, Hong Kong, Shenzhen, Shanghai, and Kuala Lumpur. U.S. investors often check the stock exchanges throughout the night to gain a hint of what might happen that day in the U.S. stock market.

14.3k Securities Exchanges (Stock Markets)

A **securities exchange** (also called a **stock market**) is a market where agents of buyers and sellers can find each other easily by providing an orderly, open plan to trade securities. Each exchange has its own rules, is subject to government regulation, and provides constant supervision and self-regulation.

The transactions were historically performed in an organized physical location, such as the New York Stock Exchange (known officially as NYSE Euronext and listed as NYX), and also known as the "**Big Board**") as well as the American Stock Exchange (known officially as NYSE MKT LLC and also owned by NYSE Euronext) Both are in New York City. You may visualize a bustling exchange that ends the trading day with a bell. However, today most stock trading occurs in a fragmented collection of 50 trading platforms, and almost all transactions are performed electronically. The market capitalization of the NYSE Euronext's over 8000 listed companies is over $16 trillion. As many as 100 billion shares trade daily on the New York Stock Exchange.

Regional stock exchanges are places where equity in publicly-held companies (often regionally located firms) is traded, and these firms do not meet the strict listing requirements of national stock exchanges. Examples are located in Boston, Chicago, Philadelphia, and San Francisco. Newer exchanges also exist like Direct Edge, in New Jersey, and BATS Exchange in Kansas; each handles about 10 percent of trades in the U.S.

OTC or Over-the-Counter Trading **Over-the-counter (OTC)** or **off-exchange trading** is done directly between two parties, without any supervision of an exchange. The electronic telecommunications network facilitates the buying and selling of securities that usually are not listed on the major exchanges through market makers.

14.3l Looking Up a Stock Price

What affects the price of a stock the most is supply and demand. When more people want to buy, the price goes up. When more people want to sell, the price goes down. If you know the company's stock symbol (search Google for "stock symbols"), the current price of any stock may be obtained by inputting the company symbol into Google or any of the other popular investment websites, such as Yahoo! Finance, MSN Money, Reuter's, and MarketWatch.

securities exchange (stock market)

Market where agents of buyers and sellers can find each other easily by providing an orderly, open plan to trade securities.

Over-the-counter (OTC) (off-exchange trading)

trading is done directly between two parties, without any supervision of an exchange.

FINANCIAL POWER POINT

Amateurs Have an Advantage over Big Stock Research Firms

Three to five years before analysts really start to follow such developments, local investors can be among the first to see the company in which they work start to really succeed. They also may see nearby new retailers in shopping malls with bright futures.

DID YOU KNOW

Crowd Funding for Startup Companies

Congress passed a law approving **crowd funding** as a way for companies to raise capital. Startup companies now may use web portals overseen by federal regulators to solicit up to $1 million annually in small amounts from lots of people, rather than solicit from a few large investors as securities laws have required.

Those with an annual income of less than $100,000 will only be allowed to invest $2000 or 5 percent of their assets, whichever is greater. Kickstarter.com is the most well known. This opens up a badly needed source of funds. However, crowd funding could turn into "crowd fleecing" if investors cannot tell the difference between a legitimate opportunity and a scam.

The millions of daily buying and selling transactions involving stocks, bonds, and mutual funds are summarized in *The Wall Street Journal*, the most widely read financial newspaper in the United States. Many daily newspapers publish abbreviated information, and security prices are quoted and traded to two decimal points. Stock quotations that might appear in *The Wall Street Journal* for Walmart, a retailer, are illustrated in Figure 14-2.

Column 1: YTD % Change. The numbers in this column report the "year to date (YTD) as a percentage" change in the price (+8.6%) of Walmart stock since January 1 of the current calendar year.

Columns 2 and 3: 52 Weeks, High and Low. This column shows that Walmart stock traded at a high price of $63.08 and a low price of $41.50 during the previous 52 weeks, not including the previous trading day.

Figure 14-2   How Stocks Are Quoted

1	2	3	4		5	6	7	8	9	10
YTD	52 WEEKS					YLD		VOL		NET
%CHG	HI	LO	STOCK (SYM)		DIV	%	PE	100S	LAST	CNG
+17.2	45.29	28.70	Walgreen	WAG	.14	.4	44	27540	39.45	+0.59
+ 3.7	20.56	14.00	WallaceCS	WCS	.66	3.4	17	714	19.70	+0.06
+ 0.1	34.50	23.00	WaddReed A	WDR	.35	1.1	25	2228	32.24	+0.04
+ 8.6	63.08	41.50	Walmart	WMT	.28	.4	42	104572	62.52	+0.82

+18.7	17.50	8.55	WacknhutCorr	WHC	...	18	448	16.45	−0.40		
+ 0.1	34.50	23	WaddiReed A	WDR	.35	1.1	25	2228	32.24	+0.04	
+17.2	45.29	28.70	Walgreen	WAG	.14	.4	44	27540	39.45	+0.59	
+ 3.7	20.56	14	WallaceCS	WCS	.66	3.4	17	714	19.70	+0.06	
+ 8.6	63.08	41.50	WalMart	WMT	.28	.4	42	104572	62.52	+0.82	
+ 9.6	14.65	7.60	Walterind	WLT	.12	1.0	12	1625	12.40	−0.10	
+ 3.1	42.99	26.52	WashMut	WM s	1.00f	3.0	11	45891	33.71	−0.45	
			WashMut	PIES	4.00	5.4	...	14	74.10	−0.40	
			WashPost B	WPO	5.60	.9	25	51	596.90	−0.60	
			WashREIT	WRE	1.33	4.9	20	590	26.99	−0.11	
			WasteMgt	WMI	.01	...	34	15675	27.46	−0.52	
			WtrPiкTch	PIK	...	...	11	51	9.48	+0.38	
			WatersCp	WAT	...	...	26	17787	32.76	+1.31	
			Watsco	WSO	.12f	.7	19	3016	17.95	+1.46	
			WatsnPharm	WPI	...	...	28	10379	30.22	+0.06	
			WatsonWyatt A	WW	...	...	18	3106	26.45	+0.95	
			Wattsind A	WTS	.24	1.5	16	3198	16.20	+0.45	
			WausaMosin	WMO	.34	2.9	62	1503	11.87	...	
			Weatherford	WFT	...	...	26	16527	46.09	−0.40	
			WeiderNutrtn A	WNI	.15	8.6	dd	251	1.75	+0.01	
			WeightWatchers	WTW n	...	...	1128	35.82	+0.62		
			WeingtnRlty	WRI	3.33f	6.5	18	943	50.87	−0.04	
			WeisMkts	WMK	1.08	3.8	18	121	28.09	−0.01	
			Wellman	WLM	.36	2.3	61	1194	15.90	−0.01	
+ 3.2	131.25	81.65	WelptHlth	WLP	...	...	19	4837	120.59	+3.09	
+12.8	51.71	38.25	WellsFargo	WFC	1.04	2.1	25	45366	49.05	+0.16	
+ 1.0	25.75	24.75	WellsFargo QUIPS	WPF n	...	...	410	25.38	−0.27		
+ 9.6	32.78	20	Wendys	WEN	.24	.8	19	5596	31.97	−0.44	
+ 6.9	63.25	45.10	Wendys	TECONS	2.50	4.0	...	15	62.25	−0.55	
+44.0	9.50	3.95	Wescoint	WCC	...	17	240	7.13	+0.37		

Column 4: Stock and Sym. This column gives the name of the stock (Walmart in this example) and its abbreviated trading symbol (WMT).

Column 5: Div. The dividend amount is based on the last quarterly declaration by the company. For example, Walmart last paid a quarterly dividend that, when converted to an annual basis, amounts to an estimated $0.28 annual dividend.

Column 6: Yld %. The figure in this column represents the yield as a percentage of dividend income, calculated by dividing the current price of the stock into the recent estimated dividend. The yield of the Walmart stock is 0.4 percent.

Column 7: PE. This figure provides the P/E ratio based on the current price. The earnings figure used to calculate the price is not published in the newspaper but is the latest available. When Walmart's "last" or closing price of $62.52 is divided by earnings, it gives a P/E ratio of 42.

Column 8: Vol 100s. This figure indicates the total volume of trading activity for the stock measured in hundreds of shares. Thus, 10,457,200 shares of Walmart were traded on that day.

Column 9: Last. The price of the last trade of the day before the market closed for Wal-Mart was $62.52.

Column 10: Net Cng. The net change, +0.82%, represents the difference between the closing price (last) on this day and the closing price of the previous trading day. Today's Walmart closing (last) price of $62.52 was up $0.82 from the previous closing price, which must have been $61.70.

14.3m Using Portfolio Tracking to Watch Your Investments

Watching your investments requires record keeping, particularly for income tax purposes, although when you sell any securities your brokerage firm will provide you with sufficient details. Recordkeeping tasks can be performed easily using the Internet. **Portfolio tracking** automatically updates the value of your portfolio after you enter the symbols of the stocks you own and the number of shares held. Online portfolio tracking services also alert you to events that may affect your stocks. Tracking helps you stay on top of your holdings so you know which stocks are performing well, which are underperforming, and which might need to be sold. For programs type in "portfolio tracker" on Google.

DID YOU KNOW

Bias toward Short-term Emotions

People engaged in investing through mutual funds have a bias toward certain behaviors that can be harmful, such as a tendency toward paying too much attention to our short-term emotions when making long-term decisions. When markets are calm, investors think they will stand pat; when they start declining they bail out, often at the worst possible moment. What to do? Set short-term goals to accomplish long-term goals you are comfortable with and stay the course, or hire an investment professional to do it for you.

portfolio tracking
Automatically updates the value of your portfolio after you enter the symbols of the stocks you own and the number of shares held.

CONCEPT CHECK 14.3

1. Give three examples of the types of website resources available to investors on the Internet.

2. List five places where you can obtain investment information on a specific stock.

3. Distinguish between the Dow Jones Industrial Average and the S&P 500.

4. Where can you go to look up stock symbols and prices?

14.4 BUYING AND SELLING STOCKS

stockbroker (account executive)

Professional who is licensed to buy and sell securities on behalf of the brokerage firm's clients.

security's street name

Securities certificates kept in the brokerage firm's name instead of the name of the individual investor.

cash account

A brokerage account that requires an initial deposit (perhaps as little as $1000) and specifies that full settlement is due to the brokerage firm within three business days after a buy or sell order has been given.

Securities transactions require the use of a licensed broker serving as a middleman between the seller and the buyer and collecting a fee on each purchase or sale of securities. A **stockbroker** (also known as an **account executive**) is licensed to buy and sell securities on behalf of the brokerage firm's clients. You can buy or sell securities through an online or human stockbroker who works for a brokerage firm that has access to the securities markets. Brokerage firms often provide investors with investment advice.

As a matter of convenience and to facilitate resale, investors prefer to leave securities certificates in the name of their brokerage firm rather than take physical possession themselves. Securities certificates kept in the brokerage firm's name instead of the name of the individual investor are known as the **security's street name**. Brokers have a duty to assess each client's suitability for particular investments. Table 14-3 shows the different types of stock brokerage firms.

14.4a Opening a Brokerage Account

To trade securities, you will need a brokerage firm to act as your agent. You can open an account at a full-service general brokerage firm or a discount brokerage firm. The firm charges a commission for any trading it conducts on your behalf. You should make clear to the brokerage firm, in writing, your investment objectives and your desired level of risk. A **cash account** is a brokerage account that requires an initial deposit (perhaps as little as $1000) and specifies that full settlement is due to the brokerage firm within three business days after a buy or sell order has been given. After each transaction, your account is debited or credited, and written confirmation is immediately forwarded.

14.4b Broker Commissions and Fees

Brokerage firms receive a commission on each securities transaction to cover the direct expenses of executing the transaction and other overhead expenses. They have established fee schedules that they use when dealing with any except the largest investors. The fees reflect a commission rate that declines as the total value of the transaction increases. For example, in lieu of a minimum commission charge of $25, a brokerage firm

general (full-service) brokerage firms

Offer a full range of services to customers, including investment advice and research.

discount brokers

Charge commissions to execute trades that are often 30 to 80 percent less than the fees charged by full-service brokers, but also offer fewer services.

online discount brokers

Such brokers, also called Internet or electronic discount brokers, have reduced the cost of executing a trade to perhaps $20 or even $10 because their primary business is online trading.

Table 14-3 **Types of Brokerage Firms**

General (Full-Service) Brokerage Firm	Offers a full range of services, including investment information and advice; research reports on companies, industries, general economic trends, and world events; an investment newsletter; recommendations to buy, sell, or hold stocks; execution of securities transactions by live brokers and online; and margin loans. Commissions and fees are higher than other firms. See Edward Jones, Raymond James, UBS, Morgan Stanley Smith Barney, and Wells Fargo Advisors.
Discount Brokerage	They charge commissions to execute trades that are often 30 to 80 percent less than the fees charged by full-service brokers. Most offer excellent research and investment tools. See Fidelity, TD Ameritrade, Charles Schwab, USAA Brokerage Services, and Vanguard.
Online Discount Brokerage	**Online discount brokers** (also called Internet or electronic discount brokers) have reduced the cost of executing a trade to perhaps $20 or even $10 because their primary business is online trading. All the discount brokers noted are also online brokers. Additional highly rated online brokers are TD Ameritrade, E*Trade, Fidelity, Scott Trade, and Vanguard.

DID YOU KNOW

About Online Day Trading

Online **day trading** occurs when an investor buys and sells stocks quickly throughout the day with the hope that the price will move enough to cover transaction costs and earn some profits. Day traders rarely own stocks overnight.

Transactions are executed online because they can be done quickly with low commissions. Day trading is a risky practice. One of billionaire Warren Buffett's commandments for getting ahead in personal finance states, "You will lose money if you trade stocks actively."

DID YOU KNOW

How to Check the Background of Your Stockbroker or Investment Advisor

You can check the background of a stockbroker (440,000) or a brokerage firm (45,000) via the Financial Industry Regulatory Authority (FINRA) (www.finra.org/investors

/toolscalculators/brokercheck/). Also check the disciplinary record of most any financial adviser who manages more than $110 million in assets at the Securities and Exchange Commission at www.adviserinfo.sec.gov. Too often the investor receives poor advice. Don't let it happen to you!

might charge 2.8 percent on a transaction amounting to less than $800, 1.8 percent on transactions between $800 and $2500, 1.6 percent on amounts between $2500 and $5000, and 1.2 percent on amounts exceeding $5000.

Transaction costs are based on sales of **round lots**, which are standard units of trading of 100 shares of stock and $1000 or $5000 par value for bonds. An **odd lot** is an amount of a security that is less than the normal unit of trading for that particular security; for stocks, any transaction less than 100 shares is usually considered to be an odd lot. When brokerage firms buy or sell shares in odd lots, they may charge a fee of 12.5 cents (called an **eighth**) per share on the odd-lot portion of the transaction, which is called the **differential**.

The payment of commissions can quickly reduce the return on any investment. A purchase commission of 2 percent is added to a sales commission of another 2 percent, for example, means that the investor has to earn a 4 percent return just to pay the transaction costs. Brokerage commissions typically range from $25 to 3 percent of the value of the transaction. The easiest way to hold down investing costs is to find a brokerage firm that charges low commissions, and that usually means using a discount or online broker.

day trading

Occurs when an investor buys and sells stocks quickly throughout a day with the hope that prices will move enough to cover transaction costs and earn some profits.

14.4c How to Order Stock Transactions

Hundreds of millions of shares of securities are traded daily on the stock markets in the United States. Every trade brings together a buyer and a seller to complete the transaction at a given price.

Types of Stock Orders Basically, there are only two types of orders—buy and sell. The stockbroker will buy or sell securities according to prescribed instructions in a process called executing an order. Those instructions can place constraints on the prices at which those orders are carried out. Table 14-4 shows the instructions that accompany stock orders.

DID YOU KNOW

Regulations Help Protect against Investment Fraud

Public trust is vital to the success of the securities industry; without it, consumers will not invest. Regulation of securities markets aims to provide investors with accurate and reliable information about securities, maintain ethical standards, and prevent fraud against investors. This regulation occurs at five levels:

1. **Securities and Exchange Commission (SEC).** *The SEC is a federal government agency that focuses on ensuring disclosure of information about securities to the investing public and on approving the rules and regulations employed by the organized securities exchanges. The SEC requires registration of listed securities with appropriate and updated information. It also prohibits manipulative practices, such as using insider information for illegal personal gain or causing the price of a security to rise or fall for false reasons. All states require registration of securities sold within their states, and they, too, regulate the securities industry.*

2. **Self-Regulatory Agencies.** *The Financial Industry Regulatory Authority (FINRA) and other self-regulatory organizations, such as the New York Stock Exchange, enforce standards of conduct for their members and their member organizations. They dictate rules for listing and for trading securities.*

3. **Brokerage Firms.** *Individual brokerage firms have established standards of conduct for brokers that govern how they deal with investors.*

4. **Security Investors Protection Corporation (SIPC).** *The SIPC is a limited insurance program to protect the investing public when an SEC-registered brokerage firm fails. Although investment losses due to fraud, misrepresentation or bad investment decisions are not covered, the SIPC protects each of an investor's accounts at a brokerage firm against financial loss as a result of unreturned securities and cash up to a total of $500,000, but no more than $100,000 in cash.*

5. **Financial Services Oversight Council (FSOC).** *The mission of the FSOC is to identify and monitor excessive risks to the U.S. financial system arising from the distress or failure of large, interconnected bank holding companies or non-bank financial companies and from risks that could arise outside the financial system. The idea is to eliminate expectations that any American financial firm is "too big to fail" and to respond to emerging threats to U.S. financial stability.*

Table 14-4 **Instructions Accompanying Stock Transaction**

Instruction	Process
Market	Buy or sell at current prevailing price
Fill-or-Kill	Immediately buy or sell at current market price or cancel
Matched	Held for minutes, hours or days until executed or cancelled
Negotiated	Buyer "bids" for best price and negotiates until accepted or cancelled
Good-til-Cancelled	Remains valid until executed or cancelled by the investor
Limit	Buy at best possible price "but not above" a specified limit or to sell at a certain price "but not below" a specified price
Stop (or Stop-Loss)	Sell at the market price if it goes below a specified price

DID YOU KNOW

The Tax Consequences of Investing in Stocks and Bonds

The government encourages investing through tax policies that favor investors.

Dividends and Interest

Taxes are low on dividend income. Funds put into regular investment accounts represent **after-tax money** (you earn an income on which you pay taxes, and then you invest some of the remaining money). Taxes are due on any interest, dividends, and capital gains in the year in which the income is received. The IRS considers as interest income any increase in the par value on bonds, including TIPS bonds. Interest is taxable at the investor's marginal tax rate. Dividend income is taxed at a maximum rate of 15 percent for most people; a zero percent rate applies to lower-income taxpayers.

Capital Gains and Losses

Capital gains taxes are low. No tax liability is incurred for any capital gains until the stock, bond, mutual fund, real estate, or other investment is sold. When you sell an investment, such as a stock, the gain or loss is calculated by analyzing what you paid for the investment plus broker commissions and loads minus the selling price minus commissions or redemption fees. Short-term gains (for investments held one year or less) are taxed at the same rates as ordinary income. Long-term gains (for investments held at least a year and a day) are taxed at special rates: The long-term capital gains rate for taxpayers below the 25 percent bracket is zero percent, the rate is 15 percent for those in the 25 percent bracket and above, and it is 20 percent for those subject to the 39.6 tax rate. Long-term capital gain rates for collectibles such as stamps and coins are 28 percent. Capital losses can be used to offset capital gains or even your regular income. See Chapter 4.

14.4d Margin Buying and Selling Short Are Risky Trading Techniques

For investors interested in taking on additional risk, there are two advanced trading techniques, and both involve using credit: (1) buying stocks on margin and (2) selling short.

Margin Trading Is Buying Stocks on Credit Some investors open a margin account with a brokerage firm in addition to their cash account so they can buy securities using credit. Opening a margin account requires making a substantial deposit of cash or securities ($2000 or more) and permits the purchase of other securities using credit granted by the brokerage firm. Both brokerage firms and the Federal Reserve Board regulate the use of margin buying, which is using a margin account to buy securities. It allows the investor to apply leverage that magnifies returns or losses.

The margin rate is the percentage of the value (or equity) in an investment that is not borrowed. The current requirement is 50 percent for common stock. Thus at least 50 percent of each dollar invested must be the investor's. The remainder may be borrowed from the broker. The securities purchased, as well as other assets in the margin account, are used as collateral.

Buying on margin also can increase returns. Those with an aggressive investment philosophy might buy on margin because it gives them the opportunity to obtain a higher rate of return. Let's say you buy a stock for $50 and the price of the stock rises to $75. If you bought the stock in a cash account and paid for it in full, you'll earn a 50 percent return on your investment ($75 − $50 = $25/50). But if you bought the stock on margin—paying $25 in cash and borrowing $25 from your broker—you'll earn a 100 percent return on the money you invested ($25/$25). Of course, you have to repay your broker $25 plus interest.

The downside to using margin is that if the stock price decreases, substantial losses can occur. Let's say the stock you bought for $50 falls to $25. If you fully paid for the stock, you'll lose 50 percent of your money. But if you bought on margin, you'll lose 100 percent, and you still must come up with the interest you owe on the loan.

margin account
Account at a brokerage firm that requires a substantial deposit of cash or securities and permits the purchase of other securities using credit granted by the brokerage firm.

margin buying
Using a margin account to buy securities; allows the investor to apply leverage that magnifies returns—or losses.

margin rate
Set by the Fed, percentage of the value (or equity) in an investment that is not borrowed—recently 25 to 50 percent.

DID YOU KNOW

The Investment That Is Best for You May Not Be Best for Your Financial Advisor

Ninety percent of financial advisors sell you what is best for them and is "suitable for you". Here is how the Securities and Exchange Commission defines the **suitability standard**. When your broker recommends that you buy or sell a particular security or she must have a reasonable basis for believing that recommendation is suitable for you. In making this assessment, your broker must consider your income and net worth, investment objectives, risk tolerance, and other security holdings.

In other words, a bond portfolio might be suitable for an older investor seeking income; a portfolio of penny stocks would not. The same bond portfolio would be *unsuitable*, however, for a young investor seeking growth.

The suitability standard also does not preclude conflicts of interest. What is best for you may not be best for the financial advisor. There could be two investments that could qualify as suitable for you, but one would pay your advisor a 1 percent commission and the other 6 percent. Which do you think he or she might recommend?

A **fiduciary standard** means that the broker must always act in the best interest of the client regardless of how it might affect the advisor. Only an investment advisor who is a **registered investment advisor** (RIA) is legally required to act as a fiduciary. Be sure to ask.

The Department of Labor is drafting a rule requiring that all financial advisors abide by fiduciary standards. The industry is fighting against the proposal.

DID YOU KNOW

Your Worst Financial Blunders in Investing in Stocks and Bonds

Based on others' financial woes, you will make mistakes in personal finance when you:

1. *Invest in stocks that do not match your investment philosophy.*
2. *Fail to use fundamental analysis when making stock investments.*
3. *Buy stocks on margin or sell stocks short.*

buying long
Buying a security (especially on margin) with the hope that the stock price will rise.

selling short
Investors selling securities they do not own (borrowing them from a broker) and later buying the same number of shares of the security at a lower price (returning them to the broker).

Here a representative of the firm will tell the investor to immediately either put up more collateral (money or other stocks) or face having the investment sold. This procedure is known as a **margin call**. If the investor fails to put up the additional cash or securities to maintain a required level of equity in the margin account, the broker will sell the securities at the market price, resulting in an even sharper financial loss to the investor. The investor is required to repay the broker for any losses.

Selling Short Is Selling Stocks Borrowed from Your Broker

Buying a security with the hope that it will go up in value—the goal of most investors—is called **buying long**. You might suspect, however, that the price of a security will drop. You can earn profits when the price of a security declines by **selling short**. In this trading technique, investors sell securities they do not own (borrowing them from a broker) and after so many days or weeks plan to buy the same number of shares of the security at a lower price (returning them to the broker). Thus, the investor earns a profit on the transaction.

Brokerage firms require an investor to maintain a margin account when selling short because it provides some assurance that the investor can repay the firm for the borrowed stock, if necessary. As a result, some or all of an investor's funds deposited in a margin account are effectively tied up during a short sale. Many brokers hold the proceeds of a short sale, without paying interest, until the customer **covers the position** by buying it back for delivery to the broker.

Only a small proportion of investors sell stocks short because this approach is so risky. Selling short and buying on margin are techniques to be used only by sophisticated investors.

 ### CONCEPT CHECK 14.4

1. Summarize the differences among discount, online, and full-service brokers.
2. Summarize the differences among types of stock orders: market, limit, and stop order.
3. Explain what selling short is and how it can go wrong for an investor.

14.5 INVESTING IN BONDS

You should consider investing in bonds if you wish to receive periodic income from a portion of your investments. While bonds usually offer a lower return to investors than stocks, there are good reasons to include bonds in one's portfolio. The primary one is to reduce market risk. Others include obtaining a regular source of predictable although low income, likelihood of profiting from possible future increases in the value of bonds, and matching some of one's assets to one's investment time horizon.

A variety of bonds are available to the investor. High quality bonds are called **investment-grade bonds** and they offer investors a reasonable certainty of regularly receiving the periodic income (interest) and retrieving the amount originally invested (principal). Only about 8 percent of the 23,000 largest U.S. companies that issue bonds meet the highest investment-grade rating standards. Bonds are usually issued at a **par value** (also known as **face value**) of $1000.

An investor typically earns a low to moderate return on bond investments, an appropriate yield when compared with the higher total returns earned on riskier stocks and stock mutual funds. Owning some bonds (or bond mutual funds) along with stocks and cash diversifies an investment portfolio.

Speculative-grade bonds pay a high interest rate. These are often derisively called **junk bonds**, and they are long-term, high-risk, high-interest-rate corporate (or municipal) IOUs issued by companies (or municipalities) with poor or no credit ratings. The interest rates paid investors on junk bonds are 3.5 to 8 percentage points more than those of Treasury bonds.

Also more elegantly called **high-yield bonds**, they carry investment ratings that are below traditional investment grade and carry a higher risk of default (not repaying the bond investors). Keep in mind that higher returns require greater risk. The **default rate** on investment grade AAA-rated bonds is ½ of 1 percent. It is 1.5% on AA bonds; 3% on A bonds; and 10% on BBB bonds. The rate is over 4% for munis. For more information, see Bond Pickers (www.bondpickers.com) or www.defaultrisk.com or search Google using "high-yield bonds."

Individual investors usually avoid buying individual junk bonds because of the substantial financial risk involved with owning too few investments. Instead, they reduce risk by diversifying their investments through a "high-yield income" bond mutual fund (see Chapter 15) that has junk bonds in its portfolio.

14.5a Corporate, U.S. Government, and Municipal Bonds

Three types of bonds are available: corporate bonds, U.S. government securities, and municipal government bonds.

Corporate Bonds Pay Reasonable Returns   Corporate bonds are interest-bearing certificates of long-term debt issued by a corporation. They represent a

---

investment-grade bonds
Offer investors a reasonable certainty of regularly receiving periodic income (interest) and retrieving the amount originally invested (principal).

speculative-grade bonds
Long-term, high-risk, high-interest-rate corporate (or municipal) IOUs issued by companies (or municipalities) with poor or no credit ratings. Also called junk bonds or high-yield bonds.

corporate bonds
Interest-bearing certificates of long-term debt issued by a corporation.

DID YOU KNOW

Money Websites for Investing in Bonds

Informative websites for investing in bonds, including the latest bond prices are:

Financial Industry Regulatory Authority (www.finra.org/)
JW Korth Shop-4-Bonds (www.shop4bonds.com)

Municipal Securities Rulemaking Board (emma.msrb.org/home)
Securities Industry and Financial Markets Association (www.investinginbonds.com)
Yahoo! Finance on bonds (finance.yahoo.com/bonds)
Wikipedia (en.wikipedia.org/wiki/Bond_(finance))

Figure 14-3 Higher Returns on Bonds Requires Greater Risk

Higher yield = (Credit quality ↓) OR (Longer maturity ↑)

needed source of funds for corporations. The dollar value of newly issued bonds is three times the dollar value of newly issued stocks. Because of tax regulations, corporations often finance major projects by issuing long-term bonds instead of selling stocks. One reason they do so is that payments of dividends to common and preferred stockholders are not tax deductible for corporations, unlike interest paid to bondholders. State laws require corporations to make bond interest payments on time. Therefore, companies in financial difficulty are required to pay bondholders before paying any short-term creditors.

The default risk varies with the issuer. To help you in appraising the risks and potential rewards of bond investments, independent advisory services, such as Moody's Investors Service, Standard & Poor's, and Fitch, grade bonds for credit risk. These firms publish what they describe as unbiased ratings of the financial conditions of corporations and municipalities that issue bonds.

bond rating

An impartial outsider's opinion of the quality—or creditworthiness—of the issuing organization.

A **bond rating** represents the opinion of an outsider on the quality—or creditworthiness—of the issuing organization. It reflects the likelihood that the issuing organization will be able to repay its debt. Ratings for each bond issue are continually re-evaluated, and they often change after the original security has been sold to the public. Investors have access to measures of the **default risk** (or **credit risk**), which is the uncertainty associated with not receiving the promised periodic interest payments as well as the principal amount when it becomes due at maturity.

default risk (credit risk)

Uncertainty associated with not receiving the promised periodic interest payments and the principal amount when it becomes due at maturity.

Table 14-5 shows the bond ratings used by Moody's, Standard & Poor's and Fitch, all well known rating services. The higher the rating, the greater the probable safety of the bond and the lower the default risk. The lower the rating of the bond the higher the stated, or effective interest rate. When bonds are reduced in price from their face amount, more risk is involved. Higher ratings denote confidence that the issuer will not default and, if necessary, that the bond can readily be sold before its maturity date. Investment-grade corporate bonds may provide returns as much as 2.5 percentage points higher than the returns available on comparable U.S. Treasury securities.

U.S. Government Securities Represent Quality and Safety U.S. Treasury securities are the world's safest investment because the government has never intentionally defaulted on its debt. U.S. Treasury securities are backed by the "full faith, credit, and taxing power of the U.S. government," and this all but guarantees the timely payment of principal and interest. The debt is held by a variety of investors, including the governments of Japan and China, the largest U.S. creditors. U.S. debt is denominated in dollars and is the cornerstone of the global financial system.

Treasury securities (Treasuries)

Known as Treasuries, securities issued by the U.S. government, including bills, notes, and bonds.

U.S. government securities are classified into two groups: (1) Treasury bills, notes, and bonds and (2) federal agency issue notes, bonds, and certificates. Treasury bills, notes, and bonds are collectively known as **Treasury securities**, or **Treasuries**. The federal government uses these debt instruments to finance the public national debt.

Treasury securities have excellent liquidity and are simple to acquire and sell. Previously issued marketable Treasury securities are bought and sold in securities markets through brokers. New issues can be purchased online using the Treasury Direct Plan (www.publicdebt.treas.gov), where they are stored electronically. Individuals may buy Treasury securities in amounts as small as $100.

Table 14-5   Summary of Bond Ratings

| Ratings | | | Credit Worthiness |
Moody's	Standard & Poor's	Fitch	
Aaa	AAA	AAA	Extremely strong capacity to meet its financial commitments.
Aa1	AA+	AA+	Strong capacity to meet its financial commitments; differs only slightly from the highest.
Aa2	AA	AA	
Aa3	AA−	AA−	Strong capacity to meet its financial commitments.
Baa1	BBB+	BBB+	Adequate capacity to meet its financial commitments.
Baa2	BBB	BBB	Adequate capacity to meet its financial commitments, but vulnerable to changing economic conditions.
Baa3	BBB−	BBB−	
Caa	CCC	CCC	Less vulnerable than lower rated bonds but faces uncertain uncertainties and exposures.
Ca	CC	CC	Currently vulnerable on good economic conditions to meet its obligations.
	C	C	
C	D	D	Currently in default with little prospect of regaining any investment standing.

The interest rates on federal government securities are lower than those on corporate bonds because they are virtually risk free. The possibility of default is near zero. Individuals with a conservative investment philosophy and overseas investors and governments are often attracted to the certainty offered by U.S. government securities. Investors can purchase these directly from the Treasury. Although interest income is subject to federal income taxes, interest earned on Treasury securities is exempt from state and local income taxes.

Treasury Bills, Notes, and Bonds Treasury bills, or T-bills, are short-term government securities with maturities ranging from a few days to just less than one year. Bills are sold at a discount from their **face value (par)**. The difference between the original purchase price and what the Treasury pays you at maturity, the gain or par, is interest. This interest is exempt from state and local income taxes but is reported as interest income on your federal tax return in the year the Treasury bill matures.

Stated as an interest rate, the return on such investments is called a discount yield. For example, if you buy a $10,000 26-week Treasury bill for $9925 and hold it until maturity, your interest will be $75 for an annual return of approximately 1.5 percent. An investor can hold a bill until maturity or sell it before it is due. When a bill matures, the proceeds can be reinvested into another bill or redeemed and the principal will be deposited into the investor's checking or savings account. The minimum purchase of T-bills is $100.

A Treasury note or bond is a fixed-principal, fixed-interest-rate government security issued for an intermediate or long term. Notes are issued for two, three, five, or ten years, and pay interest every six months. Treasury bonds have a maturity of 10 to 30 years. Notes and bonds exist only as electronic entries in accounts. The interest rate on notes and bonds is typically higher than the rates for T-bills because the lending period is longer. Interest payments are to be reported as interest income on one's federal tax return in the year received. When the security matures, the investor is repaid the principal. Investors can hold a note or bond until maturity or sell it.

Floating-rate notes are the Treasury's newest security. Their interest rates change weekly over the two-year time period, paying investors more when market rates rise and less when they fall, and they make quarterly interest payments. Interest rates are pegged to the yield on 3-month Treasury bills. Floating-rate notes may be purchased at auction or via Treasury Direct with a $100 minimum investment.

Treasury bills
Known as T-bills, U.S. government securities with maturities of less than one year.

discount yield
Difference between the original purchase price of a T-bill and what the Treasury pays you at maturity.

Treasury note (bond)
Fixed-principal, fixed-interest-rate government security issued for an intermediate term or long term. Notes mature in ten years or less; bonds mature in more than ten years.

I bonds

Nonmarketable savings bonds backed by the U.S. government that pay an earnings rate that combines two rates: a fixed interest rate set when the investor buys the bond and a semiannual variable interest rate tied to inflation that protects the investor's purchasing power.

Treasury Inflation-Protected Securities (TIPS)

Marketable Treasury bonds whose value increases with inflation. These inflation-indexed $1000 bonds are the only investment that guarantees that the investor's return will outpace inflation.

zero-coupon bonds (zeros or deep discount bonds)

Municipal, corporate, and Treasury bonds that are issued at a sharp discount from face value and pay no annual interest but are redeemed at full face value upon maturity.

I bonds are nonmarketable savings bonds backed by the U.S. government that pay an earnings rate that is a combination of two rates: (1) a fixed interest rate that is set when the investor buys the bond and (2) a semiannual variable interest rate tied to inflation that protects the investor's purchasing power. They are sold at face value, such as $25 for a $25 bond. Interest stops accruing 30 years after issue, and I bonds pay off only when redeemed. If you redeem a I bond within the first five years, you will forfeit the three most recent months' interest; after five years, you will not be penalized. All earnings on savings bonds are exempt from both state and local income taxes, while federal taxes can be deferred until the bonds are either redeemed or reach final maturity. I bonds cashed in to pay education expenses are exempt from federal income taxes.

Treasury Inflation-Protected Securities (TIPS) are marketable Treasury securities whose principal increases with changes in the Consumer Price Index (CPI). These inflation-indexed bonds are the only investment that guarantees that the investor's return will outpace inflation. TIPS bonds are sold in terms of 5, 10, and 30 years, and interest is paid to TIPS owners every six months until they mature. The interest rate is set when the security is purchased, and the rate never changes. The principal is adjusted every six months according to the rise and fall of the CPI; if inflation occurs and the CPI rises, the principal increases. The government sends the interest payment on the new principal to the investor's account. The fixed interest rate on TIPS is applied to the inflation-adjusted principal; so if inflation occurs throughout the life of a TIPS security, every interest payment will be greater than the one before it. The amount of each interest payment is determined by multiplying the inflation-adjusted principal by one-half the interest rate.

The inflation-adjusted amount added to the principal on a TIPS bond every six months is taxable, even though the investor does not receive the money until the bond matures. Thus, TIPS bonds pay "phantom taxable interest income," like **zero-coupon bonds (zeros or deep discount bonds)** (described in the Advice From a Professional box, so the investor pays federal income taxes on the interest earned each year. The investor must use other funds to pay the taxes on that income. If the TIPS are owned in a retirement account, the returns are not taxable until withdrawn.

ADVICE FROM A PROFESSIONAL

Zero-Coupon Bonds Pay Phantom Interest

Zero-coupon bonds (also called **zeros** or **deep discount bonds**) are municipal, corporate, and Treasury bonds that pay no annual interest. They are sold to investors at sharp discounts from their face value and may be redeemed at full value upon maturity. For example, a 4 percent, $1000 zero-coupon bond to be redeemed in the year 2024 might sell today for $457. Zeros pay no current income to investors, so investors do not have to be concerned about where to reinvest interest payments. The semiannual interest accumulates within the bond itself, and the return to the investor comes from redeeming the bond at its stated face value at the maturity date. In this manner, zeros operate much like Series EE savings bonds and

T-bills. The maturity date for a zero could range from a few months to as long as 30 years.

Parents often invest in zero-coupon bonds to help pay for their children's college education, and they wisely establish ownership of the zeros in the child's name. The phantom income "paid" to the child is generally so small that little, if any, income taxes are due.

People planning for retirement often buy zeros because they know exactly how much will be received at maturity. Even though the investor receives no interest money until maturity, the investor still pays income taxes every year on the interest that accumulates within the bond. Investors can avoid income taxes altogether by buying zeros in a qualified tax-sheltered retirement plan account.

Anne Ranczuch
Monroe Community College, Rochester, New York

When TIPS mature, the federal government pays the inflation-adjusted principal (or the original principal if it is greater). Investors can hold a TIPS bond until it matures or sell it before it matures. The interest on TIPS bonds can be excluded from federal income tax when the bond owner pays tuition and fees for higher education in the year the bonds are redeemed.

U.S. government savings bonds are nonmarketable, interest-bearing bonds issued by the federal government and sold at face value. They are considered a low-risk savings product that earns interest while protecting one from inflation and market risk calamities.

Series EE/E savings bonds are a secure savings product issued by the federal government that pays a fixed rate of interest for up to 30 years. The maximum amount of savings bonds you can buy in a single year is $10,000. Electronic **EE savings bonds** are sold at face value in TreasuryDirect. Paper bonds are no longer available. EE savings bonds are sold at one-half of the face value and pay no annual interest, and they may be redeemed at full value upon maturity. For example, a $100 EE savings bond might be purchased for half of its face amount, $50. The interest, compounded semi-annually, accumulates within the bond itself, and the return to the investor comes from redeeming the bond at its stated face value at the maturity date. Interest on Series EE bonds is exempt from state and local taxes. There is no federal income tax liability on the interest at redemption if the proceeds are used to fund the child's college education. (**Series HH savings bonds** [no longer sold] were originally issued at par and acquired only by exchanging Series EE bonds. Interest on Series HH bonds is exempt from state and local taxes.)

Agency Bonds Pay Slightly Better Returns than Treasuries More than 100 different bonds, notes, and certificates of debt are issued by various federal agencies that are government-sponsored enterprises but stockholder owned; these are **agency bonds**. Well-known examples of these agencies are Fannie Mae (Federal National Mortgage Association), Freddie Mac (Federal Home Loan Mortgage Corporation), and Sallie Mae (Student Loan Marketing Association). Together these make up about 40 percent of the outstanding investment-grade bonds. The first two are the government-chartered agencies responsible in part for the housing and credit debacle that went bankrupt and today are substantially owned by the federal government. Fannie and Freddie service continue to sell bonds, buy mortgages, and package home loans into securities.

Other government-chartered agencies that issue bonds include the Tennessee Valley Authority, Federal Farm Credit Banks, Federal Home Loan Banks, and Government National Mortgage Association (Ginnie Mae). Each security represents interest in a pool of loans that are sold to institutions and investors in units of $25,000, although they can also be purchased in smaller units through a mutual fund.

The assets and resources of the issuing agency back these bonds. Although the federal government does not guarantee the debt issued by such agencies, it did provide billions of dollars when Fannie Mae and Freddie Mac faced default. Agency bonds are not as widely publicized as Treasury securities, yet they pay a yield two-tenths to one full percentage point higher than the yield for comparable-term Treasury securities.

Municipal Government Bonds **Municipal government bonds** (also called **munis**) are long-term debts issued by local governments (cities, states, and various districts and political subdivisions) and their agencies. Their proceeds are used to finance public improvement projects, such as roads, bridges, and parks, or to pay ongoing expenses. Moody's Bond Record rates some 20,000 munis, and twice as many unrated securities exist. Bonds range in quality from AAA-rated state highway bonds to unrated securities issued by local governmental parking authorities.

The investor's interest income on municipal bonds is not subject to federal income taxes. This is because the U.S. Constitution requires that municipal bond interest be exempt from federal income tax. Because the

---

U.S. government savings bonds

Nonmarketable, interest-bearing bonds issued by the U.S. Treasury.

Series EE/E savings bonds

Nonmarketable, interest-bearing bonds issued by the federal government that are issued at a sharp discount from face value and pay no annual interest, and that may be redeemed at full value upon maturity.

agency bonds

Bonds, notes, and certificates of debt issued by various federal agencies that are government-sponsored enterprises but stockholder owned, such as the Federal National Mortgage Association.

municipal government bonds (munis)

Long-term debts (bonds) issued by local governments (cities, states, and various districts and political subdivisions) and their agencies.

FINANCIAL POWER POINT

Check Bond Performance Online

The bond section of the FINRA website highlights all the key questions one might have about investing in bonds (www.finra.org/Investors/InvestmentChoices/Bonds/SmartBondInvesting/Introduction/). Municipal bond prices and information is available at the Municipal Securities Rulemaking Board (emma.msrb.org/home).

DID YOU KNOW

Sean's Success Story

Sean's success in investing through the years pushed the value of his portfolio to $140,000. His old portfolio matched his aggressive investment philosophy: cash (10%), bonds (10%), and equities (80%). However, his investments took a terrible hit during the bear market crash of 2007–2009. Because of defaults, his bond values dropped from $14,000 to $11,000. The equity portion of his portfolio, which was mostly high-tech, small-cap and microcap stocks and stock mutual funds, dropped 50 percent from $112,000 to $56,000.

The first thing Sean did to try and keep his net worth figure from dropping even further was to spend less money on eating out, music, and electronics. He was scared but resisted the urge to sell low and get out of the market completely; therefore, he stayed invested throughout those two long years, which was depressing for almost all investors. Within 4 years the equities in his portfolio rose well over 60 percent to $130,000. Even though these were still shaky economic times, Sean stayed in the market, and he will continue to invest regularly as the stock markets recovers in the coming years with the slowly growing world economies. Thus by remaining invested as the market recovered, Sean recovered all of his losses, and his portfolio is up from its old high.

interest income is tax free, municipal bonds are also known as **tax-free bonds** or **tax-exempt bonds**. Interest income on munis also is exempt from state and local income taxes when the investor lives in the state that issued the bond.

Municipal bonds offer a lower stated return than other bonds. However, if your marginal tax rate is higher than 25 percent, it generally makes economic sense to invest in municipal bonds because the after-tax return on a muni might be higher than that of a corporate bond. To compare the after-tax returns of investments, see page 129.

Capital gains on the sale of munis are taxable. Such gains may be realized when bonds are bought at a discount and then sold at a higher price or redeemed for full value at maturity. Bonds bought at a premium also may appreciate to produce a gain.

14.5b   Evaluating Bond Prices and Returns

Investors can utilize the standard factors to evaluate bond prices and potential returns: interest rates, premiums and discounts, current yield, and yield to maturity.

Interest Rate Risk Results in Variable Value   A bond's price, or its value on any given day, is affected by a host of factors. These include its type, coupon rate, and availability in the marketplace; demand for the bond; prices for similar bonds; the underlying credit quality of the issuer; and the number of years before it matures.

Most important, the price also varies because of fluctuations in current **market interest rates** in the general economy. The state of the economy and the supply and demand for credit affect market interest rates. These are the current long- and short-term interest rates paid on various types of corporate and government debts that carry similar levels of risk.

market interest rates

Current long- and short-term interest rates paid on various types of corporate and government debts that carry similar levels of risk.

Long-Term Interest Rates Set by Investors Plus Occasional Fed Interventions   Long-term rates are largely set by bond investors' buying and selling decisions, primarily based on their expectations of future inflation. Short-term interest rates are manipulated by the Federal Reserve Board, which is popularly known as the "Fed." When inflation rises, the Fed often raises interest rates to discourage borrowing, which reduces consumer and business spending. When the economy slows, the Fed often lowers the interest rates on short-term Treasury issues in an attempt to stimulate economic activity by making it cheaper for companies to borrow and expand. On occasion, the

Table 14-6	**Unique Characteristics of Bonds**

DO IT IN CLASS

Coupon Rate	The bond's **coupon rate** (also known as the **coupon, coupon yield,** or **stated interest rate**) is the interest rate printed on the certificate when the bond is issued. It reflects the total annual fixed rate of interest that will be paid.
Serial or Sinking Fund	Occasionally bonds are retired serially. That is, each bond is numbered consecutively and matures according to a prenumbered schedule at stated intervals. These investments are known as **serial bonds.** Many bonds include a sinking fund through which money is set aside with a trustee each year for repayment of the principal portion of the debt.
Secured or Unsecured	A corporation issuing a secured bond pledges specific assets as collateral in the indenture (written legal agreement between debtor and lenders) the principal and interest guaranteed by another corporation or a government agency. An **unsecured bond** (or **debenture**) does not name collateral as security for the debt and is backed only by the good faith and reputation of the issuing agency.
Registered and Issued	By law, all bonds issued now are registered bonds. This provides for the recording of the bondholder's name so that checks or electronic funds transfers for payment of interest and principal can be safely forwarded when due.
Book Entry	All bonds today are issued in **book-entry form,** which means that certificates are not issued. Instead, an account is set up in the name of the issuing organization or the brokerage firm that sold the bond, and interest is paid into this account when due.
Callable	An issuer might desire to exercise a call option when interest rates drop substantially. For example, assume a company issues bonds paying a $60 annual dividend (6 percent coupon rate). When interest rates drop perhaps to 4 percent, the 6 percent bonds may represent too high a cost for borrowing to the corporation. If the bonds have a **callable** feature, the issuer can redeem the bonds before the maturity date. The issuer repurchases the bond at par value or by paying a premium, often a partial year's worth of interest. Approximately 80 percent of long-term bonds are classified as callable.

sinking fund

Bond feature through which money is set aside with a trustee each year for repayment of the principal portion of the debt at maturity.

secured bond

Pledges specific assets as collateral in indenture or has the principal and interest guaranteed by another corporation or government agency.

indenture

Written, legal agreement between bondholders and debtor that describes terms of the debt by setting forth the maturity date, interest rate, and other details.

registered bond

Bondholder's name is recorded so that checks or electronic funds transfers for payment of interest and principal can be safely forwarded when due.

call option

Stipulation in some indentures that allows issuer to repurchase the bond at par value or by paying a premium, often one year's worth of interest.

Fed buys long-term mortgage securities and Treasury bonds and notes and related debt for autos and credit cards, again to stimulate the economy.

14.5c Pricing a Bond in Today's Market

As we noted in Chapter 13, **interest rate risk** is the risk that interest rates will increase and bond prices will fall, thereby lowering the prices on older bond issues. This decline in value ensures that an older bond and a newly issued bond will offer potential investors approximately the same yield. Bonds generally have a **fixed yield** (the interest income payment remains the same) but a **variable value**.

interest rate risk

Risk that interest rates will rise and bond prices will fall, thereby lowering the prices on older bond issues.

For example, assume you own a 30-year bond with a face value of $1000 paying a semiannual coupon interest rate of 6 percent that has 20 years remaining until maturity. If interest rates in the general economy jump to 8 percent after one year, no one will want to buy your 6 percent bond for $1000 because it pays only $60 per year. If you want to sell it, the price of the bond will have to be lowered, perhaps to $802.80.

The **value of bond (or bond selling price) formula**, Equation (14.3), shows the calculation involved. If rates on similar bonds are now at 8 percent, then the discount rate is 8 percent (or 4 percent twice a year for 40 payments). The task is to calculate the present value of the interest payments and the repayment lump sum. To do so, use Appendix A.2 and Appendix A.4 and look across the interest rows to 4% and down to 40 "n" periods.

Value of Bond = Present value of interest payments + present value of lump sum

= (Annual interest payment/2 × PVIFA^{i,n}) + (Lump sum × PVIF^{i,n})

where

i = new annual **interest** rate divided by 2

n = number of years to maturity times 2 **(14.3)**

= ($60 = 2 × PVIFA$^{4\%,40}$) + ($1,000 × PVIF$^{4\%,40}$)

= ($30 × 19.7928) + ($1,000 × 0.2083)

= ($593.78 + $208.30 = $802.08

Conversely, if interest rates on newly issued bonds slip to 4 percent, the price of your 6 percent bond will increase sharply, perhaps to $1273.55. Thus, investors might be willing to pay a **bond premium** of $273.55 ($1273.55 − $1000), which is a sum of money paid in excess of the bond's face amount, to buy your $1000 bond paying 6 percent when other rates are only 4 percent. Remember that bond yields and prices move in opposite directions— as one goes up, the other goes down.

bond premium

A sum of money paid in addition to a regular price.

Premiums and Discounts When a bond is first issued, it is sold in one of three ways: (1) at its face value (the value of the bond stated on the certificate and the amount the investor will receive when the bond matures), (2) at a discount below its face value, or (3) at a premium above its face value. After a bond is issued its market price changes in order to provide a competitive effective rate of return for anyone interested in purchasing it from the original bondholder.

DO IT IN CLASS

As an example, assume that Running Paws Cat Food Company decided to issue 20-year bonds at 8.8 percent. While the bonds were being printed and prepared for sale, the market interest rate on comparable high-risk bonds rose to 9 percent. In this instance, Running Paws would sell the bonds at a slight discount to provide a competitive return. Discounts and premiums on bonds reflect changing interest rates in the economy and the number of years to maturity.

current yield

Equals the bond's fixed annual interest payment divided by its bond price.

Current Yield The **current yield** equals the bond's fixed annual interest payment divided by its bond price. It is a measure of the current annual income (the total of both semiannual interest payments in dollars) expressed as a percentage when divided by the bond's current market price. When you buy a bond at par, its current yield equals its coupon yield. For example, a bond with a 5.5 percent coupon yield purchased at par for $1000 has a current yield of 5.5 percent. As bond prices fluctuate because of interest rate changes and other factors, the current yield also changes. For example, if Sarah Jones of Denver, Colorado paid $940 for a $1000 bond paying $55 per year, the bond's current yield is 5.85 percent, as shown by the **current yield formula**, Equation (14.4).

$$\text{Current yield} = \frac{\text{current annual income}}{\text{current market price}}$$

$$= \frac{\$55}{\$940} \quad \textbf{(14.4)}$$

$$= 5.85\%$$

The current yields for many bonds based on that day's market prices are available online and are published in the financial section of many newspapers.

The total return on a bond investment consists of the same components as the return on any investment: current income and capital gains. In Sarah's case, she will receive $1000 at the maturity date (20 years from now), even though she paid only $940 for the bond; therefore, her anticipated total return (or effective yield) will be higher than the 5.85 percent current yield. How much higher is accurately revealed by the yield to maturity formula (discussed next).

Yield to Maturity Yield to maturity (YTM) is the total annual effective rate of return earned by a bondholder on a bond if the security is held to maturity. The YTM is the internal rate of return on cash flows of a fixed-income security. The YTM reflects both the current income and any difference if the bond was purchased at a price other than its face value spread over the life of the bond. The market price of a bond equals the present value of its future interest payments and the present value of its face value when the bond matures.

yield to maturity (YTM)
Total annual effective rate of return earned by a bondholder on a bond if the security is held to maturity—takes into consideration both the price at which the bond sold and the coupon interest rate to arrive at effective rate of return.

Three generalizations can be made about the yield to maturity:

1. If a bond is purchased for exactly its face value, the YTM is the same as the coupon rate printed on the certificate.
2. If a bond is purchased at a premium, the YTM will be lower than the coupon rate.
3. If a bond is purchased at a discount, the YTM will be higher than the coupon rate.

For example, because Sarah bought her 20-year bond with a coupon rate of 5.5 percent at a discount for $940, her yield to maturity must be greater than the coupon rate because she will receive $60 more than she paid for the bond when she receives the $1000 at maturity. Exactly how much greater can be determined by calculating an approximate yield to maturity when contemplating a bond purchase because bonds that seem comparable may have different YTMs.

The **yield to maturity (YTM) formula**, Equation (14.5), which is duplicated on the *Garman/Forgue* companion website, factors in the approximate appreciation when a bond is bought at a discount or at a premium:

$$\text{YTM} = \frac{I + [(FV - CV)/N]}{(FV + CV)/2} \quad \text{(14.5)}$$

where

I = **Interest** paid annually in dollars
FV = **Face value**
CV = **Current value** (price)
N = **Number** of years until maturity

If Sarah paid $940 for a 20-year bond with a 5.5 percent coupon rate, the YTM is calculated as follows:

$$\text{YTM} = \frac{\$55 + [(\$1000 - \$940)/20]}{(\$1000 + \$940)/2}$$

$$= \frac{\$58}{\$970}$$

$$= 5.98\%$$

If you plan to buy and hold a bond until its maturity, you should compare YTMs instead of current yields when considering a purchase because YTMs fairly represent all factors. The current yield on a bond is not an effective measure of the total annual return to the investor; in fact, the fewer years until maturity, the worse an indicator it becomes. As just calculated, Sarah's 20-year bond with a coupon rate of 5.5 percent and

Turn Bad Habits into Good Ones

Do You Do This?	*Do This Instead!*
Invest only in certificates of deposit	Invest in common stocks, bonds and mutual funds
Listen to tips and invest in hot stocks	Invest only in stocks with good fundamentals
Invest in speculative stocks	Utilize no more than 5 to 10 percent for speculative stocks
Invest in fewer than five stocks	Invest in more than five, or buy stock mutual funds
Ignore big changes in interest rates	Invest in bonds on interest rate shifts (but not when rates are rising)
Accept broker's advice on stock choices	Use the Internet to research stocks and bonds
Utilize full-service brokers exclusively	Buy and sell online to save on commissions
Buy on margin and sell short	Never buy on margin and sell short, as it is too risky
Avoid bonds as investments	Buy some TIPS bonds

a current yield of 5.85 percent has a YTM of 5.98 percent. If the same bond had been purchased with only ten years until maturity, the YTM would be 6.29 percent; with five years until maturity, the YTM would be 6.90 percent; and with two years until maturity, the YTM would be 8.76 percent. Exact YTMs are online and listed in detailed bond tables available at large libraries and at brokers' offices.

Six Decisions for Bond Investors Individuals interested in investing in bonds can review resources on the website of the Securities Industry and Financial Markets Association (www.investinginbonds.com). It offers a free, searchable database of the latest corporate, government, municipal, and mortgage-backed bond issues and prices. Bond investors must make six decisions:

1. **Decide on credit quality.** Consider Treasury/agency, investment-grade corporate and municipal, and below investment-grade corporate and municipal.

2. **Decide on maturity.** Consider the time schedule of your financial needs: short, medium, or long term. Bonds with a short maturity have the lowest current yield but excellent price stability. Medium maturity bonds pay close to the higher rates earned on long-term bonds and enjoy much greater price stability.

3. **Determine the after-tax return.** Assuming equivalent risk, choose the bond that provides the better after-tax return because tax-exempt securities may offer a higher after-tax return than taxable alternatives. To compare the after-tax return of investments, see page 129 in chapter 4.

4. **Select the highest yield to maturity.** Given similar bond securities with comparable risk, maturity, and tax equivalency, investors are wise to choose the one that offers the highest yield to maturity, as calculated by Equation (14.5).

5. **Instead, think about investing in bond mutual funds.** Consider whether it is smarter to invest in bond mutual funds rather than individual bonds. This topic is examined in Chapter 15.

DO IT NOW!

You know more about personal finance after reading this chapter, so get started right now by:

1. Identifying three types of stocks (See Table 14-1 on page 417) that are appropriate for your investment goals and selecting an example of each.

2. Following the price fluctuations of those stocks for two months online or via newspapers.

3. Considering a bond investment of a corporate bond by selecting one, and researching its price, and bond rating.

6. **Consider selling bonds or bond mutual funds.** Consider selling when interest rates have dropped or are expected to rise substantially in the near future, the bond rating has seriously declined, and because you can profit when rate declines push up the value of your bond.

CONCEPT CHECK 14.5

1. Distinguish between investment- and speculative-grade bonds.

2. Give some reasons why individuals often invest in corporate bonds rather than Treasuries.

3. Summarize the differences among Treasury bonds, I bonds, and TIPS bonds.

4. Give a math example of how to calculate a bond's yield to maturity that is different than the one in the book.

WHAT DO YOU RECOMMEND *NOW?*

Now that you have read the chapter on stocks and bonds, what do you recommend to Ashley Diaz in the case at the beginning of the chapter regarding:

1. Investing for retirement in 18 years?

2. Owning blue-chip common stocks and preferred stocks rather than other common stocks given Ashley's investment time horizon?

3. The wisdom of owning municipal bonds rather than corporate bonds?

4. The likely selling price of her corporate bonds, if sold today?

5. Investments that might be appropriate to fund her children's education?

BIG PICTURE SUMMARY OF LEARNING OBJECTIVES

LO1 **Explain how stocks and bonds are used as investments.**

Individual investors provide the money corporations use to create sales and earn profits. The investor shares in those profits by investing in corporations' common stock, preferred stock, and bonds.

LO2 **Describe ways to evaluate stock prices and calculate a stock's potential rate of return.**

Common stocks may be broadly classified as either income or growth stocks. The investor studies certain fundamental factors, such as the company's sales, assets, earnings, products or services, markets, and management, to determine a company's basic value. To do so, investors examine several revealing ratios such as price/earnings (P/E), price/sales (P/S), and dividend payout, as well as revealing numbers such as book value per share. Individuals also estimate the value of a company by using beta to compare its history and expected future profitability with those of competing stocks.

LO3 **Use the Internet to evaluate common stocks in which to invest.**

Individuals begin evaluating stocks by setting criteria for a stock investment. This may involve using stock-screening software; obtaining security analysts' research reports, annual reports, 10-Q and 10-K reports, and prospectuses; acquiring economic and stock market data; and using portfolio-tracking services.

LO4   **Summarize how to buy and sell stocks, as well as the techniques of margin buying and selling short.**

Securities transactions require the use of a licensed broker serving as a middleman between the seller and the buyer. You can buy or sell securities online or through a live stockbroker who works for a brokerage firm that has access to the securities markets. Many individuals use discount and online brokers rather than full-service brokers. Types of stock orders include market, limit, and stop orders. Buying on margin and selling short are risky trading techniques.

LO5   **Describe how to invest in bonds.**

Investment-grade bonds offer a reasonable certainty of regularly receiving the periodic income (interest) and retrieving the amount originally invested (principal). Junk bonds are available, too. Corporate bonds usually pay higher returns than government bonds. Interest rate risk results in variable value on bond investments.

LET'S TALK ABOUT IT

1. **Investing Today.** What counsel can you offer long-term investors who are hesitant to invest in stocks and bonds in today's economy?

2. **Common or Preferred Stock.** Make a list of the plusses and minuses of investing in either common stock or preferred stock, and give your conclusion as to which is better for you.

3. **Three Good Companies.** Make a list of three products and services that you buy on a weekly or monthly basis and the companies that sell them. Offer your initial views on whether each company would be a good place to invest money.

4. **Two Useful Measures.** The text introduced a variety of ways to measure stock performance. Name two of those measures that you might use in your own decision making. Offer reasons for selecting those measures.

5. **Would You Buy?** You have just heard that Microsoft's stock price dropped $5. If you had the money, would you buy 100 shares? Give three reasons why or why not.

6. **Interesting Stock.** Review the classifications of common stock. Based on your personal comfort level for risk, which one type of stock would be of interest to you? Give three reasons why.

7. **Sources of Information.** If you had an investment portfolio of stocks worth $20,000, identify three sources for information that you would likely use to keep abreast of current information affecting your investments.

8. **Potential Rate of Return.** Do you think anyone really calculates the potential rate of return on a particular investment? Should they? If so, offer a reason why.

9. **Invest Using Credit.** Buying on margin and selling short both involve using credit. Would you invest this way? Give two reasons why or why not.

10. **Interest in Bonds.** Do bonds interest you as an investment? Why or why not?

DO THE MATH

1. **Numerical Measures.** A stock sells at $15 per share.

   (a) What is the EPS for the company if it has a P/E ratio of 20?

   (b) If the company's dividend yield is 3 percent, what is its dividend per share?

   (c) What is the book value of the company if the price-to-book ratio is 1.5 and it has 100,000 shares of stock outstanding?

   DO IT IN CLASS
   PAGE 418

2. **Bond Selling Price.** What is the market price of a $1000, 8 percent bond if comparable market interest rates drop to 6 percent and the bond matures in 15 years?

3. **Market Price.** What is the market price of a $1000, 8 percent bond if comparable market interest rates rise to 10 percent and the bond matures in 14 years?

4. **Equivalent Taxable Yield.** For a municipal bond paying 3.4 percent for a taxpayer in the 25 percent tax bracket, what is the equivalent taxable yield? (Hint: See page 129.)

   DO IT IN CLASS
   PAGE 131

5. **Equivalent Taxable Yield.** For a municipal bond paying 3.7 percent for a taxpayer in the 33 percent tax bracket, what is the equivalent taxable yield? (Hint: See page 129.)

6. **Yield, Price, and YTM.** A corporate bond maturing in 15 years with a coupon rate of 9.9 percent was purchased for $980.

   (a) What is its current yield?

   (b) What will be its selling price in two years if comparable market interest rates drop 1.9 percentage points?

   (c) Calculate the bond's YTM using Equation (14.6) or the *Garman/Forgue* companion website.

7. **Yield, Price, and YTM.** A corporate bond maturing in 20 years with a coupon rate of 8.2 percent was purchased for $1100.

   DO IT IN CLASS
   PAGE 441

   (a) What is its current yield?

   (b) What will the bond's selling price be if comparable market interest rates rise 1.8 percentage points in two years?

   (c) Calculate the bond's YTM using Equation (14.6) or the *Garman/Forgue* companion website.

8. **Beta Calculations.** Michael Margolis is a single parent and motivational training consultant from Reno, Arizona. He is wondering about potential returns on investments given certain amounts of risk. Michael invested a total of $6000 in three stocks ($2000 in each) with different betas: stock A with a beta of 0.8, stock B with a beta of 1.7, and stock C with a beta of 2.5.

   DO IT IN CLASS
   PAGE 442

   (a) If the stock market rises 7 percent over the next year, what will be the likely value of each investment?

   (b) If the stock market declines 8 percent over the next year, what will be the likely value of each of Michael's investments?

9. **Investment Calculations.** Xiao and Shiao Jing-jian, newly weds from Rockville, Maryland, have decided to begin investing for the future. Xiao is a 7-Eleven store manager, and Shiao is a high-school math teacher. The couple intends to take $3000 out of their savings for investment purposes and then continue to invest an additional $200 to $400 per month. Both have a moderate investment philosophy and seek some cash dividends as well as price appreciation.

   Calculate the five-year return on the investment choices in the table below. Put your calculations in tabular form like that shown in Table 14-2. (Hint: When making your calculations you should

assume at the end of the first year. At the end of the first year the EPS for Running Paws will be $2.40 with a dividend of $0.66, and the EPS for Eagle Packaging will be $2.76 with a projected dividend of $0.86.)

   (a) Using the appropriate P/E ratios, what are the estimated market prices of the Running Paws and Eagle Packaging stocks after five years?

   (b) Show your calculations in determining the projected price appreciations for the two stocks over the five years.

   (c) Add the projected price appreciation of each stock to its projected cash dividends, and show the total five-year percentage returns for the two stocks.

   (d) Determine the average annual dividend for each stock, and use these figures in calculating the approximate compound yields for each.

   (e) Assume that the beta is 2.5 for Running Paws and 2.8 for Eagle Packaging. If the market went up 20 percent during the year, what would be the likely stock prices for Running Paws and Eagle Packaging?

   (f) Assume that inflation is approximately 4 percent and the return on high-quality, long-term corporate bonds is 8 percent. Given the Jing-jians' investment philosophy, explain why you would recommend (1) Running Paws, (2) Eagle Packaging, or (3) a high-quality, long-term corporate bond as a growth investment. Support your answer by calculating the potential rate of return using the information on pages 421–424 to ; or by using the *Garman/Forgue* website. The Jing-jians are in the 25 percent marginal tax bracket.

	Running Paws	Eagle Packaging
Current price	$30.00	$48.00
Current earnings per share (EPS)	$ 2.00	$ 2.30
Current quarterly cash dividend	$ 0.15	$ 0.18
Current P/E ratio	15	21
Projected earnings annual growth rate	20%	20%
Projected cash dividend growth rate	10%	10%

FINANCIAL PLANNING CASES

CASE 1

The Johnsons Want Greater Yields on Investments

The investments of Harry and Belinda have done well through the years. While the cash portion of their portfolio has risen to $16,000, it is earning a minuscule 1 percent in a money market account; thus they are seeking greater yields with bond investments.

Examine the following table, which identifies eight investment alternatives, and then respond to the questions that follow. The coupon rates vary because the issue dates range widely, and market prices are above par because older bonds paid higher interest than today's issues.

Name of Issue	Bond Denomination	Coupon Rate Percent	Years Until Maturity	Moody's Rating	Market Price	Current Yield	YTM
Corporate ABC	$1000	5.4	4	Aa	$1400		
Corporate DEF	1000	5.5	20	Aa	1550		
Corporate GHI	1000	5.9	12	Baa	1250		
Corporate JKL	1000	4.8	5	Aaa	1500		
Corporate MNO	1000	4.1	15	B	1260		
Corporate PQR	1000	5.3	11	B	1200		
Treasury note	1000	2.2	3	—	1600		
Municipal bond	1000	2.1	20	Aa	1200		

(a) What is the current yield of each investment alternative? Use Equation (14.5) or visit the *Garman/Forgue* companion website. (Write your responses in the proper column in the table.)

(b) What is the yield to maturity for each investment alternative? (Write your responses in the proper column in the table.) You may calculate the YTMs by using Equation (14.6) or by visiting the *Garman/Forgue* companion website.

(c) Knowing that the Johnsons follow a moderate investment philosophy, which one of the six corporate bonds would you recommend? Why?

(d) Given that the Johnsons are in the 25 percent federal marginal tax rate, what is the equivalent taxable yield for the municipal bond choice? Should they invest in your recommendation in part (c) or in the municipal bond? Why? You may calculate the equivalent taxable yield using the information on page 129.

(e) Which three of the eight alternatives would you recommend as a group so that the Johnsons would have some diversification protection for their $16,000? Why do you suggest that combination?

CASE 2

Victor and Maria Hernandez Wonder About Investing

Victor and Maria have decided to increase their contribution to their investment portfolio since Victor is now age 59 and

thinking about retiring in five years. For years, they have followed a moderate-risk investment philosophy and put their money in suitable stocks, bonds, and mutual funds. The value of their portfolio is now $320,000, and this is in addition to their paid-for rental property, which is worth $200,000. They plan to invest about $9000 every year for the next five years.

(a) Why should Victor and Maria consider buying common stock as an investment with the additional money?

(b) If Victor and Maria bought a stock with a market price of $50 and a beta value of 1.8, what would be the likely price of an $8000 investment after one year if the general market for stocks rose 6 percent?

(c) What would the same investment be worth if the general market for stocks dropped 8 percent?

(d) Review the types of stocks in Table 14-1 on page 417 and select 2 that you think Victor and Maria might prefer as investments. Explain why.

(e) Discuss the positives and negatives of preferred stock for Victor or Maria.

DO IT IN CLASS
PAGES 413
AND 416

CASE 3

Julia Price Seeks Rewards in the Bond Market

Julia's investments survived the Great Recession–related bear stock market declines because she was well diversified and was investing more heavily in bonds in the years preceding the decline. When it seemed like the coming recession was starting to look like a reality, Julia cashed out of some equities and moved most of that money into corporate bonds and Treasuries. As a result, over the past four years, the bond portion of her portfolio rose over 20 percent due to low inflation and declining interest rates, which pushed up the value of her bonds. Now she thinks inflation and bond prices will rise so she is selling all her bonds and investing the proceeds into equities. But the stock market prices seem too high already, so she is hesitating. Offer your opinions about her thinking.

CASE 4

An Aggressive Investor Seeks Rewards in the Bond Market

Jessica Varcoe works as a drug manufacturer's representative based in Murfreesboro, Tennessee. She has an aggressive investment philosophy and believes that interest rates will drop over the next year or two because of an expected economic slowdown. Jessica, who is in the 25 percent marginal tax rate, wants to profit in the bond market by buying and selling during the next several months. She has asked your advice on how to invest her $15,000.

(a) If Jessica buys corporate or municipal bonds, what rating should her selections have? Why?

(b) Jessica has a choice between two $1000 bonds: a corporate bond with a coupon rate of 5.1 percent and a municipal bond with a coupon rate of 3.2 percent. Which bond provides the better after-tax return? (Hint: See Equation [4.1] on page 129.)

(c) If Jessica buys fifteen, 30-year, $1000 corporate bonds with a 5.1 percent coupon rate for $960 each, what is her current yield? (Hint: Use Equation [4.1].)

(d) If market interest rates for comparable corporate bonds drop 1 percent over the next 12 months (from 5.1 percent to 4.1 percent), what will be the approximate selling price of Jessica's corporate bonds in (c)? (Hint: Use the *Garman/Forgue* companion website.)

(e) Assuming market interest rates drop 1 percent in 12 months, how much is Jessica's capital gain on the $15,000 investment if she sells? How much was her current return for the two semiannual interest payments? How much was her total return, both in dollars and as an annual yield? (Ignore transaction costs.)

(f) If Jessica is wrong in her projections and interest rates go up 1 percent over the year, what would be the probable selling price of her corporate bonds? (Hint: Use the *Garman/Forgue* companion website.) Explain why you would advise her to sell or not to sell.

CASE 5

Two Brothers' Attitudes Toward Investments

Kyle Broflovski, a guidance counselor in South Park, Colorado, has purchased several corporate and government bonds over the years, and his total bond investment now exceeds $40,000. He prefers investments with some inflation protection. His kid brother Ike, a highly paid physician, has more than $150,000 invested in various blue-chip income stocks in a variety of industries.

(a) Justify Kyle's attitude toward bond investments.

(b) Justify Ike's attitude toward stock investments.

Explain why both brothers might be happy investing some of their money in TIPS bonds.

CASE 6

A College Student Ponders Investing in the Stock Market

Ji Wu of Jefferson City, Tennessee, has $5000 that he wants to invest in the stock market. Ji is in college on a scholarship and does not plan to use the $5000 or any dividend income for another five years, when he plans to buy a home. He is currently considering a small company stock selling for $25 per share with an EPS of $1.25. Last year, the company earned $900,000, of which $250,000 was paid out in dividends.

(a) What classification of common stock would you recommend to Ji? Why?

(b) Calculate the P/E ratio and the dividend payout ratio for this stock. Given this information and your recommendation, would this stock be an appropriate purchase for Ji? Why or why not?

(c) Identify the components of the total return Ji might expect, and estimate how much he might expect annually from each component.

(d) Review the section titled "You Should Use Corporate Earnings and Other Measures" on pages 418–420 and select two that you think Ji would utilize to evaluate when investing in stocks. Explain why.

BE YOUR OWN PERSONAL FINANCIAL MANAGER

1. **Your Stock Preferences.** Complete Worksheet 54: My Preferences Among Stocks from "My Personal Financial Planner" by identifying, for each of the seven types of stock, **MY PERSONAL FINANCIAL PLANNER** those that are of interest to you, what you do or do not like about them, and those in which you might invest during your own investing life.

2. **Compare Different Stocks as Investments.** Learn about the stocks of three publically traded companies of interest to you, perhaps General Motors, Ford Motor Company, and **MY PERSONAL FINANCIAL PLANNER** Google, by visiting the website for Kiplinger at www.kiplinger.com. Then complete Worksheet 55: Comparing Stocks as Investments from "My Personal Financial Planner" by recording for each company each of the several performance variables.

3. **Preference Among Types of Bond.** Complete Worksheet 56: My Preference Among Bonds from "My Personal Financial Planner" by marking for each of the nine types one **MY PERSONAL FINANCIAL PLANNER** characteristic you do or do not like about each and which might be of interest to you as an investor.

4. **Taxable Versus Tax-Free Income.** Complete Worksheet 57: Comparing Taxable and Tax-Free Income from "My Personal Financial Planner" by inserting a realistic rate of investment **MY PERSONAL FINANCIAL PLANNER** return and tax rate and then performing the appropriate calculations.

5. **Current Yield on a Bond.** Complete Worksheet 58: The Current Yield on My Bond Investment from "My Personal Financial Planner" by inserting realistic different **MY PERSONAL FINANCIAL PLANNER** current market prices on two existing bonds (perhaps $980 and $910) and different annual interest payments (perhaps $70 and $80) for two bonds and calculating the current yields.

6. **Current Value of a Bond.** Complete Worksheet 59: The Current Value on My Bond Investment from "My Personal Financial Planner" by going online to find the current **MY PERSONAL FINANCIAL PLANNER** market prices of two existing bonds, perhaps individual issues of General Motors and Ford Motor Company, and then inserting the following information in the places provided: annual interest payment and years to maturity. Look online elsewhere for a current market interest rate on comparable securities, or perhaps use 7%, and complete the calculations required.

7. **Yield to Maturity on a Bond.** Complete Worksheet 60: The Yield to Maturity on My Bond from "My Personal Financial Planner" by going online to find the following information **MY PERSONAL FINANCIAL PLANNER** about two bonds: current market price, face value, number of years until maturity, and annual interest in dollars.

ON THE NET

Go to the Web pages indicated to complete these exercises.

1. **Latest Financial Information.** Go to Kiplinger.com and determine the top three news items that you think are related to personal investing. Note how you can use that information in making a good investment decision.

2. **Stock Quotes.** Visit the website for Kiplinger at www.kiplinger.com, where you can find stock quotes for most publicly traded companies. Type in the symbols for the following companies: Coca-Cola (KO), Google (GOOG), Microsoft (MSFT), and Disney (DIS). Evaluate these four firms on the basis of EPS, dividend yield, and P/E ratio. What do these data suggest to you about the relative attractiveness of these companies for investors?

3. **Stock Screener.** Visit the website for Yahoo! Finance, where you can find a stock-screener utility at www.screener.finance.yahoo.com/stocks.html. Search among the S&P 500 stocks for companies with a $50 minimum share price. How many companies meet this criterion? Select again using a P/E ratio from 0 to 20. How many companies meet this new criterion? Why is this list longer? Do you recognize any of the companies on either list?

4. **Recent Treasury Prices.** Visit the website for the U.S. Treasury Department at www.treasurydirect.gov and enter its Institutional section, where you will find the results of recent auctions for Treasury notes and bonds. What do the results of the auctions over the past year tell you about market expectations for movement of interest rates in the future? (Hint: Compare auction rates for bonds and notes with similar maturity periods.)

5. **Find Bond Ratings.** Visit the Standard and Poor's website at www.standardandpoors.com and look up the current bond ratings for General Motors and Ford Motor Company. Summarize your findings.

6. **Bond Calculator.** Go to Investopedia's Bond Calculator to input illustrative pricing data on bonds (www .investopedia.com/calculator/BondPrice.aspx). Write what you think of this tool.

7. **Beta Values.** Go to Calculator Edge (www.calculatoredge .com/finance/betas.htm) and input basic information on any stock to calculate its beta. Use 2 percent or a lower figure as the risk-free interest rate.

ACTION INVOLVEMENT PROJECTS

1. **Answer Seven Questions.** Review the box "Did You Know? Seven Questions Every Investor Needs to Answer" on page 424 and write down your responses to each question.

DO IT IN CLASS
PAGE 424

2. **Latest Stock Market Values.** Using a resource like *The Wall Street Journal* or the Internet in general, find the latest values for the following market indexes and indicate how each has performed over the past 12 months: DJIA, S&P 500, NASDAQ Composite, and Dow Jones Wilshire 5000 Index.

3. **Prices of Popular Stocks.** Find the latest values for the following stocks and indicate how each has performed over the past 12 months: American Express, AT&T, Caterpillar, Coca-Cola, Dell, Merck, Walmart, and Walt Disney.

4. **Characteristics of Bonds.** Review the section "Unique Characteristics of Bonds" on pages 443, select 2 that would be critically important to you as a bond investor. Explain why.

Visit the Garman/Forgue companion website at www.cengagebrain.com.

15

Investing through Mutual Funds

YOU MUST BE KIDDING, RIGHT?

Twins Huan-yue and and Hao Wang invest in mutual funds. Huan-yue majored in English in college. For more than 20 years, she invested in managed funds, counting on professional financial advisers to select the winning companies more often than not. Hao majored in Finance; he invested in unmanaged index mutual funds that achieve the same return as a particular market index by buying and holding all or a representative selection of securities in the index. After 20 years of investing, what are the odds that Huan-yue's investment portfolio balance will be better than Hao's?

A. zero   **C.** 20%

B. 10%   **D.** 30%

The answer is A. Managed mutual funds generally do not earn returns for investors that exceed the overall market indexes. The fact is the average mutual fund manager earns a lower return at least 90 percent of the time over 5-year time periods. Finding a mutual fund investment manager who can consistently beat the market is very challenging!

LEARNING OBJECTIVES

After reading this chapter, you should be able to:

1. Describe the features, advantages, and unique services of investing through mutual funds.

2. Differentiate mutual funds by investment objectives.

3. Summarize the fees and charges involved in buying and selling mutual funds.

4. Establish strategies to evaluate and select mutual funds that meet your investment goals.

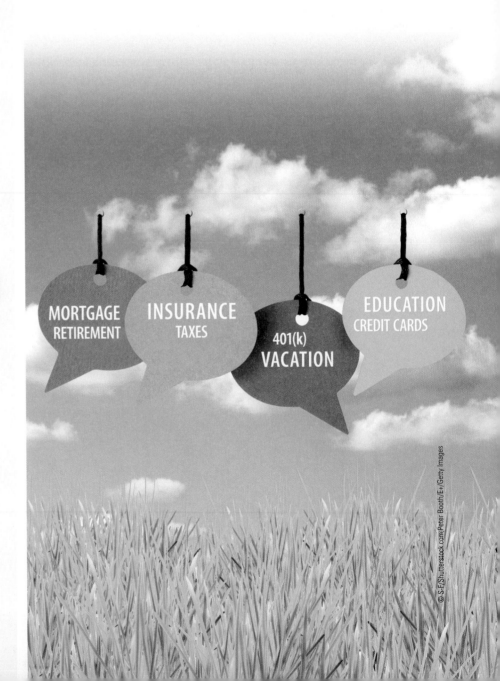

MORTGAGE
RETIREMENT

INSURANCE
TAXES

401(k)
VACATION

EDUCATION
CREDIT CARDS

© S-E;/Shutterstock.com/Peter Booth/E+/Getty Images

WHAT DO YOU RECOMMEND?

Tyler and Samantha Gent, a couple in their early 30s, have a 2-year-old child and enjoy living in a moderately priced downtown apartment. Tyler, a library director, earns $60,000 annually. Samantha earns $69,000 as a merchandise buyer for a specialty store. They are big savers: Together they have been putting $1000 to $2000 per month into CDs, and the couple now has a portfolio worth $120,000 paying about 2 percent annually. The Gents are conservative investors and want to retire in about 20 years.

What do you recommend to Tyler and Samantha on the subject of investing through mutual funds regarding:

1. Redeeming their CDs and investing their retirement money in mutual funds?

2. Investing in growth and income mutual funds instead of income funds?

3. Buying no-load rather than load funds?

4. Buying mutual funds through their employers' 401(k) retirement accounts rather than saving through a taxable account as they have been doing?

YOUR NEXT FIVE YEARS

In the next five years, you can start achieving financial success by doing the following related to investing through mutual funds:

1. *Match your investment philosophy and financial goals to a mutual fund's objectives.*

2. *Save regularly, pick an asset mix of mutual funds that matches your goals, and keep investment costs low by avoiding 12b-1 fees and high management fees.*

3. *Use your criteria to screen mutual fund investments using free online software.*

4. *Invest regularly in mutual funds through your employer's retirement plan.*

5. *Sign up for automatic reinvestment of your mutual fund dividends.*

LEARNING OBJECTIVE 1

Describe the features, advantages, and unique services of investing through mutual funds.

Most investors prefer to avoid buying individual stocks and bonds because of the high financial risk associated with owning too few investments like two or three stocks or bonds. The average investor usually cannot accumulate a portfolio diversified enough to minimize the risk linked to the failure of a one or two holdings. They often also lack both the ability and the time required to research individual securities and manage such a portfolio. In an effort to avoid these problems, many people invest *in* the stock and bond markets *through* mutual funds, which typically buy hundreds of different stocks and bonds. Mutual funds make it easy and convenient for investors to open an account and continue investing throughout their lives. Half of all households invest through mutual funds.

15.1 WHY SHOULD YOU INVEST IN MUTUAL FUNDS?

A **mutual fund** is an investment company that pools funds obtained by selling shares to investors and makes investments to achieve the financial goal of income or growth, or both. Mutual funds invest in a diversified portfolio of stocks, bonds, short-term money market instruments, and other securities or assets.

The fund might own common stock and bonds in such companies as AT&T, IBM, Google, or Running Paws Cat Food Company (our fictional example from Chapter 14). The combined holdings are known as a **portfolio**, as we noted in Chapter 13 and as shown graphically in Figure 15-1. The mutual fund company owns the investments it makes and the mutual fund investors own the mutual fund company. Unlike corporate shareholders, holders of mutual funds have no say in running the company, although they have equity interest in the pool of assets and a residual claim on the profits.

15.1a The Net Asset Value Is the Price You Pay for a Mutual Fund Share

One measure of the investor's claim on assets is the net asset value. The **net asset value (NAV)** is the price one pays (excluding any transaction costs) to buy a share of a mutual fund. It is the per-share net worth of the mutual fund. It is calculated by summing

Figure 15-1 **How a Mutual Fund Works**

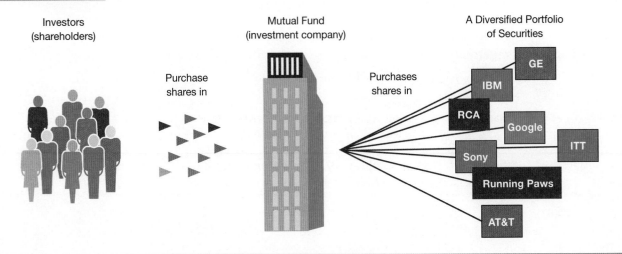

the values of all the securities in the fund's portfolio, subtracting liabilities, and then dividing by the total number of shares outstanding.

$$\text{Net asset value} = \frac{\text{market value of assets} - \text{market value of liabilities}}{\text{number of shares}} \quad \text{(15.1)}$$

For example, a mutual fund has 10 million shares outstanding and a portfolio worth $100 million, and its liabilities are $5 million. The net asset value of a single share is

$$\text{Net asset value} = \frac{\$100,000,000 - \$5,000,000}{10,000,000} = \frac{\$95,000,000}{10,000,000} = \$9.50 \text{ per share}$$

The NAV rises or falls to reflect changes in the market value of the investments held by the mutual fund company. This value is calculated daily after the U.S. stock exchanges close, and a new NAV is posted in the financial media. If the stocks and bonds held in a mutual fund increase in value, the NAV will rise. For example, if a mutual fund owns IBM and General Electric common stocks and the prices of those stocks increase, the increased value of the underlying securities is reflected in the NAV of fund shares. This is price appreciation. Some time later when investors sell shares at a net asset value higher than that paid when they purchased the shares (after transaction costs), they will have a capital gain.

The type of mutual fund that is the focus in this chapter is an **open-end mutual fund**. Accounting for more than 90 percent of all funds, open-end mutual funds issue redeemable shares that investors purchase directly from the fund (or through a broker for the fund). They are always ready to sell new shares of ownership and to buy back previously sold shares at the fund's current NAV. Open-end mutual funds, numbering more than 13,000, total more than the stocks listed on the New York Stock Exchange (approximately 2800). Table 15-1 lists advantages of investing through mutual funds.

15.1b Dividend Income and Capital Gains Distributions Result from the Mutual Fund's Earnings

A **mutual fund dividend** is income paid to investors out of profits that the mutual fund has earned from its investments. The dividend represents both ordinary income dividend distributions and capital gains distributions. **Ordinary income dividend distributions**

Table 15-1	Advantages of Investing Through Mutual Funds
Diversification	Many investors find it easier to achieve diversification through ownership of mutual funds that own hundreds of stocks and bonds rather than picking and then owning individual stocks and bonds.
Affordability	Individuals can invest in mutual funds with relatively low dollar amounts for initial purchases, such as $250 or $1000. Subsequent purchases can be as little as $50.
Professional Management	The fund's investment advisers have access to excellent research, and they select, buy, sell, and monitor the performance of the securities purchased; they oversee the portfolio.
Liquidity	You can very easily convert mutual fund shares into cash without loss of value because the investor sells (or **redeems**) the shares back to the investment company by using a telephone, wire, fax, mail, or online.
Low Transaction Costs	Because mutual funds trade in large quantities of shares, they pay far less in brokerage commissions than stock investors. Shares bought and sold are at the NAV plus any fees and charges that the fund imposes, and these are often quite low.
Uncomplicated Investment Choices	Selecting a mutual fund is easier than selecting specific stocks or bonds because mutual funds state their investment objectives, allowing investors to select funds that almost perfectly match their own objectives.

mutual fund
Investment company that pools funds by selling shares to investors and makes diversified investments to achieve financial goals of income or growth, or both.

net asset value (NAV)
Per-share value of a mutual fund.

open-end mutual fund
Investment that issues redeemable shares that investors purchase directly from the fund (or through a broker for the fund).

mutual fund dividend
Income paid to investors out of profits earned by the mutual fund from its investments.

ordinary income dividend distributions
Distributions that occur when the fund pays out dividends from the stock and interest from the bonds it hold in its portfolio; these are passed onto the investor quarterly.

DO IT IN CLASS

redeems
When an investor sells mutual fund shares.

capital gains distributions

Distributions representing the net gains (capital gains minus capital losses) that a fund realizes when it sells securities that were held in the fund's portfolio.

occur when the fund pays out dividends from the stock and interest from the bonds it hold in its portfolio. These are passed onto the investor quarterly. **Capital gains distributions** represent the net gains (capital gains minus capital losses) that a fund realizes when it sells securities that were held in the fund's portfolio. Mutual funds distribute capital gains once a year, even though the gains occur throughout the year whenever securities are sold at a profit. When a fund pays out these distributions, the NAV drops by the amount paid.

15.1c   Capital Gains Can Result When You Sell Mutual Fund Shares

When you sell your shares in the mutual fund, you receive the NAV of the share at its current market price. If the price is higher than the price you originally paid, you have a capital gain due to the increase in the NAV although your gain is reduced by transaction costs.

Reinvesting income greatly compounds share ownership. Figure 15-2 illustrates the positive results obtained by reinvesting dividends.

15.1d   Unique Mutual Fund Services

mutual fund family

Investment management company that offers a number of different funds to the investing public, each with its own investment objectives or philosophies of investing.

A **mutual fund family** is an investment management company that offers a large number of different mutual funds to the investing public, each with its own investment objectives. There are more than 400 mutual fund families (see biz.yahoo.com/p/fam/a-b.html).

Mutual funds, as shown in Table 15-2, offer a number of valuable services that are unique to this type of investment and that are helpful and appealing to investors. More than 40 percent of the total return of the S&P 500 over the past 80 years has come from reinvested dividends. Enrolling in an automatic reinvestment program is a smart and easy way of accumulating wealth over time.

Figure 15-2   The Wisdom of Automatic Dividend Reinvestment

The initial $10,000 investment in S&P 500 Index Fund grew to $58,000 over 20 years, instead of $40,000, because of the reinvestment of dividends.

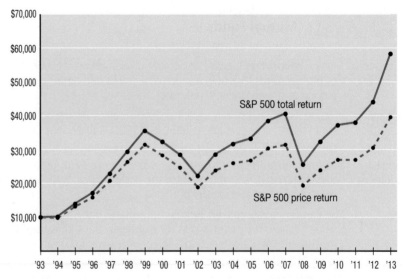

Source: The S&P 500 index is proprietary to and is calculated, distributed and marketed by S&P Opco, LLC (a subsidiary of S&P Dow Jones Indices LLC), its affiliates and/or its licensors and has been licensed for use. S&P® and S&P 500®, among other famous marks, are registered trademarks of Standard & Poor's Financial Services LLC, and Dow Jones® is a registered trademark of Dow Jones Trademark Holdings LLC. © 2013 S&P Dow Jones Indices LLC, its affiliates and/or its licensors. All rights reserved.

Table 15-2   Unique Mutual Fund Services

Convenience	Funds make it easy to open an account and invest in and sell shares. Fund prices are widely quoted. Services include toll-free telephone numbers, detailed records of transactions, checking and savings alternatives, and the paperwork and record keeping, including accounting for fractional shares.
Ease of Buying and Selling Shares	Opening an account with a mutual fund company is as simple as opening a checking account. After making your initial investment, you can easily buy more shares. Shares can be bought or sold at any time. Each is redeemed at the closing price—the NAV—at the end of the trading day.
Check Writing and Electronic Transfers	Mutual funds often offer interest-earning, check-writing money market mutual funds in which investors can accumulate cash, accept dividends, or hold their money. Investors can electronically transfer funds to and from mutual funds and banks.
Automatic Reinvestment of Income and Capital Gains	Mutual funds allow investors to choose to receive current income payments or have them automatically reinvested to purchase additional fund shares (often without paying any commissions). This is **automatic reinvestment**, as illustrated in Figure 15-2.
Exchange Privileges	An **exchange privilege** permits mutual fund shareholders to easily swap shares on a dollar-for-dollar basis for shares in another mutual fund managed by the same mutual fund family, usually at no cost.
Automatic Investment Program (AIP)	Funds often allow investors to make periodic monthly or quarterly payments using money automatically transferred from their bank accounts or paychecks to the mutual fund company. You can invest as little as $25 monthly or quarterly.
Effortless Establishment of Retirement Plans	An employee can fill out a one-page form that directs his or her employer to transfer a specified dollar amount from every paycheck to a mutual fund to buy shares for a 401(k) plan. Similarly, individuals can fill out a one-page form to buy shares for their individual retirement accounts.
Beneficiary Designation	A **beneficiary designation** enables the shareholder to name one or more beneficiaries so that the proceeds go to them without going through probate.
Withdrawal Options	Mutual funds offer **withdrawal options** (also called **systematic withdrawal plans**) to shareholders who want to receive income on a regular basis from their mutual fund investments. The minimum withdrawal amount is $50 at regular intervals. You may make regular withdrawals by (1) taking a set dollar amount each month, (2) cashing in a set number of shares each month, (3) taking the current income as cash, or (4) taking a portion of the asset growth.

automatic reinvestment
Investor's option to choose to automatically reinvest any interest, dividends, and capital gains payments to purchase additional fund shares.

exchange privilege
Allowance for mutual fund shareholders to easily swap shares on a dollar-for-dollar basis for shares in another mutual fund within a mutual fund family. Also called switching, conversion, or transfer privilege.

beneficiary designation
Allowance of fund holder to name one or more beneficiaries so that the proceeds bypass probate proceedings if the original shareholder dies.

withdrawal options (systematic withdrawal plans)
Arrangements with a mutual fund company for shareholders who want to receive income on a regular basis from their mutual fund investments.

DID YOU KNOW

Types of Investment Companies

The federal Investment Company Act distinguishes among investment companies. Open-end mutual funds are by far the most widely owned investment companies. Four other types exist:

1. **Closed-end mutual funds. Closed-end mutual funds** issue a limited and fixed number of shares at inception and do not buy them back. These companies operate with a fixed amount of capital. Closed-end shares are bought and sold on a stock exchange or in the over-the-counter market. After the original issue is sold, the price of a share depends primarily on the supply and demand in the market rather than the performance of the investment company assets. Closed-end shares of about 600 companies are actively traded like common stocks and bonds, primarily on the New York Stock Exchange.

2. **Real estate investment trusts.** A special kind of closed-end investment company is a **real estate investment trust (REIT)**. REITs invest in a portfolio of assets as defined in the trust agreement, such as properties, like office buildings and shopping centers (called an equity REIT), or mortgages (a mortgage REIT). Hybrid REITs invest in both. REITs have no predetermined life span. There are about 160 REITs traded on the New York Stock Exchange.

3. **Unit investment trusts.** A **unit investment trust (UIT)** is a closed-end investment company that makes a one-time public offering of only a specific, fixed number of units. A UIT buys and holds an unmanaged fixed portfolio of fixed-maturity securities, such as municipal bonds, for a period of time. This could be a few months or perhaps 50 years. Each unit represents a proportionate ownership interest in the specific portfolio of perhaps 10 to 50 securities. Sold by brokers for perhaps $250 to $1000 a unit, there is no trading of these securities, although brokers may repurchase and resell them. There are about 5800 UITs.

4. **Exchange-traded funds.** An **exchange-traded fund (ETF)** is a basket of passively managed securities structured like an index fund as it owns all or a representative set of securities that duplicate the performance of a market segment or index. In effect, ETFs ditch the fund manager and pass the savings on to the investor. There are ETFs for the S&P 500, called Spiders; the Dow Jones Industrial Average, called Diamonds; and Qubes based on the NASDAQ 100. There are about 1200 ETFs, and their prices are set by market forces since they are listed on securities markets (primarily on the American Stock Exchange) and traded throughout the day. ETFs give investors an easy way to track an index without buying an index fund. ETFs are available for nearly every index, from large U.S. companies to health care and foreign bonds.

CONCEPT CHECK 15.1

1. Explain how net asset value is calculated and how it is used by mutual funds.

2. List five advantages of investing in mutual funds.

3. Name five services that are unique to mutual funds.

15.2 MUTUAL FUND OBJECTIVES

LEARNING OBJECTIVE 2

Differentiate mutual funds by investment objectives.

index mutual funds (or index funds)

are those funds whose investment objective is to achieve the same return as a particular market index by buying and holding all or a representative selection of securities in it.

Most mutual funds are **managed funds**, meaning that professional managers are constantly evaluating and choosing securities using a specific investment approach. On a daily basis, active managers select the stocks and bonds in which to invest and sell them when they deem appropriate. The managers earn a fee often up to 2 percent, for their services, and ultimately their choices are responsible for the performance of the fund.

These also are **index mutual funds** (or **index funds**) whose investment objective is to achieve the same return as a particular market index by buying and holding all or a representative selection of securities in it. Index funds are called **unmanaged funds** because their managers do not evaluate or select individual securities. An S&P 500 index fund would effectively mirror the companies in the index, which are primarily large-cap U.S. stocks. Annual management fees are extremely low, perhaps only 0.07 to 0.30 percent.

DID YOU KNOW

Money Websites on Mutual Funds

Informative websites for investing through mutual funds, including online screens to compare funds are:

Business Week Online on funds (www.businessweek.com/markets-and-finance/mutual-funds-and-etfs)

CNNMoney.com on funds (money.cnn.com/pf/funds/index.html)

Kiplinger's Personal Finance (www.kiplinger.com/fronts/special-report/mutual-funds/index.html)

Kiplinger's model portfolio (www.kiplinger.com/article/investing/T033-C009-S001-kiplinger-25-model-portfolios.html)

MarketWatch (www.marketwatch.com/investing/mutual-funds?link=MW_Nav_INV)

Motley Fool (www.foolfunds.com)

Vanguard (www.vanguard.com)

Wikipedia (en.wikipedia.org/wiki/Mutual_fund)

Yahoo! Finance (finance.yahoo.com/funds)

Yahoo! Finance's fund screener (screener.finance.yahoo.com/funds.html)

Before investing in any specific mutual fund, you need to decide whether the fund's investment objectives are a good fit for your own investment philosophy and financial goals. The SEC requires funds to disclose their investment objective. Mutual funds may be classified in one of three categories: (1) income, (2) growth, and (3) growth and income. Each type has different features, risks, and reward characteristics, and the name of a fund gives a clue to its objectives.

15.2a Income Objective

A mutual fund with an **income objective**, such as money market and bond funds, invests in securities that pay regular income in dividends or interest.

Money Market Funds Mutual fund companies and brokerage firms offer **money market funds (MMFs)**. They invest in highly liquid, relatively safe securities with very short maturities (always less than one year), such as CDs, Treasury bills, and commercial paper (i.e., short-term obligations issued by corporations). To enhance liquidity, regulations require that MMFs keep 10 percent of their assets in cash or investments that can be converted easily to cash within one day. You can write checks or use an ATM card to access a money market fund account. Issuers keep the NAV (the price of each share of the fund) at $1.

Money market funds (and there are about 580 of them) pay a higher rate of return than accounts offered through banks and credit unions. They are considered extremely safe. **Tax-exempt money market funds** limit their investments to tax-exempt municipal securities with maturities of less than 60 days, and their earnings are tax free to investors. **Government securities money market funds** appeal to investors' concerns about safety by investing solely in Treasury bills and other short-term securities backed by the U.S. government.

Bond Funds **Bond funds** (also called **fixed-income funds**) aim to not incur undue risk while earning current income higher than a money market fund by investing in a portfolio of bonds and other investments, such as preferred stocks and common stocks that pay high dividends. They also earn some capital gains because bond fund prices fluctuate with changing interest rates. Today's nearly 2000 bond funds are categorized by what they own and the maturities of their portfolio holdings.

- **Short-term corporate bond funds** invest in securities maturing in one to five years.

- **Short-term U.S. government bond funds** invest in Treasury issues maturing in one to five years.

money market funds
are those that invest in highly liquid, relatively safe securities with very short securities, always less than one year.

tax-exempt money market funds
Funds that limit their investments to tax-exempt municipal securities with maturities of 60 days or less.

bond funds (fixed-income funds)
Fixed-income funds that aim to earn current income higher than a money market fund without incurring undue risk by investing in a portfolio of bonds and other low-risk investments that pay high dividends and offer capital appreciation.

- **Intermediate corporate bond funds** invest in investment-grade corporate securities with five- to ten-year maturities.
- **Intermediate government bond funds** invest in Treasuries with five- to ten-year maturities.
- **Long-term corporate bond funds** specialize in investment-grade securities maturing in 10 to 30 years.
- **Long-term U.S. government bond funds** invest in Treasury and zero-coupon bonds with maturities of ten years or longer.
- **Mortgage-backed funds** invest in mortgage-backed securities issued by agencies of the U.S. government, such as Fannie Mae (Federal National Mortgage Association) and Freddie Mac (Federal Home Loan Mortgage Corporation).
- **Junk bond funds** invest in high-yield, high-risk corporate bonds.
- **Municipal bond (tax-exempt) funds** invest in municipal bonds that provide tax-free income. Both investment-grade and high-yield municipal bond funds exist.
- **Single-state municipal bond funds** invest in debt issues of only one state.
- **World bond funds** invest in debt securities offered by foreign corporations and governments.

aggressive growth funds (maximum capital gains funds)

Funds that invest in speculative stocks with volatile price swings, seeking the greatest long-term capital appreciation possible. Also known as maximum capital gains funds and capital appreciation funds.

growth funds

Funds that seek long-term capital appreciation by investing in common stocks of companies with higher-than-average revenue and earnings growth, often the larger and well-established firms.

growth and income funds

Funds that invest in companies that have a high likelihood of both dividend income and price appreciation; less risk-oriented than aggressive growth funds or growth funds.

value funds

Funds specializing in stocks that are fundamentally sound whose prices appear to be low (low P/E ratios) based on the logic that such stocks are currently out of favor and undervalued by the market.

15.2b Growth Objective

A mutual fund that has a **growth objective** seeks capital appreciation. It invests in the common stock of companies that have above average growth potential, firms that may not pay a regular dividend but have the potential for large capital gains. Growth funds carry a fair amount of risk exposure, and this is reflected in substantial price volatility. Growth funds are categorized by what they own and their investment goals.

Aggressive growth funds (also known as **maximum capital gains funds**) seek the greatest long-term capital appreciation. Also known as **capital appreciation funds**, they make investments in speculative stocks with volatile price swings. They may employ high-risk investment techniques, such as borrowing money for leverage, short selling, hedging, and options. Lots of buying and selling occurs to enhance returns.

Growth funds seek long-term capital appreciation by investing in the common stocks of companies with higher-than-average revenue and earnings growth, often the larger and well-established firms. Such companies (like Walmart, Microsoft, and Coca-Cola) tend to reinvest most of their earnings to facilitate future growth.

Growth and income funds invest in companies that have a high likelihood of both dividend income and price appreciation.

Value funds specialize in stocks that are fundamentally sound and whose prices appear to be low (low P/E ratios), based on the logic that such stocks are currently out of favor and undervalued by the market.

DID YOU KNOW

Bond Funds Drop in Value When Interest Rates Rise

Extremely low interest rates—like those during and following an economic recession—are eventually replaced by rising interest rates because subsequent economic growth eventually results in inflation. When inflation goes up, the value of a bond mutual fund decreases. For every 1 percentage point change in interest rates, the value of the bond fund changes by the amount of the duration of maturity. For example, if a bond fund has an average duration of seven years and interest rates rise 1 percentage point, the value of the bond fund will drop by 7 percent. Should today's interest rates rise 3 percent over the next few years, the net asset value of a bond mutual fund is likely to decline in value by 21 percent.

Large-cap funds invest in the stocks of companies with a market capitalization of more than $10 billion.

Midcap funds invest in the stocks of midsize companies with a market capitalization of $2 to $10 billion in size that are expected to grow rapidly.

Small-cap funds (or **small company growth funds**) invest in lesser-known companies with a market capitalization of $300 million to $2 billion in size that offer strong potential for growth.

Microcap funds invest in high-risk companies with a market capitalization of $50 to $300 million.

Sector funds concentrate their investment holdings in one or more industries that make up a targeted part of the economy that is expected to grow, perhaps very rapidly, such as energy, biotechnology, health care, and financial services.

Regional funds invest in securities listed on stock exchanges in a specific region of the world, such as the Pacific Rim, Australia, or Europe.

Precious metals and gold funds invest in securities associated with gold, silver, and other precious metals.

Global funds invest in growth stocks of companies listed on foreign exchanges as well as in the United States, usually multinational firms.

International funds invest only in foreign stocks throughout the world.

Emerging market funds seek out stocks in countries whose economies are small but growing. Fund prices are volatile because these countries tend to be less stable politically.

15.2c Growth and Income Objective

A mutual fund that has a combined **growth and income objective** seeks a balanced return made up of current income and capital gains. Such funds primarily invest in common stocks. They seek a return not as low as offered by funds with an income objective but not as high as that offered by funds with a growth objective. They invite less risk than growth funds. There are a variety of growth and income funds.

Growth and income funds invest in companies expected to show average or better growth and pay steady or rising dividends.

ADVICE FROM A PROFESSIONAL

Invest Only "Fun Money" Aggressively

Once the investor has his or her financial plan in place, taking on more risk is acceptable—but *only* within the limits of the individual's "fun money." **Fun money** is a sum of investment money that you can afford to lose without doing serious damage to your total portfolio. You might, for example, resolve to trade with a specific sum, such as $5000, or perhaps no more than 2 or 3 percent of your portfolio. Keep such fun money in a separate account from your long-term investments. Decide mentally that if and when the money is gone, it has been spent on an activity that you enjoyed trying, but accept that the money lost is lost forever. Avoid the temptation to "throw good money after bad" by investing more money in an effort to try to recover your losses.

Speculative investing is not much different from gambling. The biggest danger of fun-money investing is that you might be successful. Success can give you the confidence— albeit probably false confidence—that you are a great investor. While you might be the next billionaire investor like Warren Buffett, such success is likely to tempt you to aggressively invest even more of the assets in your total portfolio. That approach can result in disaster. As financial columnist Jane Bryant Quinn observes, "The money you really need for life is better off in broadly diversified mutual funds, where a mistake is not forever."

Robert O. Weagley
University of Missouri–Columbia

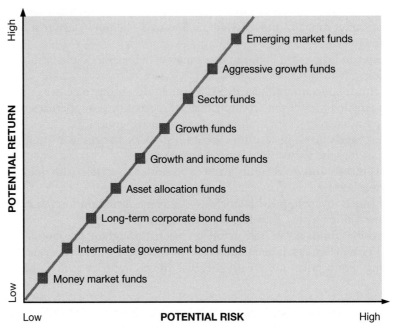

Figure 15-3   **Balancing Risk and Returns on Mutual Funds**

Note that increasing the potential for higher returns also increases the risk to the investor's capital.

Stable-value fund

Mutual fund that offers attractive returns and liquidity without market risk to defined contribution plan participants (and some 529 tuition savings plans) because they have contracts with banks and insurance companies designed to permit redemption of shares at book value regardless of market prices.

ADVICE FROM A PROFESSIONAL

Stable-Value Funds Are Available Only through Employers

Stable-value funds are only available through employer-sponsored retirement plans.

They offer attractive returns and liquidity without market risk to defined contribution plan participants (and some 529 tuition savings plans) because they have contracts with banks and insurance companies designed to permit redemption of shares at book value regardless of market prices. Over the past ten years, stable-value funds returned 3.0 to 5.0 percent annually. GIC funds increased in value during the worst of the Great Recession while virtually all others declined. Stable-value funds invest in high-quality, intermediate-term bond funds, including **guaranteed investment contracts (GICs)** offered by insurance companies. A GIC guarantees the owner a fixed or floating interest rate for a predetermined period of time, and the return of principal is guaranteed.

Dana Wolff
Southeast Technical Institute, Sioux Falls, SD

Equity-income funds invest in well-known companies with a long history of paying high dividends as they emphasize income and capital preservation.

Socially responsible funds invest in companies that meet some predefined standard of moral and ethical behavior. Criteria could be progressive employee relations, strong records of community involvement, an excellent record on environmental issues,

DID YOU KNOW

Bias toward Inertia in Investment Decisions

People engaged in investing through mutual funds have a bias toward certain behaviors that can be harmful, such as a tendency toward inertia or the tendency to not change. Once an employee selects a 401(k) plan contribution rate many never increase it, and only 20 percent of employees ever rebalance their investments. What to do? One day there will be a lot of money for you to manage in your 401(k) retirement account so regularly ratchet up your savings contribution, perhaps when you get a raise each year, and rebalance at least annually.

respect for human rights, and safe products, as well as no "sinful" products such as tobacco, guns, alcohol, and gambling. See examples at The Forum for Sustainable and Responsible Investment (www.ussif.org/).

Balanced funds (or **hybrid funds**) keep a set mix of stocks and bonds, often 60 percent stocks and 40 percent bonds, in order to earn a well-balanced return of income and long-term capital gains.

Blend funds invest in a combination of stocks and money market securities, but no fixed-income securities, such as bonds.

Asset allocation funds invest in a mix of assets (usually stocks, bonds, and cash equivalents and sometimes international assets, gold, and real estate), and they buy and sell regularly to reduce risk while trying to outperform the market. The asset mix may be based on risk tolerance (aggressive, moderate, and conservative).

Target-date retirement funds (life-cycle funds) are asset allocation funds that offer investors premixed portfolios of stocks, bonds, and cash that investors of a certain age and risk tolerance might prefer. They are often named for the year one plans to retire, for example, the "Fidelity Freedom Fund 2030." These are targeted to people in their 30s, 40s, and 50s. Target-date funds shift assets from aggressive to moderate to a more conservative mix of securities as the retirement target date approaches. They seek to first grow and then preserve the portfolio assets. This is a no-hassle, "set-it-and-forget-it" approach to investing for retirement. Regulations require target-date funds to provide investors with information that shows the projected allocations over the life of the fund.

Mutual fund funds earn a return by investing in other mutual funds. This provides extensive diversification, but expenses and fees are higher than average.

balanced funds
Funds that keep a set mix of stocks and bonds, often 60 percent stocks and 40 percent bonds, in order to earn a well-balanced return of income and long-term capital gains.

asset allocation funds
Investments in a mix of assets (usually stocks, bonds, and cash equivalents and sometimes international assets, gold, and real estate); they buy and sell regularly to reduce risk while trying to outperform the market.

target-date retirement funds (life-cycle funds)
Asset allocation funds that offer investors premixed portfolios of stocks, bonds, and cash that investors of a certain age and risk tolerance might prefer, and they are often named for the year one plans to retire.

DID YOU KNOW

For the Lowest Fees Invest in ETFs and Index Mutual Funds

Instead of looking for a needle in a haystack when investing—finding the best mutual fund—why not buy the whole haystack? The lowest costs in investing can be found among the nation's 373 index funds and 1200 exchange traded funds (ETFs). These are unmanaged baskets of passively managed securities that own a representative set of securities that duplicate the performance of an index or market segment. ETFs trade throughout the day and index funds close after the end of the business day.

One in four investors has ETFs in their portfolios partly because of the extremely low costs (0.36% annual management fee on average), which are lower than similar index mutual funds (0.76% on average). The lowest annual fee of all ETFs is Vanguard Total Stock Market ETF (VTSAX), only

(continued)

0.07 percent, which tracks 3000 stocks, while Schwab's U.S. Broad Market ETF (SCHB) tracks 2500 stocks with an annual fee of 0.08 percent.

The average annual gain of 9.6 percent on stock investments over the long-term is measured by the MSCI USA equity index from 1970 forward. It consists of 3.37 percent from dividends and 6.23 percent in capital gains. Stock pickers who are employed by managed funds have to actively trade and as a result they must obtain a return of 11 percent on average to achieve the same result as unmanaged index investment, because their fees and expenses often add up to 2 percent.

There is absolutely no scientific evidence that active fund management outperforms index funds and ETFs. Beating an unmanaged index investment may be remotely possible, but in reality it is highly unlikely.

CONCEPT CHECK 15.2

1. What are the three basic types of mutual fund objectives?

2. Distinguish among mutual funds with an income objective, growth objective, and growth and income objective.

3. Explain why investors like index mutual funds and exchange traded funds.

15.3 MUTUAL FUND INVESTING FEES AND CHARGES

LEARNING OBJECTIVE 3

Summarize the fees and charges involved in buying and selling mutual funds.

Individuals who invest through mutual funds pay transaction costs that often are less than those associated with buying individual stocks, bonds, and cash equivalent securities. However, the fees and charges associated with investing in mutual funds are many, and they can be confusing.

15.3a Load Versus No-Load Funds

All mutual funds are classified as either load or no-load funds. This refers to whether or not they assess a sales charge, or load, when shares are purchased. There are also other fees assessed on load and no-load funds that can be avoided through careful research.

Load Funds Are "Sold" and Always Charge Transaction Fees Funds that levy a sales charge for purchases are called **load funds**. Load funds are generally "sold" by stock brokerage firms, banks, and financial planners rather than marketed directly to investors by a mutual fund company. The load is the commission used to compensate sellers for their time and expertise in recommending appropriate funds for clients.

This commission, often called a **front-end load**, typically amounts to a level sales charge of 3 to 8.5 percent of the amount invested. This reduces the amount available to purchase fund shares. For example, assume that you and your stockbroker have discussed the investment potential of the Conglomerate Cat and Dog Food Mutual Fund and you decide to invest $10,000. Because this load fund charges a commission of 8.5 percent (the maximum permitted by the SEC), the stockbroker receives $850 ($10,000 × 0.085). As a result, only $9150 of your money is actually available to purchase shares.

The sales charge may be shown either as the stated commission or as a percentage of the amount invested. The **stated commission** (8.5 percent in our example) is always somewhat misleading. The "percentage of the amount invested" is a more accurate figure because it is based on the actual money invested and working. A stated commission of 8.5 percent actually amounts to 9.3 percent of the amount invested: $10,000 − $9150 = $850; $850 ÷ $9150 = 9.3%. If you want to invest a full $10,000 in this load fund, you will need to pay out $10,930 [$10,930 − ($10,930 × 8.5%) = $10,000]. Investments of $10,000 or more often receive a discount on the load.

load funds

Mutual funds that always charge a "load" or sales charge upon purchase; the load is the commission used to compensate brokers.

front-end load

A sales charge paid when an individual buys an investment, reducing the amount available to purchase fund shares.

stated commission

The sales charge as a percentage of the amount invested.

So-called **low-load funds** may carry a sales charge of perhaps 1 to 3 percent. These funds may also be sold by brokers and are sometimes sold via mail and through mutual fund retailers located in shopping centers.

Many No-Load Funds Also Assess Back-end Loads and Redemption Fees
A **back-end load** (or **contingent deferred sales charge**) is a sales commission that is imposed only when shares are sold. Deferred loads are often on a sliding scale. The fee may decline 1 percentage point for each year the investor owns the fund. For example, a fund might charge a 6 percent fee if an investor redeems the shares within one year of purchase, and then the fee declines on an annual basis, until it reaches zero after six more years.

A **redemption charge** (or **exit fee**) is lower and is usually 1 percent of the value of the shares redeemed. A fund assesses such a charge to reduce excessive trading of fund shares. The fee disappears after the investment has been held for six months or a year. Long-term investors for retirement do not need to be concerned about paying about back-end loads and exit fees, as these largely disappear over time.

All No-Load Funds Assess Fees
A **no-load fund** sells shares at the net asset value without the addition of sales charges. These mutual fund companies let people purchase shares directly from the mutual fund company without the services of a broker, banker, or financial planner. Interested investors simply seek out advertisements for these funds in financial newspapers, magazines, and the Internet and make contact through toll-free telephone numbers, online, or mail. However, the SEC does allow funds to be called "no-load" even though they assess a service fee of 0.25 percent or less when shares are purchased. No-load funds are usually the best mutual funds in which to invest.

About One-half of No-Load Funds Also Assess Expensive 12b-1 Fees
A **12b-1 fee** (named for the SEC rule that permits the charge) is an annual charge deducted by the fund company from a fund's assets to compensate underwriters and brokers for fund sales as well as to pay for advertising, marketing, distribution, and promotional costs. A 12b-1 fee is also known as a **distribution fee**. This fee also pays for **trailing commissions**, which is compensation paid to salespeople for months or years in the future.

Although the funds do not call 12b-1 fees "loads" because they are not charged up front, they have the same effect as loads—that is, they reduce the investor's return, often quite dramatically. Over 60 percent of funds assess 12b-1 fees, including many no-load funds.

These fees are hidden and they decrease a shareholder's earning power *each year* without being described as a sales commission. A 12b-1 fee is actually a "perpetual sales load" because it is assessed on the initial investment as well as on reinvested dividends, every year, forever. The SEC caps 12b-1 fees at 0.75 percent, although recall that the SEC also permits a 0.25 percent service fee, which brings the total to 1 percent. Some funds stop assessing 12b-1 fees after four to eight years. The 12b-1 fee is supposed to be replaced in 2017 with a 12b-2 fee to pay for "distribution activities, again capped at 0.25 percent annually.

low-load funds
Funds carrying sales charges of perhaps 1 to 3 percent; sold by brokers, via mail, and sometimes through mutual fund retailers located in shopping centers.

back-end load (contingent deferred sales charge)
A sales commission that is imposed only when shares are sold; often charges are on a sliding scale, with the fee dropping 1 percentage point per year that the investor stays in the fund.

redemption charge (exit fee)
Similar to a deferred load but often much lower; used to reduce excessive trading of fund shares.

no-load funds
Funds that allow investors to purchase shares directly at the net asset value (NAV) without the addition of sales charges.

12b-1 fees (distribution fees)
Annual fees that some "no-load" fund companies deduct from a fund's assets to compensate salespeople and pay other expenses.

trailing commission
Compensation paid to salespeople for months or years in the future.

DID YOU KNOW

Bias toward Worrying about the Wrong Things

People engaged in investing through mutual funds have a bias toward certain behaviors that can be harmful, such as a tendency toward worrying about the wrong things. Many investors focus on returns and passively ignore high investment fees associated with active account management, especially when they are automatically deducted from an account. What to do? Realize that high fees—which can be totally avoided—will reduce the growth of your assets 30 percent or more over many years, so steer clear of them!

FINANCIAL POWER POINT

Avoid Managed Funds because Low Fees and Expenses Mean Higher Returns

The investment balances 20 years later if an investment earns a 7 percent annual return on a $10,000 investment are as follows:

- Actively managed mutual fund (1.9 percent; $29,190)
- Index mutual fund (0.70 percent; $33,936)
- Index ETF (0.07 percent; $38,193)

Over 20 years that is $9,003 or a 31 percent higher return ($38,193 − $29,190 = $9,003/$29,190) for investing in an Index ETF compared to an actively managed mutual fund. Smart investors avoid managed funds!

standardized expense table
SEC-required information that describes and illustrates mutual fund charges in an identical manner so that investors can accurately compare the effects of all of a fund's fees and other expenses relative to other funds.

expense ratio
Expense per dollar of assets under management.

FINANCIAL POWER POINT

High Fees Will Cost You a Fortune

Mutual funds found in 401(k) plans can vary greatly in expense ratio fees. Here is how much the fees will be on $50,000 invested in certain lifecycle funds often found in 401(k) plans, as stated in *Consumer Reports*: Vanguard Target Retirement 2030 Investor, $3,531; TIAA-CREF Lifecycle 2030 Institutional, $9,416; Fidelity Freedom K 2030, $12,199; Blackrock LifePath 2030 Portfolio Class K, $13,104; T. Rowe Price Retirement 2030 Class R, $14,529. Be certain to find out how much the fees are before investing!

15.3b Mutual Fund Share Classes—Designed to Confuse—Are Sold to You

A single mutual fund may be available to investors in more than one class of shares: Class A, B, or C, and they all are falsely sold as "no load" funds. They all invest in the same portfolio of securities and have the same investment objectives but have different fee and expense patterns. Class A shares normally have a front-end sales charges paid at the time of the initial purchase. Class B shares have back-end sales charges paid when selling the shares within a specified number of years, and they might (if held long enough) allow automatic conversion to share with a lower 12b-1 fee. Class C shares might have a 12b-1 fee and a redemption charge.

Moreover, the performance results for each class will differ depending on how long you hold the shares. These shares are sold by brokers and financial planners and can be avoided by investors who choose to invest in no-load funds.

15.3c Use FINRA's Website to Compare Mutual Fund Fees

To compare the costs of various funds and share classes for your expected holding period and estimated returns, see the Financial Industry Regulatory Authority's Mutual Fund Expense Analyzer (www.apps.finra.org/fundanalyzer/1/fa.aspx). This tool estimates the value of the funds and impact of fees and expenses on your investment and also allows you to look up applicable fees and available discounts for thousands of funds.

The SEC requires that mutual funds provide investors with a summary prospectus— in plain English—of information needed to help make investment decisions, and it appears at the front of a fund's full prospectus. It must include a **standardized expense table** that describes and illustrates in an identical manner the effects of all of its fees and other expenses. Look for the fund's **expense ratio**, the expense per dollar of assets under management. Expense ratios average 1.26 percent for managed diversified stock funds (which is way too expensive) and easily as low as 0.25 percent for index funds (much lower costs).

15.3d What's Best: Load or No Load? Low Fee or High Fee?

The best choice is to invest in no-load mutual funds or ETFs with low fees. Investors can almost guarantee a poorer return than others if they put their money into a load fund with high management fees. Experts agree that "If you pick your own funds, sales charges and high management fees are a total waste of money." The SEC says that for a long-term investor a 1 percent fee that increases at 4 percent a year will devour one-third of your total return! And 1 percent is much less than the average set of fees.

Sales Commissions Reduce Returns　The sales commissions charged by load funds indisputably reduce total returns. When investment results are adjusted to account for the effects of sales charges, no-load mutual funds always have an initial advantage because the investor has more money at work. Many are perplexed at the stubbornness of actively managed funds that have not reduced their fees in years, even though countless investors have moved to low- or no-load funds.

12b-1 Fees Kill Long-Term Returns　Annual 12b-1 charges are very costly over the long run. If you pay 1 percent per year in 12b-1 fees for a mutual fund in which you invest for ten years, you will be giving up nearly 10 percent of your investment amount in trailing commissions. Yikes!

DID YOU KNOW

Learn More about Mutual Funds

Information on mutual fund investing is vast, especially on the Internet, and excellent information about mutual funds is available from numerous sources.

Personal Finance Magazines

Kiplinger's Personal Finance, Money, Business Week, Consumer Reports, Forbes, Fortune, and *Worth.* Comprehensive examinations of the performance of numerous mutual funds are featured every year in the late August issue of Forbes, the October issue of Money, a late February issue of *Business Week,* and the September issue of *Kiplinger's Personal Finance.*

Financial Press

The Wall Street Journal Barron's, Investor's Business Daily, and the business sections of newspapers such as *The New York Times* and *USA Today.*

Online News and Quote Services

CompuServe, Dow Jones News/Retrieval-Private Investor Edition, Farcast, Personal Journal, Quote.com, and Reuters Money Network.

Mutual Fund Investment Publications and Websites

Morningstar Mutual Funds, Morningstar No-Load Funds, Mutual Funds Update, Investment Companies Yearbook, IBC/Donoghue's Mutual Funds Almanac, Standard & Poor's, Lipper Mutual Fund Profiles, Moody's, and *The Value Line Mutual Fund Survey.* Dozens of newsletters that specialize in mutual funds are available, too. Morningstar (www .morningstar.com) and the Investment Company Institute (www.ici.org) provide information on thousands of funds. Some charge fees, and others are free.

Avoiding High Fees Is Critical to Investment Success Research has found that over five-year periods, lower-cost funds *always* deliver returns better than those offered by higher-cost funds. It's even harder if you're paying 1.9 percentage points a year for active management. That's like carrying a couple of heavy barbells during a marathon. The equally fast runner without the barbells is going to win over the long run.

CONCEPT CHECK 15.3

1. Give three examples of fees or charges associated with load funds.

2. Which is better for most investors, load or no-load funds? Why?

3. Summarize the effects of loads and fees on investment returns.

15.4 HOW TO SELECT THE FUNDS IN WHICH YOU SHOULD INVEST

Selecting mutual funds in which to invest is a do-it-yourself effort for no-load investors and it is easy to do. Brokers are not needed because a tremendous amount of objective information is available to help investors evaluate and select funds. To explain the process of selecting funds, let's follow Catalina Garcia's decision making. She is in her late twenties, lives in San Jose, California, and earns $51,000 annually in her sales management job. Figure 15-4 illustrates the process of selecting mutual fund investments, and Table 15-3 contains performance data for a number of large-cap mutual funds from *Kiplinger's Personal Finance.*

LEARNING OBJECTIVE 4

Establish strategies to evaluate and select mutual funds that meet your investment goals.

Figure 15-4   **The Process of Selecting Mutual Funds**

1. Review your investment policy	Conservative Moderate Aggressive
2. Review your investment goals	Goal Time horizon Return Taxes
3. Eliminate funds inappropriate for your investment goals	Income Growth Growth and income Specific fund types
4. Choose low load or no load	Low or no-load
5. Determine if investment advice is needed	For immediate investments For later portfolio review
6. Screen and compare funds that meet your investment criteria	Fund-screening tools Fees and charges Performance Services
7. Monitor your mutual fund portfolio	Portfolio monitoring Fund quotations in newspapers

DO IT IN CLASS

Table 15-3   **Mutual Fund Performance**

20 Largest Stock Mutual Funds Ranked by Size

Rank/Name	Symbol	Assets† (in billions)	Total return through Dec. 31* 1 yr.	3 yrs.	5 yrs.	Max. sales charge	Toll-free number
1. Vanguard Total Stock Market Idx Inv@	VTSMX	$296.4	33.3%	16.1%	18.7%	none	800-635-1511
2. Vanguard 500 Index Inv@	VFINX	155.3	32.2	16.0	17.8	none	800-635-1511
3. American Growth Fund of America A@	AGTHX	136.5	33.8	15.3	18.3	5.75%	800-421-0180
4. American EuroPacific Growth A@	AEPGX	121.2	20.2	7.4	13.5	5.75	800-421-0180
5. Fidelity Contrafund@	FCNTX	111.1	34.1	15.9	18.7	none	800-544-9797
6. Vanguard Total Intl Stock Idx Inv@	VGTSX	109.7	15.0	5.1	12.0	none	800-635-1511
7. American Capital Income Builder A@	CAIBX	88.9	14.9	9.7	11.6	5.75	800-421-0180
8. American Inc Fund of America A@	AMECX	87.6	18.3	11.8	14.3	5.75	800-421-0180
9. Franklin Income A@	FKINX	84.6	14.2	10.1	15.3	4.25	800-632-2301
10. American Capital World Gro & Inc A@	CWGIX	83.7	24.8	11.2	14.4	5.75	800-421-0180
11. Vanguard Wellington@	VWELX	79.3	19.7	11.8	13.7	none	800-635-1511
12. American Balanced A@	ABALX	69.7	21.7	13.0	14.6	5.75	800-421-0180
13. Fidelity Spartan 500 Index Inv@	FUSEX	69.5	32.3	16.1	17.9	none	800-544-9797
14. American Washington Mutual A@	AWSHX	69.4	31.9	16.7	16.5	5.75	800-421-0180
15. American Invstmt Co of America A@	AIVSX	68.7	32.4	14.6	16.2	5.75	800-421-0180
16. American Fundamental Inv A@	ANCFX	65.9	31.5	14.8	18.1	5.75	800-421-0180

20 Largest Stock Mutual Funds Ranked by Size

Rank/Name	Symbol	Assets† (in billions)	Total return through Dec. 31*			Max. sales charge	Toll-free number
			1 yr.	3 yrs.	5 yrs.		
17. Vanguard Emerging Mkts Stock Idx@	VEIEX	64.5	−5.2	−3.0	13.8	none	800-635-1511
18. BlackRock Global Allocation A@	MDLOX	59.1	14.4	6.6	10.1	5.25	800-441-7762
19. American New Perspective A@	ANWPX	55.1	26.8	12.3	17.0	5.75	800-421-0180
20. Dodge & Cox Stock	DODGX	53.9	40.5	18.0	19.6	none	800-621-3979
S&P 500-STOCK INDEX			32.4%	16.2%	17.9%		
MSCI EAFE INDEX			23.3%	8.7%	13.0%		

*Annualized for three and five years. †For all share classes combined. @Rankings exclude share classes of this fund with different fee structures or higher minimum initial investments.

Source: © 2014 Morningstar, Inc. All Rights Reserved. The information contained herein: (1) is proprietary to Morningstar and/or its content providers; (2) may not be copied or distributed; (3) does not constitute investment advice offered by Morningstar; and (4) is not warranted to be accurate, complete or timely. Neither Morningstar nor its content providers are responsible for any damages or losses arising from any use of this information. Past performance is no guarantee of future results. Use of information from Morningstar does not necessarily constitute agreement by Morningstar, Inc. of any investment philosophy or strategy presented in this publication.

15.4a Review Your Investment Philosophy and Investment Goals

Catalina began by reviewing her investment philosophy and financial goals. These topics were examined in Chapter 13. Catalina has a moderate investment philosophy, and she has a written investment plan (Figure 13-7 on page 405). The investment goal she is interested in investing for now is retirement, and her investment time horizon is the next 30 years or longer. She anticipates an annual return of at least 4 to 5 percent. She does not care about income taxes because these investments will be made within Catalina's tax-deferred 401(k) retirement plan at work, where her earnings will grow tax-free.

Catalina does not have any lump sums available in a savings or money market account to use for investing. To help fund her retirement plan, she decided to have $200 a month withheld from her paycheck to invest in a mutual fund with a growth investment objective. Catalina's employer's 401(k) plan offers about 20 funds as well as company stock.

15.4b Eliminate Funds Inappropriate for Your Investment Goals

Catalina began by reviewing all fund classifications (pages 459–463) and balancing the risks and returns of various funds as illustrated in Figure 15-3 on page 464. She aims to eliminate mutual funds inappropriate for her retirement investment goal.

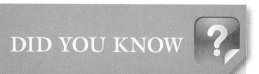

DID YOU KNOW

Your Worst Financial Blunders in Investing Through Mutual Funds

Based on others' financial woes, you will make mistakes in personal finance when you:

1. *Buy funds with high fees and expenses.*
2. *Withdraw cash dividends rather than reinvesting.*
3. *Chase short-term performance by investing in "hot" funds.*

DID YOU KNOW

Turn Bad Habits into Good Ones

Do You Do This?

Have only a few investments like stocks and bonds

Find it difficult to reinvest dividends and interest

Buy load funds or those with 12b-1 fees

Seem confused about the right funds in which to invest

Find it difficult to monitor your investments

Do This Instead!

Diversify by investing in mutual funds

Invest in funds that reinvest automatically

Invest in no-load funds or ETFs

Use a free online fund-screening tool

Manage your fund portfolio free online

Catalina recognizes that increasing the potential for higher returns also increases the risk to the investor's capital. Therefore, she eliminated the following types of funds: sector funds, emerging markets funds, and aggressive growth funds, as well as stock in the company where she works. She also realizes that investing too conservatively invites the risk of failure to achieve her goal of a financially successful retirement. Therefore, Catalina eliminated money market funds.

15.4c Create a Portfolio of Funds in Which to Invest

Instead of simply investing in "this and that" funds, Catalina smartly decided to create a portfolio of mutual funds tailored to her needs. At www.kiplinger.com/article/investing/T033-C009-S001-kiplinger-25-model-portfolios.html she found 25 portfolios recommended by *Kiplinger's Personal Finance* editors and writers. They are customized for different situations and stages of life. On that website, she can get updated returns and track the performance of her investments with the benchmark portfolios.

15.4d Choose No-Load Funds with Low Fees

The sales commissions charged by load funds indisputably reduce total returns. Catalina reasoned that since no-load mutual funds have an initial advantage—the investor has more money at work—she preferred no-load funds. Because her $200 a month was going into investment for retirement, she also thought that 12b-1 fees would be very costly over the long term. For the same reason, she wanted to avoid high management fees. She did not care about back-end loads and exit fees, as these largely disappear over time. Catalina decided to invest in one or more no-load mutual funds with no 12b-1 fees and very low management expense ratios. Catalina will have to look up some of this information on the Internet since data in Table 15-3 is quite limited.

15.4e Obtain Investment Information and Advice

limited management account
An account at an investment firm whereby, for a fee, they sell and buy your mutual fund assets, usually quarterly, on your behalf to automatically rebalance your portfolio back to your specific standards.

Because Catalina is going to invest in no-load funds, she figured she did not need the services of a broker or financial planner. Instead, she plans to use the tremendous resources that are available via the Vanguard website (www.vanguard.com)—information, education, and professional advice. Vanguard is the largest mutual fund family in the country. Catalina's employer offers investing and retirement planning seminars and workshops provided by Ernst & Young, Vanguard, T. Rowe Price, and other companies. Significant others are welcome to attend. Employer-sponsored financial advice may cover an employee's entire financial situation, including debt reduction, college planning, spousal assets, real estate, and other investments. Once Catalina's retirement assets build up to a substantial amount, perhaps $50,000 or more, she would be wise to seek professional financial advice.

Catalina's employer offers retirement plan participants access to services that automatically rebalance their retirement assets known as a **limited management account**, first discussed in chapter 13. For an annual fee of perhaps as little as $20 annually, the firm sells and buys her mutual fund assets on a quarterly basis to rebalance her portfolio back to her specific standards.

DID YOU KNOW ?

How to Ease into Investing Cautiously

Investors who are fearful of investing in the stock market can try these techniques: (1) Start by buying shares of a diversified stock mutual fund using monthly purchases for 12 months or (2) Purchase a life cycle or target date mutual fund that contains a premixed allocation of stocks and bonds.

15.4f Screen and Compare Funds That Meet Your Criteria

When comparing the track records of mutual funds, there are a number of criteria to consider. These may include expenses; net asset value; minimum initial purchase; size of fund; ratings; past performance (perhaps one, three, five, and ten years); best and worst performance in up and down markets (volatility); fund manager tenure; and services. Catalina is interested in stock funds, international funds and global funds, low management fees, and no 12b-1 fees.

DID YOU KNOW

Sean's Success Story

Sean's superb financial life continues. He increased his 401(k) contributions from 6 to 8 percent so the $90,000 in mutual funds in the account will total over $100,000 by December. That figure will be a milestone for Sean's retirement planning. While the return on his mutual fund portfolio was only 2 percent between 2007 and 2009, it did not decline; it more than doubled since then. Sean figures that the stock market is bound to go up even more as the economy grows and unemployment declines. Therefore, he has decided to move his investments completely into stock mutual funds.

Since today's share prices go up and down quite considerably during any one year, Catalina checked the volatility ratings of funds. **Volatility** characterizes a mutual fund's (or any security's) tendency to rise or fall in price over a period of time. A measure of volatility is the **standard deviation**, which gauges the degree to which a security's historical return rises above or falls below its own long-term average return—and therefore may be likely to do so again in the future. A standard deviation is a probability indicator, not an economic forecast. The bigger an investment's standard deviation, the more volatile its price may be in the future. High volatility suggests greater long-term rewards but a greater-than-normal risk of short-term losses during economic downturns. Other common measures of risk are beta, the Sharpe Ratio, and R-squared. Publications like *Kiplinger's Personal Finance* and *Money* provide volatility ratings for mutual funds.

Catalina started searching for mutual fund investments at Vanguard (www.personal .vanguard.com/us/FundsMFSIntro?%20FROM=VAN), which is considered one of the best mutual fund screening websites, and she began by typing in the fund symbols in "search." A **fund screener** or **fund-screening tool** permits an individual to screen all of the mutual funds in the market. Other mutual fund screening tools are available at the following websites:

- Yahoo! Finance (www.screener.finance.yahoo.com/funds.html)
- Kiplinger.com (www.kiplinger.com/tool/investing/T052-S001-search-and-compare-stocks-equities/index.php)
- Fidelity (www.fidelity.com/fund-screener/evaluator.shtml#!&ntf=Y)
- **Vanguard** (www.personal.vanguard.com/us/FundsMFSBasicSearch ?FROM=VAN)

Catalina focused on large-cap funds, including those shown in Table 15-3. She researched funds using the Vanguard fund screener. She obtained online a profile prospectus from Vanguard on each of the funds she liked. A **profile prospectus** (or **fund profile**) describes the mutual fund, its investment objectives, and how it tries to achieve its objectives. Written in lay language, it offers a two- to four-page summary presentation of information contained in an SEC-required legal prospectus that answers 11 key investor questions, including risks, fees, and details about the fund's ten-year performance record.

After reading fund details, looking at the numbers, and comparing performance, Catalina decided to split her monthly $200 investment between Vanguard Total Stock Market Index (VTSMX) and Vanguard Emerging Markets Stock Index (VEIEX), partly because of their low to nil expense ratios. (In addition, any minimum initial investment fees are waived for investments via her employer's retirement plan.) Catalina thinks the fund managers will beat the average market returns, such as a S&P 500 index like Vanguard's 500 Index (VFINX). Catalina might be right, or she might be wrong, but she is probably correct.

fund screener (fund-screening tool)
Permits investors to screen all of the mutual funds in the market to gauge performance.

profile prospectus (fund profile)
Publication that describes the mutual fund, its investment objectives, and how it tries to achieve its objectives in lay terms rather than the legal language used in a regular prospectus.

DID YOU KNOW

The Tax Consequences of Mutual Fund Investing

Ordinary income dividend distributions, capital gains distributions, and realized gains from the sale of mutual funds are generally subject to taxation.

1. In regular investment accounts:

   • When you buy and hold mutual fund shares, you owe income taxes on any ordinary income dividends and on the fund's capital gains in the year you receive or reinvest them.

   • When you sell shares, you owe taxes on the capital gains earned on the difference between what you paid for the shares and the selling price (less transaction costs).

• Before purchasing a mutual fund toward the end of the year, like in December, determine whether the fund has already made its end-of-year capital gains distribution. If you buy the fund before the **record date** (the date established by an issuer to determine who is eligible to receive a dividend or distribution), you will receive the income but you also will owe capital gains taxes for the whole year. Buying after the record date avoids that tax because you will not have received the distribution.

2. Interest from a tax-exempt municipal bond fund is exempt from federal income taxes.

3. In retirement accounts (such as a 401[k] or traditional IRA account), all taxes are deferred until funds are withdrawn from the account.

The next step is for Catalina to contact the human resources department at her employer and sign the documents to withhold $200 a month from her paycheck and invest $100 into each of the two funds. Catalina also knows that for every dollar invested, she gets an immediate 50 percent return because her employer's policy is to match 401(k) contributions 50 cents on the dollar for the first 6 percent of earnings. Catalina's 401(k) balance in 12 months, therefore, will show $2400 in contributions and $1200 in employer matching contributions (that's an immediate 50 percent return on her $2400!), plus whatever gain occurs (hopefully not a loss) in NAV. Catalina's 401(k) balance this time next year is likely to be more than $3600.

15.4g Monitor Your Portfolio of Mutual Fund Investments

Tracking your portfolio is imperative because investors do not want to keep any underperforming mutual funds in their portfolio for very long. If Catalina wants to invest outside of her 401(k) plan in the same or other no-load funds, she can purchase funds directly from mutual fund investment companies, such as family fund companies like Fidelity, T. Rowe Price, or any other mutual fund, like Gabelli, Neuberger, or Calvert.

Use Portfolio Monitoring on the Internet Monitoring a mutual fund portfolio is easy using any of the top-rated mutual fund websites cited earlier. Some services charge nominal fees.

Check Fund Quotations in Newspapers You can check closing prices online any time on the financial websites cited earlier or read quotes in newspapers. See Figure 15-5 for an illustration. Newspapers' quotations for no-load mutual funds list the name of the fund followed by columns for its net asset value, net change from the previous day, and year-to-date percentage return.

It is easy to research mutual funds on the Internet.

sandy young / Alamy

Figure 15-5 How Mutual Funds Are Quoted

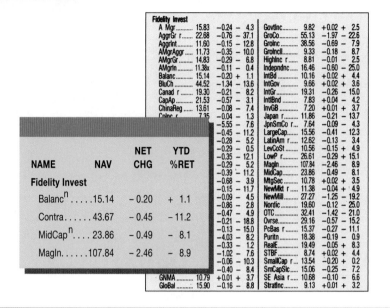

NAME	NAV	NET CHG	YTD %RET
Fidelity Invest			
Balanc[n]	15.14	– 0.20	+ 1.1
Contra	43.67	– 0.45	– 11.2
MidCap[n]	23.86	– 0.49	– 8.1
MagIn	107.84	– 2.46	– 8.9

mutual fund bid price

Shareholders receive this amount per share when they redeem their shares, which is the same dollar amount as the NAV.

mutual fund ask (or offer) price

Price at which an investor can purchase a mutual fund's shares; current NAV per share plus sales charges.

For example, within the group listing for Fidelity Investments mutual funds, the Balanced Fund (abbreviated as Balanc) has a net asset value (NAV) of $15.14, a change in the net asset value (NET CHG) of −$0.20 from the closing price of the previous trading day, and a year-to-date percentage return (YTD %RET) of 1.1 percent.

Mutual Fund Bid Price In mutual funds, the NAV is also known as the **mutual fund bid price**. Shareholders receive this amount per share when they redeem their shares—that is, the company is willing to pay this amount to buy the shares back. Also, the NAV is the amount per share an investor will pay to purchase a fund, assuming it is a no-load fund. A no-load fund is indicated as such by the alphabetic letter *n* at the end of the fund's name.

Mutual Fund Ask Price The **mutual fund ask price** (or **offer price**) is the price at which a mutual fund's share can be purchased by investors. It equals the current NAV per share plus sales charges, if any. If you wanted to buy or sell shares of Fidelity Balanced Fund, a no-load (note the superscript *n* in Figure 15-5) mutual fund, the price would be $15.14 per share. The funds listed without an *n* are load funds. The SEC requires that appropriate footnotes appear in newspaper listings of mutual funds to indicate other expenses and charges.

DO IT NOW!

You know more about personal finance after reading this chapter, so get started right now by:

1. *Identifying five unique services provided by mutual funds (see page 459) that appeal to you.*

2. *Identifying two of your long-term financial goals and determining whether you would seek a fund with a growth objective or growth and income objective for each goal.*

3. *Selecting one mutual fund from those listed in Table 15-3 on page 470 to follow for two or three months, then reassessing your selection if warranted.*

CONCEPT CHECK 15.4

1. Explain why it is important to review your investment philosophy and goals when selecting mutual fund investments.

2. Explain how you would eliminate funds inappropriate for your investment goals.

3. How might you go about monitoring your mutual fund investments?

WHAT DO YOU RECOMMEND *NOW?*

Now that you have read the chapter on mutual funds, what do you recommend to Tyler and Samantha Gent in the case at the beginning of the chapter regarding:

1. Redeeming their CDs and investing their retirement money in mutual funds?

2. Investing in growth and income mutual funds instead of income funds?

3. Buying no-load rather than load funds?

4. Buying mutual funds through their employers' 401(k) retirement accounts, rather than saving through a taxable account as they have been doing?

BIG PICTURE SUMMARY OF LEARNING OBJECTIVES

LO1 **Describe the features, advantages, and unique services of investing through mutual funds.**
A mutual fund is an investment company that pools funds obtained by selling shares to investors and makes investments to achieve the financial goal of income or growth, or both. The net asset value (NAV) is the per-share value of the fund. Advantages of mutual funds include diversification, affordability, and professional management. Unique services include ease of buying and selling, check writing, and easy establishment of retirement plans.

LO2 **Differentiate mutual funds by investment objectives.**
A mutual fund with an income objective invests in securities that pay regular income in dividends or interest. A fund that has a growth objective seeks capital appreciation. A fund that has a combined growth and income objective seeks a somewhat balanced return made up of current income and capital gains. The name of a fund, such as aggressive growth fund, typically gives a clue to its objectives.

Index funds and ETFs are popular because they earn almost exactly the same return as a particular market index.

LO3 **Summarize the fees and charges involved in buying and selling mutual funds.**
Individuals who invest through mutual funds pay annual fund operating expenses—management fees—that are deducted from fund assets before earnings are distributed to shareholders. Investors must make decisions on load and no-load funds, 12b-1 fees, deferred load, and redemption fees.

LO4 **Establish strategies to evaluate and select mutual funds that meet your investment goals.**
The process of selecting no-load mutual funds in which to invest is a do-it-yourself effort. The steps are (1) review investment philosophy and investment goals, (2) eliminate funds inappropriate for your investment goals, (3) create a portfolio of funds in which to invest, (4) choose no-load funds with low fees, (5) obtain investment information and advice, (6) screen and compare funds that meet your investment criteria, and (7) monitor your mutual fund investments.

LET'S TALK ABOUT IT

1. **Investing in Tough Economic Times.** Comment on this statement: "A great time to invest is during times of economic turmoil when assets are undervalued."

2. **One Fund of Interest.** Review the three objectives of mutual funds. Based on your investment philosophy, which one type of fund would be of most interest to you if you were saving to buy a home several years from now? Give reasons why.

3. **Two Funds.** Assume you graduated from college a few years ago, have a job paying $75,000 annually, and want to invest $300 per month in mutual funds for retirement. Which combination of two or more mutual funds (see pages 468–469) would you think appropriate? Give reasons for each of your selections.

4. **Spread Your Money into Funds.** Assume that your uncle gave you $50,000 to invest solely in mutual funds. Based on your point in the life cycle and your investment philosophy, identify your investment goals and explain how you would spread your money among different funds. (See pages 469–469.)

5. **Good Choices.** Identify the types of mutual funds that would be good choices to meet the following four investment objectives: emergency fund, house down payment, college fund for 2-year-old child,

and retirement fund for a 25-year-old. (See pages 469–469.) Give two reasons why each one of your recommendations would be appropriate.

6. **Load or No-Load.** Which is a better choice for you, load or no-load mutual funds? Give some reasons.

7. Review Table 15-1 on the "Advantages of Investing in Mutual Funds" on page 457, and select two that would be important to you as an investor. Explain why.

DO THE MATH

1. **Profits and Taxes.** A year ago, George Jetson, from Orbit City, Texas, invested $1000 by buying 100 shares of the Can't Lose Mutual Fund, an aggressive growth no-load mutual fund. George reinvested his dividends, so he now has 112 shares. So far, the NAV for George's investment has risen from $10 per share to $13.25.

   (a) What is the percentage increase in the NAV of George's mutual fund?

   (b) If George redeemed the first 100 shares of his mutual fund investment for $13.25 per share, what would be his capital gain over the amount invested?

   (c) Assuming George pays income taxes at the 25 percent rate, how much income tax will he have to pay if he sells those first 100 shares?

2. **Mutual Fund Sales.** Two years ago, Izabella Martinez, from Denver, Colorado, invested $1000 by buying 125 shares ($8 per share NAV) in the Can't Lose Mutual Fund, an aggressive growth no-load mutual fund. Last year, she made two additional investments of $500 each (50 shares at $10 and 40 shares at $12.50). Izabella

reinvested all of her dividends. So far, the NAV for her investment has risen from $8 per share to $13.25. Late in the year, she sold 60 shares at $13.25.

   (a) What were the proceeds from Izabella's sale of the 60 shares?

   (b) To use the Internal Revenue Service's "average-cost basis method" of determining the average price paid for one share, begin by calculating the average price paid for the shares. In this instance, the $2000 is divided by 215 shares (125 shares + 50 shares + 40 shares). What was the average price paid by Izabella?

   (c) To finally determine the average-cost basis of shares sold, you multiply the average price per share times the number of shares sold—in this case, 60. What is the total cost basis for Izabella's 60 shares?

   (d) Assuming that Izabella has to pay income taxes on the difference between the sales price for the 60 shares and their cost, how much is this difference?

FINANCIAL PLANNING CASES

CASE 1

The Johnsons Decide to Invest Through Mutual Funds

After learning about mutual funds, the Johnsons are confident that they are a great way to invest, especially because of the diversification and professional management that funds offer. The couple has a financial nest egg of $9500 to invest through mutual funds. They also want to invest another $300 per month on a regular basis.

 DO IT IN CLASS PAGES 469–471

Although not yet completely firm, Harry and Belinda's goals at this point are as follows:

- They want to continue to build their retirement income to retire in about 36 years.

- They will need about $10,000 in six to eight years to use as supplemental income if Belinda has a baby and does not work for six months.

- They might buy a luxury automobile requiring a $10,000 down payment if they decide not to have a child.

Knowing that the Johnsons have a moderate investment philosophy, that they live on a reasonable budget, and that they have a well-established cash-management plan, advise them on their mutual fund investments by responding to the following questions:

(a) Some comparable mutual fund performance data on stock funds are shown in Table 15-3. Using only that information and assuming that you are recommending some funds for the Johnsons' retirement needs, which two funds would you recommend? Why?

(b) How would you divide the $9500 between the two stock funds? Why?

(c) How much of the $300 monthly investment amount would you allocate to each of the stock funds? Why?

(d) Assume that both funds increase in value over the next ten years. Another bear market then occurs, causing the NAVs to drop 25 percent from the previous year. Would you recommend that the Johnsons sell their accumulated shares in the funds? Why or why not?

(e) Determine the value of the shares purchased with their $9500 original investment in ten years, assuming that the two funds' NAVs increase 6 percent annually for the ten years. (Hint: Use Appendix A.1 or the *Garman/Forgue* companion website.)

CASE 2

Victor and Maria Invest for Retirement

Victor and Maria Hernandez plan to retire in less than 15 years. Their current investment portfolio is distributed as follows: 40 percent in growth mutual funds, 40 percent in corporate bonds and bond mutual funds, and 20 percent in cash equivalents. They have decided to increase the amount of risk in their portfolio by taking 10 percent from their cash equivalent investments and investing in some mutual funds with strong growth possibilities.

DO IT IN CLASS
PAGES 469–471

(a) Of the stock mutual funds listed in Table 15-3, which two would you recommend to meet the Hernandezes' goals? Why?

(b) Would you recommend that the Hernandezes remain invested in those two funds during their retirement years? Why or why not?

CASE 3

Julia Price Is Going to Invest Big in Mutual Funds

It has been over 25 years since Julia graduated with a major in aeronautical engineering, and she has been quite successful in her career as well as in managing her personal finances. She has moved up the career ladder, earns a high salary, has $50,000 in equity in her condo, and has an investment portfolio valued at $300,000 that includes $200,000 in retirement assets through her employer's 401(k) plan. She wants to liquidate her $300,000 investment portfolio now invested in stocks, bonds, and gold and put everything into mutual funds. Julia is optimistic about the future of investing. After serious research, Julia has decided to invest $300,000 into ETFs and index mutual funds rather than actively managed funds. Offer your opinions about her thinking.

CASE 4

Matching Mutual Fund Investments to Economic Projections

Joshua Wickler, an automobile salesperson for the past ten years in Albuquerque, New Mexico is divorced and contributes to the support of his two children. He is interested in investing in mutual funds. Joshua wants to put $20,000 of accumulated savings into a stock index mutual fund and then continue to invest $200 monthly for the foreseeable future, perhaps using the money for retirement starting in about 25 years. Joshua has limited his choices solely to the index mutual funds listed in Table 15-3.

DO IT IN CLASS
PAGES 469–471

(a) In Table 15-3, note that there are two index funds based on the S&P 500 Index. Suggest a reason why Joshua should invest in one or the other, noting that the returns for the Vanguard 500 Index Fund slightly lagged the Fidelity Spartan Index Fund.

(b) Given that Joshua plans to invest $2400 annually for the next 25 years, which of the other two index funds (Vanguard Total Stock Market Index Fund or Vanguard Emerging Markets Stock Fund) would you recommend, and why?

CASE 5

Selection of a Mutual Fund as Part of a Retirement Plan

Lola Garcia, a single mother of a 6-year-old child, works for a utility company in Chestertown, Maryland, and is willing to invest $3000 per year in a mutual fund. She wants the investment income to supplement her retirement pension starting in approximately 30 years, and she has a moderate investment philosophy. Lola is concerned about not investing too conservatively because she expects to live a long life, given that her eldest relatives lived well into their 80s and early 90s. Advise Lola by responding to the following questions:

(a) If Lola invests $3000 annually into two growth mutual funds, which two types would you recommend and why? See the list on pages 460–461.

(b) Alternatively, if Lola invests $3000 annually into two growth and income funds, which two would you recommend and why? See the list on pages 461–463.

(c) Summarize why these four types of mutual funds might be suitable for Lola.

BE YOUR OWN PERSONAL FINANCIAL MANAGER

1. **Your Mutual Fund Preferences.** Review the section "Mutual Fund Objectives" and then complete Worksheet 61: My Mutual Fund Preferences from "My Personal Financial Planner." For each of the types of mutual funds listed, identify which are of interest to you and one characteristic you like about them, and note those in which you might invest during your own investing life.

2. **Comparing Mutual Fund Investments.** Learn about three stock mutual funds that might be of interest to you, such as Vanguard Target Retirement 2055 Fund (VFFVX), Vanguard Target Retirement 2050 Fund (VFIFX), and Spartan 500 Index – Investor Class (FUSEX), by going online. Then complete Worksheet 62: Comparing Mutual Funds as Investments from "My Personal Financial Planner" by recording the facts requested.

3. **Calculating Mutual Fund Returns.** Use the information for the exercises immediately above and complete Worksheet 63: Calculating the Return on Mutual Fund Investments from "My Personal Financial Planner," which will help you deter mine the return from income and capital gains after you make some assumptions, such as a 5-year holding period and the like.

4. **Evaluating My Investment Returns.** Complete Work sheet 64: Evaluating the Performance (Gain or Loss) of My Investments from "My Personal Financial Planner" using one example for which you make the assumptions. Perhaps you can use the Spartan 500 Index – Investor Class (FUSEX) in which you invested $3000 two years ago for $66.50 and its present price of $7.90.

ON THE NET

Go to the Web pages indicated to complete these exercises.

1. **Low Cost Mutual Funds.** Visit the Kiplingers website for low-cost mutual funds (www.kiplinger.com/tool/investing/T041-S000-kiplingers-25-favorite-fund/index.php). Summarize why they think these are good investments.

2. **Which ETFs for You?** Visit the website for Vanguard Investments and read its section on exchange-traded funds (ETFs) (www.personal.vanguard.com/us/funds/etf). Summarize why you think ETFs might or might not be a good investment for you.

3. **Mutual Fund Information.** Visit the website for CNNMoney. Go to the page titled "What Is a Mutual Fund" at www.money.cnn.com/retirement/guide/investing_mutualfunds.moneymag/index.htm. Review the dozen or so short articles and compare what you read there with what you read in this chapter. List two things that are new to your understanding.

4. **FINRA on Mutual Funds.** Visit the website for the Financial Industry Regulatory Authority (FINRA) at www.finra.org/Investors/SmartInvesting/Choosing Investments/MutualFunds/, where you will find a section titled "Mutual Funds." Review the several paragraphs there and compare what you read with what you read in this chapter. List two things that are new to your understanding.

ACTION INVOLVEMENT PROJECTS

1. **Review Some Mutual Fund Portfolios.** Go to Kiplinger's article on model portfolios at www.kiplinger.com/article/investing/T033-C009-S001-kiplinger-25-model-portfolios.html?si=1 and review the three illustrative portfolios that might fit your needs. Summarize your findings.

2. **Using a Fund Screener.** Go to the fund screener of Yahoo! Finance (finance.yahoo.com/funds) and look up three funds of interest to you, perhaps using some of the names of funds you found in the exercise immediately above. Summarize your findings.

3. **Reviewing ETFs.** Go to Fidelity's ETF fund screener website (www.research2.fidelity.com/fidelity/screeners/etf/landing.asp?) and click on the "Learn More" section of "ETF Portfolio Builder." Compare what you learn there with what is in this book.

4. **Unique Mutual Fund Services.** Review Table 15-2 on "Unique Mutual Fund Services" on page 459 and select 2 that would be important to you as a mutual fund investor. Explain why.

**DO IT IN CLASS
PAGE 459**

Visit the Garman/Forgue companion website at www.cengagebrain.com.

16 Real Estate and High-Risk Investments

YOU MUST BE KIDDING, RIGHT?

Friends Nicholas Belisle and Joseph Sanders both have aggressive investment philosophies. Nicholas invests primarily in residential real estate, and Joseph invests in commodities futures contracts. As longtime investors, they consider themselves experts, but occasionally, each has experienced financial losses. What are the odds that the typical investor will make money investing in commodities futures contracts?

A. 50%   **C.** 20%

B. 30%   **D.** 10%

The answer is D. Ninety percent of individual investors in futures contracts lose money. Funds used for these investments should be only those that one can afford to lose!

LEARNING OBJECTIVES

After reading this chapter, you should be able to:

1 Demonstrate how you can make money investing in real estate.

2 Recognize how to take advantage of beneficial tax treatments in real estate investing.

3 Calculate the right price to pay for real estate and how to finance your purchase.

4 Assess the disadvantages of investing in real estate.

5 Summarize the risks and challenges of investing in the alternative investments of collectibles, precious metals, and gems.

6 Explain why options and futures are risky investments.

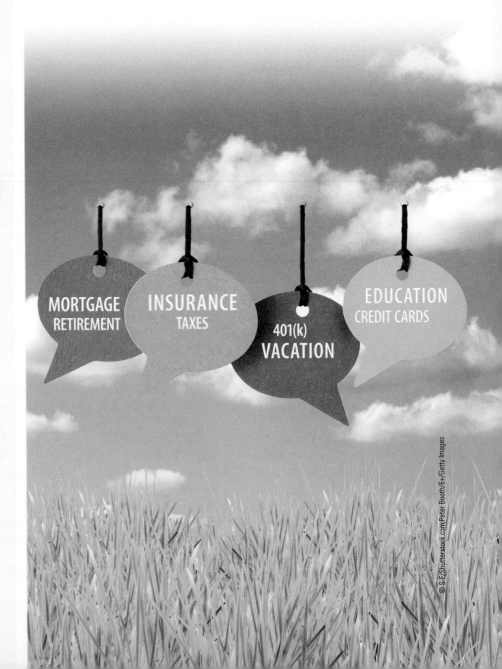

MORTGAGE RETIREMENT
INSURANCE TAXES
401(k) VACATION
EDUCATION CREDIT CARDS

© S-E/Shutterstock.com/Peter Booth/E+/Getty Images

WHAT DO YOU RECOMMEND?

© 2010 Fuse/Jupiter Images Corporation

Britanny Day, a 37-year-old marketing manager for a large corporation in Long Beach, California, earns $110,000 per year. She saves an additional about $800 each month beyond her contributions to her employer's 401(k) retirement plan. Her total 401(k) holdings are worth $260,000.

Ever since her grandfather gave her some stocks as a child, Britanny has loved investing—and she has enjoyed a good track record with her efforts. Britanny is an active trader, often trading every three or four weeks, primarily in the oil, technology, and pharmaceutical prescription drug industries. Every year, she has some losses as well as gains. Her private portfolio is currently worth $160,000. Britanny has never bought or sold options or futures contracts, but her stockbroker suggested that she consider them. Britanny also has a friend who owns several residential rental properties that she bought when prices were low who has asked her to consider investing as her partner in her next real estate venture.

What do you recommend to Britanny on the subject of real estate and alternative investments regarding:

1. **Investing in real estate?**

2. **Putting some of her money in an alternative investment, like a collectible or gold?**

3. **Investing in options and futures contracts?**

YOUR NEXT FIVE YEARS

In the next five years, you can start achieving financial success by doing the following related to real estate and high-risk investments:

1. *Before deciding to invest in real estate, carefully consider the disadvantages of such investments.*

2. *Invest only in real estate properties that have a positive cash flow.*

3. *Finance real estate investments with conventional mortgages, not mortgages with adjustable interest terms.*

4. *Use the price-to-rent ratio and discounted cash-flow methods to help determine the right price to pay for a real estate investment.*

5. *Do not put any of your long-term investment money into real estate or high-risk investments are they are not suitable.*

real estate (or housing) bubble

Rapid and unsustainable increases in home prices followed by sharp declines in values.

high-risk (or alternative) investments

Present potential for significant fluctuations in return, sometimes over short time periods.

LEARNING OBJECTIVE 1

Demonstrate how you can make money investing in real estate.

real estate

Property consisting of land, all structures permanently attached to that land, and accompanying rights and privileges, such as crops and mineral rights.

A home tends to accomplish more than just putting a roof over your head. It is also an investment, because historically housing values have increased about 3 percent annually over the long term. A **real estate** (or **housing) bubble** for residential markets occurred in the United States in the middle of the last decade. The bubble saw rapid increases in home valuations (10 or 20 percent, or more, a year) until they were unsustainable.

Then the real estate market crashed as home values plummeted 40 or 50 percent or even more in some communities. The "for sale" signs on millions of foreclosed homes also pulled down the values of nearby homes. Today over 10 percent of all mortgage holders owe more on their homes than they are worth (they are "under water"), making it extremely difficult for them to sell. Unemployment and underemployment also makes it difficult for many others to buy homes. Fortunately, the real estate market has started to recover, thus there are some reasonable investment choices available.

Investors with an aggressive investment philosophy who seek high returns and are willing to accept greater risks might consider owning alternative assets such as collectibles, precious metals, gems, options, and futures contracts. All these are referred to as **high-risk** (or **alternative**) **investments** because they have the potential for significant fluctuations in return, sometimes over short time periods.

Many investment advisors today recommend that people put 10 percent of their money into alternative investments as a way to diversity their money, recommending for example that someone in their twenties have a portfolio of 65% stocks, 15% bonds, 10% alternatives, and 10% cash. They are wrong. Real estate and alternative investments are not suitable investments for long-term investing program, such as for your retirement, because they are too risky for you too diversify appropriately Think about it? How many real estate investments can you make? How many precious metals can you own? How many options and future contacts can you buy?

16.1 HOW TO MAKE MONEY INVESTING IN REAL ESTATE

Real estate investing is not the same as buying a home in which to live, which was the subject of Chapter 9. Investing in real estate might provide you with extra income now and give a boost to your future retirement plans. But you have to do a lot of things right.

Real estate investing is complicated given today's market conditions, thus you must become smart about taxes, financing, insurance, and community economics. Real estate investments are complex, and they are much riskier than investing in mutual funds and stocks. People often do not possess the mental toughness that it takes because investing in real estate is a job. Most people are not cut out to be a do-it-yourself landlord. Dealing with tenants requires a business attitude, not a willingness to view tenants as friends.

Real estate is property consisting of land, all structures permanently attached to that land, and accompanying rights and privileges, such as crops and mineral rights. For example, you can invest directly as an individual or jointly with other investors to buy properties designed for residential living, such as houses, duplexes, apartments, mobile homes, and condominiums. You also could invest in commercial properties designed for business uses, such as office buildings, medical centers, gas stations, and motels. You might buy raw land or residential lots, although they are extremely risky and often lose money for the investor. For someone considering an investment in real estate, there are two key questions that you must answer.

16.1a   Question 1: Can You Make Current Income While You Own?

The most important consideration for real estate investors in today's real estate market is not whether the price will rise enough in a few years to make a profit. The boom days of the rapidly rising prices of the housing bubble are probably gone in most markets. The focus for real estate investors now is whether the rental income will be sufficient to make ends meet while waiting for the property to increase in value.

If you invest in a property and you are paying out more than the rental income coming in, the negative cash flow exposes you to two risks: (1) whether you can afford to continue paying out that money month after month and year after year, and (2) whether you can make up for these cash flow losses when the property sells, which you hope will be for more than you paid for it. Get either of these wrong, and you lose your invested money and maybe more.

Know the Price-to-Rent Ratio   To measure the current income in a real estate market, investors can begin by using the **price-to-rent ratio**, which is the ratio of median residential real estate prices to the median annual rents that can be earned from the real estate. The lower the ratio, the smaller the gap between annualized rental and purchase costs and the more attractive the decision to buy a home versus renting a similar one. If the price-to-rent ratio is too high, the prices for homes are likely to be too high.

Nationally the price-to-rent ratio was 15 at the peak of the housing bubble. Now it is 11, which is back to 2004 levels. For recent information on price-rent ratios see Trulia (trends.truliablog.com/category/rent-vs-buy-index/) and Altos Research (blog .altosresearch.com/single-family-home-rental/). The ratio might range from perhaps 4 in Detroit to 35 in Honolulu, or more, depending on local market conditions—meaning how low or high housing prices are.

For investors, the lower the price-to-rent ratio is in a given community and a particular property, the easier it should be to earn back your investment. For example, in San Jose, California, a condominium renting for $2600 a month might sell for the high price of $890,000 for a price-to-rent ratio of 28.5($12 \times \$2600 = \$31,200$; $890,000/\$31,200$).

> Price-to-rent ratio = Home price/annual rent
>
> $28.5 = (\$890,000/\$31,200\ [\$2,600\ \text{monthly rent} \times 12])$ **(16.1)**

Alternatively, a home in Pittsburgh, Pennsylvania, might cost $165,000 and rent for $1200 a month, thus providing a price-to-rent ratio of 11.5($165,000/\$14,400 [\$1200 \times 12])$. Investing in rental property with a high ratio will provide a profit only with a future increase in its resale value, which may be difficult to achieve in the near term.

Current Income Results from Positive Cash Flow   For an income-producing real estate investment, you pay operating expenses out of rental income. The amount of rental income you have left after paying all operating expenses is called **cash flow**. The amount of cash flow is obtained by subtracting all cash outlays from the cash income. If the property has a mortgage (a common occurrence), payments toward the mortgage principal and interest also must be made out of rental income. Operating expenses such as mortgage payments, real estate property taxes, repairs, and vacancies may eat up half or more of the rental income.

Calculate the Rental Yield   Investors also calculate the **rental yield** on properties, as shown in Equation (16.2). This is a computation of how much income the investor might pocket from rent each year before mortgage payments as a percentage of the purchase price. Most properties yield about 4 percent of income annually, although the rental yield may be as little as 1 or 2 percent and as high as 8 or 9 percent.

---

price-to-rent ratio

The ratio of median residential real estate prices to the median annual rents that can be earned from the real estate.

DO IT IN CLASS

cash flow

Amount of rental income you have left after paying all operating expenses.

rental yield

A computation of how much income the investor might pocket from rent each year (before mortgage payments) as a percentage of the purchase price; divide the annual rent by 2 and then divide by the purchase price.

DID YOU KNOW

Invest in Foreclosed Property Using a Short Sale

Foreclosure is the legal and professional procedure in which a mortgagee, or other lienholder, usually a lender, repossesses a home and sells it because the borrower has fallen behind in making payments on the loan. Prior to foreclosure, the homeowner has three options: (1) depart the property and try, for moral reasons, to repay the lender the deficiency, (2) declare bankruptcy, or (3) try to arrange a short sale. Oftentimes the remaining balance owed on the home is more than the property is worth. Unless the lender is willing to modify the terms of the loan, the lender then pursues the homeowner for the deficiency.

In a **short sale** the lender accepts less than the full mortgage amount and often forgives whatever debt is left unpaid. The **deficiency amount** is the difference between the amount owed and what the bank collects at the short sale. When a bank agrees to a short sale, the homeowner hires an agent to find a buyer. New rules require lenders to provide preapproved terms for short sales; thus, an investor's bid is more likely to be accepted. Lenders agree to absorb the loss, although they might demand the homeowner make some kind of payment or share the loss. A debt that is forgiven may be subject to income taxes. A short sale may be a buying opportunity for investors, although negotiating with banks is sometimes a cumbersome and lengthy process.

Less expensive properties often offer higher yields. The formula assumes half of rental income goes for expenses other than debt repayment.

capital improvements

Costs incurred in making value-enhancing changes (beyond maintenance and repair) in real property.

repairs

Usually tax-deductible expenses necessary to maintain property value.

$$\text{Rental yield} = \frac{(\text{rent} \div 2)}{\text{purchase price}} \quad \textbf{(16.2)}$$

	San Jose	Pittsburgh
Purchase price	$890,000	$165,000
Annual rent	31,200	14,400
Annual rent/2	15,600	7,200
Yield (annual rent/2/purchase price)	1.75%	4.36%

A slowly growing economy can lead to unfinished units and losses for real estate investors.

Bloomberg/Contributor/Getty Images

16.1b Question 2: Can You Profit When You Sell the Property?

The **capital gain** earned in a real estate investment comes from price appreciation. It is the amount above ownership costs for which an investment is sold. In real estate, **ownership costs** include the original purchase price as well as expenditures for any capital improvements made to a property prior to sale. **Capital improvements** are costs incurred in making changes in real property—beyond maintenance and repairs—that add to its value. Installing a pool and adding a room represent capital improvements.

Repairs are expenses (usually tax deductible against an investor's annual cash-flow income) necessary to maintain the value of the property. Repainting,

DID YOU KNOW

Money Websites in Real Estate

Informative websites for investing in real estate, including price-to-rent ratios in your community are:

Altos Research (blog.altosresearch.com /single-family-home-rental/)

LasVegas4Us.com discounted cash flow calculator www .lasvegas4us.com/JwwDCF/discounted_cash_flow _calculator.htm

Realtor.com (www.realtor.com/)

Trulia (trends.truliablog.com/category/rent-vs -buy-index/)

Yahoo real estate (homes.yahoo.com/)

Zillo (www.zillow.com/)

mending roof leaks, and fixing plumbing are examples of repairs, but in the eyes of the IRS they are not capital improvements.

In markets in which real estate is difficult to sell (too many properties on the market and too few buyers), perhaps because of continuing job losses in a sluggish regional economy, residential housing prices might decline 2 or 3 percent annually for a long time. That means continuing deflation in home prices in some markets year after year.

CONCEPT CHECK 16.1

1. What are the two key questions to consider before investing in real estate?

2. Distinguish between the price-to-rent ratio and the rental yield as measures of current income.

16.2 TAKE ADVANTAGE OF BENEFICIAL TAX TREATMENTS

The U.S. Congress, through provisions in the Internal Revenue Code, encourages real estate investments by giving investors five special tax treatments.

16.2a 1. Depreciation Is a Tax Deduction

Investors in real estate become successful by understanding the "numbers" of real estate investing. For example, assume that Jisue Han, a lawyer from Columbus, Ohio, invested $200,000 in a residential building ($170,000) and land ($30,000). She rents the property to a tenant for $24,000 per year. You might initially think that Jisue has to pay income taxes on the entire $24,000 in rental income. Wrong. IRS regulations allow taxpayers to deduct depreciation from rental income. **Depreciation** represents the decline in value of an asset over time due to normal wear and tear and obsolescence. A proportionate amount of a capital asset representing depreciation may be deducted against income each year over the asset's estimated life. Land cannot be depreciated.

Jisue can deduct an equal part of the building's cost over the estimated life of the property. IRS guidelines provide that residential properties may be depreciated over 27.5 years, while nonresidential properties are allowed 39 years. Jisue calculates (from Table 16-1) the amount she can annually deduct from income to be

LEARNING OBJECTIVE 2

Recognize how to take advantage of beneficial tax treatments in real estate investing.

depreciation

Decline in value of an asset over time due to normal wear and tear and obsolescence.

DID YOU KNOW

What to Do before Investing in Real Estate

1. *Set up a limited liability corporation to own your real estate investments because it protects your personal assets in case someone is injured on your rental property and sues you.*

2. *Consider investing in properties only in locales where there are thriving businesses located near good schools, supermarkets, and public transportation.*

3. *Hire an accountant experienced in real estate investing.*

4. *Line up financing options before searching for properties.*

5. *Hire an inspector to inspect the physical condition of the property.*

6. *Hire a licensed contractor for plumbing, electrical, and expensive repair jobs rather than doing them yourself.*

7. *Consider hiring a management company to tend to your property; the cost is 5 to 10 percent of rental income.*

8. *Set aside $5000 as a contingency fund for unanticipated problems with real estate investment property.*

$6182 ($170,000 ÷ 27.5). Table 16-1 shows the effects of depreciation on her income taxes, assuming Jisue pays income taxes at a combined federal and state rate of 36 percent. In this example, the depreciation deduction lowers taxable income on the property from $24,000 to $17,818($24,000 − $6182) and increases the return on the investment to 9.29 percent.

16.2b   2. Interest Is a Tax Deduction

Real estate investors incur many business expenses in attempting to earn a profit: interest on a mortgage, real estate property taxes, insurance, utilities, management bills, homeowner's association fees, capital improvements, repairs, and accounting and legal costs. The largest of these costs often is the interest expense, as properties are often purchased with a mortgage loan. Table 16-2 illustrates the effect of interest expenses on income taxes. To purchase her $200,000 investment property, assume Jisue borrowed $175,000 for 15 years at 5 percent with a monthly payment of $1383 (from Table 9-4

Table 16-1   Depreciation Reduces Income Taxes Which Increases Investor's Return

			Without Depreciation	With Depreciation
Total amount invested	$ 200,000	Gross rental income	$24,000	$24,000
Cost of land	− 30,000	Less annual depreciation expense	0	6,182
Cost of rental building	$ 170,000	Taxable income	24,000	17,818
Depreciation for 27.5 years	$ 6,182	Income taxes (36 percent combined federal and state tax rate)	8,640	6,414
		After-tax return	$15,360	$17,586
		After-tax yield (divide return by $200,000)	7.68%	8.79%

Table 16-2	Additional Effect of Interest Paid on Income Taxes on Return	
Gross rental income		$24,000
Less annual depreciation deduction		−6,182
Subtotal		$17,818
Less interest expense for the year (5 percent, $175,000 mortgage)		−7,900
Taxable income		$ 9,918
Cash flow after paying interest ($24,000 − $7900)		16,100
Less income tax liability (0.36 × $9918)		−3,570
After-tax return ($16,100 − $3570)		$ 12,530
After-tax yield [$12,530 ÷ ($200,000 − $175,000)]		50.12%

DO IT IN CLASS

on page 273). After deducting annual depreciation of $6182 and interest expenses of $7900 her taxable income is reduced to $9918. Because her income tax liability is only $3570, Jisue's after tax return of $12,530 yields 50.12 percent on her leveraged investment.

Tax laws permit investors to deduct interest expenses. The interest deduction gives Jisue a cash flow after paying mortgage interest of $16,100 ($24,000 − $7900). In essence, the $7900 in interest is paid with $2844 ($7900 × 36 percent combined federal and state income tax rate) of the money that was not sent to the federal and state governments and $5056 ($7900 − $2844) of Jisue's money.

The **loan-to-value ratio** measures the amount of leverage in a real estate investment project. It is calculated by dividing the amount of debt by the value of the total original investment. On this property Jisue's loan-to-value ratio was 87.5 percent ($175,000/$200,000) because she made a down payment of $25,000.

loan-to-value ratio

Measures the amount of leverage in a real estate investment project by dividing the total amount of debt by the market price of the investment.

$$\text{Loan-to-Value Ratio} = \frac{\text{Mortgage Amount}}{\text{Appraised Value of the Property}} \quad \textbf{(16.3)}$$
$$= \frac{\$175,000}{\$200,000}$$
$$= 87.5\%$$

16.2c 3. Capital Gains Are Taxed at Very Low Rates

Capital gains on real estate are realized through price appreciation. For most taxpayers, long-term capital gains are taxed at a rate of 15 percent.

16.2d 4. Exchange of Properties Can Be Tax Free

Another special tax treatment results when a real estate investor trades equity in one property for equity in a similar property. If none of the people involved in the trade receives any other form of property or money, the transaction is considered a **tax-free exchange** (or a **1031 exchange**).

If one person receives some money or other property, only that person has to report the extra proceeds as a taxable gain. For example, assume you bought a residential rental property five years ago for $220,000 and today it is worth much more. You trade it with your friend by giving $10,000 in cash for your friend's $280,000 single-family rental home. Your friend needs to report only the $10,000 as income this year. In contrast, you do not need to report your long-term gain, $50,000 ($280,000 − $10,000 − $220,000), until you actually sell the new property.

tax-free exchange (or 1031 exchange)

Arises when a real estate investor trades equity in one property for equity in a similar property and no other forms of property or money change hands.

16.2e   5. Taxes Can Be Lower on Vacation Home Rental Income

If you rent out your vacation property for 14 or fewer days during the year, you can pocket the income tax free because the IRS does not want to hear about this gain. The home is considered a personal residence, so you can deduct mortgage interest and property taxes just as you would for your principal residence. That same tax break is available for those who rent their primary home for 14 days or less, for example, to people attending a major sporting event in your city.

If you rent your property for 15 days or more, you are a landlord and you have turned the endeavor into a business. You may deduct expenses attributable to the rental business, such as mortgage interest, real estate property taxes, depreciation, utilities, repairs, insurance, advertising, homeowner's association fees, and property management fees, as well as auto and other travel expenses.

If you **actively participate** in the management of the property (defined as approving new tenants, deciding on rental terms, or approving repairs and capital improvements), you can deduct rental expenses up to the level of rental income you report prorated for the number of days it was rented out. When your adjusted gross income (AGI) is less than $100,000, a maximum of $25,000 of rental-related losses may be deducted each year to offset income from any source, including your salary. The $25,000 limit is gradually phased out as your AGI moves between $100,000 and $150,000. This ability to shelter income from taxes represents a terrific benefit for people who invest in real estate on a small scale.

CONCEPT CHECK 16.2

1. Summarize how depreciation is used to reduce the income from a real estate investment.

2. Briefly explain how the interest paid on the mortgage of a real estate investment reduces one's income taxes.

3. Summarize the special income tax regulations on renting out vacation homes.

16.3   PRICING AND FINANCING REAL ESTATE INVESTMENTS

discounted cash-flow method

Effective way to estimate the value or asking price of a real estate investment based on after-tax cashflow and the return on the invested dollars discounted over time to reflect a discounted yield.

Sure ways to go wrong in a real estate investment are to pay too much for the property and finance it incorrectly.

16.3a   Pay the Right Price

The **discounted cash-flow method** is an effective way to estimate the present value or appropriate price of a real estate investment. It emphasizes after-tax cash flow and the return on the invested dollars discounted over time to reflect a discounted yield. Software programs are available online to calculate the discounted cash flows. (For example, see www.lasvegas4us.com/JwwDCF/discounted_cash_flow_calculator.htm.) You also can use Appendix A-2, as illustrated in Table 16-3.

To see how this method works, assume that you require an after-tax rate of return of 10 percent on a condominium advertised for sale at $210,000. You estimate that rents can be increased about 2 percent each year for five years. After all expenses are paid, you expect to have after-tax cash flows of $4000, $4100, $4200, $4300, and $4400 for the five years. Assuming some price appreciation, you anticipate selling the property for $230,000 after all expenses are incurred. That's a conservative increase in the value of the property of less than 10 percent over 5 years. How much should you pay now to buy the property?

Table 16-3 explains how to answer this question. Multiply the estimated after-tax cash flows and the expected proceeds of $230,000 to be realized on the sale of the

Table 16-3 Discounted Cash Flow to Estimate Price

	After-Tax Cash Flow	Present Value of $1 at 10 Percent*	Present Value of After-Tax Cash Flow
1 year	$ 4,000	0.9524	$ 3,809
2 years	4,100	0.9070	3,718
3 years	4,200	0.8638	3,627
4 years	4,300	0.8227	3,537
5 years	4,400	0.7835	3,447
Sale price of property in 5 years	$230,000	0.7835	180,205
Present value of property			$198,343

*From Appendix A-2

DO IT IN CLASS

property by the present value of a dollar at 10 percent (your required rate of return). Add the present values together to obtain the total present value of the property—in this case, $198,343. The asking price of $210,000 is too high for you to earn an after-tax return of 10 percent.

Your choices are to negotiate the price down, accept a return of less than 10 percent, increase rents, hope that the sale price of the property will be higher than $230,000 five

ADVICE FROM A PROFESSIONAL

Timesharing Is a Financial Disaster as an Investment

Timesharing is the joint ownership or lease of vacation property through which the principals occupy the property individually for set periods of time. Timesharing is not an investment, although it is promoted as a way to simultaneously invest and obtain vacation housing. For $5000 to $30,000, buyers can purchase one or more weeks' use of luxury vacation housing furnished right down to the salt-and-pepper shakers. Timeshare owners pay an annual maintenance fee that averages $822 for each week of ownership. Maintenance fees increase every year, and occasionally there are special assessment fees.

With **deeded timesharing**, the buyer obtains a legal title or deed to limited time periods of use of real estate. Purchasers become secured creditors who are guaranteed continued use of the property throughout any bankruptcy proceedings. They really own their week (or two) of the property.

Nondeeded timesharing is a legal right-to-use purchase of a limited, preplanned timesharing period of use of a property. It is a long-term lease, license, or club membership permitting use of a hotel suite, condominium, or other accommodation, and the right to use usually expires in 20 to 25 years. If the true owner of the property—the developer—goes bankrupt, creditors can lock out the timeshare purchasers (technically they are tenants) from the premises. And it happens.

It is extremely hard to sell a timeshare, and sales commissions of legitimate resellers are 30 percent of the price. The Resort Property Owners Association says that the average timeshare unit languishes on the market for 4.4 years before being sold. At any point in time, 60 percent of *all* timeshares are up for sale. Timeshare sellers rarely sell for 30 percent of their original investment. As one observer said, "If someone tries to sell you a timeshare, run!"

In good economic times or bad, you can find rental lodgings in the same area at a lower price than owning. The good thing about owning a timeshare is that it forces you to take a yearly vacation, and the vacation will be at the same time and place regardless of where you live in the future. If you want variety in vacation time or place, some timeshare plans allow owners to swap their property for others in distant locations through membership in a worldwide vacation exchange such as My Resort Newwork (www.myresortnetwork.com /timeshare-exchange/) or www.RCI.com.

Philip C. Bryant
Ivy Tech Community College, Bloomington, Indiana

DID YOU KNOW

Sean's Success Story

Sean got greedy and then got smart. He greedily invested too heavily in aggressive stock mutual funds and then, because of the gyrations in the stock market, got scared and pulled out by the end of the year with his portfolio down about 10 percent. He got smarter when he decided to no longer jump in and out of the market trying to make quick profits. Thus he has decided to invest his 401(k) funds in ETF mutual funds that pretty much track the broader indexes. In addition, Sean and his brother calculated the numbers on a real estate investment with a projected 7 percent annual return, so they made a down payment on a duplex that is close to an A-rated high school. The old renters have signed new leases, and the investment produces a positive cash flow.

FINANCIAL POWER POINT

Find Out Home Prices in Seconds

To find prices on a home anywhere in the country, check out Zillo (www.zillow.com/), AOL.com (realestate.aol.com/blog/home-values/), and Trulia (www.trulia.com/home_prices/). Simply type in an address to obtain an estimate of its price. Be advised, however, that there have been complaints about accurate prices so perhaps check more than one site.

seller financing (or owner financing)
When a seller self-finances a buyer's loan by accepting a promissory note from a buyer, who makes monthly mortgage payments.

sweat equity property
Property that needs repairs but that has good underlying value; an investor buys the property at a favorable price and fixes it up to rent or sell at a profit.

years from now, or consider another investment. The discounted cash-flow method provides an effective way to estimate real estate values because it takes into account the selling price of the property, the effect of income taxes, and the time value of money.

16.3b   Financing a Real Estate Investment

Borrowing to finance a real estate investment is more expensive than borrowing to buy one's own home, often 0.5 to 1.5 percentage points above the rate for customary homebuyers. There is more risk because the investor does not live at the property. The minimum down payment for investors is often 20 or 25 percent. To make a smaller down payment and perhaps get a lower mortgage rate, some real estate investors buy a home, live in it for a year, and then rent it out as an investment.

A popular way to finance a real estate investment is through **seller financing** (or **owner financing**). This occurs when a seller is willing to self-finance a loan by accepting a promissory note from the buyer who makes monthly mortgage payments. No lending agency is involved. Investing buyers pay higher interest rates for seller financing. The seller may accept little or no down payment in exchange for an even higher interest rate, perhaps 1½ to 2½ percent above conventional mortgage rates. Owner-financed deals can be transacted very quickly for investors.

Another way to start in real estate investing is to purchase **sweat equity property**. With this approach, you seek a property that needs repairs but has good underlying value. You buy this fixer-upper at a favorable price and "sweat" by spending many hours cleaning, painting, and repairing it to rent or sell at a profit.

CONCEPT CHECK 16.3

1. Summarize how the discounted cash-flow method helps determine the right price to pay for a real estate investment.

2. Comment on the wisdom of buying a timeshare as an investment.

3. List three ways to finance a real estate investment.

16.4 DISADVANTAGES OF REAL ESTATE INVESTING

Real estate investing can be profitable. But it does have some significant disadvantages.

- **Business risk.** It is quite possible to lose money in real estate investments, as lots of investors found out in recent years. A local recession, perhaps because a large employer closed, can depress housing prices. Zoning changes can slash housing values. Rents cannot keep up with costs in communities in which industries and jobs are moving elsewhere or in deteriorating neighborhoods.

- **Foreclosures.** In communities where there are many foreclosures, other sellers have to lower their home prices to compete. This depresses the values of all comparable housing—no matter how wonderful the location or condition—thus making it more difficult for anyone to sell at a reasonable price.

- **Illiquidity.** Besides being expensive, the market for investment property is much smaller than the securities market. As a result, it is common to experience trouble in selling. It may take months or even a year or more to find a buyer, arrange the financing, and close the sale of a real estate investment.

- **Complex Assumptions.** Real estate investments require much more investigation than do most other investments. Numerous assumptions about financial details such as projected rents and the cost of repairs in the future also must be made.

- **Large initial investment.** Direct investment in real estate generally requires many thousands of dollars, often with an initial outlay of $15,000, $30,000, $50,000, or more.

- **Lack of diversification.** So much capital is required in real estate investing that spreading risk is almost impossible.

- **Dealing with tenants.** Picking the wrong tenants can quickly turn a real estate property into a big financial loss. Someone has to screen rental applicants for their credit histories, criminal records, work references, and experience with previous landlords. Lexisnexis.mysmartmove.com runs credit and criminal background checks. State laws may make it impossible to evict a deadbeat tenant for several months or a year or more.

- **Time-consuming management demands.** Managing a real estate investment requires time for conducting regular inspections of the property, dealing with insurance companies, making repairs, and collecting overdue rents. It's a job.

- **Low current income.** Expenses may reduce the cash-flow return to less than 2 percent or even generate a net loss in a given year.

- **Unpredictable costs.** Estimating costs is problematic. Investors cannot control increasing real estate tax assessments or accurately predict when a central air-conditioning unit might break down.

- **Interest rate risk.** When interest rates rise or unemployment grows, fewer people can afford to buy homes, and this puts downward pressure on prices and rents.

- **Legal fees.** The services of a real estate attorney will be needed to help handle the real estate purchase, sale, building inspections, zoning issues, tenant problems, insurance disputes, accounting, and any liability issues. Title insurance is a critically important expense to investors, particularly when allegations suggest that lenders may or may not have properly inspected the seller's legal documents.

- **High transfer costs.** Substantial transfer costs, often representing 6 to 7 percent of the property's sale price, plus money for fix-up costs, may be incurred when real estate is bought or sold.

DID YOU KNOW

The Tax Consequences of an Income-Producing Real Estate Investment

When you are considering a real estate investment, you use the investment amount (purchase price or down payment) to begin the process of estimating the likely rate of return. This calculation result may then be compared with other investment alternatives. Because some of the many assumptions in real estate calculations could be incorrect, caution is warranted in real estate analyses.

The following table shows five-year estimates for a hypothetical residential property in Denver, Colorado located close to a well-respected high school with a purchase price of $200,000. The building will be purchased with a $150,000 mortgage loan, so the buyer has to make a $50,000 down payment plus pay $8000 in closing costs. The gross rental income of $18,000 annually is projected to rise at an annual rate of 5 percent, vacancies and unpaid rent at 10 percent, real estate taxes at 7 percent, insurance at 8 percent, and maintenance at 10 percent. Virtually the entire payment for the 30-year, $150,000, 6½ percent, fixed-rate mortgage loan is assumed to be interest during these early years. For income tax purposes, the land is valued at $20,000, and the building is depreciated over 27.5 years.

The amount of annual straight-line depreciation is calculated to be $6546 ($200,000 − $20,000 = $180,000; $180,000 ÷ 27.5 = $6546).

Note (in line D) how challenging it is to earn current income from rental properties. During the first two years, the total cash flow (line D) is projected to be positive ($976 and $652), but for the following three years, the cash flow is expected to be negative (−330, −$10, and −$305). However, because the income tax laws permit depreciation (line E, $6546) to be recorded each year as a real estate investment expense, even though it is not an out-of-pocket cost, the investor calculates a total taxable loss (line F) for each of the five years of expected ownership (−$5570 the first year).

These losses can be deducted on the investor's income tax returns. Because the investor pays a 30 percent combined federal and state income tax rate, the loss results in a first-year annual tax savings of $1671 (line G). Therefore, instead of sending the $1671 to the government in taxes, the investor can use that amount to help pay the operating expenses of the investment. Consequently, the net cash-flow income (line D) of $976 is enhanced by tax savings (line G) of $1671 to result in a net cash-flow gain after taxes of $2647 ($1671 + $976).

Estimates for a Successful Real Estate Investment

		Year			
	1	**2**	**3**	**4**	**5**
A. Gross rental income	$18,000	$18,900	$19,845	$20,837	$21,879
Less vacancies and unpaid rent	1,800	1,890	1,985	2,084	2,188
B. Projected gross income	$16,200	$17,010	$17,860	$18,753	$19,691
C. Less operating expenses					
Principal and interest (P + I)	$11,376	$11,376	$11,376	$11,376	$11,376
Real estate taxes (T)	2,600	2,782	2,977	3,185	3,408
Insurance (I)	800	804	933	1,008	1,089
Maintenance	2,400	2,640	2,904	3,194	3,513
Total operating expenses	$17,176	$17,662	$18,190	$18,763	$19,386
D. Total cash flow	$ 976	$ 652	$ (330)	$ (10)	$ (305)
E. Less depreciation expense	(6,546)	(6,546)	(6,546)	(6,546)	(6,546)
F. Taxable income (or loss) (D − E)	$(5,570)	$(5,894)	$(6,876)	$(6,556)	$(6,851)
G. Annual tax savings (30 percent marginal rate)	1,671	1,768	2,062	1,966	2,055
H. Net cash-flow gain (or loss) after taxes (G + D)	$ 2,647	$ 2,420	$ 1,732	$ 1,956	$ 1,750

Assume that the property appreciates in value at an annual rate of 4 percent and will be worth $243,330 (line K) in five years ($200,000 × 1.04 × 1.04 × 1.04 × 1.04 × 1.04).

If it is sold at this price, a 6 percent real estate sales commission of $14,599 ($243,330 × 0.06) would reduce the net proceeds to $228,731 ($243,330 − $14,599).

Now we can calculate **the crude annual rate of return** on the property, as shown in the second table. A crude annual rate of return is a rough measure of the yield on amounts invested that assumes that equal portions of the gain are earned each year. The total return in this example was substantial. The investor made out-of-pocket cash investments of $50,000 for the down payment and $8000 in closing costs, and we subtract the accumulated net cash flow (line N) of $10,505 (adding all the numbers across line H because the investor already has received that money) for a total investment (line O) of $47,495. The investor has a capital gain (line M) of $53,461. After dividing to determine the before-tax total return (line R) to obtain 112 percent, the crude annual rate of return (line S) is 22.4 percent annually over the five years (112 percent ÷ 5 years).

Crude Rate of Return on a Successful Real Estate Investment

Taxable cost

I.	Purchase price ($50,000 down payment; $150,000 loan)	$200,000
	Closing costs	8,000
	Subtotal	208,000
J.	Less accumulated depreciation	32,730
	Taxable cost (adjusted basis)	$175,270

Proceeds (after paying off mortgage)

K.	Sale price	$243,330
	Less sales commission	14,599
	Net proceeds	$228,731
L.	Less taxable cost (J)	175,270
M.	Taxable proceeds (capital gain)	$ 53,461

Amount invested

	Down payment	$ 50,000
	Closing costs	8,000
N.	Less accumulated net cash-flow gains	(10,505)
O.	Total invested	$ 47,495

Crude annual rate of return

P.	Total invested	$ 47,495
Q.	Taxable proceeds (capital gain from M)	$ 53,461
R.	Before-tax total return ($53,461/$47,495)	112%
S.	Crude before-tax annual rate of return (112 percent ÷ 5 years)	22.4%

CONCEPT CHECK 16.4

1. Summarize why foreclosures and illiquidity are disadvantages in real estate investing.

2. Comment on why real estate investors often have time-consuming management demands.

16.5 INVESTING IN COLLECTIBLES, PRECIOUS METALS, AND GEMS

LEARNING OBJECTIVE 5

Summarize the risks and challenges of investing in the alternative investments of collectibles, precious metals, and gems.

Investors often think of assets as something they would like to own for the long term. When investing in collectibles, precious metals, and gems, the investor owns illiquid real assets, not intangible items represented by pieces of paper. While an asset may be bought for its long-term investment potential, profits might be earned in the short term.

A **speculator** buys in the hope that someone else will pay more for an asset in the not-too-distant future. Speculators often buy or sell in expectation of profiting from market fluctuations. If you put money into these illiquid assets, limit your speculative investing to no more than 5 to 10 percent of your total investment portfolio, and buy only what you truly adore. Don't consider collectibles, precious metals, and gems as part of your savings plan for retirement. When investing for retirement you should only use long-term strategies as outlined in Chapter 13.

speculator
An investor who buys in the hope that someone else will pay more for an asset in the not-too-distant future.

16.5a Collectibles

Collectibles are cultural artifacts that have value because of their beauty, age, scarcity, or popularity. They include baseball cards, posters, sports memorabilia, guns, photographs, paintings, prints, ceramics, comic books, watches, lunchboxes,

collectibles
Cultural artifacts that have value because of their beauty, age, scarcity, or popularity, such as antiques, stamps, rare coins, art, baseball cards, and so on.

DID YOU KNOW

Bias toward Being Reluctant to Invest Again after a Loss

People engaged in real estate and high-risk investments have a bias toward certain behaviors that can be harmful, such as a tendency toward the pain of losing money. People often avoid strong growth investment opportunities because they have lost in investments in the past. Research shows that an investment loss packs twice the emotional blow of a gain and among retirees the impact is tenfold. What to do? Set your focus on how much of a gain or loss you are willing to accept on a future investment and then accept reality by selling when those gains or losses actually occur.

FINANCIAL POWER POINT

Search for Collectibles Prices at Christie's and Sotheby's Online

The giant auction houses of Christie's (www.christies.com) and Sotheby's (www.sothebys.com) offer big selections of prints, photographs, watches, wines, furniture, diamond jewelry, and other collectibles. Check out their catalogs and videos on their websites, and consider signing up for text messages and the ability to bid by phone or online.

matchbooks, glassware, spoons, stamps, rare coins, art, rugs, fine wine, cars, and antiques. The collectible markets are fueled by nostalgia, limited availability, and "what is hot to own today." Prices for collectibles often lag other investments and continue to lag. Collectibles won't beat the return of stocks over the long term, but they are lots of fun to own.

Making a Profit on Collectibles Is Not Easy One key to success in collectibles is to invest in quality—the higher the better. Think about the highest value collectibles as being equivalent to blue-chip stocks. Although buying collectibles can be easy, turning a profit may not. The only return on collectibles occurs through price appreciation, and you must sell to realize a profit. That could be hard for you to do if the collectibles give you pleasure. If you sell, the IRS requires that you pay a 28 percent income tax rate (or your tax bracket, whichever is lower) on collectibles rather than a 15 percent tax on capital gains.

Items that are almost certain to lose value include those that are mass produced and marketed as collectibles or limited editions. You often see these kinds of collectibles advertised on television and in newspapers and magazines. Another risk is the wholesale-to-retail price spread, which could be 50 or 100 percent. If you buy from a dealer, you'll probably pay a markup of about 40 to 50 percent. Investors generally get more for their money buying at an auction, but realize that professional dealers are always bidding there too.

DID YOU KNOW

Scams Abound in Collectibles, Precious Metals, and Gems

The average investor can't tell a diamond from a cubic zirconium or a Monet from a Manet. The values of collectibles, gold, other precious metals, and precious gems rely in part upon the authority of "experts" who purport to determine their worth. Such blind trust invites risk for potential investors. When an asset does not generate a readily quantifiable return (such as rent, interest, or dividends) its value is determined by supply and demand—as well as lies and rumors. Scams, forgeries and frauds abound with these investments, as promoters and telemarketers tell tales about skyrocketing prices and high profit potentials to encourage their purchase. Collectibles, precious metals, and gems are not wise choices for the casual investor.

Prices on collectibles vary greatly from item to item and year to year. Markets are fickle. If the investor needs to convert the asset to cash, a sale may take days, weeks, or months, and the seller may be forced to accept a lower price.

Buying and Selling Collectibles on the Internet You can buy collectibles on the Internet, using eBay for example, purchasing in minutes what you might never have found even after searching for years in magazines, junk shops, flea markets, and auctions. Buying collectibles on the Internet is efficient and convenient, and it is easy to compare products and prices. It is hard to inspect the collectible before purchase, however. Search Google for "collectibles," but realize that this is a risky way to invest particularly with lots of fakes in existence.

16.5b Gold and Other Precious Metals

There is an allure to owning gold. You can own and hold it with pride, and it is beautiful to look at. Gold is a uniquely private, personal, and portable way to hold some genuine wealth. For purposes of investing, however, the reasons for owning it often do not add up. For example, gold does not generate current income while you own it. Its value is determined solely by supply and demand at the time of sale. Thus, investing in gold is speculating. Some other metals beside gold have a similar appeal to investors.

Fear Pushes Up Gold Prices Fear is what pushes up the price of gold. Some of the world's worried investors purchase gold reasoning that if their national economies crash they will be able to trade gold even if their country's paper currency is devalued. Others who buy gold are concerned about such things as high inflation, rising interest rates, countries seen as printing too much money, economic collapse, possible wars, excessive government borrowing, collapse of the credit system, and international trade wars.

The fear that gripped investors around the globe during the Great Recession has moved "gold fever" from the fringes of the investing world to the mainstream. Prices soared, and gold hoarders, who are often criticized as crackpots, for a while appeared to be smart speculators. They thought that a wave of inflation would overcome the nation due to the growing national debt and the Federal Reserve's actions to stimulate the economy.

Gold Prices Were Stagnant and Then Soared and Crashed Again Back in 1976 when there were serious concerns about extremely high inflation in the United States, gold prices jumped in 4 years from $100 an ounce to more than $800 in 1980. Then the price dropped to $400 before sliding even lower to $280 by 2001.

This roller coaster price ride for gold has happened again. After many years of little change, gold prices began to rise slowly until they hit $1000 in March of 2008 during the worst of the Great Recession and then sharply dropped to $700 a few months later. As the U.S. and world's economies continued to struggle, gold prices climbed to $1895 in 2011. Then gold prices dropped 9.4 percent in one day. Prices have since slipped to below $1200 an ounce. That's about a 37 percent loss in just a few months for those who got in late and bought near the high of $1895.

While the increase over the past ten years in gold prices may make gold sound like an appealing speculative investment, consider further that if you bought $10,000 in gold in 1980, it would have been worth $10,600 in 2013. If you invested the same $10,000 in 1980 in a mutual fund that tracks the S&P 500, you would have over $200,000 by 2013. These are not the kind of data that a gold promoter earning sales commissions wants investors to see.

Can the fear and greed of doomsayers, conspiracy theorists, and gold promoters keep gold prices rising, or is this the same kind of price bubble that happened before? Like any alternative investment, gold is subject to a meltdown. The smart investor proceeds with caution even when speculating.

DID YOU KNOW

Bias toward Chasing Hot Investments

People engaged in real estate and high-risk investments have a bias toward certain behaviors that can be harmful, such as a tendency toward recent performance. People often see investments as good or bad based on recent performance and chase hot investments expecting to cash in as they continue to rise even higher only to see them drop in price. What to do? Avoid speculation and in the future invest only on fundamentally sound information, not what is hot.

gold bullion

A refined and stamped weight of precious metal.

gold bullion coins

Various world mints issue these coins, which contain 1 troy ounce (31.15 grams) of pure gold.

16.5c You Can Invest in Gold in Several Ways

An initial investment in gold need not be expensive, although buying gold directly can be. There are many ways to invest in gold or other precious metals.

Gold Bullion Gold bullion is often thought of as the large gold "bricks" that weigh about 28 pounds that people imagine are stored in Fort Knox. Each brick is worth more than $100,000 at today's prices. All the gold in the world would create a heavy cube only 67 feet square.

The term **bullion** simply means a refined and stamped weight of precious metal. Gold bullion is traditionally purchased and traded in 1- and 10-ounce gold bars. Gold as bullion is expensive to own. There are fees for refining, fabricating, and shipping bullion. A sales charge of 5 to 8 percent is common. There are storage costs. When gold is sold, the bank or dealer buying it from an investor may insist on reassaying its quality, yet another cost for the investor. The investor should purchase insurance against fire, theft, and fraud because such transactions are not government regulated.

Gold Bullion Coins Some costs of investing in gold can be avoided by those wanting to take physical possession of gold bullion itself by owning modern **gold bullion coins**, each containing 1 troy ounce (31.15 grams) of pure gold issued by the various world mints. The most popular coins are the South African Krugerrand, Canadian Maple Leaf, and the U.S. Gold Eagle. Other gold bullion coins are available, including the Great Britain Sovereign, Australian Kangaroo Nugget, and Chinese Panda. Minimum orders are ten coins, and commissions are 5 to 6 percent when buying and 1 to 2 percent when selling. These gold bullion coins do not need to be tested for purity, are portable, and have worldwide liquidity. Investors need to store and insure their coins. Visit www.usmint.gov for a list of U.S. Gold Eagle dealers.

Collectible Gold Coins People who buy collectible gold coins buy them in part because of their intrinsic beauty and scarcity. They face high markups, difficulty in grading coins (or must pay to hire a grading service), and costs for storage and insurance. Major coin graders include American Numismatic Association Certification Service (www.anacs.com), Numismatic Guaranty Corporation (www.ngccoin.com), and

Gold and other precious metals are highly volatile investments.

DID YOU KNOW

Bitcoin Is a "Fad" Virtual Currency

Bitcoin is a peer-to-peer experimental decentralized digital cash currency based on an open source cryptographic protocol. You can buy them at an exchange and you store them in a "wallet" on your computer. Bitcoins can be transferred through a computer or smartphone without an intermediate financial institution. The purchasing power is zero thus Bitcoin has no intrinsic value. It is not protected by a central bank and governments will never confer the status of legal currency on a private currency.

Bitcoin is accepted in trade by some merchants and individuals in parts of the world. A large share of its commercial use is believed to be for illicit goods, including marijuana, cocaine, prescription painkillers, and gambling transactions. Promoters say Bitcoin helps users avoid taxes, regulations and government seizures of assets. The lack of regulations allows everything to happen, including fraud.

Many have criticized Bitcoin's highly volatile market value as prices jumped in 3 months from $17 to $230. Then in 2 days it plunged to $68 before returning to a price of $77 a week later. Subsequently it went over $1200, and then dropped to $380 in one day. Critics argue that Bitcoin is volatile, inflexible, and minimally used in commerce. The largest Bitcoin exhange in Tokyo went bankrupt after several hundred million dollars of Bitcoins disappeared. The Internal Revenue Service does not treat Bilcoin as a currency rather it is classified as "property," hence buying and selling transactions are capital gains.

Professional Coin Grading Service (www.pcgs.com). The World Gold Council (www.gold .org/) maintains a list of firms that buy and sell gold. Note that the long-term capital gains tax on collectibles, like gold, is 28 percent (or your tax bracket, whichever is lower).

Gold Mining Stocks, Mutual Funds, and ETFs Investors wanting to capitalize on world crises, economic fears, and rising gold prices by investing in smaller amounts may choose to put speculative cash in the stocks of gold mining companies, in mutual funds that own gold companies, and in specialized exchange-traded funds (ETFs). For example, you may have heard of the now defunct Homestake Gold Mine, one of the early enterprises associated with the Gold Rush of 1876 in the northern Black Hills of what was then Dakota Territory. Today, there are a handful of gold mining companies in the United States and dozens around the world.

Popular gold mutual funds include Van Eck International Investors (INIVX), USAA Precious Metals and Minerals (USAGX), Oppenheimer Gold & Special Metals A (OPGSX), and Vanguard Precious Metals and Mining (VGPM). Gold stock prices are much more volatile than the price of gold itself as they can readily swing up or down 50 percent in a matter of months. During 2013 the average gold stock price dropped 50 percent. The largest gold exchange-traded fund (ETF) is SPDR Gold Shares (GLD). Other popular gold ETFs are iShares COMEX Gold Trust (IAU) and Market Vectors Gold Miners ETF (GDX).

16.5d Investing in Other Metals—Silver, Platinum, Palladium, and Rhodium

Some other metals also appeal to certain investors. Silver, platinum, palladium, and rhodium are metals used industrially and occasionally in jewelry. The values of these metals rise and fall with changes in demand. An investor might reason that since palladium is used in auto production that when demand in China and India for vehicles increases substantially, the price of the metal will soar. Prices can drop, too. When gold prices dropped recently silver declined 25 percent in just 4 days. Illustrative specialized ETFs in these precious metals include iShares Silver Trust (SLV), ETFS Physical Platinum (PPLT), and ETFS Physical Palladium Shares (PALL).

Bitcoin

A peer-to-peer experimental digital cash currency based on an open source cryptographic protocol that can be bought at an exchange and transferred through a computer or smart phone without an intermediate financial institution.

DID YOU KNOW

Money Websites in Gold

American Numismatic Association Certification Service (www.anacs.com)

Kitco gold prices (www.kitco.com/)

Numismatic Guaranty Corporation (www.ngccoin.com)

Professional Coin Grading Service (www.pcgs.com)

World Gold Council (www.gold.org/)

USA Gold (www.usagold.com/)

U.S. Mint (www.usmint.gov)

16.5e Precious Stones and Gems

Precious stones and gems, such as diamonds, sapphires, rubies, and emeralds, are also examples of alternative investments. Investors purchase investment-grade gems as "loose gems" rather than as pieces of jewelry. Wholesale firms, not jewelers, sell the best-quality precious gems. The gem certification process may be touted as a science, but it is not; rather it is educated guesswork. Obtaining two assessments of a stone's quality, particularly on stones of less than 1 carat, is likely to result in a variation of 10 to 20 percent.

Sales commissions on precious stones are high, and reselling is very difficult. Novice investors often buy at retail and then wind up trying to sell at retail, and then selling at or near wholesale. This approach is the opposite of smart investing—that is, buying low and selling high. Losing 20 to 50 percent of one's investment in precious stones upon selling them is not uncommon.

CONCEPT CHECK 16.5

1. Identify one collectible that might be an interesting investment, and explain why it might be difficult to make a profit.

2. Explain why some investors buy gold and other precious metals, and tell why choosing one type of investment might be appealing or unappealing to you.

3. Identify some risks of investing in precious stones and gems.

16.6 INVESTING IN OPTIONS AND COMMODITY FUTURES CONTRACTS

A **derivative** (or **derivative security**) is an instrument used by people to trade or manage more easily the asset upon which these instruments are based. Derivative securities are available for commodities, equities, bonds, interest rates, exchange rates, and indexes (such as a stock market index, consumer price index, and weather conditions). Investors choose derivatives to either reduce risk by hedging against losses or taking on additional risk by speculating. The investor's returns are derived solely from changes in the underlying asset's price behavior. Two of the most common derivative instruments are options and futures contracts.

DID YOU KNOW?

Your Worst Financial Blunders in Real Estate and High-Risk Investments

Based on others' financial woes, you will make mistakes in personal finance when you:

1. *Assume that real estate prices will go up and interest rates will not increase.*

2. *Do not set enough money aside for maintenance, repairs, unanticipated capital improvements, and rising real estate taxes on rental property.*

3. *Invest some retirement money in these risky investments: margin trading, short selling, options, commodity futures, gold, precious metals, and gems, currencies, and timeshares.*

16.6a Options Allow You to Buy or Sell an Asset at a Predetermined Price

An **option** is a contract to buy or sell an asset at some point in the future at a specified price. The most common type of option is a **stock option**. This derivative gives the holder (purchaser) the right, but not the obligation, to buy or sell a specific number of shares (normally 100) of a certain stock at a specified price (the **striking price**) before a specified date (the **expiration date**, typically three, six, or nine months).

Two types of option contracts exist: calls and puts. A **call option** gives the option holder (buyer) the right, but not the obligation, to buy the optioned asset from the option writer at the striking price. A **put option** gives the option holder (buyer) the right, but not the obligation, to sell the optioned asset to the option writer at the striking price.

DID YOU KNOW ?

How to Make Sense of Option Contracts

The two principal players in the options game are the option writer and the option holder.

	Calls	
Option holder has the right to buy or sell.	**Call option** Has option to buy stock at a specific price	**Call obligation** Is obligated to sell stock at a specific price	**Option writer** has possible obligation to sell or buy.
	Put option Has option to sell stock at a specific price	**Put obligation** Is obligated to purchase stock at a specific price	
	Puts	

Most option contracts expire without being exercised, and the option seller is the only person to earn a profit. The profit results from the option premium charged when the option was originally sold. Buying and selling options are techniques used by all types of investors.

Conservative Investors Make Money on Options Selling a call option can be a fairly safe way to generate income by conservative option writers who own the underlying asset (the stock). When they sell a call, it is described as a **covered option** because the writer owns the underlying stock. If the writer does not own the asset, it is a **naked option**, a speculative position. When used effectively by conservative option writers, calls can potentially pick up an extra return of perhaps 1 to 2 percent every three months and minimize risk at the same time. In effect, this conservative investor protects himself financially by hedging his investment against loss due to price fluctuation. You also can conservatively profit by selling a call on stock already owned, giving the buyer the right to purchase your shares at a certain price any time during a relatively short period at a fixed strike price, which is higher than the current price.

covered option
Occurs when an option writer who owns the covered option sells the call.

futures contract
The obligation to make or take delivery of a certain amount of a commodity by a set date.

Aggressive Investors Profit with Options Aggressive investors in the options market attempt to profit in two ways. First, the investor can hope for an increase in the value of the option. For example, if the price of a stock is rising, the holder of a call option might sell it to another investor for a higher price than that originally paid. Second, the investor can exercise the option at the striking price, take ownership of the underlying securities, and sell them at a profit.

16.6b Buying and Selling Commodities Futures Contracts

A **futures contract** is the obligation to make or take delivery of a certain amount of a commodity by a set date. A futures derivative contract

DID YOU KNOW ?

Money Websites in Options

Informative websites for investing in options, including suggestions from professionals are:

Options Industry Council
(www.optionscentral.com)

Chicago Board Options Exchange
(www.cboe.com)

OptionsXpress (www.optionsxpress.com)

TradeKing (www.tradeking.com)

DID YOU KNOW

About Hedge Funds

Hedge funds are freewheeling risky investment pools for the extremely wealthy that use unconventional investment strategies. They are global companies, beyond most of the regulations of the U.S. government. Hedge funds trade options and commodities sell short, use leverage, risk arbitrage, buy and sell currencies, and invest in undervalued mature companies, often those in or nearing bankruptcy. Hedge funds can profit in times of market volatility as well as in a falling market. The investors are partners.

Fees charged by the hedge fund manager typically are 2 percent of assets under management and 20 percent of the upside (the "performance fee") of the fund. Most managers assess no full fees until the profits are above 8 percent. None of the 8000 hedge funds can be offered or advertised to the general investing public in the United States. They are limited to "accredited investors and purchasers" who have incomes over $200,000 and a net worth over $1 million and who own more than $5 million in investments. The small investor can buy shares in publicly traded firms, like Blackstone (BX) or Kohlberg Kravis Roberts (KKR), which are parent companies of hedge funds. A number of hedge funds have had catastrophic losses and have gone bankrupt.

hedge funds

Freewheeling risky investment pools for the extremely wealthy that use unconventional investment strategies such as trading options and commodities, selling short, using leverage and arbitrage, buying and selling currencies, and investing in undervalued mature companies.

requires the holder to buy the asset on the date specified. If the holder does not want to buy the asset, he or she must sell the contract to some other investor or to someone who wants to actually use the asset.

Conservative Economic Needs Creates Futures Markets Farmer Geraldo Esperanza who planted a 10,000-bushel soybean crop in Chana, Illinois, might want to sell part of it now to ensure the receipt of a certain price when the crop is actually harvested. Similarly, a food-processing company might want to purchase soybeans now to protect against sharp price increases in the future. And an orange juice manufacturer might want to lock in a supply of oranges at a definite price now rather than run the risk that a winter freeze would push up prices. These economic needs create futures markets. You can trade futures on an organized market for lots of commodities, such as coffee, sugar, corn, pigs, plywood, metals, energy, foreign currencies, gold, and other precious metals.

DID YOU KNOW

Turn Bad Habits into Good Ones

Do You Do This?

Avoid investing in real estate

Buy collectibles, precious metals, and gems

Invest in options and commodity futures for quick profits

Do This Instead!

Do the math to see if it might be profitable

Never put long–term investment money into these assets

Be prepared to lose money

Speculators Trade in Futures Markets The speculative investor who buys or sells a commodity contract is hoping that the market price of the commodity will rise (or fall) before the contract matures, usually 3 to 18 months after it is written. These derivatives offer the potential for extremely high profits because such contracts often are highly leveraged. Depending on the commodity, the volatility of the market, and the brokerage house requirements, an investor can put up as little as 5 to 15 percent of the total value of the contract. Some contracts require a deposit of only $300. Commissions average about $20 for each purchase and sale.

Futures Are a Zero-Sum Game In each futures transaction a winner and a loser will emerge. A buyer of a futures contract benefits if the price of the commodity increases, but the seller suffers. When prices decline, the reverse is true. An estimated 90 percent of investors in the futures market lose money. Five percent (mostly the professionals) make profits from the losers and the remaining 5 percent break even.

Trading in futures is a zero-sum game in which the wealth of all investors remains the same. The trading simply redistributes the wealth among those traders. Each profit must be offset by an equivalent loss; therefore, the average rate of return for all investors in futures is zero. The return actually becomes negative if transaction costs are included. Most investors do not belong in commodities.

DO IT NOW!

You know more about personal finance after reading this chapter, so get started right now by:

1. *Imagining what you would do if you came into $50,000 that you could invest without any concern about losing the money. Would you invest all or some of it in alternative investments? Explain why or why not.*

2. *Searching your local newspaper for opportunities to buy a house as rental property, assuming that real estate is an option for your investment. Find out the price-to-rent ratio for an average home in your community and then estimate the asking price for a particular property, the rate of interest you could expect for a mortgage, the likely rent you could charge, and other factors.*

3. *Then calculating the net present value of the property to determine the price you might offer for the property.*

CONCEPT CHECK 16.6

1. Distinguish between a call and a put for the options investor.

2. Summarize one way a person with a conservative investment philosophy can profit in options.

3. Explain how a speculative options investor can make a lot of money.

4. Offer reasons why futures contracts are not appropriate for the average long–term investor.

WHAT DO YOU RECOMMEND *NOW?*

Now that you have read the chapter on real estate and high-risk investments, what do you recommend to Britanny on:

1. Investing in real estate?

2. Putting some of her money in an alternative investment, like a collectible or gold?

3. Investing in options and futures contracts?

BIG PICTURE SUMMARY OF LEARNING OBJECTIVES

LO1 **Demonstrate how you can make money investing in real estate.**

The key questions for real estate investors are: "Can you make current income while you own?" and "Can you profit when you sell the property?" To help find answers, investors calculate the price-to-rent ratio and rental yield.

LO2 **Recognize how to take advantage of beneficial tax treatments in real estate investing.**

The Internal Revenue Service offers the investor five beneficial tax treatments, including depreciation, interest that is deductible, low tax rates on capital gains, tax-free exchanges of real estate, and special tax breaks on renting and vacation homes.

LO3 **Calculate the right price to pay for real estate and how to finance your purchase.**

The discounted cash-flow method is an effective way to estimate the value or asking price of a real estate investment. It takes into account the selling price of the property, the effect of income taxes, and the time value of money. There are various ways to finance a real estate investment.

LO4 **Assess the disadvantages of investing in real estate.**

There are many disadvantages in real estate investing, such as large initial investment, lack of

diversification, dealing with tenants, low current income, unpredictable costs, illiquidity, and high transfer costs.

LO5 **Summarize the risks and challenges of investing in the alternative investments of collectibles, precious metals, and gems.**

When investing in collectibles, precious metals, and gems, the investor owns illiquid real assets, not intangible items represented by pieces of paper. The investor's only return comes from price appreciation, as they do not pay interest or dividends. While prices are set by supply and demand, promoters hype these alternative investments. Changing investor tastes and rumors also influence prices.

LO6 **Explain why options and futures are risky investments.**

Derivatives, such as options and commodity futures, are instruments used by market participants to trade or manage more easily the asset upon which these instruments are based. While all types of investors can profit in options, only speculators with an aggressive investment philosophy should consider trading in futures. Most investors in derivatives lose money, and losses can accumulate quickly.

LET'S TALK ABOUT IT

1. **Invest in Real Estate.** Describe what would encourage you to invest in real estate given that in recent years many communities prices have declined severely.

2. **Two Questions.** Which of the two questions in real estate investing is more important? Explain why.

3. **Beneficial Tax Treatments.** Review the five beneficial tax treatments of real estate and explain which one seems most important to you as a real estate investor.

4. **Reasons to Invest.** Assume you have $30,000 in cash. Give reasons why you might want to invest that money in a real estate investment. Offer two reasons why others might not be willing to invest in real estate.

5. **Manage Tenants.** Do you think you could successfully deal with tenants and the management demands required in real estate investing? Why or why not?

6. **Disadvantages of Real Estate.** Review the list of "Disadvantages of Real Estate Investing," and identify one that you think is most important. Explain why.

7. **Timeshares as an Investment.** Explain why timeshares should not be considered an investment. Why do some people buy timeshares?

8. **Put Some Money into Alternative Investments.** What percentage of your portfolio, if any, do you think should be invested in alternative investments? Explain.

9. **Invest in Gold?** Would you invest in gold today? Explain why or why not.

10. **Options and Futures.** Both options and futures are risky investments. Identify one that seems like an unwise idea, and explain why it is unappealing.

DO THE MATH

1. **Price-to-Rent Ratios.** Calculate the price-to-rent ratios for the following properties arranged by price of home followed by likely annual rental income: (a) *$400,000/$40,000*; (b) *$300,000/$36,000*; (c) *$200,000/30,000.*

DO IT IN CLASS
PAGE 483

2. **Real Estate Investment Returns.** Austin Sandler, an electrician and his teacher spouse Emily from Laramie, Wyoming, are interested in the numbers of real estate investments. They have reviewed the figures in Table 16-2 and are impressed with the potential 50.12 percent return after taxes. Austin and Emily are in the 25 percent marginal tax bracket. Answer the following questions to help guide their investment decisions:

DO IT IN CLASS
PAGE 487

(a) Substitute the Sandler's 25 percent marginal tax bracket (his state has no state income tax) in Table 16-2, and calculate the taxable income and return after taxes.

(b) Why does real estate appear to be a favorable investment for Austin and Emily?

(c) What one factor might be changed in Table 16-2 to increase their return?

(d) Calculate the after-tax return for Austin and Emily, assuming that they bought the property and financed it with a 7 percent, $175,000 30-year mortgage with annual interest costs of $11,971.

3. Review the math in Table 16-3, on page 489, Discounted Cash Flow to Estimate Price, and give your opinion on which part of the assumptions (price increases or sales price) is more subject to poor thinking.

DO IT IN CLASS
PAGE 489

FINANCIAL PLANNING CASES

CASE 1

The Johnsons Consider a Real Estate Investment

Harry and Belinda Johnson are considering purchasing a residential income property as an investment. The Johnsons want to achieve an after-tax total return of 7 percent. They are considering a property with an asking price of $190,000 that should produce $27,000 in gross rental income and $15,000 in net operating income.

(a) Calculate the price-to-rent ratio on the property.

(b) Calculate the present value of after-tax cash flow for the property, assuming that the after-tax cash-flow numbers are $8000 for the first year, $8400 for the second year, $8800 for the third year, $9200 for the fourth year, and $9600 for the fifth year, and that the selling price of the property will be $210,000 in five years. Prepare your information in a format similar to Table 16-3, using Appendix A-2 or the *Garman/Forgue* companion website to discount the future after-tax cash flows to their present values.

(c) Give the Johnsons your advice on whether they should invest in the property at its current price of $190,000.

CASE 2

Victor and Maria Consider Selling Maria's Mother's Home

Victor and Maria Hernandez are thinking about selling her mother's home, which she recently inherited, and use the proceeds to enhance their investments for retirement. It's price declined about $30,000 in recent years to today's value of $170,000. The home is fully paid for.

(a) If the rent is $1000 a month, what is the rental yield?

(b) If they sold the home, should they invest the proceeds into any alternative investments, such as gold?

CASE 3

Julia Price Wants to Try Alternative Investments

Julia continues to be a hard worker and, at age 50, has saved and invested wisely for her planned financially successful retirement. She has an extra $15,000 in a cash management account beyond what she needs for emergency savings. She rejected options and commodity futures as too risky but is considering gold. Julia wonders if the price volatility of gold over the past few years will continue, and she has always thought about investing in antique furniture. Offer your opinions about her thinking.

CASE 4

Real Estate or Stocks?

Junhee Chang, a senior research analyst in St. Clairsville, Ohio, has bought and sold high-technology stocks profitably for years. Lately some of her stock investments have done quite poorly, including one company that went bankrupt. Emily, a longtime friend at work, has suggested that the two of them invest in real estate together because property values in some neighborhoods have been rising in anticipation of a large manufacturing company's plans to substantially increase its workforce. Emily has looked at three small office buildings and some residential duplexes as possible investments.

(a) Contrast the wisdom of investing in commercial office buildings versus the attraction of investing in residential properties.

(b) List three of the advantages associated with real estate investments.

(c) List three things that can go wrong for real estate investors.

CASE 5

From Real Estate to Options and Futures

Jonathan Williams and Cody Richardson, longtime partners in Lawton, Oklahoma, have bought and sold real estate properties for ten years. They have profited on many transactions, although they did have some substantial losses during the Great Recession. Their portfolio of real estate is worth about $4.7 million, on which they owe $2.9 million. Jonathan has read about investing in options and futures contracts, and last week, he talked with a stockbroker about the possibilities.

(a) Offer some reasons why Jonathan want to invest $100,000 or more in options and futures contracts.

(b) List some of the risks of options trading for Jonathan and Cody.

(c) From an investor's point of view, contrast trading in futures contracts with buying highly leveraged real estate.

BE YOUR OWN PERSONAL FINANCIAL MANAGER

1. **Foreclosure and Short Sales.** Given that there are so many foreclosed homes on the market, tell why you might or might not be interested in buying one as an investment. Write a summary of your conclusions.

2. **Before Investing in Real Estate.** Review the information in the Did You Know? Box titled "What to do Before Investing in Real Estate" and identify two suggestions that you definitely would follow if you invested in real estate. Write a summary of your conclusions.

3. **Disadvantages of Real Estate Investing.** Review the list in the "Disadvantages of Real Estate Investing" section and identify two disadvantages that you think might keep you from personally investing in real estate. Write a summary of your conclusions.

4. **Real Estate ETFs.** Go to the "Real Estate ETF" page for StockEncyclopedia.com (etf.stock-encyclopedia.com /category/real-estate.html) and select three illustrative companies, such as ProShares UltraShort Real Estate Fund. Write a brief report comparing those three ETFs.

ON THE NET

1. **Research Home Prices.** To find prices on homes in your community, go to Zillo (www.zillow.com/). Input addresses of homes on five nearby streets and summarize your price information findings.

2. **Research Mortgage Rates.** Find out current mortgage rates for 15- , 20- , and 30-year loans for both residential and investment loans. See LendingTree.com, Quickenloans.com, BankRate.com, and Loan.com. Write a brief report on your findings.

3. **Current Prices of Metals.** Find out the current prices of five popular metals, such as gold, silver, nickel, aluminum, cobalt, copper, lead, palladium, platinum, and silver, at websites like Kitco (www.kitco.com/) and USA Gold (www .usagold.com/). Write a brief report on your findings.

4. **Gold ETFs.** Go online and search "gold prices per ounce" on Google or Bing. Click on five websites, including Wikipedia's "Gold ETFs," and review what is written, especially about predictions of future prices. Prepare a report summarizing your findings.

5. **Collectibles Websites.** Search the Internet for two websites featuring one type of collectible that interests you (such as coins, toys, watches, or sports memorabilia). Write a brief report comparing the types of information and features available for buyers of these collectibles.

6. **Research Hedge Funds.** Go online and research two large hedge funds (such as JP Morgan Chase, Bridge-water Associates, Paulson & Co., Brevan Howard, and Soros Fund Management) by inserting "hedge fund" after the company name. Write a report comparing what services the two funds perform, participation requirements, and investment returns.

ACTION INVOLVEMENT PROJECTS

1. **Community Real Estate Prices.** Telephone two real estate brokers to determine if the prices of single-family dwellings in your community have been decreasing or increasing over the past four or five years, and ask why. Inquire about homes located near your college as well as those farther away from campus. Prepare a brief report of your findings including reasons for the change in prices.

2. **Invest in Commercial Real Estate.** Research current commercial properties for sale in your college community by reviewing the real estate section of newspapers. How many listings do you find? How many duplexes?

   How many small apartment buildings? Select one and prepare a report analyzing the property using the price-to-rent ratio and rental yield.

3. **Tax Consequences of Real Estate Investment.** Select a possible commercial real estate investment in your community and make a "first attempt" to prepare an analysis similar in format to that in the Did You Know? box titled "The Tax Consequences of an Income-Producing Real Estate Investment." Make any reasonable assumptions you desire and calculate the numbers. Prepare the table and a brief report of your findings.

Visit the Garman/Forgue companion website at www.cengagebrain.com.

17

Retirement and Estate Planning

LEARNING OBJECTIVES

After reading this chapter, you should be able to:

1 Estimate your Social Security retirement income benefit.

2 Calculate the amount you must save for retirement in today's dollars.

3 Distinguish among the types of employer-sponsored tax-sheltered retirement plans.

4 Explain the various types of personally established tax-sheltered retirement accounts.

5 Describe how to avoid penalties and make your retirement money last.

6 Plan for the distribution of your estate and, if needed, use trusts to lower estate taxes.

MORTGAGE RETIREMENT

INSURANCE TAXES

401(k) VACATION

EDUCATION CREDIT CARDS

©S-F/Shutterstock.com/Peter Booth/E+/Getty Images

WHAT DO YOU RECOMMEND?

Juliana Pérez Rodríguez, age 48, worked for a previous employer for eight years. When she left that job, Juliana left her retirement money in that employer's defined-contribution plan. It is now worth $120,000. After getting divorced and remarried four years ago, she has been working as an assistant food services manager for a convention center in Chicago, earning $70,000 per year. Juliana contributes $233 each month (4 percent of her salary) to her account in her employer's 401(k) retirement plan. Her employer provides a 100 percent match for the first 4 percent of Juliana's salary contributions. Company rules allow her to contribute a total of 8 percent on her own. Juliana's 401(k) account balance at her new employer is $21,000. Her husband Fernando, with whom she shares the same birthday, is a computer programmer working on contract for various companies and earns about $90,000 annually. When Juliana returned from a vacation with her husband, she found that her father had suffered a serious stroke. Despite undergoing physical therapy, he is now in a nursing home and likely will be there the rest of his life. Juliana is hoping that she and Fernando can retire when they both are age 65.

What do you recommend to Juliana and Fernando on the subject of retirement and estate planning regarding:

1. How much in Social Security benefits can each expect to receive?

2. How much do they each need to save for retirement if they want to spend at a lifestyle of 80 percent of their current living expenses?

3. In which types of retirement plans might Fernando invest for retirement?

4. What withdrawal rate might they use to avoid running out of money during retirement?

5. What three types of actions might they take to go about transferring their assets by contract to avoid probate?

YOUR NEXT FIVE YEARS

In the next five years, you can start achieving financial success by doing the following related retirement and estate planning:

1. *Save continuously within a tax-sheltered employer-sponsored retirement plan at least the amount required to obtain the full matching contribution from your employer.*

2. *Accept enough risk in investing to increase the likelihood that you will have enough money in retirement.*

3. *Contribute to Roth IRA accounts to supplement your employer-sponsored plans.*

4. *Keep your hands off your retirement money. Do not borrow it. Do not withdraw it. When changing employers, roll over the funds into the new employer's plan or a rollover IRA account.*

5. *To ease the transfer of your assets upon your death, learn how to use contracts to avoid probate court and make a valid will.*

retirement

The time in life when the major sources of income change from earned income (such as salary or wages) to employer-based retirement benefits, private savings and investments, income from Social Security, and perhaps part-time employment.

estate planning

The definite arrangements you make during your lifetime that are consistent with your wishes for the administration and distribution of your estate when you die.

Estimate your Social Security retirement income benefit.

Retirement is the time in life when the major sources of income from earned income (such as salary or wages) changes to sources like employer-based retirement benefits, private savings and investments, income from Social Security, and perhaps income from part-time employment. Retirement often is a gradual transition from the workforce rather than sudden cessation. Today, 30 percent of people age 65 to 69 are still working.

Planning for retirement has changed dramatically over the years. Yesterday's employers provided pensions for a lifetime that were commonly a reward for 20 or 30 years of working for one company, but today fewer than one out of five employers still offer them. Instead, half of today's employers offer voluntary retirement plans to which employees may or may not choose to contribute; the other half do not offer a retirement plan. The biggest mistake people make in planning for retirement is they spend too much on other things instead of saving for retirement. Enjoying financial security during 20 or more years of retirement is not a matter of luck. It takes planning and action. The wise financial manager's philosophy should be to save now so you can play later during your golden years.

But many young people do not make such efforts early enough in life. Two-thirds of workers age 25 to 34 are not saving at all for retirement through their employers. The one-third that does save has not saved much. Sixty percent say they have a balance of less than $10,000, reports the Employee Benefits Retirement Institute. A recent survey shows that 34 percent of Americans report that they will work until they are at least 80 or until they are too sick or die.

This is a crazy way to live: spending all one's money to pay for day-to-day consumption expenses instead of saving for retirement. Such people need to learn how to budget, save, and invest. They also need to create a financial plan because if they had a plan, they will save three times more than those without a plan, thus better managing their financial futures.

Saving and investing 10 percent of your pay starting at age 25 can provide a lump sum of $1,540,000 at age 65, while saving just 6 percent will provide only $924,000, more than one-third less. These calculations are based on a salary of $40,000 with 3 percent annual pay increases and investments that earn an 8 percent annual return.

The fact today is that you—and only you—are responsible for meeting your retirement needs. In addition, the responsibility of investing funds for retirement and the risk of making poor investments with these funds have been shifted from the employer to the employee. And if your employer does not offer a retirement plan, you can set one up yourself.

While starting a retirement program is important at a young age so too is the process of estate planning. **Estate planning** comprises the specific arrangements you make during your lifetime for the administration and distribution of your assets when you die. You need to learn how to transfer assets in such a way that they go to your desired heirs and avoid unnecessary probate court procedures. Most of your assets can be set up to transfer automatically. For the remainder, you need to prepare a will. Estate planning need not be overly complicated but you do need to do it. Details on all these topics are in this chapter.

17.1 UNDERSTANDING YOUR SOCIAL SECURITY RETIREMENT INCOME BENEFITS

The whole retirement and estate planning process must begin with improving your understanding of Social Security. This is the program that fully one-half of young workers do not believe will be around for them when they retire. Don't worry because it will be! Older people are voters, too, and they (as well as young people) will push to keep Social Security. In fact, some politicians are arguing that the benefits should be expanded and increased.

The Social Security program has become the most successful and popular domestic government program in U.S. history. Funding for Social Security benefits comes from a compulsory payroll tax split equally between employees and employers. Social Security taxes withheld from wages are called **FICA taxes** (named for the Federal Insurance Contributions Act). The amounts withheld are put into the Social Security trust fund accounts from which benefits are paid to current program recipients by the Social Security Administration (SSA).

17.1a Your Taxes Support Social Security and Medicare Benefits

Wage earners pay both FICA and Medicare taxes to the SSA. The FICA tax is paid on wage income up to the **maximum taxable yearly earnings (MTYE)**, which comprises the maximum amount to which the FICA tax is applied. The MTYE figure—$117,000 for the most recent year—is adjusted annually for inflation. The FICA tax rate is 12.4 percent, consisting of 6.2 percent paid by employees and 6.2 percent paid by employers for their workers. Self-employed workers pay a FICA tax rate of 12.4 percent, twice that of wage earners, because they are their own employers.

Wage earners and their employers also each pay a 1.45 percent **Medicare tax** on all earnings. The MTYE limit does not apply to the Medicare tax; thus the 1.45 rate applies to all employment income. Most workers pay 7.65 (6.2 + 1.45) percent of their earnings to the SSA. For example, a person earning $50,000 pays a combined FICA and Medicare tax of $3825 ($50,000 × 0.0765), and a person earning $100,000 pays $7650 ($100,000 × 0.0765).

17.1b It Takes a Minimum of Ten Years to Qualify for Full Social Security Retirement Benefits

The Social Security program covers nine out of every ten U.S. employees, although employees of some state governments are exempt and instead are covered by their state's plan. To qualify for Social Security retirement, survivors, or disability insurance benefits for you and your family, you must accumulate sufficient credits for employment in any work subject to the FICA taxes. The periods of employment in which you earn credits need not be consecutive. Military service also provides credits. You earn **Social Security credits** for a certain amount of work covered under Social Security during a calendar year. For example, workers receive one credit if they earned $1200 (for the most recent year) during any time during the year. You receive a maximum of four credits if you earned $4800 (4 × $1200) during the year. The dollar figure required for each credit earned is raised annually to keep pace with inflation.

The number of credits you have earned determines your eligibility for retirement benefits and for disability or survivors benefits if you become disabled or die. The SSA recognizes four statuses of eligibility.

1. Fully Insured **Fully insured** status requires 40 credits (10 years of work) and provides the worker and his or her family with eligibility for benefits under the retirement, survivors, and disability programs. Once obtained, this status cannot be lost even if the person never works again. Although it is required to receive retirement benefits, "fully insured" status does not imply that the worker will receive the maximum benefits allowable.

2. Currently Insured To achieve **currently insured status**, six credits must be earned in the most recent three years. This status provides for some survivors or disability benefits but no retirement benefits. To remain eligible

FICA taxes
A 6.2 percent tax paid by both the worker and employer on the worker's employment income up to the maximum taxable yearly earnings.

maximum taxable yearly earnings (MTYE)
The maximum amount to which the FICA tax is applied.

Medicare tax
A 1.45 percent tax paid by both the worker and employer on all the worker's employment income.

Social Security credits
Accumulated quarterly credits to qualify for Social Security benefits obtained by paying FICA taxes.

fully insured Social Security status
Requires 40 credits and provides workers and their families with benefits under the retirement, survivors, and disability programs; once status is earned, it cannot be taken away even if the eligible worker never works again.

FINANCIAL POWER POINT

Financing Social Security

Based on the Social Security Administration Trustees' best estimate, program costs are projected to allow 100 percent of scheduled benefits until 2033. While it is true that the Social Security system has a long-term deficit, there is zero chance that the program will be eliminated in its entirety. While many young people doubt that Social Security will provide them with benefits, there are solutions to the problem. Simple fixes that actually will work and are favored by people of both political parties and all age groups are to increase the wage cap, increase the payroll tax, and change the benefit formula.

for these benefits, a worker must continue to earn at least six credits every three years or meet a minimum number of covered years of work established by the SSA.

3. Transitionally Insured **Transitionally insured** status applies only to retired workers who reach the age of 72 without accumulating 40 credits (ten years). These people are eligible for very limited retirement benefits.

4. Not Insured Workers younger than age 72 who have fewer than six credits of work experience are **not insured**.

17.1c   You Can Obtain an Estimate of Your Social Security Retirement Benefits

Social Security Estimate

Online information that the Social Security Administration makes available to all workers, which includes earnings history, Social Security taxes paid, and an estimated benefit amount.

The Social Security Administration makes available your **Social Security Estimate** that includes a record of your earnings history, a record of how much you and your various employers paid in Social Security taxes, and an estimate of the benefits that you and your family might be eligible to receive now and in the future. You can request a Social Security Estimate at www.ssa.gov/estimator/.

The actual dollar amount of your eventual Social Security retirement benefits will be based on the average of the highest 35 years of earnings during your working years. In these calculations, your actual earnings are first adjusted, or **indexed**, to account for changes in average wages since the year the earnings were received. The SSA then calculates your average monthly indexed earnings during the 35 years in which you earned the most. The agency applies a formula to these earnings to arrive at your **basic retirement benefit** (or **primary insurance amount**). This is the amount you would receive at your **full-benefit retirement age**—currently 67 for those born in 1960 or later.

basic retirement benefit/ primary insurance amount

Amount of Social Security benefits a worker would receive at his or her full-benefit retirement age, which is 67 for those born after 1960.

full-benefit retirement age

Age at which a retiree is entitled to full Social Security benefits; 67 for those born in 1960 or later.

You have three options regarding when to begin receiving Social Security retirement benefits.

1. Begin Receiving Benefits at Your Full-Benefit Age Once you have reached your full-benefit retirement age, you are eligible to receive your basic monthly retirement benefit. You can begin collecting these benefits even if you continue working full- or part-time. Your level of employment income will not affect your level of benefits, although it may affect the income taxes that you pay on your Social Security benefits and the amount of your Medicare premiums.

2. Begin Receiving Reduced Benefits at a Younger Age You can choose to start receiving retirement benefits as early as age 62, regardless of your full-benefit retirement age. If you do so, however, your basic retirement benefit will be permanently reduced approximately 6 percent for each year you start early. Thus, if your full-benefit retirement age is 67, your benefits will be permanently reduced 30 percent (5 years × 6 percent). If you choose to take the earliest Social Security retirement benefits, you will be ahead financially if you do not survive to about age 80. Sixty percent of retirees elect to take their Social Security benefits early.

People considering early Social Security retirement benefits need to be aware that their checks will be further reduced if they have earned income above the annual limit ($15,120 for the most recent year). The reduction is $1 in benefits for every $2 in earnings. A person entitled to $1000 per month ($12,000 per year) in early retirement benefits who has an earned income of $20,000, for example, will be penalized $2440 in benefits on the income above $15,120 ($20,000 − $15,120 = $4880/2). It is possible to earn enough to completely eliminate your benefits, so the decision to take Social Security benefits early requires careful analysis.*

FINANCIAL POWER POINT

Verify Online the Accuracy of Your Social Security Statement

You have only three years to correct any errors in your Social Security Statement. You should make sure that the SSA's records are up to date and accurate by checking them online. Open an account at the Social Security Administration at www.ssa.gov/myaccount/ and check your Statement.

---

* In the year you reach your full retirement age, you can earn up to $40,080 between January and your birthday without penalty. Above that amount, your Social Security check will be reduced by about 33 cents for every dollar earned. Also, once you reach full retirement age, your benefits may be recalculated to a higher amount to account for your increased earning record.

3. Begin Receiving Larger Benefits at a Later Age You can delay taking benefits beyond your full-benefit retirement age. In such a case, your benefit would be permanently increased by as much as 8 percent per year. Once you reach age 70 the benefit amount will no longer increase so there is no need to delay receiving benefits beyond that age. You can continue to work even after you begin taking these delayed benefits. Again, your level of employment income will not affect your level of benefits, but it may affect the income taxes that you pay on your Social Security benefits and your Medicare premiums.

You can compute your own retirement benefit estimate using a program that you can download to your computer from www.ssa.gov/OACT/anypia/index.html. To determine which option is best for you, you can do the calculations for an early, on-time, or delayed beginning start date. Also see kiplinger.socialsecuritysolutions.com to determine the optimal strategy for claiming benefits.

CONCEPT CHECK 17.1

1. List the key financial planning actions that individuals must take during their working lives to prepare for retirement.

2. Summarize how workers become qualified for retirement Social Security benefits.

3. Distinguish between the benefits provided under Social Security for a worker who is fully insured and a worker who is currently insured.

4. Explain what happens if you choose to retire earlier than your full retirement age, which is probably 67.

17.2 HOW TO CALCULATE THE AMOUNT YOU MUST SAVE FOR RETIREMENT IN TODAY'S DOLLARS

To plan for a financially successful retirement, you first need to set a goal. Otherwise, as one of the most quoted figures in sports, baseball legend Yogi Berra, says, "If you don't know where you are going, you will end up somewhere else." Your **retirement savings goal**, or **retirement nest egg**, is the total amount of accumulated savings and investments needed to support your desired retirement lifestyle. Financial planners often say that people need 80 to 100 percent of their pre-retirement gross income (including Social Security benefits) to meet their expenses in retirement and maintain their lifestyle. This amount includes what you have to pay in income taxes.

Setting a personally meaningful retirement dollar goal helps motivate people to take the necessary saving and investing actions. If you begin to save and invest for retirement early in life, the compounding effect on money over time will make it fairly easy for you to reach your retirement savings goal. If you start late, it will be difficult.

> **LEARNING OBJECTIVE 2**
> Calculate the amount you must save for retirement in today's dollars.

> **Retirement savings goal (retirement nest egg)**
> *Total amount of accumulated savings and investments needed to support a desired retirement lifestyle.*

17.2a Projecting Your Annual Retirement Expenses and Income

"How large a retirement nest egg do I need?" To calculate this amount, you can fill out the Run the Numbers worksheet, "Estimating Your Retirement Savings Goal in Today's Dollars" (page 514). Each spouse in a married couple should prepare a worksheet rather than combine income and savings amounts.

17.2b An Illustration of Retirement Needs

Consider the case of Erik McKartmann, aged 35 and single, the manager of a weight loss and fitness center in South Park, Colorado. Erik currently earns $50,000 per year. He has been contributing $165 per month ($1980 annually) into an IRA

DO IT IN CLASS

DID YOU KNOW

Women Should Save More for Retirement than Men

Women save less in their 401(k) accounts than men resulting in smaller balances at retirement. Women participate in 401(k) plans at the same rate as men but they save only 6.9 percent compared to 7.6 percent for men, according to consulting firm Aon Hewitt. Women, more than men, also often fail to take advantage of the full matching contribution from their employers.

More than 20 percent of workers are not saving enough in their retirement accounts to take advantage of the company match.

Even in the 21st century women still do not earn as much, on average, as men. Because of their lower incomes and longer longevity women receive less Social Security income than men (about $13,100 annually compared with over $17,200 annually for men). Women reaching age 65 are expected to live, on average, an additional 21.4 years compared to 19.1 for men; therefore women should save more for retirement than men.

account he set up several years ago before beginning his current job. Erik hopes to retire at age 62.

1. Erik has chosen not to develop a retirement budget at this time. Instead, he simply multiplied his current salary by 80 percent to arrive at an estimate of the annual income (in current dollars) needed in retirement of $40,000 ($50,000 × 0.80). This amount was entered on line 1 of the worksheet. If Erik wants to increase the amount of dollars to support a higher retirement lifestyle, he can simply increase the percentage in the calculation.

2. Erik checked the Social Security Administration to estimate his benefits in today's dollars. At age 62, he could expect a monthly benefit of $1100 (in current dollars). Multiplying by 12 gave an expected annual Social Security benefit of $13,200 (in current dollars), which Erik entered on line 2 of the worksheet.

3. Line 3 of the worksheet, which calls for Erik's expected pension benefit, is appropriate for defined-benefit plans. After discussing his expected employer pension with the benefits counselor at work, Erik found that his anticipated benefit under the plan would amount to approximately $5800 annually, assuming that he remained with the company until his retirement, so he entered that figure on line 3.

4. Erik adds lines 2 and 3 to determine his total estimated retirement income from Social Security and his employer pension. The amount on line 4 would be $19,000 ($13,200 + $5800).

5. Subtracting line 4 from line 1 reveals that Erik would need an additional income of $21,000 ($40,000 − $19,000) in today's dollars from savings and investments to meet his annual retirement income needs.

6. At this point, Erik has considered only his annual needs and benefits. Because he plans to retire at age 62, Erik will need income for 20 years based on his life expectancy. (Of course, Erik could live well into his 80s, which would mean that he would need to save even more.) Using Appendix A-4 and assuming a return that is 3 percent above the inflation rate, Erik finds the multiplier 14.8775 where 3 percent and 20 years intersect. He then calculates that he needs an additional amount of $312,427 (14.8775 × $21,000) at retirement. That's a big number! And it is in current dollars. The number does not dissuade Erik from saving because he knows he has time and the magic of compounding on his side.

7. Erik's current savings and investments can be used to offset the $312,427 he will need for retirement. Erik has zero savings in his employer's 401(k) account; however, he does have some money invested in an IRA ($24,000), plus some other investments ($13,000). These amounts are totaled ($37,000) and recorded on line 7E.

8. If left untouched, the $37,000 that Erik has built up will continue to earn interest and dividends until he retires. Because he has 27 more years until retirement, Erik can use Appendix A-1 and, assuming a growth rate of 3 percent over 27 years, find the factor 2.2213 and multiply it by the total amount in line 7. Erik's $37,000 should have a future value of $82,188 at his retirement, so he puts this amount on line 8.

9. Subtracting line 8 from line 6 reveals that Erik's retirement nest egg will need an additional $230,239 ($312,427 − $82,188) at the time of retirement.

10. Using Appendix A-3 and a growth rate of 3 percent over 27 years, Erik finds a factor of 40.7096. When divided into $230,239, it reveals that he needs savings and investments of $5656 per year until retirement.

11. Erik records his current savings and investments of $1980 per year on line 11.

12. Erik subtracts line 11 from line 10 to determine the additional amount of annual savings that he should set aside in today's dollars to achieve his retirement goal. His shortfall totals $3676 per year. By saving an extra $306 each month ($3676 ÷ 12), he can reach his retirement goal established in step 1.

Understanding your Social Security and employer-based retirement benefits is a first step in retirement planning.

17.2c Suggestions for Funding Erik's Retirement Goal

Erik needs to continue what he is doing—saving and investing—plus save a little more so he can enjoy his lifestyle when his full-time working career ends. Erik should discuss with his benefits counselor how much he can save and invest via the company's new 401(k) program.

Erik needs to save more for retirement. He should contribute an additional $3676 per year, which is only another $306 per month, into his employer's 401(k) plan—that is, about 7.3 percent of his salary. To create an extra

DID YOU KNOW

Online Retirement Planning Calculators

Research suggests that those who calculate how much they need to save often end up having a more financially successful retirement. In your assumptions, perhaps use a 5 percent long-term rate of return minus a 3 percent annual inflation rate, and try more than one calculator:

- AARP (www.aarp.org/work/retirement-planning /retirement_calculator.html)
- American Savings Education Council's Ballpark Estimate (www.choosetosave.org/ballpark/)
- CNNMoney.com (www.money.cnn.com/calculator /retirement/retirement-need/)

- E*Trade (www.us.etrade.com/e/t/plan/retirement/quickplan? vanity=quickplan)
- Fidelity (www.fidelity.com/calculators-tools/retirement -quick-check)
- The Motley Fool (www.partners.leadfusion.com/tools /motleyfool/retire02a/tool.fcs?v=76620)
- MarketWatch.com (www.marketwatch.com/retirement /tools/retirement-planning-calculator)
- T. Rowe Price's (www3.troweprice.com/ric/ricweb /public/ric.do?WTAFeaturedResult=retirement%20 calculator)

RUN THE NUMBERS

Estimating Your Retirement Savings Goal in Today's Dollars

This worksheet will help you calculate the amount you need to set aside each year in today's dollars so that you will have adequate funds for your retirement. The example here assumes that a single person is now 35 years old, hopes to retire at age 62, has a current income of $50,000, currently saves and invests about $1980 per year, contributes zero to an employer-sponsored retirement plan, anticipates needing a retirement income of $40,000 per year assuming

a spending lifestyle at 80 percent of current income ($50,000 × 0.80), and will live an additional 20 years beyond retirement. Investment returns are assumed to be 3 percent after inflation—a reasonable but conservative estimate for a typical portfolio. The financial needs would differ if the growth rate of the investments were less than 3 percent. This approach simplifies the calculations and puts the numbers to estimate retirement needs into today's dollars. The amount saved must be higher if substantial inflation occurs.

		Example	Your Numbers
1.	Annual income needed at retirement in today's dollars (Use carefully estimated numbers or a certain percentage, such as 70% or 80%.)	$ 40,000	_____
2.	Estimated Social Security retirement benefit in today's dollars	$ 13,200	_____
3.	Estimated employer pension benefit in today's dollars (Ask your retirement benefit adviser to make an estimate of your future pension, assuming that you remain in the same job at the same salary, or make your own conservative estimate.)	$ 5,800	_____
4.	Total estimated retirement income from Social Security and employer pension in today's dollars (line 2 þ line 3)	$ 19,000	_____
5.	Additional income needed at retirement in today's dollars (line 1–line 4)	$ 21,000	_____
6.	Amount you must have at retirement in today's dollars to receive additional annual income in retirement (line 5) for 20 years (from Appendix A-4, assuming a 3% return over 20 years, or 14.8775 × $21,000)	$312,427	_____
7.	Amount already available as savings and investments in today's dollars (add lines 7A through 7D, and record the total on line 7E)		
	A. Employer savings plans, such as a 401(k), SEP-IRA, or profit-sharing plan	0	_____
	B. IRAs and Keoghs	$ 24,000	
	C. Other investments, such as mutual funds, stocks, bonds, real estate, and other assets available for retirement	$ 13,000	
	D. If you wish to include a portion of the equity in your home as savings, enter its present value minus the cost of another home in retirement	0	
	E. Total retirement savings (add lines A through D)	$ 37,000	
8.	Future value of current savings/investments at time of retirement (using Appendix A-1 and a growth rate of 3% over 27 years, the factor is 2.2213; thus, 2.2213 × $37,000)	$ 82,188	_____
9.	Additional retirement savings and investments needed at time of retirement (line 6–line 8)	$230,239	_____
10.	Annual savings needed (to reach amount in line 9) before retirement (using Appendix A-3 and a growth rate of 3% over 27 years, the factor is 40.7096; thus, $230,239/40.7096)	$ 5,656	_____
11.	Current annual contribution to savings and investment plans	$ 1,980	_____
12.	Additional amount of annual savings that you need to set aside in today's dollars to achieve retirement goal (in line 1) (line 10–line 11)	$ 3,676	_____

margin of safety he could save even more of his salary, if the rules of his employer's retirement plan permit it. His employer might also make a matching contribution (discussed later) of some or all of Erik's 401(k) contributions.

One of the reasons Erik needs to save more is that he plans to retire at age 62. If he were instead to plan to retire at 67 (his full-benefit Social Security retirement age), he could save about $1500 less per year and have income until age 87 rather than 82. This is a decision he can defer until he gets older. If he is in good health at age 62, he can consider waiting to retire.

The additional $3676 in current dollars assumes that the growth of Erik's investments will be 3 percent higher than the inflation rate. As his income goes up, Erik should continue saving about 7.3 percent of his income to reach his goal of retiring at age 62. In this way, he will have a larger amount of income at retirement, thereby replacing his higher level of employment income. Redoing the calculations every few years will help keep Erik informed and on track for a financially successful retirement. If Erik has a paid-for home at retirement, he will need less income.

CONCEPT CHECK 17.2

1. List the steps in the process of estimating your retirement savings goal in today's dollars.

2. In the text example, what can Erik do to save more for his retirement?

17.3 ACHIEVE YOUR RETIREMENT GOAL BY INVESTING THROUGH EMPLOYER-SPONSORED RETIREMENT PLANS

17.3a The Basics of Tax-sheltered Retirement Accounts

The funds you put into regular investment accounts represent **after-tax money**. Assume, for example, that a person in the 25 percent tax bracket earns an extra $1000 and is considering investing those funds. She will pay $250 in income taxes on the extra income, which leaves only $750 in after-tax money available to invest. Furthermore, the earnings from the invested funds are also subject to income taxes each year as they are accrued.

The situation is much different when you invest in **tax-sheltered retirement accounts**. The contributions may be "deductible" from your taxable income in the year they are made. Here you pay zero taxes on the contributed amount of income in the current year. This means that you are investing with **pretax money**, and the salary amount you defer, or contribute, to a tax-sheltered retirement account comes out of your earnings before income taxes are calculated. Thus, you gain an immediate elimination of part of your income tax liability for the current year. The advantage of using tax-deductible contributions is illustrated in Table 17-1.

In addition, income earned on funds in tax-sheltered retirement accounts accumulates **tax deferred**. In other words, the individual does not have to pay income taxes on the earnings (interest, dividends, and capital gains) every year as they accrue as long as they are reinvested within the retirement account. Contributors to tax-deferred accounts often assume that they will be in a lower tax bracket when retired and making withdrawals.

A **tax-free withdrawal** is a removal of assets from an account with no taxes assessed. IRS regulations permit tax-free withdrawals from certain after-tax retirement accounts, such as the Roth IRA, which is discussed later. **Tax-free** means that withdrawals are not taxed. Tax-free withdrawals sometimes occur for certain medical and education expenses and for first-time homebuyers. Details are later in the chapter.

LEARNING OBJECTIVE 3

Distinguish among the types of employer-sponsored tax-sheltered retirement plans.

after-tax money
Funds put into regular investment accounts after paying income taxes.

tax-sheltered retirement accounts
Retirement account for which all earnings from the invested funds are not subject to income taxes.

pretax money
Investing before income taxes are calculated, thus gaining an immediate elimination of part of your income tax liability for the current year.

tax deferred
The individual does not have to pay current income taxes on the earnings (interest, dividends, and capital gains) reinvested in a retirement account.

tax-free withdrawals
Removal of assets from a retirement account with no taxes assessed.

Table 17-1	**Samantha Smarty Invests $6300 in Employer's 401(k) Plan and Earns 41 Percent, Really!**

Samantha Smarty participates in her employer's 401(k) retirement plan, and contributes 7 percent, or $6300, of her $89,000 income. Since her contributions are tax deductible and she is in the 25 percent federal tax bracket, this reduces her federal income taxes by $1575 ($6300 × .25 = $1575), and it reduces her state income tax another $252 ($6300 × 0.04 = $252). Thus, for a net outflow of $4473 ($67,334 − $62,861), Samantha gets to invest $6300. That's a 41 percent return ($6300 − $4473 = $1827/$4473) on her "investment." Whoa! What a great deal!

	Not Participating in 401(k) Plan	**Participating in 401(k) Plan**
Income	$89,000	$89,000
Contribution to plan	– 0 –	6,300
Taxable income	89,000	82,700
Federal income tax*	18,106	16,531
State income tax (4%)	3,560	3,308
Take-home pay	$67,334	$62,861

* From Table 4-2 on page 114.

17.3b Employer-Sponsored Retirement Plans Are Government Regulated

employer-sponsored retirement plan

An IRS-approved retirement plan offered by an employer (also called qualified plans).

Employee Retirement Income Security Act (ERISA)

Regulates employer-sponsored plans by calling for proper plan reporting and disclosure to participants in defined-contribution, defined-benefit, and cash-balance plans.

An **employer-sponsored retirement plan** is an IRS-approved plan offered by an employer. These are called **qualified plans**, meaning that they qualify for special tax treatment under regulations of the **Employer Retirement Income Security Act (ERISA)**. They are also known as **salary-reduction plans** because the contributed income is not included in an employee's salary. In effect, the contributions to an employer-sponsored retirement plan are an interest-free loan from the government to help you fund your retirement.

ERISA does not require companies to offer retirement plans, but it does regulate those plans that are provided. ERISA calls for proper plan reporting and disclosure to participants. Participating in a plan, such as a 401(k) plan, can serve as the cornerstone of your retirement planning.

Beneficiary Designation and Account Trustee When you open a retirement account, you must sign a **beneficiary designation form**. This document contractually determines who will inherit the funds in that retirement account in case you die before the funds are distributed. This designation contractually overrides any provisions in a will.

A special rule applies to 401(k) plans and other qualified retirement plans governed by the ERISA federal law. Your spouse is entitled to inherit all the money in the account unless he or she signs a written waiver, consenting to your choice of another beneficiary. It is not enough just to name someone else on the beneficiary form that your employer provides you.

The contributions into an employee's retirement account are deposited with a **trustee** (usually a financial institution, bank, or trust company that has fiduciary responsibility for holding certain assets), which according to the employee's instructions invests the money in various securities, including mutual funds, and sometimes the stock of an employer. Each employee's funds are managed in a separate account.

Vesting The worker always has a legal right to own the amount of money he or she contributes to his or her account in the employer's plan. This also means that the employee determines how the funds are to be invested and withdrawn.

vesting

Ensures that a retirement plan participant has the right to take full possession of all employer contributions and earnings.

Vesting is the process by which employees accrue non-forfeitable rights over their employer's contributions that are made to the employee's qualified retirement plan account. Some employers permit immediate vesting, or ownership, although most employers delay the vesting of their contributions to the employee for three to four years.

According to ERISA, the employer can require that the worker must work with the company for three years before vesting begins or he or she will lose any employer contributed money. Employers sometimes permit no vesting for the first two years and then one is fully vested after the third year. This is known as **cliff vesting**. Or it can choose to have the 20 percent of the contributions vest each year over five years, known as **graduated vesting**.

If an employee has not worked long enough for the employer to be vested before leaving his or her job, the employer's contributions are forfeited back to the employer's plan. The employee has no rights to any of those funds.

There are three common types of employer-sponsored retirement plans: (1) defined-contribution, (2) defined-benefit, and (3) cash-balance.

17.3c Type 1: Defined-Contribution Retirement Plans Are Most Common Today

A **defined-contribution retirement plan** voluntarily offered by an employer is designed to provide a retiring employee a lump sum at retirement. This is the most popular retirement plan today, and it is offered by close to half of all employers. It is distinguished by its "contributions"—that is, the total amount of money put into each participating employee's individual account. The eventual retirement benefit in such an employer-sponsored plan consists solely of assets (including investment earnings) that have accumulated in the various individual accounts.

Contributory and Noncontributory Plans In a **noncontributory plan**, money to fund the retirement plan is contributed only by the employer. In a **contributory plan**, money to fund the plan is provided by both the employer and the participant or solely by the employee. Most plans are contributory.

In a contributory plan the employer chooses to make a **matching contribution** that may fully or partially match (up to a certain limit) the employee's contribution to his or her employer-sponsored retirement account. The matching contribution may be up to a certain dollar amount or a certain percentage of compensation. For example, the match might be $1.00 for every $1.00 the employee contributes up to the first 3 percent of pay. More common is $0.50 per $1.00 up to the first 6 percent of pay. Better employers contribute $1 for every $1 you contribute up to 6 percent, or more. The employer contributions effectively increase your income without increasing your tax liability because you pay no income taxes on matching contributions until they are withdrawn during retirement.

When your employer makes a contribution to your account every time you do, you in effect obtain an "instant return" on your retirement savings. Saving $4000 a year with a $0.50 employer match immediately puts $2000 more into your retirement account, giving you a 50 percent return ($2000/$4000). This concept is illustrated in Table 17-2, arguing strongly that you should work only for companies whose policy is to offer healthy matching employer retirement contributions. Employers sometimes reduce or eliminate their matching contributions to retirement plans during times of poor profits. That is when employees often leave for other employment opportunities.

Some employers make their contributions in lump-sum payments to employees' accounts, at the end of the year rather than at the time of each paycheck As a result, all employees miss out on compounding for 12 months and those who leave during the year never receive the funds.

Automatic Enrollment Many employers offer **automatic enrollment**, which is a feature in a retirement plan that allows an employer to "enroll" all eligible employees in the employer's plan. As a result, part of the employees' wages are contributed to the retirement plan on the their behalf. An employee may affirmatively choose not to contribute at the plan's default

---

graduated vesting

Schedule under which employees must be at least 20 percent vested after two years of service and gain an additional 20 percent of vesting for each subsequent year until, at the end of year six, the account is fully vested.

defined-contribution retirement plan

A retirement plan designed to provide a lump-sum at retirement; it is distinguished by its "contributions"— the total amount of money put into each participating employee's individual account.

contributory plan

The most common type of employee-sponsored defined-contribution retirement plan; accepts employee as well as employer contributions.

matching contribution

Employer benefit that offers a full or partial matching contribution to a participating employee's account in proportion to each dollar of contributions made by the participant.

FINANCIAL POWER POINT

Save 12 to 15 Percent for Retirement Including Employer Contributions

People who start saving and investing for retirement during their 20s should aim to reserve 12 to 15 percent of their pretax income every year, *including* employer contributions, for this purpose. Those who have delayed planning for retirement until their late 30s or 40s should begin investing 20 to 25 percent annually in an effort to catch up. They have no choice.

Table 17-2　Only Work for Companies Who Offer Healthy Matching Employer Retirement Contributions

You should make contributions to your employer-based retirement account at least up to the amount where you obtain the largest matching contribution from your employer. The matching 100 percent employer contributions shown below increase the retirement account balance after 30 years from $317,000 to $476,000 with a 2 percent match and to $634,000 with a 4 percent match. By increasing the employee's contribution from 4 percent ($70,000 × 0.04 = $2800) to 6 percent ($70,000 × 0.06 = $4200) to obtain the full 100 percent employer match on the first 6 percent of salary, the sum rises to almost $1 million after 30 years earning an 8 percent annual return. Be smart. Work only for employers who offer healthy matching contributions to your retirement account.

Salary $70,000	Zero Employee Contribution	100% Match of 2% of Salary	100% Match of 4% of Salary	100% Match of 6% of Salary
Employee contributions	$2,800	$2,800	$2,800	$4,200
Employer contributions	$0	$1,400	$2,800	$4,200
Total annual contributions	$2,800	$4,200	$5,600	$8,400
Account balance after 30 years earning 8%	$317,000	$476,000	$634,000	$952,000

percentage rate or to contribute a different amount. The default percentage could start at 3 percent and gradually increase annually.

self-directed

In defined-contribution plans, employees control the assets in their account—how often to make contributions to the account, how much to contribute, how much risk to take, and how to invest.

Self-Directed Defined-contribution retirement plans are described as **self-directed** because the employee controls where the assets in his or her account are invested. The individual typically selects where to invest, how much risk to take, how much to invest, how often contributions are made to the account, as well as when to buy and sell. Over time, the balance amassed in such an account consists of the contributions plus any investment income and gains, minus expenses and losses. The contributions devoted to the account are specified ("defined"). The future amount in the account at retirement will not be known until the individual decides to begin making withdrawals. This uncertainty occurs because the sum available to the retiree depends on the success of the investments made. At retirement, the retiree thus has a lump sum to manage and spend down during the rest of his or her lifetime.

Risks of Defined Contribution Plans Defined contribution plans are not without risks. In fact, they are considerable because you must decide how much to save, how to

ADVICE FROM A PROFESSIONAL

Buy Your Retirement on the Layaway Plan

The large retirement savings goal dollar amount scares some people. To allay such concerns, the following novel approach to thinking about retirement saving has been suggested. You can look at your retirement as something you "buy." The "retail price" is the retirement nest egg goal itself. From that amount, you can subtract "discounts" for anticipated income from Social Security, employer-sponsored

retirement accounts, personal retirement accounts, and any other funds you expect to have accumulated. Then you identify the difference—the shortfall indicated on line 9 of the Run the Numbers worksheet—and buy it on a "layaway plan." The additional amounts you periodically save and invest are, therefore, the "layaway payments" with which you "buy" your retirement. This is smart thinking!

Dennis R. Ackley
Ackley & Associates, Kansas City, Missouri

invest, and how much to withdraw in retirement so you do not run out of money. And you do not know what the stock markets will do over the next 30 or 40 years.

Names of Defined-Contribution Plans Several types of employer-sponsored defined-contribution plans exist. These include the 401(k), 403(b), and 457 plans (named after sections of the IRS tax code) and the SIMPLE IRA and SIMPLE 401(k). Each plan is restricted to a specific group of workers. You may contribute to these plans only if your employer offers them.

The **401(k) plan** is the best-known defined-contribution plan. It is designed for employees of private corporations. (You can compare the quality of your employer's 401(k) plan with others at BrightScope (www.brightscope.com). Eligible employees of nonprofit organizations (colleges, hospitals, religious organizations, and some other not-for-profit institutions) may contribute to a **403(b) plan** that has the same contribution limits. Employees of state and local governments and non–church controlled tax-exempt organizations may contribute to **457 plans**; only employees (not employers) make contributions to 457 plans. An employer offering 401(k), 403(b), and 457 plans may also offer Roth versions of these plans calling for after-tax (rather than tax-deferred) contributions but with provisions for tax-free withdrawals during retirement.

When the employing organization has 100 or fewer employees, it may set up a **Savings Incentive Match Plan for Employees IRA (SIMPLE IRA)**. Employers with 25 or fewer employees can offer a **Salary Reduction Simplified Employee Pension Plan (SARSEP)** plan similar to a 401(k) plan. Regulations vary somewhat for each type of plan.

Limits on Contributions There are limits on the maximum amount of income per year that an employee may contribute to an employer-sponsored plan. The maximum contribution limit to 401(k), 403(b), 457, and SIMPLE IRA plans is $17,500.

Catch-Up Provision A **catch-up provision** permits workers age 50 or older to contribute an additional $5500 to most employer-sponsored plans. Millions of people who are getting a late start on saving—including women who have gone back to work after raising children—can put more money away for retirement.

401(k) plan

Defined-contribution plan designed for employees of private corporations.

DID YOU KNOW

Enormous Hidden 401(k) Fees Reduce Employee's Returns

A median-income, two-earner household will pay nearly $155,000 over the course of their lifetime in 401(k) fees, according to an analysis by Demos, a public policy organization. *Retirement Savings Drain: The Hidden and Excessive Costs of 401(k)s,* details how savers are vulnerable to losing almost one-third of their investment returns to inefficient stock and bond markets.

Many working employees are not aware that their employer's 401(k) retirement plan charges them fees for recordkeeping, administrative services, and trading and transaction costs. All employers assess fees that are deducted each year from each account before employees see their net returns. According to the Investment Company Institute the average is 0.72% for bond mutual funds and 0.95% for stock mutual funds. That amounts to $72 to $95 in fees on every $10,000

of your 401(k) balance every year! Small employers' 401(k) fees average 1.33% compared to 0.15% for large employers.

High fees can reduce one's ending total 401(k) balance by 15 to 20 percent. That cuts $150,000 to $200,000 from an expected balance of $1,000,000, which over the years reduces your account to $800,000 to $850,000. If this hidden fee issue impacts you, contact your employer's human resource department to find out how much in fees you pay each year, what the fees pay for, and what it will take to get them reduced.

All investors are similarly challenged. If you start with $10,000 and invest $500 a month for 30 years into a low-fee index fund charging only 0.2 percent annually and it grows at 8 percent each year, your account will total $818,000. If the fund charges a moderate 1.2 percent, your account total will reach $663,000. That's $155,000 less money because 23 percent of the total went to fees!

DID YOU KNOW

Relying on Today's Voluntary 401(k)/IRA Retirement Saving Plans Has Been a Failure

According to the Center for Retirement Research, only half of the nation's 115 million private sector employees work for an employer that offers a 401(k) plan. More than one-third have no retirement coverage through their employers at all throughout their working lives. Thirty-eight million working-age households do not have any money saved for retirement.

Seventy-five percent of Americans nearing retirement have less that $30,000 in their retirement accounts. Data from the Employee Benefit Research Institute show that only 22 percent of workers 55 or older have more than $250,000 put away for retirement account. A full 60 percent of workers in that age bracket have less than $100,000 in a retirement account. Even with Social Security pension payments, $100,000 is not going to last very long, certainly not 20 more years.

Of all those who have saved in 401(k) retirement plans, 30 percent have taken out loans for an average of 20 percent of the sum in the account. Plus, two-thirds of those who leave their jobs are unable to pay off the balance borrowed. Their loans then are in default, thus triggering additional income taxes and a 10 percent tax penalty.

Fifty percent of workers who are eligible to save and invest in a retirement plan don't save at all. And 56 percent of younger workers (ages 18 to 34) don't either. Less than 3 percent of all eligible employees contributed the maximum amount to their employee-sponsored retirement accounts.

The 401(k) plans are a retirement account that was supposed to help workers end up with enough money for a person or couple to retire on. The trouble is that it is clear that the shift from defined-benefit plans to 401(k)s has been a gigantic failure. Employers took advantage of the switch to increase profits by cutting retirement benefits. Millions do not manage or invest their money wisely. The returns on investments for workers have been far less than they were told to expect.

The 401(k) program seems to have been designed to fail and it has. As a result, we are facing a looming retirement crisis, with tens of millions of Americans facing a sharp decline in living standards at the end of their working lives. Many will choose to work until they cannot continue or until they die.

Just as a voluntary Social Security system would have been a disaster, relying on today's do-it-yourself, voluntary 401(k)/IRA retirement savings system has been a failure for the American society.

Avoid the disaster by getting as smart as you can about investing. You can and must plan for retirement, save, and invest as much as possible, and keep your fingers crossed for good luck. Maybe one day Congress will require that employers again offer defined-benefit plans to workers. Or, as *Bloomberg's Business Week* says in "Australia Gets Retirement Right" that increased contributions now required by both employers and employees will assure all Australians financially successful retirements.

---

portability

Upon termination of employment, employees with portable benefits can keep their savings in tax-sheltered accounts, transferring retirement funds from employer's account directly to another account without penalty.

Portability An added benefit of employer-sponsored plans is portability. **Portability** means that upon termination of employment, an employee can transfer the retirement funds from the employer's account to another tax-sheltered account without taxes or penalty.

DOL's Lifetime Income Calculator The Department of Labor (DOL) is considering proposing a rule that would require companies to provide estimated income illustrations for workers participating in defined contribution pension plans such as 401(k)s and 403(b)s. Simply put, you would get a snapshot of how your savings in these plans would work out to a monthly dollar amount, given certain assumptions. Instead of waiting, check out the DOL's draft "Lifetime Income Calculator" (www.dol.gov/ebsa/regs/lifetimeincomecalculator.html).

Blackrock's CoRI™ Retirement Income Planning Tool A major challenge facing those saving for retirement is "How much to save?" Blackrock's CoRI™ helps savers calculate how much they need to save to generate a specific lifetime income starting at age 65. See www.blackrock.com/cori-retirement-income-planning.

17.3d Type 2: Defined-Benefit Plans Are Yesterday's Standard

The second type of employer-sponsored retirement plan, a **defined-benefit retirement plan (DB)**, pays lifetime monthly payments to retirees based on a predetermined formula. Defined-benefit plans are commonly called pensions. A **pension** is a sum of money paid regularly as a retirement benefit. The Social Security Administration, various government agencies, and some employers pay pensions to retirees, and sometimes to their survivors.

Defined-benefit plans were the standard retirement plan for previous generations, but today such pensions are offered by only 15 percent of employers. DB plans were offered by 38 percent of U.S. companies 35 years ago. These employers guaranteed employer-paid monthly retirement payments for life.

Pension benefits in defined-benefit plans are based on the years of service at the employer, average pay during the last few working years, and a percentage. For example, an employee might have a defined annual retirement benefit of 2 percent multiplied by the number of years of service and multiplied by the average annual income during the last five years of employment. In this example, a worker with 20 years of service and an average income of $48,000 over the last five years of work would have an annual pension benefit of $19,200 (20 × 0.02 × $48,000), or $1600 per month.

Since the employer contributes all the money, it assumes all the investment risks associated with creating sufficient funds to pay future benefits. Some better employers still offer a non-optional defined-benefit retirement plan *and* a voluntary defined-contribution plan to their employees.

Critics of defined-benefit plans incorrectly claim that recipients of such a retirement plan, such as firefighters, policemen, and teachers, are bankrupting states and localities. In fact it is the politicians who over the years and despite signed agreements have failed to vote to contribute to the plans each and every year. Pensions currently take up only 3.8 of state resources annually while states give away over 4 times that amount each year in corporate subsidies.

Should You Take Normal or Early Retirement Under a Defined-Benefit Plan? The earlier you retire, the smaller your monthly retirement pension from a defined-benefit plan will be because you will likely receive income for more years as a retired person. To illustrate, assume you are eligible for a full retirement pension of $28,800 per year at age 65. Your benefit may be reduced 3 percent per year if you retire at age 62. Smaller monthly pension payments are paid to the early retiree in a defined-benefit plan so that he or she will receive, in theory, the same present value amount of pension benefits as the person who retires later.

The financial advantage of taking early retirement depends in part on the person's life expectancy and the rate at which benefits are reduced. People who expect to live for a shorter period than the average expectancy may achieve a better financial position by retiring early.

Disability and Survivors Benefits Survivors and disability benefits also represent concerns for workers who have spouses or children or are financially responsible for caring for others. A person's full retirement pension forms the basis for any benefits paid to survivors and, when part of a retirement plan, for disability benefits as well. **Disability benefits** may or may not be paid to employees who become disabled prior to retirement. People receiving either survivors or disability benefits from a company pension are entitled to an amount that is substantially less than the full retirement amount. For example, if you were entitled to a retirement pension benefit of $2000 per month, your disability benefit might be only $1100 per month.

defined-benefit retirement plan (DB)
Employer-sponsored retirement plan that pays lifetime monthly annuity payments to retirees based on a predetermined formula.

disability benefits
Substantially reduced benefits paid to employees who become disabled prior to retirement.

DID YOU KNOW

Tax Consequences in Retirement Planning

Tax-deferred retirement plans, like 401(k) plans and traditional IRAs, provide these benefits:

- *Your contributions are tax deductible and are not subject to federal, state, and local income taxes.*

- *No income taxes are due on any earnings on the assets until withdrawn.*

- *Withdrawals are subject to income taxes at your marginal tax rate, which in retirement may be lower than your tax rate today.*

- *Other retirement income, such as from Social Security, pensions, employment, interest, dividends, and capital gains, is subject to income taxes.*

- *When you die, any qualified beneficiary may choose to roll your 401(k) and IRA assets into an IRA tax-free.*

If a survivor is entitled to benefits the pension amount must be paid over two people's lives instead of a single person's life; consequently, the monthly payment is different. Using the benefit described in the preceding example, if your surviving spouse is five years older than you, he or she might be entitled to $1300 per month. In contrast, if your spouse is five years younger, he or she might be entitled to only $900 per month.

A qualified **joint and survivor benefit** (or **survivor's benefit**) is an annuity whose payments continue to the surviving spouse after the participant's death, often equal to at least 50 percent of the participant's pension benefit. This requirement can be waived if desired, but only after marriage—not in a prenuptial agreement. Federal law dictates that a spouse or ex-spouse who qualifies for benefits under the plan of a spouse or former spouse must agree in writing to a waiver of the spousal benefit.

This **spousal consent requirement** protects the interests of surviving spouses. If the spouse does waive his or her pension survivor benefits, the worker's retirement benefit will increase. Upon the worker's death, the spouse will not receive any survivor benefits when a waiver has been signed. Unless a spouse has his or her own retirement benefits, it is usually wise to keep the spousal pension benefit.

**joint and survivor benefit/
survivor's benefit**

*Annuity whose payments continue
to a surviving spouse after the
participant's death; often equals
at least 50 percent of participant's
benefit.*

spousal consent requirement

*Federal law that protects the surviving
rights of a spouse or ex-spouse to
retirement or pension benefits unless
the person signs a waiver of those
rights.*

17.3e   Type 3: Cash-Balance Plan Is a Hybrid Employer-Sponsored Retirement Plan

A third type of retirement plan is a hybrid of the defined-contribution and defined-benefit plans. A **cash-balance plan** is a defined-benefit plan that gives each participant an interest-earning account credited with a percentage of pay on a monthly basis. It is distinguished by the "balance of money" in an employee's account at any point in time. The employer contributes 100 percent of the funds, and the employee contributes nothing.

cash-balance plan

*Defined-benefit plan funded solely
by an employer that gives each
participant an interest-earning
account credited with a percentage
of pay on a monthly basis.*

DID YOU KNOW

Retirement Plan Insurance

ERISA established the Pension Benefit Guaranty Corporation (PBGC; www.pbgc.gov). The nation's 27,500 employer-sponsored defined-benefit pension plans pay insurance premiums to the PBGC, which guarantees a certain minimum amount of benefits of up to $4900 a month to 44 million eligible workers should those plans become financially unable to pay their obligations. The PBGC has taken over about 3800 plans. PBGC insurance never insures defined-contribution plans, but it does insure some cash-balance plans.

DID YOU KNOW

How Poorly Prepared Are Today's "Near Retirees"?

One-third of people age 55 to 64 have not saved a penny for retirement. The National Institute on Retirement Security reports that 90 percent of American workers will not be able to afford to retire on savings and Social Security. These people cannot catch up financially. Time, not money, is still the most important concept in saving and investing for retirement. You do not want to become one of these statistics. So, begin to start saving early in life for your retirement. Prepare today by saving to do tomorrow what you love.

The Pension Protection Act regulates the percentage earned on such accounts. The employer contributes a straight percentage of perhaps 4 percent of the employee's salary every payday to his or her specific cash-balance account. Interest on cash-balance accounts is credited at a rate guaranteed by the employer, and the employer assumes all the investment risk. As a result, the amount in the account grows at a regular rate. Employees can look ahead 5 or 25 years and calculate how much money will be in their account.

17.3f   Additional Employer-Sponsored Retirement Plans

Some employers offer other supplemental savings plans to employees.

ESOP   An **employee stock-ownership plan (ESOP)** is a benefit plan through which the employer donates company stock into a trust, which are then allocated into accounts for individual employees. When employees leave the company, they get their shares of stock and can sell them. In effect, the retirement fund consists of stock in the company.

Profit-Sharing Plan   A **profit-sharing plan** is an employer-sponsored plan that shares some of the profits with employees in the form of end-of-year cash or common stock contributions into employees' 401(k) accounts. The level of contributions made to the plan may reflect each person's performance as well as the level of profits achieved by the employer.

employee stock-ownership plan (ESOP)
Benefit plan in which employers make tax-deductible gifts of company stock into trusts, which are then allocated into employee accounts.

profit-sharing plan
Employer-sponsored plan that allocates some of the employer profits to employees in the form of end-of-year cash or common stock contributions to employees' 401(k) accounts.

DID YOU KNOW ?

Money Websites for Retirement and Estate Planning

Informative websites for retirement planning, including calculators to estimate how much to save are:

AARP on estate planning (www.aarp.org/money/estate-planning/)

American Savings Education Council's ballpark estimate (www.choosetosave.org/ ballpark/)

Blackrock's CoRI retirement income planning tool (www.blackrock.com/cori-retirement-income-planning)

BrightScope (brightscope.com)

EstatePlanning.com (www.estateplanning.com/)

Nolo on wills, trusts and estates (www.nolo.com/legal-encyclopedia/wills-trusts-estates)

Pension Benefit Guaranty Corporation (PBGC; www.pbgc.gov)

QuickAdvice (www.guidedchoice.com/quickadvice/)

Social Security Administration (www.ssa.gov and www.ssa.gov/estimator/)

T. Rowe Price (troweprice.com)

Vanguard (vanguard.com)

CONCEPT CHECK 17.3

1. Distinguish among after-tax money put into investments, pretax money, and vesting.

2. Explain what is meant by tax-sheltered investment growth on money invested through qualified retirement accounts.

3. Summarize the main differences between defined-contribution and defined-benefit pension plans.

4. Explain why defined-contribution retirement plans are called self-directed.

5. Offer your impressions of working for an employer that offers a sizable matching contribution compared with one that does not.

17.4 ACHIEVE YOUR RETIREMENT SAVINGS GOAL THROUGH PERSONALLY ESTABLISHED RETIREMENT ACCOUNTS

If you do not have access to an employer plan, you easily can, and should, set up your own plan. IRS regulations allow you to take advantage of personally established, self-directed tax-sheltered retirement accounts such as an individual retirement account (IRA). The total maximum annual contribution you may make to any IRA account is $5500 (or $6500 for those over age 50). These personally established retirement accounts include Roth IRA accounts, IRAs, and Keogh and SEP-IRA plans.

If your employer does not have a retirement plan, you must open one or more accounts to fund your own retirement. You are required to make a contribution before April 15th of the tax year following the year you will take the tax deduction.

17.4a Roth IRA Accounts Provide Tax-Free Growth and Tax-Free Withdrawals

Roth IRA

IRA funded with after-tax money (and thus it is not tax deductible) that grows on a tax-deferred basis; withdrawals are not subject to taxation.

A **Roth IRA** is a nondeductible, after-tax IRA that offers significant tax and retirement planning advantages, especially for those who expect to be in a lower tax bracket in retirement. Contributions to Roth IRAs are not tax deductible, but funds in the account grow tax-free. You do not pay taxes each year on capital gains, dividends, and other distributions from securities held within a Roth IRA account.

Withdrawals from a Roth IRA also are tax-free if taken at age 59½ or later (or if you are disabled) from an account held at least five years. Tax-free withdrawals may be made for qualifying first-time homebuyer costs, medical expenses, or to pay for educational expenses. Once you remove money from a Roth IRA, it is a withdrawal (not a loan), and you cannot put it back. There is no mandatory withdrawal schedule for Roth IRAs, and money in the account can pass to an heir free of estate taxes. You may open a Roth IRA even if you (or your spouse) have a retirement plan at work. About half of employers offer Roth IRAs, and some employers offer Roth 401(k) accounts.

17.4b Individual Retirement Accounts (IRAs) Result in Tax-Free Growth and Taxable Withdrawals

individual retirement account (IRA)

Personal retirement account to which a person can make contributions that provide tax-deferred growth.

An **individual retirement account (IRA)** is a personal retirement account into which a person can make one or more annual contributions. An IRA is not an investment but rather an account in which to hold investments, like stocks and mutual funds. It is much like any other account opened at a bank, credit union, brokerage firm, or mutual fund company. You can invest IRA money almost any way you desire, including collectibles like art, gems, stamps, antiques, rugs, metals, guns, and certain coins and metals. You may invest once and never do it again or you may contribute regularly for many years, and you may change investments whenever you please.

DID YOU KNOW

MyRAs is a Starter Savings Opportunity

The Obama Administration created a new type of employer-based, no-fee savings account for retirement called MyRAs (pronounced "My-R-As"). It is aimed at the more than half the civilian labor force lacking access to a work-based retirement plan. The minimum after-tax investment is $25 and payroll deductions may be $5 or more. Funds in the account earn a rate of interest comparable to a federal government securities program, and the principal cannot be lost. Once the account balance reaches $15,000, or after 30 years, the funds must be moved to a Roth IRA account. MyRA rules are the same as for Roth IRA accounts. Distributions are always penalty free.

To fund the account, you may make a new contribution or transfer a lump-sum distribution received from another employer plan or another IRA account to your IRA account. Taxpayers can even opt on their federal tax return to allocate part or all of their refund for direct deposit into an IRA account. You may not borrow from an IRA.

A **traditional** (or **regular**) **IRA** offers tax-deferred growth. Your contributions may be tax deductible, which means that you can use all or part of your contributions to reduce your taxable income. If you (or your spouse) have a retirement plan at work, your contributions to an IRA account may be limited.

A nonworking spouse can make a deductible IRA contribution to a **spousal IRA** account of up to $5500 ($6500 if age 50 or older) as long as the couple files a joint return, and the working spouse has enough earned income to cover the contribution. The IRS requires that withdrawals from all types of IRA accounts begin no later than age 70½.

traditional (regular) IRA
Account that offers tax-deferred growth; the initial contribution may be tax deductible for the year that the IRA was funded.

spousal IRA
Account set up for spouse who does not work for wages; offers tax-deferred growth and tax deductibility.

17.4c Keoghs and SEP-IRA Accounts Are for Self-Employed Individuals

A **Keogh** (pronounced "Key-oh") is a tax-deferred retirement account designed for high-income self-employed and small-business owners. Depending on the type of Keogh established (defined benefit or defined contribution), an individual may save as much as 25 percent of self-employment earned income, with contributions capped at

Keogh
Tax-deferred retirement account designed for high-income self-employed and small-business owners.

DID YOU KNOW

Sean's Success Story

Sean is now 52 years old. He has held four jobs, and two of his employers offered no retirement plan. When working at those jobs, he made monthly deposits into a Roth IRA account with low-fee mutual fund investments. He participated fully in the plans offered by the other two employers. Total annual contributions to retirement savings usually totaled about 12 percent, including the matches from his employers who offered retirement plans. When Sean changed employers, he always transferred the vested amounts in his retirement accounts to a rollover IRA account, which now has a value of $412,000.

Sean has been with his current employer for ten years, and his 401(k) account balance is $175,000. He has been careful to diversify his retirement investments. He started investing almost solely in stock funds, especially stock index funds. During the last two years, Sean started to move some of his money into lower risk options by focusing on high-rated bond funds. His current allocation is about 60 percent equities, 30 percent bonds, and 10 percent in a money market fund. His target percentages at a planned retirement at age 65 are 45 percent equities, 40 percent bonds, and 15 percent money market. Sean is looking forward to retirement in about 12 years with a nest egg of about $2 million.

DID YOU KNOW

How to Invest Your Retirement Money

When you open any kind of defined-contribution retirement plan, you may invest in a number of alternatives. Options within employer-based plans are usually mutual funds and employer stock. With mutual funds, you will likely have, at a minimum, a stock fund, a growth stock fund, an index fund, a bond fund, and a money market fund from which to choose. You will want to pay close attention to the costs of each investment as well as stock index funds.

In Chapter 13, we described several long-term investment strategies employed by wise investors (pages 392–401). The most notable of these for retirement investing is the buy and hold philosophy funded by a dollar-cost averaging approach with broad diversification using an asset allocation strategy.

One important principle in investing for retirement is to recognize that you can accept more risk in your investments the farther away you are from retirement. Investing too conservatively almost guarantees low returns and not enough funds at retirement.

Here are some examples of accepting more risk. A young, risk-tolerant, long-term 401(k) or IRA investor with an aggressive investment philosophy might have a portfolio with 100 percent in a growth stock fund. A more moderate approach might have a stock fund/bond fund/money market fund portfolio allocated at 60/30/10 percent, respectively.

If you are just starting out in a 401(k) plan or have no other retirement assets, you might consider investing in a low-fee "target-date retirement fund" (see Chapter 15). These funds are the ultimate in disciplined, hands-off investing. To start, you pick a date that matches the year you plan to retire, perhaps in 2054. The fund will place your money in a diversified portfolio that automatically shifts the asset mix away from equities and toward more conservative fixed-income investments as you approach the year of your retirement. Be sure to avoid high fees!

Instead of being a do-it-yourself investor, a worker can sign up for the services of a "limited managed account" (see Chapter 13). You and your advisor decide on your preferred asset allocation. Then the company on your behalf sells and buys your mutual fund assets, usually quarterly, to adjust your portfolio back to your specified asset allocation percentages. You can do this for less than $100 annually.

When investing for retirement you should never be jumping in and out of investment choices. Relax and be confident that plenty of money will be available for retirement if you save and invest using long-term investment approaches described in Chapter 13. The key suggestion is that you must start to save early in life and choose to invest in low-cost index mutual funds and/or exchange-traded funds and hold them forever.

$52,000 per participant. If the income comes from self-employment, contributions can still be made after age 70½.

A **simplified employee pension–individual retirement account (SEP-IRA)** is a retirement savings account for a sole proprietor's self-employment income and those with one or more employees who are looking to save only in profitable years. A SEP-IRA is easier to set up and maintain than a Keogh. The total contribution to a SEP-IRA account should not exceed the lesser of 25% of income or $52,000. All employees must receive the same benefits under a SEP plan.

CONCEPT CHECK 17.4

1. Why should workers choose to save for retirement through a personally established retirement account?

2. Summarize the importance of low-cost investment fees to long-term retirement success.

3. List two differences between a Roth IRA and a traditional IRA.

4. Who would use a Keogh rather than a SEP-IRA to save for retirement?

17.5 AVOID PENALTIES AND DO NOT OUTLIVE YOUR MONEY

Once you have accumulated a substantial retirement nest egg, you can congratulate yourself. For many years, you sacrificed some of your spending and instead saved and invested. However, retirement planning does not end when retirement saving ends.

You will also need to plan your retirement *spending* so you—and perhaps a significant other—can live during retirement without running out of money. To do so, you must avoid withdrawing your money early, carefully manage your retirement assets, plan appropriate account withdrawals once you do retire, and consider purchasing an annuity with a portion of your retirement funds at retirement.

> **LEARNING OBJECTIVE 5**
>
> Describe how to avoid penalties and make your retirement money last.

17.5a Avoid Withdrawing Tax-Sheltered Retirement Money Early

For many people, the money accumulated in a 401(k) or IRA retirement account represents most—if not all—of their retirement savings. Withdrawing money early from a retirement account or borrowing some diverts the funds from their intended purpose, and the money is no longer there to grow tax-deferred. When other financial needs present themselves, there is often a desire to tap into the funds for nonretirement purposes. Such uses were not the intent of Congress when it set up the tax-favored status of the accounts. Making early withdrawals means that you either must retire later or retire at a lower level of living. You want to avoid both.

Beware of the Negative Impacts of Early Withdrawals Early **withdrawals**—typically defined as a premature distribution before age 59½—are taxed as ordinary income. When money is directly withdrawn from a tax-sheltered retirement account before the rules permit—perhaps to buy a car, take a vacation, remodel a home, or pay off a credit card debt—three bad things happen:

1. **More taxes are due to the government.** The IRS's **20 percent withholding rule** applies whenever a participant takes direct possession of the funds grown from pretax contributions to a retirement account. This amount is forwarded to the IRS to prepay some of the income taxes that will be owed on the withdrawn funds. You may avoid the 20 percent withholding rule by transferring

DID YOU KNOW

How Long Will You Live?

People routinely underestimate the number of years they will be retired. This is because their life expectancy at birth is not the same as their life expectancy as they get older. Your life expectancy at birth is age 74 if you are a man (it's 79 for women).

If you are among the 80 percent of Americans who reach age 65, your life expectancy is now 81 if you are a man (84 for women). Half will live to that long (81 or 84) and half will not. A 65-year-old couple faces a 4 in 5 chance that one of them will live to age 85. The chance that one will reach age 97 is 1 in 4.

Contrary to popular thinking only 4 percent of the elderly are in nursing homes.

Planning an active retirement can include working part-time at something you enjoy.

Fabio Cardoso/Flame/Corbis

the money into a **rollover IRA**, which is an account set up to receive such funds. You must make a **trustee-to-trustee rollover** whereby the funds go directly from the previous account's trustee to the trustee of the new account, avoiding any payment to the employee.

Assume William Wacky, a 35-year-old with $25,000 in a tax-sheltered retirement account, withdraws $8000 out of the account. If he pays federal and state income taxes at a combined 30 percent rate, his $8000 withdrawal must be included as part of his taxable income. That will cost him an extra $2400 ($8000 × 0.30) in income taxes. Twenty percent of the $8000 will be withheld by William's employer.

trustee-to-trustee rollover

Retirement funds go directly from the previous account's trustee to the trustee of the new account, with no direct payment to the employee occurring, thereby deferring taxation and the early withdrawal penalty.

early withdrawal penalty

A ten percent penalty over and above the taxes owed when money is withdrawn early from a qualified retirement account.

2. **Penalties are assessed.** The IRS assesses a 10 percent **early withdrawal penalty** on such withdrawals. Because William withdrew $8000, he must also pay a penalty tax of $800 ($8000 × 0.10).

3. **The investment does not grow.** Withdrawing money means that the investment can no longer accumulate. The lost time for compounding will substantially shrink one's retirement nest egg. William's withdrawal of $8000 out of the account that could have grown at 8 percent over the next 30 years costs him the forgone return of a whopping $80,502 (from Appendix A-1).

Summing up this example, William's early withdrawal of $8000 nets him only $4800 after taxes and penalties ($8000 − $2400 − $800), and he gave up a future value of more than $80,000 in his retirement account. Never withdraw funds early from your retirement account!

Some Penalty-Free Withdrawals Do Exist The IRS imposes no penalty for early withdrawals in three situations:

1. **Expenses for medical, college, and home buying.** You can make penalty-free withdrawals from an IRA account (but not an employer-sponsored plan) if you pay for medical expenses in excess of 7.5 percent of your adjusted gross income, you pay medical insurance premiums after being on unemployment for at least 12 weeks, you are disabled, you pay for qualified higher-education expenses, or

DID YOU KNOW

Taking Money Out of Your Retirement Plan When Changing Jobs Is A Huge Mistake!

More than 60 percent of workers age 18 to 34 take all the money out of their employer's tax-sheltered retirement account when they change jobs. Taking out perhaps $30,000 to pay for a wedding or to buy a car results in

perhaps $10,000 in income taxes and penalties leaving you a net of $20,000. Worse, you forever have lost over $300,000 to use during retirement (Appendix A-1, 8%, 30 years: 10.0627 × $30,000). Early withdrawals are a big mistake!

DID YOU KNOW

What To Do With Your Retirement Money When Changing Employers

When changing employers or retiring, you may have four choices:

1. *Leave it.* *You may be able to leave the money invested in your account at your former employer (about half do) until you wish to begin taking withdrawals.*

2. *Transfer it.* *You may be able to transfer the money to a retirement account at a new employer.*

3. *Transfer it.* *You can transfer the money to a rollover IRA.*

4. *Take it.* *You can take the money in cash and pay income taxes and penalties.*

Options 2, 3, and 4 result in a **lump-sum distribution** because all the money is removed from a retirement account at one time. Such a transfer must be executed correctly according to the IRS's rollover regulations or the taxpayer will be subject to a substantial tax bill and perhaps a need to borrow money to pay the IRS. A **rollover** is the action of moving assets from one tax-sheltered account to another tax-sheltered account or to an IRA within 60 days of a distribution. This procedure preserves the benefits of having funds in a tax-sheltered account.

the distribution of less than $10,000 is used for qualifying first-time home-buyer expenses.

2. **Account loan.** You may borrow up to half of your accumulated assets in an employer-sponsored account, not to exceed 50 percent of your vested account balance, or $50,000, whichever is less. The borrower pays interest on the loan, which is then credited to the person's account. Loans must be repaid with after-tax money. If the employee changes employers, he or she must repay the unpaid balance of the loan within 30 days. Otherwise, the loan is reclassified as a withdrawal, which will result in additional taxes and penalties.

3. **Early retirement.** You may avoid a penalty if you retire early (but not earlier than 59.5 years) or are totally or permanently disabled and you are willing to receive annual distributions according to an IRS-approved method for a time period of no less than five years.

DID YOU KNOW

Bias Toward Overreacting

People engaged in retirement and estate planning have a bias toward certain behaviors that can be harmful, such as a tendency toward overreacting to both investment gains and losses in retirement accounts. What to do? Retirement is a long-term goal so never think short-term at all. Instead automate the investments in your retirement plan and hire a company to regularly rebalance your account.

DID YOU KNOW

Turn Bad Habits into Good Ones

Do You Do This?	*Do This Instead!*
Put off saving for retirement	Save early and often
Avoid risk when saving for retirement	Accept risk knowing that you have time to ride out the highs and lows of the stock market
Rely only on your employer's plan when saving for retirement	Contribute to a Roth IRA to supplement your employer-sponsored plans if necessary to reach your calculated retirement savings goal
Withdraw or borrow money from your retirement accounts when money is desired for other reasons	Keep your hands off your retirement money
Put off writing your will and keeping it up to date	Go online and create a will and revise when needed

17.5b Figure Out How Many Years Your Money Will Last in Retirement

As you near retirement, you will want to ask "How long will my retirement nest egg last?" The answer to this question will depend on three factors: (1) the amount of money you have accumulated, (2) the real (after inflation) rate of return you will earn on the funds, and (3) the amount of money to be withdrawn from the account each year.

Appendix A-4 provides factors that can be divided into the money in a retirement fund to determine the amount available for spending each year. Consider the example of Wayne and Melodee Neu, young retirees from Prescott, Arizona, who want their $500,000 retirement nest egg to last 20 years. They assume that the nest egg will earn a 6 percent annual return in the future and assume an annual inflation rate of 3 percent. The present value factor in the table in the "20 years" column and the "3 percent (6 percent investment return minus 3 percent inflation)" row in Appendix A-4 is 14.8775. Dividing $500,000 by 14.8775 reveals that Wayne and Melodee could withdraw $33,608, or $2800 per month ($33,608 ÷ 12 months), for 20 years before the fund was depleted.

Because they adjusted their rate of return for inflation, the Neus can safely increase their income by two or three percent each year to safeguard the spending power of their retirement income. But what if they live for 30 more years? The factor for 30 years is 19.6004, and the answer is $25,510, or $2126 per month; almost $700 less initially.

One of the mistakes that new retirees make is withdrawing money too fast. Table 17-3 shows how long one's retirement money will last using various withdrawal rates.

DID YOU KNOW

Bias Toward Loss Aversion

People engaged in retirement and estate planning have a bias toward certain behaviors that can be harmful, such as a tendency toward avoiding losses. Research suggests that losses are twice as powerful, psychologically, as gains. Many of us are too willing to give up the potential upside of better paying investments just to be confident the downside is protected. What to do? When investing for retirement take some risk so you earn higher returns and redo the calculations of retiring on a lump sum with a 2 percent withdrawal rate instead of 4 percent.

DO IT IN CLASS

Table 17-3 **How Long Will My Retirement Money Last?**

The higher your withdrawal rate, the more likely it is that your portfolio will not last until you die. The basis for the following calculations is research by T. Rowe Price, Vanguard, and other online retirement planning websites. Here are the rates of withdrawals and the likelihood that a diversified portfolio earning a long-term historical rate of return will last through retirement, assuming 3 percent annual increases in withdrawals for inflation.

Withdrawal Rate Amount	Years in Retirement and Likelihood Money Will Last		
	20	30	40
3%	99%	99%	93%
4%	99%	86%	68%
5%	93%	61%	41%
6%	74%	35%	18%

17.5c   You Can Use an Annuity to "Guarantee" a Portion of Your Retirement Income

The fear of running out of money in retirement looms large for people approaching retirement and during retirement. How can you be sure that declines in the stock market will not cause you to have to significantly decrease your level of living as you age? Rather than continuing to manage their own investments and withdrawals in an effort to make the money last, some people use a portion of their retirement nest egg (such as one-third or one-half) to buy an annuity.

An **annuity** is a contract made with an insurance company that provides for a series of payments to be received at stated intervals (usually monthly) for life or a specified time period. For retirees who buy an annuity, this means that an insurance company will receive a portion of their retirement nest egg and, in return, promise to send monthly payments according to an agreed-upon schedule, usually for the life of the person covered by the annuity (the **annuitant**).

Payments Start Right Away When You Buy an Immediate Annuity   Retirees typically buy an **immediate annuity** at or soon after retirement. The annuity income payments will then begin at the end of the first month after purchase and any gains will accumulate tax-deferred. You do pay income taxes on the payments.

Fixed and Variable Annuities   Annuities offer several options for receiving the annuity benefits. With a **fixed annuity**, the insurance company guarantees a specified rate of return on your invested funds. The rate is relatively low, perhaps 2 or 4 percent. This is a low investment risk to the company. Because of such low payment rates, fixed annuities do have substantial inflation risk to the recipient annuitant.

In the following examples of hypothetical fixed income payments, assume that a 70-year-old retiree has purchased an annuity for $100,000. A **straight annuity** might provide a lifetime income of perhaps $790 monthly for the rest of the life of the annuitant only. An **installment-certain annuity** might provide a payment of $680 monthly for the rest of the life of the annuitant with a guarantee that if the person dies before receiving a specific number of payments, his or her beneficiary will receive a certain number of payments for a particular time period (such as ten years in this example). A **joint-and-survivor annuity** might provide $640 monthly for as long as one of the two people—usually a husband and wife—is alive.

A more common type of annuity sold by insurance salespeople is called a **variable annuity**. This is an annuity whose value rises and falls like mutual funds. Variable annuities do carry investment risk but are better able than fixed annuities to protect against inflation risk. Annuities are sold aggressively because sellers earn very high commissions and the insurance company charges substantial annual fees. An investor may have to wait 15 to 20 years before a variable annuity becomes as efficient as a equivalent investment in a mutual fund. When buying a variable annuity, make sure that you fully understand the fees, commissions, and other rules of the contract.

Annuities Carry Sales Commissions and Fees   All annuities charge a variety of fees which reduce the amount of income paid out. First-year sales commissions exceeding 10 percent are typical. Annual expenses are often 3 percent or more. The trade-off the consumer makes is between the guaranteed payouts from an annuity that often carry high costs and the potential substantial risks of managing one's own retirement investments, such as making poor investment choices.

The company knows that in a given pool of 100,000 annuitants that half will die before they reach median life expectancy, and half after. People often do not buy annuities because they prefer to keep money for their heirs. Anyone considering the purchase of an annuity might be wise to begin with Vanguard, Fidelity or TIAA-CREF, all of which are low-fee industry leaders.

annuity
Contract made with an insurance company that provides for a series of payments to be received at stated intervals (usually monthly) for a fixed or variable time period.

immediate annuity
Annuity, often funded by a lump sum from the death benefit of a life insurance policy or lump sum from a defined-contribution plan, that begins payments one month after purchase.

joint-and-survivor annuity
Provides monthly payments for as long as one of the two people—usually a husband and wife—is alive.

variable annuity
Annuity whose value rises and falls like mutual funds and pays a limited death benefit via an insurance contract.

DID YOU KNOW ?

What Happens If You Don't Save for Retirement?

If you do not save for retirement or do not save enough, there are consequences. You must begin by accepting the fact that how you are living today is not they way you are going to live in retirement. You will be poorer. Your choices will be to:

1. *Reduce your level of living in retirement, perhaps by eliminating cable television and vacations;*

2. *Delay filing for Social Security retirement benefits until past your normal full-benefits age, perhaps to 70, to obtain a larger monthly benefit;*

3. *Sell your home and move into a smaller, cheaper place, perhaps in a rural community;*

4. *Move to a geographic area that has a lower cost of living, such as a state with no state income taxes and low real estate property taxes;*

5. *Delay your retirement and continue working full-time in your present job;*

6. *Work part-time for your present employer or in a grocery store; and/or*

7. *Work until you are 80+ years of age or in failing health, or until you die.*

Alternatively, you could begin saving for retirement early in life and, therefore, invest enough to live on during your retirement. Plus, you could gain an extra $2000 a month in retirement income by paying off your home and car and getting out of credit card debt *before* you retire.

CONCEPT CHECK 17.5

1. What are some negative impacts of taking early withdrawals from retirement accounts?

2. Name two types of penalty-free withdrawals from retirement accounts.

3. Summarize how long one's retirement money will last given certain withdrawal rates.

4. Offer some positive and negative observations on the wisdom of buying an annuity with some of your retirement nest egg money when you retire.

DO IT IN CLASS

LEARNING OBJECTIVE 6

Plan for the distribution of your estate and, if needed, use trusts to lower estate taxes.

---

probate

Court-supervised process that allows creditors to present claims against an estate and ensures the transfer of a decedent's assets to the rightful beneficiaries according to a properly executed and valid will or, when no will exists, to the people, agencies, or organizations required by state law.

nonprobate property

Does not go through probate; includes assets transferred to survivors by contract (such as beneficiaries listed on retirement accounts and bank accounts held with another person).

17.6 HOW TO PLAN FOR THE DISTRIBUTION OF YOUR ASSETS

Estate planning comprises the specific arrangements you make during your lifetime for the administration and distribution of your estate when you die. It involves both financial and legal considerations, and a primary goal is to minimize both taxes and legal expenses. It is both smart and practical to take the fundamental steps while you are young and then update them as your life progresses.

Upon your death your surviving family members will not conduct the distribution of your assets. Most of these procedures are set up before your death, as described below. Others are set up through **probate** by which a special **probate court** allows creditors, such as a credit card company, an auto financing company or a mortgage lender, to present claims against an estate and ensures the transfer of a decedent's assets to the rightful beneficiaries. The probate court will make the distributions according to a properly executed and valid will or, when no will exists, to the people or organizations as required by state law.

17.6a Start Right Now by Setting Up Most of Your Assets as Nonprobate Property

Figure 17-1 illustrates the different ways that your property can be distributed after your death. Importantly, **nonprobate property** is not transferred by the probate court. Nonprobate property includes assets transferred to survivors by contract such as by

Figure 17-1   How Your Estate Is Distributed After Your Death

YOUR ENTIRE ESTATE

Most of your assets are transferred after your death by:	Your probate property is transferred by the probate court in accordance with:

1. Contracts you set up before death, including
 	
   Payable-on-death clauses in bank accounts
 	
   Assets owned by joint ownership with rights of survivorship
 	
   Beneficiary designations in life insurance and retirement plans
 	
2. Setting up trusts that designate who will receive the property, including
 	
   Living trusts established while you are still alive
 	
   Testamentary trusts designed to take effect at your death
	Your wishes as outlined in your will
	
	OR
	
	If you have no will, the intestate succession laws in your state

naming a beneficiary for your retirement plan or by owning assets with another person through joint tenancy with right of survivorship. Trusts (discussed below) can also be used to transfer assets outside of probate court.

One of the primary benefits of setting up assets as nonprobate property is time. Nonprobate property transfers immediately upon your death, whereas probate can take between 6 months and a year, or longer if there is no will. Avoiding probate court may also save money since your estate pays the cost of the probate process based on the value of the assets it must distribute, and this ranges from hundreds to perhaps thousands of dollars. Avoiding probate also maintains your privacy because a public record is maintained of the probate process.

17.6b   Most Assets Are Transferred by Contract

People of average economic means should be able to transfer by contract most or all of their assets outside of probate. Transferring your estate by contract is an easy, do-it-yourself project. You just have to take a few minutes of time to fill out the appropriate forms. There are three ways to transfer assets by contract:

1. Transfers by Beneficiary Designation When you open up investment accounts, you are given a form to complete in order to name your beneficiaries. Changes are made in the same way; you complete a new beneficiary designation form. Examples of accounts like this are IRAs, 401(k) plans, Keogh plans, pension plans, bank and credit union accounts, stock brokerage accounts, mutual funds, annuities, and life and disability income insurance policies.

A **beneficiary** is a person or organization designated to receive a benefit. A **beneficiary designation** is a legal form signed by the owner of an asset providing that the property goes to a certain person or organization in the event of the owner's death. The form also contains a place to designate a **contingent (or secondary) beneficiary** in case the first-named **beneficiary**, also known as the primary beneficiary, dies after the form is filled out. If no one has been named as beneficiary for a particular asset or if that person and a named contingent beneficiary has died, the property will go to one's estate and to probate court for distribution. The lesson here: Be certain to name contingent beneficiaries as well as beneficiaries in contracts.

2. Transfers by Property Ownership Designation Joint tenancy with right of survivorship (also called **joint tenancy**; see page 152) is the most common form

contingent (or secondary) beneficiary
The beneficiary in case the first-named beneficiary has died; also called the secondary beneficiary.

joint tenancy with right of survivorship/joint tenancy
Most common form of joint ownership, especially for husbands and wives, in which each person owns the whole of the asset, such as a bank account or home, and can dispose of it without the approval of the other owner(s).

of joint ownership of assets, especially for husbands and wives. In this case, each person owns the whole of the asset, such as a bank account or home, and can dispose of it without the approval of the other owners. Assets owned in this way often include bank accounts, stocks, bonds, real estate, mutual funds, government bonds, and other assets.

Upon the death of one owner, the surviving owners receive the property by operation of law rather than through the provisions of a will. Simply stated, the surviving owner(s) owned the entire asset before the death and own all of it after death. The lesson here: If you want an asset to immediately transfer to a particular person upon your death, own it as joint tenants with right of survivorship.

3. Transfers by Payable-on-Death Designation With a **payable-on-death designation** on a bank account the beneficiary has no rights to the funds until you pass on. Until that time, you are free to use the money kept in the bank account, to change the beneficiary, or to close the account. The named beneficiary simply needs to present a copy of your death certificate to the bank and show proper identification, and access to the account will be granted.

payable-on-death designation
Status granted to individuals who are not joint tenants and who might need to access accounts without going through probate; the deceased signs the designation before death, and the designee simply presents a death certificate to access the accounts.

17.6c The Rest of Your Estate Can Be Transferred via Your Will

Your **probate property** is simply all assets other than nonprobate property. Your probate property consists of what you owned individually and totally in your name, as well as the value of assets jointly owned through tenancy in common. In the latter case, your heirs will receive your share, but not the co-owner's share.

probate property
All assets other than nonprobate property.

Transfers with a Will Go to Your Desired Heirs A will (defined below) is the smartest way to transfer your nonprobate assets upon your death. You definitely need a will unless all of your property is nonprobate property and/or will be transferred by contract. A will is not estate planning. It is written after all the other aspects of estate planning are completed.

will
Written document in which a person tells how his or her remaining assets should be given away after death; without a will, the property will be distributed according to state probate law.

A **will** is a written document in which a person, the **testator**, tells how his or her remaining assets should be given away after death. In your will, you name an **executor** (or **personal representative**). The executor identifies assets, collects any money due, open up an estate bank account, pays off debts, obtains life insurance proceeds, liquidates assets, files for Social Security burial benefits, prepares final income tax and estate tax returns, and with the court's permission distributes the balance of any remaining money and property to the beneficiaries.

executor/personal representative
Person responsible for carrying out the provisions of a will and managing the assets until the estate is passed on to heirs.

Relatives and friends are not necessarily the best choice to perform the executor's duties, and many people name an accountant or attorney to play this role since the work is time consuming and challenging for novices and may require the hiring of experts. The person should ideally live in the state where the will is to be probated. A legal background is not necessary, but honesty and maturity are key attributes of a good executor. The executor's basic fee for carrying out these complicated tasks is about 6 percent of the estate (more for smaller estates or less for larger ones) plus a corpus commission of perhaps 5 percent of the value of the estate. Or they can charge an hourly fee.

A simple will that is prepared by an attorney can cost $125 to $400. Minor changes in a will may be made with a **codicil** instead of revoking the existing will and writing a completely new one, as you would when making major changes.

codicil
Legal instrument with which one can make minor changes to a will.

heir
Person who inherits or is entitled by law or by the terms of a will to inherit some asset.

A Valid Will Is Not Likely to Be Challenged If you die with a valid will, the probate court will transfer or distribute your property according to your wishes. A person who inherits or is entitled by law or by the terms of a will to inherit some asset is called an **heir**. A will that is properly drafted, signed, and witnessed

DID YOU KNOW

Writing a simple will is not that complicated. Here is how Harry Johnson from this book's Harry and Belinda continuing case wrote his.

Last Will and Testament of Harry Johnson
1 Introduction
Being of sound mind and memory, I Harry Johnson, do hereby publish this as my Last Will and Testament. I am married to Belinda Johnson, and my mother is Melinda Johnson.

2 Payment of Debts and Expenses
I hereby direct my Executor to pay my medical expenses, funeral expenses, debts, and the costs of settling my estate.

3 Distribution of Assets
I give my wife one-half of my possessions and all my personal effects. I give my mother one-quarter of my possessions. I give to Common Cause, a nonprofit organization, one-quarter of my possessions. If my wife, Belinda Johnson, predeceases me, I give her share to my mother, Melinda Johnson.

4 Simultaneous Death of Beneficiary
If any beneficiary of this Will, including any beneficiary of any trust established by this Will, other than my wife, shall die within 60 days of my death or prior to the distribution of my estate, I hereby declare that I shall be deemed to have survived such person.

5 Appointment of Executor and Guardian
I appoint my father-in-law, Martin Anderson, to be the Executor of this will and my estate, and provide if this executor is unable or unwilling to serve then I appoint the Trust Department of the Bank of America as alternate Executor. My Executor shall be authorized to carry out all provisions of this Will and pay my just debts, obligations, and funeral expenses.

6 Power of the Executor
The executor of this will has the power to receive payments, buy or sell assets, and pay debts and taxes owed on behalf of my estate.

7 Payment of Taxes
I direct my executor to pay all taxes imposed by governments.

8 Execution
In witness therefore, I hereby set my hand to this last Will and Testament, which consists of one page, this 31st day of January 2015.

_____   _____
Signature   Date

9 Witness Clause
The above-named person signed in our presence and in our opinion is mentally competent.

_____ _____ _____
Witness 1   Address   Date
_____ _____ _____
Witness 2   Address   Date

DID YOU KNOW

Checklist for Topics to Include in Your Will
- Decide what property to include.
- Decide who will inherit which assets.
- Identify an executor.
- Choose a guardian for your children.
- Select someone to manage children's inherited assets.
- Sign your will in front of witnesses who also will sign.
- Store your original will in an attorney's office or safe deposit box.

is unlikely to be successfully challenged by someone who is dissatisfied with the intended distribution of assets, thus reducing the likelihood of family disputes. If you have a complicated estate, you should seek the assistance of an attorney who specializes in estate planning.

FINANCIAL POWER POINT

Prepare Your Will Online

People who know exactly what they want to do with their property upon their death can use software and online programs to prepare an uncomplicated will. Examples include BuildaWill.com, LegacyWriter, LegalZoom, Kiplinger's Quicken Will-Maker, and WillPower. Some excellent resources for estate planning are on the Web: American Bar Association (www.americanbar.org/portals/public_resources.html), Cornell Law School (www.law.cornell.edu/), National Association of Estate Planners & Councils (www.naepc.org/home/for-public), and Nolo (www.nolo.com/).

You Need to Appoint a Guardian in Your Will if You Have Minor Children If you have minor children, you should appoint a legal **guardian** for each child in your will. This person is responsible for caring for and raising any child under the age of 18 and for managing the child's estate. The guardian should be someone who shares your values and views on child rearing. You might avoid as potential guardians those who are too old, too ill, or too tired from raising their own children, and those who don't really know the children. Consider naming an alternate candidate in case your first choice cannot take on this responsibility. If you have not taken steps to name a legal guardian, the court will appoint one, perhaps someone you do not know.

Without a Will, State Law Determines the Distribution of Your Property If you do not care about what happens to your property, children, and favorite pieces of jewelry, the state will make those decisions. When a person dies without a valid will, the deceased is assumed to have died **intestate**. Dying intestate can cost much more in taxes and cause legal, bureaucratic, and emotional struggles for survivors. In such a case, the probate court first ensures that the debts, income taxes, and expenses of the deceased are paid. Then, the probate court will divide all property and transfer assets to the legal heirs according to state law. If no surviving relatives exist, the estate will go to the state by **right of escheat**. One's friends and charities will get nothing.

guardian

Person responsible for caring for and raising any child under the age of 18 and for managing the child's estate.

intestate

When a person dies without a legal will.

17.6d Spouses Have Legal Rights to Each Other's Estates

The **partnership theory of marriage rights** is an assumption in state law that presumes that wedded couples share their fortunes equally. Thus, property acquired during the marriage and titled in the name of only one partner (other than property acquired by gift or inheritance) becomes the property of both spouses.

A decedent who disinherits a surviving spouse or who leaves that person with less than a fair share of the estate is judged to have reneged on the partnership. A surviving spouse disinherited in this manner has some claim in probate court to a portion of the decedent's estate if he or she chooses to elect that option. All states give a surviving spouse the right to claim one-fourth to one-half of the other spouse's estate, no matter what a will provides. The remaining portion may pass to other heirs.

In states with **community property laws**, the law assumes that the surviving spouse owns half of everything that both partners earned during the marriage, no matter how much was actually contributed by either partner and even if only one spouse held legal title to the property. States with community property laws provide the same spousal rights for marriages that end in divorce.*

trust

Legal arrangement between you as the creator of the trust and the trustee, the person designated to faithfully and wisely manage any assets in the trust to your benefit and to the benefit of your heirs.

grantor

Creator of a trust—the person who makes a grant of assets to establish a trust. Also called the settler, donor, or trustor.

17.6e Who Should Consider Setting Up a Trust?

People who should consider setting up a trust include those who have complex estates, hold relatively few liquid assets, desire privacy for their heirs, fear a battle over the provisions of a will, or live in a state with high probate costs or cumbersome probate procedures.

Use Trusts to Transfer Assets Trusts may be created to safeguard the inheritances of survivors, fund a child's education, provide the down payment on someone's home, provide financial assistance for minor children, manage property for young children or disabled elders, and provide income for future generations. They also can reduce estate taxes (the subject of the following section.) Properly drawn trusts can save you and your family time, trouble, and money. These laudable objectives can be achieved only with the assistance of an experienced attorney who specializes in carefully drafting, planning, and executing strategies and techniques in estate planning.

---

* Community property jurisdictions include Arizona, California, Idaho, Louisiana, Nebraska, Nevada, New Mexico, Puerto Rico, Texas, Washington, and Wisconsin.

A **trust** is a legal arrangement between you as the **grantor** or creator of the trust and the **trustee**, the person designated to control and manage any assets in the trust. The agreement requires the trustee to faithfully and wisely manage and administer the assets to the benefit of the grantor and others. Trusts can be established to take effect during the grantor's life as well as upon his or her death.

Living Trusts Are Established while Grantor Is Alive There are two types of trusts: (1) **living trusts** that take effect while the grantor is alive and (2) testamentary trusts (see next section) that go into effect upon death.

Revocable Living Trusts A **revocable living trust** is used to protect and manage a person's assets. The person creating the trust maintains the right to change its terms or cancel the trust at any time, for any reason, during his or her lifetime. Thus, living trusts often establish the grantor as the trustee. A revocable living trust can provide for the orderly management and distribution of assets if the grantor becomes incapacitated or incompetent. A new trustee can easily be named. A revocable living trust operates much like a will and proves difficult to contest. Its assets stay in the estate of the grantor at his or her death.

Use an Irrevocable Charitable Remainder Trust to Boost Your Current Income Effective use of an **irrevocable charitable remainder trust (CRT)** is popular for people who want to leave a portion of their estate to charity because doing so can boost one's income during the grantor's lifetime. You set up the trust and irrevocably give it assets. The trust then pays you income from the assets in the trust for a set period, usually for life, and possibly your spouse's life as well. The charity eventually receives the assets of the CRT when you (and your spouse, if so arranged) die. For example, Brianna Winston, a widow from San Jose, California, increased the after-tax income on her $600,000 investment portfolio from $1800 to $4800 per year by creating a CRT, thus giving the assets to the National Wildlife Federation. According to her attorney, Benjamin Pauly, the CRT then reinvested the proceeds, thus earning a higher return for the organization and providing more to Brianna.

A CRT works well for people who show wealth on paper because of appreciated assets. The projected future value of the gift can be discounted to a present value. This amount can then be written off as a charitable contribution on Brianna's current income tax return, saving her even more money. It is wise to give to a CRT because the donor can avoid capital gains taxes while still realizing the full benefit of the asset's current value.

Irrevocable Living Trusts An **irrevocable living trust** is an arrangement in which the grantor relinquishes ownership *and* control of property. Usually this involves a gift of the property to the trust. It cannot be changed or undone by the grantor during

trustee
Person charged with carrying out the trust for the benefit of the grantor(s) and heirs.

living trust
A trust that takes effect while the grantor is still alive.

revocable living trust
Grantor maintains the right to change the trust's terms or cancel it at any time, for any reason, during his or her lifetime.

irrevocable living trust
Arrangement in which the grantor permanently gives up ownership and the right to control of the property, to change the beneficiaries, and to change the trustees.

DID YOU KNOW ?

Money Questions to Discuss with Mom and Dad

Parents usually do not want their children to know about how they spend every nickel and dime, but there are some basic money questions that are worthwhile discussing so you all can avoid financial problems in the future:

1. *How much total income do they expect to have in retirement, including 401(k)s, IRAs, pensions, and Social Security?*
2. *How much do they have in reserve in cash and other investments?*
3. *Do they think they will need financial support from their children?*
4. *What kinds of insurance do they have (e.g., life, health, disability, long-term care, and where are the policies)?*
5. *Are the beneficiaries on life insurance and investment accounts (mutual funds, brokerage, IRAs, 401(k)s, pensions) up to date and as they want them to be?*
6. *Where is a list of parents' financial accounts, passwords, financial institutions, safe deposit box (and key), and contact information for advisors, brokers, accountants, and lawyers?*

his or her lifetime. The grantor gives up three key rights under an irrevocable living trust: (1) control of the property, (2) change of the beneficiaries, and (3) change of the trustees. Because irrevocable trusts are generally considered separate tax entities, the trust pays any income taxes due. Transfers to a trust made within three years of death may be brought back into the decedent's estate.

Testamentary Trusts Go into Effect Only Upon the Death of the Grantor The other broad category of trusts used in connection with estate planning comprises **testamentary trusts**. A testamentary trust becomes effective upon the death of the grantor according to the terms of the grantor's will or a revocable living trust. Such trusts can be designed to provide money or asset management after the grantor's death, to provide income for a surviving spouse and children, and to give assets to grandchildren or great-grandchildren while providing income from the assets to the surviving spouse and children, among other things.

testamentary trust

Becomes effective upon death of the grantor according to the terms of the grantor's will or a revocable living trust. Such trusts can provide money or asset management after the grantor's death for the heirs' benefit.

17.6f Your Letter of Last Instructions Provides Guidance to Those Left Behind

Many people prepare a **letter of last instructions** along with their will that may contain preferences regarding funeral and burial instructions, organ donation wishes, material to be included in the obituary, contact information for relatives and friends, and other information useful to the survivors, such as the location of important documents. Family members and others are not legally bound by details in a letter of last instructions, but such a letter relieves them of the stress of making some emotional decisions. A letter of last instructions may specify that certain pieces of jewelry or art not specified in your will that have more sentimental than monetary value are to go to specific people. If the will contains different instructions on these matters, the will prevails.

Your letter of last instructions and original will should be kept in a safe place, such as a lockable filing cabinet or home safe or at an attorney's office. Copies may be given to certain family members or friends.

letter of last instructions

Nonlegal instrument that may contain preferences regarding funeral and burial, material to be included in the obituary, and other information useful to the survivors, such as the location of important documents.

17.6g Estate Taxes Impact Only 3500 People Each Year Out of a Population of 321 Million

Only about 3500 of the nation's wealthiest estates each year are required to pay federal estate taxes as each owner dies, thus 99.9999 percent are exempt. The **federal estate tax** is assessed against the estate of a deceased person before property (real estate, stocks and bonds, business interests, and so on) is transferred to heirs or assigned according to terms of a will or state intestacy laws. It is a tax on the deceased's estate, not on the beneficiary who is to receive the property.

federal estate tax

Assessed against a deceased person's estate before property (real estate, stocks and bonds, business interests, and so on) is transferred to heirs or assigned according to terms of a will or state intestacy laws.

17.6h Basic Exclusion Amount Is $5.34 Million

The **estate and gift tax exemption** is the amount that one can give away during a lifetime or bequest at death without being subject to the federal estate tax. The tax law exempts the first $5,340,000 of an individual's gifts made and estates of decedents dying. This is also called

DID YOU KNOW

Your Worst Financial Blunders in Retirement and Estate Planning

Based on others' financial woes, you will make mistakes in personal finance when you:

1. *Wait until your thirties, or worse, your forties to start saving for retirement.*

2. *Forget to update forms that contractually award assets upon your death, like life insurance and retirement and checking accounts.*

3. *Invest in mutual funds that charge high fees and expenses.*

the **basic exclusion amount.** The tax rate on estates valued above this amount is 40 percent.

The law also offers "portability" of the exemption between married couples as it allows them to add any unused portion of the $5.34 million estate tax exemption of the first spouse to die to carry forward to the surviving spouse's estate tax exemption. Thus married couples may pass $10.68 million on to their heirs free from estate taxes with no planning whatsoever.

17.6i State Estate Taxes and Inheritance Taxes

Nineteen states and the District of Columbia also have a **state estate tax**, and most are coupled with the federal estate tax. So, when the federal estate tax is zero, those taxes are also zero. States with estate taxes typically exempt much less per estate from their tax and impose a top rate of 12 to 19 percent. Like the federal estate tax, bequests to a spouse are tax-free.

Once the executor of the estate has divided up the assets and distributed them to the beneficiaries, the inheritance tax comes into play. Eight states* impose an **inheritance tax** assessed by the decedent's state of residence on beneficiaries who *receive* inherited property. This tax is based on how much the beneficiaries get and their right to receive it, and the rates range from 15 to 18 percent. However, transfers to spouses, children, parents, and other close relatives may be either exempt or subject to a lower state inheritance tax rate. The beneficiaries are responsible for paying inheritance taxes.

* Indiana, Iowa, Kentucky, Maryland, Nebraska, New Jersey, Pennsylvania and Tennessee.

DID YOU KNOW ?

Gift Tax Exclusion Is $14,000 Annually

People with extremely high asset values may reduce the total of their estate by donating up to $14,000 annually to a relative or a friend. This is called the **exclusion amount**. When paid directly to an institution the funds could pay for someone's school tuition and/ or medical expenses, including insurance premiums. There are no tax consequences for gifts up to $14,000 to a recipient or up to $28,000 if members of a couple give individually to a recipient.

inheritance tax

A tax imposed by eight states that is assessed on the decedent's beneficiaries who receive inherited property.

CONCEPT CHECK 17.6

1. What is probate, and give three examples of how people should transfer assets by contract to avoid probate.

2. Distinguish between probate and nonprobate property.

3. What topics go into a properly drafted will?

4. Distinguish between an irrevocable living trust and testamentary trusts?

5. What is the likelihood of average people paying estate or inheritance taxes?

WHAT DO YOU RECOMMEND *NOW?*

Now that you have read the chapter on estate planning, what do you recommend to Juliana and Fernando on the subject of retirement and estate planning regarding:

1. How much in Social Security benefits can each expect to receive?

2. How much do they each need to save for retirement if they want to spend at a lifestyle of 80 percent of their current living expenses?

3. In which types of retirement plans might Fernando invest for retirement?

4. What withdrawal rate might they use to avoid running out of money during retirement?

5. What three types of actions might they take to go about transferring their assets by contract to avoid probate?

© iStockphoto.com/iisafx

BIG PICTURE SUMMARY OF LEARNING OBJECTIVES

LO1 **Estimate your Social Security retirement income benefit.**

You can and, indeed, must save adequately for your retirement. To do so, during your working years you should diversify your investments, keep investment costs low, and live below your means so you can save and invest. The Social Security program is funded through FICA taxes on employees and employers, and the amounts withheld are put into trust fund accounts from which benefits are paid to current program recipients. You must be fully insured under the Social Security program before retirement benefits can be paid.

LO2 **Calculate the amount you must save for retirement in today's dollars.**

Your retirement nest egg is the total amount of accumulated savings and investments needed to support your desired retirement. This is calculated by projecting your annual retirement expenses and income and determining the amount of annual savings you need to set aside in today's dollars to achieve your retirement goal.

LO3 **Distinguish among the types of employer-sponsored tax-sheltered retirement plans.**

The three major types of employer-sponsored retirement plans are defined-contribution, defined-benefit, and cash-balance. Some employers make matching contributions to their employees' accounts. To receive benefits, an employee must be vested in an employer-sponsored retirement plan.

LO4 **Explain the various types of personally established tax-sheltered retirement accounts.**

IRS regulations allow you to take advantage of personally established tax-sheltered retirement plans, including the traditional individual retirement account, or IRA, for which contributions are tax deductible and withdrawals are taxed. After-tax contributions may be made to Roth IRAs in which earnings accumulate tax-free and withdrawals are not taxed. Keogh plans and SEP-IRA plans are available for the self-employed and small business owners.

LO5 **Describe how to avoid penalties and make your retirement money last.**

You can save on taxes and make sure your retirement money is maximized by not withdrawing it prior to retirement. Then, your choices at retirement are to carefully manage your retirement account withdrawals and consider purchasing an annuity with a portion of your retirement funds. There are tables and techniques to calculate how long your money will last.

LO6 **Plan for the distribution of your estate and, if needed, use trusts to lower estate taxes.**

Nonprobate property, which does not go through the court process of probate, includes assets transferred to survivors by contract, such as naming a beneficiary for your retirement plan or with bank accounts owned with another person through joint tenancy with right of survivorship. Assets can be transferred by beneficiary designation, by property ownership, and by payable-on-death designation. By creating one or more trusts, portions of an estate can be transferred in a contractual manner to others in a way that avoids probate. A trust is a legal arrangement between you as the grantor or creator of the trust and the trustee, the person designated to control and manage any assets in the trust. Recognize that relatively few people, about 3500, pay federal estate taxes and only 8 states have inheritance taxes on recipients.

LET'S TALK ABOUT IT

1. **Retirement Investing Today.** What are your thoughts on this comment? "Younger workers today face some serious challenges in deciding where to invest their retirement funds."

2. **Why Calculate?** Do you know anyone who has estimated his or her retirement savings goal in today's dollars? Offer two reasons why many people do not perform those calculations. Offer two reasons why it would be smart for people to determine a financial target.

3. **Retirement Planning Mistakes.** Of all the mistakes that people make when planning for retirement, which one might be likely to negatively affect your retirement planning? Give two reasons why.

4. **Wills for College Students.** Do college students really need a will at this point in their lives? Why or why not? What probably would happen to the typical college student's assets if he or she died without a will?

5. **Writing a Letter of Last Instructions.** Identify topics that you would cover in your letter of last instructions.

DO THE MATH

1. **Tax-Sheltered Returns.** Irad Liu, of Commerce, Texas, is in the 25 percent marginal tax bracket and is considering the tax consequences of investing $2000 at the end of each year for 30 years in a tax-sheltered retirement account, assuming that the investment earns 8 percent annually.

   (a) How much will Irad's account total over 30 years if the growth in the investment remains sheltered from taxes?

   (b) How much will the account total if the investments are not sheltered from taxes? (Hint: Use Appendix A-3 or the *Garman/Forgue* companion website.)

2. **Withdrawal Amount.** Over the years, Samuel and Elizabeth Paget, of Elon, North Carolina, have accumulated $200,000 and $220,000, respectively, in their employer-sponsored retirement plans. If the amounts in their two accounts earn a 6 percent rate of return over Samuel and Elizabeth's anticipated 20 years of retirement, how large an amount could be withdrawn from the two accounts each month? Use the *Garman/Forgue* companion website or Appendix A-4 to make your calculations.

3. **Savings Amount Needed.** Stephanie and Cody Riley, of Newport, Rhode Island, desire an annual retirement income of $40,000. They expect to live for 30 years past retirement. Assuming that the couple could earn a 3 percent after-tax and after-inflation rate of return on their investments, what amount of accumulated savings and investments would they need? Use Appendix A-4 or the *Garman/Forgue* companion website to solve for the answer.

4. **Annual Earnings.** Isabel and Juan Selenas, of Edison, New Jersey, hope to sell their large home for $380,000 and retire to a smaller residence valued at $150,000. After they sell the property, they plan to invest the $230,000 in equity ($380,000 − $150,000, omitting selling expenses) and earn a 4 percent after-tax return. Approximately how much will this nest egg be worth in five years when they retire? Use Appendix A-4 or the *Garman/Forgue* companion website to solve for the answer.

DO IT IN CLASS PAGE 19

5. **Twins Invest.** Rachael Ake, of Omaha, Nebraska, plans to invest $3000 each year in a mutual fund for the next 25 years to accumulate savings for retirement. Her twin sister, Rebecca, plans to invest the same amount for the same length of time in the same mutual fund. However, instead of investing with after-tax money, Rebecca will invest through an employer-sponsored retirement plan. If both mutual fund accounts provide an 8 percent rate of return, how much more will Rebecca have in her retirement account after 40 years than Rachael? How much will Rebecca have if she also invests the amount saved in income taxes? Assume both women pay income taxes at a 25 percent rate. Use Appendix A-3 or the *Garman/Forgue* companion website to solve for the answer.

6. **More Aggressive Investing.** Shanice Johnson, of Philadelphia, Pennsylvania, wants to invest $4000 annually for her retirement 30 years from now. She has a conservative investment philosophy and expects to earn a return of 3 percent in a tax-sheltered account. If she took a more aggressive investment approach and earned a return of 5 percent, how much more would Shanice accumulate? Use Appendix A-3 or the *Garman/Forgue* companion website to solve for the answer.

FINANCIAL PLANNING CASES

CASE 1

The Johnsons Consider Retirement Planning

Harry Johnson's father, William, was recently forced into early retirement at age 63 because of poor health. In addition to the psychological drawbacks of the unanticipated retirement, William's financial situation is poor because he had not planned adequately for retirement. His situation has inspired Harry and Belinda to take a look at their own retirement planning. Together they now make about $100,000 per year and would like to have a similar level of living when they retire. Harry and Belinda are both 27 years old and recently received their annual Social Security Benefits Statements indicating that they could expect about $28,000 per year in today's dollars as retirement benefits at age 67. Although their retirement is a long way off, they know that the sooner they put a plan in place, the larger their retirement nest egg will be.

(a) Belinda believes that the couple could maintain their current level of living if their retirement income represented 75 percent of their current annual income after adjusting for inflation. Assuming a 4 percent inflation rate, what would Harry and Belinda's annual income need to be over and above their Social Security benefits when they retire at age 67? (Hint: Use Appendix A-1 or visit the *Garman/Forgue* companion website.)

DO IT IN CLASS
PAGE 19

(b) Both Harry and Belinda are covered by defined-contribution retirement plans at work. Harry's employer will contribute $1170 per year, and Belinda's employer will contribute $1140 per year in addition to the $4620 total that Harry and Belinda can contribute. Assuming a 7 percent rate of return, what would their retirement nest egg total 40 years from now? (Hint: Use Appendix A-3 or visit the *Garman/Forgue* companion website.)

(c) For how many years would the retirement nest egg provide the amount of income indicated in Question (a)? Assume a 4 percent return after taxes and inflation. (Hint: Use Appendix A-4 or visit the *Garman/Forgue* companion website.)

DO IT IN CLASS
PAGE 530

(d) One of Harry's dreams is to retire at age 55. What would the answers to Questions (a), (b), and (c) be if he and Belinda were to retire at that age?

(e) How would early retirement at age 55 affect the couple's Social Security benefits?

(f) What would you advise Harry and Belinda to do to meet their income needs for retirement?

CASE 2

Victor and Maria's Retirement Plans

Victor, now age 61, and Maria, age 59, plan to retire at the end of the year. Since his retail management employer changed from a defined-benefit retirement plan to a defined-contribution plan ten years ago, Victor has been contributing the maximum amount of his salary to several different mutual funds offered through the plan, although his employer never matched any of his contributions. Victor's tax-sheltered account, which now has a balance of $144,000, has been growing at a rate of 7 percent through the years. Under the previous defined-benefit plan, Victor is entitled to a single-life pension of $360 per month or a joint and survivor option paying $240 per month. The value of Victor's investment of $20,000 in Pharmacia stock eight years ago has now grown to $56,000.

Maria's earlier career as a medical records assistant provided no retirement program, although she did save $10,000 through her credit union, which was later used

to purchase zero-coupon bonds now worth $28,000. Maria's second career as a pharmaceutical representative for Pharmacia allowed her to contribute about $37,000 to her retirement account over the past nine years. Pharmacia matched a portion of her contributions, and that account is now worth $130,000; its growth rate has ranged from 6 to 10 percent annually. When Maria's mother died last year, Maria inherited her home, which is rented for $900 per month; the house has a market value of $170,000. The Hernandezes' personal residence is worth $180,000. They pay combined federal and state income taxes at a 30 percent rate.

(a) Sum up the present values of the Hernandezes' assets, excluding their personal residence, and identify which assets derive from tax-sheltered accounts.

(b) Assume that the Hernandezes sold their stocks, bonds, and rental property, realizing a gain of $238,000 after income taxes and commissions. If that sum earned a 7 percent rate of return over the Hernandezes' anticipated 20 years of retirement, how large an amount could be withdrawn each month? How large an amount could be withdrawn each month if they needed the money over 30 years? How large an amount could be withdrawn each month if the proceeds earned 6 percent for 20 years? For 30 years?

(c) Victor's $144,000 and Maria's $130,000 in retirement funds have been sheltered from income taxes for many years. Summarize the advantages the couple realized by leaving the money in the tax-sheltered accounts. Offer them a rationale to keep the money in the accounts as long as possible before making withdrawals.

CASE 3

Julia Price Thinks About Retirement

Julia is now in her early 50s. She has had two jobs in her career so far and participated fully in the defined-contribution plans offered by both employers. When she left her first position, she rolled her retirement account over to the account at her new employer, and it is currently worth about $380,000. Now she is about to change jobs again. But this time, she is taking a job with the Consumer Financial Protection Agency in Washington, DC. She will also be taking about four months off from working before starting that government job. The federal government retirement program is a defined-benefit plan. That means she cannot transfer her private sector plan to the government plan and therefore must decide whether to leave the funds within her current employer's plan or open a rollover IRA account into which to transfer the funds tax- and penalty-free. Another alternative available to her is to withdraw the $380,000 from her current account, pay income taxes on it this year (probably at a high federal marginal tax rate of 39.6), and invest the proceeds (about $228,000) in a new Roth IRA account. Offer your opinions about her thinking.

CASE 4

Calculation of Annual Savings Needed to Meet a Retirement Goal

Jasmine Amberlin, age 40, single, and from Victorville, California, is trying to estimate the amount she needs to save annually to meet her retirement needs. Jasmne currently earns $30,000 per year. She expects to need 80 percent of her current salary to live on at retirement. Jasmine anticipates that she will receive $800 per month in Social Security benefits. Using the Run the Numbers worksheet on page 514, answer the following questions.

DO IT IN CLASS PAGES 511–514

(a) What annual income would Jasmine need for retirement?

(b) What would her annual expected Social Security benefit be?

(c) Jasmine expects to receive $500 per month from her defined-benefit pension at work. What is her annual benefit?

(d) How much annual retirement income will she need from her retirement funds?

(e) How much will Jasmne need to save by retirement in today's dollars if she plans to retire at age 65 and live to age 90?

(f) Jasmine currently has $5000 in a traditional IRA. Assuming a growth rate of 8 percent, what will be the value of her IRA when she retires?

(g) How much additional money will she still need to save for retirement?

(h) What is the amount she needs to save each year to reach this goal?

CASE 5

A Couple Considers the Ramifications of Dying Intestate

Morgan Merryweather of Sioux Falls, South Dakota, is a 34-year-old police detective earning $58,000 per year. She and her husband, Joshua, have two children in elementary school. They own a modestly furnished home and two late-model cars. Morgan also owns a snowmobile. Both spouses have 401(k) retirement accounts through their employers, and their employers also provide them with $50,000 group term life policies. Morgan also has a $50,000 term life policy of her own. The couple has about $5000 in their joint checking account. Neither has a will.

DO IT IN CLASS PAGES 532–536

(a) List four negative things that could happen if either Morgan or Joshua were to die without a will.

(b) What would be the most important negative consequence of not having a will if both Morgan and Joshua were to die together in a car accident?

(c) Which assets could be jointly owned so that they will automatically transfer to the other spouse if either Morgan or Joshua dies?

(d) What qualities should Morgan and Joshua look for when naming the executors of their wills?

(e) Once they have completed and signed their wills, where should the Merryweathers keep the original documents and any copies?

BE YOUR OWN PERSONAL FINANCIAL MANAGER

1. **Income Needed in Retirement Adjusted for Inflation.** Based on your expected income in your field after you graduate, make an estimate of the dollar amount you would need to make today to live comfortably as a retiree. Then assume that inflation will average 3 per cent per year until you are age 67. Use Appendix A-1 to calculate the dollar amount you would need that year to live at the level of living you estimate as being comfortable today.

2. **Calculate Your Retirement Nest Egg.** Use the Run the Numbers worksheet and material on pages 511–515 or Worksheet 65: My Estimated Retirement Savings Goal in Today's Dollars from "My Personal Financial Planner" to estimate the amount you must save each year to reach your retirement goals.

   MY PERSONAL FINANCIAL PLANNER

3. **How Long Will Your Retirement Money Last?** If you currently have begun a retirement savings nest egg and/or are currently setting aside funds into an account each year, use Appendix A-1 (for the nest egg) and Appendix A-2 (for the annual deposits) to estimate your full nest egg at an age that you would like to retire. Then use the material on page 530 and Worksheet 66: How Long Will My Retirement Money Last? from "My Personal Financial Planner" to estimate how long that money will last based on the result you obtained for item 1 above.

   MY PERSONAL FINANCIAL PLANNER

4. **Questions to Ask About an Employer's Retirement Plan.** Are you currently employed and eligible to participate in an employer-sponsored retirement plan? Use the material on pages 511–515

   MY PERSONAL FINANCIAL PLANNER

and Worksheet 67: Questions to Ask About Your Employer's Retirement Plan from "My Personal Financial Planner" to assess the plan and make decisions about your enrollment in the plan.

5. **Beneficiary Designations.** Complete Worksheet 68: My Assets to Be Transferred by Beneficiary Designations

MY PERSONAL FINANCIAL PLANNER

in "My Personal Financial Planner" by recording your intended beneficiaries for the dozen or more types of assets you either own now or would expect to own in a few years.

ON THE NET

Go to the Web pages indicated to complete these exercises.

1. **Calculate Your Benefits.** Visit the website for the Social Security Administration. There you will find a quick benefits calculator at www.socialsecurity.gov/estimator/ that can be used to estimate your Social Security benefit in today's dollars. Use an income figure that approximates what you expect to earn in the first full year after graduating from college. When the calculator provides

your answer, click on "What's the best age?" to see when you would be better off if you had waited until age 67 to begin taking benefits rather than age 62.

2. **Charitable Remainder Trusts.** View an example of a charitable remainder trust and read the logic behind the donors making such a gift (www.futurefocus.net /crutexample.htm). What are your thoughts about the value to both the donor and the recipient?

ACTION INVOLVEMENT PROJECTS

1. **Views Concerning Social Security.** Talk to five fellow students who are not taking your personal finance class. Ask them to explain their feelings about the degree to which Social Security will meet their income needs during retirement. Then ask them how they plan to meet their retirement income needs beyond what Social Security might provide. Make a table that summarizes your findings. Then compare their views and plans with what you have learned from reading this chapter.

2. **What Is It Like to Be Retired?** Survey three individuals or couples who have been retired for more than one year. Ask them how financially well prepared they felt before they retired. Then ask them to assess the financial realities of retirement at the current point in time. Include a discussion of how their investment mix (mutual funds, stocks, bonds, annuities) may or may not have changed since they have retired. Write a summary of their responses and how their experiences may affect your thinking about being retired.

3. **Feelings About Approaching Retirement.** Survey three individuals or couples who are about 10 to 15 years away from retirement. Ask them to explain what steps they have taken to prepare for retirement and how prepared they feel. Also ask them to describe what they will do financially in the next decade to get ready for retirement. Write a summary of their responses and how their experiences impact your own thinking about getting ready for retirement.

4. **Retirement Savings Behavior Early in One's Career.** Survey three individuals or couples who are less than ten years into their professional careers. Ask them if they have started saving for retirement and, if not, why not. Also ask them

about the types of investments (mutual funds, stocks, bonds) that they are using or would use to save for retirement. Write a summary of their responses and how their efforts, or lack thereof, impact your thinking about saving for retirement.

5. **Letter of Last Instructions.** Inventory what you own, including items of sentimental value, and write a letter of last instructions telling heirs who gets what items. Sign and date the form. It is not necessary to have it witnessed, but you can if you wish.

6. **Loss of Defined-Benefit Plans.** What do you think of the long-term trend of employers largely moving away from offering employees defined-benefit retirement plans to defined-contribution plans? Write up you comments.

7. **Low-Cost Fees.** Review the box "Invest Retirement Money Only in "Low-Cost" Choices to Earn 28 Percent More" on page 525 and offer some comments about the wisdom of its conclusion.

8. **How Long Will Money Last?** Review Table 17-3 on page 530, and offer your comments on what you see.

9. **Transfers.** Make a short list of your assets and determine if upon your death they all will transfer to beneficiaries by contract, property ownership designations, or by payable-on-death designations.

10. **Letter of Last Instructions.** Create a letter of last instructions by giving your personal representative or family member the information needed concerning your personal and financial matters (funeral arrangements, location of will, insurance policies, location of documents, etc.).

APPENDIXES

© S.Dashkevych/Shutterstock.com

Appendix A

PRESENT AND FUTURE VALUE TABLES

Many problems in personal finance involve decisions about money values at varying points in time. These values can be directly and fairly compared only when they are adjusted to a common point in time. Chapter 1 introduced the basic time value concepts. This appendix offers more details about the time value of money. In addition, it provides tables listing the future and present value of $1 with which to make calculations. Four assumptions must be made to eliminate unnecessary complications:

1. Each planning period is one year long.
2. Only annual interest rates are considered.
3. Interest rates are the same during each of the annual periods.
4. Interest is compounded and continues earning a return in subsequent periods.

Tables of present and future values can be constructed to make these adjustments. **Future values** are derived from the principles of compounding the dollar values ahead in time. **Present values** are derived by discounting (which is the inverse of compounding) the dollar values and transferring them to an earlier point in time.

It is usually unnecessary to precisely identify whether the interest is paid/received at the *beginning* of a period or at the end of a period, or to know whether interest compounds daily or quarterly instead of annually. (These calculations require even more tables.) The following present and future value tables assume that money is accumulated, received, paid, compounded, or whatever at the *end* of a period. The tables can be used to compute the mathematics of personal finance with high certainty and to confirm (or reject as inaccurate) what people tell you about financial matters.

The most significant task is to find the correct table. Accordingly, each table is clearly described here, and illustrations of its use appear on the facing page where possible. In addition, the appropriate mathematical equation is shown and can be easily solved using a calculator.

Illustrations Using Appendix A-1: Future Value of a Single Amount ($1)

To use Appendix A-1 on page A-4, locate the future value factor for the time period and the interest rate.

1. You invest $500 at a 15 percent rate of return for 12 years. How much will you have at the end of that 12-year period?

   The future value factor is 5.350; hence, the solution is $500 × 5.350, or $2675.

2. Property values in your neighborhood are increasing at a rate of 5 percent per year. If your home is presently worth $190,000, what will its worth be in 7 years?

   The future value factor is 1.407; hence, the solution is $190,000 × 1.407, or $267,330.

3. You need to amass $40,000 in the next 10 years to make a balloon payment on your home mortgage. You have $17,000 available to invest. What annual interest rate must be earned to realize the $40,000?

   $40,000 ÷ $17,000 = 2.353. Read down the periods (*n*) column to 10 years and across to 2.367 (close enough), which is found under the 9 percent column. Hence, the $17,000 invested at 9 percent for 10 years will grow to a future value of slightly more than $40,000.

4. An apartment building is currently valued at $160,000, and it has been appreciating at 8 percent per year. If this rate continues, in how many years will it be worth $300,000?

   $30,000 ÷ $160,000 = 1.875. Read down the 8 percent column until you reach 1.851 (close enough to 1.875). This number corresponds to a period of 8 years. Hence, the $160,000 property appreciating at 8 percent annually will grow to a future value of $300,000 in slightly more than 8 years.

5. You have the choice of receiving a down payment from someone who wants to purchase your rental property as $15,000 today or as a personal note for $25,000 payable in 6 years. If you could expect to earn 8 percent on such funds, which is the better choice?

   The future value factor is 1.587; hence, the future value of $15,000 at 8 percent is $15,000 × 1.587, or $23,805. Thus, it would be better to take the note for $25,000.

6. How much will an automobile now priced at $20,000 cost in 4 years, assuming an annual inflation rate of 5 percent?

   Read down the 5 percent column and across the row for 4 years to locate the future value factor of 1.216. Hence, the solution is $20,000 × 1.216, or $24,320.

7. How large a lump-sum investment do you need now to have $20,000 available in 5 years, assuming a 10 percent annual rate of return?

   The $20,000 future value is divided by 1.611 (10 percent at 5 years), resulting in a current lump-sum investment of $12,415.

8. You have $5000 now and need $10,000 in 9 years. What rate of return is needed to reach that goal?

   Divide the future value of $10,000 by the present value of the lump sum of $5000 to obtain a future value factor of 2.0. In the row for 9 years, locate the future value factor of 1.999 (very close to 2.0). Read up the column to find that an 8 percent return on investment is needed.

9. How many years will it take your lump-sum investment of $10,000 to grow to $16,000, given an annual rate of return of 7 percent?

   Divide the future value of $16,000 by the present value of the $10,000 lump sum to compute a future value factor of 1.6; look down the 7 percent column to find 1.606 (close enough). Read across the row to find that an investment period of 7 years is needed.

An alternative approach is to use a calculator to determine the future value, *FV*, of a sum of money invested today, assuming that the amount remains in the investment for a specified number of time periods (usually years) and that it earns a certain rate of return each period. The equation is

$$FV = PV(1.0 + i)^n \quad \textbf{(A.1)}$$

where

$$FV = Future\,Value$$
$$PV = Present\,Value \text{ of the investment}$$
$$i = Interest \text{ rate per period}$$
$$n = Number \text{ of periods the } PV \text{ is invested}$$

Appendix A-1

Future Value of a Single Amount ($1 at the End of n Periods) (Used to Compute the Compounded Future Value of a Known Lump Sum)

n	1%	2%	3%	4%	5%	6%	7%	8%	9%	10%	11%	12%	13%	14%	15%	16%	17%	18%	19%	20%
1	1.0100	1.0200	1.0300	1.0400	1.0500	1.0600	1.0700	1.0800	1.0900	1.1000	1.1100	1.1200	1.1300	1.1400	1.1500	1.1600	1.1700	1.1800	1.1900	1.2000
2	1.0201	1.0404	1.0609	1.0816	1.1025	1.1236	1.1449	1.1664	1.1881	1.2100	1.2321	1.2544	1.2769	1.2996	1.3225	1.3456	1.3689	1.3924	1.4161	1.4400
3	1.0303	1.0612	1.0927	1.1249	1.1576	1.1910	1.2250	1.2597	1.2950	1.3310	1.3676	1.4049	1.4429	1.4815	1.5209	1.5609	1.6016	1.6430	1.6852	1.7280
4	1.0406	1.0824	1.1255	1.1699	1.2155	1.2625	1.3108	1.3605	1.4116	1.4641	1.5181	1.5735	1.6305	1.6890	1.7490	1.8106	1.8739	1.9388	2.0053	2.0736
5	1.0510	1.1041	1.1593	1.2167	1.2763	1.3382	1.4026	1.4693	1.5386	1.6105	1.6851	1.7623	1.8424	1.9254	2.0114	2.1003	2.1924	2.2878	2.3864	2.4883
6	1.0615	1.1262	1.1941	1.2653	1.3401	1.4185	1.5007	1.5869	1.6771	1.7716	1.8704	1.9738	2.0820	2.1950	2.3131	2.4364	2.5652	2.6996	2.8398	2.9860
7	1.0721	1.1487	1.2299	1.3159	1.4071	1.5036	1.6058	1.7138	1.8280	1.9487	2.0762	2.2107	2.3526	2.5023	2.6600	2.8262	3.0012	3.1855	3.3793	3.5832
8	1.0829	1.1717	1.2668	1.3686	1.4775	1.5938	1.7182	1.8509	1.9926	2.1436	2.3045	2.4760	2.6584	2.8526	3.0590	3.2784	3.5115	3.7589	4.0214	4.2998
9	1.0937	1.1951	1.3048	1.4233	1.5513	1.6895	1.8385	1.9990	2.1719	2.3579	2.5580	2.7731	3.0040	3.2519	3.5179	3.8030	4.1084	4.4355	4.7854	5.1598
10	1.1046	1.2190	1.3439	1.4802	1.6289	1.7908	1.9672	2.1589	2.3674	2.5937	2.8394	3.1058	3.3946	3.7072	4.0456	4.4114	4.8068	5.2338	5.6947	6.1917
11	1.1157	1.2434	1.3842	1.5395	1.7103	1.8983	2.1049	2.3316	2.5804	2.8531	3.1518	3.4785	3.8359	4.2262	4.6524	5.1173	5.6240	6.1759	6.7767	7.4301
12	1.1268	1.2682	1.4258	1.6010	1.7959	2.0122	2.2522	2.5182	2.8127	3.1384	3.4985	3.8960	4.3345	4.8179	5.3503	5.9360	6.5801	7.2876	8.0642	8.9161
13	1.1381	1.2936	1.4685	1.6651	1.8856	2.1329	2.4098	2.7196	3.0658	3.4523	3.8833	4.3635	4.8980	5.4924	6.1528	6.8858	7.6987	8.5994	9.5964	10.6993
14	1.1495	1.3195	1.5126	1.7317	1.9799	2.2609	2.5785	2.9372	3.3417	3.7975	4.3104	4.8871	5.5348	6.2613	7.0757	7.9875	9.0075	10.1472	11.4198	12.8392
15	1.1610	1.3459	1.5580	1.8009	2.0789	2.3966	2.7590	3.1722	3.6425	4.1772	4.7846	5.4736	6.2543	7.1379	8.1371	9.2655	10.5387	11.9737	13.5895	15.4070
16	1.1726	1.3728	1.6047	1.8730	2.1829	2.5404	2.9522	3.4259	3.9703	4.5950	5.3109	6.1304	7.0673	8.1372	9.3576	10.7480	12.3303	14.1290	16.1715	18.4884
17	1.1843	1.4002	1.6528	1.9479	2.2920	2.6928	3.1588	3.7000	4.3276	5.0545	5.8951	6.8660	7.9861	9.2765	10.7613	12.4677	14.4265	16.6722	19.2441	22.1861
18	1.1961	1.4282	1.7024	2.0258	2.4066	2.8543	3.3799	3.9960	4.7171	5.5599	6.5436	7.6900	9.0243	10.5752	12.3755	14.4625	16.8790	19.6733	22.9005	26.6233
19	1.2081	1.4568	1.7535	2.1068	2.5270	3.0256	3.6165	4.3157	5.1417	6.1159	7.2633	8.6128	10.1974	12.0557	14.2318	16.7765	19.7484	23.2144	27.2516	31.9480
20	1.2202	1.4859	1.8061	2.1911	2.6533	3.2071	3.8697	4.6610	5.6044	6.7275	8.0623	9.6463	11.5231	13.7435	16.3665	19.4608	23.1056	27.3930	32.4294	38.3376
21	1.2324	1.5157	1.8603	2.2788	2.7860	3.3996	4.1406	5.0338	6.1088	7.4002	8.9492	10.8038	13.0211	15.6676	18.8215	22.5745	27.0336	32.3238	38.5910	46.0051
22	1.2447	1.5460	1.9161	2.3699	2.9253	3.6035	4.4304	5.4365	6.6586	8.1403	9.9336	12.1003	14.7138	17.8610	21.6447	26.1864	31.6293	38.1421	45.9233	55.2061
23	1.2572	1.5769	1.9736	2.4647	3.0715	3.8197	4.7405	5.8715	7.2579	8.9543	11.0263	13.5523	16.6266	20.3616	24.8915	30.3762	37.0062	45.0076	54.6487	66.2474
24	1.2697	1.6084	2.0328	2.5633	3.2251	4.0489	5.0724	6.3412	7.9111	9.8497	12.2392	15.1786	18.7881	23.2122	28.6252	35.2364	43.2973	53.1090	65.0320	79.4968
25	1.2824	1.6406	2.0938	2.6658	3.3864	4.2919	5.4274	6.8485	8.6231	10.8347	13.5855	17.0001	21.2305	26.4619	32.9190	40.8742	50.6578	62.6686	77.3881	95.3962
26	1.2953	1.6734	2.1566	2.7725	3.5557	4.5494	5.8074	7.3964	9.3992	11.9182	15.0799	19.0401	23.9905	30.1666	37.8568	47.4141	59.2697	73.9490	92.0918	114.4755
27	1.3082	1.7069	2.2213	2.8834	3.7335	4.8223	6.2139	7.9881	10.2451	13.1100	16.7386	21.3249	27.1093	34.3899	43.5353	55.0004	69.3455	87.2598	109.5893	137.3706
28	1.3213	1.7410	2.2879	2.9987	3.9201	5.1117	6.6488	8.6271	11.1671	14.4210	18.5799	23.8839	30.6335	39.2045	50.0656	63.8004	81.1342	102.9666	130.4112	164.8447
29	1.3345	1.7758	2.3566	3.1187	4.1161	5.4184	7.1143	9.3173	12.1722	15.8631	20.6237	26.7499	34.6158	44.6931	57.5755	74.0085	94.9271	121.5005	155.1893	197.8136
30	1.3478	1.8114	2.4273	3.2434	4.3219	5.7435	7.6123	10.0627	13.2677	17.4494	22.8923	29.9599	39.1159	50.9502	66.2118	85.8499	111.0647	143.3706	184.6753	237.3763
40	1.4889	2.2080	3.2620	4.8010	7.0400	10.2857	14.9745	21.7245	31.4094	45.2593	65.0009	93.0510	132.7816	188.8835	267.8635	378.7212	533.8687	750.3783	1051.668	1469.772
50	1.6446	2.6916	4.3839	7.1067	11.4674	18.4202	29.4570	46.9016	74.3575	117.3909	184.5648	289.0022	450.7359	700.2330	1083.657	1670.704	2566.215	3927.357	5988.914	9100.438

Illustrations Using Appendix A-2: Present Value of a Single Amount ($1)

To use this table, locate the present value factor for the time period and the interest rate.

1. You want to begin a college fund for your newborn child; you hope to accumulate $30,000 by 18 years from now. If a current investment opportunity yields 7 percent, how much must you invest in a lump sum to realize the $30,000 when needed?

    The present value factor is 0.296; hence, the solution is $30,000 × 0.296, or $8880.

2. You hope to retire in 25 years and want to deposit a single lump sum that will grow to $250,000 at that time. If you can now invest at 8 percent, how much must you invest to realize the $250,000 when needed?

    The present value factor is 0.146; hence, the solution is $250,000 × 0.146, or $36,500. The present value of $250,000 received 25 years from now is $36,500 if the interest rate is 8 percent.

3. You have the choice of receiving a down payment from someone who wants to purchase your rental property as $15,000 today or as a personal note for $25,000 payable in 6 years. If you could expect to earn 8 percent on such funds, which is the better choice?

    The present value factor is 0.630; hence, the solution is $25,000 × 0.630, or $15,750. Thus, the present value of $25,000 received in 6 years is greater than $15,000 received now, and the personal note is the better choice.

4. You own a $1000 bond paying 8 percent annually until its maturity in 5 years. You need to sell the bond now, even though the market rate of interest on similar bonds has increased to 10 percent. What discounted market price for the bond will allow the new buyer to earn a yield of 10 percent?

    First, compute the present value of the future interest payments of $80 per year for 5 years at 10 percent (using Appendix A-4): $80 × 3.791, or $303.28. Second, compute the present value of the future principal repayment of $1000 after 5 years at 10 percent: $1000 × 0.621, or $621.00. Hence, the market price is the sum of the two present values ($303.28 + $621.00), or $924.28.

An alternative approach is to use a calculator to determine the present value, *PV*, of a single payment received some time in the future. The equation, which is a rearrangement of the future value Equation (A.1), is

$$PV = \frac{FV}{(1.0 + i)^n} \quad \text{(A.2)}$$

where

$$PV = \textit{Present Value} \text{ of the investment}$$
$$FV = \textit{Future Value}$$
$$i = \textit{Interest} \text{ rate per period}$$
$$n = \textit{Number} \text{ of periods the } PV \text{ is invested}$$

Appendix A-2

Present Value of a Single Amount ($1) (Used to Compute the Discounted Present Value of Some Known Future Single Lump Sum)

n	1%	2%	3%	4%	5%	6%	7%	8%	9%	10%	11%	12%	13%	14%	15%	16%	17%	18%	19%	20%
1	0.9901	0.9804	0.9709	0.9615	0.9524	0.9434	0.9346	0.9259	0.9174	0.9091	0.9009	0.8929	0.8850	0.8772	0.8696	0.8621	0.8547	0.8475	0.8403	0.8333
2	0.9803	0.9612	0.9426	0.9246	0.9070	0.8900	0.8734	0.8573	0.8417	0.8264	0.8116	0.7972	0.7831	0.7695	0.7561	0.7432	0.7305	0.7182	0.7062	0.6944
3	0.9706	0.9423	0.9151	0.8890	0.8638	0.8396	0.8163	0.7938	0.7722	0.7513	0.7312	0.7118	0.6931	0.6750	0.6575	0.6407	0.6244	0.6086	0.5934	0.5787
4	0.9610	0.9238	0.8885	0.8548	0.8227	0.7921	0.7629	0.7350	0.7084	0.6830	0.6587	0.6355	0.6133	0.5921	0.5718	0.5523	0.5337	0.5158	0.4987	0.4823
5	0.9515	0.9057	0.8626	0.8219	0.7835	0.7473	0.7130	0.6806	0.6499	0.6209	0.5935	0.5674	0.5428	0.5194	0.4972	0.4761	0.4561	0.4371	0.4190	0.4019
6	0.9420	0.8880	0.8375	0.7903	0.7462	0.7050	0.6663	0.6302	0.5963	0.5645	0.5346	0.5066	0.4803	0.4556	0.4323	0.4104	0.3898	0.3704	0.3521	0.3349
7	0.9327	0.8706	0.8131	0.7599	0.7107	0.6651	0.6227	0.5835	0.5470	0.5132	0.4817	0.4523	0.4251	0.3996	0.3759	0.3538	0.3332	0.3139	0.2959	0.2791
8	0.9235	0.8535	0.7894	0.7307	0.6768	0.6274	0.5820	0.5403	0.5019	0.4665	0.4339	0.4039	0.3762	0.3506	0.3269	0.3050	0.2848	0.2660	0.2487	0.2326
9	0.9143	0.8368	0.7664	0.7026	0.6446	0.5919	0.5439	0.5002	0.4604	0.4241	0.3909	0.3606	0.3329	0.3075	0.2843	0.2630	0.2434	0.2255	0.2090	0.1938
10	0.9053	0.8203	0.7441	0.6756	0.6139	0.5584	0.5083	0.4632	0.4224	0.3855	0.3522	0.3220	0.2946	0.2697	0.2472	0.2267	0.2080	0.1911	0.1756	0.1615
11	0.8963	0.8043	0.7224	0.6496	0.5847	0.5268	0.4751	0.4289	0.3875	0.3505	0.3173	0.2875	0.2607	0.2366	0.2149	0.1954	0.1778	0.1619	0.1476	0.1346
12	0.8874	0.7885	0.7014	0.6246	0.5568	0.4970	0.4440	0.3971	0.3555	0.3186	0.2858	0.2567	0.2307	0.2076	0.1869	0.1685	0.1520	0.1372	0.1240	0.1122
13	0.8787	0.7730	0.6810	0.6006	0.5303	0.4688	0.4150	0.3677	0.3262	0.2897	0.2575	0.2292	0.2042	0.1821	0.1625	0.1452	0.1299	0.1163	0.1042	0.0935
14	0.8700	0.7579	0.6611	0.5775	0.5051	0.4423	0.3878	0.3405	0.2992	0.2633	0.2320	0.2046	0.1807	0.1597	0.1413	0.1252	0.1110	0.0985	0.0876	0.0779
15	0.8613	0.7430	0.6419	0.5553	0.4810	0.4173	0.3624	0.3152	0.2745	0.2394	0.2090	0.1827	0.1599	0.1401	0.1229	0.1079	0.0949	0.0835	0.0736	0.0649
16	0.8528	0.7284	0.6232	0.5339	0.4581	0.3936	0.3387	0.2919	0.2519	0.2176	0.1883	0.1631	0.1415	0.1229	0.1069	0.0930	0.0811	0.0708	0.0618	0.0541
17	0.8444	0.7142	0.6050	0.5134	0.4363	0.3714	0.3166	0.2703	0.2311	0.1978	0.1696	0.1456	0.1252	0.1078	0.0929	0.0802	0.0693	0.0600	0.0520	0.0451
18	0.8360	0.7002	0.5874	0.4936	0.4155	0.3503	0.2959	0.2502	0.2120	0.1799	0.1528	0.1300	0.1108	0.0946	0.0808	0.0691	0.0592	0.0508	0.0437	0.0376
19	0.8277	0.6864	0.5703	0.4746	0.3957	0.3305	0.2765	0.2317	0.1945	0.1635	0.1377	0.1161	0.0981	0.0829	0.0703	0.0596	0.0506	0.0431	0.0367	0.0313
20	0.8195	0.6730	0.5537	0.4564	0.3769	0.3118	0.2584	0.2145	0.1784	0.1486	0.1240	0.1037	0.0868	0.0728	0.0611	0.0514	0.0433	0.0365	0.0308	0.0261
21	0.8114	0.6598	0.5375	0.4388	0.3589	0.2942	0.2415	0.1987	0.1637	0.1351	0.1117	0.0926	0.0768	0.0638	0.0531	0.0443	0.0370	0.0309	0.0259	0.0217
22	0.8034	0.6468	0.5219	0.4220	0.3418	0.2775	0.2257	0.1839	0.1502	0.1228	0.1007	0.0826	0.0680	0.0560	0.0462	0.0382	0.0316	0.0262	0.0218	0.0181
23	0.7954	0.6342	0.5067	0.4057	0.3256	0.2618	0.2109	0.1703	0.1378	0.1117	0.0907	0.0738	0.0601	0.0491	0.0402	0.0329	0.0270	0.0222	0.0183	0.0151
24	0.7876	0.6217	0.4919	0.3901	0.3101	0.2470	0.1971	0.1577	0.1264	0.1015	0.0817	0.0659	0.0532	0.0431	0.0349	0.0284	0.0231	0.0188	0.0154	0.0126
25	0.7798	0.6095	0.4776	0.3751	0.2953	0.2330	0.1842	0.1460	0.1160	0.0923	0.0736	0.0588	0.0471	0.0378	0.0304	0.0245	0.0197	0.0160	0.0129	0.0105
26	0.7720	0.5976	0.4637	0.3607	0.2812	0.2198	0.1722	0.1352	0.1064	0.0839	0.0663	0.0525	0.0417	0.0331	0.0264	0.0211	0.0169	0.0135	0.0109	0.0087
27	0.7644	0.5859	0.4502	0.3468	0.2678	0.2074	0.1609	0.1252	0.0976	0.0763	0.0597	0.0469	0.0369	0.0291	0.0230	0.0182	0.0144	0.0115	0.0091	0.0073
28	0.7568	0.5744	0.4371	0.3335	0.2551	0.1956	0.1504	0.1159	0.0895	0.0693	0.0538	0.0419	0.0326	0.0255	0.0200	0.0157	0.0123	0.0097	0.0077	0.0061
29	0.7493	0.5631	0.4243	0.3207	0.2429	0.1846	0.1406	0.1073	0.0822	0.0630	0.0485	0.0374	0.0289	0.0224	0.0174	0.0135	0.0105	0.0082	0.0064	0.0051
30	0.7419	0.5521	0.4120	0.3083	0.2314	0.1741	0.1314	0.0994	0.0754	0.0573	0.0437	0.0334	0.0256	0.0196	0.0151	0.0116	0.0090	0.0070	0.0054	0.0042
40	0.6717	0.4529	0.3066	0.2083	0.1420	0.0972	0.0668	0.0460	0.0318	0.0221	0.0154	0.0107	0.0075	0.0053	0.0037	0.0026	0.0019	0.0013	0.0010	0.0007
50	0.6080	0.3715	0.2281	0.1407	0.0872	0.0543	0.0339	0.0213	0.0134	0.0085	0.0054	0.0035	0.0022	0.0014	0.0009	0.0006	0.0004	0.0003	0.0002	0.0001

Illustrations Using Appendix A-3: Future Value of a Series of Equal Amounts (an Annuity of $1 per Period)

To use this table, locate the future value factor for the time period and the interest rate.

1. You plan to retire after 16 years. To provide for that retirement, you initiate a savings program of $7000 per year in an investment yielding 8 percent. What will the value of the retirement fund be at the beginning of the seventeenth year?

   Your last payment into the fund will occur at the end of the sixteenth year, so scan down the periods (n) column for period 16, and then move across until you reach the column for 8 percent. The future value factor is 30.32. Hence, the solution is $7000 × 30.32, or $212,240.

2. What will be the value of an investment if you put $2000 into a retirement plan yielding 7 percent annually for 25 years?

   The future value factor is 63.250. Hence, the solution is $2000 × 63.250, or $126,500.

3. You are trying to decide between putting $3000 or $4000 annually for the next 20 years into an investment yielding 7 percent for retirement purposes. What is the difference in the value of investing the extra $1000 for 20 years?

   The future value factor is 41.0. Hence, the solution is $1000 × 41.0, or $41,000.

4. You will receive an annuity payment of $1200 at the end of each year for 6 years. What will be the total value of this stream of income invested at 7 percent by the time you receive the last payment?

   The appropriate future value factor for 6 years at 7 percent is 7.153. Hence, the solution is $1200 × 7.153, or $8584.

5. How many years of investing $1200 annually at 9 percent will it take to reach a goal of $11,000?

   Divide the future value of $11,000 by the lump sum of $1200 to find a future value factor of 9.17. Look down the 9 percent column to find 9.200 (close enough). Read across the row to find that an investment period of 7 years is needed.

6. If you plan to invest $1200 annually for 9 years, what rate of return is needed to reach a goal of $15,000?

   Divide the future value goal of $15,000 by $1200 to derive the future value factor 12.5. Look across the row for 9 years to locate the future value factor of 12.49 (close enough). Read up the column to find that you need an 8 percent return.

   An alternative approach is to use a calculator to determine the total future value, *FV*, of a stream of equal payments (an annuity). The equation is

$$FV = \frac{[(1.0 + i)^n - 1.0] \times A}{i} \quad \text{(A.3)}$$

where

$FV = $ *Future Value* of the investment

$i = $ *Interest* rate per period

$n = $ *Number* of periods the *PV* is invested

$A = $ *Amount* of the annuity

Appendix A-3

Future Value of a Series of Equal Amounts (an Annuity of $1 Paid at the End of Each Period)
(Used to Compute the Compounded Future Value of a Stream of Income Payments)

n	1%	2%	3%	4%	5%	6%	7%	8%	9%	10%	11%	12%	13%	14%	15%	16%	17%	18%	19%	20%
1	1.0000	1.0000	1.0000	1.0000	1.0000	1.0000	1.0000	1.0000	1.0000	1.0000	1.0000	1.0000	1.0000	1.0000	1.0000	1.0000	1.0000	1.0000	1.0000	1.0000
2	2.0100	2.0200	2.0300	2.0400	2.0500	2.0600	2.0700	2.0800	2.0900	2.1000	2.1100	2.1200	2.1300	2.1400	2.1500	2.1600	2.1700	2.1800	2.1900	2.2000
3	3.0301	3.0604	3.0909	3.1216	3.1525	3.1836	3.2149	3.2464	3.2781	3.3100	3.3421	3.3744	3.4069	3.4396	3.4725	3.5056	3.5389	3.5724	3.6061	3.6400
4	4.0604	4.1216	4.1836	4.2465	4.3101	4.3746	4.4399	4.5061	4.5731	4.6410	4.7097	4.7793	4.8498	4.9211	4.9934	5.0665	5.1405	5.2154	5.2913	5.3680
5	5.1010	5.2040	5.3091	5.4163	5.5256	5.6371	5.7507	5.8666	5.9847	6.1051	6.2278	6.3528	6.4803	6.6101	6.7424	6.8771	7.0144	7.1542	7.2966	7.4416
6	6.1520	6.3081	6.4684	6.6330	6.8019	6.9753	7.1533	7.3359	7.5233	7.7156	7.9129	8.1152	8.3227	8.5355	8.7537	8.9775	9.2068	9.4420	9.6830	9.9299
7	7.2135	7.4343	7.6625	7.8983	8.1420	8.3938	8.6540	8.9228	9.2004	9.4872	9.7833	10.0890	10.4047	10.7305	11.0668	11.4139	11.7720	12.1415	12.5227	12.9159
8	8.2857	8.5830	8.8923	9.2142	9.5491	9.8975	10.2598	10.6366	11.0285	11.4359	11.8594	12.2997	12.7573	13.2328	13.7268	14.2401	14.7733	15.3270	15.9020	16.4991
9	9.3685	9.7546	10.1591	10.5828	11.0266	11.4913	11.9780	12.4876	13.0210	13.5795	14.1640	14.7757	15.4157	16.0853	16.7858	17.5185	18.2847	19.0859	19.9234	20.7989
10	10.4622	10.9497	11.4639	12.0061	12.5779	13.1808	13.8164	14.4866	15.1929	15.9374	16.7220	17.5487	18.4197	19.3373	20.3037	21.3215	22.3931	23.5213	24.7089	25.9587
11	11.5668	12.1687	12.8078	13.4864	14.2068	14.9716	15.7836	16.6455	17.5603	18.5312	19.5614	20.6546	21.8143	23.0445	24.3493	25.7329	27.1999	28.7551	30.4035	32.1504
12	12.6825	13.4121	14.1920	15.0258	15.9171	16.8699	17.8885	18.9771	20.1407	21.3843	22.7132	24.1331	25.6502	27.2707	29.0017	30.8502	32.8239	34.9311	37.1802	39.5805
13	13.8093	14.6803	15.6178	16.6268	17.7130	18.8821	20.1406	21.4953	22.9534	24.5227	26.2116	28.0291	29.9847	32.0887	34.3519	36.7862	39.4040	42.2187	45.2445	48.4966
14	14.9474	15.9739	17.0863	18.2919	19.5986	21.0151	22.5505	24.2149	26.0192	27.9750	30.0949	32.3926	34.8827	37.5811	40.5047	43.6720	47.1027	50.8180	54.8409	59.1959
15	16.0969	17.2934	18.5989	20.0236	21.5786	23.2760	25.1290	27.1521	29.3609	31.7725	34.4054	37.2797	40.4175	43.8424	47.5804	51.6595	56.1101	60.9653	66.2607	72.0351
16	17.2579	18.6393	20.1569	21.8245	23.6575	25.6725	27.8881	30.3243	33.0034	35.9497	39.1899	42.7533	46.6717	50.9804	55.7175	60.9250	66.6488	72.9390	79.8502	87.4421
17	18.4304	20.0121	21.7616	23.6975	25.8404	28.2129	30.8402	33.7502	36.9737	40.5447	44.5008	48.8837	53.7391	59.1176	65.0751	71.6730	78.9791	87.0680	96.0217	105.9306
18	19.6147	21.4123	23.4144	25.6454	28.1324	30.9057	33.9990	37.4502	41.3013	45.5992	50.3959	55.7497	61.7251	68.3941	75.8364	84.1407	93.4056	103.7403	115.2659	128.1167
19	20.8109	22.8406	25.1169	27.6712	30.5390	33.7600	37.3790	41.4463	46.0185	51.1591	56.9395	63.4397	70.7494	78.9692	88.2118	98.6032	110.2846	123.4135	138.1664	154.7400
20	22.0190	24.2974	26.8704	29.7781	33.0660	36.7856	40.9955	45.7620	51.1601	57.2750	64.2028	72.0524	80.9468	91.0249	102.4436	115.3797	130.0329	146.6280	165.4180	186.6880
21	23.2392	25.7833	28.6765	31.9692	35.7193	39.9927	44.8652	50.4229	56.7645	64.0025	72.2651	81.6987	92.4699	104.7684	118.8101	134.8405	153.1385	174.0210	197.8474	225.0256
22	24.4716	27.2990	30.5368	34.2480	38.5052	43.3923	49.0057	55.4568	62.8733	71.4027	81.2143	92.5026	105.4910	120.4360	137.6316	157.4150	180.1721	206.3448	236.4384	271.0307
23	25.7163	28.8450	32.4529	36.6179	41.4305	46.9958	53.4361	60.8933	69.5319	79.5430	91.1479	104.6029	120.2048	138.2970	159.2764	183.6014	211.8013	244.4868	282.3618	326.2368
24	26.9735	30.4219	34.4265	39.0826	44.5020	50.8156	58.1767	66.7648	76.7898	88.4973	102.1741	118.1552	136.8315	158.6586	184.1678	213.9776	248.8075	289.4945	337.0105	392.4842
25	28.2432	32.0303	36.4593	41.6459	47.7271	54.8645	63.2490	73.1059	84.7009	98.3471	114.4133	133.3339	155.6196	181.8708	212.7930	249.2140	292.1048	342.6035	402.0424	471.9811
26	29.5256	33.6709	38.5530	44.3117	51.1135	59.1564	68.6765	79.9544	93.3240	109.1818	127.9988	150.3339	176.8501	208.3327	245.7120	290.0883	342.7626	405.2721	479.4305	567.3773
27	30.8209	35.3443	40.7096	47.0842	54.6691	63.7058	74.4838	87.3508	102.7231	121.0999	143.0786	169.3740	200.8406	238.4993	283.5688	337.5024	402.0323	479.2211	571.5223	681.8527
28	32.1291	37.0512	42.9309	49.9676	58.4026	68.5281	80.6977	95.3388	112.9682	134.2099	159.8173	190.6989	227.9499	272.8892	327.1041	392.5027	471.3778	566.4808	681.1116	819.2233
29	33.4504	38.7922	45.2188	52.9663	62.3227	73.6398	87.3465	103.9659	124.1354	148.6309	178.3972	214.5827	258.5834	312.0937	377.1697	456.3032	552.5120	669.4474	811.5228	984.0679
30	34.7849	40.5681	47.5754	56.0849	66.4389	79.0582	94.4608	113.2832	136.3075	164.4940	199.0209	241.3327	293.1992	356.7868	434.7451	530.3117	647.4390	790.9479	966.7121	1181.882
40	48.8864	60.4020	75.4013	95.0255	120.7998	154.7620	199.6351	259.0565	337.8824	442.5925	581.8260	767.0914	1013.704	1342.025	1779.090	2360.757	3134.522	4163.212	5529.829	7343.856
50	64.4632	84.5794	112.7969	152.6671	209.3480	290.3359	406.5289	573.7701	815.0834	1163.908	1668.771	2400.018	3459.507	4994.522	7217.714	10435.65	15089.50	21813.09	31515.33	45497.17

Illustrations Using Appendix A-4: Present Value of Series of Equal Amounts (an Annuity of $1 per Period)

To use this table, locate the present value factor for the time period and the interest rate.

1. You are entering into a contract that will provide you with an income of $1000 at the end of the year for the next 10 years. If the annual interest rate is 7 percent, what is the present value of that stream of payments?

   The present value factor is 7.024; hence, the solution is $1000 × 7.024, or $7024.

2. You expect to have $250,000 available in a retirement plan when you retire. If the amount invested yields 8 percent and you hope to live an additional 20 years, how much can you withdraw each year so that the fund will just be liquidated after 20 years?

   The present value factor for 20 years at 8 percent is 9.818. Hence, the solution is $250,000 ÷ 9.818, or $25,463.

3. You have received an inheritance of $60,000 that you invested so that it earns 9 percent. If you withdraw $8000 annually to supplement your income, in how many years will the fund run out?

   Solving for *n*, $60,000 ÷ $8000 = 7.5. Scan down the 9 percent column until you find a present value factor close to 7.5, which is 7.487. The row indicates 13 years; thus, the fund will be depleted in approximately 13 years with $8000 annual withdrawals.

4. A seller offers to finance the sale of a building to you as an investment. The mortgage loan of $280,000 will be for 20 years and requires an annual mortgage payment of $24,000. Should you finance the purchase through the seller or borrow the funds from a financial institution at a current rate of 10 percent?

   $280,000 ÷ $24,000 = 11.667. Scan down the periods (*n*) column to 20 years and then read across to locate the figure closest to 11.667, which is 11.470. The column indicates 6 percent; thus, seller financing offers a lower interest rate.

5. You have the opportunity to purchase an office building for $600,000 with an expected life of 20 years. Looking over the financial details, you see that the before–tax net rental income is $90,000. If you want a return of at least 15 percent, how much should you pay for the building?

   The present value factor for 20 years at 15 percent is 6.259, and $90,000 × 6.259 = $563,310. Thus, the price is too high for you to earn a return of 15 percent.

An alternative approach is to use a calculator to determine the present value, *PV*, of a stream of payments. The equation is

$$PV = \frac{[1.0 - (1.0/1.0 + i)^n] \times A}{i} \quad \text{(A.4)}$$

where

PV = *Present Value* of the investment

i = *Interest* rate per period

n = *Number* of periods the *PV* is invested

A = *Amount* of the annuity

Appendix A-4

Present Value of a Series of Equal Amounts (an Annuity of $1 Received at the End of Each Period)
(Used to Compute the Discounted Present Value of a Stream of Income Payments)

n	1%	2%	3%	4%	5%	6%	7%	8%	9%	10%	11%	12%	13%	14%	15%	16%	17%	18%	19%	20%
1	0.9901	0.9804	0.9709	0.9615	0.9524	0.9434	0.9346	0.9259	0.9174	0.9091	0.9009	0.8929	0.8850	0.8772	0.8696	0.8621	0.8547	0.8475	0.8403	0.8333
2	1.9704	1.9416	1.9135	1.8861	1.8594	1.8334	1.8080	1.7833	1.7591	1.7355	1.7125	1.6901	1.6681	1.6467	1.6257	1.6052	1.5852	1.5656	1.5465	1.5278
3	2.9410	2.8839	2.8286	2.7751	2.7232	2.6730	2.6243	2.5771	2.5313	2.4869	2.4437	2.4018	2.3612	2.3216	2.2832	2.2459	2.2096	2.1743	2.1399	2.1065
4	3.9020	3.8077	3.7171	3.6299	3.5460	3.4651	3.3872	3.3121	3.2397	3.1699	3.1024	3.0373	2.9745	2.9137	2.8550	2.7982	2.7432	2.6901	2.6386	2.5887
5	4.8534	4.7135	4.5797	4.4518	4.3295	4.2124	4.1002	3.9927	3.8897	3.7908	3.6959	3.6048	3.5172	3.4331	3.3522	3.2743	3.1993	3.1272	3.0576	2.9906
6	5.7955	5.6014	5.4172	5.2421	5.0757	4.9173	4.7665	4.6229	4.4859	4.3553	4.2305	4.1114	3.9975	3.8887	3.7845	3.6847	3.5892	3.4976	3.4098	3.3255
7	6.7282	6.4720	6.2303	6.0021	5.7864	5.5824	5.3893	5.2064	5.0330	4.8684	4.7122	4.5638	4.4226	4.2883	4.1604	4.0386	3.9224	3.8115	3.7057	3.6046
8	7.6517	7.3255	7.0197	6.7327	6.4632	6.2098	5.9713	5.7466	5.5348	5.3349	5.1461	4.9676	4.7988	4.6389	4.4873	4.3436	4.2072	4.0776	3.9544	3.8372
9	8.5660	8.1622	7.7861	7.4353	7.1078	6.8017	6.5152	6.2469	5.9952	5.7590	5.5370	5.3282	5.1317	4.9464	4.7716	4.6065	4.4506	4.3030	4.1633	4.0310
10	9.4713	8.9826	8.5302	8.1109	7.7217	7.3601	7.0236	6.7101	6.4177	6.1446	5.8892	5.6502	5.4262	5.2161	5.0188	4.8332	4.6586	4.4941	4.3389	4.1925
11	10.3676	9.7868	9.2526	8.7605	8.3064	7.8869	7.4987	7.1390	6.8052	6.4951	6.2065	5.9377	5.6869	5.4527	5.2337	5.0286	4.8364	4.6560	4.4865	4.3271
12	11.2551	10.5753	9.9540	9.3851	8.8633	8.3838	7.9427	7.5361	7.1607	6.8137	6.4924	6.1944	5.9176	5.6603	5.4206	5.1971	4.9884	4.7932	4.6105	4.4392
13	12.1337	11.3484	10.6350	9.9856	9.3936	8.8527	8.3577	7.9038	7.4869	7.1034	6.7499	6.4235	6.1218	5.8424	5.5831	5.3423	5.1183	4.9095	4.7147	4.5327
14	13.0037	12.1062	11.2961	10.5631	9.8986	9.2950	8.7455	8.2442	7.7862	7.3667	6.9819	6.6282	6.3025	6.0021	5.7245	5.4675	5.2293	5.0081	4.8023	4.6106
15	13.8651	12.8493	11.9379	11.1184	10.3797	9.7122	9.1079	8.5595	8.0607	7.6061	7.1909	6.8109	6.4624	6.1422	5.8474	5.5755	5.3242	5.0916	4.8759	4.6755
16	14.7179	13.5777	12.5611	11.6523	10.8378	10.1059	9.4466	8.8514	8.3126	7.8237	7.3792	6.9740	6.6039	6.2651	5.9542	5.6685	5.4053	5.1624	4.9377	4.7296
17	15.5623	14.2919	13.1661	12.1657	11.2741	10.4773	9.7632	9.1216	8.5436	8.0216	7.5488	7.1196	6.7291	6.3729	6.0472	5.7487	5.4746	5.2223	4.9897	4.7746
18	16.3983	14.9920	13.7535	12.6593	11.6896	10.8276	10.0591	9.3719	8.7556	8.2014	7.7016	7.2497	6.8399	6.4674	6.1280	5.8178	5.5339	5.2732	5.0333	4.8122
19	17.2260	15.6785	14.3238	13.1339	12.0853	11.1581	10.3356	9.6036	8.9501	8.3649	7.8393	7.3658	6.9380	6.5504	6.1982	5.8775	5.5845	5.3162	5.0700	4.8435
20	18.0456	16.3514	14.8775	13.5903	12.4622	11.4699	10.5940	9.8181	9.1285	8.5136	7.9633	7.4694	7.0248	6.6231	6.2593	5.9288	5.6278	5.3527	5.1009	4.8696
21	18.8570	17.0112	15.4150	14.0292	12.8212	11.7641	10.8355	10.0168	9.2922	8.6487	8.0751	7.5620	7.1016	6.6870	6.3125	5.9731	5.6648	5.3837	5.1268	4.8913
22	19.6604	17.6580	15.9369	14.4511	13.1630	12.0416	11.0612	10.2007	9.4424	8.7715	8.1757	7.6446	7.1695	6.7429	6.3587	6.0113	5.6964	5.4099	5.1486	4.9094
23	20.4558	18.2922	16.4436	14.8568	13.4886	12.3034	11.2722	10.3711	9.5802	8.8832	8.2664	7.7184	7.2297	6.7921	6.3988	6.0442	5.7234	5.4321	5.1668	4.9245
24	21.2434	18.9139	16.9355	15.2470	13.7986	12.5504	11.4693	10.5288	9.7066	8.9847	8.3481	7.7843	7.2829	6.8351	6.4338	6.0726	5.7465	5.4509	5.1822	4.9371
25	22.0232	19.5235	17.4131	15.6221	14.0939	12.7834	11.6536	10.6748	9.8226	9.0770	8.4217	7.8431	7.3300	6.8729	6.4641	6.0971	5.7662	5.4669	5.1951	4.9476
26	22.7952	20.1210	17.8768	15.9828	14.3752	13.0032	11.8258	10.8100	9.9290	9.1609	8.4881	7.8957	7.3717	6.9061	6.4906	6.1182	5.7831	5.4804	5.2060	4.9563
27	23.5596	20.7069	18.3270	16.3296	14.6430	13.2105	11.9867	10.9352	10.0266	9.2372	8.5478	7.9426	7.4086	6.9352	6.5135	6.1364	5.7975	5.4919	5.2151	4.9636
28	24.3164	21.2813	18.7641	16.6631	14.8981	13.4062	12.1371	11.0511	10.1161	9.3066	8.6016	7.9844	7.4412	6.9607	6.5335	6.1520	5.8099	5.5016	5.2228	4.9697
29	25.0658	21.8444	19.1885	16.9837	15.1411	13.5907	12.2777	11.1584	10.1983	9.3696	8.6501	8.0218	7.4701	6.9830	6.5509	6.1656	5.8204	5.5098	5.2292	4.9747
30	25.8077	22.3965	19.6004	17.2920	15.3725	13.7648	12.4090	11.2578	10.2737	9.4269	8.6938	8.0552	7.4957	7.0027	6.5660	6.1772	5.8294	5.5168	5.2347	4.9789
40	32.8347	27.3555	23.1148	19.7928	17.1591	15.0463	13.3317	11.9246	10.7574	9.7791	8.9511	8.2438	7.6344	7.1050	6.6418	6.2335	5.8713	5.5482	5.2582	4.9966
50	39.1961	31.4236	25.7298	21.4822	18.2559	15.7619	13.8007	12.2335	10.9617	9.9148	9.0417	8.3045	7.6752	7.1327	6.6605	6.2463	5.8801	5.5541	5.2623	4.9995

Appendix B

ESTIMATING SOCIAL SECURITY BENEFITS FOR ITS THREE MAJOR PROGRAMS

The Social Security Administration (SSA) provides basic benefits for your retirement, for a period of disability, or for your survivors. To qualify, you must have earned the number of credits required for each benefit program. Last year a worker would earn one credit for each $1,200 of income subject to Social Security taxes (this figure is adjusted upward each year for inflation) up to a maximum of 4 credits per year. Once you qualify, the actual dollar level of benefits received is based on your income in years past that was subject to the Federal Insurance Contributions Act (FICA) taxes, commonly known as Social Security taxes. Benefits increase each year based on a cost of living adjustment (COLA) announced by the SSA each October for the following year.

You can obtain a personalized estimate of your benefits from the Social Security Administration at *http://www.ssa.gov/mystatement/* or http://www.ssa.gov/planners /calculators.htm. However, if you have not yet earned 40 credits, your personalized estimate will underestimate your likely benefits. You can use Appendix B.1 and the income you might expect to make per year at age 30 for a somewhat more accurate estimate. The amounts are for a 30-year-old worker but would not differ significantly for workers up to ten years older.

Social Security Retirement Benefits

To qualify for Social Security retirement benefits, any worker born after 1928 must have earned 40 credits of coverage. Others may be eligible to collect benefits based on the covered earnings of the retired worked: dependent children, spouses caring for dependent children, and retired spouses at age 62 (including former spouses if not remarried and if the marriage lasted at least ten years). See http://www.ssa.gov/pgm/ retirement.htm for more information.

Social Security Disability Benefits

To qualify for disability benefits, workers age 31 or older need at least 40 credits of coverage. At least 20 of the credits must have been attained in the most recent ten years (depending on your age). Workers younger than age 31 must have attained at least six credits, or, one more than one-half of the total credits possible after age 21, whichever is greater. (For example, a 26-year-old worker would have 20 possible credits (4 × 5 years), and would need eleven credits of coverage.) Social Security will pay disability benefits to certain family members of an eligible worker. These include dependent children up to age 18 (or 19, if the child is still in high school), a spouse caring for a dependent child who is younger than age 16 or disabled, and a spouse age 62 or older. (even if divorced, but not remarried, provided that the marriage lasted ten years). See http://www.ssa. gov/disabilityssi/ for more information.

Social Security Survivor's Benefits

For a family to qualify for Social Security Survivor's benefits, the deceased worker must have accrued at least 40 credits of coverage or an average of one credit per year since age 21 to be "fully insured." Other individuals may be considered "currently insured" if they have six credits of coverage in the previous 13 possible calendar credits. The survivors of currently insured workers receive limited types of benefits compared to those available to fully insured workers. Social Security will pay benefits to surviving children younger than age 18 (or 19, if the child is still in high school), to a surviving spouse (even if divorced from the deceased, but not remarried) caring for surviving children who are younger than age 16, and to a surviving spouse (even if divorced, if the marriage lasted at least ten years) aged 60 or older. See http://www.ssa.gov/pgm/survivors.htm for more information.

Appendix B.1   Estimates of Social Security Benefits for Its Three Major Programs

	Present Annual Earnings					
	$35,000	**$45,000**	**$55,000**	**$75,000**	**$95,000**	**$115,000**
Monthly Retirement Benefits at Age 67 in Today's Dollars						
Per month	$ 1,430	$ 1,700	$ 1,900	$ 2,270	$ 2,530	$ 2,770
Per year	$ 17,160	$20,400	$ 22,800	$ 27,240	$ 30,360	$ 33,240
As a percentage of preretirement income	49%	45%	41%	36%	32%	29%
Monthly Retirement Benefits at Age 67 in Future Dollars (for a 30-year old worker)						
Per Month	$ 5,880	$ 6,980	$ 8,060	$ 9,440	$ 10,480	$ 11,440
Per Year	$70,560	$83,760	$96,720	$113,280	$125,760	$137,280
Monthly Disability Benefits if You Became Disabled in this year						
Individual benefit per month	$ 1,340	$ 1,550	$ 1,770	$ 2,120	$ 2,270	$ 2,530
Individual benefit per year	$16,080	$18,600	$21,240	$ 25,440	$ 27,240	$ 30,360
As a percentage of income	46%	41%	39%	34%	29%	26%
Maximum family benefit per month	$ 2,400	$ 2,720	$ 2,840	$ 3,400	$ 3,520	$ 3,800
Maximum family benefit per year	$28,800	$32,640	$34,080	$ 40,800	$ 42,240	$ 45,600
As a percentage of predisability income	82%	72%	62%	54%	44%	40%
Monthly Survivor's Benefits if You Died this year						
Individual benefit per month	$ 1,040	$ 1,230	$ 1,420	$ 1,660	$ 1,840	$ 2,020
Individual benefit per year	$12,480	$14,760	$17,040	$ 19,920	$ 22,080	$ 24,240
As a percentage of income	36%	33%	31%	27%	23%	21%
Maximum family benefit per month	$ 2,580	$ 3,010	$ 3,400	$ 3,880	$ 4,190	$ 4,540
Maximum family benefit per year	$30,960	$36,120	$40,800	$ 46,560	$ 50,280	$ 54,480
As a percentage of predeath income	88%	80%	74%	62%	53%	47%

Glossary

10-Q report A report required by the SEC prepared by the company showing its financial results for the quarter, a discussion from management, a list of material events and other risk factors that have occurred, forecasts of the company's future, and notes of any significant changes or events in the quarter.

12b-1 fees (distribution fees) Annual fees that some "no-load" fund companies deduct from a fund's assets to compensate salespeople and pay other expenses.

401(k) plan Defined-contribution plan designed for employees of private corporations.

above-the-line deductions Adjustments subtracted from gross income whether taxpayer itemizes deductions or not.

acceleration clause Part of a credit contract stating that after a specific number of payments are unpaid (often just one), the loan is considered in default, and all remaining installments are due and payable upon demand of the creditor.

activities of daily living (ADLs) Insurance companies use the inability to perform a certain number of such activities as a criterion for deciding when the insured becomes eligible for long-term care benefits.

actual cash value (of personal property) Represents the purchase price of the property less depreciation.

add-on interest method Interest is calculated by applying an interest rate to the amount borrowed times the number of years to arrive at the total interest to be charged.

adjustable-rate mortgage (ARM)/variable-rate mortgage Mortgage in which the borrower's interest rate fluctuates according to some index of interest rates based on the rising or falling cost of credit in the economy—thus transferring interest rate risk to the borrower.

adjusted capitalized cost (adjusted cap cost) Subtracting the capitalized cost reductions from the gross capitalized cost.

adjusted gross income (AGI) Gross income less any exclusions and adjustments.

adjustments to income Allowable subtractions from gross income.

advance medical directives Treatment preferences and the designation of a surrogate decision maker in the event that a person should become unable to make decisions on her or his own behalf.

after-tax dollars Money on which an employee has already paid taxes.

after-tax money Funds put into regular investment accounts after paying income taxes.

after-tax profit Money left over after a firm has paid expenses, bondholder interest, and taxes.

after-tax yield The percentage yield on a taxable investment after subtracting the effect of federal income taxes that will need to be paid on the investment.

agency bonds Bonds, notes, and certificates of debt issued by various federal agencies that are government-sponsored enterprises but stockholder owned, such as the Federal National Mortgage Association.

aggressive growth funds (maximum capital gains funds) Funds that invest in speculative stocks with volatile price swings, seeking the greatest long-term capital appreciation possible. Also known as maximum capital gains funds and capital appreciation funds.

aggressive investment philosophy (risk seeker) Investors with this philosophy primarily seek capital gains, often with a short time horizon.

all-risk (open-perils) policies Cover losses caused by all perils other than those that the policy specifically excludes.

alternative dispute resolution programs Industry- or government-sponsored programs that provide an avenue to resolve disputes outside the formal court system.

amended return A special tax return form (Form 1040X) that may be filed to obtain a deserved refund or correct any tax filing mistakes on an original or previously filed return for the previous three years.

American opportunity tax credit A partially refundable tax credit of up to $2500 a year to help defray college expenses for the first four years of postsecondary education.

amortization Loan repayment method in which part of the payment goes to pay interest and part goes to repay principal. Extra payments toward principal shorten the life of the loan and decrease the total amount of interest paid.

amortization schedule List that shows all the monthly payments, the portions that will go toward interest and principal, and the debt remaining after each payment is made throughout the life of the loan.

annual fees Charges levied against cardholders for the privilege of having an open account but that are not included in the advertised APR.

annual percentage rate (APR) Expresses the cost of credit on a yearly basis as a percentage rate.

annual percentage yield (APY) Return on total interest received on a $100 deposit for 365-day period, given the institution's simple annual interest rate and compounding frequency.

annual report Legally required yearly report about financial performance, activities, and prospects sent to major stockholders and made available to the general public.

annuity A stream of payments to be received in the future, or a contract made with an insurance company that provides for a series of payments to be received at stated intervals (usually monthly) for a fixed or variable time period.

any-occupation policy Provides full benefits only if the insured cannot perform any Occupation.

appraisal fee Fee charged for a professionally prepared estimate of the fair market value of the property by an objective party.

approximate compound yield (ACY) A measure of the annualized compound growth of any long-term investment stated as a percentage.

aptitudes The natural abilities and talents that individuals possess.

as is Way for the seller to get around legal requirements for warranties; the buyer takes all risk of nonperformance or other problems despite any salesperson's verbal assurances.

asset allocation Form of diversification in which the investor decides on the proportions of an investment portfolio that will be devoted to various categories of assets.

asset allocation funds Investments in a mix of assets (usually stocks, bonds, and cash equivalents and sometimes international assets, gold, and real estate); they buy and sell regularly to reduce risk while trying to outperform the market.

asset management account (AMA, or central asset account) Multiple-purpose, coordinated package that gathers most monetary asset management vehicles into a unified account and reports activity on a single monthly statement to the client.

assets Everything you own that has monetary value.

ATM transaction fee Payments levied each time an automated teller machine (ATM) is used.

automatic premium loan Provision that allows any premium not paid by the end of the grace period to be paid automatically with a policy loan if sufficient cash value or dividends have accumulated.

automatic reinvestment Investor's option to choose to automatically reinvest any interest, dividends, and capital gains payments to purchase additional fund shares.

automobile bodily injury liability Occurs when a driver or car owner is held legally responsible for bodily injury losses that other people, including pedestrians, suffer.

automobile insurance Combines the liability and property insurance coverages that most car owners and drivers need into a single-package policy.

automobile medical payments insurance Insurance that covers bodily injury losses suffered by the driver of the insured vehicle and any passengers, regardless of who is at fault.

automobile property damage liability Occurs when a driver or car owner is held legally responsible for damage to others' property.

average-balance account Checking account for which service fees are assessed if the account's average daily balance drops below a certain level during a specified time.

average daily balance Sum of the outstanding balances owed each day during the billing period divided by the number of days in the period.

average share cost Actual cost basis of the investment used for income tax purposes, calculated by dividing the total amount invested by the total shares purchased.

average share price Calculated by dividing the share price total by the number of investment periods.

back-end load (contingent deferred sales charge) A sales commission that is imposed only when shares are sold; often charges are on a sliding scale, with the fee dropping 1 percentage point per year that the investor stays in the fund.

back-end ratio Compares the total of all monthly PITI expenditures plus auto loans and other debts with gross monthly income.

balanced funds Funds that keep a set mix of stocks and bonds, often 60 percent stocks and 40 percent bonds, in order to earn a well-balanced return of income and long-term capital gains.

balance sheet or net worth statement Snapshot of assets, liabilities, and net worth on a particular date.

balance transfer Full or partial payment on the balance of one credit card using a cash advance from another.

balloon automobile loan A loan that has a low monthly payment similar in amount to that required if the vehicle had been leased and with a large final payment similar in amount to the residual value under a lease.

bank credit card account Open-ended credit account with a financial institution that allows the holder to make purchases almost anywhere.

bankruptcy Constitutionally guaranteed right that permits people (and businesses) to ask a court to wipe out all their debts.

basic retirement benefit/primary insurance amount Amount of Social Security benefits a worker would receive at his or her full-benefit retirement age, which is 67 for those born after 1960.

bear market Market in which securities prices have declined in value by 20 percent or more from previous highs, often over the course of several weeks or months.

below-average costs Average costs of an investment if more shares are purchased when the price is down and fewer shares are purchased when the price is high.

beneficiary designation Allowance of fund holder to name one or more beneficiaries so that the proceeds bypass probate proceedings if the original shareholder dies.

beneficiary Person who receives life insurance proceeds, as per the policy.

benefit period The maximum period of time for which benefits will be paid under a disability income or other insurance policy.

best buy Product or service that, in the buyer's opinion, represents acceptable quality at a fair or low price for that quality level.

beta value (beta coefficient) A measure of stock volatility; that is, how much the stock price varies relative to the rest of the market.

Bitcoin A peer-to-peer experimental digital cash currency based on an open source cryptographic protocol that can be bought at an exchange and transferred through a computer or smart phone without an intermediate financial institution.

biweekly mortgage A form of growing-equity mortgage (GEM) that calls for payments of half of the normal payment to be made every two weeks; the borrower thus makes 26 payments a year and reduces the principal amount by one full payment each year; this reduces the mortgage term to about 20 years on a 30-year mortgage.

blue-chip stocks Stocks that have been around for a long time, have a well-regarded reputation, dominate its industry, and are known for being solid, relatively safe investments.

bond A debt instrument issued by an organization that promises repayment at a specific time and the right to receive regular interest payments during the life of the bond.

bond funds (fixed-income funds) Fixed-income funds that aim to earn current income higher than a money market fund without incurring undue risk by investing in a portfolio of bonds and other low-risk investments that pay high dividends and offer capital appreciation.

bond premium A sum of money paid in addition to a regular price.

bond rating An impartial outsider's opinion of the quality—or creditworthiness—of the issuing organization.

book value per share Reflects the book value of a company divided by the number of shares of common stock outstanding.

book value (shareholder's equity) Net worth of a company, determined by subtracting total liabilities from assets.

broker's commission Largest selling cost in selling a home; these commissions often amount to 6 percent of the selling price of the home.

budget estimates Projected dollar amounts to receive or spend in a budgeting period.

budget exceptions When budget estimates differ from actual expenditures.

budget Paper or electronic document used to record both planned and actual income and expenditures over a period of time.

budget variance Difference between amount budgeted and actual amount spent or received.

bull market Market in which securities prices have risen 20 percent or more over time.

business cycle/economic cycle Business cycles can be depicted as a wavelike pattern of rising and falling economic activity; the phases of the business cycle include expansion, peak contraction (which may turn into recession), and trough.

business-cycle risk The fact that economic growth usually does not occur in a smooth and steady manner, and this impacts profits as well as investment returns.

buy and hold/buy to hold Investment strategy in which investors buy a widely diversified mix of stocks and/or mutual funds, reinvest the dividends by buying more stocks and mutual funds, and hold onto those investments almost indefinitely.

buyer's order Written offer that names a specific vehicle and all charges; only sign such offers after the salesperson and sales manager have signed first.

buyer's remorse A myth pertaining to the buyer's supposed legal right to change his or her mind and return a vehicle after signing a purchase contract.

buying long Buying a security (especially on margin) with the hope that the stock price will rise.

cafeteria plan (flexible benefits plan) A type of employee benefit plan where employees choose their benefits from a "menu" of taxable and tax reducing benefits, thereby providing a funding mechanism by which employees may pay for some of the benefits they choose on a pretax basis.

call option Stipulation in some indentures that allows issuer to repurchase the bond at par value or by paying a premium, often one year's worth of interest.

capital gain Increase in the value of an initial investment (less costs) realized upon the sale of the investment, or the net income received from the sale of an asset above the costs incurred to purchase and sell it.

capital gains distributions Distributions representing the net gains (capital gains minus capital losses) that a fund realizes when it sells securities that were held in the fund's portfolio.

capital improvements Costs incurred in making value-enhancing changes (beyond maintenance and repair) in real property.

capital loss Decrease in paper value of an initial investment; only realized if sold.

card registration service Firm that will notify all companies with which you have debit and credit cards if your cards are lost or stolen.

career fairs University-, community-, and employer-sponsored events for job seekers to meet with many employers quickly to screen potential employers.

career goal Identifying what you want to do for a living, whether a specific job or field of employment.

career ladder Describes the progression from entry-level positions to higher levels of pay, skill, responsibility, or authority.

career plan A strategic guide for your career through short-, medium-, longer-, and long-term goals as well as future education and work-related experiences.

career planning Can help you identify an employment pathway that aligns your interests and abilities with the tasks and responsibilities expected by employers over your lifetime.

career The lifework chosen by a person to use personal talent, education, and training.

cash account A brokerage account that requires an initial deposit (perhaps as little as $1000) and specifies that full settlement is due to the brokerage firm within three business days after a buy or sell order has been given.

cash advance (or convenience) checks A check-equivalent way to take a cash advance on a credit card.

cash-balance plan Defined-benefit plan funded solely by an employer that gives each participant an interest-earning account credited with a percentage of pay on a monthly basis.

cash basis Only transactions involving actual cash received or cash spent are recorded.

cash dividends Cash profits that a firm distributes to stockholders.

cash flow Amount of rental income you have left after paying all operating expenses.

cash-flow calendar Budget estimates for monthly income and expenses.

cash-flow statement or income and expense statement Summary of all income and expense transactions over a specific time period.

cash surrender value Represents the cash value of a policy minus any surrender charges.

cash-value life insurance Pays benefits at death and includes a savings/investment element that can provide a level of benefits to the policyholder prior to the death of the insured person.

certificate of deposit (CD) An interest-earning savings instrument purchased for a fixed period of time.

certificate of insurance Document or booklet that outlines group health insurance benefits.

Chapter 7 of the Bankruptcy Act (straight bankruptcy) Provides for the liquidation of assets with proceeds applied to paying off excusable debts to the degree possible.

Chapter 13 of the Bankruptcy Act (wage earner or regular income plan) Bankruptcy plan designed for individuals with regular incomes who might be able to pay off some or all of their debts given certain court protections.

chargeback The amount of the transaction is charged back to the business where the transaction originated in the case of a dispute or challenge by the cardholder.

checking account At depository institutions, allows depositors to write checks against their deposited funds, which transfer deposited funds to other people and organizations.

child and dependent care credit A nonrefundable tax credit that may be claimed by workers who pay employment-related expenses for care of a child or other dependent if that care gives them the freedom to work seek work, or attend school full time.

chronological format Resume that provides your information in reverse order, with the most recent first.

claims adjuster Person designated by the insurance company to assess whether the loss is covered and to determine the dollar amount that the company will pay.

closed-end lease/walkaway lease Agreement in which the lessee pays no charge if the end-of-lease market value of the vehicle is lower than the originally projected residual value.

closing costs Include fees and charges other than the down payment and typically vary from 2 to 7 percent of the mortgage loan amount.

COBRA rights The Consolidated Omnibus Budget Reconciliation Act of 1985 allows a former employee to remain a member of a group health plan for as long as 18 months if the employee worked for an employer with more than 20 workers.

codicil Legal instrument with which one can make minor changes to a will.

coinsurance clause A clause in a health care plan that requires the participant to pay a proportion of any loss suffered.

coinsurance Method by which the insured and the insurer share proportionately in the payment for a loss.

collectibles Cultural artifacts that have value because of their beauty, age, scarcity, or popularity, such as antiques, stamps, rare coins, art, baseball cards, and so on.

collision insurance Reimburses insureds for losses to their vehicles resulting from a collision with another car or object or from a rollover.

commercial banks a type of bank that provides services such as accepting deposits, making business loans, and offering basic investment products.

commissions Fees or percentages of the selling price paid to salespeople, agents, and companies for their services in buying or selling an investment.

common stock Most basic form of ownership of a corporation.

comparison shopping Process of comparing products or services to find the best buy.

compounding The addition of interest to principal; the effect of compounding depends on the frequency with which interest is compounded and the periodic interest rate that is applied.

compound interest Compound interest is earning of interest on interest and arises when interest is added to the principal so that, from that moment on, the interest that has been added also earns interest.

comprehensive automobile insurance Protects against property damage losses to an insured vehicle caused by perils other than collision and rollover.

condominium (condo) Form of ownership with the owners holding legal title to their own housing unit among many, with common grounds and facilities owned by the developer or homeowners association.

conservative investment philosophy (risk aversion) Investors with this philosophy accept very little risk and are generally rewarded with relatively low rates of return for seeking the twin goals of a moderate amount of current income and preservation of capital.

consumer finance company/small-loan company Firm that specializes in making relatively small secured or unsecured loans that require monthly installment payments.

consumer price index (CPI) A broad measure of changes in the prices of all goods and services purchased for consumption by urban households.

consumer statement Your version of disputed information in your credit report when the credit bureau refuses to remove the disputed item.

contents replacement-cost protection Option sometimes available in homeowner's insurance policies (including the renter's form) that pays the full replacement cost of any personal property.

contingency clauses Specify that certain conditions must be satisfied before a contract is binding.

contingent (or secondary) beneficiary The beneficiary in case the first-named beneficiary has died; also called the secondary beneficiary.

contributory plan The most common type of employee-sponsored defined-contribution retirement plan; accepts employee as well as employer contributions.

conventional mortgage A fixed-rate, fixed-term, fixed-payment mortgage loan.

convertible preferred stock Can be exchanged at the option of the stockholder for a specified number of shares of common stock.

convertible term insurance Offers policyholders the option of exchanging a term policy for a cash-value policy without evidence of insurability.

cooling-off rule A Federal Trade Commission rule that gives consumers three days to cancel a contract of $25 or more after signing it for a sale made anywhere other than a seller's normal place of business.

cooperative (co-op) Form of ownership in which the owner holds a share of the corporation that owns and manages a group of housing units as well as common grounds and facilities.

co-payment A variation of a deductible that requires you to pay a specific dollar amount each time you use your benefits for a specific covered expense item.

corporate bonds Interest-bearing certificates of long-term debt issued by a corporation.

corporate earnings The profits a company makes during a specific time period that indicate to many analysts whether to buy or sell a stock.

countercyclical stock The stock of a company whose profits are greatly influenced by changes in the economic business cycle.

Coverdell education savings account (or education savings account) An IRS-approved way to pay the future education costs for a child younger than age 18 whereby the earnings accumulate tax-free and withdrawals for qualified expenses are tax-free.

covered option Occurs when an option writer who owns the covered option sells the call.

cover letter A letter of introduction sent to a prospective employer to get an interview.

credit An arrangement in which goods, services, or money is received in exchange for a promise to repay at a future date.

credit agreement Contract that stipulates repayment terms for credit cards.

credit application Form or interview that provides information about your ability and willingness to repay debts.

credit bureau Firm that collects and keeps records of many borrowers' credit histories.

credit cards Cards that allow repeated use of credit as long as the consumer makes regular monthly payments.

credit card blocking Occurs when hotel or other service providers place a hold on a card holder's account to reflect the anticipated cost of services.

credit counseling agency (CCA) Agency that can arrange payment schedules with unsecured creditors for overly indebted consumers and can provide individuals with credit counseling.

credit history Continuing record of a person's credit usage and repayment of debts.

credit limit Maximum outstanding debt that a lender will allow on an open-ended credit account.

credit (or periodic) statement The monthly bill on a credit card account showing the charges and payments made, minimum payment required, and due date among other information.

credit receipt Written evidence of any items returned that notes the specific amount and date of the transaction.

credit repair company (credit clinic) Firm that offers to help improve or fix a person's credit history for a (usually hefty) fee.

credit report Information compiled by a credit bureau from merchants, utility companies, banks, court records, and creditors about your payment history.

credit score (risk score) Statistical measure used to rate applicants based on various factors deemed relevant to creditworthiness and the likelihood of repayment.

credit union (CU) Member-owned, not-for-profit, insured financial institutions that provide checking, savings, and loan services to members.

cumulative preferred stock Preferred stock for which dividends must be paid, including any skipped dividends, before dividends go to common stockholders.

current income Money received while you own an investment; usually received regularly as interest, rent, or dividends.

current rate Rate of return the insurance company has recently paid to policyholders.

current yield Equals the bond's fixed annual interest payment divided by its bond price.

custodial care Suitable for people who do not need skilled nursing care but who nevertheless require supervision (for example, help with eating or personal hygiene).

day trading Occurs when an investor buys and sells stocks quickly throughout a day with the hope that prices will move enough to cover transaction costs and earn some profits.

dealer holdback/dealer rebate A percentage of the total MSRP that the manufacturer holds and then gives back to the dealer, often at the end of the year or quarter.

dealer invoice price (base invoice price) The amount the automaker charges the dealership for new vehicles at the time the dealer buys them; it does not reflect some discounts that the dealer gets.

death benefit Amount that will be paid to the beneficiary when the insured dies.

debts Lending investments that typically offer both a fixed maturity and a fixed income.

debt collection agency Firm that specializes in collecting debts that the original lender could not collect.

debt-consolidation loan A loan taken out to pay off several smaller debts.

debt limit Overall maximum you believe you should owe based on your ability to meet repayment obligations.

debt management plan (DMP) Arrangement whereby the consumer provides one monthly payment (usually somewhat smaller than the total of previous credit payments) that is distributed to all creditors.

debt payments-to-disposable income method Percentage of disposable personal income available for regular debt repayments aside from set obligations.

debt-to-equity ratio Ratio of your consumer debt to the equity in your assets.

declining-balance method Interest calculation method in which interest is assessed during each billing period (usually each month) based on the outstanding balance of the installment loan that billing period.

deductibles An initial portion of any loss that must be paid before collecting insurance benefits, or clauses in health care plans that require the participant to pay an additional portion of health expenses annually before receiving reimbursement.

deductible clause Requires that the policyholder pays an initial portion of any loss.

deed Written document used to convey real estate ownership.

default Occurs when a borrow fails to make a payment when due or fails to meet other requirements of the credit agreement (contract).

default risk (credit risk) Uncertainty associated with not receiving the promised periodic interest payments and the principal amount when it becomes due at maturity.

defect disclosure form A state required form that discloses problems that could affect the property's value or desirability, such as a basement that floods in heavy rains.

deficiency balance Occurs when money raised by the sale of repossessed collateral doesn't cover the amount owed on the debt plus any repossession expenses.

defined-benefit retirement plan (DB) Employer-sponsored retirement plan that pays lifetime monthly annuity payments to retirees based on a predetermined formula.

defined-contribution retirement plan A retirement plan designed to provide a lump-sum at retirement; it is distinguished by its "contributions"—the total amount of money put into each participating employee's individual account; or an IRS-approved retirement plan sponsored by employers that allows employees to make pretax contributions that lower their tax liability.

deflation A broad, sustained decline in prices of goods and services that is hard to stop once it takes hold, causing less consumer spending, lower corporate profits, declining home values, rising unemployment, and lower incomes.

deleveraging A time period when credit use shrinks in an economy instead of expanding as during normal economic times.

dependent A relative or household member for whom an exemption may be claimed on one's income taxes.

depository institutions Organizations licensed to take deposits and make loans.

depreciation Decline in value of an asset over time due to normal wear and tear and obsolescence.

direct sellers Companies that market insurance policies through salaried employees, mail-order promotions, newspapers, the Internet, and even vending machines.

disability benefits Substantially reduced benefits paid to employees who become disabled prior to retirement.

disability income insurance Insurance that covers a portion of the income lost when you cannot work because of illness or injury.

discharged debts Debts (or portions thereof) that are excused as a result of a bankruptcy.

discount brokers Charge commissions to execute trades that are often 30 to 80 percent less than the fees charged by full-service brokers, but also offer fewer services.

discounted cash-flow method Effective way to estimate the value or asking price of a real estate investment based on after-tax cash-flow and the return on the invested dollars discounted over time to reflect a discounted yield.

discount method Interest is calculated based on a discount rate multiplied by the amount borrowed and by the number of years to repay. Interest is then subtracted from the amount of the loan and the difference is given to the borrower. In this method, interest is paid up front before any part of the payment is applied to the principal.

discount yield Difference between the original purchase price of a T-bill and what the Treasury pays you at maturity.

discretionary income Money left over after necessities such as housing and food are paid for.

disposable income Amount of income remaining after taxes and withholding for such purposes as insurance and union dues.

diversification Process of reducing risk by spreading investment money among several different investment opportunities.

dividend payout ratio Dividends per share divided by earnings per share (EPS); helps judge the likelihood of future dividends.

dividends per share Translates the total cash dividends paid out by a company to common stockholders into a per-share figure.

dividend yield Cash dividend to an investor expressed as a percentage of the current market price of a security.

dollar-cost averaging/cost averaging Systematic program of investing equal sums of money at regular intervals, regardless of the price of the investment.

Dow Jones Industrial Average (DJIA) The most widely reported of all stock market indexes that tracks prices of only 30 actively traded blue-chip stocks, including well-known companies such as American Express and AT&T.

down payment An initial payment made in the context of buying expensive items on credit, such as a vehicle or home.

dunning letters Notices that make insistent demands for repayment.

early withdrawal penalty A ten percent penalty over and above the taxes owed when money is withdrawn early from a qualified retirement account.

earned income Compensation for performing personal services.

earned income credit (EIC) A refundable tax credit that may be claimed by workers with a qualifying child and in certain cases by childless workers.

earnest money Funds given to the seller as a deposit to hold the property until a purchase contract can be negotiated.

earnings per share (EPS) A firm's profit divided by the number of outstanding shares.

earnings yield The earnings per share of a stock divided by its price; an inversion of the price/earnings ratio; helps investors more clearly see investment expectations.

economic growth A condition of increasing production (business spending) and consumption (consumer spending) in the economy and hence increasing national income.

economic indicator Any economic statistic, such as the unemployment rate, GDP, or the inflation rate, that suggests how well the economy is doing now and how well it might be doing in the future.

effective marginal tax rate The total marginal rate reflects all taxes on a person's income, including federal, state, and local income taxes as well as Social Security and Medicare taxes.

electronic funds transfers (EFTs) Funds shifted electronically (rather than by check or cash) among various accounts or to and from other people and businesses.

employee benefit Compensation for employment that does not take the form of wages, salaries, commissions, or other cash payments.

employee benefits Forms of remuneration provided by employers to employees that result in the employee not having to pay out-of-pocket money for certain expenses; also known as nonsalary benefits.

Employee Retirement Income Security Act (ERISA) Regulates employer-sponsored plans by calling for proper plan reporting and disclosure to participants in defined-contribution, defined-benefit, and cash-balance plans.

employee stock-ownership plan (ESOP) Benefit plan in which employers make tax-deductible gifts of company stock into trusts, which are then allocated into employee accounts.

employer-sponsored retirement plan An IRS-approved retirement plan offered by an employer (also called qualified plans).

employment agency Firm that locates employment for certain types of employees.

endorsement An addition to a standard insurance policy designed to expand coverage for a special area of need.

envelope system Placing exact amounts into envelopes for each budgetary purpose.

equities Ownership equities such as common or preferred stocks, equity mutual funds, real estate, and so on that focus on capital gains more than on income.

escrow account Special reserve account at a financial institution in which funds are held until they are paid to a third party—in this case, for home insurance and for property taxes.

essential health benefits A list of ten categories of benefits that all health care plans sold on the health insurance exchanges must Provide.

estate planning The definite arrangements you make during your lifetime that are consistent with your wishes for the administration and distribution of your estate when you die.

estimated taxes People who are self-employed or receive substantial income from an employer that is not required to practice payroll withholding (such as lawyers and owners of rental property) are required by the IRS to estimate their tax liability and pay their taxes in advance in quarterly installments.

estimate of the required rate of return on an investment A calculation that multiplies the beta value of an investment by the estimated market risk and adds the risk-free T-bill rate that suggests to investors the return required to put their money at risk.

excess mileage charge Fees assessed at the end of a lease if the vehicle was driven more miles than originally specified in the lease contract.

exchange privilege Allowance for mutual fund shareholders to easily swap shares on a dollar-for-dollar basis for shares in another mutual fund within a mutual fund family. Also called switching, conversion, or transfer privilege.

exclusions Income not subject to federal taxation.

executor/personal representative Person responsible for carrying out the provisions of a will and managing the assets until the estate is passed on to heirs.

exemption (or personal exemption) Legally permitted amount deducted from AGI based on the number of people that the taxpayer's income supports.

expenses Total expenditures made in a specified time such as reported on a cash-flow statement.

expense ratio Expense per dollar of assets under management.

extended warranty/service contract/maintenance agreement/ buyer protection plan Agreement between the seller and buyer of a product to repair or replace covered product components for some specified time period; purchased separately from the product itself.

face amount Dollar value of protection as listed in the policy and used to calculate the premium.

Fair Credit Billing Act (FCBA) Helps people who wish to dispute billing errors on revolving credit accounts and permits chargebacks.

Fair Credit Reporting Act (FCRA) Requires that credit reports contain only accurate relevant information and allows consumers to challenge errors or omissions of information in their reports.

Fair Debt Collection Practices Act (FDCPA) Prohibits third-party debt collection agencies from using abusive, deceptive, or unfair practices to collect past-due debts.

fed The Federal Reserve Board, an agency of the federal government.

federal deposit insurance Insures deposits, both principal amounts and accrued interest, up to $250,000 per account for most accounts.

federal estate tax Assessed against a deceased person's estate before property (real estate, stocks and bonds, business interests, and so on) is transferred to heirs or assigned according to terms of a will or state intestacy laws.

federal funds rate The short-term rate at which depository institutions lend balances at the Federal Reserve to other depository institutions overnight.

Federal Housing Administration (FHA) Part of the U.S. Department of Housing and Urban Development (HUD) that insures loans that meet its standards to encourage home ownership.

FICA taxes A 6.2 percent tax paid by both the worker and employer on the worker's employment income up to the maximum taxable yearly earnings.

fiduciary standard A financial advisor must always act in the best interest of the client regardless of how it might affect the advisor.

filing status Description of a taxpayer's marital status on the last day of the tax year.

final expenses One-time expenses occurring just prior to or after a death.

finance charge Total dollar amount paid to use credit.

financial goals Specific objectives addressed by planning and managing finances.

financial happiness The experience you have when you are satisfied with your money matters, which is in part a result of practicing good financial behaviors.

financial literacy Knowledge of facts, concepts, principles, and technological tools that are fundamental to being smart about money.

financial planner An investment professional who evaluates the personal finances of an individual or family and recommends strategies to set and achieve long-term financial goals.

financial ratios Calculations designed to simplify evaluation of financial strength and progress.

financial records Documents that evidence financial transactions.

financial responsibility Means that you are accountable for your future financial well-being and that you strive to make wise personal financial decisions.

financial risk Possibility that an investment will fail to pay a return to the investor.

financial security The comfortable feeling that your financial resources will be adequate to fulfill any needs you have as well as most of your wants.

financial services industry Companies that provide monetary asset management and other services.

financial statements Snapshots that describe an individual's or family's current financial condition.

financial strategies Pre-established action plans implemented in specific situations.

financial success The achievement of financial aspirations that are desired, planned, or attempted, as defined by the person who seeks it.

fixed expenses Expenses that recur at fixed intervals.

fixed income Specific rate of return that a borrower agrees to pay the investor for use of the principal (initial investment).

fixed maturity Specific date on which a borrower agrees to repay the principal to the investor.

flat tax An income tax having but a single rate for all taxpayers regardless of income level and type.

flexible spending account (FSA) An employer-sponsored account that allows employee-paid expenses for medical or dependent care to be paid with an employee's pretax dollars rather than after-tax income.

floater policies Provide all-risk protection for accident and theft losses to movable property regardless of where the loss occurs.

foreclosure Process in which the lender sues the borrower to prove default and asks the court to order the sale of the property to pay the debt.

front-end load A sales charge paid when an individual buys an investment, reducing the amount available to purchase fund shares.

front-end ratio Compares the total annual PITI expenditures for housing with the loan applicant's gross annual income to assess the borrower's ability to pay the mortgage.

FSA debit card (also known as Flexcard) A card used to access and spend funds from a flexible spending account.

FSBO For sale by owner; commonly pronounced "fizbo"; home sold directly by the homeowner to save on sales commission paid to a real estate broker.

full-benefit retirement age Age at which a retiree is entitled to full Social Security benefits; 67 for those born in 1960 or later.

full warranty Warranty that meets three stringent promises: the product must be fixed at no cost to the buyer within a reasonable time, the owner will not have to undertake an unreasonable task to return the product for repair, and a defective product will be replaced with a new one or the buyer's money will be returned if the product cannot be fixed.

fully insured Social Security status Requires 40 credits and provides workers and their families with benefits under the retirement, survivors, and disability programs; once status is earned, it cannot be taken away even if the eligible worker never works again.

functional format Resume that emphasizes career-related experiences.

fundamental analysis School of thought in market analysis that assumes each stock has an intrinsic (or true) value based on its expected stream of future earnings.

fund screener (fund-screening tool) Permits investors to screen all of the mutual funds in the market to gauge performance.

futures contract The obligation to make or take delivery of a certain amount of a commodity by a set date.

future value The valuation of an asset projected to the end of a particular time period in the future.

garnishment Court-sanctioned procedure by which a portion of debtors' wages are set aside by their employers to pay debts.

general (full-service) brokerage firms Offer a full range of services to customers, including investment advice and research.

gold bullion A refined and stamped weight of precious metal.

gold bullion coins Various world mints issue these coins, which contain 1 troy ounce (31.15 grams) of pure gold.

good-faith estimate Lender's list of all the costs associated with the loan, including the annual percentage rate (APR), application and processing fees, closing costs, and any other charges that must be paid when the deal is legally consummated.

grace period Period of time during which an overdue premium may be paid without a lapse of the policy.

graduated vesting Schedule under which employees must be at least 20 percent vested after two years of service and gain an additional 20 percent of vesting for each subsequent year until, at the end of year six, the account is fully vested.

grantor Creator of a trust—the person who makes a grant of assets to establish a trust. Also called the *settler, donor*, or *trustor*.

gross capitalized cost (gross cap cost) Includes vehicle price plus the cost of any extra features such as insurance or maintenance agreements.

gross domestic product (GDP) The nation's broadest measure of economic health; it reports how much economic activity (all goods and services) has occurred within the U.S. borders during a given period.

gross income All income in the form of money, goods, services, and/or property.

group health plan Sold collectively to an entire group of people rather than to individuals, such as the group health care policies offered by employers.

growth funds Funds that seek long-term capital appreciation by investing in common stocks of companies with higher-than-average revenue and earnings growth, often the larger and well-established firms.

growth and income funds Funds that invest in companies that have a high likelihood of both dividend income and price appreciation; less risk-oriented than aggressive growth funds or growth funds.

growth stock The stock of a company that offers the promise of much higher profits tomorrow and has a consistent record of relatively rapid growth in earnings in all economic conditions.

guaranteed insurability (guaranteed purchase option) Permits the cash-value policyholder to buy additional stated amounts of cash-value life insurance at stated times in the future without evidence of insurability.

guaranteed minimum rate of return Minimum rate that, by contract, the insurance company is legally obligated to pay.

guaranteed renewable term insurance Protects you against the possibility of becoming uninsurable.

guardian Person responsible for caring for and raising any child under the age of 18 and for managing the child's estate.

hazard Any condition that increases the probability that a peril will occur.

health care plan Generic name for any program that pays or provides reimbursement for health care expenditures; an employee benefit designed to pay all or part of the employee's medical expenses.

health care proxy A legal document in which individuals designate another person to make health care decisions on their behalf if they are rendered incapable of making their wishes known.

health insurance Provides protection against direct medical expenses resulting from illness and injury based on the concept of payment after an expense occurs.

health insurance exchange (HIX) Stat-by-state mechanisms established by the ACA through which consumers can purchase a health care plan.

health maintenance organizations (HMOs) Health insurance plans that provide a broad range of health care services for a set monthly fee on a prepaid basis.

health savings account (HSA) Tax-deductible savings accounts into which individuals or employers can deposit tax-sheltered funds to pay medical bills; special savings account intended for people who have a high-deductible health care plan (with annual deductibles of at least $1000 for individuals and $2000 for families).

hedge funds Freewheeling risky investment pools for the extremely wealthy that use unconventional investment strategies such as trading options and commodities, selling short, using leverage and arbitrage, buying and selling currencies, and investing in undervalued mature companies.

heir Person who inherits or is entitled by law or by the terms of a will to inherit some asset.

herd behavior When emotion, not logic, rules investing decisions and investors decide to copy the observed decisions of other investors or movements in the markets rather than follow their own beliefs and information.

high-balling Sales tactic in which a dealer offers a trade-in allowance that is much higher than the vehicle is worth.

high-deductible health plan (HDHP) A plan that requires individuals to pay a higher deductible to cover medical expenses before insurance plan payments begin; chosen to save money on premiums.

high-risk (or alternative) investments Present potential for significant fluctuations in return, sometimes over short time periods.

home inspection Conducted to ensure that the home is physically sound and that all operating systems are in proper order.

homeowner's equity Dollar value of the home in excess of the amount owed on it.

homeowner's general liability protection Applies when you are legally liable for another person's losses, other than those that arise out of use of vehicles or your professional duties.

homeowner's insurance Combines liability and property insurance coverages that homeowners and renters typically need into single-package policies.

I bonds Nonmarketable savings bonds backed by the U.S. government that pay an earnings rate that combines two rates: a fixed interest rate set when the investor buys the bond and a semiannual variable interest rate tied to inflation that protects the investor's purchasing power.

immediate annuity Annuity, often funded by a lump sum from the death benefit of a life insurance policy or lump sum from a defined-contribution plan, that begins payments one month after purchase.

impulse buying Buying too quickly without fully considering priorities and alternatives.

income stock A stock that may not grow too quickly, but year after year pays a cash dividend higher than that offered by most companies.

incontestability clause Places a time limit on the right of the insurance company to deny a claim.

indenture Written, legal agreement between bondholders and debtor that describes terms of the debt by setting forth the maturity date, interest rate, and other details.

indexing Yearly adjustments to tax brackets that reduce inflation's effects on tax brackets.

index of leading economic indicators (LEI) A composite index reported monthly by the Conference Board that suggests the future direction of the U.S. economy.

individual retirement account (IRA) Investment account that reduces current year income, and the funds in the account accumulate tax-free; or personal retirement account to which a person can make contributions that provide tax-deferred growth.

inflation A steady and sustained rise in general price levels across economic sectors; measured by the changing cost over time of a "market basket" of goods and services that a typical household might purchase.

inheritance tax A tax imposed by eight states that is assessed on the decedent's beneficiaries who receive inherited property.

insolvent When a person owes more than he or she owns and the person has a negative net worth.

installment credit (closed-end credit) Credit arrangement in which the borrower must repay the amount owed plus interest in a specific number of equal payments.

insurance Mechanism for transferring and reducing pure risk through which a large number of individuals share in the financial losses suffered by members of the group as a whole.

insurance agents Representative of an insurance company authorized to sell, modify, service, and terminate insurance contracts.

insurance claim Formal request to the insurance company for reimbursement for a covered loss.

insurance dividends Surplus earnings of the insurance company when the difference between the total premium charged exceeds the cost to the company of providing insurance.

insurance policy Contract between the person buying insurance (the insured) and the insurance company (the insurer).

insured Individual whose life is insured.

interest Charge for borrowing money; investors in bonds earn interest.

interest-adjusted net payment index (IANPI) If a policy will remain in force until death, this method allows you to effectively measure the cost of cash-value insurance. The lower the IANPI, the lower the cost of the policy.

interest-earning checking account Any account on which you can write checks that pays interest.

interest inventories Scaled surveys that assess career interests and activities.

interest rate risk Risk that interest rates will rise and bond prices will fall, thereby lowering the prices on older bond issues.

intermediate-term goals Financial targets that can be achieved within one to five years.

intestate When a person dies without a legal will.

investing Putting saved money to work so that it makes you even more money.

investment/capital assets Tangible and intangible items acquired for their monetary benefits.

investment-grade bonds Offer investors a reasonable certainty of regularly receiving periodic income (interest) and retrieving the amount originally invested (principal).

investment philosophy Investor's general approach to tolerance for risk in investments, whether it is conservative, moderate, or aggressive, given the investor's financial goals.

investment plan An explanation of your investment philosophy and your logic on investing to reach specific goals.

investment policy statement A written document that spells out the relationship between an investor and his or her financial advisor and guides how the advisor will invest the person's money; it should detail the person's investment philosophy, financial situation, and the risks he or she is willing to take, as well as what tasks the advisor will perform.

investments Assets purchased with the goal of providing additional future income from the asset itself.

investment risk The possibility that the yield on an investment will deviate from its expected return.

irrevocable living trust Arrangement in which the grantor permanently gives up ownership and the right to control of the property, to change the beneficiaries, and to change the trustees.

itemized deductions Tax-deductible expenses.

job boards A website devoted to helping employers find suitable new employees by providing job listings, job sites, job search tips, job search engines, and related articles; some allow posting of resumes.

job interview Formal meeting between employer and potential employee to discuss job qualifications and suitability.

job referral The act recommending someone to another by sending a reference for employment.

joint-and-survivor annuity Provides monthly payments for as long as one of the two people—usually a husband and wife—is alive.

joint and survivor benefit/survivor's benefit Annuity whose payments continue to a surviving spouse after the participant's death; often equals at least 50 percent of participant's benefit.

joint tenancy with right of survivorship/joint tenancy Most common form of joint ownership, especially for husbands and wives, in which each person owns the whole of the asset, such as a bank account or home, and can dispose of it without the approval of the other owner(s).

Keogh Tax-deferred retirement account designed for high-income self-employed and small-business owners.

large-loss principle A basic rule of risk management that encourages us to insure the risks that we cannot afford and retain the risks that we can reasonably afford.

law of large numbers As the number of members in a group increases, predictions about the group's behavior become increasingly accurate.

layering term insurance policies Purchasing level-premium term policies so that coverage grows when you need it most and then can be decreased as your needs change.

leading economic indicators Statistics that change before the economy changes, thus helping predict how the economy will do in the future, such as the stock market, the number of new building permits, and the consumer confidence index.

lease Rental of a product while ownership title remains with the lease grantor; or a contract specifying both tenant and landlord legal responsibilities.

lemon laws State laws that provide guidelines for arbitrators to use to order a dealer's buyback of a "lemon" as defined under the law—commonly a car that has been in the shop four or more times to fix the same problem.

letter of last instructions Nonlegal instrument that may contain preferences regarding funeral and burial, material to be included in the obituary, and other information useful to the survivors, such as the location of important documents.

level-premium term insurance Term policy with a long term under which premiums remain constant. Also called guaranteed level-premium term insurance.

leverage Using borrowed funds to invest with the goal of earning a rate of return in excess of the after-tax costs of borrowing.

liabilities What you owe.

liability insurance Protection from financial losses suffered when you are held liable for others' losses.

lien A legal right to seize and dispose of (usually sell) property to obtain payment of a claim. Once the loan is paid, the lien is removed.

life insurance policy A contract between an insured (insurance policy holder) and an insurer or assurer, where the insurer promises to pay a designated beneficiary a sum of money (the "benefits") upon the death of the insured person.

lifestyle trade-offs Weighing the demands of particular jobs with your social and cultural preferences.

lifetime learning credit A nonrefundable tax credit that may be claimed every year for tuition and related expenses paid for all years of postsecondary education undertaken to acquire or improve job skills.

limited managed account An account at an investment firm whereby, for a fee, they sell and buy your mutual fund assets, usually quarterly, on your behalf to automatically rebalance your portfolio back to your specific standards.

limited-pay whole life insurance Whole life insurance that allows premium payments to cease before the insured reaches the age of 100.

limited warranty Any warranty that offers less protection than the three conditions for full warranty.

liquidity The speed and ease with which an asset can be converted to cash.

liquidity risk The risk that a given security or asset cannot be traded quickly enough in the market to prevent a loss (or make the required profit).

listing agreement Agreement that brokers require homeowners to sign that permits the broker to list the property exclusively or with a multiple-listing service.

living trust A trust that takes effect while the grantor is still alive.

living will Allows you to document in advance your specific wishes concerning medical treatments in an emergency or during end-of-life health care.

load funds Mutual funds that always charge a "load" or sales charge upon purchase; the load is the commission used to compensate brokers.

loan Consumer credit that is repaid in equal amounts over a set period of time.

loan commitment Lender's promise to grant a loan.

loan-to-value (LTV) ratio Original or current outstanding loan balance divided by the home value; measures the amount of leverage in a real estate investment project by dividing the total amount of debt by the market price of the investment.

long-term care insurance Provides reimbursement for costs associated with custodial care in a nursing facility Or at home.

long-term gain/loss A profit or loss on the sale of an asset that has been held for more than a year.

long-term goals Financial targets to achieve more than five years in the future.

long-term (noncurrent) liability Debt that comes due in more than one year.

loss control Designing specific mechanisms to reduce loss frequency and loss severity.

low-balling A sales tactic where the seller quotes an artificially low price to obtain a verbal agreement from a buyer and then attempts to raise the negotiated price when it comes time to finalize the written contract.

low-load funds Funds carrying sales charges of perhaps 1 to 3 percent; sold by brokers, via mail, and sometimes through mutual fund retailers located in shopping centers.

manufacturer's suggested retail price (MSRP) The retail price set by the manufacturer and posted on the federally required side window sticker.

margin account Account at a brokerage firm that requires a substantial deposit of cash or securities and permits the purchase of other securities using credit granted by the brokerage firm.

margin buying Using a margin account to buy securities; allows the investor to apply leverage that magnifies returns—or losses.

margin rate Set by the Fed, percentage of the value (or equity) in an investment that is not borrowed—recently 25 to 50 percent.

marginal cost The additional (marginal) cost of one more incremental unit of some item.

marginal tax bracket (MTB)/marginal tax rate One of seven income-range segments at which income is taxed at increasing rates. Also known as marginal tax rate.

marginal tax rate The tax rate at which your last dollar earned is taxed.

marginal utility The extra satisfaction derived from gaining one more incremental unit of a product or service.

market correction A short term price decline in the stock markets of at least 10 percent in a stock, bond, commodity or index to adjust for a recent price rises.

market efficiency The speed at which new information is reflected in investment prices suggesting that security prices are reflective of their true value at all times because publicly available information has driven market prices to the correct level.

market interest rates Current long- and short-term interest rates paid on various types of corporate and government debts that carry similar levels of risk.

market price The current price of a share of stock that a buyer is willing to pay a willing seller.

market risk/systematic risk/undiversifiable risk The possibility for an investor to experience losses due to unknown factors that affect the overall performance of the financial markets.

market timers Investors who attempt to predict the short-term movements of various markets (or market segments) and, based on those predictions, move capital from one segment to another in order to capture market gains and avoid market losses.

market volatility The likelihood of large price swings in securities due to a company's success (or lack of it) and various market conditions.

market-volatility risk The fact that all investments are subject to occasional sharp changes in price as a result of events affecting a particular company or the overall market for similar investments.

matching contribution Employer benefit that offers a full or partial matching contribution to a participating employee's account in proportion to each dollar of contributions made by the participant.

maturity date Date upon which the principal is returned to the bondholder.

maximum taxable yearly earnings (MTYE) The maximum amount to which the FICA tax is applied.

Medicaid A government health care program for low-income people funded jointly by the federal and state governments.

Medicare The federal government's health care program for the elderly.

Medicare tax A 1.45 percent tax paid by both the worker and employer on all the worker's employment income.

mentor An experienced person, often a senior coworker, who offers friendly career-related advice, guidance, and coaching to a less experienced person.

minimum-balance account Checking account that requires customers to keep a certain minimum amount for a specified time period to avoid fees.

minimum payment Lowest allowable monthly payment required by the lender; or payment that must be made to a credit account each month to cover interest and a portion of the amount owed.

moderate investment philosophy (risk indifference) Investors with this philosophy accept some risk as they seek capital gains through slow and steady growth in investment value along with current income.

monetary asset (cash) management How you handle your monetary assets.

monetary assets/liquid assets/cash equivalents Assets that can be used as cash.

money market account Interest-earning accounts that pay relatively high interest rates and offer limited check-writing privileges.

money market deposit accounts Government-insured money market account with minimum-balance requirements and tiered interest rates.

money market funds Those funds that invest in highly liquid, relatively safe securities with very short securities, always less than one year.

money market mutual fund (MMMF) Money market account in a mutual fund rather than at a depository institution.

Monte Carlo analysis Technique that performs a large number of trial runs of a particular portfolio mix of investments, called simulations, to find an optimal allocation for a particular investor's goals and risk tolerance.

mortgage broker Individual or company that acts as an intermediary between borrowers and lenders.

mortgage insurance Insures the difference between the amount of down payment required by an 80 percent LTV ratio and the actual, lower down payment.

mortgage loan Loan to purchase real estate in which the property itself serves as collateral.

municipal government bonds (munis) Long-term debts (bonds) issued by local governments (cities, states, and various districts and political subdivisions) and their agencies.

mutual fund Investment company that pools funds by selling shares to investors and makes diversified investments to achieve financial goals of income or growth, or both.

mutual fund ask (or offer) price Price at which an investor can purchase a mutual fund's shares; current NAV per share plus sales charges.

mutual fund bid price Shareholders receive this amount per share when they redeem their shares, which is the same dollar amount as the NAV.

mutual fund dividend Income paid to investors out of profits earned by the mutual fund from its investments.

mutual fund family Investment management company that offers a number of different funds to the investing public, each with its own investment objectives or philosophies of investing.

named-perils policies Cover only losses caused by perils that the policy specifically mentions.

need Item thought to be necessary.

needs-based approach A superior method of calculating the amount of insurance needed that considers all of the factors that might potentially affect the level of need.

negotiating/haggling Process of discussing actual terms of agreement with a seller, usually on higher-priced items.

net asset value (NAV) Per-share value of a mutual fund.

net surplus Amount remaining after all budget classification deficits are subtracted from those with surpluses.

net worth What's left when you subtract liabilities from assets.

new-vehicle buying service Organization that arranges discount purchases for new-car buyers who are referred to nearby participating automobile dealers that have agreed to charge specific discount prices.

no-load funds Funds that allow investors to purchase shares directly at the net asset value (NAV) without the addition of sales charges.

nominal income Also called money income; income that has not been adjusted for inflation and decreasing purchasing power.

nonforfeiture values Amounts stipulated in a life insurance policy that protect the cash value, if any, in the event that the policyholder chooses not to pay or fails to pay required premiums.

nonprobate property Does not go through probate; includes assets transferred to survivors by contract (such as beneficiaries listed on retirement accounts and bank accounts held with another person).

nonrefundable tax credit A tax credit that can reduce one's tax liability only to zero; however, if the credit is more than the tax liability, the excess is not refunded.

online discount brokers Such brokers, also called Internet or electronic discount brokers, have reduced the cost of executing a trade to perhaps $20 or even $10 because their primary business is online trading.

open-ended (revolving) credit Arrangement in which credit is extended in advance of any transaction so that borrowers do not need to reapply each time they need to use credit.

open-end mutual fund Investment that issues redeemable shares that investors purchase directly from the fund (or through a broker for the fund).

opportunity cost The opportunity cost of any decision is the value of the next best alternative that must be forgone.

ordinary income dividend distributions Distributions that occur when the fund pays out dividends from the stock and interest from the bonds it hold in its portfolio; these are passed onto the investor quarterly.

overindebted When one's excessive personal debts make repayment difficult and cause financial distress.

over-the-counter (OTC) (off-exchange trading) Where trading is done directly between two parties, without any supervision of an exchange.

owner/policyholder Retains all rights and privileges granted by the policy, including the right to amend the policy and the right to designate who receives the proceeds.

paid up Point at which the owner of a whole life policy can stop paying premiums.

participating policies Life insurance policies that pay dividends.

Patient Protection and Affordable Care Act (ACA) The law passed by Congress in 2010 to provide affordable health insurance for all US citizens and reduce the growth in health care spending.

pay yourself first Treating savings as the first expenditure after— or even before— getting paid rather than simply the money left over at the end of the month.

payable-on-death designation Status granted to individuals who are not joint tenants and who might need to access accounts without going through probate; the deceased signs the designation before death, and the designee simply presents a death certificate to access the accounts.

payroll withholding The IRS requirement that an employer withhold a certain amount from an employee's income as a prepayment of that individual's tax liability for the year. It is sent to the government where it is credited to the taxpayer's account.

PEG ratio (price-earnings growth) A way to rationalize buying a stock that has high growth is to calculate by dividing the P/E ratio by the company's projected growth rate.

perils Any event that can cause a financial loss.

periodic interest rate The monthly rate applied to the outstanding balance of a loan.

periodic statements Monthly reports that show all electronic transfers to and from accounts, fees charged, and opening and closing balances.

personal finance The study of personal and family resources considered important in achieving financial success; it involves how people spend, save, protect, and invest their financial resources.

PITI Elements of a monthly real estate payment consisting of principal, interest, real estate taxes, and homeowner's insurance.

point/interest point Fee equal to 1 percent of the total mortgage loan amount.

policy limits Specify the maximum dollar amounts that will be paid under the policy.

portability Upon termination of employment, employees with portable benefits can keep their savings in tax-sheltered accounts, transferring retirement funds from employer's account directly to another account without penalty.

portfolio Collection of investments assembled to meet your investment goals.

portfolio diversification Practice of selecting a collection of different asset classes of investments (such as stocks, bonds, mutual funds, real estate, and cash) that are chosen not only for their potential returns but also for their dissimilar risk-return characteristics.

portfolio tracking Automatically updates the value of your portfolio after you enter the symbols of the stocks you own and the number of shares held.

potential return Determined by adding anticipated income (from dividends, interest, rents, or other sources) to the future value of investment and then subtracting the investment's original cost.

pre-emptive right Right of common stockholders to purchase additional shares before a firm offers new shares to the public.

preferred provider organization (PPO) Group of health care providers (doctors, hospitals, and other health care providers) who contract with a health insurance company to provide services at a discount.

preferred stock Type of fixed-income ownership security in a corporation that pays fixed dividends.

premium quote service Offers computer-generated comparisons from among 20 to 80 different companies.

premiums The monthly or annual cost of a health care plan.

prepayment penalty Special charge assessed to the borrower for paying off a loan early.

preshopping research Gathering information before actually beginning to interact with sellers.

pretax dollars Money income that has not been taxed by the government.

pretax money Investing before income taxes are calculated, thus gaining an immediate elimination of part of your income tax liability for the current year.

price/earnings (P/E ratio) (or multiple) The current market price of a stock divided by earnings per share (EPS) over the past four quarters; used as the primary means of valuing a stock.

price/sales ratio (P/S ratio) Tells the number of dollars it takes to buy a dollar's worth of a company's annual revenues; calculated by dividing company's total market capitalization by its sales for the past four quarters.

price-to-book ratio (P/B ratio) Current stock price divided by the per-share net value of a firm's plant, equipment, and other assets (book value).

price-to-rent ratio The ratio of median residential real estate prices to the median annual rents that can be earned from the real estate.

principal Face amount of a bond; the original amount invested.

principle of indemnity Insurance will pay no more than the actual financial loss suffered.

private mortgage insurance (PMI) Mortgage insurance obtained from a private company.

probate Court-supervised process that allows creditors to present claims against an estate and ensures the transfer of a decedent's assets to the rightful beneficiaries according to a properly executed and valid will or, when no will exists, to the people, agencies, or organizations required by state law.

probate property All assets other than nonprobate property.

professional abilities Job-related activities that you can perform physically, mentally, artistically, mechanically, and financially.

professional interests Long-standing topics and activities that engage your attention.

professional liability insurance/malpractice insurance Protects individuals and organizations that provide professional services when they are held liable for their clients' losses.

professional networking Making and using contacts with individuals, groups, and other firms to exchange career information.

profile prospectus (fund profile) Publication that describes the mutual fund, its investment objectives, and how it tries to achieve its objectives in lay terms rather than the legal language used in a regular prospectus.

profit Money left over after a firm pays all expenses and interest to bondholders.

profit-sharing plan Employer-sponsored plan that allocates some of the employer profits to employees in the form of end-of-year cash or common stock contributions to employees' 401(k) accounts.

progressive tax A tax that progressively increases as a taxpayer's taxable income increases.

projected P/E ratio (forward price/earnings ratio) Because investors need to look to the future rather than the past, this measure divides price by projected earnings over the coming four quarters. Also known as forward price/earnings ratio.

promissory note (note) Contract that stipulates repayment terms for a loan.

property insurance Protection from financial losses resulting from the damage to or destruction of your property or possessions.

prospectus Highly legalistic information presented by a firm to the SEC and to the public with any new issue of stock.

purchase contract/sales contract Formal legal document that outlines the actual agreement that results from the real estate negotiations.

purchase offer/offer to purchase Written offer to purchase real estate.

purchasing power Measure of the goods and services that one's income will buy.

random/unsystematic risk Risk associated with owning only one investment of a particular type (such as stock in one company) that, by chance, may do very poorly in the future due to uncontrollable or random factors that do not affect the rest of the market.

rate of return/yield Total return on an investment expressed as a percentage of its price.

real estate Property consisting of land, all structures permanently attached to that land, and accompanying rights and privileges, such as crops and mineral rights.

real estate (or housing) bubble Rapid and unsustainable increases in home prices followed by sharp declines in values.

real estate broker (agent) Person licensed by a state to provide advice and assistance, for a fee, to buyers or sellers of real estate.

real income Income measured in constant prices relative to some base time period. It reflects the actual buying power of the money you have as measured in constant dollars.

real rate of return Return on an investment after subtracting the effects of inflation and income taxes.

recession A recurring period of decline in total output, income, employment, and trade, usually lasting from six months to a year and marked by widespread contractions in many sectors of the economy.

record keeping Recording sources and amounts of dollars earned and spent.

redeems When an investor sells mutual fund shares.

redemption charge (exit fee) Similar to a deferred load but often much lower; used to reduce excessive trading of fund shares.

redress Process of righting a wrong.

refundable tax credit A tax credit that can reduce one's income tax liability to below zero with the excess being refunded to the taxpayer.

registered bond Bondholder's name is recorded so that checks or electronic funds transfers for payment of interest and principal can be safely forwarded when due.

release Insurance document affirming that the dollar amount of the loss settlement is accepted as full and complete reimbursement.

rent Cost charged for using an apartment or other housing space.

rental yield A computation of how much income the investor might pocket from rent each year (before mortgage payments) as a percentage of the purchase price; divide the annual rent by 2 and then divide by the purchase price.

renter's contents broad form (HO-4) Named-perils policy that protects the insured from losses to the contents of a rented dwelling rather than to the dwelling itself.

repairs Usually tax-deductible expenses necessary to maintain property value.

replacement-cost requirement Stipulates that a home must be insured for 80 percent of its replacement value (some companies require 100 percent) in order for any loss to be fully covered.

repossession/foreclosure Legal proceeding by which the lender seizes an asset.

residual claim Common stockholders have a right to share in the income and assets of a corporation after higher-priority claims are satisfied.

residual clause Feature of own-occupation policies that allows for some reduced level of disability income benefits when a partial— rather than full—disability strikes.

residual value Projected value of a leased asset at the end of the lease time period.

résumé Summary record of your education, training, experience, and other qualifications.

retail credit cards Allow customers to make purchases on credit at any of the outlets of a particular retailer.

retained earnings Money left over after a firm has paid expenses, bondholder interest, taxes, preferred stockholder dividends, and common stockholder dividends.

retirement savings goal (retirement nest egg) Total amount of accumulated savings and investments needed to support a desired retirement lifestyle.

retirement The time in life when the major sources of income change from earned income (such as salary or wages) to employer-based retirement benefits, private savings and investments, income from Social Security, and perhaps part-time employment.

reverse mortgage/home-equity conversion loan Allows a homeowner older than age 61 to continue living in the home and to borrow against the equity in a home that is fully paid for and to receive the proceeds in a series of monthly payments, often for life.

revocable living trust Grantor maintains the right to change the trust's terms or cancel it at any time, for any reason, during his or her lifetime.

revolving savings fund Variable budgeting tool that places funds in savings to cover emergency or higher-than-usual expenses.

risk Uncertainty about the outcome of a situation or event.

risk averse In investments, one who tends to dislike risk and is unable to put money into investments that seem risky.

risk management Process of identifying and evaluating purely risky situations to determine and implement appropriate management.

risk premium (or equity risk premium) The difference between a riskier investment's expected return and the totally safe return on the T-bill.

risk reduction Includes mechanisms, such as insurance, that reduce the overall uncertainty about the magnitude of loss.

risk retention Accepting that some risks simply arise in the course of one's life and consciously retaining that risk.

risk tolerance An investor's willingness to weather changes in the value of your investments, that is, to weather investment risk.

Roth IRA An individual retirement account of investments made with after-tax money; the interest on such accounts is allowed to grow tax-free, and withdrawals are also tax-free.

Roth IRA IRA funded with after-tax money (and thus it is not tax deductible) that grows on a tax-deferred basis; withdrawals are not subject to taxation.

Rule of 70 A formula to determine how long it will take for the value of a dollar to decline by one-half.

Rule of 78s method/sum of the digits method A common method of calculating the prepayment penalty on a loan that uses the add-on method for calculating the interest.

sales finance company Seller-related lender whose primary business is financing sales for its parent company.

savings Income not spent on current consumption.

secured bond Pledges specific assets as collateral in indenture or has the principal and interest guaranteed by another corporation or government agency.

secured loan Loan that is backed by collateral or a cosigner.

securities Assets suitable for investment, including stocks, bonds, and mutual funds; negotiable instruments of ownership or debt, including common stock, preferred stock, and bonds.

securities exchange (stock market) Market where agents of buyers and sellers can find each other easily by providing an orderly, open plan to trade securities.

securities markets Places where stocks and bonds are traded (or in the case of electronic trading, the way in which securities are traded).

securities market index Measures the average value of a number of securities chosen as a sample to reflect the behavior of a more general market.

security's street name Securities certificates kept in the brokerage firm's name instead of the name of the individual investor.

self-directed In defined-contribution plans, employees control the assets in their account—how often to make contributions to the account, how much to contribute, how much risk to take, and how to invest.

seller financing (or owner financing) When a seller self-finances a buyer's loan by accepting a promissory note from a buyer, who makes monthly mortgage payments.

selling short Investors selling securities they do not own (borrowing them from a broker) and later buying the same number of shares of the security at a lower price (returning them to the broker).

Series EE/E savings bonds Nonmarketable, interest-bearing bonds issued by the federal government that are issued at a sharp discount from face value and pay no annual interest, and that may be redeemed at full value upon maturity.

settlement options Choices from which the policyholder can choose in how the death benefit payment will be structured.

shareholder (stockholder) Each person who owns a share of a company's stock holds a proportionate interest in firm ownership and, therefore, in the assets and income of the corporation.

short-term goals Financial targets or ends that can be achieved in less than a year.

short-term (current) liability Obligation paid off within one year.

single-family dwelling Housing unit that is detached from other units.

sinking fund Bond feature through which money is set aside with a trustee each year for repayment of the principal portion of the debt at maturity.

skills format Resume that emphasizes your aptitudes and qualities.

Social Security credits Accumulated quarterly credits to qualify for Social Security benefits obtained by paying FICA taxes.

Social Security Disability Income Insurance Under this government program, eligible workers can receive some income if their disabilities are total, meaning that they cannot work at any job.

Social Security Estimate Online Information that the Social Security Administration makes available to all workers, which includes earnings history, Social Security taxes paid, and an estimated benefit amount.

Social Security rider Provides an extra dollar amount of protection if a person fails to qualify for Social Security disability benefits (70 percent of all applicants are rejected).

Social Security survivor's benefits Government program benefits paid to a surviving spouse and children.

special (homeowner's insurance) form (HO-3) Provides open-perils protection (except for the commonly excluded perils of war, earthquake, and flood) for four types of property losses.

speculative risk Involves the potential for either gain or loss; equity investments might do either.

speculative-grade bonds Long-term, high-risk, high-interest-rate corporate (or municipal) IOUs issued by companies (or municipalities) with poor or no credit ratings. Also called junk bonds or high-yield bonds.

speculator An investor who buys in the hope that someone else will pay more for an asset in the not-too-distant future.

sponsor A powerfully positioned champion who "leans in" with an employee by advocating on their proteges' behalf and guiding them toward key players and assignments.

spousal consent requirement Federal law that protects the surviving rights of a spouse or ex-spouse to retirement or pension benefits unless the person signs a waiver of those rights.

spousal IRA Account set up for spouse who does not work for wages; offers tax-deferred growth and tax deductibility.

stable-value fund Mutual fund that offers attractive returns and liquidity without market risk to defined contribution plan participants (and some 529 tuition savings plans) because they have contracts with banks and insurance companies designed to permit redemption of shares at book value regardless of market prices.

standard deduction Fixed amount that all taxpayers may subtract from their adjusted gross income if they do not itemize their deductions.

standard of living Material well-being and peace of mind that individuals or groups earnestly desire and seek to attain, to maintain if attained, to preserve if threatened, and to regain if lost.

standardized expense table SEC-required information that describes and illustrates mutual fund charges in an identical manner so that investors can accurately compare the effects of all of a fund's fees and other expenses relative to other funds.

stated commission The sales charge as a percentage of the amount invested.

statement/billing/closing date The last day of the month for which any transactions are reported on the credit statement.

STEM majors Academic majors in science, technology, engineering, and mathematics.

stockbroker (account executive) Professional who is licensed to buy and sell securities on behalf of the brokerage firm's clients.

stocks Shares of ownership in a business corporation's assets and earnings.

stock-screening tools Enable you to quickly sift through vast databases of hundreds of companies to find those that best suit your investment objectives.

stop-payment order Notifying your bank not to honor a check when it's presented for payment.

subleasing An arrangement in which the original tenant leases the property to another tenant.

subordinate budget Detailed listing of planned expenses within a single budgeting classification.

subrogation rights Allow an insurer to take action against a negligent third party (and that party's insurance company) to obtain reimbursement for payments made to an insured.

surplus (or net gain or net income) When total income exceeds total expenses such as reported on a cashflow statement.

sweat equity property Property that needs repairs but that has good underlying value; an investor buys the property at a favorable price and fixes it up to rent or sell at a profit.

take-home pay/disposable income Pay received after employer withholdings for such things as taxes, insurance, and union dues, and it is available for budgeting for spending, saving, investing, and donating.

tangible/use/lifestyle assets Personal property used to maintain your everyday lifestyle.

target-date retirement funds (life-cycle funds) Asset allocation funds that offer investors premixed portfolios of stocks, bonds, and cash that investors of a certain age and risk tolerance might prefer, and they are often named for the year one plans to retire.

taxes Compulsory government-imposed charges levied on citizens and their property.

tax avoidance Reducing tax liability through legal techniques.

tax credit Dollar-for-dollar decrease in tax liability; also known as credit.

tax deferred The individual does not have to pay current income taxes on the earnings (interest, dividends, and capital gains) reinvested in a retirement account.

tax evasion Deliberately and willfully hiding income from the IRS, falsely claiming deductions, or otherwise cheating the government out of taxes owed; it is illegal.

tax losses Created when deductions generated from an investment (such as depreciation and net investment losses) exceed the income from an investment.

tax planning Seeking legal ways to reduce, eliminate, or defer income taxes.

tax refund Amount the IRS sends back to a taxpayer if withholding and estimated payments exceed the tax liability.

tax sheltered Income, dividends, or capital gains that are allowed to grow without taxes until distributions are taken.

taxable income Income upon which income taxes are levied.

tax-exempt income Income that is totally and permanently free of taxes.

tax-exempt money market funds Funds that limit their investments to tax-exempt municipal securities with maturities of 60 days or less.

tax-free exchange (or 1031 exchange) Arises when a real estate investor trades equity in one property for equity in a similar property and no other forms of property or money change hands.

tax-free withdrawals Removal of assets from a retirement account with no taxes assessed.

tax-sheltered (or tax-deferred) income Income exempt from income taxes in the current year but that will be subject to taxation in a later tax year.

tax-sheltered investments A financial arrangement that results in a reduction or elimination of taxes due.

tax-sheltered retirement accounts Retirement account for which all earnings from the invested funds are not subject to income taxes.

tax-sheltered retirement plan Employer-sponsored, defined-contribution retirement plans including 401(k) plans and similar 403(b) and 457 plans.

teaser rate Low interest rate that lenders sometimes use to lure buyers; these rates will be low for the first year or so and then will rise to more realistic rates.

technical analysis Method of evaluating securities that uses statistics generated by market activity, such as past prices and volume, over time to determine when to buy or sell a stock.

term life insurance "Pure protection" against early death; pays benefits only if the insured dies within the time period (term) that the policy covers.

testamentary trust Becomes effective upon death of the grantor according to the terms of the grantor's will or a revocable living trust. Such trusts can provide money or asset management after the grantor's death for the heirs' benefit.

tiered interest A way to calculate interest where the account that pays lower interest on smaller deposits and higher interest on larger balances.

time value of money A method by which one can compare cash flows across time, either as what a future cash flow is worth today (present value) or what an investment made today will be worth in the future (future value). Also, the cost of money that is borrowed or lent; it is commonly referred to as interest and adjusts for the fact that dollars to be received or paid out in the future are not equivalent to those received or paid out today.

title Legal right of ownership interest to real property.

title insurance Protects the lender's interest if the title search is later found faulty.

total income Compensation from all sources.

total return Income an investment generates from current income and capital gains.

trade-off Giving up one thing for another.

traditional (regular) IRA Account that offers tax-deferred growth; the initial contribution may be tax deductible for the year that the IRA was funded.

trailing commission Compensation paid to salespeople for months or years in the future.

trailing P/E ratio Calculated using recently reported earnings, usually from the previous four quarters.

transaction fee A small charge levied each time certain types of transactions occur, such as for cash advances and balance transfers.

Treasury bills Known as T-bills, U.S. government securities with maturities of less than one year.

Treasury Inflation-Protected Securities (TIPS) Marketable Treasury bonds whose value increases with inflation. These inflation-indexed $1000 bonds are the only investment that guarantees that the investor's return will outpace inflation.

Treasury note (bond) Fixed-principal, fixed-interest-rate government security issued for an intermediate term or long term. Notes mature in ten years or less; bonds mature in more than ten years.

Treasury securities (Treasuries) Known as Treasuries, securities issued by the U.S. government, including bills, notes, and bonds.

trust Legal arrangement between you as the creator of the trust and the trustee, the person designated to faithfully and wisely manage any assets in the trust to your benefit and to the benefit of your heirs.

trustee Person charged with carrying out the trust for the benefit of the grantor(s) and heirs.

trustee-to-trustee rollover Retirement funds go directly from the previous account's trustee to the trustee of the new account, with no direct payment to the employee occurring, thereby deferring taxation and the early withdrawal penalty.

Truth in Lending Act (TIL) Requires lenders to disclose to credit applicants both the interest rate expressed as an annual percentage rate (APR) and the finance charge.

umbrella (excess) liability insurance Catastrophic liability policy that covers liability losses in excess of those covered by any underlying homeowner's, automobile, or professional liability policy.

unearned income Investment returns in the form of rents, dividends, capital gains, interest, or royalties.

uniform settlement statement Lists all of the costs and fees to be paid at the closing.

uninsured and underinsured motorist insurance Coverage that an insured can purchase as part of automobile insurance that covers the insured in an accident when an uninsured or underinsured driver is at fault.

universal life insurance Provides the pure protection of term insurance and the cash-value buildup of whole life insurance, along with face amount variability, rate of cash-value accumulation, premiums, and rate of return.

unsecured loan/signature loan Loan granted based solely on borrower's good creditworthiness.

upside down A situation where the owner of a financed asset owes more than it is worth, thus creating negative equity.

U.S. government savings bonds Nonmarketable, interest-bearing bonds issued by the U.S. Treasury.

use-it-or-lose-it rule An IRS regulation requiring that unspent dollars in a flexible spending account at the end of a calendar year be forfeited, unless the employer allows a 2 ½-month grace period for spending the funds.

values Fundamental beliefs about what is important, desirable, and worthwhile.

value-added tax A federal retail sales tax on the estimated "value added" to a product or material at each stage of manufacture or distribution.

value funds Funds specializing in stocks that are fundamentally sound whose prices appear to be low (low P/E ratios) based on the logic that such stocks are currently out of favor and undervalued by the market.

value stock A stock that tends to trade at a low price relative to its company fundamentals (dividends, earnings, sales, and so on) and thus is considered undervalued by a value investor.

variable annuity Annuity whose value rises and falls like mutual funds and pays a limited death benefit via an insurance contract.

variable expenses (or flexible expenses) Expenses over which you have substantial control.

variable interest rates Interest rates that change monthly or annually according to general interest rate changes in the economy as a whole.

variable-rate (adjustable-rate) loans Loans for which the interest rate varies with the monthly payment going up or down, allowing the loan to be paid off by the original end date.

variable-universal life insurance Form of universal life insurance that gives the policyholder some choice in the investments made with the cash value accumulated by the policy. Also called flexible-premium variable life insurance.

vesting Ensures that a retirement plan participant has the right to take full possession of all employer contributions and earnings.

voting rights Proportionate authority to express an opinion or choice in matters affecting the company.

waiting period (elimination period) The time period between the onset of a disability and the date that disability benefits begin.

waiver of premium A clause in an insurance policy that waives the policyholder's obligation to pay any further premiums should he or she become seriously ill or disabled.

want Item not necessary but desired.

warranty Sellers' assurances that goods are as promised and that certain steps will be taken to rectify problems if they arise.

whole life insurance Form of cash-value life insurance that provides lifetime life insurance protection and expects the insured to pay premiums for life. Also called straight life insurance.

will Written document in which a person tells how his or her remaining assets should be given away after death; without a will, the property will be distributed according to state probate law.

withdrawal options (systematic withdrawal plans) Arrangements with a mutual fund company for shareholders who want to receive income on a regular basis from their mutual fund investments.

work-style personality Your own ways of working with and responding to job requirements, surroundings, and associates.

yield to maturity (YTM) Total annual effective rate of return earned by a bondholder on a bond if the security is held to maturity—takes into consideration both the price at which the bond sold and the coupon interest rate to arrive at effective rate of return.

zero-coupon bonds (zeros or deep discount bonds) Municipal, corporate, and Treasury bonds that are issued at a sharp discount from face value and pay no annual interest but are redeemed at full face value upon maturity.

Index

Note: Boldface type indicates key terms defined in text.